A GRAMMAR OF THE PRĀKRIT LANGUAGES

R. PISCHEL

A Grammar of the Prākrit Languages

Translated from German by
SUBHADRA JHĀ

MOTILAL BANARSIDASS PUBLISHING HOUSE
SINCE 1903

MOTILAL BANARSIDASS
PUBLISHING HOUSE • DELHI
Email: mlbd@mlbd.in • Website: www.mlbd.in

2nd Reprint : Delhi, ***2021***
Second Revised Edition : Delhi, 1981

ISBN: 978-93-91430-74-0

Printed & Published by
Rajendra P Jain *for*
Motilal Banarsidass Publishing House
A-44, Naraina Industrial Area, Phase I,
New Delhi–110 028 (INDIA)
Email: mlbd@mlbd.in
Website: www.mlbd.in

Dedicated
to
Dr. Rajendra Prasad
The First President of India
as a token of respect and admiration.

PREFACE TO THE REVISED EDITION

Richard Pischel's Grammar of the Prākrit Languages was first published in the year 1900 in German. Since then it had been held as the most elaborate and comprehensive work on the subject. This translator in 1955 first brought out its English translation. This translation was reprinted in 1965 and then in it was included the complete Index of Prākrit words of Late M. de Zilva Wickremsinghe published later in the Indian Antiquary by Grierson. But in the said index the Prākrit words were printed in types different from those of the main body of the translation; in addition the number of printing errors was quite considerable.

In the form in which this work is now put before the readers, the translation has been thoroughly revised and so also the index. In this work the translator's son Shri Bhāskara Jhā has largely contributed and this thing deserves mention.

By now a considerable amount of work in Prākrit has come to light—inscriptions have been published and so many such books in Apabhraṁśa have appeared as were not available to Pischel. Further different Prākrit languages, especially of the inscriptions, and different Apabhraṁśa dialects have been analysed by competent scholars like Tagare and others. In the light of these publications the work of Pischel has become out of date and requires an over all supplementation and alterations. The present translator has for sometime been working in this line and it is hoped that in the next edition of this work necessary additions and alterations will be incorporated.

But the proposed work would require years of labour and in case this was to be necessary changes were to be made in it, publication of the work would have been delayed by years.

With obvious short-comings, this work is placed before the world of scholars with the hope that they would be content with this, however with due apology to them, following the maxim *abhāve śālicūrṇaṁ vā.*

Nāgadah, Madhubani
March 19, 1981.

SUBHADRA JHĀ

TRANSLATOR'S NOTE

The following changes have been made in the system of Romanisation of Indian words :—

(a) *ṃ* has been replaced by *ṁ*.
(b) Small letters have been substituted for capital letters in proper nouns printed in Italics.

It is regretted that certain letters in Italics with diacritical marks have been printed with two different types joined together and that, as in the original, diacritical marks went off in course of printing in a number of places.

I must express my deep sense of gratitude to the Late Dr. Batakrishna Ghosh, whose English translation of the first chapter of the Introduction, under the title "Pischel on the Characteristics of the Prakrit Languages", has been of great help to me.

Āśvina, 5, *Śakābda* 1879. Subhadra Jhā

CONTENTS

I. INTRODUCTION.

A. The Prākrit Languages.

§ 1. By the term Prākrit, the Indian grammarians and rhetoricians comprehend a multitude of literary languages as the common characteristic whereof they consider Sanskrit their origin. Therefore, they generally derive the word *prākṛta* from *prakṛti*, "element", "basis", and according to them this basis is Sanskrit. So says Hemacandra, 1, 1, *prakṛtiḥ saṁskṛtam ı tatra bhavaṁ tata āgataṁ vā prākṛtam*, "Sanskrit is the basis, what originated from it or what is derived from it, is called Prākrit". Likewise Mārkaṇḍeya fol. 1: *prakṛtiḥ saṁskṛtam ı tatrabhavaṁ prākṛtamucyate*; so Dhanika on Daśarūpa 2, 60 : *prakṛter āgataṁ prākṛtam ı prakṛtiḥ saṁskṛtam*; Siṁhadevagaṇin on Vāgbhaṭālaṁkāra, 2, 2 : *prakṛteḥ saṁskṛtādāgataṁ prākṛtam*; Prākṛtacandrikā in PETERSON, Third Report 343, 7 : *prakṛtiḥ saṁskṛtam ı tatrabhavatvāt prākṛtaṁ smṛtam.* Cf. Narasiṁha, Prākṛtaśabdapradīpikā, p. 1 : *prakṛteḥ saṁskṛtāyāstu vikṛtiḥ prākṛti matā*, and Prākṛtasañjīvanī in Vāsudeva on Karpūramañjarī, ed. Bomb. 9, 11 : *prākṛtasya tu sarvameva saṁskṛtaṁ yoniḥ.* For other etymologies see § 16.

§ 2. The Rasikasarvasva in Nārāyaṇa on Gītagovinda, 5, 2, teaches : *saṁskṛtāt prākṛtam iṣṭaṁ tato'pabhraṁśabhāṣaṇam*, "it is taken for granted that from Sanskrit originated Prākrit, whence the Apabhraṁśa language". A quotation in Śaṅkara on Śakuntalā, 9, 10[1] limits this view, *saṁskṛtāt prākṛtaṁ śreṣṭhaṃ tato'pabhraṁśabhāṣaṇam*, "from Sanskrit originated the best Prākrit, and from this the Apabhraṁśa language". According to Daṇḍin, Kāvyādarśa, I, 34, Māhārāṣṭrī (§ 12) is the best Prākrit : *mahārāṣṭrāśrayāṁ bhāṣāṁ prakṛṣṭaṁ prākṛtaṁ viduḥ.* It is explained from the fact that Māhārāṣṭrī is considered to be nearest to Sanskrit. When the Indians speak simply about Prākrit, they almost always thereby mean Māhārāṣṭrī.[2] According to them Māhārāṣṭrī has the credit of being the basis of the other Prākrit languages,[3] and in the manuals written by the native grammarians Māhārāṣṭrī occupies the first place. The oldest grammarian Vararuci devotes nine chapters, having 424 rules, to Māhārāṣṭrī, and only one chapter to each of the other three languages treated by him, and that only with 14, 17 and 32 rules respectively, and at the end (12, 32) he announces that, whatever, with regard to the lastly dealt with three Prākrits, remains unsaid, with respect to that these dialects have common characteristics with Māhārāṣṭrī : *śeṣaṁ māhārāṣṭrivat.* So do the other grammarians.

1. PISCHEL, De Gr. Pr. p. 1 — 2. LASSEN, Inst. p. 7, 11 f.; MUIR, OST. 22, 43 ff. — 3. Mārkaṇḍeya fol. 4. Somewhat differently Vararuci 10, 2; 11, 2; but compare MUIR, l. c.

§ 3. With regard to what we are to understand broadly by the term Prākrit, the Indian grammarians differ from one another. Vr. considers Māhārāṣṭrī, Paiśācī, Māgadhī and Śaurasenī as Prākrit. Hc. would include in it also Ārṣa (§ 16), Cūlikāpaiśācī, and Apabhraṁśa. He is followed by Trivikrama, Siṁharāja, Narasiṁha and Lakṣmīdhara, with this difference that Trivikrama excludes Ārṣa, while Siṁharāja, Narasiṁha and Lakṣmīdhara take no notice of it. Mārkaṇḍeya, fol. 2ff., divides Prākrit into four classes: *bhāṣā*, *vibhāṣā*, *apabhraṁśa*, *paiśāca*. He includes Māhārāṣṭrī, Śaurasenī, Prācyā, Āvantī and Māgadhī under *bhāṣā*, whilst in a polemic against some unnamed author, he rejects Ardhamāgadhī, which, according to him, is nothing but a form of Māgadhī, that is not very much different from Śaurasenī, Dākṣiṇātyā, which has no special characteristic, and Bālhīkī which belongs to Māgadhī. Under the *vibhāṣāḥ* he includes the following five dialects: Śākārī, Cāṇḍālī, Śābarī, Ābhīrikī, Śākkī, and denies the status of being considered as a *vibhāṣā* to Oḍrī and Drāviḍī. He then traces back the 27 kinds of Apabhraṁśa to three only, namely to Nāgara, Vrācaḍa, and Upanāgara, the 11 Paiśācī dialects to the three Nāgaras : Kaikeya, Śaurasena, and Pāñcāla.[2] Rāmatarkavāgīśa[3] teaches in the same manner. All the grammarians consider Māhārāṣṭrī, Śaurasenī, Māgadhī, and Paiśācī as the different Prākrit languages.

1. He is not Bharata, as may be concluded from the fact that the stanza dealing with the Vibhāṣāḥ is almost identical with the one given in Bhāratīyanāṭyaśāstra, 17, 49. All the other stanzas show deviations from those of Bharata. The stanza is quoted also in Prākṛtacandrikā of Kṛṣṇapaṇḍita, in PETERSON, Third Report, p. 346 ff. Cf. also Rāmatarkavāgīśa in LASSEN, Inst. p. 21. — 2. The text was partly published by AUFRECHT, Cat. Oxon, p. 181. — 3. LASSEN, Inst. p. 19-23; cf. Kramadīśvara 5, 99, and Bhāratīyanāṭyaśāstra 17, 48ff.

§ 4. Vr. does not mention Apabhraṁśa at all (§ 3). It would, however, be wrong to conclude therefrom, with LASSEN[1], that this dialect is younger than Vr.[2] Therefore, with Bloch,[3] Vararuci should not needlessly be accused of inaccuracy and superfluity. The reason is that Vr. along with others does not consider Apabhraṁśa to be Prākrit. As Namisādhu on Rudraṭa, Kāvyālaṁkāra 2, 11 remarks, some postulate three languages : Prākrit, Sanskrit and Apabhraṁśa: *yaduktaṁ kaiścid yathā* । *prākṛtaṁ saṁskṛtaṁ caitadapabhraṁśa iti tridhā*. To this group belongs Daṇḍin, who in his Kāvyādarśa 1, 32, distinguishes between four kinds of literary works, (1) those that are in Sanskrit, (2) those that are in Prākrit, (3) those that are in Apabhraṁśa, and finally, (4) those that are written in languages, more than one (*miśra*).[4] Under Apabhraṁśa Daṇḍin includes the language of the Ābhīras etc., when used in poetical works (*kāvyeṣu*) : in treatises (*śāstreṣu*) they call everything, whatever is different from Sanskrit, Apabhraṁśa. Mārkaṇḍeya fol. 2 in a citation includes the language of the Ābhīras under the *vibhāṣāḥ* (§ 3), rather than among the dialects of Apabhraṁśa, of which he names 26; such as Pāñcāla, Mālava, Gauḍa, Oḍra, Kāliṅgya, Kārṇāṭaka, Drāviḍa, Gurjara, and so on. Consequently, he uses the term Apabhraṁśa for popular languages of Aryan and non-Aryan origins. Against this Rāmatarkavāgīśa remarks that Apabhraṁśa should not be included under the *vibhāṣāḥ* in view of the fact that they are used in dramas etc. : only the actually spoken languages of the people are to be called Apabhraṁśa. According to him, Māgadhī, as a literary language, is a *bhāṣā*, and an Apabhraṁśa as a popular language.[3]

Ravikara, in Bollensen on Vikr. p. 509, distinguishes between two kinds of Apabhraṁśa. The one is based on Prākrit and differs slightly from it in flexion, composition and word-formation, and the other is a popular dialect (*deśabhāṣā*).[6] Whilst Sanskrit and Prākrit follow the rules that are framed about their form, Apabhraṁśa is dominated by the speech of the common people. The older Vāgbhaṭa holds a similar opinion about Apabhraṁśa. In Vāgbhaṭālaṅkāra 2, 1 he names four languages: Sanskrit, Prākrit, Apabhraṁśa and Bhūtabhāṣita i.e. Paiśācī (§ 27) and under 2, 3 he remarks that Apabhraṁśa is the pure language of the different countries : *apabhraṁśastu tacchuddhaṁ tattaddeśeṣu bhāṣitam.* The younger Vāgbhaṭa in Alaṁkāratilaka 15, 3 differentiates between Sanskrit, Prākrit, Apabhraṁśa and Grāmyabhāṣā. In an inscription from Valabhī, Guhasena is praised on account of the high degree of skilfulness shown by him in his works written in three languages, namely Sanskrit, Prākrit and Apabhraṁśa[7] CIA. 10,284. Rudraṭa, Kāvyālaṁkāra 2, 12, names six languages; Sanskrit, Prākrit, Māgadhabhāṣā, Piśācabhāṣā, Śūrasenī and Apabhraṁśa, which has several divisions according to the difference in locality : *ṣaṣṭho'tra bhūribhedo deśaviśeṣād apabhraṁśaḥ.* The same six different kinds of languages are mentioned also by Amaracandṛa, Kāvyakalpalatāvṛtti p. 8.

1. IAlt.2², 1169. -- 2. Weber, IStr. 2, 57; Pischel, KB. 8, 145. — 3. Vararuci und Hemacandra (Gütersloh 1893), p. 14 f. = KZ. 33, 332 f. — 4. He is followed by Kavicandra in Kāvyacandrikā, in Lassen, Inst. p. 32. The number is not clear in Bhojadeva, Sarasvatīkaṇṭhābharaṇa 2, 7 ff., p. 56. — 5. Lassen, Inst., p. 21 f.; cf. Muir, OST. 2², 46. — 6. Somadeva in his Kathāsaritsāgara, 6, 148 mentions *saṁskṛtam*, *prākṛtam* and *deśabhāṣā* as the different languages; *bhāṣātrayaṁ yanmanuṣyeṣu saṁbhavet.* Cf. Kṣemendra, Bṛhaṭkathāmañjarī, 6, 47. 52. 7 Text — sūrasenī.

§ 5. Accordingly we have to consider as Apabhraṁśa the popular languages of India. Undoubtedly there were written in it literary works of every kind already in time much earlier than that of the literary monuments, that are still preserved for us. For the drama the Bhāratīyanāṭyaśāstra accepts this, whilst it permits the actors to use, beside Śaurasenī, the language of the drama, a provincial language optionally : *śaurasenaṁ samāsritya bhāṣā kāryā tu nāṭake athavā chandataḥ kāryā deśabhāṣā prayoktṛbhiḥ.* We need not take into consideration the artificially regulated dramas of the classical period, particularly the popular theatres of the type of *yātrā* of Bengal[1] or the musical plays of Hindusthān[2] and the popular theatres of Almora[3] and Nepal[4], a sample whereof occurs in the Hariścandranṛtyam[5]. This Apabhraṁśa has never been called Prākrit, but probably Apabhraṁśa which, according to Daṇḍin, could be used in literary poetry and according to Ravikara, deviates just slightly from Prākrit (§ 4), to which it can be traced back ultimately (§ 2). It is presented before us in some of the Prākrit grammarians, who treat Apabhraṁśa as well, in Piṅgala and in some other works (§ 29). The Indians always understand by the term Prākrit the literary languages. Pṛthvīdhara, in the introduction to his commentary on Mṛcchakaṭikā, p. v, ed. Stenzler = p. 493 ed. Godabole[6] says expressly: *māhārāṣṭryādayaḥ kāvya eva prayujyante*. Hc. 2, 174, p. 68. says that the words that are not used by earlier poets (*pūrvaiḥ kavibhiḥ*) in Prākrit are to be avoided. Daṇḍin, Kāvyādarśa 1, 35 remarks that Śaurasenī, Gauḍī, Lāṭī and others of the kind would be used in conversation under the name Prākrit, and Rāmatarkavāgīśa forbids inclusion of Apabhraṁśa among the *vibhāṣāḥ*, when they are used in dramas etc. (§ 4). We have, therefore, to differentiate between the Śaurasenī-Apabhraṁśa, the old popular language of Śūrasena, from which evolved the modern Gujarātī and Mārwārī[7], and Śaurasenī Prākrit, the artificial language, that is the language of prose of theatres, and whose all the characteristics resemble those of Sanskrit. But Śaurasenī-Apabhraṁśa would be used in lyrical poems too, now and then and that on the model of Māhārāṣṭrī, the Prākrit of lyrics and of artificial epics, remodelled for the purpose of song and recitation with its chief dialectical peculiarities left untouched. Hc. 4, 446 gives an example : Ap. *kaṇṭhi pālambu kidu radie*, which in Śaurasenī Pkt. would be *kaṇṭhe pālambaṁ kidaṁ radie*, but in Māhārāṣṭrī, with the elision of *d* it would be *kaṇṭhe pālambaṁ kaaṁ raie*. Erroneously Hc. lays down that Apabhraṁśa generally follows Śaurasenī Prākrit throughout (§ 28). Likewise there existed one Mahārāṣṭra-Apabhraṁśa, whence has developed the modern Marāṭhī[8], in addition to Mahārāṣṭra-Prākrit, *i. e.* Māhārāṣṭrī of the grammarians, as well as Māgadha-Apabhraṁśa (§ 4), which through the Lāṭa-dialect has essentially continued to this day as the dialects of Bihar and of West Bengal[9] and a Māgadh-Prākrit, *i.e.* Māgadhī of the grammarians[10]. For Paiśācī see § 27, and for Ārṣa see § 16.

1. WILSON, Select Specimens of the Theatre of the Hindus 2³, 412 ff.; NISIKANTA CHATTOPĀDHYĀYA, Indische Essays (Zürich 1883) p. 1 ff. — 2. F. ROSEN, Die Indarsabhā des Amānat (Leipzig 1892), Einleitung. — 3. S. v. OLDENBURG, Zapiski Vostočnāgo Otdelnija Imperatorskago Russkago Archeologičescago Obsščestva 5, 290 ff. — 4. KLATT, De trecentis Cānakyae poetae Indici sententiis (Halle 1873) p. 1 ff.; PISCHEL, Katalog der Bibliothek der DMG. (Leipzig 1881) 2, 5 ff. — 5. Das Hariçcandranṛtyam, Ein altnepalasisches Tanzspiel, published by A. Conardy (Leipzig 1891). — 6. From this springs the quotation from Lalitadikṣita in GOḌABOLE, p. 1. — 7. PISCHEL, Academy 1873, p. 398; HOERNLE, Comp. Gr. p. XXV. — 8. GARREZ, JA. VI. 20, p. 203 ff. (Paris 1872); wrongly HOERNLE, Comp. Gr. p. XXII. — 9. HOERNLE, Comp. Gr. p. XXIV. In Academy l. c. I have wrongly designated Pāli as Māgadha-Apabhraṁśa, against which E. KUHN, Beiträge zur Pāli Grammatik rightly (Berlin 1875) p. 8. I corrected the mistake in Jenaer Literaturzeitung, 1875, p. 316. — 10. The theory enunciated by me in the Academy, 1873, p. 379 f. has been here improved upon on various points. HOERNLE, Comp. Gr. p. XVII ff. is substantially in agreement with me. In very many details I differ from him, as is shown in the following paragraphs too. SHANKAR PĀNDURANG PANDIT has confused Apabhraṁśa with Prākrit in Gaūḍavaho p. 4 LV. ff.

§ 6. So the Prākrit languages are artificial dialects in so far as they are considerably altered from literary view-points by poets. But they are not artificial dialects, if thereby it is meant that they are the result of efforts of poets[1]. What is true with these dialects is equally true with Sanskrit, which by itself in fact is not the commonly spoken language of cultured Indians, does not have these at the base[2], but certainly goes back to one of the popular dialects, which on political or religious grounds was raised to the status of a literary medium[3]. But the difference is that it is wholly impossible to trace back all Prākrits to one common source. At least they could not have developed out of Sanskrit, as is generally held by Indian scholars and HOEFER[4], LASSEN[5], BHĀṆḌĀRKAR[6], and JACOBI[7]. All the Prākrit languages have a series of common grammatical and lexical characteristics with the Vedic language, and such are significantly missing from Sanskrit. Such correspondences are : the comparatively greater freedom in saṁdhi-rules , the change of the intervocalic *ḍ, ḍh* to *ḷ, ḷh*; the suffix *-ttaṇa* = Ved. *-tvana*[8], the svarabhakti, the gen. sing of the fem. bases in *-āe* = Ved.*-āyai*; the ins. plur. in *-ehiṁ* = Ved. *-ebhiḥ*; the imperative *hohi* = Ved. *bodhi*; *tā. jā, ĕttha* = Ved. *tāt, yā., itthā*; *te, me* as accusative; *amhe* = Ved. *asme*; Prākrit *pāso* "eye" = Ved. *paś*[9]; AMg. *vaggūhiṁ* = *vagnubhiḥ*; *saddhiṁ* = *sadhrim*; A *dive dive* = Ved. *dive dive*; J. Ś. A. *kidha*, AMg. A. *kiha* = Ved. *kathā́*; *māiṁ*, Ved. *mā́kim*; *ṇāiṁ* = Ved. *nákim*; AMg *viū* = *viduḥ*[10]; Mg. *-āho*, *-āhu*, A. *-ahŏ* = Ved. *āsaḥ*; M. JM. A. *kuṇai*, JŚ. *kuṇadi* = *kṛṇoti*; AMg JM. *sakkā* = Ved. *śakyāt*; A. *sāhu* = Ved. *śaśvat*; AMg. *ghiṁsu* = Ved. *ghraṁsa*; M. AMg. JM. Ś. A. *khambha* = Ved. *skambha*; M. AMg. JM.Ś. *rukkha* "tree" = Ved. *rukṣa*; future *sŏcchaṁ* from Ved. *śruṣ*; the (AMg.) infinitive in *-ae*, *-ttae* = Ved. *-tavai*; the absolutive (A.) in *-ppi*, *-pi*, *-vi* = Ved. *-tvi*, in = *ppiṇu* = Ved. *tvinam*, etc., what have been described in relevant places in this grammar. These alone make the hypothesis that Sanskrit was the source of the different Prākrits impossible[11].

1. BEAMES, Comp. Gr. 1, 201, 223; SORENSEN, Om Sanskrits Stilling i den almindelige Sprogudvikling i Indian (Kobenhavn 1894, p. 220 ff. PISCHEL De gr. Pr. p. 30 ff. should be corrected accordingly.— 2. FRANKE, BB. 17, 71. I doubt if ever there was a living language of the cultured people for the whole of Āryāvarta. Cf. also WACKERNAGEL, Altind. Gr. p. XLII, note 7.—3. In GGA. 1884, p. 512, I had suggested that classical Sanskrit was based on the dialect of Brahmāvarta. Cf. WACKERNAGEL, Altind. Gram. p. XXVI, note 11 for further literature on this topic. — 4. De Prakrita dialecto § 8. — 5. Inst. p. 25 ff.; IAlt. 2[2], 1163, note 5. — 6. JBoAS., 16, 315. — 7. KZ. 24, 614, wherein he says that Pāli and Prākrit are essentially a later form of Sanskrit. — 8. v. BRADKE, ZDMG. 40, 673. — 9. PISCHEL and GELDNER, Ved. Stud. 1, p. XXXI, note 2. — 10. Ved. 2, 235 f. — 11. WEBER goes too far when he (IS. 2, 111) does not see in Prākrit anything, but a degenerated old Vedic dialect. Cf. § 9.

§ 7. The affinity of the Prākrit languages with the middle and new Indo-Aryan popular dialects is not less closer than that with the Vedic language. The inscriptions of Aśoka provide us with specimens of at least four middle Indian popular dialects. The inscriptions, dating between the 2nd and 3rd centuries A. D., that are found in caves, stūpas, plates, etc., prove that there was a popular dialect that was equally intelligible in a considerably greater part of India. SENART has designated the language of these inscriptions the "Prākrit monumental[1]". This is misleading, since it suggests that Pkt. developed purely as an artificial language. We have little ground to accept this view or to agree with KERN[2] that Pāli is an artificial language, though both Pāli and Prākrit, like Ārṣa (§ 16), underwent various forms of changes as literary languages. I propose to name the Prākrit dialect of most of these inscriptions, as they are found in caves, as L e ṇ a -d i a l e c t, after *leṇa* = Skt. *layana* "hole", which occurs so often in these inscriptions. A parallel is met with in the name of the L ā ṭ a-d i a l e c t from *lāṭa* = Pkt. *laṭṭhi* = Skt. *yaṣṭi* "pillar". All these dialects are continuations not of Sanskrit, but of sister dialects thereof, and their characteristics, in a great measure, correspond to those of different Prākrits. Some examples in connection with Aśoka's first edict may here be enough. We find in the first edict the participle of the causative of *likh* in Girnār *lekhāpitā*, in Shāhbāzgarhī *likhapitu*, in Jaugaḍa *likhāpitā*, and in Mansehra [*l*]*ikhapita*, a form that occurs in the pillar edicts as well, (SENART 2, 597). The Leṇa-dialect has similar formations from roots ending in a consonant: *ba*[*ṁ*]*dhāpayati*, *kiḍāpayati*, *piḍāpayati*, *va*[*ṁ*]*dāpayati*, (Hāthigumphā Inscription p. 155. 158. 160. 163)[3], likewise Pāli: *likhāpeti*, that is very often found also in Prākrit [§ 552;] Aśoka's *likhāpita* corresponds to JM. *lihāviya* (Erz. 63, 31), Aśoka's *likhāpayisaṁ* (Girnār 14, 3), Mg. *lihāvaïśśaṁ* (Mṛcch. 136, 21). — Girnār *prajūhitavyaṁ*, from *hu* (to offer a sacrifice) with *pra*[4], shows an extension of the present stem, as is usual in Pāli and Prākrit. — In Girnār, *samājamhi* and *mahānasamhi* the ending of the pronominal declension occurs in the nominal loc.; Shāhbāzgarhī and Khālsī have *mahanasasi*, *mahānasasi*, that is *mahānasaṃsi*, a form that occurs very often in the pillar and stray edicts. In the Leṇa-dialect are found *ja*[*m*]*budipamhi* (Karle Inscription, No. 1)[5] *thuvamhi* = *stūpe*,[6] *anugāmimhi* (Nāsik No 6ª)[7], *tiraṇhumhi* (Nāsik No. 11ᵇ.19),[8] also *tiraṇhumi*, that is to say *tiraṇhummi*[9]. To this corresponds in Prākrit M. JM. JŚ. AMg. the localtive in *-mmi*, AMg. *-ṁsi*. One notices further the use of *asti* in the plural, as in Prākrit *atthi* (§ 498), and that of *se*, that is exactly so found in AMg. I shall, from the Leṇa-dialect, refer only to the declension of stems in *i-* and *u-*, whereof the gen. sing. ends in *-no* and *-sa*, *i. e.* in as, *-ssa*; it is so in Prākrit, where the gen. sing. of the *n-* stem ends in *-sa* too. On all these points, as on very many others, whereof no correspondence is to be found in Sanskrit, Prākrit agrees with the middle Indian popular-dialects.

1. Les inscriptions de Piyadasi, 2, 488. He is followed by SORENSEN, I. c. p. 187.— 2. Over de Jaartelling der zuidelijke Buddhisten (Amestrdam 1873), p. 14 f. — 3. Actes du Sixième Congrès International des Orientalistes (Leide 1885), 3, 2. — 4. PISCHEL GGA. 1881, 1323 f. — 5. Inscriptions from the Cave-Temples of Western India. By JAS. BURGESS and BHAGWANLAL INDRAJI (Bombay 1881) p. 28. — 6. SENART, l. c. 2, 472. — 7. Arch. Survey of Western India 4, 101. — 8. Arch S. of W. I, 4, 106. 114. — 9. Arch. S. of W.I. 4. 99.

§ 8. On account of the analytical character of the new Indian dialects naturally it is no more possible to demonstrate the affinity of Pkt., in the matter of flexion, with them. But this relationship is more striking in phonology and morphology, as also in the case of the Middle Indian. Patañjali, Vyākaraṇamahābhāṣya 1, p. 5, 21 f. remarks: of each correct word there are many of incorrect formations (*apabhraṃśāḥ*); thus for example of the word *gauḥ* (cow), the *apabhraṁśāḥ* are *gāvi*, *goṇi*, *gotā*, *gopotalikā*[1]. Of these, in Prākrit, the most usual form is *gāvi*; of JM. *goṇi*, the masculine is *goṇo* (§ 393). Under Pāṇini 1, 3, 1 (p. 259) Kātyāyana mentions *āṇapayati*, to which Patañjali adds *vaṭṭati* and *vaḍḍhati*; Patañjali under Pāṇini 3, 1, 91 (2, 74) records a form *supati*, and Kaiyaṭa expressly considers all such verbal forms as Apabhraṁśa[2]. The inscriptions of Aśoka (SENART 2,559) and the Leṇa-dialect (Arch S. of W. I., 4,104.110) have *ānapayati*; to it corresponds Ś. Mg. *āṇavedi* (§ 551), whereas Pāli has *āṇāpeti*. KIELHORN has already noted that Pāli has similarly sounding equivalent forms for *vaṭṭati*, *vaḍḍhati* and *supati*. The Prākrit equivalents to these are: M. AMg. JM. *vaṭṭaï*, JŚ. Ś. *vaṭṭadi*, M. AMg. JM. *vaḍḍhaï*, Ś. *vaḍḍhadi* (§ 289. 291), M. *suvaï, suaï*, JM. *suyaï* (§ 497). The Indian grammarians and rhetoricians divide Prākrit words into three classes : 1) *saṁskṛtasama*, "Sanskrit-like" (C. 1, 1; Sr. in PISCHEL, De gr. Pr. p. 40), commonly designated as *tatsama*, "that-like (that is to say like Sanskrit)", (Triv. in PISCHEL, l. c., p. 29; Mk. fol. 2; Daṇḍin, Kāvyādarśa 1, 32; Dhanika on Daśarūpa 2, 60), and also referred to as *tattulya* (Vāgbhaṭālaṁkāra 2, 2; and *samānaśabda* (Bhāratīyan. 17, 3); 2), *saṁskṛtabhava*, "originated from Sanskrit" (Sr.), commonly designated as *tadbhava* (Triv.; Mk; Daṇḍin.; Dhanika), also as *saṁskṛtayoni* (Hc. I, 1; C.), *tajja* (Vāgbhaṭa), and *vibhraṣṭa* (Bhāratīyan. 17, 3); and 3) *deśya* (Hc.,; Triv.; Sr.; Mk.; Vāgbhaṭa) or *deśi* (Deśīn. p. I. 2; Daṇḍin; Dhanika), also *deśiprasiddha* (C.) and *deśimata* (Bhāratīyan. 17, 37)[3]. The words that have the same form both in Prākrit and in Sanskrit are *tatsama* words. Thus for example, *kara, komala, jala, soma*, etc. The *tadbhava* words are classed as *sādhyamānasaṁskṛtabhavāḥ*, and *siddhasaṁskṛtabhavāḥ*. To the former class belong the Prākrit words that presuppose Sanskrit words from which they are derived in their unfinished form without an affix or suffix. This especially refers to the flexion by which a word is first of all made fit according to the rules of grammar for use (*sādhyamāna*). BEAMES has appropriately called them "early tadbhavas"[4]. They are the independent basic elements of Prākrit. The latter class includes the Prākrit words that are derived from grammatically complete (*siddha*) Sanskrit words; as AMg. *vandittā* = Skt. *vanditvā*. Although a large number of tatsama and tadbhava words are found in all the new Indian languages, it is not correct to presume that all such kinds of words originated from Sanskrit alone. The fact that all new Indian languages do not go back to Sanskrit today needs no more proof.

1. WEBER, IS. 13, 365. — 2. KIELHORN, ZDMG, 39, 327. SORENSEN, l. c., p. 180f.— 3. Cf. also BEAMES, Comp. Gr. 1, 11 ff; PISCHEL, De gr. Pr. p. 30ff.; BB. 3, 235; HORENLE, Comp. Gr. p. XXXVIII ff. Designated as the fourth class by Bhuvanapāla in WEBER, IS. 16 59 are the words that depend upon the *sāmānyabhāṣā*. — as Saṁskṛtasama and Deśaja. Bhoja, further Sṛṅgāraprakāśa, p. 102 divides Prākrit, as Sahaja, Lakṣita and Śliṣṭa.

4. Comp. Gr. 1, 17. — 5. PISCHEL on Hc. 1. 1.

§ 9. The Indians include under the *Deśya* or *Deśi* class very heterogeneous elements. They consider all such words to belong to this class as they cannot trace back to Sanskrit either in form or in meaning. It depends upon their knowledge of Sanskrit and ability in etymologising that some of them call a word to be *Deśya*, while others include it either among the tatsamas or among the tadbhavas. So we have many words that are classed as Deśī, even though they go back to genuine Sanskrit roots, simply-because they do not have closely corresponding Sanskrit words; thus for example *pāso* (eye; Triv. in BB. 6, 104) or *pāṣaṃ* (Deśīn 6, 75) from AMg. *pāsaï* = Skt. *paśyati*; or *sivvī* (needle; Deśīn, 8, 29; Triv. in BB. 3,260) from Skt. *sīvyati*. Further, there are some compound words whose individual component parts are true Sanskrit, nevertheless the special meaning ascribed to them in Prākrit is not to be found in that language : thus *acchivaḍaṇaṁ* (closing of the eyes; Deśīn. I, 39 with commentary; Triv. in BB. 13, 5) = *akṣi+patana*; or *sattāvisaṁjoaṇo* (the moon; Deśīn. 8,22; C. 1, 1 p. 39) = Siṁhadevagaṇin on Vāgbhaṭālaṁkāra 2, 2) = *saptāviṁśati+dyotana*[1]. Then there are words for which there is no root in Sanskrit. Thus *joḍaṁ* (constellation; Deśīn. 3. 49), *joḍo* (Triv. in BB. 13, 17 f.); or *tuppo* (anointed Pāiẏal. 233; Deśīn. 5, 22; Hāla 22 v. l. 289. 520), that is connected to Marāṭhī *tūpa* (clarified butter; ghee)[2]. Lastly there are words that exhibit some rare phonetic law, as *gaharo* (vulture; Pāiẏal. 126; Deśīn. 2, 84; Triv. in BB. 6. 93), by Trivikrama rightly equated as = *gṛdhra*, or *vihuṇḍuo* (Rāhu; Deśīn. 7, 65; Triv. in BB. 3, 252) = *vidhuṁtudaḥ*[3]. Among the *Deśi* words are included the largely numerous verb-forms that are designated as dhātvādeśa, "root subsitutes" by grammarians, and they cover much space in Indian grammars (Vr. 8, 1 ff.; Hc. 4, 1 ff.; Kī. 4, 46 ff.; Mk. fol. 53 ff.). Here Sanskrit fails miserably in rendering any help, though correspondence with New Indian languages is most rigorous[4]. As the name indicates, by *Deśya* people have come to understand also "provincialisms". In Hemacandra's Rāẏaṇāvalī. (§ 36), the largest collection of these provincialisms, the Dhātvādeśas have not been mentioned (Deśīn. I, 3), and Hc. (I, 4), in clear terms, excludes all such provincialisms as are not current in Prākrit. Many such Deśī words, either from Apabhraṁśa or from Prākrit, have been taken into Sanskrit dictionaries and Dhātupāṭhas also[5]. It is possible that stray non-Aryan words may have been got included in the Deśī words, but the bulk of such elements is Proto-Aryan, though our search for them in Sanskrit is fruitless. Namisādhu on Rudraṭa, Kāvyālaṁkāra 2, 12, gives an etymology of the word Prākrit, according to which the basis (*prakṛti*) of Prākrit and Sanskrit is the natural current language of the people, that cannot be fashioned according to the rules of grammar, or this Prākrit itself is this current language (§ 16). As already shown, such an assumption is unjustified. Sanskrit forms the chief constituent of individual Prākrit dialects, especially of Māhārāṣṭrī of poetical works, such as Gaüḍavaho and Rāvaṇavaho, that are composed according the model of Sanskrit. In them, therefore, the number of Deśī words is diminishingly small, while[7] they are very significant in JM. I agree entirely with SENART,[8] that all the Prākrits go back to popular dialects as their source and that their all the essential elements originally developed from the living speeches, but such of these dialects, as were raised to the status of literary languages, exactly like Sanskrit, underwent significant alterations.

1. Not perhaps..*yojana*. The 27 *nakṣatras* are meant. — 2. WEBER, ZDMG, 28, 335. — 3. Cf. Deśīn. I, 3; BÜHLER, Pāiẏalacchī p. 11 ff.; SORENSEN, l. c. 225 ff. — 4. Many

examples are to be found in the translation of Hc. and in WEBER's, observations on Hāla. — 5. ZACHARIAE, Beiträge zur indischen Lexicographie (Berlin 1883), p. 53 ff. Cf. also WACKERNAGEL. Altind. Gr. p. LI ff. — 6. BENFEY, Vollständige Grammatik § 140, 2; PISCHEL, BB. 3, 236, 264; 6, 84; BÜHLER, WZKM. 8, 17 ff.; 122 ff.; FRANKE, ibid. 321 ff. — 7. PISCHEL, GGA. 1880, p. 326, wherein it has been remarked that in the notes on Rāvaṇavaho there is much valuable material. SHANKAR P. PANDIT, Gaüḍavaho p. LVI. — -8. L'épigraphie et l'histoire-linguistique de l'Inde. Extracts from the reviews of the Séance de l' Académie des Inscriptions et Belles Lettres (Paris 1886), p. 17 ff.; Les inscriptions de Piyadasi 2. 530 ff. SENART has not, however, as already mentioned under section 7, note 1, above, taken Prākrit in its strictly correct sense.

§ 10. The inscriptions that are preserved for us in Prākrit are the documents of gift of the Pallava king Śivaskandavarman, those of the queens of the Pallava Yuvarāja Vijayabuddhavarman[1], the Ghaṭayāla inscription of Kakkuka, and the fragments of Somadeva's Lalitavigraharājanāṭaka. The first one was published by BŪHLER, EI. 1, 2 ff; certain improvements were made in it by LEUMANN, ibid 2,483ff. and PISCHEL, GN. 1895, 210 ff. I indicate them by PG. = Pallava Grant. BÜHLER has expressed the opinion that in these inscriptions there are certain characteristics that appear only in literary Prākrit. Thus the change of *ya* into *ja* in *kāravĕjjā, vaṭṭeja, hoja, jo, saṁjutto*; the more frequent change of dental *n* into cerebral *ṇ* : the occurrence of voiced consonants in place of unvoiced ones, thus *kassava aṇuvaṭṭhāveti, vi, bhaḍa, kaḍa*; the writing of doubled consonants, such as in *aggiṭṭhoma, assamedha, dhamma, savattha, raṭṭhika* etc.[2] All these peculiarities are found in a scattered manner also in one or the other inscription in the Leṇa-dialect.[3] But there is no other inscription in which these characteristics, all taken together, and in such large quantities, occur in so far as the language may be regarded as Prākrit. But it no way is absolutely pure Prākrit. *ya* stands beside *ja*: *na* is often retained; surds mostly remain unmodified; even doubled consonants are written in a simple manner : *sivakhaṁdavamo, gumike, vadhamike* etc.[4] The following are gross irregularities against Prākrit : *kāṁcipurā*: (5, 1) for *kaṁcipurā*; *ātteya°* (6, 13) for *atteya°*; *vatsa°* (6, 22) for *vaccha°*, *cāttāri* (6, 39) for *cattāri*; unusual are *vitarāma* (5, 7) for *vitarāmo*; *dūdha* (6, 31) for *duddha*, *°dattaṁ* (6, 12) for *°diṇṇaṁ*; *datā* (7, 48), i. e. *dattā* for *diṇṇā*. It can clearly be seen that the language is an artificial one.[5] For history of Prākrit, the inscription is not without interest and worth, and it has been, therefore, used regularly in this grammar, although the Leṇa-dialect and the so called Gāthā-dialect[6] are beyond its sphere. The inscription of Kakkuka, indicated by KI., was published by Munsiff DEBI PRASĀD, JRAS. 1195, p. 513 ff.[7] It is written in Jaina Māhārāṣṭrī (§ 20).

1. Published by FLEET, IA. 9, 100 ff. Almost unusable. Cf. BÜHLER. EI. 1, 2, note. — 2. BÜHLER, l. c. 2ff. — 3. SENART, Piyadasi 2, 489ff. 518ff. — 4 BÜHLER l. c. p. 2ff. — 5. To it applies even more accurately what SENART, l. c. 2, 494, says on the Leṇa-dialect: this language is, then, neither wholly popular nor entirely regulated. — 6. That this name is not appropriate has been remarked correctly by SENART, l. c. 2, 469ff. His suggestion to call the language "mixed Sanskrit" would, however, meet with little approval. Further literature in WACKERNAGEL, Altind. Gr. p. XXXIX f.

§ 11. The fragments of Somadeva's Lalitavigraharājanāṭaka are found also in two basalt-plates, discovered in Ajmīr. They have been published by KIELHORN, IA, 20, 201 ff. and recently in GN. 1893, 552 ff. In them, occur three Prākrit dialects, Māhārāṣṭrī, Śaurasenī, and Māgadhī. KONOW[1] has shown, exactly, as I had remarked in my first study of Prākrit,[2] that the Prākrit forms closely correspond to the rules of Hemacandra. But Hemacandra was hardly the authority, whose views were honoured by Somadeva. Hc. 4, 271 prescribes the absolutive in *-dūṇa* in Śaurasenī; Somadeva has the Māhārāṣṭrī form in *-ūṇa*; Hc. 4,280 requires *yyeva*, whereas Somadeva has *jjeva*; in Māgadhī in consonant-groups, Somadeva has *ś*, whereas Hc. 4,289 prescribes *s* ; the former lays down *śta* for *rth*, against *st* of Hc. 4,291 and *śka* for *hka* against *ska* of Hc. 4, 296. 297.[3] Hence it follows that the absolutive in *-ūṇa* may be an error committed by Somadeva himself; even *-dūṇa* may be wrong (§584); *śta* for *sta* as well may be an error committed in course of transmission, inasmuch as in 566,9 we find *yahastaṁ* = *yathārtham*. But as regards *śka* for *hka*, *ska* could hardly, with KONOW,[4] be considered to be a slip on the part of a scribe, since the examples are numerous. However, we cannot assess a higher value for this inscription than for any unique manuscript. It is full of gross errors against the dialects concerned, just like any manuscript of a drama. To the list of errors picked up by KONOW (l.c. p. 479) I add the following : Ś. *tujjha* (554, 4; see § 421); *jjeva* (554, 4; 555, 18) for *jeva* after anusvāra ; *ṇimmāya* (554, 13; see § 591); the passive *viloijjanti*, *pĕkkhijjanti* (554, 21. 22.) *kijjadu* (562, 24), *jaṁpijjadi* (568,6), the forms that are admitted by Hc. for *viloianti*, *pĕkkhianti*, *kariadu*, *jampiadi* (§ 535); *kitti* (555, 4) for *kiṁ ti*; *rayaṇāiṁ* (555, 15), *raaṇa* (560, 19) for *radaṇāiṁ* and *radaṇa*; *gihida* (560, 20) for *gahida*; *eārisaṁ* (563,3) for *edārisaṁ*. The dialectical inaccuracies in Māgadhī are :—*pĕśkiyyaṁdi* (565, 13) *pĕśkianti*, *pĕśkiyyasi* (565, 15) for *pĕśkiasi*, *yāṇiyyadi* (566, 1) for *yāṇiadi*, *pacakkhikadaṁ* (566, 1) for *paccaśki°*; *yahastaṃ* (566.9) for *yadhastaṁ*; *nijjhala*, *yujjha* (566, 9.11) for *ṇiyyhala*, *yuyyha* (cf. § 280, 284) ; *eva* (567,1) for *yeva*. These are the types of errors that always occur in manuscripts, just as *tamāpasara* (555, 11), *pacakkhāiṁ* (555, 14), *śśalūvaṁ* (565, 9). Moreover, most of these, if not all, would certainly disappear, if we had a few more manuscripts of the drama at our disposal. The presence of the absolutive in *-ūṇa*, and the passive in Ś. *-ijja*, and Mg. *-iyya*, may be mistakes committed by the author himself, as even Rājaśekhara, (§ 22) and later poets often mix up the dialects with one another. The writing of *n* in place of *ṇ* and insertion of *ẏ*[5] suggest Jaina influence. A second fragment, found in Ajmīr, of Haṙakelināṭaka, is ascribed to Vigraharājadeva himself and is dated November 22, 1153.[6] The grammar of Hemacandra at the earliest would have been completed towards the end of the Vikrama year 1197,[7] i.e. 1140 A.D. Consequently Somadeva and Hemacandra were contemporaries. Notwithstanding the errors these fragments are of the greatest importance for Māgadhī, that, here only has been handed down to us in a form, that is in agreement with the rules laid down by grammarians (§ 23).

1. GGA. 1894. 478ff. — 2. IA. 20, 204. — 3. KONOW, l.c., p. 581. — 4. l.c., p. 482.

— 5. KONOW, l.c., p. 480. — 6. KIELHORN, IA. 20, 201. — 7. BÜHLER, Über das Leben des Jaina Mönches Hemachandra (Wien 1889), p. 18.

§ 12. When one refers to the Prākrit language in general terms it is Māhārāṣṭrī (§ 2), that derives its name from Mahārāṣṭra, the land of the Marāṭhās, that is thereby meant. It is considered to be the best Prākrit. As shown by GARREZ) (§ 5) Māhārāṣṭrī, no doubt, has unmistakable points of contact with the Marāṭhī language.[1] No other dialect has been phonetically modified to such an extent for ornate purposes. The dropping of consonants had in M. been so extensive, as has been seen nowhere else, so that a large number of words that were phonetically quite different have assumed the same form. Thus :—M. *kaa* = *kaca* and *kṛta*; *kai* = *kati*, *kapi*, *kavi*, *kṛti* ; *kāa* = *kāka*, *kāca*, *kāya* ; *gaā* = *gatā*, *gadā*, *gajāḥ* ; *maa* = *mata*, *mada*, *maya*, *mṛga*, *mṛta*; *vaa* = *vacas*, *vayas*, *vrata*, *pada*; *sua* = *śuka*, *suta*, *śruta*, etc.[2] Therefore, it was not without reason that BEAMES designated M. the 'emasculated stuff'.[3] It was admitted long ago that its sound system was essentially determined by the fact that M. above all was used for musical stanzas. Such stanzas are the *gāhās* = *gāthās*, that are, for us, collected in the Sattasaī of Hāla, and the Vajjālagga of Jayavallabha,[4] and are scattered in the writings of authors on rhetorics, and are inserted in dramas as well. They were expressly designated as *gāhā*, 'song', 'musical stanza' thus for example H. 3, 500. 600. 698. 708, 709. 815; Vajjālagga 3 4. 9.10; p. 326, 6. The stanza that is written in the purest M. in Mudrār. 83, 2.3 and is addressed by Virādhagupta, who appears as a snake-charmer and Prākrit poet, to the minister Rākṣasa, is called by him *gāthā*, and Viśvanātha, Sāhityadarpaṇa 432, says that the women that are not of lowly origin speak Śaurasenī in dramas and that in their songs (*āsameva tu gāthāsu*) they should speak Māhārāṣṭrī. Priyaṁvadā calls the stanzas 55, 15, 16 of Śak. *gidaaṁ* = *gitakam* in 54, 8; Śakuntalā 55, 8 calls it *gidiā* = *gitikā*; the verses recited by the spy in Mudrārākṣasa 34, 6 ff. are called after 35, 1 *gidāiṁ*, " songs". The actress sings (*gāyati*) her song in M. : thus for example Śak. 2, 13; Mallikām. 19, 1; Kāleyak. 12, 6 (*viṇāṁ vādayanti gāyati*); Unmattar. 2, 17; cf. Mukund. 4, 20 ff.; about the stanzas that are recited from behind the stage it is said *nepathye giyate*; e. g. Śak. 95, 17; Viddhaś. 6, 1; Kāleyak. 3, 6; Karṇas. 3. 4. This use of M. in lyrics meant for musical purposes is undoubtedly the oldest, and in these the dropping of consonants in such large proportions is in the first place to be attributed to this cause.[5]

1. I do not think that it is correct to say like E. KUHN (KZ. 33, 478) that the oldest form of Māhārāṣṭri Prākrit is to be found in Pāli. — 2. Some examples have been given by SHANKAR P. PANDIT, Gaüḍavaho p. LVI., LVIII. —3. Comp. Gram. 1, 223. 4. BHĀṆḌĀRKAR, Report 1883, 84 (Bombay 1887), p. 17, 324ff. The correct name is *Vajjālagga* (3. 4. 5; (p. 326, 9) from which originated *Vajjālaya* (p. 326, 5). The word is derived from *vajjā* = *vrajyā* (B. R. s. v.); WEBER, Hāla,[2] p. XXXVIII; PISCHEL, Die Hofdichter des Lakṣmaṇasena (Göttingen, 1893), p. 30f.), and *lagga* (indication, mark; Deśin. 7, 17) = Skt. *lagna*. Its translation as *Padyālaya* is wrong. — 5. WEBER, IStr. 3, 159f.; 279; *Hāla*[2] p. XX.

§ 13. For a knowledge of M. the most essential work is the Sattasaī of Hāla. The first 370 stanzas were already published by WEBER under the title "Über das Saptaśatakam des Hāla, Leipzig, 1870.[1] WEBER brought out the addenda and corrigenda to his edition of the work in the ZDMG 26, 735 ff; 28, 345 ff., which were followed by a complete edition with a German translation and word-index : Das Saptaśatakam des Hāla, Leipzig, 1881. WEBER dealt upon Bhuvanapāla's commentary on Chekoktivicāralīlā in IS. 16, 1 ff. DURGĀ PRASĀD and KĀSĪNĀTH PĀṆḌURAṄG PARAB have, moreover, provided us with an edition of the work that is indispensable on account of the complete printed commentary and several good readings : The Gāthāsaptaśatī of Sātavāhana with the commentary of Gaṅgādharabhaṭṭa, Bombay, 1889 (Kāvyamālā 21). WEBER fixes as the earliest limit to the date of the collection as the 3rd. century A.D., and in any case, according to him, it was compiled earlier than the 7th century, and he has, in the introduction to his complete edition, dealt elaborately with the six different recensions of the work, of which the recension of Bhuvanapāla is the seventh (p. xxvii ff.). We gather from the Sattasaī that there was in M. a literature that was very extensive. Originally the name of the author of each of the stanzas was appended to it (H. 709). Of these names unfortunately we know only a few, many whereof are in corrupt form, and the tradition varies to a great measure in the matter of division of the verses into words. The commentators of the vulgata have given 112 names, Bhuvanapāla gives 384, considering Sātavāhana, (Śātavāhana, Śālivāhana, Sālāhaṇa) and Hāla to be one and the same person. Two of these poets, H a r i v ṛ d d h a (H a r i u ḍ ḍ h a) and P ŏ ṭ ṭ i s a were mentioned also by Rājaśekhara, Karp. 19. 2, where, moreover, occur the names of N a n d i u ḍ ḍ h a = N a n d i v ṛ d d h a and Hāla as well," and in the v. l. P ā l i t t a a, C a m p a a r ā a and M a l a a - s e h a r a are also named.[2] Of them, P ā l i t t a a is credited with the authorship of ten verses of this anthology by Bhuvanapāla. In case P ā l i t t a is to be equated to P ā d a l i p t a, as was done by WEBER[3], this Pālitta might be identical with P ā d a l i p t ā c ā r y a, who is referred to by Hc., Deśīn. 1, 2 as the author of a manual of Deśī (*deśiśāstra*). The actual name of the last mentioned poet is now proved by the v. l. with certainty to be M a l l a s e h a r a in KONOW and M a l a y a s e k h a r a, i. e. °ś e k h a r a in Bhuvanapāla. According to Bhuvanapāla, A b h i m ā n a, whose full name was A b h i m ā n a c i h n a, who was perhaps the author of H. 518, was, like P ā d a l i p t a, also the author of a *Deśiśāstra*, that had a *vṛtti* to each *sūtra*, and in which Abhimāna gave his own examples (Deśīn. 1, 144; 6, 93; 7, 1; 8, 12. 17). This holds good equally for D e v a r ā j a, who according to Bhuvanapāla, was the author of H. 220. 369, and according to Deśīn. 6. 58. 72; 8, 17, was a writer on Deśī, and also for Sātavāhana, who is mentioned among the sources of Hc. on Deśī in Deśīn. 3, 41; 5, 11; 6, 15. 18. 19. 112. 125. A p a r ā j i t a whom Bhuvanapāla describes as the author of H. 756 is different from Aparājita, who according to Karp, 6, 1 wrote M ṛ g ā ṅ k a l e k h ā k a t h ā, and was a contemporary of R ā j a ś e k h a r a. It remains still undecided whether this younger Aparājita did not mainly use Sanskrit, because it is likely that Rajaśekhara himself might have translated into Prākrit the passage under reference, and in fact, we find in the Subhāṣitāvali, a Sanskrit strophe, i.e. no. 1024, cited from him. Sarvasena, to whom, according to the authority of Bhuvanapāla, belong the verses, H. 217 and 234, composed, according to Ānandavardhana, Dhvanyāloka, 148, 9, Harivijaya, wherefrom is quoted a stanza, namely 127, 7, that is cited also by Hemacandra, Alaṅkāracūḍāmaṇi, fol. 7ᵇ (MS KIELHORN, Report, Bombay 1881, p. 102, Nr. 265).[4] In both the lists, one of the famous poets is Pravarasena. Further, in Bhuvanapāla occurs also the name of Vākpatirāja. None of the quoted passages, however, is found either in Rāvaṇavaho or in Gaüḍavaho. Because this Vākpatirāja had written a second ornate poem, i.e. Mahumahaviaa, according to G. 69, and Madhumathanavijaya, according to Ānandavardhana, Dhvanyāloka, 152, 2; Someśvara, Kāvyādarśa, fol. 31 (MS KIELHORN, Report, p. 87, No. 66. Hemacandra, Alaṅkāracūḍāmāṇi fol. 7ᵇ), it is likely that both of the stanzas might have been derived from the latter source. But the two lists often go against each other and are not reliable. However, the fact remains that the Sattasaī presupposes a very rich literature in Prākrit, in the formation of which women too took active part. Only futurity will tell whether or not stray stanzas were taken only occasionally into Sanskrit literature, as in the dramas.[5]

1. An excellent review thereof has been published by GARREZ in JA. VI, 20, 197ff. — 2. PISCHEL, GGA. 1891, 365; v. l. to Karp. 19, 2. — 3. IS. 16, 24 note 1. — 4. PISCHEL, ZDMG. 39, 316. — 5. The two editions by WEBER are respectively indicated as H¹ and H² in places where necessary, H. however, indicates the second edition.

§ 14. That Prākrit has had a rich literature is presupposed also by the second anthology, the Vajjālagga of Jayavallabha (§ 12), a Jaina belonging to the Śvetāmbara sect. According to BHĀṆḌĀRKAR, l.c. p. 17, it is divided into 48 sections and contains 704 stanzas, whereof the authors are unfortunately not named. Stanza 2 = H. 2; none of the stanzas, nos. 6 to 10, found at p. 325, occurs in H.; an immediate publication of Vajjālagga is very much desirable. A chāyā thereof was written by Ratnadeva in the Vikrama-year 1393 = 1336 A.D. Moreover, the actual name of the collection is Jaavallahaṁ according to p. 324, 26. A large number of stanzas in M. are further quoted by writers on rhetorics. Of the 67 stanzas, that WEBER collected in the supplement to H.¹, p. 202-ff., from Dhanika's commentary on Daśarūpa, Śāhityadarpaṇa and Kāvyaprakāśa, 32 are found in different recensions of Sattasaī, so that H² p. 509 ff. has yet the remaining 35. Of them the one bearing no. 968 *de ā pasia* is quoted also in Dhavanyāloka, 22, 2 in Alaṅkārac. fol. 4ᵇ and also elsewhere: the one bearing no. 969 *aṇṇaaṁ laḍahattaṇaaṁ* (so it is to be read) is cited in Ruyyaka, Alaṅkārasarvasva 67, 2; Alaṅkārac. fol. 37 etc.; the stanza no. 970 is quoted by Jayaratha, Alaṅkāravimarśinī fol. 24ᵇ (MS BÜHLER, Detailed Report Nr. 230); the stanza no 971 is cited in Śobhākara, Alaṅkāraratnākara fol. 20 (MS BÜHLER, Det. Rep. Nr. 227), and so also are the other stanzas quoted by this or that writer on poetics. The stanzas, nos. 979 *jo* (so it is to be read) *parhariuṁ*, 988 *taṁ tāṇa*, the oft-quoted 989, *tāta jāanti* and 999 *homi vahatthiareho* were taken from Ānandavardhana's Viṣamabāṇalīlā, a poem which Ānandavardhana himself quotes in Dhvanyāloka, 62, 3; 111, 4; 152, 3; 241, 12.20, and which according to 241, 19 was written for guidance of the poets (*kavivyutpattaye*). Cf. 222, 12 with the commentary of Abhinavagupta. The origin of stanza no. 979 is given by Someśvara, Kāvyādarśa, fol. 52 (MS KIELHORN, Report 1880-81, p. 87, No. 66) and Jayanta, Kāvyaprakāśadīpikā, fol. 65 (MS BÜHLER Det. Rep. Nr. 244), both of them designate this poem as a Pañcabāṇalīlā; 988 and 989 are cited by Ānandavardhana himself, Dhvanyāloka p. 111. 62[1]; stanza no. 999 is quoted by Abhinavagupta on Dhvanyāloka 152, 18 (completely mutilated in the printed edition); and it is noted by Someśvara l.c. fol. 62 and by Jayanta l.c. fol. 79 that this is from Viṣamabāṇalīlā. Further Ānandavardhana, Dhvanyāloka 241, 13 directly quotes from it also the stanza *ṇa a tāṇa ghaḍaï*. The stanza no. 243, 20[2] proves that he wrote also in Apabhraṁśa. Abhinavagupta on Dhvanyāloka p. 223, 13 cites also a Prākrit stanza of his teacher, Bhaṭṭendurāja, who has been well-known as a Sanskrit poet from a very long time.[3] The Sarasvatīkaṇṭhābharaṇa, a treatise on Rhetorics, contains the largest number of Prākrit stanzas; they number nearly 350 according to ZACHARIAE[4], of which nearly 150, and according to JACOB[5] nearly 113, are taken from Sattasaī, nearly 30[6] are from Rāvaṇavaho; besides there are stanzas in M. from Kālidāsa, Śrīharṣa, Rājaśekhara, etc. Moreover, there are in it many stanzas from sources that are still unknown. The statement of BOROOAH[7] that there existed in a poem Satyabhāmāsaṁvāda or a similar poem on the same subject is apparently based on the stanzas *kuviā ca saccahāmā*, 322, 15 and *surakusumehi kalusiaṁ*, 327, 25, which are addressed by Satyabhāmā to Rukmiṇī according to the following elucidation. Cf. also 340, 9; 369, 21; 371, 8. But according to all that we know up till now these stanzas might have been taken from Harivijaya of Sarvasena or from Madhumathanavijaya of Vākpatirāja (§ 13). It has already been noted above (§ 12) that even the dramas contain Gāthās in M.

1. 989 also Jayanta, l. c. fol 25; cf. PISCHEL, BB. 16, 172, d. — 2. It is wholly mutilated in the Kāvyamālā edition. On the evidence of the MSS it approximately reads as *mahu mahu tti bhaṇantiaho vajjaï kālu jaṇassu* 1 *to vi ṇa deu jaṇaddaṇaü goarihoi maṇassu*. — 3. AUFRECHT, Cat. Cat. 1. 59, s. v. Indurāja Bhaṭṭa. — 4. GGA. 1884, p. 309. — 5. JRAS. 1897, p. 304. AUFRECHT in WEBER, Hāla,[2] p. LVIII, note 1, has identified no. 78. — 6. ZACHARIAE, l. c. — 7. In his edition (Calcutta 1883), Preface p. IV f.

§ 15. Māhārāṣṭrī is also the language of ornate epics of which up till now two have been published, the R ā v a ṇ a v a h o, and the G a ü ḍ a v a h o. The author of R ā v a ṇ a v a h o, designated also as D a h a m u h a v a h o, mostly referred to by its Sanskrit title Setubandha, is unknown. According to tradition its author is P r a v a r a s e n a, whereby probably they mean[1] King Pravarasena II of Kashmir, under whose patronage the poem might have been written. This work had already become famous by the time of Bāṇa, that is to say, therefore, in the 7th century A.D.; so it is proved by Harṣacarita 14, the introduction. The fact that it has been referred to by Daṇḍin, Kāvyādarśa I, 34, would seem to suggest a still earlier date. Rāvaṇavaho has been handed down to us in three recensions : the existence of a fourth one is presupposed by its Sanskrit translation Setusaraṇi.[2] The vulgata was commented upon by R ā m a d ā s a, who lived under Akbar (1556-1605); he has very often misunderstood the text. HOEFER was the first scholar to have occupied himself with this work. Already in 1846 he had in view an edition of it.[3] But it was PAUL GOLDSCHMIDT who edited all the poems contained in the first two of the 15 Āśvāsas in 1873. The complete text with a German translation was published by SIEGFRIED GOLDSCHMIDT : Rāvaṇavaha oder Setubandha, Strassburg 1880 (and the translation appeared in 1883).[4] A new edition, based upon that of SIEGFRIED GOLDSCHMIDT, but containing the complete commentary of Rāmadāsa, and therefore, quite indispensable, has been published by ŚIVADATTA and PARAB : The Setubandha of Pravarasena. Bombay 1895 (=Kāvyamālā 47). The author of G a ü ḍ a v a h o is B a p p a ï r ā a, in Sanskrit V ā k p a t i r ā j a. He lived under Yaśovarman, the king of Kānykubja, therefore, is to be dated towards the end of the seventh or the beginning of the 8th century A.D.[5] He mentions in 799 ff. Bhavabhūtī, Bhāsa, Jvalanamitra, Kāntideva, Kālidāsa, Subandhu and Haricandra as his predecessors. As distinct from the other Mahākāvyas, the Gaüḍavaho alone enumerates continuously its stanzas, whereof it contains 1209 in the Āryā metre. Even this poem is represented in several recensions that often differ from one another to a great extent in number and order of sequence of the stanzas.[6] The commentary of H a r i p ā l a explains merely the principal points, on account of which it is called also G a ü ḍ a v a d h a s ā r a ṭ i k ā.[7] Very often it is nothing better than its Sanskrit paraphrase. Gaüḍavaho with the commentary of Haripāla and a word-index has been published under the title "The Gaüḍavaho, a Historical Poem in Prākrit, by Vākpati. Bombay 1887 (=Bombay Sanskrit Series Nr. XXXIV)[8] by SHANKAR PĀṆḌURANG PAṆḌIT. It has already been mentioned above (§ 13) that Vākpatirāja composed another epic in Prākrit, i.e. M a h u m a h a v i a a. One of its stanzas is found in the commentary of Abhinavagupta on Dhvanyāloka 152, 15, two others perhaps in Sarasvatīk, 322, 15; 327, 25 (§ 14). The text, in PAṆḌIT's edition, as of course in Hemacandra, is given in accordance with the Jaina mode of writing, where initially *na* occurs and there are cases of doubling as well as of *yaśruti*, because the MSS are Jaina manuscripts. Similarly is quoted the text of Sattasaī in Bhuvanapāla's commentary. This mode of orthography has not been taken into consideration in this grammar, and here the words have been quoted in pure Māhārāṣṭrī form. The Rāvaṇavaho and the Gaüḍavaho are very strongly influenced by Sanskrit patterns (§ 9) and are written in thoroughly high-flown and polished language, sometimes with unending compounds, as are found also in the dramas of Bhavabhūti and occasionally in Mṛcchakaṭikā[9] as well. The Gaüḍavaho, the Sattasaī of Hāla and the Rāvaṇavaho are the most important sources of our knowledge of Māhārāṣṭrī. Because they are furnished with excellent word-indexes, they will be referred, mostly in the section on phonology, by G. H. R. In H[1] (§ 13, note 5) p. 29 ff. WEBER has given an outline of the grammar of M., as far as it was possible with the parts of Sattasaī published till that time.

1. MAX MÜLLER, Indien in seiner Weltgeschichtlichen Bedeutung (Leipzig 1884) p. 272 ff. The assumption that Kālidāsa was the author of the Rāvaṇavaho is based entirely on recent sources. — 2. S. GOLDSCHMIDT, Rāvaṇavaho, Introduction, p. v ff. — 3. Annual Report of DMG, of the year 1845, (Leipzig 1846) p. 176; Zeitschrift für die Wissenschaft der Sprache 2, 488ff. — 4. Cf. also the recension of PISCHEL, GGA. 1880, p. 321 ff. — 5. PAṆḌIT, Gaüḍavaho, Introduction p. LXIV ff. The research of JACOBI, GGA. 1888, p. 68 f., with regard to the solar eclipse, mentioned in the stanza no. 829, that took place in 733 A.D., as indicative of the date of the downfall of Yaśovarman is wrong. The context does not permit us to consider it a reference to Yaśovarman's defeat. The type of description is very common with the writers of mahākāvyas and is of not of any historical value. — 6. PAṆḌIT, Gaüḍavaho p. VIII f.; 345 ff. — 7. Other, but wrong, explanations are given in PAṆḌIT, Gaüḍavaho p. VII f. ; JACOBI, GGA. 1888, p. 63. — 8. Review by JACOBI, GGA. 1888, p. 61 ff. — 9. Vākpatirāja is very much overrated by PAṆḌIT, Gaüḍavaho, p. p. LII ff., and JACOBI, GGA. 1888, p. 65.

§ 16. The two dialects used by the Jainas are usually considered to be closely connected to Māhārāṣṭrī. They have been differentiated from one another by JACOBI[1] by calling them Jaina Māhārāṣṭrī and Jaina Prākrit. By Jaina Māhārāṣṭrī (JM.) he means the language of the commentators and poets[2] and by Jaina Prākrit the language of the older books of the Jaina canon[3] and that of the older Sūtras.[4] The name Jaina Prākrit that was first used by E. MŪLLER[5] is not a happy one, and the statement that this Jaina Prākrit is an older or archaic Māhārāṣṭrī is wrong.[6] The Indian grammarians usually call the language of the old Jainasūtras Ārṣam, i.e. "the language of the ṛṣis." Hc, 1, 3 announces that for Ārṣa all the rules of his grammar are subject to exceptions, and in 2, 174 he states that the limitations recorded above do not hold good for Ārṣa and that there all types of forms are permissible. Trivikrama[7] excludes Ārṣa like Deśya (§ 9) from his grammar altogether, because it is of independent origin (*rūḍhatvāt*, i.e. because it does not have Sanskrit as its source and as it abides mostly by its own rules (*svatantratvācca bhūyasā*). In a quotation in Premacandra Tarkavāgīśa on Daṇḍin, Kāvyādarśa I, 33, two types of Prākrit are distinguished : the one is that which originated from Ārṣa, and the other is that which is almost exactly the same as Ārṣa : *ārṣottham ārṣatulyaṁca dvividhaṁ prākṛtaṃ viduḥ*. Namisādhu on Rudraṭa, Kāvyālaṁkāra 2, 12 thus derives the word Prākrit : that its basis (*prakṛtiḥ*) is the natural language of intercourse of all beings and it is not regulated according to grammar etc. : it is called Prākrit because it is derived from this language or is itself the same. Or it may be that *prākṛta* stands for *prāk kṛtā*, "created before, in earlier period (*pūrvam*)", for it is called *prākṛta*. The Prākrit of the Ārṣa canon, i.e. the Ardhamāgadhā, is the language of gods : *ārisavayaṇe siddhaṁ devānām addhamāgahā vāṇī*. Accordingly Prākrit is the language that is easily understood by children, women, etc. and is the basis of all languages. Like rain-water it had one and the same form in former times, but it became diversified on account of difference in locality and grammatical modifications, and has come to be known as Sanskrit and other languages mentioned by Rudraṭa 2, 12, (§ 4). Therefore, Prâkrit has been made the source of Sanskrit as well. It is to be explained by the fact that like the Buddhists, the Māgadhi[8], the Jainas consider Ardhamāgadhī, the Ārṣa of the grammarians, the original language from which all the other languages have sprung up, because Mahāvīra is supposed to have preached in that language. Thus describes the Samavāyāṅgasutta 98[9] *bhagavaṁ ca ṇaṁ addhamāgahīe bhāsāe dhammaṁ āikkhaï* I *sā vi ya ṇaṁ addhamāgahī bhāsā bhāsijjamāṇī tesiṁ savvesiṁ āriya-m-aṇāriyāṇaṁ duppaẏacaüppaẏamiẏapasupakkhisarisivāṇaṃ appappaṇo hiẏasivasuhadāẏa bhāsattāe pariṇamaï.* "The Lord propagated the law in the Ardhamāgadhī language : this peace happiness-and-bliss-giving Ardhamāgadhī undergoes modifications when it is spoken by the Aryans, the non-Aryans, the bipeds, the quadrupeds, the wild and tamed animals, the birds and the worms." Vāgbhaṭa, Alaṅkāratilaka 1, 1 : *sarvārdhamāgadhīṁ sarvabhāṣāsu pariṇāmiṇīm* I *sārviyāṁ*[10] *sarvato vācaṁ sārvajñīṁ praṇidadhmahe* "we salute *Vāc* that is fully Ardhamāgadhī and which modifies herself into all the different languages and is perfect and omniscient". In the Paṇṇavaṇāsutta 59f. the Aryans are divided into nine classes : of them the sixth one is the *bhāsāriẏā*, "those that are Aryans by language". About them it is said, p. 62[11] : *se kiṁ taṁ bhāsāriẏā* I *bhāsāriẏā je ṇaṁ addhamāgahāe bhāsāe bhāsanti jattha vi ẏa ṇaṁ bambhī livī pavattaï*, "what is meant by 'Aryans by speech' ? Aryans by speech are they who speak the Ardhamāgadhī language and who use the Brāhmī alphabet". That Mahāvīra preached in Ardhamāgadhī is mentioned, besides in the passage quoted above from the Samavāyāṅgasutta, also in the Ovavāiẏasutta § 56; it runs thus : *tae ṇaṁ samaṇe bhagavaṁ mahāvīre...adhamāgabāe...bhāsāe bhāsaï | arihā dhammaṁ parikahei | tesiṁ savvesiṁ āriya-m-aṇāriẏāṇaṃ agilāe dhammaṁ āikkhaï | sā vi ẏa ṇaṁ addhamāgahā bhāsā tesiṁ savvesiṁ āriẏa-m-aṇāriẏāṇaṁ appaṇo sabhāsāe pariṇāmeṇaṁ pariṇamaï.* The same idea is emphasized also by Abhayadeva on Uvāsagadasāo p. 46 and Malaẏagiri on the Sūriẏapannatti, in Weber, Bhagavatī, 2, 245; cf. also Hc., Abhidhānacintāmaṇi 59 with commentary. In a passage quoted in Hc. 4, 287, it is said that the older Suttas are composed in Addhamāgahabhāsā[12] : *porāṇaṁ addhamāgahabhāsāniẏaẏaṁ havaï suttaṁ.* Thereon, remarks Hc.— although this is the tradition also of the older people, Ardhamāgadhī follows its own rules and not the rules he would frame later for Māgadhī.[13] The second of the illustrative examples cited by him, *se tārise dukkhasahe jiindie* **is** = Dasaveẏāliẏasutta 633, 19, would read in Māgadhī as *śe tāliśe dukkhaśahe yidindie.*

1. Kalpasūtra, p. 17; Ausgewählte Erzählungen in Māhārāṣṭrī (Leipzig. 1886), p. xi f. — 2. Kalpasūtra, p. 17. — 3. Erzählungen p. xii. — 4. Kalpasūtra, p. 17. — 5. Beiträge zur Grammatik des Jainaprākrit (Berlin 1876). — 6. See below § 18. — 7. First in Pischel, De gr. Pr., p. 29. — 8. D'Alwis,, An Introduction to Kachchāyana's Grammar of the Pàli Language (Colombo 1863) p. cvii; Muir, OST. 2², 54; Fryer, Proc. ASB. 1879, 155f. — 9. The text has been published in also Weber, Verzeichniss 2, 2, 406; cf. further below the passage quoted from the Ovavāiyasutta. — 10. So do the MSS; the printed edition (Bombay 1894=Kāvyamālā 43) reads *sarvapām.* — 11. The text was

published by WEBER also, IS. 16, 399, and Verzeichniss 2, 2, 562. — 12. LEUMANN, Das Aupapātika Sūtra (Leipzig 1883), p. 96 s. v. Addhamāgahā bhāsā suggests *niẏaẏaṁ=nijaka*, "to hold". But Hc. himself explains it as *niyata*, and that is demanded by the sense. — 13. Wrongly explained by HOERNLE. The Prākrita-Lakshaṇam or Chaṇḍa's Grammar of the Ancient (Ārṣha) Prākrit (Calcutta 1880), p. XIX, note.

§ 17. It follows, therefore, that Ārṣa and Ardhamāgadhī are identical, and that according to tradition, the language of the older Jaina-Sūtras was A r d h a m ā g a d h ī,[1] and in fact, as demonstrated by the passage from Dasaveẏāliẏasutta quoted in Hc. (§ 16), it was used not merely in prose but also in poetry. But in spite of all the correspondences there is a greater amount of difference, between the language of prose and that of poetry. The chief characteristics of Māgadhī are :— change of *r* into *l* and of *s* into *ś*, and the nom. sing of *a*-stems ending in *-e* instead of in *-o* as well as of the consonant stems that are reduced to *a*-stems in declension. Ardhamāgadhī retains both *r* and *s*, but it has the nom. in *-e*; and according to Abhayadeva on Samav. p. 98[2] and Uvās. p. 46, it derives its name "Half Māgadhī" on that account ; *ardhamāgadhi bhāṣā yasyāṁ rasor laśau māgadhyām*[3] *ityādikaṁ māgadhabhāṣālakṣaṇaṁ paripūrṇaṁ nāsti.* As already suggested by STEVENSON,[4] WEBER[5] has proved that the contact of Ardhamāgadhi with Māgadhī is "not very close". Besides the nom. in *-e*, the only feature that is common to both is *ḍa*=Skt. *ta* in the past passive participle of roots in *-ṛ*, but that too is not the only possible form in Mg. (§ 219). The preponderance of *ẏa* must be considered as a characteristic common to both, although the conditions under which it comes in are not quite similar. Further we may consider the change of *ka* into *ga* (§ 202), that occurs in Mg. in sporadic cases only, and the frequent pluti in the voc. sing. of *a*-stems (71), that takes place in Ḍh. as well as in A. Had the literary monuments of Mg. been more numerous and handed down to us in a better condition, the contact could undoubtedly be further illustrated. At the present time, however, it is chance that decides the issue. Thus AMg. *usiṇa*=Skt. *uṣṇa*, is equivalent to Mg. *kośiṇa*=*koṣṇa* (§ 133), and it is very much remarkable that both AMg. and Mg. use likewise the Sanskrit genitive form *tava*, that is wanting in other dialects (§ 421). From the Lāṭa-dialect comes the loc. sing. in *-ṁsi*[6] of *a*-stem. In poetry even in Ardhamāgadhī in the nomin. sing. of *a*-stem the forms in *-o* abound instead of those in *-e*; in our texts forms in both are retained near one another. Thus Āẏār. p. 41, 1, *abhivāẏamiṇe*, but 2 *haẏapuvvo*, 3 *lūsiẏapuvvo* ; p. 45, 19, *nāo*, but 20 *se mahāvire*, 22 against *aladdhapuvvo* and *gāmo*; p. 46, 3 *dukkhasahe*, *apaḍinne*, 4 *sūro*, 5 *saṁvuḍe*, 6 *paḍisevamāṇo*, 7 *acale*, 14 *apuṭṭhe*, 15 *puṭṭho*, *apuṭṭho*. In such cases the manuscript-tradition is faulty which, should have been corrected by the editors. The Calcutta edition has, 45, 22, *gāme*, 46, 6, *paḍisevamāṇe*, besides the forms in *-o*. Here, in all these places *-e* must be written. But in other metrical passages undoubtedly, the original form is the nomin. sing. in *-o*, as in Āẏār. p. 127ff.; instead of °*maüḍe*, p. 128, 3, as in MS B. it should have been written °*maüḍo*. It is repeated in all the pieces written in verse, as in Sūẏagaḍaṅgasutta, in Uttarajjhaẏaṇasutta, in Dasaveẏāliẏasutta, etc. Further, the language of poetry shows many other remarkable deviations in phonology and morphology, from that of prose, and very often approaches M. and JM., the second dialect of the Jainas, but, however, without, coinciding with either. Thus for example the Skt. word *mleccha* is written as *milakkhu* in AMg. in prose, but in poetry, as in M., JM., Ś., and A., it is written as *mĕccha* (§ 84). AMg. has only in verses, like M. and JM., the verbal form *kuṇaï*, from √*kṛ* (§ 508). In AMg. the absol. forms in *-tūṇa* and *-ūṇa* are almost, if not all exclusively, limited to poetry, though they are supreme in M. and JM. (§ 584). In construction of Sandhi, in flexion and in vocabulary, the metrical works stand in contrast with those in prose. Consequently many of the grammatical peculiarities may be noticed only in works like Dasav., Uttar. and Sūyag. The characteristics of the poetical dialect almost tally with those laid down by Kramadīśvara, who in 5, 98 says that AMg. is a mixture of Māhārāṣṭrī and Māgadhī : *māhārāṣṭrī-miśrārdhamāgadhī.*[7] This may, therefore, be considered to be a third dialect of the Jainas. Further, it is noteworthy that though in Pāli the language of poetry has a series of archaic and peculiar forms unknown in prose they are not sufficient to give the former the status of a separate dialect. In the same way, as the dialect of poetry doubtlessly agrees with that of prose fundamentally, I have designated both of them by the traditional name Ardhamāgadhī (AMg.). In Bhāratīyanāṭyaśāstra 17, 48 Ardhamāgadhī is mentioned by the side of Māgadhī, Āvantī, Prācyā, Śūrasenī, Bāhlīkā and Dākṣiṇātyā, as one of the seven bhāṣās, and again in the same work 17, 50 = Sāhityadarpaṇa, p. 173, 3 is said that it is used in dramas, as the language of menials, Rājputs and bankers : *ceṭānāṁ rājaputrāṇāṁ śreṣṭhināṁ cārdhamāgadhī.* But our dramas do not conform to this, and Mārkaṇḍeya rejects, as already stated above (§ 3), the existence of Ardhamāgadhī as an independent dialect beside Māgadhī. We may expect that in dramas wherein the Jainas may appear they speak AMg. LASSEN, Inst. pp. 410 ff., has even attempted to describe the characteristics of Ardhamāgadhī on the basis of Prab. and Mudrār., and he holds the view that the language of the barber in Dhūrtas. is Amg. In Mudrār. pp. 174-178 ; 183-187; 190-194 there appears the beggar-monk (*kṣapaṇaka*) Jīvasiddhi, about whom Ḍhuṇḍhirāja in his commentary on this work, p. 40 explicitly remarks : *kṣapaṇako jainākṛtiḥ* : in the dialect of this Kṣapaṇaka, the nominative sing. forms ending in *-e* agree with those of AMg. : thus *kuvide, bhadante* (178, 4), also in the neuter *adakkhiṇe ṇakkhatte* (to be read as °*hkh*°; 176.1.2) ; further there occurs also the change of *ka* into *ga* in *śāvagāṇaṁ* (175, 1; 185, 1; 190, 10); in the voc. sing. *śāvagā* (175, 3; 177,2; 183, 5 etc.), wherein has to be noted also the lengthening of the final vowel (§ 71), in the nom. sing. *śāvage* (178,2; 193,1, it is to be so read), and in *hage* = **ahakaḥ* (§ 142. 194. 417). Otherwise, however, his dialect is Māgadhī, and Hc. 4,302 cites from it examples of Mg. In Prab. also appears a Kṣapaṇaka, who is designated as a Digambara, pp. 46-64. Rāmadāsa correctly remarks that his dialect is Mg., and notes that Māgadhī is the language spoken by the Bhikṣus, the Kṣapaṇakas, the Rākṣasas, and the servants employed in female apartments. Then there appears a Digambara also in Laṭakamelaka, pp. 12-15, 25-28, who likewise speaks Mg. It must not be overlooked that wherever a Digambara appears his dialect does not immaterially differ from that of a Śvetāmbara and it agrees with Mg. in an essential phonological characteristic (§ 21). We do not find any trace of AMg. in the dramas.

1. WILSON, Select Works 1, 289; WEBER, Bhagavatī 1, 392, 2. Published by WEBER, Verzeichniss 2, 2, 406, note 8. — 3. WEBER, l. c. correctly remarks that the quotation is from the same hitherto unknown grammar. Namisādhu on Rudraṭa, Kāvyālaṅkāra 2, 12 also quotes it, but he reads *māgadhikāyām* for *māgadhyām*. Caṇḍa, 3, 39 reads it as *māgadhikāyāṁ rasayorlasau*. WEBER's view (Verzeichniss 2, 3, XIV, note 7) that *addhamāgahā bhāsā* "expresses too little and is qualitatively inaccurate" is wrong. — 4. The Kalpasūtra, and Nava Tattva (London 1848), pp. 137 ff. — 5. Bhagavatī 1, 393 ff. — 6. E. MÜLLER, Beiträge, p. 3. The other points of resemblance mentioned by MÜLLER are found also in other dialects. — 7. HOERNLE, Caṇḍa, p. XIX wrongly assumes Ardhamāgadhī + Māhārāṣṭrī = Ārṣa.

§ 18. COLEBROOKE[1] called the language of the canon of the Jainas to be Māgadhī and opined that this Prākrit did not differ much from the language used by the dramatical authors in their works and which they assigned to women. It is considered to be derived from Sanskrit, like Pāli in Ceylon. LASSEN[2] considered it to be identical with Māhārāṣṭrī, and HOEFER[3] asserted that many of the particularities found in the Prākrit of the Jaina books are generally foreign to common Prākrit, and that on the whole the former appears to be one and same language as the latter. JACOBI finds it to be older or archaic Māhārāṣṭrī[4] and remarks further that on a comparison of the Jaina Prākrit, particularly in its earliest available form with Pāli, on one hand, and with the Prākrit of Hāla, Setubandha, etc., on the other, we find that Jaina Prākrit is more akin, to Pāli than it is to later day Prākrit,[5] and that it is an old Indian dialect, that is closely allied to Pāli, but it is decidedly later than it[6]. Against this WEBER denies the existence of any close relationship between AMg. and M. and is more critical about its kinship with Pāli and holds, as was already said before by SPIEGEL[7] and after him by JACOBI[8], that AMg. is considerably later than Pāli. AMg. differs from M. in phonetics, morphology and vocabulary so significantly that it is wholly impossible to regard it as an older. M. JACOBI[9] himself had collected together a number of points of such differences and E. MÜLLER[10] has collected still more. He rejects the idea of inclusion of AMg. under M. and will like to connect it with Māgadhī of the inscriptions. The nom. sing. in *-e* alone will fully suffice to distinguish AMg. from M. It is not a case of phonetic change that can be explained on the hypothesis of difference in time, but it is due to local dialectical peculiarity as the history of Indian linguistics clearly shows. It assigns AMg. much further to the east than M. It is likely that at the time of compilation of the canon, either in the council held at Valabhī under Devarddhigaṇin or in the council of Mathurā under Skandilācārya, the original dialect got a western colouring. At Valabhī particularly the influence of M.[11] might have been quite considerable. But such an influence could not have been significant, ecause even by it the basic character of AMg. was not touched. To M. are unknown, thus for example, the phonetic laws like the lengthening of *-am* into *-ām* before *eva* (§ 68), the weakening of *iti* into *i* (§ 93), the dropping of *-i* of the prefix *prati* in cases like *paḍucca, paḍuppanna, paḍoẏāra,* etc. (§ 163), the substitution of dentals for palatals (§ 215), the dropping of *ya* in *ahā=yathā* (§ 335) and the use of the sandhi-consonants (§ 353); further the dative in *-ttāe* (§ 364), the instrumental in *-sā* (§ 364), the locative in *-ṁsi* (§ 366), the nom. sing. of the *t*-stem in *-ṁ* (§ 396), the instrumental forms like *kammuṇā* and *dhammuṇā* (§ 404), the peculiar types of numerals, the inflection of many verbs like *āikkhaï* from *khyā* (§ 492), *pāuṇaï* from *āp* with *pra* (§ 504), *kuvvaï* from *kṛ* (§ 508), the strong and the *s*-aorists (§ 516 ff.), the infinitive in *-ṭṭu,-ittu* (§ 577), in *-ttae* (§ 578), the absolutive in *-ttā* (§ 582), *- ttāṇaṁ* (§ 583), *-ccā, -ccāṇaṁ, -ccāṇa* (§ 587), *-ẏāṇaṁ, -ẏāṇa* (§ 592). The process of cerebralization has in AMg. a wider sphere than in M. (§ 219. 222. 289. 333); and likewise the change of *ra* into *la* (§ 257). The phonetic laws that are usual in AMg. are found to hold good just sporadically in M.: such are the use of the separation-vowel (§ 132), retention of long vowels and simplification of consonant-groups in the case of the suffix *-tra* (§ 87), and in that of *kṣa* (§ 323), the change of *ka* into *ga* (§ 202), and of *pa* into *ma* (§ 248), etc. These, the *ẏaśruti* (§ 187), the often wholly different vocabulary and many other grammatical peculiarities irrefutably demonstrate that AMg. and M. have been fundamentally different dialects from the beginning. Due to its elevation to the status of a literary language AMg. did not escape the fate of the other dialects, and on account of the dropping of consonants, it has become fundamentally changed. The nom. in *-e* shows that in the matter of fixation of the linguistic boundary of AMg. we need not go further in the west beyond Allāhābād.[12] At present it is not possible to determine its region more accurately.

1. Misc. Essays, 21, 213. — 2. Inst., pp. 1, 42. 43. — ZWSpr. 3, 371. — 4. Kalpasūtra, p. 18; cf. p. 19 and Erz., p. XII; WEBER, Verzeichniss 2, 3, XIV note 7. — 5. SBE. XXII, p. XLI. — 6. Aẏāraṅga Sutta, p. VIII. — 7. Bhag. I, 396 f. — 8. Münchener gelehrte Anzeigen 1849, p. 912. — 9. Kalpasūtra p. 17 f., Erz. p. XII. — 10. Beiträge pp. 3 ff. — 11. JACOBI, Kalpasūtra, pp. 15 ff., SBE XII, pp. XXXVII ff.; WEBER, IS. 16, 218. — 12. Suggestion of JACOBI, Erz. p. XII. — 13. See § 24.

§ 19. WEBER, in IS. 16, 211-479; 17, 1-90, has studied in detail the holy scriptures of the Śvetāmbaras written in AMg. These essays were further supplemented by copious extracts that WEBER included in the catalogue of Sanskrit and Prākrit manuscripts preserved in the Royal Library of Berlin, 2, 2, 355-823; therein he has also specified all Indian and European editions of all such works[1] as were published till that time. In this grammar the entire literature that has been published has been utilized. Unfortunately there do not still exist many strictly critical editions : many of the published texts are almost unusable for grammatical purposes. The most important prose text for our purpose is the first Aṅga, the Āẏāraṅgasutta[2], which has the most antiquated language of all. After it comes into consideration particularly the second Aṅga, the Sūyagaḍaṅgasutta, of which the first book, predominantly metrical, is for the poetic language what Āẏār. is for prose. The fourth Aṅga, the Samavāẏaṅga, is essential for a knowledge of the numerals. The sixth, the Nāẏādhammakahāo, the seventh Uvāsagadasāo,[3] the eleventh, the Vivāgasuẏa, as well as particular portions of the fifth, the Vivāhapannatti contain continuous narratives and, therefore, offer much more information with regard to declension and conjugation than do others. The same is true also of two of the Upāṅgas, namely the Ovavāiẏasutta and the Niraẏāvaliẏāo, and also the first section of the Kappasūẏa among the Chedasūtra. Among the Mūlasūtras the Uttarajjhaẏaṇasutta, that is written almost entirely in verse, is of the highest importance; it contains plenty of peculiar and archaic forms : and of significance is the Dasaveẏāliẏasutta, although its language is very much degenerated. Endless repetitions of the same words and phrases render it possible to ascertain the correct reading even of the corrupt texts in several cases ; but in other cases it was not possible to reach any certainty and much has to be left out of consideration, because the sources were inadequate. Nevertheless, it is now possible to draw a clear and correct picture of AMg., and it is now proved that AMg. is the most important of all the Prākrit dialects,[4] because it is best preserved and is most copious. First of all, it was STEVENSON, Kalpa Sūtra, pp. 131 ff., who gave an incomplete and erroneous information about AMg. ; HOEFER ZWSpr. 3, 364 ff. furnished something additional ; herein he pointed out some of the chief characteristics of the language such as the ẏaśruti, the separation-vowel, the change of *ka* into *ga*, etc. Of fundamental importance for AMg. was the work of WEBER; Über ein Fragment der Bhagavatī, Theil 1.2 (Berlin 1866, 1867) = Abhandlungen der Kgl. Akademischer Wissenschaften zu Berlin, 1865, p. 367-444; 1866, p. 155-352. It was here that WEBER first of all treated the peculiar orthography of the Jaina manuscripts, attempted to determine (of course, in many places wrongly) the sound value of certain letters of the alphabet and gave the outlines of a grammar, which is still valuable and also specimens of the language. It may be noted here that the Bhagavatī is the fifth Aṅga and its canonical name is the Vivāhapannatti, by which title it will be referred to in this grammar : it will be quoted simply as Bhagavatī whenever the reference is to WEBER's above mentioned essay. The work of E. MÜLLER, the author of Beiträge zur Grammatik des Jainaprākrit, Berlin 1876, does not take us much further, although the writer in it, has made several improvements upon WEBER in respect of phonology. JACOBI in Āẏār., pp. VIII-XIV gave a cursory resumé of the grammar in comparison with that of Pāli.

1. A list of utilized editions and translations along with abbreviations has been given at the end of this grammar. — 2. It is due to the objectionable practice that has become a customary that the Jaina texts like Kalpasūtra, Aupapātikasūtra, Daśavaikālikasūtra, Bhagavatī, Jītakalpa, etc. are designated by their Sanskrit titles. Only HOERNLE in his edition of Uvāsagadasāo made a noteworthy exception. In this grammar, the Sanskrit titles will be used only when reference will be made to the remarks of the editors concerned who have named them as such, and this has been done with a view to avoid error. — 3. The

edition of HOERNLE (Calcutta 1890, Bibl. Ind.) remains upto the present day the only edition of a Jaina work with its text and the commentary critically edited. Without extracts from commentaries, the text often remains unintelligible. — 4. PISCHEL, ZDMG, 52, p. 95.

§ 20. The dialect used in non-canonical writings of the Śvetāmbaras differs from AMg. significantly. As already stated above (§ 16) JACOBI has called it Jaina Māhārāṣṭrī. More suitable perhaps would have been Jaina Saurāṣṭrī, that was suggested by JACOBI[1] earlier, if it could be assumed that Māhārāṣṭrī and Saurāṣṭrī were closely allied dialects. But that, however, is a hypothesis that cannot be established and, therefore, the name Jaina Māhārāṣṭrī may be retained, because undoubtedly this dialect is very close to Māhārāṣṭrī, even though in no way it is fully identical with it. JACOBI[2] wrongly supposes that M. of Hc. is not identical with M. of Hāla, Setubandha and dramas. All the traceable quotations in Hc. go back to Hāla, Rāvaṇavaho, Gaüḍavaho, Viṣamabāṇalīlā and Karpūramañjarī. Hc. had simply extended the orthography of the Jainas also to these works as it was so in the original Jaina manuscripts (§ 15). But in fact, it appears that Hc. had taken into consideration some specific works in JM. besides those in AMg. At least, it must be noted that not a small number of his rules may as yet be instanced only in JM. AMg. too has not remained without any influence on JM. Of the characteristics of AMg. enumerated under § 18 many are to be found also in JM. : thus for example, the saṁdhi-consonants, the nom. ending in *-m* from *t*-stems, the infinitives in *-ittu*, the absolutive in *-tta*, and the change of *ka* into *ga*. Therefore, JM. is not pure M., but in fact it is so close to it that, after all, it may be called M. The most important text in JM. is Die Āvaśyaka Erzählungen published by ERNST LEUMANN, Heft I, Leipzig, 1897. Lack of a commentary makes understanding of the text extremely difficult, and much remains completely obscure. But even these few sheets of paper show that out of these JM. texts we may expect many new and important things notably lexicographical, for in this respect JM. is perhaps the most promising dialect. The later-day texts, in a greater part, are contained in the Ausgewählte Erzählungen in Māhārāṣṭrī, zur Einführung in das studium des Prākrit. Grammatik, Text, Wörterbuch, Herausgegeben von HERMANN JACOBI, Leipzig 1886. The introductory elementary grammar contains also a section on syntax, but that is confined only to the forms that occur in the stories concerned. Besides we have to take into consideration the Kakkuka-inscription (§ 10) and the smaller pieces, like the Kālakācāryakathānaka, ZDMG. 34, 247 ff.; 35, 675; 37, 493ff., the legends of the fall of Dvāravatī, ZDMG. 42, 493ff, and of the stūpa of Mathurā SWA 137, the Ṛṣabhapañcāśikā, ZDMG. 33, 445 ff, and in the Kāvyamālā, Part VII (Bombay, 1890), pp. 124 ff., and the extracts in the Reports, that are mostly unfit for use. Probably in JM. was written also the rhetorical work of Hari, from whom Namisādhu on Rudraṭa, Kāvyālaṅkāra, 2, 19 cites a stanza.[3]

1. Kalpasūtra, p. 18. — 2. Kalpasūtra, p. 19. — 3. PISCHEL, ZDMG. 39, p. 314. In the commentary on 1, 2 for Rudra read Hari.

§ 21. We are not as yet sufficiently acquainted with the language of the canon of the Digambaras. This language does not insignificantly differ from that of the canon of the Śvetāmbaras[1]. If a conclusion has to be drawn on the basis of the non-canonical writings, it will be said that in one important aspect, as it respects phonology, i.e., so far as the change of *ta* into *da*, and of *tha* into *dha*, is concerned, it is closer to Māgadhī, than to the AMg. of the Śvetāmbaras. In any case, the later day writings of the Digambaras as well obey this phonetic law. For instance the Gāthās, in the Gurvāvali, referred to by JACOBI,[2] and the extracts from Kundakundācarya's Pavaẏanasāra and Kārttikeyasvāmin's Kattigeẏāṇupĕkkhā, that has been published by BHĀṆḌĀRKAR[3] (§ 203). Śaurasenī also observes the same phonetic law; and as the nom. sing. of *a*-stem ends in *o*, in the language of the scriptures of the Digambaras, this dialect may be designated as J a i n a Ś a u r a s e n ī. But here we have to be more cautious than even in the case of JM., so as always to remember that this designation merely serves as a convenient term, even though it is by no means accurate. Even a preliminary examination of the dialect will show that it has such forms and words as are altogether foreign to Śaurasenī, though, however, they are found partly in M. and partly in AMg. Thus typically M. is the loc. sing. ending in *-mmi*, from *a*-stems as in *dāṇammi*, *suhammi*, *asuhammi*, *ṇāṇammi*, *daṁsaṇamuhammi* (Pav. 383, 69; 385, 61; 387, 13), *kālammi* (Kattig. 400, 322) and the use of *-vva* = *iva* (Pav. 383, 44). The root *kṛ* is inflected, always showing *da* = *ta*, partly like-M. *kuṇaḍi* (Kattig. 399, 310. 319; 402, 359. 367. 370. 371; 403, 385; 404, 388. 389. 391), and partly like AMg. *kuvvadi* (Kattig. 399, 313; 400, 329; 401, 340) and *kuvvade* (403, 384), side by side with forms that are Ś. e.g. *karedi* (Pav. 384, 59; Kattig. 400, 324; 402, 369; 403, 377. 378. 383) and M. JM. AMg. *karadi* (400, 332). The form of the passive is *kīradi* (Kattig. 399, 320; 401, 342. 350,) as in M. JM. The absolutive mostly ends in *-ttā*, as in AMg. *cattā* = *tyaktvā* (Pav. 385, 64; Kattig. 403, 374); *jāṇittā* (Pav. 385, 68; Kattig. 401, 340. 342. 350); *viẏāṇittā* (Pav. 387, 21); *ṇamaṁsittā*, *niruñjhittā* (Pav. 386, 6.70); *ṇihaṇittā* (Kattig. 401, 339); also in *-ẏa* as in *bhaviẏa* (Pav. 380, 12; 387, 12); *āpiccha* = *āpṛcchya* (Pav. 386, 1); *ādāẏa* (Pav. 386, 6); *āsijja*, *āsĕjja* = *āsādya* (Pav. 386, 1. 11); *samāsiijja* (Pav. 379, 5); *gahiẏa* (Kattig. 403, 373); *pappa* (Pav. 384, 49), and in *-ccā* as in *kiccā* (Pav. 379, 4; Kattig. 402, 356. 357. 358. 375. 376); *ṭhiccā* (Kattig. 402, 355); *soccā* (Pav. 386, 6). Side by side with such forms are found also the absolutive in *-dūṇa*; *kādūṇa*, *ṇedūṇa* (Kattig. 403, 374. 375), wrongly[4] also in *-ūṇa* : *jāiūṇa*, *gamiūṇa*, *gahiūṇa*, *bhuñjāviūṇa* (Kattig. 403, 373. 374. 375. 376). Such Digambara texts may have been the source, according to which Hc. allows even in Ś forms in *-ttā* and *-dūṇa* and such other forms as are not found in Śaurasenī of the dramas, (§ 22. 266. 365. 475. 582. 584). Side by side with AMg. *pappodi* = *prāpnoti* occurs the commonly found *pāvadi* (Pav. 380, 11; Kattig. 400, 326; 403, 370); by the side of Ś. *jāṇādi* (Pav. 382, 25) is seen *jāṇadi* (Kattig. 398, 302. 303; 400, 323) as well as *ṇādi* (Pav. 382, 25); moreover, here are used forms like *muṇadi* (Kattig. 398, 303; 399,

313. 316. 337), *muṇedavvo* (the MS has °*eya*°, Pav. 380, 8), that are unknown in Ś. Mg. In this way there occur many other forms from M. AMg. Ś. side by side. From what has seen up till now it seems that JŚ. has much more of common characteristics with AMg. than with JM., and is partly more archaic. Both the texts are in verse.

1. BHĀṆḌĀRKAR, Report on the Search for Sanskrit Manuscripts in the Bombay Presidency during the year 1883-84 (Bombay 1887), pp. 106 ff.; WEBER, Verzeichniss 2, 2, 823 f. — 2. Kalpasūtra, pp. 30. — 3. l.c. pp. 379 — 389; 398 — 404. The references are given according to page and verse : cf. also PETERSON, Fourth Report, pp. 142 ff. — 4. In the manuscripts, exactly as in those of the dramas, very often M. forms are given in lieu of those of Ś.

§ 22. Among the Prākrit dialects that are used in the prose of the dramas, Śaurasenī occupies the first place.[1] As its name indicates, its basis is the dialect of Śūrasena, of which the capital city was Mathurā.[2] According to Bhāratīyanāṭyaśāstra 17, 46 the dialect of the dramas should be based on that of Śaurasena and according to 17, 51, the heroines of the drama and their lady-friends should speak Śūrasenī. According to Sāhityadarpaṇa, p. 172, 21, cultured women, not of lowly origin, speak Ś. and according to p. 173, 11f, it is spoken also by maid-servants who are not too low, eunuchs, children, lower grade-astrologers, the insane and the sick. Śaurasenī is mentioned as the language of women also by Daśarūpa 2,60. According to Bharata 17, 51; Sāhityadarpaṇa 173, 4; Pṛthvīdhara on Mṛcch., p. V, ed. STENZLER = p. 493, ed. GOḌABOLE the Vidūṣaka speaks P r ā c y ā,[3] which according to MK. fol. 72, is prescribed also for other comic characters. MK. refers to Bharata and remarks that Prācyā is grammatically derived from Śaurasenī; *prācyāyāḥ siddhiḥ śaurasenyāḥ*. The manuscripts are so corrupt that it is not possible to decipher all that MK. describes as characteristics of Prācyā. They are very meagre and mostly of lexicographical nature. It is said that for *mūrkha* should be used *murukkha*; the voc., sing. of *bhavati* is *bhodi*; for *vakra* is prescribed a form that deviates from Ś.[4]; the voc. sing. of *a*-stems may have pluti; the Vidūṣaka uses *hi, hī, bho* to express his joy, *hī, māṇahe* to express wonder (*adbhute*) and *avida* to express dismay. There appear to be some special rules to regulate *ṇaṁ, eva*, and perhaps also for the future. Pṛthvīdhara refers as a characteristic to the repeated use of *kaḥ svārthe*. Hc. 4, 285 *hī hī vidūṣakasya* prescribes Ś. directly for the Vidūṣaka, and 4, 282 *hī māṇahe vismayanirvede* is likewise recorded as Ś., and that is certainly correct. Śaurasenī is the language of the Vidūṣaka as well as of a number of other characters that appear in dramas. The older grammarians deal with Śaurasenī very briefly. Vr. 12,2 says — its basis is Skt. For it he gives 29 rules, with which the texts mostly agree,[5] and under 12, 32 he remarks that in other respects it agrees with M. *śeṣaṁ māhārāṣṭrīvat*. Hc. 4, 60-286 has 27 rules of which the last one reads *śeṣaṁ prākṛtavat* and corresponds to Vr. 12, 32. In other respects Hc. and Vr., differ strongly from one another, a thing which, to a great extent, is to be explained by the fact that Hc. has taken into consideration also the Śaurasenī of the Digambaras (§ 21), the peculiarities of which the Jainas have carried over to Śaurasenī of the dramas with the result that the Śaurasenī texts of the latter have become corrupt and later writers have been misled.[6] Even Kī. 5, 77-85 says little on this topic. Contrary to this, later grammarians, e.g. MK. fol. 65-72, and Rv. fol. 34 ff. say much more thereon. The manuscripts of these works that are available in Europe are so corrupt that in this case as well as we can use only a part of the material contained in them. Their verification is rendered difficult on account of most of the editions of the dramas being uncritical. Of the editions that have appeared in India only a few are of any use : one such is BHĀṆḌĀRKAR's edition of Mālatīmādhava (Bombay 1876), and even among the texts printed in Europe not many are of any use for the purpose of linguistic study.[7] In every case new editions do not show any improvement upon older ones. Thus : the edition of Mudrārākṣasa by TELANG (Bombay 1884), is worse than the one printed in Majumdār's series and edited by TĀRĀNĀTHA TARKAVĀCASPATI (Calcutta Saṁvat 1926); BOLLENSEN's edition of Mālavikāgnimitra (Leipzig 1879) is deplorably a retrograde step. In spite of all this, I have cited from both of them, because in them the readings are often correctly reproduced from MSS and, therefore, they are indispensable. Very often it has been possible to arrive at a decision only after consulting the highest possible number of texts of one and the same drama.[8] Many of the editions show a noteworthy admixture of dialects. It is in this way that the first Prākrit words in Kāleyakutūhala, 2, 4 *bho kiṁ ti tue hakkārido hage maṁ khu eṇhiṁ* (text *ehṇiṁ*) *chuhā bāhei* contain three dialects : *hakkārido* is Ś., *hage* is Mg., *eṇhiṁ* and *bāhei* are M., subsequently the text is much more in M. than in Ś. In Mukundān. 58, 14. 15 both Ś., *kadua* M. *kāūṇa* stand near one another in the same stanza. Here this may have been due to editor's error. In other cases it is clear that poets themselves did not know how to distinguish strictly between the different dialects. For instance Somadeva (§ 11) and Rājaśekhara. The critical edition of Karpūramañjarī by KONOW shows that the manuscripts are not always responsible for the dialectical errors committed by Rājaśekhara, particularly when the same mistakes are repeated also in the Bālarāmāyaṇa and Viddhaśālabhañjikā. Thus, all the MSS of Karpūramañjarī, 7, 6 ed. KONOW = 11, 2 ed. Bombay, have *ghĕttūṇa* in place of the only Ś. form *gĕṇhia*, an error that recurs also elsewhere (§ 584); 9, 5 = 13, 5 ed. Bom. has the dative form *suhāa*, that is wrong in Ś (§ 361). ; further the following are dialectical irregularities : *tujjha* 10, 9 = 14, 7 and *majjha* 10, 10 = 14, 8 (§ 421. 418), *vva* 14, 3 = 17, 5 for *via* (§ 143), locative like *majjhammi* 6, 1 = 9, 5 for *majjhe*, *kavvammi* 16, 8 = 19, 10 for *kavve* (§ 366), ablatives like *pāmarāhiṁto* 20, 6 = 22,9 for *pāmarādo* (§ 365), etc.[2] In Rājaśekhara, we further find many dialectical errors in the use of Deśī words. According to MK. fol. 50 Rājaśekhara's M. had its own peculiarities. He says *rājaśekharasya māhārāṣṭryāḥ prayoge ślokeṣvapi dṛśyata iti kecit*, whereby, as it appears, is meant substitution of *da* for *ta* in lieu of its dropping. The manuscripts of his dramas show repeatedly many of the forms with elision instead of those with *da* in Ś. Due to the mixing up of dialects in the Devanāgarī and the South Indian recensions of the Śakuntalā and in the South Indian recension of the Vikramorvaśīya,[9] these works do not serve any purpose in settling critical questions. In spite of all these difficulties, it is, however, possible to obtain on the whole a fairly correct picture of Ś. In phonology, the most striking characteristic is the change of *ta* into *da* and of *tha* into *dha* (§ 203); in declension and conjugation a host of forms of M. AMg. JM. JŚ. have been very much simplified. Similarly in the case of the *a*-stems only the abl. sing. in *-do* and the loc. sing. in *-e* are used : in the plur. only such forms of all the stems are nasalised at the end as are found to have been used in the ins., in the gen., as well as in the loc.; the *i*- and *u*- stems have in the gen. sing. only *-ṇo*, and not also *-ssa*; in respect of verbs, the Ātmanep. forms had by then disappeared almost completely; the opt. had only the endings *-eaṁ* (I. sing.) and *-e* ; many verbs have stem forms that deviate from those of M.; the future is formed only from *i*-stems; the passive is obtained only in *-ia*; the absolutive, against M., is found almost exclusively in *-ia*=Skt. *-ya*, etc..[10] In flexion and in vocabulary, in which Ś. greatly deviates from M., it approaches Skt. very closely, as rightly observed by Vr.[11]

1. Also Śūraseni, often wrongly called Sūraseni. — 2. LASSEN, IAlt. 1², 158, note 2; 796 note 2; 2², 512; CUNNINGHAM, The Ancient Geography of India (London 1871) 1, 374. — 3. PISCHEL, Die Recensionen der Śakuntalā (Breslau 1875), pp. 16f. — 4. PISCHEL on Hc. 1, 26. — 5. PISCHEL, KB. 8, 129 ff. — 6. That Hc. had utilized the texts of the Digambaras, even though he was a Śvetāmbara Jaina, has been shown by LEUMANN, IS. 17, 133, note 1. — 7. PISCHEL, Hemacandra, 1, xif. Since 1877 unfortunately there has been little change in the circumstance. For the purpose of grammar, primarily the materials can be drawn only from Mṛcchakaṭikā, ed. STENZLER, Śakuntalā, ed. PISCHEL, and Vikramorvaśīya, ed. BOLLENSEN; in the second line comes the Ratnāvali, ed. CAPPELLER, which in fact is the best edition of the drama, although it gives no variants, it has been planned somewhat very systematically. I could use the excellent edition of Karpūramañjari by KONOW, when the present work was in the press. But Rājaśekhara, as already pointed out above, is no authority for Ś. — 8. A list of texts used along with necessary notes is given at the end of this grammar. — 9. PISCHEL, KB. 8, 129 ff. Die Recensionen Śakuntalā, pp. 19 ff. Monatsberichte der Kgl. Akademie der Wissenschaften zu Berlin 1875, pp. 613 ff. Wrongly WEBER, IS. 14, 39 ff., 161 ff. A collection of incorrect forms was made by BURKHARD, Flexiones Prācriticae quas editioni suae Sâcuntâli Pro Supplemento adjecit. Vratislaviae 1874. — 10. PISCHEL, Jenaer Literaturzeitung 1875, pp. 794 ff.; JACOBI, Erzählungen, pp. LXX ff. Further details have been furnished in relevant paragraphs of this grammar. 11. On the nature and style of Prākrit used in modern dramas cf. GRIERSON, IA. XXIII, p. 110. So has indeed been the case for many centuries.

§ 23. Māgadhī has been transmitted to us in a still worse condition than Śaurasenī. According to Kohala in MK. fol. 74 Mg. is spoken by Rākṣasas, beggars, Kṣapaṇakas, servants, etc. ; according to Bharata 17, 50 = Sāhityadarpaṇa p. 173, 2 Mg. is used also by people frequenting the ladies' apartments of the princes, by which term according to Daśarūpa 2, 42; Sāhityad. 81, eunuchs, Kirātas, dwarfs, Mlecchas, Ābhīras, Śakāras, chamberlains etc., and according to Bharata, 24, 50-59 eunuchs, snātakas, and chamberlains are to be understood. According to Daśarūpa 2,60 the Piśācas and all the low-class people speak Mg. and according to Sarasvatīk. 56, 18 the people of lower status speak it. In dramas chamberlains always speak Skt. (Śak. 93 ff., Vikr. 37 ff., Veṇīs. 17ff.; Nāgān. 61 ff.; Mudrār 78ff.; 110 ff.; Anarghar. 109 ff.; Pārvatīp. 36 ff.; Prīyad. 2f.; 28ff.; Pratāpar. 132 ff.). The following speak Mg. : in Mṛcch., the Śakāra, his servant, Sthāvaraka, the masseur, who later becomes a Bhikṣu, Kumbhīlaka, the servant of Vasantasenā, Vardhamānaka, the servant of Cārudatta, the two Cāṇḍālas, Rohasena, the little son of Cārudatta;[2] in Śak. 113ff., both the constables and the fishermen, 154 ff., Sarvadamana, the little son of Śakuntalā; in Prab. 28 — 32, the disciple of Cārvāka and the messenger from Orissa ; in 46 — 64, the Digambara Jaina; in Mudrār. 153f., the servant who prepares seats; in 174-178, 183-187, 190-194 the Jaina monk; in 197 the messenger;[3] in 256-269 Siddhārthaka and Samiddhārthaka as Cāṇḍālas, while they in another rôle in pp. 224 ff. speak Ś.; in Lalitav. 565 — 567, the bards and the spy, who, however, also speaks Ś., in another rôle at p. 567 f.; in Veṇīs. 33-36 the Rākṣasa and his wife; in Mallikām. 143.144 the elephant-drivers; in Nāgān. 67-68 and Cait. 149 f. the servants; in Caṇḍak. 42. 43 the scoundrel, in 60-72, the Cāṇḍālas; in Dhūrtas. 16 the barber; in Hāsyārṇava 31 Sādhuhiṁsaka; in Laṭakam. 12ff., 25ff., the Digambara Jaina; in Kaṁsavadha 48-52, the humpbacked; and in Amṛtodaya 66 the Jaina monk. With the exception of Mṛcch., only short pieces are written in Mg., and they in Indian editions have come down in such a mutilated form that often it is hardly possible to recognize the dialect. It is unfortunate that even after such a long time Prabodhacandrodaya has not appeared, though it was announced long ago by the Bombay Sanskrit Series. The edition of BROCKHAUS is worthless, and I have constantly used the Pūnā, the Madras and the Bombay editions, as they are better. Of all these texts only the Lalitav. appears to be essentially in agreement with the rules of the grammarians; among other stray texts, like those of Mṛcch. and Śak., the MSS show agreement with the rules for the different dialects. Usually they are so strongly influenced by Ś., which according to Vr. 11, 2, is the basis of Mg., and according to Hc. 4, 302, mostly coincides with it, that the character of the dialect is very much effaced. The rule Hc. 4,288 *rasor laśau* is followed rigorously; according to 4, 287 the nom. sing. of *a*-stem ends in *-e*; according to 4, 301 = Vr. 11.9 *hage* is substituted for *aham*, and more rarely also for *vayam*. On the other hand no text other than Lalitav. conforms to Hc. 4, 292 = Vr. 11, 4.7 that prescribes retention of *ya* and substitution of *ya* for *ja* and of *yya* for *dya*, *rya* and *rja*. There can be no doubt that this, like all other rules of grammarians, has to be followed against the manuscripts. All the grammarians from Vr. downwards are substantially in agreement[4] on the essential points. Hc. finds these peculiarities, according to 4, 302 in Mudrār., Śak., and Veṇīs., though in our manuscripts only a part of them is found, and even the manuscripts of Hc. are lacking at this place. The more the manuscripts become available to us the more the variants become noticeable that go against our existing texts. In Mṛcch. 22, 4 for instance, in STENZLER's edition, which, as usual, is followed here in 61, 5 in GODABOLE's edition, occurs the passage *tava jjeva haśte ciśṭadu*. According to grammarians it should be read as *tava yyevva haste ciṣṭhaü*. The MSS DH in Goḍabole read *ěvva*, C. *jjeva*; almost all MSS have *haśte* and *ciṣṭadu*, i.e. *ciṣṭhadu* as in J. It is repeated throughout. Mudrār. 154, 3, E, reads, as Hc. 4, 302, *yyeva*, and 264, 1 the majority of the MSS has *ěvva*; likewise Veṇīs. 35, 7; 36, 5. The rule Hc. 4,295, according to which for an intervocalic *cha* is substituted *śca*, I have strictly observed in the Śakuntalā, for it was suggested by the MSS and also because the MSS of the Mṛcch. prove this (§ 233), which also partially conform to Hc. 4,291 prescribing the change of *stha* and *rtha* into *sta* (§ 310. 290). The characteristics of Mg. in phonology are transformation of *ra* into *la*, of *sa* into *śa*, retention of *ya*, change of *ja* into *ya*, of *dya*, *rja* and *rya* into *yya*, of *ṇya*, *nya*, *jña*, *ñja* into *ñña*, of *ccha* into *śca* of *ṭṭa* and *ṣṭha* into *sṭa* etc. (§ 24), and in inflection, especially of nouns, the formation of the nom. sing. of *a- stem* in *-e*; in other respects, as regards flexion, Mg. strictly agrees with Ś., with which it agrees also in the transformation of *ta* into *da* and of *tha* into *dha*.

1. It is not clear as to what is meant in Bharata by *aupasthāyikanirmuṇḍāḥ*. — 2. It is attested by Pṛthvīdhara, in Stenzler, p. v. and Goḍabole, p. 493. In the printed edition he speaks, but the MSS throughout indicate Mg. as in 161, 9, they have *ale ale*, in 161, 16 *māledha*, in 165, 25 *ale* and in DH in Goḍabole p. 449 9 too there occurs *māleda*. In the introductory scene there is 327, 10=484 12 ed. Goḍabole H. *āvutte*. Wrongly analysed by Bloch, Vr. und Hc. p. 4. Cf. § 42. — 3. Cf. Hillebrandt, ZDMG. 39, 130. 4. Cf. § 24 and the relevant paragraphs of this grammar.

§ 24. According to Pṛthvīdhara on Mṛcch. in Stenzler, p. V = p. 494 ed. Goḍabole the brother-in-law of the king speaks Śākārī, a dialect that is mentioned as a form of Apabhraṁśa. It is mentioned also by Kī. 5,99; Rv. in Lassen, Inst. p. 21; Mk. fol. 76; Bharata 17,53; and Sāhityad. p. 173.6. Lassen, Inst., pp. 422 ff. has attempted to determine the peculiarities of this dialect and has come to the conclusion (p. 435) that Śākārī is a Māgadhī dialect. This conclusion is quite correct, as Mk. fol. 76 readily derives it form Mg. : *māgadhyāḥ śākārī | sādhyatiti śeṣaḥ*. Further Pṛthvīdhara on Mṛcch. 9, 22, ed. Stenzler p. 240 = p. 500, ed. Goḍabole has shown that in this dialect a *y* was pronounced before the palatals, viz. *yciṣṭha* = *tiṣṭha* (§ 217). This *y* was so weak that it could not gain, therefore, any importance from the view-point of metre. According to Mk. this phonetic rule was valid for Mg. and Vrācaḍa Apabhraṁśa as well (§ 28). Other peculiarities like the change of *ta* into *ḍa* in certain past passive participial forms (§ 219) and the genitive sing. of *a*-stems in *-āha* besides in *-aśśa* (§ 366) are found in the language of other persons also; the loc. in *-āhiṁ* (366) and the voc. plur. in *-āho* (§ 372) are met with perhaps just sporadically in the dialect of Śakāra. In respect of the last three forms this dialect coincides with Apabhraṁśa, and consequently the classification of Pṛthvīdhara is not without justification. The grammarians and the rhetoricians mentioned above name Cāṇḍālī as a separate dialect, which, according to Mk. fol. 82 is derived from Māgadhī and Śaurasenī and is rightly considered likewise by Lassen, Inst. p. 420 to be a form of Māgadhī. Kk. fol. 81 derives again Śābarī from Cāṇḍālī. Accordingly the basis of the former would be S., Mg. as well as Śākārī. Cf. LASSEN, Inst. § 162. According to Mk. fol. 3 to the Māgdhī dialects belongs also B ā h l ī k ī, which is assigned by Bharata, 17, 52=Sāhityad. p. 173, 7 to gamesters and by others to the Piśāca countries. (§ 27). Undoubtedly Mg. was not a homogeneous language, on the other hand, it was dialectically diversified. It is thus that we can explain the development of *kṣa* sometimes as *hka* and sometimes as *śka*., of *rṭha* sometimes as *sta* and sometimes as *śta*; and of *ṣka*, sometimes as *ska* and sometimes as *śka*. All the dialects that have *ya* for *ja*, *la* for *r* and *ś* for *s*, and form the nom. sing. of *a*-stems in *-e* should be regarded as Mg. It has already been shown above (§ 17. 18) that the boundary of the *-e* dialect extended beyond the frontiers of Magadha. Bharata 17, 58 asserts that the languages of all the provinces lying between the Gaṅgā and the sea are full of *-e* forms. But we can conclude nothing from such a vague statement. HOERNLE[1] has divided all the Prākrits into two groups : "the Śaurasenī Prākrit tongue" and the "Māgadhī Prākrit tongue" and has drawn a line of demarcation between the two groups from Khālsī, extending in the North over Bairāt, and Allahabad, and in the South through Ramgaṛh upto Jaugaḍa.[2] GRIERSON[3], who is in agreement with HOERNLE, assumes that the two groups of Prākrit gradually come closer and calls the resultant obtained from a mixture of the two a third Prākrit, namely Ardhamāgadhī, and he assigns it to the land lying about Allāhābād and that of the Marāṭhās. I do not believe that these assumptions are tenable. The Lāṭa-dialect shows significant vestiges of dialects, so much so that even between Dhaulī and Jaugaḍa,[4] there exist dialectical differences, but generally it seems to be a homogeneous language, which perhaps was also the language of the empire and was, therefore, understood rather than spoken over a wide area in the North, the West and the South.[5] Consequently the inscriptions of Aśoka found at Khālsī, Delhi, and Mirāt and the inscription of Bairāt as well as others furnish us with no information about the language of the country. In earlier days, as it happens today, certain individual dialects, which need not be called Prākrit (§ 5), it is true, gradually shaded into each other. Ardhamāgadhī is a strong proof of this. There is no connecting link between modern Mg.[6] and the old Mg.

1. Comp. Grammar, p. XVII ff. — 2. Caṇḍa, p. XXI. — 3. Seven Grammars of the Dialects and Sub-dialects of the Bihari Language, Part I (Calcutta 1883), p. 5. ff. — 4. SENART, Piyadasi, 2, 432 ff. — 6. GRIERSON, Seven Grammars, PartI II, (Calcutta 1883)

§ 25. In Mṛcchakaṭikā p. 29-39, Māthura, the keeper of the house of gambling, and his fellow player speak the dialect, called Ḍhakkī, named after Ḍhakka that is in Bangla Desh. Mk. fol. 81, Rv. in LASSEN, Inst. p. 5, and Pṛthvīdhara on Mṛcch. p.-V=p. 493, ed. GOḌABOLE, record Ḍhakkī along with Śākārī, Cāṇḍālī and Śābarī among the dialects of Apabhraṁśa. Corresponding to its geographical situation it seems that Ḍhakkī was a transition-dialect between Māgadhī and Apabhraṁśa. According to Pṛthvīdhara this dialect is phonetically characterized by preponderance of *la* and the use of the two sibilants, namely the dental *s* and the palatal *ś* : *lakāraprāyā*[1] *ḍhakkavibhāṣā saṁskṛtaprāyatve dantyatālavyasaśakāradvayayuktā ca.* It is to be understood from this that in it, as in Mg., *ra* is changed into *la*, and *ṣa* into *sa*, which as well as *ś* remains, however, unchanged in places where it occurs in Sanskrit. In the texts the mode of writing is not always consistent, but the manuscripts preserve very often fairly correct reading. STENZLER reads in 29, 15 and 30, 1 *are re*; in 30, 7 *re*; in 30, 11 *are*, but GOḌABOLE reads in 82, 1; 84, 4; 86, 1, *ale*; in 85, 5 *le* according to most of his manuscripts and it is read otherwise everywhere as in STENZLER (30, 16; 31, 4. 9. 16; 35, 7. 12; 36, 15; 39, 16). Further this rule is corroborated by *luddhu*=*ruddhaḥ* (29, 15; 30, 1), *palivevida*=*parivepita* (30, 7), *kulu kulu*=*kuru kuru* (31, 16), *dhāledi*=*dhārayati* (34, 9; 39, 13), *puliso*=*puruṣaḥ* (34, 12). But in more cases *ra* remains in texts and manuscripts. So throughout we have *jūdiara* (29, 15; 30, 1. 12; 31, 12; 36, 18), but only in 36, 18=106, 4 ed. GOḌABOLE, the word is found with *la* (v. l.); likewise in the Calcutta ed. Śaka 1792 p. 85, 3 there is *jūdakalassa* and in Calcutta ed. 1829 p. 74, 3 *muṭṭhipahāleṇa* against °*reṇa* found in all others ; while all the editions in the following line have *ruhirapahaṁ aṇusarĕmha* in stead of the expected reading *luhilapadhaṁ aṇusalĕmha.* In the verse 30, 4, 5 by the side of *salaṇaṁ* for which the Calcutta edition of 1792 rightly has *śalaṇaṁ*, there is *ruddo rakkhiduṁ taraï* in lieu of *luddo lakkhiduṁ taladi.* Other cases are : *aṇusarĕmha* (30, 13) *māthuru* (32, 7; 34, 25), *pidaraṁ, mādaraṁ* (32, 10. 12), *pasaru* (32, 16), *jajjara* (34, 11 beside *puliso* !), *uarodheṇa* (36, 24), *ahareṇa raï* (39, 8). Likewise the manuscripts oscillate in the use of the sibilants. Beside the correct forms *daśasuvaṇṇāha* (29, 15; 30, 1), *daśasuvaṇṇaṁ* (31, 4; 32, 3; 34, 9. 12 etc.), *śuṇṇu* (30, 11), *śela* (30, 17), there occur the wrong forms like *jasaṁ* (30, 9), *ādaṁsaāmi* (34, 25), *paḍissudia* (35, 5); the palatal sibilant has been wrongly used in forms like *śamaviśamaṁ, sakaluśaaṁ* (30, 8. 9), where GOḌABOLE has correctly used *samavisamaṁ, aïkasaṇaṁ* (read *adi*°), although he has erred in using *kaśśa* (114, 9) for *kassa*, as found in the ed. of STENZLER (39, 8). With *la* and *śa* Ḍhakkī becomes close to Mg., and with the endings *-u*=*-aḥ*, and *-am*, as well as/in the second person singular of the imperative it comes close to Apabhraṁśa. Here also manuscripts are not wholly dependable. Beside *deulu* (30, 11), there occurs *deulaṁ* (30, 12) ; by the side of *esu*=*eṣaḥ* (31, 12; 34, 35, 15) there is *eso* (30, 10); beside *pasalu*=*prasara* (32, 16), there is *geṇha* (29, 16; 30, 2) as well as *paaccha*=*prayaccha* (31, 4. 7. 9; 32, 8. 12. 14; 34, 24; 35, 7); by the side of the nom. in *-u*, as in *luddhu*=*ruddhaḥ* (29, 15; 30, 1), *vippadivu pādu*=*vipratipaḥ pādaḥ* (30, 11), *dhuttu mādhulú ṇiuṇu*=*dhūrto, māthuro, nipuṇaḥ* (32, 7), *vihavu*=*vibhavaḥ* (34, 17), the texts have the nominatives in -o, as in *baddho* (31, 12), °*ppāvuḍo puliso*=°*prāvṛtaḥ puruṣaḥ* (34, 12), *ācakkhante*° (§ 499) (34, 24), °*vutto*=°*vṛttaḥ* (31, 3), and in *-e*, such as *pāḍhe*=*pāṭhaḥ* (30, 25; 31, 1), *laddhe gohe*=*labdhaḥ puruṣaḥ* (31, 3). That here we have just cases of blunders committed in manuscript-tradition and that such forms do not present special dialectical peculiarities are clearly demonstrated by the presence of the word *baddho* (31, 14) in Mg. for the correct word *baddhe*, that is not to be found in any of the editions. Certainly erroneous is *tha* in *māthuru* (32, 7; 34, 25), for which should be read *mādhulu*, as for *pāṭhe* too all the editions (30, 25; 31, 1) and also in Mg. (31, 2) the manuscripts DH in GOḌABOLE p. 88 read *pāḍe*, K has *pāḍhe*, a form which including the ending is correct only in Ḍh. So stands in 30, 16 *kadhaṁ* = *katham*, but in 36, 19 *ruhirapahaṁ* = *rudhirapatham*. The correct form would be *luddhilapadhaṁ*. As in Ś. and Mg[2]. so in Ḍh. too the manuscripts are not reliable and there is no hope that with the limited number of texts, that we have, we shall ever be able to obtain a clear description of this dialect.[3] Cf. § 203.

1. So correctly reads STENZLER; GOḌABOLE reads at p. 2 p. 494 *vakāraprāyā*, — 2. So correctly reads GOḌABOLE, — 3. LASSEN, Inst. p. 414 ff., holds that the gambler speaks Dākṣiṇātyā and Māthura, the Āvantī dialect. See § 26. BLOCH's opinion is wrong, in Vr. und Hc. p. 4.

§ 26. Likewise it is difficult to get a clear idea about the other dialects mentioned by the grammarians. According to Pṛthvīdhara in Mṛcchakaṭikā the two police officers, Vīraka and Candanaka, pp. 99-106, speak the dialect of Avantī. About this dialect all that he says is that it has *sa* and *ra*, and that it is full of proverbial expressions : *tathā* I *śauraseny-avantijā prācyā*| *etāsu dantyasakāratā* I *tatrāvantijā rephavatī lokoktivahulā*. The quotation from Pṛthvīdhara is = Bharata 17, 48. According to Bharata 17, 51 = Sāhityad. p. 173, 4, Avantijā is to be spoken in dramas by the *dhūrtāḥ*, whereby according to the scholiast in LASSEN, Inst. p. 36 are meant the dice-players. LASSEN, Inst. p. 417-419, therefore, considers as the language of Māthura, as Āvantī, but this is wrong. Mk. fol. 3, like Ki. 5, 99, considers Āvantī as a *bhāṣā* and defines it in fol. 73 as an admixture of Māhārāṣṭrī and Śaurasenī. This admixture is found in one and the same sentence : *āvanti syānmāhārāṣṭrī śaurasenyāstu saṁkarāt anayoḥ saṁkarād āvantībhāṣā siddhā syāt* I *saṁkaraścaikaṣminneva vākye boddhavyaḥ*. In this dialect are found, for instance *hoi* = *bhavati*, *pĕcchadi* = *prekṣate*, *darisedi* = *darśayati*, etc. This description is in accord with the dialect of the two police officers, as it is given in MSS. In the stanzas 99, 16. 17 there are found Ś. *acchadha* and M. *bhĕttūṇa* and *vaccaï*, side by side; similarly at 99, 24. 25 Ś. *āacchadha-* and M. *turiaṁ*, *jatteha*, *karĕjjāha* and *pahavaï*; at 100, 4 there is *darisesï*; at 100, 12 M. *jaha* and Ś. *khuḍido* occur side by side; again at 100, 19; 101, 7; 105, 9 is found *vaccadi*, a mixture of M. *vaccaï* (99, 17) and Ś. *vajjadi*, as also *vajjaï* (100, 15); at 103, 15 there is *kahijjadi* and at 16 *sāsijjaï*; the second one is a pure M. form and the first one an admixture of M. *kahijjaï* and Ś. *kadhīadi*; many other examples are to be found in prose and poem. Accordingly the definition enunciated by Pṛthvīdhara may appear to be correct. But so far as it respects Candanaka the latter's own statement, as given at 103, 5 goes against him: *vaaṁ dakkhiṇattā avvaṭṭabhāsiṇo...mlecchajātīnām anekadeśabhāṣābhijñā yatheṣṭaṁ mantrayāmaḥ* "we southerners speak unintelligibly, because we are expert in languages of many barbarian countries, we speak just as we like." Candanaka, therefore, describes himself as a Southerner (*dākṣiṇātya*), that is proved also by his own statement found at 103, 16: *kaṇṇāḍakalahappaoaṁ katemi*, "I proceed to fight in the manner of Karṇāṭa." Therefore, it is very much improbable that the language in which he should have spoken is Āvantī; on the other hand, it is to be assumed that his language is Dākṣiṇātyā, which Bharata 17, 148 calls as one of the seven *bhāṣāḥ* and which according to 17, 52 = Sāhityad. p. 173, 5 is spoken by hunters and police officers in the drama. Mk. fol. 3 (cf. fol. 76) rejects it as an independent language, because it does not have any distinctive characteristic (*lakṣaṇākaraṇāt*). LASSEN, Inst. pp. 414-416 assigns the Dākṣiṇātyā language to the unnamed gambler in Mṛcch. and he is inclined to believe that in the language of the police officers in Śak. pp. 113-117 there are vestiges of this dialect. Both of his views are wrong. The dialect used by the gambler is Ḍhakkī (§ 25) and the language of the police officers in Śak. does not differ on any point from common Ś, as already observed by BÖHTLINGK.[1] As some of the manuscripts of the Bengali recension show doubling of the aspirates, I believed earlier[2] that this must have been the distinctive characteristic of Dākṣiṇātyā. But doubling is found also in Mg. in one of the manuscripts, and it is in no way linguistically important, rather it is just an orthographical device (§ 193). So far as we have been able to see up till now, it seems that Dākṣiṇātyā must have been very close to Āvantī which is spoken by Vīraka, and that both of them were very much akin to Ś. Apart from dialectical admixture, there are a number of forms that are against idiomatic usage in Ś. Thus : *vaaṃ* for *amhe*, *do* = *dvau*, and wholly remarkable is the change of *tya* into *tta* in *dakkhiṇattā* (§ 281). The form *darisaanti* occurs in Ś. too in Mṛcch. 70, 25.

1. In his edition of Śak, p. 240. — 2. GN. 1873, p. 212 ff.

§ 27. One of the very archaic dialects is P a i ś ā c ī. Vr., 10, 1 ff. knows only one dialect of this name; likewise Kī., 5, 96 and Siṁhadevagaṇin on Vāgbhaṭālaṁkāra, 2, 3, where this dialect is called Paiśācika, and Namisādhu on Rudraṭa, Kāvyālaṁkāra, 2, 12 calls it Paiśācika and in a grammatical quotation he refers to it by the name Paiśācikī: Hc. 4,303 — 324 deals with Paiśācī and appends to it, 325 — 328, Cūlikāpaiśācika. Hc. is followed by Triv. 3, 2, 43 ff. and Sr. fol. 63 ff., and both of them call the second dialect Cūlikāpaiśācī. An unknown author (§ 3 note I) referred to by Mk. fol. 2 describes eleven types of P. *kāñcideśiyapāṇḍye ca pāñcālagauḍamāgadham* । *vrācaḍaṃ dākṣiṇātyaṁ ca śaurasenaṁ ca kaikayam* । *śābaraṁ drāviḍaṁ caiva ekādaśa piśācakāḥ*. Mk. himself, as per fol. 3, treats only 3 Paiśācīs., namely Kaikeya, Śaurasena and Pāñcāla; because they alone were used as literary dialects : *kaikeyaṁ śaurasenañca pāñcālam iti ca tridhā* । *paiśācyo nāgarā yasmāt tenāpyanyā na lakṣitāḥ*......Kaikeya according to MK. fol. 86 is based on Sanskrit, and Śaurasena upon Śaurasenī: the only difference that Pāñcāla maintains in comparison with Śaurasena consists in the former having as its characteristic change of *ra* into *la*. RV. in LASSEN, Inst. p. 22 recognizes only two classes of Paiśācī: Kaikeyapaiśācam and the second one, whose name has been handed down to us in the corrupt form Caska. In any case, in accordance with the grade of purity, these are again divided into sub-classes, of which according to LASSEN, Inst.

Appendix p. 6 Māgadha and Vrācaḍa (read thus for Brāvḍa) are called Paiśācika. Lakṣmīdhara in LASSEN, Inst. p. 13 derives the name P. from the countries of the Piśācas in which it is spoken, and is named as such according to the opinion of the people of the earlier age : these countries are Pāṇḍya, Kekaya, Bāhlīka, Sahya, Nepāla, Kuntala, Gāndhāra and four others whose names have been transmitted to us in their corrupt forms : Sudeṣa, Bhoṭa, Haiva and Kanojana. These names point towards the north and the west of India. A nation is referred to as Piśāca in the Mahābhārata 7, 121, 14. But the Indians understand by the word Piśāca only demons, (*bhūta*) of this name (Kathāsaritsāgara, 7, 26. 27). Thus it is referred to by Bhāmaha in his commentary on Vr. 10, 1: *piśācānāṁ bhāṣā paiśāci*, and, therefore, he calls it also *bhūtabhāṣā* "the language of the demons", (Daṇḍin, Kāvyādarśa 1, 38; Sarasvatīk. 95, 11. 13; Kathāsaritsāgara 7, 29; 8, 30; HALL, Vāsavadattā p. 22 note) or even *bhūtabhāṣita* as well as *bhautika* (Vāgbhaṭālaṁkāra 3, 1. 3), *bhūtavacana* (Bālarāmāyaṇa 8, 5 = Sarasvatīk. 57, 11). There is the popular belief that the unmistakable identifying characteristic of a bhūta is that he speaks with a nasal accent, and thereupon CROOKE[1] assumes that like modern English this language too for that reason has been called a Piśācabhāṣā. The grammarians make no mention of this phonetic characteristic and I deem it probable that originally P. also like M. Ś. Mg. was named as such after the name of some people or country and the name of this country or people was similar in sound to *piśāca* and that on account of this the language as well began to be referred to as the dialect of the Piśācas, meaning demons. The nation of the Piśāca or Paiśāca, except in the passage of the Mahābhārata referred to above, is nowhere mentioned, even though individual tribes like the Kaikeya or Kekaya, Bāhlīka, to whom Mk. clearly assigns as their language a Mg. dialect (§ 24), Kuntala and Gāndhāra are mentioned very frequently. According to Daśarūpa 2, 60 the Piśāca or Māgadha language is especially spoken by the Piśācas, the people of lowly origin etc. According to Sarasvatīk. 56, 19; Sāhityad. p. 173, 10 P. is the language of the Pisāca; Bhojadeva, Sarasvatīk. 57, 25 forbids the use of pure P. by high class characters : *nātyuttamapātraprayojyā paiśāci śuddhā*. The example given by him is found in Hc. 4, 236 as that of Cūlikāpaiśācika. High characters, who do not appear in the highest rôles, according to Sarasvatīk. 58, 15, speak in a language that is Sanskrit and Paiśācī at the same time, by means of the popular play of words *bhāṣāśleṣa*, which is comparatively easier in Paiśācī than in any other Prākrit dialect inasmuch as P., of all the Pkt. dialects, is most akin to Sanskrit. Vr. 10, 2, it is true, says that Śaurasenī is the basis of P. and Hc. 4, 323 agrees with him; but as shown by Hc. 4, 324, in phonology, it stands closer to Skt., Pāli and the dialect of PG. The characteristic of P. and in addition of that of CP. as well, the two dialects that the grammarians do not strictly differentiate (§ 191), is the change of the voiced consonants into the voiceless ones, e. g. P. CP. *matana* = *madana*; *tāmotara* = *dāmodara*; P. *patesa* = *pradeśa*; CP. *nakara* = *nagara*; *kiri* = *giri*; *mekha* = *megha*; *khamma* = *gharma*; *rācā* = *rājā*;

cimūta=jimūta etc. (§ 190. 191). Another characteristic feature is the retention in unchanged form of most of the consonants including *na* into which is transformed also as *ṇa* and the change *la* into *ḷa*. HOERNLE[2] on account of mutation of the voiced mutes and change of *ṇa* into *na* and *la* into *ḷa* assumes that P. is a form of the Aryan language that developed in the mouth of the Dravidian people, when the latter wanted to speak an Aryan language. SENART[3] was perfectly correct in rejecting this view. Against the hypothesis of HOERNLE that in none of the Aryan dialects of India even a trace of the devocalization of voiced mutes is visible it has to be noted that in a number of sporadical cases this mutation is noticeable in the dialect of Shâhbâzgarhī[4], in the Lāṭa[5]-dialect and in the Leṇa-dialect[6]; in the NIA languages the mutation of the aspirate voiced mutes takes place in the Dardū, Kâfir, and Gypsy languages[7], and this suggests that the home of P. has to be searched for in the north-west in India.[8] P. is so much peculiar and independent that it began to be considered as the fourth language, besides Sanskrit, Prākrit and Apabhraṁśa (Kathâsarits. 7, 29; cf. 6, 148, Bṛhatkathām. 6, 52; Bāḷarāmāyaṇa 8, 4.5; Vāgbhaṭālaṁkāra 2, 1). Perhaps P. is understood also by *grāmya-bhāṣā*, in which, according to Vāgbhaṭa, Alaṁkāratilaka 15, 13 was composed Bhīmakāvya. It is deplorable that we have to depend exclusively on a few and insufficient statements of the grammarians for a knowledge of P. Bṛhatkathā was written in P. by Guṇāḍhya,[9] whose time has been calculated by BŪHLER[10] as the first or second century A.D. The only connected fragments in this dialect are found in Hc. 4, 310, 316. 320. 322. 323[11] and perhaps also in 326. According to the annals of the northern Buddhists there lived 116 years after the death of Buddha four Sthaviras who belonged to four different castes and spoke four different languages, namely Sanskrit, Prâkrit, Apabhraṁśa and Paiśācī respectively. The Sthaviras forming one of the four chief schools of Vaibhāṣikas are said to have used Paiśacī.[12]

1. An Introduction to the Popular Religion and Folklore of Northern India (Allahabad 1894) p. 149. — 2. Comp. Grammar, p. XIX f. — 3. Piyadasi 2, 501, (note 1). 4. JOHANSSON, Shâhbâzgarhī 1, 172 ff. — 5. SENART, Piyadasi 2, 375 (*kaṁboca*), 376 *paṭipātayachaṁ* etc.); 397 (*tuphe*, etc.) — 6. HULTZSCH, ZDMG. 37, 549; 40, 66, note 5.— 7. MIKLOSICH, Beiträge, zur Kenntniss der Zigeunermundarten I, II (Wien 1874) p. 15 ff.; IV. (Wien 1878) p. 51. Cf. also Gyp. *khūl*=Hindi *ghūr* in PISCHEL, Beiträge zur Kenntnis der deutschen Zigeunner (Halle a. S. 1894) p. 42 and Kalaṣa *khās*=Gyp. *khas*=Hindi *ghās*, Skt. *ghāsa*. — 8. PISCHEL, Deutsche Rundschau XXXVI (Berlin 1883) p. 368. The hypothesis that Guṇāḍhya was a Kashmirian is incorrect. He was a South-Indian, but his work was popular in Kashmir, as is proved by its abridgments by Somadeva and Kṣemendra. HALL. Vāsavadattā (Calcutta 1859) p. 22f. note.; BÜHLER, IA 1, 302 ff., LÉVI, JA., 1885, VI. 412 ff. Cf. Namisâdhu on Rudraṭa, Kāvyālaṁkāra 2, 12. — 10. Detailed Report p. 47. — 11. PISCHEL, De gr. Pr. p. 33. I am unable to find the passage in Somadeva's work. Kaṭhāsarits. 11, 48. 49 agrees in certain places but not sufficiently accurately. — 12. WASSILJEW, Der Buddhismus, seine Dogmen, Geschichte und Literatur. Translated from the Russian (by TH. BENFEY) 1, 248, note 3; 295 (St Petersburg, 1860).

§ 28. Apabhraṁśa, in the widest sense of the term, is indicative of any language that in any manner deviates from the correct one, i.e.

Sanskrit. Consequently it is the common name for all the Indian popular dialects (§ 4), and only remotely does it signify a particular form of Prākrit dialects that were remodelled from the popular dialects to the status of literary languages according to the usual practice that obtained in Prākrit (§ 5). Hc., 4, 329 — 446 treats A. as a uniform language. But from his rules it appears that under the name A. have been included together a number of several differing dialects. The forms *dhruṁ*, *traṁ* (4, 360), *tudhra* (4, 372), *prassadi* (4, 393), *brŏppiṇu*, *brŏppi* (4,391), *gṛhanti*, *gṛṇhĕppiṇu*, (4,341. 394. 438), *vrāśu* (4,399) with their *r* and *ṛ* belong to a dialect altogether different from the one that has been described in most of the other rules. The rule 4, 396, which prescribes that in A. the sounds *ka*, *kha*, *ta*, *tha*, *pa*, *pha* generally become *ga*, *gha*, *da*, *dha*, *ba*, *bha* respectively, stands as much in contradiction to by far most of the other rules and examples : thus for instance 4, 446, according to which A. should mostly be dealt with like Ś.[1] The language of Piṅgala has gone much further than A. towards disintegration in Vikramorvaśī of Kālidāsa and in Hc. The anonymous author cited by Mk., fol. 2 recognizes 27 different dialects of A., among which are included all the sub-classes mentioned under Paiśācī (§ 27). Similarly Rv. in Lassen, Inst. App. p. 5. Mk. on account of the differences being of insignificant character (*sūkṣmabhedatvāt*) confines A. only to three varieties, *nāgara*, *vrācaḍa* and *upanāgara*, a classification that is adopted also in Kī. 5, where the second variety has been designated as *vrācaṭa*. The chief variety of A. is Nāgara, and according to Mk. this was the language of Piṅgala as well, as is evident from the fact that he (Mk.) cites passages from this work under it. From Nāgara is derived Vrācaḍa, which according to Mk. fol. 85, originated in Sindh : *sindhudeśodbhavo vrācaḍopabhraṁśaḥ*. Among its peculiarities Mk. notes the development of *y* before *c* and *j* and the change of *ṣa* and *sa* into *śa* — the phonetic characteristics that are ascribed by him also to Mg. — and by Pṛthvīdhara to the dialect of Śakāra (§ 24). Further the optional change of the initial *ta*, *da* into *ṭa*, *ḍa*, and as it seems, the retention of *ṛ*, with the exception of *bhṛtya* etc., occur as other characteristics. The rest is all corrupt in the MSS. From an admixture of Nāgara and Vrācaḍa springs Upanāgara. Kī. 5, 70 is not clear. According to Mk., fol. 81 Hariścandra considered also *Śākki* or *Śakki* as an Apabhraṁśa dialect, but Mk. himself describes it as an admixture of Skt. and Ś., and includes it in his list of Vibhāṣāḥ in fol. 3. The words *ehu je* = *eṣo*[2] *yadi* in Piṅgala 1, 4[a], according to Ravikara in Bollensen on Vikr. 527 belong to the Vārendrī bhāṣā, which, therefore, point towards Bengal.[3] On Ḍhakkī, see § 25. Thus it is clear that A. extended from Sindh to Bengal, and this is in conformity with its nature as a popular language. Only a small portion of the many A. has again been turned into Prākrit. Lakṣmīnāthabhaṭṭa on Piṅgala 1. 1. 29.61 calls the language of Piṅgala to be A v a h a ṭ ṭ h a b h ā ṣ ā[4] = Apabhraṣṭabhāṣā, but at p. 22, 15 he says that he would like to describe, in short, V a r ṇ a m a r k a ṭ ī, that has been overlooked by Piṅgala and other teachers, by *śabdaiḥ prākṛtaiḥ avahaṭṭhakaiḥ*. Hc. in Deśīn. 1, 37 says that *avajjhāo* = *upādhyāyaḥ* has not been mentioned by him as it has *prākṛtam apabhraṣṭam iva rūpam*; in 1, 67 he quotes the view of some teacher according to whom the Apabhraṁśa word *āsiao* is equivalent to *āyasikaḥ*, and in Kathāsaritsāgara, 17, 141 the pure Māhārāṣṭrī words *eso ṭhiŏ kkhu majjāro*[5] are said to be *apabhraṣṭa*. The literary A., therefore, actually is *prākṛto'pabhraṁśaḥ*, "Prākrit-Apabhraṁśa". In spite of the phonetic disorder and the incredible freedom with which poets, at their sweet will for the sake of rhyme alter the vowels, drop endings, suppress entire syllables, confuse gender, case, number and voice with one another, A. has remained extraordinarily important and interesting, and it shows affinities with the Vedic language not in a small measure (§ 6).

1. PISCHEL, Hc. 1, IX. — 2. BOLLENSEN has *eho* in the text and *eha* in the commentary; in the Bombay edition the text has *eo*. — 3. B. R. s. v. Varendra and Vārendra. — 4. The Bombay edition has everywhere °*ha*. Cf. Sarasvatīk. 59, 9. — 5. BROCKHAUS gives the wrong form *majjāo*; DURGĀPRASĀD and PARAB (Bombay 1889) correctly read *khu*.

§ 29. For a knowledge of A. up to this date the most important source is Hc. 4,329 — 446 whom follows Triv. 3, 3, 1ff. Besides the materials utilized in my edition of this work, I have used also the Vyutpattidīpikā of Udayasaubhāgyagaṇin and that both in the Pūṇā MSS.[1] The work is designated as Haimaprākṛtavṛttiḍhuṇḍhikā and is confined to the etymological explanation of individual words on the basis of Hc.'s rules. Therefore, it is worthless for the most part. Unfortunately even the text is not essentially improved by these two MSS, because they too have all the defects of the manuscripts[2] used by me earlier. Like Trivikrama, Udayasaubhāgyagaṇin has added Sanskrit equivalents to the examples of A.; this makes the understanding of the subject extraordinarily easy and has proved to be of great advantage to me. We can say nothing about the sources whence Hc. collected his examples. They, however, create the impression of having been drawn from an anthology of the type of Sattasaī. As already noted by ZACHARIAE,[3] the stanzas quoted under Hc. 4,357, 23 are found along with an elaborate Skt. gloss also in Sarasvatīk. p. 76; further, Hc. 4,353 is found also in Caṇḍa 1 11[a] (p. 36), 4,330,2 also in Caṇḍa 2, 17[g] (p. 47), and in 2, 27' (p. 47) he quotes an A. stanza of his own (see § 34 note 4). Hc. 4,420,5 is found also in Sarasvatīk., p. 158, and Hc. 4,367,5 is found even in Śukasaptati, p. 160. Next after Hc. comes into consideration the A. stanzas found in Vikramorvaśī pp. 55-72. Unfortunately SHANKAR P. PAṆḌIT[4] and BLOCH[5] have declared these metrical passages to be spurious. But they are found in all the manuscripts which are not of a South Indian source, in which even other works have been systematically abridged,[6] and, as shown by KONOW[7] are thoroughly free from suspicion as it respects their genuineness. The Piṅgalachandaḥsūtra will make rich materials available to us when we shall have a critical edition of it. A beginning of the work had already been made by BOLLENSEN in the appendix to his edition of the Vikramorvaśī, pp. 520 ff. The materials collected by him have been taken over to Berlin by SIEGFRIED GOLDSCHMIDT,[8] who had planned an edition of the work, and other materials are to be found abundantly in India.[9] The Bombay edition (1894) in the

Kāvyamālā (41) of Prākṛita-Piñgala-Sūtras with the commentary of Lakṣmīnātha Bhaṭṭa by Śivadatta and Kāśīnāth Pāṇḍuraṅg Parab is hardly usable. I have compared the text of Piṅgala of this edition with that of Goldschmidt upto 2, 140[10]. In several places this text has been found useful to me. Generally it agrees with the Bombay edition, even in respect of errors, and this shows that the material found in Europe is not sufficient for a critical edition. It is true, that the text of Goldschmidt was not meant for printing, and it is evident from the MS itself that it was the result of researches carried for private use. There still remains much to be done here, and without an edition furnished with all the critical materials and the oldest and best commentaries this A. work is useful to a very limited extent. Besides detached A. stanzas are met with here and there. Thus in Erz. edited by Jacobi, pp. 157 f.; in Kk. 260, 43 ff.; 272. 34 - 38; in Dvār. 504, 26-32; in Sarasvatīk. p. 34 59. 130. 139. 140. 165. 166. 167. 177. 214. 216. 217. 219. 254. 260f.; in the commentary on Daśarūpa 139; 11; 162, 3; in Dhvanyāloka, 243, 20 of Ānandavardhana (§ 14 with note 2); in Śukasaptati. Textus simplicior. Published by Richard Schmidt (Leipzig 1893) pp. 32. 49. 76. 122. 136. 152 note; 160 with note; 170 note; 182 note; 199; in Vetālapañcaviṁśatikā, ed. Uhle, p. 217, No. 13: 220 No. 20; in Siṁhāsanadvātriṁśikā, IS. 15, 394; in Prabandhacintāmaṇī (Bombay 1888) pp. 17. 46. 56. 59. 61. 62. 63. 70. 80. 109. 112. 121. 141. 157. 158. 159. 204. 228. 236. 238. 248., and in Beames, Comp. Grammar 2, 284. Most of these stanzas are so much corrupt that we can utilize only particular words from them. In Alaṅkāratilaka, 15, 13 Vāgbhaṭa mentions Abdhimathana as a work written in A.

1. Shridhar R. Bhāṇḍārkar, A Catalogue of the Collections of Manuscripts deposited in the Deccan College (Bombay 1888), p. 68, No. 276; p. 118, No. 788. — 2. Hc. 1, IX. — 3. GGA. 1884. p. 309. — 4. Vikramorvaśiyam (Bombay 1879) p. 9 ff. — 5. Vararuci und Hemcandra p. 15 ff. — 6. Pischel GN. 1874, 214: Monatsberichte der Akad. zu Berlin 1875, 613. Even in the case of Pañcatantra and the Mahābhārata the South Indian recensions are the shortest and by no means the oldest. — 7. GGA, 1894, 475.—8. Weber, Verzeichniss 2, 1, 269ff. — 9. Aufrecht, Cat. Cat. 1, 336 ff.; 2, 75, where it has been correctly remarked that in our texts spurious passages are found in quite a good number. Thus for example a quotation from Karpūramañjari p. 199. 200. 211. — 10. Weber, Verzeichniss 2, 1, 270, Nr. 1711.

§ 30. According to Bhāratīyanāṭyaśāstra 17, 31-44[1]; Daśarūpa 2, 59. 60; Sāhityad. 432 in the drama men of high rank and, among women, nuns, chief queens, ministers' daughters, and courtesans, according to Bharata also female artists speak Sanskrit; all other women speak Prākrit; the apsarases on the earth can speak the language of their choice. Generally these statements are in conformity with the practice obtaining in dramas. Yet everywhere the chief queen speaks Prākrit; Mālatī and Madayantikā, the daughters of the minister, speak Prākrit in Mālatīmādhava; the harlot Vasantasenā speaks mostly in Prākrit in Mṛcchakaṭikā, but at pages 83 — 86 she speaks in verses in Sanskrit. It was assumed in the case of harlots that they were well-versed in both the languages; it is noteworthy that in order to become a fully qualified harlot, she must be adept in 64 arts, be endowed with all the 64 kinds of accomplishments and be conversant with the 18 popular languages[2] : *gaṇiyā......caüsaṭṭhikalāpaṇḍiyā caüsaṭṭhi gaṇiyāguṇovaveyā......aṭṭhārasdeṣibhāsā visārāyā* (Nāyādh. 480; Vivāgas. 55 ff.). Prosperity in the profession was concomitant with this. In Kumārasaṁbhava 7, 90 Priestess Sarasvatī praises the married pair, Śiva and Pārvatī in two languages, Śiva in Sanskrit and Pārvatī in an easily intelligible language, i.e. in Prākrit. Rājaśekhara, Karp. 5, 3.4 says that a work in Skt. is rough and that it is sweet in Pkt.; accordingly the difference between the two languages is the same as that between a man and a woman. In Mṛcch. 44, 1ff. the Vidūṣaka says that two things make him laugh: one is a Sanskrit-speaking woman and the other a man who sings in a low voice ; the woman who speaks Sanskrit makes the sound *su su* like a heifer through whose nose a cord has been passed and the man who sings in a low voice resembles an aged family-priest who mutters his prayer with a dry garland of flowers worn over his head. The director of the play in Mṛcch., who subsequently plays the rôle of the Vidūṣaka, speaks in Sanskrit in the beginning, but as soon as he begins to talk to a woman he (2, 14), "according to the circumstance and usage", expresses his readiness to speak in Prākrit. In support of the statement that a man should speak to a woman in Prākrit Pṛthvīdhara (495, 13) gives a quotation : *striṣu nā prākṛtaṁ vadet.* From all this it is gathered that Prākrit is characterized as the proper language of women, as has been prescribed by the authors on rhetorics. Besides, they not only understand Skt., but they speak it as well the moment they have to say something in verse. So speak Vicakṣaṇā in Viddhaś. pp. 75. 76; Mālatī in Mālatīm. pp. 81. 84; Lavaṅgikā p. 253; Sītā in Prasannarāghava, pp. 116-118 even in prose and at pp. 120. 121. 155 in verse; Kalahaṁsikā in Anarghar. p. 113; the girl-friend of the heroine in Karṇas. p. 30, and the heroine herself, p, 32; Sindūrikā in Bālar. pp. 120. 121; in *Chardi*, Jīvān. 20, in Subhadrāh. p. 2 the actress, and Subhadrā, p. 13; in Mallikām., Mallikā, pp. 71, 17; 75, 4; 81, 12; 82, 1; 85. 9; Navamālikā 72, 8; 75, 10; Sārasikā 78, 14; 251, 3; Kālindī 82, 24; 84, 10; 91, 15; in Dhūrtas. p. 11f., Anaṅgasenā, also in prose; and sometimes also women in Cait. Buddharakṣitā cites Mālatīm. p. 242, Kāmasūtra 199, 17f. Even the men who speak usually Pkt. now and then cross over to Skt., when they have to say in verses. So the Vidūṣaka, in Viddhaś. p. 25, who declares Pkt. to be the proper medium of expression for people of his class (*amhārisajaṇajogge pāudamagge*), in Karṇas. p. 14, and Jivān. pp. 53. 83; similarly in Kaṁsavadha p. 12, the gate-keeper, in Dhūrtas. p. 9, and in Hāsy. p. 23, 33. 38, the snātaka, and at p. 28 also the barber. In Jīvān. p. 6 ff. Dhāraṇā speaks to herself in Pkt. but in the guise of a female ascetic she speaks to the minister in Skt., in Mudrār., Virādhagupta in the guise of a snake-charmer at pp. 70 ff., speaks Pkt., but to himself, pp. 73ff. 84 and to Minister Rākṣasa, p. 85 he speaks in Skt.; at p. 82. 2 he introduces himself as a Prākrit poet. An unknown poet complains that even in his time many people are not capable of reading a Prākrit poem,[3] and another one (H. 2 = Vajjālagga, 324, 20) asks why should they not be ashamed of themselves who cannot read and understand the nectar-like poetry in Prākrit and still trouble themselves about true love. We as yet do not know if in Sarasvatīk. 57, 8 Nāṭyarājasya is the correct reading, and the person who has been designated by this term is also unknown. Likewise we are not sure about the identity of Śahasāṅka referred to in 57, 9. Perhaps in the kingdom of the former there was nobody who could speak in Pkt. and in that of the latter there was none who did not speak Skt.[4] Notwithstanding the praise of Prākrit expressed here and there it has always, in comparison with Skt., been considered to be a language of inferior status, and perhaps for that reason the word Prākṛta, even as the name of the language, signifies very appropriately "common", "general", "inferior" which is also commonly denoted by the word. It is useless to carry an investigation into the antiquity and succession of the dialects (§ 32).

1. Bharata furnishes further details, and here I have entered into them only to a limited extent, because the text is very often doubtful. — 2. The number of popular dialects is mentioned to be 18 also in Ovav. § 109; Nāyādh. § 121; and Rāyap. § 291. In Kāmasūtra 33, 9 only the deśabhāṣāḥ in general are referred to. — 3. In PISCHEL, Hc. 2, p. 44, on Hc. 1, 181. — 4. Both of the following verses, i.e. 57, 10. 11 literally are= to Bālar. 8, 4. 5; 57, 13, resemble Bālar. 8, 7. Since Rājaśekhara lived a century earlier than Bhoja, it is the author of Sarasvatīk. who has borrowed them from him.

B. THE PRĀKRIT GRAMMARIANS.

§ 31. At the top of the list of the names of indigenous workers in the field of Prākrit must be placed the name of Bharata, in case, by this name, we, with the Indians, mean the mythical author of Indian dramaturgy. Mk. fol. 1 refers to Bharata among his sources. Neither the quotation found at fol. 4 nor the others, cited by scholiasts,[1] are to be found in our text of the Bhāratīyanāṭyaśāstra[2]; in adhyāya 17 thereof, the different languages have been treated, and in stanzas 6-23 there is a short and very faulty presentation of Prākrit grammar. Besides chapter 32 of the work contains a number of examples in Prākrit, and all these are thoughtlessly distorted. A second work, that is ascribed to Bharata, is Saṅgītanṛtyākara.[3] According to DEVĪPRASĀDA[4] this work is very rare. There are found hardly any citations from that work, on the other hand, they are all from another recension of Nāṭyaśāstra. Mk. fol. 1 mentions Ś ā k a l y a and K o h a l a side by side with Bharata. According to Mk. fol. 48 Śākalya, beside *tujjhesu* and *tumbhesu*, teaches also *tujjhisuṁ* and *tumbhisuṁ*, which were not acceptable to many (*etat tu na bahusammatam*), and according to fol. 71 in Ś. beside *bhodi* occurs also *hodi*.[5] The quotation from Kohala is given in § 23. It cannot be affirmed if both of them are identical with the ancient grammarians.[6] Likewise nothing can be said with certainty with regard to P ā ṇ i n i, who is credited with the authorship of P r ā k ṛ t a l a k ṣ a ṇ a, a Prākrit grammar by Kedārabhaṭṭa in Kavikaṇṭhapāśa[7] and Malayagiri.[8] He is credited also with the authorship of two epics, namely Pātālavijaya and Jāmbavatīvijaya.[9] In view of the fact that from the first are cited the forms *gṛhya* and *paśyati*, that go against Pāṇini's own rules 7, 1, 37. 81 KIELHORN[10] and BHĀṆḌĀRKAR[11] are doubtful about the identity of the poet with the grammarian Pāṇini. But we know that the antiquity of Indian epics goes back to a period, far earlier than hitherto supposed to be.[12] The word *gṛhya* is quite common in the Mahābhārata and the Rāmāyaṇa and likewise the forms of the participle ending in *-ati*, instead of those in *-anti* are not rare.[13] It is highly improbable to hypothesize that Pāṇini might not have known the Mahābhārata. His grammar does not codify the language of poetry, but the correct Skt. of the Brāhmaṇas and Sūtras,[14] and it does not follow from this that many of the forms that have not been mentioned in his grammar either did not exist from before his time or that he as a poet could not use them. According to tradition Pāṇini, the poet, was identical with Pāṇini, the grammarian,[15] and I do not see any reason to doubt its correctness. It seems probable that Pāṇini might have written a grammar of Prākrit as well and that perhaps as a supplement to his Skt. grammar which was the original work. However, the Prākrit grammar of Pāṇini is said to be very bad. Along with the names of earlier writers Mk. fol. 171 mentions also one K a p i l a.

1. PISCHEL, De gr. Pr. p. 1f. — 2. Besides the edition of ŚIVADATTA and PARAB (Bombay 1894=Kāvyamālā 42), I have used both the MSS of Pūnā; they are transcriptions from the same archetype and constitute the basis of the printed edition. The edition of GROSSET (Lyon 1897) extends up to the end of the fourteenth adhyāya only. — 3. AUFRECHT, Cat. Cat. 1, 396. 686. — 4. A Catalogue of Sanskrit Manuscripts existing in Oudh for the year 1883 (Allahabad 1884) p. 10 of.—5. PISCHEL, De gr. Pr. p. 2. 3. — 6. AUFRECHT, Cat. Cat. 1, 130 mentions one Kohala, who was a writer on music. He might have been identical with the Prākrit grammarian. Cf. also WEBER IS. 8, 272 f., IS tr. 2, 59; B.R. s. v. — 7. A work bearing this title is often referred to without any mention of its author (AURECHT, Cat. Cat. 1, 86; 2, 16). It is ascribed to Kedārabhaṭṭa by D'ALWIS An introduction to Kachchâyana's Grammar of the Pâli Language (Colombo, 1863) p. xxv. Cf. WEBER, IStr. 2, 325, note 2. — 8. WEBER IStr. 2, 325, note 2 ; IS. 10, 227, note 1; KLATT, ZDMG. 33, 472; LEUMANN Actes du Sixième Congrès International des Orientalistes (Leide 1885) 3, 2, 557 f. — 9. AUFRECHT, ZDMG. 14, 581 f., 28, 113; 36, 366 ff., Halāyudha s. v. sṛkvan; PETERSON, Subhāṣhitāvali (Bombay, 1886) p. 54 ff., who has rightly remarked that both of them may have been the names of the same epic; PISCHEL, ZDMG. 39, 95 ff. 316. — 10. GN. 1885, 185 ff. — 11. JBoAS. 16, 343 ff. — 12. BÜHLER, Die indischen inschriften und das Alter der indischen Kunstpoesie. Wien 1890. Cf. BHĀṆḌĀRKAR l. c. — 13. HOLTZMANN, Grammatisches aus dem Mahābhārata (Leipzig. 1884); BÖHTLINCK. BKSGW. 1887, 213ff. on WHITNEY § 449. 990. — 14. LIEBICH, Pāṇini (Leipzig 1891) p. 47 ff. The conclusion drawn by him from the Bhagvadgitā p. 32 ff., as shown above, cannot be proved. — 15. AUFRECHT, ZDMG, 36, 365ff., PISCHEL, ZDMG. 39, 97f.

§ 32. The oldest of the Prākrit grammars that we possess is Prākṛtaprakāśa of V a r a r u c i. Of the several persons bearing this name[1] the grammarian is distinguished from others by his gotra name Kātyāyana. This appellation was given to him by the unknown[2] author of the commentary Prākṛtamañjarī, who in his introduction interchanges Kātyāyana and Vararuci throughout and under 2, 2 uses the name Kātyāyana in lieu of Vararuci.[3] This sort of inconsistency is noticeable also in the case of the name of Vararuci, the author of the Vārttika. That he too was called Vararuci is reported by Somadeva, Kathāsaritsāgara 2, 1, and Kṣemendra, Bṛhatkathāmañjarī, 1, 68; 2, 15. Besides, the tradition goes as back as

Guṇāḍhya[4] and reaches down upto Sāyaṇa[5], and the lexicographers[6] fix him in the middle course. The anthology, Saduktikarṇāmṛta contains a stanza composed by Vārttikakāra[7], a term that can denote Kātyāyana and Kātyāyana alone[8], and Patañjali, on Pāṇini, 4, 3, 101 (2, 315 ed. KIELHORN) mentions *vārarucaṁ kāvyam*[9]. From this it appears probable that our Vārttikakāra was not a simple dry grammarian, but also a poet like his successor Patañjali[10] and his predecessor Pāṇini (§ 31). This makes it clear that Kātyāyana could be confused with Vararuci, who, according to the tradition, was a contemporary of Kālidāsa and was one of the nine jewels in the court of Vikramāditya[11]. WEBER[12] has attributed the same sort of confusion also with regard to the author of Prākṛtamañjarī, and he[13], WESTERGAARD[14] and BLOCH[15] have expressed the opinion on the question of identity of Vārttikakāra with the Prākrit grammarian, that is against the view of COWELL[16], MAXMÜLLER[17], PISCHEL[18] and KONOW[19]. When even Vr. could be surpassed by Hc. and the south Indian grammarians in the art of criticism, there is no reason to push him upwards just on account of his critical acumen, upto Vārttikakāra referred to above, "the stubborn castigator of Pāṇini"[20]. By the time Prākrit grammar of Hc. had already made great progress as compared with the time of Vr., and it is one thing to improve upon a work that has been ready from before and it is quite another to plan a work all new. After all it was a fact that Patañjali found one Kātyāyana to criticize and improve upon him. That the dialects taught by Vr., more particularly Māhārāṣṭrī, have forms that are phonetically much later than those of the language of the inscriptions of Aśoka and that of the Nāsika inscriptions proves nothing at all[21]. Because the Prākrits are merely artificial dialects and existed by the side of the popular and official dialects, it is wholly wrong to draw a chronological sketch of the Prākrit languages on the basis of the inscriptions. If the Sattasaī be the work of a s i n g l e author, it is wholly wrong to suppose, as opined by JACOBI and BLOCH, that Māhārāṣṭrī did not come into common use before the beginning of the 3rd century A.D. The names of 318 poets that have been transmitted to us through the medium of this anthology alone presuppose that there existed from before a rich literature in Prākrit (§ 13), which up to the time of Govardhanācārya and therefore, till up to the 12th century A.D. was the only literary dialect employed in composing aphoristic musical stanzas, mostly depicting love-themes and written in the Āryā metre, that might have later been collected together in the form of an anthology[22]. The Gītagovinda of Jayadeva goes back to an original work written in Apabhraṁśa[23], besides it may be noted that several Sanskrit works, of course not rarely, are found to be just imitations of some earlier works in Prākrit[24]. The assumption of BLOCH that Vr. cannot have lived before the 5th century A.D. is in no way important on lingusitic grounds. On the other hand, the possibility is not altogether ruled out that the author of Prākṛtamañjarī confused the two Vararucis, although a reference in his work to the grammarian is to be taken less lightly than that in the work of the Tibetan Tārānātha. Then there is the tradition that Kātyāyana was a Prākrit grammarian too and it seems to me that the name Vārttikārṇava-bhāṣya, a work taken to be a grammar of Prākrit and mentioned by Appayadīkṣita, Prākṛtamaṇidīpa 5, among his sources of information immediately after *vāraruca granthāḥ* corroborates it. The identity of Kātyāyana with Vararuci cannot naturally be looked upon as certain.

1. Aufrecht, Cat. Cat. 1, 551. — 2. In Oppert, Lists of Sanskrit Manuscripts in Private Libraries of Southern India, (Madras 1880. 1885) 1, 290, No. 3426 and 2, 371, No. 6341 Kātyāyana is mentioned as the author. — 3. Pischel, De gr. Pr. 10 f. — 4. Konow, GGA. 1894, 473 — 5. Cowell, The Prákṛta-Prakáśa, Second Issue. Advertisement ; Pischel, De gr. Pr. p. 9. Cf. also Prakriyākaumudīprasāda in Bhāṇḍārkar, Report 1883/84. p. 362, 18. — 6. B. R. s. v. Kātyāyana. — 7. Aufrecht, ZDMG. 36, 524 — 8. Pischel, ZDMG. 39. 98. The Prākṛtamañjarī speaks about *mahākavi Kātyāyana*. — 9. In what respect does this sort of reference to this *kāvyam* in the Mahābhāṣya warrants the statement, "that this reference to bhagavān Kātyaḥ, as the author of this Kāvya, does not hold good for Vararuci as its author" (Weber, Istr. 3, 227), I do not understand. — 10. Aufrecht, ZDMG. 36. 370. — 11. Konow, GGA. 1894, 474. — 12. Instr. 3, 378. — 13. IStr. 2,53ff. 3, 277 ff. — 14. Ueber den ältesten Zeitraum der indischen Geschichte mit Rücksicht auf die Litteratur (Breslau 1862) p. 86. — 15. Vr. und Hc. p. 9 ft. — 16. The Prākṛita-Prakāśa2, p. vi. — 17. HASL. p 148, 239 ff. — 18. — De gr. Pr. p. 9. ff. — 19. GGA. 1894, 473. — 20. Weber, Istr. 3, 278. — 21. Westergaard l. c.; Jacobi, Erzählungen, p. xiv f.; Bloch, Vr. und Hc. p. 12 f. — 22. Pischel, Hofdichter p. 30. — 23. Pischel, l. c. p. 22. — 24. Pischel, Rudraṭa's Śṛṅgāratilaka (Kiel 1886) p. 13 note 1.

§ 33. In any case, if Vararuci is not the oldest, he is one of the oldest Prākrit grammarians. The title of his grammar is Prākṛtaprakāśa, that was published with notes and a translation by Cowell: The Prákṛita Prakáśa : or The Prákṛit Grammar of Vararuci, with the Commentary (Manoramá) of Bhámaha. Second Issue, London 1868 (printed for the first time, Hertford, 1854). A reprint of the text has recently been brought out by Rama Shastri Tai-langa (Benares 1899). Vr. treats in Paricchedas 1-9, M., in 10 P., in 11 Mg., and in 12 Ś. The text has come down to us partly in a very mutilated condition, and in several places its recensions differ strongly, and this goes to prove its antiquity. The oldest of its commentators was B h ā m a h a, an inhabitant of Kashmir, who was also a rhetorician as well as poet.[2] His time has been determined only to this extent that he is older than Udbhaṭa, who lived under King Jayāpīḍa of Kashmir (779 — 813 A.D.) and wrote a commentary on the rhetorical work of Bhāmaha[3]. Bhāmaha's commentary on the Prākṛtaprakāśa bears the title Manoramā[4] and is lacking in Pariccheda 12. Undoubtedly Bhāmaha misunderstood Vr. now and then. The most striking proof of this is furnished by 4, 14[5] It is uncertain if he had ever understood the gaṇas[6] exactly as they were conceived by Vr. A distinction that is to be seen throughout in the grammar has to be rigorously maintained between the sūtras and the commentary. We can just have an idea as regards the sources of information of Bhāmaha from the significant passages quoted by him. Such passages occur under Vr. 8, 9; 9, 2. 4 - 7.9 - 17 ; 10, 4, 14; 11, 6. Of them, under 9, 2 is given *hūṁ sāhasu*[7] *sabbhāvaṁ* = H. 453 (cf. the v. 1), where none of the MSS has *huṁ*. According to Bhuvanapāla (IS. 16, 153) the writer of this stanza is V i ṣ ṇ u n ā t h a : under 9, 9 occurs *kiṇo dhuvasi*

= H. 369, it is also cited in Hc. 2,216, and according to Bhuvanapāla (IS. 16, 120) it is of Devarāja. I cannot trace the remaining ones : the examples given under 10, 4. 14 have been taken from Bṛhatkathā. In 9, 4 the Gāthās are generally referred to. A later day commentary is the Prākṛtamañjarī, of which the unknown author (cf. § 32, note 2) wrote in verses and who is evidently a South Indian. The manuscript in the Malayālam character, utilized by me, of the Royal Asiatic Society, London[8], is incomplete and extends upto Vr. 6, 18. The author evidently knew Bhāmaha. The examples given by both of them mostly tally, nevertheless the number of examples quoted by the anonymous writer is often smaller than that of those given by Bhāmaha, though sometimes a few are added by him here and there; his text differs in many places from that of Cowell[9]. The commentary is not of a high value.

1. Cowell, p. 97 ; Pischel, De gr. Pr. p. 10. 13; Bühler, Detailed Report p. 75 ; Hoernle, Proc. ASB. 1879, 79 f. — 2. Aufrecht, IS. 16, 207 f., Cat. Cat. 1. 405 f.; Peterson, Subhāṣitāvali p. 79; Pischel, Rudraṭa p. 6 f. — 3. Pischel, Rudraṭa p. 13. — 4. Aufrecht, Cat. Cat. 1, 360 wrongly calls it Prākṛtamanoramā. Wrong is also the statement that it is called Prākṛtacandrikā as well. Both the statements are based on Kielhorn, A Catalogue of Sanskrit MSS existing in the Central Provinces (Nagpur 1874) p. 84. No. 44. All other sources quoted by Aufrecht have Manoramā. The manuscript referred to by Hoernle, Proc. ASB. 1879, 79f. ascribes it to Vararuci himself. — 5. Bloch Vr. und Hc. p. 28. — 6. It is not, therefore, certain that the gaṇas did never have a fixed number of words as was supposed by Bloch, Vr. und Hc. p. 31. As in Sanskrit, so in Prākrit as well, the schools were differing from one another. — 7. We must read as such in lieu of *sāhusu* in Cowell and *kadhehi sāhusu* in Tailanga and in the translation it is to be changed into *sādhuṣu*. — 8. Noted by Aufrecht, Cat. Cat. 1, 360. — 9. The more important ones in Pischel, De. Gr. Pr. p. 10-16.

§ 34. The opinions differ very widely with regard to Caṇḍa, whose Prākṛtalakṣaṇam has been published by Hoernle : The Prákṛita Lakṣaṇam or Chaṇḍa's Grammar of the Ancient (Arsha) Prákrit. Part I. Text with a critical introduction and indexes. Calcutta, 1880. Hoernle is of the view that Caṇḍa had treated Ārṣa (§ 16. 17). He bases his edition on the manuscripts AB which give the least of the texts : he is of the opinion that the MSS CD contain later interpolations. He considers C. older than Vr. and Hc., and as such, generally speaking, he considers him to be the oldest of the known Prākrit grammarians. Against this Bloch[1] thinks "the grammar of Caṇḍa is an inaccurate and superficial abridgment of another work, may be perhaps even of Hemacandra." Both the views are incorrect. That Caṇḍa is not so old as he is considered to be by Hoernle is proved by the introductory stanza I, in which the author states that he will fashion his work on the basis of the views of earlier writers (*vṛddhamatāt*). This stanza is found in all the manuscripts of Hoernle, also in Peterson, Third Report (Bombay 1887), p. 265, and in Bhāṇḍārkar, Lists of Sanskrit Manuscripts in Private Libraries in the Bombay Presidency. Part I (Bombay 1893) p. 58, and, therefore, cannot persumably be considered, in agreement with Hoernle, p. 1, note*, to be a later adaptation. It is doubtful as to how far the work can generally be considered to be an adaptation. It is true that the manuscript C, in the commentary, appears to have received many additions. But all the rules that C and D, rather B,C, and D have in common cannot be denied to be of the original work. C evidently deals with M. JM. AMg. JŚ. side by side. This is demonstrated by the rules; thus in 1, 5 the genitive in *-āṇaṁ* is mentioned by the side of that in *-āhaṁ*; in 2, 10, the nominative in *-e* is taught close to that in *-o*; in 2, 19 the absolutive in M. JM. AMg. JM. JŚ. as well as in A. is treated; in 3, 11, 12 the rules relating to M. AMg. and JŚ. are combined into one[2]. This peculiarity is noticeable to a far greater extent in C.D. Thus in 1, 26* (p. 42) occurs A. *haũ* by the side of *haṁ* and *ahaṁ* in 2, 19, CD add forms of M. A. to those of the absolutive of M. AMg. JM. JŚ. and A.; likewise in 2, 27[e-l] the forms of A. are preponderant and in 27[l.k] also of JŚ.; in 3, 6 (p. 48) the forms from JŚ., AMg. and JM. are mixed up together; 3, 11[a] furnishes supplementary forms from CP. in addition to those given in 3, 11, 12. Hence the assertion that 3, 6 (p. 48) is fully in keeping with the characteristics of the work and that 3, 39[a] is wrong may be an impossibility. Sometimes the additions appear going back to Hc. as the source: Thus the definition of Prākṛta in C. in 1, 1 is verbally Hc. 1, 1, but the former gives just the beginning; 1, 11[a] (p. 36) is = Hc. 4, 353; 2, 1[e] (p. 37) is = Hc. 1, 6, but the former is shorter; 3, 11[a] (p. 48) corresponds to Hc. 4, 325; but here also the former is shorter. Thus everywhere C. is shorter, and in certain cases, such as in 3, 34 (p. 51) = Hc. 1, 177, in spite of so much of correspondences, the distinction is so great that C. cannot be considered the borrower. As against what has been said above, it is noteworthy that Hc. 3, 81 seems to have referred to C. 1, 17 as noted by HOERNLE, p. XXII. There C. teaches that *se* is used also in the genitive plural, and Hc. 3, 81 remarks that some author desires the use of *se* in the genitive plural as well : *idantador āmāpi se-ādeśaṁ kaścid icchati.* BLOCH[3], in fact is of the opinion that reference in C. by the singular form *kaścit* in Hc. is indicative of the fact that no great importance is to be attached to him. But the entire thesis of BLOCH with regard to the manner of giving citations in Hc. and in other Indian grammarians is essentially wrong. When Hc. says *kaścit,* thereby he means to refer to one more authority. Besides there is no grammarian other than C., who is known to have framed an identical rule; thus the greatest possibility is that in places where C. and Hc. have an identical rule, the borrower is not C., but Hc. All other such cases have been correctly put together by HOERNLE p. XXII ff.[4] I shall, however, just add the example *caüvisaṁ...pi...*given under C. 2. 12[a] (p. 44) which is much more detailed in C. than in Hc. 3, 137. Further, the terminology employed by both of them is not identical throughout. Thus in C. 2, 1[b] (p. 37) the vowel that remains after elision of a consonant is called *uddhṛta*, but in Hc. 1. 8 it is designated *udvṛtta*; C. 2, 10 has Visarjanīya, but Hc. 1, 37 has Visarga; C. under 2, 15 (p. 45) uses Ardhānusvāra, but Hc. in 3, 7 Anunāsika; etc. Moreover, sometimes C. gives us quotations that Hc. does not have. Thus 2, 21. 22. 24; 3, 38. 39 where the second example given under 1. 1 (p. 39) is quoted also by Siṁhadevagaṇin on Vāgbhaṭālaṅkāra, 2, 2 (§ 9); further those given under 2, 24 (p. 46), under

2, 27[b] and 2, 27[1] (p. 47). In no way C. had desired to treat Ārṣa alone. The so called archaisms, such as retention of *t*, *th*, the lengthening of the vowel in the endings *-āṁ*, *-iṁ*, *-ūṁ* etc. are errors committed by the scribe like the so many errors that are quite common in Jaina-MSS[5]. Even in the case of the manuscripts of C., it is noteworthy that all of them do not mostly have such errors in them and seldom do they have these all at the same places. The dialect mainly taught by C. is M., and along with it he himself mentions expressly Apabhraṁśa in 3, 37, Paiśācikī in 3, 38, Māgadhikā in 3, 39, Ārṣa in 2, 13[a-b] (p. 44), which, as already noted, is referred to several times also in the A and B recensions; Śaurasenī is mentioned in 3, 39[a] (p. 52). The example quoted in D 2, 1[c] (p. 37) is= Gaüḍavaho 220 and is found also in Hc. 1, 6; the second example given in C D under 1 26[a] (p. 42) *teṇa ahaṁ viddho* is clearly Hāla 441[6]. Because these examples are not found in all the manuscripts, it is risky to depend on them for determination of the age of C. The text has been handed down to us in such a mutilated condition that it can be used only with great caution and that also after a careful examination of the variants. In any case this much seems to be certain that C. was older than Hc. and that he is among his authorities. The very fact that C. is preserved in several recensions goes to suggest his comparatively earlier antiquity. Deviating from all other grammarians, C. begins with the nominal and pronominal flexion (*vibhakti-vidhāna*); in the second section he treats the vowels (*svaravidhāna*) and in the third the consonants (*vyañjanavidhāna*). The C D recension bifurcates the third section after 3, 36 and designates the remaining portion beginning from 3, 37 up to 3, 39 the fourth section and gives to it the heading *bhāṣāntara-vidhāna* "Rules on other languages"; corresponding to its name, this section deals with other Prākrit dialects like M. JM. AMg. and JŚ. and therefore, it was wrong to consider this alone to be an entire work Prākṛtabhāṣāntara-vidhāna as in BÜHLER (ZDMG. 42, 556) and BHĀṆḌĀRKAR (Lists, p. 58); BÜHLER and BHĀṆḌĀRKAR call the author of this to be Candra[7]. The extract quoted in BHĀṆḌĀRKAR shows that they meant by it the same work. The introduction in C D is certainly correct. Now there remains little scope for the doubt about this as the manuscript of BHĀṆḌĀRKAR has the same colophon as in A. B. C. does not at all treat the verb; perhaps this is just the legacy of transmission of the text. That the grammar was really very short is suggested by one of its name, P r ā k ṛ t a s ā r o d d-d h ā r a v ṛ t t i ḥ, which is given in the MS in PETERSON, Third Report, p. 265.

1. Vr. und Hc. p. 8. — 2. This could be applied to Ś. also in lieu of JŚ. But the very nature of the grammar, particularly 3, 6 in C D (p. 48) refers to JŚ. — 3. Vr. und Hc. p. 8. — 4. That the forms were comprehended under 2, 27 (p. 47) by C. as those of common Prākrit, as was considered by HOERNLE, p. XXIII, is wrong. The stanza is composed in pure Apabhraṁśa. It has to be read as :—*kālu laheviṇu joiā jiŭa, jiŭa mohu galei tiva tiŭa daṃsaṇu lahaï jo ṇiamem̐ appu muṇei*, "the measure in which, with the passage of time he dissolves his delusion, the yogin, who comes to know the self by penance, attains enlightenment' *joiā* is not=*jāyāyāḥ* but=*yogikaḥ*=*yogī* from *yogin*. — 5. On t cf. § 203. — 6. cf. 417, note 2. — 7. Caṇḍa is the most authentic form of the name; by it we must never under-

stand that it refers to Candra, i.e. Candragomin, (LIEBICH, Panini p. 11), since it has been proved that according to KIELHORN, IA. 15. 184 the terminology used by Candragomin is quite different from the one used by Caṇḍa.

§ 35. As a lexicographer of Pkt. there was the energetic D h a n a p ā l a, whose dictionary of synonyms, the P ā i ẏ a l a c c h ī that is Prākṛtalakṣmīḥ has been published by BÜHLER : The Pāiẏalachchhī Nāmamālā, a Prakrit Kosha, by Dhanapāla. Edited with critical notes, an introduction and a glossary by GEORG BÜHLER Göttingen 1878 (=BB. 4, 70-166[a]). According to his own statement (stanzas 276 — 278) Dhanapāla composed his work at Dhārā in the year 1029 of the Vikrama era=972 A.D., that is during the period when Mānyakheṭa was sacked in a series of attacks by a Mālava prince, for his younger sister Sundarī[1]. In stanza I he calls his work a Nāmamālā and in 278 he designates it as Desī=Deśī. As already pointed out by BÜHLER (p. 11) the Deśīs constitute only a quarter of the words of the lexicon, all others are either tatsamas or tadbhavas (§ 8), and, therefore, this work is not of any great value[2]. It contains 279 stanzas in the Āryā metre, and the first one is the maṅgalācaraṇa, and the last four constitute a statement of the event referred to above. Each object takes one complete strophe in stanzas 1-19, a verse in 20-94 a half verse in 95-202; the stanzas 203 — 275 contain single words that are explained sometimes by means of synonyms and sometimes by half of a verse. Dhanapāla is acknowledged by Hc., Deśīn. 1, 141; 3, 22; 4, 30; 6, 101; 8, 17 as one of the sources of his information. But sometimes the citations are not traceable at all in Pāīẏalacchī (3, 22; 4, 30; 8, 17), or partly they do not accord with the statement of Hc. (1, 141; 6, 101). Therefore, rightly conjectures BÜHLER (p. 15) that Dhanapāla had written another work of the same type. After his conversion to Jainism Dh. wrote Ṛṣabhapañcāśikā[3] as well.

1. Details in BÜHLER, p. 5 ff. — 2. BÜHLER, p 13ff. — 3. Vide § 20; BÜHLER, p. 9; KLATT, ZDMG. 33, 445. On Dh.'s other literary activities see BÜHLER, p. 10; AUFRECHT, ZDMG. 27, 41; Cat. Cat. 1, 267.

§ 36. Of the Prākrit grammars that have as yet come to light by far the most important is that of Hemacandra (1088 — 1172 A.D.). His Prākrit grammar constitutes the eighth section of the S i d d h a h e m a c a n d r a, i.e. grammar dedicated to Siddharāja and written by Hemacandra[1], whereof the first seven sections are devoted to the Sanskrit language. Hc. himself wrote thereupon a commentary in two recensions, one, the Bṛhatī and the other, the Laghu-vṛtti[2]; of them the Laghuvṛtti bears the name Prakāśikā and has been printed in the editions of Mahābala Kṛṣna, Bombay Saṁvat 1929 and PISCHEL : Hemacandra's Grammatik der Prākritsprachen (Siddhahemacandram Adhyāya VIII), herausgegeben, übersetzt und erlaütert, Teil 1. II. Halle a . S. 1877. 1880. On the Vṛtti, Udayasaubhāgyagaṇin wrote an etymological commentary Haimaprākṛtavṛttiḍhuṇḍhikā, under the title Vyutpattidīpikā, (§ 29), and on the eighth chapter. Narendracandrasūri wrote a running commentary named Prākṛtaprabodha[3]. Hc. has divided his grammar into four sections : of them the first two are devoted to Phonetics, the third one contains rules on Morphology, and in the fourth under 1-258 he gives root-substitutes, the classification of the roots that differ in conjugation from those of Sanskrit and detached rules for forming the passive, in rule 259 he makes certain observations on the meaning of roots: he deals with Śaurasenī in 260 — 286, Māgadhī in 287 — 302, Paiśācī in 303 — 324. Cūlikāpaiśācikā in 325-328, Apabhraṁśa in 329 — 446 and finally in 447 — 448 he passes some general remarks. The language taught by Hc. in 1, 1. 4, 259 is preponderantly M. But by the side of it he carries by force also JM. and occasionally even AMg. and that without differentiating strictly between these dialects everywhere. In 260 — 286, he has in view also JŚ. (§ 21). Nothing can as yet be said about his predecessors whose works were utilized by Hc. in his grammar. He refers by name only to H u g g a 1, 186, not as a grammarian, but as a lexicographer[4], and that with reference to Skt. only; otherwise he refers to his sources simply in general terms as *kaścit* (2,80 : 3,81); *kecit* (1, 67. 209; 2, 80. 128. 138. 145. 188; 3, 19. 25. 103. 153); *anyaḥ* (3, 103. 117); *anye* (1, 35. 88; 2, 163, 174. 207; 3, 177); *anyaiḥ* (4, 2); *anyeṣām* (4, 327) *eke* (1, 35). JACOBI[5] is of the opinion that Hc. used the sūtras of Vr. as the basis of his grammar in the same manner as Bhaṭṭojidīkṣita had the sūtras of Pāṇini the basis of his Siddhāntakaumudī. The sūtras of Vr. were irrefutably held in high esteem, and their exposition, relatively restricted, had become the main task for Prākrit grammarians. That Hc. stands to Vr. in a relation similar to that of Kātyāyana to Pāṇini is all wrong[6] as has been shown in detail by BLOCH[7]. We cannot determine with certainty if Hc. has even utilized the work Vr. at all. It is just probable that he may have done so, but it cannot be proved. It has already been noted above (§ 34) that presumably he knew Caṇḍa. Besides his grammar, Hc. has written also a dictionary of Deśīs, the D e ś ī n ā m a m ā l ā or the D e ś ī ś a b d a s a ṁ g r a h a , that was designated as Rayaṇāvali = Skt. Ratnāvali by the author himself (8, 77). According to the evidence available at pp. 1, 4ff. he wrote it after his grammar and according to 1, 3 he wrote a supplement also to it. The text has been published by PISCHEL : The Deśīnāmamālā of Hemchandra Part I. Text and critical notes. Bombay 1880.[8] Like Dhanapāla (§ 35) Hc. also included tatsamas and tadbhavas under Deśī, but in proportion to the volume of the work their number is very small, and for a knowledge of Prākrit it is extraordinarily essential. The Deśīnāmamālā is divided into eight alphabetically arranged vargas. The words are divided into two classes. In the beginning occur the words arranged according to the number of syllables that have only one meaning (*ekārthāḥ*), then follow the similarly arranged ones having more than one meaning (*anekārthāḥ*). To the first class of words are added illustrative examples in verses which were composed by Hc. himself; most of them are silly : it was so because Hc. was obliged to collect together in single verses words of different meanings. They serve as mnemotechnical auxiliaries and contain sometimes, by the side of Deśīs, furthermore, words and forms that are not usually included in Pkt. Besides, it is not rarely that this book helps us in ascertaining the exact meaning of several Deśī words.[9] Hc. has written a commentary to his Deśīn.

as well. Hc. makes no claim that his work is not based on other sources, on the other hand, he admits that his work is nothing but a compilation from earlier works of similar pattern. In 1, 37 he leaves the problem of deciding whether *ambasami* or *ambamasi* is the correct form to the learned, (*ambamasīti kecit paṭhanti tatra keṣāṁ cid bhramobhrahmo veti bahudṛśvāna eva pramāṇam*); in 1, 41 he is not clear either with regard to the form or the meaning of *acchiharullo*, and that because even authors differ from one another, he leaves it to the well informed ones to decide (*tad evaṁ granthakṛdvipratipattau bahujñāḥ pramāṇam*); in 1, 47 he distinguishes between the words *avaḍāhia* and *avaḍakkia*, which others have explained as synonyms on the basis of observation of the materials found in the best writings on Deśīs (*asmābhis tu sāradeśinirīkṣaṇena vivekaḥ kṛtaḥ*); in 1, 105 he firmly holds that *uḍḍuhia* in lieu of *uttuhia* remains due to scribe's error; likewise in 6, 8 *bora* occurs in lieu of *cora*. In support of his own decision he refers to many works in Deśī in 2, 28; to the best writings in it in 3, 12, 33; in 8, 12 he scolds modern writers on Deśī and their commentators; in 8, 13 he leaves again the decision to judicious people (*kevalaṁ sahṛdayāḥ pramāṇam*). After 1, 2 the merit of the work lies in its alphabetical arrangement. According to 1,49 he does it for students. Hc. refers by name to Abhimānacihna (1, 144; 6, 93; 7, 1; 8, 12. 17); Avantisundarī (1, 81. 157); Devarāja (6, 58. 72; 8, 17); Droṇa or Droṇācārya (1, 18. 50; 6, 7; 8, 17); Dhanapāla (1, 141; 3, 22; 4, 30; 6. 101; 8, 17); Gopāla (1, 25. 31. 45; 2 82; 3, 47; 6, 26. 58. 72; 7, 2. 76; 8. 1. 17. 67) Pādalipta (1. 2); Rāhulaka (4, 4); Śīlāṅka (2, 20; 6, 96; 8, 40); Sātavāhana (3, 41; 5, 11; 6, 15. 18. 19. 112. 125). Of them, Abhimānacihna, Devarāja, Pādalipta and Sātavāhana appear also as Prâkrit poets in the Sattasaī (§ 3) as well; about Avantisundarī BÜHLER[10] conjectures that she might have been identical with Sundarī, the younger sister of Dhanapāla, for whom he wrote Pāiẏalacchī. When she herself could write and actually wrote on Deśī it appears improbable. Rather she might have been identical with Avantisundarī, the wife of Rājaśekhara, on whose inducement, according to Karp. 7, 1, the Karpūramañjarī, a drama wholly written in Prâkrit, was presented on the stage and in fact it is she who is cited by Hc. in his grammar. Rāhulaka is referred to as a Sanskrit poet in Śārṅgadharapaddhati and Subhāṣitāvali. From among the writers in Sanskrit Hc. refers by name to Kālāpāḥ (1, 6), Bharata (8, 72), Bhāmaha (8, 39), and without naming he cites Halāyudha (1, 5; 2, 98). Mostly he refers to his sources in some general terms : thus *anye* (1, 3. 20. 22. 35. 47. 52. 62. 63. 65. 66. 70. 72. 75. 78. 87. 89. 99. 100. 102. 107. 112. 151. 160. 163; 2. 11. 12. 18. 24. 26. 29. 36. 45. 47. 50. 51. 66. 67. 69. 77. 79. 89; 3, 3. 6. 8. 28. 40. 41. 58. 59.; 4, 3. 4. 6. 7. 18. 22. 23. 26. 33. 44. 47; 5, 9. 30. 33. 36. 40. 45. 50. 61; 6, 14. 15. 16. 21. 24. 25. 26. 28. 42. 48. 53. 54, 61. 63. 75. 81. 86. 88. 91. 93. 94. 97. 99. 105. 106. 116. 121. 132. 134. 140. 145; 7, 2. 16. 17. 18. 21. 31. 33. 37. 44. 45. 48. 62. 68. 69. 74. 75. 76. 88. 91; 8, 10. 15. 18. 22. 27. 35. 36. 38. 44. 45. 59. 67); *eke*

(2, 89; 4, 5. 12; 6, 11; 7, 35; 8, 7); *kaścit* (1, 43; 2, 18; 3, 51; 5, 13; 8, 75); *kecit* (1, 5. 26. 34. 37. 41. 46. 47. 67. 79. 103. 105. 117. 120. 129. 131. 153; 2, 13. 15. 16. 17. 20. 29. 33. 38. 58. 87. 89; 3, 10. 12. 22. 23. 33. 34. 35. 36. 44. 55; 4. 4. 10. 15. 45; 5, 12. 21, 44. 58; 6, 4. 55. 80. 90. 91. 92. 93. 95. 96. 110. 111; 7, 2. 3. 6. 47. 58. 65. 75. 81. 93; 8, 4. 51. 69. 70); *pūrvācāryāḥ* (1, 11. 13); *yad āha* (1, 4. 5. [Halāyudha]. 37. 75. 121. 171; 2, 33. 48. 98 (Halāyudha); 3, 23, 54 [Skt.]; 4, 4. 10. 21. 24. 45; 5, 1. 63; 6, 15. 42. 78. 81. 93. 140. 142; 7, 46. 58. 84; 8, 1. 13. 43. 68); *yad āhuḥ* (1, 5; 3,6 4, 15); by some other expressions (1, 18. 94. 144. 174; 3, 33;34, 37; 6, 8. 58. 93; 8, 12. 17. 28). In spite of so much of care taken by him in utilization of the writings of his so many predecessors Hc. could not always avoid gross blunders for the simple reason that he drew his materials from secondary sources : thus in 2, 24 he says that *kaṇṭhadiṇāra* means "an opening in a fence" (*vṛtivivara*), and again in 6, 67 he teaches that *paero* also means "an opening in a fence" (*vṛtivivara*) in addition to "a particular ornament" (*kaṇṭhadiṇāra*). Clearly he read somewhere in some verse referred to in 6, 67 the nom. *kaṇṭhadiṇāro*, in lieu of the locative °*re*, and with the help thereof he construed 2, 24; but later he found the correct reading of 6, 67 and gave the right meaning, but he did not take notice of the error committed by him earlier. *kaṇṭhadiṇāra* is certainly an ornament made from Denar that is worn about the neck. *poālo* "steer" (6. 62) is really the same word as *vovālo* (7, 79), which as a second member of a compound needed its preceding form[11]. As far as I can see the Deśīn. constitutes an "authority of the first rank"[12] that shows to us that there still remains much to be known about the valuable contributions made in Indian languages and that we still do not know much about the rich literature that exists in Prākrit.

1. BÜHLER, Ueber das Leben Das Jaina Mönches Hemachandra (Wien 1889) p. 15. — 2. BÜHLER, l.c. p. 72. note 34. — 3. In AUFRECHT, Cat. Cat. 1, 360 the author is said to be Naracandra. According to PETERSON, Det. Report (1883), p. 127, No. 300 and BHĀṆḌĀRKAR, A Catalogue of the Collections of MSS deposited in the Deccan College (Bombay 1888) p. 328, No. 300 he calls himself Narendracandrasūri. The MS was lent out when I wanted to utilize it. — 4. PISCHEL on Hc. 1, 186; ZACHARIAE, GGA. 1889, 99 6, note 1; Die indischen Wörterbücher (Kośa) (Strassburg 1897; Grundriss 1. 3³) p. 7; Epilegomena zu der Ausgabe des Maṅkhakośa, (Wien 1899), p. 17 ff. 5. Jenaer Literaturzeitung 1876, 797. — 6. PISCHEL on Hc. 2, 145. — 7. Vr. und Hc. p. 21 ff. — 8. Found by BÜHLER, IA.2, 17 ff. — 9. BÜHLER had desired to publish the second part that would have contained the dictionary, PISCHEL Deśīn. p. 8. — 10. Pāiyalacchī- p. 7 ff. — 11. Other examples in SIEGFRIED GOLDSCHMIT, Deutsche Literaturzeitung 2, 1109. — 12. SIEGFRIED GOLDSCHMIDT, l.c.

§ 37. Undetermined remains the age of Kramadīśvara. Scholars have attempted to place him between Hc. and Bopadeva. ZACHARIAE[1] has correctly remarked that we cannot prove that Kī. lived later than Hc. and that we do not find any strong reason to support the untenable proposition that Kī. had written his grammar before Hc. Kī.'s grammar Saṁkṣiptasāra, like that of Hc., is divided into eight chapters (pādas), whereof the last chapter (Prākṛtapāda) deals with Pkt. This is a thing that also is in agreement with Hc. But in other respects the two grammarians have nothing in common. The arrangement of the subject-matter, the technical terms etc. are altogether different.[2] As regards the antiquity of Kī., it is noteworthy that a quotation in his Skt. grammar cannot be dated earlier than the eighth and later than the beginning of the ninth century A.D. The latest of the authors cited by him is Murāri,[3] about whom we now definitely know that he was anterior to Ratnākara, the author of Haravijaya,[4] who lived in about the middle of the ninth century A.D. With respect to finding a later limit to the age of Kī., it may be noted that he, like some later grammarians, gives names of more dialects than those mentioned by Hc. LASSEN, Inst. p. 15 ff. 393. 440 ff. 449 ff., Appendix 39 — 58, was the first scholar to give a detailed account of Kī. The chapter on the Root has been published by DELIUS: Radices Pracriticae (Bonnae ad Rhenum 1839) pp. 10-12. A complete edition of the Prākṛtapāda is said to have been published by RĀJENDRALĀLA MITRA in the Bibliotheca Indica-Series.[5] It could not be possible for me to procure it. I have before me pp. 17 — 24 of the text and pp. 141 — 172 of the Word-Index. from *bhāduko* up to *saddāviadi*,[6] and pp. 1-8 of the English translation. If I am allowed to draw my conclusion on the basis of the proof-sheets, I shall say that the edition had been very bad. A new edition of the eighth pāda had been printed in Calcutta, 1889. I got it through the courtesy of BLOCH, and it is from this that I have given the quotations in this grammar. This too is a very bad edition, and therefore, I have constantly taken into consideration the extracts given in LASSEN. Kī. closely follows Vr., but has, as the review given in LASSEN, Inst., App. pp. 40. ff., demonstrates certain deviations that point to some other source, thus for instance his treatment of A. is well in contrast to that of Vr. Kī. himself wrote a short commentary to his Saṁkṣiptasāra, whereof the Rasavatī of Jumaranandin is a careful exposition and elucidation.[7] The Prākṛtadīpikā of Caṇḍīdevaśarman[8] is a second commentary on the Prākṛtapāda only. RĀJENDRALĀLA MITRA[9] names a third one : The Prākṛtapādaṭīkā of Vidyāvinoda "son of Nārāyaṇa, grand'son of Bāṇeśvara and great grand'son of Jaṭādhara." He is followed by AUFRECHT[10] who, as already remarked elsewhere,[11] calls the author Vidyāvinodācārya. I had utilized the Oxford MS as the Saṁkṣiptasāra had, by then, not been printed.[12] The introduction, that RĀJENDRALĀLA MITRA has got published on the basis of a MS that is better than that of AUFRECHT, seems to suggest that at the end of the different chapters and in the colophon the author calls himself V i d y ā v i n o - d ā c ā r y a and admits that he has annotated upon an older writing of N ā r ā y a ṇ a, son of Bāṇeśvara, who was a son of Jaṭādhara, and perhaps whose brother's name was Sumeru. Nārāyaṇa had written a bigger work, but that was destroyed by some wicked person: the work that is before us is an abridgement of the work of Vidyāvinoda.[13] It has nowhere been mentioned in the work itself that the Prākṛtapāda is a commentary on Kī. In the subscripts the author always calls himself Vidyāvinodācārya[14] and his work Prākṛtapāda; thus it is still doubtful if the hypothesis of RĀJENDRA-

LĀLA MITRA is authentic. The author follows Vr. most closely, but his work is devoid of any of his merits.

1. BB. 5, 26 — 2. ZACHARIAE, BB. 5, 26. At the end of the eighth Pāda Ki. treats briefly Metrics and Rhetorics. — 3. ZACHARIAE, BB. 5. 58. — 4. PETERSON, Subhāṣitāvali p. 91. — 5. RĀJENDRALĀLA MITRA, A Descriptive Catalogue of Sanskrit MSS. in the Library of the Asiatic Society of Bengal, Part first, Grammar. (Calcutta 1877) p. 75; BHĀṆḌĀRKAR, JBoAS. 16, 250. — 6. This index does not belong to the book proper, rather it contains a number of Prākrit words quoted from Vr. Mṛcch. Śak. Vikr. Mālav., Ratn. Veṇis. Mālatim. Uttar. Mahāv. Cait. Piṅgala. Sāhityadarpaṇa. — 7. LASSEN Inst. p. 15; ZACHARIAE, BB. 5, 22 f.. AUFRECHT, Cat. Cat. 1, 684. — 8. LASSEN, Inst. p. 16; AUFRECHT, Cat. Cat. 1, 684. — 9. Notices of Sanskrit MSS. 4, 162 ff. (Calcutta 1878). — 10. Cat. Cat. 1, 684. — 11. Cat. Oxon. p. 181. — 12. De gr. Pr. p 19. — 13. The introduction is very much obscure, and it is doubtful if the foregoing explanation is correct. Cf. AUFRECHT, Cat. Oxon. p. 181. In the Cat. Cat. 2, 212, AUFRECHT has the explanation quoted by me, and that clearly in following PETERSON's Ulwar Catalogue that is not available. The work is there designated simply as Prākṛtavyākaraṇa.

§ 38. Fully depending on Hc. is Trivikramadeva in the commentary to his Prākṛtavyākaraṇa. He was a son of Mallinātha and grand'son of Ādityavarman. I have utilized two MSS of his work, the one, a transcription of the Tanjore MS preserved in the India Office Library, Burnell Collection. No 84 in Grantha, and the other, a Devanāgarī transcription of the Tanjore MS No. 10006 collated in the Sūtra with 10004,[1] that BURNELL had arranged to be prepared for me, besides the printed edition on the Granthapradarśanī Series, Nos. 1 — 32. It extends up to the end of the first adhyāya only. In his grammar[2], Triv. has employed a special type of technical terms that he has explained in the beginning of the work.[3] From 1, 1, 17 he, in his Vṛtti on the Sūtras, has everywhere verbally followed Hc. whom in the introduction he mentions as his authority, so much so that I have referred to him very rarely. In my edition of Hc., I have sometimes quoted the corresponding rules from his grammar in the margin. His special contributions are the topics 1, 3, 106; 1, 4, 121; 2, 1, 30; 3, 1, 132 and 3, 4, 71 in which he has collected together the words that cannot be regulated according to the rules of grammar and, in a great measure, belong to the category of Deśī; thus for instance in 3, 4, 71 they are expressly designated Deśyāḥ. I have published and reviewed the first two chapters in BB. 325 ff.; 6, 84 ff.; 13, 1 ff. The age of Trivikrama has been determined to the extent that he lived after Hc. (+1172 A. D.) and before Kumārasvāmir, son of Kolācala Mallinātha, inasmuch as he, in his commentary on Pratāparudrīya of Vidyānātha (ed. Madras 1868), refers to him by name in 218, 21 and without naming in 62, 19 ff.; 201, 21; 214, 4.[4] Pratāparudra II, to whom Vidyānātha dedicated his work, reigned from 1295 to 1323 A.D.[5] At 123, 1 ff. Kumārasvāmin describes the coronation of Pratāparudra as having taken place long ago (*purā kila*). His father Kolācala Mallinātha cites Bopadeva,[6] who lived in the court of Mahādeva of Devagiri who ruled from 1260 to 1271 A.D.[8] Thus we see that the hypothesis of AUFRECHT that Mallinātha could not have lived before the 14th century A.D.[9] is confirmed. Therefore, Trivikrama may probably be placed in the 13th century.

1. BURNELL, Classified Index 1. 43. — 2. Trivikrama is the author of the Sūtras as well. In De gr. Pr. p. 29, I had wrongly interpreted *nija* in *nijasūtramārgam* as referring to Trivikrama himself. The title of the work is Prākṛtavyākaraṇa and not °vṛtti as is shown by an inscription that occurs in the commentary itself — 3. Communicated by PISCHEL, De gr. Pr. pp. 34 — 37. — 4. PISCHEL, De gr. Pr. p. 38. — 5. SEWELL, A Sketch of the Dynasties of Southern India (Madras 1883), p. 33. — 6. AUFRECHT, Cat. Oxon. p. 113. — 7. AUFRECHT, Cat. Cat. 1, 616. — 8. SEWELL, l. c. p. 114. — 9. Cat. Oxon p. 113.

§ 39. Siṁharāja, son of Samudrabandhayajvan, based his Prākṛtarūpāvatāra on the grammar of Trivikramadeva. Of this work, I have utilized two manuscripts belonging to the Royal Asiatic Society in London : one of them, i.e. No. 159, is a palm-leaf manuscript in the Malayālam character, and the other, i.e. No. 57, is a paper manuscript in the same character : the latter is a transcription of the former. Siṁharāja, following the style of Kaumudī, has rearranged the grammar of Trivikrama. It begins, after a brief description of the technical terms (*saṁjñāvibhāga*, *paribhāṣāvibhāga*) and a *saṁhitāvibhāga* on the *saṁdhi* and *lopa*, immediately followed by declension (*subantavibhāga*; fol. 4 — 46), whereunder he treats the indeclinables as well; then follows the conjugation (*tiṅantavibhāga*, fol. 46 — 59) including *dhātvādeśāḥ* to which are added the rules for Ś. Mg.P. CP. A. (*śaurasenyādivibhāga*; fol. 59 — 74). He provides with a paradigm for each class of noun: *vṛkṣa* for the *a*-stems, *agni* for the *i*-stems, *taru* for the *u*-stems, *khalapū* for the *ū-stems* and *bhrātṛ* for the *ṛ*-stems. He further shows the method of forming Prākrit stems from these words and teaches the endings and the process of combining them. He treats the feminine and neuter nouns ending in vowels and consonants, the pronouns *yuṣmad* and *asmad*, the verbs whereof he gives *has* and *sah* as paradigms in the same manner.[1] The Prākṛtarūpāvatāra is not without importance for a knowledge of declension and conjugation particularly because sometimes Sr. gives more forms than do Triv. and Hc., though it is true that many of such forms are possible in theory only, but in view of the fact that they are formed strictly according to the rules, they are not devoid of interest. Following the method of Sr. on the sūtras of Triv., Raghunāthaśarman has rearranged the sūtras of Vr. in the Prākṛtānanda. — Similar is the treatment of Lakṣmīdhara in Ṣaḍbhāṣācandrikā[3] and of the wholly recent writer Nāgobā in Ṣaḍbhāṣā-subantarūpādarśa, a "superficial tract"[4] on declension.

1. Details in PISCHEL, De gr. Pr. p. 39 — 43. — 2. HOERNLE, Proc. ASB. 1880. 100 ff. — 3. BURNELL, Classified Index p. 43. Cf. LASSEN, Inst. p. 11 — 15. — 4. BURNELL l. c., p. 44.

§ 40. For a knowledge of the dialects other than M. JM. AMg. JŚ. important is the Prākṛtasarvasva of Mārkaṇḍeya Kavīndra. I have utilized two of its manuscripts. One of them belongs to the India office and is written on palm-leaves in the Nāgarī character. It is Mackenzie MS No. 70, foll. 98. It has wooden binding whereupon was formerly inscribed Piṁgalavyākaraṇa (Nāgarī-script) and Pengala Prakrota Surva Bhala Vakaranaḥ (Roman script). There was also an endorsement that has by now disappeared : It read as Pengala praukrota Surva Bhausha

Vyacaranum. The following line occurs on the first leaf in the Nāgarī script : *śrīrāmaḥ piṁgalaprākṛtasarvasvabhāṣāvyākaraṇaṃ.* The second is the Oxford MS mentioned in AUFRECHT, Cat. Oxon. p. 181. No. 412. Both the manuscripts are of the same source and are hopelessly so much corrupt that they can be utilized only in parts. Particularly for Ś., it is deplorable that it is so in view of the fact that MK. has given more details about this dialect than they are to be found in the grammar of any other writer and that MK. has drawn a line of sharp distinction between Ś. and M., MK. has been referred to according to the London MS that I could use once again at Halle through the courtesy of TAWNEY. From the colophon of the MS that has been published by AUFRECHT, l.c. it is proved that MK. wrote this work in Orissa during the period of reign of one Mukundadeva. HULTZSCH conjectures that this refers to Mukundadeva, who, according to STERLING, ruled in 1664 A.D. But we can say nothing about his age with certainty. MK. in the introduction mentions as an authority one V a s a n - t a r ā j a in addition to Śākalya, Bharata, Kohala, Vararuci and Bhāmaha (§§ 31 — 33). This refers to Vasantarāja, the author of P r ā k ṛ t a Sañjīvanī which, as assumed by COWELL[1] and AUFRECHT,[2] is not a commentary on Vr., but an independent work that follows Vr. It has been cited by Vāsudeva on Karp. 9, 11, ed. Bombay : *tuduktaṁ prākṛtasaṁjivinyāṁ prākṛtasya tu sarvameva saṁskṛtaṁ yoniḥ* (§ 1). That this Vasantarāja is identical with King Kumāragiri Vasantarāja,[3] brother-in-law of Kāṭayavema,[4] yet seems to me[5] to be very much possible. This Kāṭayavema is mentioned as the author of a Nāṭyaśāstra, Vasantarājīyam,[6] hence his occupation with Pkt. seems to be very much probable. We have the inscriptions of Kāṭayavema dated 1391, 1414 and 1416 A.D.[7] If the two Vasantarājas were identical, in all events the age of MK. must have been later than the first quarter of the 15th century. Vasantarāja, who wrote Śākuna, is, with HULTZSCH,[8] to be differentiated from the Prākrit grammarian. MK. mentions in his work one Aniruddhabhaṭṭa, the Bhaṭṭikāvya, Bhojadeva, Daṇḍin, Hariścandra, Kapila, Piṅgala, Rājaśekhara, Vākpatirāja, the Saptaśatī and the Setubandha[9] as well. Chronologically the youngest of the above-mentioned authors is Bhojadeva, the writer of Rājamṛgāṅka, the famous treatise on Karaṇa. He lived in about Śaka-Saṁvat 964 = 1042-3 A.D.[10] MK. begins with a preamble containing an introduction on the Prākrit dialects from which all that is essential has been detailed in the foregoing paragraphs. In the beginning he describes M. in 8 pādas (fol. 4^{b} — 65^{b}). This section, that is the largest one, is divided on the model of Vr., is less exhaustive than Hc., and is in many respects independent. Then follows Ś. in the 9th pāda (fol. 65^{b} — 72^{b}) that is divided into 9 prakaraṇas. Prācyā is described in the 10th pāda, Āvantī and Bāhlīkī in the 11th, and Mg. with a reference to AMg. in the 12th (§ 3). The entire section, pādas 9 — 12, bears the title B h ā ṣ ā v i v e c a n a m. It is followed in pādas 13 — 16 by *vibhāṣāḥ* (§ 3), in 17.18 by A., and in 19. 20 by P. A portion of the 17th pāda has been anticipated in the 13th pāda, and this has not altered the numbering of the folios. Next to Saurasenī the language described most accurately is Apabhraṁśa. Unfortunately the condition of the MS. is so deplorable that it is not possible to utilize fully the valuable materials contained in it.

1. Vr. p. x f. — 2. Cat. Cat. 1, 360. — 3. That Kumāragiri was the name of the king and his surname was Vasantarāja shows EI. 4, 318 ff. Cf. particularly HULTZSCH, p. 327. — 4. The name Kāṭayavema was established by me first of all, GN. 1873, 201 f. AUFRECHT, Cat. Cat. 2, 237 changes the correct name into a wrong one, i.e. to Kātavema The inscriptions, EI. 4, 318 ff., do not leave any doubt about the name § 40. p. 47. Mṛcchakaṭikā is mentioned as Mṛcchakaṭam by Mk. (fol. 82) and Bhāgīrathīvardhamāna, (fol. 79, 82). As communicated to me by KIELHORN, the first part of the name Kāṭayavema is written also as-Kāṭa and Kāṭama and the second also as Vemaya in the South Indian inscriptions. Accordingly Kāṭavema perhaps may not be wrong. — 5. De gr. Pr. p. 18. From the fact that Kātayavema, in his commentary on the dramas, does not mention Prākṛta-saṁjīvani, it cannot be concluded that, in case both the persons are identical, Vasantarāja wrote his commentary after his treatise on Rhetorics and later than K. — 6. De gr. Pr. p. 18; EI. 4, 327, strophe 17. — 7. HULTZSCH, EI. 4, 328. — 8. Prolegomena zu des Vasantarāja Sākuna nebst Text proben (Leipzig 1879) p. 29. — 9. PISCHEL, De gr. Pr. p. 17. — 10. THIBAUT, Astronomie, Astrologie und Mathematik (Strassburg 1899; Grundriss III. 9), § 37.

§ 41. Very much similar to the grammar of Mārkaṇḍeya, particularly in the section on dialects other than M., is the P r ā k ṛ t a k a l p a t a r u of R ā m a t a r k a v ā g ī ś a. The only known MS of this work, the Bengali manuscript No. 1106 of the India Office, is so much mutilated that it can hardly be utilized. LASSEN has dealt with it in Inst. p. 19 — 23. From p. 20 it is proved that Rv. worked on the model of an earlier treatise of Laṅkeśvara, whereby is meant the P r ā k ṛ t a k ā m a d h e n u of R ā v a ṇ a, that is known also as Prākṛtalaṅkeśvararāvaṇa, or shortly also as Laṅkeśvara.[1] Of the Prākṛtakāmadhenu we have as yet found only fragments.[2] If this Laṅkeśvara be identical with the author of Śivastuti, published in the Kāvyamālā 1, 6 — 8, he is older than Appayadīkṣita, who in the Kuvalayānanda, 73, 1 (ed. Benares Saṁvat 1928) cites[3] its fifth stanza, therefore, his age must have been earlier than the close of the 16th century A.D.[4] and, therefore, younger than Rāmatarkavāgīśa. A worthless selection from Trivikrama is P r ā k ṛ t a ś a b d a p r a d ī p i k ā of N a r a s i ṁ h a, whereof the beginning[5] has been published in the Granthapradarśanī Nos. 3. 4. Besides the famous treatises a large number of them are known in the form of manuscripts. We know nothing about many of them except their titles and names of the authors, or only one of the two. Ś u b h a c a n d r a wrote one Ś a b d a c i n t ā m a ṇ i, which according to HOERNLE[6] contains two adhyāyas, each of which has four pādas, and notedly follows Hc. Like South Indian Trivikramadeva and Siṁharāja (§ 38. 39) he begins his grammar with a number of Saṁjñāsūtras. Perhaps it is this very work that is referred to by RĀJENDRALĀLA MITRA[7] as Audāryacintāmaṇi and is ascribed by him to one Śubhasāgara.[8] An incomplete work in verses with a prose commentary is the P r ā k ṛ t a c a n d r i k ā of K ṛ ṣ ṇ a p a ṇ ḍ i t a alias Ś e ṣ a k ṛ ṣ ṇ a, from which PETERSON, Third Report p. 342-348 has given extracts. According to 343, 5 his teacher was Nṛsiṁha, or according to 348, 21 Narasiṁha, whereby perhaps the author of Prākṛtaśabdapradīpikā is to be understood. According to 343, 6 it was written for children (*śiśuhitaṁ kurve prākṛtacandrikām*), according to 343, 19 he seems to hold Ārṣam identical with M., because he does not mention them there notwithstanding the fact that he treats them all separately. The illustrative examples quoted by him show that he had utilized Hc. thoroughly well. His quotations from different dialects and their assignment to individual characters pp. 346—348, are in the greatest measure taken word for word from earlier authors, like Bharata and Bhojadeva. Recent is Bhāradvāja p. 348. One P r ā k ṛ t a c a n d r i k ā was written by V ā m a n ā c ā r y a, who calls himself Karañjakavisārvabhauma and is the author of a commentary on the Prākṛtapiṅgala (§ 29) as well.[9] A compendium for beginners is P r ā k ṛ t a m a ṇ i d ī p a of A p p a y a d ī k ṣ i t a[10], the polyhistor, who lived in the second half of the 16th century. He mentions Trivikrama, Hemacandra, Lakṣmīdhara, Bhoja, Puṣpavananātha, Vararuci, a Vārttikārṇavabhāṣya and or of Appayajvan (§ 32) as his authorities . In fact, however, his work is nothing better than a wholly fragmentary selection from Trivikrama devoid of all of its merits; a small portion of it, i.e. up to 1, 4, 99 has been published as Nos. 3. 5. 6. 8-10. 13 in the Granthapradarśanī Series. Elsewhere are referred to P r ā k ṛ t a k a u m u d ī,[11] a P r ā k ṛ t a v y ā k a r a ṇ a of S a m a n t a b h a d r a,[12] etc. A B h ā s ā r ṇ a v a was written by C a n d r a ś e k h a r a , father of Viśvanātha, according to Sāhityadarpaṇa 174, 2: Candraśekhara refers to one P r ā k ṛ t a s ā h i t y a r a t n ā k a r a in his commentary on Śakuntalā 175, 24, ed. PISCHEL, where under 180, 5 he quotes one B h ā ṣ ā b h e d a, which perhaps was a work on Prākrit. From One D e ś ī p r a k ā ś a, quotes Pṛthvīdhara on Mṛcch. 14, 5 p. 244, ed. STENZLER = 40, 5 p. 503, ed. GOḌABOLE: *kāṇeli kanyakāmātā*. In the works of the scholiasts are found here and there Prākrit sūtras whereof it is not possible to trace the source.

1. To me this seems to be a reasonable statement. In RĀJENDRALĀLA MITRA, Notices 9, 239. No. 3157 the author is explicitly mentioned in the introduction as Rāvaṇa, and the colophon reads as *iti rāvaṇakṛtā prākṛtakāmadhenuḥ samāptā*. In No. 3158 in the colophon the author calls it Prākṛtalaṅkeśvararāvaṇa. LASSEN, Inst. p. 9. considers according to COLEBROOKE, Prākṛtalaṅkeśvara to be the name of the work, which according to him is different from Prākṛtakāmdhenu, whose authorship, he, in agreement with LEYDEN, ascribes to Vidyāvinoda. In Rāmatarkavāgīśa (LASSEN. Inst. p. 20) the author is said to be Laṅkeśvara. The author of Śivastuti and Kālāgnirudropaniṣad (AUFRECHT Cat. Cat. 1, 542) too is so named. It is clearly a synonym of Rāvaṇa. That this Rāvaṇa "is obviously distinct from the ten-headed monster" as he is usually believed to be, can with RĀJENDRALĀLA MITRA be easily accepted. — 2. The Nos. 3157 and 3158 of the Notices 9, 238 f. clearly contain different parts of the same work, which, according to 239, 5. 6, seems to be a selection from a larger work. The first section seems to be treating the Apabhraṁśa of Piṅgala. — 3. DURGĀPRASĀD and PARAB, Kāvyamālā 1, 7, note 1. — 4. Kāvyamālā 1, 91 note 1; EI. 4, 271. — 5. According to AUFRECHT, Cat. Cat. 2, 81 it could be assumed that the work existed in a complete form. Up till now only 8 pages have been printed. — 6. 1 A. 2, 29. — 7. Proc. ASB. 1875. 77. — 8. Cf. AUFRECHT, Cat. Cat. 1, 952. — 9. AUFRECHT Cat. Cat. 1, 337. 360. 364. From RĀJENDRALĀLA MITRA, Notices 4, 172, No. 1608 it is proved that Prākṛtacandrikā is an earlier and more voluminous work. — 10. AUFRECHT, Cat. Cat. 1, 22; 2. 5. who has erred in respect of time. HULTZSCH, Reports on Sanskrit

Manuscripts in Southern India 1, 67, No. 265 assigns the work to Cinabommabhūpāla, as is proved also by the colophon. Cf. also the printed edition pp. 21. 27. — 11. AUFRECHT, Cat. Cat. 1, 360. — 12. AUFRECHT Cat. Cat. 1, 361.

§ 42. With regard to the merit of indigenous grammarians of Prākrit, BLOCH has arrived at a quite wrong conclusion that he has summarized in four sentences : "(1) Since we do not possess any manuscript of so earlier a time and presumably because we shall never come by any of them, we alone can utilize the grammarians of Pkt. only with limitations. (2) The only means to check the correctness of their statements are our MSS. (3) In places where our MSS differ from their statement it is the latter that is to be considered wrong till a verification is made with the help of some good MSS. (4) We should not admit that such forms of our MSS as they pass over in silence did not exist in their time. The argumentum ex silentio is not valid for any of the Pkt. grammarians." It is only the fourth hypothesis that is partly correct, the other three are basically wrong. The grammarians are not to be corrected with the help of MSS but the MSS are to be improved upon with the help of the grammarians. In this connection I may refer to the remarks made above (§§ 22-25) with regard to Ś. Mg. Śākārī and Ḍhakkī. Only with the help of the statements of the grammarians we are able to draw even an outline sketch of these dialects : the manuscripts are mostly disappointing. According to BLOCH[2] for example, the situation that Rohasena, son of Cārudatta, speaks Mg. in Mṛcch. according to Pṛthvīdhara, but Ś. in STENZLER would prove how little the scholiasts are to be relied upon. But as already shown above (§ 23, note 2), such vestiges in the MSS prove that they are not contributions of the scholiasts. Up to the time of publication of my edition of the Śakuntalā it was accepted that Saravadamana, pp. 155-162 spoke Ś., if no notice was taken of 155, 15; 158, 15 ed. CHE'ZY. The critical notes in any edition point to the vagueness of these vestiges of Mg., and notwithstanding this, nobody doubts today that against majority of the MSS Mg. has to be reconstructed here. CAPPELLER[3], therefore, had quite correctly drawn a parallel between Sarvadamana and Rohasena. Surely it is true that the teachings of the grammarians require a detailed examination and further elaboration.[4] Besides, I do not find any reason to revise my opinion on Hc.[5] Moreover, we should never forget that up to the present time only a small portion of the literature that the grammarians had before them has come to be known and that works like those of Hc. are based upon several earlier works. The few specimens of JŚ. (§ 21) make forthwith so much of disclosure for us regarding the sources from which Hc. came by the forms, in the section on Ś., that were not known to the older grammarians and were not found in the dramas. LASSEN, in 1837, could cover an endless number of forms from grammarians alone, the forms that, to-day in a great measure, are abundantly found in literature, and I think that in course of time we, in our turn, shall have the same experience about ourselves. It is true that through carelessness grammarians had committed monstrous blunders that have been corrected in the exegesis of the Veda with the help of tradition and in the case of Sanskrit lexicography with the assistance of the native lexicographers. It is necessary that, instead of undervaluing them, efforts should be made to bring out critically edited texts as much as possible.

1. Vr. und Hc. p. 48. — 2. Vr. und Hc. p. 4. — 3. Jenaer Literaturzeitung1877, 124. — 4. JACOBI, GGA. 1888, 71. — 5. Hc. 2, p. vi.

§ 43. HOEFER was the first scholar to handle the grammar of Pkt. in De Prakrita dialecto libri duo, Berolini 1836[1]. Almost about the same time appeared LASSEN's Institutions linguae Pracriticae, Bonnae ad Rhenum 1837, based on more richly abundant materials. A supplement thereto, die Radices Pracriticae was published by DELIUS, Bonnae ad Rhenum 1839. Up to that time none of the indigenous grammars had been published, and of the entire Pkt. literature there had appeared only a small portion, of the dramas, Mṛcch., Śak., Vikr., Ratn., Prab., Mālatīm., Uttarar. Mudrār., besides Kāvyaprakāśa and Sāhityadarpaṇa, all in wholly bad uncritical editions. Therefore, LASSEN was able to describe mainly Ś. only, M. in accordance with the statements of the grammarians and Mg. on the basis of Mṛcch., Śak., and Prab. Under these circumstances LASSEN's work is an admirable performance. With his sagacity he has effected improvements in an excellent method in numberless places in the corrupt texts, correctly utilized them and laid the foundation on which the edifice of later research could be raised up. In spite of all such qualities up till now he has found no follower. The works of WEBER on M., AMg., of EDUARD MÜLLER on AMg., of JACOBI on JM. are devoted to individual dialects; they will be referred to in appropriate places. COWELL, A short Introduction to the Ordinary Prákṛit of the Sanskrit Dramas, with a list of common irregular Prákṛit words, London 1875 is based upon Vr.; it is all elementary and does not go a long way towards attainment of its goal.[2] RISHIKESH (rather more correctly Hṛṣīkeśa) SASTRI, A Prakrita Grammar with English translation, Calcutta 1883, attempts to re-arrange the indigenous grammars on an European pattern. But as he has used very defective texts (more correctly probably on) manuscripts, without working at them critically, his grammar is not at all usable, especially because he has referred to mostly only known rules. All new are his extracts from the Prākṛtakalpalatikā, that is otherwise unknown. HAAG, in his Vergleichung des Prakrit mit den Romanischen Sprachen, Berlin 1869, discusses a number of phonetical phenomena, that are common to known languages. HOERNLE[3] has given a general survey of the history of Prākrit — Philology and WEBER[4] of the recent publications (1870 — 1881).

1. Cf. BENARY, Jahrbücher für wissenschaftliche Kritik 1836, 863 ff. — 2. cf. PISCHEL, Jenaer Literaturzeitung 1875, 794 ff. — 3. A Sketch of the History of Prakrit Philology, Calcutta Review, October 1880. Cf. Centenary Review of the ASB. Calcutta 1885) II, p. 157 ff. — 4. Hāla² (Leipzig 1881) p. vii f. with note.

§ 44. In this grammar an attempt has been made for the first time to treat the different Prākrit dialects beside one another and to utilize the entire available materials. Subsequent to LASSEN, we have come to know of AMg. JM. and almost the whole of M., and as a matter of that, all the most important dialects with correlated literature. Here have been introduced all new Ḍh. D. Ā. JŚ. whereof we have up till now come by only a few specimens. Ś. and M. have undergone a thorough revision. As already remarked above (§§ 19. 22. 23), most of the texts in AMg. Ś. Mg. have not as yet been critically edited and published; many not usable for grammatical purposes. Hence the main task, at least with regard to Ś. and Mg., has been to obtain admissible materials, and for this purpose I have utilized three to four different editions of many dramas, a task that has been tedious, and more unfortunately not always fruitful. But this has not been possible for AMg., and as it respects this dialect, the critical issues will later require many emendations. Nevertheless I hope to have paved the way, in spite of the materials being very often faulty. As already remarked above, although Sanskrit is not the only source of Prākrit, a complete description of the latter has to be independently based upon it. Pāli, the Aśokan dialects, the Leṇa-dialect and the modern Indian languages have been quoted very sparingly for the purpose of comparison, though I have had plenty of materials in hand, as the present volume, which exceeds much beyond the scope of the scheme of the Grundriss, would have become still bigger. Consequently linguistic hypotheses have been scrupulously avoided. In the first place it provides a sure philological grounding, and I think that I have succeeded in my efforts for most of the dialects. Necessary quotations have been amply furnished. But the knowledge of Pkt. and its literature is limited to such a small circle of scholars that to me it appears wistful to shift evidences accurately in support of the rules and to make at the same time a beginning of a lexicon.

II. PHONETICS.

§ 45. The phonetic system of Pkt. differs from that of Classical Skt. to the extent that there exist in Pkt. *ĕ*, *ŏ*[1], *ḷa* (§ 226), and dialectically also the independent *ñ* (§ 237), *lha* (§ 242) and the composite sounds *ñña* (§ 282), *yca*, *yja* (§ 217), *yha* (§ 331), *lha* (§ 330), *śka*, *śkh*, *ḫka* (§§ 302.324), *śta* (§ 310), *śṭa*, *śṭha* and *sṭa* (§ 303), and that on the contrary in all the Pkt. dialects the sounds *ḷr*, , *ai*, *au*[2], *ṣa* except in Mg. *ciṣṭhadi* = *tiṣṭhati* (§ 303), *ḥ*, voiceless non-conjunct consonants are wanting, besides most of them do not have *ṛ*, *na*, *ya*, *śa* and conjunct consonants of non-homogeneous classes. Generally conjunctions of homogeneous consonants occur only when the first member is a nasal.[3] In places of consonants that drop inside a word, between two vowels there develops as a weakly articulated sound, *ya* that is written in all the dialects in Jaina manuscripts, and it is a distinctive feature of AMg., JM. and JŚ. (§ 187). In this grammar it has been transcribed by *ẏa*.

1. S. Goldschmidt, Prākṛtica, p. 28 ff., denies the existence of *ĕ* and *ŏ*. Against that Jacobi, KZ. 25, 292 ff.; Pischel, GGA., 1880, 325. — 2. In Pkt. *ai* has been retained only in the interjection *ai*, see § 60. — 3. C. 2. 14 pp. 18. 44; Hc. 1, 1; Triv. and Sr. in Pischel, De gr. Pr. p. 34 ff.; Kṛṣṇapaṇḍita in Peterson, Third Report 344, 1 ff.; Kalpacūrṇi in Leumann, Āv. 6, Note 4; Lakṣmīnāthabhaṭṭa on Piṅgala 1, 2, p. 3, 4 ff., where in the fifth line *bha* for *ma* is to be read, besides *saărapuṭṭhe hi be bi*, and in the sixth line something like *pāue ṇatthi* for *pāḍave ṇa hvaranti*, because very often *atthi* stands for the plural

santi (§ 498). Neither *hvavanti* not *honti-bhavanti* fits in metrically. In line 6 read *bha* for *ma* and in line 7 read *au aḥ ba ya*. Accordingly *ba* as well should be wanting in Pkt. On this see § 201.

§ 46 The accent-system of M. AMg. JM., of poetical A. and presumably also of JŚ. corresponds to that of the language of the Vedas essentially. Since in Pkt. takes place weakening, dropping as well as raising of vowels; besides there occurs doubling of consonants in certain cases, therefore, it could not be purely musical, on the other hand it must have been preponderantly expiatory. In Ś. Mg. Ḍh., besides, the system of accent is the same as that in Classical Skt. which mostly corresponds to that of Latin.[1] The relevant paragraphs furnish the details.

1. PISCHEL, KZ. 34, 568 ff.; 35, 140 ff. Besides JACOBI, ZDMG. 47, 574 ff.; KZ. 35, 578 ff.; GRIERSON, ZDMG. 49, 395 ff.

A. SONANTS AND VOWELS

1. SONANTS

§ 47. *ṛ* was retained just dialectically only in A. (Hc. 4, 329; Kī. 5. 16; Namisādhu on Rudraṭa, Kāvyālaṅkāra 2. 12, p. 15, 9); *tṛṇu* = *tṛṇam* (Hc. 4, 329; Namisādhu l.c.); *sukṛdu* (Hc. 4, 329), *sukṛdaṁ* (Ki. 5, 16) = *sukṛtaṁ*; *gṛṇhaï* = *gṛhṇāti*, *gṛhanti* = *gṛhṇanti*, *gṛṇhĕppiṇu* = **gṛhṇitvinam* (§ 588) = *gṛhitvā* (Hc. 4, 336. 344, 2. 394. 438, 1); *kṛdantahŏ* = *kṛtāntasya* (Hc. 4, 370, 4). In most of the Apabhraṁśa dialects *ṛ* is unknown as in all the Prākrit languages. CP. *khṛta* = *ghṛta* in Kī. 5. 102 may be an incorrect reading for *khata*, as *taṭhahitapaka* = *dṛḍhahṛdayka* 5, 102) shows. In LASSEN, Inst. p. 441 the example does not occur. As a sonant *ṛ* might be pronounced with a tinge of *a*+, *i*+ and *u*+. Like the consonantal *r* (§ 287-295) the sonantal *ṛ* is assimilated to the preceding consonant, so that only the vowel remains. Thereafter, *ṛ* following a consonant is transformed into *a*, *i*, and *u* in Pkt. and A. On initial *ṛ*, see § 56, 57, and on *ĕ* for *ṛ*, § 53.

1. MAHLOW, Anzeiger für deutsches Altertum und deutsche Literatur, 24, 10. Cf. JOHANNES SCHMIDT, Zur Geschichte des indogermanischen Vocalismus 2, sf.; Kritik der Sonantentheorie p. 175 ff.; BECHTEL, Die Hauptprobleme der indogermanischen Lautlehre seit Schleicher, p. 128 ff. Further literature in WACKERNAGEL, Alt. Gram. 28, who shows that the original pronunciation was a *r*- vowel.

§ 48. As the vowel pronounced with *ṛ* was not definite it vacillated in the same words not only in different dialects, but even within the same dialect. The native grammarians consider the change of *ṛ* to *a* as usual, and they have enumerated under gaṇas the words that show a change of *ṛ* into either *i* or *u* (Vr. 1, 27-29; Hc. 1, 126-139; Kī, 27.30. 32; Mk. fol. 9. 10; Pkl., p. 31 ff.; no classification in C. 2, 5 p. 15. 43) instead of into *a*. Generally the texts illustrate their statements with examples taken by preference from M., and they are to be considered accordingly. The examples, so far as possible, have been given in the following pages in conformity with the practice adopted by grammarians.

§ 49. *a* develops for *ṛ*, e. g. in M. *ghaa* = *ghṛta* (H. 22; read so with the variant reading), AMg. JM. *ghaya* (C.2.5) [read so with the variant reading]; Hc. 1, 126; Pāiyal. 123; Āyār. 2, 1, 4, 5; 2, 6, 1, 9, 12; 2, 13,4; Vivāhap.

910; Uttar. 170, 432; Kappas; Āv. 12, 12; T. 6, 4. 7; Erz.), but Ś. Mg. *ghida* (Mṛcch. 3, 12; 117, 8; 126, 5 [read so for *ghia*]). — PG. *taṇa* = *tṛṇa* (6, 33, likewise M. (Bh. 1, 27; Hc 1, 126; Kī 1, 27; G. H. R.), AMg. (Āyār. 1, 1, 4, 6; 1, 6, 3, 2; Sūyag. 129. 810. 812; Vivāhap. 120. 479. 500. 645.658. 1245. 1250; Uttar. 106. 219. 371. 582. 695. 1048; Jīv. 356. 464. 465; Paṇṇav. 33, 43 etc.), *taṇaga* = *tṛṇaka* (Āyār. 2, 2, 3, 18; Dasav. 623,1), *taṇaïlla* (grassy; Jīv. 355); JM. (KI. 12; Dvār. 502, 31; 504, 13; Erz.), Ś. (Śak. 106. 13), A. (Hc. 4,329. 334. 339); but also AMg. *tiṇa* (Vivāhap, 1526), JM. (Erz.), JŚ. (Kattig. 399, 313), Ś. (Vikr. 15, 11), A. (Hc. 4, 329. 358, 2. — M. *kaa* = *kṛta* (Bh. 1, 27; Hc. 1, 126; Pāiyal. 77; G. H. R.); PG. *adhikate* = = *adhikṛtān* (5, 5), *kaḍa* (7, 51); AMg. *kaya* (Uvās.; Ovav.) and *kaḍa* (Āyār. I, 8, 4, 11; Sūyag. 46. 74. 77. 104. 106. 133. 136. 151. 282. 368. 465; Nirayāv.; Bhag; Kappas.), also in compounds, such as in *akaḍa* (Āyār. 1, 2, 1, 3,5, 6), *dukkaḍa* (Āyār. 1, 7, 1, 3; Sūyag. 233 f. 275. 284. 359; Uttar. 33), *vigaḍa, viyaḍa* (Āyār. 1, 8, 1, 7; Sūyag. 344; Uttar. 53), *sukaḍa* (Āyār. 1, 7, 1, 3; 2, 4, 2, 3; Uttar. 76), *saṁkhaya* = *saṁskṛta* (Sūyag. 134. 150; Uttar. 199), *purekaḍa* = *puraskṛta* (§ 306. 345), *āhākaḍa* = **yāthākṛta* (§ 335); JM. *kaya* (Erz. ; Kk.), *dukkaya* (Pāiyal. 53; Erz.); JŚ. Ś. *kada* (Pav. 384, 36 (Text *kaya*), Mṛcch. 3, 19; 41, 18; 52, 12; Śak. 36, 16; 105, 15; 140, 13; Vikr. 16, 12; 21, 9; 23. 8), Mg. *kada* (Mṛcch. 40, 5; 133, 8; 159, 22) and *kaḍa* (Mṛcch. 17, 8; 32, 5; 27, 23. 24 etc), *kaḷa* (Mṛcch. 11, 1 ; 40, 4); P. *kata* (Hc. 4, 322. 323); A. *kaa* (Hc. 4, 422, 10), *kaaü* = *kṛtakaḥ* = *kṛtaḥ* (Hc. 4, 429, 1). But in Ś. Mg. the best texts and MSS have very often *kida*, e.g. Ś. (Mṛcch. 2, 21; 36, 4; 68, 12; Śak. 124, 7; 154, 9; 161, 5; Vikr. 33, 11; 35, 6; 72, 16; 84, 21), Mg. (Mṛcch. 112, 16; 121, 6; 165, 2), a form, that perhaps alone is correct in these dialects, and in any case that must remain in cases where *kṛta* constitutes the second member of a compound. thus Ś. *siddhikida* (Mṛcch. 6, 11. 13; 7, 5). *purākida* (Śak. 162, 13), *paccakkhīkida* (Vckr. 72, 12), Mg. *duskida* (Mṛcch. 125, 1. 4). So also M. in *duhāia* = *dvidhākṛta* (Hc. 1, 126; R. 8, 106), *dohāia* (R.), whereas elsewhere *kia* in M. is incorrect. A. has also *i* beside *a* for *ṛ* : *akia* = *akṛta* (Hc. 4, 396, 4), *kiaü* = *kṛtakam* = *kṛtam* (Hc. 4, 371), *kidu* (Hc. 4, 446). Cf. § 219. — *vasaha* = *vṛṣabha* (Bh. 1, 27; C. 2, 5 p. 43; 3, 13; Hc. 1, 126; Pāiyal. 151); so. M. (G. R.); AMg. Vivāhap. 225; Uttar. 338; Kappas. § 4.32. 61; Nāyādh. § 47), also *vasabha* (Āyār. 2, 10, 12; 2, 11, 7. 11; Vivāhap. 1048; Paṇṇav. 122; Aṇuog. 502; Kappas. § 114. 118); JM. *vasaha* (Dvār. 498, 24: Kk., Erz.) and *vasabha* (Erz.); JŚ. *vasaha* (Pav. 382, 26. 43); but Ś. always has *vusaha* (Mṛcch. 6. 7; Mālav. 65, 8; Bālar. 73. 18; 93, 10; 287, 15; Pras. 44, 13), which occurs wrongly also in M. (H. 460. 820; in the first place in the variant reading and in the ed. Bombay there occurs correctly *va*°). — AMg. *ghaṭṭha* = *ghṛṣṭa* (Hc. 1, 126; Āyār, 2, 2, 1, 3; 2, 5, 1, 3; 2, 10, 5; Paṇṇav. 96, 110; Jīv. 439. 4, 5. 447. 449. 453. 483 ff.; Ovav. — AMg. JM. *maṭṭiyā*, Ś. *maṭṭiā* = *mṛttikā* (Āyār. 2, 1, 6, 6; 2, 1. 7, 3; 2, 3, 2, 13; Vivāhap. 331. 447. 810. 1253. 1255; Ṭhāṇ. 321; Paṇhāv. 419. 494; Uttar. 758; Nāyādh. 621; Rāyap. 176; Uvās.; Ovav.; Erz.; Mṛcch. 94, 16; 95. 8. 9; Śak. 79. 1; 155, 10; Bhartṛharinirveda 14, 5). — AMg. *vaṭṭ* = *vṛtta* (round; Hc. 2, 29; Āẏār. 1, 5, 6, 4; 2, 4, 2, 7, 12; Sūẏag. 590; Ṭhāṇ. 20; Vivāhap. 942; Uttar. 1022; Paṇṇav. 9 ff.; Uvās. ; Ovav. ; Kappas.). — AMg. *vaṇhi* = *vṛṣṇi* (Uttar. 666; Nāẏādh. 1262), *andhagavaṇhi* = *andhakavṛṣṇi* (Uttar. 678 = Dasav. 613, 33; Vivāhap. 1394; Antag. 3).

§ 50. In all dialects *ṛ* is most frequently represented by *i*, which corresponds today to *ri*, the most usual pronunciation of *ṛ* in India. Such words are grouped under the *ṛṣyādi* class in Vr. 1, 28; Kī. 1, 32; Mk. fol. 9 f.; Pkl. p. 31 and under the *kṛpādi* class in Hc. 1, 128, without an attempt to enumerate them exhaustively. Thus : M. AMg. Ś. *kisa* = *kṛśa* (Hc. 1, 128; H. ; Uttar. 750; Uvās.; Śak. 53, 9). — M. AMg. Ś. Mg. *kiviṇa* = *kṛpaṇa* (Hc. 1, 128; G. H.; Kappas.; Kāleyak. 26, 1 (text °*va*°); Mṛcch. 19, 6; 136, 18. 19). — AMg. *giddha* = *gṛdhra* (greedy; Sūẏag 105; Vivāhap. 450. 1128; Uttar. 593; Nāẏādh. 433. 606); JM. Ś. Mg. (vulture; Vr. 12, 6; Mk. fol. 9; Erz.; Vikr. 75, 11; 79, 15; 80, 20; Mālav. 28, 12; Śak. 116,3) — AMg. *giddhi* = *gṛddhi* (Hc. 1, 128; Sūẏag. 363. 371. 406; Uttar. 933. 939. 944. 954 etc.), *giddhiẏa* = *gṛddhika* (Paṇhāv. 150). — M. AMg. JŚ. Ś. A. *diṭṭhi* = *dṛṣṭi* (Bh. 1,28; Hc. 1, 128; Kī. 1, 32; Mk. fol. 10; G. H. R.; Bhag.; Uvās.; Erz.; Kk.; Pav. 388, 5; Mṛcch. 57, 3. 10. 17; 59, 24; 68, 22; 152, 25; Śak. 53, 8; 59, 7; 77, 10 etc.; Hc. 4, 330, 3). — M. *viṁchua* (Bh. 1, 28; H. 237), *viṁcua* (C. 2, 15; Hc. 1, 128; 2, 16. 89; Kī. 2, 68 (text *viñcao*, ed. Rāj. *viccuo*)), *viṁchia* (Hc. I, 26; 2, 16); *vicchua* (Mk. fol. 10), AMg. *vicchuẏa* (Ṭhāṇ. 311. 312; Paṇhāv 47. 537; Nāẏādh. 755; Vivāhap. 522; Jīv. 257), *vicchiya* (Uttar. 1064)[1] = *vṛścika*. — M. *siāla* = *sṛgāla* (Bh. 1, 28; Hc. 1, 128; Kī. 132; Mk. fol. 9); AMg. JM. *siẏāla* (Āẏār. 2, 1, 5, 3; Sūẏag. 296; Paṇṇav. 49. 367. 369; Jīv. 356; Kk.), *siẏālaga* (Nāẏādh. 511), *siẏālattāe* (Ṭhāṇ. 296), *siẏāli* (Paṇṇav. 368); Ś. *siāla* (Mṛcch. 72, 22; Śak. 35,9); Mg. *śiāla* (Mṛcch. 22, 10; 113, 20; 120, 12; 122, 8; 127, 5; Śak. 116, 3), *śiāli* (Mṛcch. 11, 20). — M. AMg. JM. A. *siṅga* = *śṛṅga* (Hc. 1, 130; Pāiẏal. 210; G.H.; Vivāhap. 326. 1042; Uvās,; Ovav.; Kappas. ; Erz.; Hc. 4, 337), according to Hc. 1, 130 also *saṅga*. — M. Ś. Mg. A. *hiaa* = *hṛdaya* (Bh. 1, 28; Hc. 1, 128; Kī. 32, ; M k. fol. 10; G. H. R.; Mṛcch. 17, 15; 27, 4. 19.21; 37, 16 etc. Mg. Mṛcch. 29. 21; 128.2; 169. 6; Prab. 63, 15 [so read with M.]; Hc. s. v.); AMg. JM. *hiẏaẏa* (Bhag.; Uvās.; Nāẏādh.; Kappas.; Ovav.; etc.; Etz.; Kk.); Mg. mostly *haḍakka* (§ 194) also *halaka, halaa* (§ 244); P. *hitapa*, *hitapaka* (§ 191).

1. It will be possible to determine accurately in individual cases the correct form of this word when more critical editions will come into existence.

§ 51. We find *u* for *ṛ* preferably before a labial consonant, or (§57) when there is *u* in the following syllable. All grammarians group together the words which have *u* under the *ṛtvādi* class. Thus: M. *ṇihua* = *nibhṛta* (Hc. 1, 131; Deśīn. 5, 50; Mk. fol. 10; H. R.); AMg. JM. *nihuẏa* (Pāiẏal. 15; Uttar. 627; Ovav. ; Erz.); Ś. *ṇihuda* (Śak. 53, 4, 6; Mudrār. 44, 6; Karṇas 18, 19; 37, 16). — M. *ṇivvua* = *nirvṛta* (Bh. 1, 29; Hc. 1, 131; G. H. R.; Śak. 96, 2); AMg. JM. *nivvuẏa* (Kappas.; Erz.); Ś. *ṇivvuda* (Śak. 70; 4; 98, 7; Vikr. 53, 1 (read so with the South Indian recension 651, 2 ed. PISCHEL Mudrār. 103, 7). Cf. § 219. — M. AMg. JM. *pucchaï* = *pṛcchati* and other forms of the root (Hc. 4, 97; H. R. ; Uvās.; Bhag.; Kappas.; etc.; Erz.); Ś. *pucchadi*, (Mṛcch. 27, 17; 105, 8; 142, 9; Vikr. 18, 8); Mg. *puścadi* (Hc. 4, 295), *puścāmi* (Prab. 51, 1; 62, 6); A. *pucchimi* (Vikr. 65, 3), *pucchahu* (Hc. 4, 364, 422. 9). — M. *puhaī*, *puhavī* = *pṛthvī* (§ 115. 139; Bh. 1, 29; C. 3, 30 p. 50; Hc. 1, 131; Kī. 1, 30; Mk. fol. 10; G. H. R.); AMg. JŚ. *puḍhavī* (Ṭhāṇ. 135; Uttar. 1034. 1036; Sūyag. 19. 26. 325. 332; Āyār. 1, 1, 2, 2, ff.; Vivāhap. 920. 1099; Paṇṇav. 742; Dasav. 630, 17; Uvās. etc.; Kattig. 401, 346); so also JM. (Erz.); Ś. (Śak. 59, 12) beside *puhavī* (Erz.; Kk; Dvār. 501, 23; Vikr. 11, 4; Prab. 39, 6), as also Mg. (Mṛcch. 38, 7) and A. (Piṅgala 1, 30; Vikr. 35, 18) p. 50 have.— AMg. *phusaï* = *spṛśai* (§ 486). — M. AMg. Ś. A. *muṇāla* = *mṛṇāla* (Bh. 1, 29; Hc. 1, 131; Kī. 1, 30; Mk. fol. 10; G. H. R.; Śak. 88. 2; Jīv. 290; Rāyap. 55; Ovav.; Mṛcch. 68. 24; Sak. 63, 2. 15; Karp. 41, 1; Vṛṣabh. 50, 1; Hc. 4, 444, 2). — M. *muiṅga* = *mṛdaṅga* (Hc. 1, 46. 137; Mk. fol. 10); AMg. JM. *muiṅga*, *muyiṅga* (Paṇhāv. 512; Ṭhāṇ. 481; Vivāhap. 797 (so the commentary). 920; Rāyap. 20, 231; Jīv. 251; Paṇṇav. 99. 101; Erz.); Ś. *midaṅga* (Mālav. 19, 1; v. l. *maiṅga*); according to Hc. 1, 137; Mk. fol. 10 also *miṅga*; Mg. *miḍaṅga* (Mṛcch. 122, 8; variant reading *mudaṅga* and so GOḌABOLE 337, 7). — J.M. S. *vuttanta* = *vṛttānta* (Bh. 1, 29; Hc. 1, 131; Erz., Kk. Śak. 43, 6; Vikr. 52. 1; 72. 12; 81, 2). — AMg. JM. *vuṭṭhi* = *vṛṣṭi* (Hc. 1, 137; Pāiyal. 227; Vivāhap. 331; Kappas.; Erz.); M. also *viṭṭhi* (Hc. 1, 137; Kī, 1, 32; H. 261); *vuṭṭha* = *vṛṣṭa* (Hc. 1, 137; M. *uvvuṭṭha* (G. 3 75); AMg. *silāvuṭṭha* (Dasav. 630, 21); Ś. *pavuṭṭha* (Śak. 139. 15). — M. JM. A., sporadically in AMg., *kuṇai* JŚ. *kuṇadi* = **kṛṇāti* = Vedic * *kṛṇoti* (§ 508). On °*mūsā*°, *mosā*°, beside *musā*° = *mṛṣā*° = see §78.

§ 52. The vowel differs in the same words in many cases other than those mentioned above. So M. AMg. JM. Ś. Mg. *daḍha* and JŚ. S. A *diḍha* = *dṛḍha* (§ 242). — *dhaṭṭha* (Hc. 1, 130) and *dhiṭṭha* = *dhṛṣṭa* 1, 130; C. 1, 24 p. 41). — M. *ṇiatta* = *nivṛtta* (Hc. 1, 132; G. H. R.) and *ṇivutta* (Hc. 1, 132). — AMg. JM. *maccu* = *mṛtyu* (Hc. 1, 130; Sūyag. 45; Paṇhāv, 401; Dvār. 501, 25; Erz.) and Ś. *miccu* (Hc. 1, 130; Mālav. 54, 16; Karṇas. 32, 17). — M. AMg. JM. Ś. = *masiṇa* = *masṛṇa* (Hc. 1, 130; Kī. 1, 32; Mk. fol. 10; Pāival. 261; G. H. R., Ovav.; Erz.; Uttarar. 11, 8; 163, 4) and *masaṇa* (Hc. 1, 130). — AMg. Ś. *miu* = *mṛdu* (Vivāhap. 943. 949; Ovav.; Kappas.; Vṛṣabh. 13, 13 (Text *midu*)), but always M. *maüa* AMg. *maüya* = *mṛduka* (Hc. 1, 127); H. R. ; Vivāhap. 943. 954; Uttar. 1022; Jīv. 350, 549; Aṇuog. 268; Nāyādh.); AMg. *maüga* (Jīv. 508); M. *maüia* = **mṛdukita*, *maüī* = *mṛdvī* (G.). — *vandāraa* (Hc. 1, 132) and *vundāraa* = *vṛndāraka* (Hc. 1, 132; Kī. 1, 30). — AMg. *vaga* = *vṛka* (Āyār. 2, 1, 5, 3; Vivāhap. 282. 484 (text *vagga*, commentary *viga*); Paṇṇav 367), *vagī* = *vṛkī* (Paṇṇv. 368) and AMg. *viga* (Āyār. 2, 1, 8, 12 (cf. the variant reading), Nāyādh. 344), Ś. *via* (Uttarar. 105, 12). Cf. § 219. According to Hc. 2, 110 *kṛṣṇa* in the sense of "black" becomes *kasaṇa*, *kasiṇa*, *kaṇha* and as a proper name it becomes only *kaṇha*, according to Bh. 3, 61 in the sense of "black" it always becomes *kasaṇa* in the sense of "Kṛṣṇa" it becomes *kaṇha* only; according to Kalpal. p. 33, as a proper noun it becomes *kaṇha* and *kiṇha*;

Mk. for. 29 and Kī. 2, 56 make no distinction between *kasaṇa* and *kaṇha*. In the sense of "black" it occurs as M. Ś. *kasaṇa* (G. H. R.; Pracaṇḍap. 47, 4; Mṛcch. 2, 21; Vikr. 21. 8; 51, 10; 67, 18; Ratn. 311, 21; Mālatīm. 103, 6; 224, 3; Mahāv. 98, 4) Veṇīs. 61, 10). AMg. JM. *kasiṇa* (Paṇṇav. 101; Paṇhāv. 285; Sūyag. 282; Uttar. 644; Ovav., Bhag.; Dvār. 503, 6; Erz.; Ṛṣabhap.), also probably wrong, in M. (G. 563, the variant reading excepted), and Ś. (Mallikām. 122, 6); M. AMg. Ś. *kaṇha* (G.; Āyār. 2, 4, 2, 18; Paṇṇav. 496 ff.; Jīv. 320; Caṇḍak. 86, 8. 9. 10 (in *kaṇhāhi*; text *kahṇa* and *kahva*)), AMg. also *kiṇha* (Āyār. 2, 5, 1, 5; Vivāhap. 1033; Rāyap. 50. 51. 104. 120. 126. 228; Paṇhāv. 285 (beside *kasiṇa*) Paṇṇav. 496 ff. (always interchanging with *kaṇha*); Jīv. 255. 272. 274. 453. 457); as a proper noun M. AMg. JM. Ś. *kaṇha* (H.; Āyār. p. 126, 1, Paṇṇav. 61; Nirayāv. § 2, where also in the proper nouns *sukaṇha*, *mahākaṇha*, *vira-kaṇha.*, *rāmakaṇha*, *seṇakaṇha mahāseṇakaṇha*; p. 80; Ovav.,; Kappas.; Dvār. 497; 6, 33; 498; 34; 499; 37, etc. Cait. 75, 14; 77, 3; 78, 10; 79; 6. 1 4; 92. 13 (mostly printed as *kanha*, °*ḍa*, *kahna*); Vṛṣabh. 9, 4; 18, 15; 23, 18 etc. (mostly printed as *kanha*)). Wrong is *kisaṇa* (Bālar. 141, 3; Karp. 50, 12 ed. Bomb. where the variant reading in KONOW, p. 48 has only *kasaṇa*) and *kiṇha* (Nirayāv. 79). Cf. also *kasaṇīya* = *kṛṣṇāyita*, *kasaṇapakkha* = *kṛṣṇapakṣa* Pāiyal. 198. 268), *kasaṇasia* = ;**krāṇasita* "the black-white" = Balabhadra (Deśīn. 2, 23). — *vṛddhi* in the sense of "growth" becomes *vuḍḍhi* (Hc. 1, 131; 2, 40; Mk. fol. 24; AMg. Uvās. § 50), and in the sense of "interest" it becomes AMg. *vaḍḍhi* (Uvās). However we find also M. *parivaḍḍhi* (Mk. fol. 24; R. 5, 2) and JM. *viddhi* (growth : KĪ. 20). Cf. § 53.

§ 53. Sometimes dialectically all the three vowels occur even in the same words. Thus : *prākṛta* becomes *pāyaya* in AMg. (Hc. 1, 67; Nāyādh. § 145; variant reading *pāgaya*), *pāgaya* in JM. (Erz. 2. 28) and *pāyaya* (Hc. 1, 67); Kalpacūrṇī on Av. 6, 29), *pāia* in M., *pāiya* in JM. (cited under Hc. 1, 181; Vajjālagga 325. 2; Pāiyal. 1) and *pāua* in M. (H. 2 [v. l. *pāia*, Vajjālagga 324, 20]698; Karp. 5, 3). *pāuda* in Ś. (Karp. 5. 1; Mudrār. 82, 2. 5; Viddhaś. 25, 8 (read so everywhere) *pākida* in Mg. (Veṇīs. 34, 20). — *pṛṣṭha* becomes in M. *paṭṭhi* (Hc. 1, 131; G.), *puṭṭha* (Bh. 4, 20; R.), *puṭṭhī* (Bh. 4, 20; H. R.; Karp. 57. 6), in AMg. *piṭṭha* (Hc. 1, 35, Sūyag. 180. 285. 286; Nāyādh. §65; p. 938 958, 959, 964, 1107; Uttar. 29, 69; Uvās.; Ovav.), *piṭṭhi* (Hc. 1, 35. 129. Āyār. 1, 1, 2,5; Nāyādh. 940; Dasav. 632, 24), *puṭṭha* (Nirayāv. § 17), *puṭṭhi* (Sūyag. 292), in JM. *piṭṭha*, *piṭṭhi puṭṭhi* (Erz.), in Ś. D. *piṭṭha* (Vikr. 39, 3; Mālav. 33, 2; 59, 3; 69. 61; Mallikām. 145; 21; 191, 5; Mudrār. 254, 1; Mṛcch. 105, 25), *piṭṭhi* (Kaṁsav. 57, 9), *puṭṭha* (Pras. 44, 14; Ratn. 316, 22), *puṭṭhi* (Bālar. 238, 10), in Mg. *pisṭa* (Mṛcch. 99, 8; 130, 1; Veṇīs. 35. 5. 10), *pisṭi* (Mṛcch. 165, 9 and in A. *paṭṭhi*, *piṭṭhi*, *puṭṭhi* (Hc. 4, 329). According to Hc. 1, 129, in *pṛṣṭha* *ṛ* is changed to *a* only when the word occurs at the end of a compound. So M. JM. *mahivaṭṭha* (Hc. 1, 129); Pratāpar. 214. 9 (°*pa*'); Āv. 12, 23); Ś. *dharaṇivaṭṭha* (Uttarar. 63, 12; Bālar. 248, 5; 287, 16); however, also probably wrong is JM. *dharaṇiviṭṭha* (Sagara 7, 12), Ś. *dharaṇipiṭṭha* (text. °*ṇipiṭhṭha*; Bālar. 245, 15). The printed texts and the MSS of Veṇīs.

64, 18 waver between *kālapuṭṭha*, *°vuṭṭha*, *°piṭṭha*. –– *bṛhaspati* forms *bahapphaï*, *bihapphaï*, *buhapphaï* (C. 2, 5 p. 43; Hc. 1, 138; Sr. fol. 36) and a number of other forms with a similar variation in vowels (§ 212). We find also AMg. *bahassaï* (Sūyag. 709 (text *va°*), Ṭhāṇ. 82; Paṇṇav. 116 (text *va°*)), *bihassaï* (Aṇuog. 356 (text *vi°*). Ovav. § 36 (text°*va°*)); Ś. *bahappadi* (Mallikām. 57, 3; 184, 3 (text *va°*)); *bihapphadi* (Ratn. 310, 29). — In all the dialects *vṛddha* becomes *vuḍḍha* (C. 2, 5; 3, 16 p. 49; 3, 26; Hc. 1, 131; 2, 40. 90; Mk. fol. 24; H.; Āyār. 2, 2, 3, 24; Ovav.; Erz.,) Ś. Mṛcch. 44, 4; 69; 20; 71, 22; Anarghar. 156, 5; Mg., Mṛcch. 117, 23; 120, 9; 124, 4 etc.), according to Bh. 1, 27 also *vaddha*, and according to Hc. 1, 128; 2, 40 also *viddha*. — *vṛnta* forms AMg. *viṇṭa* (Hc. 1, 139, Samav. 98); Paṇṇav 40 (text *bi°*), *tālaviṇṭa* (Paṇhāv. 33), *pattaviṇṭa* (Jīv. 681); commonly also *veṇṭa* with change of *i* to *ĕ* before a double consonant (§ 119); so M. *vĕṇṭa* (Hc. 1, 139; 2, 31; Mk. fol. 26; H.; Śak. 119. 6), *tālavĕṇṭa* (Karp. 82,2); AMg. (Jīv. 329 [text *bĕ°*]; Paṇṇav. 40 [text *bĕ°*]), *tālavĕṇṭa* (Nāyādh. § 136), *pattavĕṇṭa* (Jīv. 549 [text °*bĕ°*]); Ś. Viddhaś. 14, 13), *tālavĕṇṭa* (Vikr. 75, 10; Uttarar. 16,7; Viddhaś. 61, 1; Veṇīs. 92, 22 (so to be read); Bālar. 131, 13 (so to be read), *tālmĕṇṭaa* (Mṛcch. 38, 4; 59, 7); Mg. Mṛcch. 21, 16). Hc. 1, 67 has *talavĕṇṭa* too by the side of *tālavĕṇṭa* (2, 31). Bh. (1, 10) has *talavĕṇṭaa* by the side of *tālavĕṇṭaa*. Further Hc. (1, 139 teaches also *vŏṇṭa*; 1, 67, *tālavŏṇṭa* along with *talavŏṇṭa* i.e. **vuṇṭa* with the change of *u* to *ŏ* before a double consonant (§ 125). In AMg. frequent is *tāliyaṇṭa* (Āyār. 2, 1, 7, 5; Paṇhāv. 236. 533; Aṇuttar. 10; Nāyādh. 277; Vivāhap. 807, 831. 964; Ovav. § 52 (so to be read); Dasav. 616, 38; 626, 3) *tāliyaṇṭaka* (Paṇhāv. 448 = **tālivṛnta* with a change of *ṛ* into *a*, as in Pāli *vaṇṭa*.

§ 54. BOLLENSEN[1] has propounded the law of assimilation, according to which, for example, only *miatiṇhiā* or *maataṇhiā* = *mṛgatṛṣṇikā* has to be declared as the correct form. PAUL GOLDSCHMIDT[2], on the reverse has postulated dissimilation in cases like *miaṅka* = *mṛgāṅka* beside *maïnda* = *mṛgendra*, *visaṁkhala* = *viśṛṅkhala* beside *siṅkhalā* = *śṛṅkhalā* (§ 213). Taking into consideration the great divergence between statements of grammarians and manuscripts, it is not possible to frame any such strict rule. In M. they say *maataṇhā* (R.), *maataṇhiā* (Sarasvatīk. 172, 18) beside *mudhamia*), Ś. *miataṇhā* (Dhūrtas. 11, 6; v. l. *maatiṇhā*), *miatiṇhā* (Anarghar. 60, 4), *maataṇhiā* (Vikr. 17, 1), *maatiṇhiā* (Viddhaś. 47, 9; but ed. Calc. 36, 1 *miataṇhiā*), *miatiṇhiā* (Viddhaś. 115, 5); further, indeed M. *maïnda* (G. R.), M. Ś. *maalañchaṇa*, JM. *mayalañchaṇa* = *mṛgalāñchana* (H.; Karp. 65, 10; 105, 7; Mṛcch. 169, 14; Vikr. 43, 11; 45, 20[3]; Pāiyal. 5; Dvār. 500, 18, Erz.), but beside *maaṅka* (Hc. 1, 130; also in A. 4, 396, 1), JM. *mayaṅka* (Erz.), in M. D. Ś. Mg. common *miaṅka* (Hc. 1, 130; G. H. R.; Karp. 60, 1; 84, 8; D. Mṛcch. 101, 11; Ś. Vikr. 58, 10; Viddhaś. 109, 5; Karp. 105, 7; Mg. Mṛcch. 37, 25); JM. has also *miyaṅka* (Erz.). Beside Ś. *maa* = *mṛga* stand *miaā* = *mṛgayā* (Śak. 29, 2. 3) and M. S. *mai* = *mṛgi* (Śak. 85, 2; Prab. 67, 12); Ś. *maavahū* = *mṛgavadhū* (Śak. 86, 4), beside S. *sāhāmia* = *śākhāmṛga* (Mṛcch. 69, 11); Vikr. 81, 13), AMg. *ihāmiya* (Jīv. 481. 492. 508; Nāyādh. 721,

Rāẏap 58 [°*ga*]); likewise AMg. generally only *miga*, *miẏa* 3 (Āẏār. 2, ; 3, 3; 2, 5, 1, 5; Vivāhap. 119 ff.; Uttar. 338. 412. 499. 595. 601; Dasav. N. 648, 7; Sūẏag. 52. 54. 56. 317; Ovav. § 37) *miẏasirāo*=*mṛgaśirāḥ* (Ṭhāṇ. 81), *migavva*=*mṛgavya* (Uttar. 498) speak against JM. *maẏa* (Dvār. 501, 13), *mayacchi*=*mṛgākṣi* (Ṛṣabhap. 26), M. *maacchi* (Karp. 65, 4). In compounds it is euphony that has undoubtedly assisted in the choice of vowels.

1. On Vikr. 17, 1, p. 216. — 2. Specimen des Setubandha (Göttingen 1873) p. 83 on 2, 2. — 3. The v. l. has *mia*° and so stands in Viddhaś. 63, 4 too.

§ 55. The *ṛ* of nouns ending in *ṛ* becomes *u* before the suffix -*ka*, and also when such a noun is the first member of a compound (Hc. 1, 134); PG. *jāmātukasa*=*jāmātṛkasya* (6. 14), *bhātukāṇa*=*bhrātṛkāṇām* (6.18); M. *jāmāua*=*jāmātṛka* (Bh. 1, 29; Hc. 1, 131; Mk. fol. 10; H.); JM. *jāmāuẏa* (Erz.); Ś. *jāmādua* (Mahāv. 27, 22; Mallikām. 209, 22); *jāmādusadda*=*jāmātṛśabda* (Mallikām. 209, 1); JM. *bhāuvacchala*=*bhrātṛvatsala* (Dvār. 503, 38; 507, 30), *bhāughāẏaga*=*bhrātṛghātaka*, *bhāuẏa*=*bhrātṛka* (Erz.), Ś. *bhādusaa*=*bhrātṛśata* (Veṇīs. 59,3); Ś. *bhādua* (Vikr. 75, 8); Mg. *vañcidabhāduka*=*vañcitabhrātṛka* (Mṛcch. 129, 6); AMg. *puttanattupariẏāra*=*putranaptṛparivāra* (Vivāhap. 482), *ammāpiusantie* (Āẏār 2, 15, 15), *ammāpiussūsaga* (Vivāhap. 608), *māupiusujāya* (Sūẏag. 585; Ovav§ 11), *māuoẏa*, *piusukka*=*mātrojaḥ*, *pitṛśukra* (Sūẏag. 817.822; Ṭhāṇ. 159; Vivāhap. 111), *māuẏa* (Nāẏādh. 1430); Ś. *mādughara* (Mṛcch. 54, 4) Mg. *mādukā* (Mṛcch. 122, 5); M. *piuvaha*=*pitṛvadha* (G. 484), JM. *nattuẏa*=*naptṛka* (Āv. 8, 31); AMg. *nattui* =*naptṛki* (Kappas. § 109). However, *i* too does not occur rarely: M. *ṇattia*=*naptṛka* (Hc. 1, 137; Sarasvatīk. 8, 13), *taṭṭhighaḍaṇā*=*tvaṣṭṛghaṭanā* (G. 704), *māihara* (Hc. 1, 135); AMg. *māimaraṇa*, *bhāimaraṇa* (Sūẏag. 787), *mātrākkhiẏa* (Ovav. § 72); Ś. *mādivacchala* (Śak. 158, 12); AMg. *peiẏa*=*paitṛka* (Vivāhap. 113); JM. *bhāivacchala*, *bhāighāẏaẏa* (Dvār. 501, 3. 38), *bhāivahaga*=*bhrātṛvadhaka* (Erz. 14, 28; 23, 19). *bhāisoga*=*bhrātṛśoka* (Erz. 53, 11; AMg. *ammāpiisamāṇa*, *bhāisamāṇa* (Ṭhāṇ. 284); A. *piimāimosaṇa*=*pitṛmātṛmoṣaṇa* (Erz. 158, 3); AMg. *bhaṭṭidāraẏa*=*bhartṛdāraka* (Paṇṇav. 366), S. *bhaṭṭidāraa* (Mahāv. 28, 2; 32, 22); Ś. *bhaṭṭidāriā* (Lalitav. 560, 9; 561, 6. 12; 562. 22; 563, 5; Mālatīm. 72, 2. 4. 8; 73, 5; 85, 3; Nāgān. 10, 9. 13; 12, 5. 10; 13, 4, etc.). In declension masculine nouns are inflected like those of *a*-, *i*- and *u*-stems, the feminine ones, like *ā*- stems; and *mātṛ* also is declined like those of *ī*- and *ū*-stems (§ 389 — 392).

§ 56. Generally the initial *ṛ* becomes *ri* (Vr. 1, 30; C. 2, 5; Hc. 1, 140; Kī. 1, 28; Mk. fol. 11), and *li* in Mg. So M. AMg. JM. JŚ. Ś. A. *riddhi*=*ṛddhi* (Pāiẏal. 62; G. H., Sūẏag. 954; Ovav.; Kl. 12; Erz. Kk.; Ṛṣabhap.; Kattig. 400, 325; 403, 370; Mṛcch. 6, 4; 21. 7; 77, 10; 94. 19; Hc. 4, 418, 8). — M. AMg. JM.Ś. *rikkha* (Hc. 2. 19; Pāiẏal. 96; H.; Nāẏādh.; Ovav.; Kappas.; Erz.; Bālar. 221, 5; 250, 18) and M. AMg. Ś. *riccha*=*ṛkṣa* (Vr. 1, 30; 3, 30; Hc. 1, 140; 2, 19; Pāiẏal. 128; R.; Rāẏap. 124; Śak. 35, 9; Anarghar. 156, 5). — M. JM. *riṇa*=*ṛṇa* (Bh. 1, 30; C. 2, 5; Hc. 1, 141; Mk. fol. 11; H.; Kk.); Ś. *ariṇa*=*anṛṇa* (Mṛcch. 64, 22; Śak. 24, 13; 141, 10); Mg. *līṇa* (Mṛcch. 21, 19) with metrical lengthening of *i* (§ 73). — AMg *riu* = *ṛtu* (Hc. 1, 141. 209; Pāiyal. 208; Samav. 119; Nirayāv. 81); Ś. *ridu* (Bālar. 131, 12). — AMg. *riuvveya* = *ṛgveda* (Ṭhāṇ. 166; Vivāhap. 149. 787; Nirayāv. 44; Ovav. § 77 [so to be read]; Kappas. § 10). — M. AMg. *risaha* = *ṛṣabha* (C. 2, 5 p. 43; Hc. 1, 141; R. [as a proper noun]; Paṇhāv. 270; Vivāhap. 10; Uvās.; Ovav.), AMg. Ś. also. *risabha* (Ṭhāṇ. 266 [as a proper noun]; Śak. 95. 7). — Ś. *ricāiṁ* = *ṛcaḥ* (Ratn. 302, 11). —AMg. JM. Ś. *risi* = *ṛṣi* (Hc. 1, 141; Pāiyal. 32; Sūyag. 202; Erz.; Mṛcch. 326, 14 (interpolation); Mg. *liśi* (Prab. 46, 15. 16; 47, 1); AMg. *mahārisi* (Sūyag. 203; Nāyādh. 1475). In cases, like AMg. *rāyarisi* = *rājarṣi* (Vivāhap. 908. 915. 916; Nāyādh. 600 ff. 1022; Uttar. 279 ff. 563), *māhaṇarisi* = *brahmarṣi* (§ 250; Nirayāv. 48, 50 ff.), JM. *maharisi* = *maharṣi* (Erz.), Ś. *sattarisi* = *saptarṣi* (Viddhaś. 49, 4. 6. 8), JM. *divāyaṇarisi* = *dvipāyanarṣi* (Dvār. 496, 7. 38; 497. 3) the existence of a separation-vowel (§ 137) has to be assumed; all these forms, therefore, directly go back to Sanskrit.

§ 57. An initial *ṛ* develops, not seldom into *a*, *i*, *u*, besides into *ri*. So M. AMg. JM. Ā. A. *acchaï*, P. *acchati* = *ṛcchati* (§ 480). — AMg. *accha* = *ṛkṣa* (Āyār. 2, 1, 5, 3; Vivāhap. 282. 484; Nāyādh. 345 by the side of *riccha*; Paṇṇav. 49. 367), *acchi* (Paṇṇav. 368); cf. Skt. *achabhalla*. — AMg. *aṇa* = *ṛṇa* (Hc. 1, 141; Paṇhāv. 150). — AMg. JM. *iḍḍhi* = *ṛddhi* (Ṭhāṇ. 80. 178; Uttar. 116. 666; Vivāhap. 55. 221; Nāyādh. 990; Ovav. § 33. 69; Uvās.; Kappas.; Nirayāv. § 16; Dasav. 635, 38; 640, 5; Dasav. N. 652, 28). As LEUMANN (Aup. S. s. v. *riddhi*) remarks rightly *iḍḍhi* is the form that occurs in older texts and *riddhi*, in later texts. The same holds good for AMg. as well in the case of other forms with *ri°* that are found by the side of such as have some vowel. — AMg. Ś. *isi* = *ṛṣi* (Vr. 1, 28; C. 2. 5; Hc. 1, 141; Kī. 1, 32; Mk. fol. 10; Paṇhāv. 448 (*suisi*); Uttar. 375. 377. 630; Vivāhap. 795. 851; Śak. 41, 1; 61, 11; 70, 6; 79, 7; 98, 8; 155, 9; Vikr. 80, 17; Uttarar. 123, 10; Unmattar. 3, 7 etc.); in proper nouns AMg. *isigutta*, *isiguttiya*, *isidatta*, *isipāliya* (Kappas.), and in compounds like AMg. Ś. *mahesi* = *maharṣi* (Sūyag. 74. 137; Uttar. 717. 720. 815; Anarghar. 151, 10; Unmattar. 4, 18); M.Ś. *rāesi* = *rājarṣi* (G.; Śak. 19, 5; 20, 12; 21, 4; 50, 1; 52, 16; 57, 12; Vikr. 6, 13. 16; 7. 2; 8, 14; 10, 2. 4. 14 etc.). — AMg. *uu* = *ṛtu* (Hc. 1, 131. 141. 209; Vivāhap. 423. 798; Paṇhāv. 464. 534; Nāyādh. 344. 912. 916. 918; Aṇuog. 242. 432; Dasav. 627, 11; Dasav. N. 648, 14); Ś. *udu* (Śak. 2, 8). Cf. § 157. On the ostensible M. *udu* see § 204. — AMg. Ś. *ujju* = *ṛju*, (Hc. 1, 131. 141; 2, 98; Paṇṇav. 847; Aṇuog. 541. 542. 552. 633; Uttar. 698. 699; Ovav.; Kaṁsav. 37, 20), AMg. *ujjukaḍa* = *ṛyukṛta* (Āyār. 1, 1, 3, 1); usually found *ujjua* = *ṛjuka* (Vr. 3, 52); so M. (H.R.); Ś. (Mṛcch. 88, 18; 90, 21;[1] Śak. 80. 4; 130, 5; Ratn. 302, 19; 308, 7; Mudrār. 192, 13; Anarghar. 113, 9; Karṇas. 20, 13, etc.), *adiujjua* (Ratn. 309, 24; Priyad. 43, 15); AMg. *ujjuga* (Paṇhāv. 381; Uvās.), *ujjuya* (Pāiyal. 175; Āyār. 2, 1, 5, 3; 2, 3, 2, 14, 16; Uttar. 170; Ovav.; Kappas.), *aṇujjuya* (Uttar. 990). — *usaha* = *ṛṣabha* (C. 2, 5p. 43; 3, 34 p. 51; Hc. 1, 131. 133); AMg. *usabha* (Āyār. 2, 15, 21; Nāyādh.; Ovav.; Kappas.); AMg. JM. *usabha* (Hc. 1, 24; Kappas.; Āv. 46, 21; Erz.); JM. *usabhaya* (Āv. 46, 21), AMg. *usabhadatta* (Āyār. 2, 15, 2;

Kappas.); AMg. *usabhasena* (Kappas.). — According to Kī. 1, 31 *ṛṇa* always becomes *uṇa*. We find in the text also *riṇa* (§ 56) and *aṇa* (§ 57) only.

1. So to be read; cf. PISCHEL, on Hc. 2. 98. GODABOLE 249, 9; 256, 1 writes *ujjaa*, what the scholiast translates by *ujjvala* and *udyata*.

§ 58. Corresponding to the development of *ṛ* into *i*, *u*, in the declension of *ṛ*-stems, *ṝ*-develops into *i*, *ū*: AMg. *ammāpūṇaṁ*, *ammāpiūṇaṁ*, *māiṇaṁ* (§ 391, 392). Skt. *īr* and *ūr* originating from earlier *ṝ* are regularly treated according to the phonetic law of Pkt: M. JM. *tīraï*, *tīra-tiyate* (§ 537); M. *païṇṇa* = *prakīrṇa* (G.H.R.), *viiṇṇa* = *vikīrṇa* (H.), *vivaïṇṇa* = *viprakīrṇa* (H.R.); JM. *viiṇṇa* = *vitīrṇa* (Erz.); M. *pūrraï* = *pūryate* (§ 537); M. AMg. JM. Ś. *puṇṇa* = *pūrṇa* (H. R.); Uvās.; Kappas.; Kk.; Prab. 57, 2). By the side of M. Ś. *jiṇṇa* = *jīrṇa* (Hc. 1, 102; H.; Pratāp. 201, 13; Mṛcch. 93, 9), Mg. *yiṇṇa* (Mṛcch. 162, 23) there is found very frequently M. AMg. JM. Ś. *juṇṇa* = Vedic *jūrṇá* (Hc. 1, 102; G. H.; Karp. 88, 3; Āyār. 2, 16, 9, Vivāhap. 1308; Nāyādh. 321. 983. 985. 987; Uttar. 440; Rāyap. 258f.; Aṇuog. 292; Āv. 37, 26; 40, 16; Erz.; Śak. 35. 9; Karp. 53, 5; Viddhaś. 114, 6; Mallikām 88, 23; Hāsy. 25, 5); AMg. *parijuṇṇa* (Āyār. 4, 7, 6, 1; Ṭhāṇ. 540; Uttar. 63); AMg. *juṇṇiya* (Nāyādh. 348); JM. *juṇṇaga* (Āv. 41, 1). By the side of *tittha* = *tīrtha*, M. has *tūha* = **tūrtha* (Hc. 1, 104; H; Sarasvatīk. 44, 12); *uttūha* = **uttūrtha* (up-flowing fountain; Deśīn. 1, 94). PG. *tūthike* = **tūrthikān* = *tīrthikān* (5, 5); AMg. *aṇṇaütthiya* = **anyatūrthika*[1] (Vivāhap. 129. 130. 137. 139. 142. 178. 323. 324 etc.; Nāyādh. 984 ff.; Ṭhāṇ. 147; Ovav.), *paraütthiya* = **paratūrthika*.[3] It is wrong[3] to derive[4] *tūha* directly from earlier *tṝtha*.

1. WEBER, IS. 16, 46, 299. Note 2: LEUMANN, Aup. S. p. 95. — 2. LEUMANN l.c.— 3. BARTHOLOMAE, ZDMG. 50, 680.—4. WACKERNAGEL, Alt. Gr. 24.

§ 59. Following a consonant *l* develops into *ili*: *kilitta* = *kḷpta* (Vr. 1, 33; Hc., 145; Kī. 1, 33; Mk. fol. 11); *kilitti* = *kḷpti* (Kī. 1, 33; Mk.fol. 11). According to Kī. 5, 16, in A it either remains or develops into *a* : *kḷtta*, *katta* = *kḷpta*. (Hc. 1, 145; 4, 329) accepts the presence of *l* in *klinna* "moistened" too (PISCHEL on Hc. 1, 145). The forms *kiliṇṇa* and A. *kiṇṇa* quoted by him, are explained as having originated from *klinna* (§ 136). Single *ḷ* develops into *li* in *ḷiāra* (Mk. fol. 11), *likāra* (Kalpal. p. 36) = *ḷkāra*

2. VOWELS.

(a) THE DIPHTHONGS *ai* and *au*

§ 60. In Pkt., *ai* has been retained as an interjection only, and that also in poetry only (Hc. 1, 169); usually in its place is used also M. Ś. *aï* = Skt. *ayi* (Vr. 9, 12; Hc. 1, 169; 2, 205; H.; Mṛcch. 63, 13; 64, 25; 87, 21; Vikr. 28, 10; 42, 19; 45, 2; Mālatīm. 74, 5; 247, 1; 264, 3 etc.). Some scholars according to Hc. 1, 1 = Prākṛtacandrikā 344, 5; C. 2, 14 p. 37 in Pkt. too permit *ai* in words like *kaiava* = *kaitava*, *airāvaṇa* (Bhaṭṭikāvya 13, 33). In fact, however, the places where *ai* is found the text gives an incorrect reading (PISCHEL on Hc. 1. 1). Mk. fol. 12 rejects it expressly. Generally *ai* develops into *e*, and before a double consonant, into *ĕ* : PG. *vijayavejayike* = *vijayavaijayikān* (6, 9). — M. AMg. JM. Ś. *erāvaṇa* = *airāvaṇa*

(Bh. 1, 35; Vr. 2, 11; Hc. 1, 148. 208; Kī. 2, 31; Mk. fol. 15; R.; Sūyag. 317; Kappas.; Erz.; Mṛcch. 68, 14); A. *erāvaï* = *airāvata* (Piṅgala 1, 24); cf. § 246. — AMg. *esajja* = *aiśvarya* (Ṭhāṇ. 450). — JŚ. *eyagga* = *aikāgrya* (Pav. 388, 1). — Ś. *edihāsia* = *aitihāsika* (Lalitav. 555, 2). — M. *keḍhaba* = *kaiṭabha* (Vr. 2, 21. 29; Hc. 1, 148. 196, 240; Kī. 2, 11; Mk. fol. 16). — M. *geria* = *gairika* (Karp. 80, 10), AMg. *geruya* = **gairuka* (Āyār. 2, 1, 6, 6; Sūyag. 834; Paṇṇav. 26; Dasav. 619, 41). — AMg. *neyāuya* = **naiyāuka* = *naiyāyika* (Sūyag. 117. 361; 994; ff. (*ṇe°*); Nāyādh. § 144; Uttar. 158, 180. 238. 324; Ovav.), *aṇeyāuya* (Sūyag. 736). — AMg. *mehuṇa* = *maithuna* (Āyār. 2, 1, 3, 2. 9, 1; 2, 2, 1, 12. 2, 10; Sūyag. 409. 816. 822 f. 923. 994. Bhag.; Uvās.; Ovav.), JM. *mehuṇaya* (Erz.), JŚ. *medhuṇa* (Kattig. 399, 306; text *°hu°*). — M. *vehavva* = *vaidhavya* (G.H.R.). — AMg. JM. *veyaḍḍha* = *vaitāḍhya* (C. 2. 6; Vivāhap. 479; Ṭhāṇ. 73; Vivāgas. 91; Nirayāv. 79; Erz.). — M. AMg. JM. *sela* = *śaila* (Bh. 1, 35; Pāiyal. 50; G. R.; Mṛcch. 41, 16; Karp. 49. 6; Āyār. 2, 2, 2, 8; 2, 6, 1, 2; Kappas; Ovav.; Erz.; Ṛṣabhap.), but CP. *saïla* (Hc. 4, 326). — M. AMg. JM. Ś. Mg. *tĕlla* = *taila* (§ 90). — M. JM. AMg. *cĕtta* = *caitra* (Kārp. 12, 4. 9; Viddhaś. 25, 2; Kī. 19; Āyār. 2, 15. 6; Kappas.). — M. JM. *mĕttī* = *maitrī* (H. R.; Kī. 7; Erz.). — M. JM. Ś. *vĕjja* = *vaidya* (Hc. 1, 148; 2, 24; H.; Āv. 16, 8; Erz.;-Vikr. 47. 2; Mālav. 26, 5; Karp. 104, 7). — M. Ś. *sĕṇṇa* = *sainya* (§ 282). — On the development of *i* for *ĕ* from *ai*, see § 84.

§ 61. The grammarians permit the use of *aï* compulsorily in the case of some words and optionally in that of others in lieu of *e*. The words in which there must be *aï* have been grouped by them under the *daityādi* class (Vr. 1, 36; Hc. 1, 151; Kī 1, 37; Mk. fol. 12; Pkl. p. 36). But common to all of them are only the words M. *daïcca* = *daitya* (Pāiyal. 26, 99; G.); *vaïdeha* (Kī. *°hi*) = *vaideha*; AMg. *vaïsāha* = *vaïśākha* (Āyār. 2, 15, 25 (beside *ve°* !); Vivāhap. 1426; Nīrayāv. 10; Uttar. 768; Kappas.). Further Hc. and C. 2, 6 also have *aïsaria* = *aiśvarya*, for which AMg. has *esajja* (§60); Hc. alone has *daïnna* = *dainya*, *vaïjavaṇa* = *vaijavana*; *daïvaya* = *daivata*; *vaïāila* *vaitāliya*; *vaïdabbha* = *vaïdarbha*; *vaïssāṇara* = *vaïśvānara*; *vaïsāla* = *vaiśāla*. Bh. Hc. Mk. Pkl. add also *saïra* = *svaira*, which Pāiyal. 13. 15 also has; Bh. Hc. Mk. have *vaïesa* = *vaideśa*, Bh. Hc. Mk. Pkl. M. *kaïava* (G. H.) JM. *kaiyava* (Pāiyal. 157; Erz.). Kī. and Pkl. have in addition, AMg. *vaïssa* = *vaiśya* (Vivāgas. 152; Uttar. 754), by the side whereof AMg. has *vĕssa* (Sūyag. 373), further *vaïdesia* = *vaideśya* and *vesaïa* = *vaiṣayika*; besides Kī. alone has *vaïsamma* = *vaïṣamya*, Pkl. *khaïtta* = *kṣaitra*. In the case of all other words the statements of the grammarians are at variance. Vr. 1, 37 and Kī. 1, 38 permit both *ai* and *e*, side by side, only in *daiva*. Hc. 1, 153 has a special rule with regard to this word, and he knows yet others with a similar phonetic alteration; besides like Pkl. p. 37 and Triv. 1, 2, 102 he includes all such words in the *vairādi* group, wherein Triv. includes also *daiva*. Mk. fol. 12 has a *daivādi* class. According to Bh. on Vr. 1, 37 the word *daiva* is pronounced as *daïva*, but according to Vr. 3, 52 the word on account of development of *e* with reduplication of *v* becomes *dĕvva*. Both of them are found in Kī. as well, whilst Hc. had *dĕvva*, *daïva* and *daïvva*; Mk. seems to prescribe *dĕvva* and *daïvva*. But *dĕvva* and *daïvva* are = *daïva*; A. *daïva* (Hc. 4, 331; 340, 1; 889). According to Mk. fol. 66 and Rv. (PISCHEL on Hc. 1, 153) *aï* is not used in this word in Ś. that is mainly concluded by exclusion of *aï* from Ś. in Rv. And in fact, according to the best MSS (PISCHEL on Hc. 1, 148) *ai* in Ś. and Mg. develops into *e* only; and never into *aï*, not even in the words in which the other dialects must have only *aï*. Thus : *kedava* = *kaitava* (Śak. 106, 6), *veśāha* (Viddhaś. 77, 7), *sera* = *svaira* (Mṛcch. 143, 15; Mukund. 70, 18. 19). In the words showing alteration between *aï* and *e* Ś. and Mg. always have *e*. So Ś. Mg. *dĕvva* (Mṛcch. 20, 24; Śak. 60, 17; 71, 4; 161, 12; Mālav. 57, 19; Ratn. 317, 32; Mṛcch. 140, 10). — According to Bh. 1, 35 *kailāsa* becomes *kelāsa*, but according to Hc. Mk. and Pkl. it becomes *kaïlāsa* or *kelāsa*; Pāiẏal. 97 has *kaïlāsa*, M. (G.R. Bālar. 181, 14) and Ś. (Vikr. 41, 3; 52, 5; Viddhaś. 25, 9) have *kelāsa*. According to Bh. 1, 36, C. 2, 6 *vaira* becomes *vaïra*, and according to Hc., Mk. and Pkl. it becomes also *vera*. So JM. *vaïra* (Erz.), *vaïri-* = *vairin* (Erz.; Kk.) by the side of M. AMg. JM. Ś. *vera* (R.; Sūẏag. 16, 359. 375. 406. 872. 891 : Āẏār. 1, 2, 5, 5; Bhag.; Erz., Kk.; Mṛcch. 24, 4; 148, 1; Mahāv. 52, 18. 19; Prab. 9, 16); Mg. *vela* (Mṛcch. 21, 15. 19; 133, 8; 165, 2); M. JM. *veri-* (G.; Erz.; Kk.); JM. *veriẏa* = *vairika* (Kk.), A. *veria* (Hc. 4, 439, 1), Mg. *velia* (Mṛcch. 126, 6). — According to Kī. *kairava* forms *kaïrava*, and according to Hc. Mk. Pkl. also *kerava*. — For *caitra*, Kī. prescribes *caïtta*, but Hc. Mk. Pkl. also *cĕtta*, and it is found in M. AMg. JM. (§ 60); for *jaitra*, Mk. has *jaïtta* and *jĕtta*, and for *bhairava*, Bh. Hc.Kī. have *bhaïrava*, and Mk. Pkl. have *bherava* as well. In M. is found *bhaïravī* (G.), in AMg. JM. *bherava* (Sūẏag. 129. 130; Āẏār. 1, 6, 2, 3; 1, 7, 6, 5; 2, 15, 15; Ovav.; Kappas.; Erz.), in Ś. *mahābheravī* (Prab. 65, 4; 66, 10 (it is to be read as such)), Mg. *mahābhelava* (Prab. 58, 18 [so to be read]). In the proper noun *bhairavānanda* (Karp. 24, 2 ff.) the MSS, as in the Bombay edition 25, 4 ff., mostly have *bhaïra°*, which was rightly corrected to *bhera°* by KONOW, as it stands in Kāleyak. 16, 14. According to Bh.Kī. Mk. Pkl. *vaiśampāyana* forms *vaïsampāaṇa*, according to Hc. *ve°* too, *vaiśravaṇa*, according to Hc., becomes *vaïsavaṇa* and *ve°*, and so AMg. JM. *vesamaṇa* (Nāẏādh. 852 853; Uttar. 677; Bhag,; Ovav.; Kappas; Erz.). Hc. prescribes interchange between *aï* and *e* also in the case of *vaitālika* and *vaiśika*, the words in which according to Bh. there is *aï*; AMg. has *vesiẏa* (Aṇuog.). All the gaṇas of the grammarians are ākṛtigaṇas, and they are to be augmented further from literature, like AMg. *vaïroẏaṇa* = *vairocana* (Sūẏag. 306; Bhag.); *vaïkuṇṭha* = *vaikuṇṭha* (Pāiẏal. 21) etc.

§ 61.[a] Like *ai*, there are some words that, according to Hc. 1, 1 = Prākṛtacandrikā, 344, 5; C. 2, 14 p. 37, permit also *au* : *sauaria* = *saudarya*, *kaurava*, *kaulava* (C.) = *kaurava*. Such errors of transcription are numerous in MSS. Generally *au* develops into *o* (Vr. 1, 41; C. 2, 8; Hc. 1, 159; Kī. 1, 39; Mk. fol. 13), and into *ŏ* before double consonants; PG. *kolikā* = *kaulikāḥ* (6, 39), *kosika* = *kouśika* (6, 16); M. *kosia* (Hc.; G. 306), Ś. *kosia* (Śak. 20, 12). — Ś. *orasa* = *aurasa* (Vikr. 80, 4). — AMg. *avamma* = *aupamya* (Ovav.). — M. AMg. JM. JŚ. Ś. *osaha* = *auṣadha* (§ 223). — AMg. JM.

kouya, kouga = *kautuka* (Pāiyal. 156; Sūyag. 730; Ovav.; Kappas.; Erz. — M. AMg. JM. *komui* = *kaumudi* (Bh. 1, 41; Hc.; Kī.; H.; Ovav.; Erz.), Ś. *komudī* (Vikr. 23, 20; Priyad. 19, 11; 40, 5). — Ś. *kosambi* = *kauśāmbi* (Bh.; Hc; Ratn. 310, 21), Ś. *kosambiā* = *kauśāmbikā* (Ratn. 308, 29). — M. AMg. JM. *koūhala* = *kautūhala* (G.; Uttar. 631; Erz.; Kk.), Ś. *kodūhala* (Mṛcch. 68, 14; Śak. 19, 3; 121, 10; 129, 1; Vikr. 19, 7; Mālatīm. 257, 1; Mudrār. 43, 5; Viddhaś. 15, 2; Pras. 19, 4; Cait. 42, 1; 44, 12), *kodūhalilla* (Bālar. 168, 3); M. AMg. JM. *kouhalla* = *kautūhalya* (Hc. 1, 117. 171; 2, 99; Pāiyal. 156; G. H.; Karp. 57, 3; Vivāhap. 11, 12. 812), AMg. JM. also *koūhalla* (Ovav.; Kk.). On *kohala* see § 123. — M. AMg. JM. D. A. *do* = *dvau* (§ 436) = — JM. *dovaï* = *dyauṣpati* (Kk.)— AMg. *dovai* = *draupadi* (Nāyādh. 1228), Mg. *dovadi* (Mṛcch. 11, 7; 16, 23; 128, 14 (so to be read throughout with most of the MSS; *dŏppadi* (129.6) is not = *draupadi*, but = *duṣpatiḥ*). — JŚ. *dhoda* = *dhauta* (Pav. 379, 1). — M. AMg. *porāṇa* = *paurāṇa* (H. Ovav.; Kappas.; Rāyap. 74, 139; Hc. 4, 287), JM. *porāṇaya* (Erz.). — M. AMg. JM. Ś. *sohagga* = *saubhāgya* (G. H. R.; Ovav.; Erz.; Mṛcch. 68, 17; Śak. 71, 8; Vikr. 32, 17; Mahāv. 34, 11; Prab. 37, 16; 38, 1; 39, 6). — M. JM. *kŏtthuha* = *kaustubha* (Bh.; Hc.; G. H. R.; Erz.). — M. AMg. JM. Ś. A. *jovvaṇa* = *yauvana* (§ 90) — M. *docca* — *dautya* (H. 84). — M. Ś. *dŏbballa* = *daurbalya* (G. H. R.; Śak. 63, 1) — JM. *pavŏtta* = *prapautra* (Av. 8, 31). — M. Ś. *mŏttia*, JM. *mottiya* = *mauktika* (G. H. R.; Mṛcch. 70, 25; 71, 3; Karp. 73, 5; 82; 8; Viddhaś. 108, 2; Erz.). — M. AMg. JM. JŚ. Ś. A. *sŏkkha* = *saukhya* (Mk. ; G. H. R.; Ovav.; Kappas.; Erz.; Kī. 9; Pav. 381, 19, 20; 383, 75; 385, 69; Kattig. 402, 361. 362. 269; Mālatīm. 82, 3; Uttarar. 121, 4; Hc. 4, 332, 1), Mg. *śŏkkha* (Prab. 28, 15; 56, 1; 58, 16). — M. JM. Ś. *sŏmma* = *saumya* (G. R.; KI. 7; Ratn. 317, 31; Mahāv. 6, 8; Uttarar. 31, 20; 62, 8; 71, 8; 92, 8; Anarghar. 149, 9; Kaṁsav. 9, 2), by the side of AMg. JM. *soma* (Nāyādh.; Kappas.; Erz.). — Like the development of *ai* into *aï*, a number of words show a change of *au* into *aü*. The grammarians have collected them together in the *paurādi* ākṛtigaṇa (Vr. 1, 42; Hc. 1, 162; Kī. 1, 41; Mk. fol. 13; Pkl. p. 38). But there is the difference that while the number of words that have *aï* beside *e* for *ai* is large the number of words that have aü along with *o* for *au* is very small. Bh. on Vr. 1, 42 permits *kosala* by the side fo *kaüsala*, which alone is found in Hc. Kī. Mk.; Hc. 1, 161, 162. has *kŏccheaya* by the side of *kaücheaya* : Mk. fol. 13 permits *moṇa* by the side of *maüṇa*, which Hc. has, and *moli* by the side of *mauli*, which Hc. and Pkl. too have, even though he refers to Karp. 6, 9. According to Mk. *aü* does not occur in Ś. in *kaurava* and *gaurava*, according to Pkl. not in *paura* and *kaurava*. In lieu of *o* is prescribed *aü* in *paura* by Bh. Hc. Kī. Mk. Pkl. in *kaurava* by Bh. C. Hc. Kī. Mk. Pkl, in *pauruṣa* by Bh. Hc. Mk. Pkl., in *saura* and *kaula* by Hc. C., in *gauḍa* by Hc. Pkl., in *kṣaurita* by Mk. Pkl., in *saudha* by Hc., in *kṣaura* by Mk., and in *aucitya* by Pkl. The instances met with are : M. *kaüla* (G.) and *kola* (Karp. 25, 2 = Kāleyaka. 16, 21 (text *kau°*)). — M. *gaüḍa* (G.), but AMg. A. *goḍa* (Paṇhāv. 41 (text *gau°*, but cf. WEBER, Verzeichniss 2, 2, 510); Piṅgala 2, 112. 138). — M. JM. *paüra* = *paura* (G.; KI. 12; Erz.,

Ṛsabhap.), but Ś. *pora* (Śak. 138, 11; Mudrār. 42, 10 (text *pau°*); 161, 1; Mālatīm. 288, 3; Uttarar. 27, 3; Bālar. 149, 21; Kāleyak. 22, 5), Mg. *pola* (Mṛcch. 167, 1, 2 [edition *pau°*]); therefore, in Mṛcch. 160, 11 *paülā* is to be corrected as *polā*. — Bh. Hc. Mk. Pkl. have *paürisa* = *pauruṣa*, but JM. *porisa* (Erz.), AMg. *porisī* (Āyār. 1,8,1, 4; Samav. 74; Uvās.; Kappas.), *porisīya* (Sūyag. 281), *aporisīya* (Vivāhap. 447; Nāyādh. 1113). Cf. § 124.— *maüṇa* = *mauna* (Hc. Mk.) and so in Ś. (Viddhaś. 46, 11) is certainly an error for *moṇa*, as in M. AMg. JM. (Mk.; H.; Āyār. 1, 2, 4, 4; 1, 2, 6, 3; Sūyag. 120. 123. 495. 502; Paṇhāv. 403; Erz.; Ṛṣabhap.). — M. AMg. JM. *maüli* = *mauli* (G.; Karp. 2, 5; Sūyag. 730. 766. Ṭhāṇ. 480; Ovav. § 33; Kk.) and M. *moli* (Karp. 6, 9). In Ś. *moli* (Karp. 112, 3; Mallikām. 183, 5; Pras. 33. 6 (text *mau°*)), but *maüli* (Vikr. 75, 11; Mālatīm. 218, 1). But in the Bombay edition (1888) of Vikr. (122, 1) and as a v. l. in Sankar P. Paṇḍit (131, 4), in Mālatīm., the MS N. and the Madras edition, there is *moli*, which occurs in the Bombay 1892 edition as *mauli* (167, 2). Presumably in both the places the correct form would be *moli*. Hc. has *saüha* = *saudha*, but Ś. *sodha* (Mālatīm. 292, 4). The variation, therefore, is far more dialectical than assumed by grammarians. For Ś. Mg. only *o* should be correct. According to Vr. 1, 43; Hc. 1, 163; Kī. 1, 42 *gaurava* develops into both *gaürava* and *gārava*, and according to Mk. fol. 13, it develops also into *gorava*, which he alone assigns to Ś. JM. has *gaürava* (Erz.), M. Ś. *gorava* (H.; Adbhutad. 54, 10), M. AMg. JM. *gārava* (G. H. R.; Dasav. 635, 38; Paṇhāv. 307; Uttar. 902; Erz.); JM. *ya* (KĪ. 6). To Pāli *garu* belongs *gārava*. Pkt. *garua*, *garuya* = *guruka* (§ 123), Skt. *garīyas*, *gariṣṭha*. On *u* for *ŏ* from *au* see § 84.

(*b*) Lengthening of Short Vowels.

§ 62. A short vowel before *r* + consonant, especially a sibilant or a sibilant + following *ya*, *ra*, *va* or another sibilant, is very often lengthened and the consonant group is simplified. The cases of lengthening are more frequent in M and, especially in AMg. and JM., than in Ś. Mg. which often retain the short vowel and assimilate the consonants. Thus :— *r* + consonant : PG. *kātūṇaṁ*, P. *kātūnaṁ*, AMg. JM. *kāūṇaṁ* = **kartvāṇam* (§ 585, 586); VG. *kātūṇa*, JŚ. *kādūṇa* (§ 21), M. JM. *kāūṇa* = **kartvāna* (§ 586); M. AMg. JM. *kāuṁ*, Ś. Mg. *kāduṁ* = *kartum* (§ 574); M. *kāavva*, AMg. JM. *kāyavva*, JŚ. Ś. Mg. *kādavva* = *kartavya* (§ 570). — *gāyarī* = **gāgarī* = *gaggarī* = Skt. *gargarī* (Deśīn. 2, 89). — M. *dūhava* = *durbhaga* (Hc 1, 115. 192; Karp. 86, 2), and on its analogy Ś. *sūhava* = *subhaga* (Hc. 1, 113, 192; Mallikām. 126, 2). — AMg. JM. *niṇei* = *nirṇayati* (Nirayāv. § 17; Uttar. 578, Erz.); JM. *niṇeha* = *nirṇayata* (Dvār. 496, 5); *niṇijjanta*, *niṇijjamāṇa* = *nirṇiyamāna* (Āv. 24, 4; 25, 34), *niṇehii* = *nirṇeṣyati*, *ṇineūṇa* = *nirṇīya* (Erz.); AMg. JM. *ṇirṇīya* = *nirṇīta* (Nāyādh. 516; Erz.). — A *sāva* = *sarva* (Hc. 4, 420, 5 = Sarasvatīk. 158, 22). — In the case of *r* + stop or nasal generally the vowel remains short and the consonants are assimilated. — AMg. *parimāsi* *parimarśin* (Ṭhāṇ. 313) — AMg., JM., JŚ. *phāsa* = *sparśa* (Hc. 2, 92; Āyār. 1, 2, 3, 2; 1, 4, 2, 2. 3, 2; 1, 5, 4, 5; 1, 6, 3. 2; Sūyag. 170. 172. 257.

337; Paṇṇav. 8. 10. 380; Aṇuog. 268; Ovav.; Kappas. ; Erz.; Pav. 384. 47). — M. AMg. JM. *vāsa*=*varṣa* (Hc. 1, 43; H.; Sūẏag. 148; Vivāhap. 427. 479, 1243; Uttar. 673; Dasav. 632, 42; Samav. 166; Uvās.; Erz.); AMg. *vāsaï*=*varṣati* (Daśav. N. 648, 7. 13. 14), *vāsiukāma*=*varṣitukāma* (Ṭhāṇ. 155), but Ś. *vassāridu*=*varṣartu* (Viddhaś. 99, 1; v. l. *vāsā°*); Mg. *vaśśadi* (Mṛcch. 79, 9). — AMg. *sāsava*=*sārṣapa* (Āẏār. 2, 1, 8, 3). In AMg. Sometimes the vowel followed by *l* + consonant is also lengthened: AMg. *phāguṇa*= *phalguna* (Vivāhap. 1426) by the side of *phagguṇa*, *phaggumitta* (Kappas), *phagguṇī* (Uvās.), M. *phaggu* (H.), Ś. *uttaraphagguṇī*, *phagguṇa* (Karp. 18, 6; 20, 6; Dhanaṁjayav. 11, 7); AMg. *vāgala*=*valkala* (Nāẏādh. 1275; Niraẏāv. 54), *vāga*=*valka* (Ovav. § 74; text *vāka*), but M. Ś. *vakkala* (G.; Śak. 10. 12; 27, 10; Vikr. 84. 20; Anarghar. 58, 11). M. *avavakkala*=*apavalkala* (G.), Mg. *ṇivvakkala*=*nirvalkala* (Mṛcch. 22, 7).

§ 63. A sibilant + *ya*: AMg. *nāsasi*=*naśyasi* (Uttar. 712); M. *ṇāsaï*, *ṇāsanti*, *ṇāsasu* (H. R.); JM *nāsaï nāsanti* (Erz), by the side of AMg *nassāmi* (Uttar. 713), AMg *nassaï* (Hc. 4, 178, 230; Āẏār 1, 2, 3, 5 [v.l. *nāsaï*], *nassamāṇa* (Uvās), *viṇassaï* (Āẏār 1, 2, 3, 5); JM. *nassāmo*, *ṇassa* (Erz.); Ś. *ṇassadi* (Śak. 95, 8); Mg. *viṇaśśadu* (Mṛcch. 118, 19). — AMg. JM. *pāsaï*=*paśyati* (Āẏār. 1, 1, 5, 2; Sūẏag. 91; Vivāhap. 156, 231, 274, 275. 284. 1325 ff.; Vivāgas. 139; Nandīs. 363, 371; Rāẏap. 21. 240; Jīv. 339 ff.; Dasav. 463, 13 etc.; Erz.); AMg. *pāsiẏavvaṁ na pāsaï pāsiukāme na pāsaï pāsittā vi na pāsaï* (Paṇṇav. 667), *aṇupassiẏā* (absol., Sūẏag. 122); *pāsa* (eye; Deśīn. 6, 75; Triv. in BB. 6, 104). — AMg. *kisanti*=*kliśyante* (Uttar. 576)), but JM. *kilissa* (Erz.), Ś. *adikilissadi* (Mālav. 7, 17)— AMg. JM. *sisa*=*śiṣya* (Hc. 1, 43; 4, 265; Pāiẏal. 101; Dasav. N. 645, 12. 13; Kappas.; Āv. 40, 8ff.; 41, 11; Dvār. 499, 13; Erz.); *siṣaga*=*śiṣyaka*. (Āv. 40, 22; Dvār. 498, 13), by the side of JM. Ś. *sissa* (Āv. 33, 21; Priyad. 35, 5; Hāsy. 25, 13; 27, 19; 34, 3. 6. 10; Mallikām. 156, 23; Kāleyaka. 18, 3. 9; 19, 13; 24, 14; incorrect *sisa* 16, 8); Ś. *susissa*=*suśiṣya* (Śak. 77, 11), *sissā*=*śiṣyā* (Mallikām. 219, 20); AMg. *sissaṇī* (girl-disciple; Vivāhap. 342 (text *°ssī°*); Nāẏādh. 1498; Samav. 241).— M. *tūsaï* (Vr. 8. 46; Hc. 4, 236; Kī. 4. 68; H.), JŚ. *tūsedi* (Kattig. 400, 335), but Ś *tussadi* (Mālav. 8, 3). AMg. JM. *maṇūsa*=*manuṣya* (Hc. 1, 43; Sūẏag. 180; Vivāhap. 79. 341. 361. 425; Uttar. 175; Paṇṇav. 706; Dasav. N. 653, 11; Ovav.; Āv. 26, 34; Erz.), AMg. *maṇūsi* (Paṇṇav. 706), but also *maṇussa* (Vivāhap. 362. 717. Paṇṇav. 367; Uvās.), and so also JŚ. (Kattig. 399, 308) and always M. Ś. (1,2 26ᵇ p. 42; Pāiẏal. 60; H.; Mṛcch. 44, 2. 3; 71, 9; 117; 18; 136, 7). Mg. *maṇuśśa* (Mṛcch. 11, 24; 13, 4; 17, 17; 30, 21; 125, 21; 164, 6), *maṇuśśaa* (Mṛcch. 131, 10), *maṇuśśaka* (Mṛcch. 113, 21). — The same lengthening takes place in Mg. in the genitive forms like *kāmāha* from **kāmāsa*=*kāmasya*, *cālittāha* =*cāritrasya*, *śalilāha*=*śarīrasya*, while in A. *kaṇaaha*=*kanakasya*, *caṇḍālaha*= *caṇḍālasya*, etc. show subsequently shortened *a* (§ 264. 315 366); further in the genitive like A. *kāsu*, *jāsu*, *tāsu*=*kasya*, *yasya*, *tasya* (§ 425) and in the forms of the future like A *kariṣu*= **kariśyaṃ*=*kariṣyāmi*, *pāvisu*= **prāpiṣyam* =*prāpsyāmi*, *pĕkkhāhimi*= **prekṣiṣyāmi*=*prekṣiṣye*; *sahihimi*=*sahiṣye*; *karihisi*= *kariṣyasi* (§ 315. 520. 525. 531. 533).

§ 64. Sibilant + *ra* : M. *sāsū* = *śvaśrū* (H.), Ś. *sāsue* = **śvaśrūke* (Bālar. 153, 20). — M. *mīsa* = *miśra* (Hc. 1, 43; 2, 170; H); AMg. *mīsajāya* = *miśrajāta* (Ovav.), *mīsaya* = *miśraka* (Ṭhāṇ. 129 f.; Kappas.), *mīsijjaï* (Uvās.) *mīsiya* (Kappas.); *mīsālia* (Hc. 2, 170); but *missaï* (Hc. 4, 28); Ś. *missa* (Mṛcch. 69, 12; Śak. 18, 3), *missiā* = *miśrikā* (Śak. 142, 10), *missida* (Prab. 29. 8); Mg. *miśśa* (Mṛcch. 11, 6; 117, 8). — AMg. *vīsa* = *visra* (Sūyag. 753). — M. JM. *vīsamaï* *viśrāmyati* by the side of Ś. *vissamiadu* (§ 489). — M. *vīsambha* = *visrambha* (Hc. 1, 43; H. R.), but Ś. *vissambha* (Mṛcch. 74, 8 [so it is to be read with v. l. and ed. GOḌABOLE 213, 1]; Śak. 19, 4; Mālatīm. 105; [So AD.]; 210, 7 (So N.) — Ś. *ūsā* = *usrā* = (Lalitav. 555, 1). — AMg. *ūsaveha* = *ucchrapayata* from **utśrapayata* (Vivāhap. 957), *ūsaviya* = **ucchrapita* (Ovav.; Kappas.): AMg. JM. *ūsiya* = *ucchrita* (Sūyag. 771. 958 [text *u*°]; Paṇhāv. 287; Nāyādh. 481; Uttar. 664; Nandīs. 63. 68; Ovav.; Kappas.; Erz.), but AMg. *ussiya* (Sūyag. 309), *samussiya* (Sūyag. 275) beside °*ūsi*° Sūyag. 281), *ussaviya* (Āyār. 2, 1, 7, 1), Ś. *ussāvedi* = *ucchrāpayati* (Uttarar. 61, 2). — Sibilant + *va* : M. AMg. JM. *āsa* = *aśva* (Bh. 1, 2; Hc. 1, 43; R.; Āyār. 2, 1. 5, 3; Vivāhap. 503; Vivāgas. 61; Uttar. 195. 217. 336. 500. 501; Nāyādh. 731. 780. 1233. 1266. 1388. 1456; Paṇṇav. 367; Aṇuog. 507; Nirāyāv.; Ovav., Āv. 35, 12. 13. 16. 21. 24; Erz.; Kk.), beside *assa* (Bh. 1, 2; Āyār. 2, 10, 12; 2, 11, 11. 12; 2, 15, 20; Sūyag. 182; Uttar. 617; Āv. 11, 18 ff.), as Ś. always has (Mṛcch. 69, 10; Bālar. 238, 8). — M. *ṇīsāsaï.*; AMg. *nīsasanti*; JM. *nīsasiūṇa* = *niḥśvasya* (Erz.); Ś. *ṇīsasadi*, Mg. *nīśaśadu*; M. *ūsasaï*, AMg. *ūsasanti*; Mg. *ūśaśadu*; M. *vīsasaï*; AMg. *vīsase*; Ś. *vīsasadi*; also AMg, *ussasaï*, *nissasaï*, from *śvas* preceded by *niḥ*, *ud*, *vi* (§ 327ᵃ. 496). — AMg. JM. Ś. *vīsattha* = *viśvasta* (Ovav. Kappas.; Erz.; Mṛcch. 99, 24; 100, 4; 105, 1; Śak. 70, 9; Vikr. 8, 8; 23, 6; 47, 1). — A. *sāha* = *śaśvat* (Hc. 4, 366. 422, 22), equated to *sarva* by Hc. — Sibilant + sibilant, originating through the process of assimilation in Pkt. in Skt. = *ḥ* + sibilant : M. AMg. JM. Ś. *ūsava*, *ūsaa* = *utsava* from **ussava*, **ussaa* (§ 327ᵃ). — M. *ūsua* = *utsuka*, by the side of AMg. JM. *ussuya*, Ś. *ussua* (§ 327ᵃ). — M. *vīsaria* = **vismarita* = *vismṛta*, JŚ. *vīsarida*, beside JM. *vissariya* (§ 478). — M. *ṇīsaṅka* = *niḥśaṅka* (G.H.), AMg. *nīsaṅka* (Āyār. 1, 5, 5, 2,) A. with metrical shortening *ṇisaṅka* (Hc. 4, 396, 1; 401,2) by the side of JM. *nissaṅka* (Erz.). — M.S. *ṇīsaha* = *niḥsaha* (Hc. 1, 4, 3; G. H. R.; Uttarar. 92, 10) by the side of *nissaha* (Hc. 1, 13. — M. JM. Ś. A. *dūsaha* = *duḥsaha* (Hc. 1, 13. 115; Kī. 2, 113; Pāiyal. 234; H. R.; Āv. 12, 31.; Karp. 82, 7; Mālatīm. 79, 2; Vikr. 60, 18), Ś. *dūsahattaṇa* = *duḥsahatva* (Mālatīm. 81, 2) by the side of Ś. *dussaha* (Hc. 1, 13. 115; Kī. 2, 113; Prab. 44, 1) and poetical M. *dūsaha* (Hc. 1, 115; G. H.) — AMg. *teyākama* - = *tejaḥkarman.* (Ovav.) — *maṇāsilā* = *manaḥśilā* (Hc. 1, 26. 43) by the side of *maṇośilā*, *maṇasilā* (§ 347) and *maṇaṁsilā* (§ 74).

§ 65. In other cases lengthening of vowels is exceptional, partly just dialectical. AMg. JM. *gāuya* = *gávyūta* (§ 80). — M. AMg. JM. JŚ. Ś. *jīhā* = *jihvā* (Vr. 1, 17; Hc. 1, 92; 2, 57;-Kī. 1, 17; Mk. fol. 7; Pāiyal. 251; G. H. R.; Āyār. p. 137, 7. 9; Vivāhap. 943; Paṇṇav. 101; Jīv. 883; Uttar. 943 (by the side of *jibbhā* § 332); Uvās.; Ovav.; Kappas.; Erz. Kk.; Kattig.

403. 381; Vikr. 15, 3; 16, 12; 18, 10; Karp. 66, 5; Vṛṣabh. 20, 9; Caṇḍak. 17, 3; Mallikām. 90, 23; Kaṁsav. 7, 17); Mg. *yihā* (Mṛcch. 167, 3). — M. AMg. JM. Ś. *dāhiṇa* from **dākhiṇa* (§ 323) = *dakṣiṇa* (Hc. 1, 45; 2, 72; G. H. R.; Ratn. 293, 3; Āyār. 1, 7, 6, 2; 2, 1, 2, 6; Jīv. 345; Bhag.; Ovav.; Kappas.; Erz.; Mṛcch. 97, 15; 117, 18; Veṇīs. 61, 6; Bālar. 249, 7); AMg. *dāhiṇilla* (Ṭhāṇ. 264 ff.; 358; Vivāgas. 180; Paṇṇav. 102 f; Vivāhap. 218. 880. 1288 ff. 1331 ff. 1874; Nāyādh. 333. 335. 867. 1349; Jīv. 227ff. 345; Rāyap. 72. 73); AMg. *āyāhiṇa*, *payāhiṇa* = *ādakṣiṇa*, *pradakṣiṇa* (Sūyag. 1017; Vivāhap. 161. 162; Nirayāv. § 4; Uvās.; Ovav. (text ādā°)), *pāyāhiṇa* (Uttar. 302); by the side of PG. *dakhiṇa* (6, 28), M. AMg. JM. Ś. Ā. *dakkhiṇa* (Hc. 1, 45; 2, 72; G. H. R.; Pratāpar. 215, 19; Sūyag. 574; Erz.; Mṛcch. 9, 9; 155, 4; Vikr. 20, 2; 31, 5; 45, 2; 76, 17; Bālar. 264, 4; 278, 19; Mṛcch. 99, 19), Mg. *daḥkhiṇa* (Mṛcch. 130, 5; 164, 7; 168, 18; Caṇḍak. 64, 9; 66, 13; 71, 9), Ś. *dakkhiṇā* (Caṇḍak. 3, 16); AMg. *dakkhiṇilla* (Samav. 144; Nāyādh. 866. 921. 929. 930. 1350). — PG. *dūdha—dugdha* (6, 31). — M. *dhūā*, AMg. JM. *dhūyā*, Ś. Mg. *dhūdā* (daughter) = ** dhuktā*, **dhūtā*, with a going over to the *ā* - declension (§ 212. 392). — AMg. JM. *bhāsa-* = *bhasman* (Ṭhāṇ. 589; Paṇhāv. 507; Antag. 68; Vivāhap. 171. 1033. 1232. 1247. 1254. 1281. 1282; Kappas.; Sagara 4, 9), but Ś. *bhassa* (Hāsy. 27, 19; 41, 4). — *rāyagaï* (leech; Deśīn. 7, 5) from **rātagati* = **raktagati*.

§ 66. *ĕ* and *ŏ* too, according to § 119. 122. 125 developed from *i*, *u*, *ī*, *ū*, whether original or going back to *ṛ*, before consonant-groups are, in certain dialects, lengthened, and in such cases the consonant-groups are simplified. AMg. *koḍha* from **kŏṭṭha* = **kuṭṭha* = *kuṣṭha* (Nāyādh. 1046. 1047. 1177; Uvās. § 148; Vivāgas. 33, 34 [text *kŏḍḍhu*]. 198), *koḍdhi-* (Paṇhav. 523) from and by the side of *koṭṭhi-* (Āyār 1, 6, 1, 3), *kuṭṭhi-* (Āyār. 2, 4, 2, 1) = *kuṣṭhin*, *koḍhiya* = **kuṣṭhika* (Vivāgas 177). — AMg. *gehi* (greed) from **gĕddhi* = *giddhi* (§ 50) = *gṛddhi* (Āyār. 1, 6, 2, 2; Sūyag. 97. 321. 348; Paṇhāv. 147. 148. 323; Samav. 83. 113; Vivāhap. 1026; Uttar. 217). — *ṇelaccha* (eunuch.; Pāiyal. 235; Hc. 1, 174; Deśīn. 4, 44) from **ṇĕllaccha*, **ṇillaccha* = *nirlakṣa* (BÜHLER, Pāiyal. s. v.), however, *lakṣa* = *lakṣaṇa* "sex mark". — AMg. *dehaï* (Uttar. 571) = *dĕkkaï* from **dikkhaï* = **dṛkṣati* (§ 554), *dehe* = **dṛkṣet* (Dasav. 631, 22), *dehae—*dṛkṣate* (Sūyag. 52), *dehamāṇi* (Vivāhap. 794 f.); A. *drehi* (glance; Hc. 4, 422, 6). — AMg. JM. *seḍhi* (series), from **seṭṭhi* for **siṭṭhi* = *śliṣṭi* (Ṭhāṇ. 464. 546. 588; Paṇhāv. 271. 272; Samav. 220; Vivāhap. 410. 481. 991. 1308. 1669. 1675ff. 1870. 1875ff. Rāyap. 49. 90. 258; Jīv. 351. 456. 707. 709; Aṇuog. 218. 221ff. 245ff. 381 etc., Paṇṇav. 396. 398. 401ff., 627. 847; Nandīs. 165. 371; Uttar. 829. 882. 887; Ovav., Erz.); AMg. *seḍhiya* (Paṇṇav. 846; Ovav.), *aṇuseḍhi* (Vivāhap. 1680 f. 1877 ff.), *paseḍhi* (Rāyap. 49. 90), *viseḍhi* (Vivāhap. 1680 f.; 1877ff.; Nandīs. 373).[1] — M. *soṇāra* (H. 191) from **sŏṇṇāra* = *suṇṇāra* (v. l. to H. 191) = *svarṇakāra*.[2] — *ohala* (mortar; Hc. 1, 171; Mk. fol. 8) from *ŏkkhala* (Vr.), 1, 21; Hc. 1, 171; Kī., 1, 24) = AMg. *ukkhala* (Deśīn. 1, 30; Mk. fol. 9, Paṇhāv. 34), AMg. *ukkhalaga* (Sūyag. 250) = *udūkhala*, which becomes also AMg. *udūhala* (Āyār. 2, 1, 7, 1) and M. *uūhala* (Hc. 1, 171).[3]

The long vowel in M. AMg. JM. *chūḍha*=*kṣubdha* (Hc. 2, 19. 92. 127; H. R.; Paṇhāv. 201; Dasav. 641, 15; Uttar. 758; Āv. 14, 18; 18, 13; 25, 4; 41, 7; Erz.) and in the compound words M. AMg. *ucchūḍha* (Hc. 2, 127; H. v. 1.; Paṇhāv. 268; Nāẏādh. § 4. 46; Uvās.; Ovav.); AMg. *paliucchūḍha* =*paryutkṣubdha* (Ovav. p. 30, 3 [so to be read]); AMg. JM. *nicchūḍha* (Vivāgas. 84. 143; Nāẏādh. 825. 833. 1174. 1313. 1411; Paṇṇav. 828. 835; Nandīs. 380; Paṇhāv. 151; Āv. 16, 1; 21, 5 (so to be read with the MSS)), M. *paricchūḍha* (Deśīn. 6, 25; R.), M. *vicchūḍha* (Pāiẏal. 84; G. R.), M. *vicchūḍhavva* (R.) are to be explained as having developed due to analogy with *ūḍha, gūḍha, mūḍha, rūḍha.* AMg., in fact. has *bha* in the root in words like *chubhanti* (Paṇhāv. 56; text °*bbh*°), *chubhĕjja* (Dasav. (652, 24), *chubhittā* (Uttar. 499), *ucchubhaï* (Nāẏādh. 325), *ucchubha* (Paṇhāv. 59; cf. the commentary), *nicchubhaï* (Nāẏādh. 1411; Vivāhap. 114; Paṇṇav. 827, 832. 834), *nicchubhanti* (Nāẏādh 516; Vivāgas. 84), *nicchubhāvei* (Nāẏādh. 823. 824. 1313; Vivāgas. 86. 143), *nicchubhāviẏa* (Nāẏādh. 823; Vivāgas. 87), *vicchubha* (Paṇhāv. 59; cf. the commentary), and it is occasionally found in JM. also, as in *chubhaï* (Erz.) and in the passive *chubhbaï* (Āv. 2, 3), *nicchubbhaï* (Āv. 42, 35), but JM. has also *chuhāmi, chuhaï* (Erz.), M. has throughout *vicchuhaï* (H. R.), *vicchuhire* (Hc. 3, 142), and wherefrom is deduced the root *chuh,* from which the participles are formed on analogy.[4] The normal development of Skt. *kṣubdha* is into *chuddha* (Bh. 3. 30). Cf. *jaḍha* § 67. 565. — *mūsala* (mallet; Hc. 1, 113), by the side of the usual *musala* (H. R.), is derived from the present stem *musya-*, *musya-* (Dhātupāṭha 26, 111, *musa, muṣa khaṇḍane*) and, therefore, = **muṣyala*.[5]

1. *seḍhi* is throughout explained by commentators as *śreṇi* and has been taken also as *śreḍhi* (Hc., Liṅgānuśāsana, 2, 25, Uṇādigaṇasūtra 631), *śreḍhī* (B.R. s. v.) into Skt. — 2. Thus more correctly than KZ. 34, 573; *u* is to be explained according to § 152, and the contraction, according to § 167. — 3. Mk. fol. 8f. has *uḍukhala*; cf. § 148. — 4. S. GOLDSCHMIDT questions association of *chuhaï* and *kṣubh*, Prakritica p. 20 on insufficient grounds. Cf. LEUMANN, Aup. S. s. v. *ucchūḍha*; PISCHEL, BB. 15, 123f. and § 120. — 5. Cf. Puruṣottama. Dvirūpakośa 3 with v. l.

§ 67. In contrast to *ĕ, ŏ* before consonant groups sometimes *a* is not lengthened when the consonant groups are simplified. In such cases the accent originally fell on the ending. M. *maraḍhi*=NIA. *marāṭhi*= *māhāraṣṭrī* (Karp. 10, 5; cf. § 354). —*jaḍha* (forsaken), AMg. *vijaḍha*, *vippajaḍha* for **jāḍha*, from the root *jah*, inferred from the present form *jahaï*=*jahāti* of *hā* (§ 565). — AMg. *aḍha*=*aṣṭá* (8), AMg. JM. *aḍhaẏālisaṁ*, AMg. *aḍhaẏāla* (48), *aḍhasaṭṭiṁ* (68), A *aḍhāisa* (28), *aḍhaālisa* (48), AMg. *aḍhārasama* (18) (§ 442. 449). — In compound words formed with *sṛṣṭá*, from *sṛj* : AMg. *ūsaḍha*=*utsṛṣṭa*, "separation", "selection", "expelled", "isolated", (Āẏār. 2, 2, 1, 7), "exquisite", "preferable" (Āẏār. 2, 4, 2, 6. 16; Dasav. 623, 13); AMg. *ṇisaḍha*=*nisṛṣṭa* (Nāẏādh. 1276); M. *visaḍha*=*visṛṣṭa*, "released" (R. 6, 66), "given up" (R. 11, 89), "unequal", "uneven" (Hc. 1, 241; Pāiẏal. 207), "non-violent" or "healthy", (Deśīn. 7, 62);[1] AMg. JM. *samosaḍha*=*samavasṛṣṭa* "what has occurred", "what has come (e.g. Vivāhap. 211. 257. 622; Nāẏādh. 558. 567. 619. 671. 874.

967. 1331. 1446. 1454 f. etc.; Vivāgas. 103; Niraẏāv. 41. 43. 74; Dasav. 624, 21; Uvās.; Āv. 16, 20; Dvār. 497, 27).[2]

1. Hc. traces the word in the sense of "uneven" to *viṣama*; S. GOLDSCHMIDT in R. assigns to it the meanings "self-released", "tried" and explains it as = **viśratha* = *viślatha*. — 2. The Indian editions mostly write *samosaḍḍha* (e.g. Vivāhap. 511. 514. 788ff. 912. 934. 971. 978. 988. etc.; Vivāgas. 160. 200. 214. 248; Nāẏdh. 973. 982. 1018. 1025 etc.), also °*saṭṭa* (Rāyap. 12. 232) and °*sadda* (Rāyap. 233). Cf. § 235.

§ 68. In AMg., before the enclitic *eva*, on account of which the preceding word becomes more prominent, the *a* of the syllable *am* of such a preceding word very often undergoes lengthening and thereby, against § 348, *m* gets retained : *evāmeva* (Vivāhap. 162; Uvās. § 219); *khippāmeva* = *kṣiprameva* (Āẏār. 2, 6, 2, 3; p. 130, 1; Vivāhap. 106. 154. 241; Samav. 100; Uvās. ; Niraẏāv.; Nāẏādh.; Kappas.); *bhogāmeva* (Āẏār. 1, 2, 4, 2); *pavvāmeva* = *pūrvameva* (Āẏār. 2, 1, 2, 4); *juttāmeva* = *yuktameva* Vivāhap. 503. 790; Uvās.; Niraẏāv.); *saṁjaẏāmeva* = *saṁyatameva* (Āẏār. 2, 1, 1, 2. 4, 4. 5, 2. 4. 6 etc.). This takes place also before pure Prākrit *ṁ*, that is changed into *m*, as in *tāmeva jāṇappavaraṁ* = *tadeva yānapravaram* (Uvās. § 211), and also before the first secondary anusvāra, which too is changed into *m*, as in *jeṇāmeva cāugghaṇṭe āsarahe teṇāmrva uvāgacchaï* = *yenaiva caturghaṇṭo'śvarathas tenaivopāgacchati* (Nāyādh. § 133); *jeṇāmeva rāẏagihe ṇaẏare jeṇāmeva guṇasilae ceie teṇāmeva uvāgaccgaï* (Nāẏādh. 373); *jeṇāmeva sohamme kappe......teṇāmeva uvāgacchaï* (Kappas. § 29). In this case the original *ā* remains against § 83 : *jāmeva disaṁ pāubbhūẏā tāmeva disaṁ paḍigayā* = *yāmeva diśaṁ prādurbhūtāstāmeva diśaṁ pratigatāḥ* (Vivāhap. 190; Vivāgas. 38 [where there is *disiṁ*], more often in the feminine = °*bhūtā*, °*gatā* (Vivāgas. 4; Uvās. § 61. 211. 249; Niraẏāv. § 5; Ovav. § 59; Nāẏādh. § 5); cf. further Sūẏag. 1012; Ovav. § 60. 61; Kappas. P. 62 § 28; *tāmeva païsĕ jjaṁ* = *tāmeva patiśayyām* (Ovav. § 62). The same lengthening takes place also in AMg. before *avi* : *kisāmavi* = *kṛśamapi* (Suẏag. 1); *taṇāmavi* = *tṛṇamapi* (Uttar. 219); *annaẏarāmavi* = *anyataramapi*, *aṇudisāmavi* = *anudiśamapi* (Daśav. 625, 15. 37).

§ 69. A short vowel is lengthened in declensional forms before the ablative sing. forming suffixes Skt. *-tas*, Pkt. *-hi*, *-hiṁto*; and *i* as well as *u* is lengthened in such cases even before a plural ending beginning with a consonant (§ 365, 379. 381). In derivative words used adverbially the original short *a* remains mostly before *-tas* : AMg. JM. *aggao* (Hc. 1, 37; Nāẏādh. 1107; Uvās.; Kappas.; Erz.), Ś. *aggado* (Mṛcch. 40, 14; 151, 18; 327, 1; Śak. 37, 7; 131, 10; Vikr. 25, 15; 33, 4; 41, 11; 42, 18; Ratn. 317, 12. 14), Mg. *aggado* (Mṛcch. 119, 3. 6; 121, 10; 126, 14; 132, 3; 136, 21). — Ś. Mg. D. *aṇṇado* = *anyataḥ* (Śak. 17, 4; Mṛcch. 29, 33; 96, 25; 102, 18). — Used as pure abl. AMg. *piṭṭhāo* = *pṛṣṭhāt* (Nāẏādh. 938. 964) and *piṭṭhāhi* (Nāẏādh. 958. 959), but in an adverbial sense *piṭṭhao* (Sūẏag. 180. 186. 204. 213; Nāẏādh. § 65; p. 1107; Uttar. 29. 69; Uvās.; Ovav.); likewise JM *piṭṭhao* (Erz.), Ś. D. *piṭṭhado* (Mālav. 33, 2; 59, 3; 69, 6; Mallikām. 145, 21; Mudrār. 254, 1; Mṛcch. 105, 25), Ś. *puṭṭhado* (Ratn. 316, 22), Mg. *pisṭado* (Mṛcch. 99, 8; 130, 1; Veṇīs. 35, 5. 10). — AMg. *davvao khĕttao kālao bhāvao guṇao* = *dravyataḥ kṣetrataḥ kālato bhāvato guṇataḥ* (Vivāhap. 203. 204; and except *guṇao* 157; Uttar. 1014; Ovav. § 28; Kappas. 118), *davvao vaṇṇao* *gandhao rasao phāsao* (Vivāhap. 29), *soẏao ghāṇao phāsao = śrotrato ghrāṇataḥ sparśataḥ* by the side of *cakkhūo, jibbhāo, jihāo = cakṣustaḥ, jihvātaḥ* (Āẏār. 2, 15, 5, 1-5). — Ś. *jammado = janmataḥ* (Ratn. 298, 11). — But always Ś. *kāraṇādo*, Mg. *kālaṇādo = kāraṇataḥ* (Mṛcch. 39, 14. 22; 55, 16; 60, 25; 61, 23; 74, 14; 78, 3; 147, 17. 18 etc.; Mg. 133, 1; 140, 14; 158, 21; 165, 7); JM. *dūrāo* (Erz.), Ś. *dūrādo* (Hc. 4, 276), P. *tūrāto* (Hc. 4, 321), but Mg. *dūlado* (Mṛcch. 121, 11); M. *pacchao* (R.), commonly found *pacchā* (G. H. R.) = *paścāt*, but Ś. *pacchādo* (Mṛcch. 71, 22). In Mṛcch. 9, 9 occur *dakkhiṇādo, vāmādo* in connection with the abl. of the feminine *chāā = chāyā*; besides elsewhere there occurs Ś. Mg. *vāmado* (Mṛcch. 14, 8; 13; 25; 14, 7). On the shortening of vowels in pure ablative see § 99.

§ 70. A final short vowel is sometimes lengthened in formation of a compound. So in AMg. JM. before the suffixes *-maya*, *-*mayika*. Thus : AMg. *raẏaẏāmaya = rajatamaya* (Uvās.), *phalīharaẏaṇāmaẏa = sphaṭikaratnamaya* (Vivāhap. 253); AMg. JM. *savvarayaṇāmaẏa* (Vivāhap. 1322. 1323. 1448; Jīv. 483; Kappas.; Ovav.; Erz.) and °*maïẏa* (Ṭhāṇ. 266); AMg. *vaïrāmaẏa vajramaya* (Vivāhap. 1441; Jīv. 494. 563. 883; Samav. 102. 132; Rāẏap. 63. 69. 105; Ovav.), *riṭṭhāmaẏa = ariṣṭamaya* (Jīv. 549; Rāẏap. 105), *veruliyāmaẏa = vaiḍūryamaya* (Jīv. 494; Rāẏap. 105), *savvaphāliẏāmaẏa = sarvasphāṭikamaya* (Paṇṇav. 115); *āgāsaphāḷiyāmaya = ākāśasphāṭikamaya* (Samav. 97; Ovav.). But JM. *raẏaṇamaẏa* (Erz.) by the side of °*ṇā*° (T. 5, 12); AMg. *ṇāṇāmaṇimaẏa* (Jīv. 494), *āhāramaïya* (Dasav. 631, 24), *purāṇuvittimaïya* (Dasav. N. 661, 5); JŚ. *puggalamaïẏa, uvaogamaẏa, pŏggaladavvamaẏa = *pudgalamayika, upayogamaya, pudgaladravyamaya* (Pav. 384, 36. 49. 58), *asuimaya* (Kattig. 400, 337); *vārīmaï* by the side of *vārimaï = vārimayi* (Hc. 1, 4); M. *ṇehamaïa = *snehamaẏika* (H. 450). Lengthening takes place further, in compounds with numerals for 5, 6, 7 and 8: *pañcā, chā*°, *sattā*°, *aṭṭhā*° (§ 440 ff.), likewise with *aüṇā*° = *aguṇa* and *aḍḍhā*° *ardha*° (§ 444. 450); similar is the case with the final vowel of the prefixes, especially of *pra*, in which already in Skt. the quantity of the vowel underwent variation, as in *pradeśa, prādeśa* (Puruṣottama, Dvirūpakośa 25). So M. *paaḍa* (G.) and M. Mg., *pāaḍa = prakaṭa* (Bh. 1, 2; Hc. 1, 44; Kī. 1, 1; Mk. fol. 4. 5; G. H. R.; Vajjāl. 325, 23; Mṛcch. 40, 6); JM. *paẏaḍa* (Erz.; Kk.); AMg. : *pāgaḍa* (Ovav.; Kappas.); M. *pāaḍia = prakaṭita* (H.); AMg. *pāgaḍiẏa* (Ovav.). — M. *pāroha = praroha* (Hc. 1, 44; G. H. R.). — M. *pasutta* and *pāsutta* (Bh. 1, 2; Hc. 1, 44; Kī. 1, 1; Mk. fol. 4, 5; G. H. R.), but Ś. only *pasutta* (Mṛcch. 44, 18; 50, 23). — *pasiddhi = prasiddhi* (G.) and *pāsiddhi* (Bh. 1, 2; Hc. 1, 44; Kī. 1, 1; Mk. fol. 4. 5). — AMg. *pāvaẏaṇa = pravacana* (Hc. 1, 44; Bhag.; Uvās.; Ovav.). — Also M. *pāsiijaï = prasvidyate* (H. 771) and AMg. *pāsavaṇa = prasravana* (Uvās.) may more appropriately be put here than under § 64. — AMg. *abhīi = abhijit* (Kappas.), *viīvaïttā = *vyativrajitvā* (Ovav. § 63), *viīvayamāṇe* (Uvās. § 79; so to be read; see § 151). In many cases the lengthening is purely metrical, as in M. *diṭṭhīpahammi = dṛṣṭipathe* (H. 456), *ṇāhīkamala = nābhikamala, araīvilāsa = arativilāsa* (G. 13. 111; AMg. *girīvara* (Sūẏag. 110); JM. *verulīẏamaṇimŏlla = vaiḍūryamaṇimaulya* (Erz. 29, 28). So also *paīhara = patighara* (Hc. 1, 4) by the side of *païhara*, Ś. *padighara* (Mālatīm. 243, 4); *velūvaṇa* by the side of *veluvaṇa* = *veṇuvana* (Hc. 1, 4). In the dialect of Śakāra in Mṛcch. *a* appears to have sometimes been lengthened before the suffix *-ka* : *cāludattāke* (127. 23; 128, 6; 149, 25); *cāludattākaṁ* (127, 25; 166, 18); *cāludattākeṇa* (133, 1; 137, 1; 151, 23); *vāsudevākaṁ* (121, 16); *guḍāha* = *guḍaka* (116, 25; cf. § 206); *śaputtākaṁ* = *saputrakam* (166, 18). The same lengthening is found also in AMg. *muhuttāga* = *muhūrtaka* (Āẏār. 1, 8, 2, 6), *piḷāga* = *piṭaka* (Sūẏag. 208), *khuḍḍāga, -ẏa* = *kṣudraka* (Vivāhap. 1851ff.; Ovav.; Āẏār. 2, 1, 4, 5; cf. § 294), and in the frequent AMg. *aṇādiya, aṇāiẏa* = *anādika* (Sūẏag. 84. 867; Ṭhāṇ. 41, 129; Paṇhāv. 302; Nāẏādh. 464. 471; Vivāhap. 39. 848. 1128) by the side of *aṇādiẏa, aṇāiẏa* (Sūẏag. 787; Uttar. 842; Vivāhap. 160), also JM. (Erz. 33, 17; cf. v. 1); JŚ. *ādiya* (Kattig. 401, 353); PG. *ādika* (5, 4; 6, 34). Cf. Vedic *jahāka* by the side of *jahaka* (Ved. Stud. 1, 63) and § 73. 97.

§ 71. Final vowels used in the voc. sing. and in the paricles employed in calling somebody from a distance are lengthened (pluti) : *re re capphalaẏā, re re nigghiṇaẏā, he harī, he gurū, he pahū* (Hc. 3, 38); AMg. *āṇandā* (Uvās. § 44. 84), *kālāsā* (Vivāhap. 132), *goẏamā* (Hc. 3, 38; Vivāhap. 34ff. 1311. 1315. 1416; Ovav. § 66ff.; Uvās. etc.), *kāsavā* (Hc. 3, 38; Vivāhap. 1237f.), *camarā asurindā asurarāẏā appatthiẏapatthịiyā* = *camara asurendra aśurarāja aprārthyaprārthika* (Vivāhap. 254), *hantā mandiẏaputtā* (Vivāhap. 268), *puttā* = *putra* (Uvās.; Nāẏādh.), *hantā* = *hanta* (Bhag.; Uvās.; Ovav.), *subuddhī* (Nāẏādh. 997, 998. 1003), *maharisī* (Sūẏag. 182), *mahāmuṇī* = *mahāmune* (Sūẏag. 419), *jambū* (Uvās.); Ś. *dāsieuttā* = *dāsyāḥputra* (Mṛcch. 4, 9; 80, 13. 23; 81, 12; 82, 4; 108, 16), *are re kaṇelisudā rāasālasaṁṭhāṇaā ussaṁkhalaā* = *kaṇelisuta rājaśyālasaṁsthānka ucchṛṅkhalaka* (Mṛcch. 151, 16f.); Mg. *haṇḍe kumbhilaā* = *haṇḍe kumbhilaka* (Śak. 113. 2), *le gaṇṭhiścedaā* = *re granthicchedaka* (Śak. 115, 4), *le calā* = *re cara* (spy ! Lalitav. 566, 14. 18). *puttakā haḍakkā* = *putraka hṛdayaka* (Mṛcch. 114, 16); and so the *a-* stem always in Mg. according to Vr. 11, 13, to which, however, the texts do not conform; *vāśū* (girl ? Mṛcch. 9, 24; 17, 1; 127, 7); Ā. *are re pavahaṇavāhaā* (Mṛcch. 100, 17); Ḍh. *vippalambhaā* = *vipralambhaka*, *palivevidaṅgaā* = *parivepitāṅgaka, khalantaā* = *skhalan, kalĕntaā* = *kurvan* (Mṛcch. 30, 6ff.); A. *bhamarā* = *bhramara* (Hc. 4, 387, 2), *mittaḍā* = *mitra* (Hc. 4. 422, 1), *haṁsā* (Vikr. 61, 20), *hiaḍā* = *hṛdaya* (Hc. 4, 357, 4. 422, 12. 23. 439, 1). In this place a mention should be made also of the lengthening of the final *a* in the imperative in cases like AMg. *kuvvāhā* = **kurvata* = *kuruta* (Āẏār. 1, 3, 2, 1), *pāsahā* = *paśyata* (Āẏār. 1, 6, 5, 5; Sūẏag. 144. 148.), *saṁbujjhahā* = *saṁbudhyadhvam* (Sūẏag. 335). After dropping of the final consonant the lengthening takes place in cases like JM. *dhī* = *dhik* (Dvār. 501, 33); Ś. *haddhī haddhī* = *hā dhik ha dhik* (e.g. Mṛcch. 12, 6; 16, 6; 50, 23; 170; 3; Śak. 27, 1; 62, 5; 72 7; Vikr. 25, 14; 75, 10). See also § 75. Frequent is the lengthening of *u* of *hou* = *bhavatu* before the enclitic *ṇaṁ* in AMg. *hoū ṇaṁ* = *bhavatu nanu* (Nāẏādh. 1084. 1228. 1351; Ovav. § 105).

§ 72. After dropping of *ḥ*, *i* and *u* of the endings *-iḥ* and *-uḥ* of the nom. are always lengthened in the sing. of masculine and feminine words ending in *-i* and *-u* M. *aggi* = *agniḥ* (H. 163), AMg. *agaṇi* (Sūyag. 273. 281. 291), Mg. *lośaggi* = *roṣagniḥ* (Mṛcch. 123, 2); M. AMg. *asī* = *asiḥ* (G. 239; Sūyag. 593), Mg. *aśi* (Mṛcch. 12, 17); JM. *sahi* = **sakhiḥ* = *sakhā* (KI. 14); Ś. *pīdi* = *prītiḥ* (Mṛcch. 24, 4); M. JŚ. Ś *diṭṭhī* = *dṛṣṭiḥ* (H. 15; Pav. 388, 5; Mṛcch. 57, 10); D. *seṇāvai* = *senāpatiḥ* (Mṛcch. 101, 21); M. JM. *tarū* = *taruḥ* (Hc. 3, 19; H. 913; Erz. 4, 29); AMg. Ś. *bhikkhū* = *bhikṣuḥ* (Āyār. 1, 2, 5, 3; Mṛcch. 78, 13); JM. *gurū* = *guruḥ* (KI. 14), *bindū* = *binduḥ* (Āv. 15, 18); JM. D. *viṇhū* = *viṣṇuḥ* (Āv. 36, 41; Mṛcch. 105, 21). Some grammarians, according to Hc. 3, 19, permit even nasalisation of the vowel instead of its lengthening (§ 178); *aggiṁ*, *ṇihiṁ vāuṁ*, *vihuṁ*. In the instrumental plural in *-bhiḥ*, and, along with it, in all the dialects other than A., in the abl. plur. in *-bhyaḥ*, which dropped with it, the lengthening never takes place after elision of *ḥ*, but there develops by the side of the short vowel also a nasal vowel : *-hi*, *-hiṁ*, *-hĩ*, (§ 178), A. in the abl *-hu*, *-huṁ*, *-hũ* (§ 368. 369. 381. 387 etc.). In Ś. Mg. is used *-hiṁ* only.

§ 73. A short vowel is lengthened in a large number of cases exclusively on account of metrical consideration in medial and final syllables, especially in AMg. and in A. Thus : M. *aṁsū* = *aśru* (H. 153): AMg. *dhiīmao* = *dhṛtimataḥ* (Āyār. 2, 16, 8), *maimaṁ* = *matimān* (Sūyag. 397), *maīmayā* = *matimatā* (Āyār. 1, 8, 2, 16); Sūyag. 373), *amaimayā* = **amatimatkāḥ* (Sūyag. 213), *pañjalīo* = *prāñjalikaḥ* (Dasav. 634, 23), *jāijarāmaraṇehiṁ* = *jātijarāmaraṇaiḥ* (Sūyag. 156), *pavvaie* = *pravrajitaḥ* (Sūyag. 495), *mahiḍḍhiyā* = *maharddhikāḥ* (Āyār. 2, 15, 18, 4); *soṇiaṁ* = *śoṇitam* (Āyār. 1, 7, 8, 9), *sāhiyā* = *sādhikā* (Ovav. § 174); Mg. *līṇe* = *ṛṇam* (Mṛcch. 21, 19). Particularly frequent are the cases of lengthening of the final *i* in verbal forms, especially at the end of a half verse or of a complete verse: AMg. *sahaī* = *sahate* (Āyār. 1, 2, 6, 3), *saraī* = *smarati* (Sūyag. 172; Uttar. 277), *kuvvaī* = **kurvati* = *karoti* (Dasav. 623, 33), *bhāsaī* = *bhāṣate* (Sūyag. 106), *maraī* = **marati* = *mriyate* (Uttar. 207), *kiccaī* = *kṛtyate* (Sūyag. 106), *bajjhaī* = *badhyate* (Uttar. 245), *karissaī* = *kariṣyati* = (Dasav. 627, 24), *jāṇantī aṇuhŏntī* = *jānanti, anubhavanti* (Ovav. § 179. 188), *accehī* = *atyehi* (Sūyag. 148); AMg. JM. *bhuñjaī* = *bhunakti* (Sūyag. 133; Āv. 8, 4. 24); Mg. *ovaggadī* = *apavalgati* (Mṛcch. 10, 5). Further, very often in AMg. and JM. the final *a* of the absolutive in *-ya* is lengthened in poetry. AMg. *paḍilehiyā* = *pratilekhya*, *muṇiyā* = *jñātvā*, *sāpehiyā* = *saṁprekṣya*, *vihūṇiyā* = *vidhūya* (Āyār. 1, 7, 8, 7. 13. 23. 24); AMg. JM. *pāsiyā* = **paśya* (Uttar. 361; Erz. 38 35); AMg. *viyāṇiyā* = *vijñāya* (Dasav. 637; 5; 642, 12) etc. (§ 590. 591). Lengthening of final vowels occurs in many sporadic cases like AMg. *jagaī* = *jagati* (Sūyag. 104), *keī* = *kecit* (Ovav. 63, 20); JM. *kayāī* = *kadācit* (Āv. 8, 7; 37. 37).

§ 74. In lieu of a lengthened vowel there comes in a short nasal vowel before one of the simplified consonants of a consonant-group. Here the rules § 62-65 apply. The grammarians (Vr. 4, 15; Hc. 1, 26; Mk. fol. 34; Pkl. p. 10) enumerate together such words under the *vakrādi* or (Kī. 2, 122) *aśrvādi* group. Thus : *kaṁkoḍa* (Hc.), M. *kaṁkoḷa* (Śukasaptati 123, 2; text °*la*) and M AMg. *kakkoḷa* (G. 582; Paṇhāv. 527; text °*la*) = *karkoṭa* (cf. § 238). — M. AMg. JM. JŚ. Ś.A. *daṁsaṇa* = *darśana* (Bh. Hc. Kī. Mk. Pkl.; G. H. R.; Sūẏag. 312, 314; Bhag.; Nāẏādh.; Uvās.; Kappas. etc.; Erz.; Kk.; Ṛṣabhap.; Pav. 379, 2; 380, 6; 387, 13; 389, 9. 4; Kattig. 400, 328. 329; Lalitav. 554, 7. 8; Mṛcch. 23, 14. 21; 29, 11; 97, 15; 169, 14; Śak. 50, 1; 73, 9; 84, 13; Vikr. 16, 15; 19, 3 etc.; Hc. 4, 401, 1), Mg. *daṁśaṇa* (Mṛcch. 21, 9; 37, 10; Prab. 52, 6; 58, 16); likewise in *daṁsi.* = *darśin* (Vikr. 8, 11), *daṁsaï*, *daṁsei* (§ 554) and in others — M.Ś. *phaṁsa* = *sparśa* (Bh. Kī. Mk. Pkl. ; G. H. R.; Vikr. 51, 2; Mālatīm. 217, 5; 262, 3; Uttarar. 92, 9; 93, 7; 125, 7; 163, 4; Viddhaś. 70, 10; Bālar. 202, 9), Ś. *pariphaṁsa* (Bālar. 202, 16), Mg. *sphaṁśa* (Prab. 58, 8); *phaṁsaï* (Hc. 4, 182). — *paṁsu* = *parśu* (Hc.). — M. *ṇihaṁsa* = *nigharṣa* (G.), *ṇihaṁsaṇa* = *nigharṣaṇa* (G.R.). — A. *baṁhiṇa* = *barhin* (Vikr. 58, 8). — *l* + consonant in *suṁka* = *śulka* (Mk.), AMg. *ussuṁka* (Kappas. § 102) [so to be read]. 209; Nāẏādh. § 112; p. 1388 [so to be read]. Vivāgas. 230 has *sukka*. — Sibilant + *ya* : AMg. *namaṁsaï* = *namasyati* (Āẏār. 2, 15, 19; Nāẏādh. § 7; p. 292; Uvās. Bhag.; Kappas.; cf. Ovav. § 20. 38. 50 etc.), JŚ. *ṇamaṁsittā* = **namasyitvā* (Pav. 386, 6). JM. *niẏaṁsaha* = *nivasata* (Erz. 59, 30) from **nivasyata*, presupposes a similar formation in the present wherefrom are derived the causative forms AMg. *niẏaṁsei* (Jīv. 611), *niẏaṁseha* (Vivāhap. 1262), *niẏaṁsittā* (Jīv. 611), *niẏaṁsāvei* (Āẏār. 2, 15, 20), and from such a form of the present are derived the substantives M. *ṇiaṁsaṇa* (Mk. H.), *viṇiaṁsaṇa* (H.), AMg. *niẏaṁsaṇa* (Paṇṇav. 111 [so to be read with the commentary]; Rāyap. 81; Ovav. § 35); *viṇiaṁsaṇa* (Mk.); *paḍiṇiaṁsaṇa* (night dress; Deśīn. 6, 36). — M. *vaaṁsa* = *vayasya* (Hc. Mk. Pkl.) *vaaṁsi* = **vayasyi* (Karp. 46, 8), JM. *vayaṁsa* (Erz.), A. *vaaṁsiahu* = **vayaśyikābhyaḥ* (Hc. 4, 351), by the side of M. *vaassa* (H.), as always in Ś. (e.g. Mrcch. 7, 3. 14. 19; Śak. 29, 3; 30, 6; Vikr. 16, 11; 18, 8). — Sibilant + *ra* : M. JM. A. *aṁsu* = *aśru* (Bh. Hc. Kī. Mk. Pkl.; G. H. R.; Karṇas. 44, 20; Erz.; Dvār. 501, 32; Piṅgala 1, 61[a]), but Ś. *assu* (Veṇīs. 66, 7; Subhadr. 17, 3; Mukund. 15, 1), and so probably to be read for *aṁsu* in Vikr. 83, 13 [see v. l.; ed. Bomb. 133, 2; ed. PAṆḌIT 150, 12., ed. PISCHEL 666, 3]; Mudrār. 260, 3 [see v. l.]; Viddhaś. (79, 6; 80, 2). — AMg. *maṁsu* = *śmaśru* (Bh. Hc. Kī. Mk.; Pāiẏal. 112; Āẏār. 1, 8, 3, 11, 2, 8, 5; Paṇhāv. 351; Bhag.; Ovav.), *nimmaṁsu* = *niḥśmaśru* (Aṇuttar. 12; text °*sa*); JŚ. *maṁsuga* = *śmaśruku* (Pav. 386, 4). Cf. § 312. — M. AMg. *taṁsa* = *tryasra* (Bh.; Hc.; Mk.; Karp. 37, 7; 40, 3; Āẏār. 1, 5, 6, 4; Sūẏag. 590; Ṭhāṇ. 445. 493); AMg. *caüraṁsa* = *caturasra* (Āẏār. 1, 5. 6, 4; Sūẏag. 590; Ṭhāṇ. 20. 493; Uvās.; Ovav.), *chaḷaṁsa* = *ṣaḍasra* (Ṭhāṇ. 493), *chaḷaṁsiya*, *aṭṭhaṁsa* = *ṣaḍasrika*, *aṣṭāsra* (Sūẏag. 590). — Sibilant + *va* : *aṁsa* = *aśva* (Bh.) and so AMg. *aṁsŏttha* = *aśvattha* (Vivāhap. 1530), but *assŏttha* (Ṭhāṇ. 555), *āsŏttha* (Āẏār. 2, 1, 8, 7; Paṇṇav. 31), *āsattha* (Samav. 233). — M. *maṇaṁsi-* = *manasvin* (Hc. Mk. H.), *maṇaṁsiṇi* = *manasvinī* (Bh. Kī. Pkl.) and M. Ś. *māṇaṁsiṇi* (Hc.; H.; Bālar. 142, 3; 242, 4). Likewise in other adjectives ending in *-vin* in AMg., as in *oẏaṁsi-* = *ojasvin* (Āẏār. 2, 4, 2, 2; Nāẏādh.; Ovav.), *jasaṁsi-* = *yaśasvin*, *teẏaṁsi-*, *tejaṁsi-* = *tejasvin* (Āẏār. 2, 4, 2, 2; Nāẏādh.), *vaccaṁsi-* = *varcasvin* (Nāẏādh.; Ovav.). — *haṁsa* = *hrasva* (Bh.; see § 354). — Visarga + sibilant : *maṇaṁsilā*

=*manaḥśilā* (Hc) by the side of *maṇāsilā, maṇosilā, maṇasilā* (§ 64. 347). Besides in AMg. this phonetic law comes into force sometimes elsewhere too when one of the conjunct consonants is a sibilant. Thus in the case of *ṣ*+*k* in *saṁkuli*=*śaṣkuli* (Āyār. 2, 1, 4, 5; Paṇhāv. 490), by the side of *sakkuli* (Thāṇ. 259 (commentary *saṁkulī*); Dasav. 621, 2); in the case of *ṣ*+*m* in *pāṇiṁsi*= **pāṇiṣmin*=*pāṇau, leluṁsi*= **leṣṭuṣmin*=*leṣṭau* (§ 312. 379) and that in *s*+*m* in *aṁsi*=*asmi* (§ 313. 498), and in the pronominal locative singular and in the nominal locative singular formed on the analogy thereof, like *kaṁsi, jaṁsi, taṁsi*=*kasmin, yasmin, tasmin*; *logaṁsi*=*loke*; *tārisagaṁsi vāsagharaṁsi*=*tādṛśake vāsagṛhe* (§ 313. 366[a]. 425ff.); in the case of *k*+ *ṣ* in *pilaṁkhu*=*plakṣa* (Āyār. 2, 1, 8, 7, for which is printed *pilakkhu* (Vivāhap. 609, 1530 °*ka*), *pilukkha* (Paṇṇav. 31), *piluṁka* (Samav. 233), also the v. l. in Āyār. has *pilakkhu*; further in *paṁkha*=*pakṣa* (Uttar. 439), *paṁkhi-*=*pakṣin* (Rāyap. 235), *paṁkhiṇi*=*pakṣiṇī* (Uttar. 445); in the case of *t*+*s* in *giṁchā* =*jighatsā* (Uttar. 48. 50; commentary *dighañchā*), *vitigiṁchā* (Āyār. 1, 3, 1; 1, 5, 5, 2), *vitigiṁchaï* Sūyag. 727 f.), *vitigiṁchiya* (Vivāhap. 150)=*vicikitsā, vicikitsati, vicikitsita* (§ 215, 555); in the case of *p*+*s* in *dugaṁchā*=*jugupsā* (Ṭhāṇ. 151; Vivāhap. 110; Uttar. 960), *duguṁchā* (Paṇhāv. 537), *duguṁchaṇa* (Āyār. 1, 1, 7, 1; Uttar. 628 [°*ga*°]), *dogaṁchi-*=*jugupsin* (Uttar. 51. 219 [°*gu*°]), *dugaṁchaṇijja* (Uttar. 410), also JM. *dugaṁchā* (Pāiyal. 245; Erz.), AMg. *duguṁchaï, duuṁchaï, duguṁchamāṇa*, °*gu*° (§ 215. 555), *paḍidugaṁchi-*=*pratijugupsin* (Sūyag. 133). So also in the case of *ṣ*+*ṭ* in *gaṁṭhi* (Mk.), *giṁṭhi* (Hc.), *guṁṭhi* (Bh.)=*gṛṣṭi*, but Ś. *giṭṭhi* (Mṛcch. 44, 3), that is taught by Hc. too. The cases in which a nasal vowel has developed without one of the consonants being *r* or a sibilant are : *guṁcha* =*guccha* (Hc.), but Ś. *guccha* (Ratn. 300, 18). — M. *piṁcha*=*piccha* (G. R.), but also M. AMg. Ś. *piccha* (Karp. 46, 12; Āyār. 1, 1, 6, 5; Aṇuog. 507; Uvās.; Vikr. 32.7). — *puṁcha*=*puccha* (Hc. Mk. Pkl.), but AMg. *puccha* (Āyār. 1, 1, 6, 5), Mg. *puśca* (Mṛcch. 10, 4). — In AMg. JM. *saṇaṁkumāra* =*sanatkumāra* (Ṭhāṇ. 90. 200; Samav. 9. 16. 18; Paṇhāv. 314; Paṇṇav. 123. 124; Vivāhap. 241. 242; Ovav.; Erz.) the anusvāra is to be assumed according to § 75. In AMg. *mahaṁsa*=*mahāśva* (Vivāhap. 830; Ovav.) *mahaṁ*, with LEUMANN, is to be explained as having developed from the original stem *mahant*, which was pronounced as *mahanta* also. Cf. therewith § 182. AMg. JM. *miṁjā*= Pāli *miṁjā*= Skt. *majjā* with *i*, according to § 101 (Āyār. 1, 1, 6, 5; Sūyag. 771; Ṭhāṇ. 186. 431; Paṇhāv. 26; Paṇṇav. 40; Vivāhap. 112. 113. 280. 926; Jīv. 464; Uvās.; Ovav., Erz.), *miṁjiyā* (Paṇṇav. 529; Vivāhap. 448) may be going back to the original form **mazjā, *mazjikā*. In formation and in meaning *buṁdha*=*budhna* corresponds to Latin *fundus* and is, therefore, correctly written as *bundha*. M. AMg. JM. A. *vaṁka*=*vakra* (Vr. Hc. Kī. Mk. Pkl.; H.; Āyār. 1, 1, 5, 3; Paṇṇav. 479. 482; Nirayāv.; Erz.; Kk., Piṅgala 1, 2; Hc. 4, 330, 3. 356. 412), along with M. *vaṅkia*=*vakrita* (R.), M. A. *vaṅkima* ((Viddhaś. 55, 7 [so to be read with v. l.] ; Hc. 4, 344), A. *vaṅkuḍaa* (Hc. 4, 418, 8) is connected with Vedic *vaṅku* and to the root *vaki kauṭilye*, (Dhātup. 4. 14) and, therefore, it is to be written as *vaṅka*. Ś. *vakka* (Ratn. 302, 19; 308. 7; Vṛṣabh. 24, 7; 26, 9;

Mallikām. 233, 12; Kaṁsav. 7, 18), *vakkadara* (Pras. 140, 1), *vakkida* (Bālar. 246, 14), *aṇuvakka* (Mālav. 48. 19) are formed from *vakra*. AMg. *vakkaya* = *vakraka* (Ovav.). The use of *vaṅka* in Ś. (Karṇas. 22, 19) is wrong. The feminine *vaṅkuṇi* from *vaṅkuṇa* has been used in Pras. 46, 5, and is found in the proper noun *tivaṅkuṇi* (Kaṁsav. 55, 11))[2] as well. Cf. § 86. On *viṁchua*, *viṁchia*, *viṁcua* see § 301.

1. Aup. S. s. v. — PISCHEL on Hc. 1, 26; GELDNER, Ved. Stud. 2, 164. 258.

§ 75. In the final syllable, besides in the case of pluti (§ 71), after the dropping off of the final consonant, sometimes dialectically lengthening alternates with anusvāra (cf. § 181). AMg. JM. *visā* and *visaṁ* = **viṁśat* = *viṁśati*, *tisā* and *tisaṁ* = *triṁśat*, *cattālisā* and *cattālisaṁ* = *catvāriṁśat*, A., with shortening of the final vowel, *visa*, *caüālisa*, *coālisa* by the side of *tisā* (§ 445); AMg. *tiriyā tiryak* (Hc. 2, 143) by the side of *tiriyaṁ* (Āyār. 1, 1, 5, 2; 1, 5, 6, 2; 1, 7, 1, 5; 1, 8, 4, 14; Sūyag. 191, 273. 304. 397. 428. 914. 931; Uttar. 1031; Pāṇṇav. 381; Kappas.), also in compounds like *tiriyaṁvāya* = *tiryagvāta*, *tiriyaṁbhāgi-* = *tiryagbhāgin* (Sūyag. 829); AMg. *samiyā* = *samyak* (Sūyag. 918; Āyār. 1, 4, 2, 6; 1, 5, 2, 2. 5, 3) by the side of AMg. *samiyaṁ* (Āyār. 1, 5, 5, 3; Sūyag. 304), and AMg. JM. JŚ. Ś. *sammaṁ* (Hc. 1, 24; Āyār. 1, 2, 1, 5; 1, 5, 5, 1. 6, 1; Sūyag. 844. 958. 994. 996; Ṭhāṇ. 243; Vivāhap. 163. 165. 238; Uttar. 450; Erz.; Kk.; Pav. 389, 3; Kattig. 399, 308. 309; Kāleyak. 21, 15; 24, 18); AMg. also *samiyāe* (Āyār. 1, 5, 5, 3. 5). Cf. § 114. In poetry in AMg. is found *jaṁsī* by the side of *jaṁsi* = *yasmin* and *yasyām* (Sūyag. 137. 273. 297), in A., *jahī* by the side of *jahiṁ* = *yasmin* (Piṅgala 2. 135, 277) and *kī* by the side of *kiṁ*, *ki* (Piṅgala 2. 138). Perhaps these forms go back directly to *jassiṁ*, *jahiṁ*, *kiṁ*, but seemingly the lengthening is purely prosodical.

§ 76. A short nasal vowel is sometimes, before an immediately following *ra* or a sibilant or *ha*, lengthened, and there takes place elision of the nasalisation. Thus: AMg. *visā*, *visaṁ* = **viṁśat*, *viṁśati*, *tisā*, *tisaṁ* = *triṁśat*, *cattālisā*, *cattālisaṁ* = *catvāriṁśat*, and others; A. *visa*, *tisā*, *caüālisā*, *coālisā* (§75. 445). — Pāli *dāṭhā*, CP. *tāṭhā* (Hc. 4, 325), M. AMg. Ś. *dāḍhā* = *daṁṣṭrā* (Vr. 4, 33; C. 3, 11; Hc. 2, 139; Kī. 2, 117; Mk. fol. 39; G. H. R.; Āyār. 1, 6, 5; 1, Jīv. 883; Aṇuog. 507; Uvās.; Kappas., Mālatīm. 251, 5; Caṇḍak. 17, 8; Bālar. 249, 8; 259, 17; 270, 6; AMg. Ś. *dāḍhi-* = *daṁṣṭrin* (Aṇuog. 349; Veṇīs. 24. 7 [so to be read]). — M. AMg. JM. A *sīha* = *siṁha* (Vr. 1, 17; Hc. 1, 29. 92. 264; Kī. 1, 17; Mk. fol. 7; Pāiyal. 43; G. H. R.; Āyār. 2, 15, 21; Sūyag. 225. 414. 748; Paṇṇav. 367; Rāyap. 114: Uttar. 338; Dasav. N. 647, 36; Erz.; Kk., Hc. 4, 406, 1; 418, 3), AMg. *sīhī* *siṁhī* (Paṇṇav. 368), by the side of *siṁgha* (§ 267) and *siṁha*, as in Ś. (Bālar. 209, 11 *siṁhaṇāda*; 234, 8 *ṇarasiṁha*; Caṇḍak. 17, 1 *vaṇasiṁha*), in compounds correspondingly Hc. 1, 92 has *siṁhadatta*, *siṁharāa*; so also Mg. *śiṁhaśāvaa* = *siṁhasābaka* (Śak. 154, 6), but AMg. *sīhaguhā* (Nāyādh. 1427 ff.). In Bālar. 50, 11 stands in Ś. *sīhasaṁhā* [sic.; read °*saṁghā*]; Mallikām. 143, 14 in Mg. *śīhamuha* 144, 3 but *śiṁghamuha* [sic] = *siṁhamukha*. — *kesua* from **keṁsua* (§ 119) = *kiṁsua* (G. H.; Karp. 10, 7) = *kiṁśuka* (Hc. 1, 29. 86), Sindhī *kesū*. — *pisaï*, Ś. *pisedi* = **piṁsati* = *pinaṣṭi* (§ 506;-Hc. 4, 185; Mṛcch.

3, 1. 21); AMg. *pisaṇa* = **piṁsana* (Paṇhāv. 77). — AMg. *vūhae* from **vuṁhae* = *vṛṁhayet* (Sūyag. 894), *aṇuvūhaï* (Nāyādh.; Kappas.), *duppaḍivūhaṇa*, *paḍivūhaṇa* (Āyār. 1, 2, 5, 4. 5). Especially frequent are the cases of lengthening of *a* in the prefix *sam* in AMg. in words like *sārakkhaṇa* = *saṁrakṣaṇa* (Ṭhāṇ. 556), *sārakkhaṇayā* = *saṁrakṣaṇatā* (Ṭhāṇ. 333), *sārakkhi-* = *saṁrakṣin* (Ṭhāṇ. 313), *sārakkhamāṇa* (Āyār. 1, 5, 5, 1; Uvās.; Nirayāv.), also in JM. *sārakkhaṇijja*, *sārakkhantassa* (Āv. 28, 16. 17); AMg. *sārohi* = *saṁrohin* (Ṭhāṇ. 314); *sāharaï* = *saṁharati* (Kappas.), *sāharĕjjā* (Vivāhap. 1152), *sāharanti* (Ṭhāṇ. 155), *sāhaṭu* = **saṁhartu* (§ 577), *paḍisāharaï*, (Paṇṇav. 841; Nāyādh.; Ovav.); *sāhaṇanti*, *sāhaṇittā* (Vivāhap. 137. 138. 141). Thus is explained also M. *sakkaa*, AMg. JM. *sakkaya*, Ś. *sakkada* = *saṁskṛtá* (C. 2, 15 p. 18; Hc. 1, 28; 2, 4; Mk. fol. 35; Karp. 5, 3; Vajjāl. 325, 20; Mṛcch. 44, 2; Karp. 5, 1), AMg. JM. *asakkaya* (Paṇhāv. 137; Vajjāl. 325, 20); further *sakkāra* = *saṁskāra* (Hc. 1, 28; 2, 4; Mk. fol. 35; R. 15, 91), JM. *sakkāriya* = *saṁskārita* (Erz.). The route is *saṁskṛta*, **sāṁskṛta*, **sākkaa*, *sakkaa*. Cf. § 306. According to Mk. fol. 35 and Vāmanācārya in Rishikesh p. 12 note, a mention should here be made also of *satthua* = *saṁṣtuta* and *satthava*, *satthāva* = *saṁstāva*, *saṁstava*. But AMg. *saṁthuya* (Āyār. 1, 2, 1, 1). Cf. *kohaṇḍi*, *kohaṇḍa* § 127.

c) Elevation of Vowels

§ 77. The first vowel of a prefix is sometimes elevated in synthetic formations in Skt. *abhijāti* and *ābhijāti*; *pariplava* and *pāriplava*; *prativeśya* and *prātiveśya* Pkt. exhibits the same phenomenon (Vr. 1, 2; Hc. 1, 44; Kī. 1, 1; Mk. fol. 4. 5; Pkl. p. 19). *ahijāi* and M. *āhijāi* (H.), *āhiāi* (R.) = *abhijāti*; M. *paḍivaā* = *pratipad* (H.) and *pāḍivaā*; M. AMg. *pāḍiĕkka* = *pratyeka* (§ 163); *paḍipphaddhi-* and *pāḍipphaddhi-* = *pratispardhin* (Hc.; Kī. 1, 1; 2, 101); *paḍisiddhi* and *pāḍisiddhi* = **pratiṣiddhi* (competition; also 2, 174; Deśīn. 6, 77; Ś. Karp. 18, 1; 21, 5; 44, 9); *paḍisāra* and *pāḍisāra* = **pratismāra* (cunning; Deśīn. 6, 16); M. JM. *samiddhi* (G. H.; Ṛṣabhap.) and M. *sāmiddhi* = *samṛddhi* (H.); AMg. JM. *ajjhovavanna*, °*vaṇṇa* = *adhyupapanna* (Āyār. 1, 1, 6, 6; 2, 1, 7, 2; Śūyag. 185. 210. 751. 923; Nāyādh. 1069. 1387. 1461. 1469; Vivāgas. 87. 92; Uvās.; Āv. 26, 25; 30, 26; Erz.), *ajjhovavajjaha*, *ajjhovavajjaï* (Nāyādh. 841. 1390), *ajjhovavajjihii* (Ovav.); AMg. *abbhovagamiyā* = *ābhyupagamikī* (Bhag.; cf. Aup. S. s. v. *āhevacca*). The final vowel of the prefix appears to have been elevated in M. *veāriuṁ*, *veārijjasi* = *vitārayitum*, *vitārayase* (H. 286. 909); *veāria* (expanded; hair; Deśīn. 7, 95); AMg. *āhevacca* = *ādhipatya* (Samav. 134; Nāyādh. 257. 310. 329. 481. 529. 1417. 1507; Vivāgas. 28, 57 [*a*°]; Paṇṇav. 98. 100. 103; Antag. 3 [a°]; Ovav.; Kappas.), In cases like AMg. *aṇovāhaṇaga*, °*ya* = **anupānahanaka* (Sūyag. 759; Vivāhap. 135; Ovav.); AMg. JŚ. *aṇovama* = *anupama* (Paṇṇav. 136; Ovav.; Pav. 380, 13); AMg. *aṇouya* = *anṛtuka* (Ṭhāṇ. 369), *aṇovaṇihiya* = *anupanihita* (Aṇuog. 228. 241. 242), *aṇovasaṁkha* = *anupasaṁkhya* (Sūyag. 454) elevation of the vowel has not to be assumed, but as firstly shown by S. Goldschmidt[1] there is the negative *aṇa-* which occurs also in AMg. *aṇaii* = *aniti*[2]; *aṇaüdaya* (Kattig. 399, 309), M. *aṇahiaa* = *ahṛdaya* (H. R.), *aṇohŏnta* = *abhavat* (H.); *aṇarasia* (H.), *aṇadīhara* = *adīrgha* (R.); *aṇamilia* = *amilita* (Deśīn. 1, 44); *aṇarāmaa* = **arāmaka* = *arati* (Deśīn. 1, 45) and others[3]. Cf. § 70.

1. ZDMG. 32, 99ff.; KZ. 24, 426. — 2. LEUMANN, Aup. S. s. v. — 3. PISCHEL BB. 3, 243ff.; WEBER on H. 41. Cf. JOHANNES SCHMIDT, KZ. 23, 271 ff.

§ 78. Prākrit shows vocalic elevation that deviates from that of Skt. in many other cases as well. Thus : *pārakera* = *parakīya* (Hc. 1, 44), but Ś. *parakera* (Mālav. 26, 5), *parakeraa* (Śak. 96, 10), Mg. *palakelaa* (Mṛcch. 37, 13; Śak. 161, 7); M. *māṇaṁsi-*, *māṇaṁsiṇī* = *manasvin*, *manasviṇī* (§ 74); M. JM. JŚ. *sāriccha* (Bh. 1, 2; Hc. 1, 44; Kī. 1, 1; Mk. fol. 5; Pkl. p. 19; H.; Erz.; Kk.; Kattig. 401, 338). = **sādṛkṣa*[1], corresponding to *tādṛkṣa*, *yādṛkṣa*; AMg. *cāuranta* = *caturanta* (Hc. 1, 44; Sūyag. 787. 789; Ṭhāṇ. 41. 129. 512; Samav. 42; Paṇhāv. 302; Nāyādh. 464. 471; Uttar. 339. 842. 869; Vivāhap. 7. 39. 160. 848. 1049. 1128 etc.), *cāukkoṇa* = *catuṣkoṇa*. (Nāyādh. 1054; Jīv. 289, 478), *cāugghaṇṭa* (Nāyādh. § 130; p. 731. 780. 784. 826. 1060. 1233. 1266. 1456; Vivāhap. 114. 801. 802. 830; Rāyap. 231. 237. 239; Nirayāv. § 21), *cāujjāma* = *caturyāma* (Vivāhap. 135), *cāuraṅgiṇī* (Nāyādh. § 65. 100. 103; p. 538. 541; Ovav. Nirayāv.). AMg. *teicchā* = *cikitsā* (§ 215). The secondary vowels originating from *ṛ*, either by contraction or by ablaut or by insertion, show the same elevation. Thus : AMg. *gāhāvaï* = *gṛhapati*, simultaneously accompanied with lengthening of the penultimate *a* according to § 70 (Āyār. 1, 7, 2, 1. 2; 3, 3; 5, 2; 2, 1, 1 ff.; Sūyag. 846. 848. 850. 957 ff.; Vivāhap. 162. 227. 345. 346. 1207 ff.; Nirayāv. 41. 43; Uvās.; Kappas.), *gāhāvaïṇī* = *gṛhapatnī* (Vivāhap. 1266. 1270. 1271; Nāyādh. 530; Uvās.). By the side of AMg. *musaṁ* = *mṛṣā* (Sūyag. 74. 340. 489; Dasav. 614. 29; Uttar. 116), *musāvāda* (Sūyag. 207; Uvās. § 14 [text *mūsā°*]. 46 [*°vāya*]), *musāvādi-* (Āyār. 2, 4, 1, 8) there occurs the too frequent *mosa* (Uttar. 373. 952. 957), *mosa*, *saccāmosa*, *asaccāmosa* (Āyār. 2, 4, 1, 4; Paṇṇav. 362; Ṭhāṇ. 203; Ovav. § 148. 149), *taccamosa* (Ṭhāṇ. 152; Paṇṇav. 362), *māyāmosa* (Ṭhāṇ. 21; Vivāhap. 126; Paṇhāv. 86; Paṇṇav. 638; Kappas. § 118; Ovav.). — *rovaï*, *dhovaï*, *sovaï* from *ru*, *dhau*, *svap* (§ 473. 482. 497); *sovaṇa* (sleep; Deśīn. 8, 58); AMg. *asovaṇi* = *avasvāpani* (Kappas. § 28), *sovaṇi* = *svāpaṇi* (Nāyādh. 1288); AMg. *vesalaga* = *vṛṣalaka* (Sūyag. 729), *sovāga* = *śvapāka* (Āyār. 1, 8, 4, 11; Uttar. 349. 371. 402. 409. 410), *sovāgi* = *śvapāki* (Sūyag. 709); AMg. *gelanna* = *glānya* (Ṭhāṇ. 369) from *gilāṇa* = *glāna* (§ 136). On M. AMg. JM. *bāhiṁ* = *bahiḥ* see § 181. Elevation of the final vowel after elision of a consonant at the end of word takes place in AMg. *puḍho* for **puḍhu* = *pṛthak* (Āyār. 1, 1, 2, 1. 2; 3, 4ff., 1, 2, 6, 2 etc.; Sūyag. 81. 123; Ṭhāṇ. 332), *puḍhochanda* (Āyār. 1, 5, 2, 2; cf. Sūyag. 412), *puḍhosiya* = *pṛthakśrita* (Āyār. 1, 1, 2, 2; 6, 3; Sūyag. 332. 468), *puḍhojiya* = *pṛthagjīva* (Sūyag. 46). *puḍhosatta* = *pṛthaksattva* (Sūyag. 425; cf. 401). In **puḍhu* for *puḍha* the second vowel is assimilated to the first one, as in *puhutta* = *pṛthaktva* (Ṭhāṇ. 212; Aṇuog. 45. 405 ff.; Nandīs. 160. 163. 168 f.), for which is found also *puhatta* (Paṇṇav. 602. 744; Vivāhap. 181. 182. 1057)[2], also *pohatta* (Samav. 71; Vivāhap. 178), *pohattiya* (Paṇṇav. 639. 640. 664) with elevation of the first *u*. Pāli *puthu*[3] shows the course of development; there is correspondence between Pāli *puthujja* and AMg. *puḍhojaga*=*pṛthagjaka* (Sūyag. 104. 342), as well as between *putthujjana* and AMg. *puḍhojaṇa* (Sūyag. 166). According to Hc. 1, 24. 137. 188 *pihaṁ*, *puhaṁ*, *pidhaṁ* and *pudhaṁ* are also used; so JM. *pihappihaṁ* (Āv. 7, 8. 17), AMg. *pihajjaṇa*=*pṛthagjana* (Ṭhāṇ. 132).

1. At the end of a compound *sāriccha* mostly=**sādṛksya* may be taken to be a substantive. That it was also an adjective is proved by instances like those found in Erz. 71, 33. Cf. § 245. — 2. That the MSS have *puhutta* also has been shown by WEBER, Bhag. 2, 260, Anm. 1. — 3. ERNST KUHN, Beiträge p. 23; E. MÜLLER, Simplified Grammar p. 6.

d) SHORTENING OF LONG VOWELS.

§ 79. In M. AMg. JM. JŚ. A., and more rarely in other dialects, long vowels are often shortened and *e* is changed into *i*, when the accent originally fell on the long vowel of the preceding or following syllable. Such words as have their *ā* shortened to *a* have been classed under *yathādi*-ākṛtigaṇa by Vr. 1, 10; Kī. 1, 9; Mk. fol. 6; Pkl. p. 22 : Hc. 1, 67 divides them into two groups; adverbs in general (*avyaya*) and the *ākṛtigaṇa utkhātādi* and in 1, 68 he further teaches that such words as are formed by the kṛta - suffix -*á* (*ghañ*) and show vṛddhi have their *ā* shortened to *a*, as in *pravāhá*, *prahārá*, *prakārá*, etc. He is followed by Triv. and Ad. 1, 2, 37. 38. The words with-*ī* arer gouped under *pāṇiyādi* gaṇa by Vr. 1, 18; Hc. 1, 101; Pkl. p. 28; and under the *gṛhitādi* class by Mk. fol. 8. Triv. and Ad. 1, 2, 51 set up the *gabhiraga* gaṇa and group the words like *pāṇiya*, *alika*, *kariṣa*, *upanita*, *jivati* that show *i* also under the *pāṇiyādi* class (1, 11). Inversely Kī. groups under *pāṇiyādi* (1, 11) the words that require shortening of ī compulsorily and under the *gabhirādi* class those in which it is optional (1, 12). Hc. permits general exceptions to his rule. The grammarians have not set up a *gaṇa* for the words with *ū*.

§ 80. A vowel is shortened if the accent fell on the preceding syllable: M. *ukkhaa*, JM. *ukkhaẏa*=*útkhāta* (Grr.; G. R. Erz.), M. *samukkhaa* (H.) by the side of M. *ukkhāa* (H.); AMg. *kulala*=*kúlāla* (an owl; Sūẏag. 437; Uttar. 447; Dasav. 632; 37); M. *ṇisaha*=*niḥśākha* (H.); M. *varai*=*várāki* (H.) by the side of the more frequent *varāa*, *varāi* (H.), *sāmaa* (Hc. 1, 71) =*śyámāka* (Śāntanava, Phiṭsūtra 2, 23; 3, 18), according to Śrīharṣa, Dvirūpakośa 48 also in Skt. *śyāmaka*. — AMg. *aṇiẏa*=*ánika* (Ṭhāṇ. 357; Ovav.), *aṇiẏāhivaï*=*anikādhipati* (Ṭhāṇ. 125. 357), *pāẏāṭṭāṇiẏa*, *piḍhāṇiẏa*, *kuñjarāṇiẏa*, *mahisāṇiẏa*, *rahāṇiẏa* (Ṭhāṇ. 357), by the side of *aṇiẏa* (Niraẏāv.; Ovav.; Nāẏādh.); M. *alia*, AMg. JM. *aliẏa*=*álika* (Grr.; G. H. R.; Vivāhap. 352. 687; Paṇhāv. 134; Uttar. 19; Dvār. 497, 19; Erz.), also Ś. (Mṛcch. 24, 25; 57, 14. 15; 95, 17; 153, 18; Vikr. 30, 21; Mālav. 41, 18; Ratn. 324, 9; Caṇḍak. 9, 17; 52, 10; 86, 10; 87, 13. 16 etc.) and Mg. (Mṛcch. 145, 16; 165, 1). But for Ś. Mg., except in poetry (Mṛcch. 145, 16; 153, 18) often *alia* also is good; this has been partly better accredited inasmuch as *alia* is permitted by grammarians and occurs in Ś. (Prab. 37, 6 [against *aliattaṇa* 38, 1] ; Nāgān. 45, 11; 103, 3; Mudrār. 59, 1; Pras. 37, 17; 44, 11; 46, 14; 47, 11; 120, 1; Veṇīs 24, 4; 97, 9; 107, 4 etc.), and JM. *aliẏa* in Erz.; M. *osianta*-=*ávasidat* (R.), *pasia*=*prásida* (Hc.; H.), but Ś. *pasida* (Mṛcch.

4, 5; Prab. 44, 2; Nāgān. 46, 11; 47, 6), Mg. *paśida* (Mṛcch. 9, 24; 131, 18; 170, 18; 176, 9); AMg. *karisa* = *kárīṣa* (Grr.; Uvās.), but also M. *karīsa* (G.); AMg. *vammiya* (Hc.; Sūyag. 613; cf. Vivāhap. 1226ff. [mostly °*i*°]) and M. *vammia* (G.) = *vál̥mīka* (Ujjvaladatta on Uṇādisūtra 4, 25); according to Puruṣottama = Dvirūpakośa 8 there occurs *vālmika* as well, and according to Śrīharṣa, Dvirūpakośa 51 *valmika* also is found in Skt.; *sirisa* = *śirīṣa* (Hc.), but also M. *sirīsa* (Śak. 2, 15). — M. *ulua*, AMg. *uluga* = *úlūka* (Sarasvatīk. 16, 10; Sūyag. 695); AMg. JM. *gāuya* = *gávyūta* (Ṭhāṇ. 83. 88. 89; Vivāhap. 425. 1529; Jīv. 276; Aṇuog. 381. 385. 397, 403; Paṇṇav. 52. 601. 602; Nandīs. 160. 163. 168; Ovav.; Erz.); M. Ś. *verulia*, AMg. JM. *veruliya* = *vai'ḍūrya* (Hc. 2, 133; Kī. 2, 117; [text °*ṇi*°]; Mk. fol. 39; Pāiyal. 119; G.; Mṛcch. 70, 25; 71, 3 [so to be read]; Karp. 33, 1; Sūyag. 834; Ṭhāṇ. 75. 86. 514. 568; Paṇhāv. 440; Vivāhap. 1146. 1322. 1324; Paṇṇav. 26. 540; Nandīs. 72; Rāyap. 29. 58. 69; Jīv. 217. 494. 549; Uttar. 629. 981. 1042; Erz.); cf. § 241. — *viruva* = *vírūpa* (Deśīn. 7, 63). — *caviḍā*, *cavilā* = *cápeṭā* (Hc. 1, 146. 198) by the side of M. AMg. *caveḍā* (Hc.; H.; Uttar. 596).

§ 81. A vowel becomes short if the accent fell on the following syllable : AMg. JM. *āyariya* = *ācāryá* (§ 134)[1]; AMg. *amāvasā* = *amāvāsyá* (Kappas.); M. AMg. JM. *ṭhavei* = *sthāpáyati* and other causatives (§ 551. 552); M. JM. *kumara* = *kumārá* (Grr.; Erz.), M. *kumarī* = *kumārī́* (G.; Karp. 80. 6), M. *kumaravāla* = *kumārapāla* (Deśīn. 1, 104) 88), by the side of M. JM. A. *kumāra*, *kumārī* (G. H.; Erz.; Hc. 4, 362), as always in Ś. *kumāra* (Vikr. 52. 16; 72, 15. 21; 79, 15; Mudrār. 44, 3; Pras. 35, 2. 7), *kumāraa* (Śak. 41, 2; 155, 9 [so to be read]; 156, 6, 14. Mudrār. 43, 5; 44, 1), *kumārī* (Mālav. 68. 10), in Mg. *kumāla* (Nāgān. 67, 1. 14 [so to be read]); *khaïa*, JM. *khaïya* = *khāditá* (Bh. Mk. Pkl.; Erz.); *khaïra* = *khādirá* (Grr.); A *taïsa* = *tādṛśá*, *jaïsa* = *yādṛśá* (Hc. 4, 403. 404); AMg. JM. *pajjava* = *paryāyá* (Āyār. 1, 3, 1, 4; 2, 15, 23; Paṇṇav. 237ff.); Jīv. 238. 262. 450. 451; Uttar. 797. 895; Aṇuog. 270; Vivāhap. 128; Ovav.; Āv. 43, 4. 9), JŚ. *pajjaya* (Pav. 388, 4; Kattig. 398, 302); M. *pavaha* = *pravāhá* (Grr.; G. H. R.), by the side of M. JM. *pavāha* (Grr.; G.; Erz.; Kk.), as in Ś. (Mṛcch. 2, 20); M. *maṁjara* (§ 86) *mārjārá* (C. 2, 15; Hc. 2, 132; H. 286), *majjara* (Mk. fol. 6), by the side of *maṁjāra* (Hc. 1, 26) and AMg. JŚ. Ś. *majjāra* (Paṇhāv. 20. 64. 528; Nāyādh. 756; Kattig. 401, 347; Śák. 145, 9), M.Ś. *majjārī* (Pāiyal. 150; Deśīn. 1, 98, 82; Viddhaś. 114, 6), *majjāriā* (Karp. 53, 5); A. *sahū̃* = *sākám* (§ 206); M. *halia* = *hāliká* (Grr.; H.). — M. JM. *gahira* = *gabhīrá* (Grr.; G. R.; Erz.) by the side of *gahira* (G.); M. *ṇia* = *nītá* (R.), AMg. *niya* (Uttar. 617, and the words more frequently found in compounds like *aïṇia* = *atinīta* (Deśīn. 1, 24), M. *āṇia* (Grr.; G. H. R.), JM. *āṇiya* (Dvār. 496, 30. 32; Erz.), M. *samāṇia* (H.) M. *uṇṇia* (R.), *uvaṇia* (Hc.; Mk.; R.); AMg. JM. *niṇiya* (Nāyādh. 516; Erz.), by the side of M. *ṇia* (H.), JM. *nīya* (Erz.); always with a long vowel in Ś. *ṇīda* (Mṛcch. 95; 7 : Śak. 127. 9), *avaṇīda* (Vikr. 87, 4), *paccāṇīda* (Vikr. 10, 4), *uvaṇīda* (Mṛcch. 17, 14; 25; 14; 69, 7; Śak. 19, 7), *pariṇīda* (Śak. 76. 10), *duvviṇīda* (Śak. 17, 4), *aviṇīda* (Śak. 135, 2; 154, 7), and in Mg. *ṇīda* (Mṛcch. 162, 19), *avaṇīda* (Mṛcch.

109), 16), *āṇida* (Mṛcch. 99, 2; 124 19; 175, 15). In Triv. and Ad. 1, 2, 51, lengthening of vowel, in *ānita* is limited to the feminine. The example quoted by Triv., viz. *āṇidā bhuvaṇabbhudĕkkajaṇaṇī* = *ānītā bhuvanādbhutaikajananī* is regulated according to either JŚ. or Ś. — *tuṇhia* = *tūṣṇiká* (Bh. 3, 58; Hc. 2, 99), by the side of AMg. JM. *tusiṇiya* (Āyār. 2, 3, 1, 16 ff.; Āv. 25, 20); M. *viḷia vriḍitá* (Grr.; Deśīn. 1, 20; 7, 65; R. 1, 6 v. 1.; Acyutaś. 82), *viḍia* (R.), AMg., *saviḷiya* (Nāyādh. 958); AMg. *sarisiva* = *sarisṛpá* (Āyār. 2, 4, 2. 7 [so to be read with v. l.]; Sūyag. 105. 747; Jīv. 263. 264 [here °*ri*°]; also *sarisava* (Āyār. 2, 3, 3, 3; Sūyag. 129. 944; Samav. 98) and *sirisiva* (Sūyag. 339; Rāyap. 228 [°*sa*°]. 235). — M. AMg. JM. *iṇa* = *ená* (§ 431); M. *viaṇā*, JM. *viyaṇā* = *vedaná*' (Vr. 1, 34; Hc. 1, 146; Kī. 1, 34; Mk. fol. 11; Pāiyal. 161; G. H. R.; Erz.).

1. Wrongly Jacobi, KZ. 23. 598; 35, 569. The separation-vowel *it* and the sonants are without influence on the working of the accent. Cf. 8. 131.

§ 82. Shortening of vowels takes place on account of stress accent also in other cases in which we have the accent no more. Thus: M. *ahira* = *abhīra* (H. 811); *kaḷaa* beside *kaḷāa* = *kalāda* (goldsmith : Triv. and Ad. 1, 2, 37 for *kālaa* = *kālaka* in Hc.); *marala* (Mk. fol. 6) = *marāla*; JM. *mahua* by the side of *mahūa* = *madhūka* (Vr. 1, 24; Hc. 1, 122; Kī. 1, 13; Mk. fol. 9; Kī. 18); AMg. *saraḍuya* = *śalāṭuka* (Āyār. 2, 1, 8, 6). The double-forms in Pkt. have as their basis the multitude of forms with different accents in Skt. So *khāira* = *khā'dir*, but *khaïra* = *khādirá*; *devara* is = *dévara* (Phiṭsūtra 3, 18), but M. *diara* (Vr. 1, 34; Hc. 1, 146; Kī. 1, 34; Mk. fol. 11; H.), JM. *diyara* (Pāiyal. 252) = *devará* (Uṇādisūtra 3, 132); AMg. *pāyaya*, JM. *pāgaya*, *pāyaya*, M. *pāia*, JM. *pāiya*, M. *pāua*, Ś. *pāuda*, Mg. *pākida* (§ 53) are = *prā́kṛta*, but *paaa* (Hc. 1, 67; Triv. 1, 2, 37), *paüa* (Bh. 1, 10; Kī. 1, 9; Mk. fol. 6) = *prākṛtá* (cf. *sáṁskṛta* and *saṁskṛtá*). *balaā* (Hc. 1, 67; Triv.; Ad. 1, 2, 37) by the side of *balāā* = *bālā'kā* presupposes the accent as in **ba'lākā* or **balākā'* as AMg. *suhuma* = *sūkṣma* (§ 131), where the accent seems to be as in **sūkṣmá*, whilst in the Uṇādis. 4, 176, it is transmitted as *sū́kṣma*. The ordinals *duia* (Bh. 1, 18; Hc. 1, 94. 101; Kī. 1, 11; Mk. fol. 8), JM. *duiya* (Erz.), Ś. *dudia* (Mṛcch. 51, 10; 69, 5. 6; 78, 8; Śak. 137, 2; Vikr. 5, 12; 10, 1; 19, 8; Mahāv. 52, 17 etc.)[1], Mg. *dudia* (Mṛcch. 81, 5; 134, 2); M. *biia* (Hc. 1, 94; G. 1081; R.), AMg. JM. *biiya* (Sūyag. 177; Uvās.; Nāyādh.; Kappas. and very often in colophons, as in Āyār. p. 3. 8. 15. 29. 34 etc.; Erz.), M. *taïa* (Bh. 1, 18; Hc. 1, 101; Kī. 1, 11; Mk. fol. 8; G.), AMg. JM. *taïya* (Ovav. § 105. 144; Uvās.; Nirayāv.; Kappas, and often in colophons, as in Āyār. p. 4. 10. 16. 17. 20. 24 etc.; Erz.; Ṛsabhap.), Ś. *tadia* (Mṛcch. 69, 14. 15; Mudrār. 41, 7 [so to be read; see v. l.]), Mg. *tadia* (Mṛcch. 166, 24 [text *taïa*]) do not go back to *dvitī'ya*, *tṛtīya*, but to **dvityá*, **trityá*.[2] In cases like M. *jiaï* = *jivati*, M. AMg. JM. *āruhaï* = *ārohati*, there is transition over to the 6th class (§ 482).[3] On *pāṇia* see § 91, on *gahia* = *gṛhītá* § 564. Long contracted vowels, except before double consonants and in A., are never shortened : *kālāsa* from *kālāasa* = *kālāyasá* (§ 165); *kumbhāra* from *kumbhaāra* = *kumbhakārá* and other compound words formed with *kāra* added to them (§ 167); *cakkāa* = *cakkāa* = *cakkaāa* = *cakravāká*

(§ 167); *pāikka* from *pādātiká* (§ 194); *bia, tia* from *biia, *tiia* = **dvitiya*, **tṛtiya* (§ 165) : So probably also *ṇarāa* by the side of M. *ṇārāa* (R.), AMg. JM. *nārāya* (Uvās.; Ovav. Prabandhac. 100, 7; Erz.) = *nārāca* (Hc. 1, 67).[4] On AMg. *paḍiṇa* see § 99.

1. The texts often have *dudīa*, as in Mudrār. 41, 7; Mālatim. 31, 6; 71, 3; 72, 4; 103, 8; Bālar. 174, 10; Aṇarghar. 61, 6; Vṛṣabh. 23, 9 etc. The v. l. in Mālatim. has mostly the correct reading. — 2. JACOBI on Kalpas. p. 103, note 28. Cf. PISCHEL, KZ. 35, 144; JACOBI, KZ. 35, 570 f. — 3. JACOBI objects to assumption of such a transition, KZ. 35. 569 f., of course on insufficient grounds. — 4. According to JACOBI, KZ. 35, ,65, note 1, the theory of contraction lacks proof as such. It is still to be proved. In PW the accent is shown as in *nārāca'* probably according to Vedic. *narācī'* In BW. the accent is rightly wanting. Perhaps there existed the double forms *nārāca* and *narāca*. Cf. under § 79-82 in general, PISCHEL KZ. 34, 568 ff.; 35, 140 ff. Against this, wrongly JACOBI, KZ. 35, 363 ff.

§ 83. Long vowels are shortened in close syllables (Hc. 1, 84). PG. : *raṭṭhika* = *rāṣṭrika* (5, 4); *amacce* = *amātyān* (5, 5); *vatthavāṇa* = *vāstavyānām* (6, 8); *bamhaṇāṇaṁ* (6, 8.2 7. 30. 38); *puvva* = *pūrva* (6, 12. 28) etc. Sanskritisms in PG. are : *kāṁcipurā* for *kaṁcipurā* = *kāñcipurāt* (5, 1) and *ātteya* for *atteya* = *āttreya* (6, 13); faulty is also *cāttāri* for *cattāri* = *catvāri* (6, 39). — PG. M. AMg. JM. Dh. *kaṭṭha* = *kāṣṭha* (PG. 6, 33; H.; Ovav.; Erz.; Mṛcch. 30, 16)ī.[1] M. JM. Ś. *kavva* = *kāvya* (G. H. R.; Erz.; Vikr. 31, 11; 35, 5. — M. JM. AMg. *gatta* = *gātra* (R.; Ovav.; Erz.). — M. AMg. JM. Ś. *rajja* = *rājya* (H. R.; Nāẏādh.; Niraẏāv.; Ovav.; Erz.; Vikr. 75. 5). — JŚ. *uvasanta* = *upaśānta* (Kattig. 403, 377). — Mg. *śanta* = *śrānta* (Mṛcch. 13, 7). — A. *kanta* = *kānta* (Hc. 4, 345. 351. 357, 1; 358, 1; Vikr. 58, 9). — M. AMg. JM. A. *kitti* = *kirti* (Vr. 3, 24; Hc. 2, 30; Kī. 2, 34; Mk. fol. 22; G. R.; Uvās; Ovav. Kappas.; Erz.; Hc. 4, 335); Ś. *kittiā* = *kirtikā* (Vikr. 12, 14).— AMg. JM. JŚ. Ś. A. *tittha* = *tirtha* (Ovav.; Kappas.; Erz.; Pav. 379, 1; Śak. 79, 1; 105, 4; 118, 10; Hc. 4, 441, 2). — M. AMg. Ś. Mg. A. *gimha* = *griṣma* (G. H. R.; Ovav.; Kappas.; Mṛcch. 80, 23; Śak. 10, 1; Hc. 4, 357, 3). — M. JM. Ś. Mg. A. *uddha* = *ūrdhva* (G. H. R.; Erz.; Mṛcch. 39, 2; 41, 22; 136, 16; Hc. 4, 444, 3), AMg. JM. *uḍḍha*, JM. *ubbha* (§ 300). — M. AMg. *kumma* = *kūrma* (G.; Uvās.; Ovav.; Kappas.). — M. AMg. JM. Ś. Mg. A. *cuṇṇa* = *cūrṇa* (G. H. R.; Āẏār. 2, 1, 8, 3; 2, 2, 3, 9; Kappas.; Kk.; Mṛcch. 68, 25; 117, 7; Hc. 4, 395, 2). — M. AMg. JŚ. Ś. *mulla* = *mūlya* (H.; Karp. 73, 10; Ovav.; Kattig. 400, 335; Mṛcch. 55, 15; 78, 3; 82, 15; 88, 21 ff.; Śak. 116, 12). — All the syllables that are accompanied with a nasal vowel or anusvāra are governed by the same law, whether they existed already in Skt. (Hc. 1, 72) or if this anusvāra is secondary in Pkt. having originated from *m* according to § 348; M. Ś. *kaṁsatāla* = *kāṁsyatāla* (G.; Mṛcch. 69, 24; Karp. 3, 3 v. 1.). — M. AMg. JM. Ś. *paṁsu* = *pāṁsu* (G. R.; Vivāgas. 155; Bhag.; Erz., Mālatīm. 142, 1; Mallikām. 253, 18; 336, 9). — M. AMg. JM. JŚ. Ś. *maṁsa* = *māṁsa* (H.; Sūẏag. 281; Dasav. 632, 24; Uvās.; Ovav.; Erz.; Āv. 27, 12; Kattig. 400, 328; Śak. 29, 6), Mg. *maṁśa* (Mṛcch. 10, 1; 21, 17; 117; 9; 123, 7; 126, 5; 163, 9; Veṇīs. 33. 6; 34, 2; *maṁśae* 33, 12). — The rule frequently becomes operative in the final syllables ending in *-ām*, *-īm*, *-ūm*, *-ān* of Skt. declensional forms, as in M. *puttāṇaṁ* = *putrāṇām*, *aggiṇaṁ*

= *agninām*, *vāūṇaṁ* = *vāyūnām*, *mālaṁ* = *mālām*, *sahiṁ* = *sakhīm*, *vahuṁ* = *vadhūm*; AMg. *mahaṁ* = *mahān*, *āyavaṁ* = *ātmavām*, etc. (§ 370 ff. 396); further in adverbs like *dāṇiṁ* = *idānim* (§ 144), AMg. JM. *saddhiṁ* = *sadhrim* (§ 103). In the case of interjections the rule does not hold good : Ś. Mg. *āṁ* = *ām* (Mṛcch. 27, 10; Śak. 71, 13; 134, 14; Vikr. 13, 2; 35, 9; 75, 6; Mālav. 6, 3; 80, 8; Bālar. 123, 17; Mṛcch. 136, 19). In A. *kahāṁ*, *jahāṁ*, *tahāṁ*, in the sense of *kutaḥ*, *yataḥ*, *tataḥ* (Hc. 4, 355) the lengthening is to be explained according to § 68.

1. In connection with the rules of this type, that are to be covered times without number, the examples from M. AMg. JM. have been selected from the texts that are provided with word-indices, as far as possible, for the sake of brevity and the examples are confined chiefly to words that possibly occur uniformly in many dialects.

§ 84. Before a consonant group *e* becomes *ĕ* and *o* becomes *ŏ*. In M. AMg. JM. sometimes there enter *i* and *u* in lieu of *ĕ* and *ŏ*. Thus : M. AMg. JM. *pĕcchaï* = *prekṣate* (Hc. 4, 181; H. G. R.; Ovav.; Erz.), AMg. *pĕcchaṇijja* = *prekṣaṇiya* (Nāyādh.; Ovav.; Kappas.), *pĕcchaga* = *prekṣaka* (Vivāhap. 929) and AMg. JM. *picchaï* (Kappas.; Kk.), AMg. *picchaṇĕjja* (Jīv. 353), JŚ. *pĕcchadi* (Pav. 384, 48), Ś. *pĕkkhadi* (Śak. 13, 6; Vikr. 84, 5), Mg. *pĕskadi* (Hc. 4, 295, 297; Mṛcch. 80, 4; 112, 17); M. *avĕkkhi-* = *apekṣin* (G.); M. *duppĕccha* = *duṣprekṣya* (R.), Ś. *duppekkha* (Prab. 45, 11), Mg. *duspĕska* (Mṛcch. 116, 7). — *dubbhĕjja* = *durbhedya* (Mṛcch. 68, 19). — AMg. JM. Ś. A. *mĕccha* = *mleccha* (Ovav. § 183 [v. l. *mi°*] ; Āv. 39, 2; Mudrār. 229. 9; Cait. 38, 6 [text *malĕccha*] ; Piṅgala 1, 77ᵃ. 117ᵃ; 2, 272) and *milĭccha* (Hc. 1, 84), AMg. *miccha* (Paṇṇav. 136). — M. *chĕtta* = *kṣetra* (Bh. 3, 30; Hc. 2, 17; G. H.), AMg. *chitta* (Ovav. § 1), AMg. JM. JŚ. Ś. *khĕtta* (Āyār. 1, 2, 3, 3; Sūyag. 628; Vivāhap. 97. 157. 203 f. 583 ff.; Uttar. 355 ff.; Dasav. N. 653, 14; Erz.; Pav. 379, 3; 387, 21; Kattig. 401, 352; Mṛcch. 120, 7; Anarghar. 261, 5), AMg *khitta* (Uttar. 576. 1014). — M. AMg. JM. *oṭṭha* = *ŏṣṭha* (G. H. R.; Karp. 8, 3; 58, 5; Paṇhāv. 63; Āv. 41, 6; Erz.) and JM. *uṭṭha* (Erz.), AMg. *huṭṭha* (Āyār. 1, 1, 2, 5). — M. AMg. JM. Ś. *aṇṇŏṇṇa* = *anyonya* (G. H. R ; Sūyag. 137; Ovav.; Erz.; Mṛcch. 24, 16; 71, 1. 13; Śak. 56, 15; Vikr. 51, 16) and M. *aṇṇuṇṇa* (Hc. 1, 156; G.), wrongly also in Ś. Bālar. 217, 8. — M. AMg. Ś. *paŏṭṭha* = *prakoṣṭha* (Mk. fol. 13; Karp. 47, 6; Ovav.; Mṛcch. 68, 23; 69, 5 ff.; 70, 5 ff.; 71, 11. 12; 72, 1; Bālar. 80, 1; Viddhaś. 126, 3) and M. *paüṭṭha* (Hc. 1, 156; G.). — AMg. *maṇunna* = *manojña* (§ 276). — The rule holds good also for the secondary *e*, *o* that originated from *ai*, *au* (§ 60 ff.), by saṁprasāraṇa (§ 153. 154), and those that originated from *aï* and *aü* (§ 166). As *i* from *ĕ*, there occurs *ai* always in AMg. JM. *ikkhāga* = *aikṣvāka* (Āyār. 2, 1, 2, 2; Ṭhāṇ. 414. 458; Nāyādh. 692. 729. 1505; Paṇṇav. 61.; Uttar. 532; Ovav.; Kappas.; Āv. 46, 19; Erz.), wrongly equated as = *ikṣvāku* by Leumann and Jacobi : Ś. *mitteya* = *maitreya* (Mṛcch. 4, 22. 23; 6, 3; 17, 20; 22, 15; 53, 18; 74, 19; 150, 12), likewise Mg. (Mṛcch. 45, 1); *sindhava* = *saindhava* (Vr. 1, 38; Hc. 1, 149; Kī. 1, 36; Mk. fol. 12); M. AMg. *saṇiccara* = *śanaiścara* (Hc. 1, 149 with note; Paṇhāv. 312; Paṇṇav. 116; Ovav.). AMg. *śaṇiṁcara* (Ṭhāṇ. 82, 399; Bhag. 2, 225), as in Triv. 1, 2, 94 in my MSS against *saṇicchara* of the printed edition, is explained either according to § 74 or from **saṇiaṁcara*, from M. Ś. *ṣaṇiaṁ*, AMg. JM.

saṇiyaṁ, Pāli *sanikaṁ*, *saniṁ* (Hc. 2, 168; Pāiyal. 15; G. H.; Āyār. 2, 15. 19. 20. 22; Vivāhap. 172. 173; Uvās.; Erz.; Mālatīm. 239. 3; Uttarar. 32, 8; Paiyad. 17, 13; Pras. 45, 3; Mallikām. 242, 1). In Viddhaś. 120, 9 stands in Ś. *saṇiccara* except in the v. 1. — Mk., fol. 12 teaches besides *saindhava* also *bhaikṣājīvika*, *naiyāyika* and *paiṇḍapātika*. Consequently *bhikkhājīvia* can be traced back to *bhikṣājīvika*, *piṇḍavāia* goes back to *piṇḍapātrika* ; *naiyāyika* becomes *neyāuya* in AMg. (§ 60). The words which always show *u* from *o* for *au* have been grouped by grammarians (Vr. 1, 44; Hc. 1, 160; Kī. 1, 43; Mk. fol. 13; Pkl. p. 37) under the *saundaryādi* class, which, according to Mk. and Pkl., who almost always agree with one another, is an ākṛtigaṇa. Triv. 1, 2, 97, who is followed by Ad., has the ākṛtigaṇa *śauṇḍaga*, and the examples are the same as those in Hc. To this gaṇa belong *sundera* = *saundarya* (M. Karp. 66, 7; Ś. Dhūrtas. 10, 9), for which Pratāp. 220, 9 has *sŏndajja*, and Hc. teaches *sundaria*; also *uvariṭṭhaa* = *aupariṣṭhaka* (Mk. Pkl.); *kukkheaa* = *kaukṣeyaka* (Bh. Kī. Mk. Pkl.), for which Hc. 1, 161 and Triv. 1, 2, 96 teach *kuccheaa* and *kŏccheaa*; *duvāria* = *dauvārika* (Bh. [read so for *duvvā*°], Hc. Kī. Mk. Pkl.) is rather *dvārika*; *dussāhia* = *dauḥsādhika* (Mk. Pkl.); *pulomi* = *paulomī* (Hc. Mk. Pkl.); *pussa* = *pauṣya* (Mk. [*pauṣa*]); Pkl. [*pauruṣa*]); *muñja* = *mauñja* (Mk. Pkl.); *muñjāaṇa* = *mauñjāyana* (Bh. Hc. Kī. Mk.); *suṇḍa* = *śauṇḍa* (Bh. Hc. Kī. Mk. Pkl.); *suṇḍia* = *śauṇḍika* (Kī. Mk. Pkl.), and so Mg. *śuṇḍikāgāla* = *śauṇḍikāgāra* (Śak. 118, 7); *suddhoaṇi* = *śauddhodani* (Hc.). — *suvaṇṇia* = *sauvarṇika* (Hc.) is rather = **suvarṇika*, *sugandhattaṇa* = *saugandhya* Hc.) = **saugandhatvana*.

§ 85. The *e* occurring at the end of a word, and the original as well as secondary *o* (§ 342 ff.) before the enclitics, that begin with double consonants, except in A., become *ĕ* and *ŏ* and not *i* and *u*, : M. *tumhĕttha* = Ved. *yuṣme stha* (R. 3, 3), *sāarĕtti* = *sāgara iti* (R. 4, 39), *aṇurāŏ tti* = *anurāga iti* (G. 715), *piŏtti* = *priya iti* (H. 46); JM. *purisŏ tti* = *puruṣa iti* (Āv. 13, 2), *gaŏtti* = *gata iti* (Āv. 17, 6), *kālŏvva* = *kāla iva* (Erz. 71, 27. 35); JŚ. *samŏtti* = *sama iti* (Pav. 380, 7). Wrong readings are AMg. *mu tti* (Āyār. 1, 1, 3, 4) for *mŏtti*, as it is correctly in the Calcutta edition, = *sma iti*, JŚ. *māyācāruvva* for *māyācārŏ vva* (Pav. 383, 44), AMg. *lohabhāruvva*, *gaṁgasouvva* for °*bhārŏvva*, °*soŏvva* (Uttar. 583), and elsewhere. See § 346. (sometimes even before a single consonant *o* appears as *u* : M. *tulaṇe* = Skt. *tolane* G. 50) Ś. *avahidŏmhi* = *avahitosmi* (Vikr. 78, 14), *bamhaṇŏjjĕvva* = *brāhmaṇa eva* (Mṛcch. 27, 14); Mg. *eśĕ kkhu* = *eṣa khalu* (Mṛcch. 40, 9), *puttakĕtti* = *putraka iti* (Śak. 161, 7). Against this, in M. *e* and *o* are always changed into *i* and *u* in the final syllable of case endings after long vowels, when the metre requires a short vowel : *pucchiāi muddhāe* = *pṛṣṭāyā mugdhāyāḥ* (H. 15); *golāi tūhāiṁ* = *godāyastīrthāni* (H. 58); *gāmataruṇiu hiaaṁ* = *grāmataruṇyo hṛdayam* (H. 546); *uahiu ṇiggaaṁ* = *udadhernirgatam* (G. 56). Just apparently sometimes in all MSS are written *ĕ* and *ŏ*, that are permitted by grammarians in Pkt. and A. (Āv. p. 6, note 4; Saṁgītaratnākara 4, 55. 56; Piṅgala 1, 4), thus — *jasoāĕ*, *cumbiaṁ* = *yaśodāyāścumbitam* (G. 21), or *kŏtthuhakiraṇāantiŏ kaṇhassa* = *kaustubhakiraṇāyamānāḥ kṛṣṇasya* (G. 22). The MSS mostly waver, thus even the best manuscript of G. 44, for *harāliṅgaṇalajjiyāĕajjāĕ* of the text, has °*lajjiȳāi ajjāi*. Examples of this sort are preponderant.[1] For AMg. JM. JŚ. as well the same rule holds good : however, in AMg. and JM. the texts, sometimes even after long vowels, have *ĕ* and *ŏ*, probably wrongly. Thus : AMg. *savvakammāvahāŏ* = *sarvakarmāvahāḥ* (Āȳār. 1, 8, 1, 16), but the Calc. edition gives the correct reading °*hāu*; *levamāȳāĕ saṁjae* = *lepamātrāyāṁ saṁyataḥ* (Dasav. 622. 13); *nigganthattāŏ bhassaī* = *nirgranthavād bhraśyati* (Dasav. 624, 33); JM. *buddhiĕ caüvvihāĕ juo* = *buddhyā caturvidhayā yutaḥ* (Āv. 7, 23), *muddāĕ aṅkio* = *mudrayāṅkitaḥ* (Āv. 8, 14), *jūhāo paribhaṭṭho* = *yūthāt paribhraṣṭaḥ* (Erz. 69, 14). In AMg. JM., even before vowels and simple consonants, *e* and *o*, in many other cases in poetry, measure short : thus in AMg. *unnaĕ vā paoe* = *unnato vā payodaḥ*, *vuṭṭhĕ balāhaĕ tti* = *vṛṣṭobalāhaka iti* (Dasav. 629, 31. 32), *alolŏ bhikkhū* = *alolo bhikṣuḥ* (Dasav. 640, 3); JM. *mannĕ esa* = *manya eṣa* (Āv. 7, 30), *niŏ ujjeṇiṁ* = *nīta ujjayinīm* (Āv. 8, 14). In poetry, for the enclitic *me*, in AMg., is used *mi*, for *se* in AMg. JM. is used *sĕ*, and in AMg., *si* (§ 418. 423), in Mg. Mṛcch. 43, 6 ff., in verse there occurs *śakki* for *śakke* = *śakyaḥ* etc. (§ 64). In AMg. *utāho* becomes *udāhu* (Uvās.) or *uȳāhu* (Āȳār. 1, 4, 2, 6). Cf. also § 346. In A. *e* and *o*, in all cases, could become either short or *i* and *u* in the final position: *piĕ diṭṭhaï* = *priye* **dṛṣṭake* (Hc. 4, 365, 1); *hiaï* = *hṛdaye* (Hc. 4, 330, 3. 395, 4. 420, 3) ; *piĕ pavasantĕ* = *priye pravasati* (Hc. 4, 422, 12); *kalijugi dullahahŏ* = *kaliyuge durlabhasya* (Hc. 4, 338); *aṅguliu jajjariāu* = *aṅgulyo jarjaritāḥ* (Hc. 4, 333); *diṇaaru khaagāli* = *dinakaraḥ kṣayakāle* (Hc. 4, 377); *kṛdantaho* = *kṛtāntasya* (Hc. 4, 370, 4), Cf. § 128. 130. 346. Sometimes *a* is written wrongly before double consonants in lieu of *ĕ* and *ŏ*. So M. *pamhaṭṭha mhi* for *pamhaṭṭhŏmhi* = *prasmṛtavānasmi* (R. 6, 12; already in Hc. 3, 105); Ś. *hadamhi* for *hadŏmhi* = *hato'smi* (Śak. 29, 9); Mg. *kadamhi* for *kadĕmhi* (Mṛcch. 38, 15).[2] Cf. § 92 ff. 392 ff.

1. § 365. 375. 385, LASSEN, Inst. p. 148. WEBER; ZDMG. 28, 352; S. GOLDSCHMIDT, Prākṛtica p. 29.—2. PISCHEL, GGA 188 , 342 ff. Wrongly S. GOLDSCHMIDT, Prākṛtica p. 17.

§ 86. A long vowel, before a group of several consonants, one of which is *r*, sometime becomes a short nasal vowel and the consonant-group is simplified : M. *maṁjara* (§ 81), *vaṁjara* (Hc. 2, 132), *maṁjāra* (Hc. 1, 26), by the side of *majjara*, AMg. JŚ. Ś. *majjāra* = *mārjāra* (§ 81). — *muṁḍha-* = *mūrdhan* (Hc. 1, 26; 2, 41), noticed only AMg. JM. *muddha-* (§ 402; Erz.), that does not appear to have been used in M. Ś. (PISCHEL on Hc. 2, 41). — AMg. *mĕṁḍha* (buck : Ṭhāṇ. 250), *miṁḍha* (Ṭhāṇ. 205; Sūȳag. 708), *mĕṁḍhaga* (Ṭhāṇ. 260), *miṁḍhaga* (Ovav. § 107*), *miṁḍhaȳa* (Samav. 131) = *meḍhra*, *meḍhraka*, that, as *meṇḍhaka*, *meṇḍha* and *meṇḍhra*, have entered into Skt. as well; fem. *meṁḍhī* (Deśīn. 6, 138), *miṁḍhiȳā* (Pāiȳal. 219), and according to Deśīn. 6, 138 also *meṇṭhī*.

§ 87. In case a long vowel, that occurs before an original consonant-group, is retained, there appears a single consonant out of the double consonants originating through assimilation or in particular cases, its phonetic substitute, elision (Hc. 2, 92). Such cases mostly occur when one of the consonants is either *r* or a sibilant. Thus : *āsa* = *āsya* (Hc.). — AMg. JM. *īsara* = *īśvara* (Hc.; Uvās.; Kappas.; Erz.), Mg. *īśala* (Mṛcch. 17, 4;

Śak. 116, 2), by the side of *issara* (Bh. 3. 58). — M. JM. Ś. *isā* = *irṣyā* (G.H. R.; Erz.; Mṛcch. 69, 25), but also Ś. *issā* (Prab. 39, 2. 3). Mg. *iśśā* (Prab. 47, 1). — M. AMg. JM. Ś. *dīha* = *dīrgha* (Bh. 3, 58; Hc. 2, 91; G. H. R.; Nāẏādh.; Kappas.; Erz.; Mṛcch. 39, 2; 41, 22; 69, 8; 78, 25; Ratn. 307, 318, 26; Mālatīm. 76, 5; Mṛcch. 116, 17; 168, 20; Hc. 4, 330, 2); Ś. *dīhiā* = *dīrghikā* (Priyad. 11, 2, 5; 12, 12; Vṛṣabh. 39, 3), AMg. JM. *dīhiẏā* (Āẏār. 2, 3, 3, 2; Ovav.; Erz.), by the side of *diggha* (Bh. 3, 58; Hc. 2, 91). Ś. Mg. *digghiā* (Ratn. 299, 12; Nāgān. 51, 6; Priyad. 8, 13; 12, 2; 19, 17; 23, 11 24. 9. 15; Mg. Mṛcch. 134, 7). — M. AMg. JM. Ś. *pāsa* = *pārśva* (Hc. 2, 92; G. H. R.; Āẏār. 1, 1, 2, 5; Ovav.; Kappas.; Erz.; Vikr. 17, 11; 24, 4, 5; 36, 12; 75, 15; Prab. 64, 2; Priyad. 8, 14). — AMg. JM. *pehaï* = *prekṣate* (§ 323). — M. JM. Ś. A. *bāha* (tears), by the side of *bappha* (smoke), Ś. *bappa* (tears) = *bāṣpa* (§ 305). — AMg. *lūha* by the side of *lukkha* = *rūkṣa*, *lūhei* = *rūkṣayati* (§ 257). — *leḍhukka* = *leṣṭuka* (§ 304). — AMg. JŚ. *loḍha* = *loṣṭa* (§ 304). — M. *veḍhaï*, AMg. JM. *veḍhei*, Ś. *veḍhida* = Pāli *veṭhati*, *veṭhita* = Skt. *veṣṭate veṣṭita*, (§ 304). M. AMg. JM. Ś. A. *sīsa—śīrṣa* (Hc. 2, 92; G. H. R.; Āẏār. 1, 1, 2, 6; Uvās.; Erz.; Mṛcch. 24, 14. 16. 17; 68, 14; 74, 5; 78, 10; Śak. 39. 4; Hc. 4, 389, 446), Mg. *śīśa* (Mṛcch. 12. 18; 13, 9; 40, 6; 113, 1; 127, 12), °*śīśaka* (Mṛcch. 20, 17). — AMg. JM. *soma* = *saumya* by the side of M. Ś. *sŏmma* (§ 61[a]). — Cf. § 284. In AMg., as against in all other dialects, long vowels remain very frequently before the suffix *-tra*, that develops into *-ẏa* from *-ta*. So : *gāẏa* = *gātra* (Āẏār. 1, 8, 1, 19; 2, 2, 3, 9; Ṭhāṇ. 289; Nāẏādh. 267; Vivāhap. 822. 1257. 1261; Uttar. 61. 106. 109; Uvās.; Ovav.; Kappas.); *goẏa* = *gotra* (Āẏār. 1, 2, 3, 1; 2, 2, 3, 4; Paṇṇav. 716; Uttar. 966; Ovav.; Kappas.), by the side of *gŏtta* (Dasav. 628. 3; Uvās.; Ovav.; Kappas.); *dhāī* = *dhātrī* (Hc. 2, 81; Āẏār. 1, 2, 5, 1; 2, 15, 13; Sūẏag. 255; Vivāgas. 81; Vivāhap. 959; Nāẏādh. § 117; Rāẏap. 288; Ovav. [§ 105]); *pāẏa* = *pātra* (Āẏār. 1, 8, 1, 18; 2, 6, 1, 1 ff.; Sūẏag. 194; Uttar. 219; Ovav.), *pāī* = *pātrī* (Sūẏag. 783), *kaṁsapāī* = *kāṁsyapātrī* (Ṭhāṇ. 528; Kappas.); *lohiẏapūẏapāī* = *lohitapūyapātrī* (Sūẏag. 281); *māẏā* = *mātrā* (Āẏār. 1, 2, 5, 3; Ovav.), *māẏanna* = *mātrājña* (Āẏār. 1, 2, 5, 3; 1, 7, 3, 2; 1, 8, 1, 19; Dasav. 623, 15; Uttar. 51), *taṇamāẏa* = *tṛṇamātra* (Sūẏag. 608); *mūẏa* = *mūtra* (Āẏār. 1, 6, 1, 3); *soẏa* = *śrotra* (Āẏār. 1, 2, 1, 2, 5; Sūẏag. 639). Only in *rātri* (Bh. 3, 58; Hc. 2, 88; Mk. fol. 28) the rule is not restricted merely to AMg. as *rāī* (Vivāhap. 936. 938), *rāībhoẏaṇa* = *rātribhojana* (Ṭhāṇ. 180; Ovav.), *rāīṁdiẏa rātriṁdiva* (Ṭhāṇ. 133; Nāẏādh. 347; Vivāhap. 1293; Kappas.), *rāẏa* = °*rātra* (Kappas.), °*rāiẏa* = °*rātrika* (Sūẏag. 731; Ovav.; Kappas.); but there occurs also in M. *rāī* (H.), by the side of *ratti* (H. R.; Śak. 55, 15), JŚ. *rāibhoẏaṇa* (Kattig. 399, 306) by the side of *rattiṁ* (Kattig. 103, 374. 375), *rattidivahaṁ* (Kattig. 402, 364), Ś. *rādi* (Mṛcch. 93, 12. 15) by the side of the usual *ratti* (Mṛcch. 93, 6. 7; 147, 16; 148. 2; Śak. 29, 7), Mg. *latti* (Mṛcch. 21. 18), *lattiṁ*, *lattiṁdivaṁ* (Mṛcch. 45, 21; 161, 4).

§ 88. The prefix *ā* remains often before the root *khyā*, and always before *jñā*, and the initial syllable of the roots is treated as if it were a medial one. AMg. *āghaṁ* = *ākhyān* (Sūẏag. 397), *āghāẏa* = *ākhyāẏa* (Sūẏag. 375), *āghāvei*, *āghavemāṇa*, *āghaviẏa*, *āghavittae*, *āghavijjanti* (§ 551), *āghavaṇā* = *ākhyā-*

panā (Nāyādh. § 143; p. 539; Uvās. § 222); Ś. *paccākhādum̐* = *pratyākhyātum* (Vikr. 45, 5). Ḍh. *akkhanto* (Mṛcch. 34, 24) is an incorrect reading for *ācakkhanto* (§ 491. 499). But also AMg. *akkhāi*, *akkhanti*, *paccakkhāi* (§ 491). AMg. JM. *āṇavei*, Ś. Mg. *āṇavedi* = *ājñāpayati* (§ 551); M. AMg. JM. *āṇā* = *ājñā* (Vr. 3, 55; Hc. 2, 92; Kī. 2, 109; Mk. fol. 27; G. H R ; Samav.; 134; Ovav.; Kappas.; Āv. 8, 17, 18; Kk.; Ṛṣabhap.); VG. M. AMg. Ā. Ś. Mg. *aṇatti* = *ājñapti* (Bh. 3, 55; Hc. 2, 92; Kī. 2, 109, Mk. fol. 27; VG. 102, 16; R.; Nirayāv.; Priyad. 11, 10; Mṛcch. 105, 1; 166, 21; 171, 17; Veṇīs. 36, 6); AMg. *āṇattiyā* (Uvās.; Ovav.; Nirayāv.), *āṇavaṇa* = *ājñāpana* (Hc. 2, 92; Uvās.), *āṇamaṇi* = **ājñāpani* (Paṇṇav. 363. 369). In other cases the usage wavers : thus : M. *āsasaï* = *āśvasiti*, but Ś. *samassasadu*, Mg. *śamaśśaśadu* = *samāśvasitu* (§ 496). In Ś. *akkandāmi* = *ākrandāmi* (Uttarar. 32, 1), *akkandasi* (Mudrār. 263, 4), Mg. *akkandāmi* = (Mṛcch. 162, 17) the printed editions (except that of STENZLER) with the majority of the manuscripts have *ākka*°, so that it could be read as *āka*° also. But M. JM. *akkamaï*, *akkanta*, *samakkanta* (G. H. R.; Erz.; Kk.) always have the shortened vowel, which also is explained better with the help of *krand*. Besides, a long vowel remains before a consonant-group formed without *r* or a sibilant only seldom, and it is so preserved dialectically : JŚ. *āda-* = *ātman* (Pav. 380, 8. 12; 381, 15. 16; 382, 23. 24. 25; 383, 70. 24), AMg. *āya-* (Āyār. 1, 1, 1, 3, 4, 5; 1, 2, 2 2. 5, 4; Sūyag. 28. 35. 81. 151. 231. 838; Vivāhap. 76. 132. 283. 1059 ff. [the text mostly *āta-*] ; Uttar. 251). — AMg. *sāmali* = *śālmali* (Sūyag. 315; Ṭhāṇ. 88. 555; Paṇhāv. 274; Aṇuttar. 9; Ovav. § 16; *kūḍasāmali* (Uttar. 626), dialectical *sāmari* (Pāiyal. 264; Deśīn. 8, 23.; Triv. 1, 3, 105 = BB. 3,259; cf. § 109). — M. AMg. A. *thāha*, "ground : bottom" (Pāiyal. 249; Deśīn. 5, 30; R.; Paṇhāv. 380; Nāyādh. 904. 1112. 1341; Hc. 4, 444, 3), according to Hc. also "deep water" and "broad" by the side of *thaha* (residence; Deśīn. 5, 24) and *thaggha* (deep; Pāiyal. 249; Deśīn. 5, 24); AMg. *atthāha* (groundless; deep; Deśīn. 1.54; Nāyādh. 1112; Vivāhap. 104. 447) by the side of *atthaggha* (Deśīn. 1, 54) = **stāghya*,* *astāghya*. Cf. § 333.

1. In Deśīn. 5, 24, the words are to be read as *thaggho 'gādhe* and *thaggho 'gādhaḥ*. The scholiasts connect it to *stāgha*. Improvement has been effected according to this GGA. 1880, 334.

§ 89. Against § 83, sometimes a long nasal vowel is retained dialectically, and in such cases the nasal sound disappears : *kāsa* = *kāṁsya*, *pāsu* = *pāṁsu* (Hc. 1, 29. 70); M. *māsa* = *māṁsa* (Vr. 4, 16; Hc. 1, 29. 70; Mk. fol. 34; G. R.), *māsala* = *māṁsala* (Hc. 1, 29; G. R.), *māsalaanta*, *māsalia* (G.). The same thing takes place also in the case of secondary nasal vowels in Pāli *pekhuṇa*, *pĕkkhuṇa*, M. AMg. *pehuṇa* = **preṅkhuṇa*, **prĕṁkhuṇa*, **prĕkhuṇa* = Skt. *preṅkhaṇa* (wandering = swing, wing; Pāiyal. 126; Deśīn. 6, 58; G. H. R.; Āyār. 2, 1, 7, 5; Paṇhāv. 33. 489. 533; Paṇṇav. 529; Nāyādh. 500; Jīv. 464). The derivation from *pakṣman* (CHILDERS, s. v. *pĕkhuṇa*; S. GOLDSCHMIDT, KZ. 25, 611) or from *pakṣa* (WEBER, IStr. 3,396) is lniguistically impossible. So also the accusative plural forms in *-ā*, *-i*, *-ū*, in M. AMg. A., such as M. *guṇā* = *guṇān*, AMg. *rukkhā* = *rūkṣān*, A. *kuñjarā* = *kuñjarān*, AMg. *mallai* = *mallakin.*, *bahū* = *bahūn* (§ 367. 381) can be traced back to the Skt. forms through **guṇā̃ṁ*, **guṇā*, **bahū̃ṁ*, **bahū̃*, etc., as having developed due to gradual weakening of the nasals. Perhaps Mg. *dālaṁ* = *dārān* (§ 367a) developed in the same manner. Cf. also *kesua* from **kĕṁsua* = *kiṁśuka* and *kohaṇḍi*, *kohaṇḍa* from **kŏmhaṇḍi*, °*ṇḍa* = *kūṣmāṇḍi*, °*ṇḍa* (§ 76, 127).

§ 90. When the original word had its accent on the final syllable, a long vowel preceding a simple consonant is often shortened and the simple consonant is duplicated. Sometimes doubling of consonants takes place even after an originally short vowel (§ 194). The words in which doubling is obligatory have been grouped under the ākṛtigaṇa *niḍādi* (Vr. 3, 52; Kī. 2, 111; Mk. fol. 27) and under *tailādi* (Hc. 2, 98; Triv. 1, 4, 93;), the cases, in which lengthening is optional, are included in the ākṛtigaṇa *sevādi* in Vr. 3, 58; Hc. 2, 99; Kī. 2, 112; Mk. fol. 27, and under the *daivaga* class in Triv. 1, 4, 92. Not very many examples of application of this rule, notably in Bh. and Mk., are to be found. — M. Ś. Mg. Ḍh. *ĕvvaṁ* = *evám* (H.; Mṛcch. 4, 20; 9, 1; 12, 25 etc.; Vikr. 6, 15; 13, 18; 8 etc.; Mg. Mṛcch. 31, 17; 39, 20; 80, 18 etc.; Ḍh. Mṛcch. 30, 14. 18; 31, 19. 22; 35, 17) by the side of *evaṁ*. — Ś. *kacca* = *kācá* / (Karp. 19, 8). — AMg. JM. *kiḍḍā* = *krīḍā́* (Āyār. 1, 2, 1, 3; Sūyag. 81; Jīv. 577; Jīyak. 45; Uttar 483; Nāyādh.; Āv. 15, 13), AMg. JM. *khĕḍḍa* (n.; Hc. 2, 174; Triv. 1, 3, 105 = BB. 3, 253; Ovav.; Erz.); A. *khĕḍḍaa* (Hc. 4, 422, 10); beside AMg. JM. *kiḍā* (Uvās.; Erz.); AMg. *kiḷaṇa* (Ovav.), *kiḷāvaṇa* (Rayap. 288; Ovav.); M. Ś. *kiḷā* (G.; Cait. 69. 9); Ś. *kiḷāpavvada* = *krīḍāparvata* (Vikr. 31, 17; Mallikām. 135, 5; Adbhutad. 61, 20 [text °*ḍā*°], *kiḷaṇaa* = *krīḍanaka* (Śak. 155, 1). Cf. § 206. 240. — *khaṇṇu* by the side of *khāṇu* (Hc. 2, 99; Mk. fol. 21. 27) = **skhāṇú*, an allied dialectical form of *sthāṇú* (§ 120. 309); M. *khaṇṇua* (H.). — AMg. JM. *khatta* = *khātá*, *ukkhatta* by the side of M. *ukkhāa*, *ukkhaa* (§ 566). — Ś. *jĕvva*, P. Mg. *yĕvva* = *evá*, by the side of *jeva*, *yeva* (§ 95. 335). — M. AMg. JM. Ś. A. *jŏvvaṇa* = *yauvaná* (Grr.; G. H. R.; Āyār. 1, 2, 1, 3; Sūyag. 212; Ṭhāṇ. 369; Paṇhāv. 288; Paṇṇav. 100; Vivāhap. 825. 827; Dasav. 641, 16; KI. 13; Erz.; Mṛcch. 22, 22; 141, 15; 142, 12; 145, 12; Śak. 11, 4; 13, 2; Prab. 41, 5; [so it is to be read]; Dhūrtas. 15, 8; Mallikām. 221, 2; Hc. 4, 422, 7; Vikr. 68, 22), AMg. *jŏvvaṇaga* (Vivāhap. 946), but always *juva-*, *jua-* = *yúvan* (§ 402), and so also M. JM. *juvaï*, *juvai* = *yuvatì*, *yuvatí* (G. H. R.; Śak. 120, 7; Ratn. 293, 5; Pratāp. 218, 11; Erz.), Ś. *juvadi* (Mṛcch. 69 23; 73, 9), Mg. *yuvadi* (Mṛcch. 136, 13).[1] — *ṇĕḍḍa* = *nīḍá* (Grr.), by the side of M. *ṇiḍa* (G. H.).[2] — M. JM. *tuṇhikka* = *tūṣṇīká* (H. R.; Āv. 38, 2; Erz.), by the side of *tuṇhia*, AMg. JM. *tusiṇiya* (§ 81). M. AMg. JM. Ś. Mg. *tĕlla* = *tailá* (Grr.; H.; Āyār. 2, 1, 4, 5. 9, 3; 2, 6, 1, 9. 12; 2, 7, 1, 11; 2, 12, 4. 15, 20; Sūyag 248. 935; Paṇhāv. 381; Vivāgas. 235; Vivāhap. 1288. 1327. 1329; Rāyap. 167. 175; Uvās.; Ovav.; Kappas.; Erz.; Mṛcch. 69, 7. 12; 72, 10; Śak. 39, 4; Mṛcch. 25, 19; 117, 8), also AMg. *tilla* (Paṇṇav. 63; Uttar. 432. 806). — *thiṇṇa* by the side of *thiṇa* = *styāná* (Hc. 1, 74), M. *thiṇṇaa* = *styānaka* (R.). — AMg. JM. *thulla* by the side of AMg. JŚ. Ś. *thūla* = *sthūlá* (§ 127). — *thŏkka* = *stoká* (Hc. 2, 125) beside the common *thova*, *thoa* (§ 230). — AMg. *dugulla* = *dukūlá* (Hc. 1, 119; Pāiyal.

266; Āẏār. 2, 5, 1, 4; Paṇhāv. 238; Vivāhap. 791. 941. 962; Jīv. 508; 559; Ovav.; Kappas.), according to Vr. 1, 25; Hc. 1, 119, Kī. 1, 25; Mk. fol. 9 also *dualla*, beside M. Ś. *duūla* (Hc., Mk., H.; Mallikām. 68, 5; 69, 13). — AMg. *dhatta—dhmātá* (Nāẏādh. § 61). M. AMg. JM. Ś. A. *pĕmma = premán* (Grr.; G. H. R.; Ratn. 299, 18; Viddhaś. 6. 3; Bālar. 122, 13. 16; Sūẏag. 771; Erz.; Mṛcch. 72, 25; Vikr. 45. 2; 51, 16; Viddhaś. 59, 1; Anarghar. 297, 14; Vṛṣabh. 9, 1; 29, 6; 43, 8; Mallikām. 225, 1; Hc. 4, 395, 3. 423, 1; Vikr. 64, 4), also AMg. JM. *pimma* (Rāẏap. 252; Erz.) and AMg. *pema-* (Sūẏag. 923. 958; Dasav. 631. 19; Uvās.; Ovav.). — *mukka* beside *mūa = mūká* (Hc. 2, 99). — M. *lajjā = lājāḥ* (H. 814). — AMg. *viḍḍā = vriḍá* (Hc. 2, 98; Deśīn. 7, 61; Niraẏāv. § 13). Cf. § 240. — *sevvā = sĕvā'* (Grr.), beside M. JM. *sevā* (G. H.; Erz.). The same accent is seen in AMg. *pāẏatta = pādāta* (Nāẏādh.; Ovav.; Kappas.).

1. According to Kī. 2, 111 *va* in *yuvan* too is doubled. The texts do not attest it, and it is against the rule. Jacobi, KZ. 35, 565 considers that it is curious that in *yauvana*, it is not *na*, but *va*, that is doubled. But this, however, takes place only in the case of the consonant that occurs immediately after a long vowel! The entire polemic of Jacobi, KZ. 35. 575 ff. against Pischel, KZ. 35, 140 ff. does not alter in the least the situation, which may be explained by stating that a consonant is often doubled before a tonic syllable. — 2. Pischel on Hc. 1, 106.

§ 91. The same rule holds good in the optative in *-jjā*, *-jja*, *-ĕjjā* *-ĕjja*, *-ijjā*, *-ijja* in AMg. JM., as in *kujjā = kuryā't*; *dĕjjā = dĕyā't*; *hŏjjā = bhūyā't*; *bhuñjejjā = *bhuñjiyā't = bhuñjyā't*; *jāṇijjā*, *jāṇĕjjā = janīyā't*, a flexion that the verbs of the first conjugation too have (§ 459 ff.); and further in the passive in *-ijja*, *-jja* in M. AMg. JM. JŚ. D. A., in *-yya*, *-iyya* in P., as in words like M. JM. A. *dijjaï*, JŚ. *dijjadi*, P. *tiyyate = diyáte*,[1] AMg. *kahijjaï*, D. *kahijjadi = kathyáte* (§ 535 ff). While Ś. *karaṇia*, *ramaṇia*, Mg. *kalaṇia*, *lamaṇia* and the similarly formed participia nec. and adjectives are traceable to Skt. *karaṇíya*, *ramaṇíya* and so forth, the corresponding forms like M. JM. AMg. *karaṇijja*, *ramaṇijja* and other similar ones (§ 571) presuppose forms of the type **karaṇá*, *ramaṇya'* A. *ravaṇṇa* (Hc. 4, 422, 11) etc., likewise the substantively used M. Ś. Mg. A. *pāṇia*, AMg. JM. *paṇiya = pāniya* (Vr. 1, 18; Hc. 1, 101; Kī. 1, 11; Mk. fol. 8; Pkl. p. 28; H. R.; Nāẏādh. 1009, 1011. 1013. 1032. 1053. 1058. 1375. 1386; Uvās.; Ovav.; Āv. 25, 3; 40. 6; 42, 7. 12; Mṛcch. 45, 9; 77, 11; Laṭakam. 4.12; Mg. Mṛcch. 45, 7; 113, 21; 115, 1.2; 136, 11; Hc. 4, 396, 4. 418, 7. 434. 1) presuppose one **pānyà* or **pānyá*[2]. In Ś. occurs *pāṇia* (Hāsy. 37, 7), in AMg. *pāṇiẏa* for metrical reason (Uttar. 895). — M. *biijja* (Hc. 1, 248), *tiijja* (Kī. 2, 36), A. *taïjji* (Hc. 4, 339) are to be explained like M. *biia*, AMg. JM. *biiẏa*, M. *taïa*, AMg. JM. *taïẏa*, Ś. Mg. *tadia* (§ 82). The words in *-éya*, *-ya* as well follow the analogy of those in *-īya-*, as AMg. JM. *nāmadhĕjja = nāmadhéya* (§ 252), AMg. *pĕjja = péya* (§ 572), in such cases *e* was pronounced very weak, because in a great measure the accent fell on the final syllable. (Whitney, Sanskrit Grammar § 1216 a): this is so also in the case of a few forms of the comparative degree like AMg. *pé'jjaṁ = préyas*, AMg. JM. *bhujjo = bhū́yaḥ* (§ 414). Cf. § 252. — *tiṇṇi = triṇi* (§ 438) is formed on the basis of the genitive *tiṇṇaṁ = triṇā'm*, and on the model of *tiṇṇi* have been regulated *dŏṇṇi*, *bĕṇṇi*, *biṇṇi = dvau*, *dve*; likewise *dŏṇṇaṁ* is formed on the model of *tiṇṇaṁ* (§ 436). In a number of isolated words that appear to be exceptions to the rule duplication of consonants is evidently due to a different cause. So in A. *adhiṇṇa* = *adhī́na* (Hc. 4, 427); the common dialectical form *ĕkka* = *ĕka* beside AMg. JM. *ega* (§ 435); AMg. *kavalla, kabhalla* = *kapā'la* or *kápāla*, Pāli *kapalla* (§ 208); Pāli, M. *chĕppa* = *śĕpa* (§ 211); M. *sŏtta* = *srótas* (Bh. 3, 52; Hc. 2, 98; Mk. fol. 27; G. H. R.); AMg. *paḍisŏttagāmi-* = *pratisrotogāmin* (Uttar. 441), *visŏttiyā* = **visrotaskā* (Āyār. 1, 1, 3, 2), beside *soya* (Ovav.), *paḍisoya, vissoasiyā* (Hc. 2, 98). M. AMg. JM. *maṇḍukka* (Hc. 2, 98; Kī. 2, 112; Mk. fol. 27; Pāiyal. 131; Sarasvatīk. 34, 17; Ṭhāṇ. 311. 312; Paṇhāv. 18; Vivāhap. 552. 553. 1048; Āv. 7, 29), AMg. *maṇḍukkiyā* (Uvās. § 38) may be traced back to *maṇḍuka* (Śrīharṣa, Dvirūpakośa 35), whereof the accent has not been transmitted, and not to *maṇḍū́ka*, that gives AMg. *maṇḍūya* (Paṇṇav. 480), Ś. A. *maṇḍūa* (Mṛcch. 9, 11; so more correctly GOḌABOLE 25, 6; Piṅgala 1, 67).

1. According to JACOBI, KZ. 35, 575 the reduplication of *ya* in the passive goes against the rule, because except in the first person singular of the indicative present, it is not the final syllable that is accented, but the *ya* that occurs before the personal ending. Evidently here the question can be only of (cf. § 90, note 1) the syllable immediately following a long vowel, therefore, of the last syllable of the stem. — 2. PISCHEL, KZ. 35, 142.

§ 92. A final long vowel followed by an enclitic is often shortened; when this takes place the single initial consonant of the enclitic is reduplicated; M. *appaṇa ccea* = *ātmanā caiva* (G. 83), *taṇha ccia* = *tṛṣṇā caiva* (H. 93), *gharasāmiṇi ccea* = *gṛhasvāminī caiva* (H. 736), *ummillanti ccia* = *unmīlantī caiva* (R. 12, 24); AMg. *hiri cceva* = *hrīścaiva* (Ṭhāṇ. 76); JM. *sa cceva sā* (Āv. 18, 19), *abhaṇanta ccia* = *abhaṇantaścaiva* (Ṛṣabhap. 13), *sahasa cciya* = *sahasā caiva* (Erz. 83, 37); M. *gaaṇĕccia* = *gagane caiva* (G. 319), *muŏccea* = *mṛtaścaiva* (H. 497), *āvāĕ ccia* = *āpāte caiva, tĕccea* = *te caiva, sŏccea* = *sa caiva* (R. 1, 58; 5, 67; 6, 67). — PG. *bĕ tti* = *dve iti* (6, 39), *hoja tti* = *bhūyād iti* (7, 48), *kaḍa tti* = *kṛteti* (7, 51); M. *sahasa tti* = *sahaseti, bhikkhatti* = *bhikṣeti* (H. 459. 554), *ṇiatti* = *nīteti* (R. 5, 6), *tumhārisa tti* = *tvadṛśā iti* (G. 706), *māṇiṇitti* (H. 807), *mahi tti* (R. 5, 20), *sāarĕ tti* = *sāgara iti* (R. 4, 39), *aṇurāŏ tti* = *anurāga iti* (G. 715); AMg. *taha tti* = *tatheti* (Uvās. § 67.87.120 etc.), *cāi tti* = *tyāgīti* (Dasav. 613, 18. 20), *antakaḍĕ tti* = *antakṛd iti* (Āyār. 2, 16, 10. 11), *tasakāŏ tti* = *trasakāya iti* (Dasav. 615, 12); JM. *sā sā satti* (Āv. 16, 26), *kā esā kamalāmela tti* (Āv. 30, 5), *savannu tti* = *sarvajña iti* (Āv. (16, 21), *silogŏ tti* = *śloka iti* (Āv. 8, 56.) — M. *soṇāratula vva.* — *suvarṇakāratuleva* (H. 191), *soha vva, vaṇamāla vva, kittivva, āṇa vva* = *śobheva, vanamāleva, kīrtiriva, ājñeva* (R. 1, 48), *vaṇahatthiṇi vva* = *vanahastinīva* (R. 4, 59), *aïppahāe vva, antavirasŏ vva* = *atiprabhāta iva, antavirasa iva* (H. 68); AMg. *giri vva* = *girir iva* (Āyār. 2, 16, 3), *milakkhu vva* = *mleccha iva* (Sūyag. 57), *dīvĕ vva* [text *va*] = *dīpa iva* (Sūyag., 304), *ayakŏṭṭhao vva* = *ayaḥkoṣṭhaka iva* (Uvās. § 94); JM. *thambhiya vva lihiya vva kīliya vva taṅkukkariya vva* = *stambhiteva likhiteva kīliteva ṭaṅkotkīrṇeva* (Erz. 17, 8), *jaṇaṇi vva* = *jananīva* (KI. 9), *taṇaŏ* = *tanaya iva* (KI. 14), *candŏ vva, mahi vva* = *candra iva, mahīva* (Erz. 84, 20); in A. *va* also occurs on account of metre in *piapabbhaṭṭha va* = *priyaprabhraṣṭeva* (Hc. 4, 436). In AMg. JM. as a rule a long vowel is retained before *ceva*. In Ś. Mg. neither *ceva* nor *va* occurs. The cases where they are found are examples of error against the dialect : as in Ś. *gosammi ccea*=*gose caiva*, *taṁ cea*=*tac caiva*, *paaṭṭaṁ cea*=*pravṛttaṁ caiva* (Kāleyak. 2, 5. 17; 2, 12); Ś. *nāmeṇa vva* (Lalitav. 560, 22), *bhaṇidaṁva* (Vikr. 26, 13; ed. PAṆḌIT 47, 2 and ed. Bombay 46, 2 also the false *evva*; it is rightly wanting in BP., ed. Calc. 1830, p. 35, 1; ed. LENZ., 25, 10; ed. PAṆḌIT 632, 18), *suttadhāli vva*, Mg. *śuttadhāli vva* (Mṛcch. 21, 9; 23, 21), Mg. *cale vva*=*cara iva*, *amhadeśiya vva*=*asmaddeśiyā iva*, *deśiyĕ vva*=*deśiya iva* (Lalitav. 565, 8. 12. 14), *goṇa vva* (Mṛcch. 112, 17) and so often in Indian editions. (Extraordinary case :—*timirammiva*, v. l. °*mi*°=*timiramiva* [RB 5].

§ 93. In AMg. a long vowel, before *iti*, if it is a pluti-vowel and in enumeration before *iti vā*, is retained. In such cases *iti* becomes *i*[1] through *ti* : *āyampulā i* (Vivāhap. 1260; text *ti*); *sihā i* (Vivāhap. 1268; text *di*); *goyamā i* (Vivāhap. 1311. 1315; text *di*; Uvās. § 86); *āṇandā i* ((Uvās. § 44); *kāmadevā i* (Uvās. § 118); *kāli i* (Nirayāv. § 5; text *ti*); *ajjo i* (Uvās. § 119. 174). — *māyā i vā piyā i vā bhāyā i vā bhayiṇi i vā bhajjā i vā puttā i vā dhūyā i vā suṇhā i vā*=*mā teti vā piteti vā bhrāteti vā bhaginiti vā bhāryeti vā putrā iti vā duhiteti vā snuṣeti vā* (Jīv. 355; cf. Sūyag. 750; Nāyādh, 1110); *uṭṭhāṇe i vā kamme i vā bale i vā vīrie i vā purisakkāraparakkame i vā*=*uttānam iti vā karmeti vā balam iti vā vīryam iti vā puruṣakāraparākrama iti vā* (Vivāhap. 67. 68; Uvās. § 166ff). Cf. further Sūyag. 747. 758. 857; Vivāhap. 41.70; Ovav. § 96.112.165; Kappas. § 109. 210).

1. The MSS and printed editions very often wrongly have *ti* and also *di*. Cf. WEBER, Bhag. 1, 495, 2, 256 note, *290, note 12.

§ 94. In Mg. and Ś. before the particle *khu*, which originates from *khalu* (§ 148) under the influence of the pretone, whereby *khu* becomes *kkhu*, *e* and *o* are shortened : Ś. *asamaĕ kkhu*=*asamaye khalu* (Śak. 14, 6), *edĕ kkhu* (Mṛcch. 8, 2; Śak. 41, 1; 79, 6), *maĕ kkhu*=*mayā khalu* (Vikr. 26, 15); Ś. *mahantŏ kkhu* (Vikr. 45, 1; 73, 11; 81, 20; Mālatīm. 22, 2), Mg. *mahantĕ kkhu* (Prab. 58, 9)=*mahān khalu*; Ś. *kāmŏ kkhu* (Mṛcch. 28,1), *maaṇŏ kkhu* (Vikr. 23, 2); Mg. *hagĕ kkhu* (Śak. 113, 9), wrongly *hage khu* (Lalitav. 566, 6)=*ahaṁ khalu*, *dukkalĕ kkhu*=*duṣkaraḥ khalu* (Mṛcch. 43, 4). The rest of the long vowels remain in all the dialects (for P. and CP. material is not available) and in M. AMg. JM. JŚ. A., after any vowel *khu* mostly becomes *hu*. In Ś. Mg. after a long vowel, other than *e* or *o*, *khu* remains, and after a short vowel it becomes *kkhu*, and only seldom and incorrectly it becomes *hu* in all MSS as Ś. *ṇa hu* (Mṛcch. 60, 1. 24; 61, 23; 117, 16, 17; 150, 18; 153, 2; 327, 4), *ṇu hu* (Mṛcch. 59, 22), Mg. *ṇa hu* (Mṛcch. 161. 17, in the same line with *lāaṇioĕ* [so it is to be read] *kkhu* !), *ṇu hu* (Mṛcch. 133, 14. 15. 22; 169, 18). Otherwise in the text or in the variants there occurs everywhere *ṇa kkhu* or *ṇu kkhu*; as throughout in the text in Śak., where in 50, 2 only for *ṇa hu* of the text, with the best MSS we should read *ṇa kkhu*. It is only in verses that even in Ś. (Mṛcch. 40, 25) and in Mg. (Mṛcch. 9, 25; 21, 17. 19; 29, 22; 43, 3; 161, 14; Śak. 114, 6) *hu* is correct.[1] Even after a short vowel, therefore, occurs in M. A. *ṇa hu* (G. 718. 864. 900. 908. 911. 1004. 1135; H.; R. 3, 7; 6, 16; 7, 6; Hc. 4, 390; Vikr. 72, 11); so also Dh. (Mṛcch. 30, 17; 31, 1); AMg. JM. *na hu* (Uttar. 583, 743; Āv.

11, 2; Erz. 79, 14; 81, 35), but Ś. Mg. *ṇa kkhu* (Śak. 13, 7; 60, 14. 17; 72, 9; 156, 14; Prab. 14, 17; Śak. 160, 10); M. *ṇu hu* (G. 183. 996), but Ś. Mg. *ṇu kkhu* (Śak. 18, 10; 19, 1; 39, 12; 77, 1; 86, 8 etc.; Mg. 113,7); AMg. *mā ẏa hu* (Āẏār. 1, 2, 5, 5,); M. AMg. JM. *vi hu* (G. 865. 885. 886 etc.; H.; R. 1, 15; 5, 70; 7, 63; Dasav. 634. 2; Erz. 80, 7; Kk. 272, 1; 277, 23); AMg. *hoi hu* = *bhavati khalu* (Uttar. 628. 629); JŚ. *havadi hu* (Pav. 380, 9); but Ś. *atthi kkhu* = *asti khalu* (Śak. 127, 14), *arihadi kkhu* = *arhati khalu, lajjāmi kkhu* (Śak. 58, 13; 164, 5), *sumaresu kkhu* = *smara khalu, bhāāmi kkhu* = *bibhemi khalu* (Vikr. 13, 4; 24, 13). In Rājaśekhara occurs *ṇa hu* (e.g. Karp. 22, 7; 32, 10; 33, 1) against *ṇu kkhu* (Karp. 93, 4) — an error against the dialect. After long vowels : M. AMg. *mā hu* (H. 521, 607; R. 8, 14; Uttar. 440 [*hū*]. 617), but Ś *mā khu* (Mṛcch. 54, 21; Śak. 153, 13; 159, 7; Vikr. 48, 3; 49, 1); M. *ko khu* (Hc. 2, 198), *ko hu* (H. 384; v. 1. *kkhu*), but Ś. *kŏkkhu* (Mṛcch. 64, 18); M. *so khu* (H. 401; v. 1. *kkhu, hu*), JŚ. *so hu* (Kattig. 399, 317. 318; 400, 323), but Ś. *sŏ kkhu* (Mṛcch. 28, 20; 142, 10); AMg. *se hu* (Āẏār. 1, 1, 1, 7. 2, 6; 1, 2, 6, 2; 1, 6, 5, 6; 2, 16. 9. 10), but Mg. *śĕ kkhu* (Mṛcch. 12, 20). Wrong is Ś. *so khu* (Lalitav. 560. 19), **as** *aṇiruddheṇa khu* occurring in the same place (555, 1). JM. *sā hū* (Erz. 77, 23); AMg. *eso hu* (Uttar. 362), but Ś. *esŏ kkhu* (Mṛcch. 18, 8; 23, 19); Mg. *eśĕ kkhu* (Mṛcch. 40, 9; Veṇīs. 36, 4); AMg. *vimukkā hu* = *vimuktāḥ khalu* (Āẏār. 1, 2, 2, 1), *siyā hu* = *syāt khalu* (Uttar. 297; Dasav. 634, 5); JM. *visamā hu* = *viṣamā khalu* (Ṛṣabhap. 17); Ś. *abalā khu* (Mṛcch. 12, 21), *akkhamā khu* = *akṣamā khalu, bahuballahā khu* = *bahuvallabhāḥ khalu, esā khu* = *eṣā khalu, rakkhaṇiā khu* = *rakṣaṇiyā khalu* (Śak. 53, 2; 58, 1; 67, 1; 74, 8), *parihāsasilā khu* = *parihāsaśilā khalu* (Karp. 40, 9), *mandabhāiṇi khu* = *mandabhāgini khalu* (Mṛcch. 22, 25), *dūravattiṇi khu* = *dūravarttini khalu* (Śak. 85, 7); Mg. *āadā khu* = *āgatā khalu* (Mṛcch. 99, 7), *avśalovaśappaṇiā khu lāāṇo* = *avasaropasarpaṇiyāḥ khalu rājānaḥ* (Śak. 115, 10), *ṇiadi khu* = *niyatiḥ khalu* (Mṛcch. 161, 5). Accordingly in Śak. 99, 16 the reading has to be emended as *daṁsaṇiākidi khu* = *darśaniyākṛtiḥ khalu*. In PG. *tasa khu* (7, 41) and *sa ca khu* (7, 47) *khu* may, following the mode of orthography of the inscription, be allowed to remain in the place of *kkhu*. CAPPELLER, in his editions, against the manuscripts, that mostly have *kkhu*, even after long vowels, has shortened all such vowels[2]. Thus for example he writes *esa kkhu* for *esā khu* (Ratn. 292, 31; 295, 8; 297, 24; 300, 4 etc.), *sa kkhu* for *sā khu* (Ratn. 302, 2; 318, 11; 320,1), *ma kkhu* for *mā khu* (Ratn. 301, 17; 325, 13), *muhara kkhu* for *muharā khu* = *mukharā khalu* (Ratn. 305, 19); *maaṇajjarāula kkhu* = *madanajvarāturā khalu* (Hāsy. 25, 25), *mahadi kkhu* = *mahatī khalu, puḍhavi kkhu* = *pṛthivi khalu* (Ratn. 299, 5; 328, 27) etc. It is equally wrong, as sometimes it is in some other good editions of dramas, to write *kkhu* for *khu* after anusvāra, as in Ś. *kiṁ kkhu* (Mṛcch. 13, 3), *uakidaṁ kkhu* = *upakṛtaṁ khalu, kahiṁ kkhu* = *kutra khalu, amadaṁ kkhu* = *amṛtaṁ khalu* (Vikr. 8, 15; 9, 3. 11). After anusvāra *khu* only is correct, as Mk. fol. 72 for Ś. explicitly teaches, and as M. AMg. too have : e. g. M. *taṁ khu* = *tat khalu* (G. 860, 879; H. 142); AMg. *evaṁ khu* (Sūẏag. 95. 176), *eyaṁ khu* = *etat khalu* (Uttar. 106)[3]. In M. AMg. and especially in JM.; however, *khu* and *hu* are proportionately rarer. AMg.

mostly uses *khalu* which is found also in JŚ. (Pav. 380, 7; 381, 18.21; Kattig. 401, 343), more rarely also in JM. in which occurs the combination *taṁ seyaṁ khalu* = *tac chreyaḥ khalu* (Erz. 33, 18) that occurs frequently in AMg. (e. g. Nāyādh. 333. 482; Vivāgas. 218; Uvās. § 66. 138. 140. 151; Nirayāv. § 12. 14. 18. 20. 23; Ovav. § 85. 86; Kappas. § 21) and many other similar ones have been taken over into JM. Both the forms of the particle stand side by side in AMg. *appā hu khalu duddamo* = *ātmā khalu durdamaḥ* (Uttar. 19).

1. Not quite correctly LASSEN, Inst. p. 192, 7; BOLLENSEN on Vikr. 11, 2, p. 196. — 2. CAPPELLER, Jenaer Literaturzeitung 1877, p. 125. Already correctly, LASSEN l. c. and STENZLER on Mṛcch. 2. 19. — 3. The hypothesis that *kkhu* should be written everywhere (PISCHEL on Śak. p. 210) already goes back to Hc. 2, 198.

§ 95. The same rules, as for *khu* (§ 94), hold good also for Ś. *jeva jĕvva*, P.Mg. *yĕva*, *yĕvva* (§ 336) also. After short vowels and after *e*, *o*, which may become short, the initial consonant is doubled : Ś. *ajjassa jjĕvva* = *āryasyaiva* (Mṛcch. 4, 8. 12), *aïreṇa jjeva* = *acireṇaiva* (Lalitav. 562, 23); *idha jjeva* (*jjĕvva*) = *ihaiva* (Śak. 12, 4; Ratn. 293, 25; Mg. Mṛcch. 114, 21), *disadi jjĕvva* = *dṛśyata eva* (Ratn. 295, 10), *saṁpajjadi jjeva* = *saṁpadyata eva* (Śak. 120, 2), *saṁtappadi jjĕvva* = *saṁtapyata eva* (Mṛcch. 63, 24); Mg. *tava yyĕvva* = *tavaiva* (Mṛcch. 22, 4), *teṇa yyĕvva* = *tenaiva* (Mṛcch. 133, 7); P. *savvassa yyeva* = *sarvasyaiva* (Hc. 4, 316), Ś. *bhūmiĕjjĕvva* = *bhūmyāmeva* (Mṛcch. 45, 15), *muhĕjjeva* = *mukha eva*, *sujjodaĕjjeva* = *sūryodaya eva* (Śak. 77, 11; 79, 9), *idŏjjĕvva* = *ita eva* (Mṛcch. 4, 22; 6, 13), *jŏ jjĕvva jaṇo....sŏ jjĕvva* = *ya eva janaḥ...sa eva* (Mṛcch. 57, 13), *so saccŏ jjeva siviṇae diṭṭhŏtti* = *sa satya eva svapne dṛṣṭa iti* (Lalitav. 555, 1); Mg. *daṁśaantĕ jjeva* = *darśayann eva* (Śak. 114, 11), *aṇācaskidĕyyĕvva* = **anācakṣita eva*, *pisṭado yyĕvva* = *pṛṣṭhata eva*, *bhasṭālakĕ yyĕvva* = *bhaṭṭāraka eva* (Mṛcch. 37, 21; 99, 8; 112, 18); P. *tūrātŏ-yyĕva* = *dūrādeva* (Hc. 4, 323). Other long vowels remain before the particle: Ś. *amhasāmiṇā jeva* = *asmatsvāminaiva*, *tadhā jeva* = *tathaiva*, *ṇikkampā jeva* = *niṣkampā eva* (Śak. 116, 8; 126, 10. 14; 128, 6); Mg. *diśanti yĕvva* = *dṛśyamā-naiva* (Mṛcch. 14, 11). CAPPELLER wrongly writes a short vowel in such cases also (cf. § 94); e. g. Ratn. 291, 1; 295, 23, 296, 24 etc., as also in Lalitav. 554, 5. 6. 21, which wrongly has *jjeva* also after anusvāra (554, 4; 555, 18), and at 567, 1 even *eva*. Wrong is also Mg. *śahaśa jjĕvva* (Mṛcch. 96, 24) for *śahaśā yĕvva*.

§ 96. All final long vowels are shortened before the enclitic forms of √*as* (to be) beginning with a conjunct consonant. M : *ṭhia mhi* = *sthitāsmi*, *dūmia mhi* = *dūnāsmi* (H. 239. 423), *asaï mha* = *asatyāḥ smaḥ*, *khavia mho* = *kṣapitāḥ smaḥ*, *roāvia mha* = *roditāḥ smaḥ* (H. 417. 423. 807), *tumhĕ ttha* = *yuṣme stha* (R. 3, 3); JM. *parisantŏ mhi* = *pariśrānto'smi* (Erz. 6, 25); Ś. *uva vasida mhi* = *upoṣitāsmi*, *alaṁkida mhi* = *alaṁkṛtāsmi* (Mṛcch. 4, 6; 23, 25), *āatta mhi* = *āyattāsmi*, *edāvattha mhi* = *etadavasthāsmi*, *asahāiṇi mhi* = *asahāyinyasmi* (Śak. 25, 3; 52, 8; 59, 11), *virahukkaṇṭhida mhi* = *virahotkaṇṭhitāsmi*, *vimharida mhi* = *vismṛtāsmi* (Vikr. 82, 16; 83, 20), *avaraddha mha* = *aparāddhāḥ smaḥ*, *ṇivvuda mha* = *nirvṛtāḥ smaḥ* (Sak. 27, 6; 58, 6), *alaṅghaṇiā kada mha* = *alaṅ-ghanīyāḥ kṛtāḥ smaḥ*, *uagada mha* = *upagatāḥ smaḥ* (Vikr. 23, 8, 14). On *ĕ*, *ŏ* and the incorrect forms like M. *pamhuṭṭha mhi*, Ś. *hada mhi*, Mg. *kada mhi* see § 85. The reading like M. *vĕtti* for *va tti*, *sahasĕtti* for *sahasa tti* (H. 885. 936), *piĕtti* for *pia tti*, *ṇisaṇṇĕtti* for *ṇisaṇṇa tti*, *dhīrĕtti* for *dhīra tti*, *pelavĕtti* for *pelava tti*, *taṇuĕtti* for *taṇua tti* (R. 5, 5. 6. 8), *vihiṇĕvva* for *vihiṇa vva* (R. 14, 16); JŚ. *mamĕtti* for *mama tti* (Pav. 388, 27); Ś. *piadarĕtti* for *piadara tti*, *vĕtti* for *va tti*, *paḍivādaṇijjĕtti*, *ṇiddĕtti* (Śak. ed. Böhtlingk, 9, 8; 37, 13; 43, 14; 83, 6), and M. *galia vva* for *galiĕ vva* = *galita iva*, *candaavva* for *candaĕ vva*, *seubandha vva* for *seubandhŏ vva* (R. 1, 2; 3, 48; 15, 19)[1] are based on Sanskritisms, though they stand in MSS, they are wrong.

1. Pischel, De Kālidāsae Śākuntali recensionibus p. 53; GGA. 1880.325 f.; Burkhard, Sacuntala, Glossarium p. 36, note*, Bollensen, Mālavikāgnimitra p. xiv; cf. Weber, IS, 14, 298. Wrong : Hoefer, De Prakrita dialecto p. 44; Lassen, Inst. p. 188; S. Goldschmidt, Prākṛtica p. 27 f.

§ 97. In M. AMg. JM a final JŚ. long vowel is frequently shortened in the formation of a compound (Vr. 4, 1; Hc. 1, 4; Kī. 2, 143, Mk. fol. 31). This takes place often especially in the case of stems ending in-*ī*, which have wholly collapsed together with the stems in -*i* (§ 384) and more rarely in the case of those in-*ā* and -*ū*. Ś. Mg. always retain long vowels in prose. M. *gāmaṇiutta* = *grāmaṇīputra* (H. 31); M. *ṇaïpūra* = *nadīpūra*, *ṇaïṇiuñja* = *nadīnikuñja*, *ṇaïpheṇa* (H. 45. 218. 671) beside *ṇaïkaccha* = *nadīkakṣa* (H. 416); *ṇaïaḍa* = *nadītaṭa* (G. 407), *ṇaïsŏ tta* = *nadīsrotas* (R. 1, 54); AMg. *naïtalāya*° = *nadītaḍāga*° (Nāyādh. § 128) beside *naïtīra* (Kappas. § 120); but Ś. only *ṇaīvea* = *nadīvega* (Śak. 32, 1), Mg. *śoṇiaṇaīdaṁśaṇa* = *śoṇitanadīdarśana* (Veṇīs. 35, 7); AMg. *itthiveya* = *strīveda* (Sūyag. 234; Vivāhap. 179. 180; Uttar. 960) beside *itthīveya* (Sūyag. 237); *itthibhāva* (Uvās. § 246), *itthilakkhaṇa* = *strīlakṣaṇa* (Nāyādh. § 119), *itthisaṁsagga* = *strīsaṁsarga* (Dasav. 633, 1) beside JŚ. *itthīsaṁsagga* (Kattig. 402, 358), AMg. *itthīvayaṇa* = *strīvacana* (Āyār. 2, 4, 1, 3), *itthīviggaha* = *strīvigraha* (Dasav. 632, 38); JM. *itthī lola* (Āv. 16, 30) beside *itthirayaṇa* = *strīratna* (Erz. 3, 33; 13, 5); but Ś. only *itthīkallavatta* = *strīkalyavarta* (Mṛcch. 60, 19), *itthīradaṇa* = *strīratna* (Śak. 38, 5; 103, 6), *itthījaṇa* (Ratn. 298, 14); AMg. *puḍhavisattha* = *pṛthvīśāstra* (Āyār. 1, 1. 2, 2. 3. 6). *puḍhavikamma*— = *pṛthvīkarman* (Āyār. 1, 1, 2, 2. 4. 6), *puḍhavijīva* (Dasav. 620, 34), *puḍhavisilāpaṭṭaya* = *pṛthvīśilāpaṭṭaka* (Ovav. § 10; Uvās. § 164. 166. 170); JM. *puhavimaṇḍala* (Erz. 41, 24), *puhavivikkhāya* (Erz. 64, 23), beside M. *pahaïvaï* = *pṛthvīpati* (G.); JŚ. *puḍhavītoyāṇā* (Kattig. 401, 346), Ś. *puḍhavīṇādha* = *pṛthvīnātha* (Śak. 59, 12). — AMg. *accharagaṇa* = *apsarāgaṇa* (Paṇhāv. 315; Paṇṇav. 96. 99; Nitayāv. 78; Nāyādh. 562; Ovav. [§ 38] beside *accarākoḍi* (Vivāhap. 254); Ś. only *accharātittha* = *apsarātīrtha*, *accharāsaṁbandha* (Śak. 118, 10; 158, 2), *accharākāmua* = *apsarākāmuka*, *accharāvāvāra* = *apsarāvyāpāra*, *accharāvirahida* (Vikr. 31, 14; 51, 13; 75, 10), *accharājaṇa* (Pārvatīp. 9, 9; 10, 2); AMg. *kiḍḍakara* = *krīḍākara* (Ovav.); M. *jăuṇaaḍa* beside *jauṇāaḍa* (Bh. 4, 1; Hc. 4. 1; Mk. fol. 31) *jăuṇā saṁgaa* (G. 1053); Ś. *jamuṇāsaṁgama* (Vikr. 23, 13); M. *bhicchaara* = *bhikṣācara* (H. 162); AMg. *bhikkhakāla* (Dasav. 618, 17); AMg. *muttajāla*, *muttadāma*, beside *muttājāla* (Ovav.). — M. *vahumāā* = *vadhūmātā* (H. 508); *vahumuha* beside *vahūmuha* = *vadhūmukha* (Bh. 4, 1, Hc. 1, 4; Mk. fol. 31); but JM. *vahūsahijja* = *vadhūsahāya* (Erz. 6, 12); Ś. *ṇavavahūkeṣakalāva* = *navavadhūkeśakalāpa* (Mṛcch. 410), Cf. § 70.

§ 98. The vowel of the word *śrī* is shortened in all the dialects, both when it is employed as a proper noun or is prefixed to another noun as an appellative or as an epitheton ornans; it so happens also in the case of *hrī* in AMg. (Kī. 2, 57). M. *sirithaṇa* = *śrīstana* (G. 28), *sirisevia* = *śrīsevita* (R. 1, 21), *siridaṁsaṇa* = *śrīdarśana* (G. 514); AMg. *sirigutta* = *śrīgupta*, *sirihara* = *śrīdhara* (Kappas.); JM. *sirikantā* = *śrīkāntā*, *sirimaī* = *śrīmatī* (Erz.); Ś. *siripavvada* = *śrīparvata* (Ratn. 297, 31; Mālatīm. 30, 2. 8 [so it is to be read with v. l. to 8 of ed. LASSEN 11, 6; 12, 2; of ed. Calc. 1866, p. 12 3; of ed. Bomb. 1892, p. 18, 11; 19, 6; of ed. Madras 21, 9; 22, 1]). — M. *mahusiripariṇāma* = *madhuśripariṇāma* (G. 791), *ṇahasirikaṇṭha* = *nabhaḥśrikaṇṭha* (H. 75), *rāasiribhāaṇa* = *rājaśrībhājana* (R. 4, 62); AMg. JM. *sirivaccha* = *śrīvatsa* (Ovav.; Kappas.; Erz.); AMg. *sirighara* = *śrīgṛha* (Vivāhap. 820. 962), *hirisiriparivajjiya* (Vivāhap. 250), *hirisiridhiikittiparivajjiya* = *hriśrīdhṛtikīrtiparivarjita* (Uvās. § 95), *sirisamudaya* (Kappas. § 42); JM. *sirisūyaga* = *śrīsūcaka* (Erz. 67, 32), *sirikaya* = *śrīkaca* (Kk. 276, 13;) A. *siriāṇanda* (Hc. 4, 401, 3). — M. *sirijasavamma* = *śrīyaśovarman* (G. 99), *sirihāla* (H. 698), *śirikamalāuha* (G. 798), *sirirāasehara* (Karp. 6, 5); JM. *sirilakkhaṇa* = *śrīlakṣmaṇa*, *sirihariandа* = *śrīharicandra*, *sirirajjila*, *siriṇāhaḍa*, *siribhillua*, *sirikakka*, *sirikakkuya* (KI. 2.3. 4. 5. 6. 20. 22); Ś. *sirikhaṇḍadāsa* (Ratn. 297, 31), *siricārudatta* (Mṛcch. 94, 5; to be read so with GOḌABOLE 267, 5; Mg. *śiliśomeśalaeva* = *śrīsomeśvaradeva* (Lalitav. 566, 6); JM. *sirisamaṇasaṁgha* = *śrīśramaṇasaṅgha* (Kk. 266, 3; 270. 5. 38). — The long vowel is sometimes retained if required by the metre : thus in M. *śirisamullāsa* (G. 856) and so it is also in AMg. in prose *sirisamāṇavesāo* = *śrīsamānaveśyāḥ* (Nāyādh. § 65; Ovav. [§ 38] beside *sirisamāṇavesāo* (Vivāhap. 791). In Kappas. § 35, for *vayaṇasirīpallava* we have to read °*siri*° with the v. l. In *śrika*, the vowel wavers : AMg. *siriya* (Kappas.), *sirīya* Nāyādh.), *sasiriya* (Paṇṇav. 96), but *sasirīya* (Paṇṇav. 116); the mostly found and probably the only correct form in prose *sassiriya* (Samav. 213. 214; Paṇhāv. 263; Vivāhap. 168. 194 f.; Jīv. 502. 504. 506; Nāyādh. 369; Nirayāv.; Ovav.; Kappas.); Ś. *sassiria* (Śak. ed. BÖHTLINGK 62, 13; Vikr. 41, 4; so it is to be read),[1] but *sassiriadā* (Mṛcch. 68, 21; 73, 8. 11; 107, 2), *sassiriattaṇa* (Ratn. 292, 12; text. *sasi*°; ed. Calc. *sassiriadā*). AMg. *hiripaḍicchāyaṇa* = *hripraticchādana* (Āyār. 1, 7, 7, 1); *sirihiri*° (Nirayāv. 73); *hiri*° (Ṭhāṇ. 151). The word that, in AMg., is used as a proper noun too, as in *hiri cceva* = *hrireva*, (Ṭhāṇ. 76), and in the plural *hirīo* (acc. plur. beside *sirīo*; Vivāhap. 962) is not attested in other dialects[2]. This word *hiri* occurs, beside *ahirīmāṇe* (Āyār. 1, 6, 2, 2,), as an adjective; the reading *harime* for *hrīmān* (Uttar. 961) is to be corrected to *hirime*; likewise for Ś. *ohariāmi* (Uttarar. 23. 12) should be read *ohiriāmi* = *apahriye*; so stands Ś. *hiriāmi* (Śak. ed. BÖHTLINGK 108, 21). The Bengal recension (164, 5) has the form *lajjāmi* corresponding to the dialect; whereas the Kashmir recension wrongly has *arihāmi* = *arhāmi*. Cf. § 135. 195.

1. Wrongly BÖHTLINGK on Śak. 62, 13; BOLLENSEN on Vikr. 41, 4. — 2. PISCHEL on Hc. 2, 104.

§ 99. The original short of *i* and *u* is sometimes retained in verses against § 69. M. *diabhūmisu* = *dvijabhūmiṣu* (Hc. 3, 16 = G. 727); *añjalihiṁ*

= *añjalibhiḥ* (H. 678), *°ppaṇaïsu* = *°praṇatiṣu*, *virahisu* = *virahiṣu*, *caüsaṭṭhisu suttisu* = *cauḥsaṣṭyāṁ śuktiṣu* (Karp. 2, 3; 38, 5; 72, 6); AMg. *pakkhihiṁ* = *pakṣibhiḥ* (Uttar. 593), *vagguhiṁ* = *vagnubhiḥ* (Samav. 83), *heuhiṁ* = *hetubhiḥ* (Dasav. 635, 34), *pāṇiṇaṁ* = *prāṇinām* (Āẏār. p.15, 33; Sūẏag. 365; Uttar. 312. 715. 717 ff.), *kukammiṇaṁ* = *kukarmiṇām* (Sūẏag. 341), *pakkhiṇaṁ* = *pakṣiṇām* (Uttar. 601), *tāiṇaṁ* = *trāyiṇām* (Uttar. 692), *girisu* = *giriṣu* (Sūẏag. 310), *jāisu* = *jātiṣu*, *gārisu* = *agāriṣu*, *jantusu* = *jantuṣu*, *joṇisu* = *yoniṣu*, *guttisu* = *guptiṣu* (Uttar. 155. 207. 446. 574. 992); JM. *vakkhāṇāisu* = *vyākhyānādiṣu* (Āv· 41, 28 in a quotation from Viśeṣ. 1, 1466). So throughout AMg. JM. in *caühiṁ*, *caüsu* = *caturbhiḥ*, *caturṣu* (§ 439). On the other hand in verses long vowels of Skt. and Pkt. are not infrequently shortened in declension. So in the abl. sing. AMg. *thāṇao* = *sthānāt*, *saṁjamao* = *saṁyamāt* (Sūẏag. 46), *kulalao* = *kulālāt*, *viggahao* = *vigrahāt* (Dasav. 632, 37. 38), *sirio* = *śriyāḥ* (Dasav. 641. 28); JŚ. *uvasamado* = *upaśamāt* (Kattig. 399, 308). Cf. § 69. In the nom. and acc. plural : M. *divvosahio* = *divyauṣadhāyaḥ* (Mudrār. 60, 9); AMg. *osahio* (Dasav. N. 648, 10), *itthio* = *striyaḥ* (Āẏār. 1, 8, 1, 16; Sūẏag. 218. 222. 237. 540. 542; Uttar. 76, 921, also *itthiu* (Uttar. 373), *nārio* (Uttar. 679 [text *°ī°*] = Dasav. 613, 35; 635, 14), *koḍio* = *koṭayaḥ* (Uttar. 502; text *°ī°*), *rāio* = *rātrayaḥ* (Sūẏag. 100; Uttar. 416. 436)*i*; in the instr. plur.: AMg. *itthihiṁ* = *stribhiḥ* (Uttar. 570); in the gen. plur. : AMg. *isiṇaṁ* = *ṛṣiṇām*, *bhikkhuṇaṁ* = *bhikṣūṇām*, *muṇiṇaṁ* = *munīnām* (Uttar. 375. 377. 409. 921); in the loc. sing. AMg. *rāẏahāṇie* = *rājadhānyām* (Uttar. 86; text *°ī°*, the correct form occurs in the commentary), *kāsibhūmie* = *kāśibhūmyām* (Uttar. 402); in the loc. plur. AMg. *itthisu* = *strīṣu* (Sūẏag. 185 [text *°ī°*); Uttar. 204). So also A. *radie* = *ratyā* (Hc. 4, 446). In Mg. shortening in the stem has taken place in *ahiśālianti* for *ahiśālianti* = *abhisāryamāṇā* (Mṛcch. 11, 19), even in AMg. *paḍiṇaṁ* for *paḍīṇaṁ* = *pratīcīnam* (§ 165; Dasav. 625, 37) against § 82. According to Śrīharṣa, Dvirūpakośa, 152 : *prācinaṁ prācinaṁ ca syāt* the corresponding shortening occurs also in Skt.

§ 100. In A. in verses long and short vowels interchange according to metre and rhyme. The rhyme often determines even the pitch of the vowel. The language of Piṅgala goes furthest in this respect. Hemacandra: *sāmalā dhaṇa suvaṇṇareha* = *śyāmalā dhanyā suvarṇarekhā* (4, 330, 1), *sakaṇṇī bhalli* = *sakarṇā bhalliḥ* (4, 330, 3), *phala lihiā* = *phalāni likhitāni* 4, 335); *paḍia sila* = *patitā śilā* (4, 337), *addhā valaā mahihī gaa addhā phuṭṭa* = *ardhāni valayāni mahyāṁ gatānyardhāni sphuṭitāni* (4, 352); *vihi viṇaḍaü pīḍantu gaha* = *vidhir vinaṭayatu pīḍantu grahāḥ* (4, 385); Kālidāsa, Vikr. : *parahua mahurapalāviṇi kantī.....bhamantī* = *parabhṛte madhurapralāpini kānte* = = *bhramantī* (59, 11. 12), *sā paï diṭṭhī jahaṇabharālasa* = *sā tvayā dṛṣṭā jaghanabharālasā* in rhyme with *gaïlāsa* = *gatilālasam* (62, 12), *kīlanti dhaṇia ṇa diṭṭhi paī* = *krīḍant dhanikā na dṛṣṭā tvayā* (63,5); Piṅgala : *sūi meru ṇisaṅku* = *sūcyate merurniḥśaṅkam* (1, 40), *mahihara taha a suraaṇā* = *mahīdharāstathā ca surajanāḥ* (1, 80), *jasu..... kaṇṭhaṭṭhia visā pindhaṇa disā saṁtāria saṁsārā* = *yasya kaṇṭhe sthitaṁ viṣaṁ pidhānaṁ diśaḥ santāritaḥ saṁsāraḥ* (1, 81), *varisae* for *varisaï* = *varṣati* in rhyme with *disae* = *dṛśyate* (1, 142), *ṇaccanti saṁhāro dūrittā hammāro* = *nṛtyanti saṁharatu duritam asmadīyam* (2, 43) etc. See also § 85. 128.

(e) Single Vowels

§ 101. Skt. *a* may become *i* (Schwā) in syllables before the accent. Hc. 1, 46 puts the words in which this phonetic alteration is obligatory in the ākṛtigaṇa *svapnādi* and in 1, 48 adds also *madhyama* and *katama*, he allows option in 1, 47 for *pakva, aṅgāra, lalāṭa*, in 1, 49 for *saptaparṇa*. Vr. 1, 3; Kī. 1, 2; Mk. fol. 5 restrict this to *īṣat, pakva, svapna, vetasa, vyajana, mṛdaṅga* and *aṅgāra*. It appears most frequently in M. AMg. JM., Ś. and Mg. always retain *a* in certain cases, as Mk. lays this down expressly for *aṅgāra* and *vetasa*. So : AMg. *asiṇa*=*aśaná* (Āyār. 2, 1, 5, 1); JM. *uttima*=*uttama'* (Hc. 1, 46; KI 9), AMg. JM. *uttimaṅga*=*uttamāṅga* (Paṇhāv. 274. 285; Ovav.; Erz.), beside JM. *uttamaṅga* (Pāiyal. 111; Erz.), M. AMg. JM. *uttama* (G.; Nāyādh.; Kappas.; Erz.). — M. *kaïma*=*katamá* (Hc. 1, 48; H. 119), but Ś. Mg. *kadama* (Mṛcch. 39, 6; Śak. 132, 7; Vikr. 35, 13; Mg. Mṛcch. 130, 3). — M. Mg. A. *kiviṇa*=*kṛpaṇá* (Hc. 1, 46; G. H.; Mṛcch. 19, 6; 136, 18. 19; Hc. 4, 419, 1 [so to be read], Ś. *akiviṇa* (Mṛcch. 55, 25). — AMg. *ghiṁsu*=*ghraṁśa* (§ 105). — AMg. JM. JŚ. *carima*=*caramá* (Paṇṇav. 65 ff.; Vivāhap. 113. 173. 598 f. 1254. 1262; Erz.; Kattig. 401, 348), *acarima* (Paṇṇav. 66ff.). — AMg. *nigiṇa*=*nagná* (§ 133). — M. AMg. Ś. *pikka*=*pakvá* (Grr.; H.; Karp. 67, 8; Vivāhap. 1185; Bālar. 292, 13), AMg. *vivikka* =*vipakva* (Ṭhāṇ. 377. 378), Ś. *paripikka* (Bālar. 142, 2; 209, 7); beside AMg. Ś. *pakka* (Hc. 1, 47; Āyār. 2, 4, 2, 14. 15; Ṭhāṇ. 218; Paṇṇav. 483; Dasav. 628, 29; 629, 8; Dhūrtas. 12, 9), Ś. *supakka* (Mṛcch. 79, 25), *paripakka* (Ratn. 301, 19). — M. *pusia*=*pṛṣatá* (gazelle; H. 631), AMg. *phusiya* (§ 208; drop; Āyār. 1, 5, 1, 1, Nāyādh.; Kappas.; gazelle; Āyār. 2, 5, 1, 5). — M. AMg. JM. *majjhima*=*madhyamá* (Hc. 1, 48; H.; Ṭhāṇ. 128. 141. 152. 175; Sūyag. 334; Paṇṇav. 76; Jīv. 175, 408; Vivāhap. 1412; Aṇuog. 266; Uvās.; Ovav.; Kappas.; Erz.), AMg. *majjhimaya*=*madhyamaka* (Uvās.; Kappas.), feminine *majjhimiyā* (Jīv. 905ff.), *majjhimilla* (Aṇuog. 383), but Ś. only *majjhama* (Vikr. 6, 19; Mahāv. 65. 5; 133, 9; Veṇīs. 60, 6; 63, 4; 64, 23; 99, 12). — AMg. JM. *miṁjā*=*majjā'* (§ 74). — AMg. JM. *muiṅga*=*mṛdaṅgá* (Āyār. 2, 11, 1; Sūyag. 731; Paṇhāv. 512; Paṇṇav. 99. 101; Jīv. 251; Vivāhap. 797 [text *muyaṅga*, correctly in the commentary]; Rāyap. 20 [v. l.]. 231; Uvās.; Ovav.; Kappas.; Erz.), also *miiṅga* (Hc. 1, 137), but Ś. *mudaṅga* (Mālav. 19, 1); Mg. *midaṅga* (Mṛcch. 122, 8; Goḍabole, 337, 7 more correctly *mudaṅga*). Cf. § 51. — M. *veḍisa*=*vetasá* (Grr.; H.), but P. *vetasa* (Hc. 4, 307), Ś. *vedasa* (Śak. 31, 16; 105, 9). — M. AMg. JM. *sĕjjā* from *sijjā* (T. 5, 15 and often v. l. § 107)=*śayyā'* (Vr. 1, 5; 3, 17; Hc. 1, 57;2, 24; Kī. 1, 4; 2, 70; Mk. fol. 5. 21, G.; Karp. 25, 1; 39, 3; 70, 6; Āyār. 2, 2, 1, 1. 3, 24 ff.; Sūyag. 97. 771; Paṇhāv. 372. 398. 410. 424; Vivāhap. 135. 185. 839. 1310; Paṇṇav. 844; Uttar. 489. 495; Dasav. 642, 36; Ovav.; Kappas.; Erz.); Mg. *śeyyā* (Cait. 149, 19; text *sĕjjā*); AMg. *nisejjā* (Dasav. 642, 36), *nisijjā* (Kappas. § 120), *paḍisĕjjā* (Vivāhap. 964); JM. *sĕjjāyara* (Kk.), *sijjāyarī* (T. 4, 17).[1]

1. Pischel, KZ. 34, 570. According to Jacobi, KZ. 35, 572, *kaïm* probably received its *i* through its contamination with *kati*; *antima* (as it is also in Sanskrit), *uttima, carima* and *majjhima* have developed their *i* through the influence of analogy with *paścima* and *sijjā, ṇisijjā, sāhijjā, miṁjā*, under the influence of *jja*.

§ 102. Exceptions to the rule are just apparent : M. *aṅgāra* (Hc. 1, 47; Pāiyal. 158), *aṅgāraa* (H. 261), *aṅgārāanta-* = *aṅgārāyamāṇa* (G. 136), Ś. Mg. *aṅgāla* (Pras. 120, 2. 13; 121. 8; Jīvān. 43, 9 [probably to be read as °*ra*°] ; Mṛcch. 10, 1), Ś. *aṅgāraka* (Mālav. 48, 18), AMg. *aṅgāra* (Paṇhāv. 202. 534), *aṅgāraka* = (Paṇhāv. 313; Ovav. § 36), *aṅgāraga* (Paṇṇav. § 116), *aṅgāraya* (Ṭhāṇ. 263) = Skt. *áṅgāra, aṅgāraka* (charcoal; the planet Mars), beside AMg. *iṅgāla* (Grr., also C. 2, 4; Pāiyal. 158; Āyār. 2, 2, 2, 8; 2, 10, 17; Sūyag. 270, 783; Ṭhāṇ. 230. 391. 478; Paṇṇav. 28; Vivāgas. 108, 141; Nāyādh. 371; Vivāhap. 237. 254. 322 f. 348. 480. 609. 883. 1286. 1293; Jīv. 51. 257. 293. Nirayāv. 47; Uttar. 1053 [text °*ra*]; Dasav. 616, 32; 618, 29; 630, 25; Uvās. § 51), *saïṅgāla, viiṅgāla* (Vivāhap. 450. 451), *iṅgālaga* (Ṭhāṇ. 82), also taken into Sanskrit (ZACHARIAE, GGA. 1894, 820), *aṅgua* beside *iṅgua* = *iṅguda* (Hc. 1, 89), Ś. *iṅgudī* (Śak. 39, 4), *aṅgālia* beside *iṅgāli* (a piece of sugar-cane; Deśīn. 1, 28. 79) are related to one another like *aṅgati* and *iṅgati, aṭati* and *iṭánt, addhá* and *addhá*, that originally stood in an ablaut relation with one another probably. From *īṣát* the Prākṛtamañjarī, in PISCHEL, De gr. Pr. p. 13, mentions *īsa, īsi, isi.* Of these we have Ś. *īsa* in Mālatīm. 239, 3 in all the editions : *īsa maṇṇuṁ* (v. l. *maṇṇe*) *ujjhia*, and so we have to read also in Veṇīs. 12, 10; 61, 15 *īsa vihasia* with the v. l. to 12, 10 and in M. *cirehi īsa tti* (Pratāp. 206, 11; text *īsi*), *pāvaï īsisa* (H. 444; correctly in the v. l. and ed. Bomb.; or *isaṁpi* with v. l.); correct is *īsīsa*........... *maṇaṁ kuṇanti* (Karp. 8, 9; cf. v. l.), because *īṣat* here stands by itself. Elsewhere it occurs throughout in the beginning of compounds; thus in M. *īsijalapesiaccha* = *īṣajjalaprekṣitākṣa* *īsiraabhiṇṇa* = *īṣadrajobhinna*, *īsiṇiha* = *īṣannibha*, *īsiviatta* = *īṣadvivṛtta* (R. 2, 39; 11, 43; 12, 48; 13, 70), *īsidiṭṭha* = *īṣaddṛṣṭa* (Bālar. 120, 5), *īsasaṁcaraṇacañcura* (Karp. 86, 1; the v. l. has *īsaṁ*, the ed. Bomb. 85, 10 reads *īsa saṁcaraṇabandhurā*), *īsubbhijjanta* [text *īsubbhiṇṇandaṁ*] = *īṣadudbhidyamāna* (Mallikām. 239, 5); JM., *īṣtviāsaṁ* = *īsadvikāsam* (KI. 7); Ś. *īsiparissantā* = *īṣatpariśrāntā* (Śak. 133, 1), *īsiviasida* = *īṣadvikasita* (Mālatīm. 121, 5), *īsimaülida* = *īṣanmukulita, īsimasiṇa* = *īṣanmasṛṇa* (Mahāv. 22, 20; 24, 6), *īsivirala* (Uttarar. 73, 5), *īsivalida* (Nāgān. 8, 15), *īsadāradesadāvida* = *īṣaddvāradeśadāpita* (Mudrār. 43, 8), *īsiṇiddāmuddida* = *īṣannidrāmudrita* (Bālar. 220,6) ; *īsitiricchi* (text °*ra*°) = *īṣattiryak, īsisvṇijjanta* = *īṣacchrūyamāṇa, īsicaüria* = *īsaccaturita* (?), *īsimaülanta-* [text °*mmu*°] = *īṣanmukulāyamāna*, etc. (Mallikām. 74, 2; 123, 5; 141, 8, 225, 8); also *īsīsi* in M. *īsīsivalanta-* (H. 370) and Ś. *īsīsijaraḍhāamāṇa* (Karp. 38, 1); falsely independent in Ś. *īsīsi veaṇā samuppaṇṇā* (Karp. 73, 6), which has been correctly emended as *īsīsa* by Konow. The *ī* is, therefore, explained from the cases in which *īṣat*, as the first member of a compound, became accentless according to Pāṇini 6, 2, 54. Cf. Hc. 2, 129. The Prākṛtamañjarī l. c. teaches also *isi*, which occurs often in MSS. Bh. 1, 3; Mk. fol. '5, and several times also in Indian editions : *isisicumbia* occurs in Śak. 4, 9 ed. BÖHTLINGK. Ś. *īsasaṁkamida* (Jīvān. 43, 8) for *īsi*°, *īsi samīve hohi* = *īṣat sāmīpe bhava, īsi vilambia* = *īṣadvilambya, īsi uttāṇaṁ kadua* = *īṣad uttānaṁ kṛtvā* (Mallikām. 87, 18; 124, 5; 222, 8) for *īsa*°, and JM. *īsi hasiūṇa* (Erz. 57, 17) for *īsiṁ hasiūṇa* are false readings, as AMg. JM. have the nasalized form *īsiṁ* always used in independent words and generally in compound words (Ṭhāṇ. 135, 297, Āẏār. 2, 15, 20 [*isi*°]. 21 [*isi*°]. 22 [*isi*°]; Paṇṇav. 846; Nāẏādh. 1284; Vivāhap. 239. 248. 920 [*isi-*], Jīv. 444. 501. 794. 860; Ovav. § 33. 49, VII [so read everywhere for *isi*;] Kappas. § 15; Āv. 48, 14; Erz.). AMg. has also an adjective *isiya* = **iṣatka* (Nāẏādh. 990).

§ 103. Corresponding to the rule *i* occurs in forms like JŚ. A. *kidha* (Pav. 384, 47; 388, 2.5; Hc. 4, 401, 1), AMg. JM. A. *kiha* (Āẏār. 1, 6, 1; 6; Āv. 10, 23; 35, 18; 46, 31; Erz.; Hc. 4, 401, 3) = Vedic *kathā'*. On its analogy are formed A. *jidha, tidha, jiha, tiha* = *yáthā, táthā* (Hc. 4, 401), as reversely the short of the final of *ā* has been brought in on the analogy of M. AMg. JM. A. *jaha, taha*, JŚ. *jadha, tadha* (§ 113). In a similar manner are to be explained also AMg. JM. *tise, jise*, M. *tissā, jissā* = *tasyāḥ, yasyāḥ* as formed on the analogy of *kise, kissā* (§ 425 ff.)[1].—*ghisaï* (Vr. 8, 28 [read as such]; Hc. 4, 204) = *ghásti* = *ghásati* has been taken over to the sixth conjugation (§ 482). — M. A. *candimā* (brilliance of the moon; Vr. 2, 6; Hc. 1, 185; Kī. 2, 25; Mk. fol. 14; Pāiẏal. 244; G. H. 609 [read as such], R.; Hc. 4, 349) is to be identified neither with the native grammarians with *candrikā*, nor with LASSEN[2], E. KUHN[3], S. GOLDSCHMIDT[4] and JACOBI[5] with *candrámas* against which are the accent, gender and meaning, but with **candriman*[6] which according to Hc. 1, 35, might become feminine, and has been taken over into Skt. as *candrimā* (B. -R. s. v.). Pāli *candimā* (nom. sing.), AMg. *candima-* (Niraẏāv. 38; Ovav.; Kappas.), AMg. A. nomin *candimā* (Sūẏag. 433 (text °*da*°). 460; Dasav. 627, 11; Piṅgala 1, 30 [text -*da-*]) are masculine and mean "the moon', and are secondary derivatives from *candimā* (fem.) with dependence upon *candramas*. *candrikā* becomes Ś. *candiā* (Cait. 40, 15; Adbhutad. 71, 9). — According to Hc. 1, 49. 265; Mk. fol. 18 besides *chattavaṇṇa* we may say *chattivaṇṇa* (Vr. 2, 41; Kī. 2, 46). The Indian grammarians equate these words as = *saptaparṇa*, which is to be accented as *saptáparṇa*. But *saptán* nowhere shows *ch* initially and the *a* originating from *an* never becomes *i*, as we learn from *pañcama, sattama, aṭṭhama, ṇavama, dasama*, etc. (§ 449)[7]. *chattavaṇṇa*, therefore, is *not* = *saptaparṇa*, but = *chattraparṇa*, and *chattivaṇṇa* = **chatriparṇa* from *chattri* (Hc., Uṇādigaṇas, 446) = *chattra*. In AMg. the word occurs as *sattavaṇṇa* (Paṇṇav. 31; Nāẏādh. 916; Vivāhap. 41. 1530; Ovav. § 6) and *sattivaṇṇa* (Ṭhāṇ. 266 [commentary *satta*°]. 555; Vivāhap. 289), which, if the reading be correct, is formed on the analogy of *chattivaṇṇa*; Ś. has *chattavaṇṇa* (Śak. 18, 5; cf. v. l.) and *sattavaṇṇa* (Priyad. 10, 13). — AMg. JM. *puvviṁ* [e.g. Āẏār. 1, 2, 1, 2. 3. 4; Sūẏag. 202. 203 [text here °*aṁ*°]; Dasav. 641, 4; Nāẏādh.; Uvās.; Ovav.; Kappas.; Erz.) is not = *pū́rvam*, but = **pūrvī'm*; cf. AMg. *puvvāṇupuvviṁ* (Nirayāv. § 1), which has already been shown by WARREN as = *pūrva* + *ānupūrvim*. — AMg. JM. *saddhiṁ* (e.g. Āẏār. 1, 2, 1, 2. 3. 4; Nāẏādh.; Uvās.; Ovav. § 15. 16; Kappas. etc.; Erz.) is not = *sārdhám*, but = Vedic *sadhrī́m*.[8] We cannot determine the accent in *avaiaṁsa, avataṁsaka*, which in AMg. become *vaḍiṁsa* (Rāẏap. 102), *vaḍiṁsaga* (Samav. 10. 12. 16. 23; Rāẏap. 103. 139; Vivāhap. 41; Uvās.; Ovav.; Kappas.), and *vaḍiṁsaẏa* (Uvās.; Nāẏādh.; Kappas.); *i* and the dropping of the initial *a* point to an accent on the final syllable (§ 142). The exceptions to the rule are AMg. *kuṇima* = *kúṇapa* and *viḍima* = *viṭa'pa* (§ 248) only which presuppose accentuation on the final. On M. AMg. JM. Ś. *ṇiḍāla*, M. AMg. *ṇilāḍa* = *lalāṭa* see § 260; on AMg. *āikkhaï*, § 492, on *diṇṇa* § 566, and on AMg. JM. *appiṇaï* § 557.

1. Franke opines differently with regard to the genitive forms like *tissā*, GN. 1895, 529, note 1. — 2. Inst. p. 203. — 3. Beiträge p. 22. — 4. Rāvaṇavaho p. 156, note 1. — 5. Kalpasūtra. s. v. KZ. 35, 573. — 6. Pischel KZ. 34, 572. — 7. Jacobi has not taken these into consideration, KZ. 35, 572. — 8. Pischel, Ved. Stud. 2, 235.

§ 104. Before and after a labial sometimes *a* becomes *u*: *puḍhama*, *paḍhuma*, *puḍhuma* = *prathama* (C. 3, 9 p. 48; Hc. 1, 55). The common form found in all the dialects is *paḍhama*. So M. (G. H. R.); AMg. (Āyār. 2, 2, 3, 18; 2, 5, 1, 6; Sūyag. 45; Uvās.; Nāyādh.; Kappas.; Nirayāv. etc.); JM. (Kl. 1; Erz. ; Kk.); JŚ. (Kattig. 398, 304; 400. 332; 401. 332, 344); Ś. (Mṛcch. 68, 23; 94, 3; 138, 15; Śak. 43, 6; 50, 1; 67. 11; Vikr. 22, 20; 27, 13); Mg. (Mṛcch. 130, 13. 18; 139, 10; 153, 21); D. (Mṛcch. 102, 19); A. (Piṅgala 1, 1. 10. 23. 40 etc.). *puḍhama* stands in M. (H. 832), in Ś. (Mudrār. 182, 3; 204, 4. 6), in Mg. (Mudrār. 185, 4); but the best and most of the MSS of Mudrār. have *paḍhama*, as in 253, 4 in the text (v. l. *pu*°). S. Goldschmidt has *paḍhuma* several times in R.; likewise Bollensen in Vikr. 23, 19; 24, 1; 83, 19. In this respect as well the manuscripts waver, and so is the case with other texts, and it would, perhaps, be better to read *paḍhama*, everywhere in M.Ś. Mg.[1] P. has *pudhuma* (Hc. 4, 316). The South Indian manuscripts and the printed editions based on them generally write *puḍama*.[2] — M. *pulaaï*, *pulaei*, *pulaïa* (Vr. 8, 69; Hc. 4, 181; Pāiyal. 78; H. R.), M. *puloei*, *puloia* beside *paloei*, *paloia* (Hc. 4, 181; H. R.; Pras. 113, 19); Ś. *puloedi*, *puloanta*, *puloida*, and so on and so forth (Mahāv. 99, 3; 100, 10; Bālar. 76, 1; Vṛṣabh. 14, 9; 15, 1; 17, 1; 22, 9; 24, 2; 42, 10; 48, 10; 55, 3; 57. 1; 59, 17; Pras. 11, 14; 12, 1; 13, 14; 16, 17; 35, 7; 41, 3; 115, 17 [here they often write *pulovedi* and so forth]) = *pralokayati*. — A. Mg. *pāuraṇa* (Hc. 1, 175; Triv. 1, 3, 105; Āyār. 2, 5, 1, 5; Paṇhāv. 534; Uttar. 489) = Pāli *pāvuraṇa*, *pāpuraṇa* = *prāvaraṇa*; AMg. *kaṇṇapāuraṇā* = *karṇaprāvaraṇāḥ* (Paṇṇav. 56; Ṭhāṇ. 260; *pāuraṇī* (coat of mail; Deśīn. 6, 43) = **prāvaraṇī*.[3] — M. *uppei*, *uppia* (Hc. 1, 269; G. s. v. *ṛ*; Karp. 48, 4) = *arpayati*, *arpita* beside *appei*, *appia*, *ŏppei*, *ŏppia* (§ 125; Hc. 1, 63). — AMg. *ummuggā* = **unmagnā* (rising above the surface; Āyār. p. 15, 32; 27, 9), beside *ummaggā* (Uttar. 235), *omugganimuggiya* (Āyār. 2, 3, 2, 5, read so with the v. l.) = **avamagnanimagnita*. — AMg. *kammuṇā*, *kammuṇāu*, *kammuṇo*, *kammuṇaṁ*, *dhammuṇā*, JM. *kammuṇā* = *karmaṇā*, *karmaṇaḥ*, *karmaṇām*, *dharmaṇā* (§ 404). — AMg. JM. *paṇuvisaṁ*, *paṇuvisā* = *pañcaviṁśati* (§ 273). — M. AMg. *vŏcchaṁ* from **vucchaṁ* (§ 125) = *vakṣyāmi*, M. AMg. JM. *vŏttuṁ* from **vuttuṁ* = *vaktum* (§ 529. 574). — A. *vuñaï* = Mg. *vaññadi* = **vrajñāti* from *vraj* (§ 488). — *vŏjjhaa*, *vŏjjhaamalla* for *vu*° (§ 125; burden; Deśīn. 7, 80) is traceable to AMg. *vŏhjja* = *vahya* (§ 572). — AMg. *susāṇa* from **śmuśāna* = *śmaśāna* (Hc. 2, 86; Āyār. 2, 2, 2, 8; Paṇhāv. 177. 419; Uttar. 1006; Ovav.; Kappas.; Āv. 31, 24); but M. Ś. *masāṇa* (Vr. 3, 6; C. 3, 23; Hc. 2, 86, Kī. 2, 53; Mk. fol. 21; Pāiyal. 158; G. H.; Karp. 101, 7; Mṛcch. 72, 8; 155, 4; Mālatīm. 30, 4; 224, 3; Anarghar. 279, 10; Caṇḍak. 86, 7; 92, 11); Mg. *maśāṇa* (Mṛcch. 168, 18; Mudrār. 267, 2; Caṇḍak. 61, 11; 63, 11; 64, 9; [°*ṇaa*]; 66, 13; 71, 9. 11). On M. JM. AMg. *muṇaï*, JŚ. *muṇadi* see § 489 on. A. *jhuṇi*, Ś. *dhuṇi* = *dhvani*, § 299. Cf. also § 337.

1. Pischel on Hc. 1, 55. — 2. Pischel, Die Recensionen der Śakuntalā p. 13; e. g. Vikramorvaśiya, ed. Pischel 629, 26; 630, 18. 20; 633, 18; Pārvatip. 28, 22 ed. Glaser; Mallikām. which, beside *puḍhama* (152, 18), has also *paḍama* (56, 11). On the variation between *pa* and *pu*°, in MSS in Ś. cf. the v. l. e. g. also on Mālav. 39, 5. 6. 7. — 3. Pischel, BB. 3, 247.

§ 105. Dialectically several nouns in *-a* have become *u-* stems. This takes place especially in compounds with *-jña*, *-jñaka* in M. AMg. JM. JŚ. when *jña* becomes *ṇṇa*, in AMg. also *nna* (Hc. 1, 56; Mk. fol. 20). Thus : M. *akaaṇṇua* = *akṛtajñaka* (H. R.), *aṇṇua* = *ajñaka* (H.); *ahiṇṇu-abhijña* (Hc. 1, 56), but Ś. *aṇahiṇṇa* (Śak. 106, 6; Mudrār. 59, 1 [*bhi*°]); *āgamaṇṇa* = *āgamajña* (Hc. 1, 56); M. *guṇaṇṇua* = *guṇajñaka* (G.), *guṇaaṇṇua* (H.), but Ś. *guṇaṇṇa* (Kāleyak. 25, 22); AMg. *dosannu* = *doṣajña* (Dasav. 627, 36); AMg. *paḍirūvaṇṇu* = *pratirūpajña* (Uttar. 694), *parakkamaṇṇu* = *parākramajña* (Sūẏag. 576. 578); AMg. *vinnu* (Āẏār. 2, 16, 1.2; Sūẏag. 26), M. *viṇṇua* (Mk. fol. 20) = *vijña*, *vijñaka*; AMg. *vihinnu* = *vidhijña* (Nāẏādh. § 18); M. AMg. JM. JŚ. *savvaṇṇu* = *sarvajña* (Hc. 1, 56; Vajjāl. 324; 9; Āẏār. 2, 15, 26; Vivāhap.. 916; Aṇuog. 95. 518; Uttar. 689; Dasav. N. 655, 8; Ovav.; Kappas.; Dvār. 495, 9; 497, 38; Erz.; Pav. 381. 16; Kattig. 398, 302, 303 [text *savvaṇhu*]), but Mg. *śavvañña* (Hc. 4, 293). P. *savvañña* (Hc. 4, 303). Cf. § 276. The following also have become *u-* stems : AMg. *ghiṁsu* = *ghraṁsá* (§ 101; Sūẏag. 249; Uttar. 58, 109); AMg. *pāṇu* = *prāṇá*, when it means a unit of time[1] (Vivāhap. 423; Aṇuog. 431. 432; Ovav.; Kappas.), *āṇāpāṇu* (Ṭhāṇ. 173; Aṇuog. 242; Dasav. N. 654, 2; Ovav.); AMg. *pilaṁkhu*, *pilakkhu* = *plakṣá* (§ 74); AMg. *manthu* = *manthá* (Āẏār. 1, 8, 4, 4; 2, 1, 8, 7; Uttar. 249; Dasav. 622, 8; 623, 10); AMg. *milakkhu* = *mlecchá* (Āẏār. 2, 3, 1, 8; Sūẏag. 56. 57. 817 [cf. 816 *milukkhaẏa*]. 928; Paṇṇav. 58; Paṇhāv. 41 [text °*lu*°; cf. Weber, Verzeichniss 2, 2, 510]) = Pāli *milakkhu* (§ 233) beside *milíccha*, AMg. JM. Ś. A. *mĕccha*, AMg. *miccha* (§ 84). Cf. *pāvāsu*, *pavāsu* § 118. All these words are accented at the end and undoubtedly the colouring of the vowel is associated therewith. The base *āryā'*, in the meaning "mother-in-law", also becomes an *u-stem*, = *ajjū* (Hc. 1, 77) and *āryakā*, in the meaning "mistress", Ś. *ajjuā* (Mṛcch. 27, 2 ff.; 28, 2 ff.; 29, 1 ff.; 36, 4; 37, 3ff. etc.), Mg. *ayyuā* (Mṛcch. 10, 2; 39, 20. 24. 25; 40, 4, 10), *ayyukā* (Mṛcch. 13, 8). In Mg. *ayyuā* means "mother" also (Śak. 158, 11, where Śaṅkara, following Candraśekhara, remarks : *ajjukāśabdo mātari deśiyaḥ*). On AMg. *āhu*, *udāhu*, *addakkhu*, *niṇṇakkhu* etc. in the sense of the third person singular see § 516.

1. Leumann, Aup. S. s, v., *pāṇu*, and especially Aṇuog. 431.

§ 106. A final *a* becomes *u* in A. in the genitive singular of nouns in *-a*, and of similarly formed pronominal forms of the pronouns of the first and second persons, in the second person singular of the imperative, the second person plural of the indicative and the imperative and in some adverbs : *suaṇassu* = *sujanasya*, *piassu* = *priyasya*, *khandhassu* = *skandhasya*, *kan-*

tassu = *kāntasya* (Hc. 4, 338. 354. 445. 3), *tassu, tāsu, tasu, jāsu, jasu, kassu, kāsu, kasu* = *tasya, yasya, kasya* (§ 425. 427. 428); *parassu* = *parasya* (Hc. 4,338. 354); *mahu, majjhu* in the sense of *mama*; *taü* for **tavu* = *tava, tuhu* [so it is to be read], *tujjhu* in the sense of *tava* (Hc. s. v. *ma-, tu*); *piu* = *piba* (Hc. 4, 338 1], *piahu* = *pibata* (Hc. 4, 422, 20); *bhaṇu* = *bhaṇa* (Hc. 4, 401, 4; Piṅgala 1, 120; and read so everywhere for *bhaṇa*); *sikkhu* = *śikṣa* (Hc. 4, 404); *icchahu* = *icchatha, pucchahu* = *pṛcchatha* (Hc. 4, 384. 422, 9), *kuṇehu* = *kṛṇuta* = *kuruta* (Piṅgala 1,89. 118), *dehu* = *dayata* (Hc. 4, 384; Piṅgala 1, 10), *jāṇehu* = *jānita* (Piṅgala 1, 5, 14. 38), *vivāṇehu* = *vijānita* (Piṅgala 1, 25. 50); *ṇamahu* = *namata* (Hc. 4, 440); *ĕtthu, jĕtthu, tĕtthu* in the sense of *atra, yatra, tatra*, (§ 107; Hc. s. v.; Piṅgala 1, 114); *jattu, tattu* = *yatra, tatra* (Hc. 4, 404); *ajju* = *adya* (Hc. 4, 343, 2. 418. 7 and read so everywhere for *ajja*).

§ 107. Only apparently *e* has sometimes taken the place of *a*. The extremely frequent *ĕttha* of M. AMg. JM. Ś. Mg. PG. (5, 7), D. (Mṛcch. 102, 18; 103, 16; 105, 15), Ā. (Mṛcch. 102, 25; 103, 4), A. *ĕtthu* (§ 106) neither go back to *atra* (Hc. 1, 57)[2] nor to **itra*[2] or **etra*[3], but they relate to *iha*, like *taṭtha* to *taha, jattha* to *jaha, kattha* to *kaha* : so stands for **ittha* = Vedic. *ithā'*[4] Cf. A. *ithi* (GOLDSCHMIDT *ethi*), *ithi* (GOLDSCHMIDT *itthi* = *atra* Piṅgala 1, 5[a]86), and AMg. JM. A. *kiha*, JŚ. A. *kidha* = *kathā'* (§ 103). A. *kĕtthu*, beside *kidha, kiha* = *kathā*, has its consonant doubled according to § 194; for the rest, the pronouns have mutually influenced one another even here both in inlaut as well as in auslaut (cf. § 103). — M. *ukkera* (gift, heap; Bh. 1, 5; Hc. 1, 58; Kī. 1, 4; Mk. fol. 5; Deśīn. 1, 96; Pāiyal. 18. G.; Karp. 69, 6; Viddhaś. 11, 6), that occurs also in Ś. (Bālar. 129, 6. 7, 167, 10; 210, 2), against *ukkara* (Caṇḍak. 16, 17), and is found in M. and AMg. also (G.; Nāyādh. Kappas.) is not = *utkara*[5], but must be equated, with LASSEN[6] either as = **utkarya*, or be connected with *utkirati*. In Bālar. 234, 9 the word *vaïera* = *vyatikara* is wrongly printed : the correct form is *vadiara*(Śak. 13, 2) .— M. Ś. *gĕndua* (Viddhaś. 56, 2; 58; 6; Mallikām. 134, 21. 23 (text *gā°*), A. *gindu* (Piṅgala 1, 125) cannot with Hc. 1, 57. 182 be traced back to *kanduka* that forms M. Ś. *kandua* (G. 752; Mālav. 68, 10), but belongs with *gĕṇḍuī* (game : Deśīn. 2, 94), Pāli *geṇḍuka*, as well as *genduka, ginduka, gĕṇḍu, geṇḍuka gĕṇḍūka* that have forced their way into Sanskrit, but to the now extinct root **gid*, **giḍ*, present **giṇḍaï, gĕṇḍaï* "to play". Cf. *jhĕṇḍua* "ball" (Deśīn. 3, 59). — *ghe ppaï* stands for **ghippat* and does not go back to *grabh*, but to **ghṛp* (§ 212. 518). *dhêṁkuṇa* (bug : Desīn. 4, 14; Triv. 1, 3, 105, 60) beside *ḍhaṁkuṇa* (Deśīn. 4, 14) stands for AMg. *ḍhiṁkuṇa* (Jīv. 356; Uttar. 1064 (text *°ka°*)), as Skt. *diṅka* also makes probable, and is = **daṁkhuṇa*, and can be traced back to **daṁkhá'*, connected to *daṁś* (§ 212. 267)[7]. — M. *velli* (Creeper : Bh. 1, 5; Hc. 1, 58, Mk. fol. 5; G. H.) is not = *valli*, but stands for **villi*. With *vĕllā* (creeper), *vĕlla* (hair; a small lock, amusement-: Deśīn. 7, 94), *vili* (wave; Deśīn. 7, 73; Triv. 1, 3, 105, 80), *vĕllarī* (courtesan; Deśīn. 7, 96), M. Ś. *vĕllira*, (automatically moving : G. 137; Viddhaś.55, 8. [text *cĕ°*]; Bālar. 203, 13), A. *uvvĕllira* (Vikr. 56, 6), M. Ś. *uvvĕlla* = **udvilna* (§ 566; G. R.; Karp. 37, 5; Mālatīm. 201, 1; 258, 2; Mahāv. 29, 19) go back to a root, **vil* (to be moved), to which *velu* = *veṇu* (§ 243) also has to be referred.[8] M. A. *vĕllaï* with its composita *uvvĕllaï, ṇivvĕllaï, saṁvĕllaï* (G. H. R.; Pratāp. 119, 11; Bālar. 180, 7; 182, 2; Vikr. 67. 19), Ś. *vĕllamāṇa* (Bālar. 168. 3), *uvvĕllida* (Ratn. 302, 31), *uvvĕllanta-* (Mālatīm. 76, 3; 125, 4; 129, 2), which is frequent also in later day Sanskrit, is either a denominativum from *vĕlla* = **vilna*, or derived from **vilyati* **vilvati*. — *sĕjjā* = *śayyā* is regularly derived from *sijjā* (§ 101). — M. *suhĕllī* (Pāiẏal. 159; Deśīn. 8, 36; H.) is to be explained from **suhillī* = *sukha*+suffix *-illa*, while its synonym *suhallī* (Deśīn. 8, 36) goes back to *sukha*+suffix *alla* (§ 595)[9]. — AMg. JM. *hĕṭṭhā* = *adhástāt* (Samav. 101; Ovav. § 10. 152; Erz.) presupposes **adheṣṭāt*, corresponding to *purĕkkhaḍa* = **pureṣkṛta*, which has already been compared by WEBER.[10] It is only in this manner that we can explain the cerebralization. The word, which occurs in Pāli too, cannot be separated from *adhastāt*: therefore, the assumption of one **adheṣṭha*[11] is wrong : On AMg. *ahe* = *adhaḥ*, *pure* = *puraḥ* see § 345. From *hĕṭṭhā* is derived in AMg. JM. an adjective *hĕṭṭha*, wherefrom we have AMg. *hĕṭṭhaṁ* (Hc. 2, 141; Ṭhāṇ. 179. 492; text *heṭṭhiṁ*), JM. *hĕṭṭheṇa* (Erz.) AMg. JM. *hĕṭṭhao* (Vivāgas. 143; Erz.) = Pāli *hĕṭṭhato*, M. *hĕṭṭhammi* (H. 365); JM. *hĕṭṭhaẏammi* (Erz.), *hĕṭṭhaṭṭhia* (Hc. 4, 448), also *hiṭṭha* (Deśīn. ī8, 67, *hiṭṭhaṁ* (Ṭhāṇ. 179; text *-iṁ*) written with *i*, according to § 84; and from it, as in Pāli, a superlative AMg. *hĕṭṭhima* (Ṭhāṇ. 197; Samav. 66, 68. 72; Vivāhap. 524. 529. 1412; Aṇuog. 266), *heṭṭhimaya* (Vivāhap. 82), *hiṭṭhima* (Paṇṇav. 76; Ṭhāṇ. 197 [6><beside 1><*hĕ°*]; Uttar. 1086), and a very frequent adjective AMg. *hĕṭṭhilla* (Ṭhāṇ. 341. 545; Samav. 136 ff.; Paṇṇav. 478; Nāẏādh. 867; Vivāhap. 128. 347. 392 ff. 437. 1101. 1240. 133 1 ff. 1777; Aṇuog. 427 ff.; Jīv. 240 ff. 710; Ovav.). Cf. § 308. — A. *hĕlli* (O female friend ! Hc. 4, 379, 1, 422, 13) beside JM. *halí*, A. *hali*, M. Ś. *halā* (§ 375) goes back to **hillī* = **hali*' with doubling of the *la* according to § 194.

1. So also CHILDERS, s. v.; S. GOLDSCHMIDT, Prākṛtica p. 6. — 2. LASSEN, Inst. p. 129; JOHANSSON, Shāhbāzgarhi 1, 133 ff. — 3. FAUSBÖLL, Dhammapada p. 350. — 4. PISCHEL, Ved. Stud. 2, 88. —5 . BÜHLER, Pāiẏal. s. v. — 6. Inst. p. 118. — 7. PISCHEL, BB. 3, 255 f. — 8. PISCHEL, BB. 3, 263ff. Cf. JOHANSSON, IF. 3, 249f. — 9. Impossible is the derivation from *sukhakeli*, which according to the translation of the scholiasts is approved of by WEBER, Hāla[1] p. 40; 2 s. v. — 10. Bhag. 1, 404; Cf. E. KUHN, Beiträge p. 21. — 11. JOHANSSON, IF. 3, 218. As Pāli has also *pure, purĕkkhāra, sve, suve* etc. (KUHN p. 58), it is unnecessary to hypothesize the existence of a "Proto-Pāli *e*."

§ 108. Sometimes *ā* becomes *i* (Schwā) in the post-tonic syllable. This especially takes place in the plur. of pronouns and in the first person plur. of the pres. indic. of paraśmaipada in M. AMg. JM. JŚ. A. Thus : AMg. JM. *tesiṁ* = *téṣām*, *tāsiṁ* = *tāsām*, *eesiṁ* = *etéṣām*, *eẏāsiṁ* = *etāsām*, *jesiṁ* = *yéṣām*, *jāsiṁ* = *yāsām*, *kesiṁ*, = *kéṣām*, *imesiṁ*, *imāsiṁ* from the stem *imá*, *aṇṇesiṁ* = *anyéṣām*, *aṇṇāsiṁ* = *anyāsām*. Their analogy is followed by the rest of pronouns, as the very rare M. *seiṁ* = *eṣā́m*, *paresiṁ* = *páreṣām*, *savvesiṁ* = *sárveṣām* (§ 425 ff.).[1] — M. *jampimo* = *jálpāmaḥ*; M. AMg. *ṇamimo*, *námāmaḥ*; M. JM. *bhaṇimo- bháṇāmaḥ*; M. JM. *vandimo* = *vándāmahe*; A. *lahimu* = *lábhāmahe* etc. Their analogy is followed in *pucchimo* = *pṛcchā́maḥ*, *lihimo* = *likhā́maḥ*; *suṇimo* = **śruṇā́maḥ*, and so forth (§ 455).[2] This sort of transformation rarely occurs also in the first pers. sing. of the ind. pres. in M., and of the ind. pres. and fut. in A. (§ 454.520). The grammarians teach forms also in *-ami, -ama, -ima, -amo, -amu*, of which those in *-ami* are found in JM. A. § 454). M. JM. AMg. *sāhijja, sāhĕjja = sắhāyya* (Pāiẏal. 215; G. 1116; Vivāhap. 502; Erz.)[3] correspond to the rule.

1. PISCHEL, KZ. 34. 570f. — JACOBI, KZ. 35, 574, who wrongly assumes that I had given only three examples, whereas I have there five, and overlooks the genit. plur. forms of the pronouns *ta-, eta-, ya-, ka-, ima-* only are frequently used, and those of the other pronouns more rarely. He offers no explanation of his own of *i*. — 2. JACOBI, KZ. 35, 574 f. appears to think that the examples cited by me, KZ. 34. 571, are all that are available. He arrives at a quite wrong decision with regard to *gamimo, jāṇimo*. Cf. § 455. According to him. *-ima* may have been borrowed from an Apabhraṁśa dialect, in which till now *-imo* has not been found at all. — 3. According to JACOBI, KZ. 35, 573, 575, here it would be *jja*, as in *sijjā, nisijjā, miñjā*, the origin of *i*. It is the old view that was represented for example, by WEBER, Hāla[1] p. 38, who assumes the influence of *ya*. But *jja* has not influenced in the least the preceding vowel; cf. §§ 280. 284. 287.

§ 109. Even in the syllable preceding the accented one *ā*, like *a* (§ 101), sometimes becomes *i* : it takes place, evidently after it is at first changed into *a*. So according to Hc. 1, 81, °*mātrá* may become °*matta* or °*mĕtta*, from °*mitta*, thus for example AMg. *vihatthimitta = vitastimātra* (Sūẏag. 280), *itthāmitta = itthāmātra* (Śūẏag. 339), *vinnāẏapariṇaẏamitta = vijñātapariṇayamātra* (Nāẏādh. § 27—Kappas. § 10. 52. 80), *sāẏaṇamitta = svādanamātra* (Kappas. S. § 26) almost always stands with the v. l. °*mĕtta*, as the word occurs in M. (G. H. R.), AMg. (Vivāhap. 203.204. 452 f. 1042), JM. (Erz.; Kk.), Ś. (Śak. 39, 12; 60, 15; 96, 2; Vikr. 7, 12; 41, 13; 80, 13; 84, 6; Uttarar. 21, 10; 100, 1 etc.), °*mĕttaka* (Śak. 31, 11 [read as such]; 76, 7), *adimĕttaṁ = atimātram* (Mṛcch. 89, 4; -90, 13. 21); Mg. *yādamĕttaka = jātamātraka* (Mṛcch. 114, 8).[1] On *mahāmĕttha = mahāmātra*, and *mĕtthapurisa*, see § 293. — *bhisaï* is = **bhāsáti*, **bhasáti* for *bhắsati* with crossing over to the 6th class (§ 482). M. AMg. Ś. *gĕjjha*, Mg. *duggeyha*, M. A. *duggĕjjha = grắhya, durgrāhya* is formed from the present stem, therefore, = **gṛhya*, **durgṛhya*, and so stands for **gijjha*, **duggijjha* (§ 572). — *śālmali* forms in AMg. *sāmali*, dialectically *sāmari* (§ 88). The other form *simbali*, that occurs beside it is AMg. (Pāiẏal 264; Desīn. 1, 146; Vivāhap. 447 f.; Uttar. 590 (so correctly given in the commentary); Dasav. 621 ,5 (text *sa*°)), *ĕkkasimbali = śāmalipuṣpair navaphalikā* (Deśīn. 1. 146) belongs to Vedic *śimbalá* (flower of the cotton tree[2]). The form *kuppisa* beside *kuppāsa = kūrpāsa* (Hc. 1, 72) points to the accent **kū́rpāsa*.

1. Cf. BRUGMANN, KZ. 27, 198. — So correctly GELDNER, Ved. Stud. 2, 159 according to Sāyaṇa. BÜHLER has already referred to Vedic *śimbali* (sic), Pāiẏal see under *simbaliṁ*.

§ 110. In the ending *-māna* of the ātmanep. pres. participle *i* sometimes occurs for *ā*. So in M. *meliṇa* from *melaī* from *mil*, and especially in the oldest AMg., as in *āgamamiṇa, samaṇujāṇamiṇa, āḍhāẏamiṇa*, etc. (§ 562). — *khalliḍa = khalvāṭa* (Hc. 1,74), which, as *khalliṭa* and *khalliṭa* has gone over to Skt. also, presupposes an accent *khalvāṭá* (Pāṇini, 5, 2, 125; Hc., Uṇādigaṇas. 148). In A. *khallihaḍaü* (Hc. 4, 389) *h* seems to go back to *ḍha* (§ 207) against § 242. Cf. § 138.

§ 111. For *ā* occurs *u* in *suṇhā* for **saṇhā = sāsnā* (Hc. 1, 75). ; *thuvaa*

(Hc. 1,75) is not = *stāvaka*, but = **stuvaka* = **stuván* from the pres. stem. *thuva-*, whence originates also the passive *thuvvaï* (§ 494). — M. AMg. Ś. *ulla* (Hc. 1, 82; Pāiyal. 185; G. H.; Pracaṇḍap. 47, 6; Āyār. 2, 1, 6, 5. 6; 2, 1, 7. 9;-2, 3, 2, 6. 11. 12 [*udaülla*] ; Uttar. 758; Kappas.; Mālatīm. 107.6 (*rasŏllŏlla*)), M. *ullaa* (R.; Vikr. 53, 6 [read *jalŏllaaṁ* with ed. Bomb. 89,5]) with the denominative M. *ullei* (G. H.), JM. *ullĕttā* (Erz.), AMg. *ullaṇa*, *ullaṇiyā* (Uvās.), and with *ŏ* according to § 125. M. AMg. *ŏlla* (H. R.; Karp. 27, 12; 69, 4; 94, 6; 95, 11; Dasav. 619, 18; 622, 8), M. *ŏllaa* (R.), M. *ŏllei* (H.), *ŏllaṇa* (R.), Ś. *ŏllavida* (Mṛcch. 71, 4) are not to be equated with Hc. with *ārdra*, but with WEBER[1] with *ud, unda* (to moisten), *udan, udaka* (water), and consequently they correspond to **udra* which occurs in *udrá* (otter), *anudrá* (waterless), and *udrín* (watery)[2]. — *ārdra* becomes M. AMg. JM. Ś. *adda* (Hc. 1, 82; Mk. fol. 22; G.; Karp. 45, 7; Ovav.; Erz.; Bālar. 125, 13), M. AMg. also *alla* (Hc. 1, 82; Mk fol. 22; H.; Nirayāv.; Uvās). — AMg. JM. *devāṇuppiya* is not, with WEBER,[3] LEUMANN,[4] WARREN,[5] STEINTHAL[6] and JACOBI[7] to be equated as = *devānāṁpriya*, but with HOERNLE[8] as = *devānupriya* = *deva*+*anupriya*, that in Pāli becomes *aṇuppiya*.[9] — *ūsāra* (rain; Hc. 1, 76) is not = *āsāra*, that remains in M, Ś. A. as *āsāra* (G. R.; Caṇḍak. 16, 18; Vikr. 55, 17), but = **utsāra*. On *ajjū* = *āryā* see § 105.

1. ZDMG. 26, 741; H. s. v., falsely H1. p. 261; cf. Haripāla on G. 527 *ulliam tti deśī dhātur ārdrībhāve*. — 2. P. GOLDSCHMIDT on Specimen 2, 8, p. 84. — 3. Bhag. 1, 405. — 4. Aup. S. s. v.; WZKM. 3, 44. — 5. Nirayāv. s.v. — 6. Specimen s. v. 7. — Kalpas. and Erz. s. v.; cf. also E. MÜLLER, Beiträge p. 15. 8. — Uvās., Appendix III, p. 31. — 9. MORRIS, Journal of the Pāli Text Society, 1886, p. 117.

§ 112. AMg. *pārevaya* (Hc. 1, 80; Paṇṇav. 54. 526; Jīv. 459; Rāyap. 52 [text *pāreva*] ; Uttar. 981), *pārevayaga* (Paṇhāv. 24.57), fem. *pārevaī* (Vivāgas. 107) = Pāli *pārepata* is a dialectical side-form of M. *pārāvaa* (Hc. 1, 80; Pāiyal. 124; G. H.; Karp. 87. 10), Ś. *pārāvada* (Mṛcch. 71, 14; 79, 24; 80, 4; Śak. 138, 2; Viddhaś. 111, 3) = Skt. Pāli *pārapata*. *pāre* is a locative as in *pāregaṅgam*, *pāretaraṅgiṇi*, etc. AMg. *pārevaya* "date-palm" (Paṇṇav. 483. 531) is = *pārevata*. — AMg. *pacchekamma* = *paścātkarman* (Hc. 1,79) is technically formed on the analogy of *purekamma-* (§ 345). In Paṇhāv. 492, occurs *pacchākammaṁ purekammaṁ*. — *dera* (door; Hc. 1,79) beside *dāra*, *bāra*, *duvāra*, *duāra* (§ 298.300.139) = Singhalese *dera* is perhaps = **darya*; cf. *darī* (cave.). — AMg. *ukkosa*, which the scholiasts translate by *utkarṣa*, whereafter WEBER explains it as having developed from **ukkāsa*, and which WARREN[2] tries to consider as a writer's mistake, is = **utkoṣa* from *kuṣa niṣkarṣe* (Dhātup. 31,46), that in Skt. is accidentally not attested with *ud*. Generally its instrumental form *ukkoseṇaṁ* "at the highest", "at most" is used with its converse *jahanneṇaṁ* "at the lowest" (Aṇuttar. 3; Ṭhāṇ. 106.133; Samav. 8. 9. 11; Paṇṇav. 52, 205ff; Vivāhap. 26ff. 59.60 143. 182.272ff. 358.373 etc.; Jīv. 18. 35, 39. 49 etc.; Aṇuog. 161 ff.; 398 ff.; Uttar. 201; Ovav.), more seldom there occurs its synonym, the accusative form *ukkosaṁ* (Vivāhap. 180.371.390 f.; Uttar. 312 ff.). As an adjective (Paṇhāv. 29), beside *majjhima jahanna* (Ṭhāṇ. 128.141.152.175). the grammarians (Hc. 4,258; Triv. 3, 1, 132) and the scholiasts equate it as = *utkṛṣṭa*; *ukkosiya* (Ṭhāṇ. 505; Vivāhap. 83.93; Uttar. 976; Kappas) is neither with WEBER[3] = *utkarṣika*, nor with JACOBI[4] = *utkṛṣṭa*, but is to be equated as = **utkoṣita*. —On *dhovaī* = *dhāvati* see § 482.

1. Bhag. 1, 443; cf. LEUMANN, Aup. S. s. v. — 2. Over de goodsdienstige en wijsgeerige Begrippen der Jaina's (Zwolle 1875) p. 43, note 1. — 3. Bhag. 1, 443. — 4. Kalpas. s. v.

§ 113. A final unaccented *ā* of adverbs, very often in M. and sometimes also in AMg. JŚ. JM. A. in verses, is shortened (Grr. see § 79); M. *aṇṇaha* = *anyáthā* (H.), beside M. JM. *aṇṇahā* (G.; Kk.), JŚ. *aṇṇadhā* (Pav. 385,63; text °*hā*); Ś. only *aṇṇadhā* (Mṛcch. 24,4; 51,24;52,13; 64,25; Śak. 52,16; 73,8; 76,5; Vikr. 18,8; 40, 16), likewise Mg. (Mṛcch. 165, 4); M. AMg. JM. *jaha, taha* = *yáthā, táthā* (G. H. R.; Uvās.; Kappas.; Erz.; Kk.); JŚ. *jadha,* (Pav. 386, 4; 387, 24 [°*ha*]), *tadha* (Pav. 379, 4; 381, 16 [°*ha*] ; Kattig. 398, 304 [°*ha*]); A. *jiha, jidha, tiha, tidha* (Hc. 4, 401) with *i* on the analogy of AMg. JM. A. *kiha*, JŚ. A. *kidha* = Vedic *kathá*, which owes the shortness of *a* in Pkt. to *jaha, taha* and M. *kaha* (G. H. R.) (§ 103). Ś. Mg. have, in prose only *tadhā, jadhā* (Mg. *yadhā*), *kadhaṁ* (never *kadhā*). Ā. has in verse *jaha* (Mṛcch. 100, 12). For Mg. *taha* (Mṛcch. 123, 7), in verse, read *tadha*, as in JŚ. — M. JM. AMg. *va* = *vā* (G. H. R.; Erz.; Kk.; Dasav. 618, 25; 620, 32.33); Ś. Mg. in prose only *vā*. The metre decides the quantity, and, therefore, both of the forms sometimes do occur in one and the same verse : thus M. *jaha...ṇa tahā* (H. 61); JM. *kiṁ calidvva... kiṁ vā jalio* (Erz. 71, 22); JŚ. *guṇe ẏa jadhā tadha bandho* (Pav. 384, 48); AMg. *paḍisehie va dinne vā* (Dasav. 622. 37). In M. AMg. JM. *saï* = *sádā* (Vr. 1, 11; Hc. 1, 72; Kī. 1, 10; Mk. fol. 7; Pāiẏal. 87; G. R.; Pratāp. 225, 14; Acyutaś. 1. 20. 22. 62. 66. 69. 93; Dasav. 622. 23; Kk. 259, 24[1]) *i* is regularly substituted according to § 108. Rare in M. is *saā* (H. 861). Bh. 1, 11 teaches the same phonetic change also for *jaï* = *yadā'* and *taï* = *tadā'*. This presupposes an accentuation **yádā*, **tádā*, as in the ṚV., after a negative the word *kadā* is accented as *kádā*, on which is based M. *kaï* (H,), that may have influenced *jaï, taï*. *taïaṁ*, which according to JACOBI[2] is a counter example demonstrating the rule of substitution for *i* for *ā* in a post-accentual syllable and may be = *tadā*', is not known to me at all. Even if it existed, in any case, it would be explained according to § 114, as a side-form of *taïā*, that is like *kāïā, jaïā* found in M. (Vr. 6, 8; Hc. 3, 65; Mk. fol. 46; G. H. R.; *kaïā* also Acyutaś. 86, 91), AMg. *taïẏā* (Uttar. 279); *jaïā* has not been found. These words are = **kaẏidā*, **taẏidā*, **yaẏidā* from *káyā, táyā, yáyā* + *dā* a§ 121) and, therefore, strictly conform to the rule. Shortening takes place also in Ś. M. Ḍh. *ka'dua, gadua* for **ka'duvā*, **gaduvā* = *kṛtvā, gatvā* (§ 581).

1. Wrongly explained by JACOBI as = *svayam*. — 2. KZ. 35, 575. The word has been quoted by JACOBI probably from the word-index to Hc., where *taïaṁ* = *tṛtīyam* and *taïā* = *tadā* occur under one another.

§ 114. In an adverb there develops dialectically an anusvāra by the side of *ā* that is either final or has come into being due to elision of a consonant; in A. there develops also an anunāsika. M. AMg. JM. *jahā*, A. *jihā̃* = *yathā* (Hc. 4, 337). Beside *mā*, that occurs in all the dialects, A. has *mā, maṁ* (read so everywhere for *ma* according to Hc. 4,418, *mā̃* when a short and *maṁ* when a long syllable is required; see the Wortzeichniss zu Hc.), beside *viṇā* of all the dialects A. *viṇu* (Hc. s.v.) = **viṇaṁ*- (§ 351). — *maṇā* = *manāk* (Hc. 2, 169), beside M. Ś. *maṇaṁ* (Mk. fol. 39; H.; Śak. 146. 8; Karṇas. 31. 9); JM. *maṇāgaṁ* (Erz.) A. *maṇāũ* (§352), also JM. *maṇayaṁ* (Hc. 2, 169; KI. 10), and *maṇiyaṁ* (Hc. 2, 169). — AMg. *musaṁ* beside *musā*° = *mṛṣā* (§ 78). AMg. *sakkhaṁ* = *sākṣāt* (Hc. 1, 24; Uttar. 116. 370; Ovav.), beside Ś. *sakkhā* (Mallikām. 190, 19). AMg. *hĕṭṭhaṁ* beside AMg. JM. *hĕṭṭhā* (§ 107) is an accusative beside ablative, as it may be the case in *sakkhaṁ* also. In AMg., beside *tahā* we have also *tahaṁ* before a vowel in the phrase *evaṁ eyaṁ taham eyaṁ avitaham eyam* = *eyaṁ evametattathaitad avitathametad* (Vivāhap. 946; Uvās. § 12; Ovav. § 54; Kappas. § 13. 83). This *taham* stands for *tahaṁ* (§ 349) and corresponds to one **tatham* beside *tathā*, like *kathám* beside Vedic *kathā́*. So can A. *jihā̃* too be referred to **yathám* beside *yáthā*, Cf. § 72. 74. 75. 86. So also AMg. *sŏccam*, *dissam* occurring before as vowel for *sŏccaṁ*, *dissaṁ*, beside *sŏccā*, *dissā* = *śrutvā dṛṣṭvā* (§334.349). Final *ā* in the inst. sing. and *ā* originating from -*āḥ* of the abl. and of the gen. as well as of the therewith connected locative of the feminines in *i*, *ī*, *u* or *ū* are often shortened in M. : *bandia* = *bandyā*; *koḍia* = *koṭeh*; *ṇaaria* = *nagaryām*; *vahūa* = *vadhvā* (§ 385). The corresponding forms in -*a* of the feminine in -*ā*, which are mentioned by some grammarians, are not to be found. In places where they stood earlier in Karp. thence they have been eliminated in the critical edition of Konow (§ 375).

§ 115. A transition from *i* to *a*, which the grammarians mention (Vr. 1, 13, 14; Hc. 1, 88—91; Kī. 1. 18. 19; Mk. fol. 7) has not really taken place. Thus for example *paḍaṁsuā* (Hc. 1, 26. 88. 206), *paḍaṁsua* (Mk. fol. 34) is not = *pratiśrut*, *pratiśruta*, but = **pratyāśrut*, **pratyāśruta*, as is shown by *pratyāśrāva*. *pratiśrut* in AMg. forms *paḍiṁsuyā* (Ovav. s. v.); for *pratiśruta* is found *paḍiṁsuda* (Bh. 4, 15). — In M. JM. Ś. Mg. A. *puhavi*, AMg. JŚ. JM. Ś. *puḍhavi* (§51) *a* is a separation vowel like *u* in *puhuvī* (§ 139), both, therefore, = *pṛthvī*. — *baheḍaa* (Hc. 1, 88) is not = *vibhītaka*, but = *baheṭaka* (Vaijayantī 59. 351; cf. BÖHTLINGK s. v. *vahedaka*. — *saḍhila* (Hc. 1, 89), AMg. *pasaḍhila* (Hc. 1, 89; Paṇṇav. 118) go, like M. AMg. Ś. *siḍhila* (Vr. 2, 28; Hc. 1, 89. 215. 254; Kī. 2, 17; G. H. R.; Āyār. 1, 5, 3, 4; Nāyādh. 949; Rāyap. 258 f.; Vivāhap. 39. 136. 382 f. 1308; Uttar. 196; Śak. 132. 12; Vikr. 30, 4), M. *siḍhilattaṇa* = **śithilatvana* (G.), *siḍhiladā* (Śak. 63, 1), M. Ś. *siḍhilei*, °*di* (R.; Śak. 11, 1; Bālar. 36, 5; Caṇḍak. 58, 10), M. AMg. Ś. *pasiḍhila* (G. H. R. Vivāhap. 806; Uttar 773; Nāyādh.; Ovav.; Viddhaś. 64, 5), back to the original **śṛthila*', *a* and *i*, therefore, represent an original *ṛ* as elsewhere (§ 52), — In *haladdā*, *haladdī* (Grr.) beside M. AMg. JM. *haliddā* (Hc. 1. 88. G. H.; Uttar. 982, 1050; Rāyap. 53; Erz.), M. *haliddī* (Hc. 1.88. 254; G.; Karp. 69, 3) = *haridrā*, AMg. *hālidda* = *hāridra* (Āyār. 1, 5, 6, 4 [read thus] Paṇṇav. 525; Samav. 64; Jīva 224; Ovav.; Kappas.) *a* and *i* are presumably separation-vowels. On *aṅgua* beside *iṅgua* = *iṅguda* see § 102.

1. S. GOLDSCHMIDT, R. s. v. *siḍhila*; cf. B.-R. s. v. *śithira* and WACKERNAGEL Altind. Gr. § 16.

§ 116. For the second *i* of *iti* = Latin *ita*, there has been preserved in M. AMg. JM. an old *a*, when *iti* stands independently in the beginning of a sentence, in AMg. also in the beginning of a compound : M. *ia* (Vr. 1, 14; Hc. 1, 91; Kī. 1, 19; Mk. fol. 7; G. H. R.; Bālar. 113, 17; Karp. 6. 4; 48, 14; 57, 7; Viddhaś. 64, 7; Acyutaś. 22, 45, 82, 93. 103; AMg. JM. *iẏa* (C. 2, 28; Pāiẏal. 224; Āẏār. 1. 2, 1, 1; 1, 2, 3, 1. 5; 1, 4, 3, 2 (v. 1. everywhere *iti*); Ovav. § 184. 186; KI. 14; Kk.); AMg. *iẏaccheẏa*, *iẏaniuṇa*, *iẏanayāvādi-*, *iẏaüvaesaladdha*, *iẏaviṇṇāṇapatta* = *iticcheka*, *itinipuṇa*, *itinayavādin*, *ityupadeśalabdha*, *itivijñānaprāpta* (Uvās. § 219). Mostly the texts have in AMg. *ii* for *iẏa* (ẏag. 137. 203 [*iti*] ; Uttar. 63. 99. 116. 311. 508. 512. 513; Dasav. 626. 11, 630, 14; Uvās. § 114). As *i* and *ẏa* are always interchanged in Jaina MSS, it is doubtful if here we have simply a case of error of MSS or not. JŚ., however, has *idi* (Pav. 385, 65, 387, 18. 24; Kattig. 399, 314;) it has it whether rightly or wrongly is yet to be decided. In Ś. there wrongly occurs *ia* (Kāleyak. 27, 16). As an enclitic *iti* becomes *ti*, *tti* (§ 92), AMg. also *i* (§ 93).

§ 117. Sometimes *i* becomes *u* through assimilation to an *u* of the following syllable : M. AMg. JM. *ucchu* = *ikṣú* (Vr. 1, 15; Bh. 3, 30; Hc. 1, 95; 2, 17,; Kī. 1, 22; Mk. fol. 7; Pāiẏal, 143: G. H.; Āẏār. 2, 1, 8, 9. 12; 2, 1, 10, 4; 2, 7, 2, 5; Paṇhāv. 127; Uttar. 590; Dasav. 614, 13; 621, 5. 41; Dasav. N. 660, 4; Ovav.; Āv. 23, 24; Erz.). By the side thereof AMg. has also *ikkhu* (Hc. 2. 17; Sūẏag. 594; Paṇṇav. 33, 40; Jīv. 356; Vivāhap. 1526), *ikkhūẏa* (Paṇṇav. 33. 40), and similarly in Ś. we must read *ikkhu* with the MSS instead of *ucchu* in Śak. 144, 12 against Candraśekhara 206, 17, as stands in Rukmiṇīp. 42, 14. In M. JM. occurs *icchu* H. 740. 775; KI. 18; but it is hardly correct. On AMg. JM. *ikkhāga* = *aikṣvāka*, see § 84. — AMg. *usu* = *íṣu* (Sūẏag. 270, 286. 293; Vivāhap. 121. 122. 348. 505. 506. 1388; Rāẏap. 257; Niraẏāv. § 5); AMg. *usugāra* (Ṭhāṇ. 86), *usuẏāra* (Ṭhāṇ. 383; Uttar. 421. 422. 449; Paṇhāv. 317 [text *ikkhu*°, but cf. the commentary)) = *iṣukāra* (name of a hill). Yet AMg. JM. have also *isattha* = *iṣuśāstra*[1] (Paṇhāv. 322; Ovav. § 107, p. 78, 4; Erz. 67, 1. 2); AMg. *isāsaṭṭhāṇa* = *iṣvāsasthāna* (Niraẏāv. § 5 beside *usu*); M. *isu* (Pāiẏal. 36; G. 1145 [*kāmesu*] ; Karp. 12, 8; 94, 8; [*pañcesu*] . — AMg. *susu* = *śiśu* in *susumāra* = *śiśumāra* (Sūẏag. 821; Paṇhāv. 19; Vivāgas. 50. 186), more frequently *suṁsumāra* (Paṇṇav. 47. 48; Jīv. 71; Nāẏādh. 510; Uttar. 1072; Vivāhap. 1285 [text °*sa*°]), *suṁsumārī* (Jīv. 111); but AMg. *sisupāla* (Sūẏag. 161), *sisunāga* (Uttar. 205); M. *sisu* (Pāiẏal. 58) ; Ś. *sisubhāva* (Viddhaś. 21, 12), *sisuāla* = *śiśukāla* (Cait. 37, 7).

1. So correctly Abhayadeva on Paṇhāv. 322. Wrongly equated as = *iṣvastra* by LEUMANN, Aup. S. s. v. and JACOBI, Erz. s. v.

§ 118. The *i* of the prefix *ni* becomes *u* before *ma*, that has originated from *pa* according to § 248 and from *va* according to § 251 : *ṇumajjaï* = *nipadyate* (Hc. 1. 94; 4, 123; Kī. 4, 46), *ṇumaṇṇa* = *nipanna* (Hc. 1, 94, 174). The forms referred by Grr. to *sad* cannot be separated from one another. The v. 1. *ṇuvaṇṇa* (G. 1161) and its meaning "fallen asleep" (Deśīn. 4, 25) clearly points to the origin of *ma* from *pa*. Derivation from *majj* is factually and linguistically impossible. In H. 530. 608. 669 WEBER reads with the MSS *ṇimajjasu*, *ṇimajjanta*, *ṇimajjaï*, *ṇimajjihisi*. But at another place (under 669) he refers °to *ṇu* that occurs in a stanza quoted by Hc., in Dhvanyāloka p. 20 and in Kāvyaprakāśa, p. 123 in the best old Sāradā MSS,[1] Śobhākara, Alaṁkāraratnākara fol. 67ᵇ (MS BÜHLER, Det. Report, No. 227). Hemacandra, Alaṁkāracūḍāmaṇi fol. 4ᵇ (MSS KIELHORN, Report, Bombay 1881, p. 102, No. 265), Mammaṭa, Śabdavyāpāravicāra fol. 6ᵃ, Jayanta, Kāvyaprakāśadīpikā-fol. 6ᵇ. 22ᵇ, whereas Sāhityadarpaṇa p. 5 reads *ṇi*°. Everywhere *nu*° should be read, *ṇumanta*, explained in Triv. 1, 2, 48 by *nimantra*, is a mistaken reading from *ṇumanna* in Hc. — *ṇumaï* (Hc. 4, 199) beside *ṇimaï* (Hc. 4, 199), M. *ṇimei* (R.) "throw down" is = *vi* "to throw" (Dhātup. 24, 39) with *ni*. Therefore, the v. l. *ṇivia* (R. 12, 30) beside *ṇimia*[2]. — Sometimes dialectically the suffix *-uka* steps in for the Skt. suffix *-ika*, so that apparently *u* stands for *i*. So M. *viṁchua*, *viṁcua*, *vicchua*, AMg. *vicchuya*, beside M. *viṁchia*, AMg. *vicchiya* = *vṛścika* (§ 50); AMg. *geruya* beside M. *geria* = *gairika*; AMg. *neyāuya* = *naiyāyika* (§ 60); M. *jāṇua* = **jñānika*; (H. 286), *akaajāṇua* = *akṛtajña*, *vijāṇua* = *vijña*, *dĕvvajāṇua* = *daivajña* etc. (Mk. fol. 20), probably also in the proper names Ś. *jāṇua*, Mg. *yāṇua* (Śak. 115, 1. 9. 11); *pāvāsua*, A. *pavāsua* *prāvāsika* (Hc. 1, 95; 4, 395; 4), also *pāvāsu*, *pavāsu* = *prāvāsin* (Hc. 1,44), that probably goes back to **pavāsu* = *pravāsá* (§ 105), whence may have originated also *pāvāsua*. — AMg. JM. *duruhaï* (§ 482) is not = *adhirohati*[3], but = **udruháti* = *udrohati*,[4] however, not by metathesis of *ud* to *du* as HOERNLE thinks, but with a separation-vowel and falling out of the initial *u* from **uduruhaï* (§139, 141). — *yudhiṣṭhira*, according to Hc. 1, 96. 107. 254, may become *jahuṭṭhila*, *jahiṭṭhila* (also Bh. 2, 30; Kī. 2, 35; Mk. fol. 17). It is not clear what was the origin of *jahu* and *jahi*. In the text we find AMg. *juhiṭṭhila* (Antag. in ZDMG. 42, 528; Nāyādh. 1287 ff. (text, more often °*illa*); Ś. A. *juhiṭṭhira* (Karp. 18, 4; Veṇīs. 102, 4; Pracaṇḍap. 29, 12; 31, 13; 34, 8; Piṅgala 2, 102).

1. For Hc. and Kāvyaprakāśa the remark made already by WEBER on H. 530 is without any result. Wrong is the derivation from *nimi*, particularly from *ṇimia* = *nimita*, in GOLDSCHMIDT, R. s. v. *ṇima*. — 3. WEBER, Bhag. 1, 411; LEUMANN, Aup. s. s. v. STEINTHAL, Specimen s. v.; E. MÜLLER, Beiträge p. 34. — 4. HOERNLE, Uvās. Translation p. 38, note 103.

§ 119. Before a consonant-group *i* may become *ĕ* (Vr. 1, 12; Hc. 1, 85; Kī. 1, 16; Mk. fol. 7; Pkl. p. 25; Deśīn. 1, 174) : PG. M. AMg. JM. Ś. Mg. P. D. Ā. *ĕttha*, A. *ĕtthu* = *itthá* (§ 107); AMg. *āgamĕssa* = *āgamiṣyant* (Āyār. 1, 4, 3, 2); *cĕndha*, beside *cindha* = *cihna* (§ 267; ; Bh. 1, 12); *ṇĕddā*, beside *ṇiddā* = *nidrā* (Bh. 1, 12); *dhammĕlla*, beside *dhammilla* (Grr.); *peṇḍa*, beside *piṇḍa* (Grr.); *pĕṭṭha* beside *piṭṭha* = *piṣṭa* (Grr.); AMg. *lĕcchaï* = *licchavi* (Sūyag. 495. 585; Vivāhap. 800; Nirayāv.; Ovav.; Kappas.); PG. AMg. *vĕṭṭhi* (PG. 6, 32; Uttar 792), beside *viṭṭhi* = *viṣṭi* (Kī.; Mk.); *vĕṇhu*, beside *viṇhu* = *viṣṇu* (Grr.); AMg. *vĕbbhala* = *vihvala* (Paṇhāv. 165); *sĕndūra*, beside *sindūra* (Grr.). So also *kesua* from,* *kĕṁsua* = *kiṁśuka* (§ 76.) This rule is more frequently illustrated by cases having a secondary *i*, particularly that which has developed from *ṛ* : °*mĕtta* from °*mitta* = °*mātra* (§ 109); *gĕṇhaï*, beside *giṇha* = *gṛhṇāti* (§ 512); *gĕjjha* from **gijjha* = **gṛhya* for *grāhya* (§ 109. 572); *vĕṇṭa* beside *viṇṭa* = *vṛnta* (§ 53); AMg. *gĕddha* (Ovav. § 70), beside *giddha* (§ 50) = *gṛdhra*; AMg. *gehi* (§ 60) from **gĕddhi* = *giddhi* (§ 50) = *gṛddhi*. According to Mk. fol. 66 *e* never occurs in Ś. in any of the words included in the ākṛtigaṇa *piṇḍasama* by Vr. Pkl. and under the *piṇḍādi* by Mk. Kī. in which Bh. Kī. Mk. like Hc. in his rule 1, 85, include *piṇḍa, dhammilla, sindūra, viṣṇu, piṣṭa*, Hc. and Mk. also *bilva*, which forms *bĕlla, billa* (§ 296), Bh. also *nidrā, cihna*, Mk. Kī. *viṣṭi*, Kī. *kiṁśuka* which Hc. has in a special rule, and for which Mk. likewise forbids *e* in Ś. This is attested by the texts in which there occur, par ex. Ś. *piṇḍa* (Mṛcch. 41, 11; 69, 12; Prab. 49, 4), also Mg. (Mṛcch. 125. 5; Prab. 46, 14), Mg. *ciṇha* (Mṛcch. 159, 23); Ś. *ṇiddā* = *nidrā* (Mṛcch. 45, 24; Vikr. 24, 17; Prab. 17, 1; 38. 2.6; 39; 8); Ś. *viṇhudāsa* (Mudrār. 243, 2; 247, 1; 248, 7; 249, 5. 6; 259, 7). In the optative in *-ĕjjā, -ijjā* in AMg. and JM. (§ 91.459 ff.) *ĕ* occurs for and beside *i*. — *te* in the numerals, such as AMg. JM. *terasa*, A. *teraha* (13), AMg. JM. *tevisaṁ*, A. *teisa* (23), AMg. JM. *tĕttisaṁ* (33), JM. *teyālisaṁ* (43), AMg. JM. *tesaṭṭhiṁ, tevaṭṭhiṁ* (63) etc. (§ 443 ff.), as well as in AMg. *teindiya, tendiya* (§ 438) is perhaps not = *tri*, but = *traya*: *terasa*, therefore = **trayadaśan*. — AMg. *teicchā* = *cikitsā* beside *vitigicchā vitigiṁcchā* (§ 215) has strengthened reduplication, like Skt. *cekite, cekitat, cekitāna*.

§ 120. In *haraḍai* = *harītakī, haritakī* (Hc. 1, 99.206) *a* is probably a separation-vowel like *i*, in Skt. The *ḍa* of Pkt. points to a basic form **hartakī*. —*ā* for *i* is taught by Hc. 1.100; 2, 60; 60.74 in *kamhāra, kambhāra* = *kaśmira*, for which we should, with Triv. 1, 2, 50, read *kāśmira*; cf. Skt. *kambhārī* beside *kāśmirī* "gmelina arborea". Ś. has *kamhīra* (Mudrār. 204, 2). — On *i* for *ī* see § 79ff. — AMg. *uṭṭhubhaha* "spit" (Vivāhap. 1263), *uṭṭhubhanti* "they spit"; (Vivāhap. 1264; text °*bhahanti*), AMg. *aṇiṭṭhubhaya* "not spitting", (Paṇhāv. 350; Ovav. § 30, V), dialectical *ṇiṭṭhuhia* (loudly spat out; Deśīn. 4, 41) as well as Pāli *niṭṭhuhati, nuṭṭhuhati, ṇuṭṭhubhi, niṭṭhubhana* have nothing to do with *ṣṭhiv*, with which it had hitherto been considered to be associated, but all these belong to the root √ *stubh* (to drive out; *stunbhu niṣkoṣaṇe*, Dhātup. 31, 7), which in Skt. is used for voice only = "to emit a sound". The parallel root is *kṣubh* (*stubh* : *kṣubh* = *stambh* : *skambh* = Skt. *sthāṇu* : Pkt. *khāṇu* = *duttha* : *dukkha* [hinder portion; Deśīn. 5, 42] ; § 90.308.309) which occurs in Pkt. AMg. JM. *chubhai*, M. JM. *chuhaï* and in composita (§ 66). Pāli *nicchubhati* "springs forth" (from the sea)[1], shows transfer of meaning, which we find also in Skt. *nirasana* (throwing outside, to throw out, spit forth). — *hūṇa* (Hc. 1, 103), M. AMg. JŚ. A. *vihūṇa* (Hc. 1. 103; Śukasaptati 15, 3; Nāyādh. 950; Vivāhap. 202. 1123. 1816f. 1825; Nirayāv. 44; Uttar. 357. 439. 633. 809; Pav. 380, 7; 381, 17; 387, 12; Piṅgala 1, 7), AMg. *vippahūṇa* (Sūyag. 271.282; Nāyādh. 322; Paṇhāv. 56) are not to be equated with Hc. as = *hīna, vihīna, viprahīṇa*, but they belong to *dhūna* (Kāśikā on Pāṇini. 8, 2,44) from *dhu, dhū* "to shake off" which forms in AMg. *dhuṇāï* and in M. AMg. *dhuṇaï, vihuṇaï* (§ 503). In all the dialects *hā* regularly forms *hīṇa*. So M. AMg. JŚ. Ś. *hīṇa* (G. H.; Uvās.; Pav. 382, 24. 25; 388, 2; Vikr. 24, 20), JM. *aihīṇa* (Kk.); M. JM. JŚ. *parihīṇa* (H.; KI. 8; Erz.; Kk., Kattig. 400, 329); AMg. *pahīṇa* (Bhag.); Ś. *avahīṇa* (Śak. 30, 2), M. *aṇohīṇa* (R.); JŚ. Ś. *vihīṇa* (Kattig. 404, 387.389; Mṛcch. 18, 10). — On *juṇṇa* = *jūrṇa* and *tūha* = *tīrtha* see § 58.

1. KERN, Bijdrage tot de-Verklaring van eenige Woorden in Pāli-Geschriften voorkomende (Amesterdam 1886) p. 18; FAUSBØLL, Nogle Bemaerkninger om enkelte vanskelige Pâli-Ord i Jātaka-Bogen (Kopenhagen 1888) p. 19. Not correctly TRENCKNER, Milindapañho p. 423 f.

§ 121. Most of the dialects, beside *i*, partly have *e* in *idṛśa, idṛkṣa, kidṛśa, kidṛkṣa* : Aśoka *edisa, hedisa heḍisa* (Khālsi) *ediśa, hediśa*; Pāli *edisa, erisa, edikkha, erikkha* beside *idisa, irisa, idikkha,* but only *kīdisa, kīrisa, kīdikkha, kīrikkha*; M. AMg. JM. Ś. *erisa* (Vr. 1, 91.31; Hc. 1, 105.142; Kī. 1, 15; Mk. fol. 8.11; H. 10; R. 11, 104; Sūẏag. 197; Dasav. 626, 27; Ovav.; Niraẏāv.; Bhag.; Āv. 24, 3ff.; 25, 31. 32; 27, 2, 6.25; Dvār. 508, 6; Erz.; Kk. Lalitav. 555, 6; 562, 22; Mṛcch. 151.20.155,5; Śak. 50, 4; Prab. 4, 9); AMg. JM; *erisaẏa* (Naẏādh. 1284; Āv. 24, 10); A. *erisia* (Piṅgala 2, 185); AMg. *elisa* (C. 2, 5 p. 43), *aṇelisa* (Āẏār. 1, 6, 1, 1; 1, 7, 2, 4; 1, 7, 8, 1, 17; 1. 8, 1, 15; 2, 16, 2; Sūẏag. 301. 434 [text *aṇā°*]. 533. 544. 546. 549. 869); P. *etisa* (Hc. 4, 317.323); Ś. mostly *idisa* (Mṛcch. 24, 20; 39, 11; 54, 1; 72, 19; 90, 9; 82, 12; 88, 16; 151. 16; Śak. 103, 5; 104, 7; 123, 12; 127, 7; 130, 1; 135, 15; Vikr. 20, 6; 44, 13; Ratn. 317, 33; 318, 16.22; Karp. 19, 6; 21, 4 etc.), Mg. only *idiśa* (Mṛcch. 38, 7;129, 7; 131. 7; 158, 24; 165, 13; 166, 21; 177, 10); AMg. *elikkha* (Uttar. 237), *elikkhaẏa* (Āẏār. 1, 8, 3, 5); M. AMg. JM. Ś. *kerisa* (Grr.; H. 374 [read so with v. 1.] ; Niraẏāv.; Bhag.; Erz.; Mṛcch. 141, 7; Vikr. 50, 6; 52, 3; Prab. 10, 15; 39, 13), JM. . *kerisaẏa* (Kk.), Mg. *keliśa* (Prab. 46, 14.16; 50, 14; 53, 15.16; 56, 1; Veṇīs. 35, 3); Ś. also *kīdisa* (Mṛcch. 27, 18; Śak. 39, 6; Vikr. 28, 19; Mudrār. 58, 6; 184, 5). Doubtful forms are M. *irisaa* (H.940), JM. *iisa* (Erz.), Ś. *irisa* (Uttarar. 26,6 beside *idisa* 26, 8; Mālav. 6, 1; 44, 18; 47, 3; Mahāv. 119, 12. 14. 20; Mudrār. 233, 1), *kirisa* (Mālav. 5, 3.17)[1], Mg. *kiliśa* (Mṛcch. 125, 2.4; 132, 9; GOḌABOLE 344, 7; 345, 1 has *keliśa,* only 363, 2 also *kiliśa*). According to the testimony of the best manuscripts only *erisa, kerisa* and *idisa, kīdisa* will be correct in Ś.; in Mg. the correct forms would be **eliśa, keliśa* and *idiśa,* **kīdiśa* (the v.l often has *keliśa*). Cf. § 244.245. The hitherto unexplained[2] *e* goes back to *-ayi, -aï.* From Vedic *ka'yā+dṛś* has developed *kerisa*; *erisa* comes from Vedic *ayā́+dṛś,* like *kaïā, taïā, jaïā* from *kā́yā+dā, tā́yā+dā, yā́yā=dā* (§ 113). *ayā́* is influenced by *kā́yā.* In A. *aïsa=idṛśa, kaïsa=kidṛśa* (Hc. 4, 403) it is better to consider them as formation on the analogy of A. *taïsa=tādṛśa, jāïsa=yādṛśa,* as the intermediate forms for the development of *erisa, kerisa.* Cf. Vedic *kayasya* and AMg. *aẏaṁsi,* M. *aammi* and A. *āammi* (§ 429). On *ĕddaha, kĕddaha, tĕddha, jĕdaaha* see § 122. Beside *piyūṣa,* Skt. has *peyūṣa,* so too Pkt. Ś. *piūsa* (Bālar. 266, 19) and M. Ś. *peūsa* (Hc. 1, 105; H.; Ś.Karp. 82, 5; Bālar. 150,19; 223, 294, 10; Mallikām. 245, 6). On *baheḍaa=vibhītakā* see § 115; in Paṇṇav. 31, in AMg. we have *vibhelae=vibhedakaḥ* (§ 244).

1. An uncritical collection in BOLLENSEN on Mālav. 5, 2 —5, p. 122. — 2. Literature in JOHANSSON, Shāhbāzgarhi 1, 134.

§ 122. Like *i* (§ 119), *ī* also may become *ĕ* before consonant-groups : AMg. JM; *kiḍḍā,* AMg. *kheḍḍā* dialectical *khĕḍḍā,* A. *khĕḍḍaa=krīḍā* (§ 90); *nĕḍḍa* beside *ṇiḍa* (§ 90); AMg. JM. *jāṇijjā, jāṇĕjjā=jāniyāt* (§ 91); M. *ĕddaha=idṛśa,*[1] with reduplication according to § 90 and *ha* for *śa* according to 262 (on Vr. 4, 25 and Appendix B. p. 101; Hc. 2, 157; Mk. fol. 40; Deśīn. 1, 144; H.; also in Ś. Viddhaś. 71, 1, everywhere *ĕddahamĕtta* = *īdṛśamātra*); *kĕddaha* = *kidṛśa* and on its analogy *tĕddaha* = *tādṛśa*, *jĕddaha* = *yādṛśa* (Grr.). Similarly is explained also *e* in AMg. M. JM. *āmeḷa* (garland; braid of hair; Vr. 2, 16; Hc. 1. 105. 202, 234; Kī. 1. 15; 2, 9; Mk. fol. 8. 16; Pāiẏal. 140; Deśīn. 1, 62; G. 112; Paṇṇav. 111; Ovav.; JM. in *kamaḷāmeḷā*, (Āv. 29, 18ff.), M. *āmeḷiaa* (R. 9, 21), AMg. *āmeḷaga* (Rāẏap. 111), *āmeḷaẏa* (Uvās. § 206; read as such; Ovav.). *āmeḷa* is = **āpiḍya*, which passes through the stages **āpiḍḍa*, **āpĕḍḍa*, **āpeḍa* with *ma* for *pa* according to § 248, *e* for *ĕ* according to § 66 and *ḷa* for *ḍa* according to § 240[2]. Ś. *āpiḍa* (Mālatīm. 207, 4); according to Hc. 1, 202 there occurs dialectically also as *āveḍa*. In the same way we must explain *ṇimeḷa* (gums; Deśīn. 4, 30) from **nipiḍya*, and AMg. *veḍa* from **vĕḍḍa* for **vriḍya* of the present stem *vridya*-; cf. § 240. Doubtful is the origin of *e* in *peḍha* (Hc. 1, 106), beside the common *pīḍha* = *pīṭha*. M. *peḍhāla* (G. 731) has been falsely derived by Haripāla from *pīṭhayukta*. It means "broad" or "round" (Pāiẏal. 84; Deśīn. 6, 7) and perhaps is connected with *piṇḍa*, *e* never appears in the passive in *-ijja* and the participles nec. and adjectives in *-aṇijja* in M. AMg. JM. JŚ. (§ 91).

1. The grammarians explain it by *etāvat*, Hc. Deśīn. 1, 144 by *iyat*. 2. — WEBER has correctly connected it with *īdṛśa*, H' p. 59. The grammarians equate *āmeḷa* as = *āpīḍa*; likewise LASSEN, Inst. p. 207; S. GOLDSCHMIDT, Prakritica p. 15; LEUMANN, Aup. S. s. v.; BÜHLER, Pāiẏal s. v. In that case it is only *e* that remains unexplained. In Triv. 1, 2, 56, the printed edition has °*la* and the MSS have °*ḷa*.

§ 123. In Pkt. there appears several times *a* in place of Skt. *u*, especially in the first syllable of a word of which second syllable likewise contains *u*. In most of such cases *a* might have been the original vowel and the forms with *u* might have been formed analogically (Vr. 1, 22; Hc. 1, 107; Kī. 1, 6; Mk. fol. 9); M. Ś.Ā.A. *garua*, AMg. JM. *garuẏa* = *guruka* (G.H.R.; Sūẏāg. 692. 747. 750; Paṇṇav. 8. 10; Vivāhap. 126. 436; Aṇuog. 268; Nāẏādh.; Erz.; Śak. 10, 3; Mālav. 34, 9; 37, 8; Priyad. 4, 7; Ā. Mṛcch. 148, 1; A. Hc. 4, 340, 2), feminine AMg. *garui* (Grr.; G.; Nāẏādh.; cf. § 139), and in derivatives like M. *garuattaṇa* = **gurutvana* (G.H.R.), *garuia* (G. R.), *garuei* (G.), JM. *garukka* = *gurutva* (KI. 13; cf. § 299); Ś. *garuadā* (Priyad. 31, 12), *agaruadā* (Mahāv. 54, 19). Cf. *gārava* and *gorava* § 61[a]. As Hc. 1, 109 explicitly teaches, *a* has come in only with the addition of the suffix *-ka*; in all the dialects *guru* retains its *u*.[1] — A. AMg. JM. *agaru* (Grr.; G.; Sūẏag. 248; Uvās.; Erz.), also in Skt. beside *aguru* (M. Karp. 87, 9); AMg. also *agaluẏa* (Ovav.); M. *kālāaru* (G.), AMg. *kālāgaru* (Ovav.; Kappas.). — *gaḷoi* = *guḍūci* (§ 127). — M. AMg. JM. Ś. *maüḍa* = *mŭkuṭa* (Grr.; G.; Āẏār. 2, 13, 20; p. 128. 3; Paṇhāv. 160. 234. 251. 440; Paṇṇav. 100. 101. 117; Vivāgas. 161; Nāẏādh. § 35. 92; p. 269. 1274; Jīv. 605; Rāẏap. 21; Ovav.; Kappas.; Erz.; Veṇīs. 59, 22). — *maüra* = *mukura* (Grr.), but Ś. *radaṇamuura* (Mallikām. 194, 4; text *raa*-). — M. AMg. JM. Ś. *maüla* = *mukula* (Grr.; G.H.R.; Anarghar. 20, 3; Kaṁsav. 9, 3; Paṇhāv. 284; Paṇṇav. 111; Uvās.; Ovav.; Erz.; Mudrār. 46. 7 [to be read as such]; Mālav. 69, 2), and in the derivatives like M. *maülia* (G.H.R.), AMg. *maüliẏa* (Ovav.; Kappas.), Ś. *maülida* (Śak. 14, 6; Mahāv. 22, 20; Uttarar. 163. 5) = *muku*-

lita; M. *maülāia* (Ratn. 293, 2); Ś. *maülāanta* (Mālatīm. 121, 5; 254, 2); Ś. *maülāvijjanti* (Priyad. 11, 3; read °*vianti*); Mg. Ś. *maülĕnti* (Mṛcch. 80, 21; 81, 2); AMg. *maüli* = *mukulinaḥ* (Paṇhāv. 119)[2]. In a similar manner is explained also *kohala* = *kutūhala* (Hc. 1, 171) from **katūhala*, **kaūhala*, beside M. AMg. JM. *koūhala*, Ś. *kodūhala* (61[a]), and M. *somāra* (H.R.), *somāla* (Bh. 2, 30; Hc. 1, 171. 254; Pāiẏal. 88; Lalitav. 563, 2) from **sakumāra*, **saümāra* (§ 166) = *sukumāra*, while AMg. *sūmāla* (Āẏār. 2, 15, 17; Niraẏāv.; Kappas.) goes back to AMg. *sukumāla* (Vivāhap. 822. 946; Antag. 7. 16. 21; Jīv. 350, 549. 938; Paṇhāv. 278. 284; Ovav. § 48 etc.). M. has also *suumāra* (Śak. 2, 14), Ś. only *suumāra* (Mṛcch. 37, 5; Śak. 19, 6; 54, 4), *sukumāra* (Vikr. 5, 9), JM. *sukumāraẏā* = °*ratā* (Erz.). *somāla* has been taken over to Skt. as well[3]. *soamalla* = *saukumārya* (§ 285) presupposes a transition of the second *u* to *a*, as AMg. JM. too have *dugaṁchā*, beside *duguṁchā* = *jugupsā* (§ 74). Assimilation to the vowel of the following syllable on account of accent takes place in M. *avariṁ* = *upári* (Grr.; G.), beside M. AMg. JM. *uvariṁ* (Hc. 1, 108; H.R.; Paṇṇav. 90ff.; Samav. 101; Rāẏap. 62; Vivāhap. 198; Ovav.; Āv. 8. 12; Erz.), M. JM. Ś. *uvari* (G.H.R.; Erz.; Mṛcch. 41, 22; Śak. 30, 1; Mālav. 66, 2; Prab. 38, 8), Ś. *uvaridaṇa* (Mṛcch. 42, 13), Mg. *uvali* (Mṛcch. 134, 8), AMg. *uppiṁ*. (§ 148). To *avariṁ* belongs M. *avarilla* (upper garment; Hc. 2, 166; Pāiẏal. 175) as well as *varilla* (Karp. 56, 7; 70, 8; 95, 11). In the same way is explained *a* in M. *avahovāsa*, *avahoāsa* (Bh. 4, 33; Hc. 2, 138; H.R.)[4], beside AMg. *ubhaopāsaṁ* (Samav. 151; Ovav.), *ubhaẏopāsaṁ* (Paṇhāv. 258), *ubhaopāsiṁ* (Samav. 98; Jīv. 496f. 500. 502. 504; Nāẏādh. 275; Vivāhap. 826. 830), *ubhaopāse* (Kappas. p. 96, 24), *ubhayokālaṁ* (Hc. 2. 138), *ubhaokūleṇam* (Ovav.) *ubhao* (Vivāhap. 941; Nāẏādh.; Kappas.) is = **ubhatas* for *ubhayatas*[5] from *ubhá*, *avaho* = **ubáthas* (§ 212), wherefrom is derived *avaha*, and according to some (Hc. 2. 138) is derived also *uvaha*. So also *bhamaẏā* = **bhruvakā* (§ 124) and *avajjhāa* = *upādhyāya* (Deśīn. 1. 37; cf. § 28). — *tarakṣu*, in AMg. has become an *a*-stem : *taraccha* (Āẏār. 2, 1, 5, 3; Paṇṇav. 49. 367. 369; Vivāhap. 282. 484; Nāẏādh. 345), feminine *taracchī* (Paṇṇav.368). On *kattha* = *kutra*, *kao*, *kado*, *katto*, *kaohiṁto* = *kutaḥ* see § 293. 428, on *jahiṭṭhila*, *jahuṭṭhila* = *yudhiṣṭhira*, §118.

1. BOLLENSEN wrongly says on Mālav. p. 172 that when it is an adjective, it is *garu*, and when a substantive, it is *guru*. In Jīv. 224, *garu* is a false reading, likewise Śak. ed. BÖHTLINGK 79, 9; 86. 3. — 2. On *maūḍa* and *maūla* cf. also KUHN, KZ. 31, 324. — 3. ZACHARIAE, BB. 10, 135ff. — Cf. P. GOLDSCHMIDT, Specimen p. 81; WEBER, ZDMG. 28, 390 — LEUMANN, Aup. S. s. v.

§ 124. Beside *tumburu* (Diospyros embryopteris) there occur dialectically *ṭimbaru* (Deśīn. 4, 3) and *ṭimbaruẏa* (Pāiẏal. 258). In lieu of *u* there appears *i* as a separation-vowel[1] in all the dialects in *purisa*, Mg. *puliśa* = *puruṣa* (Vr. 1, 23; Hc. 1, 111; Kī. 1. 26; Mk. fol. 9; e.g. M.; G.H.R.; AMg.: Āẏār. 1, 3, 3, 4; Sūẏag. 202. 203; Paṇhāv. 222; Ṭhāṇ. 360 and very often; JM. : Erz.; JŚ. : Kattig. 401, 345; Ś. : Mṛcch. 9, 10; 17, 19; 24, 35; 29, 3; Śak. 126, 14; 141, 10; Vikr. 35, 12; Prab. 39, 13; Mg. : Lalitav. 565, 13; Mṛcch. 113, 21; 116, 17; 157, 14; Prab. 51, 8; 53, 11; 62, 7; D. : Mṛcch. 104, 7); *paürisa* (Grr.), JM. *porisa*, AMg. *porisī*, *porasiẏa*, *aporisīẏa* (§ 61[a]). False is AMg. JM. *porusa* in Uttar. 17; Erz. 17, 35. In Ś. *purusŏttama* (Vikr.

35, 15) the *u* has been intentionally retained on account of similarity of sound with that of *purūrava-*, therefore, it falsely occurs also in Mālatīm. 73, 6. Elsewhere it is always *purisŏttama* (Mālatīm. 266, 4. Veṇīs. 97, 9) in Ś., and *pulišŏtta na* in Mg. (Prab. 32, 7. 14). In M. AMg. JM.Ś. *bhiuḍi* (Hc. 1, 110; G.H.R.; Vivāgas. 90. 121. 144. 157; Nāẏādh. 753. 1310. 1312; Vivāhap. 237. 254; Uvās.; Niraẏāv. ; Āv. 12, 27; Erz.; Veṇīs. 60, 5; 61, 18; Bālar. 270, 5, AMg. also in *bhiguḍi* (Paṇhāv. 162. 285) *i* is not = *u* of *bhrukuṭi*, but = *ṛ* of *bhṛkuṭi*. False is M. *bhuuḍi* (Pratāp. 220, 20) as well as *huuḍi* (Acyutaś. 58). On the other hand *a* stands for *u* according to § 123 in *bhamaẏā* (Hc. 2, 167) against AMg. *bhamuhā* (§ 206; Pāiẏal. 251; Āẏār. 1, 1, 2, 5; 2, 13, 17 [neuter] ; Jīv. 563; Rāẏap. 165; Ovav.; Kappas.), A. *bhŏhā* (Piṅgala 2, 98; § 166. 251), and M. *bhumaā* (Bh. 4. 33; Hc. 1, 121; 2, 167; Kī. 1, 117; Mk. fol. 39; G.H.R.), AMg. *bhumaẏā* (Pāiẏal. 251; Uvās.; Ovav.), *bhumagā* (Paṇhāv. 272. 285 [text *bhū*°] ; Uvās.); *bhumā* (Ovav. s.v. *kŏkkuiẏa*). Cf. § 206. 254. 261. — AMg. *chiẏa* (one who has enjoyed; Hc. 1, 112; 2. 117; Nandīs. 380) is not = *kṣuta*, but onomatopoetically = **chita*, corresponding to German *tsi* ! In addition AMg. *chiẏamāṇa* (convalescent; Āẏār. 2, 2, 3, 27). In the same way is to be explained *chikka* (Deśīn. 3, 36); cf. Skt. *chikkā*, *chikkana*. — On *sūhava* = *subhaga* see § 62, on *mūsala* = *musala*, § 66.

1. Zimmer, KZ. 24, 220 f.; S. Goldschmidt, KZ. 25, 615; Wackernagel, Altind. Gr. § 51.

§ 125. Like *i* becoming *ĕ*, (§ 119), before consonant-groups *u* may become *ŏ* (Vr. 1, 20; Hc. 1, 116; Kī. 1, 23; Mk. fol. 8; Pkl. p. 31). According to Mk. fol. 66, this change does not take place in Ś. except in *muktā* and *puṣkara*, and this is attested substantially by the texts. PG. *khaṁdakŏṁḍisa* = *skandakuṇḍinaḥ* (6, 19); M. *gŏccha* = *guccha* (H. R.), *gŏcchaa* (H.), M. *tŏṇḍa* (Grr.; H. 402 [read as such]), but Mg. *tuṇḍa* (Mṛcch. 112, 8); *mŏṇḍa* (Grr.), but M.Ś.Mg. *muṇḍa* (G.; Mṛcch. 80, 20; Prab. 49, 4; Mg. Mṛcch. 122, 7; Prab. 53, 14); Ś. *pŏkkhara* = *puṣkara* (Grr.; Mṛcch. 2, 16; 54, 2; 95, 11), and AMg. JM. *pukkhara* (Kappas.; Erz.), Ś. *pukkharakkha* = *puṣkarākṣa* (Mudrār. 204, 3); AMg. Ś. *pŏkkhariṇi* (Āẏār. 2, 3, 3, 2 [text °*ra*] ; Nāẏādh. 1060; Dhūrtas. 5, 10) and AMg. JM. *pukkheriṇi* (Sūẏag. 565, 613; T. 4, 9); Mg. *pŏskaliṇi* (Mṛcch. 112, 11) and *puskaliṇi* (Mṛcch. 113, 22); AMg. *pŏṇḍariẏa* (Sūẏāg. 813; Paṇṇav. 34; Ovav.), and JM. *puṇḍariẏa* (Erz.), Ś. *puṇḍaria* (Mālatīm. 122, 2); JM. *kŏṭṭima* (Grr.; Erz.), beside M. *kuṭṭima* (R.); Ś. *pŏtthaa* = *pustaka* (Grr.; Mṛcch. 69, 17; Karp. 12, 11), AMg. *pŏtthaẏa* (Ovav.) NPK. *lŏddhaa* = *lubdhaka* (Grr.; Pāiẏal. 248); M. *mŏtthā* = *mustā* (Hc. 1, 116; Sarasvatīk. 16, 9); M. Ś. *mŏggara* = *mudgara* (Grr.; R.; Bālar. 245, 18; 251, 3) beside *muggara* (R.); AMg. JŚ. *pŏggala* = *pudgala* (Hc. 1, 116; Āẏār. 2, 1, 10, 6; Bhag.; Uvās.; Ovav; Kappas.; Pav. 384, 58), beside JŚ. Mg. *puggala* (Pav. 384, 36. 47. 59; Prab. 46, 14); M.Ś. *mŏttā* (Bh.; Kī.; Mk.; Pkl. R.; Vikr. 40, 18), beside M. Ś. *muttā* (G.R.; Mṛcch. 69, 1; Karp 72,2), Ś. *muttāhala* = *muktāphala* (Karp. 72, 3. 8; 73, 9), M. *muttāhalilla* (Karp. 2, 5; 100, 5). On the lengthening of such a secondary *ŏ*, see § 66 and cf. §127.

§ 126. Beside *duūla*, AMg. *dugulla*, according to grammarians, there occurs also *duulla* (§ 90). — AMg. *uvviḍha*, which according to Hc. 1, 120 = *udvyūḍha*, belongs rather to *uvvihaï* = *udvidhyati* from *vidh* (*vyadh*) with *ud* (§ 489), as is clear from Vivāhap. 1388 : *se jahā ṇāmae ke i puriṣe...usuṁ... uvvihaï uvvihittā...tassa usussa...uvviḍhassa samāṇassa.* It has, therefore, been formed on the analogy of *liḍha*, from *lih*, *mīḍha*, from *mih*, from the secondary root *vih* = *vidh*. *udvyūḍha* forms regularly M. AMg. *uvvūḍha* (Hc. 1, 120; Śak. 88, 2; Jīv. 826). On *u* for *ū* see § 80-82. For *nūpura*, all the dialects have *ṇeura*, Mg. *ṇeula*, that go back to the side-form preserved in modern Indian languages as *nepūra*, *nepura*, which may be set side by side with Skt. *keyūra*, Pkt. *keūra* : cf. Ś. *ṇeurakeūraṁ*, (Bālar. 248. 17), A. *ṇeurakeurao* (Piṅgala 1, 26). So M.Ś. *ṇeura* (Vr. 1, 26; Hc. 1, 123; Kī. 1, 5; ; Mk. fol. 9; G.H.R.; Mṛcch. 41, 2; Vikr. 31, 7; Mālav. 40, 7; Ratn. 294, 32; Prab. 39, 8 [read as such with PM] ; Pras. 39, 18; 114, 9; Karp. 21, 1; Bālar. 248, 17), M. *ṇeurilla* = *nūpuravat* (G.); *saṇeura* (Mālav. 37, 15; 43. 2); AMg. JM. *neura* (C. 2, 4 [read as such with A] ; 3, 34 p. 35; Pāiyal. 118; Paṇhāv. 236, 514; Nāyādh. § 65. 102; p. 948; Vivāhap. 791; Ovav.; Āv.12, 6); Mg. *ṇeula* (Mṛcch. 99, 7. 10); A. *ṇeura* (Piṅgala 1, 17. 22. 26). Hc. 1, 123; Deśīn. 4, 28 known also *ṇiura* and 1, 123 *ṇūura*; Pratāp. 220, 14 has certainly a false reading *ṇūvurāiṁ*.

§ 127. Like *u* (§ 125), before consonant-groups *ū* too may become *ŏ* : AMg. *kŏppara* = *kūrpara* (Hc. 1, 24; Vivāgas. 90), beside M. *kuppara* (G.); AMg. JM. *mŏlla* = *mūlya*[1] (Hc. 1, 124; Āyār. 2, 5, 1, 4; 2, 6, 1, 2; p. 128, 6; Āv. 31, 10; Erz.), M. *amŏlla* (G.), beside the more frequent *mulla* (§ 83). Like *ŏ* from *u* (§ 66), the *ŏ* from *ū* is also lengthened, when an original consonant-group is simplified. Thus may be explained, AMg. *toṇa* = *tūṇa* (Hc. 1, 125; Paṇṇav. 72. 79. 81. 83; Vivāgas. 112; Nāyādh. 1426), beside Ś. *tūṇi-* (Veṇīs. 62, 4; Mukund. 69, 14); M. *toṇira* = *tūṇira* (Hc. 1, 124; Karp. 47, 8); *thoṇā* beside *thūṇā* = *sthūṇa* (Hc. 1, 125). They go back to **tŏṇṇa*, **tŏṇṇira*, **thŏṇṇā* from **tulna*, **tulnira*, **sthulnā*[2]. A similar explanation holds good for M. *thora* from **thŏrra* = *sthūra'* (Hc. 1, 124, 255; 2, 99; G.H. R.; Sarasvatīk. 171, 22; Karp. 50, 11; 64, 2; 74, 7; 81. 4) beside AMg. JM. *thulla* = *sthūlá* (Hc. 2, 99; Āyār. 2, 4, 2, 7; Āv. 22, 15, 42), *aïthulla* (Āv. 22, 35) and AMg. JŚ. Ś. *thūla* (Āyār. p. 133, 33; 136, 3; Sūyag. 286; Paṇhāv. 437; Kattig. 398, 303. 305; Karp. 72, 1; Hāsy. 32, 1 [read as such with v. l., while Āv. 22, 34 *thulla*, 22, 33 *aïthulla* should be corrected]). Further for AMg. *ṇaṅgola* = *lāṅgūla* (Nāyādh. 502), *ṇaṅgoli-* = *lāṅgūlin* (Jīv. 345), *ṇaṅgoliya* = *lāṅgūlika* (Jīv. 392), beside *ṇaṅgula* (Jīv. 883. 886. 887), *goṇaṅgula* (Vivāhap. 1048), *ṇaṅgūli-* (Aṇuog. 349), and M. AMg. JM. JŚ. Ś. *tambola* = *tāmbūla* (Hc. 1, 124; Mk. fol. 8; G.; Aṇuog. 61; Uvās.; Ovav.; Erz.; Kattig. 401, 350; Mṛcch. 71, 6; Mālatīm. 201, 2 [read as such] ; Karp. 98, 4; Viddhaś. 28, 7; Kaṁsav. 55, 13) [text *tambŏlla*)), AMg. *tambolaya* (Sūyag. 250), *tamboli* (Jīv. 487; Rāyap. 137). The *o* presupposes final accentuation of *lāṅgūla* and *tāmbūla*, in which case *l* is doubled according to § 90, as in *thulla*, *dugulla*. The line of development was, therefore : *tāmbūlá*, **tambulla*, **tambŏlla*, *tambola*.[3] In *kohaṇḍi* = *kūṣmāṇḍi*, (Hc. 1, 124; 2, 73; Kī. 2, 73; Pāiyal. 14, 6), AMg. *kohaṇḍa* = *kūṣmāṇḍa* (Paṇṇav. 111), beside *kūhaṇḍa* (Paṇhāv. 172. 230. 312) and *kuhaṇḍa* (Paṇṇav. 115; probably wrongly) too *o* is secondary. For Ś. *kohaṇḍa* (Karp. ed. Bomb. 99, 3), that is forbidden by Mk. for Ś. KONOW 103, 1 reads *kumbhaṇḍa*, and we must read as such also in Viddhaś. 23, 2. The stages were : **kumhaṇḍi*, **kŏmhaṇḍi*, **komhaṇḍi*, *kŏhaṇḍi*, *kohaṇḍi* (§ 76. 89. 312), *kohaḷi* (Hc. 1, 124; 2, 73), *kohaliyā* (Pāiyal. 146) may in the same way be derived from *kŏhŏḍi*. Cf. Marāṭhī. *kohaḷeṁ*, *gaḷoi*=*guḍūci* (Hc. 1, 107. 124; § 123) may be going back to **goḍŏcci*.

1. JACOBI, Erz. s. v. *mŏlla*, wrongly equates it as=*maulya*, which is a back formation from Pkt. — 2. WINDISCH, KZ. 27, 168, HÜBSCHMANN, ZDMG. 39, 92ff., FORTUNATOV, KZ. 36, 18. Wrongly BARTHOLOMAE, IF.3, 157 ff.; WACKERNAGEL, Altind. Gram. § 146 d note, 172 d note; JOH. SCHMIDT, Kritik der Sonantentheorie p. 1, note. — 3. Impossible is the derivation from *tāmragula* in LEUMANN, Aup. S. p. 165.

§ 128. In the syllable preceding and following the accented one *e* sometimes becomes *i* (§ 79-82); before a consonant-group it becomes *ĕ*, *i* (§ 84), in the auslaut before enclitics with a double consonant in the anlaut it becomes *ĕ*, and dialectically, however, sometimes, after a long vowel it becomes *i* also (§ 85). A secondary *ĕ* is sometimes lengthened and the consonant-group, simplified (§ 66. 122). In A. *e* is shortened also in the inst. sing. in *-ena* and in the inst. plur. in *-ehiṁ*, occasionally (cf. Saṅgītaratnākara 4, 56). So *bŏllieṇa* (Hc. 4, 383, 2; read as such); *pāṇiĕṇa* (Hc. 4, 434); *khaṇĕṇa* (Hc. 4; 419,1; read as such); *amhĕhĩ*, *tumhĕhĩ*. (Hc. 4, 371), *vaṅkĕhĩ loaṇĕhĩ* (Hc. 4, 356; read as such); *atthĕhĩ*, *satthĕhĩ*, *hatthĕhĩ* (Hc. 4, 358; read as such), *dentĕhĩ* (Hc. 4, 419, 5; read as such). Since the manuscripts vary so greatly, it is doubtful whether one should or should not in such cases do as I have done in my edition of Hemacandra and write *bŏllieṁ*, *pāṇieṁ*, *vaṅkehĩ* or with the v. l. *vaṅkihĩ*, *loaṇihĩ* etc. It is true that we often find without any variant the instrumental plural forms in *-ahiṁ*, *-ahĩ*, that are formed from the stems in *a-* (§ 308). Beside the loc. plur. of the pronouns of the first and second persons in *-esu*, some grammarians prescribe the loc. forms in *-asu*, and Śākalya teaches also *tujjhisuṁ* and *tumbhisuṁ* (§ 415. 422). JM. *eiṇā*, Ś. Mg. *ediṇā*, JM. Ś. Mg. *imiṇā*, beside *eeṇa*, Ś. Mg. *edeṇa*, *imeṇa* (§ 426. 430) are best explained with LASSEN (Inst. § 107) as formed from an *i*- stem, which is certainly the case for *kiṇā*=*keṇa*, on the analogy of which are formed *jiṇā* and *tiṇā* (§ 428). — AMg. JM. *aüṇa*°, *aüṇa*[a] are not=*ekona*, but=*aguṇa* (§ 444). On JM. *āṇasu*, A. *āṇahi* see § 474, and on the causative in *-a* instead of in*-e*, § 491.

§ 129. For *e* occurs *a* in *ṇāliara*=*nālikera* (Deśīn. 2, 10), beside M. *ṇālieri* (G.), Ś. *ṇāriela* (Śak. 78, 12), and *pavaṭṭha*=*praveṣṭa*, equated by Grr. (Vr. 1, 40; Hc. 1, 156; Kī. 1, 40; Mk. fol. 13) as=*prakoṣṭha*,[1] which evidently forms M. AMg. *paŏṭṭha* (Karp. 47, 6; Ovav.) and *paüṭṭha* (G.; Kappas.); in Ś., as Mk. expressly teaches, it forms only *paŏṭṭha'* (Bālar. 80, 1; Viddhaś. 126, 3; in the meaning "house", Mṛcch. 68, 23 ff.). — *thūṇa* (Hc. 1, 147; Deśīn. 5, 29) beside *theṇa*, AMg. *teṇa* (§ 307)=*stena*, cannot be separated from *thūṇa* (horse; Deśīn. 529) and may be equated as=*tūrṇa* for **stūrṇa* "quick", "fast"; cf. *theṇilla* "fearful" (Deśīn. 5, 32) and *veḷu* "thief" § 243. —AMg. JM. JŚ. *dosa* (hatred; Deśīn. 5, 56; Triv. 1, 4, 121; for example

Āẏār. 1, 3, 4, 4; Sūẏag. 198; Paṇṇav. 638; Dasav. N. 653, 6; Uttar. 199. 446, 648. 707. 822. 876. 902. 910 ff.; Vivāhap. 125. 832. 1026; Erz.; Ṛṣabhap.; Pav. 384, 54; 385, 61; Kattig. 404, 389), AMg. JM. JŚ. *padosa, paosa* (Sūẏag. 81; Uttar. 368; Erz.; Pav. 385, 69) are not = *dveṣa, pradveṣa*[2], but = *doṣa, pradoṣa* with a change of meaning.[3] Further also *dosākaraṇa* (anger; Deśīn. 5. 51); *dveṣa* becomes *besa* (§ 300).

1. So wrongly also LASSEN, Inst. p. 136, note*. — 2. CHILDERS, s. v.; WEBER, Bhag. s. v.; JACOBI, Kalpasūtra s. v.; Erz. p.xxv, note 1; LEUMANN, Aup. S. s. v.; KLATT Ṛṣabhap. s. v., E. MÜLLER, Beiträge p. 23. — 3. PISCHEL, BB. 13, 14 ff.

§ 130. *o* becomes *ŏ*, *u* before consonant-groups (§ 84), in the auslaut before enclitics with double consonants in the anlaut *ŏ*, dialectically elsewhere also *ŏ*, *u* (§ 85. 346). The secondary *ŏ* is sometimes lengthened and the consonant-group, simplified (§ 66. 127). In A. *o* becomes *u* not only in the auslaut (§ 85. 346), but occasionally in the inlaut as well, as in *viueṁ* for *vioeṁ* = *viyogena* (Hc. 4, 419, 5). — M. *aṇṇaṇṇa* (Hc. 1, 156; G. H.), JM. *annanna* (Erz.) is not = *anyonya*, that becomes *aṇṇŏṇṇa, aṇṇuṇṇa* (§ 84), but = Vedic *anyānya*. — *āvajja* is not = *ātodya* (Hc. 1, 156), which becomes *āŏjja, āujja*, Ś. *pakkhāujja* = *pakṣātodya* (Karp. 3, 3), but = **āvādya*. — *a* for *o* is seen in *pulaaï, pulaei, pulaïa* beside *puloei, paloei, puloia, paloia* = *pralokayati, pralokita* (§ 104) and *pallaṭṭaï* beside *palŏṭṭaï* (to upset; Hc. 4, 200), *pallaṭṭa* (Hc. 2, 47. 68), beside *palŏṭṭa* (Hc. 4, 258). Probably these words are derived from different roots. On *pavaṭṭha*, ostensibly = *prakoṣṭha*, see § 129. — AMg. JM. *theva* (a drop. a little; Pāiyal. 164; Hc. 2, 125. Deśīn. 5, 29; Dasav. N. 652, 32; Kl. 7; Āv. 45, 2; Erz.), has nothing to do with *thova* = *stoka* (§ 230), but it with *thippaï*. (Hc. 4, 175) is derived from the roots *stip, step* (Dhātupāṭha 10, 3. 4), as has correctly been shown by CHILDERS for Pāli *theva*.

(f). SEPARATION-VOWELS

§ 131. Consonant-groups are often separated in Pkt. by a separation or epenthetic vowel, and the individual consonants are then treated according to the phonetic rules holding good for the different dialects. Vocalic development takes place only when one of the consonants is *y, r, l* or a nasal. The exact quality and quantity of the separation-vowel is indefinite so that they appear as *a, i* and *u*. Metrically it is sometimes without any value. Thus in AMg. *a* in *agaṇi* : *nivvāvao agaṇī nivāaĕjja, ṇa paṇḍie agaṇī samārabhĕjjā* (Sūẏag. 330); in *garahio*; *musāvāo ẏa lagammi savvasāhūhi garahio* (Dasav. 625. 3); cf. Sūẏag. 912. 914; *i* in *kiriẏākiriẏaṁ veṇaïẏāṇuvāẏaṁ* (Sūẏag. 322) in *kiṁpurisa* : *asogo kiṁṇarāṇaṁ ca kiṁpurisāṇaṁ ca campao* (Ṭhāṇ. 505; Abhayadeva on Samav. 21); in *arihaï* : *bhikkhū akkhāum arihai* (Dasav. 631. 8) so *bhāsium arihaï kiriẏavādaṁ* (Sūẏag. 476; also in *kiriya°*); in *āẏariẏa* : *āaẏari ẏassa mahappaṇo* (Dasav. 631, 33)[1]. It does not even hinder shortening of a long vowel under the influence of accent, as AMg. JM. *āẏariẏa* = *ācārya* (§ 81. 134), M.Ś. *verulia*, AMg. JM. *veruliẏa* = *vaiḍūrẏa* (§ 80), Ś. *murukkha* = *mūrkhá* (§ 139), AMg. *suhuma* = *sūkṣma* (§ 82; C. 3, 30; Hc. 1, 118; 2, 113; Āẏār. 2, 4, 1, 7; 2, 15, 3; p. 131. 32; Sūẏag. 128. 217. 493;

Paṇṇav. 72. 79. 81. 83; Paṇhāv. 274; Jīv. 39. 41. 313; Aṇuog. 260, 391. 392; Vivāhap. 105. 943. 1385. 1438; Uttar. 1040; Ovav.; Kappas.),[2] nor the doubling of the consonants according to § 195, nor the change of *a* into *i* according to § 101, as in AMg. *nigiṇa* = *nagná* (§ 133), nor the transformation of *tya* to *cca* and *dhya* to *jjha* (§ 280).

1. More examples in Jacobi, KZ. 23, 594ff. — 2. In Sūyag. 174 (= 3, 2, 1) the printed edition reads *ah' ime suhamā saṅgā*, in the beginning certainly correctly so that with Jacobi, KZ. 23,595, *suhmā* is not to be accepted. Cf. § 323.

§ 132. Only in AMg. and A. *a* is more frequently a separation-vowel : it so occurs much more rarely in other dialects. AMg. *agaṇi* = *agni* (Hc. 2, 102; e.g.-Āẏār. 1, 1, 4, 6; Sūẏag. 273; Vivāgas. 224; Vivāhap. 120; Dasav. 616, 32 and unusually often); AMg. *abhikkhaṇaṁ* = *abhikiṣṇam* (Kappas.); AMg. *garahā* = *garhā* (Vivāhap. 132), *garahaṇā* = *garhaṇā* (Ovav.), *garahāmo, garahai* (Sūẏag. 912. 914), *garahaha* (Vivāhap. 132. 332), JM. *garahasi* (Erz. 55, 29), AMg. JM. *garahiẏa* (Sūẏag. 504; Dasav. 625, 3; Erz. 35, 15), AMg. *vigarahamāṇa* (Sūẏag. 912), JŚ. *garahaṇa* (Kattig. 400, 331), beside *gariha* (Vr. 3, 62; Kī. 2, 59), AMg. *garihā* (Hc. 2, 104; Mk. fol. 29; Pāiẏal 245; Ṭhāṇ. 40), *garihāmi* (Vivāhap. 614), *garihasi* (Sūẏag. 912; read °-*ra*° JM. *garihasu* (Erz. 42, 18); AMg. *raẏaṇi* = *aratni* (§ 141);[1] AMg. *rahassa* = *hrasva*; M. AMg. Ś.A. *dihara* = *dirgha* (§ 354); AMg. *sakahāo* = *sakthini* (§ 358); AMg. *haraẏa* = *hrada* (Hc. 2, 120; Āẏār. 1, 5, 5, 1; 1, 6, 1, 2; Sūẏāg. 123; Uttar. 376f.; Vivāhap. 105. 194. 270). A. *garāsa* = *grāsa* (Piṅgala 2, 140), *tarāsaī* = *trasyati* (P. 2, 96), *paramāṇa* = *pramāṇa* (P. 1, 28), *parasaṇṇa* = *prasanna* (P. 2, 49), *parāvahĩ* = *prāpnuvanti* (Hc. 4, 442, 1). From other dialects some examples are : M. *raaṇa* = *ratna* (Vr. 3, 60; Kī. 2, 55; Mk. fol. 29; G. H.R.), AMg. JM. JŚ. *raẏaṇa* (§ 70; C. 3, 30; Hc. 2, 101; Kattig. 400, 325); Ś. *radaṇa* (Mṛcch. 52, 9; 68, 25; 70, 24; 71, 1; Śak. 38, 5; 103, 6; 117, 7; Vikr. 77, 15 etc.[2] D. *radaṇa* (Mṛcch. 101,1 2; Mg. *ladaṇa*, 146, 4; 159, 12; 164, 20; Śak. 113, 3; 117, 5), Ś. *sattuhaṇa* = *śatrughna* (Bālar. 310, 15; Anarghar. 317, 17), beside *sattuggha* (Bālar. 151, 1); M. Ś. *śalāhā* = *ślāghā* (Vr. 3, 63. Hc. 2, 101; Kī. 2, 57; Mk. fol. 30; G.; Caṇḍak. 95, 8), M. *salāhaṇa* = *ślāghana* (H.); *salahaï* (Hc. 4, 88), M. *salāhamāṇa* (H.), *ahisalāhamāṇa* (G.), *salāhaṇijja* (H.), Ś. *salāhaṇia* (Mṛcch. 128, 4; Prab. 4, 8 [read so] ; Ratn. 304. 18; 319, 15; Mālatīm. 82, 8 [so to be read], Mg. *śalāhaṇia* (Mṛcch. 38, 1 [read so]); Ś. *salāhiadi* (Ratn. 309, 5; Prab. 12, 11 [read so]); A. *salahijjosu, salahijjaï* (Piṅgala 1, 95. 117); JM. *bhasama-* = *bhasman* (Erz.); P. *dharamapatani* = *dharmapatni* (Mk. fol. 87). The dialect remains undetermined in the case of *gahara* from **gṛdhara* = *gṛdhra* (Pāiẏal. 126; Deśīn. 2, 84); *palaakkha* = *plakṣa* (C. 3, 30; Hc. 2, 103), for which AMg. has *pilaṁkhu, pilakkhu* § 74. 105); *sāraṅga* = *śārṅga* (Vr. 3, 60; Hc. 2, 100; Kī. 2, 55; Mk. fol. 29). According to Hc. 4, 270 in Ś. and according to 4, 323 in P. *purava*, and according to 4, 302, in Mg. *pulava* = *pūrva* are used.[3] Against the principal rule is P. *kasaṭa* = *kaṣṭa* (Vr. 10, 6; Hc. 4. 314; Kī. 5,109; ed. *kasṭam*; cf. Lassen, Inst. p. 441). False is Ś. *parāṇa* = *prāṇa* (Cait. 54, 10) for which read *pāṇa*, as for example Mṛcch. 155, 18; 166, 9. 14. 15. Cf. also §140.

1. For AMg. *ahārāiṇiyāe*=*yathāratnikāya* (Ṭhāṇ. 355. 356) is to be read as *ahārāyaṇiyāe*. — 2. The printed editions write almost without exception *raaṇa* in Ś. *laaṇa* in Mg., that is a blunder committed against the dialects concerned. — 3. For in Ś. and in Mg.; these are not attested by the texts (PISCHEL on Hc. 4, 270). Probably by Ś. here is meant JŚ. too.

§ 133. Most frequently appears as a separation-vowel *i*. In AMg. it is so found in many cases where the remaining dialects show assimilation of consonants. 1) One of the consonants is a nasal : AMg. *usiṇa*=*uṣṇa* (Āẏār. 2,1, 6, 4; 2, 2, 1, 8; 2, 2, 3, 10; Sūẏag. 132. 590; Thāṇ. 131. 135; Paṇṇav. 8.10.786ff.; Jīv. 224. 295; Vivāhap. 194. 195. 250. 436; 465. 1470ff.; Aṇuog. 268; Uttar 48.57), *accuṣina*=*atyuṣṇa* (Āẏār. 2, 1, 7, 5), *siẏosiṇa*=*śītoṣṇa* (Āẏār. 1,3,1,2; Vivāhāp. 862.863), beside *siuṇha* (Sūẏag. 134;) Mg. *kośiṇa*=*koṣṇa* (Veṇīs. 34.4). Cf. 312. AMg. *kasiṇa*=*kṛtsna* (Hc. 2, 75 104; Sūẏag. 26.28.172.292.416.439. 460; Vivāhap. 205; Aṇuog. 104; Uttar. 251; Ovav.; Kappas.) and=*kṛṣṇa*, beside *kasaṇa, kaṇha, kiṇha* (§ 52); AMg. JM. *tūsiṇiẏa*=*tūṣṇika*, beside *tuṇhia, tuṇhikka* (§ 81. 90); AMg. *dosiṇā* =*jyotsnā*, Ś *dosiṇi*=*jyautsni* (§ 215) : AMg. *nigiṇa*=*nagna* (Āyār. 2, 2, 3, 11; 2, 7, 1, 11; Sūẏag. 108 [text *nigaṇa*]) with *i* in the first syllable according to § 101, beside *nagiṇa* (Āẏar. 1,6,2,3; Sūẏag. 169; Dasav. 627, 1), *nagiṇiṇa* (sic; Uttar. 208) *nāganiẏa*=Sūẏag. 344)=*nagnatva*; AMg. *pasiṇa*=*praśna* (Āẏār. 2, 3, 2, 17, Sūẏag. 383.918; Nāẏādh. 301, 577. 578; Vivāhap. 151. 973. 978. 1251. 1261. 1408; Nandīs, 471; Uttar. 513; Uvās.; Ovav.); AMg. *siṇāṇa*=*snāna* (Mk. fol. 29; Āẏār. 2, 1, 6, 2; 2, 2, 1, 8; 2, 7, 1, 11; Sūẏag. 344. 382; Dasav. 626, 40; probably incorrectly also in Ś. Cait. 44, 4; 92, 14; 134, 9; 150, 7; 260, 4); AMg. *asiṇāṇa* (Dasav. 626, 39), *pāosiṇāṇa*=*prātaḥsnāna* (Sūẏag. 337), *siṇāi*=*snāti* (Mk. fol. 29; Sūẏag. 340); *asiṇāittā* (Sūẏag. 994) *siṇāẏanta-, siṇāẏanti* (Dasav. 626, 37. 38), probably incorrectly also Ś. *siṇāvĕnti* (Cait. 44, 13), *siṇāẏaga*=*snātaka* (Sūẏag. 929. 933. 940), *siṇāẏaẏa* (Uttar. 755; text *siṇāio*); P. *sināta*=*snāta* (Hc. 4, 314), *katasinānena*=*kṛtasnānena* (Hc. 4, 322; read so); *siviṇa, simiṇa, suviṇa, sumiṇa*=*svapna* (§ 177). *i* is a separation-vowel also in the declension of *rājan*, as in inst. sing. JM. *rāiṇā*, P. *rāciñā* (§ 399).

§ 134. 2) If one of the consonants is *ya*, except in AMg. JM. JŚ. it drops after the separation vowel *i* : AMg. JM. *ceiẏa*=Pāli *cetiya*=*caitya* (Āẏār. 2, 21; 23,3, 1; 2, 10, 17; 2, 15, 25; Sūẏag. 1014;-Ṭhāṇ. 266; Samav. 101. 233; Paṇhāv. 521; Vivāhap. 5. 164. 934; Rāẏap. 154; Jīẏak. 6; Uvās.; Ovav.; Kappas.; Niraẏāv.; T. 6, 24; Erz.; Kk.); AMg. *ciẏatta*=**tiyakta*=*tyakta*, *jhiẏāi*=*dhyāti* (§ 280); AMg. *teṇiẏa*=*stainya* (§ 307); AMg. *bāliẏa*=*bālya* (Vivāhap. 132); AMg. JM. *bahiyā*=*bāhẏāt* (Āẏār. 1, 1, 7, 1; Sūẏag. 954; Uvās.; Ovav.; Kappas.; Āv. 14, 10); AMg. *viẏaggha*=*vyāghra* (Paṇhāv. 20); Ś. *diṭṭhiā*=*diṣṭyā* (Hc. 2, 104; Mṛcch. 68, 2; 74, 11; Śak. 52, 10; 167,7; Vikr. 10, 20; 26, 15; 49, 4; 75, 2 etc.); *hijjo*=*hyas* (Deśīn. 8, 67; Pāiẏal. 211; Triv. 1, 3, 105; cf. BB. 3, 251), Ś. *hio* (Mālav. 51, 7; Priyad. 19, 12); in words of all classes, as in the absolutives in *-ya* for example AMg. *pāsiẏa*, JM *pĕcchiẏa*, Ś. *pĕkkhia*, Mg. *peskia*, Ḍh. *paḍissudia* (§ 590, 591), the optatives in *-yā*, as AMg. *siā*=*sẏāt*, *hanyāt* (§ 465), *bhuñjĕrjjā*=*bhuñjyāt*, *karejjā*= **karyāt* (§ 459), the participia nec. and the adjectives in *-ijja*, as *karaṇijja*, *ramaṇijja* (§ 91. 571), the numerals, as M. *biia, biijja*, AMg. JM. *biiya*; M. *taïa*, AMg. JM. *taïya*, Ś.Mg. *tadia*, A. *taïjji* (§ 82. 91. 449). The separation-vowel *i* is especially frequent in the consonant-group *rya*. The words of the type are classed by Vṛ. 3, 20; Hc. 2, 107; Kī. 2, 81 under the ākṛtigaṇa *cauryasama*. A long vowel is mostly common before *rya*. Thus AMg. *āriya* = *ārya* (Āyār. 1, 2, 2, 3; 1, 2, 5, 2. 3; 1, 4, 2, 5; Sūyag. 54. 204. 363. 914; Paṇṇav. 59ff.; Samav. 98; Vivāhap. 1246; Uttar. 109. 509; Ovav.); *aṇāriya* (Āyār. 1, 4, 2, 4; Sūyag. 56. 68. 208. 210. 437. 439. 923. 931. 935; Samav. 98; Uttar. 511. 990); AMg. JM. *āyāriya* = *ācārya* (Hc. 1, 73; Āyār. 2, 1, 10,1; 2, 3, 3, 3ff.; Samav. 85; Ṭhāṇ. 157. 286; Nandīs. 512ff.; Dasav. 633. 41; 634, 19ff.; Uttar. 43; Nāyādh ; Uvās ; Ovav.; Kappas.; Āv, 33, 17; 38 13. 18; 40, 9ff.; Erz. Kk;), also *āiriya* (C. 1, 5 p. 40; Hc. 1, 73. 2, 107) Ś. *ācāria* (Cat, 45 5; 89, 12; 127, 13), Mg. *ācālia* (Prab, 28, 14; 29, 7; 58, 17; 61, 5; 62,. 1.2. 6; Cait. 149, 17. 19; 150, 2. 3. 13); M.Ś. *coria* = *caurya* (Grr.; H.; Cait. 81, 1), AMg. JM. *bhāriyā* = *bhāryā* (Hc. 2, 107; Sūyag. 176; Uvās.; Kappas.; Erz.); AMg. JŚ. *vīriya* = *vīrya* (Sūyag. 351. 360. 365. 442; Vivāhap. 67. 68. 125; Uvās.; Ovav.; Kappas.; Pav. 379, 2; 381, 19; 386, 1); M.Ś. *verulia*, AMg. JM. *veruliya* = *vaiḍūrya* (§ 80); AMg. *sūriya* (Hc. 2, 107; Sūyag. 306, 310. 312; Vivāhap. 452. 1040. 1273. 1282; Ovav. § 163; Kappas.), *asūriya* (Sūyag. 273); *soria* = *śaurya* (Bh. 3, 20; Hc. 2, 107; Kī. 2, 81). Hc. 2, 87 has also the examples *theria* = *sthairya*, *gambhīria*, *gahīria* = *gāmbhīrya*, and after the short vowel *sundaria* = *saundarya*, *varia* = *varya*, *bamhacaria* = *brahmacarya*. Corresponding to AMg. *moriyaputta* = *mauryaputra* (Samav. 123. 151; Bhag.), JM. *moriyavaṁsa* = *mauryavaṁśa* (Āv. 8, 17): Mg. has *molia* *maurya* (Mudrār. 268, 1). After a short vowel *i* has entered into the group *rya* in AMg. *tiriyaṁ* = *tiryak* (Āyār. 1, 1, 5, 2. 3; 1, 2, 5, 4; Sūyag. 191. 273. 304. 397. 428. 914. 931; Kappas.), *tiriyā* (Hc. 2, 143), AMg. JM. JŚ. *tiriya* (Bhag.; Uvās.; Ovav.; Erz.; Pav. 380, 12; 383, 70. 27); AMg. *pariyāga* = *paryāya* (Vivāgas. 270; Vivāhap. 235, 796. 845; Uvās.; Ovav.; Kappas.). often beside *pariyāya*; AMg. *vippariyāsa* = *viparyāsa* (Sūyag. 468. 497. 498).

§ 135. 3) Consonant-groups with *r* excepting *rya* (§ 134); PG. *pariharitavaṁ* = *parihartavyam* (6, 36); M. *kiriā*, AMg. JŚ. *kiriyā* = *kriyā* (Vr. 3, 60 Hc. 2, 104; G.; Sūyag. 322. 412. 445. 460; Bhag.; Nāyādh.; Ovav.; Pav. 381, 21; 386, 6. 10; Kattig. 403, 373, 374); AMg. *darisaṇa* = *darśana* (Hc. 2, 105; Mk. fol. 29; Sūyag. 43; Bhag.; Ovav.), *darisi-* = *darśin* (Nandīs. 388; Bhag.; Uvās.; Kappas.), *darisaṇijja* = *darśaniya* (Paṇṇav. 96. 118. 127; Uvās.; Ovav.; Nāyādh.; Bhag.); *darisaï*, JM. *darisei*, Ā.D. *darisedi* = *darśayati* (§ 554); *āarisa* (Hc. 2, 105; Mk. fol. 29), AMg. *ādarisa* (Ovav.) = *āsdarśa*; M. AMg. *pharisa* = *sparśa* (Vr. 3, 62; Mk. fol. 29; Pāiyal. 240; H.R.; Āyār. 1, 1, 7, 4; Nāyādh.; Ovav.); AMg. *pharisaga* = *sparśaka* (Kappas.), *dupparisa* = *duḥsparśa* (Paṇhāv. 508); *pharisaï* = *sparśayatï* (Hc. 4, 182); *marisaï*. = *marṣayati* (Vr. 8, 11; Hc. 4. 235); M. *amarisa* = *amarṣa* (Hc. 2, 105; G. R); M.Ś. *āmarisa* = *āmarṣa* (Acyutaś. 53; Uttarar. 20, 11), Mg. *āmaliśa* (Mallikām. 143, 11); Ś. *parāmarisa* (Hc. 2, 105; Mṛcch. 15, 6; 70, 1), *marisedu* Mṛcch 3, 19; Mālav. 86, 8), *marisehi* (Mālav. 38, 4; 55, 12); cf. Śak. 27, 6; 58, 9. 11; 73. 6; 115, 2; M. AMg. JM. Ś. *varisa* = *varṣa* (Hc. 2, 105; G.H.;

Ovav.; KI. 19; Āv. 13. 25; 14, 12; Erz.; Ṛṣabhap.; Bālar. 276, 3; Veṇīs. 65, 3; Mallikām. 225, 2; 259, 6); AMg. *varisā* = *varṣāḥ* (Hc. 2, 105; Nirayāv. 81); *varisaṇa* = *varṣaṇa* (Mk. fol. 29); Ś. *varisi-* = *varṣin* (Veṇīs. 60, 6; Karp. 71, 6); AMg. A. *varisaï* (Vr. 8, 11; Hc. 4, 235; Dasav. N. 648, 10; Piṅgala 1, 62); A. *varisei* (Vikr. 55, 2); JM. *varisiuṁ* = *varṣayituṁ* (Āv. 40, 4); Ś. *varisiduṁ* (Mālav. 66, 20), *varisanta-* (Prab. 4, 3; Caṇḍak. 16. 18); Mg. *valiśa* (Veṇīs. 33, 4); AMg. *sarisava* = *sarṣapa* (Paṇṇav. 34. 35; Nāyādh. § 61; Vivāhap. 1424ff. 1526; Ovav. §73); M. AMg. JM.Ś. *harisa* = *harṣa* (Vr. 3, 62; Hc. 2, 105; Kī. 2. 59; G.H.R.; Nirayāv.; Ovav.; Kappas.; Erz.; Kk.; Ratn. 300, 21; Mudrār. 263, 6; Veṇīs. 62, 12; 65, 7); AMg. *lomaharisa* (Paṇṇav. 90); Ś. *saharisa* (Mṛcch. 71, 19; Veṇīs. 65, 7); *harisaï* = *harṣati* (Hc. 4, 235), AMg. *harise* = *harṣet* (Āyār. 1, 2, 3, 2), Ś. *harisāvida* (Bālar. 242, 6); AMg. *vaïra* = *vajra* (Sūyag. 834; Ṭhāṇ. 265; Vivāhap. 499. 1326; Uttar. 589. 1041; Kappas.), *vaïrāmaya* = *vajramaya* (§ 70). On *siri* = *śri* and *hiri* = *hri* (Vr. 3, 62; C. 3. 30; p. 50; Hc. 2, 104; Kī. 2, 57; Mk. fol. 29) see § 98. 195.

§ 136. One of the consonants is *l* (Vr. 3, 60. 62; Hc. 2, 106; Kī. 2, 59. 104; Mk. fol. 29) : M. *kilammaï* = *klāmyati* (Hc. 2, 106; G. R.), AMg. *kilāmĕjja* = *klāmyet* (Āyār. 2, 1, 7, 1), Ś. *kilammadi* (Śak. 123, 8; Mālatīm. 135, 5; Mallikām. 69. 7; 133, 14; 159, 8; (text °*aï*)), M. A. *kilāmia* = **klāmita* (G.R.; Vikr. 60, 16); M. AMg. JM. Ś. Mg. *kilanta* = *klānta* (Grr.; G.R. Vivāhap. 1308; Rāyap. 258; Kappas.; Erz.; Uttarar. 18, 12 [text *kilinta*] ; Mṛcch. 13, 7. 10 [text *kilinte*] ; see v. l. in GOḌABOLE); JM.Ś. *kilammanta* (Erz.; Mālatīm. 81, 1); Ś. *kilammida* = **klāmita* (Karṇas. 47, 12; text°*li*°), *adikilammida* (Mālatīm. 206, 4); JM. *kilissaï* = *kliśyati* (Erz.), AMg. *samkilissaï* = *saṁkliśyati* (Ovav.; Ś. *adikilissadi* (Mālav 7, 17), *kilissanta* (Ratn. 304, 30); JM. *kiliṭṭha* (Grr.; Erz.), AMg. *saṁkiliṭṭha* (Ovav.) *asaṁkiliṭṭha* (Dasav. 642, 41); Ś. *kilesa* = *kleśa* (Grr.; Mṛcch. 68, 8. 10, Lalitav. 562, 22); M.Ś. *kiliṇṇa* = *klinna* (Hc. 1, 145; 2, 106; G.; Mukunda 15, 1); A. *kilinnaü* (Hc. 4, 329), beside *kiṇṇaü* (cf. § 59); AMg. *kiliva* = *kliba*. (Āyār. 2, 1, 3, 2); AMg. *gilāi, vigilāi* = *glāyati, viglāyati* (Hc. 2, 106; Sūyag. 200. 215; Ovav.; Kappas.); AMg. *milāi* (Hc. 2, 106; 4, 18, Āyār. 1, 1, ,5, 6);. M. JM.Ś. *milāṇa* = *mlāna* (Grr. ; G.H.; Erz.; Mṛcch. 2, 16; Vikr. 26, 13; Cait. 73, 9), Ś. *milāanta* (Mālatīm. 249, 4), *milāamāṇa* (Vikr. 51, 10; Mālav. 30, 7); for Ś. *pammalāadi* (Mālatīm. 120, 2) with ed. Madras 105, 3 and ed. Bombay 1892, p. 92, 2 we have to read *parimilāadi* (§ 479); *miliccha*, AMg; *milakkhu*, beside AMg. JM. Ś.A. *mĕccha*, AMg. *miccha* = *mleccha* (§ 84. 105); *silimha-* = *śleṣman* (Hc. 2, 106); AMg. JM. *siliṭṭha* = *śliṣṭa* (Grr.; Ovav.; Kappas.; Āv. 38, 10. 12), *asiliṭṭha* (Āv. 38, 8); Ś. *susiliṭṭha* (Mṛcch. 71, 13, Mālatīm. 234, 3), *dussiliṭṭha* (Mahāv. 23, 19); AMg. *silesa* = *śleṣa* (Hc. 2 106; Vivāhap. 658); AMg. JM. *siloga* = *śloka* (Sūyag. 370. 497. 938; Aṇuog. 557; Dasav. 637, 31. 44; 638, 8; 641, 7; Ovav.; Erz.), AMg. *siloya* (Sūyag. 405. 417. 506), Ś. *siloa* (Hc. 2, 106; Lalitav. 554, 13; Mudrār. 162, 6; Viddhaś. 117, 13; Karṇas. 30, 3. 5); *suila* (Hc. 2, 106), AMg. *sukkila* = *śukla* (Hc. 2, 106 [read as such] ; Ṭhāṇ. 569; Jīv. 27. 33. 224. 350. 457. 464. 482. 554. 928. 938; Aṇuog. 267; Uttar. 1021. 1024. 1041; Ovav.; Kappas.[1]; JM. *sukkiliya* (Āv. 7, 16).

1. The Indian editions very frequently write *sukkilla* (e. g. Ṭhāṇ. 339. 345. 348. 349 406. 568, Vivāhap. 436, 532. 535. 544. 1033. 1322. 1323. 1421. 1451. 1456; Paṇṇav. 8.11ff. 46. 241. 379. 380. 481. 525, Paṇhāv. 167; Samav. 64; Rāyap. 50.55. 104. 110. 120 (*sukilla*) etc. Sometimes both the forms stand printed side by side, thus Ṭhāṇ. 568 *sukkilla*, but 569 *sukkila*, Aṇuog. 267 *sukkila*, but 269 *sukkilla*. According to Hc. 2, 106, the correct form is *sukkila* in agreement with § 195.

§ 137. The separation-vowel *i* sometimes comes in after a secondary *b* developed in between *mr* and *ml* (§ 295); *ambira* = *āmra* (Hc. 2, 56; Deśīn. 1, 15); M. *tambira* = *tāmra* (Hc. 2, 56; H. 589 [read as such]); M. *āambira* = *ātāmra* (G. H.); *tambirā* (rust of wheat; Deśīn. 5, 5); AMg. JM. *ambila* = *amla* (Hc. 2, 106; Āyār. 1, 5, 6, 4; 2, 1, 7, 7; 2, 1, 11, 1; Ṭhāṇ. 20; Paṇṇav. 8. 10. 12ff.; Vivāhap. 147. 532; Jīv. 224; Uttar. 1021; Dasav. N. 656, 29; Kappas.; Āv. 24, 18); AMg. *aṇambila* (Āyār. 2, 1, 7, 7), *accambila* (Dasav. 621, 14); *ambiliyā* (tamarind; Pāiyal. 145); AMg. *āyambila* = *ācāmla*[1] (Vivāhap. 223; Nāyādh. 1292; Ovav.; Dvār. 498, 2), *āyambilaya* = *ācāmlaka*) (Ṭhāṇ. 352; Ovav. [text °*bilie*]). For Mg. *tikkhābilakeṇa* (Mṛcch. 163, 19), according to the v. l. in GODABOLE p. 442, we should read *tikkhambilakeṇa*.

1. So the word is mostly explained by scholiasts. Improbable assumption with regard to its origin in LEUMANN, Aup. S. s. v. *āyambiliya* and in WEBER, IS. 16, 305, note 12.

§ 138. In Ś. Mg. *i* appears as a separation-vowel in the passive in -*ia* as in *paḍhiadi* = Pāli *paṭhiyate* = *paṭhyate*, against M. AMg. JM. JŚ. *paḍhijjaï*, P. *paḍhiyyate* (§ 535 ff.), in the participia nec. and adjectives in -*aṇia* as in Ś. *karaṇia*, Mg. *kalaṇia* = *karaṇiya*, Ś. *ramaṇia*, Mg. *lamaṇia* = *ramaṇiya*, against M. AMg. JM. JŚ. *karaṇijja*, *ramaṇijja* = **karaṇya'*, **ramaṇyá* (§ 91. 134. 571), and in M. AMg. in the ending -*miṇa* = Skt. -*māna* as in AMg. *āgamamiṇa* (§ 110. 562). The separation-vowel oscillates between *i* and *i* in M.Ś. *accharia* JM. *acchariya* = *āścarya* (Vr. 12, 30 for Ś.; Hc. 1, 58; 2, 67; Mk. fol. 22; G.; Mṛcch. 172, 6; Mālav. 69, 2; 85, 8; Vikr. 9, 12; Prab. 4, 1; Mālatīm. 25, 1; Lalitav. 562, 19 etc.[1]; Pāiyal. 165; Kk.), Mg. *aścalia* (Lalitav. 565, 11 [*ya*°] ; 566, 3; Veṇīs 34, 6) and Ś. *accharia* (Hc.; Mṛcch. 73, 8; Śak. 14, 4; 157, 5; Ratn. 296, 25; 300, 7. 13; 306, 1; 313, 23; 322, 23 etc.); M. AMg. also *acchera* (Bh. 1, 5; 3, 18. 40; Hc. 1, 58; 2. 67; Kī. 1, 4; 2, 79; Mk. fol. 22; H.; Paṇhāv. 380 [text *acchara*]), AMg. JM. *accheraya* (Nāyādh. 778f. 1376; Kappas.; Āv. 29, 23; Erz., Kk.), AMg. *accheraga* (Paṇhāv. 288), according to Hc. also *acchariija*, a form which points to accentuation as *āścaryà* and *acchaara*, whose origin is still obscure. Beside M. *pilosa* (G. 589; [read as such]) = *ploṣa*, *piluṭṭha* = *pluṣṭa* (Hc. 2, 106), we have also *piluṭṭha* (Deśīn. 6, 51). M. Ś. *jiā* (Vr. 3, 66; Hc. 2, 115; Kī. 2, 61; Mk. fol. 30) is not = *jyā*, but = *jivā*. In PG. *āpiṭṭityaṁ* for-*āpaṭṭiyāṁ* = *āpiṭṭyām* (6, 37), and in inscriptions *i* frequently stands for *i*.

1. In many editions of the drama falsely written as *acca*° Cf. § 301.

§ 139. If one of the conjunct consonants is a labial or *va*, the more usual separation-vowel is *u*: M. *uddhumāi* = **uddhmāti* (Vr. 8, 32; Hc. 4, 8), *uddhumāa* = *uddhmāta* (G.R.), *uddhūmāia* (R.); *khuluha* = *kulpha* (Deśīn. 2, 75; Pāiyal. 250; cf. § 206); AMg. *chaüma-* = *chadman* (Hc. 2, 112), especially in *chaümattha* = *chadmastha* (Āyār. 1, 8, 4, 15; Ṭhāṇ. 50. 51. 188; Vivāhap. 78. 80; Uttar. 116. 805. 812; Ovav.; Kappas.); *tuvaraï* = *tvarate* (Vr. 8, 4; Hc. 4, 170,) M.Ś. *tuvara* = *tvarasva* (H.; Śak. 77, 3; 79, 6). Ś. *tuvaradi*

(Mṛcch. 97, 9; Vikr. 9, 12); *tuvaradu* (Mṛcch. 160, 14; Śak. 64, 11; Ratn. 313, 7), *tuaradu* (Mālav. 39, 11), *tuvaramha* (Ratn. 293, 31), *tuvaranta* (Mālatīm. 119, 4), *tuvarāvedi* (Mālatīm. 24, 4), *tuarāvedi* (Mālav. 33, 7; 39, 13), *tuarāvedu* (Mālav. 27, 19), *tuvarāanti* (Mālatīm. 114, 5); Mg. *tuvaladu* (Mṛcch. 170, 5), *tuvaleśi* (Mṛcch. 165, 24); AMg. JM.Ś. *duvāra* = *dvāra* (Hc. 2, 112; Mk. fol. 31; Pāiẏal. 235; Āẏār. 2, 1, 5, 4ff.; Vivāhap. 1264; Nāẏādh.; Āv. 25. 34; Erz.; Kk.; Mālatīm. 238, 6; Mudrār. 43, 8 [read as such with the v. l. for *dāra*] ; Ratn. 303, 2; 309, 10; 312, 22; Mālav. 23, 6; 62, 18; 65, 7; Bālar. 35, 6; Priyad. 37, 9; 38, 7), *duāra* (Mṛcch. 39, 3; 50, 23; 70, 9; 72, 13; 81, 25; Śak. 115. 5; Viddhaś. 78, 9; 83, 7); *duāraa* (Mṛcch. 6, 6; 44, 25; 51, 10; 68, 21; 99, 18; Mahāv. 100, 6); Mg. *duvāla* (Prab. 46, 12), *duāla* (Mṛcch. 43, 11; Cait. 150, 1), *duālaa* (Mṛcch. 45, 2; 97, 17); AMg. JM. *duvālasa* = *dvādaśa* (§ 244); M. AMg. Ś. Mg. *duve*, A. *dui* = *dve* (§ 437); M. AMg. JM.Ś. *paüma* = Pāli *paduma* = Skt. *padma* (Vr. 3, 65; Hc. 2, 112; Kī. 2, 62; Mk. fol. 31; Acyutaś. 36, 44. 90. 94 [text *paduma*] ; Ṭhāṇ. 75ff.; Uvās.; Ovav.; Kappas.; Erz.; Kk.; Priyad. 13, 16 [°*du*°]); Ś. *paü.-marāa* = *padmarāga* (Mṛcch. 71, 1); AMg. Ś. *paüminī* = *padminī* (Kappas. Mṛcch. 77, 13); AMg. *paümāvaī* = *padmāvatī* (Niraẏāv.), Ś. *padumāvadī* (Priyad. 24, 8); Ś. *puruvva* = *pūrva* (Mṛcch. 39, 23; 89, 4; Nāgān. 49, 10); AMg; *riuvveẏa* = *ṛgveda* (Ṭhāṇ. 166; Vivāhap. 149. 787; Niraẏāv. 44; Kappas.), M. AMg. JM. *sumaraï*, Ś. *sumaradi*, Mg. *śumaladi* = *smarati* (§ 478); AMg. *suve* (C. 3, 30 p. 50; Hc. 2, 114), *sue* (Āẏār. 2, 5, 1, 10; Uttar. 103; Dasav. 639, 15), Ś. *suvo* (Mukund. 14, 18) = *śvaḥ*. The separation-vowel *u* appears regularly in the feminine of the adjectives in -*u* (Vr. 3, 65; C. 3, 30 p. 50; Hc. 2, 113; Kī. 2, 62; Mk. fol. 30 f.), as *guruvī* (Grr.) = *gurvī*, while *garuī* belongs to *garua* = *guruka* (§ 123), consequently in Hc. 2, 113 the word with *b* is to be corrected as *guruvī*; *taṇuvī* = *tanvī*; (Grr.), M. *taṇuī* (H.); *lahuvī* = *laghvī* (Grr.); M.Ś. *lahuī* (G.; Mṛcch. 73, 11); *maüvī* = *mṛdvī* (Grr.), M. *maüī* (G.); *bahuvī* = *bahvī* (Grr.); *sāhuī* = *sādhvī* (Mk.). The feminine of *pṛthu* is *puhuvī*, when it is used adjectively (Hc. 1, 131; 2, 113), against which M. JM. Ś.A. *puhavī*, *puhaī*, AMg. JM. Ś. JŚ. *puḍhavī* in the meaning "the earth" (§ 51. 115). In the same way is explained also the absolutive Ś. Mg. Ḍh. *kadua* = *kṛtvā*, *gadua* = *gatvā* from **kaduvā*, **gaduvā* (§ 581), and the absolutive in -*tuāṇaṁ*, -*tuāṇa*, such as *kāuāṇaṁ*, *kāuāṇa* = **kartvānam* (§ 584). — Sometimes *u* is brought in when the syllable preceding or following the consonant-group contains *u* or *o*. Thus *murukkha* = *mūrkha* (§ 131; Hc. 2, 112), which according to Mk. belongs to the *prācyā bhāṣā*, that is to be spoken by the Vidūṣaka (§ 23), and which occurs in Pras. 48. 1 in Ś. [text *murukha*] , whilst elsewhere *mukkha* is used (e.g. Ś. Mṛcch. 52, 11. 15; 81, 4; Karp. 13. 8; Priyad. 18, 5. 14; 38, 1. 8; Cait. 82. 7; Mg. Mṛcch. 81, 17. 19; Prab. 50, 13); P. *sunusā* = *snuṣā* (Hc. 4, 314), to which *suṇhā* and *sŏṇhā* of the rest of the dialects go back (§ 148); *suruggha* = *srughna* (Hc. 2, 13); AMg. *duruhaï* = **udruhati* (§ 118. 141. 482).

§ 140. The separation-vowel oscillates between *a* and *i* in *kasaṇa*, *kasiṇa* = *kṛṣṇa* (§ 52); M.Ś. *barahi*-, AMg. Ś. *barahiṇa* (§ 406) = *barhin*, beside *bariha* = *barha* (Hc. 2, 104); A. *barihiṇa* = *barhin* (Hc. 4, 422, 8); *saṇeha* = *sneha*

(2, 102), A. *sasaṇehi* (Hc. 4, 367, 5), *saṇiddha* = *snigdha* (Hc. 2, 109), elsewhere M. JM. Ś. *siṇeha*, that is not mentioned by Vr. and Hc., though it is the only form found in dramas and occurs very frequently (Kī. 2, 58; Mk. fol. 26; G.H.R.; Erz.; Mṛcch. 27, 17; 28, 10; Śak. 9, 14; 56, 15; 90, 12; 132, 1; Mālav. 39, 6; Mālatīm. 94, 6; Uttarar. 68, 8; Ratn. 327, 13); Ś. *ṇissiṇeha* (Mṛcch. 25, 21), M. AMg. JM. Ś. *siṇiddha* = *snigdha* (Hc. 2 109; G.; Ovav.; Kappas.; Erz.; Mṛcch. 2, 22; 57, 10 [to be read as such]; 59, 24; 72, 7; Śak. 53, 8; 84, 11; 132, 11; Mālav. 5, 10; 60, 6); M. *siṇiddhaaṁ* (Vikr. 51, 7; 53, 5); AMg. *sasiṇiddha* = *sasnigdha* (Āẏār. 2, 1, 6, 6. 7. 9 [*sasa°* v. l.]; Kappas.). Beside these forms, we have also M. A. *ṇeha*, AMg. JM. *neha*, AMg. JM. *niddha*, M. *ṇiddha* = *sniḍḍha* (§ 313). The separation-vowel oscillates between *a* and *u* in *puhavī*, *puhai*, *puḍhavī* and *puhuvī* (§ 139); AMg. *suhuma* (§ 131) and AMg. *suhama* (Hc. 2, 101; Sūẏag. 174); Ś. *sakkaṇomi* and *sakkuṇomi* = *śaknomi* (§ 505). Dialectically *a*, *i* and *u* are exchanged in *arh*, *arha* and *arhant* (Hc. 2, 104. 111); AMg. *araha-* (Sūẏag. 321; Samav. 111; Uvās.; Ovav.; Kappas.); AMg. JŚ. *arahanta-* (Sūẏag. 322; Ṭhāṇ. 288; Vivāhap. 1. 1235; Ovav.; Kappas.; Pav. 379, 3. 4 (here the text has °*ri*°); 383, 44; 385, 63); AMg. JM. M. *arihaï* (Āẏār. 1, 3, 2, 2; Sūẏag. 178; Dasav. 631, 8; Erz.; Śak. 120, 6), Ś. *arihadi* (Śak. 24, 12; 57, 8; 58, 13; 73, 8; Ratn. 323, 1), Mg. *alihadi* (Śak. 116, 1); Ś. *ariha* = *arha* (Vr. 3, 62; Mukund. 17, 4); *arihā* = *arhā* (Kī 2, 59); AMg. JM. *mahariha* = *mahārha* (Vivāgas. 128; Rāyap. 174; Ovav.; Erz.), JM. *jahāriha* = *yathārha* (Erz.; Kk.), Ś. *mahāriha* (Śak. 117, 7), Mg. *mahāliha* (Śak. 117, 5); Mg. *alihanta-* (Prab. 46, 11; 51, 12; 52, 7; 54, 6; 58, 7; 59, 9; 60, 13; Mudrār. 183, 2 [to be read as such]; Laṭakam. 12, 13; 14, 19; Amṛt. 66, 2); JM *aruha* (Hc. 2, 111; Dvār. 502, 27, beside *arahantāṇaṁ*, (v. l. °*ri*°). The reading *aruhadi* found in Devanāgarī and South Indian recensions of the Śak. (Böhtlingk on 17, 7. 8 of his edition), and Mālav. (33, 1; 65, 2), and in the Priyad. 34, 20, based on South Indian manuscripts, in Ś. assuredly is wrong. — *aruhanta-* (Hc. 2, 111).

g) Dropping off and Addition of Vowels.

§ 141. Originally a vowel, at the beginning of a word, dropped off only when it was not accented. So in words having more than two syllables with final accentuation: AMg. *daga* = *udaká* (Sūẏag. 203. 209. 249. 337. 339. 340; Ṭhāṇ. 339. 400; Paṇhāv. 353. 531; Vivāhap. 942; Dasav. 619. 27; 630, 13; Ovav.; Kappas.), beside *udaga*, *udaẏa* (Ovav. § 83ff.; Uvās.; Nāẏādh.), sometimes both occur beside one another as in Sūẏag. 337 *udageṇa* [= *dageṇa*] *je siddhiṁ udāharanti sāyaṁ ca pāyam udagaṁ phusantā*[1] [*udagassa*] = *dogassa phāseṇa siyā ẏa siddhī sijjhiṁsu pāṇā bahave dagaṁsi*. The rest of the dialects do not have this dropping off: M. *uaa* (G.H.R.), JM. *udaẏa* (Erz.), Ś. *udaa* (Mṛcch. 37, 23; Śak. 10, 1; 18, 3; 67, 4; 72, 13; 74, 9; Vikr. 53, 13), Mg. *udaa*, (Mṛcch. 45, 12; 132, 10; 133, 7; 7; 134, 7). AMg. *duruhaï* = **udruháti* (§ 118. 139. 482). — AMg. *pāhaṇāo* = *upānáhau* °(Sūẏag. 384 [text *pāṇahāo*]; Ṭhāṇ. 359 [text °*vā*°, commentary °*pā*°]; Paṇhāv. 487 [text °*vā*°] 1212 [text *vāṇahāo*]; Ovav. °*pā*° and °*vā*°), beside Ś. *uvāṇaha*

(Mṛcch. 72, 9), AMg.; *chattovāhaṇa* (Sūyag. 249 [text °*vāṇaha*]; Vivāhap. 153), *aṇovāhaṇaga, °ya* (§ 77). — AMg. JM. JŚ. *posaha* = *upavasathá* (Antag. 19; Sūyag. 771. 994; Uvās.; Nāyādh.; Bhag.; Ovav. Kappas.; Erz.; Kattig. 402, 359; 403, 376); AMg. *posahiya* = *upavasathika* (Nāyādh.; Uvās.).— AMg. *rayaṇi* = *aratní* (§ 132; Vivāhap. 1563; Ovav.). — AMg. *lāū* = *alābū'*, *lāu* = *alábu* (Hc. 1, 66; Āyār. 2, 6, 1, 1; Aṇuttar. 11; Ovav. § 79, VII [to be read as such]), *lāuya* = *alábuka* (Āyār. 2, 6, 1, 4; Ṭhāṇ. 151; Vivāhap. 41. 1033; Paṇṇav. 31), also *lāuṁ* (Hc. 1, 66), beside AMg. *alāu* (Sūyag. 245), *alāuya* (Sūyag. 926. 928 [°*bu*°]), Ś. *alāvū* (Hc. 1, 237; Bālar. 229, 21).

§ 142. We must also presuppose final accentuation in AMg. *gāra* = *agāra* (Āyār. 1, 5, 3, 5; Sūyag. 126. 154. 345), *gārattha* = *agārastha* (Sūyag. 642. 986; Uttar. 208), *gāri-* = *agārin* (Uttar. 207), beside *agāra* (Āyār. 1, 2, 3, 5; Nāyādh.). — M. AMg. *rahaṭṭa* = *araghaṭṭa* (H. 490; Paṇhāv. 67), beside M. JM. *arahaṭṭa* (G. 685; Ṛṣabhap. 30. 47; wrongly the ed. Bomb. 47 *palliā rahaṭṭa vva*). — M. *vaaṁsa* = *avataṁsa* (H. 439), AMg. *vaḍiṁsa*, *vaḍiṁsaga* (§ 103), beside M. *avaaṁsa* (H. 173. 180), *avaaṁsaanti* (Śak. 2, 15). — Mg. *hage, hagge* = **ahakaḥ*; A. *haũ* = *ahakam* (§ 417). AMg. JM. *hĕṭṭhā* = *adhástāt* and derivatives (§ 107). — To this further belong the cases like AMg. *tiya* = *atita* (Sūyag. 122. 470; Ṭhāṇ. 173. 174; Vivāhap. 24. 155; Uttar. 833; Uvās.; Kappas). — AMg. *piṇidhattae* = **apinidhātave* (Ovav. § 79, X). — AMg. *pūha* = **apyūha* (§ 286). — AMg. *vakkamaï* = *apakrāmati* beside *avakkammaï*, Ś. Mg. *avakkamadi* (§ 481), AMg. *vakkanta* = *apakrānta* (Paṇṇav. 41; Kappas.), *vakkanti* = *apakrānti* (Kappas.); M. *valagganti* = *avalagyanti* (G. 226. 551); Ś. *vaṭṭhida* = *avasthita* (Mṛcch. 40, 14); *vamhala* = *apasmāraḥ* (Hc. 2, 174), where also the shortening of *ā* points to a final accentuation.—Agreeing with Skt. is M. AMg. *piṇaddha* = *pinaddha* (G.H. R.; Rāyap. 81f.; Ovav.; Nāyādh.). An accentuation differing from that of Skt. is presupposed in M. AMg. JM. A. *raṇṇa* = *áraṇya* (Vr. 1, 4; Hc. 1, 66; Kī. 1, 3; Mk. fol. 5; G.H.R.; Nāyādh. 1117. 1439; Ovav.; Erz.; Vikr. 58, 9; 71, 9; 72, 10). beside the rarer *araṇṇa* (G.H.; Āyār. p. 133, 32; Kappas.; Erz.), which is the usual form in Ś. (Śak. 33, 4; Ratn. 314, 32; Mālatīm. 30, 9; Uttarar. 190, 2; Dhūrtas. 11, 12; Karṇas. 46, 12; Vṛṣabh. 28, 19; 50, 5; Caṇḍak. 17, 16; 95, 10); against the dialect is *pāraddhiraṇṇa* (Viddhaś. 23, 9). — M.A. *riṭṭha* = *ariṣṭa* (R. 1, 3; Piṅgala 2, 72), JM. *riṭṭhanemi* = *ariṣṭanemi* (Dvār. 496, 2; 499, 13; 502, 505; 27), beside AMg. JM. *ariṭṭhanemi* (Kappas.; Dvār. 495, 9; 497, 26; 504, 19; 505, 5); AMg. *riṭṭha* (a gem; Jīv. 218; Rāyap. 29; Vivāhap. 212. 1146; Nāyādh.; Ovav.; Kappas.) = *áriṣta*, Pāli *ariṭṭha*,[1] AMg. *riṭṭhaga* (Nāyādh. § 61; Uttar. 980), *riṭṭaya* (Ovav.) = *ariṣṭaka*, *riṭṭhāmaya* = *ariṣṭamaya* (Jīv. 549; Rāyap. 105), beside *ariṭṭha* (a tree; Paṇṇav. 31). Cf. *ariṣṭatáti*. Probably to this group belongs also M. AMg. JM. Mg. A. *to*, which the grammarians and, with them, S. GOLDSCHMIDT[2], connect with *ta-*, but which could better be derived from *átas*.

1. WINDISCH, ZDMG. 49,285 against whose explanation goes Pkt.—2 Prākṛtica p. 22.

§ 143. The initial vowel particularly frequently drops off in enclitics under the influence of loss of accent. When the words are not used enclitically, the vowel is retained. Thus : *api* after an anusvāra becomes *pi*, after a vowel, *vi*, as PG. *anne vi* = *anyān api* (5, 6), *amhehi vi* = *asmābhirapi* (6, 29); M. *maraṇaṁ pi* (H. 12), *taṁ pi* (G. 430), *caḍulaṁ pi* (R. 2, 18), *ajja vi* = *adyāpi* (H. s. v. *vi*), *taha vi* = *tathāpi* (R. 1, 15), *ṇimmalā vi* = *nirmalā api* (G. 72), *amhe vi* = *asme api* (H. 232), *appavaso vi* = *alpavaśo'pi* (H. 265). So also the other dialects. At the beginning of a sentence *a* remains : PG. *api* (6, 37), M. AMg. JM. Ś. *avi* (R.; Āẏār. 1, 8, 1, 10; Dasav. 632; 42; Kk. 270, 46; Mṛcch. 46, 5; 57, 6; 70, 12; 82, 12; Śak. 49, 8; often in *avi a* and *avi ṇāma*), so in verses after *m*, when a short syllable is required as AMg. *muhuttam avi* (Āẏār. 1, 2, 1, 3), *kālagam avi* (Kappas. Th. 13, 3), and when in AMg. *-ām* remains against the rule (§68); further in AMg. JM. *puṇar avi* = *punar api* (§ 342) and in AMg. JM. *ẏāvi* = *ẏa*+*avi*+*cāpi* (e.g. Āẏār. 1, 1, 1, 5; 1, 1, 5, 3; Sūẏag. 120; Uvās.; Kappas.; Āv. 8, 13; Erz. 34, 15), in cases like M. Ś. *keṇāvi* (H. 105; Vikr. 10, 12 [to be read as such]), JM. Ś. *teṇāvi* (Erz. 10, 25; 17, 17; 22, 9; Mālatīm. 78, 8), Ś. *ĕttikeṇāvi* (Śak. 29, 9); Ś. Mg. *mamāvi* (Mṛcch. 65, 19; Śak. 9, 13; 19, 3; 32, 3; 50, 4; Mṛcch. 140, 1); Ś. Mg. *tavāvi* (Mālatīm. 92. 4; Mṛcch. 124, 20); AMg. *khaṇam avi* = *kṣaṇam api* (Nāẏādh. § 137); JM. *evam avi* (Āv. 16, 24); JM. *saẏalam avi jīvaloẏaṁ* (Kappas. § 44); M. *piāttaṇeṇāvi* = **priẏātvanenāpi* (H. 267); Ś. *jīvidasavvas-seṇāvi* = *jīvitasarvasvenāpi* (Śak. 20, 5). In all such cases particular emphasis is to be laid on the word standing before *avi*[1]. On AMg. *app* see § 174. — After anusvāra *iti* becomes *ti*, after vowels *tti*; and long vowels are shortened before it (§ 92) : PG. *ca tti* = *ceti* (6, 37); *jīviaṁ ti* = *jīvitam iti* (R. 5, 4), *ṇatthi tti* = *nāstīti* (G. 281); AMg. *iṇaṁ ti* = *enad iti* (Āẏār. 1, 3, 1, 3), *aṇupari-ẏaṭṭaï tti* = *anuparivartata iti* (Āẏār. 1, 2, 3, 6); Ś. *laheaṁ ti* = *labheyam iti* (Śak. 13, 9), *pĕkkhadi tti* = *prekṣata iti* (Śak. 13, 6). So in all dialects. On AMg. *i* see § 93, on M. *ia*, AMg. JM. *iẏa* at the beginning of the sentence see § 116, on AMg. *icc* § 174. In M. AMg. JM. after anusvāra and short vowels *iva* becomes *va*, after long vowels that are shortened (§ 92); in verses sometimes even after short vowels it becomes *vva* : M. *kamalaṁ va* = *kamalam iva* (G. 668), *uaassa va*+*udakasyeva* (H. 53), *pakkhehi va* = *pakṣair iva* (H. 218), *ālā-ṇakkhaṁbhesu va* = *ālānastambheṣviva* (R. 3, 1), *mahumahaṇeṇa vva* = *madhu-mathaneneva* (H. 425), *samūsasanti vva* = *samucchvasantīva* (H. 625), *dāru vva* = *dārviva* (H. 105); AMg. *puṁchaṁ va* = *puccham iva* (Uvās. 94); JM. *puttam va* = *putram iva* (Erz. 43, 34), *kaṇagaṁ va* = *kanakam iva* (Kk. 258, 23). Ś. Mg. do not have this word, but they substitute *via* for it (Vr. 12, 24). In M. AMg. JM. occurs also *iva*: M. (G.); AMg. *ṭaṅkaṇā iva* (Sūẏag. 198), *meham iva* = *megham iva* (Uvās. § 102); cf. § 345; JM. *kiṃnaro iva* (Āv. 8, 28), *tiṇam iva* = *tṛṇam iva*, *vammaho iva* = *manmatha iva* (Erz. 24, 34; 84, 21). On A. *jiv̄a*, M. AMg. JM. P. *piva*, *viva*, *miva* see § 336.

1. BOLLENSEN, Vikr. p. 156f. wrongly rejects writings of this sort.

§ 144. In Ś. Mg. *idānim* is very often used enclitically in the weakened sense of "well", "now", "then", and then it becomes *dāṇiṁ* (Hc. 4, 277. 302). S. *vāvaḍo dāṇiṁ ahaṁ* = *vyāpṛta idānim aham* (Mṛcch. 4, 24), *jo dāṇiṁ*... *so dāṇiṁ* (Mṛcch. 6, 4. 8; 147, 16. 17), *kiṁ khu dāṇiṁ* = *kiṃ khalvidānim* (Mṛcch. 13, 3), *ko dāṇiṁ so* = *ka idānim saḥ* (Mṛcch. 28, 13), *aṇantarakara-*

ṇiaṁ dāṇim āṇavedu ajjo = *anantarakaraṇīyam idānīm ājñāpayatu āryaḥ* (Hc. 4, 277 = Śak. 2, 5); Mg. *āyiviā dāṇiṁ śaṁvuttā* = *ājīvikedanīṁ saṁvṛttā* (Mṛcch. 37, 6), *śe dāṇim, ke dāṇiṁ* (Mṛcch. 37, 19. 25), *ĕttha dāṇīṁ* (Mṛcch. 162, 18), *tośide dāṇīṁ bhaṭṭā* = *toṣita idānīṁ bhartā* (Śak. 118, 1). In other dialects this use is rare, as PG. *ĕttha dāṇi* (5, 7); M. *aṇṇam dāṇiṁ bohiṁ* = *anyām idānīṁ bodhim* (Hc. 4, 277), *kiṁ dāṇi* (H. 390), *to dāṇi* (R. 11, 121). In the beginning of a sentence and when emphasis is to be laid on the meaning "now", the *i* is retained in Ś. Mg.[1] too : *idāṇiṁ* (Mṛcch. 50, 4; Śak. 10, 2; 18, 1; 25, 3; 56, 9; 67, 6; 77, 6; 87, 1; 139; 1; Vikr. 21, 12; 22, 14; 24, 1; 27, 4 etc. (read so everywhere). M. hardly uses the word, but it employs *iṇhiṁ, ĕṇhiṁ, ĕttāhe*, that are quite foreign to Ś. and Mg. AMg, JM, JŚ, have *iyāṇiṁ, idāṇiṁ* even inside sentences (e.g. Āyār. 1. 1. 4, 3; Uvās. § 66; Ovav. § 86. 87; Āv. 16, 14; 30, 10; 40, 5; Pav. 384, 60), metrically also AMg. *iyāṇi* (Dasav. N. 653, 40).

1. CAPPELLER, Jenaer Literaturzeitung 1877, p. 125, who in his edition of Ratn. rightly maintains the distinction.

§ 145. An initial *a* generally drops in the sing. indic. pres. of the root *as* "to be" in the first and second persons when the forms are used enclitically : AMg. JM. *mi* (§ 498), M. JM. Ś. *mhi, si*, Mg. *smi* [text *mhi*], *śi*. Thus for example AMg. *vañcio mi tti* = *vañcito'smiti* (Uttar. 116); JM. *viddho mi tti* = *viddho'smīti* (Āv. 28, 14); M. *ṭhia mhi* = *sthitāsmi* (H. 239); Ś. *iaṁ mhi* = *iyamasmi* (Mṛcch. 3, 5; Śak. 1, 8; Ratn. 290, 28 [read so]; Nāgān. 2, 16 [and so on]; Pārvatīp. 1, 18 [and so on]; Mg. *kilantĕ smi-* = *klānto'smi* (Mṛcch. 13, 10); cf. § 85. 96. — M. *ajja si* = *adyāsi* (H. 861), *taṁ si* = *tvam asi* (G.H.R.), *diṭṭhā si* = *dṛṣṭāsi* (R. 11, 129) *mūḍho si* (G. 487); JM. *kā si* (Erz., 8, 4, 12), *mukko si* = *mukto'si* (Kk. 266, 25), *taṁ si* = *tvam asi* (Ṛṣabhap. 15); *paccādiṭṭho si* = *pratyādiṣṭo'si* (Mṛcch. 5, 3), *pucchidā si* = *pṛṣṭāsi* (Mṛcch. 28, 21), *dāṇiṁ si* (Mṛcch. 91, 18) *sariraṁ si* (Mālav. 38, 5); Mg. *śante śi kilante śi* = *śrānto'si klānto'si* (Mṛcch. 13, 7), *eśa śi* = *eṣāsi* (Mṛcch. 17, 1). — *atthi* = *asti*, never used enclitically, as it is generally employed in the pregnant sense = "there is", "it exists" stands, whilst as copula is used M. AMg. JM. *hoi*, JŚ. *hodi*, Ś. Mg. *bhodi* = *bhavati*, as already pointed out by LASSEN, Inst. p. 193. On AMg. *namo 'tthu ṇaṁ* see § 175. 498, on M. JM. *kiṁ tha* § 175, on AMg. JM.Ś. Mg. Ḍh. *ṇaṁ* = *nūnám* § 150.

§ 146. Final *a* has dropped off in the ins. sing. of the *a-* stem in A.: *aggiĕ* = *agnikena, vāeṁ* = *vātena* (Hc. 4, 343, 1); *eṁ ciṇheṁ* = *ena cihnena* (Vikr. 58, 11); *koheṁ* = *krodhena* (Piṅgala 1, 77*a*); *daïeṁ* = *dayitena* (Hc. 4, 333.342); *daïveṁ* = *daivena* (C. 4, 331); *pahāreṁ* = *prahāreṇa* (Vikr. 65, 4); *bhamanteṁ* = **bhramantena* = *bhramatā* (Vikr. 58, 9; 69, 1; 72, 10); *rūeṁ* = *rūpeṇa* (Piṅgala 1.2*a*); *sahajeṁ* = *sahajena* (Piṅgala, 1, 4*a*). In the ins. sing. of *i-* and *u-* stems, *ā*, after its transition into *a*, (§ 100) has dropped off likewise : *aggiṁ*, beside *aggiṇa* from *aggiṇā* = *agninā* (Hc. 4, 343). On *ṁ* from *n* see § 348. In A *a* has fallen in the absolutive in *-i* from *-ia* = *ya*, as *daī* = Ś. *daïa-* (§ 594).

§ 147. The flexion of *strī* shows that originally the word was disyllabic. In AMg. JŚ. JM. Ś. *itthī* (Hc. 2, 130; examples in § 97. 160), AMg. JM. *itthiyā* (Dasav. 628, 2; Dvār. 507, 2; Āv. 48, 42); Ś. *itthiā* (e.g. Mṛcch.

44, 1. 2; 148, 23; Vikr. 16, 9; 24, 10; 45, 21; 72, 18; Mālav. 39, 2; Prab. 17, 8 [read so]; 38, 5; 39, 6 etc.), also Ā. (Mṛcch. 148, 22), Mg. *istiā* (§ 310) = *strikā*, the *i* is, therefore, the remnant of an old vowel, as correctly noticed by JOHANSSON[1]. In M. *itthī* is rare and it is only in the later-day poets that it is visible (Acyutaś. 15; Pratāp. 220, 9; Sāhityad. 178, 3), *itthiajaṇa* (Śukasaptati 81, 5), as also Vr. 12, 22 correctly requires *itthī* for Ś.[2]. In AMg. we also find, mostly in verses, also *thī* (Hc. 2, 130; Āẏār. 1, 2, 4, 3; Uttar. 482, 483, 485) and *thiẏā* = *strikā* (Sūẏag. 285) used; yet the usual form even in verses is AMg. *itthī*. A. too has *thī* (Kk. 261, 4).

1. Shāhbāzgarhi 1, 149. But his etymology is wrong; Correctly BEZZENBERGER, GN, 1878, 271 ff. — 2. PISCHEL on Hc. 2, 130; cf. S. GOLDSCHMIDT, ZDMG. 26, 745; WEBER H.[2] p. 454.

(h) — DROPPING OFF OF VOWELS.

§ 148. Unaccented vowels, especially *a*, are sometimes pushed off in the interior of words : *katta* "married wife" (Triv. 1, 3, 105; cf. BB. 3, 251) = *kálatra*, **kaltra*; AMg, *piusiẏā* = *pitṛṣvasṛkā* from **piusasiẏā* (Hc.) 1, 134; 2, 142), M. *piussiā* (Mk. fol. 40), AMg. *piussiẏā* (Vivāgas. 105; Dasav. 627, 40), AMg. *māusiẏā* (Hc. 1, 134, 2, 142; Pāiẏal. 253; Vivāgas. 105 [text *māsiẏā*; correctly the commentary]; Dasav. 627, 39 [text *māu siu tti*], M. *māussiā* [Mk. fol. 40; MS *māussāā*] = *mātṛṣvasṛkā*. M *piucchā*, *māucchā* (Hc. 1, 134; 2, 142; Mk. fol. 40; Pāiẏal. 253; H.), AMg. *piucchā* (Nāẏādh. 1299. 1300. 1348), Ś. *māducchaa*, *māducchiā* (Karp. 32, 6. 8; cf. v. l.) presuppose a change of *sa* into *cha* according to § 211. *pupphā*, *pupphiā* = *pitṛṣvasā* (Deśīn. 6, 52; Pāiẏal. 253) remain unexplained notwithstanding BÜHLER, ZDMG. 43, 146; E. KUHN. KZ. 33, 478f., because the dropping off of *i* is without an analogy. M. *pŏpphala* = *pūgaphalá* from **pūgphala*, **pupphala* (§ 125, 127; Hc. 1, 170; Karp. 95, 1), beside AMg. *pūẏaphala* (Sūẏag. 250), M.Ś. *pŏpphalī* = *pūgaphalī* (Hc. 1, 170; Śukasaptati 123, 9; Viddhaś. 75, 2 [text *pophalli*]); AMg. *saṇapphaẏa* = *sánakhapada* (Sūẏag. 288. 822; Ṭhāṇ 322; Paṇṇav. 49; Paṇhāv. 42; Uttar. 1075)[1]; AMg. *subbhi* = *surabhi'* (Āẏār. 1, 6, 2, 4; 1, 8, 2, 9; 2, 1, 9, 4; 2, 4, 2, 18; Sūẏag. 409. 590; Ṭhāṇ. 20; Samav. 64; Paṇṇav. 8. 10ff.; Paṇhāv. 518. 538; Vivāhap. 29. 532. 544; Uttar. 1021. 1024), according to which has been formed *dubbhi*, which mostly occurs beside it. Vivāhap. 29 has *subbhi durabhi*, Āẏār. 1, 5, 6, 4 has *surabhi durabhi* side by side. In *khu*, *hu* = *khálu* (§ 94) the dropping off of *a* is explained through **khlu*, by the enclitic use of *khalu*. AMg. *uppiṁ* (e.g. Ṭhāṇ. 179. 492; Vivāgas. 117. 216. 226. 227. 235. 253; Vivāhap. 104, 199. 233. 250. 410. 414. 797. 846; Jīv. 439. 483 etc.) presupposes the accentuation **úpari* or **upari'*, whilst *upári* becomes M. JM. Ś. *uvari*, M. AMg. JM. *uvariṁ*, Mg. *uvali*, M. also *avariṁ* (§ 123). — *ā* has disappeared in JM. *bhāujjā* = *bhrātṛjāyā* (Deśīn. 6, 103; Āv. 27. 18 [read so; see v. l.]). — *i* has dropped off. in M.S. *majjhaṇṇa* = *mādhyáṁdina* (Vr. 3, 7; Hc. 2, 84; Kī. 2, 54; Mk. fol. 21; H. 839 [read so]; Mālav. 27, 18; Nāgān. 18, 2; Mallikām. 67, 7; Jīvān. 42, 20 (cf. also ? *ṇha* 46, 10. 17]), Mg. *mayyhaṇṇa* (text *majjhaṇṇa*; Mṛcch. 116, 6; Mudrār. 175, 3), *mayyhaṇṇika* (Mṛcch. 117, 14), beside Ś. *majjhaṁdiṇa*

Śak. 29, 4). The grammarians derive *majjhaṇṇa* from *madhyāhna*, and they have been followed by all European scholars. BLOCH[2] has characterized the form as false, that has been rightly rejected by WACKERNAGEL[3]; however, he himself quite wrongly explains the development of the form through the tendency of allowing two aspirates to follow one another, since this tendency is unknown in Pkt. (§ 214). — *u* has dropped off in AMg. JM. *īsattha* = *iṣuśāstra* (Samav. 131; Paṇhāv. 322 [text *i*°]; Ovav. § 107; Erz. 67, 1.2)[4] AMg. *challuẏa* = *ṣaḍulūka* (Ṭhāṇ. 472; Kappas. Th. § 6 [read so], with shortening of *ū* of *úlūka*, according to § 80; JM. *dhiẏā*, Ś. Mg. *dhidā* (Prākṛtamañjarī on Vr. 4, 33 *dhidā ca duhitā matā*), mostly in the compounds JM. *dāsiedhiẏā*, Ś. *dāsiedhidā*, Mg. *dāśiedhidā* (§ 392) = **duhitā́* for *duhitā́*[5]; M. AMg. JM.Ś. *suṇhā* (Hc. 1, 261; H.; Āẏār. 1, 2, 1, 1; 2, 2, 1, 12; Sūẏag. 787; Antag. 55; Jīv. 355; Nāẏādh. 628. 631. 633. 634. 647. 660. 820. 1110; Vivāgas. 105; Vivāhap. 602; Āv. 22, 42; Bālar. 168, 5 [read so], M. *sŏṇhā* with *ŏ* according to § 125 (Vr. 2, 47; Kī. 2, 91; Mk. fol. 39; H.), in Kāleyak. 14, 7 also in Ś. [text *sohṇā*] = *snuṣā*, from P. *sunusā* (§ 139), **suṇuhā* (§ 263)[6]; so also AMg. *suṇhatta* = **snuṣātva* (Vivāhap. 1046), beside AMg. *ṇhusā* (Sūẏag. 377) and Ś. *susā* (Hc. 1, 261; Bālar. 176, 15 [correct?]). — *ū* has dropped off in *ohala*, *ŏkkhala*, AMg. *ukkhala* = *udūkhala* (§ 66), which presupposes an accentuation other than *ulū'khala*.[7] On *ĕtto*, *aṇṇo* see § 197.

1. The texts often write the word wrongly. KZ. 34, 573 I have blundered in considering the word an avyayībhāva. JACOBI, KZ. 35, 571 rightly rejects this, but he forgets to note that the word is a bahuvrīhi, on account of which, in fact, nothing is altered—2. Vr. and Hc. p. 33f. — 3. KZ. 33. 575 f., Altind. Gr. § 105, note; § 108, note — 4. LEUMANN, Aup. Ś. s. v. and JACOBI, Erz. s. v. explained the word with *iṣvastra*, that is factually and linguistically impossible, Abhayadeva on Paṇhāv. 322 rightly equates it as = *iṣuśāstra* Cf. § 117 HOEFER, De Prākrita dialecto p. 61 and BARTHOLOMAE, ZDMG. 50, 693 derive the word from *dhītā* from √ *dhai*, BOLLENSEN on Mālav. p. 172, derives with others the word from *duhidā*...Skt. *duhitā*, wherein *ī* remains unexplained. — 6. Wrongly JACOBI, Erz. p. XXXII, note 3, has understood the word *suṇhā* to have developed from *ṇhusā* through metathesis. AMg. proves that *ṇhusā* was not objectionable. Cf. also E. KUHN, KZ. 33, 479. In Ki. 2, 91 there occurs also *ṇohā* beside *sŏṇhā*. — 7. Wrongly JACOBI, ZDMG. 47, 582; PISCHEL, KZ. 34, 573 f.

(i) DROPPING OFF AND WEAKENING OF SYLLABLES.

§ 149. Disappearance of the syllable *ya* occurs in M. A. *atthamaṇa* = *astama'yana* (H.; Hc. 4, 444, 2); the form has crossed also into Skt. as *astamana*; A. *ṇimma* = *niyamá* (Piṅgala 1, 104. 143) with reduplication of *ma* according to § 194; *ṇisaṇi*, *ṇisaṇiā* (ladder; Deśīn. 4, 43) = *niḥśrayaṇi*, *niḥśrayaṇikā*, beside AMg. *nisseṇi* (Āẏār. 2, 1, 7, 1; 2, 2, 1, 6). — *va* has dropped in *aḍa* = *avaṭá* (Hc. 271; Pāiẏal. 130); AMg. JM. *em* = *evám* in AMg. *em ee* = *evam ete* (Ṭhāṇ. 576, 579; Dasav. 613, 9). JM. *emāi* = *evamādi* (Erz.; Śagara 8, 12), M. *emea* (G. H.), AMg. JM. *emeva* (Hc. 1, 271; Pāiẏal 166 [*emeẏa*]; Āẏār 2, 1, 6, 4. 7, 5; 2,5, 1, 11; Uttar. 442. 633. 804; Dasav. N. 646, 9; 650, 28; 652, 21; 660, 29; 662, 43; Āv. 19, 37). In JM. *evaḍḍa*, *evaḍḍaga* (so big; Āv. 45, 6. 7), AMg. *emahālaẏa*, femin. *emahāliẏā* (Vivāhap. 412. 415 [femin.] 1041; Uvās. § 84), *emahiḍḍhiẏa* (Vivāhap. 214), *esuhuma* (Vivāhap. 1191f.; Ovav. § 140) *e* should not with HOERNLE[1] be equated as = *evam*, but with

WEBER[2] as = *tyat*, more correctly **ayat* (§ 153), to which AMg. *evaïya* (Vivāhap. 212. 214. 1103; Kappas.), *evaïkhutto* (Kappas.) and the parallel *kemahāliyā* (Paṇṇav. 599 ff.; Jīv. 18. 65; Aṇuog. 401 ff.; Vivāhap. 415), *kemahiḍḍhiya, kemahajjuïya, kemahābala, kemahāyasa, kemahāsŏkkha, kemahāṇubhāga* (Vivāhap. 211), *kemahesakkha* (Vivāhap. 887), *kevaïya* (Āyār. 2, 3,2, 17; Vivāhap. 17. 26. 209. 211. 239. 242. 734. 738. 1076 ff.), *kevaciraṁ* (Vivāhap. 180. 1050; Paṇṇav. 545 ff.), *kevacciraṁ* (Jīv. 108. 128ff.), M. *kĕccira, kĕcciraṁ* (R. 3, 30. 33)[3], Ś. *kĕcciraṁ* (Mālatīm. 125, 2 [read so]; 278, 8; Viddhaś. 18, 11; 61, 8; Kāleyak. 9, 22), *kĕcciréṇa* (Mālatīm. 276, 6) point. WEBER has likewise already compared Vedic. *ivat*; Vedic *kīvat* stands in the same relation to *keva-*. Cf. also § 153. 261. 434. Dropping off of *va* occurs in *kalera* (rib; Deśīn. 2, 53; Triv. 1, 3, 105) from *kalevara* = *kalebara*[4]. An isolated case is *duggāvi* = *durgādevi* (Hc. 1, 270). [Dropping takes place sometimes in the medial position :—M *daṇuindu* = *danujendra* (RB 2).

1. Uvās. s.v. *emahālaya*.—2 Bhag. 1,422.—3 S. GOLDSCHMIDT, Prākṛtica, p.23, note 1.—4 PISCHEL, BB. 695.

§ 150. Dropping off of the initial syllable occurs in AMg. JM. Ś. Mg. Dh. Ā. *ṇaṁ* = *nūnám* (Hc. 4. 283, 302; e.g. Āyār. 1. 6. 3. 1; 7, 1, 5. 3, 1. 4, 1. 2. 6, 1. 3 etc; Ovav. §2 ff.; Uvās.; Nāyādh.; Nīrayāv.; Kappas.; Āv. 15, 3; 16, 17; 17, 12; Erz.; Kk.; Mṛcch. 4, 12; 17, 22; 23, 10; Śak. 3, 4; 27, 5; 37, 7; Mg. Mṛcch. 12, 16; 22, 5; 31, 2; 81, 15; Ḍh. Mṛcch. 32, 23; Ā. Mṛcch. 103, 10. 13). The usual derivation of the word from *nanú*[1], which Hc. 4, 283 even has, fails because of the accent, since *ṇaṁ* in Ś. Ḍh. is used even in the beginning of a sentence and, therefore, was not always an enclitic. To regard AMg. *ṇaṁ*, with WEBER[2], as the remnant of an old pronominal stem *na* and to separate it from the *ṇaṁ* of the dramas is impossible, because their use in other respects is similar. Further, AMg. sometimes employs *nūṇaṁ* otherwise exactly like *ṇaṁ*; e.g. *se nūṇaṁ* (Uvās. § 118. 173. 192) as against *se ṇaṁ* (Āyār. 2, 3, 1, 17ff). Sometimes *ṇūṇaṁ* as well stands at the beginning of the sentence, e.g. JM. *ṇūṇaṁ gaheṇa gahia tti teṇa tie mamaṁ dinnā* (Āv. 12, 28); Ś. *ṇūṇaṁ esa de attagado maṇoradho* (Śak. 14, 11); Mg. *ṇūṇaṁ. . , takkemi* (Mṛcch. 141, 1), as elsewhere in Ś. Mg. *ṇaṁ*. That in AMg. JM. *ṇaṁ* is always written with cerebral *ṇa* (§224) is also an argument for its having been originally used within a word, although it may have its source in enclisis. — M. *ḍhilla* = *śithilá* (§ 194; Karp. 8, 5; 70, 8) as in Modern Indian[3], beside *saḍhila, siḍhila* (§ 115). Identical with it is *ḍhĕlla* (poor; Deśin. 4, 16), with *ĕ* for *i* according to § 119. Dropping off of the final syllable occurs in *ova* (elephant-trap; Deśīn. 1, 49) = **a'vapata*, AMg. *ovā* (Āyār. 2, 1, 5, 4), beside *oāa* (Deśīn. 1, 166) = *avapāta*; *kisala* = *kiśálaya* (Hc. 1, 269); cf. *pisalla* (§ 232); M. AMg. JM. *je*, A. *ji* for *jeva* = *eva* (§ 336); M. *dā* for *dāva* = *tāvat* in *mā dā* (R. 3, 10, 27) against the dialect (§ 185); Mg. *ghaḍukka* = *ghaṭotkaca* (Mṛcch. 29, 20). In *sahia* = *sahṛdaya* (Hc. 1, 269) we should not assume dropping off of a syllable. The word is = **sahṛd* with a regular descent to the *a-* declension. Likewise is *hia* (Mk. fol. 33), AMg. *hiya* (Āyār. 1, 1, 2, 5) = *hṛd*, Mg. *haḍakka* (§ 194) = **hṛdaka*.

1. LASSEN, Inst. p. 173; BÖHTLINGK on Śak., 4.4 p. 149, etc.—2 Bhag. 1, 422 ff.—3 PISCHEL on Hc. 1, 89.

(j) SAMPRASĀRAṆA

§ 151. Saṁprasāraṇa takes place in Pkt. in the same cases as in Skt.; *ya* in an unaccented syllable becomes i, and *va* becomes *u* : Ś. *iṭṭhi* = *iṣṭi* from *yaj* (Śak. 70, 6); M. *utta* = *upta* from *vap* (G.); M. AMg. JM. *sutta* = *supta* from *svap* (H.; Kappas.; Erz.). Pkt. has, however, this change of sound also in a number of cases in which Skt. shows *ya* and *va*. Thus *ya* becomes *i* : AMg. *abhintara* = *abhyantara* (Nāẏādh.; Ovav.; Kappas.); AMg. JM. *tirikkha* = **tiryakṣa* from *tiryak* (Thāṇ. 121. 336; Sūẏag. 298; Bhag.; Uvās.; Ovav.; Kappas.; Erz.); M. Ś. A. *tiricchi* (Hc. 2, 143; 4, 295; Karp. 37, 5; Mallikām. 74. 2 [text °*ra*°]; Hc. 4, 414, 3.420, 3), Mg. *tiliśi* (Hc. 4, 295 [so it is to be read]); Ś. *tiriccha* (Bālar. 68, 14; 76; 19; 246, 9; Viddhaś. 34, 10; 124, 3); AMg. *vitiriccha* (Vivāhap. 253); AMg. *paḍiṇiẏa* = *pratẏanika* (Ovav. § 117; *viaṇa* = *vyajana* (Vr. 1, 3; Hc. 1. 46; Kī. 1, 2; Mk. fol. 5); M. *vilia* = *vyalika* (Hc. 1, 46; H.); in future such as *kāhmi* from **karṣyāmi*, *dāhimi* from **dāsyāmi*, and the endings *-ihisi*, *-ihii* in M. AMg. JM. (§520ff.). On *bāhiṁ* see §181. In AMg. sometimes even the secondary *ya* which has taken the place of some other consonant becomes *i* : *āiriẏa* beside *āẏariẏa* = *acāryà* (§81. 134), *rāiṇṇa* for **rāẏaṇṇa* = *rājanyà* (Ṭhān. 120; Samav. 232; Vivāhap. 800; Ovav.; Kappas.)[1]. *ya* has become *i* in AMg. *viikkanta* = *vyaṭikrānta* (Āẏār. 2, 15, 2, 25 [text *vi*°]; Nāẏādh.; Kappas. s. v. *viikkaṁta*; Uvās. s. v. *vaikkanta*); *viiẏamāṇa* = *vyativrajamāna* (Nāẏādh.; Kappas.); *viivaïttā* = **vyativrajitvā* (Ovav.)[2]. For *yā* has developed *i* in *thiṇa*, *ṭhiṇa* = *styāna* (Hc. 174; 2, 33. 99), beside *thiṇṇa*, M. *thiṇṇa a* (R.).

1. So more correctly than in KZ. 34,570; falsely JACOBI, KZ. 35,573. The frequent interchange of *ya* and *i* in Jaina manuscripts need not be assumed here, because the word is always written with *i*, and for *āiriya* the change to *i* has been explicitly taught by grammarians.—2. From the v.l. I feel assured to admit that it is *vī*, and not *vi* or *va* that is to be written. The lengthening for the second *ī* is explained according to § 70.

§ 152. *va* is changed to *u*, before double consonants also to *ŏ* (§125) AMg. *aṁsŏttha*, *assŏttha*, *āsŏttha* = *aśvatthá* (§ 74); *gaüā* = *gavayá*, femin. *gaüā* (Hc. 1, 54. 158; 2, 174; 3, 35); A. *jāũ* = *yā́vat*, *tāũ* = *tā́vat* (Hc. 4, 406, 423, 3; 426, [read *jāũ*]); M. A. *turia* = *tvaritá* (Vr. 8, 5; Hc. 4, 172; G.H.R. Piṅgala 1, 5), AMg. JM. *turiẏa* (Pāiẏal. 173; Vivāhap. 949; Nāẏādh.; Ovav.; Kappas.), Ś. *turida* (Mṛcch. 40, 24; 41, 12; 170, 4; Ram. 297, 12; Veṇīs. 22, 20; Mālatīm. 284, 11; 289, 6 etc.), Mg. *tulida* (Mṛcch. 11, 21; 96, 18; 97, 1; 98, 1.2; 117, 15; 133, 11; 171, 2; Caṇḍak. 43, 8), A. D. Ā. *turia* (Vikr. 58, 4; Mṛcch. 99, 24; 100, 3.11); *visuṁ* = *viṣvak* (Hc. 1, 24. 43. 52); M. *suaï*, *suvaï*, JM. *suẏaï* **svapáti* = *svapìti*, JM. Ś. *suvāmi*, A. *suahĩ* (§ 497), AMg. *suviṇa*, *sumiṇa*. A. *suiṇa* = *svápna* (§ 177) in connection with the verb; M. Ś. *sŏtthi* = *svasti* (Kī. 2, 148; H.; Mṛcch. 6, 23; 25, 4; 54, 11. 19; 73, 18; Vikr. 15, 16; 29, 1; 44, 5 etc.) *sŏtthivāaṇā* = *svastivācana* (Vikr. 43, 14; 44, 13), *sŏtthivāaṇaa* (Vikr. 26, 15), AMg. *sŏtthiẏa* = *svastika* (Paṇhāv. 283. 286; Ovav.); AMg. *souṇiẏa* = *śauvanika* (dog-keeper; Sūẏag. 714; but *sovaṇiẏa* 721). Also secondary *va*, which has first arisen in Pkt., sometimes becomes *u* through ablaut in the prefix *upa* (§ 155); further in A. *ṇāü* from **ṇāvaṁ* = *nāma* (Hc. 4, 426. 1). Secondary *u* is sometimes also elevated, as in *sovaï*, JM. *sovĕnti*, *souṁ*, A. *soevā*; *sovana*, AMg. *asovaṇi*, *sovaṇi* from *svap* (§78. 497); AMg. *sovāga* = *śvapāka*, *sovāgi* = *śvapāki* (§ 78), and *ŏ* arising from *u* is elevated, as in M. *soṇāra* = *svarṇakāra* (§66). — *vā* appears as *ū* in the absolutely in PG. M. AMg. JM. *-tūṇaṁ*, P. *-tūnaṁ*, M. AMg. JM. *-ūṇaṁ*, M. AMg. JM. *-tūṇa*, P. *-tūna*, JŚ. *-dūṇa*, M. AMg. JM. *-ūṇa* = Vedic *tvānam*, as in PG. *kātūṇaṁ*, P. *kātūnaṁ*, AMg. JM. *kāūṇaṁ*, JŚ. *kādūaṇ*, M. JM. *kāūṇa* = **kartvānam*, **kartvāna* (§ 584 ff.). On *do*, *du* apparently = *dvī*, see § 435.

§ 153. Under the law of saṁprasāraṇa falls also the change of *aya* into *e* and of *ava* into *o*. Thus *aya* becomes *e* in verbs of the 10th class, causatives and similarly formed denominatives, such as PG. *aṇuvaṭṭhāveti* = *anuprasthāpayati*, AMg. *ṭhāvei*, M. AMg. JM. *ṭhavei* = *sthāpayati* (§ 551 f.); M. AMg. *kahei*, Mg. *kadhedi* = *kathayati*, Ś. *kadhedu* = *kaṭhayatu* (§490); Ś. *sidalāvedi* = *śitalāyati* (§ 559). Further in cases like M. *ṇei*, JM. *nei* = *nayati*, Ś. *ṇedu* = *nayatu* (§ 474); M. JM. *dei*, Ś. *dedi* = **dayati*, Mg. *dedha* = **dayata* (§474); AMg. *terasa*, A. *teraha* = **trayadaśa* = *trayodaśa* (§ 443), AMg. JM. *tevisaṁ*, A. *teisa* = **trayaviṁśati* = *trayoviṁśati*; AMg. JM. *tĕttisaṁ*, *tittisaṁ* = *trayastriṁśat* (§ 445); AMg. *nisseṇi* = *niḥśrayaṇi* (§149). — AMg. *leṇa* = *layana* (Sūyag. 658; Ṭhāṇ. 490. 515; Paṇhāv. 32. 178. 419; Vivāhap. 361 f. 1123. 1193; Ovav.; Kappas.). — M. Ś. A. *ĕttia* (Hc. 2, 157; G. H.; Mṛcch. 41, 19; 60, 12; 77, 10. 24; Vikr. 45, 4; Mālav. 26, 10; Mālatīm. 82, 9; Uttarar. 18, 2; 66; 1; 72, 6; Hc. 4. 341. 2), JM. *ĕttiya* (Āv. 18. 6; Erz.), Ś. Mg. *ĕttika* (Śak. 29, 9; 59; 3; 70, 10; 71, 14; 76, 6; Vikr. 25, 7; 46, 8; 84, 9; Mg. Mṛcch. 125, 24; 165, 14; Śak. 114. 11), *ittia* (Hc. 2, 156) can neither with Lassen[1] be referred directly to **ati* nor with S. Goldschmidt with the support of Hc. directly to *iyat*, but it presupposes one **ayat* from which was derived **ayattya*, with a separation-vowel **ayattiya*, corresponding to Skt. *ihatya*, *kvatya*, *tatratya*. In the same way M. Ś. A. *kĕttia* (Hc. 2, 157; H.; Mṛcch. 72, 6; 88, 20; Vikr. 30, 8; Hc. 4, 383, 1), JM. *kĕttiya* (Erz.) = **kayattya*, **kayattiya* from the stem *kaya-*. So we must explain *e-* and *ke-* also in the first member of compounds in AMg. M. Ś. (§149). Analogous formations are M. *jĕttia* (Hc. 2, 157; G.H.R.), Mg. *yĕttika*, *yĕttia* (Mṛcch. 132, 13; 139. 11); *jittia* (Hc. 2, 156), M. Mg. A. *tĕttia* (Hc. 2, 157; G.H.R.; Mṛcch. 139, 12; Hc. 4, 395, 7), Mg. *tĕttika* (Mṛcch. 132, 14); *tittia* (Hc. 2, 156). Derivatives are *ĕttila*, *kĕttila*, *jĕttila*, *tĕttila* (Hc. 2, 157), JM. *ĕttilliya* (Āv. 45, 7), A. *ĕttula*, *kĕttula*, *jĕttula*, *tĕttula* (Hc. 4, 435).

1. Inst p. 125. — 2. Prākṛtica p. 23.

§ 154. *ava* becomes *o* through *aü*, e.g. in M. *oaraṇa* = *avataraṇa* (G.H.); M. *oāra* (G.H.), Ś. *odāra* (Śak. 21, 8), beside *avadāra* (Vikr. 21, 1) = *avatāra*, Ś. *odaradi* = *avatarati*, Mg. *odala* = *avatara* (§ 477); JŚ. *ŏggaha* = *avagraha* (Pav. 381, 21); AMg. *oma* = *avama* (Ṭhāṇ. 328; Uttar. 352. 768. 918), *aṇoma* = *anavama* (Āyār. 1, 3, 2, 3), *omāṇa* = *avamāna* (Uttar. 790), *vodāṇa* = *vyavadāna* (Sūyag. 523), and so very frequently in all the dialects in the prefix of the *ava* (Vr. 4, 21; Hc. 1, 172; Mk. fol. 35); AMg *osā* = *avaśyā*

(Sūyag 829; Uttar. 311; Dasav. 616, 21), also *ussā* for *ŏssā* (Ṭhāṇ. 339; Kappas. S. §45; v.l. *osā*, as should be read everywhere), *bahuosa* (Āyār. 2, 1, 4, 1), *apposa* (Āyār. 1, 7, 6, 4; 2, 1, 1, 2); M. Ś. *osāa*=*avaśyāya* (R. Vikr.; 15, 11 [read so with v. l. and the Drāviḍa recension 625, 11, ed. PISCHEL]); M. AMg. JM. *ohi*=*avadhi* (H.; Uvās.; Ovav.; Kappas.; Erz.); AMg. *joṇiyā*=*yavanikā* (Vivāhap. 792; Ovav.; Nāyādh.), but *javaṇa* (Paṇhāv. 41; Paṇṇav. 58), *javaṇiyā* (Kappas.); M. Ś. *ṇomāliā*=*navamālikā* (Hc. 1, 170; H.; Mṛcch. 73, 10; Lalitav. 560 9. 17. 20 [a proper noun]; Mālatīm. 81, 1; Śak. 9, 11; 12, 13; 13, 3; 15, 3), *ṇomalliā*=*navamallikā* (Vr. 1, 7); M. *ṇohaliā*=*navaphalikā* (Hc. 1. 170; Kī. 2, 148 [°*aṁ*]; H.); M. AMg. JM. A. *loṇa*=*lavaṇa* (Vr. 1, 7; Hc. 1, 171; Kī. 1, 8; Mk. fol. 6; G.H.; Kāleyak. 14, 13; Āyār. 2, 1, 6, 6. 9; 2, 1, 10, 7; Sūyag. 337. 834. 935; Dasav 614, 15. 16; 625, 13; Āv. 22, 39; Hc. 4, 418, 7. 444, 4), PG. JM. *aloṇa*=*alavaṇa* (6, 32; Āv. 22, 39), JM. *loṇiya aloṇiya* (Āv. 22, 14. 30. 31). According to Mk. fol. 66 Ś. has *lavaṇa* only. M. AMg. JM. A. *hoi*, JŚ. *hodi*, Ś. Mg. *bhodi*=*bhavati* (§ 475f.). The secondary *ava* derived from *apa* too may become *o* (Vr. 4, 21; Hc. 1, 172; Mk. fol. 35), as M. JM. *osaraï*=*apasarati*, JM. Ś. *osara*=*apasara*, Mg. *ośaladi*=*apasarati* (§477). — *āva* appears as *o* in M. *oli*=*āvali* (Hc. 1, 83, who equates it as=*āli*; G.H.R.) and in *lŏṇṇa*=*lāvaṇya* (Mk. fol. 6), A. also *saloṇa*=*salāvaṇya* (Hc. 4, 444,4) in rhyme with *loṇa*=*lavaṇa*. According to Mk. fol. 66 Ś. has *lāvaṇṇa* only, and so it occurs in Śak. 158, 10.

§ 155. According to Hc. 1, 173, *upa* may become either *ū* or *o*. His examples are : *ūhasiaṁ*, *ohasiaṁ*, *uvahasiaṁ*=*upahasitam*; *ujjhāo*, *ŏjjhāo*, *uvajjhāo*=*upādhyāyaḥ*; *ūāso*, *oāso*, *uvavāso*=*upavāsaḥ*. Mk. fol. 35 mentions that these do occur according to somebody (*kasyacinmate*). *ujjhāa*, that is found in poetry in JM. (Erz. 69, 28; 72, 39), stands for **ūjjhāa* from **uujjhāa*=M. Ś. *uvajjhāa* (H.; Karp. 6, 3; Vikr. 36, 3. 6. 12; Mudrār. 35, 9; 36, 4, 6; 37, 1; Priyad. 34, 14. 17. 21; 35, 15), AMg. JM. *uvajjhāya* (Āyār. 2, 1, 10, 1; 2, 3, 3, 3ff.; Samav. 85; Ṭhāṇ. 354f. 366. 384ff.; Erz.) =*upādhyāya*. There arises, therefore, *u* from *va* according to §152 and the two colliding *u*'s have been contracted into one. The same process is effective in *ūhasia* (Hc.) from **uuhasia*=*uvahasia*=*upahasita*, beside the dialectical *ūhaṭṭha* (laughter; Deśīn. 1. 140)=**upahasta*; further in *ūāsa* (Hc.)=**uuāsa*=*uvaāsa*=*upavāsa*; *ūṇandia* (overjoyed; Deśīn. 1, 141)= =**upanandita*; *ūyaṭṭha*=**upavṛṣṭa* (Pāiyal. 197); *ūsitta*=*upasikta* (Pāiyal. 187)[1]. Against these there occur the parallel forms with *o*, not going back to *upa*. In *ŏjjhāa*, from which is derived NI. *ojhā*[2], *ŏ* is to be explained according to § 125, in AMg. *paḍoyāra*=*pratyupacāra*, *paḍoyārei*=*pratyupacārayati* (§ 163) *o*, if the reading is correct, must be explained according to §77; in all other cases *o*=*ava* or *apa* according to § 154, even when no corresponding word is found in Skt. Thus :—*ohasia* (Hc.)=*apahasita*, as *ohaṭṭha* (Deśīn. 1, 153)=**apahasta*, *oāsa* (Hc.) is=**apavāsa*; *ositta* (Deśīn. 1, 158)=*avasikta*. *ua* never becomes *o*, for Pāli, M. *o* (R.), that is equated by Hc. 1, 172 and most of the scholiasts to=*uta*, and by others is explained with *atha vā*[3], is=Pāli *ādu*[4], AMg. *adu* (Sūyag. 118. 172, 248.

253. 514; Uttar. 90), *adu vā* (Sūẏag. 16, 46. 92. 142; Uttar. 28. 116. 180. 328; Samav. 82. 83), *adu va* (Sūẏag. 182. 249; Samav. 81), Ś. Mg. *ādu* (Mṛcch. 2, 23; 3, 14; 4, 1; 17, 21; 51, 24; 73, 4; Mālatīm. 77, 3; Priẏad. 30, 13; 37, 14; Adbhutad. 53, 3; Mg. Mṛcch. 21, 14; 132, 21; 158, 7), which, as sometimes *o*, is explained as = *atha vā*. *o* has, therefore, developed from **āu *aü*.[5]

1. In the last two examples *ū* can be equated also as = *ud*, as usually it is according to § 64. 327a. — 2. CROOKE, An Introduction to the Popular Religion and Folklore of Northern India (Allahabad 1894) p. 96 note. False with others, PISCHEL, GGA. 1894, 419, note 1. — 3. S. GOLDSCHMIDT. Rāvaṇavaho s. v. *o*. — 4. KERN, Bijdrage tot de Verklaring van eenige Woorden in Pāli-Geschriften voorkomende (Amsterdam 1886) p. 25 wrongly equates the word as = Vedic *ād u*. Cf. also FAUSBØLL, Nogle Nemaerkniger om enkelte vanskelige Pāli-Ord i Jātaka-Bogen (Kopenhagen 1881) p. 25ff. The words do have nothing in common in meaning. — 5. Falsely JACOBI ZDMG. 47, 578; KZ. 35, 578. Pāli *oka* = *udaka* is to be explained from **ukka*, **ŏkka* according to § 66. AMg. *adu* cannot be = *ataḥ* (WEBER, Bhag. 1, 422; E. MÜLLER, Beiträge p. 36), because *ta* does not become *da* in AMg. Cf. § 203. 204.

(*k*) VOCALIC SAṀDHI

§ 156. Similar vowels, when they meet together in compounds, are contracted mostly as in Skt. : *a*, *ā*+*a*, *ā* becomes *ā*; *i*, *ī*+*i*, *ī* = *ī*; *u*, *ū*+*u*, *ū* = *ū*. PG. *mahārajādhirājo* (5, 2), *ārakkhādhikate* = *ārakṣādhikṛtān* (5, 5), *sahassātireka* = *sahasrātireka* (7, 42), *vasudhādhipataye* = °*patin* (7, 44), *narādhamo* (7, 47); M. *kaāvarāha* = *kṛtāparādha* (H. 50); AMg. *kālākāla* (Āẏār. 1, 2, 1, 1); JM. *iṅgiẏākāra* (Āv. 11, 22); JŚ. *surāsura* (Pav. 379, 1); Ś. *kilesāṇala* = *kleśānala* (Lalitav. 562, 22); Mg. *yūdialāvamāṇa* = *dyūtakarāvamāna* (Mṛcch. 39, 35); A. *sāsāṇala* = *śvāsānala* (Hc. 4, 395, 2); M. *puhavīsa* = *pṛthivīśa* (H. 780); A. *aṁsūsāsahĩ* = *aśrūcchvāsaiḥ* (Hc. 4, 431). So also in the secondary vowel in M. *isīsa*, *isisi*[1] = *iṣat*+*iṣat* (§ 102). Before double consonants a long vowel is shortened according to §83 : M. *uddhaccha* = *ūrdhvākṣa* (H. 161). *kaïnda* = *kavīndra* (Karp. 6, 9); JŚ. *adindiẏatta* = *atīndriyatva* (Pav. 381, 20); AMg. *guṇaṭṭhi-* = *guṇārthin* (Āẏār. 1, 2, 1, 1); JM. *rattaccha* = *raktākṣa* (Āv. 12, 27); Ś. *jammantare* = *janmāntare* (Mṛcch. 4, 5); Mg. *aṇṇaggāmantala* = *anyagrāmāntara* (Mṛcch. 13, 8); PG. *aggiṭṭhomavājapeyassamedhayāji* (5, 1). So also in the verse before a simple consonant in AMg. *rāẏamacca* = *rājāmātya* (Sūẏag. 182; Dasav. 624, 22). In AMg., more rarely in JM. JŚ., however, similar vowels often remain uncontracted, particularly in dvandva compounds. Thus :—*a*+*a* : AMg. *smaṇamāhaṇāaīhi*° = *śramaṇabrāhmaṇātithi*° (Āẏār. 2, 1, 11, 9; 2, 2, 1, 2. 2, 8; cf. 2, 10, 4), *puvvavidehaavaravideha*° (Jīv. 161. 174f. 210; Aṇuog. 396. 397; Bhag.), *saaṅga* = *svāṅga* (Sūẏag. 364), *saaṭṭha* = *sārtha* (Sūẏag. 579), *kharapharuasasiṇiddhadittaaṇiṭṭhaasubhaappiẏaakantavaggūhi ẏa* = *kharaparuṣāsnigdhadīptāniṣṭāśubhāpriyākāntavagnubhiś ca* (Nāẏādh. 757), *puḍhavidagaagaṇi*° = *pṛthvyudakāgni*° (Paṇhāv. 353), *indaṇilaaẏasikusuma* = *indranilātasikusuma* (Ovav. § 10), *maṇaagutti*, *kāẏaagutti* = *manogupti*, *kāẏāgupti* (Vivāhap. 1462); AMg. *suraasurā* = *surāsurāḥ*, JM. *suraasuramaṇuẏamahiẏā* = *surāsuramanujāmahitāḥ* (Āẏār. 2, 15, 12; Kk. 269, 26); JM. *egaakkhara*[2] = *ekākṣara* (Āv. 7, 27), *aïregaaṭṭhavāsa* = *atirekāṣṭavarṣa* (Āv. 8, 9) *saẏalaatthamiẏajiẏaloa* = *sakalāstamitajīvaloka*

(Āv. 8, 22); JŚ. *savvaatthesu* = *sarvārtheṣu*, *vandaṇaatthaṁ* = *vandanārtham* (Kattig. 399, 313; 402, 356). — *a*+*ā* AMg. *akiriẏaāẏā* = *akriyātmānaḥ* (Sūẏag 410; — *a* for *ā* according to §97), *selagajakkhaāruhaṇa* = *śailakayakṣārohaṇa* (Nāẏādh. 966). — *ā*+*a* : AMg. *mahāaḍavī* (Nāẏādh. 1449), beside JM. *mahāḍavī* (Erz.); JM. *dhammakahāavasāṇa* = *dharmakathāvasāna* (Āv. 7, 27), *mahāakkanda* = *mahākranda* (Dvār. 505, 20). — *i*+*i* : AMg. *maīiḍḍhigārava* = *matyṛddhigaurava* (Dasav. 635. 38), where, therefore, the second *i* is secondary. — *u*+*u* : AMg. *bahuujjhiẏadhammiẏa* = *bahūjjhitadhārmika* (Āẏār. 2, 1, 10, 4. 11, 9; Dasav. 621, 6), *bahuudaga* = *bahūdaka* (Sūẏag. 565), beside *bahūdaẏa* (Ṭhāṇ. 400), *bahuuppala* = *bahūtpala* (Nāẏādh. 509), *devakuruuttarakuru*° (Jīv. 147. 174. 194. 205, 209. 211; Aṇuog. 396), °*kuruga* (Vivāhap. 425), *devakuruuttarakurāo* (Samav. 111), °*kuraẏāo* (Samav. 114), *suuddhara* (Dasav. 737, 30), *suujjuẏāra* = *svṛjukāra* (Sūẏag. 493), in which the second *u* is secondary. The vowels remain uncontracted in M. very rarely, somewhat more frequently in Ś. as M. *pavālaaṅkuraa* = *pravālāṅkuraka* (H. 680), *piāahara* = *priyādhara* (H. 827), *dhavalaaṁsua* = *dhavalāṁśuka* (R. 9, 25; cf. also the v. l.); Ś. *piaṁvadāaṇusūāo* = *priyaṁvadānuśūye* (Śak. 67, 6), *puñjikadaajjaüttakitti*° = *puñjikṛtāryaputrakīrti*° (Bālar. 289, 20), *aggisaraṇaālindaa* = *agniśaraṇālindaka* (Śak. 97, 17), *ceḍiāaccaṇāa* = *ceṭikārcanāya* (false dative), *pūāariha* = *pūjārha* (Mukund. 17, 12, 14). So also in A. *addhaaddha* = *ardhārdha*, *biaaddha* = *dvitīyārdha* (Piṅgala 1, 6. 50). In cases like Piṅgala 1, 24. 25 we must not assume a composition, but the stem, used as nominative. Too common is Hc. 1, 4.

§ 157. *a*, *ā* with short dissimilar vowels before single consonants in compounds undergo, the same saṁdhi as prescribed in Skt. : *a*, *ā*+*i* become = *e*; *a*, *ā*+*u* = *o*. Thus for example M. *disebha* = from *disā* = **diśā* = *dig* = *ibha* (G. 148), *saṁdaṭṭebhamŏttia* = *saṃdaṣṭebhamauktika* (G. 236), *pañcesu* = *pañceṣu* (Karp. 12, 8; 94, 8), *kisoarī* = *kṛśodarī* (H. 309), *sāmoaa* = = *śyāmodaka* R. 9, 40. 43. 44), *girilulioahi* = *girilulitoodadhi* (G. 148). Likewise the other dialects. Contraction takes place also in the case of secondary *i* and *u*, so AMg. Ś. *mahesi* from *mahā*+*isi* = *ṛṣi*, M.Ś. *rāesi* from *rāa* = *rāja*+*isi* = *ṛṣi* (§57); AMg. *savvouẏa* from *savva* = *sarva*+*uvẏa* = *ṛtuka* = *sarvartuka* (Paṇhāv. 259; Samav. 237; Vivāgas. 10; Vivāhap. 791; Nāẏādh. 527; Paṇṇav. 111; Ovav.; Kappas.), *ṇiccouga*, °*ẏa* = *nityartuka* (Samav. 233; Ṭhāṇ. 369), *aṇouẏa* = *anṛtuka* (§77; Ṭhāṇ. 369). In AMg. the vowels often remain uncontracted : *savvaüvarilla* (Jīv. 878f.), beside *savvupparilla* (Jīv. 879); *paḍhamasamaẏaüvasanta* = *prathamasamayopaśānta* (Paṇṇav. 65); *kakkolaüsira* (Paṇhāv. 527); *āẏariẏaüvajjhāẏa* = *ācāryopādhādhyāya* (Ṭhāṇ. 354f. 366, 384ff.; Samav. 85); *hĕṭṭhimaüvarima* (Samav. 68; Ṭhāṇ. 197 [*hi*°]); *vāẏaghaṇaüdahi vātaghanodadhi*(Vivāhap. 102); *kaṇṭhasüttaürattha* = *kaṇṭhasūtrorahstha* (Vivāhap. 791); *appaüdaẏa* = *alpodaka* (Āẏār. 2, 3, 2, 17), *divadisāüdahiṇaṁ* = *dvipadigudadhinām* (Vivāhap. 82). *mahāudaga* = *mahodaka* (Uttar. 714); also in the secondary second vowel : *ihāmigaüsabha* = *ihāmṛgarṣabha* (Jiv. 481. 492. 508; Nāẏādh. 721 [°*ha*]; Ovav. § 10; Kappas. §44); *khaggaüsabha* = *khaḍgarasabha* (Ovav. §37). In other dialects the vowels seldom remain uncontracted, such as in JM. *pavaẏaṇaüvaghāẏaga* = *pravacano-*

paghātaka, saṁjamaüvaghāya = *saṁyamopaghāta* (Kk. 261, 25. 26); Ś. *vasantussavaüvāaṇa* = *vasantotsavopāyana* (Malav. 39, 10; uncertain ; cf. v. l.); and in the secondary second vowel Ś. *visajjïdaïsidāraa* = *visarjitarṣidāraka* (Uttarar. 123. 10).

§ 158. If the second member of a compound begins with *i, u,* followed by a double consonant, or with either original or secondary *i, ū,* the final *a, ā* of the first member is, as a rule, discarded. (C. 2, 2; of Hc. 1, 10). So M.A. *gaïnda* = *gajendra* (G.H.R.; Vikr. 54, 1), A. *gaïndaa* (Vikr. 59, 8; 60, 21; 63, 2); JŚ. Ś. A. *ṇarinda* = *narendra* (Kattig.). 400, 326; Mālatīm. 206,7, [so to be read]; 292, 4; Piṅgala 1, 21. 24), Mg. *ṇalinda* (Mṛcch. 40, 6); AMg. Ś. Mg. *mahinda* = *mahendra* (Ṭhāṇ. 266; Mālatīm. 201, 5; Mṛcch. 128.8); AMg. JŚ. *devinda* = *devendra* (C. 2, 2; Hc. 3, 162; Kattig. 400, 326); AMg. *joisinda* = *jyotiṣendra* (Ṭhāṇ. 138); AMg. JM. JŚ. *jiṇinda* = *jivendra* (Ovav. § 37; Āv. 7, 24; Erz.; Kk.; Pav. 382, 42); Ś. *maïnda* = *mṛgendra* (Śak. 155, 1 [to be so read]; 156,7 and so many compounds with *indra* in all the dialects (cf. § 159); JM. *māindajāla* = *māyendrajāla* (Āv. 8, 53); AMg. *egindiya* = *ekendriya* (Vivāhap. 100. 109. 144); AMg. *soindiya, ghāṇindiya, jibbhindiya, phāsindiya* = *śrotrendriya, ghrāṇendriya, jihvendriya, sparśendriya* (Ṭhāṇ. 300; Vivāhap. 32; Ovav. p. 40. VI; Uttar. 822), A. *jibhindia* = *jihvendriya* (Hc. 4,427 [so to be read]); M. *taddiasindu* = *taddivasendu* (G. 702); *tiasisa* = *tridaśeśa* (Hc. 1, 10); JM. *rāisara* = *rājeśvara* (Erz.); *pavvadisara* = *parvateśvara* (Mudrār. 40, 6; 46, 9; 216, 13); M. *kaṇṇuppala* = *karṇotpala* (G. 760), AMg. JM. *niluppala*, Ś. *ṇiluppala* = *nilotpala* (Uvās. § 95; Ovav. § 10; KI. 18 [*ṇi*°]; Erz. 79, 8; Priyad. 15, 8; 33, 2; 39, 2); Mg. *ṇahuppala* = *nakhotpala* (Mṛcch. 122, 19); M. *khandhukkheva* = *skandhotkṣepa* (G. 1049), CP. *pātukkheva* = *pādotkṣepa* (Hc. 4, 326); AMg. *gandhuddhuya*, A. *gandhuddhua* = *gandhoddhuta* (Ovav. § 2; Vikr. 64, 16); JM. *rayaṇujjala* = *ratnojjvala* (Āv. 8, 4); Ś. *mandamāruduvvĕllida* = *mandamārutodvellita* (Ratn. 302, 31; cf. Mālatīm. 76, 3), *pavvadummūlida* = *parvatonmūlita* (Śak. 89, 13); Mg. *śavvuyyāṇa* = *sarvodyāna* (Mṛcch. 113, 19); M. *kaūsāsa* = *kṛtocchvāsa*, *liḍhūsa* = *liḍhoṣa* (G. 387. 536), *gamaṇūsua* = *gamanotsuka* (R. 1, 6); AMg. *egūṇa* = *ekona* (§144), *pañcūṇa* (Śamav. 208; Jīv. 219), *desūṇa* (Samav. 152. 219), *bhāgūṇa, kosūṇa* (Jīv. 228. 231); M. *gāmūsava* = *grāmotsava* (G. 598); M. JM. Ś. *mahūsava* = *mahotsava* (Karp. 12, 9; Erz. Mṛcch. 28, 2; Ratn. 292, 9. 12; 293, 13; 295, 19; 298, 30; Mālatīm. 29, 4; 119, 1; 142, 7; 218, 3 etc.; Uttarar. 108, 2; 113, 6; Caṇḍak. 93, 6; Anarghar. 154, 3; Nāgān. 42, 4 [text °*ūssa*°]; 53, 19; Vṛṣabh. 11, 2; Subhadr. 11, 5. 17); Ś. *vasantūsava* = *vasantotsava* (Śak. 121, 11; Vikr. 51, 14; Mālav. 39, 10 [so to be read]). So also in the case of secondary second vowel : AMg. *uttamiḍḍhi* = *uttama* + *ṛddhi* (Ṭhāṇ. 80), *deviḍḍhi* (Uvās. *mahiḍḍhi* (Ṭhāṇ. 178), *mahiḍḍhiya* (Ovav.); very seldom before a simple consonant, as in JM. *visesuvaogo* = *viśeṣopayoga* (Kk. 277, 9) and A. *addhuia* = *ardhodita* (Mṛcch. 100, 12).

§ 159. In the cases mentioned in § 158 contraction takes place, sometimes, when the second member begins already in Skt. with *i, ū* and a simple consonant follows it : Ṣ. *vāderida* = *vāterita* (Śak. 12, 1); M. *kariaroru* = *kariara* + *ūru* = *karikaroru* (H. 925), *piṇoru* = *pina* + *ūru* (R. 12, 16), *pāaḍoru* = *prakaṭoru* (H. 473), *valioru* = *valitoru* (G. 1161); AMg. *varoru* (Kappas. 33. 35), *pivaroru*, *disāgaïndoru* = *diggajendroru* (Kappas. § 36), *egoruẏa* = *ekoruka* (Paṇṇav. 56), but *egūruẏa* (Jīv. 345ff.; Vivāhap. 717); JM. *karikaroru* (Erz. 16, 12); Ś. *mantharoru* (Mālatīm. 108, 1), *pivaroru* (Mālatīm. 260, 3 [so to be read]). If the first member is a prefix, the vowels in contact are always contracted : Mg. AMg. JM. *pĕcchaï*, JŚ. *pĕcchadi*, Ś. *pĕkkhadi*, Mg. *pĕskadi* = *prekṣate* (§ 84); M. *aṇavĕkkhia* = *anapekṣita* (R.), JM. *avĕkkhaï* (Erz.); Ś. *avĕkkhadi* = *apekṣate* (Śak. 43, 10; 130, 2); M. *uvĕkkhia* = *upekṣita* (H.); M. *pĕllia* = *prerita* (G.H.). Also in the case of *i*, *u* with double consonants following, contraction occurs, but only seldom without a v. l. Thus M. *ṇisāarenda* = *niśācarendra* (R. 7, 59); M. Mg. *mahenda* = *mahendra* (R. 6, 22; 13, 20; Mṛcch. 133, 12); M. *rakkhasenda* = *rākṣasendra* (R. 12, 77); Ś. *ṇarenda* = *narendra* (Mālatīm. 90, 4; 179, 5); *rattŏppala* = *raktotpala* (Mṛcch. 73, 12). JŚ. *pañcendiẏa* = *pañcendriya* (Pav. 388, 9) must be an error. Beside it, almost always is found also the v. l. with *i*, *u*, as for example for Ś. *mahenda* (Vikr. 5, 10; 6, 19; 8. 11. 13; 36, 3; 83, 20; 84, 2) the Bengāli manuscripts always have *mahinda*, as is found elsewhere too in Ś. (§ 158)[1]; for Ś. *ṇiṇṇŏṇṇada* = *nimnonnata* (Śak. 131, 7) we should read *ṇiṇṇuṇṇada* with the v.l., as there stands in M. *ṇiṇṇuṇṇaa* (G. 681); for Ś. *uṇhŏṇha* (Śak. 29, 6), the correct form will be *uṇhuṇha*, for Ś. *maddalŏddāma* = *mardaloddāma* (Ratn. 292, 11), *maddaluddāma*[2]. Contraction might correctly be required in cases like JM. *ahesara*, *khaẏaresara*, *naresara* (Erz.); Ś. *paramesara* (Prab. 14, 9; 17, 2), which were probably first contracted with secondary *isara*, and certainly in Ś. *purisŏttama*, Mg. *pulisŏttama* = *puruṣottama* (§ 124), since as a proper noun, it has directly been taken from Skt. Elsewhere one says AMg. *purisuttama* (Dasav. 613, 40 [the original passage in Uttar. 681 has °*so*°]; Kappas. § 16 [so it is to be read with v. l.]; Ovav. §20 [so it is to be read; cf. the following *loguttama*]).

1. In any case Bollensen is wrong when he, on Vikr. 8, 11 p. 176, considers that *mahinda* has transgressed the boundary of high Pkt., by which he means Ś. — 2. Explanation of ŏ in such cases, according to § 125, does not appear likely in the face of a large number of counter-examples. Presumably in cases of this sort we have examples of Sanskritism that are to be corrected. Cf. Lassen, Inst. p. 175, note.

§ 160. In AMg. *a*, *ā* is often retained, even when a double consonant follows *i*, *u*, as in the case of single consonants (§ 157; cf. § 156). So AMg. *kakkeẏaṇaïndaṇila* = *karkatanendranila*, *māḍambiẏaïbbha* = *māḍambikebhya*, *koḍumbiẏaïbbha* = *kauṭumbikebhya* (Ovav. § 10. 38. 48); *pisāẏaïnda* = *piśācendra* (Ṭhāṇ. 90), but *pisāinda* (Ṭhāṇ. 138. 229); *bhūẏaïnda* = *bhūtendra* (Ṭhāṇ. 90), but *bhūinda* (Ṭhāṇ. 229), beside *jakkhinda*, *rakkhasinda*, *kiṁnarinda* etc. (Ṭhāṇ. 90; cf. § 158); *annāyaüñcha* = *ajñātoñcha* (Dasav. 636, 17); *lavaṇasamuddaüttaraṇa* = *lavaṇasamudrottaraṇa* (Nāẏādh. 966); *pehuṇaükkhevaga* = *preṅkhaṇotkṣepaka* (Paṇhāv. 533); *nāvāussiñcaẏa* = *nāvotsiñcaka* (Āẏār. 2, 3, 2, 19. 20); *indiẏaüddesa* = *indriyoddeśa*, *dugullasukumālaüttarijja* = *dukūlasukumārottariya*, *aṇegaüttama* = *anekottama*, *bhaẏaüvvigga* = *bhayodvigna*, *sohammakoppaüḍḍhaloẏa* = *saudharmakalpordhvaloka* (Vivāhap. 177f. 791, 809. 835. 920); *āẏāmaüsseha* = *āyāmotsedha* (Ovav. § 10). Very rarely the vowels remain beside one another in other dialects, as M. *paṇaṭṭhaüjjoa* = *pranaṣtoddyota*, *khaüppāa* = *khotpāta* (R. 9, 77. 78).

piṇatthaṇaütthambhiāṇaṇa = *pinastanotthāmbhitānana* (H. 294), *muhaüvvūḍha* = *mukhodvyūḍha* (Śak. 88, 2). False is Ś. *mŏttiaüppatti* = *mauktikotpatti* (Viddhaś. 108, 2), for which we should read *mŏttiuppati* [v. l. °*ŏppa*°]; as for example M. *piāmahuppati* = *pitāmahotpatti* (R. 1, 17), AMg. *aṅkuruppatti* (Paṇṇav. 848) remain, and in Prab. 17, 2 Ś. *pabohŏppatti* = *prabodhotpatti* is to be corrected to *pabohuppatti*. Hiatus is the rule in all dialects in *itthi* = *strī* (§ 147): AMg. *asurakumāraītthio*, *thaṇiẏakumāraītthiẏo*, *tirikkhajoṇiẏaītthio*, *maṇussaītthio*, °*devaītthio* (Vivāhap. 1394); JŚ. *paraītthiāloa* = *parastryāloka* (Kattig. 401, 344), *bhūsaṇaītthisaṁsagga* (Kattig. 402, 358); Ś. *anteurāītthi* (Śak. 38, 5). However, there occurs also AMg. *maṇussitthio*, *devitthio*, beside *tirikkhajoṇitthio* (Ṭhāṇ. 121); JŚ. *purisitthī* (Kattig. 401. 345).

§ 161. Falling out of *a*, *ā* is also to be assumed before original or secondary *e*, *o*, but not before the *e*, *o* going back to Skt. *ai*, *au*[1] : *gāmeṇi* (goat; Deśīn. 2,84) = *grāma*+*eṇi*; M. *ṇavelā* = *nava*+*elā*, *phullelā* = *phulla*+*elā* (R. 1, 62. 63), *ukkhaṇḍiĕkkapāsa* = *utkhaṇḍitaikapārśva* (R. 5, 43); Ś. *avalambiderāvaṇahattha* = *avalambitairāvaṇahasta* (Mṛchh. 68, 14), *silādalĕkkadesa* = *śilātalaikadeśa* (Śak. 56, 11), *karuṇĕkkamaṇa* = *karuṇaikamanas* (Mālatīm. 251, 7); M. *kusumŏtthaa* = *kusumāvastṛta* (R. 10, 36), *paḍhamosaria* = *prathamāpasṛta* (H. 351), *bāhomaṭṭha* = *bāṣpāvamṛṣṭa* (R. 5, 21), *jāloli* from *jāla* = *jvāla*+*oli* = *āvali* (§ 154; H. 589), as *vaṇoli* = *vana*+*āvali* (Hc. 2, 177 = H. 579, where *vaṇāli*), *vāoli* = *vāta*+*āvali*, *paholi* = *prabhā*+*āvali* (G. 555,1008); AMg. JM. *udaŏlla* from *udaka*+*ŏlla* = **udra*, (§ 111; Dasav. 625, 27; Āv. 9, 3), beside AMg. *udaülla* = *udaka*+*ulla* (Āẏār. 2, 1, 6, 6; 2, 6, 2, 4); AMg. *vāseṇŏlla* = *varṣeṇa*+*ŏlla* = (Uttar. 673); AMg. *mālohaḍa* = *māla* (platform; pedestal; Deśīn. 6, 146)[2]+*ohaḍa* = *avahṛta* (Āẏār. 2, 1, 7, 1; Dasav. 620, 36), *maṭṭiolitta* = *maṭṭiā* = *mṛttikā*+*olitta* = *avalipta* (Āẏār. 2, 1, 7, 3); JM. *jaloha* = *jalaugha* (Erz. 3, 26), *saṁṭhāṇosappiṇi*° = *saṁsthānāvasarpiṇi*° (Ṛṣabhap. 47); Ś. *guḍodaṇa* = *guḍaudana* (Mṛcch. 3, 12), *vasantodāra* = *vasantāvatāra* (Śak. 21, 8), *kararuhorampa* = *kararuha* = *orampa* (seizure; Mālatīm. 261, 2; so to be read; cf. Deśīn. 1, 171; Pāiẏal. 198). Sometimes the vowels remain beside one another, as M. *vāandolaṇaoṇavia* = *vātāndolanāvanamita* (H. 637); AMg. *khuḍḍagaegāvali* = *kṣudrakaikāvali* (Ovav. [§ 38]), *vippahāiẏaolamba* = *viprabhājitāvalamba* (Ovav. § 4); JM. *sabhāovāsa* = *sabhāvakāśa* (Āv. 15, 12).

1. In cases like *ṇavelā*, *jaloha*, *guḍodaṇa* one may be in doubts. The proposition is proved with the help of the compounds with secondary *ĕ*, *ŏ*, *o*, that have, therefore, been selected as examples copiously. — 2. Cf. JACOBI, SBE. XXII, 105 note.

§ 162. *i*, *ī*, *u*, *ū*, as a rule, do not undergo saṁdhi with a following dissimilar vowel (Hc. 1, 6) : M. *ṇahappahāvaliaruṇa* = *nakhaprabhāvalyaruṇa* (Hc. 1, 6), *rattiandhaa* = *rātryandhaka* (H. 669), *saṁjhāvahuavaūḍha* = *saṁdhyāvadhvavagūḍha* (Hc. 1, 6); AMg. *jāiāriẏa* = *jātyārya* (Ṭhāṇ. 414), *jāiandha* = *jatyandha* (Sūẏag. 438), *sattiagga* = *śaktyagra* (Dasav. 634, 11), *puḍhaviāu*° = **pṛthivyāpaḥ* (Paṇṇav. 742), *pantovahiuvaaraṇa* = *prāntopadhyupakaraṇa* (Uttar. 350), *pagaïuvasanta* = *prakṛtyupaśānta* (Vivāhap. 100. 174), *puḍhaviuḍḍhaloẏa* = *pṛthvyūrdhvaloka* (Vivāhap. 920), *kadaliūsuga* = *kadali*+*ūsuga* (middle, inside; cf. BÖHTLINGK 2, *ūṣa* 1) b) c); Āẏār. 2, 1, 8, 12), *suahijjiẏa* = *svadhīta* (Ṭhāṇ. 190. 191), *bahuaṭṭhiẏa* = *bahvasthika* (Āẏār. 2, 1, 10, 5 [to be read thus]. 6; Dasav. 621, 4), *sāhuajjava* = *sādhvārjava* (Ṭhāṇ. 356), *sualaṁkiẏa* = *svalaṁkṛta* (Dasav. 632, 39), *kavikacchuagaṇi* = *kapikacchvagni* (Paṇhāv. 537), *bahuosa* = *bahvavaśya* (Āẏār. 2, 1, 4, 1); also in the secondary second vowel, as in AMg. *suisi* = *svṛṣi* (Paṇhāv. 448), *bahuiḍḍhi* = *bahuvṛddhi* (Nāẏādh. 990). Beside AMg. *cakkhuindiẏa* = *cakṣurindriya* (Samav. 17) more frequent is *cakkhindiẏa* = *cakkha-cakṣas*+*indriya* (Samav. 69. 73. 77 ff; Vivāhap. 32; Uttar. 822; Ovav. p. 40. VI). JM. *asappiṇiussappiṇi*° = *avasarpiṇyutsarpiṇi*° (Ṛṣabhap. 47), *suaṇuẏatta* = *svanuvṛtta* (Āv. 11, 15), *meruāgāra* (7. 5. 8); Ś. *santiudaa* = *śāntyudaka* (Śak. 67, 4), *uvarialindaa* = *uparyalindaka* (Mālatīm. 72, 8; 187, 2), *uvvasiakkhara* = *urvaśyakṣara* (Vikr. 31, 11), *sarassadiuvāaṇa* = *sarasvatyupāyana* (Mālav. 16, 19), *sidāmaṇḍaviummilā*° = *sitāmāṇḍavyūrmilā*° (Bālar. 151. 1), *dehacchaviulluñcida* = *dehacchavyulluñcita* (Prab. 45, 11). Quite isolated is the dropping off of *i* in AMg. *itthattha* = *stryartha* (Dasav. 638. 18) and *kiṁcūṇa* from **kiṁciūṇa* = *kiṁcidūna* (Samav. 153; Ovav. 30, II, e), as well as of the initial *i* in AMg. *bendiẏa* (Ṭhāṇ. 275; Dasav. 615, 8), *tendiẏa* (Ṭhāṇ. 275. 322), beside *beindiẏa*, *teindiẏa* (Ṭhāṇ. 25, 122. 322 [*ve*°]; Samav. 228; Vivāhap. 30. 31. 93. 144; Dasav. 615, 8 [*te*°] = *dvindriya*, *trindriya*. AMg. *isāsa* = *iṣvāsa* (§ 117) is directly derived from Skt.

§ 163. *i* and *u*, as final sounds of prefixes, with following dissimilar vowels, undergo the same saṁdhi as prescribed in Skt. The group of sounds thus arising is treated according to the rules holding good for individual dialects. M. AMg. JM. Ś. *accanta* = *atyanta* (G.; Niraẏāv.; Erz.; Pav. 380, 12; 389, 1; Mṛcch. 60, 25; Mālav. 28, 13); AMg. *accei* = *atyeti* (Āẏār. 1, 2, 1, 3); AMg. JM. *ajjhovavanna* = *adhyupapanna* (§ 77); M. *abbhāgaa* = *abhyāgata* (H.); JM. *abbhuvagacchāviẏa*, *abbhuvagaẏa* = *abhyupagamita*, *abhyupagata* (Āv. 30, 9. 10); Ś. Mg. *abbhuvavaṇṇa* = *abhyupapanna* (Mṛcch. 28, 18; Vikr. 8, 12; Mg. Mṛcch. 175, 18); M. AMg. Ś. A. *pajjatta* = *paryāpta* (G.H.R.; Uvās.; Śak. 71, 7; Vikr. 25, 6; Hc. 4, 365, 2); M. Ś. *ṇivvūḍha* = *nirvyūḍha* (G.H.R.; Mālatīm. 282, 3); M. *aṇṇesaï*, Mg. *aṇṇeśadi* = *anveṣati* (G. ; Mṛcch. 12, 3); Ś. A. *aṇṇesanta-* = *anveṣat* (Erz.; Vikr. 52, 20; Mṛcch. 148, 7. 8). The sound-groups *ty*, *ry*, especially in AMg. JM., are often separated by separation-vowels, in which case *ẏ* disappears often in AMg. and JM., and always in other dialects, so that the vowels, as in § 162, come beside one another. M. *aïāara* (H.); JM. *aïẏāẏara* (Erz.) = **atiẏādara* = *atyādara*; AMg. *ṇāiuṇha* = *nātyuṣṇa* (Vivāhap. 954), beside AMg. *accusiṇa* (Āẏār. 2, 1, 7, 5), M. *accuṇha* (H.); M. *aïujjua* (H.), Ś. *adiujjua* (Ratn. 309, 24; Priyad. 43, 15) = *atyrjuka*; AMg. *ahiẏāsijjanti* = *adhyāsyante* (Ovav.); JM. *paḍiẏāgaẏa* = *pratyāgata* (Erz.), beside M. *paccāgaa* (H.), JM. *paccāgaẏa* (Erz.), Ś. *paccāgada* (Uttarar. 106, 10); AMg. *paḍiẏāikkhiẏa* = *pratyākhyāta*, beside *paccakkhāa* (§ 565); AM). *paḍiuccāreẏavva* = *pratyuccārayitavya* (Vivāhap. 34); AMg. *pariẏāvanna* = *paryāpanna* (Āẏār. 2, 1, 9, 6. 11, 7. 8); AMg. *paliucchūḍha* = *paryutkṣubdha* = (§ 66); M. *viola* = *vyākula* (§ 166). In AMg., and in other dialects, the *i* of *prati* too, is thrown out before a dissimilar vowel following it. Thus beside AMg. M. *pāḍiĕkka* = *pratyeka* (Hc. 2, 210; R.; Nāẏādh. 1224; Vivāhap. 1206; Ovav. [read so in all the places for *pāḍiẏakka*]) also *pāḍikka* for **pāḍĕkka* (§ 84; Hc. 2, 210); *paḍaṁsuā* = **pratyāśrut*

(§ 115); *paḍāyāṇa* = **pratyāḍāna* (§ 258); AMg. *paḍucca* for **paḍiucca* from *vaccaï* = *vrajati* (§ 202, 590), *pāḍucciya* = *prātītika* (Ṭhāṇ. 38); AMg. *paḍuppanna* = *pratyutpanna* (Āyār. 1, 4, 1, 1; Sūyag. 533, Ṭhāṇ. 173. 174; Vivāhap. 24. 78. 79. 80. 651; Jīv. 337. 338; Aṇuog. 473. 510ff.; Uvās), JM. *apaḍuppanna* (Āv. 17, 31); AMg. *paḍoyāra* = *pratyavatāra* (LEUMANN, Aup. S. s. v. and = *pratyupacāra* (§ 155; Vivāhap. 1235. 1251), *paḍoyāreu* = *pratyupacārayatu*, *paḍoyāreha* = *pratyupacārayata*, *paḍoyārĕnti* = *pratyupacārayanti*, *paḍoyarijjamāṇa* = = *pratyupacāryamāṇa* (Vivāhap. 1235. 1251). On M. *pattiaï*, JM. AMg. *pattiyaï*, Ś. Mg. *pattiāadi*, AMg. *patteya* see § 281. 487.

§ 164. A. vowel, which remains after dropping off of a consonant (§ 186), is called *udvṛtta*[1]. An *udvṛtta* vowel, as a rule, undergoes no saṁdhi with a preceding vowel (C. 2, 1 p. 37; Hc. 1, 8; cf. Vr. 4, 1). So M. *uaa* = *udaka* (G. H. R.[2]); *gaa* = *gaja* and *gata*; *paavi* = *padavi* (G.H.); *saala* = *sakala*; *aṇurāa* = *anurāga*; *ghāa* = *ghāta* (H. R.); *kaī* = *kati* (R.), = *kapi* (G.H.R.), = *kavi* (G. H.); *jaī* = *yadi*; *ṇaī* = *nadī*; *gāiā* = *gāyikā* (H.); *taüsi* = *trapuṣi* (H.); *paüra* = *pracura* (H.); *pia* = *priya*; *piaama* = *priyatama*; *piāsā* = *pipāsā* (H.); *riu* = *ripu*, *juala* = *yugala*; *rūa* = *rūpa*; *sūi* = *śūci* (G. H.); *aṇea* = *aneka* (G.H.); *joaṇa* = *yojana* (R.); *loa* = *loka*. The rule holds good also for compounds of all kinds: M. *aïra* = *acira*; *aūvva* = *apūrva*; *avaaṁsa* = *avataṁsa* (H. R.); *āaa* = *āyata* (H. R.); *uvaüḍha* = *upagūḍha*; *paāva* = *pratāpa*; *paīva* = *pradipa*; *dāhiṇāṁsaaḍa* = *dakṣiṇāṁśataṭa* (G. 104); *saaṇha* = *satṛṣṇa* (H.). *golāaḍa* = *godātaṭa* (H. 103); *disāala* = *diktala* (R. 1,7); *vasahaīndha* = *vṛṣabhacihna* = (G. 425); *ṇisiara* = *niśicara* (R.); *saürisa* = *satpuruṣa* (G. 992); *gandhaüḍi* = *gandhakuṭi* (G. 319); *golāūra* = *godāpūra* (H. 231); *viiṇṇaūra* = *vitirṇatūrya* (R. 8, 65); *guruaṇa* = *gurujana* (H.) So in all other dialects under similar conditions.

1. Hc. 1, 8 calls the vowel *udvṛetta*. In C. 2, 1 p. 37 it is called *uddhṛta* Triv. 1, 1, 22; Sr. fol. 2; Narasiṁha 1, 1, 22; Appayadikṣita 1, 1, 22 call it *śeṣa* a term that is not recommended, as Hc. 2, 89 and Triv. 1, 4, 86 employ it for the consonant that is retained out of a group. — 2. These quotations hold good for all the following words under which nothing has been noted.

§ 165. Udvṛtta vowels are sometimes contracted with preceding similar vowels. Thus *a*, *ā* with *a*, *ā* : *attamāṇa* beside *āvattamāṇa* = *āvartamāna* (Hc. 1, 271); AMg. *āra* from **aara* = *avara* (Sūyag. 106. 322) and JM. *ādara* (Kk. II; *oāava* (time of the sun-set; Deśīn. 1, 162) = **oaāava* = *apagatātapa*, whereas *ovāaa* (Triv. 1, 4, 121; ed. *oāava*; cf. also BB. 13, 13) is = *apavātaka*; *kālāsa* beside *kālāasa*, as according to Mk. always in Ś., = *kālāyasa* (Vr. 4, 3; Hc. 1, 269); A. *khāi* beside *khāaï* = *khādati* (Vr. 8, 27; one : Kī. 4, 77; Hc. 4, 228; 419, 1); A. *khanti* = *khāanti*, **khānti* = *khādanti* (Hc. 4, 445, 4), *khāu* *khādatu* (Bh. 8, 27), from which a root *khā* has been deduced, from which have been formed a future *khāhii* (§ 525), a second person singular imperative A. *khāhi* (Hc. 4, 422, 4. 16) and a past passive participle *khāa* = **khāta* (Hc. 4, 228); *gāṇa* from *gāaṇa* = *gāyana* (Deśīn. 2, 108); *gāṇi* (trough for cattle; Deśīn. 2, 8 from **gaāaṇi*, AMg. *gavāṇi* (Āyār. 2, 10, 19) = *gavādani*; Mg. *gomāo* from **gomāao* = *gomāyavaḥ* (Mṛcch. 168, 20); A. *campāvaṇṇi* = *campakavarṇi* (Hc. 4,1); *chāṇa* (clothing; Deśīn. 330, 34) = *chādana*; A. *jāi* from *jaaï* = *jayati* (Piṅgala. 1, 85a; *dhāi* beside *dhāvaï* = *dhāvati* (Vr. 8, 27; Hc. 4, 228), M. *uddhāi* = *uddhāvati* (R.), from which is deduced, as in the case of *khād*, a root *dhā*, from which are formed *dhāu* (Bh. 8, 27), *dhāha* (Hc. 2, 192), *dhāhii* (§ 525), *dhāo* Hc. 4, 228); AMg. *pacchitta* (Samav. 91; Hc. 4, 428), beside AMg. *pāyacchitta* (Jīyak. 18; Uvās.; Nāyādh.; Ovav.; Kappas.) = *prāyaścitta*; *pāvaḍaṇa*, beside M. *pāavaḍaṇa* (H. °*pa*°) = *pādapatana* (Bh. 4, 1; Hc. 1. 270; Mk. fol. 31); M. JM. Ś. *pāikka* = *pādātika* (§ 194); *pāvīḍha* beside *pāavīḍha* = *pādapīṭha* (Hc. 1, 270; Mk. fol. 31); AMg. *bhante* = *bhadantaḥ* (§ 366b); *bhāṇa* = *bhājana* (Vr. 4, 4; Hc. 1, 267; Kī. 2, 151), whilst Ś., as noted by Mk., has only *bhāaṇa* (Mṛcch. 41, 6; Śak. 72, 16; 105, 9; Prab. 59, 4; Veṇīs. 25, 3. 5; Mallikām. 289, 3; Adbhutad. 2, 15). On forms like *gāi* = *gāyati*, *jhāi* = *dhyāyati*, *jāi* = *jāyate*, *palāi* = *palāyate* see § 479. 487. 567. — *i*, *ī* get contracted with udvṛtta *i*, *ī* in M.A. *bīa* (Hc. 1, 5, 248; 2, 79; G. s. v. *viya*; H. s. v. *vīa*; R. s. v. *biia*; Piṅgala, 1, 23. 49. 56. 79. 83), A. also *bia* (Piṅgala. 1, 50), AMg. JM. *biya* (Vivāhap. 55; Uvās.; Kappas.; Kī. 21; Erz.), beside M. *biia*, AMg. JM. *biiya* (§ 82) = *dvitīya*; A. *tia* from **tiia* = *tṛtīya* (Piṅgala. 1, 49. 59. 70); AMg. *paḍīṇa*, *udīṇa* = *pratīcīna*, *udīcīna* (Āyār. 1, 4, 4, 4; 1, 6, 4, 2; Ovav. § 4), *paḍiṇa* (Vivāhap. 1675f.), also shortened prosodically *paḍiṇa* (Dasav. 625, 37; cf. § 99); AMg. *sīyā* = *śibikā* (Āyār. p. 127, 26; Nāyādh. 865ff.; 1021 f, 1074. 1097. 1189. 1497; Nirayāv. 61. 62; Vīvāhap. 275. 277. 362. 1262; Ovav.; Kappas.), beside AMg. JM. *siviyā* (Āyār. 127, 15 [to be read so]; Ovav.; Erz.); in future, as JM. *hohī* beside M. JM. *hohii* = **bhoṣyati* = *bhaviṣyati* (§ 521). JM. *viṇāsihī* (§ 527), *jarehī*, *nivārehī* (§ 528), *ehī*, A. *esī* (§ 529), JM. *dāhī* (§ 530), *sakkehī* (§ 531), AMg. JM. *kāhī* (§ 533), AMg. *nāhī* (§ 534). M. *cīa* (H. 104) is = **ciia* from **citiya* = *citya*, AMg. *cī* in *cīvandaṇa* = *caityavandana*, according to Hc. 1, 151 is = **cii* = Skt. *citi*-. — *u*, *ū* with the udvṛtta -*u*, *ū*, are contracted in AMg. *umbara* from *uumbara*, **ūmbara* = *udumbara* (Vr. 4, 2; Hc. 1, 270; Kī. 2, 152; Anuttar. 11; Nāyādh. § 137; p. 289. 439; Ṭhāṇ. 555; Jīv. 46. 494; Niryāv. 55, Paṇṇav. 31; Vivāhap. 807. 1530).

§ 166. Sometimes *a*, *ā* is contracted with an udvṛtta *i*, *ī*, *u*, *ū* too: *kelī* from **kaīli* = **kadilī* = *kadalī* with *i* according to § 101, and on the same model *kela* from **kaila* = **kadila* = *kadala* (Hc. 1, 167. 220)[1]; M. AMg. JM. Ś. *thera* from* *thaïra* = *sthavira* (Hc. 1, 166; 2, 89; Pāiyal, 2; Deśīn. 5, 29; H. 197 [to be read so]; text *ṭhera*]; Kāvyaprakāśa 73, 9 = H. 983 [to be read so according to the best MS.; text *ṭhera*]; Sarasvatīk. 8, 13 [*ṭhera*]; Acyutaś. 32 [*ṭhera*]; Ṭhāṇ. 141. 157. 286; Vivāhap. 131. 132. 169. 172. 173. 185. 792; Uttar. 786; Ovav.; Kappas.; Nāyādh.; Erz.; Kk.; Anarghar. 63, 4 [*ṭhera*]); M. Ś. also *thavira* (Prab. 38, 10 [ed. Bomb. P. M. *ṭhavira*]; Nagān. 3, 2 [v. l. *ṭhavira*, *ṭhera*]; M. *therī* (Pāiyal. 107; H. 654 [text *ṭherī*°; ed. Bomb. 7, 52 *ṭhera*°]); AMg. *theraya* (Sūyag. 176), *theraga* (Sūyag. 334), *theriyā* [Kappas.); *therāsaṇa* (lotus; Deśīn. 5, 29), *therosaṇa* (lotus; Triv. 1, 4, 121) = **sthavirāvasana*[2]; *meḍambha* from **maïḍambha* = **mṛgīdambha* (noose for catching a roe; Deśīn. 6, 139); *mehara* beside **maihara* = **matidhara* (headman; Deśīn. 6, 121); AMg. *vera* (Kappas. § 45) from *vaïra* (§ 135) = *vajra*; A. *eha*, *jeha*, *teha*, *keha* (H. 4, 402) from and beside *aïsa*, *jaïsa*, *taïsa*, *kaïsa* (Hc. 4, 403) = *idṛśa*, *yādṛśa*, *tādṛśa*, *kīdṛśa* (§ 121); A. *jĕ* for the common *jaï* = *yadi* (Piṅgala. 1, 4a. 97 [GOLDSCHMIDT *jaṁ*]); M. *de* beside *daï* = Ś. *daïa*, absolutive from *daya-* (§ 594). In AMg. A. *-aī = -ati*, the ending of the third person singular, too is sometimes contracted into *-e* in verses. So AMg. *aṭṭe* (Sūyåg. 412) from *aṭṭaī* (cf. *pariaṭṭaī* (Hc. 4, 230) = **aṭyati* from *aṭ* (not from *aṭṭa = ārta*), *kappe* = **kalpati* (Āyār. 1,8,4, 2), *bhuñje* from *bhuñjaï* (§ 507) = = *bhunakti* (Āyār. 1, 8, 4, 6. 7), *abhibhāse = abhibhāṣate*, *paḍiyāikkhe = pratyākhyāti* (§ 491), *seve* = **sevati*, *paḍiseve* = **pratiṣevati* (Āyār. 1, 8, 1, 7. 14. 17. 4, 5); A. *ṇacce = nṛtyati*, *sadde* = **śabdati = śabdayati*, *gajje = garjati*, *bolle = bŏllaī* (Hc. 4, 2), *ugge* from **uggai* = **udgāti* (to go up; Piṅgala. 2, 82. 90. 228. 268), *hose* (Prabandhac. 56, 6) from *hosaī* (Hc. 4, 388. 418, 4) = **bhoṣyati = bhaviṣyati* (§ 521). Similarly are explained also AMg. *bemi* from **baīmi* = *bravīmi* (§ 494). — A. *co = caü = catur* (Piṅgala. 1, 65; GOLDSCHMIDT, however, reads *aṭṭha vi lahuā* for *co laghu kattha vi* of the ed. Bomb.), *covisa*, *coviṣa* beside *caüvisaha = caturviṁśati*, *coālīsaha* beside *caüālisā*, AMg. *coyāloisaṁ* beside *caüyālisaṁ = catuścatvāriṁśat*, *cŏttisaṁ* — *catustriṁśat*, etc. (§ 445); M. *cŏttha* beside *caüttha = caturtha* (§ 449); *cŏddaha* beside A. *caüddaha*, AMg. *cŏddasa* beside *caüddasa = caturdaśa* (§ 443), AMg. *cŏddasama = caturdaśama* (§ 449); *cŏgguṇa* beside *caügguṇa = caturguṇa*, *cŏvvāra* beside *caüvvāra-caturvāra* (Hc. 1,171); *tovaṭṭa* beside *taüvaṭṭa trapupaṭṭa* (an ear-ornament; Deśīn. 5, 23; 6, 89); M. AMg. *pŏmma = padma* (Hc. 1, 61; 2, 112; Mk. fol. 31; Kāleyak. 14, 15; Pārvatīp. 28, 15; Uttar. 752 (text *pomaṁ*]), *pŏmmā = padmā* (H.); M. Ś. *pŏmmarāa* = *padmarāga* (Mk. fol. 31; H.; Karp. 47, 2; 103, 4 (Ś.); Viddhaś. 113, 7 (Ś.); Pras. 121, 8 [Ś.; text *pa°*]; 155, 12; Bālar. 157, 12 (Ś); 168, 4 (Ś.); M. *pŏmmāsaṇa = padmāsana* (Kāleyak. 3, 11), from and beside M. AMg. JM. Ś. *paüma*, *paümarāa* (§ 139); *bohāri* beside *baühāri* (brush; Deśīn. 6, 97; 8, 17); A. *bhŏhā* from **bhāuhā = bhamuhā* (Piṅgala 2, 98; § 124. 251); *moḍa* beside *maüḍi* (tress; Deśīn. 6, 117; Pāiyal. 57), M. AMg. JM. Ś. A. *mora* (Vr. 1, 8; Kī. 1, 7; Mk. fol. 6; Pāiyal. 42, H.; Aṇuog. 502. 507; Nandīs. 70; Paṇṇav. 526; Rāyap. 52; Kappas.; Kk.; Śak. 155, 10; 158, 13; Uttarar. 163, 10; Jīvān. 16, 12; Vikr. 72. 8; Piṅgala 2, 90), A. *moraa* (Piṅgala 2, 228), femin. M. Ś. *mori* (Śak. 85, 2; Ś. Śak. 58, 8; Viddhaś. 20, 15), Mg. *moli* (Mṛcch.) 10, 4 [to be so read), AMg. *moraga = mayūraka* (Āyār. 2, 2, 3, 18) from and beside M. AMg. JM. Ś. *maūra* (Grr.; G.; Paṇṇav. 54; Dasav. N. 662, 36; Erz.; Vikr. 32, 7; Mallikām. 220, 20), AMg. *mayūra* (Vivāgas. 187. 202), *mayūratta = mayūratva* (Vivāgas. 247), Mg. *maūlaka* (Śak. 159, 3), femin. AMg. *mayūri* (Nāyādh. 475, 490. 491). *mora* has gone into Skt. too, and consequently it has been treated as Skt. by Hc. 1, 171. M. *moha = mayūkha* (Grr. ; R. 1, 18) from and beside M. Ś. *maūha* (Grr.; Pāiyal. 47; G.H.R.; Prab. 46, 1); M. *viola* from **viāula = vyākula* (Deśīn. 7, 63; R.; cf. § 162)[4]; A. *saṁhāro* from *saṁharaü = saṁharatu* (Piṅgala 2, 43). Cf. also *kohala*, *samāra*, *somāla* § 123, *o* § 155. M. AMg. *bora = badara* (Vr. 1, 6; Hc., 1, 170; Kī. 1, 8; Mk. fol. 5; G. H.; Paṇṇav. 531; Vivāhap. 609. 1256. 1530), AMg. *bori = badari* (Hc. 1, 170; Mk. fol. 5; Pāiyal. 254; Aṇuttar. 9) presuppose one **badura*, **baduri*.[5] AMg. *būra* (v.l. *pūra*; Jīv. 489. 509. 559; Rāyap. 57; Uttar. 986; Vivāhap. 182; Ovav.; Kappas.; Nāyādh.) is not = *badara*, but = *pūra* (citron-tree) which will be the correct reading. The scholiasts generally explain it as *vanaspativiśeṣa*.[6] Obscure is *pora = pūtara* (Hc. 1, 170.).

1. PISCHEL, KZ. 34, 572; not correctly JACOBI, ZDMG. 47, 575; KZ. 35. 573. — 2. PISCHEL, BB. 13, 3 — 3. PISCHEL, Deśīn. Introduction p. 7. — 4. PISCHEL, GGA, 1880, p. 335. — 5. PISCHEL, KZ. 34, 572; falsely JACOBI, ZDMG. 47. 575; KZ. 55, 573. According to Mk. fol. 66 Ś. has *baara* only.

§ 167. In compounds too the udvṛtta vowel is sometimes contracted with the final vowel of the first member : M. A. *andhāra* = *andhakāra* (Mk. fol. 31; H.; Piṅgala.1,117[a];2,90), A. *andhāraa* (Hc. 4,349), M. *andhāria* = *andhakārita* (H.), JM. *andhāriya* (Erz.; Kk.), beside M. Ś. *andhaāra* (G.H.R.; Mṛcch. 44, 19; 80, 9; 88, 17; 138, 3; Śak. 141. 7; Priyad. 51, 12; Karp. 85, 6; Mallikām. 209, 17; Prab. 14, 17; Cait. 40, 15), Mg. *andhaāla* (Mṛcch. 14, 10, 22; 16, 22), AMg. JM. *andhayāra* (Ovav.; Kappas.; Nāyādh.; Ṛṣabhap,. JM. *andhayāriya* (Erz.); M. JM. A. *āa* from and beside *āaa* = *āgata* (Hc. 1, 268; H.; Āv. 8, 47; Piṅgala 2, 255. 264); *kaṁsāla* = *kāṁsyatāla* (Hc. 2, 92), Ś. *kaṁsatālaa* (Mṛcch. 69, 24); AMg. *kammāra* = *karmakāra* (Jīv. 295) and other compounds with *kāra*, like AMg. *kumbhāra* = *kumbhakāra* (Hc. 1, 8; Mk. fol. 32; Uvās.), besides *kumbhaāra* (Grr.), AMg. *kumbhakāra* (Uvās.), JM. *kumbhagāra* (Erz.), D. *cammaāraa* = *carmakāraka* (Mṛcch. 104, 19), M. *mālārī* = *mālākārī* (H.; Deśīn. 1, 146, 114), AMg. *lohāra* = *lohakāra* (Jīv. 293), M. *valaāraa* = *valayakāraka* (H.), *soṇāra* = *svarṇakāra* (§ 66), AMg. *dodhāra* = *dvidhākāra* (Ṭhāṇ. 401); A. *piārī* = *priyakārī* (Piṅgala 2, 37); JM. *khandhāra* = *skandhāvāra* (Mk. fol. 32; Erz.), beside *khandhavāra* (Erz.); M. *cakkāa* = *cakravāka* (Hc. 1, 8; K.. 2, 151; Mk. fol. 32; Candraśekhara on Śak. 88, 2 p. 192; G.R.; Śak. 88, 2), AMg. *cakkāga* (Paṇṇav. 54); AMg. *ṇiṇṇāra* = *nirnagara* (Vivāhap. 1277); AMg. *nimboliyā* = *nimbagulikā* (Nāyādh. 1152. 1173); *talāra* = *talavāra* (Deśīn. 5, 3; Triv. 1, 3, 105; PISCHEL, BB. 3, 261); *pāra* beside *pāāra* = *prākāra* (Hc. 1, 268); M. *pāraa* (Hc. 1, 271; H.; Ind. Stud. 16, 78, on 184) beside *pāvāraa* = *prāvāraka*; *pārāa* beside *pārāvaa* = *pārāvata* (Bh. 4, 5; cf. § 112); M. *pāvāliā* = *prapāpālikā* (H.); JM *varisāla* = *varṣākāla* (Erz.); *vāraṇa* beside *vāaraṇa* = *vyākaraṇa* (Hc. 1, 268); M. *sālāhaṇa* = *sātavāhana* (Hc. 1, 8, 211; H.); M. *sāhāra* = *sāhakāra* (Karp. 95, 1); AMg. *sūmāla* beside *sukumāla* = *sukumāra* (§ 123); *sūrisa* = beside *suurisa* = *supuruṣa* (Hc. 1, 8). As compounds are treated also M. *jālā*, *tālā* (Hc. 3, 65; Mk. fol 46; Dhvanyāloka 62, 4) too; falsely also in Ś. (Mallikām. 87, 11; 124, 14) and Mg. (Mallikām. 144, 3)—**yāt kālāt*, **tāt kālāt*, *kālā* (Hc. 3, 65; Mk. fol. 46) = **kāt kālāt* (PISCHEL, BB. 16, 172). Cf. also § 254.

§ 168. In some cases *a*, at the end of the first member of a compound, is elided before a dissimilar udvṛtta vowel in the beginning of the second member : *indova* from **indaova* = *indragopa* (Pāiyal. 150; Deśīn. 1, 81), beside AMg. *indagova* (Aṇuog. 344), *indagovaga* (Uttar. 1062), °*ya* (Paṇṇav. 45); *indovatta* = **indragopātma* (cochineal; Deśīn. 1, 81); *gharolī* from **gharaolī* = **gharagolī* = *gṛhagolī* a thousand-footed insect living in a house; Deśīn. 2, 105), AMg. *gharoliyā* = *gṛhagolikā* (Paṇhāv. 22; Paṇṇav. 53 [text *gharoila*]; *gharola* from **gharaola* = **gharagola* = *gṛhagola* (*ka*) (a kind of home-made pastry : Deśīn. 2, 106); M. AMg. JM. Ś. Mg. Ḍh. *deula* = *devakula* (Hc. 1, 271, Mk. fol. 33;

H.; Aṇuog. 387; Nāyādh. 535; T. 4, 9; 7, 18; Erz.; Mṛcch. 151, 14; Karṇas. 25, 1; Mṛcch. 29, 24; 30. 11. 12), beside and from JM. Ś. *devaüla* (Hc.; Mk.; Erz.; Viddhaś. 59, 7; Cait. 134, 10. 14), AMg. *devakula* (Āyār. 2, 2, 2, 8; 2, 10, 14; 2, 11, 8; Paṇhāv. 521; Nāyādh. 581; Kappas.); JM. *deuliyā* = *devakulikā* (Āv. 31, 10); JM. D. *rāula* = *rājakula* (Bh. 4, 1; Hc. 1, 267; Mk. fol. 32; Erz.; Mṛcch. 105, 4), Mg. *lāula* (Lalitav. 565, 7. 9. 15; 566, 13. 12; Mṛcch. 36, 22; 135, 2), falsely in Ś. (Prab. 47, 5. 9; 49, 13. 15; ed. M. has throughout *lāaüla*, ed. P. 47, 9), where *rāaüla* (Grr.) is to be read, as stands in Śak. 115, 3. 6; 119, 1; Ratn. 309, 9; Nāgān. 57, 3; Priyad. 9. 13. In Prab. 32, 9 for Mg. *lājaüla* (ed. M. *rājaüla*) we should read *lāaüla*; JM. has also *rāyaüla* (Erz.)[1]; Mg. *lāutta* from **lāaütta* = *rājaputra* (Śak. 114, 1; 115, 7. 9; 116. 9; 117, 5); *vāutta* beside *vāäütta* = *vataputra* (Deśīn. 7, 88).

1. Cf. Candraśekhara on Śak. 114, 1 (p. 197) *rāulaśabda* (so to be read) *īśvare deśī* In this sense the word stands in Prab. as in Skt. too in the inscriptions (KIELHORN, EI. 4, 312, note 7). Wholly wrong JACOBI, ZDMG. 47, 576.

§ 169. In the sentence as a rule vowels remain unchanged in the auslaut, whether they originally stood next to one another or have afterwards come together through dropping out of a consonant. PG. *kāṁcipurā aggiṭṭhoma°* = *kāñcipurād agniṣṭoma°* (5, 1), *sivakhaṁdavamo amhaṁ visaye* = *śivaskandavarmāsmākaṁ viṣaye* (5, 2), *govallave amacce ārakhādhikate* = *govallavān amātyān ārakṣādhikṛtān* (5, 5), *tti api ca āpiṭṭiyaṁ* = *ityapi cāpiṭṭyām* (6. 37). *tti eva* = *ityeva* (6, 39), *tasa khu amhe* = *tasya khalvasme* (7, 41), *sakakāle uparilikhitaṁ* = *svakakāla uparilikhitam* (7, 44); M. *ṇa a me icchāi* = *na ca ma icchayā* (H. 555), *taṁ si aviṇiddā* = *tvamasyavinidrā* (H. 66), *daṭṭhūṇa uṇṇamante* = *dṛṣṭvonnamataḥ* (H. 539), *jivie āsaṅgho* = *jīvitā āśaṁsā* (R. 1, 15), *paaṭṭaü uahi* = *pravartatāṁudadhiḥ* (R. 3, 58); *āmuaï aṅgāiṁ* = *āmuñcatyaṅgāni* (R. 5, 8), *jāo elāsurahimmi* = *yāta elāsurabhau* (G. 417), *so esa kesavo uvasamuddam uddāma°* = *sa eṣa keśava upasamudramuddāma°* (G. 1045); AMg. *atthi me āyā ovavāie* = *asti ma ātmaupapātikaḥ* (Āyār. 1, 1, 1, 3), *cattāri ee* = *catvāra ete*, (Dasav. 632, 7) *tāo ajjāo ĕjjamāṇio pāsai* = *tā āryā eyamānāḥ paśyati* (Nirayāv. 59), *ege āha* = *eka āha* (Sūyag. 74), *khiṇe āummi* = *kṣiṇa āyuṣi* (Sūyag. 212), *jo imāo disāo aṇudisāo aṇusaṁcaraï* = *ya imā diśa anudiśo'nusaṁcarati* (Āyār. 1, 1, 1, 4). So also the rest of the dialects.

§ 170. *na* (not) not rarely undergoes saṁdhi with the initial vowel of the following word, especially when the latter is a verb : M. AMg. JM. JŚ. Ś. *ṇatthi* = *nāsti* (e.g. G.H.R. s. v. *as*; Āyār. 1, 1, 1, 3; Āv. 9, 9; Pav. 380, 10; Mṛcch. 2, 24), Mg. *ṇasti* (e.g. Mṛcch. 19, 11 [text *ṇatthi*]); M. *ṇāmi* = *na*+*ami* (G. 246), *ṇalliaï* = *na*+*alliaï* (R. 14. 5); M. JŚ. Ś. *ṇāhaṁ* = *na*+*aham* (H.178; Pav. 384, 36; Vikr. 10, 13); M. *ṇāulabhāva* = *na*+*ākulabhāva* (G. 813), *ṇāgaa* = *na*+*āgata* (H. 856), *ṇālavaï* = *na*+*ālapati* (H. 647); AMg. JŚ. *neva*, *ṇeva* = *na*+*eva* (Āyār. 1, 1, 3, 3. 4, 1; Pav. 384. 59), M. *ṇea* (G.H.R.); AMg. *ṇāṇāgama* = *na*+*anāgama* (Āyār. 1, 4. 2, 2), *nābhijāṇaï* = *nābhijānāti* (Āyār. 1, 5, 1, 3), *nārabhe* = *na*+*ārabheta* (Āyār. 1, 5, 3, 4), *nābhibhāsiṁsu* = *na*+*abhi°*, *nāivattaï na*+*ativartate* (Āyār. 1, 8, 1, 6); Ś. *ṇāgadā* = *na*+*āgatā* (Mālatīm. 72, 6); Mg. *ṇāaścadi* = *na*+*āgacchati* (Mṛcch. 116, 5. 19; 117, 11); AMg. JM. *nāidūra* (Uvās. § 208; Ovas. § 33; Nāyādh. § 7; Erz. 22, 23), Ś. *ṇādidūra*

(Mālatīm. 30, 8), Mg. *ṇādidūla* (Caṇḍak. 66, 13) = *na*+*atidūra*; Ś. *ṇārihadi* = *na*+*arhati* (Śak. 24, 12); M. *ṇĕcchaī* = *na*+*icchati* (H.205), Ś. *ṇĕcchadi* (Śak. 73, 4), Mg. *ṇĕścadi* (Mṛcch. 11, 1); Ś. *ṇālaṁkidā* = *na*+*alaṁkṛtā* (Mṛcch. 18, 10), *ṇodaradi* = *na*+*avatarati* (Mṛcch. 108, 21). In such cases *na* is proclitic and is treated as the first member of a compound. This holds good also for the root *jñā* which after *na* very often drops its initial *ja* which, as in the inlaut, is changed into *ẏa* in AMg. JM. : M. *ṇa āṇāmi*, *ṇai āṇasi*, *ṇa āṇaï*, *ṇa āṇimo*, *ṇa āṇaha*, *ṇa āṇanti*; AMg. JM. *ṇa ẏāṇāmi* (Nāẏādh. 84; Āv. 29, 19), JM. *ṇa ẏāṇasi*, *ṇa ẏāṇaï*, AMg. *ṇa ẏāṇāmo*; Ś. *ṇa āṇāmi* (Mṛcch. 5?, 16; 65, 11; Vikr. 43, 14; 46, 1); Mg. *ṇa āṇāmi* (Mṛcch. 140, 12); Ś. D. *ṇa āṇādi*; D. *ṇa āṇāsi*, Ś. *ṇa āṇiadi* = *na jñāyate*; M. AMg. Ś. *ṇa āṇe* = *na jāne*. References in § 457. 510. 548. This formation is quite analogous to compounds such as Ś. *aāṇanteṇa* = *ajānatā* (Mṛcch 18, 22; 63, 24). *aāṇia* = *ajñātvā* (Śak. 50, 13), AMg. *viẏāṇāi*, Ś. Mg. *viāṇādi*, AMg. *pariẏāṇāi*, Mg. *paccabhiāṇādi* (§ 510). In most of the cases, however, *na* is not proclitic, and, therefore, as a rule it remains unchanged before all vowels, as M. *ṇa itthaṁ* = *neṣṭam* (H. 501), *ṇa isā* = *nerṣyā* (H. 829), *ṇa uttaraï* = *nottarati* (H. 271), *ṇa ei* = *naiti* (R. 14, 43), *ṇa ohasiā* = *nāvahasitā* (H. 60); AMg. *na ambile*, *na uṇhe*, *na itthī*, *na annahā* = *nāmlaḥ*, *noṣṇaḥ*, *na strī*, *nānyathā*, beside *natthi* (Āẏār. 1, 5, 6, 4), and so in all dialects.[1]

1. Cf. LASSEN Inst. p. 193; BOLLENSEN on Vikr. p. 193. 302; S. GOLDSCHMIDT, ZDMG, 32, 104.

§ 171. As sometimes in Skt., *na* is used as the first member of a compound instead of *a*, *an* in Pkt. too. M. *ṇasahiāloa* = *asoḍhāloka* (G. 364), *ṇāsahiapaḍiboha* = *asoḍhapratibodha* (G. 1162), *ṇapahuppanta-* = *aprabhavat* (G. 16, 46), *ṇapahutta* = *aprabhūta* (G. 114) for which R. 3, 57 has *ṇavahutta* with *pa* treated as a medial sound for the sake of rhyme. One may also like to consider this *na* in AMg. in cases like *taṁ maggaṁ ṇuttaraṁ* = *taṁ mārgamanuttaram* (Sūẏag. 419); *disaṁ ṇantajiṇeṇa* = *diśamanantajinena* (Āẏār. 2, 16, 6); *diṭṭhihiṁ ṇantāhiṁ* = *dṛṣṭibhiranantābhiḥ*, *muttisuhaṁ ṇantāhiṁpi* [text *vi*] *vaggavaggūhiṁ* = *muktisukham anantairapi vargavagnubhiḥ* (Paṇṇav. 135); *aggivaṇṇāiṁ ṇegaso* = *agnivarṇāny anekaśaḥ* (Uttar. 598); *egapae ṇegāiṁ padāiṁ* = *ekapade 'nekāni padāni* (Paṇṇav. 63), *ĕssanti ṇantaso* = *eṣyantyanantaśaḥ* (Sūẏag. 45. 56. 71); *bandhaṇehi ṇegehi* = *bandhanairanekaiḥ* (Sūẏag. 225); *gaṇḍavacchāsu* [text °*vatthā*°] *ṇegacittāsu* = *gaṇḍavakṣaḥsvanekacittāsu* (Uttar. 252); *itto ṇantaguṇiyā* = *ito* *'*nantaguṇikāḥ* (Uttar. 599); *virāẏae ṇegaguṇovavee* = *virājate 'nekaguṇopetaḥ* (Sūẏag. 309); *buddehi ṇāiṇṇā* = *buddhair anācīrṇā* (Dasav. 627, 16). As, however, the dropping off of the initial *a* occurs in all the analogous cases (§ 175), and the texts always write *ṇ*, never *n*, we shall have here to assume the dropping off of *a*. Hence in transcription we should write *maggaṁ 'ṇuttaraṁ*, etc.

§ 172. Besides in the case of *na*, contraction takes place within the sentence more frequently only when one of the words is a pronoun, an adverb, a preposition, or a case form of a substantive, used as a preposition, in which proclisis or enclisis of the particles has to be assumed. This contraction occurs especially in AMg. JM. So AMg. *ahāvarā* = *athāparā* (Āẏār. 2,

1, 11, 4ff.; 2, 2, 3, 19ff.; 2, 5, 1, 7ff. etc.), *ṇa ẏāhaṁ* = *na cāham* (Āẏār. 1, 7, 6, 1), *jeṇāhaṁ* = *yenāham* (Uttar. 241); JM. *jeṇāhaṁ* (Erz. 17, 14), *jeṇāṇiẏāhaṁ* = *yenānitāham* [Erz. 8, 23], *ihāḍavie* = *ihāṭavyām* (Erz. 30, 13), M. *sahasāgaassa* = *sahasāgatasya* (H. 297); AMg. *purāsi* = *purāsit* (Sūẏag. 898); JM. *sahāmacceṇa* = *sahāmātyena* (Āv. 11, 18); AMg. *dārigeẏaṁ* = *dārikeyam* (Dasav. N. 648, 2); M. *ṇa hujjalā* = *na khalūjjvalā* (on H. 993); AMg. *no hūvaṇamanti* = *no khalūpanamanti* (Sūẏag. 100);, *ĕtthovarae* = *atroparataḥ* (Āẏār. 1, 6, 2, 4); JM. *siharovari* = *śikharopari* (T. 5, 10); Ś. *mamovari* = *mamopari* (Mṛcch. 41, 22); JŚ. *jassedha* [text °*eha*] = *yasyeha* (Pav. 382, 24). On *ajjāvi, keṇāvi, teṇāvi* etc. see § 143. Contraction occurs more seldom in other cases, as AMg. *samāsajjāvitahaṁ* = *samāsādyāvitatham* (Āẏār. 1, 7, 8, 17), *jāṇittāẏariẏassa* = *jñātvācāryasya* (Uttar. 43), *kammāṇāṇaphalā* = *karmāṇyajñānaphalāni* (Uttar. 113), *tahosuẏāro* = *tatheṣukāraḥ* (Uttar. 422), *isiṇāhāra-m-āiṇi* = *ṛṣiṇāhārādini* (Dasav. 626, 6); JM. *māṇusesūvavannā, tirikkhesūvavannā* = *manusyeṣūpapannā, *tiryakṣeṣūpapannā* (Āv. 17, 22. 23), *paḍikappieṇāgao* = *pratikalpitenāgataḥ* (Erz. 32, 18), *subuddināmeṇāmacceṇa* = *subuddhināmnāmātyena* (Erz. 17, 19). In AMg. in verses sometimes even the vowels, that have come together, even secondarily, are contracted. So : *esovarae* = *eṣa uparataḥ* (Āẏār. 1, 1, 5, 1); *uvasaggā bhimāsi* = *upasargā bhimā āsan* (Āẏār. 1, 8, 2, 7); *tamhāivijjo* = *tasmād atividyaḥ* (Āẏār. 1, 4, 3, 3); *buddhāṇusāsanti* = *buddhā anuśāsati* (Uttar. 33); *parājiẏāvasappāmo* = *parājitā apasarpāmaḥ* (Sūẏag. 186); *akaẏakaraṇāṇahhigaẏā ẏa* = *akṛtakaraṇa anabhigatāś ca* (Jīẏakappa 73). Also after a toneless nasal in *maggāṇusāsanti* for *maggā aṇusāsanti* = *mārgamanuśāsati* (Sūẏag. 465. 517), *addhāṇugacchaï, panthāṇugāmie* for *addhā aṇugahaï, panthā, aṇugāmie* = *adhvānam anugacchati, panthānam *anugāmikaḥ* (Sūẏag. 59). Cf. § 173. 175

§ 173. In the auslaut vowels are often thrown out in M. JŚ., and especially in JM. AMg. before a vowel in the anlaut : M. *jeṇ' ahaṁ* = *yenāham* (H. 441), *tujjh' avarāhe* = *tavāparādhe* (H. 277); JM. *kuṇāleṇ' imaṁ* = *kuṇālenaimam* (Āv. 8, 16), *tāẏass' āṇaṁ* = *tātasyājñām* (Āv. 8, 18), *jeṇ' evaṁ* = *yenaivaṁ* [Erz. 14, 8] *ih' eva* = *ihaiva* (Āv. 29, 14; Erz. 17, 3; 20, 14), *jāv' esā* = *yāvad eṣā* (Erz. 53, 28), *tah' eva* = *tathaiva* (Āv. 12, 26; 27, 19), *tass' aṇṇesaṇatthaṁ* = *tasyānveṣaṇārtham* (Erz. 13, 18); JŚ. *ten' iha* (Pav. 387, 21) *jatth' atthi* = *yatrāsti* (Kattig. 401, 353), *teṇ' uvaïṭṭho* = *tenopadiṣṭaḥ* (Kattig. 398, 304); AMg. *akkhāẏ' aṇelisaṁ* = *ākhyāyānidṛśam* (Āẏār. 1, 8, 1, 15), *jatth' atthamie, jatth' avasappanti, jatth' agaṇi* = *yatrāstamitaḥ yatrāvasarpanti, yatrāgniḥ* (Sūẏag. 129. 181. 273), *vuḍḍheṇ' aṇusāsie* = *vṛddhenānuśāsitaḥ* (Sūẏag. 515), *ubhaẏass' antareṇa* = *ubhayasyāntareṇa* (Uttar. 32), *vinnāvaṇ' itthisu* = *vijñāpanā strīṣu* (Sūẏag. 208. 209), *jen' uvahammai* = *yenopahanyate* (Dasav. 627, 13), *jah' ĕttha* = *yathātra* (Āẏār. 1, 5, 3, 2), *vippaḍivann' ege* = *vipratipannā eke* (Sūẏag. 170), *tass' āharaha* = *tasyāharata* (Āẏār. 2, 1, 11, 2). *i* has dropped off e.g. in AMg. JM. *natth' ĕttha* = *nāstyatra* (Āẏār. 1, 4, 2, 5; Erz. 10, 21) against Ś. *ṇatthi ĕttha* (Śak. 121, 5); AMg. *jaṁs' ime* = *yasminnime* (Āẏār. 1, 2, 6, 2), *sant' ime* = *santime* (Āẏār. 1, 1, 6, 1; Sūẏag. 65; Uttar. 200; Dasav. 625, 25; 626, 36); *vaẏant' ege* = *vadantyeke* (Sūẏag. 37), *cattār' itthiẏāo* = *catasraḥ striyaḥ* (Ṭhāṇ. 247), *cattār' antaradivā* = *catvāro 'ntaradvipāḥ* (Ṭhāṇ. 260) in the verse, beside °*ri a*° in prose and *cattāri agaṇio* = *caturo 'gniṇ* (Sūyag. 274) in the verse, *kilant' anne* = *krīḍantyanye, tarant' ege* = *tarantyeke* (Uttar. 504, 567), *tinn' udahī, dŏnn' udahī* = *traya udadhayaḥ, dvāvudadhī* (Uttar. 996, 1000), *dalām' ahaṁ* = *dalayāmy ahaṁ* (= *dadāmy ahaṁ*) (Uttar. 663). *e* has dropped off for example in AMg. *s'evaṁ* = *sa evam* (Āyār. 1, 7, 3, 3; 2, 3, 1, 1), *paḍham' ittha* = *prathamo'tra* (Nandīs. 74), *tubbh' ĕttha* = *yuṣme atra, im' ee* = *ima ete, mann' erisaṁ* = *manya idṛśam* (Uttar. 358. 439. 571), *im' eyārūve* = *ayametadrūpaḥ* (Vivāgas. 116; Vivāhap. 151. 170. 171; Uvās.). *o* has dropped off in AMg. *guruṇ' antie* for *guruṇo antie* = *gurorantike* (Uttar. 29; Dasav. 632, 22). Anusvāra has dropped off after weakening of the nasal sound, for example, in AMg. *ṇiogajivāṇ' aṇantāṇaṁ* = *niyogajivānām anantānām* (Paṇṇav. 42), *cariss' ahaṁ* for *carissaṁ ahaṁ* = *cariṣyāmyahaṁ* (Sūyag. 239), *pucchiss' ahaṁ* for *pucchissaṁ ahaṁ* = *aprākṣamaham* (Sūyag. 259), *veṇaïyāṇ' u vāyaṁ* = *vainayikānām u vādam* (Sūyag. 322), *vippariyās' uvĕnti* = *viparyāsam upayanti* (Sūyag. 468. 497), *dukkhāṇ' antakaro* = *duḥkhānām antakaraḥ* (Uttar. 1005), *siddhāṇ' ogāhaṇā* = *siddhānām avagāhanā* (Ovav. 171), *paḍham'ittha* = *prathamamatra* (Kappas. Th. § 9), *im' eyārūvaṁ* = *imametadrūpaṃ* (Āyār. 2, 15, 24; Kappas. § 94), *im' erisaṁ aṇāyāraṁ* = *imamidṛśamanācāram* (Dasav. 626, 27); JM. *moriyāvaṁsāṇ' amhaṁ* = *mauryavaṁśānâmasmākam* (Āv. 8, 17), *im' erisaṁ* = *imamidṛśam* (Āv. 25, 26). Almost all the examples occur in verses. In the very frequent AMg. *no iṇ' aṭṭhe samaṭṭhe* (Sūyag. 852. 986. 992; Paṇṇav. 366; Nāyādh. 570; Vivāhap. 37. 44. 46ff. 79. 106. 112 ff. 204; Ovav. § 69, 74; Uvās. s. v. *samaṭṭha*), beside *no iṇam aṭṭhe samaṭṭhe* (Ovav. § 94) "that is not the case" *iṇ'* is to be taken, with Hc. 3, 85 as the nom. sing. of the neuter, which, elsewhere too in AMg. (§ 357), is related with the masculine.[1] Very rarely a final vowel has dropped off in other dialects, as in Ś. *etth' antare* (Mṛcch. 40, 23; also in JM. Erz. 17, 30); Mg). *tav' edeṇa* = *tavaitena* (Mṛcch. 12, 19) in the verse.

1. Not correctly WEBER, Bhag. 1, 409, where is given a collection on the saṁdhi from Vivāhap, E. MÜLLER, Beiträge p. 50, HOERNLE, Uvās. Translation, note 107. Cf. LEUMANN, WZKM. 3, 344f.

§ 174. In AMg. the final vowels of *api* and *iti*, with an initial dissimilar vowel, sometimes undergo the saṁdhi prescribed in Skt.: *app* = *apy* fuses with *eka* and **ekatya* into one word, as in Pāli: *appege* = **apyekaḥ* (Āyār. 1, 1, 2, 5), *appege* = **apyeke* (Āyār. 1, 1, 6, 5), *jaṁsi taṁsi' ppege* = *yasmin tasminn *apyeke* (Āyār. 1, 8, 2, 13), beside medial *vi ege* (Āyār. 1, 5, 4, 1), *vi ee* (Uttar. 1016), and *v' ege* (Āyār. 1, 5, 5, 2; 1, 6, 4, 1; Sūyag. 234), *v' ee* (Vivāhap. 101. 180), *v' eg' evam āhaṁsu* = **apyeka evam āhuḥ* (Sūyag. 240), *evaṁ p' ege* (Āyār. 1, 6, 1, 1. 2), *puvvaṁ p' eyaṁ pacchā v'* [so to be read] *eyaṁ* = *pūrvamapye'tatpaścādapyetat* (Āyār. 1, 5, 2, 3); AMg. *appegaïyā* = Pāli *appekacce* = **apyekatyāḥ* (Ovav.); also in JM. *io pp' eva* = *ito 'pyeva* (Āv. 19, 23). Likewise *iti*: AMg. *iccāi* = *ityādi* (Kappas. § 196ff.); *icceva* (Āyār. 1, 5, 5, 3; Sūyag. 557), *iccev' ege* (Āyār. 1, 3, 2, 2), *iccatthaṁ* (Āyār. 1, 2, 1, 1), *iccevaṁ* (Āyār. 1, 2, 1, 3), *iccee* (Āyār. 1, 1, 3, 7. 4, 7; 1, 5, 4, 5), *icceehiṁ* (Āyār. 1, 2, 1, 5), *icceyāo icceyāsiṁ* (Āyār. 2, 1, 11, 10. 11), *icceyāvanti* (Āyār. 1, 5, 6, 4). In Ś. Mg. *nu*, before *etad* becomes *nv* and then fuses with it into one word: Ś.

evaṁ (*ĕvvaṁ*) *ṇedaṁ* = *evaṁ nvetat* (Mṛcch. 22, 16; 57, 20; Śak. 2, 5; 45, 13; 71, 6; Prab. 8. 6; Ratn. 292, 8), *kiṁ ṇedaṁ* = *kiṁ nvetat* (Mṛcch. 3, 2; 27, 17; 40, 17; 54, 15; 60, 4; 97, 14; 117, 17; 169, 20; 171, 4; 172, 22; Vikr. 25. 18; 31, 4; Ratn. 301, 28), likewise Mg. (Mṛcch. 40, 8; 134, 17; 171, 5), and against the dialect (§ 429) *taṁ ṇidaṁ* = *tannvidam* (Lalitav. 566, 20).

§ 175. An initial *a* in verses, after *e*, *o*, is sometimes elided as in Skt. M. *piŏ'jja* = *priyo'dya* (H. 137); AMg. *āsiṇe'ṇelisaṁ* = *āsīno'nidṛśam* (Āẏār. 1, 7, 8, 17,) *phāse 'hiẏāsae* = *sparśānadhyāsayet* (Āẏār. 1, 7, 8, 18), *se 'bhinnāẏdaṁsaṇe* = *so'bhinnātmadarśanaḥ* (Āẏār. 1, 8, 1, 10), *sisaṁ se 'bhitāvaẏanti* = *śirṣamasyābhitāpayanti* (Sūẏag. 280, *se 'ṇutappaï* = *so 'nutapyate* (Sūẏag. 226), *uvasante 'ṇihe* = *upaśānto, nihaḥ* (Sūẏag. 365), *tippamāṇo 'hiḥāsae* = *tṛpyamāṇo 'dhyāsayet* (Āẏār. 1, 7, 8, 10), *iṇamo 'bbavī* = *idamabravīt* (Sūẏag. 259), *ābhogao 'ibahuso* = *ābhogato 'tibahuśaḥ* (Jīẏak. 44), *bālo 'varajjhaï* = *bālo 'parādhyate* (Dasav. 624, 32); Mg. *snāde 'haṁ* = *snāto 'ham* (Mṛcch. 136, 11). In prose dropping off of *a* occurs in the set formula AMg. *ṇamŏ'tthu ṇaṁ* = *namo 'stu nūnam* (§ 498) and in JM. in *aham*, as in *tie 'haṁ* = *tasyāmaham* (Erz. 12, 22), *tao 'haṁ* = *tato 'ham, jāo 'haṁ* = *jāto 'ham* (Erz. 9, 36; 53, 34). In AMg., seldom in JM. M., in verses, initial *a* too frequently drops off even after vowels other than *e*, *o*. Thus after *ā* in *pajjijjamāṇā 'ṭṭataraṁ* = *pāyyamānā ārtataram* (Sūẏag. 282); after *i* in *jāiẏarāmaraṇehi 'bhidduā* = *jātijarāmaraṇairabhidrutāḥ* (Sūẏag. 156), *ciṭṭanti'bhitappamāṇā* = *tiṣṭhantyabhitapiyamānāḥ* (Sūẏag. 274), *sūlāhi 'bhitāvaẏanti* = *śūlābhir abhitāpayanti* (Sūẏag. 280. 289), *jāvanti 'vijjāpurisā* = *yāvanto 'vidyāpuruṣāḥ* (Uttar. 215), *novalabhāmi 'haṁ* = *nopalahhe' haṁ* (Uttar. 575), *cattāri 'bhŏjjāiṁ* = *catvāryabhojyāni* (Dasav. 626, 6), *jaī 'haṁ* = *yadyaham* (Dasav. 641, 21), as M. too has (R. 15, 88), *aguṇehi 'sāhū* = *aguṇairasādhūn* (Dasav. 637, 3); after *i* in AMg. *veẏaraṇi 'bhiduggā* = *vaitaranyabhidurgā* (Sūẏag). 270), *lahaï 'bhidugge* = *labhate 'bhidurge* (Sūẏag. 277), *jaṁsi 'bhidugge* = *yasminnabhidurge* (Sūẏag. 287. 297 [°*duggaṁsi*]), *nadī 'bhiduggā* (Sūẏag. 297); after *u* in JM. *dosu 'bhiggaho* = *dvayorabhigrahaḥ* (Āv. 19, 36); also after anusvāra with weakening of the nasal sound, as in AMg. *kahaṁ 'bhitāvā* = *kathamabhitāpāḥ* (Sūẏag. 259), *veẏaraṇiṁ 'bhiduggaṁ* = *vaitaraṇimabhidurgām* (Sūyag. 270), *vayaṇaṁ 'bhiuñje* = *vacanamabhiyuñje* (Sūẏag. 529). False in prose is *tesiṁ'tie* (Āẏār. 1, 6, 4, 1), for which, according to the commentators, we have to write *tesiṁ antie*, Cf. § 171. 172. 173. Even vowels, other than *a*, sometimes drop off in AMg. after *e*, *o*; thus *i* in *je 'me* for *je ime* = *ya ime* (Sūẏag. 454), *je 'ha* for *je iha* = *ya iha* (Sūẏag. 304); *e* in AMg. *akāriṇo 'ttha* = *akāriṇo'tra* (Uttar. 290), *anno 'ttha* = *anyo 'tra* (Uttar. 791), M. *ko 'ttha* (H. 364), and after the weakened nasal sound in M. JM. *kiṁ tha* = *kiṁ ĕttha* = *kim atra* (H. s. v. *tha*; Āv. 26, 9).

(l) Epenthesis

§ 176. The separation vowel *i* in the sound-group *ry* (§ 134) has sometimes made its way into the preceding syllable, and with an *a*, *ā* of the same becomes fused into *e* : M. AMg. *acchera*, AMg JM. *accheraẏa*, AMg. *accheraga*, beside M. Ś. *accharia*, JM. *acchariẏa*, Ś. *accharia*, M. *aśalia*, dialectically *acchariјја* and *acchaara* = *āścarya* (§ 138) also; M. *kera* = *kārya*[4] (belonging to; Mk. fol. 40; Kaṁsav. 52, 11), *keraṁ* (on account of; Kāvyaprakāśa 28, 7), Ś. *amhakera* (Hc. 2, 147; Jīvān. 19, 9), *tumhakera* (Hc. 2, 147; Jīvān. 104, 6), *parakera* (Mālav. 26, 5), elswhere in Ś. *keraka, keraa* (Mṛcch. 4, 3; 38, 3; 53, 20; 63, 16; 64, 19; 65, 10. 11; 68, 11; 74, 8; 153, 2; Śak. 96, 10; 155, 9; Mālatīm. 267. 2; Mudrār. 35, 8; Priyad. 43, 16; 44, 6; Jīvān. 9, 1; Kaṁsav. 50, 11); also in Ā. *keraka* (Mṛcch. 100, 18); femin. Ś. *kerikā keriā* (Mṛcch. 88, 24 [read *kerika tti* [; 90, 14; 95, 6; Viddhaś. 83, 4), also in Ā. *kerikā* (Mṛcch. 104, 9); Ś. *parakeraattaṇa* = **parakāryatvana* (Mālatīm. 215, 3); Mg. *kelaka, kelaa* (Mṛcch. 13, 9; 37, 13; 40, 9; 96, 21. 22; 97, 2; 100, 20; 112, 10; 118, 17; 119, 5; 122, 14. 15 [read *kelakāiṁ*]; 130, 10; 132, 2; 133, 2; 146, 16; 152, 6; 173, 9; Śak. 116, 11; 161, 7), also to be mentioned here Prab. 32, 8, where *bhaṭṭālakakelakehiṁ*, according to II, 34. 115, is to be read ; femin. *kelikā, keliā* (Mṛcch. 21, 21; 132, 16; [read *kelikāe*]; 139, 16 [read *kelikā*]; 164, 3. 8; 167, 3, 21); A. *kera* (Hc. 4, 422. 373), *keraa* (Hc. 4, 359. 373); M. AMg. Ś. *peranta* = *paryanta* (Vr. 3, 18; Bh. 1, 5; Hc. 1, 58; 2, 65. 93; Kī. 1, 4; 2, 79; Mk. fol. 5, 22; Pāiẏal. 173 G.H.; Ovav.; Lalitav. 555, 11; 567, 23; Vikr. 31, 17; Mālatīm. 76, 5; 103, 3; 118, 6; 248, 5; Mahāv. 97, 13; Bālar. 49, 2; 67; 15; 76, 16; 226, 3; 278, 20; 287, 9; Anarghar. 58, 9; Mallikām. 55, 10; 57, 17). AMg. *pariperanta* (Nāẏādh. 513. 1383ff.; Vivāgas. 107); *bamhacera* (Hc. 1, 59; 2, 63, 74, 93), AMg. A. *bambhacera* (Hc. 2, 74; Āẏār. 1, 5, 2, 4; 1, 6, 2, 1; 1, 6, 4, 1; 2, 15, 24; Sūẏag. 81. 171. 318. 643. 652. 759. 866; Vivāhap. 10, 135. 722. 726; Dasav. 618, 33; Dasav. N. 649, 38; Uvās.; Ovav. § 69; Nāẏādh.; Niraẏāv.; Erz. 3, 24), beside *bamhacaria* (Hc. 2, 63. 107) = *brahmacarya*; AMg. JM. *merā* = *maryā*[2] (frontier; Hc. 1, 87; Āẏār. 2. 1, 2, 5; 2, 3, 1, 13; 2, 5, 1, 2; 2, 6, 1, 1; Āv. 47, 23, 25; Kk.); AMg. *nimmera* = *nirmarya* (Ṭhāṇ. 136. 143 [*ṇi°*]; Vivāhap. 483. 1048; Ovav.), *samera* = *samarya* (Ṭhāṇ. 136 [text *sammera*]. 143); AMg. JM. *pāḍihera* = Pāli *pāṭihāriẏa* = *prātihārya*[3] (Vivāhap. 1047. 1189; Ovav.; Āv. 14, 2), JM. *pāḍiherattaṇa* (Āv. 13, 25); AMg. *pariherage* = *parihāryaka* (Ovav.); M. Ś. *sundera* = *saundarya* (§ 84). On *ukkera* see § 107, on *dera* §112. Isolated is Mg. *śeṇaṁ* from **śaṇiaṁ* (Mṛcch. 134, 24) = M. Ś. *saṇiaṁ*, AMg. JM. *saṇiẏaṁ* = Pāli *sanikaṁ* (§ 84). Epenthesis of *u* occurs in AMg. *pora-* = *parvan* from **paurva-* (Āẏār. 2, 1, 8, 11).

1. Pischel. IA 2, 121 ff,; on He. 2, 174. Hoernle. JASB, 41, 1, 124, ff IA, 2, 210 ff. Comp. Gr §377 and Beames Comp. Gr. 2, 281 ff. derive the word from *krta*,—2. Leumann, Aup. S. s. v. *uimmera* Hc. and Triv. derive it from *mirrā*.—3. Leumann, Aup. S. s.v.

(m) Assimilation of Vowels

§ 177. Dialectically the vowels of the neighbouring syllables have sometimes been assimilated to one another. AMg. *mirii* = *márici* (Jīv. 542; Paṇhāv. 254 [text *°riẏa*]; Ovav. [§38]. 48 [so to be read]; Nāẏādh. §122), *samiriẏa* = *samaricika* (Samav. 211 [text *°ma°*]; Ovav.); AMg. *miriẏā* = *marica* (Hc. 1, 46; Āẏār. 2, 1, 8, 3; Paṇṇav. 531); M. *avariṁ* = *upári*; M. *avahoāsa avahovāsa* = **ubhathaḥpārśva* (§ 212), *avajjhāa* = *upādhyāya* (§ 123); *bhamaẏā*, beside M. *bhumaā*, AMg. *bhumaẏā* = **bhruvakā* (§ 124); M. AMg. JM. *ucchu*

= *ikṣú*; AMg. *usu* = *i'ṣu*, *suṣu* = *śiśu* (§ 117); AMg. *puhutta* = *pṛthaktva* beside *puhatta* (§ 78). As in Sanskrit, there occur beside one another AMg. *niu ramba* = *nikuramba* (Ovav.) and AMg. *niurumba* = *nikurumba* (Samav. 211; Ovav.), beside *sarisiva* = *sarisṛpa* there are often found the variants *sirisiva*, *sirisiva* (§ 81). M. Ś. *siviṇa* = *svapna* (Vr. 1, 3; 3, 62; C. 3, 15ᵃ p. 49; Hc. 1, 46. 259; 2, 108; Kī. 1, 2; 2, 59; Mk. fol. 5. 29; H. R.; Pratāp. 212, 9; Vṛṣabh. 14, 6; 17, 1. 2), M. Ś. *siviṇaa* = *svapnaka* (H. 2, 186; H.; Karp. 75, 4; Lalitav. 554, 21. 22; 555, 1; Vikr. 24, 17; Mālav. 62, 5; Mālatīm. 179, 9; Bālar. 238, 14; Karp. 70, 3. 11. 12; 71, 1; 73, 4; Veṇīs. 18, 13. 20. 21; Nagān. 12, 11; 13. 4; 23. 3; Karṇas. 16, 9. 12); M. *paḍisiviṇaa* = *pratisvapnaka* (Karp. 75, 5); *simiṇa* (C. 3, 15ᵃ p. 49; Hc. 1, 46, 259), beside AMg. JM. *suviṇa* (Sūyag. 838ff.; Vivāhap. 943ff. 1318ff.; Uttar. 249. 456; Nāyādh.; Kappas.; Erz.). A *suiṇa* (Hc. 4, 434, 1), and AMg. JM. *sumiṇa* (Hc. 1, 46; Ṭhāṇ. 567; Nandīs. 365; Samav. 26; Vivāhap. 947. 1318; Nāyādh.; Nirayāv.; Kappas.; T. 7, 16; Erz.), JM. *suviṇaga*, *sumiṇaga* (Erz.) = *svapnaka* (§ 133. 152. 248). The forms like *kilimmaī*, *kilimmihii*, *kilinta* beside *kilammaī*, *kilanta* are not to be assumed as correct with S. GOLDSCHMIDT,[1] but they rest upon the variation with the frequent v. l. *kilissai*.[2] On future forms like *bhavissidi* see § 520.

1. ZDMG. 32. 107. — 2. PISCHEL, GGA. 1880, 328 f. Cf. § 136.

3. ANUSVĀRA AND THE NASAL VOWELS.

§ 178. In addition to the anusvāra, Pkt. possesses two nasal vowels, of which one is expressed by the sign of anusvāra and the other by that of Anunāsika. The distinction between anusvāra and the first nasal vowel is not defined in all cases, particularly in the final syllable, where their treatment is mostly the same and the origin cannot be traced definitely. Thus for example in the inst. plur. in *-hiṁ*, beside which *-hĩ*, *-hi* are used. If Ś. *devehiṁ* (Śak. 21, 5) is equated to Vedic *devébhiḥ*, which I regard to be correct, a nasal vowel is to be assumed; on the other hand it is equated as = θεόφιν[1], as the usual hypothesis is and, therefore, anusvāra is more probable. Likewise a nasal vowel will have to be assumed in cases like *aggiṁ* = *agniḥ* beside *aggī* and *vāuṁ* = *vāyuḥ* beside *vāū* (§ 72); on the other hand anusvāra, for example, in the genitive plural *devāṇaṁ*, beside which occur also *devāṇâ* and *devāṇa*, exactly as *devehiṃ*, *devehi*, has to be assumed. In adverbs like *uvariṁ* beside *uvari* = *upari* anusvāra is and in *bāhiṁ* = *bahiḥ*, a nasal vowel is probable. In words where *ṁ* may be traced back to *n*, *m* I assume anusvāra, elsewhere, however, a nasal vowel, as a rule.[2]

1. The equation naturally holds good for the ending only. — 2. On anusvāra and the nasal vowel see literature in WACKERNAGEL, Altind. Gr. §223. 224.

§ 179. As in the Veda,[1] so in Pkt. too, the anunāsika is not mostly indicated in manuscripts so that in very many of the cases its existence is to be concluded only from the statements of the grammarians. Thus in H. 651, the MSS write *jāi vaaṇāi*, the Bombay edition, *jāṇi vaaṇāṇi*, whilst Hc, 3, 26 explicitly demands *jāĩ vaaṇāĩ* that does not, as WEBER thinks,[2] go against the metre, since the ardhacandra never makes position. In Śak. 116, 3 in Mg. we have *śaülāṇaṁ muhaṁ = svakulānāṁ mukham*, the MS Z reads *saaṇāṇaṁ muhaṁ = svajanānāṁ mukham*; according to Hc. 4, 300 there should be read *śaaṇāhã muhaṁ*, that no MS has. Vr. 2, 3; Kī. 2, 5; Mk. fol. 14 teach that in *yamunā* the *m* drops out. Hc. 1, 178, on the other hand, teaches, without doubt more correctly, intrusion of anunāsika : *jãuṇā*. The manuscripts and texts write in M. AMg. *jaüṇā* only, in Ś. *jamuṇā* (§ 251). In the Sattasaī, the manuscript *ψ* sometimes writes ardhacandra instead of bindu of the rest, but not always in the right place.[4] For Apabhraṁśa Hc. 4, 397 teaches entry of *v̆* for *m*, e. g. *kav̆alu* beside *kamalu = kamalam*. The manuscripts ordinarily write *mv*. Therefore, the use of ardhacandra cannot be determined from the manuscripts.

1. Max Müller on the Ṛgvedaprātiśākhya 64; Weber on the Vājasaneyiprātiśākhya 4, 9. 13. — 2. On H. 651. — 3. So I take, with Weber, H. p. 4, the mark for anunāsika. Wrongly equate B.-R. s. v., according to Weber, Die Rāma-Tāpanīya-Upanishad (Berlin 1864), p. 334, ardhacandra = anusvāra. The name for the sign for anusāvra is bindu, as has been said in the preceding and following paragraphs. — 4. Weber, H. p. 4; cf. on H. 274.289.292. 489.507. 548. 556. 572. 597 and γ on 5.

§ 180. The grammarians teach that in Pkt. and A. the syllables *-iṁ*, *-hiṁ*, *-uṁ*, *-huṁ*, *-haṁ* at the end of a pada, according to Saṁgītaratnākara *-huṁ*, *-iṁ* in A. even in the middle of a pada, may be reckoned short (Āv. p. 6, note 4; Saṁgītaratnākara 4, 55. 56; Piṅgala 1, 4; Hc. 4,411). Therefore, formerly these syllables were allowed to stand even before vowels and consonants, when a short vowel was required. Weber[1] in this case wishes to remove bindu everywhere and he is followed by all the modern European editors.[2] Sh. P. Pandit in his edition of the Gaüḍavaha puts a sign of shortness over the bindu, e.g. 1, 16 *aṅgāiṁ viṇhuṇo, bhariāiṁ va* for the same purpose Durgāprasād, Śivadatta and Parab, in their editions of the Sattasaī, Rāvaṇavaha, Piṅgala and Karpūramañjarī, have employed ardhacandra.[3] Bollensen[4] even wished to regard the ardhacandra as a sign of "elevation", that Weber[5] rightly rejects. Hc. 3, 7, 26 teaches *-hi*, *-hiṁ* and *-ĩ*, *-iṁ* and the MS. R[H] of the Rāvaṇavaha tends to write *-hĩ*, *-hĩ* when a short is required.[6] Likewise writes the edition of Samav. in the verses. p. 232. 233. 239, as *tihĩ tihĩ saehiṁ, chahĩ purisasaehĩ nikkhanto, saveiyātoraṇehĩ uvaveyā-tribhis tribhiḥ śataiḥ, ṣaḍbhiḥ puruṣaśatair niṣkrāntaḥ, savedikātoraṇair upetāḥ*. This passage, without doubt, gives the right direction with regard to the employment of the ardhacandra. It will have to be written when a short syllable is required and the following word begins with a vowel or the preceding or the following word ends in *ṁ*, as is the case in Samav. in the herein referred to two passgaes. We shall, therefore, have to write, for example *sālaṁkarāṇā gāhāṇaṁ* (H. 3); *silummūliāĩ kūlāiṁ* (H. 355); *tumhehĩ uvĕkkhio* (H. 420); °*pasāhiāĩ aṅgāiṁ* (H. 578); *paṇḍūĩ salilāĩ* (G. 577); *vevirapaoharāṇaṁ disāṇā* °*taṇumajjhāṇaṁ, ... nimīliāĩ muhāiṁ* (R. 6, 89) °*dhūsarāĩ muhāiṁ* (R. 8, 9); *khaṇacumbiāĩ bhamarehĩ uaha suumārakesarasihāiṁ* (Śak. 2, 14). The ardhacandra has to be written also in cases like *taṇāiṁ sŏttuṁ diṇṇāĩ jāĩ* (H. 379), *jāĩ vaaṇāĩ* (H. 651), that is expressly testified to by Hc. (§ 179); further in cases like A. *taruhũ vi* (Hc. 4, 3241,2); *atthĕhĩ satthĕhĩ hatthĕhĩ vi* (Hc. 4, 358, 1); *mukkāhã vi* (Hc. 4, 370, 1), where the bindu would be incorrect as instead of *vi* there would have to stand *pi* after it. *ṁ* always makes position, which ~ never does (§ 348. 350).[7]

1. On H. 3. — 2. As S. GOLDSCHMIDT, R. p.XIX. Against him KLATT, ZDMG. 33, 451f. — 3. Cf. on Hc. 1, 2, note 3. — 4. On Vikr. p. 521, note; p. 525f., note. — 5. On H. 481. — 6. S. GOLDSCHMIDT, R. p. XIX, note 2. — 7. The nasal vowel uttered with bindu is more strongly nasalized than that indicated by the ardhacandra. BOPP was not wrong to the extent meant by BERGAIGNE (Mémoires de la Société de Linguistique de Paris 2, 204, Note 1.

§ 181. After the vowels, that are final either by origin or have become so due to dropping off of a final consonant, the anusvāra is frequently added in M. AMg. JM. in adverbs except in the cases discussed in § 75. 114. M. *ajjaṁ* (H.R.) beside *ajja = adya*; AMg. JM. *ihaṁ* beside *iha = iha* (Hc. 1, 24; Āyār. 1, 1, 3, 7; Jīv. 305; Uvās. ; Nāyādh. Nirayāv. ; Kk.)[1], also *ihayaṁ* (Hc. 1, 24); AMg. JM. *isiṁ* beside M. Ś. *isi* (§ 102); AMg. JM. *pabhiim = prabhṛti* (Uvās.; Kappas.; Erz.; Kk.); AMg. *uppiṁ*, M. AMg. JM. *uvariṁ*, M. *avariṁ*, beside M. JM. Ś. *uvari*, Mg. *uvali = upari* (§ 123. 148) AMg. *saīṁ = sakṛt* (Āyār. 2, 1, 1, 5; Uttar. 201. 235), *asaīṁ = asakṛt* (Āyār. 1, 2, 3, 1; Jīv. 308; Uttar. 201); AMg. *jugavaṁ + yugapat* (Ṭhāṇ. 227; Vivāhap. 1440; Uttar. 870. 878. 881. 1032; Ovav.); AMg. *jāvaṁ, tāvaṁ = yāvat, tāvat* (Vivhāp. 268. 269. In M. AMg. JM. *bāhiṁ = bahiḥ* (Hc. 2, 140; Mk. fol. 40; Pāiyal. 224; G.; Āyār. 2, 7, 2, 1; 2, 10, 6; Sūyag. 753; Nāyādh. § 122 [so to be read]; Erz.), also in *bāhiṁsalla = bahiḥśalya* (Ṭhāṇ. 314) and *bāhiṁhiṁto* (Ṭhāṇ. 408) and in AMg. *pāuṁ = prāduḥ* (§ 341) and *muhuṁ = muhuḥ* (Uttar. 197) a nasal vowel has probably to be assumed (§ 178). Perhaps, however, *bāhiṁ* should be equated as = *bāhyam* according to §151. Since Mk. fol. 40 teaches *bahiṁ* as well, perhaps this explanation is more correct. It would, therefore be better to separate *bāhiṁ* from *bahiṁ*. Cf. also *saṇiṁcara* (§ 84) and § 349.

1. Cf. HOERNLE, Uvās., Translation, note 217.

§ 182. In M. anusvāra is sometimes added to the final *a* in the instr. sing. of the masculine and neuter of the *a*- stems (Hc. 1, 27); *sabbhāveṇaṁ = sadbhāvena* ((H. 286); *paruṇṇeṇaṁ muheṇaṁ = praruditena mukhena* (H. 354); *samaavaseṇaṁ = samayavaśena* (H. 398); °*loaṇeṇaṁ*, °*seeṇaṁ* = °*locanena*,° *svedena*: (H. 828); *kavāḍantareṇaṁ = kapāṭāntareṇa* (G. 212); *pañjareṇaṁ* (G. 301); °*visaaṁseaṁ* = °*viśadāṁsena* (R. 3, 55). This sort of addition is very frequent in AMg JM. So AMg. *teṇaṁ kāleṇaṁ teṇaṁ samaeṇaṁ = tena kālena tena samayena* (e.g. Āyār. 2, 15, 1. 6. 17. 22; Uvās. § 1ff. 9.75ff.; Nāyādh. § 1. 4. 6; Ovav. § 1. 15. 16. 23ff.; Kappas. § 1. 2. 14 etc.); AMg. *samaṇeṇaṁ bhagavayā mahāvīreṇaṁ = śramaṇena bhagavatā mahāvīreṇa* (e. g. Nāyādh. § 8 [where further 21 instrumental forms in -*ṇaṁ* follow; shortened, e.g. Uvās. § 2. 78, 91]), *koheṇaṁ māṇeṇaṁ lobheṇaṁ = krodhena mānena lobhena* (Vivāhap. 85), *sakkeṇaṁ devindeṇaṁ devaraṇṇeṇaṁ = śakreṇa devendreṇa devarājena* (Nāyādh. 852), *paravāgaraṇeṇaṁ = paravyākaraṇena* (Āyār. 1, 1, 1, 4; 1, 7, 2, 3). *hiraṇṇeṇaṁ = hiraṇyena* (Āyār. 1, 2, 3, 3); JM. *vaccanteṇaṁ = vrajatā, vaḍḍeṇaṁ saddeṇaṁ = vadreṇa śabdena, uppaheṇaṁ = utpathena, sureṇaṁ = sureṇa* (Āv. 11, 19; 23, 14; 36, 32. 37), *saṇaṁkumāreṇaṁ nāyāmaccavuttanteṇaṁ kovaṁ uvagaeṇaṁ = sanatkumāreṇa jñātāmātyavṛttāntena kopam upagatena* (Erz. 3, 29). Similarly also in adverbially used instrumental forms, like AMg. *āṇupuvveṇaṁ* = *ānupūrvyeṇa* (Āẏār. 1, 6, 4, 1; 1, 7, 7, 5; [*aṇu°*]; Niraẏāv. § 13; Nāẏādh. § 118 [*aṇu°*]) *paraṁpareṇaṁ* (Kappas. S. § 27); AMg. JM. *suheṇaṁ* = *sukhena* (Vivāgas. 81; Ovav. § 16; Niraẏāv.; Nāẏādh.; Erz.); AMg. *majjheṇaṁ* = *madhyena* (Uvās.; Nāẏādh.; Kappas.; Niraẏāv.; Vivāhap. 236; Ovav. § 17).[1] In the nomin. and acc. plural of the neuter Vr.5, 26 teaches the ending *-i*: *vaṇāi, dahīi, mahūi* = *vanāni dadhīni, madhūni*, Mk. fol. 43: *-iṁ*: *vaṇāiṁ dahīiṁ, mahūiṁ*, Kī. 3, 28 beside *-iṁ* in *dhaṇāiṁ, jasāiṁ, dahiiṁ* and according to the opinion of some in *dhaṇāṁiṁ, vaṇāṁiṁ* with anusvāra even before the ending, Hc. 3, 26, *-ĩ, -iṁ*. In prose in all the dialects there occurs only *-iṁ*, so AMg. *se jjāiṁ kulāiṁ* = *sa yāni kulāni* (Āẏār. 2, 1, 2, 2) beside *kulāṇi* (§ 367); JM. *pañca egūṇāiṁ aḍḍāgasaẏāiṁ. . . pakkhittāiṁ* = *pañcaikonāny ādarśaśatāni . . . prakṣiptāni* (Āv. 17, 15); Ś. *rāarakkhidāiṁ tavovaṇāiṁ* = *rājarakṣitāni tapovanāni* (Śak. 16, 13); Mg. *°śavalāiṁ duśśagandhiāiṁ cīvalāiṁ* = *eśabalāni dūṣyagandhikāni cīvarāṇi* (Mṛcch. 113, 22); Ḍh. *bhūdāiṁ suvaṇṇāiṁ* = *bhūtāni suvarṇāni* (Mṛcch. 36, 21). In verses *-i* is written, when the metre requires a short, certain in many cases and probably in all cases (§ 179. 180) wrongly. Hc. points to *ĩ*, and in Vr. 5. 26 *-i* is probably a false reading for *-iṁ*. The statement in Kī. 3, 28, that some scholars require *-iṁ* before the anusvāra ought to teach probably more correctly the forms *dhaṇaṁiṁ, vaṇaṁiṁ* instead of *dhaṇāṁiṁ, vaṇāṁiṁ* given in the text, corresponding to AMg. *mahaṁāsa* for *mahant+aśva* = *mahāśva* (§ 74). The anusvāra stands here instead of the long. In the loc. plur. of all stems is found form beside in *-su*, also in *-suṁ*, that dominates in Ś. Mg. (§ 367). The nom. acc. sing. of the neut. in *-i*, *-u* has frequently *-iṁ*, as in *dahiṁ, mahuṁ* beside *dahi, mahu* (§ 379), probably in dependence upon the neut. forms in *-aṁ*; according to Hc. 3, 25 some taught also *dahĩ, mahũ*. Beside *mama* M. AMg. JM. have *mamaṁ* (§ 418; H.; Vivāgas. § 121. 122; Uvās.; Bhag.; Āv. 72, 28). In the imperative in *-hi* the presses, according to the MSS,[2] print, often wrongly *-hiṁ* for *-hi* (e. g. Āẏār. 2, 1, 5, 5 *paribhāehiṁ*, read *°hi*; p. 126, 7 *pavvattehiṁ*, read *pavattehi*; Nāẏādh. 144; Vivāhap. 612. 613 *bhuñjāhiṁ*, read *°hi*; Kappas. § 114 *jiṇāhiṁ*, read *°hi*, *vasāhiṁ*, read *°hi*, *nihaṇāhiṁ*, read *°hi*; Vivāhap. 612. 613 *dalaẏāhiṁ*, read *°hi*). Sometimes anusvāra is introduced on account of metre, as in *devaṁṇāgasuvaṇṇa* = *devanāgasuparṇa* (Hc. 1, 26); AMg. *chandaṁnirohena* = *chandonirodhena* (Uttar. 195). Compounds like M. *uvariṁḍhūmaṇivesa* = *uparidhūmaniveśa* (G. 140), AMg. *uvariṁpuñchaṇio* = *uparipucchinyaḥ* (Rāẏap. 108; text *°pucchaṇiu*), according to § 181, AMg. *tiriẏaṁvāẏa* = *tiryagvāta, tiriẏaṁbhāgi* = *tiryagbhāgin* (Sūẏag. 829), according to § 75, are to be explained.

1. With these instr. in *-eṇaṁ*, perhaps both the Vedic. instr. forms *ghanénā* and *tejaneṇa* are to be compared (LANMAN, Noun-Inflection p. 331), with difficulty the instr. in *-ena* (LANMAN, l. c. p. 332). — 2. LEUMANN, Aup. S. p. 58, note p. 9

§ 183. Final *n* and *m* as a rule become anusvāra, which in AMg. M. JM. often vanishes before vowels and consonants (§ 348ff.). A short nasal vowel and anusvāra alternate more often with non-nasalized long vowels (§ 72. 74. 75. 86. 114). Before an immediately following sibilant, *r*, *h* a short nasal vowel is often lengthened with loss of the nasal tone (§ 76). A long nasal vowel and a long vowel with anusvāra following it either become shortened (§ 83), or the nasal tone vanishes (§ 89), before consonants in the auslaut also in the case of a short vowel (§ 72. 173. 175. 350).

B. THE CONSONANTS

I. CONSONANTS IN FREE POSITIONS

1. Generalities and in Relating to Whole or Several Classes

§ 184. Initial consonants other than *n*, *y*, *ś*, *ṣ* remain as a rule unchanged. In the beginning of the second member of a compound they are generally treated as in between vowels in the interior of a word according to § 186. 188; more frequently, however, the initial of verbal roots remains unchanged even after prefixes ending in a vowel[1] : M. *paāsei* = *prakāśayati* (G.); *bhamaraüla* = *bhramarākula* (H. 668) beside *mahuarakula* = *madhukarakula* (G. 468); *āiṇṇa* = *ākirṇa* (G.), *paiṇṇa* = *prakirṇa* (G.H.R.); *āaa* (H.) beside usual *āgaa* (G.H.R.) = *āgata*; *vasahaïndha* = *vṛṣabhacihna* (G). beside *aṇumaraṇamaṇḍaṇacindha* (G. 479); *karaala* = *karatala* (H. 170) beside *calaṇatala* = *caraṇatala* (R. 9, 37); *uvaïsaï* = *upadiśati* (H.); *avasāria* = *apasārita* *vihalavasāria* = *vihvalaprasārita* (R. 1, 1; 13, 27), and so against § 189 also PG. *aṇuvaṭṭhāveti* = *anuprasthāpayati* (7, 45);[2] *gahavaī* = *gṛhapati* (H.); *vaṁsavatta* = *vaṁśapattra* (H. 676) beside *aṅkollapatta* (H. 313); Ś. *ajjaütta* = *āryaputra* (e.g. Mṛcch. 53, 18) beside Mg. *ayyapuliśa* = *āryapuruṣa* (Mṛcch. 132. 23). Aspirates, according to § 188, may become *h* : M. *vālahilla* = *vālakhilya* (G.), *raīhara* = *ratighara* (H.), *jalahara* = *jaladhara* (G.H.R.), *ṇuttāhala* = *muktāphala* (G.), *thaṇahara* = *stanabhara* (H.), beside M. *sarisavakhala* = = *sarṣapakhala* (Hc. 1, 187), *palaaghaṇa* = *pralayaghana* (R. 5, 22), *vammahadhaṇu* = *manmathadhanuḥ* (R. 1, 29), *ṇimbaphala* (H. 248), *rakkhābhuaṁga* = *rakṣābhujaṁga* (G. 178). In the same way, most of the enclitics and sometimes words standing behind proclitics after vowels are treated as in inlaut: Ś. Mg. D. *adha iṁ* = *atha kim* (e.g. Ś. Mṛcch. 17, 24; 60, 6; 67, 11; Mg. Mṛcch. 14, 7; 22, 1; 118, 2, 4. 6. 25; D. Mṛcch. 101, 3); M. Ś. Mg. D.Ā.A. CP. (Hc. 4,326) *a*, AMg. JM. JŚ. *ya* = *ca*; M. *ira* = *kira* = Skt. *kila* (Vr. 9, 5; Hc. 2, 186; G.R.); M. JM. Ś. Mg. *uṇa* = *punar*, in the sense of "now", "however" (Hc. 1, 65. 177; Mk. fol. 39; G.H.R.; Āv. 8, 33; Erz.; Kk. Ś. e.g. Mṛcch. 9, 8; 13, 22; 25, 1; 29, 6 etc.; Mg. e.g. Mṛcch. 14, 22; 38, 8; 43, 4; 127, 24 etc.) also after anusvāra like M. Ś. *kiṁ uṇa* = *kiṁ punar* (H. 25. 417; R. 3, 28. 32; 4, 26; 11, 26; Mṛcch. 3, 20; 18, 3; Prab. 15, 9; 38, 6r; 42, 6); M. *eṇhiṁ uṇa* = *idāniṁ punar* (H. 307), *hiaaṁ uṇa* = *hṛdayaṁ punar* (H. 660); Ś. *sampadaṁ uṇa* = *sāmpratam punar* (Mṛcch. 18, 23), *ahaṁ uṇa* (Mṛcch. 25, 14); *tassiṁ uṇa* = *tasmin punar* (Vikr. 35, 5), *kadhaṁ uṇa* = *kathaṁ punar* (Vikr. 73, 14); Ś. Mg. *kiṁṇimittaṁ uṇa* (Mṛcch. 88, 16; 151, 2; Mg. 19, 5); *vi* = *api* (§ 143); M. *ṇa vahuttaṁ* = *na prabhūtam* (R. 3, 57) for the sake of assonance[3], beside *apahutta* (H. 277, 436). In A, the secondary *pa*, originating from *tva* (§ 300) as well is treated in the absolutive, as in *pĕkkhevinu, pĕkkhevi, pĕkkhivi* = **prekṣĕtvi, bhaṇivi* = **bhaṇitvi, piavi* = **pibatvi, ramevi* = **ramayitvī* (§ 588). M. A. *ṇavara, ṇavaraṁ*, JM. *navaraṁ*, (Erz.; Ṛṣabhap.) "only" (Vr. 9, 7; Hc. 2. 187; G.H.R.; Hc. 4, 377. 401, 6 [so to be read], P. GOLDSCHMIDT[4] conjectures = *na param*, hardly rightly, as the anusvāra appears to be secondary. Certainly wrong is the interpretation of M.A. *ṇavari* (Vr. 9, 8; Hc. 2, 188; G.H.R.; Hc. 4, 423, 2)g, JM. *navari* (Pāiẏal. 17; Erz.; Kk.) "thereon", "so forth" from *na pare*, against which is the *i* (§ 85). Very frequent is the dropping off of the *ja* after *na* in *jñā* in all the dialects; AMg. JM. have *ẏa* more often as in inlaut §170).

1. For the rules, that are common to all the dialects, for brievity, examples will be given generally only from M. — 2. PISCHEL, G.N. 1895, p. 211. — 3. Assonance was also determinant for the dropping off of the initial consonant in cases, like *ovvaṇāiṁ* for *jŏvvaṇāiṁ* (R. 7, 62), *ṇa iṇaṁ* for *ṇa dīṇaṁ* (R. 8. 61), *aṇehiṁ* for *jaṇehiṁ, ūraṁ* for *dūraṁ* (R. 8, 65). The other texts mentioned by S. GOLDSCHMIDT, (ZDMG). 32, 105) do not have "better and weightier" readings but quite false ones (PISCHEL, GGA. 1880, 327). — 4. GN. 1874. 573, note; cf. S. GOLDSCHMIDT, ZDMG. 32. 105.

§ 185. In *tāvat, tu, te* "your", "to you", "thine" and "these" *t* becomes *d* dialectically as in the initial syllable. Hc. 4, 262. 302. 323 mentions the change in *tāvat* for Ś. Mg. P. In Ś. Mg. it is the rule after all vowels and anusvāra, as Ś. *ciṭṭha dāva* (Mṛcch. 138, 16; 139, 3; Śak. 125, 1), Mg. *ciṣṭha dāva* (Mṛcch. 9, 24; 114, 12) = *tiṣṭha tāvat*; S. Mg. D. *mā dāva* = *mā tāvat* (Mṛcch. 18, 2; 29, 11; 55, 15; Mg. 117, 14; 151. 25; 170, 24, D. 100, 17); Ś. *uvaṇehi dāva* = *upanaya tāvat* (Mṛcch. 61, 10); Mg. *yāṇāhi dāva* = *jānihi tāvat* (Mṛcch. 80, 21); Ś. *citthaḍu dāva*, Mg. *ciṣṭhadu dāva* = *tiṣṭhatu tāvat* (Vikr. 34, 5; Mṛcch. 167, 21); Ś. *ajjuāe dāva* = *āryāyai tāvat* (Mṛcch. 94, 7); *tumhe dāva* = *yuṣme tāvat* (16, 20); Ś. Mg. Ā. *ido dāva* = *itastāvat* (Mṛcch. 3, 3; Vikr. 45, 17; Mg. Mṛcch. 16, 16; Ā. Mṛcch. 99, 20); Ś. *aṇaṅgaṁ dāva* (Ratn. 298, 13); *daïśśaṁ dāva* = **dayisyāmi tāvat* (Mṛcch. 35, 8); Ś. Mg. *ĕvvaṁ dāva* = *evaṁ tāvat* (Mṛcch. 12, 25; 24, 20; 29, 1; Mg. 123, 4; 126, 8). The same change occurs also in M. (H.R.), but very seldom without the variant reading *tāva*, as in R. 3, 26. 29, so that for M., as for AMg. JM., *tāva* only will be correct, which in Ś. Mg. as well always stands at the beginning of a sentence[1]. On M. *dā* see § 150. — *tu* (however) has become *du* in JŚ. after vowels (Pav. 381, 18. 20; 384, 58; 385, 64; Kattig. 404, 388); after anusvāra it remains *tu* (Pav. 382, 23), as also in M. (G. 947), AMg. (Sūẏag. 188. 414. 429. 437. 439. 497), JM. (Āv. 19, 32; 20, 8), Ś. (Vikr. 40, 20), D. (Mṛcch. 325, 19). Except in JŚ. *tu* is rare in all the dialects; it occurs more frequently in Ś. only in *kiṁ tu* (Mṛcch. 53, 20; Śak. 17, 11; 50, 11; 51, 12; 54, 9; 73, 8; 78. 7; 98, 7; 119, 2; 126. 8; Vikr. 33, 11; 40, 6) for which the Dravidian and Devanāgarī recensions of Śak. and the Dravidian recension of Vikr. wrongly write *kiṁ du.*[2] The *u*, that occurs in M. (G. 964), JM. (Āv. 7, 38; 8, 1 [*yu*]; 19, 30. 34; 20, 1. 3. 7. Erz.; Kk.) and especially in AMg. (e.g. Sūyag. 50. 170. 204. 297. 312. 316. 330. 403. 406. 410. 415. 416. 465 etc.; Uttar. 43. 219. 295. 312ff. 329f. 353; Dasav. 622, 11. 27; Niraẏāv. § 2; throughout in the verses is to be derived neither with Sh. P. PANDIT[3] and JACOBI[4] from *tu*, nor with WARREN[5] from *ca*; but it is = *u*, that occurs also in M. *kim u* (Karp. 78, 9. 13. 14).—*te* of the pronoun of the second person, in Ś. Mg. Ā. D. after vowels or anusvāra becomes *de*. So Ś. *ṇa de* =*na te* (Śak. 65, 10), *aṇubhava dāva de* (Śak. 67, 12), *mā de* (Vikr. 6, 17), *hā vi de* (Mṛcch. 5, 2), *parihiadi de*=*parihiyate te* (Śak. 91, 5), *suṭṭhu de*= *suṣṭhu te* (Mṛcch. 29, 14). *amadaṁ khu de*=*amṛtaṁ khalu te* (Vikr. 9, 11), *eso de* (Mṛcch. 7, 3), *kudo de* (Mṛcch. 36, 7), *piduṇo de*=*pituste* (Mṛcch. 95, 15; so to be read with the v. l. in GOḌABOLE, p. 271), *sāadaṁ de*=*svāgataṁ te* (Mṛcch. 3, 6), *jaṁ de*=*yat te* (Mṛcch. 55, 4; Vikr. 41, 18), *mantidaṁ de* =*mantritaṁ te* (Vikr. 44, 9); Ś. *matthaaṁ de*, Mg. *mastaaṁ de*=*mastakaṁ te* (Mṛcch. 18, 5; 21, 22); Mg. *ede vi de*=*ete 'pi te* (=*tvām*; Mṛcch. 128, 12) *tado de*=*tatas te* (Prab. 50, 14), *paṇhaṁ de*=*praśnaṁ te* (Mṛcch. 80, 18), *ĕvvaṁ de*=*evaṁ te* (=*tvām*; Mṛcch. 128, 14); Ā. *pidā vi de*=*pitāpi te*, *jadi de* =*yadi te* (Mṛcch. 104, 17; 105, 3); D. *ahiṇṇāṇaṁ de*=*abhijñānaṁ te* (Mṛcch. 105, 9). This phonetic change seems to be assumed in M. also. Without a v. l. are found *vi de*=*api te* (H. 737); *vva de*=*iva te* (R. 4, 31); *pariaṇeṇa de*=*parijanena te* (R. 4, 33); *pi de* (R. 11, 83), *a de*=*ca te* (R. 11, 126). In all other passages, with the exception of the Telugu recension of H., the v. l. has *te*, particularly even always after anusāra (H. s.v. *de*; R. s.v. *tu*) so that the correct reading remains doubtful. — After other pronominal forms *te* (these) also becomes *de* in Ś. Mg. (§ 425). So also M. *jālā de*= **yāt kālāt te* (Dhvanyāloka 62, 4=H. 989). On M. *dāvaī*=*tāpayati* see § 275.

1. CAPPELLER, Jenaer Literaturzeitung 1877, p. 125; BÖHTLINGK, Sanskrit-Chrestomathie[2] p. 369. Cf. PISCHEL on Hc. 4, 262; BOLLENSEN on Mālav. p. 122. — 2. Cf. § 275. — 3. G. s. v. — 4. Erz. s. v. — 5. Nirayāv. s. v.

§ 186. In the middle of a word, in most of the dialects, intervocalic *k, g, c, j, t, d* usually, *p, b, v* sometimes, and *y*, except in PG. VG. P. CP., are always dropped (Vr. 2, 2; C. 3, 34; Hc. 1, 177; Kī. 2, 1; Mk. fol. 14). So M. *uaa*=*udaka* (G.H.R.)[1]; *loa*=*loka*; *saala*=*sakala* (H.R.); *sua*=*śuka* (H. R.); *aṇurāa*=*anurāga*; *juala*=*yugala*; *ṇaara*=*nagara* (G.H.); *turaa*=*turaga* (G.R.); *ṇārāa*=*nārāca* (R.); *paüra*=*pracura* (H.); *vii*=*vīci* (G.R.); *gaa*=*gaja*; *ṇia*=*nija*; *bhoaṇa*=*bhojana* (H.); *raaa*=*rajata* (R.); *kaanta*=*kṛtānta* (G.R.); *ṇiamba*=*nitamba*; *rasāala*=*rasātala* (G.R.); *gaā*=*gadā* (R.); *pāa*= *pāda*; *maaṇa*=*madana* (H.R.); *hiaa*=*hṛdaya*; *ṇiuṇa*=*nipuṇa* (H.R.); *riu*= *ripu*; *rūa*=*rūpa*; *alāu, lāu*=*alābu* (§ 141); *viuha*=*vibudha* (Hc.); *chāā*=*chāyā*; *pia*=*priya*, *vioa*=*viyoga* (H. R.); *jia*=*jiva*; *diaha*=*divasa*; *lāaṇṇa*=*lāvaṇya* (G.); *vaḷaāṇala*=*vaḍavānala* (Hc.) Cf. § 199.

1. These citations hold good for all the words for which no references have been given. Cf. also § 184, note 1.

§ 187. In place of the consonants that have dropped off a weakly articulated *ya* (*laghuprayatnatara yakāra*) is uttered, that is indicated in this grammar by *ẏa* (§45; C. 3. 35; Hc. 1, 180; Kī. 3, 2). Except in MSS written by Jainas this *ẏa* is not indicated. Hc. 1, 180 teaches that it comes in between *a* and *ā* only, but he attests also *piẏaī*=*pibati* and 1, 15 *sariẏā*=Pāli *saritā*=*sarit*. Mk. fol. 14 refers to a quotation, according to which *ẏaśruti* occurs when one of the vowels is either an *a*- or an *i*- sound : *anādāv aditau varṇau paṭhitavyau yakāravad iti pāṭhaśikṣā*. In KI. *ẏa* is generally written only between *a*- sounds, as : 1 *saẏalāṇa*, 9 *paẏā*, 10 *ṇāẏa*, *maṇaẏam pi* (sic), 11 *saẏa*-

lam pi (sic); on the other hand, it is mostly wanting after an *i-* sound. But the inscription is not uniform. Beside *ṇiya* (9) stands *ṇia* (12); in 14 there is *iya* and in 13, *ṇeya* = *naiva* also. The oldest MSS write *ya* after all vowels before *a, ā* in AMg. JM. JŚ., and for these dialects *ya* is a characteristic.[1] Therefore, *indiya* = *indriya, hiyaya* = *hṛdaya*; *giya* = *gita*; *dihiyā* = *dirghikā*; *ruya ruta*; *dūya* = *dūta*; *teya* = *tejas*; *loya* = *loka* are rightly written. One says, however, only *ei* = *eti*; *loe* = *loke*; *dūo* = *dūtaḥ*, *uiya* = *ucita*, *uūiṁ* = **ṛtūni*. Numerous examples are found in the preceding and following paragraphs. The Jainas erroneously carry this and other modes of writing from AMg. JM. JŚ. over to other dialects too (§ 11. 15).

1. HOEFER ZWS, 3, 366; WEBER, Bhag. 1, 397 ff.; E. MÜLLER, Beiträge p. 4 f.; PISCHEL, Hc. 1, p. x f.; on 1, 180; KLATT, ZDMG. 33, 447; JACOBI, ZDMG. 34, 181; KZ. 25,295; STEINTHAL, Specimen p. 3.

§ 188. Aspirates, except *ch, jh, ṭh, ḍh*, mostly become *h* between vowels (Vr. 2, 27; Hc. 1, 187; Kī. 2, 14; Mk. fol. 16). So M. *muha* = *mukha* (G.H.R.)[1]; *mehalā* = *mekhalā*; *sāhā* = *śākhā*; *jahaṇa* = *jaghana*; *meha* = *megha*; *rahuṇāha* = *raghunātha* (R.); *lahua* = *laghuka*; *aha* = *atha*; *jūha* = *yūtha*; *mahumahaṇa* = *madhumathana*; *raha* = *ratha*; *ahara* = *adhara*; *ruhira* = *rudhira* (G.R.); *vahū* = *vadhū*; *sihu* = *sidhu* (G.H.); *sahara* = *śaphara* (G.); *sehāliā* = *śephālikā* (H.); *ahiṇava* = *abhinava*; *ṇaha* = *nabhas* and = *nakha*; *rahasa* = *rabhasa*; *sahā* = *sabhā* (R.); *seriha* = *sairibha* (G.H.). On *ph* see further especially § 200. In the initial syllable transition to *h* is just sporadic : *hammaī* (goes to) with the compounds *ṇihammaī*, *ṇihammaī*, *āhammai*, *pahammaī* (Hc. 4, 162), *ṇihammia* (gone out) : (Deśīn. 4, 43), M. *pahammanti* (G. 871 v. l.) = Pāli *ghammati*. The word has *h* already in Skt. and is attributed to the speech of Surāṣṭra[2], and by Haripāla on G. 871, to that of Kamboja. Dialectically initial *bh* has frequently become *h* in the root *bhū* and its compounds, which has probably resulted from the enclitically used form. So AMg. JM. *havaī*, JŚ. *havadi*, M. JM. A. *hoi*, JŚ. *hodi* = *bhavati*, M. *huvanti* = *bhavanti*, PG. *hoja*, P. *huveyya* = *bhavet*, Mg. *huviadi* = **bhūyate*, Ś. *havissadi*, Mg. *haviśśadi* = *bhaviṣyati*, AMg. JM. *hoyavva*, Ś. Mg. *hodavva*, Mg. *huvidavva* = *bhavitavya*, M. JM. *houṁ*, JŚ. *hoduṁ* = *bhavitum* (§ 475. 476. 521. 570). The Telugu recension of H. has pretty often *h* for *bh* : *haṭṭha* = *bhraṣṭa*; *haṇida* = *bhaṇita*; *haṇirī* for *bhaṇirī*; *haṇḍaṇa* = *bhaṇḍana*; *hamira* = *bhamira*; *hāā* = *bhrātā*; *huaga*, *huaṁga* = *bhujaga*, *bhujaṁga*; *humaā* for *bhumaā*; *hūsaṇa* = *bhūṣaṇa*; *hea* = *bheda*; *hoaṇa* = *bhojana*.[3] On aspirates at the beginning of the second member of a compound see § 184.

1. Cf. § 186, note 1. — Patañjali, Vyākaraṇamahābhāṣya 1, p. 9,26 ed. KIELHORN; Naighaṇṭuka 2, 14 (p. 14, 17 ed. Roth = 1, 238 ed. SATYAVRATA SĀMAŚRAMĪ); WEBER, IS. 13,363 f.; E. KUHN, Beiträge p.42.—3. WEBER, H. s.s. v.v.

§ 189. In PG. VG. all consonants, including the aspirates, with the exception of *bh* in *hoja* (§ 188), remain unchanged: PG. *ārakhādhikate gumike tūthike* = *ārakṣādhikṛtān gulmikān tirthikān* (5, 5); *udakādiṁ* (6, 29); *jāmātukasa* = *jāmātṛkasya* (6, 14); *nāganaṁdisa* = *nāganandinaḥ* (6, 25); *patibhāga* = *pratibhāga* (6, 12); *mahārājādhirājo* (5, 1); *appatihata* = *apratihata* (6, 19); *varisasatasahassātireka* = *varṣaśatasahasrātireka* (7, 42); *āpiṭṭi* (6, 8. 37); *api* (6, 37); *parihāpetavva* = *parthāpayitavya* (6, 37); *pamukhāṇaṁ* = *pramukhāṇām* (6, 27. 38);

uparilikhitaṁ (7, 44); *atha* (6, 40); *tūthike* = *tirthikān* (5,5); *assamedha* = *aśvamedha* (5, 1); *narādhamo* (7, 47); *vasudhādhipataye* = *vasudhādhipatin* (7, 44); °*cchobhaṁ* = °*kṣobham* (6, 32); *vallabhamadena* (6, 40). Exceptions are *kassava* = *kāśyapa* (6, 18); *kāravĕjjā* = Pāli *kārāpĕyya* (6, 40); *aṇuvaṭṭhāveti* = *anupras-thāpayati* (§ 184); *vi* = *api* (5, 6; 6, 29); *bhaḍa* = *bhaṭa* (5, 7; 7, 43); *koḍī* = *koṭī* (6, 10); *kaḍa* = *kṛta* (7, 51). Cf. Bühler, EI. 1, 3 and § 10.

§ 190. In P. most of the consonants remain in the initial and in medial syllables (Hc. 4, 324; Namisādhu on Rudraṭa, Kāvyālaṅkāra 2, 12); *anekapa*; *makaraketu*; *sagaraputtavacana*; *vijayasenena lapitaṁ*; *pāṭaliputta*; *patākā*; *vetasa* (Hc. 4, 307); *pāpa*; *āyudha*; *mukha*; *megha*; *sabhā*; *kamaṭha*; *maṭha*. In initial and medial syllables *da* becomes *ta* (Hc. 4, 307), according to Namisādhu, optionally : *tāmotara* = *dāmodara*; *tiṭṭha* = *dṛṣṭa* (Hc. 4, 314, 321. 323); *taṭṭhūna*, *tatthūna* (Hc. 4, 313. 323); *tātisa* = *tādṛśa*, *yātisa* = *yādṛśa* (Hc. 4, 317); *teti* = **dayati* (Hc. 4, 318); *tevara* = *devara* (Hc. 4, 324); *matana* = *madana*, *satana* = *sadana*, *patesa* = *pradeśa*, *vatanaka* = *vadanaka* (Hc. 4, 307),—*tha* becomes *dh* according to Hc. : *adha* = *atha* (Hc. 4, 323), *kadhitūna* = **kathitvāna* (Hc. 4, 312); *pudhuma* = *prathama* (Hc. 4, 316); *kadhaṁ* = *katham* (Hc. 4, 323); according to Namisādhu it is retained : *pathama* = *prathama*; *puthuvī* = *pṛthvī*.

§ 191. In CP. remain, not only, as in P, the tenues, but also the medial, as in the initial syllable, are changed into tenues (Hc. 4, 325; Kī., 5, 102)[1] : *kakana* = *gagana*; *kiritaṭa* = *giritaṭa*; *khamma* = *gharma*; *khata* = *ghṛta* (§ 47); *cāta* = *jāta*; *cimūta* = *jimūta*; *chacchara* = *jharjhara*; *chaṁkāla* = *jhaṅkāra*; *ṭamaruka* = *ḍamaruka*; *ṭimpa* = *ḍimba*; *ṭhakkā* = *ḍhakkā*; *tāmotara* = *dāmodara*; *thūli* = *dhūli*; *pāḷaka* = *bālaka*; *pisa* = *bisa*; *phakavati* = *bhagavatī*; *phūta* = *bhūta*; *nakara* = *nagara*; *mekha* = *megha*; *rāca-* = *rājan*; *taṭāka* = *taḍāga*. *kāṭha* = *gāḍha*; *matana* = *madana*; *mathura* = *madhura*; *sāthu* + *sādhu*; *raphasa* = *rabhasa*. According to Hc. 4, 325 and Kī. 5, 103 the change takes place in secondary sounds too, as in *cacaṇa* = Pkt. *jajaṇa* = Skt. *yajana*; *paṭimā* = *paḍimā* = *pratimā*; *tāṭhā* = Pkt. *dāḍhā* = *daṁṣṭrā* (§ 76). According to Hc. and Kī. conjunct consonants too undergo the change : *tukkā* = *durgā*; *makkana* = *mārgaṇa*, *vakkha* = *vyāghra*; *caccara* = *jarjara*; *nicchara* = *nirjhara*; *kaṇṭa* = *gaṇḍa*; *maṇṭala* = *maṇḍala*; *saṇṭha* = *ṣaṇḍha*; *kantappa* = *kandarpa*; *panthava* = *bāndhava*; *ṭimpa* = *ḍimba*; *ramphā* = *rambhā*. Vr. 10, 3 teaches that initial and conjunct consonants remain unaltered. Examples of this rule in Bh. are : *gakana* = *gagana*, against *kakana* in Kī. ; *gamana*; *dasavatana*; *gopinta* = *govinda*; *saṁgāma* = *saṁgrāma*; *vaggha* = *vyāghra*, against *vakkha* in Hc. Of these *nt* in *gopinta* is against Vr., but it is in accord with Hc., Kī., as also the examples of Bh. for the inlaut *mekha*, *rāca-*, *ṇicchara*, *vaṭisa* = *vaḍiśa*, *māthava* = *mādhava*, *saraphasa*, *salapha* = *śalabha*. Hc. 4,327 mentions that according to the opinion of other teachers this change does not take place in the consonants in the initial syllable and in the root *yuj* : *gati*; *ghamma*, *jimūta*; *jhacchara*; *ḍamaruka*; *ḍhakkā*; *ḍāmotara*; *bāḷaka*; *bhakavatī*; *niyojita* aganst *niyocita* in 4,325. Doubtful is the treatment of *va*. Bh. has *gopinta* = *govinda*, *kesapa* = *keśava*, but *vaṭisa* = *vaḍiśa*, *dasavatana* = *daśavadaṇa*, *māthava* = *mādhava*, *vaggha* = *vyāghra*. In Hc. the original *va* is consistently retained : *vakkha* = *vyāghra*; *panthava* = *bāndhava*;

phakavati = *bhagavati*; *vasuthā* = *vasudhā*. Kī. has 5, 108 *pala* = *vana*, but 5, 110 *vañña* = *varṇa*, and he retains it also in 5, 107 *thvalati* = *dhvanati*, *thvalita* = *dhvanita*.[2] Probably *pa* is to be written, unless here too, different dialects have got mixed up promiscuously. Secondary *va*, that originated from *ya* (§254), has becomes *pa* in P. *hitapa* = *hṛdaya* (Sr. fol. 64), *hitapaka* = *hṛdayaka* (Vr. 10, 14; Hc. 4, 310; Kī. 5, 112; Namisādhu on Rudraṭa 2, 12; Siṁhadevagaṇin on Vāgbhaṭālaṁkāra 2, 3).[3] Mk. has *pisesa* = *viśeṣa* (fol. 86), *kupa ci* = *kva cid*, *pisumaa* = *vismaya* (fol. 87) in the section on Kaikeyapaiśācikā. On *piva* see § 336, on an analogous transformation in the Gipsy, Dardu and Kāfir languages see MIKLOSICH, Beiträge zur Kenntnis der Zigeunermundarten (Wien 1874. 1878 I.II. p. 15ff.; IV. p. 51. Cf. §27 notes 7. 8.

1. It has already been noted above, § 27, that the grammarians do not sharply distinguish between P. and CP. In Vr. and Kī. by P. is obviously meant CP., while the rule for P. given in Hc. 4, 304 on *rājan* is a characteristic of CP., since Hc. 4, 304 has *rājā*, against *rācā*, *rācānaṁ* in Bh. 10, 12 and 4,323 has *rājaṁ rājā*, against that 4,325 has *rācā* for CP. In Hc 4,326 in CP. °*aggalaggapatibimbaṁ*, *luddaṁ samuddā* are in accord with 4, 327, on the other hand, °*pātukkhevena* is to be corrected to °*pena*. 2. So reads also the Paris manuscript according to LASSEN, Inst. p. 441; cf., however, § 243. — 3. For the false reading *hitaakaṁ* in Vr. (cf. v.l., where *va* has been wrongly read for *pa*) and in Kī. we have to read *hitapakaṁ*.

§ 192. In A., according to Hc., 4, 396, intervocalic *k*, *t*, *p* become *g*, *d*, *b* respectively instead of dropping off, and *kh*, *th*, *pha* become *gh*, *dh*, *bh* respectively instead of changing into *h* (§ 188). Examples of this rule are not very abundant : *khaagāli* = *kṣayakāle* (Hc. 4, 377); *ṇāagu* = *nāyakaḥ* (Hc. 4, 427); *vicchohagaru* = *vikṣobhakaram* (Hc. 4, 396, 1); *sughĕ* = *sukhe* (Hc. 4, 396, 2); *āgado* = *āgataḥ* (Hc. 4, 355. 372); *karadi*, *ciṭṭhadi* = *karoti*, *tiṣṭhati* (Hc. 4, 360); *kiḍadi* = *krīḍati* (Hc. 4, 442, 2); *kṛdantahŏ* = *kṛtāntasya* (Hc. 4, 370, 4); *ghaḍadi*, *praāvadi*, *ṭhido* = *ghaṭate*, *prajāpatiḥ*, *sthitaḥ* (Hc. 4, 404); *madi* = *mati* (Hc. 4, 372); *viṇimmavidu*, *kidu*, *radiĕ*, *vihidu* = *vinirmāpitam*, *kṛtam*, *ratyāḥ*, *vihitam* (Hc. 4, 446); *gañjidu*, *maḍidu*, *harāvidu*, *bhāmidu*, *hiṁṣidu* = **gañjitam* (= *piḍitam*; Hc. 4, 409; cf. Āryāsaptaśatī 384. 685; Gītagovinda 1, 19), *marditam*, *hāritam bhrāmitam*, *hiṁsitam* (Kk. 260, 43ff.); *sabadhu* = *śapatham*, *kadhidu* = *kathitam*, *sabhalaũ* = *saphalakam* (Hc. 4, 396, 3). By far in most cases A. follows the rules that are applicable to M.; A. of Piṅgala always observe them, except in the case of *madagala* = *madakala* (§ 202), so does that of Kālidāsa as well : hence this phonetic law can be considered to hold good just dialectically (§ 28).

§ 193. In lieu of dropping off of a consonant or of change of an aspirate to *h*, there often occurs their reduplication. The aspirates are doubled by the corresponding non-aspirate sounds, so that when doubled they appear as *kkha*, *ggha*, *ccha*, *jjha*, *ṭṭha*, *ḍḍha*, *ttha*, *ddha*, *ppha*, *bbha* (Vr. 3, 51; C. 3, 26; H. 2, 90; Kī. 2, 108; Mk. fol. 26). The preceding and the following paragraphs contain numerous examples. In PG. the doubled aspirates, in consonance with the mode of writing of the other inscriptions, are partly written as simple aspirates : *ārakhādhikate*[1] *ārakṣādhikṛtān* (5, 5); *vadhanike* = *vardhanakān* (6, 9); *dakhiṇa* = *dakṣiṇa* (6, 28); *pupha* = *puṣpa* (6, 34). The inscription, however, mostly follows the mode of writing of the manuscripts : *aggiṭṭhoma* [so to be read] = *agniṣṭoma* (5, 1); *savattha* = *sarvatra* (5, 3); *raṭṭhika* = *rāṣṭrika* (5, 4); *ĕttha* = *itthā* (5, 7); *vatthavāṇa* = *vāstavyānām* (6, 8); *raṭṭhe* = *rāṣṭre* (6, 27); *araṭṭha* = *arāṣṭra* (6, 32); *vĕṭṭhi* = *viṣṭi* (6, 32); °*cchobhaṁ* = *kṣobham* (6, 32); *kaṭṭha* = *kāṣṭha* (6, 33); *aṭṭhārasa* = *aṣṭādaśa* (6, 34); *addhikā* = *ardhakāḥ* (6, 39); *aṇuvaṭṭhāveti* = *anuprasthāpayati* (7, 45); *vigghe* = *vighnān* (7, 46); *sahattha* = *svahasta* (7, 51). In *abhatthemi* = *abhyarthayāmi* we have both the modes of writing combined. In the manuscripts, that are written in the Dravidian script and in the Nāgarī manuscripts thence transcribed, hence in the South Indian print too, the aspirates like other consonants are either printed double or are mostly hinted by a small circle in the interval before the aspirate (a somewhat rare point) as to be doubled : *aghgha* = or *aogha* = *aggha* = *arghya*; *abhbhaththaṇā* or *aobhaothaṇā* = *abbhatthaṇā* = Skt. *abhyarthanā*; *vakhkhaththala* or *vaokhaothala* = *vakṣaḥsthala*. *cha* and *dha* are most seldom written doubled; in relation to the other aspirates the manuscripts waver. In Bengali manuscripts doubling occurs very seldom; it is sometimes so also in older editions, as in that of Prabodhacandrodaya, Pūṇā śāke 1773 in some aspirates, such as *kha*, e.g. in *rakhkhasi* = *rākṣasi* (fol. 13-); *gha*, e.g. in *ughghāḍiadi* = *udghāṭyate* (fol. 12b); *ṭha*, e.g. in *suṭhṭhu* = *suṣṭhu* (fol. 19b), *pha*, in *viphphuraṁta* = *visphurat* (fol. 16b), *bha*, e.g. in *ṇibhbhatsida* (sic) for *ṇibbhacchida* = *nirbhartsita* (6a). The edition writes in Sanskrit too *ujhjhita* (fol. 13a). Evidently it rests upon a South Indian text, since it often agrees with the Telugu edition of Madras. Sh. P. PAṆḌIT has retained this orthography, strictly depending on his manuscripts, in his editions of Mālavikāgnimitra and Vikramorvaśīya in the case of all the aspirates, so that he too writes for example *puchchidum̐*, *diṭhṭhiṁ*, *ṇijhjhāanti*, *siṇidhdhaṁ* (Mālav. 5), *ubhbhiṇṇa*, *paththidā* (p. 6) etc. also[2]. Doubling also occurs in the manuscripts of Hāla and in sporadic cases especially in *bha*, also in some Calcutta editions of Jaina books, as in Paṇhāv. *khokhubhbhamāṇa* (169, 210); *pabhbhaṭṭha* (216); *labhbhā* (363. 466); *vibhbhamo* (227. 468); *abhbhuṇṇaya* (284); in Vivāgas. *tubhbhiṁ* (17); *tubhbhaṁ* (20. 21); *ukhkhatta* (214); *pām̆okhkhaṁ* (215), *pām̆okkhāṇaṁ*, *pam̆okhkhehiṁ*, *abhbhuage* (216); in Jīv. *sattakhkhutto* (621), *dakhkhiṇilla* (842), *savvabhbhantarilla* (878f.), °*ṇakkhāṇaṁ* (883, 886. 887), *majhjhimiya* (905ff.), *avaḍhḍha* (1055f.) etc. This mode of writing has only orthographic, but not a phonetic significance (§ 26).

1. So to be read; see LEUMANN, EI. 2.484.—2. Cf. PAṆḌIT, Mālav.2 (Bombay 1889) p. vf. — 3. WEBER, Hāla1 p. 26f.

§ 194. Instead of dropping off, or when aspirates become *h*, an intervocalic consonant is often doubled, if it originally stood before an accented vowel. Semivowels and nasals too undergo this doubling. So AMg. *ukkhā* = *ukhá* (Āyār. 2, 1, 2, 1); AMg. *ujju* = *ṛjú* (§ 57); A. *kĕtthu* = *kathá* (§ 107); JM. *jitta* = *jitá* (Erz. 13, 6); AMg. *ṇijjitta* = *nirjita* (Sūyag. 704); M. *ṇakkha*, AMg. *nakkha* beside *ṇaha*, *naha* = *nakhá* (Bh. 3, 58; Hc. 2, 99; Kī. 2, 212; Mk. fol. 27; Pāiyal. 109; H.R.; Uvās.); A. *ṇimma* = *niyamá* (§ 149); M. AMg. *ṇŏllaï*, *ṇullaï* = *nudáti* (§244); M. *phuṭṭaï* = *sphuṭáti* (Hc. 4, 177. 231; G.H.R.); A. *phuṭṭı* = *sphuṭeḥ* (Hc. 4, 357, 4), *phuṭṭisu* = *sphuṭi-*

ṣyāmi (Hc. 4, 422, 12); *phiṭṭaï* = **sphiṭáti* (Hc. 4, 177, 370) beside *phuḍaï*, *phiḍaï*; *sŏllaï* = *sūdáyati* (§ 244); *hatta* = *hata'* in *ohatta* = *avahata* (bent downward; Deśīn. 1, 156), *pasuhatta*, *parasuhatta* = *parśuhata*, *paraśuhata* (tree; Deśīn. 6, 29); A. *duritta* = *duritá* (Piṅgala 2, 17, 35. 43 [*dūrittā*]. 186), *mālatti* = *mālati'* (Piṅgala 2, 113), *vrattu* = *vratám* (Hc. 4, 394). The same accent is to be assumed in the suffix *-ka* in M. *sisakka* = *śirṣaka* (R. 15, 30); *leḍukka*, *leḍhukha* = *leṣṭuka* (§ 304); M. JM. Ś. A. *pāikka* = *pādātika* (Hc. 2, 138); R.; Erz.; Mālatīm. 288, 6; Bālar. 199, 10; Priyad. 44, 18 [so to be read with ed. Calc. 49, 2]; Piṅgala 1, 107. 121. 143a. 152a [*pa*°; text *paīka*]; 2, 138)[1]; Mg. *haḍakka* = **hṛdaka* (§ 150; Vr. 11, 6; Kī. 5, 89 [text *hṛdakko*; in Lassen, Inst. p. 393 *hladakko*]; Mṛcch. 79, 11; 114, 14. 16. 18; 115, 23), in verses also *haḷaka* (Mṛcch. 9, 25 [Śakāra] and *haḍaka* 30, 21); Mg. *hagge* = **ahakaḥ* (§ 142. 417); *aakka* beside *aaga* = *ajaka* (demon; Deśīn. 1, 6)[2]; A. *kālikkā* = *kālikā* (Piṅgala 2, 43); Ś. °*caccikka* = °*carcika* (Mṛcch. 73. 15); A. *ṇāakka* = *nāyaka* (Piṅgala 1, 34. 57. 116). *dipakka* = *dipaka* (Piṅgala 1, 138). *rūakka* = *rūpaka* (Piṅgala 2, 137), *sāraṅgikkā* = *sāraṅgikā* (Piṅgala 2, 71 [*sa*°]. Likewise in the suffix *-ta* in AMg. *viuvvitta* = *vikurvita* (Sūyag. 792. 806), beside the usual *viuvviya*. According to the same rule is explained the duplication of °*la* in the suffixes *-alla*, *-illa*, *-ulla* = *alá*, *-ilá*, *-ulá* (§ 595). Against the rule, and according to analogy are formed A. *paümāvatti* = *pádmāvatī* and *meṇakkā* = *ménakā* (Piṅgala 1, 116, 2, 209). The doubling is frequent also after a long vowel which is then shortened, as in *ĕvvaṁ* = *evám*; *kiḍḍā* = *kriḍá*; *jĕvva* = *evá*; *ṇĕḍḍa* = *niḍá*; *tuṇhikka* = *tūṣṇiká*; *tĕllá* = *tailá*; *dugullá* = *dukūlá* etc. (§ 90).[3] On the duplication of enclitics see § 92ff., on *ṇihitta*, *vāhitta* § 286.

1. S. Goldschmidt (Monatsberichte der Königl. Akademie der Wissenschaften zu Berlin 1879, 922), who is followed by Weber (Hāla² p. xvii) and Jacobi [Erz. s.v.], wrongly derives the word from Persian, because of the large number of cases of duplication of the suffix *-ka* were not known to him. My derivation from *pādika* (GGA. 1881, 1321) was also wrong, although linguistically that is unassailable — 2. Cf. Böhtlingk s. v. *ajaka*, and *purilladeva* = *asura* (Deśīn. 6, 55) = *daitya* (Triv. 1, 4, 121; cf. BB. 13, 12) — 3. Pischel, KZ. 35. 140ff.; otherwise Jacobi, KZ. 35, 575 ff.

§ 195. If conjunct consonants are separated by a separation-vowel, they must be simplified or be treated according to § 186. 188. Sometimes, however, in this case one of them is doubled according to the rule holding good for conjunct consonants (§ 131) : AMg. *sassiriya*. Ś. *sassiria* = *saśrika*; Ś. *sassiriadā*, *sassiriattaṇa* = *saśrikatā*, **saśrikatvana* (§ 98.135)[1]; *puruvva* = *pūrva*; *murukkha* = *mūrkha*; AMg. *riuvveya* = *ṛgveda* (§ 139); Ś. *sakkaṇomi*, *sakkuṇomi* = *śaknomi*; *sakkaṇodi*, *sakkuṇodi* = *śaknoti* (§ 140. 505); AMg. *sakkiriya* = *sakriya* (Ovav. § 30. II, 4b; so to be read with the MSS); AMg. *sukkila* = *śukla*, JM. *sukkiliya* = *śuklita* (§ 136). In JM. *namŏkkāra*, M. A. *avarŏppara*, M. AMg. JM. Ś. *parŏppara* = *namaskāra*, *aparaspara*, *paraspara*, *as* has been changed into *o*, beside *ska* into *kka*, and *spa* into *ppa* (§306. 311. 347). In M. AMg. *pŏmma* = *padma*, *pŏmmā* = *padmā*, M. Ś. *pŏmmarāa* = *padmarāga*, *a* has contracted with the udvṛtta vowel (§ 139. 166), and yet in spite of this a doubling has taken place.[2] On *-jja* for *-ya* see § 91.

1. Kāvyaprakāśa 72, 11 *jaasirī* is correct, like *jaasirīe* (G. 243), since in line 10 *balāmoḍii* is to be read (§ 238. 589). It is not, with Weber, Hāla¹ A. 22;²977, to be written as *jaassirī*. 2. Pischel, KZ. 35, 146f. On Pāli see Franke, GN. 1895-530.

§ 196. Consonant-groups standing at the beginning of the second member of a compound may be treated as if they were initial and in that case they must be simplified (§ 268; Vr. 3, 57; Hc. 2, 97; Kī. 2, 115; Mk. fol. 28); M. *vāraṇakhandha* = *vāraṇaskandha* (G. 1200) beside *mahisakkhandha* = *mahiṣaskandha* (H. 561); M. *hatthaphaṁsa* = *hastasparśa* (H. 330) beside *hatthapphaṁsa* (H. 462); Ś. *aṇugahida* = *anugṛhita* (Mṛcch. 25, 3) beside *pariggahida* = *parigṛhita* (Mṛcch. 41, 10); *ṇaīgāma* beside *ṇaïggāma* = *nadigrāma* (Bh.; Hc.); *kusumapaara* beside *kusumappaara* = *kusumaprakara* (Bh.; Hc.); *devathui* beside *devatthui* = *devastuti* (Bh.; Hc.; Kī.); *āṇālakhambha* beside *āṇālakkhambha* = *ālānastambha* (Bh.; Hc.); *harakhandā* beside *harakkhandā* = *haraskandau* (Hc.). Doubling is, however, the rule, that is to say, the treatment is as in the inlaut; and on this analogy[1], not seldom, even a single consonant has been doubled at the beginning of a compound : Ś. *akkhādia* = *akhādita* (Mṛcch. 55, 15); *addaṁsaṇa* = *adarśana* (Hc. 2, 97); M. *addiṭṭha* = *adṛṣṭa* (G.H.R.); M. *addāa*, AMg. JM. *addāga*, *addāya* = **ādāpaka*[2] (mirror; Deśīn. 1, 14; Paiyal. 119; H.; Ṭhāṇ. 284; Paṇṇav. 435f.; Nandīs. 471; Āv. 17, 10. 14. 15. 16; Erz.); M. *pabbuddha* = *prabuddha* (R. 12, 34); ; *abbuddhasiri-* = *abuddhaśri* (Deśīn. 1, 42; Triv. 1, 4, 121); M. *akkhaṇḍia* = *akhaṇḍita* (H. 689); M. *alliaī*, JM. *alliyaï*, AMg. *uvalliyaī*, M. *samalliaï*, JM. *samalliyaï* (§ 474); M. JM. *allīṇa* (G.H.R., Āv. 14, 23; 24, 17; 26, 28; Erz.), M. *aṇallīṇa* (R.), *samallīṇa* (H.) from *lī* with *ā*, *upa*, *samā*[3]; *allivaī* = **ālipáti* = *ālimpati* (Hc. 4, 39); *avallāva* = *apalāpa* (Deśīn. 1, 38); A. *uddhabbhua* = *ūrdhvabhuja* (Hc. 4, 444, 3); *ŏggāla* beside *oāla* for **ogāla* (rivulet; Deśīn. 1, 151) = **avagāla*, from *gal* with *ava*; AMg. *kāyaggirā* = *kāyagirā* (Dasav. 634, 24); M. Ś. *tĕllŏkka* (Bh. 1. 35; 3, 58; Hc. 2, 97; Kī. 2, 114; Mk. fol. 27; R.; Dhūrtas. 4, 20; Anarghar. 317, 16); Karṇas. 13, 9.11; Mahāv. 118, 3; Uttarar. 64. 8 [*tĕlloa*]; Mallikām. 133, 3), beside AMg. M. *telŏkka* (Grr.; G.; Paṇṇav. 2. 178ff. [°*lu*°]; Dasav. N. 655, 28; Uvās.; Kappas.) = *trailokya*; Mg. *pañcayyaṇa* = *pañcajanāḥ* (Mṛcch. 112, 6); *paḍikkūla* (Hc. 2, 97), beside the usual *paḍiūla* = *pratikūla*; M. *pabbala* = *prabala* (R.); *pammukka* (Hc. 2, 97) beside the usual *pamukka* = *pramukta* (§ 566); M. AMg. JM. Ś. *paravvasa* (H. R.; Paṇhāv. 136; T. 6, 14; Erz.; Lalitav. 554, 5; Vikr. 29, 12, v.l.; Nāgān, 50, 13 v.l.), Mg. *palavvaśa* (Mallikām. 143, 11; so to be read) = *paravaśa*; AMg. *aṇuvvasa* = *anuvaśa* (Sūyag. 192); *pavvāaï* = **pravāyati* = *pravāti* (Hc. 4, 18), M. *pavvāa* = *pravāta* (H. R.); M. *āṇāmĕttapphala* = *ājñāmātraphala* (R. 3, 6); *ahiṇavadiṇṇapphala* = *abhinavadattaphala* (R. 2, 37); *pāavapphala* = *pādapaphala* (R. 9, 4; cf. R. 12, 12; 13, 89; H. 576); *baddhapphala* beside *baddhaphala* (Hc. 2, 97; Mk. fol. 29); JM. *bahupphala* (Kī. 2, 116; Kk. 271, 20), beside *bahuhala* (Kī. 2, 116, cf. § 200); AMg. *purisakkāra* = *puruṣakāra* (Vivāhap. 67. 68. 125; Nāyādh. 374; Uvās. Ovav.)[4], as M. *sāhukkāra* = *sādhukāra* (R.); AMg. *tahakkāra* = *tathākāra* (Ṭhāṇ. 566); JM. *bhattibhara* = *bhaktibhara* (Kk. 269, 14); M. *maṇikkha* = *īamaṇikhacita* (Mṛcch. 41, 2); M. *malaasiharakkhaṇḍa* = *malayaśikharakhaṇḍa* (Hc. 2, 97 = R. 8, 69); M. *vaṇṇagghaa* = *varṇaghṛta* (H. 520); A. *vijjajjhara* = *vidyādhara* (Vikr. 59, 5; see § 216); A. *vippakkha* = *vipakṣa* (Piṅgala 1,138-); AMg. *sakaḍabbhi*, *sagaḍabbhi* = *svakṛtabhid* (Āyār. 1, 3, 4, 1. 4); M. *sajjia*

= *sajīva* (R. 1, 45), *sattaṇha* = *satṛṣṇa* (R. 1, 46), *sappivāsa* = *sapipāsa* (Hc. 2, 97; R. 3, 21), *sesapphaṇa* = *śeṣaphaṇa* (R. 6, 19; cf. 6, 63. 69. 72; 7, 59; 9, 14, 34. 45), *paṇḍurappheṇa* (R. 8, 9; cf. 8, 49; 13, 24. 53. 66); AMg. JŚ. *saccitta* = *sacitra* (Dasav. 622, 39; Kattig. 403, 379). In °*kkāra*, the words beginning with *kkha* and °*pphala*, the doubling is to be ascribed perhaps to an original *s*, in many other cases the duplication is purely metrical, and certainly also in M. *taṇullaā* (Karp. 27, 12), beside the usual *taṇulaā* = *tanulatā*, AMg. *rāgaddosa* (Uttar. 707; Dasav. N. 653, 6), beside the usual *rāgadosa* (§ 129), JŚ. *kuddiṭṭhi* = *kudṛṣṭi* (Kattig. 399, 318; 400, 323), beside and influenced by *saddiṭṭhi* = *saddṛṣṭi* (Kattig. 399, 317, 320) and so on.

1. Pischel, KZ. 35, 147ff. — 2. So more correctly than BB. 3, 247, as JM. *addāga* proves. On contraction cf. § 165, on *dāvaī* § 554. Incorrect Weber, Hāla[1] p. 29; on Hāla[2] 4. 204. — 3. So more correctly than BB. 13. 10f.; cf. KZ. 35, 149. — 4. Incorrectly explain Hoernle (Uvās.; Transl. p. 111, note 254) and Leumann (WZKM. 3, 345) these words as formed on the analogy of *balakkāra* = *balātkāra*. It could, with equal justification, be explained as having been formed according to *sakkāra* = *satkāra*.

§ 197. In many cases, duplication of consonants may be explained from a word-formation or a flexion deviating from Skt. So in *katto* = *kutaḥ* from **kattaḥ* = *kad* + *taḥ*; *jatto* = *yad* + *taḥ*; *tatto* = *tad* + *taḥ*; *aṇṇatto* = *anyad* + *taḥ*, on the analogy of which are formed *atto* = *átaḥ*; *ĕkkatto* = *ekataḥ*; *savvatto* = *sarvataḥ* and probably also *itto* = *itáḥ*, which, however, might have a quite regular reduplication (of *t*) according to § 194. *etto* = **etaṭaḥ* is derived from *eta* = *etad* + *taḥ*, as *aṇṇo* from *anya* = *anyad* + *taḥ* according to § 339 and with elision of *a* according § 148. On *to* see § 142[1]. The majority of the verbs of the fourth and sixth classes of Skt. verb has, according to the phonetic laws of Pkt., doubling as its consequence, as in *alliaī* (§ 196); *phuṭṭaī*, *phiṭṭaī* (§ 194); *kukkai*, *kŏkkaī* = **krukyati*; *callaī* = **calyati* = *calati*; *ummillaī* = **unmīlyati* = *unmīlati*; Ś. *ruccadi* = **rucyate* = *rocate*; *laggaï* = **lagyati* = *lagati*; Ś. *vajjadi* = **vrajyati* = *vrajati* (§ 487. 488)[2]. From the derivation of nouns from the present stems are explained the cases, like *oalla* (shivering, departure; Deśīn. 1, 165; Triv. 1, 4, 121 = BB. 13, 8) = **apacalya*; cf. *oallanti*, *oallanta-* (R.); *ujjalla* (Hc. 2, 174 [so to be read; see translation p. 89]; Triv. 1, 4, 121 = BB. 13, 7), *ŏjjalla* (Deśīn. 1, 154) "strong", *ujjallā* (violence; Deśīn. 1, 97) from **ujjvalya-*; *kŏppa* (agitation; Deśīn. 2, 45; Triv. 1,4,121 = BB. 6, 104) from *kupya-*; *sivvi* (needle; Deśīn. 8, 29; Triv. 1, 3, 105 BB. 3, 260), *sivviṇi* (Deśin. 8, 29) from *sivya-*.[3]

1. Examples in § 425ff. Cf. Pischel, KZ. 35, 149. Somewhat differently S. Goldschmidt, Prākṛtica p. 22; wrongly Jacobi, KZ. 35, 578; wrong is also Leumann Aup. S. s. v. *tatto*, who considers the reduplication as purely metrical. — 2. Pischel, BB, 13, 8ff—3. Pischel, BB. 6, 86.

§ 198. Change of tenues into mediae is the rule for the cerebrals, when they stand unconnected in the interior of a word and between vowels; *ṭ* becomes *ḍ* and *ṭha* becomes *ḍh* (Vr. 2, 20. 24; Hc. 1, 195. 199; Kī. 2, 10. 18; Mk. fol. 16). So M. *kaḍaa* = *kaṭaka* (G.H.R.)[3]; *kuḍumla* = *kuṭumba* (G.H.); *ghaḍia* = *ghaṭita*; *caḍula* = *caṭula*; *taḍa* = *taṭa*; *paḍala* = *paṭala*; *viḍava* *viṭapa*. — *kaḍhiṇa* = *kaṭhina* (G.H.); *kaḍhiṇattaṇa* = **kaṭhinatvana* (R.); *kamaḍha* = *kamaṭha* (G.H.); *paḍhaī* = *paṭhati* (H.); *pīḍha* = *pīṭha* (G.); *haḍha* = *haṭha* (G.). This change occurs exceptionally also in PG. in *bhaḍa* =

= *bhaṭa* and *koḍi* = *koṭi* (§ 189). According to Hc. 1. 195 sometimes *ṭ* remains, as in *aṭaï* = *aṭati*, which must be a false reading.

1. Cf. §184, note 1; §186, note 1.

§ 199. Instead of dropping off (§ 186), *p* mostly becomes *v*[1], not *b*, except dialectically in A. (§ 192), as scholars assumed before (Vr. 2, 15; Hc. 1, 231; Kī. 2, 8; Mk. fol. 16. M. *āava* = *ātapa* (G.H.R.)[2], *uvala* = *upala* (G.); *kova* = *kopa*; *cāva* = *cāpa*; *ṇiva* = *nipa* (R.); *diva* = *dipa*; *paāva* = *pratāpa*; *viviṇa* = *vipina* (G.); *savaha* = *śapatha* (H.); *sāvaa* = *śvāpada* (G.R.). Exceptionally in PG. too in *aṇuvaṭṭhāveti*, *kassava*, *kāravĕjjā*, *vi* (§ 189). On *va* for initial and secondary *pa* see § 184. According to Hc. 1, 231 euphony determines the elision or the change to *v*. According to Bh. on Vr. 2, 2 and Mk. fol. 14 this holds good especially for the dropping off of all the sounds mentioned in § 186.[3] Usually *p* becomes *v* before *a*, *ā*, but on the other hand drops off before *u*, *ū*; before other vowels the usage wavers. Jaina MSS often wrongly write *b* for *v*.

1. COWELL, Vararuci², p. XIV; PISCHEL, GGA. 1873, p. 52; Academy 1873, p. 398; Jenaer Literaturzeitung 1875, p. 317; P. GOLDSCHMIDT, GN. 1874,512 note ***—2. Cf. §184, note 1 and § 186, note 1,—3. PISCHEL on Hc. 2,231.

§ 200. According to Vr. 2, 26 in the medial syllable between vowels *ph* always becomes *bh*. Bh. gives as examples : *sibhā* = *śiphā*; *sebhāliā* = *śephālikā*; *sabhari* = *śaphari*; *sabhalaṁ* = *saphalam*. Mk. fol. 16 limits this change to the gaṇa *śiphādi*, in which he reckons; *sibhā* = *śiphā*; *sebha* = *śepha*; *sebhāliā* = *śephālikā*; he cites also *sabhari* = *śaphari* as used by somebody.[1] Kī. 2, 16 teaches *bh* for *śiphā* and *śaphara*. Hc. 1, 236 prescribes both *bh* and *h*; he teaches *bh* for *rebha* = *repha* and *sibhā* = *śiphā*; *h* for *muttāhala* = *muktāphala*; *bh* and *h* beside one another for *sabhala*, *sahala* = *saphala*; *sebhāliā*, *sehāliā* = *śephālikā*; *sabhari*, *sahari* = *śaphari*; *gubhaï*, *guhaï* = *guphaṭi*. The words hitherto examined have throughout *h*, or in the beginning of the second member of a compound also *ph*. Thus M. JM. Ś. *muttāhala* = *muktāphala* (G.; Karp. 73, 9; 72, 3; 73, 2; Erz.); M. *muttāhalilla* (Karp. 2, 5; 100, 5); M. *sahara*, *sahari* (G.); M. Ś. *sehāliā* (H.; Mṛcch. 73, 9 [so with the v. l. to be read]; Priyad. 11, 1; 12, 3; 13. 16); Ś. *cittaphalaa* = *citraphalaka* (e.g. Mṛcch. 57, 3; 59, 7; 69. 19; Śak. 125, 7; 133, 8; 134, 4; 142, 11; Vikr. 24, 18; Ratn. 298, 4; 303, 19; Mālatīm. 127, 11); *bahuhala* (Kī. 2, 116); Ś. *bahuphala* (Vikr. 45, 13), *saphala* (Mālav. 44, 1; 46, 11); *saggaphala* = *svargaphala* (Prab. 42, 5); Mg. *paṇaśaphala* (Mṛcch. 115, 20) etc. On A. see §192, on °*pphala*, *ū* §196. In what relation *phumaï* and *bhumaï* = *bhramati* (Hc. 4, 161) stand to one another cannot be said. Dravidian MSS write *bhaṇ* (to speak) in Skt. and Pkt. very frequently *phaṇ* (cf. e. g. Vikr. ed. PISCHEL 622, 10 v.l., 17 v. l.; 639, 8 v. l.; Mallikām. 83, 4). Cf. § 208.

1. The MS reads *saparir yāsaür* (or *yāsaḍar*) *ityādyapi kaścit*.

§ 201. *b* in the inlaut, between vowels, becomes *v* (Hc. 1, 237); M. AMg. JM. Ā. Ś. D. A. *kalevara* = *kalebara* (G.R.; Vivāhap. 1303 [°*ḍe*°). 1390 [°*ḍe*]; Rāyap. 142 [°*ḍe*°]; Erz. Mṛcch. 148, 22. 23; Piṅgala 1, 86ᵃ; Hc. 4, 365, 3), Mg. *kalevala* (Mṛcch. 168, 20); M. AMg. Ś. Mg. A. *kavala* = *kabala* (G.H.; Śak. 85, 2; Nāyādh.; Ovav.; Mṛcch. 69, 7; Hc. 4. 289. 387, 1); M. JM. A. *kavandha* = *kabandha* (R.; Erz. [text °*ba*°;] Piṅgal. 2, 230);

AMg. *kilīva* = *klība* (Āẏār. 2, 1, 3, 22); *chāva* = *śāba* (§ 11); M. *thavaa* = *stabaka* (R.), AMg. *thavaïẏa* = *stabakita* (Vivāhap. 41; Ovav.); M. *dāvaï* = Marāṭhī *dābṇeṁ* (Śak. 55, 16)[1]; M. JM. *sava* = *śaba* (G.; Āv. 36, 34); M. AMg. JM. Ś. *savara* = *śabara* (G. [text °*ba*°]; Vivāhap. 246 [text °*vva*°]; Paṇhāv. 41 [text °*ba*°]; Paṇṇav. 58; Erz.; Pras. 134, 6. 7 [text °*ba*°], M. AMg. *savari* (G. [text °*ba*°]; Vivāhap. 792 [text °*ba*°]; Nāẏādh. §117 [text °*ba*°]; Ovav. § 55 [text °*ba*°]; M. *savala* = *śabala* (H.); AMg. JM. *siviẏā* = *śibikā* (§ 165); JM. *sivira* (Erz. [text °*bi*°]), Mg. *śivila* (Lalitav. 565, 6. 8) = *śibira*[2]. Seldom *b* drops out as in AMg. *alāu*, *alāuẏa*, *lāū*, *lāu*, *lāuẏa* beside Ś. *alāvū* = *alābu*, (§ 141); *ṇiandhaṇa* = *nibandhana* (dress; Deśīn. 4, 38; Triv. 1, 4, 121)[3]; *viuha* (Hc. 1, 177); beside JM. *vibuha* (Erz.) = *vibudha*.—*v* very often remains, especially between *a*- sounds. As in the case of *p* (§ 199), so in its case as well the euphony determines the question.

1. Accordingly the remark on Śak. 55,16, p. 184 has to be amended.—2. As the examples show, the Jaina manuscripts especially very often write *b* for *v*, which is not, as JACOBI (Erz. §20,2d., p.XXVIII) assumes, supported phonetically, but it is simply an error of transcription. Likewise they sometimes write *b* instead of *v* in the initial syllable. E. MÜLLER, Beiträge p. 29). In the Lalitav., as in the MSS, with the exception of those in the Dravidian script, only *v* is written, even in places, where *b* should stand, Cf. also §45, note 3.—3. PISCHEL, BB. 13,8.

§ 202. Except in the cases mentioned in § 192. 198-200, the change of tenues to mediae and vice-versa (§ 190. 191) is only sporadic and dialectical. Instead of dropping off, *k* in AMg. JŚ. JM., very frequently between vowels, becomes *g*, especially in the case of the suffix *-ka* (Hc. 1, 177) : AMg. JM. *asoga* = *aśoka* (e.g. Vivāhap. 41; Uvās.; Nāẏādh.; Ovav.; Kappas; [read *asoga* in the Glossary]; Erz.); JM. *asoga* (Āv. 8, 2. 32); AMg. JM. *āgāsa* = *ākāśa* (Uvas.; Ovav.; Āv. 21, 15); AMg. *egamega* = *ekaika* (§ 353); AMg. JM. *kulagara* = *kulakara* (Kappas.; Āv. 46, 20. 22); AMg. JM. *jamagasamaga* = *yamakasamaka* (Uvās. § 148. 153; Kappas. § 102; Ovav. § 52; Āv. 17, 15); AMg. JM. JŚ. *loga* = *loka* (e.g. Āẏār. 1, 1, 1, 5. 7; 1, 1, 3, 2; Erz.; Pav. 381, 16; 387, 25), JŚ. *logālogaṁ* (Pav. 382, 23) beside *loẏāloẏaṁ* (Kattig. 398, 302); AMg. *sāgapāgāe śākapākāya* (Sūẏag. 247. 249), *silogagāmi-* = *ślokakāmin* (Sūẏag. 497); AMg. JŚ. *appaga* = *ātmaka* (Sūẏag. 188; Pav. 385, 66. 68); JŚ. *maṁsuga* = *śmaśruka* (Pav. 386, 4); AMg. *phalaga* = *phalaka* Sūẏag. 274; Uvās. Ovav.); JM. *tilagacŏddasaga* = *tilakacaturdaśaka* (Āv. 17, 1; 37, 29; 38, 24). For these dialects frequent retention of *g*, instead of dropping off, is also a characteristic. Change of *ka* to *ga* occurs sporadically in other dialects too. Thus Mg. always *hage*, *hagge* = **ahakaḥ* (§ 142. 194. 417); further *śāvaga* = *śrāvaka* (Mudrār. 175, 1. 3; 177, 2; 178, 2; 183, 5; 185. 1; 190, 10; 193, 1 [so to be read]), as also at Prab. 46, 13; 47, 7 *śāvagā*, 58, 15 *śāvagi*, for *sāvakā*, *śāvakā*, *sāvaki*, *śāvaki* of the text, have to read, corresponding to AMg. JM. *sāvaga* (e.g. Uvās.; Erz.). Cf. § 17. Further *ka* has become *ga* in M. A. *maragaa*, AMg. JM. *maragaẏa*, Ś. *maragada* = *marakata* (Hc. 1, 182; Mk. fol. 14; G.H.R.; Karp. 46, 8; 69, 8; Sūẏag. 834; Paṇṇav. 26; Uttar. 1042; Ovav.; Kappas.; Āv. 13, 43; Mṛcch. 71, 1 [read °*gada*]; Karp. 53, 2; 59, 1; 61, 7. 8; 62, 11; Mallikām. 201, 13;

[read °*gada*]; Hc. 4, 349), wrongly *maraaa* (Acyutaś. 43) and *maraada* (Kī. 2, 28). According to Hc. 1, 182; Mk. fol. 14 *ka* becomes *ga* in *madakala* also; a mention should be made here of A. *madagala* (Piṅgala 1, 64; Hc. 4, 406, 1), where it can be explained according to § 192. In M. occurs also *pāgasāsaṇa* = *pākśāsana* (G. 380). On *gĕndua* see § 107. -*kha* has become *gh* in AMg. *āghāvei* = *ākhyāpayati*, *āghavaṇā* = *ākhyāpanā* (§ 88. 551), and in *ṇighasa* = *nikaṣa* (§ 206). In *ahilaṅkhaī*, *ahilaṅghaī* (wishes; Hc. 4. 192) we cannot decide with certainty whether *kh* or *gh* is original. Dialectically *ca* has become *ja* in *pisāji* = *piśāci* (Hc. 1, 177). Reversely *ca* appears for *ja* in M.Ś. *cakkhaī* (eats; Vr. Appendix A. p. 99, Sūtra 20)[1], M. *cakkhia* (tasted; Hc. 4, 258; Triv. 3, 1, 132; H. 605), *acakkhia* (H. 917), *cakkhanta*- (H. 171), Ś. *cakkhia* (absol.; Nāgān. 49, 5), *cakkhijjanta*- (correctly *cakkhianta*-; Caṇḍak. 16, 16)[2] from *jakṣa*-; *maccaī* beside *majjaī* = *mādyati* from *mad* (Hc. 4, 225); A. *raccasi* = *rajyase* from *raj* (Hc. 4, 422, 23); M. JM. *vaccaī* (Vr. 8, 47; Hc. 4,225; Kī. 4,46 G.H.R.; Erz.; Kk.; Ṛṣabhap.), Ā. *vaccadi* (Mṛcch. 99, 17 [so to be read]; 100, 19; 101, 7; 148, 8; D. *vaccaī* (Mṛcch. 100, 15 [so to be read]), *vacca*, *vaccadi* (Mṛcch. 105, 4. 9), beside Ḍh. *vajjadi*, Ś. *vajjamha*, Mg. *vayyĕnti* (§ 488)[3]. To *vaccaī* belongs also AMg. *paḍucca* for **paḍiucca* (§ 163. 590), which strictly corresponds to Skt. *pratītya*, by which the scholiasts mostly explain it,[4] and A. *vicca* (road; Hc. 4, 421).

1. WEBER, Bhag. 1, 387; ZDMG. 28, 391. — 2. PISCHEL on Hc. 4, 258, where I refer to the New Indian dialects 3. *vaccaī* is perhaps a denominative from *vrātya* = **vrātayati* and *vajja* is from *vraiyā* = **vrajyati*. In that case *cca* would be phonetically quite regular. — 4. Wrongly WEBER, Bhag. 1, 381; E. MÜLLER, Beiträge p. 21.

§ 203. The presumption that in AMg. and JM. every *ta* may[1] either remain or drop off, or that between two vowels, of which the second one is *i*, *t* may be introduced[2] is erroneous. As already conjectured by WEBER[3] all these cases are to be credited to the account of the scribes, who very often inserted Skt. forms in the text, just as did the Jainas, from an orthographical point of view, and generally committed the clumsiest blunders against the dialects.[4] — *ta* becomes *da* and *tha* becomes *dha* in JŚ. Ś. Mg. Ḍh., dialectically also in A. (§ 192). So JŚ. *vandida*, *dhoda* = *vandita*, *dhauta* (Pav. 379, 1); *saṁpajjadi* = *saṁpadyate*, *bhamadi* = *bhramati*, *pĕcchadi* = *prekṣate* (Pav. 380, 6; 380; 12; 384, 48); *bhūdo*, *jādi* = *bhūtaḥ*, *yāti* (Pav. 381, 15); *ajadhāgahidatthā ede* = *ayathāgṛhitārthā ete* (Pav. 389, 1); *devadajadi* = *daivatayati* (Pav. 383, 69); *tasaghāda*, *karadi*, *kārayadi*, *icchadi*, *jāyade* = *trasaghāta*, *karoti*, *kārayati*, *icchati*, *jāyate* (Kattig. 400, 332); Ś. *adidhi* = *atithi* (Śak. 18, 1, 8; 20, 5; 23, 9; 71, 12); Ś. *kadhehi*, *kadhesu* = *kathaya*, *kathedu* = *kathayatu*, Mg. *kadhedi* = *kathayati* (§ 490); Ś. *cūdaladiaṁ* = *cūtalatikām* (Śak. 119, 9); JŚ. *jadha*, Ś. *jadhā*, Mg. *yadhā* = *yathā*, JŚ. *tadha*; Ś. Mg. *tadhā* = *tathā* (§ 113); *pāridosia*, Mg. *pālidośia* = *pāritoṣika* (Śak. 117. 1. 5); JŚ. *havadi*, *hodi*, Ś. Mg. Ḍh. *bhodi* = *bhavati* (§ 475. 476); Ś. *sāadaṁ* (Mṛcch. 3, 6; 59, 19; 80, 7; 86, 25; 94, 22; Śak. 56, 4; 80, 3), Mg. *śāadaṁ* (Mṛcch. 113, 7; 129, 18) = *svāgatam*; Ḍh. *jūdiala* = *dyūtakara* (§ 25), *jūda* = *dyūta* (Mṛcch. 30, 18; 34, 25 [so with v. l. to be read]; 35, 5 [similarly]; 39, 17), *palivevida* = *parivapita* (Mṛcch. 30, 7), *vajjadi*, *dhāledi*, *bhaṇādi*, *jiṇādi* = *vrajati*, *dhārayati*, *bhaṇati*, *jayati* (Mṛcch. 30, 10; 34, 9. 12. 22); Ś. Ḍh. *sampadaṁ* = *sāmpratam* (Mṛcch. 6, 22; 17, 19;

18, 23; Śak. 25, 2; 30, 4; 67, 12. etc.; Ḍh. ; Mṛcch. 30, 4; 31, 9; 32, 8), Mg. *śampadaṁ* (Mṛcch. 16, 20; 32, 2. 4. 5, 38, 19; 99, 11 etc.). On Ḍh. *māthuru* = *māthuraḥ* see § 25. — Vr. 12, 3 and Mk. fol. 66f. require for Ś. (and with it for Mg.) the change into *da*, *dha*; Hc. 4, 260. 267 and the grammarians following him desire *da*; they, however, wrongly allow *ha* as well beside *dha*.[5] In JŚ. Ś. Mg. Ḍh. original *da* and *dha* very often remain instead of dropping off, or of being changed into *ha* [Kī. 5, 71; Mk. fol. 66). *kada tti* = *kṛteti* in PG. 7, 51 is a printer's error in the transcription for *kaḍa tti*. On *pidhaṁ*, *pudhaṁ* beside *pihaṁ*, *puhaṁ* = *pṛthak* see § 78. On Ā.D. see § 26.

1. JACOBI, Erz. § 20, 1, note 2. — 2. E. MÜLLER, Beiträge, 5.; cf. STEINTHAL Specimen p. 2.—3. Bhag. 1,400; cf. IS. 16,234f.—4. HOERNLE Uvās. p.xviiff. The handwriting shows that in cases like *tavaṇijjamatīu kaṇagamatīu pulakāmatīu riṭṭhāmatīu vairāmatīu* (Jiv. 563), *t* is absurd. Likewise it is unthinkable that in one and the same dialect beside one another have been used *bhavati* and *bhavaī*, *bhagavatā* and *bhagavayā*, *mātaraṁ* and *piyaraṁ* (Āyār. 1,6,4,3) and so on, especially when nowhere have all the MSS *t*. When in the future *ehī* is used, it presupposes *ehii* and not *ehiti-*, as occurs in Āyār. 2,4,1,2 (§529). Not quiet correctly, therefore, LEUMANN WZKM 3,340. With the exception of Uvās. all the texts in AMg. JM. are full of numberless errors. Cf. §349.—5. On Ś. see PISCHEL, KB. 8,129 ff.—The following and preceding paragraphs give numerous examples. Cf. also §22-25.

§ 204. Vr. 2, 7; Kī. 2, 28; Mk. fol. 15 teach that in M. also in a number of cases *ta* becomes *da*. They have collected these in the gaṇa *ṛtvādi*. Bh. reckons in it : *udu* = *ṛtu*; *raada* = *rajata*; *āada* = *āgata*; *ṇivvudi* = = *nirvṛti*; *āudi* = *āvṛti*; *saṁvudi* = *saṁvṛti*; *suidi* = *sukṛti*; *āidi* = *ākṛti*; *hada* = *hata* = *saṁjada* = *saṁyata*; *viuda* = *vivṛta*; *saṁjāda* = *saṁyāta*; *sampadi* = *samprati*; *paḍivaddi* = *pratipatti*. In Kī. and Mk. the gaṇa is an ākṛtigaṇa. Kī. reckons in it *ṛtu*, *rajata*, *āgata*, *nivṛta*, *surata*, *marakata*, *sukṛta*, *saṁyata*, *vivṛti*, *pravṛti*, *āvṛti*, *ākṛti*, *vidhṛti*, *saṁhṛti*, *nivṛtti*, *niṣpatti*, *saṁpatti*, *pratipatti*, *śruta*, *khyāti*, *tāta*, *sāmpratam*. Mk. mentions :—*ṛtu*, *rajata*, *tāta*, *saṁyata*, *kirāta* (as *cilāda*), *saṁhṛti*, *susaṁgata*, *kratu*, *samprati*, *sāmpratam*; *kṛti* and *vṛti*, when provided with a prefix, as *ākṛti*, *vikṛti*, *prakṛti*, *upakṛti*, *apavṛti*, *āvṛti*, *parivṛti*, *nirvṛti*, *saṁvṛti*, *vivṛti*; *āvṛta*, *parivṛta*, *saṁvṛta*, *vivṛta*, *prabhṛti* [MS *padudi*]; *vrata*. Mk. permits the change as optional in the following sūtra in *surata*, *hata*, *āgata*, etc. (*ityādi*). Hc. 1, 209 polemises against this view. The phonetic change occurs in Ś. Mg., but not in M.; when it is found once in M. it is a case of dialectical admixture.[3] In R. *udu* occurs without a variant (1, 18; 3, 29; 6, 11; 9, 85), never *uu*. False reading is *udu* for *uu* in AMg. (Āyār. 2, 2, 2, 6; Ṭhāṇ. 527). Further R. has *maīladā*, beside *paḍiā* (3, 31); *vivaṇṇadā*, *rāmādo* in the same stanza with *araī*, *seummi* (8, 87); similarly *mandodari* in the compound *mandodarisuadūmiavāṇarapariosa°*, that is with a retained *d* and three elided *t*. The same thing occurs elsewhere too, especially in the gāthās of the dramas, as *māladī* instead of *mālaī* = *mālatī* (Lalitav. 536, 2); *adaṁsanti* = *avataṁśayanti* (Śak. ed. BÖHTLINGK 4, 10); *ladāo* = *latāḥ* (Śak. ed. BÖHTLINGK 53, 7; without v. l.; cf. v. l. 85, 3 ed. PISCHEL and 84, 15 of the Kashmir recension, ed. BURKHARD; *uvaṇaīdavvo* = *upanetavyaḥ* (Mālav. 23, 3; without v. l.); *uvaṇide* = *upanīte* (H. 827); *hodu* beside *hoi* (H. 878); *kāduṁ* = *kartum* (Hc. 924); *haṇidā* = *bhaṇitā* (H. 963) etc. All the examples from H.

occur in the Telugu recension. When Hc. declares such forms to be false in M., there is no reason for seeing in them, with S. GOLDSCHMIDT[2], "puristic prohibitions." Rather, we have here cases of errors against the dialect, as conversely in MSS forms of M. are given times without number in Ś. The information in Vr. Kī. in no way relates to M. Especially striking are *paḍivaddi* (Bh.), for which perhaps we have, with AC, to read *paḍivatti*, in spite of the remarkable *d* for *ḍ*, and *nivaddi* (sic.), *nippadi* (sic), *saṁpaddi*, *paḍipaddi* (Kī.), which perhaps rest only on a misunderstanding. On AMg. *adu*, *adu vā*, see § 155, note 5.

1. PISCHEL Vikr. p. 614f.—2 Rāvaṇavaho, p. XVII; cf. also R. 13.97. p. 309. note 4.

§ 205. In the initial and medial syllables, Pkt., deviating from Skt., has often aspirates, that in the inlaut, according to § 188, mostly become *h*. The cause of aspiration is not the same everywhere. In no case is the mere proximity of an unjoined *r* or *s* or of a conjoint *r* the reason, as has generally been assumed.[1] In the case of tenues, nasals, and *la*, aspiration generally goes back to a sibilant, that originally stood before them and has disappeared from Skt.[2] The original sound groups *ska*, *sta*, *spa*, *sna*, *sma*, in the initial syllable, according to §306 — 313, generate *kha*, *tha*, *pha*, *ṇha*, *mha*.

1. LASSEN Inst. p. 197f. 251; JACOBI Erz. § 21, 2 p. XXVIII. Cf. PISCHEL, BB. 3, 253. — 2. WACKERNAGEL, Altind. Gr. § 230 231.

§ 206. In the initial syllable Skr. *ka* appears as *kha*, often in the beginning of the second member of a compound, as *ha*, as in the medial syllable. JM. *khaṁdharā* = *kaṁdharā* (Mk. fol. 17; Erz. 1, 17), but M. Ś. *kaṁdharā* (G.; Mallikām. 192, 22; 201, 7; 220, 20); *khappara* = *karpara* (Hc. 1, 181); AMg. *khasiẏa* = *kasita* (Hc. 1, 181), *khāsiẏa* = *kāsita* (Hc. 1, 181; Nandīs. 380); AMg. JM. *khiṅkhiṇi* = *kiṅkiṇi* (Paṇhāv. 514; Rāẏap. 109. 129; 142; Jīv. 349 [text *khaṅ°*]. 443; Nāẏādh. 948 [text *khaṅ°*]; Uvās.; Ovav. Erz.); *sakhiṅkhiṇi* (Jīv. 468; Āv. 35, 25), *khiṅkhiṇiẏa* = *kiṅkiṇika* (Uvās.), *sakhiṅkhiṇiẏa* (Nāẏādh. § 93; p. 769. 861 [text *°kha°*], but M. Ś. *kiṅkiṇī* (Pāiẏal. 273; G.; Viddhaś. 56, 1; Karp. 55, 7; 56, 4; 102, 1; Veṇīs. 63, 10; Bālar. 202, 14; Ś. Karp. 17, 6; Mālatīm. 201, 6), Ś. *kiṅkiṇiā* = *kiṅkiṇikā* (Viddhaś. 117, 3); AMg. *khila* = *kīla* in *indakhila* = *indrakīla* (Jīv. 493; Ovav. § 1), beside JM. *indakila* (Dvār.); *khilaa* = *kīlaka* (Hc. 1, 181); M. AMg JM. Ś. *khujja* = *kubja* "hump-back" (Vr. 2, 34; Hc. 1, 181; Kī. 2, 40; Mk fol. 17; Pāiẏal. 155; H.; Antag. 22; Aṇuog. 250; Jīv. 87; Nāẏādh. § 117 p. 832. 837; Paṇṇav. 428; Paṇhāv. 78. 523; [text *kujja*]; Vivāgas. 226 Vivāhap. 791, 964; Ovav.; Niraẏāv. ; Āv. 21, 5, 13; Erz.; Śak. 31, 16 Mālav. 70, 8; Pras. 44, 1 ff.), AMg. *ambakhujjaẏa* = *āmrakubjaka* (Vivāhap. 116), *khujjatta* = *kubjatva* (Āẏār. 1, 2, 3, 2); *khujjiẏa* = *kubjita* Āẏār. 1, 6, 1, 3); but in the meaning "achyranthes aspera" *kujja* (Hc. 1, 81; Mk. fol. 17), AMg. *kŏjja* (Kappas. § 37), *kujjaẏa* (Paṇṇav. 32); *khuḍḍia* (cohabitation; Deśīn. 2, 75); *saṁkhuḍḍaï* (to rejoice; Hc. 4, 168) from *kurd*, *kūrd*; cf. *khurd*, *khūrd* (Dhātupāṭha 2, 21)[1]; AMg. JM. *khĕḍḍa*; A. *khĕḍḍaa* (§ 90); *khĕḍḍaï* (to enjoy oneself; Hc. 4, 168); *khĕllanti* (they play; Hc 4, 382), JM *khĕllāveūṇa* (Erz.), *khĕlla* (Erz.), AMg. *khĕllāvaṇa* (Āẏār. 2, 15, 13); Ś. *khealadi* (Mudrār. 71, 4; Viddhaś. 27, 5), *khelidum* (Mudrār. 71, 3

81, 2) *khelaṇa* (Viddhaś. 58. 6; Mallikām. 135, 5), A. *khelanta* (Piṅgala 1, 123[a]), *khĕllia* (laughter; Deśīn. 2, 76) from the root *krīḍ*[2]; AMg. *khutto*, M. *huttaṁ* = *kṛtvaḥ* (§ 451); *khuluha* = *kulpha* (Deśīn. 2, 75; Pāiyal. 250; cf. § 139); M. *ṇihasa* = *nikaṣa* (Vr. 2, 4; Hc. 1, 186. 260; Kī. 2,24; Mk. fol. 14; G.R.); AMg., with change in the media according to §202, *nighasa* (Vivāhap. 10; Rāyap. 54; Uvās.; Ovav.), M. *ṇihasaṇa* = *nikaṣaṇa* G.H.R.)[3]; cf. *khaṣ* beside *kaṣ* (Dhātupāṭha 17,35); A. *vihasanti* = *vikasanti* (Hc. 4,365 1). Corresponding to the Skt. suffix. *-ka*, (WHITNEY[1] § 199) Pkt. has a suffix *-kha*, which occurs in A. *ṇavakhī* = *navaki* (Hc. 4,420, 5). Mk. fol. 37 teaches that without change of meaning *ha* may appear (*svārthe ca*) *haś ca*; *puttaha* = *putraka*; *ekaha* = *ekaka*. To this again may be added *kaḥ svārthe* : *puttahaa*. This *-kha*, *-ha* occurs in AMg. *khahayara khahavara* = **khakacara* = *khacara* (bird; Āyār. 2, 3, 3, 3; Sūyag. 825; Aṇuog. 265. 408. 449; Jīv. 71, 83. 86. 117ff. 317. 319. 323; Nāyādh. 1179; Paṇṇav. 47. 54. 55. 302. 593ff. Samav. 132; Ṭhāṇ. 121f.; Vivāhap. 472. 479. 522f. 526. 1285. 1535; Vivāgas. 50. 108. 187. 204f.; Uttar. 1072. 1078f.; Ovav. § 118), *khahacari* (female bird; Ṭhāṇ. 121f.)[4]; Mg. *vacāhagaṇṭhī śaguḍāhaśuṇṭhī* = *vacākāgranthiḥ saguḍakaśuṇṭhī* (Mṛcch. 116, 25; cf. § 70); M. *chāhā*, *chāhī* = **chāyākā* (§ 255); AMg. *phalaha* = *phalaka* (Vivāhap. 135; Ovav.), and with reduplicated suffix *phalahaga* (Āyār. 2, 1, 7, 1; Ovav.), that has gone over to Skt. as *phalahaka*; beside AMg. *phalaga* (Āyār. 2, 2, 1 6; 2, 3, 1, 2; Uvās.; Ovav.) and *phalaya* (Āyār. 2, 7, 1, 4); M. AMg. Ś. *phaliha* = *sphaṭika* (Vr. 2, 4. 22; Hc. 1, 186. 197; Kī. 2, 24; Mk. fol. 14; G.H.R.; Vivāhap. 253; Rāyap. 33; Nāyādh.; Kappas.; Mṛcch. 68, 18; 69, 1; Vikr. 39, 2; 66; 13; Mālav. 63, 1; Nāgān. 54, 12; Karp. 54, 1; Viddhaś. 25. 9; 28, 5; 74, 7), JM. *phalihamaya* (Erz.), beside AMg. *phāliya* (Nāyādh. § 102; Ovav. [§ 38]; Kappas. § 40), *phāliyāmaya* (Paṇṇav. 115; Samav. 97; Ovav. §16, p. 31, 19), Ś. *phaḍia* (Ratn. 318, 30; Pras. 10, 20; probably to be read °*ḷia* § 238); *phalihagiri* = *sphaṭikagiri* = Kailāsa (Pāiyal. 97); AMg. *bhamuhā* = Pāli *bhamuka* = **bhravukā* for **bhruvukā* (§ 124a)[5]; JM. *sirihā* = *śrīkā* (Erz. 86, 19); M. AMg. JM. D. *suṇaha* = Pāli *sunakha* = Skt. *śunaka* (H.; Paṇhāv. 20; Nāyādh. 345; Paṇṇav. 136; Āv. 34, 20. 24; Erz.; Mṛcch. 105, 4), beside M. *suṇaa* (Hc. 1, 52; H.; Sarasvatīk. 8, 13), AMg. JM. *suṇaga* (Jīv. 356 [cf. 255, where text *suṇamaḍe*]; Nāyādh. 450; Paṇṇav. 49; Uttar. 985; Āv. 35, 6, 10), *suṇaya* (Āyār. 1, 8, 3, 4. 6; Paṇhāv. 201; Paṇṇav. 367. 369; Āv. 35, 9; 36, 28ff.; Dvār. 497, 18), *kolasuṇaya* (Sūyag. 591; Paṇṇav. 367), femin. *suṇiyā* (Paṇṇav. 368). To *suṇaha* has further *ka* been added in Mg. *śuṇahaka* (Mṛcch. 113, 20) and A. *suṇahaü* (Hc. 4, 443). Perhaps it was thought that *suṇaha* was = *sunakha* = *su* + *nakha*[6]; Ḍh. *tuhaṁ*, A. *tuhũ* = *tvakám* (§ 421) with *u* according to § 152 and *ũ* according to § 352; A. *sahũ* = *sākam* (Hc. 4, 356. 419) with *a* according to § 81 and *ũ* according to § 352. Cf. also AMg. *phaṇiha* (sic; comb; Sūyag. 250) with *phaṇaga* (sic: Uttar. 672). M. *cihura* (Vr. 2, 4; Hc. 1, 186; Kī. 2, 24; Mk. fol. 14; Pāiyal. 109; G. H.; Pracaṇḍap. 43, 15; Karp. 48, 10; Acyutaś. 35); Mg. *cihula* (Mṛcch. 171, 2 [so to be read with v.l.]), wrongly M. *ciura* (Sāhityad. 73, 4; Viddhaś. 25, 1), questionably whether correct in Ś. (Prab. 45, 1), will not be = *cikura*, which in the meaning of "a colouring material" becomes AMg. *ciura* (Nāẏādh. § 61), but is = **cikṣura*, a form derived with reduplication from √ *kṣur* (to shave) which would have to become in Pkt. **cikkhura* or **cikhura*, *cihura*. *cihura* bears the same relation to *cikura* as √ **skur* to √ **kur*. We have a reduplication of *ci* in AMg. *cikkhalla* (mud; loam; swamp; Hc. 3, 142; Deśīn. 3, 11; Paṇhāv. 47 [°*la*]; Aṇuog. 367; the explanation be *cikhhala* is uncertain; the word probably belongs to modern Indian *cikila*, *cikkaṇa* to which my attention has been drawn by E. KUHN; AMg. M. *cikkhilla* (H.R.; Paṇṇav. 89ff. [91 °*kkha*°]); Vivāhap. 658f. [commentary °*kkha*°] Paṇhāv. 164. 212 [commentary °*kkha*°]; AMg. *cikhilla* (Ovav. § 32; text °*kha*°; see v.l.) = **cikṣālya* from *kṣàl* "that which is to be washed off," "that which is to be purified"[7]. M. *ṇihāa* (multitude, crowd; Deśīn. 4, 49; Pāiẏal. 19; G.H.R.) is not = *nikāya*,[8] but = *nighāta*.[9] — *nihelaṇa* (home; Hc. 2; 174; Kī. 2, 120. Deśīn. 4, 51; 5, 37; Pāiẏal. 49 [*ni*°]; Triv. 1, 3, 105) is not = *niketana*,[10] but = *nibhelaṇa* (Kappas. § 41) and belongs to √ *bhil bhedane* (Dhātupāṭha32, 66), which occurs in AMg. *bhelaïttā* (Ṭhāṇ. 421)[11]; cf. *bil*, *bila*. — *vihala* is not = *vikala*, but = *vihvala* (§ 332). — M. *sihara* (Pāiẏal. 259; R.) is not = *śikara* (Hc. 1, 184)[12], but comes from M. *sibhara* (R.), that the grammarians (Vr. 2, 5; Hc. 1, 184; Kī. 2, 26; Mk. fol. 14) likewise derive from *śikara*, that, however, belongs to Vedic *śibham*[13].

1. PISCHEL, BB. 3, 254. — 2. PISCHEL BB. 3. 254f. *kheḷadi*, *khĕḷḷaī* have gone also into Skt. as√*khel*. Deviating from BB. 6, 92, I would now consider dropping off of *s* in most of the other words. — 3. The scholiasts mostly equate *ṇihasa* as = *nigharṣa* and *nihaṣaṇa* as *nigharṣaṇa*, a thing that is not possible linguistically, since these words would become *ṇihaṁsa*, *ṇihaṁsaṇa* — 4. Abhayadeva on Ṭhāṇ. 121 remarks *khahaṁ ti, prākṛtatvena kham ākāśam iti*. — 5. LEUMANN, Aup. S. s. v. does not rightly consider *ha* as preventer of the hiatus. — 6. That the aspiration rests chiefly on this false analogy, as TRENCKNER assumes in the case of Pali. (Pāli Miscellany p. 58. note 6), is wrong. On the reduplicated suffix. cf. AMg. *phalahaga*, *thūbhiyāgā* (§208) and Mk. fol. 37.—7. Aṇuog. 367 offers a beautiful etymology of *cikkhalla* as a sample as one may etymologize : *cicca karoti khallaṁ ca bhavati cikkhallaṁ*. A. *cikkhili* (feminine; [sic]; Prabandhac. 56. 6), is an adjective. Both the words, *cihura* (PISCHEL on Hc. 1. 186) and *cikkhalla* (ZACHARIAE, Beiträge zur indischen Lexicographie p. 56) have been taken also into Skt. — 8. BÜHLER, Pāiẏal. p. 12 and s. v. — 9. PISCHEL, BB. 6. 01. — 10. BÜHLER, Pāiyal p. 12 and s. v. — 11. PISCHEL, BB. 3, 252 ; 6. 91; E. MÜLLER, Beiträge p. 34. 12. P.GOLDSCHMIDT, GN. 1874, p. 470. — 13. PISCHEL, BB. 6. 91.

§ 207. *ṭa* has become *ḍha* through *ṭha* in AMg. *cimiḍha* = *cipiṭa* (§248); *vaḍha* = *vaṭa* (Hc. 2, 174; Triv. 1, 3, 105[1]); *saaḍha* = *śakaṭa* (Vr. 2, 21; Hc. 1. 196; Kī. 2, 11; Mk. fol. 16), but AMg. *sagaḍa* (Āẏār. 2, 3, 2, 16; 2, 11, 17; Sūẏag. 350). Ś. *saaḍiā* = *śakaṭikā* (Mṛcch. 94, 15ff), Mg. *śaaḷa* (Mṛcch. 122, 10; § 238; *saḍhā* = *saṭā* (Vr. 2, 21; Hc. 1, 196; Kī. 2, 11; Mk. fol. 16), but M. *saḍā* (R.). Cf. also A. *khallihaḍaü* (§ 110). -*ta* appears as *tha* in *thimpaï* = *tṛmpati* (Vr. 8, 22), *thippaī* (Hc. 4, 138; Kī. 4, 46), *thĕppaī* (Kī. 4, 46) = *tṛpyate* = **stṛmpati*, **stṛpyate*. Not identical with it is *thippaī* (drops down; Hc. 4, 175), that with *theva* (a drop; § 130) belongs to √*stip*, *step* (Dhātupāṭha 10, 3. 4). The suffix -*tha*, instead of Skt. -*ta* occurs in M. AMg. JM. *bharaha* = *bharata* (Vr. 2, 9; C. 3, 12 p. 49; Hc. 1, 214; Kī. 2, 30; Mk.fol. 15; G.R.; Antag. 3; Uttar. 515. 517; Ovav.; Sagara 2, 6; Dvār.; Erz.; Kk.), AMg. *dāhiṇaḍḍhabharahe* = *dakṣiṇārdhabharate*[1] (Āẏār. 2, 15, 2;

Nāẏādh. § 13.93); M. AMg. JM. A. *bhāraha* = *bhārata* (G.; Āẏār. 2, 25. 2; Ṭhāṇ. 70, 73; Vivāhap. 427. 479; Uttar. 515. 517. 532. 541; Nāẏādh.; Uvās.; Niraẏāv., Kappas.; Erz.; Hc. 4, 399); M. *bhārahī* (G.). The form *bharatha*, to which *bharaha* goes back, as *bhāraha* to **bhāratha*[2], is attested by Uṇādis. 3, 115 and Ś. *bharadha* (Mk.; Bālar. 155, 3; 310, 9 [falsely *bharada* 55, 17; 150, 21]; Anarghar. 316, 15 [text °*da*]; but ed. Calc. Śak. 1782, p. 237, 4 correctly °*dha*; Pras. 91, 12 [text °*da*], Mg. *bhāladha* (Mṛcch. 128, 13 [STENZLER °*li*,° see v. l. in GOḌABOLE, 353, 12]; 129, 3 (text °*de*)[3]. Corresponding to the suffix -*tha* in Skt. *āvasatha* = AMg. *āvasaha* (e.g. Āẏār. 1, 7, 2, 1ff.; Ovav.), Skt. *upavasatha, nivasatha, pravasatha* etc., M. AMg. JM. have *vasahi* = **vasathi* = *vasati* (Vr. 2, 9; C. 3, 12 p. 49; Hc. 1, 214; Kī. 2, 30; Mk. fol. 15; Pāiẏal. 49; G.H.R.; Paṇhāv. 136. 178. 215; Vivāhap. 152. 1123. 1193; Nāẏādh. 581; Uttar. 449. 918 [beside *āvasaha*]; Dasav. N. 647, 49; Ovav.; Āv. 27, 25; Kk.); AMg. *kuvasahi* = *kuvasati* (Paṇhāv.)[4]. -*ha*, Ś. Mg. -*dha* in the second person plural imperative likewise go back to -*tha*, since the second person plural indicative is used as the imperative (§ 471).— *kāhala* (cowardly, fearful; C. 3, 12 p. 49; Hc. 1, 214; cowardly, scoundrel; Deśīn. 2, 58), that is equated by Grr. and P. GOLDSCHMIDT[5] as = *kātara*, cannot be separated from *kāhala* (tender; weak; Deśīn. 2, 58), and *kāhali* (a tender young woman; Deśīn. 2, 26). *kāhala, kāhali* is used in Skt. also; perhaps it forced its way into it first from Pkt., and perhaps belongs M. *tharatharei*, Ś. *tharatharedi* (throbs violently [from the heart]; trembles); (§ 558), and therefore, are = *kā*+*thara, kā*, as in Skt. *kāpuruṣa kābhartṛ* etc. *kātara* becomes M. A. *kāara* (G.R.; Hc. 4, 376, 1), AMg. *kāẏara* (Nāẏādh.), Ś. *kādara* (Śak. 17, 12; 84, 16; Vikr. 27, 6; Mālav. 40, 13), Mg. *kādala* (Mṛcch. 120, 9); *kātara* and **kāthara* probably go back to the basic form **kāstara*. — According to Hc. 1, 214 *mātuliṅga* becomes *māhuliṅga*, on the other hand *mātuluṅga* becomes *māuluṅga*, as AMg. Ś. have (Āẏār. 2, 1, 8. 1; Paṇṇav. 482; Adbhutad. 68, 6 [read *mādu*°]). *māhuliṅga* (also C. 3, 12 p. 49) belongs to the same category as *madhukarkaṭikā, madhukukkuṭikā, madhujambīra, madhūjambha, madhubījapūra, madhurajambīra, madhurabījapūra, madhuravalli, madhuvalli, madhūla, mahūlaka*, all of which mean special kinds of citron. *māhuliṅga* is, therefore, = **mādhuliṅga*. In Paṇṇav. 531 AMg. *māuliṅga* is emended. AMg. *vihatthi* (Sūẏag. 280; Vivāhap. 425; Nandīs. 168; Aṇuog. 384. 413) is not = *vitasti* (C. 3, 12 p. 49; Hc. 1, 214[6], but in the root *tas s* will have dropped off; *vihatthi*, therefore, will stand for **vithatthi* = **vistasti*[7].

1. The edition in the Granthapradarśani at p. 93, for it reads *poḍo* / *doḍaḥ* / *āaṇo* / *ḍolā* / ?; see BB. 6.88ff. — 2. WARREN, Over de godsdienstige en wisjgeerige Begrippen der Jaina's (Zwolle 1875) p. 106, note. — 3. Wrongly P. GOLDSCHMIDT, GN. 1874. p. 473. — 4. PISCHEL, BB. 6. 92f. Wrongly P. GOLDSCHMIDT. GN. 1874. p. 473. — 5. GN. 1874, p. 473. — 6. P. GOLDSCHMIDT, GN. 1874. p. 473. — 7. More probably it is an adaptation of one **vihastī* (BB 6. 93).

§ 208. *pa* appears as *ph* in AMg. Ś. *phaṇasa* = *paṇasa* (Vr. 2, 37; Hc. 1, 232; Jīv. 46; Paṇṇav. 482. 531; Vivāhap. 1530; Ovav.; Bālar. 209, 78 [*pa*°]; Viddhaś. 63. 2), beside M. *paṇasa* (Karp. 115, 2), Mg. *paṇaśa* (Mṛcch. 115, 20); M. AMg. JM. *pharusa* = *paruṣa* (Vr. 2, 36; C. 3, 11; Hc. 1, 232; Kī.

2, 43; Mk. fol. 18; G.H. [so 344 to be read; see Index and the v.l. IS. 16, 104]. R.; Āyār. 1, 6, 4, 1. 2, 8; 1, 8, 1, 8; 3, 5, 13; 2, 1, 6, 3; 2, 4, 1, 6; Sūyag. 122 [text *pa°*]. 172. 485. 517. 527. 729; Jīv. 273; Nāyādh. § 135; p. 757; Paṇhāv. 393. 394. 396. 516; Vivāhap. 254. 481; Uttar. 92; Uvās. ; Ovav.; Erz.), JM. *aīpharusa* = *atiparuṣa* (Kk.); M. *pharusattaṇa* = **paruṣatvana* (R.); AMg. *pharusiya* = *paruṣita* (Āyār. 1, 3, 1, 2; 6, 4, 1 [see v.l.]); M. AM. JM. *phaliha* = *parigha* (Vr. 2, 30. 36; Hc. 1, 232. 254; Kī. 2, 43; Mk. fol. 17. 18; Pāiyal. 267; R.; Āyār. 2, 1, 5, 2; 2, 3, 2, 14, 2, 4. 2, 11; 2, 11, 5; Sūyag. 771; Vivāhap. 416; Dasav. 628, 22; Dvār. 500, 30); M. *phalihā* = *parikhā* (Vr. 2, 30. 36; Hc. 1, 232. 254; Kī. 2, 43; Mk. fol. 17. 18; Pāiyal. 240; R), AMg. *pharihā* (Nāyādh. 994. 1001ff. 1006. 1008. 1012. 1014 1023; probably to be read as *phalihā*); *phālihadda* = *pāribhadra* (Hc. 1, 232. 254); AMg. *pharasu* = Pāli *pharasu* = Skt. *paraśu* (Vivāgas. 239); but M. AMg. JM. Ś. *parasu* (G.; Nāyādh. § 135; p. 438 [text. *°ri°*]. 1438; Paṇhāv. 198 [text *°ri°*]; Nirayāv.; Erz.; Kk.; Mahāv. 29, 19), Mg. *palaśu* (Mṛcch. 157, 13), Ś *parasurāma* (Mahāv. 55, 12; 64, 20; Bālar. 36, 5. 6); AMg. *phusiya* = Pāli *phusita* = *pṛṣata* (§ 101; AMg. JM. *phāsuya* (Āyār. 2. 1, 1, 4. 6; 2, 1, 2, 1ff.; Paṇhāv. 497; Uvās.; ZDMG. 34, 291, 44; Kk.) = Pāli *phāsuka* is phonetically = *prāsuka*, which however, is certainly a false Sanskritism of the Pkt. word[1]; *aphāsuya* (Āyār. 2, 1, 1, 1. 3. 6. 11ff.); *bahuphāsuya* (Āyār. 2, 2, 3, 24ff.). *phāsuya* might belong to √*spṛś* = **sparśuka*[2] (§62). *phāḍei*, which Hc. 1, 198 equates as = *pāṭayati* = *sphāṭayati*. — Mk. fol. 18 has, moreover, *phalihi* = *paridhi* and *phalama* = *palama*, which probably ought to be *phaṇasa* = *paṇasa*. The first word may also be corrupt. In *rampaī*, *ramphaī* (hews; Hc. 4, 194) whether *pa* or *pha* is original cannot be said; cf. *raṁpa* "section" (H. 119. 120 with v. l. *rumpa*, *rumpha*[3]). — In AMg. more rarely in JM., medial *pa* in some words has become *bh* through *ph* (§200). So AMg. *kacchabha* = *kacchapa* (Jīv. 71. 290 478; Nāyādh. 510; Paṇhāv. 18. 119. 170; Paṇṇav. 47; Vivāgas. 49. 186; Vivāhap. 248. 483. 1033. 1285; Uttar. 1072), *kacchabhi* = *kacchapi* (lute, Paṇhāv. 512; Nāyādh. 1275. 1378; Rāyap. 88); AMg. *kabhalla* = *kapāla* (§ 91; Uvās. § 94; Antag. 27; Aṇuttar. 10 [text *°va°*, commentary *bha°*], beside *kavalla* (Sūyag. 275; Vivāhap. 270. 383), *kavalli* (Vivāgas. 141). *kavāla* (Āyār. 2, 1, 3, 4); to these add *kaphāḍa* (hollow; Deśīn. 2, 7); AMg. *thūbha* = *stūpa* (Āyār. 2, 1, 2, 3; 2, 3, 3, 1; Sūyag. 26; Paṇhāv. 31, 234, 286; Aṇuog. 387; Jīv. 546f.; Paṇṇav. 369; Rāyap. 153f. 195f.; Vivāhap. 560, 659. 1249; Ṭhāṇ 266). also JM. (Sagara 2, 7; T. 5, 11. 13. 16; 6, 13. 15; 7, 8; ZDMG. 34, 291, 47. 49); AMg. *thūbhiyā* = *stūpikā* (Āyār. 2, 10, 17; Jīv. 492; 495. 506; Nāyādh. Ovav.), and with reduplicated suffix *thūbiyāgā* = **stūpikākā* (Samav. 213; Paṇṇav. 116; Rāyap. 116; Nāyādh. § 122); AMg. *gothūbha* = *gostūpa* (Ṭhāṇ. 262. 268; Jīv. 715f. 718ff.; Samav. 106. 108. 113. 116f. 127. 143ff. 233 [on account of metre also *gothubha*]; Vivāhap. 198). The later form occurs in *thūha* (battlements of the palace; ant-hill; Deśīn. 5, 32). Cf. Leṇa-dialect *thuba* (Arch. Survey of W. India 5, 78, 10). — AMg. *vibhāsā* = *vipāśā* (Ṭhāṇ. 5. 44).

1. JACOBI, Kk. s. v. *phāsuya* analyses it into *pra*+*asu*+*ka*. Skt. *prāṣuka*, so for as I can see, is used by the Jainas only. — 2. HOERNLE, Uvās. s. v. Not rightly CHILDERS s. v. *phāsu*, who will equate it as=*spārha*. — 3. WEBER, ZDMG. 28, 378.

§ 209. More rarely takes place aspiration of the medials. For *ga* occurs *gha* in *ghāaṇa*=*gāyana* (singer; Hc. 2, 174; Deśīn. 2, 108; Triv. 1, 3, 105=BB. 3, 255); AMg. *siṅghāḍaga*=*śṛṅgāṭaka* (Uvās.; Nāẏādh.; Ovav.; Kappas.). *ghisaī* is not=*grasati*, but=**ghasáti* (§ 103. 482). —*ja* appears as *jha* in *jhaḍila* beside *jaḍila*=*jaṭila* (Hc. 1, 194); *jhattha* (annihilated; gone; Deśīn. 3, 61) from √*jas*; cf., however, also √*jhaṣ*. AMg. *jhūsittā* (absol.; Vivāgas. 270f.; Antag. 69 [*jhu°*]; Nāẏādh. 383. 388; Uvās.; Ovav.), *jhūsiẏa* [Ṭhāṇ. 56 [Commentary]. 187. 274; Nāẏādh. 382; Antag. 69 [*jhu°*]; Jīv. 289 [*jhu°*]), Vivāhap. 169. 173; 321; Uvās.; Ovav.), mostly explained with *kṣiṇa* or *kṣapita*[1], *jhūsaṇā* [Nāẏādh. 376, Vivāhap. 169. 173; Ṭhāṇ. 56. 187. 274; Uvās.; Ovav.), *parijhūsiẏa* (Ṭhāṇ. 202) belong to √*jhūṣ*, that is mentioned beside *jūṣ*, *yūṣ*. (Dhātupāṭha 17, 29)[2]. — *da* becomes *dha* in *dhippaï* beside *dippaï*=*dīpyate* (Hc. 1, 223); *kaüha* (Hc. 1, 225), dialectically *kakudha* (Triv. 1, 3, 105)=Pāli *kakudha*, a form parallel to *kakhubha*[3]. — *ba* appears as *bha* in AMg. *bhimbhisāra*=*bimbisāra* (Ṭhāṇ. 523; Ovav. [so to be read for *bhambha°*; cf. v.l.); M. *bhisiṇī*=*bisinī* (Vr. 2, 38; Hc. 1, 238; Kī. 2, 44; Pāiẏal. 149; H.; Sāhityad. 79, 1), Ś. has *bisiṇī* (Vṛṣabh. 39, 3; Mālav. 75, 8). According to Bh. on Vr. 2, 38 and Hc. 1, 238 aspiration does not occur in *bisa* and so M. *bisa* (Pāiẏal. 256; G. H.; Karp. 95, 12). Mk. fol. 18 teaches *bhisa*=*bisa* but quotes H. 8, where stands *bhisiṇisaṇḍaṁ*. AMg., like Pāli, has *bhisa* (Āẏār. 2, 1, 8, 10; Sūẏag. 813; Jīv. 290. 353; Paṇṇav. 35. 40; Rāẏap. 55). For *bṛsī* Bh. 1, 28 and Hc. 1, 28 teach *bisī*, the Pāiẏal, 215 *bhisī*. *bṛsikā* has aspiration : *bhisiā* (Deśīn. 6, 105), AMg. *bhisigā* (Sūẏag. 726), *bhisiẏā* (Āẏār. 2, 2, 3, 2; Nāẏādh. 1279. 1283; Ovav.). *bhukkaī* barks; (Hc. 4, 186), *bhukkiẏa* (barking; Pāiẏal. 182), *bhukkaṇa* (dog.; Deśīn. 6, 110); beside *bukkaī*=*garjati* (Hc. 4, 98), *ubbukkaī* (speaks; Hc. 4, 2), *bukkaṇa* (a crow; Deśīn. 6, 94; Pāiẏal. 44). On *bhaassaī*, *bhaappaī* etc. see § 212. — *bhibbhala*, *bhiṁbhala* (Hc. 2, 58 with translation), M. Ś. *bhĕṁbhala* (R. 6, 37; Cait. 38. 9 [text *bhemhaṇo*]), Ś. *bhĕṁbhaladā* (Cait. 44, 9), *bhĕṁbhalida* (Cait. 55, 13 [text *bhĕmha°*]) cannot, with Hc., be derived from *vibbhala*, *vĕbbhala*=*vihvala* (§ 332), since the aspiration of *v* would have given *ha* in the initial syllable as is shown by *vihala*. The words belong, with *bhaṁbhala* (block-head; later stubbornness, Deśīn. 6, 110) to √*bharbh hiṁsāyām* (Dhātupāṭha 15, 71). It is, therefore, to be written with anusvāra, as the gloss on Hc. 2, 58 tells us, and this is to be explained according to §74.

1. On the meaning see LEUMANN, Aup. S. s. v. *jhūsiya*; HOERNLE, Uvās. Translation, note 160. — 2. HOERNLE, Uvās. l. c. Overlooked by LEUMANN, Aup. S. s. v. *jhūs*, Incorrect is its association with AMg. *jhusira* (LEUMANN, WZKM. 3. 343). Cf. § 211. — 3. *kaüha* can naturally be derived from *kakubha* too. Cf. PISCHEL, BB. 3,257; v. BRADKE, ZDMG. 40, 660; WACKERNAGEL, Altind. Gram. § 156, b. Wrongly P. GOLDSCHMIDT, GN. 1874 p. 473.

§ 210. Aspiration of nasals and semivowels takes place in *ṇhāvia*=*nāpita* (Hc. 1, 230; Pāiẏal. 61), really=**snāpita*[1], as AMg. *ṇhāviẏā*=*snāpikā* (Vivāhap. 964) and other derivatives from *snā* (§ 313). Ś. Mg. have *ṇāvida*=*nāpita* (Hāsy. 28, 19; Mṛcch. 113, 10)[2]. — M. *pamhusaī*=**pras-*

mṛṣati[3] = *pramṛṣyati* (Hc. 4, 75. 184; G.), M, *pamhasijjāsu* = *pramṛṣyeḥ* (H. 348), M. *pamhusia* (G.), Ś. *pamhasida* (Mahāv. 65, 1; ed. Bomb. 1892, p. 161, 8 °*ppamusida*), M. JM. *pamhūṭṭha* (Hc. 3, 105 = R. 6, 12; Hc. 4,258; Āv. 7, 31), A. *pamhuṭṭhaü* (Hc. 4, 396, 3; so to be read), M. *pamhaṭṭha* (R.); according to Hc. 4, 158 *pamhusaī* is also = *pramuṣṇāti*, according to 4, 258 *pamhuṭṭha* also is = *pramuṣita*; A. *bhumhaḍi* = *bhūmi* (Hc. 4, 395, 6) with the suffix -*aḍa*, femin. -*aḍī* (Hc. 4, 429. 431). — AMg. *lhasuṇa* = *laśuna* (Āyār. 2, 7, 2, 6; Vivāhap. 609; Paṇṇav. 40; Jīyāk. 54), beside AMg. JM. *lasuṇa* (Āyār. 2, 1, 8, 13; Sūyag. 337 [text *lasaṇa*]; Āv. 40, 18); *lhikkaï* beside *likkaï* (hides oneself; Hc. 4, 55), a denominative from M. *lhikka* = **ślikna* (Hc. 4, 258; G.), cf. *śliku* "dependant" and § 566.

1. Weber, KB. 1, 505. — 2. Wrongly permits S. Goldschmidt, Prākṛtica p. 7, note 3, Skt. *nāpita* to be derived from Pkt. *ṇāvia*. The dropping off of the initial *s* depends upon the accent = *nāpitá*, like Vedic *paḍbhiḥ* from *spaś* (Pischel, Ved. Stud., 1, 239) — 3. Weber on Hāla[1] 358;[2] 348; ZDMG. 28, 3. 425.

§ 211. A simple initial sibilant of Skt. is sometimes aspirated in Pkt. *śha*, *ṣha sha*, then all become uniformly *cha*. The derivation of this *cha* from an original sound-group *kṣa* or *ska* is not at all certain. *chamī* = *śamī* (Hc. 1,265); AMg. *chāva* = Pāli *chāpa* = *śāba* (Hc. 1, 265; Ki. 2, 46; Sūyag. 511)[1], *chāvaa* = *śābaka* (Vr. 2, 41; Mk. fol. 18), but Mg. *śāvaka* (Mṛcch. 10, 6); AMg. *chivāḍi* = *śivāṭi* (2, 1, 1, 3.4); M. AMg. *chĕppa*, *chippa* = *śepa* (Deśīn. 3, 36; Pāiyal. 128; G. H.; Vivāgas. 69);[2] in addition to *chippālua* (tail; Deśīn. 3, 29); but Ś. *suṇasseha* = *śunaḥśepha* (Anarghar. 58, 5; 59, 12); *chippīra* (straw; Deśīn. 3, 28; Pāiyal. 142) beside *sippīra* (straw; H. 330), *sippa* (straw; Deśīn. 8, 28); in addition to this probably also *chippiṇḍi* (flour; Deśīn. 3, 37) and *chippāla* (a bullock accustomed to corn; Deśīn. 3, 28), *chui* (a female crane; Deśīn. 3, 30 = *śuciḥ*; *cha* = *ṣaṭ*, *chaṭṭha* = *ṣaṣṭha*, and *cha*°, *chal*° in numerous compounds (§ 240. 441)[3]; AMg. *chuhā* = *sudhā* (Hc. 1, 265; Deśīn. 2, 42; Vivāhap. 658f.), in addition to *chuhia* (plastered; Deśīn. 3, 30); AMg. *chirā* = *sirā* (Hc. 1, 266; Ṭhāṇ. 55; Jīv. 271; Samav. 227; Vivāhap. 89, 810), *chiratta* (Aṇuog. 12), beside *sirā* (Hc. 1, 266). On M. AMg. *piucchā*, M. *māucchā*, Ś. *māducchaa*, *māducchiā* = *pitṛṣvasā*, *mātṛṣvasā*, *mātṛṣvasṛka*, *mātṛṣvasṛkā* see § 148; on *chattavaṇṇa*, *chattivaṇṇa*, ostensibly = *saptaparṇa* see § 103. An initial sonant sibilant is presupposed by AMg. *jhusira* (full of holes; hole; Āyār. 2, 11, 4; 2, 15, 22 [p. 129, 1]; Paṇhāv. 137; Nāyādh. 752; Dasav. 620, 30; Uvās.), *ajhusira* (Jīyak. 55), *antŏjjhusira* (Nāyādh. 397) = **zuṣira* = *suṣira* or **zuṣira* = *śuṣira*[4]. Perhaps *jhalā* (mirage; Deśīn. 3, 53; Pāyial. 232) also belongs to *śal* (to prop up) = **żalā*, and *jharua* (midge; cricket; Deśīn. 3, 54), *jhāruā* (cricket; Deśīn. 3, 57), from √*śarv hiṁsāyām* (Dhātupāṭha 15, 76), *śaru* (an arrow).[5]

1. Pott, Die Zigeuner in Europa und Asien 2, 181 ff.; Pischel, GGA. 1875; p. 627 on Hc. 1, 265. Wrongly Miklosich, Beiträge zur Kenntniss der Zigeunermundarten I.II (Wien 1874) p. 26. — 2. Johansson (IF. 3, 213), with whom Wackernagel, (Altind. Gr. § 230b, p. 266) concurs, compares Latin cippus, Greek — 3. σ κ οῖ π ο s. 3—Hypotheses. on the original form of *ṣaṣ* in Hübschmann, KZ. 27, 106; Bartholomae, KZ. 29, 576. — 4. Leumann, WZKM. 3, 343. Whether *suṣira* or *śuṣira* is the more correct form of writing still remains to be probed into. Śrīharṣa, Dvirūpakośa 150 teaches *suṣi*, and *śuṣti*. Zachariae writes Śāśvata 185. against the best MSS. *suṣira*, but Hemacandra, Anekārthasaṁ-

graha 3, 607 *śuṣira*, is given as a derivative form from *śuṣ* (Uṇādigaṇasūtra 416). Connection with AMg. *jhüs* (§209) is out of consideration. Its derivation from *śuṣ* is quite uncertain. Wrongly Hoernle, Uvās, Translation, note 172. —Jiv. 273 has *susira*. — 5. The word can be connected to *kṣāraka* also.

§ 212. Aspiration appears in some cases in Pkt. in a syllable of the word different from that in Skt. In sporadic cases this may be explained by the fact that originally the initial and the final syllables of the word were aspirated, and dialectically the aspiration of a sound vanished indifferently. In most cases, however, there remains for us scarcely any assumption other than "turning-round of the breath." M. *iharā* from **itharatā*, **iharaā* = *itarathā* (§ 354); *uvaha*, M. *avaha* from **ubatha* for **ubhata*, deduced from M. *avahovāsaṁ*, *avahoāsaṁ* = AMg. *ubhaopāsaṁ* = **ubhataḥpārśvaṁ* (§ 123) *keḍhava* from **kaiṭhaba* for *kaiṭabha* (Vr. 2, 21. 29; Hc. 1, 196. 240; Kī. 2 11.27; Mk fol. 16. 17); *gaḍhaī* from **gaṭhati* = *ghaṭate* (He. 4, 112) beside the usual *ghadaī*; M. AMg JM. A. *ghĕppaī* from **ghṛpyati* = *gṛhyate* (§548), inf. M. *ghĕituṁ* = **ghṛptum* = *grahītum* (§ 574); absol. *ghĕttuāṇaṁ*, *ghĕttuāṇa* (§ 584) M. AMg. JM. *ghĕttūṇa* = **ghṛptvānam* = *grahitvā* (§586), particip. nec. *ghĕttavva* = **ghṛptavya* = *grahitavya* (§ 570), fut. JM. *ghĕcchāmo* (§534) belong to a root **ghṛp*, that is a root parallel to *gṛbh* (§ 107)[1]; *ḍhaṁkuṇa*, *ḍhĕṁkuṇa*, AMg. *ḍhiṁkuṇa* (bug) for **ḍaṁkhuṇa* belong to Marāṭhī *ḍaṁkhṇeṁ* (to bite, to sting), *ḍaṁkh* (bite, sting of a poisonous animal) = *daṁś* (§107. 267); M. *ḍhajjaī* (Jīvān. 97, 9), Ś. *ḍhajjadi* (Mālav. 28, 8; Mallikām. 90. 23 [text °*aī*]), *ḍhajjadu* (Veṇīs. 23, 18; so to be read; see v. l. 135), Mg. *ḍhayyadi* (Mṛcch. 9.25) for **ḍajjhadi*, M. AMg. JM. *ḍajjhaī* (§ 222) = *dahyate*, Ś. *viḍhajjia* = *vidahya* (Mahāv. 96, 11), *ḍhajjanta-* (Mālatīm. 79, 2; so to be read with the v. l. and ed. Madras. 67, 6; Rukmiṇīp. 20, 7; 35, 9; Mallikām. 57, 7; 133, 13); cf. v. l. *ḍhajjaï* on H. 373; M. *dihi* from **dṛthi* = *dhṛti* (Hc. 2, 131; Sāhityad. 219, 14); M. *dhūā*, AMg. JM. *dhūyā*, Ś. Mg. *dhūdā* = **dhuktā* = *duhitā* (§ 65; 392); JŚ. Ś. Mg. A. *bahiṇi* for **baghiṇi* = *bhaginī* (Hc. 2, 126; Pāiyal. 252; Kattig. 401, 338; Mālatīm. 31, 5; Mg. Mṛcch. 11, 9; 113, 19; 138, 25; 140, 1. 7; A Hc. 4, 351), mostly with *kaḥ svārthe*, Ś. *bahiṇiā* = *bhaginikā* (Mṛcch. 94, 4; 328, 5; Śak. 15, 4; 85, 4. 6; Mālatīm. 130, 3; Mahāv. 118, 18; 119, 3; Ratn. 324, 23; 327, 7. 9. 13; 328, 20; Prab. 68, 7; Cait. 88, 12; 92, 15; Karp. 33, 4, 7; 34, 3; 35, 2 etc.), A. *bahiṇuĕ* (Hc. 4, 422, 14). From *bṛhaspati* are found AMg. *bahassaī*, *bihassaī*, Ś. *bahappadi*, *bahappaī*, *bihapphadi* (§ 53). The grammarians mention these and a number of other forms : *bahassaī*, *bihassaï*, *buhassaī* (C. 2. 5. p 43; Hc. 2, 69. 137; Sr. fol. 36); *bahappaī*, *bihappaī*, *buhappaī* (C. 2, 5 p. 43; Hc. 2, 53, 137; Sr. fol. 36); *bahappaī*, *bihapphaī*, *buhapphaī* (C. 2, 5 p. 43; Hc. 1, 138; 2, 53, 69. 137); Mg. *buhaspadi* (Hc. 4, 289), *biha*ś*padī* (Namisādhu on Rudraṭa Kāvyālaṁkāra 2, 12); further with aspirated initial : *bhaassaï* (C. 2. 5 p. 43; Hc. 2, 69. 137; Sr. fol. 36), *bhiassaī*, *bhuassaī* (C. 2, 5 p. 43); *bhaappaï* (C. 2, 5 p. 43; Hc. 2, 137; Mk. fol. 38; Prākṛtamañjarī in Pischel. De gr. Prācr. p. 15; Sr. fol. 36), *bhiappaī*, *bhuappaī* (C. 2, 5 p. 43); *bhaapphaï* (Vr. 4, 30; C. 2, 5 p. 43; Hc. 2, 69. 137; K.. 2, 117; Sr. fol. 36), *bhiapphai*, *bhuapphaī* (C. 2, 5 p. 43)[2].

1. PISCHEL, KB. 8. 148f. Wrongly P. GOLDSCHMIDT, GN. 1874, p. 512; WEBER, IS. 14, 73, note 2; JACOBI, KZ. 28,253f.; JOHANSSON, KZ. 32,447. Cf. S. GOLDSCHMIDT, ZDMG. 29, 493; WEBER on Hāla 286. — 2. PISCHEL on Hc. 1, 138. The forms with initial *h* in lieu of *bh* in Triv., Sr. and in the Prākṛtamañjarī are orthographical errors of the Dravidian manuscripts. The edition of Triv. has *bh*.

§ 213. Loss of aspiration occurs in AMg. JM. Ś. *saṅkalā* = *śṛṅkhalā* (Paṇhāv. 183; Jīv. 503; Ṛṣabhap. 33; Laṭakam. 18, 4). AMg. *saṅkala* = *śṛṅkhala* (n); Hc. 1, 189; Paṇhāv. 536), AMg. JM. *saṅkaliyā* = *śṛṅkhalikā* (Sūyag 269; Āv. 14, 17), JM. *saṅkaliya* = *śṛṅkhalita* (Āv. 13, 28). So also the modern Indian languages[1]. But M. Ś. *saṅkhalā* (G.; Mṛcch. 41, 10); Ś *ussaṅkhalaa* (Mṛcch. 151, 17); M. Ś. *visaṅkhala* (R.; Mālatīm. 291, 2); Mg. *śaṅkhalā* (Mṛcch. 167, 6); M. Ś. *sinkhalā* (R.; Acyutaś. 41; Mālatīm. 129, 1; Priyad. 4, 5; Mallikām. 141, 7; Anarghar. 265, 2; 308, 9; Vṛṣabh. 38, 10; Viddhaś. 84, 9 [text °*sa*°]; 85, 3. 8)[2]. — AMg. *ḍhaṅka* = Pāli *dhaṅka* = Skt. *dhvāṅkṣa* for **ḍhaṅkha* (crow; crane; vulture; Deśīn. 4, 13; Pāiyal. 44; Sūyag. 437 508; Uttar. 593), *ḍhiṅka*, (Paṇhāv. 24), which as well as *ḍhĕṅkī* for *ḍhiṅkī* female crane; Deśīn. 4, 15), presupposes an accentuation **dhvāṅkṣá*. In the sense of a particular plant, of which the bees are fond (cf. BÖHTLNGK s.v. *dhvāṅkṣa*), occurs in M. *ḍhaṅkha* (H. 755)[3]— AMg. *bihaṇa* = *bhiṣaṇa* (Paṇhāv. 78), *bihaṇaga* = *bhiṣaṇaka* (Paṇhāv. 48. 49. 167. 177), but M. Ś. *bhisaṇa* (G. R. Vikr. 28. 8; Mahāv. 12, 1; Bālar 54, 7; Anarghar. 58, 5; Mallikām. 82, 18; 141, 9), Ś. *adibhisaṇa* (Mallikām. 183, 3). To *bhiṣ* belong also *bihai*, *biheī* (§ 501). Cf § 263 *paṇguraṇa* (clock; overcoat; Hc. 1, 175; Triv. 1, 3, 105) against Marāṭhī *pāṁgharūṇ pāṁgharṇeṁ*, *pāṁghurṇeṁ*[4]. AMg. *saṇḍeya* = * *ṣāṇḍheya* (capon; Ovav. §1) is a false reading for *saṇḍheya*, as in Skt. too *ṣaṇḍa* and *ṣaṇḍha* are interchanged in manuscripts. On secondary *kha*, *cca*, *tta*, *ppa* for *kkha*, *ccha*, *tthha*, *ppha* see § 301 ff.

1. PISCHEL on Hc. 1, 189. — 2. Cf. §54. — 3. In the stanza that was not intelligible to WEBER, *dhaṅkharaseso* = *dhvāṅkṣarasaiṣaḥ*, and the comma after *mukho* are to be erased. — 4. PISCHEL, BB. 3. 247ff.

§ 214. WEBER[1] has assumed that in Pkt. "secondary aspiration, respecting *h* direct" occurs through the influence of the preceding aspirates. The examples given by him *bhāraha*, *khila* in *dharaṇikhila*, *phalaha* have found their correct explanation in § 206. 207. On the other hand, WACKERNAGEL[2] has attributed to Pkt. a "want of tendency towards succession of two aspirates." His only example is *majjhaṇṇa*, which he wrongly equates as = *madhyāhna*, while it is = *madhyaṁdina* (§ 148). In any case, the example would prove otherwise nothing, as *majjhaṇha* is quite common (§ 330). The reference to E. KUHN, Beiträge p. 41 too proves nothing. For Pāli *majjhatta* = *madhyastha*, Pkt. says, in all the dialects in which the word can be located, M. AMg. JM. JŚ. Ś. *majjhattha* (H.R.; Āyār. 1, 7, 8, 5; Sūyag. 97; Nāyādh. 1274; T. 5, 16; Ṛṣabh. 49; Kk. 275, 45; Pav. 389, 3; Mṛcch. 68, 21; Bālar. 238, 8; Karṇas. 31, 10; Mallikām. 250. 2. 3), for Pāli *majjhattatā*, Ś. *majjhatthadā* (Śak. 27, 5; Mālav. 39, 9; Adbhutad. 4, 10). That even in Pāli the reason for the loss of aspiration is not lack of the tendency hypothesised by WACKERNAGEL, is shown by Pāli *indapatta* = *indraprastha*, *maṭṭa* beside *maṭṭha* = *mṛṣṭa*, *vaṭṭa* = *vṛṣṭa*, *atta* = *asta*, *bhaddamutta* = *bhadramusta* etc. (E. KUHN, Beiträge p. 41. 53). Pkt. *samatta* beside *samattha* = *samasta* (§307) From cases, like M. *takkhaṇukkhaaharihatthukkhittabhĕmbhalā* (R. 6, 37), *khandhukkheva* (G. 1049), AMg. *majjhabhāgattha* (Nāy̆ādh. § 92), JM *hatthikkhandha* (Āv. 25, 39), JŚ. *mohakkhohavihūṇo* (Pav. 380, 7), Ś. *phalihatthambha* (Mālav. 63, 1), words, like *khambha*, *khuhā*, *jhajjhara*, *jhaṁkhaī* *jhujjhaï*, *bhippha*, *bhibbhala*, and the numberless examples, like *ghaṭṭha*, *bhaiṭha* *hattha*,[3] *hittha*, *ḍajjhihii*, *duhihii bujjhihii* etc. it results that Pkt. does not have the disinclination attributed to it, and cannot have it according to its phonetic law. On the other hand, some of the dialects, particularly AMg., have special liking for succession of two aspirates, as in *khiṅkhiṇī*, *khahacara*, *thūbha*, *kacchabha* (§ 206. 208). That the examples adduced by JACOBI cannot be put forward in defence of a disinclination for two successive aspirates is shown in § 312 ff.

1. Bhag. 1, 411. — 2. KZ. 33. 575 f.; Altind. Gr. § 105, note. — 3. With WACKERNAGEL, I include here, among the aspirates, *ha* also, for the sake of brevity. — 4. Erz. XXXII, note 3; XXXIII, note 2.

§ 215. Dialectically guttarals interchange with labials (§ 230. 231 266.286). In place of the palatals dialectically occur dentals as well *ta* for *ca* and *da* for *ja*. AMg. *teicchā* = **cekitsā* = *cikitsā* (Āy̆ār. 1, 2, 5, 6; 1, 8, 4, 1; 2, 13, 22; Kappas. S. § 49), *tigicchā* (Ṭhāṇ. 313; Paṇhāv. 356; Nāy̆ādh 603. 605; Uttar. 106), *tigicchay̆a*, *tigicchaga* = *cikitsaka* (Ṭhāṇ. 313; Nāy̆adh. 603. 605; Uttar. 620), *tigicchaï*, *tigicchiy̆a* (§ 555), *vitigicchā* = *vicikitsā* (Ṭhāṇ. 191; Āy̆ār. 2, 1, 3, 5; Sūy̆ag. 189. 401, 445. 514. 533; Uttar. 468ff.), *vitigiṁchā*, *vitigiṁchaï*, *vitigiṁchiy̆a* (§ 74. 555), *vitigicchāmi* (Ṭhāṇ. 245), *nivvitigiccha* (Sūy̆ag. 771; Uttar. 811; Vivāhap. 183; Ovav. § 124). — AMg. *digicchantadigiṁchā* = *jighatsat*, *jighatsā*, AMg. JM. *dugaṁchā*, *duguṁchā*, AMg. *duguṁchaṇa*, *dugaṁchaṇijja*, *dogaṁchi-*, *doguṁchi-*, *paḍidugaṁchi-*, *duguṁchaï*, *duguṁchamāṇa*, *dugoṁchamāṇa*, *adugucchiy̆a* (§ 74. 555), beside the usual *jugucchā* (Bh. 3, 40), *juucchaï*, *jugucchaï* etc. (§ 555). — AMg. *dosiṇā* = *jyotsnā* (Triv. 1, 3, 105 = BB. 3. 250; Ṭhāṇ. 95; Paṇhāv. 533; Sūriy̆ap. in the index 5, 2, 574. 577), *dosiṇābhā* (Nāy̆ādh. 1523); *dosiṇi* = *jyautsni* (Deśīn. 5, 50), Ś. *baṇadosiṇi* = *vaṇajyautsni* (Śak. 12, 13); *dosāṇia* (bright; clear; Deśīn. 5. 51). — In secondary *ja*, originating from *ya* according to § 252, the change could have occurred in *dŏgga* (pair; Deśīn. 5, 49; Triv. 1. 3, 105 = BB. 3, 241), when it is to be equated as = *yugma*. It can, however, be carried over also to AMg. JM. *duga*, *dvika* (§ 451)[1].

1. AMg. *pādīṇaṁ*...*prācīnam* (Āy̆ār. 2, 1, 9, 1) is either a false reading or a printing mistake for *pāiṇaṁ*, as it rightly stands in Āy̆ār. 1. 1, 5, 2. 3; 2. 2. 2, 8). The ed. Calc. has *pāiṇaṁ*. Cf. WEBER, Bhag. 1, 413; IS. 14, 255f.; E. MÜLLER; Beiträge p. 25; PISCHEL, BB. 3. 241. 250; 6. 100f.

§ 216. Like dentals for palatals (§ 215), palatals have conversely taken the place of dentals in a number of cases. So *cacchaï* from **tyakṣati* beside *tacchaï* = *takṣati* (Hc. 4, 194). M. AMg. JM. *ciṭṭhaï*, Ś. A. *ciṭṭhadi*, Mg. *ciṣṭhadi* = *tiṣṭhati* from *sthā* (§ 483). — *cuccha* beside *tuccha* (Hc. 1, 204), according to Hc. also with an aspirated initial sound *chuccha*. — A. *vijjajjhara* = *vidyādhara* (Vikr. 59, 5). On AMg. *ciy̆atta* = *tyakta*, *ciccā*, *cĕccā* = *tyaktvā* see § 280.

§ 217. According to Pṛthvīdhara on Mṛcch. 9, 22 (p. 240) ed. STENZLER = 26, 8 (p. 500), ed. GOḌABOLE, in the dialect of Śakāra, there was pronounced a weak *ya* before *ca*, which did not make position : *yciṣṭha* = *tiṣṭha*. According to Mk. fol. 75, 85 this *ya* appeared in Mg. and in Vrācaḍa A. also before *ja*: M. *ycilaṁ* = *ciram*; *yjāā* = *jāyā*; *ycalaā* = *caraka*; A. *ycalaï* = *calati*, *yjalaï* = *jvalati* (§ 24. 28). Perhaps the rules given for Mg., Vr. 11, 5 and Kī. 5, 88, relate to this. On account of bad transmission of the text, the meaning cannot be determined with certainty. Cf. COWELL, Vr. p. 179, note 1; LASSEN, Inst. p. 393. 396 §146. 1.

§ 218. Dentals of Skt. are represented often by cerebrals in Pkt. The reverse transformation in some dialects (§ 225) proves that it was a matter of dialectically differing pronunciation and that the assumption of some other influence is erroneous. Initially *ṭa* appears for *ta* in *ṭagara* = *tagara* (Hc. 1, 205); *ṭūvara* = *tūbara* (Hc. 1,205); *ṭimbaru* = *tumburu* (Deśīn. 4, 3), *ṭimbaruẏa* = *tumburuka* (Pāiẏal. 258) to which should belong also *ṭimburiṇī* (Śukasaptati 122, 15). Cf. § 124. Medially *ṭa* appears for *ta* in CP. *paṭimā* = *pratimā* (Hc. 4, 325), for which the other dialects, according to § 198, say *paḍimā*. The words, in which *ḍa* appears for *ta* have been collected in the gaṇa *pratyādi* by Hc. 1, 206; Kī. 2, 29 and Mk. fol. 15. In Hc. it is an ākṛtigaṇa. Kī. mentions only *pratibaddha*, *prābhṛta*, *vetasa*, *patākā* and *garta*; Mk. puts together seven words in a verse : *prati*, *vetasa*, *patākā*, *haritaki*, *vyāpṛta*, *mṛtaka*, *prākṛta* for which *prābhṛta* is to be read. Change of *ta* to *ḍa* in *prati* is especially frequent in all the dialects, except P. CP. So M. AMg. JM. Ḍh. *paḍimā* = *pratimā* (C. 3, 12 p. 49; Hc. 1, 206; Pāiẏal. 217; G.H.R.; Ṭhāṇ. 266; Āẏār. 2, 2, 3, 18ff.; 2,6,1, 4ff.; 2,7,2, 8ff.; 2,8,2, ff;Uvās.; Ovav.; Erz.; Mṛcch. 30, 11. 16. 17); AMg. JM. JŚ. *paḍipuṇṇa* = *pratipūrṇa* (Nāẏādh. 449. 500; Uvās.; Kappas.; Erz.; Pav. 387. 13); M. Ś. Mg. *paḍivaaṇa* = *prativacana* (H. R.; Mṛcch. 37, 8; Vikr. 18, 11; Mg. Mṛcch. 32, 19); M. JM. Ś. *paḍivakkha* = *pratipakṣa* (Pāiẏal. 35; G.H.R.; Erz.; Vikr. 23. 7; Prab. 7, 9; 12, 5); M. AMg. Ś. *paḍibaddha* = *pratibaddha* (G.H.R.; Mṛcch. 41, 3; 68. 20. 25; Uvās.); JŚ. *appaḍibaddha* (Pav. 387, 25). Ś. *paḍibandhedha* (Śak. 113, 12), AMg. *paḍibandhaṇa* (Dasav. 643, 16); M. A. *paḍihāi*, Ś. *paḍihādi*, *paḍihāadi* = *pratibhāti* (§ 487), and so very many others. Cf. § 163. 220. In P. CP., according to Hc. 4, 307; Namisādhu on Rudrata, Kāvyālaṁkāra 2, 12, the change does not take place : *patibimba* (Hc. 4, 326); an exception is *paṭimā* (Hc. 4, 325). Other examples are M. AMg. JM. A. *paḍaï* = *patati* (Vr. 8 51; Hc. 4, 219; G.H.R.; Niraẏāv. § 11; Naẏādh. 1394; Sagara 3, 10; Hc. 4, 422, 4. 18), Mg. *paḍadi* (Mṛcch. 31, 10; 158, 7.9, 169, 5); M. AMg. *paḍaü* = *patatu* (H.; Āẏār. 2, 4, 1, 12), JM. *paḍāmo* = *patāmaḥ* (Āv. 8, 50). Mg. *paḍemi* (Mṛcch. 127, 12), M.A. *paḍia* = *patita* (G.H.R.; Hc. 4, 337). JM. *paḍiẏa* (Erz.), Ś. Mg. *paḍida* (Mṛcch. 54, 3; 81, 9; 95, 11; 120, 7; Mudrār. 104, 8; Ratn. 314, 27; Mṛcch. 10, 1; 133, 10; 169, 5; 170, 16), Ś. *ṇivaḍida* = *nipatita* (Śak. 35, 10; 77, 11), AMg. *pavaḍijja* = *prapatet*, *pavaḍemāṇa* = *prapatamāna* (Āẏār. 2, 2, 1, 7; 2, 2, 3, 2. 23; 2, 3, 2, 15), and so throughout in the root *pat* and derivatives from it, like M. JM. Mg. *paḍaṇa* = *patana* (G.H.R.; Erz.; Mṛcch. 30, 23), but CP. *nipatanti* (Hc. 4, 326).

— M. Ś. *paḍāā* = *patākā* (Grr.; G.R.; Mṛcch. 68, 17), AMg. JM. *paḍāgā* (Ṭhāṇ. 284; Jīv. 483; Naẏādh. § 122; p. 1318; Paṇhāv. 160; Rāẏap. 59. 68. 70; Vivāhap. 276. 833; Niraẏāv.; Ovav.; Kappas.; Erz.); JM. *paḍāẏā* (Pāiẏal. 68; Erz.); AMg. *sapaḍāga* (Rāẏap. 128), but P. *patākā* (Hc. 4, 307). — *pahuḍi* = *prabhṛti* (Hc. 1. 206), but Ś. Mg. *pahudi* (Mṛcch. 23, 15. 23; 73, 10; Śak. 52, 5; 85, 7; Vikr. 15. 8. 9; 45. 20; Mudrār. 253, 8; Prab. 9, 5; 28, 17; Mg. Mṛcch. 13, 25; 21, 11; 133, 21; Veṇīs. 35. 5), Ś. *pahudia* = *prabhṛtika* (Mṛcch. 71, 1). — AMg. JM. *pāhuḍa* = *prābhṛta* (Grr.; Pāiẏal. 236; Āẏār. 2, 2. 2, 10ff.; Vivāgas. 128. 132; Nāẏādh. 439. 539. 540. 774ff. 1375f. 1431, Rāẏap. 226. Aṇuog. 558; Erz.), *pāhuḍiẏā* = *prābhṛtikā* (Āẏār. 2, 2, 3, 1; Aṇuog. 558). — M. AMg. JM. Ś. Mg. D. *vāvaḍa* = *vyāpṛta* (Hc.; Mk.; H.R.; Uttar. 496; Erz.; Kk.; Mṛcch. 4, 24; 29, 21; 104, 8). JM. also *vāula* (Kk.), AMg. *vāuẏa* (Ovav.), Ś. *vāvuḍa* (Mālav. 72, 7), *vāvuḍadā* = *vyāpṛtatā* (Mṛcch. 325, 19). — M. *veḍisa*, but P. *vetasa*, Ś. *vedasa* = *vetasa* (§ 101). — *haraḍaī* = *harītakī* (§ 120).

§ 219. Cerebralization has a wider range in AMg., partly in JM. too (Hc. 1, 206), than in the other dialects. It appears especially in these dialects in the past passive participles of certain roots in *ṛ*. So : AMg. *kaḍa* = *kṛta*, *akaḍa* = *akṛta*, *dukkaḍa* = *duṣkṛta*, *sukaḍa* = *sukṛta*, *vigaḍa*, *viẏaḍa* = *vikṛta*, *pagaḍa* = *prakṛta*, *purekaḍa* = *puraskṛta*, *ahākaḍa* = *yathākṛta*, beside M.A. *kaa*, AMg. JM. *kaẏa*, PG.P. *kata*, JŚ. Ś. Mg. *kada*, Ś. Mg. A. *kida*, A. *akia* (§49; cf. § 306). — AMg. *patthaḍa* = *prastṛta* (Ṭhāṇ. 197), *vitthaḍa* = *vistṛta* (Jīv. 253; Ovav. § 56), *saṁthaḍa* = *saṁstṛta* (Āẏār. 2, 1, 3, 9; 2, 1, 6, 1), *asaṁthaḍa* (Āẏār. 2, 4, 2, 14), *ahāsaṁthaḍa* = *yathāsaṁstṛta* (Āẏār. 2, 7, 2, 14). — AMg. *maḍa* = *mṛta* (Vivāhap. 13; Uttar. 985; Jīv. 255; Kappas.), AMg. JM. *maḍaẏa* = *mṛtaka* (Hc. 1, 206; Pāiẏal. 158; Āẏār. 2, 10, 17; Āv. 24, 4), beside AMg. JM. *maẏa* (Vivāhap. 16. 1041. 1042; Dvār. 503, 5, 7; 504, 4, 17), JM. *muẏa* (Āv. 28, 8), (G.), M. *maa* (G.), *mua* (H.R.), JŚ. *mada* (Pav. 387, 18), Ś. *muda* (Mṛcch. 72, 20; Karp. 22, 9). — *vuḍa* = *vṛta* in AMg. *abhinivvuḍa* = *abhinirvṛta* (Sūẏag. 110. 117 [°*ṇi*°). 371), *nivvuḍa* = *nirvṛta* (Āẏār. 1, 4, 3, 3; Sūẏag. 550), *pāuḍa* = *prāvṛta* (Āẏār. 1, 2, 2, 1; Sūẏag. 134. 170), *parinivvuḍa* = *parinirvṛta* (Kappas.) beside *ẏa* (Ovav.; Kappas.), *parivuḍa* *parivṛta* (Ovav.), *saṁparivuḍa* = *saṁparivṛta* (Vivāhap. 186. 830; Nāẏādh. §4. 130; p. 431. 574. 724. 784. 1068. 1074. 1273. 1290. 1327; Uvās.; Ovav.; Kappas.), *saṁvuḍa* = *saṁvṛta* (Āẏār. 1, 8, 3, 13; 2, 1, 9, 1; Sūẏag. 81. 117. 144; Vivāhap. 942; Kappas.), *asaṁvuḍa* (Sūẏag. 108. 115), *susaṁvuḍa* (Sūẏag. 141), beside M. *ṇivvua*, JM. *nivvuẏa*, Ś. *ṇivvuda* (§ 51), M. *pāua* (H.), Ḍh. S. *pāvuda* (Mṛcch. 34, 12; 72, 2. 9), Ś. *avāvuda* = *apāvṛta* (Mṛcch. 16, 3. 5. 9), Ś. D. *parivuda* = *parivṛta* (Mṛcch. 6, 6; 106, 1), Ś. *saṁvuda* (Mṛcch. 15, 7), AMg. *saṁvuẏa* (Ovav.). — AMg. JM. *haḍa* = *hṛta* (Āẏār. 2, 2, 2, 4; Āv. 44, 7); AMg. *avahaḍa* = *apahṛta* (Hc. 1, 206), *abhihaḍa* (Āẏār. 1, 7, 1, 1. 2; 2, 1, 11; 2, 2, 1, 2), *āhaḍa* (Āẏār. 1, 7, 5, 4; 2, 1, 9, 2; Sūẏag. 382), *asamāhaḍa* (Āẏār. 2, 1, 3, 5), *nihaḍa* = *nirhṛta* (Āẏār. 2, 1, 1, 11; 2, 9, 7; 2, 10. 2. 4), beside M. *hia* = *hṛta* (H.R.), Ś. *avahada* = *apahṛta* (Mṛcch. 52, 13. 21; 53, 2. 21; 55, 16; 74, 12; 78, 2; 89, 9; 147, 17 154, 13; Vikr. 41, 12). According to Vr. 11, 15 cerebralization occurs also in Mg. in *kaḍa* =

kṛta, maḍa = *mṛta, gaḍa* = *gata*. So are found Mg. *kaḍa* (Mṛcch. 17, 8; 32, 5; 127, 23. 24; 132, 10. 11. 12; 149, 24; 154, 20; 164. 10); *maḍa* (Mṛcch. 119, 15), *maḍaa* (Caṇḍak. 63. 11), *gaḍa* (Mṛcch. 10.6; 13, 8; 20, 16; 36, 13), beside *kada, kida* (§ 49), *gada* (Mṛcch. 39, 20; 116, 7; 128. 2; 171, 11; (Prab. 50. 6; Caṇḍak. 70, 14; Veṇīs. 34, 9 etc.). *kaḍa* occurs also in PG. 7, 51 cf. EI. 2, 485) beside *adhikate* = *adhikṛtān* (5, 5). *maḍa* is treated as provincial in Deśīn. 6, 141. On *kaḷa, maḷa* see § 244. Other examples of cerebralization from AMg. are : *dukkaḍi-* = *duṣkṛtin* (Sūẏag. 295); *uvakkhaḍei* = **upaskṛtayati*, *uvakkhaḍāvei* (§ 559); *purĕkkhaḍa* = *puraskṛta* (Paṇṇav. 796ff.); *niẏaḍi* = *nikṛtin* (Dasav. 635. 7). *niẏaḍilla* = *nikṛtimat* (Uttar. 990), *niẏaḍillaẏā* = *nikṛtimattā* (Ṭhāṇ. 338; Vivāhap. 687; Ovav.); *saṁkhaḍi* = *saṁskṛti* (Āẏār. 1, 8, 1, 18), *pagaḍi* = *prakṛti* (Ṭhāṇ. 216; Vivāhap. 74), JŚ. *paẏaḍi* (Kattig. 399, 308), beside *pagaī* (Ovav.; Kappas.), M. *paaī* (H.R.), Ś. *païdi* (Śak. 35, 8; 66, 8; 117, 11; 153, 14; Vikr. 73, 12; 75, 4), *vaḍiṁsa, vaḍiṁsaga, vaḍiṁsaẏa* = *avataṁsa, avataṁsaka* (§ 103); *veẏāvaḍiẏa* beside *veẏāvacca* = *vaiẏāpṛtya* (LEUMANN, Ovav. s. v. *veẏāvacca*). Doubtful is the meaning of Mg. *viḍatta, ppaḍavadi* (Mṛcch. 165, 11). Lalitadīkṣita's interpretation as *vitapta, pratapati* in GOḌABOLE p. 448 is forced. Presumably we should read : *viḍhatte ceḍe kiṁ ṇa ppalavadi* = *vidaghaścetaḥ kiṁ na pralapati*. On *viḍhatta* cf. M. *ḍhajjaī*, Ś. *ḍhajjadi, viḍhajjia*, Mg. *ḍhayyadi* (§ 212), on *ppalavadi*, the v.l. *ppatabadi* in GOḌABOLE.

§ 220. In some cases cerebralization does not take place as a rule : M. AMg. JM. Ś. *païṇṇā* = *pratijñā* (Hc. 1, 206; G.R.; Ovav.; Kappas.; Erz.; Kk.; Mālav. 66, 18; 69, 5), beside AMg. *apaḍinna* = *apratijña* (Āẏār. 1, 8, 1, 19. 22; 1, 8, 2, 5. 11. 16; 1, 8, 3, 9. 12. 14; 1, 8, 4, 6. 7. 14); AMg. JM. *païṭṭhāṇa* = *pratiṣṭhāna* (Ṭhāṇ. 513; Nāẏādh. 623; Vivāhap. 418, 447; Ovav.; Kappas.; Erz.), also in the proper name of the town JM. Ś. *païṭṭhāṇa* (Āv. 21, 1; Kk. 269, 44 [so to be read in place of *paẏa*°); Vikr. 23, 14; 73, 11 [so to be read with all MSS (p. 255), the Indian editions and the Dravidian recension]), as also in the Leṇa-dialect *païṭhāṇa* beside *patiṭhāṇa* (Arch. Survey of Western India 5, 76, 8); AMg. *païṭṭhā* = *pratiṣṭhā* (Hc. 1, 206); AMg. JM. *païṭṭhiẏa* = *pratiṣṭhita* (Uvās.; Ovav., Kappas.; Erz.; Kk.), beside M. *paḍiṭṭhia* (G.R.), AMg. *paḍiṭṭhiẏa* (Ovav.); AMg. *païṭṭhāvaẏa* = = **pratiṣṭhāpaka* (Ovav.), JM. *païṭṭhāviẏa* = *pratiṣṭhāpita* (T. 7, 2; Erz.), beside M. *paḍiṭṭhāvia* (R.), Ś. *paḍiṭṭhāvehi* = *pratiṣṭhāpaya* (Ratn. 295, 26); JM. *païdiṇaṁ* = *pratidinam* (Erz.; Kk.), *païdiẏahaṁ* = *pratidivasam* (Kk.), *païsamaẏaṁ* = *pratisamayam* (Hc. 1, 206), *païvarisaṁ* = *prativarṣam* (7 1); also in idependently standing *prati*, JM. *paï* (Kk.), Ś. *padi* (Cait. 88, 12; 90, 4. 5); *paiva* = *pratipa* (Hc. 1, 206; Pāiẏal. 154), beside Mg. *vippadiva* = *vipratipa* (Mṛcch. 29, 23), Ḍh. *vippadiva* (Mṛcch. 30, 11. 12; cf. GOḌABOLE p. 86, 1.2); M. JM. *sampaï* = *sāmprati* (Hc. 1, 206; Pāiẏal. 67; G.R.; Erz.; Kk.; Ṛṣabhap.), JM. *sampaẏaṁ* = *sāmpratam* (Pāiẏal. 67; Erz., Kk.) beside Ś. Ḍh. *sampadaṁ* (e.g. Ś. Mṛcch. 6, 22; 17, 19; 18, 23; 36, 9; 42, 9; Śak. 25 2; 30.4; 67, 12; Vikr. 26, 12; 27, 21; 46, 15; Ḍh. Mṛcch. 30, 4; 31, 9; 32, 8), Mg *śampadaṁ* (e.g. Mṛcch. 16, 20; 32, 2. 4. 5; 38, 19; 99, 11; 119, 11; 53, 22; Prab. 58, 17).

§ 221. *tha*, through *ṭha*, becomes *ḍha* initially in M. *ḍhakkaï*, *ḍhakkei* (covers; disguises; closes; Hc. 4, 21; H.), JM. *ḍhakkemi* (T. 7, 9), *ḍhakkeūṇa* (Erz.; Dvār. 499, 8), Ś. *ḍhakkehi* (Mṛcch. 36, 3); Mg. *ḍhakkida*, *ḍhakkedha* (Mṛcch. 79, 17; 164, 14), also with infixed nasal *ḍhaṁkiśśaṁ* (Prab. 58, 10; so to be read; BROCKHAUS *ṭaṅkissaṁ*, ed. Bomb. P. *ḍhaṁkissaṁ*, (ed. M. *thagaïssaṁ* = Pāli *thaketi*[1], *ḍhaṅkaṇī* (cover; Deśīn. 4, 14); *ḍhakka* (covetous; Erz.); cf. § 309. Medially in M. *kaḍhaï* = *kvathati* (Vr. 8, 39; Hc. 4, 119. 220; Kī. 4. 46), *kaḍhamāṇa* (G.), *kaḍḍhasi*, *kaḍḍhasu* (H. 401; so to be read), *kaḍhia* (Karp. 40, 2), Ś. *kaḍhiamāṇa* (Anarghar. 270, 1; text °*ijja*°), *kaḍhida* (Karp. 82, 7), AMg. *sukaḍhiya* (Jīv. 823. 860f.); AMg. *gaḍhiya* = *grathita* (Āyār. 1, 2, 3, 5. 4, 2. 5, 4 [text °*ḍḍh*°]; 1, 4, 4, 2; 1, 6, 5, 5; 1, 8, 1, 9; 2, 1, 8, 2; Sūyag. 84, 601. 699. 751; Ṭhāṇ. 156; Vivāhap. 450. 1129; Nāyādh. 433. 606; Vivāgas. [text °*ḍḍh*°]. 92), *agaḍhiya* (Āyār. 2, 1, 5, 5; Paṇhāv. 359. 370); *nisiḍha* beside *nisiha* = *niśitha* (Hc. 1, 216). In Ś. occurs *ṇisiḍha* (Mallikām. 201, 6; 209, 18) as well as *ṇisiha* (Kāleyak. 26, 2) falsely for *ṇisidha*. AMg. *nijjūḍha* = *niryūtha* (expelled; singled out; Nāyādh. 323; Vivāhap. 134; Dasav. 631. 11; 644, 12. 19, 21. 22. 24), *aṇijjūḍha* (Vivāhap. 134), beside M. AMg. JM. A. *jūha* = *yūtha* (G.H.R.; Nāyādh.; Āv. 42,7; Erz.; Vikr. 56, 21), Ś. *jūdha* (Caṇḍak. 17, 12). M. *jūhiā* = *yūthikā* (G.), AMg. *jūhiyā* (Kappas.), Ś. *jūdhiā* (Vṛṣabh. 14, 9; 16, 2; 17, 2; 21, 14 [text everywhere °*hi*°]), AMg. *nijjhūhaga* = **niryūthaka*, *nijjūhiya* = **niryūthita* (Dasav. 644, 16. 17), JM. *nijjūhijjaï* (Āv. 42, 15); *paḍhama*, *paḍhuma*, *puḍhama*, *puḍhuma* beside P. *pudhuma* = *prathama* (§ 104); *puḍhavi* beside *puhavi*, *puhii* = *pṛthvi* (§ 51)[2]; AMg. *puḍho* = *pṛthak*, beside *puhutta*, *puhatta* = *pṛthaktva* (§ 78); AMg. *meḍhi* = *methi* (Hc. 1, 215; Nāyādh. 630; Uvās.); *saḍhila*, *pasaḍhila*, *siḍhila*, *pasiḍhila* = *śithila*, *praśithila* (§ 115).

1. Falsely S. GOLDSCHMIDT, Prākṛtica p. 2f. The word presupposes one Skt. **sthak*, Cf. § 309. Not quite correct PISCHEL, BB. 15, 125. — Ornate and false BARTHOLOMAE, IF. 3, 164f.

§ 222. In the initial position *da* has become *ḍa* in M. AMg. JM. in the roots *daś* and *dah* and their derivatives (Hc. 1, 217. 218; Mk. fol. 17). Vr. 2, 35 mentions *daśana* only, Kī. 2, 42, also *dahana*, for which they, like Mk., require the change compulsorily, whilst Hc. 1, 217 permits it optionally in *daśana*, *daṣṭa*, *dagdha*, *dāha*, but for the roots themselves he always prescribes it. We find JM. *ḍasaï*, but AMg. *dasamāṇa* (cf. v. l.), *dasantu* (Āyār. 1, 8, 3, 4); M. *ḍaṭṭha* (H.) and M. JM. *daṭṭha* (R.; Kk.); M. AMg. JM. *ḍakka* (§ 566); AMg. *saṁḍāsa* = *saṁdaṁśa* (Uttar. 593); *uḍḍasa* (bug; Deśīn. 1, 96); *uḍḍāsa* (pain; Deśīn. 1, 99); but AMg. JŚ. *daṁśa* = *daṁśa* Āyār. 2, 2, 3, 28; Ovav.; Kattig. 401, 353); Ḍh. *daṭṭha* (Mṛcch. 39, 8); M. *dasaṇa* (G.), and so always in Ś. according to Vr. 12, 31, which retains the dental initially even in the anlaut : *dasaṇādasaṇi* (Laṭakam. 7, 6), *daṁsaḍi* (Śak. 160, 1), *daṭṭha*, *daṁsida* (Mālav. 53, 17; 54, 6). So also *dāḍhā* = *daṁṣṭrā* (§76). — *dah* forms *ḍahaï* (H.), JM. *ḍahe* (Erz. 38, 18), AMg. *ḍahaha* (Sūyag. 596), *ḍahĕjjā* (Dasav. 634, 5), *ḍahijjā* (Sūyag. 783); M. *ḍahiūṇa* (H.R.); M. AMg. JM. *ḍajjhaï* (Hc. 4, 246; G.H.R.; Āyār. 1, 2, 3, 5, 4, 2; 1, 3, 3, 2; Sūyag. 273; Uttar. 282, 284), M. *ḍajjhasi*, *ḍajjhasu*

(H.); M. AMg. JM. *ḍajjhanti* (G.; Paṇhāv. 381; Dvār. 498, 26), M. *ḍajjhihisi* (H.); JM. *ḍajjhihii* (Āv. 32, 35); JM. *ḍajjhae* (Dvār. 498. 22); AMg. *ḍajjhantu* (Paṇhāv. 127); M. AMg. *ḍajjhanta-* (G. R.; Karp. 87. 9; Jīv. 591; Paṇhāv. 63; Paṇṇav. 99; Nāẏādh.; Kappas.), JM. *ḍajjhinti* (Dvār. 499, 23); AMg. JM. *ḍajjhamāṇa* (Sūẏag. 270. 286; Paṇhāv. 59. 217; Uttar. 446; Dvār. 498, 25), °*ṇi* (Uttar. 284; Dvār. 498, 28; 499, 7); AMg. *viḍajjhamāṇa* (Āẏār. 1, 6, 4, 1); AMg. *aḍajjha* (Ṭhāṇ. 146); M. *ḍaḍḍha* (H.R.), but only R. 3, 48 in *ḍaḍḍhaa* without a v.l., everywhere else with v.l. *daḍḍha*, as also AMg. JM. have (C. 3, 16; Sūẏag. 288. 783; Paṇhāv. 176; Paṇṇav. 848; Vivāhap. 13. 16. 617; Āv. 9, 16. 20; 19, 13. 15; Dvār. 499, 21. 22, 500, 16; 501, 34,) M. without v. l. only R. 7, 52. Cf. Kī. 2, 17. In M. the cerebralization is so preponderant, that certainly also in R. 15, 58 with v.l. should be read *ḍahiuṁ*,[1] in spite of JM. *dahiuṁ* [Erz. 24, 25). In compounds the dental seems to prevail : *vidaḍḍha* (Kī. 2, 17); M. *viaḍḍha*=*vidagdha* (G.H.; Anarghar. 20, 3); JM. *niddahaī* (Erz. 3, 17), AMg. *ṇiddhĕjjā* (Uttār. 363), JM. *niddaḍḍha* (Dvār. 504, 9. 10a; AMg. *samādahamāṇa* (Āẏār. 1, 8, 2, 14); otherwise, except in *daḍḍha*, it is testified to with outright uncertainty, as *dahijjaī* (Hc. 4, 246), AMg. *dajjhamāṇa* (Vivāhap. 13, 16. 617), probably under the influence of the adjacently standing *daḍḍha*, as JM. *dahaī* (Erz. 3, 18), through the preceding parallel *niddahaī* (Erz. 3, 17). In Ś. the dental remains, except in the cases of transimposition of breath (§ 212), throughout : *dahiduṁ* (Śak. 72, 12); *daḍḍha*=*dagdha* (Anarghar. 150. 4; text *daddha*; cf. also ed. Calc. 89, 2); *viaḍḍha*=*vidahdha* (Mālatīm. 76, 6; 250, 3; Hāsy. 25, 8; 22, 31, 17). In derivatives cerebralization is found e.g.. in M. AMg. *ḍāha* (Pāiẏal. 46; H.; Āẏār. 2, 10, 17), M. JM. *ḍahaṇa* (Pāiẏal. 6; G.; Erz.) beside JM. *dahaṇa* (Erz.; Kk.). So also *ḍaḍḍhāḍi* (way of the forest fire; Deśīn. 4, 8) from *dagdha*+*vāii* (way) with contraction according to § 167. For *da* appears *ḍa*, further in the anlaut in JM. *ḍaṇḍa*=*daṇḍa* (Vr. 2, 35; C. 3, 16; Hc. 1, 217; Kī. 2, 42; Mk. fol. 18; Āv. 47, 26ff.), beside the common *daṇḍa* in all the dialects (e.g. M. G.H.R.; AMg. Āẏār; 1, 8, 1, 7 [v.l. *ḍa*°]. 8; 1, 8, 3, 7. 10; Uvās.; Ovav.; Nāẏādh.; JM. Erz. Kk. JŚ. Kattig. 401, 345ff.; Ś. Vr. 12, 31; Mṛcch. 41, 6; 155, 5; Śak. 125. 1; 130, 4; Mālav. 71, 6. 78, 7; Prab. 4, 3; Mg. Mṛcch. 154, 10; 155, 5); *ḍabbha*=*darbha* (Hc. 1, 217), beside M. AMg. *dabbha* (G.; Śak. 85, 2; Uvās.; *ḍambha*, beside *dambha*=*dambha* (Hc. 1, 217), moreover, also *ḍambhia*=*dāmbhika* (gamester; Deśīn. 4. 8) also belongs; AMg. JM. *ḍahara*=*dahara* (young Deśīn. 4, 8; Pāiẏal. 58; Āẏār. 2, 11, 18; Sūẏag. 100. 113. 472. 515; Antag. 55; Dasav. 623. 20; 633, 28, 32, 35; 636, 14; 637, 7; Āv. 42, 16); *ḍolā*=*dolā* (Grr.; Deśīn. 4, 11; Pāiẏal. 232), beside M. Ś. *dolā* (Vr. 12, 31; Hc.; Mk.; G.; Karp. 23, 5; 54, 10; 55, 4; 57, 2. 5. 7; Mālav. 32, 12; 34, 12; 39, 7. 15; 40, 5; Karp. 54, 5; 58. 1; Viddhaś. 117, 1), M. *ḍolāia*=*dolāyita* (under H. 966), beside Ś. *dolāamāṇa* (Mṛcch. 68, 14); in addition also *ḍola* (eye; Deśīn. 4. 9; Triv. 1, 3, 105), *ḍolia* (antelope; Deśīn. 4,12)[2]; AMg. JM. *ḍohala*=*dohada* (Hc. 1, 217; Mk. fol. 18; Nāẏādh.; Erz.), beside the common M. AMg. JM. Ś. *dohala* (Vr. 2, 12; Hc. 1, 217; Mk. fol. 18; H.R.; Vivāgas. 116; Nāẏādh.; Kappas.; Niraẏāv. Erz.; Mālav. 30, 13; 34, 13;

36, 2; 40, 6; 48, 14; Karp. 20, 2. 6; 64. 9; 66, 1; Ratn. 297, 32). M. Ś. *dohaḷaa* = *dohalaka* (H., Karp. 62. 9; Viddhaś. 121, 5; Ratn. 300, 17). Cf. § 244. 436. In AMg. the anlaut of reduplication is cerebralized in *āḍahaï* = *ādadhāti* (Ovav. § 44), *āḍahanti* = *ādadhati* (Sūẏag. 286).[3] Cf. § 223.500. *dara* becomes *ḍara* in the meaning "fear", (Hc. 1, 217), as *darati* in the meaning "fears", "trembles", *ḍaraï* (Hc. 4, 198);[4] on the other hand, the dentai remains in the meaning "something", "a little", "half" : M. JM. Ś. (Hc. 1, 217; 2, 215; Deśīn. 5 33; Pāiẏal. 212; G.H.R.; Karp. 46, 14; 56, 7; 66, 11; Erz.; Mālatīm. 118, 5; Uttarar. 125, 4; Caṇḍak. 16, 16; Viddhaś. 117, 4; 126, 3). *dara* "fear" with a dental in R. 6, 56 stands for the sake of rhyme with *kandara*. In the inlaut *ḍa* appears for *da* in *kaḍaṇa* beside *kaaṇa* (Hc. 1, 217); M. *khuḍia*, Ś. *khuḍida* = **kṣudita* = *kṣuṇṇa*, M. *ukkhuḍia* = **utkṣudita* (§ 568); AMg. *tuḍiẏa* = **tudita* (§ 258); Mg. *haḍakka* = **hṛdaka* (§ 194). *saḍaï* belongs according to Hc. 4, 219, to *sad*, according Vr. 8, 51 and Kī. 4, 46, to *śad*. Probably it is to be rightly connected with *śaṭ*, in favour of which are AMg. *paḍisāḍĕnti*, *paḍisāḍittā* (Āẏār. 2, 15, 18), JM. *paḍisaḍaṇa* (Kk. 268, 22)[5].

1. Pischel, GGA. 1880, p. 327. Falsely S. Goldschmidt, Rāvaṇavaho p. 322, note 5, who completely overlooks the dialectical distinction. — 2. Pischel BB. 6, 89,— 3. Jacobi (SBE. 45, 283), with the commentary, falsely derives the form from *dah* "to burn". — 4. Pischel on Hc. 1, 217; 4, 198. — 5. So probably more correctly than on Hc. 4, 219.

§ 223. In the anlaut *dha* has become *ḍha* in M. *ḍhaṅkha*, AMg. *ḍhaṅka*, *ḍhiṅka* = Pāli *ḍhaṅka* = Skt. *dhvāṅkṣa*, *ḍhĕṅki* = *dhvāṅkṣī* (§ 213); in the inlaut in AMg. *nisaḍha*, *ṇisaḍha* = *niṣadha* (Hc. 1, 226; Mk. fol. 17; Thāṇ. 72. 75. 176; Samav. 19. 161. 162; Jīv. 583; Nāẏādh. 668; Niraẏāv. 79ff.; Paṇhāv. 243; Rāẏap. 177), but *nisaha* (Sūẏag. 313); *osaḍha* (Hc. 1, 227; Kī. 2, 1; Mk. fol. 17), beside M. AMg. JM. JŚ. Ś. *osaha* (C. 2,8; Hc. 1,227; H.; Vivāhap. 516; Uttar. 602. 918; Sūẏag. 771; Uvās.; Ovav.; Erz.; Kattig. 402, 362; Mālav. 26, 15) and Ś. *osadha* in *laddhosadha* (Śak. 56, 16) = *auṣadha*[1]. To it belongs also AMg. JM. *āḍhāi* = **ādhāti* = *ādadhāti* (§ 500)[1], causative *āḍhavaï*, *viḍhavaï*, passive causative *āḍhappaï*, *āḍhaviaï*, *viḍhappaï*, *viḍhavijjaï* (§ 286), participles M. AMg. JM. *āḍhatta*, M. *samāḍhatta*, M. JM. Ś. *viḍhatta* A. *viḍhattaũ*, (§ 565). The derivation, going back to Hc. 2, 138, of *āḍhatta*, from *ārabdha*[2], is linguistically impossible. To *dhā*, not to *dṛ*, belongs also *āḍhia* (desired : fit to be set; attractive; stable; Hc. 1, 143; Deśīn. 1, 74), JM. *āḍhiẏa* (Āv. 43, 25) = **ādhita* = *āhita*. On cerebralization may be compared *saḍḍhā* = *śraddhā*, *saḍḍha* = *śrāddha*, *saḍḍhi-* = *śraddhin* (§ 333) and AMg. *āḍahaï*, *āḍahanti* (§ 222).

1. Wrongly connects E. Müller, Beiträge p. 57, *āḍhāi* to *ārādhati*, and Hoernle, Uvās., Transl. note 306, to *ardhayati* or to *ārdhayati*. — 2. E. Müller, Beiträge p. 57; Weber, Hāla s. v. *āḍhatta*; P. Goldschmidt, GN. 1874. p. 512, note Goldschmidt. **; S. G, Rāvaṇavaho s. v. *rabh*; ZDMG. 29, 494. Wrong is also Jacobi, KZ. 28. 253.

§ 224. In all the dialects, except PG. VG. AMg. JM. JŚ. P. CP., in the anlaut, as in the inlaut, *na* is always changed into *ṇa* (Vr. 2, 42; Hc. 1, 228; Kī. 2, 106; Mk. fol. 18); M. *ṇa* = *na*; *ṇaaṇa* = *nayana* (G.H.R.)[1]; *ṇaliṇī* = *nalinī*; *ṇāsaṇa* = *nāśana* (R.); *ṇihaṇa* = *nidhana* (G.R.); *ṇihāṇa* = *nidhāna*;

ṇihuaṇa = *nidhuvana* (H.); *ṇūṇaṁ* (H.), *ṇūṇa* (G.R.) = *nūnam*. Likewise Ś. Mg. Ḍh. Ā.D.A. In AMg. JM. JŚ. single *n* in the beginning of words and doubled *n* within words may be retained. Kī. 2, 107 generally permits dental *n* in the anlaut : *ṇaī* or *naī* = *nadī*. In palm-leaf MSS even in AMg. and JM. usually, and in KI. throughout, *ṇa* is written, while the paper manuscripts, in the anlaut, and often also in the doublings, retain *n*[2]. In the particle *ṇaṁ* = *nūnám*, always *ṇ* is written, that is explained by the fact that *n* originally stood in the inlaut and that *ṇaṁ* is an enclitic (§150). The Jainas carry this orthographical device also to other dialects, so that it sometimes wrongly also in M., e.g. in Gaüḍavaho, has been retained by the editors according to the MSS. The statement, that in AMg. even a medial simple *na* is sometime retained as in *āranāla*, *anila*, *anala* in Hc. 1, 228, probably is based purely upon false readings. Inscriptionally *na* is written wrongly in Ś. *nomālie* = *navamālike* (Lalitav. 560, 9. 17 beside *ṇomālie*) and Mg. *nijjhala* = *nirjhara* 566, 9 whilst *niraṁtara* (561, 2) and *nia* (567, 1) are printing mistakes[3]. In PG., with the exception of *madena* (6, 40), *na* in the inflectional endings undergoes cerebralization throughout : *pallavāṇa* (5, 2), *vatthavāṇa* = *vāstavyānām* (6, 8), *bamhaṇāṇaṁ* = *brāhmaṇānām* (6, 8. 27. 30. 38), *kātūṇaṁ* = **kṛtvānam* (6, 10. 29), *nātūṇaṁ* = **jñātvānam* (6, 39), *likhiteṇa* (7, 51), elsewhere the single *na* in the inlaut is partly retained, as *senāpati* (5, 3), *vadhanike* = **vardhanikān* (6, 9), *aneka* (6, 10), °*ppadāyino* = °*pradāyinaḥ* (6, 11), *sātāhani* (6, 27), *vinesi* (?6, 31), partly it becomes *ṇa*, as in *maṇusāṇa* = *manuṣyāṇām* (5, 7), *dāṇi* = *idānīṁ* (5, 7), *appaṇo* = *ātmanaḥ* (6, 8), *sāsaṇassa* = *śāsanasya* (6, 10), *nivataṇaṁ* = *nivartanam* (6, 38), *aṇu*° = *anu*° (7, 45). In the anlaut, on the other hand, as also the doubled one in the inlaut, the dental *na* is always retained : *neyike* = *naiyikān* (5, 7), *kumāranaṁdi* (6, 17), *naṁdijasa* = *nandijasya* (6, 21), *nāganaṁdisa* = *nāganandinaḥ* (6, 25), *nivataṇaṁ* = *nivartanam* (6, 38), *saṁvinayika* (6, 32), *nigaha* = *nigraha* (7, 41), *narādhamo* (7, 47), *anne* = *anyān* 5, 6;7, 43). So the inscription distinguishes also in the case of the secondary simplified nasal, derived from *jña*: *āṇataṁ* = *ājñaptam* (7, 49), where *jña* is taken as in the inlaut, beside *nātūṇaṁ* = **jñātvānam* (6, 39). The inscription thus agrees on the last two points generally with the more modern Jaina manuscripts.[4] So also in VG. : *pallavāṇaṁ* (101, 2); *nārāyaṇassa* (101, 8), *vaddhaniyaṁ* (101, 8), *kātūṇa* (101, 9), *nātūṇa* (101, 10; cf. EI. 1, 2 note 2). In P. CP. *na* remains throughout : P. *dhana*, *matana* = *madana*, *satana* = *sadana*, *vatanaka* = *vadanaka*, *cintayamāni* = *cintayamānā*, *gantūna* = **gantvāna*, *natthūṇa* = **naṣṭvāna* etc., also *sināna* = *snāna*, *sināta* = *snāta*, *sunusā* = *snuṣā* : CP. *matana* = *madana*, *tanu*, *nakara* = *nagara* etc. (Vr. 4, 7. 13; Hc. 4, 304. 307. 310. 312. 313. 314. 325. 328; Namisādhu on Rudraṭa, Kāvyālaṁkāra 2, 12.

1. Cf, §186, not 1.—2. LEUMANN, Āvaśyaka-Erzählungen p.6, not 4. On the flexiblity of the manuscripts see WEBER, Bhag. 1,402f.; E, MÜLLER, Beiträge p. 29f.; JACOBI, ZDMG. 34. 181, according to whom even in the oldest manuscripts *ṇā* appears not rarely; STEINTHAL, Specimen p. 3.— KONOW, GN. 1894, 480.—Not quite correctly BÜHLER, EI. 13.

§ 225. Very rarely and only dialectically the cerebrals of Skt. become dentals. In P. *ṭu* can become *tu* (Hc. 4, 311); *kutumbaka* beside *kuṭumbaka.* In P. CP. *ṇa* becomes *na* : P. *gunaganayutta* = *guṇagaṇayukta*; *gunena* = *guṇena*; *taluni* = *taruṇī*; *visāna* = *viṣāṇa*; *gahana* = *grahaṇa* (Vr. 10, 5; C. 3, 38; Hc. 4, 306. 309. 323; Namisādhu on Rudraṭa, Kāvyālaṁkāra 2, 12); CP.; *makkana* = *mārgaṇa*, *panaya* = *praṇaya*, *nakhatappanesuṁ* = *nakhadarpaṇeṣu*, *pātukkhepena* = *pādotkṣepeṇa* (Hc. 4, 325. 326). According to Siṁhadevagaṇin on Vāgbhaṭālaṁkāra 2, 12 *ṇa* should become *n* also in Mg. *taluna* = *taruṇa.* S. has confused Mg. with P. In AMg. JM. JŚ, the manuscripts write *nna* for *ṇṇa* of the other dialects, except that of P. CP., just as for the dental *nna* (§ 224). *nisanna* = *niṣaṇṇa*; *paḍipunna* = *pratipūrṇa*; *vanna* = *varṇa*; also in the case of the secondary *ṇṇa*, as *anna* = M. Ś. *aṇṇa* = Skt. *anya* etc.

§ 226. Dentals would have occurred for cerebrals in a greater measure if the grammarians, with whom the North Indian manuscripts agree, were correct in saying that *ṭa*, *ḍa*, *ṇa* could become *la* (Vr. 2, 22. 23; C. 3, 21; Hc. 1, 197, 198. 202. 203, Kī. 2, 12. 13; Mk. fol. 16). In lieu of *la*, however, *ḷa* should always be written, as in similar cases in Pāli[1]. The North Indian manuscripts know *ḷa* as little as the anunāsika (§ 179), even not in the cases, such as Hc. 4, 308, where for P. change of *la* into *ḷa* is required[2]. Trivikrama's grantha-manuscripts write in this place 3, 2, 48 (MS B. 39) always *ḷa*, in the rule corresponding to Hc. 1, 197, 202, in the sūtra, it is true, they write *ḷa*, and in the examples, with some exceptions, that are scribe's errors, as is shown by the variations of the manuscripts,[3] only *ḷa*. The edition in the Granthapradarśanī has only *ḷa*. In the sūtra 2, 3, 24 of Trivikrama himself stands : *ṭor baḍiśādau laḥ*. The manuscripts of the texts and the print fluctuate; e.g. in Hc. 1, 202 stands *kīlaï* = *krīḍati*; in Triv. 1, 3, 30 the manuscript has A. *kīlaï*, B. *kīḷaï*; Śak. 155, 1, the Bengali and Nāgarī MSS have *kīlaṇaaṁ* = *krīḍanakam*, 155, 12 *kiliśśaṁ* or wrongly *kilissaṁ* = *krīḍiṣyāmi*. Of the South Indian manuscripts the Grantha-manuscript L[4] reads *kīḷaṇijjaṁ* = *krīḍanīyam*, but *kilissaṁ*, the Telugu-manuscript F *kīḷanijjaṁ* and *kiḷissaṁ*, P. *kilaṇaṁ*, but *kilissaṁ*, the Malayālam-manuscript V *kīḷaṇiyaṁ*, but *kilissaṁ*, the Telugu edition, Madras 1874 p. 304 *kīḷaṇiaaṁ* and p. 305 *kiḷaïssaṁ*; Vikr. 41, 7; 52, 9 has for *kiḍissaṁ kilamāṇā*, the South-Indian recension 643, 1; 650, 17 *kīḍissaṁ*, *kiḷamāṇā*, 31, 17 for *kilāpauvadaperante* = *krīḍāparvataparyante*, 636, 17 *kilāpavvade* = *krīḍāparvate*; Mālav. 60, 11 the Telugu manuscript of the India Office too has *kilissaṁ*, in Mālatīm. 142, 1 the Telugu edition 123, 8 reads *kilaṇādo* for *kiḷaṇādo* etc. Similar is the case in other words. The South-Indian texts mostly have *ḷa*, which they employ in Skt. too in the same cases in which they use *ṇa*, so that they, e.g. write *taraḷa*, *marāḷa*, *saraḷa*, etc. The Bhaṭṭiprolu-Inscription I, A[5], writes *phāḷiga* = *sphāṭika*, while PG. has *pīlā* = *pīḍā* (6, 40), for which *pīḷā* was anticipated[6]. In agreement with Pāli *ḷa* is to be assumed for Pkt. when it stands for *ṭa*, *ḍa*. Therefore, there has not occurred a change from one class to another. When *ḍa* and *ḷa* are mentioned to have a similar sound by Hemacandra on Abhidhānacintāmaṇi 258 (p. 322 ed. Böhtlingk), Sarasvatīk, p. 98, Vāgbhaṭa, Alaṁkāratilaka p. 14, Sāhityadarpaṇa 261, 11, and Kālidāsa, Raghuv. 9, 46 permits *bhujalatām* in alliteration with *jaḍatām* (*ḍalayorabhedaḥ* says Mallinātha on it), this is explained by the fact that in Classical Skt. of the North *ḷa* had vanished both in writing and speech, but it proves nothing for Pkt.[7] in relation to the modern Indian languages. Cf. § 238. 240.

1. E. KUHN p. 36f.; E. MÜLLER, Simplified Pali Grammar p. 27. — 2. See the critical notes on this. rule. — 3. So writes, e.g. in 1, 3, 30 A. *valahāmuhaṃ*, B *vaḷaāmuhaṁ*; A *galulo*, B *garuḷo* = *garuḍaḥ*; A *talāaṁ*, B *taḷāaṁ* = *taḍākam*; in 1, 3, 24 A *valisaṁ*, B *baḷisaṃ* = *baḍiśam* etc. — 4 On the notation of the manuscripts see GN. 1873, 190f. — 5. EI. 2, 324.—6. On the inscriptional occurrences of *ḷa* see BÜHLER, EI. 2, 368; FLEET, CII. 3, 4, 269 — 7. PISCHEL GGA. 1873, p. 50; on Hc. 1, 202; 4, 326.

§ 227. Except in Ḍh. and Mg. *śa* and *ṣa* have become *sa* in Pkt., so that most of the dialects have the dental sibilant only (Vr. 2, 43; Hc. 1, 260; Kī. 2, 103; Mk. fol. 18), PG. *sivakhaṁdavamo* = *śivaskandavarmā* (5, 2), *visae* = *viṣaye* (5, 3), *pesaṇa* = *peṣaṇa* (5, 6), *yaso* = *yaśaḥ* (6, 9), *sāsaṇassa* = *śāsanasya* (6, 10), *sata* = *śata* (6, 11), *kosika* = *kauśika* (6, 16), *sāka* = *śāka* (6, 34), *visaya* = *viṣaya* (6, 35) and others; M. *asesa* = *aśeṣa* (G.H.), *āsivisa* = *āśiviṣa* (R.), *kesa* = *keśa* (G.H.R.), *ghosa* = *ghoṣa* (G.H.), *pasu* = *paśu* (G.), *masi* = *maṣi* (H.R.), *mahisa* = *mahiṣa* (G.H.R.), *rosa* = *roṣa* (G.H.R.). *sisira* = *śiśira* (G.H.R.), *sisu* = *śiśu* (G.); Ś. *kidavisesaā*...*sohadi* = *kṛtaviśeṣakā*. . . *śobhate* (Mṛcch. 2, 21), *parisilidāsesadesaṁtaravvavahāro* = *pariśilitāśeṣadeśāntara-vyavahāraḥ* (Lalitav. 560, 19), *sasiseharavallahā* = *śaśiśekharavallabhā* (Lalitav. 561, 9), *sussūsidapuruvvo sussūsidavvo* = *śuśrūṣitapūrvaḥ śuśrūṣitavyaḥ* (Mṛcch. 39, 23). Likewise AMg. JM. JŚ. P. CP. Ā.D.A.

§ 228. In Ḍh. *ṣa* has become *sa*, but *śa* has been retained : *esa, esu, eso* = *eṣaḥ* (Mṛcch. 30, 10; 31, 8; 34, 17; 35, 15; 36, 23); *puliso* = *puruṣaḥ* (34, 12); *mūsido* = *mūṣitaḥ* (38, 18; 39, 1); *samavisamaṁ, sakalusaaṁ* (so to be read !) = *samaviṣamam, sakaluṣakam* (v.l. *aïkasaṇaṁ* = *atikṛṣṇam*; 30, 8. 9); however, *ādaṁśaāmi* (so to be read!) = *ādarśayāmi* (34, 25); *jaśaṁ* [so to be read] = *yaśaḥ* (30, 9); *daśasuvaṇṇa* = *daśasuvarṇa* (29, 15; 30, 1; 31, 4 etc.); *śalaṇaṁ* (to be read so!) = *śaraṇam* (30, 4); *śuṇṇu* = *śūnyaḥ* (30, 11); *śela* = *śaila* (30, 17). See § 25.

§ 229. In Mg., according to Mk. fol. 85 also in Vrācaḍa Apabhraṁśa, and as it appears, in Kaikeyapaiśācika too, *ṣa* and *sa*, when not conjoined, become *śa* in the inlaut and anlaut; *śa* itself is retained (Vr. 11, 3; C. 3, 39; Hc. 4, 288; Kī. 5, 86; Mk. fol. 74; Namisādhu on Rudraṭa, Kāvyālaṁkāra 2, 12). The rule holds good also when the sounds are combined with *ya, ra, la, va* or when they are in a consonant group split up by a separation vowel or are otherwise resolved through the phonetic laws of Pkt. : *idiśaśśa akayyaśśa* = *idṛśasyākāryasya* (Śak. 113, 5); *avaśalovaśappaṇia* = *avasaropasarpaṇiya* (Śak. 115, 10); *keśeśu* = *keśeṣu* (Mṛcch. 122, 22; Veṇīs. 35, 19); *duśśāśaṇaśśa* = *duḥśāsanasya* (Mṛcch. 12, 15; Veṇīs. 35, 12), *puliśa* = *puruṣa* (§ 124); *bhūśaṇaśadda* = *bhūṣaṇaśabda* (Mṛcch. 14, 23); *mahiśama-hāśula* = *mahiṣamahāsura* (Caṇḍak. 68, 16); *māṇuśamaṁśa* = *mānuṣamāṁsa* (Veṇīs. 33, 3); *māśalāśi* = *māṣarāśi* (Mṛcch. 14, 10); *lāeśi* = *rājarṣi* (Veṇīs. 34, 1); *lośaggi* = *roṣāgni* (Mṛcch. 123, 2); *lośāmaliśapalavvaśa* = *roṣāmarṣapara-vaśa* (Mallikām. 143, 11); *valiśaśada* = *varṣaśata* (Veṇīs. 33, 4); *viśakaṇṇaā* = *viṣakanyakā* (Mudrār. 193, 3; 194, 6); *viśeśa* = *viśeṣa* (Mṛcch. 38, 13); *viśśāvaśuśśa* = **viśvāvasuṣya* = *viśvāvasoḥ* (Mṛcch. 11, 9), *śalila* = *salila* (Mṛcch.

136, 11; 158, 13); *śalīla*=*śarīra* (Mṛcch. 124, 21; 127, 5; 140, 10; 154, 10; Veṇīs. 34, 1); *śahaśśa*=*sahasra* (§448); *śamaśśaśadu*=*samāśvasitu* (Mṛcch. 130, 17); *śamāśāśiadi*=*samāśvāryate* (Veṇīs. 34, 13); *śilaśi*=*śirasi* (Mṛcch. 116, 15); *śiliśomeśalaeva*=*śrīsomeśvaradeva* (Lalitav. 566, 6); *śivilaṇiveśa*=*śibiraniveśa* (Lalitav. 565, 6); *śoṇidavaśaśamuddaduśśaṁcala*=*soṇitavaśāsamudra-duḥsaṁcara* (Veṇīs 34. 5); *śośāveduṁ*=*śoṣayitum* (Mṛcch. 140, 9).

2. On Single Consonants.

§ 230. *ka* becomes *ca* in *kirāta* : M. *cilāa* (Vr. 2, 33 [Bh. here and under 2, 30 *cilāda*]; Hc. 1, 183. 254; Kī. 2, 35. 41; Mk. fol. 17 [*cilāda*]; R), AMg. *cilāẏa* (Paṇhāv. 42; Paṇṇav. 58), femin. *cilāī* (Ovav.), *cilāiẏā* (Vivāhap. 791, Rāẏap. 288; Nāẏādh.; Ovav.); cf. *cilātiputra* (commentary upon Ṛṣabhap. 38). In the meaning "Śiva" *ka* remains according to Hc. Mk. So M. *kirāa* (G. 35). In Ś., according to Mk., *ka* remains in tribal names : *kirāda* (Bālar. 168, 2; Karp. 90, 8). *kirāẏa* occurs in Pāiẏal. 273. — *ka* is represented by *va* in *ovāsa*=*avakāśa* (Pāiẏal. 261; G.H.R.), beside *oāsa* (Hc. 1, 172; G.H.R.), M. Ś. *avaāsa* (Hc. 1, 172; G.; Mṛcch. 44, 19; Vikr. 41, 8, Prab. 46, 2), JM. *avagāsā* (Erz.), AMg. *avagāsiẏa*=**avakāśika* (Uvās.) *ovāsaī*=*avakāśate* (Vr. 8, 35; Hc. 4, 179); M. *antovāsa*=*antaravakāśa* (G. 848; § 383)[1]. Further in AMg. *jūva*=*yūka* (Jīv. 356), beside *jūā, ūā*, AMg. *jūẏā* (§ 335); M. AMg. JM. JŚ. A. *thova*=*stoka* (Hc. 2, 125; G.; Āẏār. 1, 2, 4, 4; Sūẏag. 950; Ṭhāṇ. 238; Jīv. 798; Vivāhap. 26, 423; Uttar. 311.959; Dasav. 621, 13; Jīẏak. 92; Ovav.; Kappas.; Āv. 41, 9; 43, 3, 5; Dvār. 504, 8; Erz.; Kattig. 400, 335 [text *thū*°]; Hc. 4, 376, 1), AMg. JM. *thovaẏa*=*stokaka* (Nāẏādh.; Erz.), AMg. *thovaẏaraṁ* (Jīẏak. 92), JM. *thovāthovaṁ* (Āv. 43, 7), beside M. Ś. Mg. *thoa* (Hc. 2, 45. 115; G.H.R.; Karp. 10, 6; 37, 5; Ś. Karp. 45, 9; Mg. Mṛcch. 157, 6), *thŏkka* (§ 90)[2]; AMg. *divaḍḍha*=*dvikārdha* (§ 450). *va* probably, according to § 199, originated from *pa*, therefore, it may be a case of interchange between gutturals and labials. Cf. § 231. 266. 286. On *pavaṭṭha*, ostensibly=*prakoṣṭha* see § 129; on *candimā*, ostensibly=*candrikā* § 103; on AMg. JM. JŚ. Mg. A. *ga* for *ka*, § 192. 202; on *kha*, *ha* for *ka*, see § 206.

1. Falsely Ascoli, Kritische Studien p. 216, note 35. — 2. It is difficult to explain *v*, here, as in other cases, with Pischel, GGA. 1881 p. 1322, from the velar *k*. S. Goldschmidt, KZ. 112, note 1, wrongly thinks that it was brought in to prevent hiatus, that is prohibited in none of the dialects.

§ 231. *ga* appears as *va* in *ovāhaï* beside *ogāhaï*=*avagāhate* (Hc. 4, 205)[1]; AMg. *juvala*=*yugala* (Vivāhap. 962), *juvalaẏa*=*yugalaka* (Vivāhap. 82), *juvaliẏa*=*yugalita* (Vivāhap. 41; Ovav.); cf. § 286 *juppaī*; AMg. *taḷāva* =*taḍāga* (Vivāhap. 610; Uvās). beside AMg. JM. *taḷāga* (Āẏār. 2, 3, 3, 2; Paṇhāv. 31. 246. 437. 520; Paṇṇav. 84; Uttar. 884; Ovav.; Āv. 11, 44. 45; Erz.), AMg. *taḷāẏa* (Ovav.), *taḍāga* (Āẏār. 2, 1, 2, 3); M. *taḷāa* (Vr. 2, 23; C. 3, 21 p. 50; Hc. 1, 202; Kī. 2, 13; Mk. fol. 16; G.H. v.l.); Ś. *taḍāga* Mṛcch. 37, 23; 151, 15); M. *dūhava*=*durbhaga* (Hc. 1, 115. 192; Karp. 86, 2), and on its analogy with a lengthened vowel *sūhava*=*subhaga* (Hc. 1, 113. 192), according to Mk. fol. 39 also *duhavī*, *suhavī*=*durbhagā*, *subhagā*. Reversely *ga* occurs for *va* in AMg. JM. *agaḍa*=*avaṭa* (2, 1, 2, 3; Ovav.;

Erz.), beside *aẏaḍa* (Deśīn. 1, 18; Pāiẏal. 130) and common *avaḍa*; AMg. *ṇiṇhaga* = **naïhnava*[2] (heretic; Ovav. § 122), beside AMg. *niṇhavĕjja* (Āẏār 1,5, 3, 1), *niṇhave* (Dasav. 631, 31), *aṇiṇhavemāṇa* (Nāẏādh. § 83); cf. § 473; AMg. *aṇhaga* = *āsrava* (Paṇhāv. 324), beside *aṇhaẏa* (Āẏār. 2,4, 1, 6; Paṇhāv; 7; Ovav.)[3], *paṇhaẏa* = *prasrava* (Vivāhap. 794), AMg. *mahāṇubhāga* = *mahānubhāva* (Bhag.; Ovav.)[4]. Cf. also AMg. *pariẏāga, niẏāga* (§ 254). — M. *puṇṇāma* = *puṁnāga* (Hc. 1, 190; R.), beside AMg. *punnāga* (Āẏār. 2, 10, 21; Nāẏādh. 699. [°*ṇṇā*]), Ś. *puṇṇāa* (Mallikām. 116, 9), and *bhāmiṇī* = *bhāginī* (Hc. 1, 190), beside M. Ś. *mandabhāiṇī* (H.; Mṛcch. 22, 25; 120, 6; 170, 325; Vikr. 84, 21 and often) presuppose the process of development *puṇṇāga*; **puṇṇāva, puṇṇāma* (§ 261)[5]. Skt. *puṁnāman* is a borrowing from Pkt.— *chāla* ostensibly = *chāga*, and *chālī* = *chāgi* (Hc. 1, 191) have, according § 165, arisen from *chāgala, chāgali*. For Mg. *cheliā* (Laṭakam. 12, 14) we have to read *chāliā*. Ś. has *chāgala* (Mṛcch. 17, 15). On *gha* for *ga* see § 209 Cf. § 230.

1. Falsely Ascoli, Kritische Studien p. 216, note 35 — 2. So the word is not to be equated as = *nihnava* (Leumann, Aup. S. s. v.). *i* stands for *ai* according to § 84.—Not correctly, Leumann, Aup. S. s. v.). — 4. So correctly Leumann, Aup. S. s.v. *aṇubhāga*. Weber, Bhag. 2, 290 thinks of Skt. *anubhāga*. To me the equation of AMg. *pūsamāṇaga* = Skt. *puṣyamānava*, given by Leumann, Aup. S. s. v., is not clear. The word *vaddhamānagā*. in Ovav. § 55, mentioned earlier, makes it probable that the word is to be equated as *puṣymāṇa*+*ka*. In no case, with Leumann, we can assume dropping off of *v*. — 5. Cf. S. Goldschmidt, Prākrtica p. 15; Rāvaṇavaho, Index p. 172a, note 1, who, rather wrongly explains *va* as having been brought in to stop the hiatus. Cf. § 230, note 2.

§ 232. AMg. *auṇṭaṇa* is not, with Hc. 1, 177, to be equated as = *ākuñcana*, but as = **ākuṇṭana* from √*kuṭa kauṭilye* (Dhātupāṭha 28, 73), that is identical with √*kuṭi vaikalye* (Dhātupāṭha 9, 37). Hence it is derived from the present stem *ākuṇṭa*-, that occurs in AMg. *āuṇṭiẏa, āuṇṭĕjjā* (Vivāhap. 1151. 1152)[1]. To the same root belong Skt. *kuṭila*, Pkt. *kuḍilla kuḍillaa* (crooked; Deśīn. 2, 40; Pāiẏal. 155), *koḍilla* (bad; Deśīn. 2, 40) and *kuṇṭī* bundle; Deśīn. 2, 34). — *khasia*, according to Hc. 1, 193 = *khacita*, is rather = *kasita*, in conformity with Hc. 1, 181; cf. § 206. —AMg. *pisalla* (Paṇhāv. 79 v.l.), *sapisallaga* (Paṇhāv. 525), that Hc. equates as = *piśāca*, will be = *piśācālaya*, according to § 150. 165. 194. *piśāca* becomes regularly M. Ś. *pisāa* (H.; Prab. 46, 2; Mudrār. 186, 4 [°*ca*]; 191, 5 [°*ca*], AMg. JM *pisāẏa* (Ṭhāṇ. 90. 138. 229; Paṇhāv. 172. 230. 312; Uvās.; Ovav.; Erz.).

1. *āuṁṭāvemi* (sic; Nāẏādh. 603; commentary *āuṁṭāvemi*), *āuṁṭeha, āuṁṭehi* (sic; Nāẏādh. 605) is a false reading for *āuṭṭāvemi, āuṭṭeha, āuṭṭĕnti*, as e.g. *āuṭṭaï* (Ṭhāṇ. 152; Sūẏag. 403), *āuṭṭāmo* (Āẏār. 2, 1, 3, 2), *āuṭṭitae* (Kappas. S. § 49), *viuṭṭāmi* (Vivāhap. 614), *viuṭṭaṇa* (Sūẏag. 476) are found. The forms belong to √*vṛt*.

§ 233. *cha* remains unchanged in the anlaut. In the inlaut it becomes *ccha* after vowels, as in Skt., and after nasal vowels and nasals it remains *cha*, whether it be original or secondary. Thus M. *chala* (G.H.); *chavi* (G.R.); *chāā* = *chāyā* (G.H.R.); *chea* = *cheda* (G.H.R.); *icchaï* = *icchati* (H.R.); *ucchaṅga* = *utsaṅga* (G.H.R.); *gacchaï* = *gacchati* (H.); *pucchaï* = *pṛcchati* (R.); *mucchā* = *mūrchā* (R.); *piṁcha* = *piccha, puṁcha* = *puccha* (§ 74); *puñchaï* = *proñchati* (Hc. 4, 105). Likewise in other dialects except Mg.— AMg. *milakkhu* beside *miliccha*, AMg. JM. Ś. A. *mĕccha*, AMg. *miccha* = *mleccha*

(§ 84. 105. 136) are explained from the common basic form **mlaska*[1]. In Mg. original as well as secondary *ccha* becomes *śca* (Hc. 4, 295; Namisādhu on Rudraṭa, Kāvyālaṁkāra 2, 12); *iściadi* = **icchyate* = *iṣyate* (Śak. 118,6); *gaśca* = *gaccha* (Hc.; Lalitav. 566, 18; Śak. 115, 4), *gaścamha* = *gacchāma* Śak. 118, 7); *puścaṁde* = *pṛcchan* (Lalitav. 565, 20); *maśca* from the usual Pkt. *maccha* = *matsya* (Mṛcch. 11, 11. 12 [so to be read]; Śak. 114. 2. 9); *maścalī* (fish; Śak. 118, 2) = Gujarāti *māchalī*, Hindī *machalī*, Sindhī. *machaḍī*[2]; *āvaṇṇavaścala* = *āpannavatsala*, *piścila* = *picchila* (Hc.; Namis.); *uścaladi* = *ucchalati*, *tiliści pĕskadi* = M. *tiricchi pĕcchaï* = *tiryak prekṣate*, *puścadi* = *pṛcchati* (Hc. 4. 295); *yivantavaścā* = *jivadvatsā* (Hc. 4, 302). The texts mostly have *ccha*: nevertheless there are distinct vestiges of this rule found in the MSS. So some MSS have *gaścasi*, *gaśchasi*, *gaśca* for *gacchaśi*, *gaccha* (Mṛcch. 20, 14); Pṛthvīdhara in STENZLER p. 241 has *maścāśikā* for *macchāśikā* (Mṛcch. 10, 23); for *gaccha* (Mṛcch. 132, 16) there occur *gaśca*, *gaśśa*; for *āacchāmi* (Mṛcch. 132, 17), *āaścāmi*, *āaśvāmi*; for *āgacchadi* (Mṛcch. 133, 8), *āgaścadi*. *āgaśchadi etc.*[3] In the anlaut *cha* remains : *chāla* (Hc. 4, 295), *chāā* = *chāyā* (Mudrār. 267, 2). The *cha* of *chedaa* in *ganṭhichedaa* = *granthichedaka* (Śak. 115, 4. 12) may also be regarded as in the anlaut. The v. l. °*śchedaā* in R, however, makes here the reading **ścedaa* more probable. See also §327.

1. E. KUHN, KZ. 25, 327. — 2. PISCHEL on Śakuntalā p. 199, note 1. — 3. PISCHEL, GGA. 1881 p. 1319.

§ 234. In place of Skt. *ja* an old *ga* has been retained dialectically in the root *añj* and its derivatives in conjunction with certain prefixes : AMg. *abbhaṅgei* (Āyār. 2, 2, 3, 8; 2, 15, 20), *abhaṅgĕjja* = *abhyañjyāt*, commentary = *abhyaṅgyāt* (Āyār. 2, 2, 1, 8), *abbhaṅgĕttā* = **abhyañjitvā* (Āyār. 2, 6, 1, 9; Ṭhāṇ. 126), *abbhaṅgāvei* = *abhyañjayati* (Vivāgas. 235; text °*bbhi*°); JM. *abbhaṅgijjaha* = *abhyajyadhve* (Erz. 59, 30), *abbhaṅgiuṁ* (Erz. 57, 10); AMg. JM. *abbhaṅgiya* (Ovav. [°*bbhi*°]; Kappas.; Nāyādh. [°*bbhi*°]; Erz.); AMg. JM. *abhaṅgaṇa* = *abhyañjana* (Uvās. Ovav.; Kappas.; Erz.); Mg. *abbhaṅgida* = *abhyakta* (Mṛcch. 69, 7); AMg. *niraṅgaṇa* (Ovav.) against M. *nirañjaṇa* (G.H.). The guttural is found also in Skt. *abhyaṅga* = AMg. *abbhaṅga* (Ovav.). In Sūyag. 248 is published *muhabhiṁjāe*. In the simple root and its derivatives, in all the dialects, there occurs only *ja*. — AMg. *omugganimuggiya*, explained by the commentator as *majjanonmajiana*, is = **avamagnanimagnita*, as *ummaggā*, *ummuggā* = **unmagnā* (§ 104).

§ 235. Hc. 4, 229 teaches that *j* in the root *sṛj* becomes *r*. His examples *nisiraī*, *vosiraī*, *vosirāmi* = *vyavasṛjati*, *vyavasṛjāmi* occur very frequently in AMg. JM. So AMg. *nisirāmi* (Āyār. 2, 1, 10, 7), *nisiraï* (Paṇṇav. 384f.; Vivāhap. 120f. 212. 254. 1217. 1271 Nāyādh.), *nisirāmo* (Āyār. 2, 1, 9, 1; 2, 2, 2, 10); *nisirinti* (Sūyag. 680), *nisirĕjjā* (Āyār. 2, 1, 10, 1; 2, 5, 2, 3; 2, 6, 1, 11; Sūyag. 682; Ṭhāṇ. 590. [°*ri*°]), *nisirāhi* (Āyār. 2, 1, 10, 1), *nisira* (Dasav. 632, 28), *nisirinta-* (Sūyag. 680), *nisirittā* (absolutive : Vivāhap. 1251), *nisirijjamāṇa* (Vivāhap. 122), *nisirāvĕnti* (Sūyag. 680), substantive *nisiraṇa* (Dasav. N. 658, 33); AMg. *vosirāmi* (Āyār. p. 132, 2; 133, 6, 134,3; 136, 5; Nāyādh. 1165; Vivāhap. 173; Dasav. 614, 19; 616, 20; Ovav.); JM. *vosiraī* (Erz. 50, 37); AMg. *vosirĕjjā* (Āyār. 2, 10, 1ff). *vosire* (Āyār. 1,

7, 8. 22; Sūẏag. 214; Uttar. 737. 923; Dasav. 619. 14); JM. *vosirasu* (Erz. 42, 33); AMg. *vosirittā* (absol.; Āẏār. 2, 10, 22); JM. *vosiriẏa* (Āv. 11, 19; Erz. 50, 36); AMg. *viosire* (Āẏār. 2, 16, 1). The reference of these forms to *sṛj*[1] is impossible. Rather the AMg. JM. participle, *samosariẏa* = *samavasṛta* (Vivāgas. 151; Uvās. § 2. 9. 75. 189; Niraẏāv. § 3; Āv. 31, 22; cf. § 565) beside the more frequent *samosaḍha* = *samavasṛṣṭa* (§ 67), further AMg *samosarĕjjā samosariukāma* (Ovav.), *samosaraṇa* (Bhag.; Ovav.) shows that in AMg. JM. the roots *sṛj* and *sṛ* have coincided. *sṛ* forms *saraï* = *saráti*, in the meaning "to go", "to run", but *siraï* = **saráti* in the meaning "to cause to go", "to cause to run", "to let go" and so on. The coincidence of both the roots is proved, for example, also by AMg. *nisirijjamāṇa* beside *nisiṭṭha* (Vivāhap. 122), *nisiraï* (Vivāhap. 254) beside *nisiṭṭha* (Vivāhap. 257).

1. E. Müller, Beiträge p. 65; Leumann, Aup. S. s. v. *vosir* and *viosagga*; Jacobi' Erz. s.v. *vosiraï*.

§ 236. In Mg. *ja* becomes *ya* (Vr. 11, 4; Hc. 4, 292; Kī. 5, 90; Namisādhu on Rudraṭa, Kāvyālaṁkāra 2, 12), *yāṇidavvaṁ* = *jñātavyam*, *yāṇiśśamha* = *jñāsyāmaḥ yā* [*ṇe*] = *jāne*, *yāṇiẏyadi* = *jñāyate*, *yāṇidaṁ* = *jñātam*, *yampideṇa* = *jalpitena* (Lalitav. 565, 7. 9. 13; 566, 1. 8. 12); *yāṇadi* = *jānāti* (Hc.; Namis.); *yaṇavada* = *janapada* (Hc.; Namis.); *yalahala* = *jaladhara* (Hc. 4, 296); *yāyade* = *jāyate*, *yāā* = *jāyā* (Hc.). The MSS of the dramas, with quite rare exceptions, write in Mg. too only *ja*, since in the North-Indian dialects *ya* and *ja* have in many cases coalesced together.[1] That is simply a contribution of the scribe,[2] and for *ja*, according to the grammarians, we have to substitute *ya* throughout, as has been done in this grammar. Therefore, e.g. one has to write for *jāla* (Śak. 114,2) *yāla*, with the MS R; for *jamadaggi* (Mṛcch. 12,12), *yamadaggi*; for *jiadi* (Mṛcch. 12,20), *yiadi*; for *jāṇāśi* (Veṇīs. 34, 18), *yāṇāśi*; for *joisa* (Mudrār, 177, 4); *yoiśa* = *jyotiṣa*; for *jiṇa* (Prab. 46, 12), *yiṇa*; for *jaṇehiṁ jammantala*° (Caṇḍak. 42,11), *yaṇehiṁ yammantala*° = *janairjanmāntara*° etc. In the interior of a word simple *ja* drops out between vowels according to § 186. Corresponding to *ya* for *ja*, *yha* will have to be written in cases like *yhaṇṇayyhaṇanta*- for *jhaṇṇajjhaṇanta*- (Mṛcch. 11, 6), *yhatti* for *jhatti* = *jhaṭiti* (Mṛcch. 29, 21; 114, 21; 168, 19) and in conjunct consonants, as in *ṇiyyhala* for *nijjhala* = *nirjhara* (Lalitav. 566, 9), *uyyhia* for *ujjhia* = *ujjhitvā* (Mudrār. 178, 6); *jjh* also in Hc. 4, 302), Cf. § 217. 280. In PG. VG., where *ja* otherwise remains (§189), it has become. *ya* in PG.; *bhāraddāyo*, *bhāradāya*°, *bhāradāyasa* = *bhāradvājaḥ*, *bhāradvāja*°, *bhāradvājasya* (5, 2; 6, 16. 19); VG. *bhāraddāyassa* (101, 2, cf. EI. 1, 2, note 2). Cf. § 253. — *uvvivaï*, according to Vr. 8, 43; Hc. 4, 227; Kī. 5, 46 = *udvijate* is rather = **udvipate* = *udvepate*, as *uvvea* is not = *udvega* (Hc. 4, 227), but = **udvepa*, from √*vip*, *vepate*. On AMg. *murava* = *muraja* see § 254.

1. Beames, Comp. Gr. § 23; Hoernle, Comp. Gr. § 17. — 2. So correctly already Lassen, Inst. § 154, 3. Cf. above § 23.

§ 237. Independent *ña* occurs in CP. in declension of the word *rājan*, when the sound-group *jñ* is separated by a separation-vowel according to § 133 and becomes *ciñ* according to § 191 (cf. note 1) : *rāciñā*, *rāciño* = *rājñā*, *rājñaḥ* (Hc. 4, 304; § 399). In Bh. 10, 12 *rācinā*, *rācino*, *rācini* are read with dental *n*. Further *ñ* stands in A. *vuñaī* = **vrajñāti* = *vrajati*, absol. *vuñĕppi*, *vuñĕppiṇu* (Hc. 4, 392) = Mg. *vaññadi* (§ 488).

§ 238. As a rule *ṭ* becomes *ḍ* in the inlaut between two vowels (§ 198). *ṭa* becomes *ḷa* in lieu of *ḍa*, in M. AMg. JM. Ś. *phaḷiha* = *sphaṭika*, AMg. *phāḷiya* = *sphāṭika* (§ 206). In M. *phaḍiha* (R. s. v.; the better recension C has °*li*°), certainly, and in Ś. *phaḍia* (§ 206) probably are false. — *phālei* (causes to burst; splits) is not to be traced back to √*paṭ* with Hc. 1, 198, but to √*phal*,√*sphal*. — *capeṭā* forms also M. AMg. *caviḍā*, *caviḷā* (Hc. 1, 146. 198) besides *caveḍā* (Hc. 1, 146; H.; Uttar. 596). Cf. § 80. Dialectically *ṭa* becomes *ḷa* also, for which the North Indian MSS write *la* (§ 226). So M. AMg. *kakkoḷa* = *karkoṭa* (G.; Paṇhāv. 527); AMg. *kaḷitta* = *kaṭitra* (Ovav. § 10); AMg. *kheḷa* (saliva) = *kheṭa* (Āyār. 2, 1, 5, 2; 2, 2, 1, 7; Thāṇ. 483; Paṇhāv. 343. 505; Antag. 23; Vivāhap. 164; Uttar. 734; Kappas.), *kheḷei* = *kheṭayati* (Vivāhap. 112); AMg. *piḷaga* = *piṭaka* (Sūyag. 208); Mg. *yūḷaka* = *jūṭaka* (Mṛcch. 136, 15); M). *śaala* = *śakaṭa* (Mṛcch. 122, 10), beside Ś. *saaḍiā* = *śakaṭikā*, AMg. *sagaḍa*, dialectical *saaḍha* (§ 207). This sort of sound-change is especially frequent in the A. of Piṅgala : *ṇiaḷa* = *nikaṭa* (1, 127[a], 129[a]; 2, 84); *paaḷa* = *prakaṭa* (1, 72; 2, 97. 272); *paaḷia* = *prakaṭita* (2, 264); *phuḷa* = *sphuṭa* (2, 48); *phuḷe* = *sphuṭati*, in the sense of *sphuṭanti* (2, 230); *makkaḷa* = *markaṭa* (1, 91, 99); *vahuḷiā* = *vadhūṭikā* (2, 84). Beside *balamoḷia* = *balamoṭita* (1, 140)[a], for *moḷiā* = *moṭitaḥ* (2, 112) we have to read *moḍiā*, or for *choḍiā*, that stands in rhyme with it, (so S. GOLDSCHMIDT for *loḍiā*) we have to read perhaps *choḷiā* = *choṭitaḥ*. In M. stands *balāmoḷi*° (R. 10, 64; but the v.l. has °*ḍi*°, and so we have to read, since √*muṭ* has *ḍa* always. So M. *balamoḍi*° (H.); M. JM. Ś. *balāmoḍi* (Deśīn. 6, 92; Pāiyal. 174; Triv. 2, 1, 30; Kāvyaprakāśa 72, 10 (cf. § 589); Kk. 260, 35; Mallikām. 122, 8); Ś. *balāmoḍia* past passive participle; Mālatīm. 76, 4; 128, 8; 253, 7; absol. Mālatīm. 235, 3; Rukmiṇīp. 15, 13; 21, 6)[1], *pacchāmoḍia* (absol.; Śak. 144, 11); M. *āmoḍaṇa* (G.); Mg. *moḍaīśśaṁ*, *moḍaīśśāmi* (Mṛcch. 113, 1; 128, 14), *moḍemi*, *moḍia* (Mṛcch. 128, 2; 137, 1). To it belong also *āmoḍa*, *moḍa* (braid of hair; Deśīn. 1, 62; 6, 117) and Ś. *mŏṭṭima* (Anarghar. 152, 9; Rucipati : *mŏṭṭimaṁ balātkāre deśī*, probably also *mŏṭṭāaī* = *ramate* (Hc. 4, 168). — For *kaḍasī* (cemetery; Deśīn. 2, 6) = **kaṭaśī* from *kaṭa* (corpse; e. g. Viṣṇupurāṇa 3, 13, 10) = Pkt. *kaḍa* (vanished; dead; Deśīn. 2, 51) + *śī* (to lie), the MSS in Hc. 2, 174 have *karasī*, hence a change of *ṭa* to *ra* through *ḍa*. The same change of *ṭa* into *ra* takes place in AMg. *purabheyaṇī* (city; Uttar. 618) = Pāli *puṭabhedana*[2]. On *ḍha* for *ṭa* see § 207.

1. In *balā* we should not, with PISCHEL, GGA, 1880, p. 331f.; WEBER, Hāla[1] p. 210; BÜHLER, Pāiyal. s. v. *balāmoḍī* look for the ablative *balāt*. Rather the prefix *ā* has to be assumed, as *āmaḍa*, *āmoḍana* indicate. — Very false JACOBI, SBE. 45, 102, note 2. *puṭa* is wrongly Sanskritized into *putra* (cf. Vr. 12, 5) in *pāṭaliputra*. Cf. § 292.

§ 239. In the inlaut *ṭh* becomes *ḍh* between vowels (§ 198). Dialectically very rarely it becomes *h* : AMg. JM. *kuhāḍa* = *kuṭhāra* (Sūyag. 274; Uttar. 596; T. 6, 16. 17. 18), JM. *kuhāḍaya* (T. 7, 1); *pihaḍa* = *piṭhara* (Hc. 1, 201), AMg. *pihaḍaga* (Jīv. 251), *pihaḍaya* (Uvās. § 184), beside *piḍhara* (Hc. 1, 201; Pāiyal. 172), AMg. *piḍharaga* (Āyār. 2, 1, 11, 5). On the interchange between *ḍa* and *ra* see 241. 258. — *kaṇḍa* <*kaṇṭha* (Rāvaṇa I, 5) shows change of *ṭh* into *ḍ*.

§ 240. As a rule *ḍ* becomes *ḷ*, when it stands in the inlaut between vowels not joined together. The North Indian MSS and printed books write *l* (§ 226; Vr. 2, 23; C. 3, 21; Hc. 1, 202; Kī. 2, 13; Mk. fol. 16). Vr. C. Mk. prescribe *ḷa* for *ḍa* as obligatory; Bh. makes the rule optional and permits *ḍa* in *dāḍima, baḍiśa, nibiḍa*; Hc. requires *ḷa* for *vaḍavāmukha, garuḍa, taḍāga, kriḍati*, allows optionally *ḷa* and *ḍa* in *baḍiśa, dāḍima guḍa, nāḍi, naḍa, āpiḍa*, and teaches *ḍa* as compulsory for *nibiḍa, gauḍa, piḍita, niḍa, uḍu* and *taḍita*. With him agrees Triv., who splits the rule into two 1, 3, 24 (*baḍiśādau*) and 1, 3, 30. Kī. has, like Triv., the gaṇa *baḍiśādi*, but he limits it to *baḍiśa, nibiḍa* and *jaḍa*, which must have *ḍa* according to him. The dialects do not make any strict distinction. One says, for example : AMg. *āmeḷiya* = *āmreḍita* (Aṇuog. 37); AMg. *gaveḷaga* = *gaveḍaka* (Ovav.); AMg. JM. *guḷa* = *guḍa* (Āyār. 2, 1, 4, 5; Ovav., Erz.), Mg. *guḷodaṇa* (Mṛcch. 163, 20), also *guḍa* (Hc. 1, 202), Mg. *guḍāha* = *guḍaka* (Mṛcch. 116, 25); M. Mg. *ṇiaḷa* = *nigaḍa* (G.H.R.; Mṛcch. 109, 16; 132, 20; 162, 17), AMg. *nigaḷa* (Jīv. 349; Ovav.); M. *ṇiaḷia* = *nigaḍita* (G.R.), JM. *niyaḷiya* (Pāiyal. 197); M. *ṇiaḷāvia* (H.); Ś. *ṇigaḷavadi* (Mālav. 51, 21); AMg. *eḷaya* = *eḍaka* (Uttar. 226; Paṇṇav. 366f.; Ovav.); M. AMg. JM. *garuḷa* = *garuḍa* (Hc. 1, 202; Pāiyal. 25; G.; Ṭhāṇ. 71. 85; Sūyag. 317. 771; Āyār. 2, 15, 12. 13; Paṇhāv. 235. 311; Vivāhap. 183. 964 [°*ḍa*]; Paṇṇav. 97; Jīv. 485. 488; Nirayāv.; Ovav.; Dvār. 507, 37); beside them M. has *garuḍa* (R.), JM. *garuḍavūha* beside *garuḷasattha* (Erz.); Ś. *garuḍa* (Nāgān. 66, 10; 71, 12; 99, 1). Mg. *galuḍa* (text °*ru*°; Nāgān. 68, 4. 13); in M. stands *galuḍa* (Acyutaś. 2. 29. 34; AMg. *chaḷaṁsa* = *ṣaḍaśra* (Ṭhāṇ. 493), *chaḷaṁsiya* (Sūyag. 590), *chaḷāyayaṇa* = *ṣaḍāyatana* (Sūyag. 456), *chaḷasii* = *ṣaḍaśiti* (Vivāhap. 199; Samav. 143); cf. §211. 441; AMg. JM. *soḷasa*. A. *soḷaha* = *ṣoḍaśa* (§ 443); *vaḍavā* (Pāiyal. 226); M. *vaḍavāmuha* (R.), A. *vaḍavāṇala* (Hc. 4, 365; 2, 419, 6), beside M. *vaḷavāmuha, vaḷaāmuha* (R.), *vaḷaāṇala* (R. 2, 24; 5, 77), JM. *vaḷayāmuha* (Erz.); Ś. *dāḍima* (Bh. 2, 23; Hc. 1, 202; Viddhaś. 15, 2), M. *dāḍimi* (G.), beside AMg. *dāḷima* (Hc. 1, 202; Āyār. 2, 1, 8, 1; Vivāhap. 1530; Paṇṇav. 483, 531; Ovav.); M. AMg. JM. *āmeḷa*, M. *āmeḷiaa*, AMg. *āmeḷaga, āmeḷaya* = **āpiḍya* (§ 122), beside *āveḍa* (Hc. 1, 202), Ś. *āpiḍa* (Mālatīm. 207, 4); AMg. *taḷāga, taḷāva* beside *taḍāga* = *taḍāka* (§ 231); M. *kiḷei* (G.), AMg. *kilanti* (Rāyap. 138; Uttar. 504), *kiḷae* (Uttar. 570), *kiḷiya* (Āyār. p. 135; 17); Samav. 23), JM. *kilaï, kiḷanta-, kiḷanti, kiḷiūṇa* (Erz.), Ś. *kiḷasi* (Mṛcch. 54, 3; 95, 11), *kiḷa* (Mṛcch. 95, 23), *kiḷamha* (Ratn. 293, 25); Ś. Ḍh. Mg. *kiḷĕmha* (Mṛcch. 94, 15; 30, 18; 131, 18); Ś. *kiḷissaṁ* (Vikr. 41, 7; 47, 11 [so to be read both the times with the Dravidian recension and the v.l. to 47, 11 instead of °*ḍi*°; Mālav. 60, 11), *kiḷissasi* (Mṛcch. 94. 19; 95, 12); Mg. *kiḷiśśaṁ* (Mṛcch. 30, 23; Śak. 155, 12; Mg. Ā. *kiḷiduṁ* (Mṛcch. 100, 21; 140, 7; 148, 13); Ś. *kiḷida* (Mṛcch. 95, 7; Ratn. 293, 29) Ś. *kiḷamāṇa* (Vikr. 52, 9); A. *kiḷaï* (Vikr. 64, 5), *kiḷadi* (Hc. 4, 442, 2), *kiḷanti* (Vikr. 63, 5) from *kriḍ*; M. Ś. *kiḷā* = *kriḍā*, Ś. *kiḷaṇaa*, AMg. *kiḷaṇa, kiḷāvaṇa*, beside AMg. JM. *kiḍā, kiḍḍā* (§ 90), as well as Ś. *kheḷadi*, A. *kheḷanta* AMg. *khĕḷḷāvaṇa*, JM.

khĕllāveūṇa, khĕlla, A. *khĕllanti*, beside AMg. JM. *khĕḍḍa*, A. *khĕḍḍaa*; *khĕḍḍaï* (§ 90. 206); AMg. *tāḷei* = *tāḍayati* (Nāyādh. 1236. 1305), *tāḷĕnti* (Vivāhap. 236), *tāḷayanti* (Uttar. 360. 365), *tāḷĕjjā* (Uvās. § 200), *tāḷeha* (Nāyādh. 1305), *tāḷemāṇa* (Vivāgas. 102), *taḷijjamāṇa* (Paṇhāv. 196), *tāḷiya* (Nāyādh. 1236), *tāḷaṇa* (Paṇhāv. 535; Uttar. 582; Ovav.), Mg. of Śakāra *tāḷia* (absol.; Mṛcch. 167, 6), but elsewhere M. Mg. *tāḍaṇa* (G.H.R.; Karp. 1, 7; 65, 9; Mṛcch. 122, 20); M. *tāḍiumaṇā* (Karp. 70, 7), *tāḍia* (R.); JM. *tāḍiya, tāḍijjamāṇa* (Erz.); Ś. *tāḍedi* (Mṛcch. 79, 22), *tāḍia* (absol.; Mṛcch. 155, 4), *tāḍida* (Mṛcch. 69, 23), *tāḍaīduṁ, tāḍaïssaṁ* (Mālav. 44, 16; 65, 20), *tāḍiadi* (Mālatīm. 267, 6), *tāḍianta-, tāḍiamāṇa* (Mudrār. 211, 5; 212, 2; 203, 1); Mg. *tāḍhedha* (Mṛcch. 166, 24; 169, 22), *tāḍaïśśaṁ* (Mṛcch. 80, 5); Mg. Ā *tāḍida* (Mṛcch. 29, 19; 105, 2; 148, 10). In agreement with Hc. M. AMg. have *uḍu* (Pāiyal. 96; Karp. 36, 3; Jīv. 351); M. *gaüḍa* (G.), AMg. A. *goḍa* (Paṇhāv. 41; Piṅgala 2, 112, 138; cf. § 61*a*); M. *ṇiviḍa* (G.; on H. 996; Karp. 49, 11), *ṇiviḍia* (G.); JM. *niviḍa* (Erz.); M. *ṇiḍa, ṇĕḍḍa* (§ 90); M. JM. *taḍi* (Pāiyal. 98; G.; Erz.; 14, 22; 71, 23), AMg. *taḍiyā* (Vivāhap. 943), but A. *taḷi* (Vikr. 55, 2); M. *piḍia* (G.R.), AMg. JM. *piḍiya* (Pāiyal, 190; Uttar. 577; Erz.). Ś. *piḍida* (Mṛcch. 22, 13; Śak. 11, 1), also M. *ṇippiḍia* (R.), *saṁpiḍia* (G.), *piḍijjanta-* (H.R.), *piḍaṇa* (H.), M. JM. Ś. *piḍā* (Pāiyal. 161; G.; Erz., Mṛcch. 22, 13; Śak. 29, 9; Vikr. 18,5), Ś. *piḍiadi* (Mṛcch. 72, 15), *piḍedi* (Vikr. 16, 17). In AMg. however, *ḷa* prevails : *piḷiya* (Uttar. 590); *piḷiyaga* (Ovav.); *piḷei* (Dasav. 631, 37; Uttar. 927. 935. 940.945. 950); *āviḷae, paviḷae, nippiḷae* (Āyār. 1, 4, 4, 1); *uppiḷavĕjja* (Āyār. 2, 3, 1, 13); *paripiḷĕjja* (Sūyag. 208); *oviḷemāṇa* (Vivāgas. 102; text *u*°); *āviḷiyāṇa, paripiḷiyāṇa* (Āyār. 2, 1, 8, 1); *piḷā* (Paṇhāv. 394. 402. 426; Uttar. 675); *saṁpiḷā* (Uttar. 926. 934. 940. 945. 950), *piḷaṇa* (Paṇhāv. 537; Vivāhap. 610; Uvās.). In Uttar. 620 stands *piḍaï* beside *āviḷijja*. In Piṅgala 1, 145*a* we have to read *piḷia* with S. GOLDSCHMIDT, what is required also by the rhyme with *milia*. AMg. *eḍei* = *eḍayati* (Vivāhap. 248), *eḍanti* (Vivāhap. 236), *eḍĕnti* (Ovav.), *eḍittā* (Vivāhap. 236. 248) have always *ḍa*. Beside *viḍḍā* = *vrīḍā* (§ 90), AMg. has an adjective *viḍḍa* (Vivāhap. 1258); but the commentary reads *veḍa*, that will be correct and is connected to AMg. *veḷanaya* (Aṇuog. 333), that according to Deśīn. 7, 65 is also a substantive and regulates dialectical *velūṇā* (Deśīn. 7, 65). *e* is to be explained according to § 122. M. has *viḍia* beside *viḷia* = *vrīḍita*, AMg. *saviḷiya* (§ 81). *viddūṇā, vedūṇā* (Deśīn. 7, 65) are also adduced.

§ 241. *ḍa* has become *ra* in M. Ś. *verulia*, AMg. JM. *veruliya* = *vāiḍūrya* (§ 80). Bh. 4, 33 has *veluria*, by which *veḷuria* is meant, as by *velulia* (Deśīn. 7, 77), *veḷulia*. According to Hc. 2, 133 there occurs also *vedujja*. Further in AMg. JM. *birāla* = *biḍāla*[1] (Āyār. 2, 1, 5, 3; Paṇṇav. 367. 369; Nāyādh. 345; Uttar 918; Āv. 42, 20), A. *birālaa* (Piṅgala 1, 67; ed. Bombay. °*ḍā*°), femin. *birāli* (Nandīs. 92; Paṇṇav. 368; Āv. 42, 42), AMg. *birāliyā* (Sūyag. 824), also as a name of a plant *chirabirāli* = *kṣīrabiḍāli* (Vivāhap. 1532), *birāliya* (Āyār. 2, 1, 8, 3). For *viḍāla* (Jīv. 356) is to be read *birāla*. Ś. has *biḍāla* (Mālav. 50, 16; v.l. *vi*°; Śak. ed. BÖHTLINGK 94, 7, where the South Indian MSS and printed editions waver between *biḍāla, biḍāla*, *biḷāḷa* and *vilāḷa*, feminine *biḍāli* (Hāsy. 25, 7), *biḍāliā* (Mālav. 67, 9; v.l. *viāriā, bilāliā, vuḍāliā*); Pāli *biḷāla* and *biḷāra*.

1. Excluding Nandis. 92 and Sūẏag. 824, the texts everywhere have *vi°*. For Skt. the only authentic transcription is *bi°*, that is valid for Pkt. also.

§ 242. *ḍha* remains unchanged in all the dialects : AMg. JM. *āḍhaẏa*=*āḍhaka* (Ovav.; Erz.); AMg. *āsāḍha*=*āṣāḍha* (Āẏār. 2, 15, 2; Kappas.); M. JM. Ś. *gāḍha*=*gāḍha* (Pāiẏal. 90; G.H.; Karp. 64, 7; Erz.; Ś. Karp. 15, 5); M. AMg. JM. Ś. Mg. *daḍha* (Pāiẏal. 90; Āẏār. 1, 6, 2, 2; Sūẏag. 161. 544; Mṛcch. 69, 11; Śak. 11, 1; Vikr. 16, 16; 30, 3; Mg. Mṛcch. 116, 8), JŚ. Ś. A. *diḍha* (Kattig. 400, 329. 330, 336; 403, 370; Mṛcch. 44, 5; Vikr. 12, 20; 22, 14; Mallikām. 225, 11; Priẏad. 42, 4; 43, 6; Prab. 18, 1; Piṅgala 1, 86a)=*dṛḍha*; M. JM. *bāḍha*=*bāḍha* (Pāiẏal. 90; G.; Erz.). On A. *khallihaḍaũ* cf. § 110. 207. — Secondary *ḍha*, originating from *ṣṭa* (§ 66. 67. 304) becomes *ḷha* (written *lha*) in *kŏḷhua* (jackal; Deśīn. 2, 65; Pāiẏal. 152) from **koḍhua*=*kroṣṭuka*[1], to which belongs also *kuḷha* for **kŏṭha* (jackal; Deśīn. 2, 34)=**kroṣṭa* for *kroṣṭṛ*; *kŏḷhāhala* (fruit of momordica monadelpha; Deśīn. 2, 39)=**kroṣṭāphala*; cf. *kroṣṭuphala*, Likewise *gŏḷhā* =*gūḍhā* (momordica monadelpha; Deśīn. 2, 95), *gŏḷhāphala*=*gūḍhaphala* (Pāiẏal. 255)[2].

1. LEUMANN, GSAI. 6, 117 note. — 2. Pkt. shows that we should not be sanguine about *gūḍhaphala* with BÖHTLINGK s. v. It is assumed that *ḷha* makes a position.

§ 243. *ṇ* in *veṇu* may become *ḷ* : AMg. *veḷu* (Hc. 1, 203; Pāiẏal. 144; Sūẏag. 197. 248; Paṇṇav. 33; Rāẏap. 33. 89. 184), beside *veṇu* (Āẏār. 2, 11, 4; Sūẏag. 197. 248; Vivāhap. 1526; Paṇṇav. 40), *veṇudeva* (Sūẏag. 317); likewise *veḷuga*, *veḷuẏa*=*veṇuka* (amomum; Āẏār. 2, 1, 8, 14; Vivāhap. 1526; Dasav. 623, 4; Paṇṇav. 43). Since Pāli has *veḷu*, *ḷ* is to be assumed probably also in Pkt. Probably *veṇu* and *veḷu* gŏ back to the basic form **velnu*, which belongs to the root *vel*, *vĕll* that is much used and has widely branched off in Pkt. (§ 107). From this even the other meanings of *veḷu* "thief" and "pestle" (Deśīn. 7, 94) could be well explained; cf. *thūṇa* "thief" § 129.—In P. CP. *ṇa* becomes *na* (§ 225). Kī. 5, 107. 108 teaches that *la* enters : *phalati*=*bhaṇati*, *thvalati* [sic]=*dhvanati*, *phalitaṁ*=*bhaṇitam*, *thvalitaṁ* [sic]=*dhvanitam*, *palaṁ*=Pkt. *vaṇaṁ*=*vanam*; *phalaha* [sic]= *bhaṇata* (5, 113); *phalāmo*=*bhaṇāmaḥ* (5, 114). In the examples *kakaṇa* =*gagaṇa* (5, 102), *jajaṇa*, *cacaṇa*=*yajana* (5, 103), *calaṇa*=*caraṇa*, *usaṇa* =*uṣṇa*, *pasaṇa*=*praśna*, *sināṇa* [sic]=*snāna* (5, 109) the edition writes *ṇa*, and since *ṇa*, *na*, and *la* very often interchange in the Bengali script in the MSS the hypothesis, is, that in agreement with other grammarians *na* is to be read for *la*. According to Kī. 5, 110 *na* and *ṇa* can become also *ña* in P. : *kañaka*=*kanaka*; *vañña*=*varṇa*.

§ 244. Sometimes *ta* and *da* become *la*, and through the intermediate stages *ṭa*, *ḍa* (§ 218. 219) they become *ḷa* (§ 226. 238. 240), that the North Indian MSS likewise indicated by *la*, so that it cannot always be said with certainty whether *la* or *ḷa* is to be written : Ś. *alasī*=*atasī* (Hc. 1, 211 Mallikām. 87, 15); but AMg. *aẏasī* (Vivāhap. 41. 1526; Paṇṇav. 34. 526; Uttar. 592; Ovav.); AMg. *āsila*=*asita* (Sūẏag. 203;) *palila* (Hc. 1, 212) beside M. *palia* = *palita* (Hc. 1, 212; G.H.); M. *vijjulā* = Pāli *vidyutā* = *vidyut* (Hc. 2, 173; Mk. fol. 37; R.), *vijjulī* = **vidyutī* (Vr. 4, 26; Mk. fol. 37), M.Ś. A. *vijjuliā* = **vidyutikā*[1] (H. 584 v.l.; Vikr. 27. 13; Piṅgala 1, 142a). *vijjuā*, that Vr. 4, 9; Hc. 1, 15; Kī. 2, 129; Mk. fol. 33 forbid for M., stands in H. 584, hardly rightly, as elsewhere M. has only *vijjulā* and *vijju* (G.H.R.); Ś. has *vijjudā* (Mṛcch. 91, 19; Veṇīs. 60, 17); M. *sālavāhaṇa*, *sālāhaṇa* = *sātavāhana* (Hc. 1, 8. 211; H.; cf. § 167), yet JM. beside *sālivāhaṇa* also *sāẏavāhaṇa* (Kk.); Mg. *śūla* = *sūta* (Mṛcch. 97, 3).—AMg. *salilā* (stream; Sūẏag. 317. 460; Uttar. 342; perhaps also Vivāhap. 479) is not, with Jacobi[2] to be equated as = Pāli *saritā* = Skt. *sarit*, which always retains *r*, but is a feminine of the adjective *salila* (Āẏār. 2, 16, 10 = Sūẏag. 468) of which Skt. *salila* (water) is neuter. — *ḷa* is to be read in Mg. *kaḷa* (Mṛcch. 11, 1 40, 4), *maḷa* (Mṛcch. 118, 14. 15. 24; 132, 21) beside *kaḍa*, *maḍa* = *kṛta* *mṛta* (§ 219), JM. *vāuḷa* = *vyāpṛta* (Kk.; § 218), A. *paḷaï* for *paḍaï* (§ 218) = *patati* (Piṅgala 1, 78. 116. 120a. 123. 125. 125. 133. 135; 2, 60. 135 202. 231. 261). — *ḍa* has become *la* in M. AMg. *kalamba* = *kadamba* (Vr. 2, 12; Hc. 1, 222; Kī. 2, 20; Mk. fol. 15; Pāiẏal. 255; G.H.R.; Paṇhāv. 60; Ṭhāṇ. 321), beside *kaamba* (Hc. 1, 222), AMg. *kaẏambaga* (Nāẏādh. 354. 1045), *kaẏambaẏa*, (Kappas.; text falsely °*bu*°; v. l. *kalambaẏa*, *kalamba*, *kaẏamba*); AMg. *kālamba* (Ṭhāṇ. 505), M. *kāamba* (G.R.) = *kādamba*. — M. *goḷa* = *godā* (Hc. 2, 174; Mk. fol. 39; Deśin. 2, 104; Pāiẏal. 132; Triv. 1, 3, 105; H.), also introduced into Skt.[3] The MSS of Triv. write *ḷa*, which is attested by the v. l. *goḍā* in H. — M. AMg. *ṇŏllaï*, *ṇullaï* = *nudáti* with doubling according to § 194 (Vr. 8, 7; Hc. 4, 143; Kī. 4, 46 (text *ṇŏṇṇa*]; Mk. fol. 53); M. *ṇŏllei* (H. R.), *ṇŏllĕnti* (G.), *ṇŏllia* (R.), *paṇŏllia* (G.R.); AMg. *ṇŏllāvehinti*, *ṇŏllāviẏa* (Vivāhap. 1280), *paṇŏlla* (absol.; Sūẏag. 360), *vipaṇŏllae* (Āẏār. 1, 5, 2, 2), *paṇullemāṇa* (Nandīs. 146; commentary °*ṇo*°). — JM. *palīvei* = *pradīpayati* (Hc. 1, 221; Āv. 9, 13), *palīvesi*, *palīvehi* (Āv. 9, 19; 32, 21); [M. *palitta* = *pradīpta* (RB 5)]. JM. *palīvaï* (Hc. 4, 152; Mk. fol. 15; Erz.); M. *palīvesi*, *palīviuṁ*, *palippamāṇa* (H.), *palīvei* (R. 5, 67)[4]; M. AMg. *palitta* (Vr. 2, 12; Hc. 1, 221; Kī. 2, 20; H.R.; Nāẏādh. 1117); M. *palīvia* (H.), JM. *palīviẏa* (Pāiẏal. 16; Āv. 9, 15; 32, 22. 26); AMg. *ālīviẏa* (Vivāgas. 225); *ālīvaṇa* = *ādīpana* (Deśīn. 1, 71); JM. *palīvaṇaga* (Āv. 19, 9); but without prefix M. *dippanta-* (R.), *dippanti dippamāṇa* (G.), A. *dīvia* = *dīpita* (Vikr. 60, 19), and with prefix Ś. *uddīvanti* (Mṛcch. 2, 22), *padīvesi* (Uttarar. 83, 2; ed Calc. 1831, p. 55, 19 has °*lī*°). — AMg. JM. *duvālasa* = *dvādaśa* (Paṇhāv. 347; Vivāhap. 168. 173. 249. 608; Uvās.; Kappas.; Erz.), *duvālasaṅga* (Hc. 1, 254; Samav. 3; Ṭhāṇ. 569; Sūẏag. 616; Nandīs. 388. 394), *duvāḷasaviha* (Vivāhap. 159. 524; Paṇṇav. 30. 374; Jīv. 44), *duvālasama* (Āẏār. 1, 8, 4, 7; Sūẏag. 699). — AMg. JM. *ḍohaḷa*, M. AMg. JM. Ś. *dohaḷa* = *dohada*, M.Ś. *dohaḷaa* (§ 222), according to the information given by Pāli, to be written with *ḷa*, as is shown also by Mg. *haḷaka* (Mṛcch. 9, 25), *haḷaa* (Mṛcch. 163, 24) beside the usual Mg. *haḍakka* (§ 194). Cf. § 436. — M. *maḷaï* = *mradate* (Vr. 8, 50; Hc. 4, 126; R.), *maḷesi* (H.), *maḷei* (R.), *maḷia* (G.H.R.), *parimaḷasi* (H.), *parimaḷia* (H.R.), *vimaḷaï* (G.), *vimaḷia* (G.R.), *omaḷia* (R.), *maḷaṇa* (G.), *parimaḷaṇa*

(H.), with *la* as in Marâṭhī and Gujarātī[5]. — AMg. *elīsa* = *idṛśa*, *aṇelisa* = = *anidṛśa*, *elikkha*, *elikkhaẏa* = *idṛkṣa*, *idṛkṣaka* (§ 121). — *sŏllaï* (cooks; Hc. 4, 90) = *sūdáyati*, with doubling according to § 194, AMg. *sŏlla* (cooked; roasted; Uvās.; Niraẏāv.) *sŏllaẏa* (Uvās.) = *sūd+na*, *sūd+na+ka* (§566)[6] and from the present stem (§ 565) *sŏlliẏa* = *sūdita* (Ovav.). — *veḷūṇā* beside *bedūṇā*, *viddūṇā* (§ 240); AMg. *vibhelaẏa* = *vibhedaka* (§ 121).

1. So correctly BOLLENSEN on Vikr. 27, 13 p. 279. Not correctly, thinks WEBER on H. 584 with regard to *vidyullatā*. — 2. SBE. 45. 68, note 1. Even JACOBI's explanation of *kulala* is wrong; see § 80. — 3. PISCHEL, BB. 3, 237f. — 4. The text has *paḍivei*, in the same stanza with *palita*, for which 1, 5; 5, 87 *paḍitta*, 15, 73 perhaps *païtta* stands. Forms with *ḍa* are not attested elsewhere — 5. PISCHEL on Hc. 4, 126. — 6. Wrongly equated by HOERNLE, Uvās. s. v. as = *śūlya*, *śūlyaka*, an explanation, that is not tenable in places like as Ovav. § 74 *iṅgālasŏlliya*.

§ 245. *ta* becomes *ra* through *ḍa* (§ 218) in *sattari* = *saptati* (Hc. 1, 210); AMg. JM. *sattariṁ*, *sattari*, JM. also *saẏari* (70); AMg. *egūṇasattariṁ* (69), *ĕkkasattariṁ* (71), *bāvattariṁ* (72), JM. also *bisattari*; AMg. *tevattariṁ* (73), *covattariṁ*, JM. *caũhattari* (74) etc., A. *ehattari* (71), *chāhattari* (76) See § 446. More frequently *da* has become *ra*, Mg. *la*, through *ḍa*; AMg *urāla* = *udāra* (Āẏār. 1, 8, 1, 9; 2, 15, 14. 15 [text *o*°] [1]; Sūẏag. 95. 392. 408. 639; Ṭhāṇ. 177; Nāẏādh. § 4; p. 369. 566; Antag. 57; Vivāhap. 10. 155. 168. 170. 231. 248. 942. 1039. 1228f.; Uttar. 1052. 1058; Uvās.; Niraẏāv.; Kappas. s. v. *orāla*); *orāliẏa* = *audārika* (Paṇṇav. 397 [°*u*][1]. 461ff.; Uttar. 881; Vivāhap. 111, 146. 528ff. 620; Ṭhāṇ. 54. 55; Ovav.). — *karalī* = *kadalī* in the meaning "elephant flag", but *kaalī* in the meaning "musa sapientum" (Hc. 1, 220). False is Ś. *kaṇaakeriā* (Bālar. 131, 14) = *kanakakadalikā* against M. Ś. *kaalī* (Karp. 46. 14; 102, 6), Ś. *kadaliā* (Prab. 66, 2), AMg. JM. *kaẏalī* (Pāiẏal. 254; Āẏār. 2, 1, 8, 12 [so to be read] ; cf. v. l.]. — *gaggara* = *gadgada* (Vr. 2, 13; Hc. 1, 219; Kī. 2, 21; Mk. fol. 15). — *daśa* becomes *rasa*, *raha* in the numerals 11-13, 15, 17-18 (Vr. 2, 14; Hc. 1, 219; Kī. 2, 21; Mk. fol. 15), So : AMg. *ĕkkārasa*, A. *eāraha*, *ĕggāraha*, *gāraha*, but also A. *ĕkkadaha*, CP. *ekālasa* (11); AMg. JM. *bārasa*, A. *bāraha*, beside AMg. JM. *duvālasa* (§ 244) (12); AMg. *terasa*, A. *teraha* (13); AMg. JM. *paṇṇarasa*, A. *paṇṇaraha* (15); AMg. JM. *sattarasa* (17); AMg. JM. PG. *aṭṭhārasa*, A. *aṭṭhāraha* (18). See § 443. Likewise the ordinals (§ 449). Further *da* becomes *ra* in the adjectival and pronominal compound words formed with *-dṛś*, *-dṛśa*, *dṛkṣa*, as in M. AMg. JM. Ś. *erisa*, AMg. JM. *erisaẏa*, A. *erisia* beside AMg. *elisa*, *aṇelisa*, P. *etisa*, Ś. *īdisa*, Mg. *īdiśa* = *idṛśa* (§ 121); M. AMg. JM. Ś. *kerisa*, JM *kerisaẏa*, Mg. *keliśa* beside Ś. *kīdisa* = *kīdṛśa* (§ 121); JM. *annārisa* = *anyādṛśa* (Hc. 1, 142; Erz.), Ś. *aṇṇārisa* (Vikr. 52, 19; Mālatīm. 89, 7; 138, 10; 217, 4; Mahāv. 128. 7; Bhartṛharinirveda 4, 1), but P. *aññātisa* (Hc. 4, 317), A. *aṇṇāisa* (Hc. 4, 413); M. JM. Ś. *amhārisa* = *asmādṛśa* (Hc. 1,142; H.; Erz. Mṛcch. 4, 16. 17. 21; 18, 3; Mudrār. 36, 4; 241, 8; 259, 1; Karp.; 92, 8; Viddhaś. 25, 8), feminine Ś. *amhārisī* (Viddhaś. 71, 9; 116, 5), but P. *amhātisa* (Hc. 4, 317); M. JM. Ś. *tumhārisa* = *yuṣmādṛśa* (Hc. 1, 142; G.R.; Erz.; Viddhaś. 51, 12; 121, 9; Karp. 93. 9), but P. *yumhātisa* (Hc. 4, 317); *eārisa* = *etādṛśa* (Hc. 1, 142), Ś. *edārisa* (Viddhaś. 102, 2; so to be read);

feminine *edārisī* (Prab. 44, 13; so to be read), AMg. JM. *jārisa*=*yādṛśa* (Hc. 1, 142; Kī. 1, 29; Uttar. 794; Erz.), AMg. *jārisaya* (Nāyādh. 1284), but P. *yātisa* (Hc. 4, 317), Ś. *jādisa* (Viddhaś. 29, 3; 32, 1. 2), feminine *jādisī* (Śak. 51, 11. 12; Prab. 16, 10), A. *jaïsa* (Hc. 4, 403. 404); M. AMg. JM. Ś. *tārisa*=*tādṛśa* (Bh. 1, 31; Hc. 1, 142; Kī 1, 29; R.; Karp. 115, 4; Sūyag. 365., 429; Uttar. 794; Dasav. 633, 19=Hc. 4, 287; Āv. 27, 2. 6. 25; Erz.; Vikr. 52, 19; Mahāv. 126, 7; Prab. 44, 12 [read *tārisie*, AMg. *atārisa* (Āyār. 1, 6, 1, 6), *tārisaga* (Nāyādh.; Kappas.), Mg. *tāliśa* (Mṛcch. 37, 11), but Ś. also *tādisa* (Śak. 32, 5; Vikr. 52, 7; 53, 11; Prab. 16, 10), feminine *tādisī* (Śak. 51, 12; Viddhaś. 32, 1.2), Mg. *tādiśī* (Mṛcch. 140, 12; Prab. 62, 7), P. *tātisa* (Hc. 4, 317), A. *taïsa* (Hc. 4, 403); AMg. A. *sari*=*sadṛk* (Hc. 1, 142; Nāyādh.; Piṅgala 1, 42); M. AMg. JM. JŚ. Ś.D.A. *sarisa*=*sadṛśa* (Bh. 1, 31; Hc. 1, 142; Mk. fol. 11; G.H.R.; Uvās.; Nirayāv.; Nāyādh.; Kappas.; KI. 12; Erz.; Kattig. 399, 316; Mṛcch. 17, 18; 24, 16; 55, 4; 95, 11; 134, 18; 152, 21; Śak. 132. 1; 134, 8; Vikr. 6, 1; 8, 13 [so to be read]; 39, 12; Mālav. 6, 20 etc.; D. Mṛcch. 102, 23; 105, 4; A. Piṅgala 1, 10), AMg. *sarisaya*, feminine *sarisiyā* (Nāyādh.), Mg. *śaliśa* (Mṛcch. 154, 20; 164, 20; 176, 5), A. *sarisima*=**sadṛśiman*=*sādṛśya* (Hc. 4, 395, 1); M. Ś. *sariccha*=*sadṛkṣa* (Hc 1, 44, 142; H.; Viddhaś 23, 4), also M. JM. JŚ. *sāriccha* (§ 78), and Ś. *sārikkha* (Karp. 108, 2), *sāriccha*=**sādṛkṣya* (Hc. 2, 17; G. G. 852; see v. 1.), AMg. A. *sārikkha* (Hc. 2, 17; 4, 404); Ś. *sārikkhadā* (Karp. 109, 7. 10). Cf. also *bhavārisa* (Hc. 1, 142) against A. *avarāisa*=**aparādṛśa* (Hc. 4, 413).

1. *orāla* is likewise false, as *urāliya*. Both the words are substituted by one another in the anlaut in MSS and printed editions.

§ 246. Sometimes *va* has taken the place of *ta* and *da* just apparently. —*āvajja* is not=*ātodya* (Hc. 1, 156), but=**āvādya* (§ 130). AMg. *ujjovemāṇa* (Paṇṇav. 100. 102. 112; Uvās.; Ovav.), *ujjoviya* (Nāyādh.; Kappas.), *ujjovĕnta-* (Nāyādh.) are not=*uddyotayamāna, uddyotita uddyotayant* with the infixed *v*[1], but belong to $\sqrt{}$*dyu*, that occurs in Skt. *dyu* (day), *didyu* (thunderbolt; lightening), perhaps also in A. *joedi* (sees; Hc. 4, 422, 6 and Index of words in Hc.) and certainly in the modern Indian dialects[2]. M. *ruvaï*, M. JM. *rovaï* do not belong to *rud*, but to *ru* (§ 473). *kavaṭṭia* is not=*kadarthita* (Hc. 1, 224; 2, 29), but=*kava* in the sense of *kad* =*ku*+**ārtita*=*ārta* (§289. 428). Certain other phonetic changes assumed by the grammarians are also not tenable. *erāvaṇa* is not=*airāvata* (Vr. 2, 11; Bh. 1, 35; Kī. 2, 31; Mk. fol. 15), but=*airāvaṇa* (Hc. 1, 148. 208; § 60). *gabbhiṇa* is not =*garbhita* (Vr. 2, 10; Hc. 1, 208; Kī. 2, 31; Mk. fol. 15), but=*garbhin* with a transition to the *a*-declension (§ 406). *atimuktaka* forms, according to Hc. 1, 26. 178. 208, *aṇiuṁṭaa* beside *aïmuṁṭaa*; in AMg. it regularly becomes *aïmuttaya* (Hc. 1, 26; Ovav. § 8), in Ś. *adimŏttaa* (Mṛcch. 73, 10), as *atimukta*, JM. *aïmutta* (Pāiyal. 256), Ś. *adimutta* (Vikr. 21, 9; Vṛṣabh. 15, 17; 47, 15; Mallikām. 97, 6; 128. 15). In Mk. fol. 34 *aïmuṁta* is to be read for *aïmutta* of the MS; in Bh. 4, 15 probably *aïmuṁka* is to be read for *ahimuṁka*, which is explained by *abhimukta*. Whence comes *aṇiŭṁtaa* is not clear. On *ta* erroneously used in AMg. see § 203; on *da* for *ta*, §192.

203. 204; on *ṭa*, *ḍa* for *ta*, § 218. 219; on *ta* for *da*, § 190. 191; on *ḍa* for *da*, § 222.

1. LEUMANN, Aup. S. s. v. *ujjoy*. — 2. PISCHEL on Hc. 4, 322.

§ 247. *tha* may become *ḍha* (§ 221), *dha* may become *ḍha* (§ 223), in CP. *tha* (§ 191). AMg. *samilā* (Uttar. 592. 788) is explained by JACOBI[1] with *samidh*. That is phonetically impossible and against the sense. The explanation of the commentators by *kilikā*, *yugakilikā* points to **samitā*; cf. *samit*, *samiti*. — *na* becomes mostly *ṇa* (§ 224). In *nimba* it may become *la* : *limba* (Hc. 1, 230) = Marāṭhī *liṁba*, A. *limbaḍaa* (Hc. 4, 387, 2) = Gujarātī *liṁbaḍa*, beside M. *ṇimba* (Hc. 1, 230; H.), AMg. *nimboliyā* = *nimbagulikā* (Nāyādh. 1152. 1173; cf. §167). — On *ṇhāviā* = *nāpita* see §210.

1. SBE. 45, p. 94, note 4.

§ 248. For *pa*, which as a rule becomes *va* (§ 199), dialectically also *ba* (§ 192) and *bha* (§ 209), there may appear sometimes also *ma*: M. AMg. JM. *āmeḷa* = *āpiḍya*, *āmeḷiaa*, AMg. *āmeḷaga*, *ameḷaya* (§ 122); *ṇimeḷa* = **ṇipiḍya* (§ 122); M. *ṇumajjaï* = *nipadyate*, *ṇumaṇṇa* = *nipanna* (§ 118); AMg. *āṇamaṇi* = *ājñāpani* (Paṇṇav. 363ff. 369) beside *āṇavaṇi* (Paṇṇav. 364f.); AMg. *cimiḍha* = *cipiṭa* (Nāyādh. 751; commentary *cimiṭṭha*) against. *civiḍha* (Nāyādh. 745; text *civiṭṭha*, commentary *cimiṭṭha*, in the text, therefore, to be read *cimiḍha*, as for example in 751; cf. § 207); AMg. *kuṇima* = *kuṇapa* (Sūyag. 225. 282. 483. 811; Ṭhāṇ. 338; Paṇhāv. 179; Jīv. 255; Ovav.); AMg. *talima* = *talpa* (Deśīn. 5, 20; Pāiyal. 117. 122; Nāyādh. 1192f.); AMg. *nima*, *ṇima* = *nipa* (Hc. 1, 234; Dasav. 623 ,5; Paṇṇav. 31; Ovav.; cf. Ovav. § 6 note 12), beside AMg. *niva*, A. *ṇiva* (Hc. 1, 234; Ovav.; Piṅgala 1, 60[a]; 2, 82); AMg. *bhiṇḍimāla* = *bhindipāla* (Jīv. 257. 279; Paṇhāv. 61. 158; Ovav.), beside *bhiṇḍivāla* (Vr. 3, 46; Hc. 2, 38 [also PISCHEL], 89; Kī. 2, 65; Mk. fol. 26; AMg. *maṇāma* = Pāli *manāpa* (Ṭhāṇ. 65. 66. 527; Samav. 94; Vivāhap. 162. 480; Nāyādh.; Nirayāv.; Ovav.; Kappas.). feminine *maṇāmī* (Vivāhap. 196), *amaṇāma* (Sūyag. 630; Vivāgas. 40f.; Samav. 227; Jīv. 256; Vivāhap. 89. 117. 254); AMg. *vaṇimaga*, °*ya* = *vanipaka* (Āyār. 2, 1, 1, 13; 2, 1, 5, 1; 2, 2, 2, 8ff.; 2, 3, 1, 2; 2, 5, 1, 9ff.; 2, 6, 1, 7; 2, 10, 23; 2, 15, 11; Paṇhāv. 492; Ṭhāṇ. 397; Nāyadh. 1086; Dasav. 622, 31. 35; 626, 29; Kappas.), *vaṇimayayāe* = *vanipakatayā* (Paṇhāv. 358; text *vaṇimayāe*); AMg. *viḍima* = *viṭapa* (twig. Āyār. 2, 4, 2. 12; Paṇhāv. 437; Jīv. 548f.; Dasav. 628, 28; Ovav. §4; tree; Dasav. N. 645, 4; Rhinoceros; Deśīn. 7, 89; ovav. § 37. [37]; young roe; Deśīn. 7, 89), but M. Ś. *viḍava* (Bh. 2, 20; Kī. 2, 10; G.H.R.; Śak. 67, 2; 137, 5; Vikr. 12, 17; 22, 12; 31, 1); *viḍavi-* = *viṭapin* (Pāiyal. 54); AMg. JM. *sumiṇa* beside *suviṇa*, JM. *sumiṇaga* beside *suviṇaga*; *simiṇa* beside M. *siviṇa*, Ś. AMg. *siviṇaa* = Pāli *supina* = Skt. *svapna* (§ 177). The transition, that is almost wholly restricted to AMg. is explained by the interchange of *ma* and *va* (§ 251. 261).

§ 249. Ś. *pāraddhi* (hunting; Viddhaś. 23, 9), which is equated by Hc. 1, 235 and Nārāyaṇadīkṣita on Viddhaś. 23, 9 as = *pāpardhi*, is = *prārabdhi*; its synonym *pāraddha* (Deśīn. 6, 77), that means also reward for an act done in a former life", "oppressed" and "tortured", is = *prārabdha*.

§ 250. Like *pa* (§ 248), *ba* also sometimes becomes *ma* : *kamandha* =

kabandha (Vr. 2, 19; Hc. 1, 239; Mk. fol. 16). Hc. 1, 239; Mk. fol. 16; Prākṛtamañjari in PISCHEL, De gr. Prācr. p. 14 teach also *kayandha*, that has its origin in AMg. JM. or JŚ. and, therefore, will be = *kaẏandha*. We find in the texts also M. JM. A. *kavandha* (§ 201), which according to Mk. fol. 67 Ś. too always has. — *samara* = *śabara* (Hc. 1, 258), but M. AMg. JM. Ś. *savara*, M. AMg. *savari* (§ 201). AMg. JM. *māhaṇa* with WEBER[1], E. MÜLLER,[2] JACOBI,[3] LEUMANN,[4] S. GOLDSCHMIDT,[5] ASCOLI,[6] HOERNLE[7] to be equated as = *brāhmaṇa*, is linguistically impossible. Corresponding to AMg. JM. *bambha-* = *brahman*, *bambhaẏāri-* = *brahmacārin*, *bambhaṇṇaẏa* = *brāhmaṇyaka*, *bambhaloẏa* = *brahmaloka* etc. (§ 267) the word must be pronounced as *bambhaṇa*, as is also the case, AMg. JM. *bambhaṇa* (Uttar. 748. 753f.; Āv. 18, 15; Erz.; Kk.), AMg. *subambhaṇa* (Paṇhāv. 448). Sometimes both the words occur beside one another, as Erz. 1, 7 *māhaṇassa*, but 1, 8 *bambhaṇeṇa*; Kk. 276. 25 *baṁbhaṇarūva*, but II, 508, 19 *māhaṇarūvaga*, AMg. employs almost exclusively *māhaṇa*[8] (e.g. Āẏār. 2, 1, 1, 12. 2, 1. 3. 11, 9; 2, 2, 1, 2. 2, 8, 9; 2, 6, 1, 1; 2, 7, 2, 15, 2. 4. 11; Sūẏag. 17. 56. 74. 105. 106. 113. 118. 373. 419. 495. 553. 620. 642f.; Vivāhap. 115. 119. 343; Vivāgas. 152f.; Ovav.; Kappas.), *mahāmāhaṇa* (Uvās.), femin. AMg. JM. *māhaṇī* (Āẏār. 2, 15, 2; Nāẏādh. 1151; Vivāhap. 788; Kappas.; Āv. 12, 1), *māhaṇatta* = *brāhmaṇatva* (Uttar. 756). I derive the word from Skt. *makha* (sacrifice), *mākha* (pertaining to a sacrifice), and equate it, therefore, as = **mākhana* = "sacrificial priest."

1. Bhag. 1, 410, note 5. — 2. Beiträge p. 29. — 3. Kalpas. und Erz. s. v. — 4. Aup. S. s. v. — 5. Prākṛtica p. 15. — 6. Kritische Studien p. 221 with note 8. — 7. Uvās., Translation p. 120, note 273. — 8. Cf. Uttar. 748 *je loe baṁbhaṇo vutto... taṁ vayaṁ būma māhaṇaṁ*.

§ 251. In A. *ma*, in the inlaut, may become *v̐a* (Hc. 4, 397); *kav̐ala* beside *kamala* (Hc. 4, 397); *bhav̐ara* beside *bhamara* (Hc. 4, 397); *ṇisāv̐aṇṇa* = *niḥsāmānya* (Hc. 4, 341, 1); *pav̐āṇa* = *pramāṇa* (Hc. 4, 419, 3); beside *pamāṇa* (Hc. 4, 399, 1); *bhav̐aï* = *bhramati* (Hc. 4, 401, 2); *vajjav̐a* = *vajramaya* (Hc. 4, 395, 5); *sav̐a* = *sama* (Hc. 4, 358, 2); *suv̐arahi* beside *sumari* = *smara* (Hc. 4, 387). This phonetic transformation has become obsolete in other dialects and partly in A. itself, as either *v* has vanished behind the anunāsika or more frequently the anunāsika has disappeared before *v*, so that only ◌̃ or *v* has remained. Thus according to Hc. 1, 178 the anunāsika takes the place of *m* in *aṇiuṃtaa* = *atimuktaka* (§ 246); *kā̃ua* = *kāmuka*; *cā̃uṇḍā* = *cāmuṇḍā*; *jaū̃ṇā* = *yamunā*. According to Vr. 2, 3; Kī. 2, 5; Mk. fol. 14 *m* drops off in *yamunā*, and so has M. AMg. JM. *jaüṇā* (G.; v. l. on H. 671; Kaṁsav. 55, 5; Prabandhac. 27, 2; Ṭhāṇ. 544; Vivāgas. 208; Dvār. 495, 20; T. 4, 8). Most of the MSS have in H. 671 *jamuṇā*. as also Ś. (Vikr. 23, 13; 41. 3). The correct spelling in M. AMg. JM. will be *jaū̃ṇā* (§179). For *kā̃ua* M. Ś. have *kāmua* (H.; Mṛcch. 25, 21; 71, 6; Vikr. 21, 18; 31. 14), JM. *kāmuẏa* (Erz.); for *cā̃uṇḍā* Ś. has *cāmuṇḍā* (Mālatīm. 30, 5; Karp. 105, 2; 106, 2; 107, 1). Erroneous is M. *kuarī* for *kumarī* = *kumārī* (H. 298) and the similar v. l. in other words in WEBER, H.[2] p. LXI on the stanza 298. The same sound-change is to be assumed in A. in *thā̃u* = *sthāman* (Hc. 4, 358, 1; text *thāu*), in the sense of *sthāna*, as the scholiasts explain.

Kī. 5, 99 has *thāma sthāne*. Further in *bhõhā* from, *bhamuhā* (Piṅgala 2, 98; text *bhohā*, S. GOLDSCHMIDT *bhauṃhā*; cf. § 124. 166) and *haṇuā = hanumān* (Piṅgala 1, 63a; text *haṇũā*). — *va* has taken the place of *ma* in AMg. *aṇavadagga*, AMg. JM. *aṇavaẏagga* = Pāli *anamatagga* = *anamadagra*[1] (Sūẏag. 456 [°*ṇo*°]. 787. 789. 867; Ṭhāṇ. 41. 129; Paṇhāv. 214. 302; Nāẏādh. 464. 471; Vivāhap. 38. 39. 160. 848. 1128. 1290. 1324; Uttar. 842; Erz.) from √*nam*, which in M. JM. A. also has sometimes *va* : *ṇavaī* (Hc. 4, 226); M. *oṇavia* = **avanamita* = *avanata* (H. 637), JM *navakāra* = *namaskāra* (Erz. 35, 23, 25. 27 29); AMg. *vippaṇavanti* = *vipraṇamanti* (Sūẏag. 472); A. *ṇavahĩ* = *namanti* (Hc. 4, 367, 4), *ṇavantāhã* = *namatām* (Hc. 4, 399). In all the dialects, however, *nam* mostly retains its *m*. *ahivaṇṇu* (Hc. 1, 243), beside Mg. Ś. *ahimaṇṇu* (Hc. 1, 243; Veṇīs. 34, 12; 64, 16) ; A. *ravaṇṇa* = *ramaṇya* (Hc. 4, 422, 11); AMg. *vāṇavantara*[2] beside the usual *vāṇamantara* (Nāẏādh. 1124; Ṭhāṇ. 222; Bhag.; Ovav.; Kappas.). — In the anlaut too *ma* has sometimes become *va* : AMg. *vimaṁsā* = *mimāṁsā* (Sūẏag. 59; Ṭhāṇ. 332f.; Nandīs. 351. 381. 383. 505), *vimaṁsaẏa* = *mimāṁsaka* (Paṇhāv. 109)[3]; *vaṁjara* (Hc. 2, 132) beside *maṁjara* (§ 81. 86); M. JM. A. *vammaha* = *manmatha* (Vr. 2, 39; C. 3, 21; Hc. 1, 242; Kī. 2, 45; Mk. fol. 18; G.H.R.; Karp. 38, 11; 47, 16; 57, 6; Viddhaś. 24, 12; Dhūrtas. 3, 13; Unmattar. 2, 19; Erz.; Piṅgala 2, 88), also in Mg. in verses (Mṛcch. 10, 13: text *ba*°; cf. GOḌABOLE 28, 4 with note), but in Ś. only *mammadha*[4] (Śak. 53, 2; Hāsy. 22, 15; 3. 14; Karp. 92, 8; Mālatīm. 81, 2; 125, 2; 266, 3; Nāgān. 12, 2; Pras. 32, 12, 36, 18; 84, 3; Vṛṣabh. 29, 19; 38, 11; 42, 11; 49, 9; 51, 10; Pārvatīp. 24, 15; 26, 23; 28, 5; 30, 17; Bālar. 135, 10; Karṇas. 30, 5; Anarghar. 270, 8 etc.). On *va* from *ma* in consonant-groups see § 277. 312. Cf. also ASCOLI, Kritische Studien p. 200f. — M. A. *bhasala* (bee; H.; Karp. 10, 7. 8; 64, 5; Hc. 4, 444, 5) is to be derived neither with Hc. 1, 244. 254; Deśīn. 6, 101 from *bhramara*, nor with WEBER[5] from √*bhraṁś*, but it belongs with *bhasman* (ashes), *bhasad* (the hinder part), *bhastrā* (bellows) to √*bhas* "to blow", and therefore, designates the bee as "the humming creature."[6] The word has gone over to Skt. too.[7]

1. The correct explanation of this t.t., which, except in Vivāhap. 991, is an adjective of *saṁsāra*, probably means "whereof the beginning is not bent off" — "what does not change" = "endless." The root √*nam* has correctly been identified by JACOBI, Erz. s. v.; his other explanation is, however, wrong. False also PISCHEL, BB. 3, 245. The scholiasts explain the word as *ananta*, *aparyanta*, *aparyavasāna* and mostly consider *avadagga*, *avaẏagga* as Deśī words used in the sense of "end", and, therefore, analyse the word as *aṇ*+*avdagga*. — 2. LEUMANN, Aup. S. s. v. *vāṇamantara*. — 3. The scholiasts explain the words as *vimarśa*, *vimarśaka*. — 4. The Indian editions always write *mammaha*. Falsely they sometimes have also *vammaha* in Ś. (Bālar. 24, 11; 242, 4; Viddhaś. 23. 9, 99, 8; Rukmiṇīp. 19, 10; 20, 7; 28, 6; 30, 14; Mallikām. 122, 18; 124. 3; 158. 19 etc.). as conversely *mammaha* in M. (Acyutaś. 58; false also H. 327. 576 [cf. v. l.]. P. GOLDSCHMIDT (Specimen, p. 10) liked to write it wrongly as *bammaha*. — 5. On H. 444. — 6. PISCHEL, Ved. Stud. 2, 63. 7. PISCHEL, on Hc. 1, 244.

§ 252. Except in Mg. P. CP. *ya* becomes *ja* in the anlaut (Vr. 2, 31; C. 3, 15; Hc. 1, 245; Kī. 2, 38 ; Mk. fol. 17) : M. AMg. JM. JŚ. Ś. D. (Mṛcch. 101, 9; 102, 21; 103, 15; 105, 7). Ḍh. A. *jaï*, Ś. also often Ā (Mṛcch. 105, 3) *jadi* = *yadi*, but Mg. *ẏaï*, *yadi*; M. AMg. JM. Ā. (Mṛcch.

100, 12). A. *jaha*, JŚ. *jadha*, Ś. D. (Mṛcch. 105, 21); *jadhā* = *yathā*, but Mg. *yadhā* (§ 113); M. AMg. JM. *jakkha* = *yakṣa* (G.H.; Karp. 26, 1; Āẏār. 2, 1, 2, 3; Sūẏag. 674; Paṇṇav. 75; Ṭhāṇ. 90. 229; Nāẏādh.; Ovav.; Āv. 13, 25ff.; Erz.; JŚ. *jadi* = *yati* (Pav. 383, 69); M. AMg. JM. A. *jūha*, Ś. *jūdha* = *yūtha* (§ 221); M. AMg. JM. Ś. A. *jŏvvaṇa* = *yauvana* (§ 90); AMg. JM. *jārisa*, but P. *yātisa* = *yādṛśa*, Ś. *jādisi* = *yādṛśi* (§ 245). So also in the inlaut when it is, according to § 91, doubled in M. AMg. JM. JŚ. D.A. (Vr. 2, 17; C. 3, 25; Hc. 1, 248; Kī. 2, 36. 37; Mk. fol. 16), as M. JM. A. *dijjaī*; JŚ. *dijjadi* = *diyate*, but P. *tiyyate*, Ś. Mg. *diadi* (§ 545); AMg. JM. *hŏjjā* = *bhūyāt*, AMg. *dĕjjā* = *deyāt*, *ahiṭṭhĕjjā* = *adhiṣṭheyāt*, *pahĕjja* = *praheyāt* (§ 466); M. AMg. JM. *karaṇijja* = *karaṇiya*, but Ś. *karaṇia*; AMg. *vandaṇijja* but Ś. *vandaṇia* (§ 571); AMg. *aṅgulijjaka* = *aṅguliyoka* (Nāẏādh. [°*lĕ*°]; Ovav.; Kappas.); AMg. JM. *kañcuijja* = *kañcukiya* (chamberlain; Vivāhap. 792, 800. 963. 966; Rāẏap. 289; Nāẏādh. § 128; Ovav.; Āv. 8, 8); AMg. *kosĕjja* = *kauśeya* (Θvav.); AMg. *gevĕjja* = *graiveya* (Uttar. 1086; Nāẏādh.; Ovav.; Kappas. [°*vi*°]); AMg. JM. *nāmadhĕjja* = *nāmadheya* (Āẏār. 2, 15, 11. 15; Nāẏādh. § 92. 116; p. 1228. 1351 [°*dhi*°]; Paṇhāv. 303. 327; Ovav. § 16. 105. 165; Niraẏāv. ; Kappas.; Āv. 10, 2). As a rule *y* drops off in the inlaut according to § 186. In Mg. P. CP. *y* remains in the anlaut and inlaut, in Mg. in the inlaut only when doubled (Hc. 4, 292) : Mg. *yuga* = *yuga* (Hc. 4, 288); *yādi* = *yāti*, *yadhāśalūva* = *yathāsvarūpa*, *yāṇavatta* = *yānapattra* (Hc. 4, 292); *yutta* = *yukta* (Hc. 4, 302); *yaśka* = *yakṣa* (Namisādhu on Rudraṭa, Kāvyālaṁkāra 2, 12); *yadhā* = *yathā*, *yaṁ yaṁ* = *yad yad*, *yahastaṁ* [read °*dha*°] = *yathārtham* (Lalitav. 566, 5. 8. 9); in the inlaut : *alaśkiyyamāṇa* = *alakṣyamāṇa*, *pĕśkıyyaṁdi*, *pĕśkiyyasi* [read °*śi*] = *prekṣyante*, *prekṣyase*; *yāṇiyyadi* = *jñāyate* (Lalitav. 565, 7. 13. 15; 566, 1). As in the case of *ja* (§ 236) in this case too the manuscripts do not falsely establish the rule. P. : *yutta* = *yukta*, *yātisa*, *yumhātisa*, *yad* = *yādṛśa*, *yāṣmādṛśa*, *yad* (Hc. 4, 306, 317. 323); in the inlaut : *giyyate* = *giyate*, *tiyyate* = *diyate*, *ramiyyate ramyate*, *paḍhiyyate* = *paṭhyate*, *huvĕyya* = *bhavet* (Hc. 4, 315. 320. 323) : CP. *niyocita* = (Hc. 4. 325; cf. 327). On *dŏgga* = *yugma* see § 215, on *yeva* = *eva* § 336.

§ 253. As in the case of treatment of *na* (§ 224,), so in that of *ya* too PG. shows an extraordinary variation. In the anlaut it is retained in °*yāji* (5, 1); °*ppayutte* = °*prayuktān* (5, 6); °*yaso*° = *yaśas* (6, 9); °*yŏllaka* (?6. 31); *yo* = *yaḥ*; (7, 46); on the contrary it becomes *ja* in *jo* (7, 44) and °*saṁjutto* = °*saṁyuktaḥ* (7, 47). VG. has *yuva*° (101, 2). In the inlaut simple *ya* remains unchanged in PG. VG. : PG. °*vājapeẏa*° (5, 1); *visaye* = *viṣaye* (5, 3); *neyike* = **naiyikān* (5, 6); °*āyu*° = °*āyus*°, *vijayavejayike* = *vijayavaijaẏikān* (6, 9); °*ppadāyino* = °*pradāyinaḥ* (6, 11); *ātteya*° = *ātreya*° (6, 13); °*saṁvinayikaṁ* (6, 32); *visaya*° = *viṣaya*° (6, 35); *āpiṭṭiyaṁ* = *āpiṭṭyām* (6, 37); *bhūyo* = *bhūyaḥ* (7, 41); *vasudhādhipataye* = °*patin* (7, 44); *ajātāe* = AMg. *ajjattāe* (Kappas. Th. 2; S. 6, 7) = *adyatvāya* (7, 45)[1]; °*sahassāya* = °*sahasrāya* (7, 48); VG. *vijaya* (101, 1. 3); *nārāyaṇassa*, *āyuṁ*, *vaddhaniyaṁ* (101, 8); *gāmeyikā* (101, 10; cf. EI. 1, 2, note 2); *pariharayaṁ* (101, 11; cf. EI. 1, 2, note 2). In PG. the same variation is found in the case of duplicated *ya* as in the anlaut : at 6, 40, beside one another, there stand *karĕyya, kāravĕjjā = kuryāt, kārayet*; 7, 1 *karĕyyāma = kuryāma*, but 7, 46 *vaṭṭeja = vartayet* and 7, 48 *hoja = bhūyāt*[2]. See (§ 280). As usual, *dya* becomes *jja* in *ajātāye*; likewise *rya* would correctly and regularly become *jja* in *golasamajasa, agisamajasa, dattajasa, dāmajasa, sālasamajasa, agisamaja°* (6, 12. 13. 21. 23. 27. 37), if BÜHLER were right in equating *°aja°* as = *ārya*[3]. But *naṁdijasa* and *sāmijasa* (6, 21. 26) cannot be equated phonetically with BÜHLER as = *nandyāryasya* and *svāmyāryasya*, but are = *nandijasya, svāmijasya*. Also for the rest, therefore, *°ja* has to be assumed.

1. This is the correct explanation of LEUMANN; false PISCHEL, GN. 1895, 211.—2. Cf. BÜHLER, EI, 1, 2f. —3. l.c. 1,2.

254. In the place of *ya*, apparently *ga* has entered into AMg. *pariẏāga = paryāya* (Āẏār. 2, 15, 16; Vivāgas. 270; Vivāhap. 135. 173. 220.223. 235. 249. 796. 845. 968. 969; Nāẏādh. 1225; Uvās.; Ovav.), beside *pariẏāẏa* (Uvās.; Ovav.). To equate *pariẏāga* as = *paryāyaka* by contraction, according to § 165, with HOERNLE (Uvās. s. v.), in the case of a t.t. of prose, is improbable. I suspect that *pariẏāga* stands for **pariyāva* with *ga* for *va* according to § 231. In support of this view stands AMg. JM. *pajjava = paryāya*, which ought to be mentioned at the same time. Likewise AMg. *niẏāga* (Āẏār. 1, 1, 3, 1; Sūẏag. 665 [*ṇi°*]) = **nyāva* will stand for *nyāya* (commentary = *mokṣamārga, saṁyama, mokṣa*). — Interchange of *ya* and *va*, as in Skt.[1] and in Pāli[2], occurs in *kaīavaṁ = katipayam* (Hc. 1, 250); AMg. JM. *pajjava = paryāya* (§ 81); AMg. *tāvattisā = trayastriṁśat*, AMg. JM. *tāvattisagā, °ẏā = trayastriṁśakāḥ* (§ 438); A. *āvaï = āyāti* (Hc. 4, 367, 1. 419, 3), *āvahi* (Hc. 4, 422, 1), *āva* [GOLDSCHMIDT *āu*] = *āyāti* (Piṅgala 2, 88)[3]; A. *gāva* [GOLDSCHMIDT *gāu*] = *gāyanti* (Piṅgala. 2, 88), *gāvanta* (Piṅgala 2, 230); further in the participia necessitatis in A. *-evā, ĕvvaü, -iĕvvaü*, like *soevā = *svapeyya* (§ 497), *jaggevā = *jāgreyya* (§ 556), *kariĕvvaü = *karyeyyakam* of the passive stem (§ 547), *sahĕvvaü = *saheyyakam* (§ 570). In AMg. *murava* for **muraẏa = muraja* (Paṇhāv. 512; Vivāhap. 1102; Ovav.; Kappas. [so to be read]), *muravi = muraji* (Ovav.), beside M. Ś. *muraa* (Pāiẏal. 266; H.; Mṛcch. 69, 23) *va* has entered for the secondary *ya*. *murava* might rest also upon the popular etymology = *mu + rava*. The *pa* in P. *hitapa = hṛdaya, hitapaka = hṛdayaka* (§ 191) too goes back to a secondary *va* for *ya*, whilst *va* has become *pa*, as in *gopinta = govinda, kesapa = keśava* (§ 191).

1. WACKERNAGEL, Altind. Gr. § 188c. — 2. E. KUHN, Beiträge p. 42f.; E. MÜLLER, Simplified Pāli Grammar p. 30f. — 3. PISCHEL, on Hc. 4, 367, 1; cf., however, also √*av* (to go) and Ved. Stud. 1, 1. vi.

§ 255. Corresponding to Pāli *nahāru*, Greek νευρον, Latin nervus AMg. JM. have *ṇhāru = snāya* (Ṭhāṇ. 55; Paṇhāv. 49; Vivāhap. 89, 349. 810; Jīv. 66. 271; Erz.), AMg. *ṇhāruṇi = *snāyuni* (Āẏār. 1, 1, 6, 5; Sūẏag. 676). There occurs *ṇhāu* twice (Samav. 227). — In *yaṣṭi ya* becomes *la* (Vr. 2, 32; C. 3. 17*a* p. 49; Hc. 1, 247; 2, 34; Ki. 2, 39; Mk. fol 17); M. AMg. JM. *laṭṭhi, laṭṭhi* (H.; R.; Karp. 44, 3; 49, 12; 58, 5; 69, 8; 73, 10; 80, 10; Viddhaś. 64, 4; Āẏār. 1, 8, 3, 5; 2, 4, 2, 11; Sūẏag. 726; Paṇhāv. 282, Nāẏādh. § 135. 136; p. 1420; Vivāhap. 831; Uvās.; Ovav.; Kappas.; Erz.). According to Mk. fol. 67 Ś. has *jaṭṭhi* only and so stands Vṛṣabh. 37, 2 and is so meant in Mallikām. 129, 19, where the text has *taṇuyaṭṭi*, and at 192, 22, where it has *hārayaṭṭhi*. Rājaśekhara, however, uses *laṭṭhi* (Karp. 110, 6; Viddhaś. 42, 7; 97, 11; 122, 3 [*hāralaṭṭhi*]; Bālar. 305, 10) and *laṭṭhiā* (Viddhaś. 108, 3) in Ś. too, corresponding to M. *laṭṭhiā* (C. 3, 17a p. 49), AMg. *laṭṭhiyā* (Āyār. 2, 2, 3, 2). False is *jaṭṭhi* in M. (Sāhityadarpaṇa 73. 5). Pāli has *laṭṭhi* and *yaṭṭhi*. — *kaīvāhaṁ*, according to Hc. 1, 250 = *katipayam*, is = Pāli *katipāhaṁ* = Skt. *katipayāhaṁ* according to § 167. — M. *chāhā* (shade; shadow; Vr. 2, 18; H.), Ś. *sacchāha* (Hc. 1, 249; Mṛcch. 68, 24) and M. *chāhi* (shade, shadow; sky; Hc. 1, 249; Mk. fol. 19; Deśīn. 3, 26; Pāiyal 236; H. R.) is not = *chāyā*, but = **chāyākhā* = **chāyākā*; it stands, hence, for **chākhā*, ** chākhi* with contraction according to § 165 and with aspiration according to § 206. In the sense of "beauty" only *chāā* is used according to Hc. 1, 249, as generally *chāyā* occurs in M.Ś. Mg. only as *chāā* (G.H.R.; Karp. 69, 5; Mṛcch. 9, 9; Śak. 29, 4; 51, 6; Vikr. 51, 11; Karp. 41, 2; Mg. Mudrār. 267, 2), in AMg. JM. as *chāyā* (Pāiyal. 113. 236; Kappas.; Erz.).

§ 256. *ra* always becomes *la* in Mg. (C.3, 39; Hc. 4, 288; Kī. 5, 87; Mk. fol. 74; Namisādhu on Rudraṭa, Kāvyālaṁkāra 2, 12; Siṁhadevagaṇin on Vāgbhaṭālaṁkāra. 2, 2) and Ḍh. (§ 25). Thus Mg.: *lahaśavaśaṇamilaśulaśilavialidamandālalāyidaṁhiyuge vilayiṇe* = *rabhasavaśanamrasuraśirovicalitamandārarājitāṁhriyugo virajinaḥ* (Hc. 4, 288); *śāyaṁbhaliśalaśivila* = *sākambhariśvaraśibira*, *viggahalāaṇaleśalaśiliṇaṁ* = *vigraharājanareśvaraśriṇām* (Lalitav. 565, 6. 11); *ṇagalantala* = *nagarāntara*, *dalidda cāludattāha aṇulattā* = *daridracārudattasyānuraktā*, *andhaālapūlida* = *andhakārapūrita*, *ovālidaśalila* = *apavāritaśarira* (Mṛcch. 13, 8. 25; 14, 22; 127, 25); *mahāladaṇabhāśula* = *mahāratnabhāsura*, *udalabbhantala* = *udarābhyantara* (Śak. 113, 3; 114, 10); *śamale piabhattālaṁ luhilappiaṁ* = *samare priyabhartāraṁ rudhirapriyam* (Veṇīs. 33, 8); *bahuṇalakadukkhadāluṇapaliṇāme dukkale* = *bahunarakaduḥkhadāruṇapariṇāmo duṣkaraḥ* (Caṇḍīk. 42, 6). — Ḍh. : *ale le* = *are re*; ; *luddhu* = *ruddhaḥ*; *palivevida* = *parivepita*; *kulu* = *kuru*; *dhāledi* = *dhārayati*; *pulisa* = *puruṣa* (§ 25). — According to C. 3, 38; Kī. 5, 109; Siṁhadevagaṇin on Vāgbhaṭālaṁkāra. 2, 3 in P. too *ra* becomes *la* : *ale ale duṭṭhalakkhasā* = *are are duṣṭarākṣasāḥ* (C); *calaṇa* = *caraṇa* (Kī. 5, 109); *chaṅkāla* = *jhaṅkāra* (Kī. 5, 102) *hali* = *hari* (Kī. 5, 111); *ludda* = *rudra* (S.). Undoubtedly in C. Kī. S., P. has again been interchanged with CP. (§ 191 note 1). The examples from P. in Hc. 4, 304. 307. 314. 316. 319. 320. 321. 323. 324 have throughout *ra*, as also Kī. 5, 109 *usara* = *uṣṭra*, *kāria* = *kārya*. On the other hand Hc. 4, 326, teaches that in CP. *la* may enter for *ra* : *golicalaṇa* = *gauricaraṇa*, *ekātasatanuthalaṁ luddaṁ* = *ekādaśatanudharaṁ rudram*, *hala* = *hara* (Hc. 4, 326); *nala* = *nara*, *sala* = *saras* (Triv. 3, 2. 64). Likewise Sr. fol. 65. Most of the examples from CP. have, however, *ra*, as *nagara*, *kiritaṭa*, *rāca-*, *caccara*, *nicchara*, *chacchara*, *tamaruka*, *tāmotara*, *mathura* etc. (Hc. 4, 325), so that the examples in Hc. 4, 326 certainly originate from a third Paiśācī dialect that Mk. calls Pāñcāla (§27). Presumably the transition of *ra* into *la* in it was just as necessary as in Mg. and in Ḍh.

§ 257. In dialects other than Mg. Ḍh. Pāñcāla (§ 256) the change of *ra* into *la* is sporadic and fluctuating. Vr. 2, 30; Hc. 1, 254; Kī. 2, 35; Mk. fol. 17; Pkl. p. 52 have collected the words that take *la* under the ākṛtigaṇa *haridrādi*. The information supplied by them, however, does not hold equally good for all the dialects. They say : *haladdā, haladdī* (Grr.), M. AMg. JM. *haliddā*, M. *haliddī*, AMg. *hālidda* (§ 115); M. JŚ. Ś. *dalidda* = *daridra* (Gr.; G. 859 [so to be read : v. l.]; H.; Kattig. 404, 387; Mṛcch. 18, 9; 29, 1. 3; 54, 3; 55, 25; 70, 7), Ś. *daliddadā* (Mṛcch. 6, 8; 17, 18; 54, 1), but M. also *dariddattaṇa* (Karp. 16, 2), Ś. *dariddadā* (Mālav. 26, 15), AMg. JM. *daridda* (Kappas.; Erz.), JM. *dariddi-* = *daridrin, dariddiya* (Erz.); *jahiṭṭhila* (Grr.), *jahuṭṭhila* (Hc.), AMg. *juhiṭṭhila*, but S. A. *juhiṭṭhira* = *yudhiṣṭhira* (§ 118); M. JM. Ś. *muhala* = *mukhara* (Grr.; G.H.R.; Erz.; Prab. 39, 8); AMg. JM. *kaluṇa* = *karuṇa* (Grr.; Āyār. 1, 6, 1, 2; Sūyag. 225. 270. 273. 282. 286. 288. 289. 291; Nāyādh.; Ovav. Sagara 5, 15; Erz.; everywhere adverb *kaluṇaṁ*), beside JM. Ś.A. *karuṇa* (Erz.; Śak. 109, 9; Vikr. 67, 11) and always M. AMg. JM. *karuṇā* (pity; G.; Āyār. 2, 2, 1, 8; 2, 2, 3, 15 [text here false *kaluṇa*°]; Sagara 5, 18; Kk.); M. *karuṇaa* = *karuṇaka* (pity; G.); M. *cilāa*, AMg. *cilāya* = *kirāta*, AMg. *cilāī* = *kirātī*, *cilāiyā* = *kirātikā*, beside Ś. *kirāda* JM. *kirāya*, and M. *kirāa* in the meaning "Śiva" (§230); M. AMg. JM. *phaliha* = *parigha*, M. AMg. *phalihā* = *parikhā* (§208); *phālihadda* = *pāribhadra* (§208); *valuṇa* = *varuṇa* (Hc. 1, 254), but M. *varuṇa* (H.); Ś. *vāruṇī* (Bālar. 134, 13); AMg. *antalikkha* = *antarikṣa* (Āyār. 2, 1, 7, 1; 2, 2, 1, 7; 2, 4, 1, 13; 2, 5, 1, 20. 21; 2, 7, 1, 7; Sūyag. 294. 708; Uttar. 456. 651; Dasav. 629, 33; Nāyādh. §93; Uvās.), but Ś. *antarikkha* (Pāiyal. 27; Mṛcch. 44, 19; Mālav. 25, 14); AMg. *ruila* = *rucira* (Sūyag. 565; Samav. 25 [°*lla*]. 59; Paṇhāv. 269. 285; Paṇṇav. 116; Nāyādh.; Ovav.; Kappas.); AMg. *lūha* (Āyār. 1, 2, 6, 3; 1, 5, 3, 5; 1, 6, 5, 5; 1, 8, 4, 4; Sūyag. 165. 185. 578. 665; Paṇhāv. 348f.; Vivāhap. 279. 838; Ṭhāṇ. 198; Uttar. 56. 106; Ovav.), *sulūha* (Sūyag. 497) and *lukkha* (Āyār. 1, 5, 6, 4; 1, 8, 3, 3; 2, 1, 5, 5; Sūyag. 590; Ṭhāṇ. 198; Vivāhap. 1470ff.; Paṇṇav. 8. 11. 12. 13. 380; Aṇuog. 268; Jīv. 28. 224; Uttar. 1022; Kappas.) = *rūkṣa*, *lukkhaya* (Uttar. 1028), *lukkhatta* (Ṭhāṇ. 188; Vivāhap. 1351), *lūhei*, *lūhittā* (Jīv. 610; Nāyādh. 267; Rāyap. 185), *lūhiya* (Nāyādh.; Ovav.; Kappas.), falsely *rukkha* (Sūyag. 239), that in AMg. too always is = *rukṣa* (tree; §320); but A. *rukkha* (Piṅgala 2, 98). and so also JM. in the word-play with *rukkha* "tree" (Ṛṣabhap. 29), AMg. shows *la* also in *lāḍhā* = *rāḍhā* (Āyār. 1, 8, 3, 2) and = *rāḍhāḥ* (Āyār. 1, 8, 3. 6. 8; Paṇṇav. 61; Vivāhap. 1254) = Ś. *rāḍhā* (Karp. 9, 4) = Skt. *rāḍhā*; further in *pariyāla* = *parivāra*[1] (Nāyādh. § 130; p. 724. 784. 1273. 1290. 1327. 1460 [°*ra*]. 1465; Ovav.; Nirayāv.) beside *parivāra* (Ovav.; Kappas.); further in *sūmāla*, *sukumāla* beside M. *somāra*, also *somāla*, *suumāra*, Ś. *suumāra*, *sukumāra*, JM. *sukumārayā* (§ 123); in the numeral AMg. JM. *cattālisaṁ*, AMg. *cattālisā*, JM. *cāyālisaṁ*, *cālisa*°, A. *cālisa* = *catvāriṁśat* and in combinations with other numerals, as AMg. JM. *bāyālisaṁ* (42), *caüyālisaṁ*, *coyālisaṁ* (44) and others (§ 445). Often in AMg. *pari* becomes *pali*, especially in the oldest dialect; e.g. in *paliuñcayanti* = *parikuñcayanti* (Sūyag. 489), *paliuñciya* = *parikuñcya* (Āyār. 2, 1, 11, 1), *paliuñcaṇa* = *parikuñcana* (Sūyag. 381), *apaliuñcamāṇa* = *aparikuñcamāna*

(Āẏār. 1, 7, 4, 1; 2, 5, 2, 1); *paliyanta*=*paryanta* (Āẏār. 1, 3, 4, 1. 4; Sūẏag. 108. 172); *palei*=*paryeti* (Sūẏag. 495), *palinti*=*pariyanti* (Sūẏag. 95. 134); *paliẏaṅka*=*paryaṅka* (Āẏār. 2, 13, 19. 20; Sūẏag. 386; Ovav.); *palikkhiṇa* =*parikṣiṇa* Sūẏag. 978); *palicchinna*=*paricchinna* (Āẏār. 1, 4, 4, 2; Sūẏag. 560), *palicchindiẏa*=*paricchidya* (Āẏār. 1, 4, 4, 3; 2, 5, 2, 3. 5), *paliŏcchinna*=*paryavacchinna* (Āẏār. 1, 5, 1, 3); *palibhindiẏāṇaṁ*=*paribhidya* (Sūẏag. 243); *palicchāei*=*paricchādayati* (Āẏār. 2, 1, 10, 6); *palimaddĕjjā*= *parimardayet* (Āẏār. 2, 13; 2); *paliucchūḍha*=*paryutkṣubdha* (§66); *saṁpalimajjamāṇa* (Āẏār. 1, 5, 4, 3). Therefore, AMg. has *la* for *ra* more frequently than the other dialects have. In this respect it approximates to Mg. and is removed from M. (§ 18). According to Hc. 1, 254 there one says beside *jaḍhara*=*jaṭhara*, *vaḍhara*=*vaṭhara*, *ṇiṭṭhura*=*niṣṭhura* also *jaḍhala*, *vaḍhala* *ṇiṭṭhula*. Upto this moment the forms to be found in the text are M. Ś. *jaḍhara* (Pāiẏal. 112; G.; Mṛcch. 72, 19); M. *ṇiṭṭhura* (G.H.R.), AMg. JM. JŚ. *niṭṭhura* (Pāiẏal. 74; Ovav.; Erz.; Kattig. 400, 333 [*ṇi*°]). Hc. 1, 254 and Triv. 1, 3, 78 teach that *caraṇa* becomes *calaṇa* in the sense of "foot", and that otherwise it remains. *caraṇa*. Bh. Mk. Pkl. have *calaṇa* without limitation. So *calaṇa* "foot" in M. AMg. JM. Ś. A. (Pāiẏal. 109; G.H.R.[2]; Karp. 46, 8; 56, 1; 60, 1; 62, 8; Uvās.; Ovav.; Kappas.[3]; Ṛṣabhap.[4]; Mṛcch. 41, 4. 12; Śak. 27, 9; 62, 6; 84, 14; Mālav. 34. 12; Karp. 22, 1[5]; Hc. 4, 399), AMg. has *caraṇa* in the meaning "way of life" (Nāẏādh.), A. in the meaning "foot of a metre" (Piṅgala 1, 2. 13. 79. 80 etc.), but also in the meaning "foot" (1, 4*a*, 22. 85*a*. 116; 2, 186). In stead of *sakkāla* =*satkāra* (Hc. 1, 254) only M. AMg. JM. Ś. *sakkāra* is to be pointed to (G.R.; Nāẏādh; Niraẏāv.; Kappas.; Erz.; Kk.; Śak. 23, 8; 27, 6; Mālav. 44, 4; 70, 2; 72, 2). — On *iṅgāla* beside *aṅgāra* see § 102, on *kāhala* beside *kāara* see § 207, on *bhasala* see § 251.

1. The form conformably is *pariẏāla*, rather=*paricāra*, the meaning, however conformably is=*parivāra*. — 2. R. 6, 7; 8, 28 is with the v. l. to be read as *calaṇa*, 6, 8; 13, 49 is to be corrected as *calaṇa*. — 3. Kappas. § 36 stands *caraṇa* behind *calaṇa* of the preceding line. It is corrected as *calaṇa*. — 4. Ṛṣabhap. 28 is with the ed. Bombay to be read as *calaṇa*. — 5. Vikr. 53, 9; 72, 19 in Bollensen has *caraṇa*, the v. l. excepted. The Dravidian recension, in the first place, does not have the word; in the second place Paṇḍit with his MSS reads *caraṇa* (127, 1), however, Pischel *calaṇa* (658, 18). It is to be corrected as *calaṇa*.

§ 258. AMg. *tuḍiẏa* (Aẏār. 2, 11, 14; Paṇhāv. 513; Nāẏādh. 870; Rāẏap. 20. 21. 60. 80; Niraẏāv. ; Ovav.; Kappas.) is not, with the commentators, Jacobi[1], E. Müller[2], Warren[3] and Leumann[4], to be equated as=*tūrya*, but is=**tudita*=*tunna* from *tudaī* (Hc. 4, 116)=*tudati* with cerebralization according to § 222. Cf. Skt. *tuḍ*, *toḍi*, *toḍikā* (name of a musical mode), *toḍya*, *ātodya* (cymbal). — *kiḍi*, *bheḍa*, presumably=*kiri*, *bhera* (Hc. 1, 251) are=Skt. *kiṭi*, *bheḍa*[5]. AMg. *paḍāẏāṇa* (saddle; Hc. 1, 252) is not with Hc. to be understood as=*paryāṇa*, but as= **pratyādāna* according to § 163; cf. Skt. *ādāna* (decoration of a saddle). For *ra* has entered *ḍa* in AMg. JM. *kuhāḍa*=*kuṭhāra* and *pihaḍa*=*piṭhara* (§ 239). — AMg. *kaṇavira*=*karavira* (Hc. 1, 253; Pāiẏal. 146; Paṇṇav. 526; Rāẏap. 52 ff.; Paṇhāv. 194), *kaṇaviraẏa* (Paṇṇav. 527 ff.) is to be explained perhaps from **kaḷavira* or *kalavira* according to § 260, if a synonym **kaṇavira* does not occur. M. has *karavira* (G.), Mg. *kalavila* (Mṛcch. 157, 5). According to § 166. 167 *kaṇera* (Hc. 1, 168) too goes back to *kaṇavira*. Hc. equates it as = *karṇikāra*, and the MSS ABCE, as well as Triv. 1, 3, 3 give *kaṇṇero*, according to which it has been so written in my edition too. But F and the Bombay edition read *kaṇero*, and in Marāṭhī, Gujarātī and Urdū *kaṇera* means "Oleander"; for Hindī Bate gives the meaning "Casearea Ovata", which is in no way correct. Since *karṇikāra* may, according to § 287, form *kaṇiāra* with a simple *ṇa*, Hc has evidently interchanged the plants. JM. *kaṇeradatta* (Erz.) will, therefore, be = *karviradatta karavira, karaviraka, karavirya* are well known as proper names, but not *karṇikāra*. It is phonetically impossible to refer *kaṇera* back to *karṇikāra*[6].

1. Kalpasūtra s. v. — 2. Beiträge p. 28. — 3. Nirayāv. s. v. — 4. Aup. S. s. v.—5. Pischel on Hc. 1, 251 — 6. Jacobi, ZDMG. 47, 578.

§ 259. For Skt. *kila* dialectical *kira* has been retained in M. JM.A. *kira* (Vr. 9, 5; Hc. 2, 186; Kī. 4, 83; G.H.R.; Erz.: Piṅgala 1, 60; Hc. 4, 349). Beside it JM. has *kila* (Āv. 8, 45; Erz.) and so always Ś. (Mṛcch. 2, 24; Śak. 21, 4; 30, 1; 116, 7; 159, 12; Vikr. 52, 4; 72, 18; 80, 20 etc.). In places where in Indian editions occurs Ś. *kira*, as Pras. 46, 7; 48, 12; 101, 3; 119, 12, there is either a false reading or a case of interchange of dialects. M. *ira*, beside *kira*, (Vr. 9, 5; Hc. 2, 186; Kī. 4, 83; G.; R.) is explained according to § 184, *hira* (Hc. 2, 186) according to § 388. Otherwise *ra* for *la* is also only sporadic and dialectical: Ś. *pharaa* = *phalaka* (shield; Deśīn. 6, 82; Karp. 97, 6); AMg. *saraḍuya* = *śalāṭuka* (Āyār. 2, 1, 8, 6); *sāmari* = *śālmali* beside AMg. *sāmali* (§ 88, 109).

§ 260. In the anlaut *la* has become *ṇa*, *na* in *ṇāhala* = *lāhala* (Vr. 2, 40; Hc. 1, 256), beside *lāhala* (Hc. 1, 256); *ṇaṅgala*, AMg. *naṅgala* = *lāṅgala* (Hc. 1, 256; Kī. 2, 47; Mk. fol. 18; Pāiyal 121 [*na*°]; Āyār. 2, 4, 2, 11; Paṇhāv. 234; Dasav. N. 646, 10), beside *laṅgala* (Hc.; Mk.), *naṅgaliya* = *lāṅgalika* (Ovav.; Kappas.) AMg. *ṇaṅgula* = *lāṅgula* (Mk. fol. 18; Jīv. 883. 886. 887), *goṇaṅgula* (Vivāhap. 1048), *ṇaṅgūla* = *lāṅgūla* (Hc. 1, 256), *naṅgūli-* = *lāṅgūlin* (Aṇuog. 349), *ṇaṅgola* (Nāyādh. 502), *ṇaṅgoli-* (Jīv. 345), *ṇaṅgoliya* (Ṭhāṇ. 259); Jīv. 392 ([*na*°]), beside M. *laṅgūla* (Hc. 1, 256); G.; *ṇohala* = *lohala* (Kī. 2, 47; Mk. fol. 18), beside *lohala* (Mk.). It is seen that the texts in AMg. mostly write, *ṇa* in the anlaut. According to Mk. fol. 67 the sound-change does not take place in Ś. Corresponding to Pāli *nalāṭa*, beside *lalāṭa*, Pkt. has *ṇalāḍa* (Hc. 2. 123), M. AMg. with *i* according to § 103 *ṇilāḍa* (R.; Āyār. 1, 1, 2, 5 [*ni*°]; Nāyādh. 1310. 1312; Paṇhāv. 273 [*ni*°; commentary *niḍāla*]; Vivāgas. 90 [commentary *niḍāla*]. 121. 144. 157. 169) more frequently with transposition of the last syllables according to § 354, M. *ṇaḍāla* (Hc. 1, 257; 2, 123; Kī. 2, 117; Mk. fol. 38; G.); M. AMg. JM.Ś. *ṇiḍāla* (AMg. JM. sometimes *ni*°; Bh. 4, 33; Hc. 1, 257; H.R.; Karp. 48, 6. Nāyādh. 754. 790. 823; Vivāhap. 237; Rāyap. 113; Jīv. 351. 353; Paṇhāv. 162. 285; Uvās.; Nirayāv.; Ovav.; Āv. 12, 27; Erz.; Bālar. 101, 6; 259, 8 [text° *ḍo*°]; Caṇḍak. 87, 8; Mallikām. 195, 5); A. *ṇiḍalā* (Piṅgala 2, 98; text *ṇialā*). For Ś. the form is apparently incorrect. *lalāḍa* is made certain for Ś. by the similarly sounding *lalāḍe, lāḍesara* (Bālar. 74, 21); It occurs also in Bālar. 270, 5; Veṇīs. 60, 5 [text °*ṭa*; v. l. *ṇiḍāla, ṇiḍala, ṇiḍila*]. False in AMg. *lilāḍa* (Rāyap. 165). Mk. fol. 38 teaches also *laḍāla, ṇiḍila* is edited in Ś. in Pārvatīpariṇaya 24, 12 [ed. GLASER 23, 31 has *ṇiḍala*; cf. v. l. to Veṇīs. 60, 5]. The word has gone over to Skt. as *niṭala, niṭāla, niṭila*[1]. To *ṇaḍāla* belongs M. *ṇāḍāla* (found on the forehead; G. 29). to *ṇiḍāla* belongs the dialectical *ṇeḍāli* (a kind of head ornament; Deśīn. 4, 43). In the inlaut *l* has become *m* in *jampaï = jalpati* and derivatives (§ 296). — In P. CP. *la* becomes *ḷa* : in the inlaut P. *kamaḷa, kuḷa, jaḷa, saḷiḷa sīḷa = śīla* (Hc. 4, 308); CP. *thūḷi = dhūli*; *pāḷaka, bāḷaka = bāḷaka*; *manṭaḷa = maṇḍala, liḷā = līṭā*; *saïḷa = śaiḷa* (Hc. 4,325—327). So probably *ucchaḷḷanti* (Hc. 4, 326) too is to be written Cf. § 226.

1. According to JACOBI, KZ. 35, 573 *ṇiḍāla* cannot directly be identified with *lalāṭa* without much ado.

§ 261. In A. sometimes *va* becomes *v̐a*[1] : *ev̐a = eva* in the sense of *evam* (Hc. 4, 376, 1. 418. 1); *ev̐aï = eva + api*, in the sense of *evam eva* (Hc. 4, 332, 2.423, 2. 441, 1); *ev̐ahiṁ* in the sense of *idānīm* = Vedic *evaīḥ* (Hc. 4, 387, 3; 420, 4); *kev̐a* (Hc. 4, 343, 1. 401,1); *kiv̐a* (Hc. 4, 401, 2. 422, 14) in the sense of *katham* = **keva* (cf. § 149. 434), *kev̐aï* (Hc. 4, 390. 396, 4) = *kathamapi*; *tev̐a* (Hc. 4, 343, 1. 397. 401, 4), *tiv̐a* (Hc. 4, 344. 367, 4.376, 2. 395, 1. 397.422, 2), in the sense of *tathā* = **teva, tev̐aï* (Hc. 4, 439, 4); *jev̐a* (Hc. 4, 397. 401, 4; Kī. 5, 6 [so to be read]), *jiv̐a* (Hc. 4, 330, 3. 336. 344. 347. 354. 367, 4. 376, 2. 397 etc.; Kk. 272, 37 [text *jiva*] in the sense of *yathā* = **yeva*, **yiva* (§ 336); *jāv̐a = yāvat* (Hc. 4, 395, 3); *tāv̐a = tāvat* (Hc. 4, 395, 3). From *v̐a* a full-fledged *ma* has developed in A. *jāma = yāvat* (Hc. 4, 387, 2. 406, 1; Vetālap. p. 217, No. 13); *tāma = tāvat* (Hc. 4, 406, 1; Vetālap. p. 217, No. 13); *jāmahĩ, tāmahĩ = yāvadbhiḥ, tāvadbhiḥ* in the sense of *yāvat, tāvat* (Hc. 4, 406, 3; Erz. 86, 17ff. [text °*va*°]). The same line of development has to be assumed also for the other dialects, in which *va* is represented by *ma*: *ajjama = ārjava* (Triv. 1, 3, 105)[2]; *ohāmaï* (excels; Hc. 4, 25), *ohāmiya* (overcome; Pāiyal. 187), beside *ohāvaï* (Hc. 4, 160), *ohāia* = **ohāvia* (downcast; Deśīn. 1, 158) = **apabhāvati, apabhāvita*[3]; *gamesaï* beside *gavesaï = gaveṣati* (Hc. 4, 189); *ṇimī* beside *ṇivi = nivi* (Hc. 1, 259); *ṇumaï, ṇimaï* from √*vi* (§ 118); Ś. *damiḷa* (Mallikām. 296, 14) = *draviḍa*, AMg. *damiḷā* (Vivāhap. 792; Rāyap. 288), *damiḷi* (Nāyādh.; Ovav.) = Pāli *damiḷi* = Skt. *draviḍi*, beside AMg. *daviḷa* (Paṇhāv. 41), Ś. *daviḍa* (Mṛcch. 103, 6; Viddhaś. 75, 2) = *draviḍa*, M. *daviḍi = draviḍi* (Viddhaś. 24, 12); AMg. JM. *vesamaṇa = vaiśravaṇa* (§ 60). The same phonetic-change has taken place in the case of the secondary *va* in the passive *cimmaï* beside *civvaï* from *civ* and JM. *summaü* beside *suvvaï* from *svap* (§ 536); further in AMg. *bhumā* = **bhruvā* = *bhrūḥ*, M. *bhumaā*, AMg. *bhumayā, bhumagā, bhamuhā* = **bhruvukā* (§ 124. 206). — On the analogous change of *pa, ba* through *va* into *ma* see § 248. 250, on *va* for *ma* see § 251. 277, on *ga* for *va* see § 231, on *pa* for *va* see § 191. 254 and on *va* for *ya* see § 254.

1. The MSS almost always write *mva* for *ẏa*; more seldom *ẏa*, what perhaps is correct in the vicinity of *ẏa*. — 2. PISCHEL, BB. 76, 94. — 3. S. GOLDSCHMIDT, Prākṛtica p. 14 f., who wrongly assumes *avabhū*. Cf. 286.

§ 262. The sibilants sometimes become *ha* dialectically, especially after long vowels and diphthongs. According to Vr. 2, 44. 45; C. 3, 14; Kī. 2, 104. 105; Mk. fol. 19 in M., in *daśan* and in the numerals connected with it *śa* becomes *ha* necessarily, and in proper names it so becomes optionally; according to Hc. 1, 262 the change to *ha* is optional also in the case of the purely numeral words, with which the texts are in agreement. M. *dasa* (R. [v. l. often *daha*]; Karp. 73, 9; 87, 1), *daha* (Karp. 12, 7); *dasakaṁdhara* (G. R.); *dasakaṇṭha, dahakaṇṭha* (R.); *dahamuha, daharaha, dāsarahi, dahavaaṇa, dasāṇaṇa* (R.). *ha* occurs also in A. (Piṅgala 1, 83 [so S. GOLDSCHMIDT]. 123. 125. 156; 2, 196); however, *dasa* (Vikr. 67, 20). AMg. JM. have only *dasa* (§ 442). According to Mk. fol. 67 in Ś. *śa* in *daśan* and *caturdaśan* may become either *sa* or *ha*; on the other hand *sa* must stand in the proper names, *ha* in the remaining tens, excluding 10 itself and 14. The forms that have been located are *dasa* (Karp. 72, 3; Pras. 19, 5) and *daha* (Ratn. 292, 12); *dasakaṁdhara* (Mahāv. 118, 3); *dāsaradha* (Uttarar. 27,4 [°*ha*]; Bālar. 152, 10 [°*ha*]; Anarghar. 150, 12 [°*ha*], *dāsaradhi* (Anarghar. 157, 10 [°*hi*]), *dasamuha* (Mahāv. 22, 20; Pras. 143, 6; Bālar. 20, 15), *dasāṇaṇa* (Bālar. 57, 2; 123, 17; 125, 10; 139, 13), *dasakaṇṭha* (Bālar. 122, 15; 143, 17). Mg. Ḍh. have *daśa* only (Mṛcch. 11, 1; 32, 18; 38, 17; 121, 25; 122, 19; 133, 20; 134, 13; Ḍh. Mṛcch. 29, 15; 30, 1; 31, 4; 32. 3; 34, 9. 12. 17; 35, 7; 39, 13), Mg. *daśakaṁdhala* (Mṛcch. 12, 13). False is Mg. *daha* (Lalitav. 566, 11). In the remaining tens M.A. have *ha*, the other dialects, *sa* (§ 443). *śa* has further become *ha* in M.Ś. *ĕddahamĕtta* = *idṛśamātra*, M. *tĕddaha* = *tādṛśa*, *jĕddaha* = *yādṛśa* (§ 122); A. *eha, keha, jeha, teha* beside *aïsa, kaïsa, jaïsa, taïsa* = *idṛśa, kidṛśa, yādṛśa, tādṛśa* (§ 121. 166); A *sāha* = *śaśvat* (§ 64). According to Kī. 2, 104 *palāśa* becomes *palāha*. A mention should be made of M. AMg. Ś. *palāsa* (G. H.; Kappas.; Mṛcch. 127, 21), Mg. *palāśa* (Mṛcch. 127, 24).

§ 263. *ṣa* has become *ha* in M. *dhaṇuha* = **dhanuṣa* = *dhanus* (Hc. 1, 22; Karp. 38, 11; Pras. 65, 5), *dhaṇuho* = *dhanuṣaḥ* (Bālar. 113, 17). — M. *paccūha* = *pratyūṣa*, in the meaning "morning-sun" (Hc. 2, 14; Deśīn. 6, 5; Pāiẏal. 4; H. 606 [so to be read with v. l. and the commentary], but M. AMg. JM. JŚ.Ś *paccūsa* in the meaning "morning-twilight" [Hc. 2, 14; Pāiẏal. 46; G. H. R.; Nāẏādh.; Kappas.; Erz.; Kattig. 403. 374. 375; Śak. 29, 7; Mallikām. 57, 16; Viddhaś. 115, 4). — M. AMg. JM. *pāhāṇa* = *pāṣāṇa* (C. 3, 14; Hc. 1, 262; Kī. 2, 104; Mk. fol. 19; G.H.; Uvās. Erz.), JM. *pāhāṇaga* (Erz.), beside *pāsāṇa* (Hc.; Mk.), as according to Mk. fol. 67 always in Ś. — AMg. *bihaṇa* = *bhiṣaṇa*, *bihaṇaga* = *bhiṣaṇaka*, M. JM. *bihaï, bihei* beside M.Ś. *bhisaṇa* = *bhiṣaṇa* (§ 213. 501). A. *eho, eha, ehu* = *eṣa, eṣā*, **eṣaṁ* = *etad* (Hc. 4, 362 and Word-Index; Piṅgala 1, 4 [in BOLLENSEN on Vikr. p. 527]. 66. 81; 2, 64; Vikr. 55, 16). — A. *akkhihĩ* from **akkhisĩ* = **akṣiṣmin* = *akṣṇi* (§ 312. 379). — *chaha* = **ṣaṣa* = *ṣaṣ* with crossing over to the *a*-declension (Piṅgala 1, 95. 96. 97). So is explained *ha* also in M. AMg. JM. Ś. *suṇhā*, M. *sŏṇhā* from P. *sunusā* for **suṇuhā* (§ 148); *kāhāvaṇa* (Vr. 3. 39; Hc. 2, 71; Kī. 2, 71; Mk. fol. 25) from **kāsāvaṇa* (§ 87), *kārṣāpaṇa*, also with shortening of *ā* of the first syllable (§ 82), *kahāvaṇa* (Hc. 2, 71), AMg. *kūḍakahāvaṇa* (Uttar. 629); in future, as *kāhimi*, *hohimi*, *kāhāmi*, *kāhaṁ*, *hohāmi* = **karṣyāmi*, **bhoṣyāmi* (§ 520 ff.); in aorist, like *kāhī* beside *kāsi* (§ 516). Jacobi[1], misled by the commentators, equates AMg. *viha* (Āyār. 1, 7, 4, 2) as = *viṣa*. The word recurs in Āyār. 2, 3, 1, 11; 2, 3, 3, 14; 2, 5, 2, 7 and there it is mostly assumed by commentators as = *aṭavi*, therefore, means "forest" and probably is = *vikha* "without heaven" = "where one does not see the sky." Therefore, Āyār. 1, 7, 4, 2 is to be translated as "for the ascetic it is better that he goes into the forest alone". *viṣa* in M. AMg. JM. Ś. becomes only *visa* (G.H.R.; Uvās.; Nirayāv. Ovav.; Erz.; Ṛṣabhap.; Priyad. 51, 1.8. 15. 16; 53, 14; Mudrār. 40, 6; Mālav. 56, 8; 65, 10); Mg. *viśa* (Mṛcch. 136, 17; 164, 1; Mudrār. 193, 3; 194, 6); JM. *nivvisa* = *nirviṣa* (Sagara 6, 2).

1. SBE. 22, p. 68.

§ 264. *sa* has become *ha* in : *ṇiharaī* beside *ṇisaraī* = *niḥsarati* (Hc. 4, 79). In *divasa sa* becomes *ha* compulsorily, according to Vr. 2, 46, and optionally according to Hc. 1, 263; Kī. 2, 105; Mk. fol. 19; Prākṛtamañjarī in Pischel, De gr. Prācr. p. 14. M. has *diasa*, *divasa* (G.R.) and *diaha* (G. H.; Karp. 12, 7; 23, 7; 43, 11 etc.); AMg. only *divasa* (Nāyādh.; Uvās.; Nirayāv; Kappas.); JM. *divasa* (Erz.; Kk.), *diyasa* (Prākṛtamañjarī l. c.), *diyasayara* (Pāiyal 4), *diyaha* (Pāiyal. 157; Erz.), *aṇudiyahaṁ* (Kk.); JŚ. *divaha* (Kattig. 402, 364); Ś. only *divasa*, *diasa* (Mṛcch. 68, 4; Śak. 44, 5; 53, 9; 67, 10; 121, 6; 162, 13; Vikr. 52, 1; Mudrār. 184, 5; Karp. 33, 7; 103, 3; 110, 6), *aṇudiasaṁ* (Śak. 51, 5) against M. *aṇudiahaṁ* (H.; Karp. 116. 1 [°*hā̃*]); Mg. *diaśa* (Śak. 114, 9), falsely *diaha* (Veṇīs. 33, 5); A. *diaha* (Hc. 4, 388. 418. 4), *diahaḍa* (Hc. 4, 333. 387, 2). — *dūhala* (unhappy; Deśīn. 5, 43) beside *dūsala* (Deśīn. 5, 43; Triv. 1, 3, 105 = BB. 6, 87) = *duḥsara*. — M. JM. *sāhaī* = **śāsati*[1] (Hc. 4, 2; H. R.; Erz.). — AMg. JM. A °*hattari*, AMg. °*hattariṁ* = °*saptati*, as JM. *caühattari* (74), AMg. *pañcahattari* (75), *sattahattariṁ* (77), *aṭṭhahattariṁ* (78), A. *ehattari* (71), *chāhattari* (76); (§ 245. 446). — In future as *dāhimi*, *dāhāmi*, *dāhaṁ* = *dāsyāmi* (§ 520 ff.) and aorists as *ṭhāhī* beside *ṭhāsī* (§ 516); in the loc. sing. of the pronouns *ta-*, *ya-*, *ka-*: *tahiṁ*, *yahiṁ*, *kahiṁ* beside *tassiṁ*, *jassiṁ*, *kassiṁ* (§ 425. 427. 428) and in the loc. of nouns formed according to it in Mg. as *kulāhiṁ* = *kule*; *pavahaṇāhiṁ* = *pravahaṇe* and in A., as *antahĩ* = *ante*; *cittahĩ* = *citte*; *gharahĩ* = *ghare*; *sisahĩ* = *śirṣe* (§ 366); in the genitive plural formed likewise according to the pronominal declension with the ending *-sām* in Mg. and A., as Mg. *śaaṇāhā̃* = *svagaṇāṇām*, A. *taṇahā̃* = *tṛṇāṇām*, *mukkāhũ* = *muktānām*, *loaṇahā̃* = *locanayoḥ*, *saüṇāhā̃* = *śakunānām* (§ 370), the genitives that are found according to Hc. 4, 300 also in M., as *sariāhā̃* = *saritām*, *kammāhā̃* = *karmaṇām*, *tāhā̃* = *teṣām*, *tumhāhā̃* = *yuṣmākam*, *amhāhā̃* = *asmākam* (§ 395, 404. 419. 422); in the genitive sing. in Mg. in *āha* from *-*āsa* = -*asya*, as *kāmāha* = *kāmasya*; *calittāha* = *caritrasya*; *puttāha* = *putrasya*, and in A. in -*aha*, -*ahŏ*, as *kaṇaaha* = *kanakasya*, *caṇḍālaha* = *caṇḍālasya*, *kāmahŏ*

= *kāmasya*, *sesahŏ* = *śeṣasya* (§ 366); in A. in the 2. sing. active in *-hi* beside in *-si* as *ṇīsarahi* = *niḥsarasi*; *ruahi* = Vedic *ruvasi*; *lahasi* = *labhase* (§ 455). On *h* = *s* in consonant groups see § 312 ff.

1. P. GOLDSCHMIDT, Specimen p. 72; WEBER. ZDMG. 28, 369.

§ 265. For *ṣa* in *ṣaṣṭi* (60) and *sa* in *saptati* (70) there occurs *va* too beside *cha, sa, ha* (§ 211. 264) in conjunctions with units in AMg. JM.: *bāvaṭṭhiṁ* (62), *tevaṭṭhiṁ* (63), *caüvaṭṭhi°* (64), *chāvaṭṭhiṁ* (66), *bāvattariṁ* (72), *tevattariṁ* (73), *covattariṁ* (74), *chāvattariṁ* (76); (§ 446); AMg. *tinnitevaṭṭhāiṁ pāvāduyasayāiṁ* (363 adversaries); JM. *tiṇhaṁ tevaṭṭhāṇaṁ nayarasayāṇaṁ* (of the 363 cities); (§ 447). The *va* has probably developed on the analogy of *va* in the numerals with 50, as *egāvaṇṇaṁ* (51), *bāvaṇṇaṁ* (52), *levaṇṇaṁ* (53), *caüvaṇṇaṁ* (54), *paṇavaṇṇaṁ* (55), *sattāvaṇṇaṁ* (57), *aṭṭhāvaṇṇaṁ* (58), A. *bāvaṇṇa* (52), *sattāvaṇṇāī* (57); (§ 273), in which it regularly stands (§ 199) for *pa* of **pañcat* (§ 445). *aüṇaṭṭhiṁ* (59), *aüṇattariṁ* (69), (§ 444) *paṇṇaṭṭhiṁ* (65); (§ 446) stand for **aguṇavaṭṭhiṁ*, **aguṇaaṭṭhiṁ*, **aguṇāṭṭhiṁ*, **aguṇavattariṁ*, **aguṇaattariṁ*, **aguṇāttariṁ*; **paṇṇavaṭṭhiṁ*, **paṇṇaaṭṭhiṁ*, **paṇṇāṭṭhiṁ*, *paṇṇavaṭṭhiṁ* according to § 167. 83. Spellings like *khaḍaṅgavi* = *ṣaḍaṅgavid* (WEBER, Bhag. 1, 425), *khoḍasama* = *ṣoḍaśa* (Sūyag. 562 in the subscription), *hŏkkhaï* = **bhoṣyati* (§ 521) are Sanskritisms, with an erroneous writing of *kha* for *ṣa*, the sounds that in pronunciation have coalesced in Northern India of the present day.[1] On this is based the false reading AMg. *pākhaṇḍa* (Ṭhāṇ. 583), Mg. *pāhaṇḍa* = *pāṣaṇḍa* (Prab. 48, 1). The Madras (59, 14) and the Bombay (103, 2) editions correctly have *pāsaṇḍa*, as also AMg. (Aṇuog. 356; Uvās., Bhag.)[2] and JM. *pāsaṇḍiya* = *pāṣaṇḍika* (Kk.).

1. BEAMES, Comp. Gr. 1, 261 f.; HOERNLE, Comp. Gr. § 19 p. 24; WACKERNAGEL, Altind, Gr. §118—2. Cf. WEBER, Bhag. 2, 213, note 6; KERN, Jaartelling p. 67 note; E. MÜLLER, Beiträge p. 32 f.

§ 266. *ha* neither falls out, nor it is brought in to avoid hiatus. All the cases in which this has been assumed[1] rest partly on false readings and partly on false etymologies.[2] Where in the interior of a word, between vowels, there appears an aspirate for *h* of Skt., there we need not see "coarsening" of *h*[3], but some old phonetic conditions.[4] So Ś. Mg. Ā. *idha* = *iha* (Ś. Mṛcch. 2, 25; 4, 14; 6, 9,9; 10. 12; 24, 20; 51, 24; 57, 17; 69, 6. 15; etc.; Śak. 12, 4; 20, 3; 67, 5; 115, 5; 168, 15; Vikr. 30, 17; 48, 4; Mg. Mṛcch. 37, 10; 100, 20; 113, 17; 114, 21; 123, 21; 133, 15. 16; 164, 10; Śak. 114, 11; Ā. Mṛcch. 100, 18). Ś. Mg. sometimes falsely have *iha*, as Ś. (Mṛcch. 70, 12; 72, 13; Vikr. 21, 12), *ihaloio* (Mṛcch 4, 1), Mg. (Mṛcch. 37, 10 [beside *idha* !]; 122, 12), readings, that are to be corrected.[5] The rest of the dialects have *iha*, also D. (Mṛcch 101, 13) and JŚ. *iha* (Pav. 389, 2), *ihaloga* (Pav. 387, 25), *ihaparaloya* (Kattig. 402, 365). From this is explained the fact that Hc. 4, 268 permits in Ś. *iha* beside *idha* (§21). For Ḍh., where *ida* was expected, examples are wanting. — *dāgha* = *dāha* (Hc. 1, 264); cf. Skt. *nidāgha*. — AMg. *nibhelaṇa* beside *ṇihelaṇa*, M. *sibhara* beside *sihara* (§ 206). — AMg. *maghamaghanta*, *maghamaghĕnta* beside M. *mahamahaī*, JM. *mahamahiya* (§558). — AMg. *vebhāra* (Vivāhap. 194. 195;

Uttar. 194 f.), *vĕbbhāra* (Nāẏādh.), *vibbhāra* (Nāẏādh. 1032) = *vaihāra*, among the Jainas also in Skt. *vaibhāra*[6]. The passive *vubbhaī* = *uhyate*, *dubbhaī* = *duhyate*, *libbhaī* = *lihyate* (§ 541. 544) go back to the root-doublets **vabh*, **dubh*, **libh*. *bh* is related to the original *gh*, *gh*, as *v* is related to *k*, *g*, (230. 231), that is to say here is a case of transformation of gutturals as labials. -*rubbhaī* from *rudh* (§ 546), also in the parasmaipada *rumbhaī* in M. AMg. commonly (§ 507), is formed on the analogy of the roots in gutturals. — On *hammaī* = Pāli *ghammati* see § 188. Obscure is *bhimora* = *himora* Hc. 2,174; Triv. 1,3,105 = BB. 3,259), since a Skt. word *himora* is not known, and the meaning *bhimora* has not been transmitted.

1. WEBER, teaches dropping of, Hāla[1] p. 29;[2] on the stanzas 4,410.584; WEBER, Hāla[1] p. 29; Bhag. 1,411, P. GOLDSCHMIDT, GN. 1874, p. 478, S. GOLDSCHMIDT, Rāvaṇavaho s.v. *thāha*; and LEUMANN, Aup. S. s.v. *bhamuhā* teach insertion. — 2. PISCHEL, GGA. 1880 p. 333 f.; 3,246 f.; 6,92 f.; cf. § 296. — 3. P. GOLDSCHMIDT, GN. 1874, p. 469 ff. — 4. PISCHEL, BB. 6,91 f. — 5. PISCHEL, KB. 8, 137.

§ 267. After nasal vowels *h* may become *gh*, after nasals, the aspirates of the corresponding class of the nasals. In many cases the aspirates here as well might be older than *h*, as certainly in *saṁhaaṇa* (body; Deśīn. 8, 14; Pāiẏal, 59; Triv. 1, 3, 105 = BB. 3, 255), AMg. *saṁghaẏaṇa* (Jīv. 66; Vivāhap. 83, 89; Uvās.; Ovav.) = **saṁghatana* = *saṁghanana*, AMg. *saṁghaẏaṇi* (Jīv. 66. 87) = **saṁghatani*, Ś. *saṁghadi* = *saṁhati* (Anarghar. 290, 2). Other examples are : *saṁghāra* = *saṁhāra* (Hc. 1, 264); *siṁgha* = *siṁha* (Hc. 1, 264), beside M. AMg. JM. A. *sīha*, Ś. *siṁha*, Mg. *śiṁha* (§ 76); falsely stands in Ś. *siṅgha* (Śak. 102, 2 ed. BÖHTLINGK according to some MSS), *virasiṅgha* (Karṇas. 53, 20), *siṁghala* (Mallikām. 88, 21), M. *siṁghalī* = *siṁhalī* (Viddhaś. 24, 11). AMg. *haṁbho* (Āẏār. 1, 4, 2, 6; Sūẏag. 579; Vivāhap. 254; Dasav. 640, 27; Nāẏādh. 740. 761. 767. 769. 1337; Uvās.; Nīraẏāv.) = Ś. Mg. *haṁho* (Viddhaś. 97, 10; Mg. Mṛcch. 140, 12; 141, 1, 149; 17; 163, 2; 165, 8; 167, 2) = Skt. *haṁho*. — Behind nasals the aspirate stands for *h* in M. AMg. JM. *cindha* from **cinha* (§ 330) = *cihna* (Vr. 3, 34; Hc. 2, 50; Kī. 2, 117 [text *ciṇṇaṁ*]; Mk. fol. 25; Pāiẏal. 68. 114; G.; Āẏār. 2, 15, 18; Nāẏādh. § 64; p. 1318; Paṇṇav. 101. 117; Vivāhap. 498; Paṇhāv. 155. 167; Ovav.; Uvās.; Niraẏāv.; Āv. 13. 5; Dvār. 507, 38), JM. *cindhiẏa* = *cihnita* (Āv. 27, 1), dialectical *cindhāla* (charming; excellent; Deśīn. 3, 22), M. in compounds °*indha* (G.), beside M. Ś. Mg. A. *ciṇha* (Hc. 2, 50; R.; Nāgān. 87, 11; Mg. Mṛcch. 159, 23; Nāgān. 67, 6; A. Vikr. 58, 11). According to Mk. fol. 68 Ś. has only *ciṇha*. Bh. 1, 12 teaches beside *cindha* also *cĕndha* (§ 119). Further in AMg. JM. A. *bambha-* = *brahman* (Jīv. 912; Sūẏag. 74; Ovav.; Kappas.; Erz.; T. 5, 15; Hc. 4, 412); AMg. *bambha-* = *brahman* (Uttar. 904. 906; Dasav. N. 654, 39), *bambha* = = *brāhma* (Āẏār. p. 125. 34), feminine *bambhī* (Vivāhap. 3; Paṇṇav. 62. 63): M. *bambhaṇḍa* — *brahmāṇḍa* (G.); AMg. *bambhaloẏa* = *brahmaloka* (Uttar. 1090; Vivāhap. 224. 418; Ovav.); AMg. *bambhacāri-* (Āẏār. 2, 1, 9, 1; Uttar. 164; Uvās.), AMg. JM. *bambhaẏāri-* = *brahmacārin* (Dasav. 618, 34; 632, 38; Uttar. 353. 487. 917 f.; Nāẏādh.; Ovav.; Kappas.; Erz.); AMg. A. *bambhacera* = *brahmacarya* (§ 176); AMg. JM. *bambhaṇa* = *brāhmaṇa* (§250); AMg *bambhaṇṇaẏa* = *brāhmaṇyaka* (Ovav.; Kappas.) and others. The other dialects have only *bamha-*, *bamhaṇa* (§ 287. 330). The same phonetic alteration has taken place in the secondary *h* that originated from a sibilant (§ 262 ff.) in *āsaṁghā* = **āsaṁhā* = *āśaṁsā* (Deśīn. 1, 63), mostly with a change of gender (§ 357)[1], M.Ś. *āsaṁgha* (Trīv. 1, 3, 105 = BB. 3, 250; G. R.; Śak. 160, 14; Vikr. 11, 2; Viddhaś. 42, 7; Kaṁsav. 7, 20). Ś. *aṇāsaṁgha* (Mallikām. 93, 9); M. *āsaṁghaï* = *āśaṁsati* (Hc. 4, 35; G.R.); *saṁghaï* = *śaṁsati* (Hc. 4, 2); AMg. *ḍhiṁkuṇa*, dialectical *ḍhaṁkuṇa*, *ḍhĕṁkuṇa* = **daṁkhuṇa* from *daṁś* (§ 107. 212)[2]. Beside AMg. JM.A. *simbha-* (Hc. 2, 74; Paṇhāv. 498; Erz.; Hc. 4, 412), AMg. *sĕmbha-* (WEBER, Bhag. 1, 439), also femin. *sĕmbhā* (Mk. fol. 25) = *śleṣman* from **sĕmha-*, **simha*, AMg. *sĕmbhiẏa* (WEBER, Bhag. 1, 415; 2, 274. 274), *simbhiẏa* (Ovav.) = *ślaiṣmika*, AMg. has also, with a secondary nasal vowel, *siṁghāṇa* from *śleṣmāṇa-* (§ 403), **sĕmhāṇa-*, *simhāṇa-*, **siṁhāṇa* (Āẏār. 2, 2, 1, 7 [so to be read with v. l.]; Ṭhāṇ. 483; Paṇhāv. 505; Vivāhap. 164; Dasav. 631, 3; Uttar. 734; Sūẏag. 704; Ovav.; Kappas.; Bhag.). The word, as *śiṅghāṇa*, *śṛṅghāṇika*, has been taken into Skt. A denominative therefrom is AMg.; *siṁghāṇei* (Vivāhap. 112). A. has also *gimbha* = *grīṣma* (Hc. 4, 412). On *kambhāra* = *kāśmīra* see § 120, on *sepha* = *śleṣman* see § 312, and on *bharaï* = *smarati*, § 313.

1. BOLLENSEN on Vikr. 11, 2 p. 196; Cf. PISCHEL, De gr. Prācr. p. 5 f.; on Hc. 4, 35; BB. 3, 250 — 2. Cf. PISCHEL, BB. 3, 255; 6, 85 f.

II. CONJUNCT CONSONANTS.

§ 268. Conjunct consonants of different classes are either separated by a separation-vowel (§131-140) or assimilated. In the anlaut, with the exception of *ṇha*, *mha*, *lha*, and dialectically also of consonant+*ra*, only a simple consonant can stand : of the consonants assimilated in the inlaut only the second one enters into the anlaut. The anlaut of the second member of a compound is generally treated as inlaut (§ 196). M. *kaḍhaï* = *kvathati*; *kiḷaï* = *krīḍati*; *khandha* = *skandha*; *gaṇṭhi* = *granthi*; *jalaï* = *jvalati*; *thala* = *sthala*; *thāmatthāma-* = *sthāmasthāma-* (G.); *dia* = *dvija*; *bhamaï* = *bhramati*; *ṇhāṇa* = *snāna*; *ṇhāvia* = *snāpita*; *lhasaï* = *hrasati*. — *mhi* = *asmi*, *mha*, *mho* = *smaḥ* may since they are enclitic, be regarded as treated in the inlaut.[1] The grammarians permit a consonant+*r* in the anlaut and in the inlaut (Vr. 3, 4; Hc. 2, 80; Mk. fol. 20) : *doha*, *droha* = *droha* (Bh. 3, 4), *daha*, *draha* = *hrada* (§ 354; Hc. 2, 80); Deśīn. 8, 14); *canda*, *candra* (Grr.); *rudda*, *rudra* (Bh.; Hc.); *inda*, *indra* (Mk.); *bhadda*, *bhadra* (Hc.; Mk); *samudda*, *samudra* (Hc.). So there occurs M. *bodraha* (Pāiẏal. 62; cf. Deśīn. 7, 80) or *vodraha* (young; Hc. 2, 80; Deśīn. 7, 80; H. 392)[2]; JM. *vandra* (crowd; Hc. 1, 53; 2, 79; Deśīn. 7.32; Erz. 26, 3) or *bandra*, *bundra*[3]. Frequent is consonant+*r*, that sometimes is secondary, in A. So in Hc. : *traṁ* = *tad*, more correctly = *tyad* (4,360); *dramma* = δρχαμη' (4, 422, 4); *dravakka* (fruit; 4, 422, 4); *draha* = *hrada* (4, 423, 1); *drehi* = **dekhi* = *dṛṣṭi* (4, 422, 6; cf. §66); *dhruṁ* in the sense of *yad*, *yasmād* (4, 360. 438, 1), in Kī. 5, 49 *druṁ* = *tad*, *jruṁ* = *yad* and according to 5, 69 peculiar to Vrācaḍa Apabhraṁśa; *dhruvu* = *dhruvaṁ* (4, 418; cf. Kī. 5, 5, where *ghruva ghru* has been published); *praṅgaṇa* = *prāṅgaṇa* (4, 360. 420, 4);

pramāṇia pramāṇita (4, 422, 1); *praāvadi*=*prajāpati* (4, 404); *prassadi*=*paśyati* (4, 393); *prāiva, prāiva prāu*=*prāyaḥ* (4, 414); *pria*=*priya* (4, 370, 2. 377. 379, 2; 398. 401, 6. 417;); *bruvaha*=*brūta*; *brŏppi, brŏppiṇu*= **brūtvā* (4, 391; also Kī. 5, 58; *bhrantri*=*bhrānti* (4.360); *vratta*=*vrata* (4, 394); *vrāsa*=*vyāsa* (4, 399; Kī. 5, 5). In Kī. beside those mentioned above also *bhrāsa*=*bhāṣya* (5, 5). In the inlaut : *antraḍi*=*antra* (Hc. 4,445, 3); *bhrantri*=*bhrānti* (4,360); *putra* (Kī. 5, 2); perhaps also in *jatru, tatru*=*yatra, tatra* (Hc. 4, 404), and in *etrula, kĕtrula, jetrula, tĕtrula*=*iyat, kiyat, yāvat, tāvat* (Hc. 4, 435), where the MSS waver between *tta* and *tra*. Kī. 5, 50 has in the edition *yadru, tadru*=*yatra, tatra*. — In Mg. A. there occur dialectically in the anlaut also *yca, yja* (§ 217).

1. The relevant paragraphs supply the references. — 2. So according to Hc. 2, 80. The MSS, according to Weber on H. 392 and IS 16, 140 f., do not have *r*. — 3. Pischel on He. 1, 53.

§ 269. In the inlaut, of conjunct consonants, there can stand only : 1) the consonant doubled and with the aspirate of its own class; 2) the composite sounds *ṇha, mha, lha*; 3) dialectically consonant+*r* (§ 268); (4) nasal+consonant of its class. The MSS mostly write anusvâra in place of the nasal : the grammarians differ. According to Kī. 2, 121; Mk. fol. 34 *ṁ* comes in for *n, ṅ*, according to Vr. 4, 14, for *n, ñ* before a consonant[1]: *vaṁcaṇia*=*vañcanīya*; *viṁjha*=*vindhya*; *paṅkti, paṁti*=*paṅktiḥ*; *maṁti-*=*mantrin*. According to Hc. 1, 1 *ṅ, ñ* can remain before consonants of their own class; according to 1, 25, on the other hand, *ṅ, ñ, ṇ, n* must become *ṁ* before consonants; according to 1, 30, however, they may remain; however, according to Hc. some grammarians require them necessarily. From Deśīn. 1, 26 it is seen that *aïrimpa*, not *aïriṁpa*, was written, and Deśīn. 1, 18 makes it probable that *andhandhu*, and not *aṁdhaṁdhu* should be read.[2] The examples of the grammarians partly relate to words in which the nasal, in conformity with the phonetic laws of Pkt. goes away from its class, and in them *ṁ* must be written.[3] So Ś. *avaraṁmuha*=*aparāṅmukha* (Vikr. 44, 9); AMg. *chaṁmāsiya*=*ṣaṇmāsika* (Āyār. 2, 1, 2, 1); M. A. *chaṁmuha*=*ṣaṇmukha* (§ 441); M. Ś. *diṁmuha*=*diṅmukha* (Karp. 39. 3; Viddhaś. 34, 11; Laṭakam. 4, 3); M. *diṁmoha*=*diṅmoha* (H. 866); M. JM. Ś. *paraṁmuha*=*parāṅmukha* (G.H.R.; Erz.; Śak. 75, 15; Mahāv. 34, 12; Bhartṛharin. 22, 13); M. AMg. JM. Ś. A. *paṁti*=*paṅkti* (R.; Karp. 47, 12; 101, 1; Jīv. 446. 512; Paṇhāv. 520; Rāyap. 143; Vivāhap. 1325; Ovav.; Kappas.; Āv. 36, 36; Bālar. 49. 2; Karp. 37, 9; Piṅgala 1, 10), M.Ś. °*vaṁti* (H.; Mṛcch. 69, 1), AMg. *paṁtiyā*=*paṅktikā* (Āyār. 2, 3, 3, 2; 2, 11, 5; Aṇuog. 386; Ṭhāṇ. 94; Vivāhap. 361; Paṇṇav. 80. 84. 85); AMg. *baṁjha*=*bandhya* (Sūyag. 460, (text *va*°]), *abaṁjha* (Sūyag. 606 [text *ava*°]); M. AMg. JM. Ś. *viṁjha*=*vindhya* (G.H.R.; Mṛcch. 41, 16; Vivāhap. 1189. 1274. 1287; Erz.; Rukmiṇīp. 48, 3); Ś. *viṁjhakedu* (Priyad. 14, 6; 52, 6); M. JM.Ś. *saṁjhā*=*sandhyā* (G.H.R.; Erz.; Karp. 67, 4). In support of this stand the rules, like Vr. 3, 43=Hc. 2, 61; Kī. 2, 98; Mk. fol. 25 too, where for *nma* the change into *mma* is especially prescribed again. Whether an exception should, however, be generally made for nasal+

nasal, and, therefore, even *parammuha*, *chammāsiya* should be written, remains undetermined. 5) In Mg., in the inlaut too, are found *śca*, *yyha*, *ṣṭha*, *śka*, *śkha*, *ska*, *skha*, *śta*, *śṭa*, *sta*, *spa*, *spha*, *ẖka* (§233. 236. 271. 290. 301. ff. 331).

1. On the misunderstanding of this rule by Bhāmaha see COWELL on Vr. p. 137, note 2. — 2. PISCHEL, Deśin., Introduction p. 8. f. — 3. PISCHEL on Hc. 1, 25.

§ 270. Of the conjunct mutes of different classes the first one is assimilated to the second (Vr. 3, 1.50; C. 3, 3. 24; Hc. 2, 77. 89; Kī. 2, 49. 108; Mk. fol. 19. 26). (1) *k*+*t* becomes *tt* : M. *āsatta* = *āsakta* (G.H.); *jutta* = *yukta* (H.R.); *bhatti* = *bhakti* (G.H.); *mŏttia* = *mauktika* (G.H.R.). Likewise in other dialects[1]. *mukka* beside rare *mutta* = *mukta* is derived from **mukna*, as *ragga* beside *ratta* = *rakta* goes back to **ragṇa* (§ 566), *sakka*, which Hc. 2, 2 equates as = *śakta*, is everywhere = *śakya* (Kī. 2, 1)[2]. *nakkaṁcara* (Hc. 1, 177) is not = *naktaṁcara*, which must become *ṇattaṁcara*, but goes back to **nakkā* from **nakā'* (§ 194. 355) = Vedic *nak*[3]. — (2) *k*+*th* becomes *tth*: JM. *rittha* = *riktha* (Pāiyal. 49; Erz.; Kk.); AMg. *sittha* = *siktha* (Hc. 2, 77; Ovav.; Kappas.); *sitthaa* = *sikthaka* (Bh. 3, 1; Pāiyal. 228). — 3) *k*+*p* becomes *pp*; M. *vappaīrāa* = *vākpatirāja* (G.). — 4) *g*+*dh* becomes *ddh*; M. *duddha* = *dugdha* (G.H.); M. *muddha* = *mugdha* (G.H.R.); M. *ṇiddha* (H.R.), *siṇiddha* = *snigdha* (G.). — 5) *g*+*bh* becomes *bbh* : M. *pabbhāra* = *prāgbhāra* (G.R.)[4]. — 6) *ṭ*+*k* becomes *kk* : AMg. *chakka* = *ṣaṭka* (§ 451); AMg. *chakkaṭṭhaga* = *ṣaṭkāṣṭhaka* (Nāyādh.).—7) *ṭ*+*c* becomes *cc* : AMg. *chacca* = *ṣaṭca*; *chaccaraṇa* = *ṣaṭcaraṇa* (§441). — 8) *ṭ*+*t* becomes *tt* : AMg. *chattala* = *ṣaṭtala*; *chattisaṁ*, *chattisā* = *ṣaṭtriṁśat* (§441). — 9) *ṭ*+*p* becomes *pp* : M. *chappaa* = JM. *chappaya* = *ṣaṭpada*; AMg. *chappaṇṇaṁ*, A. *chappaṇa* = **ṣaṭpañcat* (56; § 441. 445). — 10) *ṭ*+*ph* becomes *pph*: *kappala* = *kaṭphala* (Hc. 2, 77). — 11) *ḍ*+*g* becomes *gg* : M. *khagga* = *khaḍga* (G.H.R.); M. *chagguṇa* = *ṣaḍguṇa*, Ś. *chagguṇaa* = *ṣaḍguṇaka* (§ 441). — 12) *ḍ*+*j* becomes *jj* : AMg. *chajjiva* = *ṣaḍjiva* (Āyār. 1, 1, 7, 7); *sajja* = *ṣaḍja* (Hc. 2, 77). — 13) *ḍ*+*d* becomes *dd* : AMg. *chaddisiṁ* = *ṣaḍdiśam* (§ 441). —14) *ḍ*+*bh* becomes *bbh* : AMg. *chabbhāya*, °*ga* = *ṣaḍbhāga* (§441); Ś. *chabbhua* = *ṣaḍabhuja* (Caiṭ. 42, 7). — 15) *ḍ*+*v* becomes *vv* : AMg. JM. A. *chavvisaṁ* = *ṣaḍviṁśati* (§ 441). — 16) *t*+*k* becomes *kk* : M. *ukkaṇṭhā* = *utkaṇṭhā* (G.H.); AMg. *ukkaliyā* = *utkalikā* (Ovav.); Ś. *balakkāra* = *balātkāra* (Mṛcch. 13. 22; 17, 23; 23, 23. 25; Śak. 137, 3), Mg. *balakkāla* (Mṛcch. 140. 15; 146, 17; 158, 22; 162, 20; 173, 12). — 17) *t*+*kh* becomes *kkh* : M. *ukkhaa*, JM. *ukkhaya* = *utkhāta* (80). — 18) *t*+*p* becomes *pp*: M. *uppala* = *utpala* (G.H.R.); AMg. *tappaḍhamayā* = *tatprathamatā* (Ovav.; Kappas.); M. *sappurisa* = *satpuruṣa* (G.H.). — 19) *t*+*ph* becomes *pph*: M. *upphulla* = *utphulla* (H.R.); M. Mg. *upphāla* = *utphāla* (R.; Mṛcch. 99, 10). — 20) *d*+*g* becomes *gg* : M. *uggama* = *udgama* (G.H.R.); M.Ś. *mŏggara* = *mudgara*: AMg. JŚ. *pŏggala* = *pudgala* (§125). — 21) *d*+*gh* becomes *ggh* : M. *ugghāa* = *udghāta* (G.H.R.); M. *ugghuṭṭha* = *udghuṣṭa* (R.). — 22) *d*+*b* becomes *bb* : M. *bubbua* = *budbuda* (G.); Ś. *ubbandhia* = *udbandhya* (§ 513). — 23) *d*+*bh* becomes *bbh*: M. *ubbhaḍa* = *udbhaṭa* (G.R.); M. *ubbhea* = *udbheda* (G.H.R.); M. *sabbhāva* = *sadbhāva* (G.H.R.). — 24) *p*+*t* becomes *tt* : M. *ukkhita* = *utkṣipta* (G.H.R.); M. *pajjatta* = *paryāpta* (G.H.R.); M. *sutta*

= *supta* (H). — 25) *b+j* becomes *jj*: M. AMg. JM. Ś. *khujja* = *kubja* (§206). — 26) *b+d* becomes *dd*: *adda* = *abda* (Hc. 2, 79); M. *sadda* = *śabda* (G.H. R.). — 27) *b+dh* becomes *ddh* : *āraddha* = *ārabdha* (R.); M. *laddha* = *labdha* (G.H.R.); *lŏddhaa* = *lubdhaka* (§ 125).

1. Cf. § 184, note 1.—2. BOLLENSEN, on Vikr. 12, 120; PISCHEL on Hc. 2, 2. Cf. 279. — 3. Skt. *nakṣatra* "star", "constellation" too should be equated as — **nakkṣatra* "ruling over the night." The usual explanations from **naktatra* (AUFRECHT, KZ. 8, 71; cf. WEBER, Naxatra 2, 268) or from √*nakṣ* (GRASSMANN, Wörterbuch s.v.) are in any case perverse.—4. So according to the usual interpretation. ZACHARIAE, (Beiträge zur indischen Lexicographie p. 60 ff.) sees probably rightly in *prāgbhāra* a false back-formation from *pabbhāra*. He would like to derive *pabbhāra*, that is frequent in AMg. also (e.g. Uttar. 1034; Aṇuog, 416; Vivāhap. 248. 920; Ṭhāṇ, 135.297; Ovav.; Nirayāv.). and is found also in JM. (Kk.) and Ś. (Anarghar. 149, 10), from **prahvāra*. The common meaning "crowd" points however, rather to **prabhāra* (JACOBI, Kk. s.v.) with duplication according to § 196.

§ 271. Conjunct mutes of the same class, except in the cases mentioned in § 333, undergo a change only dialectically. In Mg. *ṭṭ* becomes *sṭ* (Hc. 4, 290); *pasṭa* = *paṭṭa*; *bhasṭālikā* = *bhaṭṭārikā*; *bhasṭiṇi* = *bhaṭṭini*. STENZLER, in Mṛcch., writes *śṭ* for *ṭṭ*: *bhaśṭaka* = *bhaṭṭaka* (10, 5; 16, 18; 22, 3. 5; 114, 16; 118, 8. 12. 22; 119, 9; 122, 10; 124. 12ff.; 125, 1, 3. 8. 24; 132, 11. 15. 18); *bhaśṭālaa* = *bhaṭṭāraka* (22, 5; 32, 4; 112, 18; 119, 13; 121, 12; 154, 9; 164, 12; 165, 1.5; 176, 4); *piśṭadu* = **piṭṭadu* = *piṭṭayatu* (125, 8). GOḌABOLE, as often in other cases also, has followed him. The manuscripts almost always have *bhaṭṭaka, bhaṣṭaka, bhaṣṭhaka, bhaṭṭālaka, bhaṣṭālaka* [°*laa*], only some of the MSS have °*śṭ*° in 10, 5; 22, 3. 5; 32, 4; 119, 13; 124, 24; 132, 11. For *piśṭadu* all have *piṭṭadu*[1] or *viṭṭadu*, likewise *aṭṭhahāśaśśa* (168, 21), for which we should read *asṭa*° according to Hc. The Calcutta editions, have *ṭṭ*° throughout, likewise all the editions in Śak. 114, 12; 116, 11; 118, 4; Prab. 32, 8. 10. 11. 12; Caṇḍak. 60, 12 etc. In Mṛcch. *śṭ* may be a dialectical variant for *sṭ*, as *śk* beside *ẖk* = *kṣ*. But elsewhere according to Hc. *sṭ* should be written for *ṭṭ*[2]. Cf. § 290. — *kṛtti* (skin) becomes *kicci* according to Hc. 2, 12. In the text we find only *katti* (Pāiyal. 110; G.H.) and M. *kitti* (H.). In H. 951 the MS W has the v.l. °*kaccia* for °*kattio*; in Dhvanyāloka at 128, 6 the edition reads °*katti a* and so also Kāvyaprakāśa 329, 10 the edition and the best manuscripts, *kacci* and *kicci* presuppose Skt. **kṛtyā* = *kartyā* (scil. *tvak*) "what is to be cut off (skin)". Cf. AMg. *vigiñcaï* = **vikṛntyati* (§485). On Mg. *śca* for *ccha* see § 233.

1. *piṭṭhadu* in GOḌABOLE p. 345, note 9 is a printing error.— 2. ASCOLI, Kritische Studien p. 233 note; SENART, Piyadasi 1, 29 f.; 2, 418 ff; JOHANSSON, Shābhāzgarhi 2, 18 note 1. wrongly equate *sṭ* as = *ṭṭ*. Cf. PISCHEL, GGA. 1881, 1319 f.

§ 272. If the first of the two conjunct consonants is a nasal, the sound-group remains unchanged as a rule, when the nasal precedes : M. *aṅka* (G.H.R.); M. Ś. *saṅkhalā* = *śṛṅkhalā* (§ 213): M. *siṅga* = *śṛṅga* (G.H.); M. *jaṅghā* (G.); M. *kŏñca* = *krauñca* (G.); M. *lañchaṇa* = *lāñchana* (G.H.R.); M. *mañjarī* (G.H.); M. *kaṇṭha* (G.H.R.); M. *khaṇḍa* (G.H.R.); M. *anta* (G.H.R.); M. *manthara* (G.H.R.); *maaranda* = *makaranda* (H.R.); M. *bandha* (G.H.R.); M. *jambū* (G.H.). If the nasal quits its own class, it becomes *ṁ* (§ 269).

§ 273. Dialectically *ñca* becomes *ṇṇa* in *pañcadaśan* and *pañcāśat* (Vr. 3,, 44; Hc. 2, 43; Kī. 2, 66; Mk. fol. 25). So : *paṇṇaraha* (15; Grr.; A. Piṅgala 1, 112. 114); AMg. JM. *paṇṇarasa* (°*nna*°) (Hc. 3, 123; Kappas.; Bhag.; Erz. p. XLI), *paṇṇarasi* (Kappas.); *paṇṇāsā* (50; Vr. 3, 44; Hc. 2, 43; Mk. fol. 26; Kappas.); AMg. JM. also *paṇṇāsaṁ* (Kī. 2, 66; Ṭhāṇ. 266; Bhag.; Erz.), also *pannā* (C. 3, 32), in the remaining fifties shortened to °*paṇṇaṁ*, °*vaṇṇaṁ* : *ĕkkāvannaṁ* (ed. *ekā*°; 51; Samav. 112); *bāvaṇṇaṁ* (52); *tevaṇṇaṁ* (53); *caüvaṇṇaṁ* (54); *paṇavaṇṇaṁ* (55); *chappaṇṇaṁ* (56); *sattāvaṇṇaṁ* (57); *aṭṭhāvaṇṇaṁ* (58) (Weber, Bhagavatī 1, 426; Samav. 113-117; Erz. p. XLI) *aüṇāpaṇṇaṁ* (49; Ovav. §163); *paṇapaṇṇaīma* (55th; Kappas.); A. *bāvaṇṇa* (52), *sattāvaṇṇāī* (57) (Piṅgala 1, 87. 51). So also AMg. *paṇṇaṭṭhi* (65; Kappas.) and *pannattari* (75; Samav. 133). Before 20 — 60, in JM. AMg. *paṇṇa* is mostly weakened to *paṇa* : *paṇavisaṁ* (25); *paṇatisaṁ* (35); *paṇaẏālisaṁ* (45); *paṇavaṇṇaṁ* (55) and *paṇavaṇṇā* (C. 3, 33; [so to be read; see v. l.]; Hc. 2, 174; Deśīn. 6, 27; Triv. 1, 3, 105 = BB. 3, 245 beside *pañcāvaṇṇā*); *paṇasaṭṭhiṁ* (Weber, Bhagavatī 1, 425; Samav. 72-123; Erz. p. XLI). So also AMg. *paṇapaṇṇaīma* (55th; Kappas.) and A. *chappaṇa* (56; Piṅgala 1, 96). Corresponding to Pāli *paṇṇuvisati*, *paṇṇuvisaṁ* (25) stands AMg. *paṇuvisāhi* (Instr.; Āẏār. p. 137,25), AMg. *paṇuvisaṁ* (Rāẏap. 114 f.; Jīv. 673; Jīẏak. 19. 20); J. *paṇuvisā* (Āv. 48, 13), of which *u* is to be explained according to §104. Pāli too has *pannarasa, pannarasī, paṇṇarasa, paṇṇāsa* beside *paññāsa*. E. Kuhn has conjectured (KZ. 33, 478), that "*ññ* should be explained as arising from a dissimilation of *c* and *ś*, and accordingly it goes to back to a time, when *ś* had not yet become the dental sibilant, but in its pronunciation was still distinctly connected to *c*." That is not possible for *ṇṇa*. Pañjābī and Sindhī *paṁjāh*, P. °*vaṁjā*, S. °*vaṁjāha* (Hoernle, Comp. Gr. 259) point to the change from *ñca, to ñja ñya, nya*. Cf. Pāli *āṇā* = *ājñā*, *āṇāpeti* = *ājñāpayati* and § 274.276. 282. 283. In A. the nasal has vanished in *pacīsa* (25) and *pacaālisahĩ* (45; instr.). See § 445. On AMg. *āuṇṭaṇa* apparently = *ākuñcana* see § 232.

§ 274. According to Hc. 4, 293; Sr. fol. 62; Namisādhu on Rudraṭa, Kāvyālaṁkāra 2, 12 in Mg. *ñja* becomes *ñña* : *aññali* = *añjali*; *dhaṇaññaa* = *dhanaṁjaya*; *paññala* = *prāñjala*. According to this *ja*, as in the anlaut (236), has become *ya*. In Mṛcch. 19, 6 stands *añjaliṁ*.

§ 275. According to Hc. 4, 261. 302; Namisādhu on Rudraṭa, Kāvyālaṁkāra 2, 12; Amaracandra, Kāvyakalpalatāvṛtti p. 9 in Ś. and Mg. *nta* may become *nda*. The examples of the grammarians are : Ś. *andeura* = *antaḥpura*; *ṇiccinda* = *niścinta*; *mahanda-* = *mahat*; Mg. *mahanda-* ; presumptive Ś. *randūṇa* = *ratvā* (Hc. 4, 271) and further Trivikrama 3, 2,1 *saüṁdale* = *śakuntale*. In the inscriptions *nda* occurs throughout for *nta* in Lalitav. in Mg. : *payyaṁde* = *paryante* (565, 7); *avayyaṁdadā* = *aparyantatā* (565, 12); *pĕśkiyyaṁḍi* = *prekṣyante* (565, 13); *puścaṁde, ṇi* [*liśkaṁ*] *de* = *pṛcchan nirikṣamāṇaḥ* (565, 20); *vaññaṁdassa* = *vrajataḥ* (566, 7), whilst in Ś. *nta* exclusively remains : *viloijjaṁti* = *vilokyante* (554, 21); *pĕkkhijjaṁti* = *prekṣyante* (554, 22); *vuttaṁtā*. . .*suṇiyaṁti* = *vṛttāntāḥ*. . . *śrūyante* (555, 2); *huvaṁti* = *bhavanti* (555, 5); *peraṁtesu* = *paryanteṣu* (555, 11), *desaṁtara* =

deśāntara (560, 19) etc. HOFFFR[1] and LASSEN[2] have already collected numerous examples, from older texts, that have partly vanished in the recent editions, such as *bhakkhandi*, for which STENZLER, Mṛcch. 69, 3, with his manuscripts, reads *bhakkhanti* = *bhakṣayanti*, *sandāva*, for which stands *saṁtāpa* (Mṛcch. 78, 8; Śak. 55, 1; 68, 1; Ratn. 298, 10; 229, 10), etc. In Prab. the editions also of Pūṇā (P.), Bombay (Bb.) and Madras (M.), like that of BROCKHAUS (B.) frequently have *nda*, even in words other than in BROCKHAUS, as 39, 2 B. Bb. *ramandi*, M.P. *ramaṁdi*, 9 B. *saṁbhāvaandi*, M. P. *saṁhāvaaṁdi*, Bb. *saṁbhāvayaṁdi*, but 4 B. *ciṭhṭhanti*, M. *ciṭṭhandi*, P. *ciṭhṭhandi* Bb. *tussanti*, while all 7 read *nti* in B. *paḍichanti*, Bb. M. *paḍicchanti*, P. *paḍichanti*. The same variation occurs there often and so also in many of the editions published by Indians. Thus Sh. P. PAṆḌIT writes Mālav[2]. 27, 2 *oloanti*, 3 *antare*, but 5 *uvaārāṇandaraṁ* (BOLLENSEN 6, 9 correctly °*ntaraṁ*); 66, 1 *pañcarattabhbhandare* (BOLLENSEN 34, 13 °*ntare*), but 5 *āantavvaṁ* etc.; TĀRĀKUMĀRA CAKRAVARTI, Uttarar. 59, 5; 69, 10; 77, 4; 89, 11 *vāsandi* = *vāsanti*; TELANG, Mudrār. 36, 4 *jāṇandi*, but 38, 2 *jāṇantaṁ*; 39, 4 *sahandi*, but 7 *nivedianti* [sic.]; DURGĀPRASĀDA and PARABA, Unmattarāghava 3,2.5; 7, 4 *dīsandi*, but 5, 4 *dīsanti* = *dṛśyante*; 7, 4 *aṇṇesandie* = *anveṣantyā*, but 5, 4 *saṁbhamantā* = *saṁbhramantaḥ*; Mukund. 13, 2 *kiṁ di* = *kim iti*; 13, 18 *andareṇa* = *antareṇa*; 17, 14 *sandi* = *śānti*; 21, 12 *akkando* = *ākrāntaḥ*. Frequent is the spelling in both the editions of Pārvatīp., as *ṇirandaraṁ cindāulaṁ* (2, 15. 16), *vāsandie* (9, 3), *vāsandiā* (9, 15), *ahilasandi* (24, 16; 28, 4) and others. LASSEN was inclined to see therein a peculiarity of Ś[3]. But *nda* is found also in Mg. as well as in M. too, e.g. *jāṇandā* v.l. for *jāṇantā* (H. 821); *kiṁ deṇa* (H. 905); *bhaṇandi* (Pārvatīp. 28, 2); *ramandi* = **ramanti*, *ujjhando* = *ujjhantaḥ*, *rajjandi* = *rajyante* (Mukund. 5, 2. 23, 2). Hc. 2, 180 teaches that *haṁdi* is used to express astonishment, regret, certainty, reality and doubt, and 2, 181 teaches that *haṁda* is used in the sense "take !", "take care". *haṁda* is = *handa* = Skt. *hanta*. The example given by Hc. is H. 200, where the MSS read *gĕnhaha*, *giṇhaha*, *maṁda*, the Jaina recension R. has *haṁdi* and Bhuvanapāla (IS. 16, 70 on stanza 145) reads *haṁta*. AMg. has *haṁda ha* or *haṁda haṁ* (Āyār. 2, 1, 10, 6. 11, 1. 2; Ṭhāṇ. 354); elsewhere, however, M. AMg. JM. Ś. *hanta*, AMg. also *hantā* (G.; Āyār. 2, 5, 2, 4; Nāyādh. 1332; Vivāgas. 16; Uvās.; Bhag.; Ovav.; Kk.; Vikr. 31, 7). AMg. *haṁdi* (Sūyag. 151; Dasav. 624, 26 [*handi*]; Dasav. N. 647, 41 [*handi*]; 653; 13 [*handi*]; Ṭhāṇ. 488; Aṇuog. 323; Nāyādh. 1134), goes back to JM. *haṁti* (Kk.), that is = *ham iti*. Cf. § 185 and AMg. *haṁbho* § 267. The examples in Hc., with the exception of *handa*, are found in the Telugu recension, and like the doubled setting of the aspirates (§193), the writing of *nd* for *nt* is to be traced back to the Dravidians, who pronounce *nt* as *nd*. Hence *nd* is found frequently especially in Dravidian MSS and in the MSS which go back to the Dravidians. Sometimes the Dravidian MSS write *ntta* for *nta* in Skt. too, e.g. *śakunttalā*[4], to ensure the pronunciation *nt* thereby, and so in Pkt. too the South Indian PG. writes *mahaṁtte* (7, 43) for *mahaṁte* = *mahataḥ* (acc. plur.)[5], as also old Pkt. MSS are fond of doubling *t* after *m*[6]. Especially frequent is *saṁdāva* in M. (H. 817; Appendix 994) and Ś. (Mālatīm. 79, 1; 81, 2; 219, 1; Uttarar. 6, 1; 92, 9; 163, 5; Nāgān. 87, 12; Viddhaś. 81, 4; Priyad. 4, 7; 22, 12; 24, 7; 25, 13; Mallikām. 218, 10, 223, 6; 330. 17; Rukmiṇīp. 27, 6. 11; 33,13). *saṁdāvedi* (Priyad. 20, 7; Mukund. 73, 3 [so to be read]), *saṁdāvida* (Mālatīm. 79, 1). Śak. too has *sandāva* at 55, 1 in most of the manuscripts, at 68, 1, in two of them at 127, 7, most of them have *sandāvedi*. Since M. possesses a verb *dāvaï* = *tāpayati* (Śak. 55, 16 with note 1 at p. 184; cf. also §201, note 1), one might derive *saṁdāpa* from it. But in M. *saṁtāva* is the most accredited form, and for Ś. the only correct one. Dialectically the same phonetic change has occurred in *oandaï* = *apakṛntati* (§ 485), and *vihuṁḍua* = *vidhuṁtuda* (Deśīn. 7, 65; Triv. 1, 3, 105 = BB. 3, 252).

1. De Prakrita dialecto p. 54. — 2. Inst. p. 238; 378 note. —3. Inst. p. 238.— 4. Pischel, GN. 1873, 211 f.; KB. 8, 130 f.; Vikramorvaśīya p. 615—5. Pischel, GN. 1895. 210. — 6. S. Goldschmidt, ZDMG. 29, 494, note 1; Rāvaṇavaho p. xi.

§ 276. If the nasal stands in the second place, *ṇ*, *n* become assimilated to the preceding consonant : M *aggi* = *agni* (G.H.R.); M. AMg. JM. Ś. *uvvigga* = *udvigna* (G.H.R.; Uvās.; Erz.; Mṛcch. 150, 16; 151, 2). *uvviṇṇa*, that is equated by Hc. 2, 79 as = *udvigna* is rather = **udvṛṇṇa* from Vedic *vrad*, **vṛd* with *ud*. An original *ṛ* is pointed to by *vuṇṇa* (timid; frightened; Hc. 4, 421; Deśīn. 7, 94; Pāiyal. 76) and *uvvuṇṇa* (frightened; Deśīn. 1, 123); JM. *nagga* = *nagna* (Erz.); M. *rugga* = *rugṇa* (G.); M. *viggha* = *vighna* (R.); AMg. *sayagghi* = *śataghnī* (Uttar. 285; Ovav.); *suruggha* = *srughna* (Hc. 2, 113); AMg. *pattī* = *patnī* (Uttar. 363. 422); M. *savatta* = *sapatna* (G.R.), M. JM. Ś. *savattī* = *sapatnī* (H.; Āv. 28, 9; Anarghar. 287, 1; Veṇīs. 12, 6), Ś. *ṇisavatta* = *niḥasapatna* (Mṛcch. 5, 1), M. *paattaa* = *prayatna* (H.); AMg. *pappoi*, JŚ. *pappodi* = *prāpnoti* (§ 504). See 566. The sound-group *jña*, as a rule, becomes *ṇṇa* in the anlaut *ṇa* (Vr. 3, 44; Hc. 2, 42; Kī. 2, 102; Mk. fol. 25) : M. *ahiṇṇāṇa* = *abhijñāna* (R.); M. *jaṇṇa* = *yajña* (H.); *paṇṇā* = *prajñā* (Hc. 2, 42); M. *saṇṇā* = *saṁjñā* (R.); M. AMg. JM. *āṇā* = *ājñā*, AMg. JM. *āṇavei*, Ś. Mg. *āṇavedi* = *ājñāpayati* (§ 88); M. *ṇajjaï*, AMg. JM. *najjaï* = *jñāyate* (§548), AMg. *nāṇa* = *jñāna* (Āyār. 1, 6, 1, 6). Hc. 2, 83 permits also *ajjā* = *ājñā*; *pajjā* = *prajñā*; *saṁjā* = *saṁjñā*; *jāṇa* = *jñāna*, and beside *ṇṇa*, *ṇṇu* (§ 105) also *jja*, when *jña* forms the second member of a compound : *appaṇṇu*, *appajja*, = *ātmajña*, *ahiṇṇu*, *ahijja* = *abhijña*, *iṅgiaṇṇu*, *iṅgiajja* = *iṅgitajña*; *daïvaṇṇu*, *daïvajja* = *daivajña*; *maṇŏṇṇa*, *maṇŏjja* = *manojña*; *savvaṇṇu*, *savvajja* = *sarvajña*, but only *viṇṇāṇa* = *vijñāna*. According to Vr. 3, 5; Kī. 2, 52; Mk. fol. 20 in M. only *jja* is used in words of the type of *sarvajña*: *savvajja*, *ahijja*, *iṅgiajja*, *sujja* = *sujña*, in Ś. on the other hand, according to Vr. 12, 8 only *savvaṇṇa*, *iṅgidaṇṇa*, according to 12, 7 in *vijña* and *yajña* optionally *ñja*, according to Kī. 5, 76 *ahijjo*, and *ahiñco* optionally, according to 5, 77 *paliñcā* = *pratijñā*. The correct reading in Vr. Kī. is wholly doubtful; presumably *jja* and *ṇṇa* should be permitted. The forms found in the texts are Ś. *aṇahiṇṇa* = *anabhijña* (Śak. 106, 6; Mudrār. 59. 1) *jaṇṇa* = *yajña* (Śak. 142, 3; Mālav. 70, 15); *païṇṇā* (§ 220). In AMg. beside *ṇṇu*, *nnu* (§ 105), *ṇṇa*, *nna* also are suitable for use : *samaṇunna* = *samnujña* (Āyār. 1, 1, 1, 5); *kheyanna* = *khedajña* (Āyār. 1, 1, 4, 2; 1, 2, 3, 6;

1, 2, 5, 3; 1, 2, 6, 5; 1, 3, 1, 3. 4; 1, 4, 1, 2; 1, 5, 6, 3; Sūẏag. 234 [°*da*°] 304. 565); *māẏanna* = *mātrajña* (Āẏār. 1 2, 5, 3; 1, 7, 3, 2; 1, 8, 1, 19; Dasav. 623, 15; (Uttar. 51); *kālanna*, *balanna*, *khaṇaẏanna*, *khaṇanna*, *viṇaẏanna*, *samaẏanna*, *bhāvanna* (Āẏār. 1, 2, 5, 3; 1, 7, 3, 2); *meẏanna* (Uttar. 508); *panna* = *prajña* (Uttar. 33); *āsupanna* = *āśuprajña* (Uttar. 181); *mahāpanna* (Uttar 200); *maṇunna*, *amaṇunna* = *manojña*, *amanojña* (Āẏār. 2, 1, 10, 2. 1 2; 2, 4, 2, 6; p. 136, 7 ff.; Sūẏag. 390; Ovav. 53, 87), but Ś. *maṇŏjja* (Mallikām. 195, 5). So also AMg. *janna* = *yajña* (Uttar. 742), *jaṇṇaī* = *yajñakṛt* (Ovav). In Mg. *jña* becomes *ñña* (H. 4, 293); *avaññā* = *avajñā*; *paññāvisāla* = *prajñāviśāla*; *śavvañña* = *sarvajña*. Vr. Kī. Mk. do not have this rule, and the MSS write only *ṇṇa*. So: *jaṇṇa* = *yajña* (Mṛcch. 171, 11); *jaṇṇaśeṇi* = *yajñaseṇi* (Veṇīs. 34, 13); for which, according to Hc., should be written *yañña yaññaśenī*; *paḍiṇṇāda* = *pratijñāta* (Veṇīs. 35, 13) *viṇṇāda* = *vijñāta* (Mṛcch. 37, 21), *viṇṇavia* = *vijñāpya* (Mṛcch. 138, 25; 139, 1) etc. The rule attests *vaññadi* = **vrajñāti* (§ 448), which the copyists did not change, as they did not identify it. — In P. too *jña* becomes *ñña* (Hc. 4, 303; Namisādhu on Rudraṭa, Kāvyālaṁkāra 2, 12): *paññā* = *prajñā*; *saññā* = *saṁjñā*; *savvañña* = *sarvajña*; *ñāna* = *jñāna*; *viññāna* = *vijñāna*; *yañña* = *yajña*; *raññā*, *rañño* = *rājñā*, *rājñaḥ* (Hc. 4, 304) beside *rāciñā*, *rāciño* (§237. 399). In Vr. 10, 9. 12 the MSS give *ñja*, *jja*, which will simply be an error for *ñña*.

§ 277. If the nasal standing behind a stop is *ma*, the sound-groups are differently treated. As a rule *gma* becomes *gga* : M. AMg. *jugga* = *yugma* (Bh. 3, 2; Hc. 2, 62; Kī. 2, 51; Mk. fol. 19; Vivāhap. 275, 362); *tigga* = *tigma* (Hc. 2, 62); *vaggi-* = *vāgmin* (Bh. 3, 2); probably also *dŏgga* = *yugma* (§ 215). Dialectically, however, it becomes *mma* as well : AMg. *jumma* = *yugma* (Hc. 6, 62; Vivāhap. 1391 ff.; 1666 ff.; Ṭhāṇ. 275; Samav. 138); *timma* = *tigma* (Hc. 2, 62). — *kma* becomes *ppa* Vr. 3, 49; Hc. 2, 52; Kī. 2, 63; Mk. fol. 26); *ruppa* = *rukma* (Bh. 3, 49; Kī. 2, 63); AMg. *ruppi-* = *rukmin*, by Hc. 2, 52 equated as = *rukmiṇ* (Samav. 114. 117. 139. 144. 157. 160; Ṭhāṇ. 75; Nāẏādh. 781 ff.; Rāẏap. 177); AMg. JM. Ś. *ruppiṇī* = *rukmiṇī* (Antag. 3, 43; Nāẏādh. 529; Niraẏāv. 79; Paṇhāv. 292; Dvār. 497, 31 ff.; 502, 34; 505, 34; Pracaṇḍap. 18, 15; Mālatīm. 266, 4 [so to be read]; Nāgān. 51, 8 [v.l. = ed. Jibananda Vidyasagara 49, 7, where, however, *rukkiṇī*]. — According to Hc. 2, 52 *kuṭmala* forms in Pkt. *kumpala*, as also Pāiẏal. 54 has. Since beside it is found also *kuñcala* (Deśīn. 2, 36; Pāiẏal. 54), that cannot go back to *kuṭmala* or *kuḍmala*; *kumpala* also is comes a dialectical form, may be added beside *kuṭmala*. At Mk. fol. 26 the manuscript has *kuppala*. — *ātman* becomes almost always in M., and always in A. *appa-* (Vr. 3, 48; Kī. 2, 63; G.H.R.)[1], very rarely M. *atta-* in *attaṇo* (G. 63. 96; Karp. 82, 2). The other dialects are divergent differ (Hc. 2, 51; Mk. fol. 26). AMg. JM. have *appa-* and *atta-* beside one another even in compounds, as AMg. *ajjhappa-* = *adhyātman* (Āẏār. 1, 5, 4, 5; Paṇhāv. 437); AMg. JM. *attaẏa* = *ātmaja* (Vivāhap. 795; Erz.), AMg. *attaẏā* = *ātmajā* (Nāẏādh. 727. 1228. 1232); AMg. has also *āẏa-* for **āta-*, corresponding to JŚ. *āda-* (§ 88); by the side of it JŚ. has *appa-*; in Ś. Mg. only in the nomin. sing. *appa-* is frequent; in other cases almost only *atta-*, accus.

attāṇaaṁ; Ḍh. has *appa-* (§ 401). The prevalent form occurring in the Girnâr inscriptions, *āpta-*, which is not to be read[2] *ātpa-* with ASCOLI[3] and SENART[4], shows that *appa-*, by the route *ātma-*, **ātva-* (§ 251. 312), * *ātpa*, *āpta*, has sprung up by transposition of the stops, whilst *atta* is the regular continuation of *ātman*[5]. In *kma = ppa* we have to assume *tma*— as a transition step : *rukma*, **rutma = ruppa*. — *dma* becomes *mma* : *chamma = chadma* (Hc. 2, 112), beside the usual form *chaüma* (§ 139); *pŏmma = padma* (§ 166. 195) beside *paüma* (§ 139).

1. In H. 201 in place of *attaṇo*, as also the Bombay edition has, should be read *appaṇo* with S., likewise in G. 90 with the best manuscript J. In M. probably *appaṇo* should be read *attaṇo* everywhere. — for BHAGVANLĀL INDRAJI, IA. 10, 105; PISCHEL, GGA. 1881, p. 1317 f.; BÜHLER, ZDMG. 37, 89. — 3. Kritische Studien p. 197, note 10,—4. Piyadasi, 1, 26 ff. — 5. PISCHEL, GGA. 1881, p. 1318.

§ 278. If nasals of different classes meet together, then *ṅma*, *ṇma* become *ṁma* (§ 269), *nma* becomes *mma* (Vr. 3, 43; Hc. 2, 61; Kī. 2, 98; Mk. fol. 25), *mna* becomes *ṇṇa*, AMg. JM. JŚ. also *nna* (Vr. 3, 44; Hc. 2, 42; Mk. fol. 25) : M. *ummuha = unmukha* (G.R.), *ummūla = unmūla* (H.) *ummūlaṇa = unmūlana* (R.), *jamma- = janman* (H.R.); *mammaṇa = manmana* (Hc. 2, 42); M. JM. A. *vammaha = manmatha* (§ 251); M. *ṇiṇṇa = nimna* (Hc. 2, 42; G.), *ṇiṇṇaā = nimnagā* (G.), AMg. *niṇṇa* (Vivāhap. 1244), *isiṁṇiṇṇaẏara = iṣannimnatara* (Vivāhap. 239), *ninnagā* (Paṇhāv. 440); M.Ś. *pajjuṇṇa = pradyumna* (Bh. 3, 44; Hc. 2, 42; Ratn. 295, 26; 296, 5. 17). In *dhṛṣṭadyumna*, according to Hc. 2, 94 *mna* becomes *ṇa* : *dhaṭṭhajjuṇa*. Ś. has *dhaṭṭhajjuṇṇa* (Pracaṇḍap. 8, 19), Mg. *dhiṭṭhajjuṇṇa* (Veṇīs. 35, 19), for which should be read *dhiṭṭhayyuṇṇa*. If *dhaṭṭhjjuṇa* is not purely metri causa, it is perhaps to be equated to **dhṛṣṭārjuna*, as there occurs the synonym *arjuna* for *dyumna*.

§ 279. When a stop or nasal collides with a semi-vowel, as a rule the semi-vowel is assimilated, provided a separation-vowel is not inserted (§131-140). If the two semi-vowels collide together, usually the second is assimilated to the first. 1). One of the sounds is *ya* (Vr. 3, 2; C. 3, 2; Hc. 2, 78; Kī. 2, 51; Mk. fol. 19): *kya = kka*: Ś. *cāṇakka = cāṇakya* (Mudrār. 53, 8 ff.); *pārakka = pārakya* (Hc. 1, 44; 2, 148); AMg. *vakka = vākya* (Hc. 2, 174; Sūẏag. 838. 841. 842. 844; Uttar. 674.752; Dasav. 636, 10.16; Dasav. N. 644, 21; 649, 26. 658; 29. 31; 659, 22. 33); Ś. *sakka = śakya* (Śk. 73, 11; 155, 8; Vikr. 10,13; 12,20; 18,16; 22,14; 40,7).— *khya = kkha*: M. *akkhāṇaa = ākhyānaka* (H.); AMg. *akkhāi = ākhyāti* (§ 491); Ś. *vakkhāṇaïssaṁ = *vyākhyānayiṣyāmi = vyākhyāsye* (Viddhaś. 63, 3, Rukmiṇīp. 19, 3); M. AMg. JM. JŚ. Ś. A. *sŏkkha = saukhya* (§61). On AMg. *āghāvei* see §88. 551. — *gya = gga*; M. *jŏgga = yogya* (G.H.R.), AMg. JM. *veragga = vairāgya* (Ovav.; Erz.); M. *sohagga = saubhāgya* (G.H.R.). — *cya = cca*; AMg. *cuẏa = cyuta* (Āẏār. 1, 1, 1, 3; Kappas.); M. *muccaï = mucyate* (G.); AMg. *vuccaï*, Ś. Mg. *vuccadi = ucyate* (§ 544). — *jya = jja*; M. *jujjaï = yujyate* (H.), *bhujjanta- = bhujyamāna* (G.); *rajja = rājya* (H.R.). — *ṭya = ṭṭ* : *naṭṭaa = nāṭyaka* (Mṛcch. 70, 3); M. *tuṭṭaï* (Hc. 4. 116), M.A. *ṭuṭṭaï* (§292) = *truṭyati*; M. *lŏṭṭaï = luṭyati* (Hc. 4, 146; Karp. 39, 3). — *ḍya = ḍḍa* : *kuḍḍa = kuḍya* (Hc. 2, 78; H.); AMg. *piḍḍaï = piḍyate* (Āẏār. 1. 2, 5, 4). — *ḍhya*

= *ḍḍha* = *āḍhya* (G.; Sūẏag. 957; Uvās.; Ovav.; Niraẏāv.); AMg. JM. *veẏaḍḍha* = *vaitāḍhya* (§ 60). — *pya* = *ppa*: AMg. *appege* **apyeke*, *appegaīẏā* = **apyekatyāḥ* = Pāli *appekacce* (§174); M. *kuppaī* = *kupyati* (H. G.), *suppaü* = *supyatām* (H.). — *bhya* = *bbha*; M. *abbhantara* = *abhyantara* (G.H.R.); Ś. Mg. *abbhuvavaṇṇa* = *abhyupapanna* (§ 163); AMg. JM. *ibbha* = *ibhya* (Ṭhāṇ. 414. 526; Paṇhāv. 319; Nāẏādh. 547. 1231; Vivāgas. 82; Ovav.; Erz.). On *d* for *jy* see § 215.

§ 280. In conjunction with dentals *y* is assimilated only after it has palatalized the preceding dental. Thus *tya* becomes = *cca* (Vr. 3, 27; Hc. 2, 13; Kī. 2, 32; Mk. fol. 23), *thya* = *ccha* (Vr. 3, 27; Hc. 2, 21; Kī. 2, 92; Mk. fol. 23), *dya* = *jja* (Vr. 3. 27; Hc. 2, 24; Kī. 2, 22; Mk. fol. 23), *dhya* = *jjha* (Vr. 3, 28; Hc. 2, 26; Kī. 2, 87; Mk. fol. 23). — *tya* = *cca*: M. AMg. JM. JŚ. Ś. *accanta* = *atyanta* (§163); M. *ṇaccaī* = *nṛtyati* (Vr. 8, 47; Hc. 4, 225; H.); M. *dŏcca* = *dautya* (H.); AMg. *veẏāvacca* = *vaiyāpṛtya* (Ovav.); M. *sacca* = *satya* (G.H.). — *thya* = *ccha*: M.Ś. *ṇevaccha*, AMg. JM. *nevaccha* = *nepathya*[1] (G.R.; Vikr. 75, 14; Ratn. 309, 16 [°*ttha*]; Mālatīm. 206, 7; 234, 3 [both the times °*ttha*]; Pras. 41, 7; Mālav. 33. 18; 36, 3; 38, 3; 73, 17; 74, 17 [throughout °*ttha*]; Priyad. 27, 18; 28, 1. 4; Viddhaś. 30, 8; 120, 11 [both the times °*ttha*]; Rukmiṇīp. 37, 15; 41, 11 [°*cca*]; 42, 5; 43, 5. 9; Āẏār. 2, 15. 18 [°*ttha*]; Vivāgas. 234; Paṇhāv. 240. 459 [both the times °*ttha*]; Ṭhāṇ. 238 [°*ttha*]; Nāẏādh. § 117 [°*ttha*]; Ovav.; Āv. 27, 17; Erz.), AMg. JM. also *nevacchiẏa* (Vivāgas. 111; Paṇhāv. 196 [both the texts °*tthiẏa*]; Āv. 28. 5) = **nepathyita*; JM. *nevacchĕttā* (absol.; Āv. 26. 27); AMg. *paccha* = *pathya* (Grr.; Kappas.); M. Ś. *racchā* = *rathyā* (G. H.; Mṛcch. 2, 20; Karp. 20, 4; 30, 7). — *dya* = *jja* : PG. *ajātāye* = *adyatvāya* (§ 253); M. *ajja* = *adya* (G.H.R.); M. *ujjāṇa* = *udyāna* (G.R.), *chijjaī* = *chidyate* (R.), *vijjujjoa* = *vidyuddyota* (G. 907); M. JM. Ś. *vĕjja* = *vaidya* (§60).—*dhya* = *jjha* : M. Ś. *uvajjhāa*, AMg. JM. *uvajjhāẏa* = *upādhyāya* (§ 155) ; M. *majjha* = *madhya* (G.H.R.); M. AMg. JM. Ś. *viṁjha* = *vindhya* (§269); M. JM. Ś. *saṁjhā* = *sandhyā* (§ 269). In Mg. *dya* becomes *yya* corresponding to § 236 (Hc. 4, 292; Kī. 5, 90; Namisādhu on Rudraṭa, Kāvyālaṁkāra 2, 12) : *ayya* = *adya*; *avayya* = *avadya*; *mayya* = *madya*; *viyyāhala* = *vidyādhara*. Corresponding to this *dhya* must become *yyha*, therefore, e.g. *madhyaṁdina* becomes *mayyhaṇṇa* (§ 148. 214. 236). The MSS write throughout *jja*, *jjha*, as in the rest of the dialects; so also Lalitav. 566, 11 *yujjha* = **yudhya* = *yuddha* = M. AMg. JM. Ś. A. *jujjha* (G.H.; Bālar. 180, 5; Nāẏādh. 1311. 1313; Erz.; Lalitav. 568, 4; Bālar. 246, 5; Jīvān. 86, 10; Hc. 4, 386). The separation-vowel *i* does not hinder palatalization : AMg. *ciẏatta* from **tiẏakta* = *tyakta* (Ṭhāṇ. 528 [text *bi*°]; Kappas. § 117; cf. § 134), absol. *ciccā*, *cĕccā*, *ciccāṇa*, *cĕccāṇa* = **tiyaktvā*, **tiiktvā*, **tīktvā* = *tyaktvā* (§587), quite like *caẏaī* = *tyajati* (Hc. 4, 86; Uttar. 902; Dasav. 638, 18), *caẏanti* = *tyajanti* (Āẏār. 1, 4, 3, 1; 1, 6, 1, 2; Sūẏag. 100 [*ci*°]. 174), *cae* = *tyajet* (Āẏār. 1, 5, 4, 5), *caẏāhi* = *tyaja* (Āẏār. 1, 6, 1. 5), *caïssanti* = *tyakṣyanti* (Sūẏag. 361), *catta* = *tyakta* (Āẏār. 2, 15, 23. 24), JM. *cāī* = *tyāgī* (KJ. 5). AMg. *jhiẏāi* = *dhyāti*, as M. *jhāi* (§479).

1. As the text shows, not only the Jaina-MSS, which regularly interchange *ccha* and *ttha*, but also the MSS of the dramas particularly very often write *ttha* in this word. The v. l. has throughout the only correct form *ṇevaccha*.

§ 281. D. *dakkhiṇattā* = *dākṣiṇātyāh* (Mṛcch. 103, 5) forms an exception to § 280. See § 26. Further AMg. *ghatta* (Sūyag. 964), *aghatta* (Sūyag. 969. 983), provided these cases, with the scholiasts, are to be equated as = *ghātya, aghātya.* However, *ghatta* may also be equated as = *ghātá* according to § 90, with a change of gender according to § 357, which is more probable. Other cases too are simply apparent exceptions. *caïtta* (Hc. 1, 151; 2, 13; Mk. fol. 23) is not = *caitya*[1], but = *caitra*, in the sense of *caitya* (B. R. s.v. *caitra*). — In M. *pattiaï*, AMg. JM. *pattiyaï*, Ś. Mg. *pattiāadi* (§487) = *pratiyāti* and AMg. *patteya* = *pratyeka* (Hc. 2, 210; Āyār. 1,1, 6, 2; 1, 2 1, 5; Sūyag. 28. 783; Jīv. 44. 47. 436. 478 ff.; Paṇṇav. 30. 32. 35. 40; Rāyap. 68. 124. 126. 134. 139. 152 ff.; Nāyādh. § 42; p. 1268; Ovav.; Kappas.), *patteyabuddha* = *pratyekabuddha* (Nandīs. 245; Paṇṇav. 19) *patti* = **parati*, **parti* with separation-vowel is from *prati* (§ 132). *prati* and **parti* may, therefore, be compared with προτι' and πορτι'[2]. AMg. °*vattiyaṁ* (Ovav.) is not, with LEUMANN[3], to be equated as = *pratyayam*, but as = *vṛttikam.* On AMg. *paḍucca, paḍuppanna* etc. see § 163. — AMg. JŚ. *tacca* (Hc. 2, 21; Uvās.; Kappas.; Kattig. 400, 324) is not with Hc. and the commentary to be equated as = *tathya*, but with WEBER[4] and HOERNLE[5] as = *tattva*, more correctly through the intermediate step **tāttya* (§299). *tathya* with the separation-vowel becomes in AMg. *tahiya* = **tathiya*; it sometimes stands beside *tacca*, as *taccāṇaṁ tahiyāṇaṁ* (Nāyādh. 1006; Uvās. §85), *taccehiṁ tahiehiṁ* (Uvās. §220. 259). — *sāmattha* beside *sāmaccha* (Hc. 2, 22) is not = *sāmarthya*, but presupposes a **sāmartha.* — M. *kutthasi, kutthasu* = *kvathyase, kvathyasva* (H. 401) is a false reading (cf. the v.l.) for *kaḍḍhasi, kaḍḍhasu* passive of *kaḍhaï* = *kvathati* (§221).

1. With Hc., WEBER, ZDMG. 28, 403; on Hāla² 216. — 2. PISCHEL on Hc. 2, 210. Cf. HOERNLE, Uvās. s.v. *pattiya.* Deviating BOLLENSEN on Vikr. p. 331 f.; WEBER on Hāla² 216; E. MÜLLER, Beiträge p. 64. — 3. Aup. S. s. v. — 4. Bhag. 1,398, note 2.—5. Uvās. Translation p. 127, note 281.

§ 282. *y* is assimilated to a nasal : *ṇya, nya* become *ṇṇa*; in AMg. JM. JŚ. it is written also *nna*; in Mg. (Hc. 4, 293; Namisādhu on Rudraṭa, Kāvyālaṁkāra 2, 12), P. CP. (Hc. 4, 305) they become *ñña.* So M. *dakkhiṇṇa* = *dākṣiṇya* (G.H.R.), *puṇṇa* = *puṇya* (H.R.); AMg. *hiraṇṇa* = *hiraṇya* (Āyār. 1, 2, 3, 3; 2, 15, 10. 12. 17. 18; Uvās.; Kappas.; Nāyādh.; Erz.), Mg. *śahilaṇṇa* = *sahiraṇya* (Mṛcch. 21, 9); AMg. *pinnāga* = *piṇyāka* (Āyār. 2, 1, 8, 8; Sūyag. 926. 928. 931; Dasav. 623, 7), *panna* = *paṇya* (Sūyag. 921); M.Ś. Mg. *aṇṇa*, AMg. JM. *anna* = *anya*; M. *ṇāsa* = *nyāsa* (H.), *viṇṇāsa* = *vinyāsa* (G.); M.Ś. *maṇṇe* = *manye* (§457); M.Ś. *sĕṇṇa* = *sainya* (G.R.; Adbhutad. 56, 6. 19). — Mg. *abamhañña* = *abrahmaṇya*; *puñña* = *puṇya*; *ahimaññu* = *abhimanyu* (cf. § 283); *aññadiśaṁ* = *anyadiśaṁ*; *kaññakā* = *kanyakā*; *śāmañña* = *sāmānya*; (Hc.; Namisādhu). The MSS of the dramas have only *ṇṇa*. — P. *puñña* = *puṇya*; *abhimaññu* = *abhimanyu*; *kaññakā* = *kanyakā* (Hc.). According to Vr. 10, 10 in P. *kanyā* becomes *kañjā*, according to 12, 7 in Ś. *bhāhmaṇya* becomes *bamhañja* or *bamhaṇṇa* or *bamhañca*, *kanyā* becomes *kaṇṇā* or *kañcā.* The reading in Vr. and Kī. is very doubtful. In Ś. we find in the texts *bamhaṇṇa* (Mṛcch. 89, 12), *abbamhaṇṇa* = *abrāhmaṇya* (Śak. 142, 8. 14; Vikr. 84, 13; Karṇas. 10, 3; 33, 10); *kaṇṇaā* (Śak. 30, 3; 71, 3 [so to be read]; 134, 8; Mālatīm. 73, 8; 80, 1 [so to be read]; 223, 1, 243. 1 [so to be read [Mudrār. 40, 6 [so to be read]; Ratn. 299, 6; Nāgān. 10, 14 [°*kā*]; 11, 1. 10 etc.); in Mg. Mudrār. 193, 3; 194, 6 [so to be read]. *-mya* becomes *mma*, after a long vowel *ma*: M. *kilammaï*, Ś. *kilammadi* = *klāmyati* (§ 136); M. *tāmaï* = *tāmyati* (H.), Ś. *uttamma* = *uttāmya* (Śak. 19, 8). *uttammia* = *uttamya* (Śak. 56, 9); M.Ś. *sŏmma*, AMg. JM. *soma* = *saumya* (61a); Ś. *kāmāe* = *kāmyayā* (Mṛcch. 49, 14).

§ 283. *abhimanyu* becomes, according to Vr. 3, 17; Kī. 2, 70; Mk. fol. 21, *ahimajju*, according to Hc. 2, 25 *ahimajju*, *ahimañju*, *ahimaṇṇu*. Ś. has *ahimaṇṇu* (Mk. fol. 68; Veṇīs. 64,16, likewise Mg. Veṇīs. 34,12), for which *ahimaññu* should stand according to § 282. Beside M.Ś. *maṇṇu* (H.R.; Veṇīs. 9, 19; 11, 15; 12, 1; 61, 22) according to Hc. 2, 44 for *manyu* is used also *mantu*. This appears several times in the Telugu recension of Hāla as a v.l. for *maṇṇu*[1]. According to Pāiyāl. 165 *mantu* means "bashfulness", "unpleasantness", the meanings that in Deśīn. 6, 141 are evidently given to the connected word *mantakkha*. Skt. too has *mantu*[2], which according to the form compares with *kantu* (love; Deśīn. 2, 1).

1. Weber on Hāla 683. — 2. Bühler, Pāiyal. s.v.

§ 284. *yya* becomes *jja* (Vr. 3, 17; Hc. 2, 24; Kī. 2, 70; Mk. fol. 21): M. AMg. JM. *sĕjjā* = *śayyā* (§101, in Mg. P. CP. *yya* (§252). — *rya* becomes in all the dialects, other than Mg., *jja* (Vr. 3, 17; C. 3, 15; Hc. 2, 24; Kī. 2, 89; Mk. fol. 21): M. *ajja* = *ārya* (G.) *ajjā* = *āryā* (H.), *kajja* = *kārya* (G.H.) *majjāā* = *maryādā* (H.R.). In Ś. Mg. according to Hc. 4, 266. 302 *rya* can become *jja* or *yya*: Ś. *ayyaütta payyākulikada mhi* = *āryaputra paryākulikṛtāsmi*; *suyya* = *sūrya*; beside *ajja* = *ārya*; *pajjāula* = *paryākula*; *kajjaparavasa* = *kārya-paravaśa*; Mg. *ayya* = *ārya*. The spelling *yya* is found only sometimes in South Indian MSS. Mostly they write, however, in place of the ligature a small circle: *a*○*a* = *ārya*; *pa*○*avaṭhṭhāvehi* = *paryavasthāpaya*; *su*○*ya* = *sūrya*, an orthographic device which may either permit of a choice between the pronunciations *jja* and *yya*[1] or express an intermediate sound between the two sound-groups. The circle, as rightly remarked by Müller[2], has the same value as the real ligature of the Jaina MSS which Weber[3] wished to read as *yya*, which, however, with Jacobi[4], and E. Müller[5], is now read as *jja*. Probably it indicates a sound intermediate between both. Hc.'s rule will, therefore, be explained by the pronunciation of the Jainas. The MSS of the dramas write in both the dialects *jja*. Right is *jja* for Ś., *yya* for Mg. that are prescribed by Vr. 11, 7 : *kayya* = *kārya*, and is offered by Lalitav.; *payyaṁde* = *paryante* (565, 7), *avayyaṁdadā* = *aparyantatā* (565, 12). Instead of *jja* there occurs after *i*, *ū*, except the sound-group, which arise through the separation-vowel, *ria*, *riya* (§134), also *ra*, therefore, elision of *y* according to §87 (Vr. 3, 18. 19; Hc. 2, 63; Kī. 2, 79; Mk. fol. 22) : M. *gambhira* = *gāmbhirya* (R.); M. AMg. JM. Ś.A. *tūra* = *tūrya* (Grr.; G.H.R.; Āyār. p. 128, 32; Erz.; Vikr. 56, 5; Mahāv. 121, 7; Veṇīs. 23, 11; 64; 2; 73, 16; Bālar. 147, 18; 200, 10; Piṅgala 1,15); M. *soḍira* = *śaṇṭirya* (Mk. R.), Ś. *soḍirattaṇa* (Karp. 30,7), *sŏṇḍira* = *śauṇḍirya* (Hc.; Mallikām. 146, 6), *sŏṇḍiradā* (Mṛcch. 54, 4; 74, 12). So especially in the passive, as *jiraï* = *jiryate*, M. JM. *tiraï*, *tirae* = *tiryate*, M. JM. *hiraï* = *hriyate* (§537), M. AMg. JM. *kiraï* = *kriyate* (§547)[6]. The word *sūra*, frequent in all the dialects, Mg. *śūla*, is to be derived with Hc. 2,64 from *sūra*. In P., necessarily according to Vr. 10, 8, sometimes according to Hc. 4, 314, the separation-vowel comes in *bhāriā* = *bhāryā*. Hc. has also *sujja* = *sūrya*, for which **suyya* was expected, and *kirate* for **kiryate* = *kriyate* (4, 316). — *kacca* (business; Deśīn. 2, 2) is not = *kārya*, but = *kṛtya*.

1. Pischel, GN. 1873, p. 208; Monatsberichte der Kgl. Akademie der Wissenschaften zu Berlin 1875, p. 615 f. — 2. Beiträge p. 12. — 3. Bhag. 1,388 f. — 4. Kalpasūtra p. 18 note 1. — 5. Beiträge p. 12 f. — 6. Falsely Jacobi, KZ. 28, 250.

§ 285. Like simple *ra* (§256. 257), sometimes even *r*, that is in conjunction with *y*, is changed into *l*, to which *y* is assimilated: JM. *pallāṇa paryāṇa* (Hc. 2, 68; Kī. 2, 80; Mk. fol. 20; Erz.), whilst AMg. *paḍāẏāṇa* is = *pratyādāna* (§ 258); *soamalla* = *saukumārya* (Vr. 3, 21; Hc. 2, 68; Kī. 2, 80; Mk. fol. 22; cf. §123). M. *pallaṅka* (Vr. 3, 21; C. 3, 22; Kī. 2, 80; Mk. fol. 22; G.; Karp. 36, 3) can, like AMg. *paliẏaṅka* (§257) with Hc. 2, 68, be derived from Skt. *palyaṅka*, if it itself is not a Prākritic bye-form of *paryaṅka*. In *pallaṭṭa* (Hc. 2, 68), Ś. *pallattha* (Vr. 3, 21; Hc. 2, 68; Kī. 2, 80; Mk. fol. 22; Bālar. 243, 11; Veṇīs. 60, 10; 65, 13; Mallikām. 26, 18; 57, 9; 125, 6; 135, 16; 195, 3; Rukmiṇīp. 29, 8), M. AMg. Ś. *palhattha* (Hc. 4, 258; Triv. 3, 1, 132; G.R. s.v. *as*; Kappas.; Mṛcch. 41, 20; Mālatīm. 118, 3; 260, 5), M. *vivalhattha*, Ś. *vipalhattha* (Uttarar. 63, 13 [text °*nha*°]; 92, 10 [text °*ṇha*°]) and their denominatives *pallaṭṭaï*, *palhatthaï* (Hc. 4, 26, 200; G.R. s.v. *as*), AMg. *palhatthiẏa* (Pāiẏal. 201; Vivāhap. 282. 284; Nāẏādh. 1326; Uttar. 29), that are derived by grammarians, scholiasts and all moderners[1] from *as* (to throw) with *pari*, two roots are to be assumed. *pallaṭṭa* and *pallattha* are = *paryasta* (§308), *palhattha*, on the contrary = **prahlasta* is from *hlas* = *hras* with *pra*; cf. *nirhrasta*, *nirhrasita*. M. *palhattharaṇa* (R. 11, 108) is a false reading for *paccattharaṇa*, as CK have = **pratyāstaraṇa*; cf. *pratyāstāra* (carpet).

1. Weber Bhag. 1,409 note 2; P. Goldschmidt, GN. 1874, p. 1521; E. Müller, Beiträge p. 45.64: S. Goldschmidt, Rāvaṇavaho s.v. 2 *as*; Sh. P. Paṇḍit, Gaüḍavaho s.v. *as*; Jacobi, Kalpasūtra s.v. *palhattha*; Johansson, KZ. 32,454 f.; Hoernle, Comp. Gr. §137.143.

§ 286. *lya* becomes *lla* : M. *kalla* = *kalya* (G.H.); M. *kullāhi tullā* = *kulyābhis tulyāḥ* (Karp. 44, 6); M. AMg. JŚ. Ś. *mulla*, AMg. JM. *mŏlla* = *mūlya* (§ 83. 127). — *vya* becomes *vva* : M. *vavasāa* = *vyāvasāya* (G.R.), *vāha* = *vyādha* (G.H.), *kavva* = *kāvya* (G.H.R.); the participia necess. in -*tavya*, as AMg. JM. *hoẏavva*, Ś. Mg. *hodavva*. JŚ. Ś. *bhavidavva*, Mg. *huvidavva* = *bhavitavya* (§ 570). AMg. *pittijja* (Kappas.) is not = *pitṛvya*[1], but = **pitriya*. AMg. *pūha* (Nāẏādh. § 18; p. 331. 353. 845; Ovav.) is not = *vyūha*[2], but = **pyūha* for **apyūha* from *ūh* with *api* (§ 142). *pp* in some passive, which P. Goldschmidt[3] and S. Goldschmidt[4] try to explain from *vy*, that Weber[5] earlier regarded as erroneously written *yy*, Jacobi[6] and according to him Johansson[7] wished to derive from false analogy, has regularly arisen from *py*. M. JM. AMg. A. *ghĕppaï* is = **ghṛpyate* for **gṛbhyate* = *gṛhyate* (§ 212. 548). JM. *āḍhappaï* (Hc. 4, 254; Āv. 12, 21) beside *āḍhaviaï* (Hc. 4, 254) and M. *viḍhappaï* (Hc. 4, 251; R.) beside *viḍhavijjaï*

(Hc. 4, 251) are regular passive of *āḍhavaï* (Hc. 4, 155; Kī. 4, 46) and *viḍhavaï* (Hc. 4, 108), the causatives from *dhā* (§ 553) with cerebralization according to § 223. The past passive participle M. AMg. JM. *āḍhatta*, M. *samāḍhatta* M. JM. Ś. *viḍhatta*, A. *viḍhattaũ* (§565) may be derived from the causative, so that *āḍhatta* would be = **ādhapta*, like *āṇatta* = *ājñapta*; they are probably better derived from the present stem (§565)[8]. — *sippaï* = *snihyate* and *sicyate* (Hc. 4, 255), M. *sippanta-* (v.l. to H. 185) belongs to *simpaï* (Hc. 4, 96), which are related to Marāṭhī *śiṁpṇeṁ*, Gujarātī *śiṁpvuṁ*[9] and presuppose a root **sip*, which was parallel to *sic* from **sik*. This is, therefore, a case of interchange of gutturals and labials (§215). To **sip* belongs M. AMg. Ś. *sippī* (conch; Hc. 2, 138; Mk. fol. 40; H.R.; Karp. 2, 4; Viddhaś. 63, 8; Uvās.; Bālar. 195, 9; 264, 3; Viddhaś. 108, 2) = Pāli *sippi*, Marāṭhī *śipa*, *śiṁpa*, Gujarātī *śipa*, Hindī *sīpi*, *sipa*, Sindhī *sipa*[10]. — *vāhippaï* (Hc. 4, 253), JM. *vāhippantu* (Āv. 38, 6), which is derived, with Hc. 4, 253 from √*hṛ*, is = *vyāhriyate*, is rather = *vyākṣipyate* with a somewhat more special meaning than in Skt., as *samākṣip* occasionally has in Skt. As a proof we have M. *ṇihippanta-* (R. 8, 97) = *nikṣipyamāṇa*, which is wrongly derived from √*dhā* by S. GOLDSCHMIDT. From this may be derived M. *ṇihitta*, AMg. JM. *nihitta* (Bh. 3, 58; Hc. 2, 99; Kī. 2, 112; Mk. fol. 27; G.R.; Karp. 2, 5; Vivāhap. 116; Erz.), A. *ṇihittaü* (Hc. 4, 395, 2) and M. AMg. JM. *vāhitta* (Hc. 1, 128; 2, 99; Pāiyal. 247; H.; Uttar. 29; Āv. 38, 6)[11] = *nikṣipta*, *vyākṣipta*. Possible is also, however, the explanation from *nihita*, *vyāhṛta* according to § 194. — Hitherto several forms with *pp* have been falsely regarded as passive, which are so according to neither their form nor their meaning. *khuppaï* (sinks; immerses; Vr. 8, 68; Hc. 4, 101; Kī. 4, 51), M. *khuppanta-* (R.), past passive participle M. AMg. *khutta* (R.; Paṇhāv. 201), explained by S. GOLDSCHMIDT[12] from **khuvyaï* and derived from *khu* = *khan*, is = **kṣupyati* from √*kṣupa avasādane, sāde* (WESTERGAARD, Radices p. 333). — *juppaï* (yokes; Hc. 4, 109) is = *yupyati* from *yupa ekīkaraṇe, samīkaraṇe* (B.-R. s.v.), with which may be compared AMg. *juvala*, *juvalaya*, *juvaliya* (§231). — M. *pahuppaï* (Hc. 3, 142; 4, 63; Mk. fol. 53; G.H.R.), which has been explained by WEBER[1] as a deponentially used passive of *bhū* with *pra*, is a denominative from *prabhutva* = **prabhutvati* "exercises authority"; "is able to"; "is in a position to". This is borne out by A. *pahuccaï* (Hc. 4, 390. 491), that presupposes one **prabhutyati* with the phonetic change discussed in § 299. So too M. *ohuppanta-* (R. 3, 18) = **apabhutvant-*. The scholiasts explain it as *ākramyamāṇa* and *abhibhūyamāna*. It belongs to *ohāvaï* = **apabhāvati* = **apabhāvayati* in the sense of *ākrāmati* (Hc. 4, 160), from which spring also *ohāia*, *ohāmaï*, *ohāmiya* (§261) and *ohua* (overcome; Deśīn. 1, 158) = **apabhūta*. — M. *appāhaï* (entrusts; Hc. 4, 180), *appāhei*, *appāhĕnta-*, *appāheuṁ*, *appāhijjaï*, *appāhia* (H.R.), which S. GOLDSCHMIDT[14] artificially derives from an impossible **āvyāhṛta*, and WEBER[15] doubtfully equates as = *har* + *abhyā*, is regularly = **āprārthayati* from *pratha prakhyāne* (Dhātupāṭha 32, 19); cf. *viprathayati*, *saṁprathita*.

1. JACOBI, Kalpasūtra s. v.; E. MÜLLER, Beiträge p. 17. 35. —2. LEUMANN Aup.

S. s. v. with the scholiasts. — 3. GN. 1874, p. 512 f. — 4. ZDMG. 29, 491 ff.; Prākṛtica p. 3, 13 note 1, 17 f. — 5. ZDMG. 28, 350; Hāla[1] p. 64; cf. IS. 14, 92 f. — 6. KZ. 28, 249 ff. — 7. KZ. 32, 446 ff.; where occur further literary details. — 8. The derivation from *rabh* is linguistically impossible. — 9. PISCHEL, on Hc. 4, 96 — 10. PISCHEL on Hc. 2, 138. — 11. Cf. P. GOLDSCHMIDT, GN. 1874, p. 513 note.; JACOBI, Erz. s. v. *nihitta*. — 12. Prākṛtica p. 17 f.; against it JOHANSSON, KZ. 32, 448, note 1. — 13. On Hāla 7. — 14. Rāvaṇavaho s. v. — 15. Hāla s. v.

§ 287. II) One of the sounds is *r* (Vr. 3, 3; C. 3, 9; Hc. 2, 79; Kī. 2, 50; Mk. fol. 19); *rka* = *kka*: M. *akka* = *arka* (G.); AMg. *kakkeyaṇa* = *karketana* (Ovav.; Kappas.); Ś. *takkemi* = *tarkayāmi* (§490). On M. *kaṁkoḍa*, *kaṁkoḷa* beside M. AMg. *kakkoḷa* = *karkoṭa* see §74. — *kra* = *kka*: A. *kijjaī* = *kryaite* (§547); M. *cakka* = *cakra* (G.), *vikkama* = *vikrama* (G.). On M. AMg. JM. A. *vaṁka* = *vakra* see § 74. — *rkha* = *kkha*; Ś. Mg. *mukkha* = = *mūrkha* (§ 139). — *rga* = *gga*; Ś. *ṇiggamamagga* = *nirgamamārga* (Lalitav. 567, 24); M. *duggama durgama* (G.R.), *vagga* = *varga* (G.H.R.). — *gra* = *gga*; PG. *gāmāgāmabhojake* = *grāmagrāmabhojakān* (5, 4), *gāme* = *grāme* (6, 28), *gahaṇaṁ* = *grahaṇam* (6, 31. 33. 34), *nigaha* = *nigraha* (7, 41); M. *gaha* = *graha* (G.H.R.); AMg. JM. *naggoha*, *ṇaggoha* = *nyagrodha* (C. 3, 9; Āyār. 2, 1, 8, 5. 7; Jīv. 46; Paṇṇav. 31; Vivāhap. 41 [*ṇi*°]. 1530; Kappas. §212 [text *ṇi*°; see also the v.l.]; Āv. 48, 25; Erz.); AMg. JŚ. *niggantha* = *nirgrantha* (e.g. Āyār. 2, 15, 29; p. 132, 4. 6. 15 ff.; Uvās.; Ovav.; Kappas.; Kattig. 404, 386). — *rgh* = *ggha* : M. *ṇigghiṇa* = *nirghṛṇa* (H.), *ṇigghosa* = *nirghoṣa* (R.), Ś. Mg. *digghiā* = *dīrghikā* (§ 87). — *ghra* = *ggha*; *āigghaī* = *ājighrati*, *jigghia* = **jighrita*, M.AMg. *agghāi* = *āghrāti*, *agghāia* = **āghrāyita* (§ 408). — *rca* = *cca* : M. *accā* = *arcā* (G.); JM. Ś.D. *kucca* = *kūrca* (Erz. Śak. 134, 4; Karp. 22, 8; D. Mṛcch. 104. 7); Ś. *caccari carcari* (Ratn. 293, 17. 18). — *rch* = *cch*: M. *mucchā* = *mūrchā* (R.). — *chra* = *ccha*: Ś. *samucchida* = *samucchrita* (Mṛcch. 68, 15). — *rja* = *jja* : M. *ajjuṇa* = *arjuna* (G.), *gajjia* = *garjita* (G.H.R.), *jajjara* = *jarjara* (G.H.), *bhua* (birch; Deśīn. 6, 106) is not = *bhūrja*, but = *bhuja* (Vaijayantī 48, 89), therefore, M. *bhuavatta* (G. 641) = **bhujapattra*. In Mg. *rya* becomes *yya* (Vr. 11, 7; Hc. 4, 292); *ayyuṇa* = *arjuna*; *kayya* = *kārya*; *gayyadi* = *garjati*; *guṇavayyida* = *guṇavarjita*; *duyyaṇa* = *durjana*. MSS of the dramas have only *jja*, thus *kajja* (Mṛcch. 126, 6; 139, 23); *dujjaṇa* (Mṛcch. 115, 23). — *jra* = *jja*; M. *vajja* = *vajra* (G.H.R.). — *rjha* = *jjha*; M. *ṇijjhara* = *nirjhara* (G.H.). — *rṇa* = *ṇṇa* : M. *kaṇṇa* = *karṇa* (G.H.R.), *cuṇṇa* = *cūrṇa* (G.H.R.). *vaṇṇa* = *varṇa* (G.H.). *karṇikāra* can, beside *kaṇṇiāra*, form also *kaṇiāra* (Bh. 3, 58, Hc. 2, 95; Kī. 2, 114; Mk. fol. 27). So AMg. *kaṇiyāra* (Āyār. p. 128, 28), A. *kaṇiāra* (Hc. 4, 396, 5). The form shows accentuation on the final = **karṇikārá*. On *kaṇera* see §258. A *cūra* (Hc. 4, 337) is not = *cūrṇa*, which too becomes in A. *cuṇṇa* (Hc. 4, 395, 2), but = **cūrya*. — *rpa* = *ppa* : M. *kuppara*, AMg. *kŏppara* (§ 127); M. *kuppāsa* = *kurpāsa* (G.H.), *dappa* = *darpa* (G.H.R.). — *pra* = *ppa* : PG. : *amhapesaṇappayutte* = *asmatpreṣaṇaprayuktān* (5, 6), *appatihata* = *apratihata* (6, 10), *satasahassappadāyino* = *śatasahasrapradāyinaḥ* (6, 11), *patiebhāgo* = *pratibhāgaḥ* (6, 12 etc.) etc.; M. *pia* = *priya* (G.H. R.) *appia* = *apriya* (H.). — *rba* = *bba*: AMg. *kabbaḍa* = *karbaṭa* (Āyār. 1, 7, 6, 4; 2, 1, 2, 6; Sūyag. 684; Ṭhāṇ. 347; Paṇhāv. 175. 246. 406, 486; Nāyādh.

1278; Uttar. 891; Vivāhap. 40. 295; Ovav.; Kappas.); Ś. *ṇibbandha*=*nirbandha* (Mṛcch. 5, 4; Śak. 51, 14); M. *dŏbballa*=*daurbalya* (G.H.R.). — *bra*=*bba* : PG. *bamhaṇāṇaṁ* =*brāhmaṇānām* (6, 8. 27. 30. 38), AMg. JM. *bambhaṇa* (§ 250), Ś. Mg. *bamhaṇa* (e.g. Mṛcch. 4, 16. 18. 21. 24; 5, 5; 6, 2; Mg. Mṛcch. 45, 17; 121, 10; 127, 4; Śak. 113, 7); Ś. *abbamhaṇṇa*=*abrāhmaṇya* (§ 282). — *rbha*=*bbha* : M. *gabbha*=*garbha* (G. H. R.), *ṇibbhara*=*nirbhara* (G.H.R.); Ś. *dubbhĕjja*=*durbhedya* (Mṛcch. 68, 19). — *bhra*=*bbha*; PG. *bhātukāṇa*=*bhrātṛkāṇām* (6, 18); M. *paribbhamaī*=*paribhramati* (G.H.), *bhamara*=*bhramara* (G.H.R.). — *rma*=*mma* : AMg. *ummī*=*ūrmi* (Ovav.; Kappas.); PG. M. *dhamma*=*dharma* (5, 1; G. H. R.), PG. *dhamāyubala*° =*dharmāyurbala*° (6,9), *sivakhaṁdavamo*=*śivaskandavarmā* (5,2), Ś. *dummaṇussa* *durmaṇuṣya* (Mrcch. 18,8;40,14). — *mra*=*mma*: M. *dhummakkha*=*dhūmrākṣa* (R.); AMg. *makkhei*=*mrakṣayati* (Āyār. 2, 2, 3, 8), *makkhĕjja*=*mrakṣayet* (Āyār. 2, 13, 4). — *rla*=*lla* : M. *ṇillajja*=*nirlajja* (H.R.), *dullaha*=*durlabha* (H.). — *rva*=*vva*: PG. *savvattha*=*sarvatra* (5, 3), *puvvadattaṁ*=*pūrvadattam* (6, 12. 28); M. *puvva*=*pūrva*, *savva*=*sarva* (G.H. R.). — *vra*=*vva* : Ś. *pārivvājaa*=*parivrājaka* (Mṛcch. 41,5.7.10.17); M. *vaa*=*vraja* (H.); AMg. *vīhi*=*vrīhi* (Āyār. 2, 10. 10; Sūyag. 682. Ṭhāṇ. 134; Vivāhap 421. 1185; Jīv. 356). On *rya* see § 284. 285.

§ 288. In conjunction with dentals *r* may be regularly assimilated. *rta*=*tta*: PG. *nivataṇaṁ*=*nivartanam* (6, 38); M. *āvatta*=*āvarta* (G.R.), *kitti* =*kīrti* (G.R.; cf. §83); Ḍh. *dhutta*=*dhūrta* (Mṛcch. 30, 12; 32, 7; 34, 25; 35, 1; 36, 23); M. *muhutta*=*muhūrta* (H.R.). — *tra*=*tta*: PG. *gottasa*=*gotrasya* (6, 9 etc.); M. *kalatta*=*kalatra* (H.R.), *citta*=*citra*, *patta*=*patra*, *sattu*=*śatru* (G.H.). — *rtha*=*ttha* : M. *attha*=*artha* (G.H.R.), *patthiva*=*pārthiva* (G. R.), *sattha*=*sārtha* (G. H. R.), *samattha*=*samartha* (H. R.). — *rda*=*dda* : PG. *balivadda*=*balivarda* (6, 33); M. *kaddama*=*kardama* (G. H. R.), *daddura*=*dardura* (G.), *duddiṇa*=*durdina* (G. R.).— *dra*=*dda*. PG. *ācanda*°=*ācandra*° (6, 29); M. *inda*=*indra*, *ṇiddā*=*nidrā* (G. H. R.), *bhadda*=*bhadra* (G. H.), *samudda*=*samudra* (G. H. R.) — *rdha*=*ddha*: PG. °*vadhanike*= **vardhanikān* (6, 9); M. *addha*=*ardha* (G. H. R.), *ṇiddhūma* =*nirdhūma* (H. R.); AMg. *muddha-*=*mūrdham* (§ 402). — *dhra*= *ddha* : AMg. *saddhiṁ*=*sadhrim* (§103).

§ 289. In lieu of the dental, there occurs frequently the cerebral in the groups, in which the first member is *r*, especially in AMg. According to the grammarians (Vr. 3, 22; Hc. 2, 30; Kī. 2, 34; Mk. fol. 22) in the case of *rt* cerebralization is the rule. The words, which retain the dental, are collected by Vr. 3, 24; Hc.; Kī.; Mk. in the ākṛtigaṇa *dhūrtādi*. The dialects deviate sometimes in the case of the same words : AMg. JM. *aṭṭa*=*ārta* (Āyār. 1, 1, 2, 1; 1, 2, 5, 5; 1, 4, 2, 2; 1, 6, 1, 4; Sūyag. 401; Nāyādh.; Nirayāv.; Uvās.; Ovav.; Kappas.; Erz.); AMg. *aṭṭataraṁ* (Sūyag. 282); AMg. *aṭṭiya*= **ārtita* (Ovav.); in addition to *kavaṭṭia* (§246); but Ś. *atti*=*ārti* (Śak. 57, 4). — AMg. *kiṭṭaī*=*kirtayati* (Āyār. 1, 5, 4, 3; 1, 6, 1, 1), *kiṭṭe* (Sūyag. 661), *kiṭṭamāṇa* (Sūyag. 663), *kiṭṭittā* (Āyār. p. 137, 27; Kappas.), *kiṭṭiya* (Āyār. p. 132, 33; 137; 23; Sūyag. 578. 661), but always *kitti*=*kirti* in all the dialects (§ 83. 288). — *kevaṭṭa*=*kaivarta* (Hc.;

Mk.), *kevaṭṭaa* (Bh.). — M. AMg. JM. *cakkavaṭṭi-*= *cakravartin* (Karp. 7, 3; 79, 4; 115, 10; Ṭhāṇ. 80. 197; Samav. 42; Vivāhap. 7. 1049; Nāyādh.; Ovav.; Kappas.; Erz.), but Ś. *cakkavatti-* (Caṇḍak. 87, 15; 94, 10; Hāsy. 21, 7), as perhaps also Karp. 104, 2. 4 with the v.l. is to be read. — AMg. *naṭṭaga*=*nartaka* (Ovav.; Kappas.); *ṇaṭṭaa* (Bh. 3, 22; Mk. fol. 22); *ṇaṭṭaī* =*nartakī* (Bh. 3, 22; Hc. 2, 30).—Ś. Ḍh. *bhaṭṭā*=*bhartā* in the sense of "Lord", but in all the dialects *bhattā* in the sense of "husband", "consort" (§390); AMg. *bhaṭṭidāraya*, Ś. *bhaṭṭidāraa*, *bhaṭṭidāriā* (§55). — The root *vṛt* forms M. *vaṭṭasi* (H.), *vaṭṭaï* (R.), AMg. JM. *vaṭṭaï* (Vivāhap. 268. 1408; Erz. 6, 3). AMg. *vaṭṭanti* (Āyār. 2, 2, 2, 11. 12; Kappas. S. § 35), M. AMg. JM. *vaṭṭanta-* (R.; Uttar. 712; Erz. 22, 9), AMg. JM. *vaṭṭamāṇa* (Āyār. 2, 2, 2, 1; Vivāhap. 268; Uvās.; Ovav.; Nāyādh.; Kappas.; Erz.), JŚ. Ś. *vaṭṭadi* (Pav. 382, 27; Lalitav. 560, 15; Mṛcch. 2, 20; 3, 1. 20; 169, 21; Śak. 37, 7; 59, 12; Vikr. 21, 10; 52, 1; Caṇḍak. 86, 4; Hāsy. 21, 8; 25, 3; 28, 20 etc.), JŚ. *vaṭṭadu* (Pav. 387, 21), Mg. *vaṭṭāmi* (Mṛcch. 32, 22). Likewise with prefixes, e.g. M. *āaṭṭanta-*, *āvaṭṭamāṇa* (R.); AMg. *aṇupari-vaṭṭamāṇa* (Sūyag. 328), *aṇupariyaṭṭaï* (Āyar. 1, 2, 3, 6; 1, 2, 6, 5,) *niyaṭṭaï* (Uttar. 116), *niyaṭṭanti* (Āyār. 1, 2, 2, 1; 1, 6, 4, 1), *niyaṭṭamāṇa* (Āyār. 1, 6, 4, 1), *nivaṭṭaĕjjā* (Sūyag. 415), *uvvaṭṭĕjja* (Āyār. 2, 2, 1, 8), *uvvaṭṭĕnti* (Āyār. 2, 2, 3, 9), JM. *uvvaṭṭiya* (Erz.), Ś. *paaṭṭadi*=*pravartate* (Mṛcch. 71, 7), A. *paaṭṭaï* (Hc. 4, 347), and in derivatives, such as AMg. *pariyaṭṭaṇā* (Āyār. 1, 2, 1, 1; 2, 1, 4, 2; Ovav.), *pariyaṭṭaya* (Kappas.), but M.Ś. *pari-attaṇa*, *parivattaṇa* (G.R.; Mṛcch. 2, 20; Vikr. 31, 6), AMg. *pariyatta*= *parivarta* (Ovav.); AMg. *saṁvaṭṭaga* (Uttar. 1056). In conjunction with prefixes, as the examples form Grr. already show, the dentals predominate. Thus pro ex. M. *uvvattaï* (G.), *ṇiattaï* (G.H.R.), *pariattaï* (G.), *parivattasu* (H.), *pariattanta-*, *parivattiuṁ* (R.); AMg. *pavattaï* (Pāṇṇav. 62); Ś. *ṇiattiadi* (Vikr. 46, 19), *ṇiattiadu* (Mṛcch. 74, 25; 78, 10 [°*va*°]), *ṇivattissadi* (Vikr. 17, 2), *ṇiattaïssadi* (Śak. 91, 6), *ṇiattāvehi*, *ṇiattadu* (Śak. 91, 5. 6), *ṇiattasu* (Śak. 87. 1. 2 [to be so read]), *ṇivattamāṇa* (Vikr. 5, 11), *ṇivvattehi*, *ṇivvattedu* (Mṛcch. 27, 12. 15), *ṇivvattamha* (Śak. 74, 3) etc. Likewise in derivatives. — AMg. *vaṭṭaya*=*vartaka* (quail; Āyār. 2, 10, 12; Sūyag. 100; Uvās.), *vaṭṭaga* (Sūyag. 681. 708, 722, 747), but *vattiā*=*vartikā* (Bh.; Hc.) against *vaṭṭiā* (Mk.). — AMg. *vaṭṭi*=*varti* (Hc. 2, 30) in *gandhavaṭṭi* (Ovav.; Kappas.; Nāyādh.) against M. *vatti* (H.). — The cerebrals stand throughout in the absolutive, as AMg. *kaṭṭu*=*kartu*°, *āhaṭṭu*=*āhartu*°, *samāhaṭṭu*, *sāhaṭṭu* etc. (§ 577). On *kāuṁ*, *kāduṁ*=*kartum* etc. § 62. — Transition to the media occurs in AMg. *gaḍḍa*=*garta* (Vr. 3, 25; Hc. 2, 35; Mk. fol. 23; Vivāhap. 246. 479); *gaḍḍā*=*gartā* (Hc. 2, 35).

§ 290. *rtha* becomes *ṭṭha* in AMg. JM. *aṭṭha*=*artha* in the sense of "reason", "cause", "thing", "story", but *attha* in the sense of "wealth", "money" (Hc. 2, 33). So especially in the phrase AMg. *ṇo iṇ' aṭṭhe samaṭṭhe* (§ 173), and in adverbially used case form like AMg. *se teṇ' aṭṭheṇaṁ* (Vivāhap. 34 ff.; Uvās. § 218. 219), *se keṇ' aṭṭheṇaṁ* (Uvās. §218. 219); AMg. JM. *aṭṭhāe* (Uttar. 363; Uvās.; Ovav.; Nāyādh.; Nirayāv.; Erz.), *aṭṭhayāe* (Nāyādh.; Ovav.; Erz.,); JM. *aṭṭhā* (Erz.). However, the dental also occurs in the meaning "thing", "story" (Ovav.) and in adverbially used forms, such as AMg. *iccatthaṁ* (Āẏār. 1, 2, 1, 1), and more frequently in JM. (Erz.). The rest of the dialects have only the dental in all the meanings of the word.[1] AMg. has also *aṇaṭṭha* "aimless", "false" (Uvās.; Ovav.), *niraṭṭhaga* (Uttar. 113), *samaṭṭha* (§ 173). Beside M. AMg. JM. A. *caüttha*=*caturtha*, Hc. 2, 33 teaches also *caüṭṭha*; beside Ś. *caduttha*, there occurs also *caduṭṭha* (§ 449). AMg. *addhuṭṭha* is=*ardha*+**turtha* (§ 450). On *kavaṭṭia* said to be=*kadarthita* see § 246. 289. In Mg. *rtha* becomes *sta* (Hc. 4, 291; Namisādhu on Rudraṭa, Kāvyālaṁkāra 2, 12); *eśe aste* =*eṣo 'rthaḥ* (Namis.); *astavadi*=*arthavati*, *śastavāhe*=*sārthavāhaḥ* (Hc. 4, 291); *tista*=*tirtha* (Hc. 4, 301). So the Lalitav. 566, 9 has *yahastaṁ* (read *yadhastaṁ*) =*yathārtham*, but 566, 7 *śaśtaśśa*=*sārthasya* and 566, 8, *paśtiduṁ* =*prārthayituṁ* with *śta*. In Mṛcch. 131, 9; 133, 1; 140, 13; 146, 16; 152, 6; 168, 2 all MSS have *attha*, likewise Caṇḍak. 60, 11; Prab. 28, 14, where, however, the ed. Madras reads *palamacco*. Mṛcch. 145, 17 K in GODABOLE has *accha*, 158, 21, the very good manuscript E has *aśta*. In Mṛcch. 138, 17 MSS have *kajjaṭṭhi* for *kayyasti*; in Śak. 114, 11 there stands *vikka-atthaṁ*=*vikrayārtham*, 115, 7 *śāmippaśādatthaṁ*=*svāmiprasādārtham*, Prab. 28, 15 has *titthiehiṁ*=*tīrthikaiḥ*, 29, 7 *titthiā*=*tīrthikāḥ*. Mṛcch. 122. 14; 128, 3; 158, 19 STENZLER has *śatthavāha*=*sārthavāha*, 133, 1, *śaṭṭhavāha*. The MSS vary greatly, and at 128, 3 E in GODABOLE correctly has *śastavāha*, to which the reading *śasyastavāha* of B and *śatchavāha* of H point[2]. The manuscripts everywhere are to be corrected according to the rules of the grammarians.

1. PISCHEL on Hc. 2, 33. Not quite correctly LEUMANN, Aup. S. s. v. *attha*. — 2. PISCHEL, GGA. 1881, p. 1319 f.

§ 291. *rda* becomes *ḍḍa* in *kavaḍḍa*=*kaparda* (Hc. 2, 36; Mk. fol. 23). — *gaḍḍaha*=*gardabha* (Vr. 3, 26; Hc. 2, 37; Kī. 2, 23; Mk. fol. 23) beside *gaddaha* (Hc. 2, 37; Pāiẏal. 150), which is the only form authenticated by the texts in AMg. JM. Ś. Mg. Ḍh. and is expressly prescribed for Ś. by Mk. fol. 67 (Sūẏag. 204. 724 f. 727 [°*bha*]; Samav. 83; Uttar. 794; Kk.; Ś. Mṛcch. 45, 16; Mg. Mṛcch. 79, 13; 175, 14), JM. *gaddabhī*= *gardabhī* and *gārdabhī* (Kk.), *gaddabhilla* (Kk.), *gaddabbha*=**gārdabhya* (unharmonious, shrill; Deśīn. 2, 82; Pāiẏal. 204); *gaddaha* (Deśīn. 2, 83), *gaddahaẏa* (Pāiẏal. 39; white lotus); Ḍh. *gaddahī* (Mṛcch. 29, 19). Kāleẏak. 25, 15 *gaḍḍuho* [sic] is printed in Ś. — *chaḍḍaï*=*chardati* (Hc. 2, 36); AMg. *chaḍḍĕjjā* (Āẏār. 2, 1, 3, 1), *chaḍḍasi* (Uvās. § 95), JM. *chaḍḍijjaï* (Āv. 41, 8), *chaḍḍei*, *chaḍḍijjaï*, *chaḍḍiẏa* (Erz.); A. *chaḍḍeviṇu* (Hc. 4, 422. 3); JŚ. *chaḍḍida* (Pav. 387, 18; Text °*ẏa*); *chaḍḍi*=*chardi* (Hc. 2, 36); JM. *chaḍḍī* =*chardis* (Erz.); AMg. *chaḍḍiẏalliẏā* (Ovav.); M. JM. Ś. *vicchaḍḍa*=*viccharda* (Hc. 2, 36; Mk. fol. 23; Pāiẏal. 62; Deśīn. 7, 32; G.H.R.; Kk.; Erz.; Anarghar. 277, 3 [so with ed. Calcutta to be read]); *vicchaḍḍi*=*vicchardi* (Vr. 3, 26; Kī. 2, 23); AMg. *vicchaḍḍaïttā* (Ovav.; Kappas.); M. *vicchaḍḍia* (R.). AMg. JM. *vicchaḍḍiẏa* (Ovav.; Pāiẏal. 79), Ś. *vicchaḍḍida* (Uttarar. 20, 11; Mālatīm. 241, 5; 254, 4; 276, 6; Anarghar. 149, 10 [so to be read everywhere]). — *maḍḍaï*=*mardate* (Hc. 4, 126), but Ś. *maddiadi*=*mardyate*

(Mṛcch. 69, 9); *maḍḍia* = *mardita* (Hc. 2, 36); *saṁmaḍḍa* = *saṁmarda* (Vr. 3, 26; Hc. 2, 36; Kī. 2, 23; Mk. fol. 23), but M. JM. Ś. *saṁmadda* (G.; Erz.; Mṛcch. 325, 17); *saṁmaḍḍia* = *saṁmardita* (Hc. 2, 36). Against these Ś. *uvamadda* = *upamarda* (Mṛcch. 18, 11); AMg. *pamaddaṇa* = *pramardana* (Ovav.; Kappas.), *pamaddi-* = *pramardin* (Nāyādh.; Ovav.); *pāmaddā* = **pādamardā* (stamping asunder of corns with the feet; Deśīn. 6, 40); AMg. *parimaddaṇa* = *parimardana* (Nāyādh.; Ovav.; Kappas.), *piḍhamadda* = *piṭhamarda* (Ovav.; Kappas.); Ś. *piḍhamaddiā* (Mālav. 14, 9); Adbhutad. 72, 13; 91, 9), AMg. *vāmaddaṇa* = *vyāmardana* (Ovav.; Kappas.). — *viaḍḍi* = *vitardi* (Vr. 3, 26; Hc. 2, 36; Kī. 2, 23) = *khuḍḍia* = *kūrdita*, *saṁkhuḍḍaï* = *saṁkūrdati* (§ 206), beside AMg. *ukkuddaï* (Uttar. 788). According to Mk. fol. 23, some taught also *taḍḍū* = *tardū*. — *rdha* has become *ḍḍha* in : AMg. JM. *aḍḍha* = *ardha* beside *addha*, as other dialects only have (Hc. 2, 41; §450); *aḍḍha*, pro ex. also in AMg. *avaḍḍha* = *apārdha* (Jīv. 1055 f.; Vivāhap. 1057. 1306), *saaḍḍha*, *aṇaḍḍha* (Vivāhap. 354), *divaḍḍha* (§ 450); JM. *aḍḍhamāsa* (Erz.), beside *addha*° (Kk) and AMg. *māsaddha* (Vivāhap. 168); J.M. *aḍḍharatta* = *ardharātra* (Erz.) etc.; M. AMg. JM. Ś. Mg. Ā.A. *addha* (G.H.R.; Samav. 156. 158; Ṭhāṇ. 265; Jīv. 231. 632 f.; Vivāhap. 209. 1178; § 450; Erz.; Kk. Ṛṣabhap.; Mṛcch. 69, 16; Caṇḍak. 51, 11; Karp. 60, 11; Mg. Mṛcch. 31, 17. 20. 23. 25; 32, 5; 133, 10; 168, 20. 21; Śak. 118, 4; Ā. Mṛcch. 100, 12; A. Hc. 4, 352; Piṅgala 1, 6. 61 ff.). — M. AMg. JM. *vaḍḍhaï* = *vardhate* (Vr. 8, 44; Hc. 4, 220; Kī. 4, 46; Mk. fol. 23; H.R.; Āyār. 2, 16, 5 [°*i*]; Sūyag. 460; Vivāhap. 160; Kk.); Ś. *vaḍḍhadi* (Vikr. 10, 20; 19, 7; 49, 4; 78, 18; 88, 14; Mālav. 25, 4). Likewise with prefixes, in the causative and in derivations. The proper name *vardhamāna* becomes AMg. JŚ. Ś. *vaḍḍhamāṇa* (Āyār. 2, 15, 12; Pav. 379, 1; Mṛcch. 25, 18; 44, 24; 45, 5 etc.), but AMg. also *vaddhamāṇa* (C. 3, 26; Āyār. 2, 15, 15; Ovav.; Kappas.), as also AMg. *nandivaddhaṇa* (Āyār. 2, 15, 15; Kappas.) and *vaddhāvei* (Ovav.; Kappas.; Nirayāv.) are said. For *govardhana* Mk. fol. 24 teaches *govaddhaṇa*. Ś. has *govaḍḍhaṇa* (Vṛṣabh. 19, 5).

§ 292. *tra* has become *ṭṭa* in M.A. *ṭuṭṭaï* = *truṭyati* (R.; Piṅgala 1, 65. 68) beside AMg. *tuṭṭaï* (Sūyag. 100. 105. 148); *tuṭṭanti* (Sūyag. 539); *ṭuṭṭaï* (Hc. 4, 230); A. *tuṭṭaü* (Hc. 4, 356). According to Vr. 12, 5 in Ś. *putra* in certain cases (*kvacit*) may become *puḍa*. Perhaps it is connected with the old form of *pāṭaliputra*, which would have been **pāṭaliputa* (§238, note 2), and must have regularly become **pāḍaliuḍa*. To the Skt. form corresponds M. Mg. *pāḍaliutta* (H. 2, 150; Mṛcch. 37, 3), JM. *pāḍaliputta* (Āv. 8, 1; 12, 1. 40; Erz.), Ś. *pāḍaliputtaa* (Mudrār. 149, 3). In Mg. Stenzler writes in Mṛcch. 118, 1; 119, 11. 21; 124, 5; 129, 18; 132, 9, 164. 16; 165, 3 *puśthaka* = *putraka*. The MSS deviate very much and point rather to *pustaka* or to *puśtaka*. Almost everywhere occurs the v.l. *puttaka*, and in Mg. in Mṛcch. *putta* 19, 19; 116, 8; 129, 7; 133, 1; 160, 11; 166, 1; 167, 24; 168, 3; *puttaka* 114, 16; 122, 15; 158, 20; *śaputtāka* 166, 18. 21 stand. Stenzler likes to correct it to *puśthaka* at p. 294, on 114, 16. But only at 158, 20 some MSS have *pustake*, *puśtake*, *putthake*, otherwise all have °*tta*°, which will be correct. As at 158, 19 for *ṇattike* = *naptṛkaḥ* the vv. ll. *ṇatthike* (so STENZLER, GOḌABOLE and the Calc. editions in the text), *ṇastike, ṇaśtike* also occur, there seems to be a case of interchange with the change from *rtha* (§290). After a long vowel *tra* frequently becomes *ẏa* through *ta* in AMg., as *gāẏa* = *gātra*, *goẏa* = *gotra*; *dhāi* = *dhātrī*; *pāi* = *pātrī* (§87). In *rātrī* the same law holds in M.Ś. (§87). *dhārī* (nurse; Hc. 2, 81) is not = *dhātrī*, but is derived from √*dhai* (to suckle) with suffix *-ra* = "wet nurse". Cf. *dhāru*.

§ 293. Against § 288 *tra* apparently becomes *ttha* in adverbs ending in *-tra*, as *aṇṇattha* = *anyatra* (Hc. 2, 161; 3, 59); Ś. *attha* = *atra* in *atthabhavaṁ* (Śak. 33, 3; 35, 7; Vikr. 30, 9), *atthabhavado* (Mālav. 27, 11), *atthabhodī* (Vikr. 38, 17; 83, 13; Mālav. 26, 1); M. AMg. JM. *kattha* = *kutra* (Bh. 6, 7; Hc. 2, 161; G.H.R.; Kappas.; Ovav.; Erz.; Kk.); M. AMg. JM. JŚ. Ś.D. *jattha* = *yatra* (Bh. 6, 7; Hc. 2, 161; H.R.; Kappas.; Erz.; Kk.; Kattig.; 401, 353; Uttarar. 20, 11; 21, 10; D. Mṛcch. 100, 3); M. AMg JM. Ś. Mg. *tattha* = *tatra* (Bh. 6, 7; Hc. 2, 161; Kī. 3, 42; G.H.R.; Āẏār. 1, 1, 1, 7; 1, 1, 2, 1. 2 etc.; Nāẏādh.; Uvās.; Kappas.; Kk.; Vikr. 48, 14; Mg. Prab. 32, 6), in Ś. also in *tatthabhavaṁ* (Vikr. 46, 6; 47, 2; 75, 3. 15), *tatthabhavadā* (Śak. 30, 2; Vikr. 16, 11; 80, 14; 84, 19; Mālav. 10, 13), *tatthabhavado* (Mṛcch. 6, 4; 22, 12; Vikr. 38, 18 ; 51, 13; 79, 16), *tattha-bhodī* (Mṛcch. 88, 13; Śak. 95, 12; 125, 7; 132, 7; 134, 13; Vikr. 16, 4.7. 13; 18, 5 etc.); *iarattha* = *itaratra* (Bh. 6, 2); M. JM. *savvattha* = *sarvatra* (Bh. 6, 2; Hc. 3, 59.60; G.H.R.; Erz.). Meanwhile PG. M. AMg. JM. Ś. Mg. D. Ā. *ĕttha*, A. *ĕtthu* (§107), on account of the *e*, cannot be equated as = *atra*, but as = Vedic *itthā*. From it the rest of the adverbs cannot be separated, so that *kattha* must be derived from **katthā*, *jattha* from **yatthā* etc.[1] The regular continuation of *yatra*, *tatra* are A. *jattu*, *tattu* (Hc. 4, 404; cf. 268), of *anyatra*, Ḍh. *aṇṇatta* (Mṛcch. 36, 23; 39, 10). Mg. *atta* = *atra* (Mṛcch. 161, 17; 167, 17) is probably false. In the first place D. has *ĕttha*, in the second it is wanting in most of the MSS. The spellings *attabhavaṁ*, *tattabhavaṁ*, which the Dravidian and Devanāgarī recensions of Śak. and Mālav. have[2], and which occur occasionally elsewhere also, are erroneous[3]. On A. *kĕtthu*, *jĕtthu*, *tĕtthu* see §107. — Ś. *mahāmĕttha* = *mahāmātra* (Mṛcch. 40, 22) is a false reading for *mahāmĕtta*, as the MSS D H in GOḌABOLE p. 120 read, and *mĕtthapurisa* = **mātrapuruṣa* (Mṛcch. 69, 12) for *mahāmĕttapurisa* (cf. D in GOḌABOLE p. 196), since *mātra* becomes only *mitta*, *mĕtta* (§109). Cf. also *mĕṇṭha*, JM. *miṇṭha* (mahout, elephant-driver; Deśīn. 6, 138; Erz.), Pāli *mĕṇḍa* — M. *patthī* (H. 240), which WEBER wishes to equate as = *pātrī*, is a false reading for *pacchi* (Deśīn. 6, 1), Pāli *pacchi*; cf. v. l. ZDMG. 28, 408; JS.16, 78 on stanza 185.

1. Differently in S. GOLDSCHMIDT, Prākṛtica p. 22; R, s.v. *kattha*; WEBER on H. 240. Cf. PISCHEL BB. 3,253. — 2. BÖHTLINGK on Śak. 20,11 p. 177.—3. PISCHEL, De Kālidāsae Śākuntali recensionibus p. 34 f.

§ 294. *dra* has become *ḍḍa* in AMg. JM. *khuḍḍa* = *kṣudra* (Deśīn. 2, 74; Āẏār. 2, 2, 3, 2; Sūẏag. 414; Ṭhāṇ. 546; Uttar. 13; Jīv. 476ff.; 559. 622; 663. 1013 ff.; Kappas.; Erz.); *khuḍḍaa* (Hc. 2, 174; Triv. 1, 3, 105), AMg. JM. *khuḍḍaẏa*, femin. *khuḍḍiẏā* (Āẏār. 1, 3, 3, 2; 2, 2, 1, 4; 2, 2, 2,3; Ṭhāṇ. 67; Paṇhāv. 520; Vivāhap. 1100; Kappas.; Āv. 23, 6), AMg. *khuḍ-*

ḍaga (Sūyag. 872; Ṭhāṇ. 545; Vivāhap. 1101; Ovav.), *khuḍḍāga* (§70); rarely AMg. also *khudda* (Sūyag. 504) and *khuddāya* (Kappas.). — Like simple *da* becoming *la* (§244), *dda*, originating from *dra*, also becomes *lla* in M. AMg. *alla*, beside M. AMg. JM. Ś. *adda* = *ārdra* (§111), and *chilla* (hole; hut; Deśīn. 3, 35), *ucchilla* (hole; Deśīn. 1, 95), beside M. AMg. JM. *chidda* (H.; Uvās.; Erz.) and AMg. JM. *chiḍḍa* (Nirayāv.; Āv. 41, 4. 5; Erz. v. 1.), M. *chiddia* = *chidrita* (G.). On *culla* see §325. M. *maḷaï* is not = *mardati*, but = *mradate* (§244). The synonymous *maḍhaï* (Hc. 4, 126) is = *maṭhati* from *maṭha mardanivāsayoḥ* (Dhātupāṭha 9, 47 according to Bopadeva), which belongs to *math*, *manth*. On *dra* beside *dda* see § 268.

§ 295. *b* is inserted between *m* and *r* in *āmra* and *tāmra*. The sound-group *mbra* created in this manner either is separated by a separation vowel: *ambira*, *tambira* (§137), or in it *r* is assimilated. So M. AMg. JM. *amba* (Vr. 3, 53; C. 3, 9; Hc. 2, 56; Kī. 2, 64; Mk. fol. 27; Pāiyal. 145; H.; Āyār. 2, 1, 8, 1. 4. 6; 2, 7, 2, 2ff.; 2, 10, 21; Ṭhāṇ. 205; Paṇṇav. 482. 531; Vivāhap. 116, 1256; Erz.); AMg. *ambaga* (Aṇuttar. 11; Uttar. 231. 983ff.); AMg. *ambāḍaga* = *āmrātaka* (Āyār. 2, 1, 8, 1. 4; Paṇṇav. 482). — M. AMg. *tamba* = *tāmra* (Grr.; Pāiyal. 93; G.H.R.; Sūyag. 282. 834; Uttar. 597; Vivāhap. 1326; Ovav.; Kappas.); AMg. *tambaga* (Uttar. 1065); *tambiya* (Ovav.); M.Ś. *tambavaṇṇī* = *tāmraparṇī* (Karp. 12, 4; 71, 8; Bālar. 264, 3. 4; Anarghar. 297, 15 [so to be read]); M. *āamba*, AMg. *āyamba* = *ātāmra* (G.H.; Śak. 119, 6; (Ovav.); *tambakimi* = *tāmrakrimi* (cochineal; Deśīn. 5, 6); *tambaratti* = **tāmrarakti* (wheat-rust; Deśīn. 5, 5); *tambasiha* = *tāmra-śikha* (cock; Pāiyal. 125); M. *tambā* = *tāmrā* (cow; Deśīn. 5, 1; Pāiyal. 45; H.). — According to Mk. fol. 27 *kamra* also becomes *kamba*. — *mla* is treated in the same way. *amla* becomes either *ambila* or *amba* : AMg. *sehambadāli-yambehiṁ* = *sedhāmladālikāmlaiḥ* (Uvās. § 40); A. *ambaṇu* = *āmlatvam* (Hc. 4, 376, 2).

§ 296. III) If one of the sounds is *la* (Vr. 3, 3; C. 3; Hc. 2, 79; Kī. 2, 50; Mk. fol. 19): *lka* = *kka*: M. *ukkā* = *ulkā* (G.R.); *kakka* = *kalka* (Vivāhap. 1025); M.Ś. *vakkala* = *valkala* (§ 62). — *kla* = *kka*: AMg. *kisanti* = *kliśyanti* (Uttar. 576), *kesa* = *kleśa* (Uttar. 202. 575), *kiva* = *klība* (Ṭhāṇ. 181); *vikkava* = *viklava* (Bh. 3, 3; Hc. 2, 79). *śukla* forms beside AMg. *sukka* (Sūyag. 313; Ṭhāṇ. 25ff.) and *suila*, AMg. *sukkila* (§136) according to Hc. 2, 11 also *suṅga*. Provided this goes back to *śukla* the more correct spelling would be *suṁga*, corresponding to *suṁka* = *śulka* (§74) with transition to the media — *lga* = *gga* : M. *phaggu* = *phalgu*, AMg. Ś. *phagguṇa* = *phalguna* (§62); AMg. *vaggaï*, *vaggittā* = *valgati valgitvā* (Vivāhap. 253), *vaggaṇa* = *valgana* (Ovav.), *vaggu* = *valgu* (Sūyag. 245). — *lpa* = *ppa* : AMg. JM. Ś. *appa* = *alpa* (Sūyag. 371; Uvās.; Nāyādh.; Nirayāv.; Ovav.; Kappas.; Erz.; Kk.; Mṛcch. 150, 18); M. AMg. JM. Ś. *kappa* = *kalpa* (G.H.R.; Uvās.; Nāyādh.; Ovav.; Kappas.; Erz.; Kk.; Vikr. 11, 4); M. AMg. JM. *sippa* = *śilpa* (H.; Nāyādh.; Uvās.; Kappas.; Erz.; Ṛṣabhap.), AMg. Ś. *sippi-* = *śilpin* (Uvās.; Ovav.; Mṛcch. 152, 25; 153. 3). In *jalp* and its derivatives *l* becomes *m* : M. JM. *jampaï* = *jalpati* (Vr. 8, 24; Hc. 4, 2; Kī. 4, 46; G.H.R.; Erz.; Kk.); JM. *jampia* [sic.], *jampanteṇa* (KI. 8, 15); AMg. *jampantā*

(Sūẏag. 50); JM. *paẏaṁpae* = *prajalpate* (Erz.); Ḍh. *jampiduṁ*, *jampasi* (Mṛcch. 34, 24; 39, 9); Ś. *jampasi* (Vikr. 41, 11), *jaṁpijjadi* (Lalitav. 568, 6), *jampissaṁ* (Mālatīm. 247, 2); *jampaṇa* (disgrace; mouth; Deśīn. 3, 51); JM. *ajampaṇa* (non-betrayal; Erz. 10, 34); M.A. *jampira* (Hc. 2, 145; H.; Hc. 4, 350, 1), AMg. *aẏampira* (Dasav. 619, 22; 631, 13; 632, 28); AMg. *pajampāvaṇa* = **prajalpāpana* (teaching to learn; Ovav.); Mg. *yaṁpideṇa* (Lalitav. 566, 12), A. *pajampaha* (Hc. 4, 422, 10; so to be read). For *mpa* there often occurs *ppa*: AMg. *jappanti* (Sūẏag. 26); Ś. *jappemi* (Hāsy. 33, 21), *jappasi* (Kaṁsav. 49, 7), *jappesi* (Hāsy. 25, 10. 12; 34, 37), *jappissadi* (Pras. 144, 2), *jappiduṁ* (Hāsy. 33, 13), *jappanti* (Prab. 44, 1; so ed. Bomb. P.M.), °*jappiṇi* (Pras. 37, 16; Vṛṣabh. 26, 7), *jappida* (Pras. 120, 1) etc. Probably everywhere it is to be read *mpa*, as certainly in M. *jampieṇa* for *jappieṇa* (Ratn. 322, 4), as rightly stands *jampie* (Karp. 38, 4) as well as A. *jampiaṁ* (Piṅgala 1, 60; so Goldschmidt for *iṁ*, *aṁ*, *jaṁ*) — *pla* = *ppa*: M. *pavaṁga* = *plavaṁga*, *pavaṁgama* = *plavaṁgama* (R.), *parippavanta-* = *pariplavant-* (G.R.), *pappua* = *prapluta* (G.); AMg. *paviuṁ* = *plavitum* (Sūẏag. 508); *vippava* = *viplava* (Hc. 2, 106). — *lpha* = *ppha* : AMg. *guppha* = *gulpha* (Āẏār. 1, 1, 2, 5; Ovav.). *lba* = *bba*. : M. *ubbaṇa* = *ulbaṇa* (G. 734; text *uvvaṇa*); AMg. *kibbisa* = *kilbiṣa* (Uttar. 156 [text °*vvi*°; Dasav. 624, 11. 12), *kibbisiẏa* = **kilbiṣika* (Ovav.); *subba* = *śulba* (Hc. 2, 79). — *lbha* = *bbha* : AMg. *pagabbhaï* = *pragalbhate* (Āẏār. 1, 5, 3, 3 [°*ī*] ; Sūẏag. 134. 150), *pagabbhiẏa* (Sūẏag. 31. 146. 198), *pāgabbhiẏa* (Sūẏag. 596), *pagabbhittā* (Sūẏag. 358), *vippagabbhiẏa* (Sūẏag. 50), *pagabbhi-* (Sūẏag. 332), *pāgabbhi-* (Sūẏag. 268. 296). Hence *pagambhaï* (Uttar. 202) is a printing error for *pagabhbhaï* = *pagabbhaï*. — *lma* = *mma*: *kammasa* = *kalmaṣa* (Hc. 2, 79; Pāiẏal. 53); AMg. *kummāsa* = *kulmāṣa* (Āẏār. 1, 8, 4, 4. 13); AMg. Ś. Mg. *gumma* = *gulma* (Āẏār. 2, 3, 2, 15; Nāẏādh.; Mṛcch. 97, 22; Mudrār. 185, 8; 197, 5; Priẏad. 12, 3; 13, 3; 19, 17; 23. 14; Karṇas. 28. 7; Subhadr. 12,5; Mg. Caṇḍak. 61, 11), PG. *gumike* = *gulmikān* (5, 5); M. *vammia*, AMg. *vammiẏa* = *valmika* (§ 80); Ś. *vammii* = *vālmiki* (Bālar. 6, 15). — *mla* = *mma* : AMg. JM. Ś.A. *mĕccha* = *mleccha* (§ 84. 105). —On *lya* see § 286, on *rla* § 287. — *lva* = *lla*: Ś. *gallakka* = *galvarka* (Mṛcch. 6, 6); M. *pallala* = *palvala* (G.); AMg. *billa* = *bilva* (Hc. 1, 85; Mk. fol. 7; Pāiẏal. 148; Paṇṇav. 531; Vivāhap. 1530 [*vi*°]; Dasav. 621, 5), according to Hc. and Mk. also *bĕlla* (§119).

§ 297. IV) One of the consonants is *va* (Vr. 3, 3; C. 3, 2; Hc. 2, 79; Kī. 2, 50; Mk. fol. 19); *kva* = *kka*: M. *kaḍhaï* = *kvathati*, Ś. *kaḍhida*, AMg. *sukaḍhiẏa* (§ 221); M. *kaṇakkaṇia* = *kvaṇakvaṇita* (Karp. 55, 7); M. AMg. Ś. *pikka*, AMg. Ś. *pakka* = *pakva* (§ 101). — *gva* has become *vva* instead of *gga* in *divvāsā* = *digvāsāḥ* (Cāmuṇḍā; Deśīn. 5, 39). — *jva* = *jja* : M. *jalaï* = *jvalati*, *ujjala* = *ujjvala*, *pajjalaï* = *prajvalati* (G.H.R.); M. *jara* = *jvara* (H.). — *ṇva* = *ṇṇa*; M. *kiṇṇa* = *kiṇva* (G.); Ś. *kaṇṇa* = *kaṇva* (Śak. 9, 10; 14, 1; 15,1 etc.); Ś. *rumaṇṇado* = **rumaṇvataḥ* (Ratn. 320, 16). On *vya* see § 286, on *rva*, *vra* § 287, on *lva* § 296.

§ 298. In conjunction with dental stops *va* may be assimilated to the dental. *tva* = *tta* : PG. M. AMg. JM. *cattāri*, Mg. *cattāli* = *catvāri* (§ 439);

M.Ś. *satta* = *sattva* (H.; Śak. 154, 7); the suffix *tta* = *-tva*, as *piṇatta* = *pinatva*; AMg. *bhaṭṭitta* = *bhartṛtva*; **-ttaṇa* = *-tvana*, as M. *piṇattaṇa* = **pinatvana*, Ś. *ṇiuṇattaṇa* = *nipuṇatvana*, A. *pattattaṇa* = **pattratvana* (§ 597). — *dva* = *dda* : M. AMg. JM. *dāra* = *dvāra* (C. 3, 7; Hc. 1, 70; 2, 79, 112; G.H.R.; Sūyag. 129; Nāyādh.; Ovav.; Erz.); always M.Ś.A. *dia*, JM. *diya* = *dvija* (Hc. 1, 94; Pāiyal. 102; G.; Erz.; KI. 11 [*dia*]; Caṇḍak. 3, 16; 52, 6; 56, 6; 93, 13; Piṅgala 2, 48), *diāhama* = *dvijādhama* (the bird bhāsa ; Deśīn. 5, 39), also = *dvipa* (Hc. 2, 79); Ś. *diuṇa* = *dviguṇa* (Śak. 140, 13), *diuṇadara* = *dviguṇatara* (Mṛcch. 22, 13), *diuṇida* = *dviguṇita* (Nāgān. 18, 2); Mg. *diuṇa* (Mṛcch. 177, 10); *diraa* = *dvirada* (Hc. 1, 94); AMg. *dāvara* = *dvāpara* (Sūyag. 136), *danda* = *dvandva*, *digu* = *dvigu* (Aṇuog. 358); AMg. JM. *jambuddiva* = *jambudvipa* (Uvās.; Nirayāv.; Nāyādh.; Ovav.; Kappas.; Kk.); PG. *bharaddāyo* = *bharadvājaḥ* (5, 2), *bhāradāya*, *bhāradāyasa* (6, 16. 19); M. *saddala* = *śādvala* (G.). — *dhva* = *ddha* : *dhattha* = *dhvasta* (Hc. 2, 79), M. *uddhattha* = *uddhvasta* (G. 608; so to be read). If the prefix *ud* occurs before a word beginning with *va*, so *dva* becomes *vva*: M. *uvvattaṇa* = *udvartana* (G.H.R.), AMg. *uvvaṭṭaṇa* (Uvās.); JM. *uvvaṭṭiya* (Erz.); M. *uvvahaṇa* = *udvahana* (G. R.); M. AMg. JM. Ś. *uvvigga* = *udvigna* (§ 276).

§ 299. Dialectically sometimes *tva* becomes *cca* through *tya*, *thva* becomes *ccha* through *thya*, *dva* becomes *jja* through *dya* and *dhva* becomes *jjha* through *dhya*. *tva* = *cca* : M. AMg. JM. *catvara* = *caccara* (Hc. 2, 12; Kī. 2, 33; H.; Vivāgas. 103f.; Ovav.; Kappas.; Erz.), beside M. Ś. *cattara* (Hc. 2, 12; Kī. 2, 33; H.; Mṛcch. 6, 7; 28, 20; Bālar. 147, 20); AMg. JŚ. *tacca* = **tāttva* (§ 281); A. *pahuccaï* = **prabhutvati* (§ 286); AMg. JM. JŚ. in the absolutives, as AMg. JŚ. *kiccā* = *kṛtvā*; AMg. JM. JŚ. *sŏccā* = *śrutvā*; AMg. *bhŏccā* = *bhuktvā*; AMg. *ciccāṇa*, *cĕccāṇa* = **tyaktvāna*, *hiccāṇaṁ* = **hitvānaṁ* (§ 587). — *thva* = *ccha*: AMg. *picchi* = *pṛthvi* (Hc. 2, 15). — *dva* = *jja*; AMg. *vijjaṁ* = *vidvān* (Hc. 2, 15; Sūyag. 126. 306). — *dhva* = *jjha*: AMg. JM. *jhaya* (Hc. 2, 27; Nāyādh. § 47; Vivāgas. 61; Kappas. § 4. 32; T. 5, 10; Erz.); AMg. *isijjhaya* = *ṛṣidhvaja* (Uttar. 630); *aruṇajjhaya* (Uvās. §179; 277, 5), *indajjhaya* (Samav. 97), *mahindajjhaya* (Ṭhāṇ. 266; Jīv. 551 f.; Kappas. p. 96, 26), *maṅgalajjhaya* (Jīv. 552), *ūsiyajjhaya* = *ucchritadhvaja* (Nāyādh. 481; Ovav. § 40), *kaṇagajjhaya* (Nāyādh. 1084), *cindhajjhaya* = *cihnadhvaja* (Nirayāv. § 5), *dhammajjhaya* (Ovav. § 16), *chattajjhaya* = *chattradhvaja* (Paṇhāv. 286), *tālajjhaüvviddha* = *tāladhvajodviddha* (Paṇhāv. 249), *sajjhaya* (Samav. 97; Rāyap. 128; Ovav. § 2. 42. 49), beside M. *dhaa* (Hc. 2, 27; H. R.), JM. *dhaya* (Pāiyal. 68; Erz.), M. Ś. *maaraddhaa* (H.; Karp. 66, 11; 76, 9; 83, 1; 110, 5; Śak. 120, 5; Bālar. 289, 13; Viddhaś. 105, 8); P. *makaraddhaja* (Hc. 4, 323), but AMg. *mayarajjhaya* (Paṇhāv. 286); JM. *garuḷaddhaya* (Dvār. 507, 37), but AMg. *garuḷajjhaya* (Paṇhāv. 235); AMg. *tāladdhaya* (Samav. 236). — A. *jhuṇi* (Hc. 1, 52; 4, 432), beside Ś. *dhuṇi* (Pras. 14, 10; Kaṁsav. 9, 15; Vṛṣabh. 48, 9) = *dhvani* from **dhvuni* with *u* according to § 104. — AMg. *bujjhā* = *buddhvā* (Hc. 2. 15), *abujjha* (Sūyag. 504). — M. JM. Ś. *sajjhasa* = *sādhvasa* (Hc. 2, 26; Kī. 2, 75; Mk. fol. 23; G.; Erz.; Jīvān. 88, 14; Mālatīm. 276, 6; Pārvatīp. 12, 14. 23), beside *saddhasa* (Mk.). Nāgān. 27, 14 stands *adisaddhaseṇa*;

the ed. Calc. 1873 p. 27, 1 has *adisajjhaseṇa*. — *māukka* is not = *mṛdutva* (Hc. 2, 2; Mk. fol. 26), but = **mārdukya* from *mṛduka* (cf. § 52), as JM. *garukka* (Kī. 13) = **gukukya* from *guruka* (§123).

§ 300. However, *va* behind *ta* shifts to *pa*, behind *da* to *ba*; dialectically *tva* becomes *ppa*, *dva* becomes *bba*[1]. *tva* = *ppa* : M. *pahuppaī* = **prabhutvati* (§ 286); A. *paī* = *tvām*, *tvayā* and *tvayi* (§ 421); A. *-ppaṇa* = *-tvana*, as *vaḍḍappaṇa* beside *vaḍḍhattaṇa* = **vaḍratvana*, *maṇusappaṇa* = **manuṣatvana* (§ 597); A. absolutive in *-ppi* = *-tvī*, as *jiṇĕappi*, *jĕppi* = **jitvī*; *gampi* = *gantvi* = Vedic. *gatvī*, *gamĕppi* = **gamitvī*, and *-ppiṇu* = *-tvīnam*, as *gamĕppiṇu*, *gampiṇu* = **gamitvīnam*; *karĕppiṇu* = **karitvīnam* (§ 588). This secondary *pa* becomes *va* too, as *karevi* beside *karĕppi*; *leviṇu* beside *lĕppiṇu*; *ramevi* beside *ramĕppi* (§ 184. 588). On *ppa* from *tma* see § 277. — *dva* = *bba* : PG. M. AMg. *be*, A. *bi* = *dve*, *bĕṇṇi*, *biṇṇi* = **dveni* (436. 437); M. *biuṇa* = *dviguṇa* (Hc. 1, 94; 2, 79; G.H.R.)[2], but Ś. Mg. *diuṇa* (§ 298); AMg. JM. *bārasa*. A. *bāraha* = *dvādaśa* (§ 443), as generally AMg. JM. A. *bā°* = *dvā°* (§ 445 ff); M. *biia*, *bia*, *biijja*, AMg. JM. *biiya*, *biya*, A. *bia* = *dvitiya* (§ 82.91. 165. 449); M. A. *bāra* = *dvāra* (C. 3, 7; Hc. 1, 79; 2, 79. 112; H.; Hc. 4, 436); AMg. JM. *bāravai* = *dvāravatī* (Nāyādh. 524. 1296 ff.; Nirayāv. 79; Dvār. 495, 1 ff.); *bisaṁtava* = *dviṣaṁtapa* (Hc. 1, 177); M. *besa* = *dveṣa* (G.); M. AMg. = *dveṣya* (Hc. 2, 92; G. H.; Paṇhāv. 397; Uttar. 33), metrically also AMg. *baīssa* (Uttar. 961). *dhva* = *bbha*; JM. *ubbha* = *ūrdhva* (Hc. 2, 59; Erz.); JM. *ubbhaya* = *ūrdhvaka* (Pāiyal. 234); M. *ubbhia*, JM. *ubbhiya* = **ūrdhvita* (R.; Erz.), *ubbheha* = **ūrdhvayata* (Erz. 40, 15), beside M. JM. Ś. Mg. A. *uddha* (§ 83), AMg. JM. *uḍḍha* (Āyār. 1, 1, 1, 1. 5, 2. 3; 1, 2, 5, 4, 6. 5; 1, 4, 2, 3. 4 etc.; Sūyag. 215. 273. 288. 304. 590. 914. 931; Vivāhap. 11. 101. 105 f. 260 etc.; Erz.). — *nva* = *ṇṇa* : M. JM. *aṇṇesaṇa* = *anveṣaṇa* (G.; Erz.), Ś. *aṇṇesaṇā* = *anveṣaṇā* (Vikr. 32, 3), *aṇṇesīadi* = *anviṣyate*, *aṇṇesidavva* = *anveṣitavya* (Mṛcch. 4, 4. 21); Ś. *dhaṇṇantari* = *dhanvantari* (Bālar. 76, 1); Mg. *maṇṇantala* = *manvantara* (Prab. 50, 13; so correctly ed. Bombay. M.P.); Ś. *evaṁ*, *ṇedaṁ* = *evaṁ nv etat*; Ś. Mg. *kiṁ ṇedaṁ* = *kiṁ nv etat* (§ 174).

1. ASCOLI, Vorlesungen p. 59; Kritische Studien p. 197 ff,; PISCHEL, GGA. 1881, p. 1317 f. — 2. The Indian editions and WEBER in H. mostly write *v* in lieu of *b*.

§ 301. If the first member of conjunct consonants is a sibilant and the consonant following it, a tenuis, as a rule, the sibilant is assimilated to the tenuis and the latter gets aspirated. If, however, the sibilant stands at the end of a member of a compound, generally aspiration of the initial tenuis of the following member does not take place, particularly if the first member is a prefix[1]. *śca* = *ccha* (Vr. 3, 40; Hc. 2, 21; Kī. 2, 92; Mk. fol. 25); M. Ś. *accharia*, JM. *acchariya*, Ś. *accharīa*, M. AMg. *acchera*; *accharijja*; AMg. JM. *accheraya*, AMg. *accheraga* = *āścarya*, *āścaryaka* (§138. 176); M. AMg. JM. Ś. *pacchā* = *paścāt* (G.H.R.; Erz.; Vivāhap. 101; Uvās.; Nāyādh.; Kappas.; Mṛcch. 150, 18; Śak. 105, 14; Karp. 33, 8); A. *pacchi* = **paśce* (Hc. 4, 388); M. AMg. JM. Ā. *pacchima* = *paścima* (Grr.; G. R.; Vivāhap. 63; Uvās.; Ovav.; Kappas.; Erz.; Mṛcch. 99, 18); Ś. *pacchādāva* = *paścāttāpa* (Vikr. 33, 11; 38, 17); AMg. *pāyacchitta*, AMg. A. *pacchitta* = *prāyaścitta* (§ 165); AMg. JM. *nicchaya*, A. *ṇicchaa* = *niścaya* (Uvās.; Ovav.;

Erz.; Kk.; Hc. 4, 422, 10), but M. *ṇiccaa* (R.); AMg. JM. *nicchiya* = *niścita* Dasav. 642, 7; Nirayāv.; Erz.), Ś. *ṇicchida* (Bālar. 87, 1), but also Ś. *ṇiccida* (Mudrār. 208, 10 ed. Calc. Saṁvat. 1926; Mahāv. 55, 1 ed. Bomb.); M. Ś. A. *ṇiccala* = *niścala* (Hc. 2, 21. 77; Mk. fol. 25; G.H.R.; Mṛcch. 59, 24; Mudrār. 44, 6; Hc. 4, 436), AMg. JM. *niccala* (Uvās.; Kappas.; Erz.); M. AMg. *ṇiccĕṭṭha* = *niśceṣṭa* (R.; Nirayāv.); M. *duccaria*, JM. *duccariya*, Ś. *duccarida* = *duścarita* (H.; Erz.; Mahāv. 118, 11); AMg. *duccara* = *duścara* (Āyār. 1, 8, 3, 2), *duccaraga* (Āyār. 1, 8, 3, 6); JM. Ś. *tavaccaraṇa* = *tapaścaraṇa* (Dvār. 496, 19; 502, 36; 505, 15. 38; Mṛcch. 68, 8. 9; 72, 6; Pārvatīp. 24, 3; 25, 19; 26, 13; 27, 2. 10). — *ṇahaara* is not = *nabhaścara* (Kī. 2, 110), but = **nabhacara* (§ 347). M. JM. Ś. *harianda* (G.; KI. 3; Karp. 58, 4), JM. *hariyanda* (Dvār. 503, 16) is not = *hariścandra* (Hc. 2, 87; Kī. 2, 110 [text *harianno*, LASSEN *hariaṇḍo*]), which becomes Mg. *haliccanda* (Caṇḍak. 43, 5), but = *haricandra* like M. *hārianda* (G.) = *hāricandra*. — *cuaī* may be = **ścutáti* (Hc. 2, 77; cf. § 210, note 2), or = **cyutáti*. — In M. *viṁchua*, *viṁchia* beside *vicchua*, AMg. *vicchuya*, *vicchiya* = *vṛścika* (§ 50. 118) the nasal vowel is to be explained as in M. *piṁcha* = *piccha*; *guṁcha* = *guccha*; *puṁcha* = *puccha* (§ 74); *viṁcua* (§ 50) is treated according to the rule that holds good for compounds. — Corresponding to the change of old *ccha* to *śca* (§ 233), in Mg. *śca* remains unaltered : *aścalia* = *āścarya* (§ 138); *ṇiścaa* = *niścaya* (Mṛcch. 40, 4; text. °*cca*°); *ṇiścala* (Mṛcch. 135, 2); *paścādo* = *paścāt* (Veṇīs. 35, 10 in Hc. 4, 299; Bengal recension *paccādo*)[2]; *paścā* (Mudrār. 174, 8 [text *pacchā*; cf. v. l.]; Caṇḍak. 42, 12 [text *pacchā*]); *paścima* (Mṛcch. 169, 22; text *pacchima*; v. l. *paccima* and *pakṣima*); *śilaścālaṇa* = = *śiraścālana* (Mṛcch. 126, 7). — *ścha* becomes *ccha* : M. *ṇicchallia* = *niśchallita* (G.); AMg. *nicchoḍĕjja* = *niśchoṭeyam* (Uvās. § 200); JM. *nicchoḷiūṇa* = *niśchoḍya* (Erz. 59. 13).

1. LASSEN, Inst. p. 261. 264. — 2. PISCHEL on Hc. 4, 299.

§ 302. *ṣka* and *ṣkha* become *kkha* as a rule (Vr. 3, 29; Hc. 2, 4; Kī. 2, 88; Mk. fol. 24). *ṇikkha* = *niṣka* (Hc. 2, 4), according to Mk. fol. 24 also *ṇikka*; Ś. *pŏkkhara*, AMg. JM. *pukkhara* = *puṣkara*, AMg. Ś. *pŏkkhariṇī*, AMg. *pukkhariṇī* (§ 125); *mukkha* = *muṣka* (Bh. 3, 29); M. AMg. *vikkhambha* = *viṣkambha* (Kī. 2, 88; R.; Ovav.). In many cases, however, the aspiration does not take place, even outside the compounds, while it sometimes appears in compounds against the rule : M. Ś. *kikkindha* = *kiṣkindha* (R.; Anarghar. 262, 5); M. AMg. JM. *caükka* = *catuṣka* (Deśīn. 3, 2; G.; Āyār. 2, 11, 10; Aṇuog. 388; Paṇṇav. 702; Nāyādh. § 65; p. 1294; Ovav.; Nirayāv. Kappas.; Erz.; Kk).); Ś. *cadukkiā* = *catuṣkikā* (Bālar. 131, 16; Viddhaś. 52, 4 [text *caü*°]); AMg. JM. *turukka* = *turuṣka* (Paṇhāv. 258; Samav. 210; Paṇṇav. 96. 99. 110; Vivāhap. 941; Rāyap. 28. 36. 60. 190; Uvās.; Ovav.; Nāyādh.; Kappas.; Āv. 40, 17 [read so]); Ś. *dhāṇukka* = *dhānuṣka* (Mk. fol. 24; Bālar. 86, 15 202, 16), *dhāṇukkadā* (Bālar. 261, 1); *sakkaī* = *ṣvaṣkati* (Mk. fol. 55; WEBER on H. 608), *osakka* = **apaṣvaṣkna* (gone away; Deśīn. 1, 149; Pāiyal 178), AMg. *osakkaī* (Paṇṇav. 541), M. *osakkanta* (R.), AMg. *avasakkĕjjā* (Āyār. 1, 2, 5, 3), AMg. *paccosakkaī* = **pratyapaṣvaṣkati* (Nāyādh. 1463; Vivāhap. 1035, 1217. 1248), M. *parisakkaī*

(H. R. [text falsely *paḍi°*]), M. *parisakkaṇa* (G.R.); AMg. *sakkuli* beside *saṁkuli* = *śaṣkuli* (§ 74); AMg. JM. *sukka* = *śuṣka* (Hc. 2, 5; Aṇuttar. 11. 13; Nāẏādh. 984; Vivāhap. 270; Uttar. 758 ff.; Uvās.; Kappas.; Erz.), *sukkanti* (Deśīn. 8, 18, 23), A. *sukkahi* (Hc. 4, 427) = **śuṣkanti*, M. AMg. *parisukka* = *pariśuṣka* (G.; Uttar. 53); beside M. AMg. Ś. *sukkha* (Hc. 2, 5; H.R.; Dasav. N. 660, 16; Mṛcch. 2, 15; 44, 4), Ś. *sukkhāṇa* (Mṛcch. 18, 4) M. *sukkhanta-* (H.), *osukkha, osukkhanta-* (R.). Examples for compounds are : M. *ṇikkaïava* = *niṣkaitava* (H.); M. Ś. *ṇikkampa* = *niṣkampa* (G. R.; Śak. 126, 14; Mahāv. 32, 21); M. JM. *ṇikkāraṇa* = *niṣkāraṇa* (G. R.; Dvār.); AMg. *ṇikkaṇa* = *niṣkaṇa* (Vivāgas. 102), *nikkaṅkaḍa* = *niṣkaṅkaṭa* (Paṇṇav. 118; Ovav.); M. Ś. *ṇikkiva* = *niṣkṛpa* (Pāiẏal. 73; H.; Śak. 55, 16; Caṇḍak. 87, 2); M. AMg. Ś.A. *dukkara* = *duṣkara* (Hc. 2, 4; G.H.R.; Vivāhap. 817; Uvās.; Mṛcch. 77, 14; Hc. 4, 414, 4. 441), AMg. *dukkaḍa*, JM. *dukkaẏa* (§ 49). *nis*+*kram* forms in M. *ṇikkhamaï*, in AMg. *nikkhamaï* (§ 481), AMg. *nikkhamma* = *niṣkramya* (Āẏār. 1, 6, 4, 1; Kappas.), *nikkhamissanti, nikkhamiṁsu, nikkhamittae* (Kappas.); AMg. JM. *nikkhanta* (Āẏār. 1, 1, 3, 2; Erz.); AMg. *paḍinikkhamaï* (§ 481); AMg. JM. *nikkhamaṇa* (Kappas.; Erz.). M. has also *ṇikkamaï* (H.), *viṇikkamaï* (G.) beside *viṇikkhamaï* (G.), a point on which the manuscripts vary. Ś. has only *ṇikkamadi* (§ 481), *ṇikkamiduṁ* (Mudrār. 43, 6), *ṇikkamanta-* (Mudrār. 186, 2), *ṇikkanta* (Mṛcch. 51, 5. 8. 12), *ṇikkămaïssămi* (Mṛcch. 52, 9); Ḍh. *ṇikkamia* (Mṛcch. 36, 23); D. *ṇikkamantassa* (Mṛcch. 105, 24). — In Mg. *ṣka* becomes *ska* and *ṣkha* becomes *skha* (Hc. 4, 289) : *śuska* = *śuṣka*; *dhaṇuskhaṇḍa* = *dhanuṣkhaṇḍa*. According to Namisādhu on Rudraṭa, Kāvyālaṁkāra 2, 12, *śka* and *śkha* appear, and so the Lalitav. has *tuluśka* = *turuṣka* (565, 14. 17), *śuśke* = *śuṣkaḥ* (566, 12). The texts write *kkha, kka.* So Mṛcch. 21, 17 *śukkhe*, but MS A. *śuskhe*; 132, 24; 133, 17; *śukkha* without v. l.; 161, 7 *śukkhā*, v.l. *śuṣkā* = *śuṣkaḥ*; 133. 15. 16 *śukkhāvaïśśaṁ* without v.l.; 112, 11 *pŏkkhaliṇie*, 113, 22 *pukkhaliṇie* without v.l.; 134, 1; 165, 22; 166, 22 *ṇikkamadi, ṇikkama* with the v.l. *ṇiṣkama, ṇikkhama* 133, 21; 173, 9 *ṇikkide*, 134, 13 *ṇikkīdaṁ* = *niṣkrītaḥ*, *ṇiṣkrītam* without v. l.; 43, 4; 175, 15 *dukkala* = *duṣkara* without v. l.; 125, 1. 4 *dukkida* = *duṣkṛta* with the v.l. *dukhkhida, dukkhida, duḥkida* etc. We should read *śuska, pŏskaliṇi, ṇiskamadi, ṇiskida, duskala, duskida* etc.

§ 303. *ṣṭa* and *ṣṭha* become *ṭṭha* (Vr. 3, 10. 51; C. 3, 8. 11; Hc. 2, 34. 90; Kī. 2, 86. 49; Mk. fol. 21. 19): PG. *aggiṭṭhoma* = *agniṣṭoma* (5, 1; cf. Leumann, EI. 2, 484), *aṭṭhārasa* = *aṣṭādaśa* (6, 34), *vĕṭṭhi* = *viṣṭi* (6, 32); M. *iṭṭha* = *iṣṭa* (H.), *diṭṭhi* = *dṛṣṭi* (G.H.R.), *muṭṭhi* = *muṣṭi* (G.H.R.) — PG. *kaṭṭha* = = *kāṣṭha* (6, 33); *gŏṭṭhī* = *goṣṭhī* (G.), *ṇiṭṭhura* = *niṣṭhura* (G.H.R.), *suṭṭhu* = *suṣṭhu* (G.H.R.). Likewise the other dialects except Mg. In Mg. *ṣṭa* and *ṣṭha* become *sṭa* (Hc. 4, 289, 290) : *kasṭa* = *kāṣṭa*; *kŏsṭāgāla* = *koṣṭhāgāra*; *śusṭu* = *suṣṭhu*. Namisādhu on Rudraṭa, Kāvyālaṁkāra 2, 12 prescribes *ś* for *ṣ* in consonant-groups (cf. § 302): *kŏśṭhāgāla* (MSS *kosthā°*, *koṣṭa°*; ed. *kāsya°*). The manuscripts of the dramas vary; the texts have *ṭṭha* mostly falsely; Stenzler in Mṛcch., mostly has *śṭa*. Thus in Mṛcch. *kaśṭa* = *kaṣṭa* (29, 18; 127, 13); the MSS have *kaṣṭa, kaṭṭha, kaṭṭa*; *duśṭūṇa pabbhaśṭe* = **dṛṣṭvāna, prabhraṣṭaḥ*; (29, 21); the MSS have *daṭṭhūṇa, pabbhaṭṭhe*; *duśṭa*

= *dusṭa* (19, 5; 20, 17; 21, 8; 40, 9; 79, 17. 18; 112. 14. 21; 113, 19; 133, 19; 151, 25); the MSS have mostly *duṭṭha*, partly *dusṭa, dusṭha, duttha, duṭṭa, duha, duśṭa, ducha*; *paṇaśṭā* = *praṇaṣṭā* (14, 11); the MSS have °*ṭṭhā*, °*śṭā*, °*ṣṭā*, °*ṣṭhā*; *palāmiśṭā* = *parāmṛṣṭā* (16, 23); the MSS have °*miścā*, °*miśvā*, °*miṭṭhā*, °*miṣṭā*, °*miśṭā*, °*miṣṭhā*, °*miṭṭā*; *uvaviśṭe*, °*paviśṭā*, °*ppaviśṭaṁ* = *upaviṣṭaḥ*, °*praviṣṭam* (14, 10; 21, 12. 21. 22), the MSS have °*viśce*, °*viṭṭhe*, °*viśṭe*, °*viṣṭaṁ*, °*viṣṭa*, °*viṭṭha*, °*viśṭaṁ*, °*viṭṭhā*, °*viśṭā*, °*viṣṭā*, etc.; *laśṭia* = *rāṣṭrika* (121, 12; 125, 21; 130, 13; 138, 14), the MSS have *laṭṭhia, laṭṭia, laṣṭhia, laṣṭia, śavĕṭṭhaṇaṁ* (11, 22), but *śavĕśṭaṇeṇa* (127, 12) = *saveṣṭanam*, °*nena*; the MSS point to °*veḍha*° (see STENZLER p. 242, 301; GOḌABOLE p. 32. 35 and § 304), and so GOḌABOLE 32, 9 rightly reads *śaveḍhaṇaṁ* etc.; Prab : *miṭṭhaṁ* = *miṣṭam* (46, 17); *paṇaṭṭhassa* = *praṇaṣṭasya* (50, 14); *uvadiṭṭhe* = *upadiṣṭaḥ* (51, 2); *duṭṭha* = *duṣṭa* (51, 10); *diṭṭhānde* (sic; 51, 10; Bomb. *diṭṭhaṁdo*, M. *diṭṭhande*, P. *diṭhṭhande*); so also ed. Bombay M., whilst P, except 50, 14, has always °*ṭhṭha*°. BROCKHAUS does not give any v.l. Veṇīs. : *paṇaṭṭha* = *praṇaṣṭa* (35, 2. 7) without v.l.; Mudrār. : *pavĕṭṭhuṁ* = *praveṣṭum* (185, 6), printed *pavĕṭhṭhuṁ* for which the best MSS and the ed. Calc. 156, 8 have *pavisiduṁ* (read °*śi*°) etc. — *ṣṭha* Mṛcch. : *kośṭake* = *kŏṣṭhaka* (113, 15), the MSS have *koghaṭake* (?), *koṣṭake, kŏṭṭhake, kośake, koṣṭhake*, while in Veṇīs. 33, 6 *gŏṭṭhāgāle*, in the ed. Calc. p. 69, 1 *kŏṭhṭhāgāle* stands and the MSS have mostly *kŏṭṭhāgāle*, none of them has °*śṭa*, in the face of Hc.'s *kŏṣṭāgālaṁ*, probably taken from here and Namisādhu's *kŏśṭhāgālaṁ*; *piśṭi, puśṭi* = *pṛṣṭha* (79, 9; 165, 9), the MSS *piṭṭhi, puṭṭhi*, and so Veṇīs. 35, 5. 10 *piṭṭhado*, '*ṇupiṭṭhaṁ* = *pṛṣṭhato*, '*nupṛṣṭham*, where *pisṭado aṇupisṭam* should be read; *śuśṭu* = *suṣṭhu* (36, 11; 112, 9; 115, 16; 164, 25), the MSS *suṭṭhu, śuṣṭu*, in the face of Hc.'s *śuṣṭu*; for *śŏṭṭhakaṁ* (20, 21) we should read *śŏsṭukam* = **suṣṭhukam*; the MSS have *śoṇukkaṁ, śoṇukaṁ, śŏṭṭhikaṁ, śŏṭṭhakaṁ, śostakaṁ*, the ed. Calc. has *sŏṭṭhikaṁ*, which it explains as = *svastikam*; *śeśṭi* = *śreṣṭhi-* (38, 1), the MSS have °*ṭṭha*°, as is printed in Mudrār. 257, 5 (the ed. Calc. 212, 10 °*ṭṭi*°) etc. *ṣṭha* is retained according to Vr. 11, 14; Hc. 4, 298 in Mg. *ciṣṭhadi* = *tiṣṭhati*. STENZLER in Mṛcch. writes throughout *ciśṭadi* (pro ex. 9, 22. 24; 10, 2. 12; 79, 16; 96, 3; 97, 2 etc.), the MSS mostly have *ciṣṭha, ciṣṭa, ciṭṭha*, only quite rarely *ciśṭa*; Prab. 32, 11; in Mudrār. 185, 8; 267, 2 occurs °*ṭṭha*°, °*ṭṭa*°, °*ṭhṭha*° in the different editions. In Kī. 5, 95 the printed edition has *ciṭṭa*, LASSEN Inst. p. 393 *chiṭṭha*, P. also has the similar-form according to Kī. In Siṁhadevagaṇin on Vāgbhaṭālaṁkāra 2, 2 *ciṭṭha* is published. — In P., according to Hc. 4, 313, the dental may enter into the ending *°*ṣṭvāna* of the absol. : *ṇatthūna* beside *ṇaṭṭhūna* = **naṣṭvāna*, *tatthūna* beside *taṭṭhūna* = **dṛṣṭvāna*. On P. *kasaṭa* = *kaṣṭa* see § 132. M. *vuttha* with its compounds, as *uvvuttha, paüttha, paḍiuttha, parivuttha*; JM. *pavuttha* (§ 564) is not = **uṣṭa* (BÜHLER, Pāiyal. s.v. *vuttho*), which would have given **vuṭṭha* or **uṭṭha*, but = **vasta* with a secondary transition of *a* into *u* according to § 104. Like M. *vasia* and its compounds, such as *uvvasia, pavasia*, Ś. *uvavasida* = **vasita* (§564), so is also *vuttha* = **vasta*, formed from the present stem, beside the regular M. *usia* = *uṣita* (G.). Cf. § 337. *ālĕddhuaṁ* (Hc. 1, 24; 2, 164), *ālĕddhuṁ* (Hc. 2, 164), *āliddha* (Hc. 2, 49;

Pāiyal. 85; Deśīn. 1, 66), M. *āliddhaa* (Vikr. 51, 6) are not to be derived with Hc. from *śliṣ*, but they belong to *ālihaī* (touches; Hc. 4, 182; cf. BÜHLER, Pāiyal. s. v. *āliddhaṁ*), which = *āleḍhi* from *lih* of the 6th class with *ā*, and is = **ālihati*, and, they are = **ālegdhukam*, **ālegdhum*, **āligdha*, **āligdhaka*, *h* here is to be treated according to the analogy of roots in an old *gh*. So correctly already BOLLENSEN, Vikr. p. 364.

§ 304. In *iṣṭā* (Hc. 2, 34), *uṣṭra* (Hc. 2, 34; Mk. fol. 21) and *saṁdaṣṭa* (Hc. 2, 34) the aspiration does not take place : M. AMg. JM. *iṭṭā* = *iṣṭā* (G.; Ṭhāṇ. 478; Antag 29; T. 7, 9. 15 [so it should be read; cf. c.l. to 7, 15]), AMg. JM. *iṭṭagā* = *iṣṭakā* (Antag. 28; Paṇhāv. 128 [°*kā*]; Āv. 16, 10. 13; 19, 4), AMg. *iṭṭayagiṇi* = *iṣṭakāgni* (Jīv. 293). — AMg. *uṭṭa* = *uṣṭra* (Sūyag. 253. 724 f.; 727; Vivāgas. 163; Jīv. 356; Paṇhāv. 304; Paṇṇav. 366. 367; Uvās.; Ovav.), *uṭṭiya* = *auṣṭrika* (Uvās.), *uṭṭiyā* = *uṣṭrikā* (Uvās.; Ovav.). According to Mk. fol. 21 there occurs also *uṭṭha*. — M. *saṁdaṭṭa* = *saṁdaṣṭa* (Deśīn. 8, 18; G.R. s. v. *daṁś*, *daś*). — *daṁṣṭrā* becomes M. AMg. Ś. *dāḍhā*, CP. *tāṭhā*; *daṁṣṭrin*, AMg. Ś. *dāḍhi-* (§ 76). — *veṣṭate*, with its long vowel retained according to § 87, forms *veḍhaī* = Pāli *veṭhati* (Vr. 8, 40; Hc. 4, 221; Kī. 4, 67). So M. *veḍhia*, *āveḍhia* (H.); AMg. *veḍhemi* (Uvās § 108), *veḍhei* (Nāyādh. 621; Uvās. 110; Nirayāv. § 11; Vivāhap. 447), *veḍhĕnti* (Paṇhāv. 112), *uvvaḍhĕjja vā nivveḍhĕjja vā* (Āyār. 2, 3, 2, 2), *veḍhittā* (Rāyap. 266), *veḍhāvei* (Vivāgas. 170), *āveḍhiya*, *pariveḍhiya* (Ṭhāṇ. 568; Nāyādh. 1265; Paṇṇav. 436; Vivāhap. 706 f. 1323); JM. *veḍhĕttā*, *veḍhiya*, *veḍhiuṁ*, *veḍheuṁ* (Kk.), *pariveḍhiya* (Ṛṣabhap. 20), *veḍhiyaya* (Pāiyal. 199), *veḍhāviya*, *pariveḍhāviya* (T. 7, 15. 17); Ś. *veḍhida* (Mṛcch. 44, 4; 79, 20 [to be so read; see v.l.]; M. AMg. Ś. *veḍha* = *veṣṭa* (G.H.R.; Aṇuog. 557; Jīv. 862; Nāyādh. 1323. 1370; Rāyap. 266; Bālar. 168. 6; 267, 1); M *veḍhaṇa* = *veṣṭana* (H.R.), Mg. *śaveḍhaṇa* (Mṛcch. 11, 22; 127, 12; so it should be read; see § 303). AMg. *veḍhima* (Āyār. 2, 12, 1; 2, 15, 20; Aṇuog. 29; Paṇhāv. 490. 519; Ṭhāṇ. 339; Nāyādh. 269; Vivāhap. 823; Jīv. 348. 605; Rāyap. 186; Nandīs. 507; Dasav. N. 651, 10; Ovav.); M. AMg. *āveḍha* (R.; Paṇhāv. 185); M. *āveḍhaṇa* (G.). Likewise formed are : AMg. *koḍha* from *kŏṭṭha* = **kuṭṭha* = *kuṣṭha*, *koḍhi-* from and beside *kŏṭṭhi-*, *kuṭṭhi*, *koḍhiya* = *kuṣṭika* (§ 66); AMg. *seḍhi* from **sĕṭṭhi*, **siṭṭhi* = *śliṣṭi*, *seḍhiya*, *aṇuseḍhi*, *paseḍhi*, *viseḍhi* (§66); AMg. JŚ. *loḍha* = *loṣṭa* (Dasav. 620, 14; Pav. 389, 10), beside Ś. *lŏṭṭhaka* (Mṛcch. 79, 21), Mg. *lŏsṭaguḍiā* (Mṛcch. 80, 5). Beside the regular AMg. *lĕṭṭhu* = *leṣṭu* (Paṇhāv. 502; Ovav.; Kappas.), JM. *lĕṭṭhuya* = *leṣṭuka* (Erz.); Ś. *lĕṭṭhuā* = *leṣṭukā* (Mṛcch. 78, 12) stands *leḍhukka* (Deśīn. 7, 24; Pāiyal. 153) with reduplication of *k* according to § 194; further with dropping of the aspiration, stand *leḍu* (Pāiyal. 153), *leḍua* (Deśīn. 7, 24; Pāiyal. 153), *leḍukka* (Deśīn. 7, 29) = Pāli *lĕḍḍu*, and AMg. *leḷu* written *lelu* (§ 226; Āyār. 1, 8, 3, 10; 2, 1. 3, 4. 5, 2; 2, 10, 8; Sūyag. 647. 692; Dasav. 616. 14; 630, 17), going back to *leḍu*. Instead of *ḍha* there occurs *ḷha* (written *lha*) in *kŏḷhua* = **kroṣṭuka*, *kulha* = *kroṣṭṛ*, *kŏḷhāhala* = **kroṣṭāphala* (§ 242). The same phonetic change, without lengthening of the vowels, has taken place in M. *maraḍhī* = *māhārāṣṭri*; AMg. *aḍha* = *aṣṭa*, *ūsaḍha* = *utsṛṣṭa*, *ṇisaḍha* = *nisṛṣṭa*; M. *visaḍha* = *visṛṣṭa*; AMg. JM. *samosaḍha* = *samavasṛṣṭa* (§ 67). Cf. § 564.

§ 305. *ṣpa* and *ṣpha* become *ppha* (Vr. 85. 51; Hc. 2, 53. 90; Kī. 2, 100. 49; Mk. fol. 25, 19); PG. *pupha* i.e. *puppha*=*puṣpa* (6, 34), M. AMg. JM. Ś. *puppha* (H.R.; Āẏār. 2, 3, 3, 9; Uttar 981; Kappas.; Erz.; Hāsy. 31, 21), Ś. *pupphaka*=*puṣpaka*(Mṛcch. 68, 9); Ś.A. *pupphakaraṇḍaa*= *puṣpakaraṇḍaka* (Mṛcch. 93, 9; 107, 2; 100, 24); A. *pupphavaī*=*puṣpavati* (Hc. 4, 438, 3); *sappha*=*śaṣpa* (Bh. 3, 35; Hc. 2, 53). *bāṣpa* in the sense of "tears", according to § 87. 188, becomes *bāha* through **bāpha*, in the sense of "steam", however, it becomes *bappha* (Vr. 3, 38; Hc. 2, 70; Mk. fol. 25). So M. JM. Ś.A. *bāha* (tears : G.H.R.; Acyutaś. 60; Vikr. 51, 8; 53, 6; 54, 10; Karp. 43, 12; 44, 6; Bālar. 156, 16; Erz. 8, 9 [*vāha*]; Dvār. 507, 16; Sagara. 8, 14; Ṛṣabhap. 12; Mṛcch. 325, 15; Śak. 8 2, 11; Mālatīm. 89, 7; Uttarar. 78, 5; Ratn. 298, 26; Bālar. 281, 3; Karp. 83, 2; Mallikām. 161, 11; 196, 18 [*vā°*]; Cait. 38, 10 [*vā°*]; Hc. 4, 395, 2; Vikr. 59, 6; 60, 17; 61, 5; 69, 21); Ś. *bappha* (steam; Jīvān. 43, 10). Instead of *bappha* Mk. fol. 25 has *bappa*, as in Pāli, and as taught by him in the section on Ś. fol. 68, that in Ś. in the meaning "tears" *bappa* too may be used. Whether *bappa* is not merely an error of MSS for *bappa*, cannot be said with certainty. In Veṇīs. 62, 13; 63, 17; 76, 4, *bappha* is printed; the ed. Calc. has *bāppa*, *bāṣpa*; in Mudrār. 260, 4, there stands in the text *vāha*; but the best MSS have *bāpā*, P. *bāppha*, the ed. Calc. Saṁvat 1926 p. 214, 6 has *bāppa*; at Rukmiṇīp. 30, 1, stands *bappha*, likewise in Mallikām. 85, 14; 124, 22 [*vā°*]. The vv. ll. *vaspa*, *vāspa*, *vāppa*, *vāppha* in Śak. 140; 13 also point to *bappa* or *bappha*; and in Priẏad. 42, 4 stands *bappha* in the ed. Calc. 47, 1 *vappa*; in Cait. 44, 8 stands *vāspa*; in Śak. 82, 11 Z has *bāppha*. Consequently for Ś. *bappha* too, perhaps also *bappa*, beside *bāha* in the meaning "tears" will be correct. In Pāiẏal. 112 *bappha* and *bāha* are given in the meaning "tears". — The compounds oscillate between *ppa* and *ppha*, yet *ppa* preponderates : AMg. JM. *caüppaẏa*, AMg. *caüpaẏa*, A. *caüpaa*= *catuṣpada* (§ 439); Ś. *caduppadha*=*catuṣpatha* (Mṛcch. 25, 14; text *caüppaha*); AMg. *duppadhaṁsaga*=*duṣpradharṣaka* (Uttar. 286); M. *duppariia*=*duṣparicita* (R.); M. JM. *duppĕccha*, Ś. *duppĕkkha*=*duṣprekṣya* (R.; Erz.; Lalitav. 555, 11; Prab. 45, 11); M. *ṇippacchima*, *ṇippatta*, *ṇippivāsa*=*niṣpaścima*, *niṣpattra*, *niṣpipāsa* (H.), *ṇippakkha*=*niṣpakṣa* (G.), *ṇippaampa*, *ṇippasara*, *ṇippaha* =*niṣprakampa*, *niṣprasara*, *niṣprabha* (R.); AMg. *nippaṅka*=*niṣpaṅka* (Paṇṇav. 118; Ovav.). Beside M. *ṇippaṇṇa*=*niṣpanna* (H.), one says more usually[1] M. *ṇipphaṇṇa*, JM. AMg. *nipphanna* (R.; Erz.; Kk.; Ṭhāṇ. 525; Dasav. N. 653, 20; 657, 5; Nāẏādh.; Kappas.); *nipphesa*=*niṣpeṣa* (Hc. 2, 53); AMg. *nippāva* =*niṣpāva* (Ṭhāṇ. 398), but more frequently *nipphāva* (Bh. 3, 35; Hc. 2, 53; Sūẏag. 747, Paṇṇav. 34; JM. *nipphāiẏa*=*ṇiṣpādita* (Erz.). One always says M. Ś. *ṇipphanda*, AMg. *nipphanda*, which should be equated as=*niḥspanda* (H. R.; Antag. 48; Nāẏādh. 1383; Uvās.; Kappas.; Mahāv. 14, 20; Mallikām. 85, 14; 87, 9; 124, 6; 154, 21; 221, 12; Cait. 43, 4). — *ṣph*=*ppha* : M. *ṇipphura*=*niṣphura* (G.), M. Ś. *ṇipphala*, JM. *nipphala*= *niṣphala* (H.R.; Dvār. 501, 30; Ṛṣabhap. 14; Lalitav. 555, 8; Mṛcch. 120, 7; Mudrār. 266, 2; Caṇḍak. 8, 11; Mallikām. 181, 17; 224, 5). — In Mg. *ṣpa* becomes *spa* and *ṣpha* becomes *spha* (Hc. 4, 289); *śaspakavala*=*śaṣpa*-

kabala, *ṇisphala* = *niṣphala*. According to Namisādhu on Rudraṭa, Kāvyālaṁkāra 2, 12 *śpa* and *śpha* should be written. In Mṛcch. stands *puppha-kalaṇḍa* = *puṣpakaraṇḍa* (113, 20), *pupphakalaṇḍaa* (96, 18; 99, 4; 100, 21; 158, 22), *pupphakalaṇḍaka* (129, 5; 132, 2; 133. 2; 140, 8. 14; 146, 16; 162, 18; 173, 11). The MSS have partly *puṣpa*, *puṣpha*. At 116, 7, stands *duppĕkkhe* = *duṣprekṣyaḥ*; the v.l. is *duppĕcche*. One should read *puspa*° and *duspĕske*.

1. So correctly S. GOLDSCHMIDT, Rāvaṇavaho zu Übersetzung 4, 32; false PISCHEL, GGA. 180 p. 329.

§ 306. *ska* and *skha* become *kkha* (Vr. 3, 29. 51; C. 3, 3; Hc. 2, 4. 90; Kī. 2, 88. 49; Mk. fol. 24. 19): M. AMg. JM. *khandha* = *skandha* (G.H.R.; Āẏār. 2, 1, 7, 1. 8, 11; Uvās.; Nāẏādh.; Nīrayāv.; Ovav.; Kappas.; Erz.); PG. *khaṁdakŏṁḍisa* = *skandakuṇḍinaḥ* (6, 19); M. AMg. JM. Ś. A. *khambha* = *skambha* (G. R.; Acyutaś. 42, 51; Sūẏag. 961; Jīv. 448. 481; Paṇhāv. 279; Samav. 101; Vivāhap. 658. 660. 823; Rāẏap. 58. 144; Nāẏādh. § 21. 122; p. 1054; Ovav.; Erz.; Mṛcch. 40, 22; 68, 18; Viddhaś. 60, 2; Dhūrtas. 6, 5; Hc. 4, 399). The grammarians (Vr. 3, 14; Bh. 3, 50; C. 3, 10. 19; Hc. 1, 187; 2, 8. 89; Kī. 2, 77; Mk. fol. 21) derive *khambha* from *stambha*, since they depend upon classical Skt. It is naturally = Vedic *skambha*, *avakkhanda* = *avaskanda* (Hc. 2, 4); AMg. *amaṇakkha*, *samaṇakkha* = *amanaska*, *samanaska* (Sūẏag. 842); *makkhara* = *maskara* (Kī. 2, 88). In *skanda*, according to Hc. 2, 5; Mk. fol. 24 aspiration may not take place; *khanda* and *kanda*. As a rule it does not occur in compounds (§ 301) : *ĕkkāra* = *ayaskāra* (Hc. 1, 166); AMg. JM. *namŏkkāra* = *namaskāra* (Hc. 2, 4; Āẏār. 2, 15. 22; Erz.; Kk.), beside *ṇamoẏāra*, *ṇavaẏāra* (C. 34 p. 51) and M. *ṇamakkāra* (G.); cf. § 195; AMg. JM. *takkara* = *taskara* (Paṇhāv. 120; Nāẏādh. 1417; Uttar. 289; Uvās.; Ovav.; Erz.), AMg. *tukkarattaṇa* (Paṇhāv. 147); Ś. *tirakkāra* = *tiraskāra* (Prab. 15, 1); Ś. *tirakkariṇi* = *tiraskariṇi* (Śak. 119, 3). So reads also the Kashmir recension 112, 14, whilst the Devanāgarī recension 77, 9, ed. BÖHTLINGK and the South Indian recension 256, 17 read *tirakkhariṇi*, as also BOLLENSEN, Vikr. 24, 4; 42, 19 against his best MSS, which have °*kka*°; the ed. Bomb. 1888 has at 41, 6; 72. 1 rightly °*kka*°; the South Indian MSS of Śak. and Vikr. swing between °*kkha*° and °*kka*°. M. *sakkaa*, AMg. JM. *sakkaẏa*, Ś. *sakkada* = *saṁskṛta*, AMg. JM. *asakkaẏa* = *asaṁskṛta*, M. *sakkāra* = *saṁskāra*, JM. *sakkāriẏa* = *saṁskārita* (§ 76), AMg. *purakkaḍa* = *puraskṛta* (Sūẏag. 692), *purekaḍa* (Sūẏag. 284. 540; Dasav. 627, 7; 633. 17; Ovav.), beside AMg. *saṁkhaẏa* (§ 49), *saṁkhaḍi* = *saṁskṛti* (Kappas.), *uvakkhaḍa* = *upaskṛta* (Uttar. 355), *purĕkkhaḍa* (Paṇṇav. 796 ff.). Cf. § 49. 219. To it belongs also *ṇikkha* (thief; Deśīn. 4, 47) = **ṇiṣkṛ*. AMg. *nakka* (nose; Deśīn. 4, 46; Āẏār. 2, 3, 2, 5; Sūẏag. 280. 748) is = **nāska* from Vedic *nās* with a change of gender; in addition *nakkasirā* (nostril; Pāiẏal. 114). — *skha* = *kkha* : M. JM. *khalaï*, Ś. *khaladi* = *skhalati* (R.; Dvār. 504, 34; Śak. 131, 6), Ḍh. *khalantaā* (Mṛcch. 30, 8); M. *khalia*, JM. *khaliẏa*, Ś. *khalida* = *skhalita* (G.H.R.; Erz., Vikr.; 35, 9); M. Ś. *parikkhalanta* (H. R.; Mṛcch. 72, 3), M. *parikkhalia* (G. R.). In Mg. *ška* and *škha* are retained according to Hc. 4, 289;

maskali- = *maskarın*; *paskhaladi* = *praskhalati*. According to Namisâdhu on Rudraṭa, Kāvyālaṁkāra *s* becomes *ś*. The texts have *kkha* : *khalanti* (Mṛcch. 10, 15). *pakhhalanti* (Mṛcch. 9, 23; 10, 15), *khandheṇa* (Mṛcch. 22, 8), without any v. l. *hatthikkhandhaṁ* (Śak. 117, 4), where R. has °*skandhaṁ*. One should read *skhalanti*, *paskhalanti*, *skandheṇa*, *hastiskandhaṁ*. So in all the cases.

§ 307. *sta* and *stha* become *ttha* (Vr. 3, 12. 51; Hc. 2, 45. 90; Kī. 2, 85. 49; Mk. fol. 21. 19); M. *thaṇa* = *stana* (G.H.R.); *thui* = *stuti* (G.R.), *thoa* = *stoka* (G.H.R.), *attha* = *asta* (G.R.) and = *astra* (R.), *atthi* = *asti* (§ 498), *patthara* = *prastara* (H.), *hattha* = *hasta* (G.H.R.); PG. *vatthavāṇa* = *vāstavyānām* (6, 8), *sahattha* = *svahasta* (7, 51) *vitthaaṁ* = *vistṛtam* RV. Likewise in other dialects. In compounds aspiration does not take place as a rule : **AMg. JM.** *duttara* = *dustara* (Āẏār. 2, 16, 10; Sūẏag. 213; Erz.), M. *duttāra* = *dustāra*, *duttārattaṇa* = **dustāratvana* (R.), AMg. *suduttāra* (Ovav.); AMg. *nittusa* = *nistuṣa* (Paṇhāv. 435). So also M. AMg. *samatta* = *samasta* (Hc. 2, 45; R.; Nāẏādh.; Ovav.; Kappas.), beside M. JM. Ś. *samattha* (R.; Erz.; Kk.; Mahāv. 27, 6; 28, 1; where, however, the ed. Bomb. 59, 4; 62, 1 has *samatta*). *uraaḍa*, which Kī. 2, 110 equates as = *urastaṭa*, is explained, as already admitted by LASSEN[1], from the stem *ura-* (§ 407). Beside *theṇa* = *stena* (thief; Hc. 1, 147; Deśīn. 5, 29; Pāiẏal. 72), *theṇilla* (taken; fearful; Deśīn. 5, 32), *thūṇa* (§ 129), AMg. and JM. exclusively have *teṇa* (Āẏār. 2, 2, 2, 4; 2, 3, 1, 9. 10; 2, 4, 1, 8; Paṇhāv. 412 f.; Samav. 85; Uttar. 228. 990; Dasav. 623, 36. 40; 624, 10; 627, 34; Uvās.; Āv. 44, 7); AMg. *ateṇa* = *astena* (Āẏār. 2, 2, 2, 4), *teṇa* (Ovav.), *teṇiẏa* (Jīẏak. 87; Kappas.) = *stainya*. *theṇa* is related to *teṇa*, as *stāyu* is to *tāyu*. *tena* (theft) has gone over also to Jaina-Skt.[2] According to Hc. 2, 46; Mk. fol. 21 *tava* also may be used beside *thava* = *stava*; according to Vr. 3, 13; Hc. 2, 45; Mk. fol. 21 *stamba* becomes *tamba*. — *stha* = *ttha* : M. *thaüḍa* = *sthapuṭa* (G.), *thala* = *sthala* (G. H.), *thira* = *sthira* (G. H.), *avatthā* = *avasthā* (H. R.); Ś. *kāatthaa* = *kāyasthaka* (Mṛcch. 78, 13).

1. Inst. § 82 p. 273. — 2. E. MÜLLER, Beiträge p. 47.

§ 308. Instead of the dental *ttha*, sometimes the cerebral *ṭṭha* too occurs for *sta* and *stha*. Sometimes both of them stand beside one another, even in various forms and derivatives of the same roots and in the same dialect; it is not possible to frame a rule, as regards when one or the other sound should stand. M. AMg. JM. Ś. *aṭṭhi* = *asthi* (Vr. 3, 11; Hc. 2, 32; Kī. 2, 69; Mk. fol. 21; G. H.; Aṇuttar. 11, 12; Āẏār. 1, 1, 6, 5; 2, 1, 1, 2. 3, 4; Sūẏag. 594; Vivāgas 90; Vivāhap. 89. 112. 168. 183. 280. 926; Ṭhāṇ. 54 f. 186. 431; Uvās.; Ovav.; Kappas.; Erz.; Caṇḍak. 87, 9); M. *aṭṭhia*, AMg. *aṭṭhiẏa* = *asthika* (H.; Āẏār. 2, 1, 10, 6), Ś. *aṭṭhia* = *asthija* (Mṛcch. 69, 12; so should be read; cf. v. l.); AMg. *bahuaṭṭhiẏa* (Āẏār. 2, 1, 10, 5. 6). — *stambha* forms *thambha* and *ṭhaṁbha*, when it means "immovability", "stiffness' (Hc. 2, 9). Mk. fol. 21 has *thambha* only, and so M. (R.), JM. *gaïthambha* = *gatistambha* (Erz. 82, 21), *muhathambha* = *mukhastambha* (Erz. 82, 22), Ś. *ūrutthambha* (Śak. 27, 1; Priyad. 17, 12). In the meaning "pole", "post" one says only *thambha* in M. AMg. Ś. (C. 3, 11;

Hc. 2, 1; R.; Vivāhap. 1327; Mālav. 63, 1; Viddhaś. 74, 7). Beside *thambhijjaï* = *stabhyate*, Hc. 2, 9 teaches also *ṭhambhijjaï*. Frequently there occurs in the text the dental *tha*, as M. *thambhia*, AMg. JM. *thambhiya* (G.; Nāyādh.; Ovav.; Kappas.; Erz.; Kk.), M. *uttambhijjaï*, *uttambhijjanti* (R. G.); M. *uttambhia* (H.R.), Ś. *uttambhida* (Priyad. 4, 7); cerebral *ṭha* occurs in A. *uṭṭhabbhaï* (Hc. 3, 365; 3)[1]. On *khambha*, see § 306. — Beside *thera* there occurs more frequently *ṭhera* = *sthavira* (§ 166). — Beside AMg. *tattha* = *trasta* (Uvās.), M. *uttattha* (H.), *saṃtattha* (G.), there occurs, according to Hc. 2, 136. also *taṭṭha*. The grammarians (Vr. 8, 62; Appendix A 37; Hc. 2, 136; Deśīn. 8, 67; Pāiyal. 260; Triv. 3, 1, 132) derive M. *hittha* (H. R.) and *āhittha* (R.) as well from *trasta*. S. GOLDSCHMIDT[2] derives; *hittha* from *bhiṣ*, WEBER[3] derives it from *dhvasta* or *adhastāt*, which in M. AMg. JM. forms *hĕṭṭha*, *hiṭṭha* (§ 107) and HOEFER[4] thought of aspiration of the initial of *trasta*. Dialectically there occur also *hittha* (noun — shame; Pāiyal. 167), *hitthā* (shame; Deśīn. 8, 67), *hittha* (ashamed; fearful; Gopāla in Deśīn. 8, 67; cf. Deśīkośa on H. 386), *āhittha* (angry, confused; Deśīn. 1, 76; Pāiyal. 171), and with cerebralization *hiṭṭha*, *hiṭṭhahiḍa* (confused; Deśīn. 8, 67). The interchange of *ttha* and *ṭṭha* points to *sta*, and hence I consider the derivation from *adhastāt* as correct. — Ś. *pallattha*, beside the dialectical *pallaṭṭa*, *pallaṭṭaï* (§ 285) = *paryasta*; *pallaṭṭa* has lost its aspiration, as *samatta* beside *samattha* = *samasta* (§307). M. Ś. A *visamṭhula* = *visaṁsthula*, written in Skt. as *visaṁṣṭhula* as well (Hc. 2, 32; Mk. fol. 21; Pāiyal. 264; G.H.R.; Mṛcch. 41, 10 v.l.; 117, 19; Vikr. 60, 18; Prab. 39, 8; Mallikām. 13, 3; Hc. 4, 436).

1. PISCHEL, BB. 15, 122. — 2. Rāvaṇavaho s. v. *bhiṣ*. — 3. On Hāla 386. — 4. ZWS. 2, 518.

§ 309. The wavering between *ṭṭha* and *ttha* is especially seen in the root *sthā* and its derivatives, without one being able, with OSTHOFF[1], to explain *ṭha* by false analogy. One says: PG. *aṇuvaṭṭhāveti* = *anuprasthāpayati* (7, 45; cf. 184. 189); M. JM. *ṭhāi* = **sthāti*, M. *ṇiṭṭhāi*, *saṁṭhāi*, JM. *ṭhāha*, AMg. *abbhuṭṭhanti*; JM. *ṭhāyanti*, but A. *thanti*; A. *uṭṭhaī*, JM. *uṭṭhaha*, AMg. JM. *uṭṭhei*, JM. Ś. *uṭṭhehi*, but Ś. also *utthehi*, *utthedu*, (§ 483); M. *ṭhia*, AMg. JM. *ṭhiya*, Ś. *ṭhida* = *sthita* (G.H.R.; Āyār. 1, 6, 5, 5; Nāyādh.; Kappas.; Erz.; Kk.; Vikr. 42, 18; 52, 2), but also *thia*, Ś. *thida* (Hc. 4, 16; Vikr. 83, 20); Mg. AMg. JM. *ṭhavei*, A. *ṭhavehu*, AMg. *ṭhāvei*, JM. *ṭhāvemi*, A. *paṭhāviaī*, Ś. *paṭṭhāvia*, beside Ś. *samavatthāvemi*, *pajjavatthāvehi* (§ 551), M. *uṭṭhia*, AMg. JM. *uṭṭhiya* (Hc. 4, 16; R.; Aṇuog. 60; Vivāhap. 169; Āyār. 1. 5, 2, 2; Nāyādh.; Kappas.; Erz.), but also *utthia*, Ś. *utthida* (Hc. 4, 16; Vikr. 75, 15; v. l. °*ṭṭhi*°); *paṭṭhia* = *prasthita* (Hc. 4, 16), but M. *patthia* (H. R.), Ś. *patthida* (Śak. 136, 16; Vikr. 16, 2; 22, 17; Mālatīm. 102, 8; 104, 2, 3; 124, 6; Mudrār. 228. 5; 261, 3; Prab. 17, 9; Priyad. 8, 16; AMg. JM. *uvaṭṭhiya* = *upasthita* (Bhag.; Erz.; Kk.), but also Ś. *uvatthida* (Śak. 13, 7, 9; Vikr. 6, 19; 10, 2; 43, 3); M. AMg. JM. Ś. A. *ṭhāṇa* = *sthāna* (Hc. 4, 16; Pāiyal. 261; G.H.R.; Āyār. 1, 2, 3, 6; 2, 2, 1, 1 ff.; Sūyag. 688; Uttar. 37,5; Vivāhap. 1310; Uvās. ; Nāyādh.; Ovav.; Kappas.; Erz.; Kk.; Ṛṣabhap. 29; Pav. 383. 44; Mṛcch. 70, 25; 141, 2; Śak. 123, 7; 154, 8;

Vikr. 23, 15; 44, 7 etc.; Hc. 4, 362), but also M. *thāṇa* (Hc. 4, 16; R.); AMg. *ṭhāṇijja* (respectable; Deśīn. 4, 5; Nirayāv. § 10), beside *thāṇijja* (Deśīn. 4, 5) = *sthānīya*; M. AMg. JM. *ṭhii*, Ś. *ṭhidi* = *sthiti* (H.R.; Uvās.; Ovav.; Nirayāv.; Nāyādh.; Kappas.; Erz.), but also M. *ṭhii*, Ś. *thidi* (R.; Vikr. 28, 19; 72, 16; in Śak. 107, 12), and so many others. At the end of compounds °*stha* always becomes °*ttha*; M. *kamalattha, karattha* (H.), *dūrattha* (R.); AMg. *āgārattha* (Āyār. 1, 8, 1, 6), *gāratthiya* (Āyār. 2, 1, 1, 7); JM. *āsanattha, jŏvvaṇattha, sahāvattha, hiyayattha* (Erz.), Ś. *ekattha* (Mṛcch. 73, 3; Śak. 26, 14), *vaattha* = *vayaḥstha* (Śak. 141, 9), *païdittha* = *prakṛtistha* (Śak. 160, 13); M. AMg. JM. JŚ. Ś. *majjhattha* = *madhyastha* (§ 214). Corresponding to Skt. °*ttha*, *aśvattha* becomes AMg. *aṁsŏttha, assŏttha, āsŏttha, āsattha* (§ 74); *kapittha* becomes AMg. Mg. *kavittha* (Āyār. 2, 1, 8, 1. 6; Mṛcch. 21, 22), but mostly AMg. *kaviṭṭha* (Nirayāv. 45; Paṇṇav. 31. 482; Jīv. 46; Dasav. 623, 8; Uttar. 983 f.). — *sthāṇu*, according to Vr. 3, 15; Hc. 2, 7; Kī. 2, 78; Mk. fol. 21, becomes **thāṇu* in the meaning "Śiva", but in the meanings "stump", "flock" it becomes *khāṇu*. So M. *thāṇu* "Śiva" (Pāiyal. 21; G.); AMg. *khāṇu* "stump", "flock" (Paṇhāv. 509; Nāyādh. 335; Uttar. 439), but JM. also *thāṇu* "stump of a tree", "flock" (Pāiyal. 259; Dvār. 504, 9), *khāṇu*, beside which *khaṇṇu* also is said (Hc. 2, 99; Mk. fol. 21. 27) ; this goes back to a side-form '**skhāṇu*'. *thāṇu* is related to *khāṇu* as *stubh* to *kṣubh*, *stambh* to *skambh*, Pkt. *duttha* to *dukkha* (§ 90. 120. 306. 311). — *sthag* has in M. a dental in the beginning : *thaei* (R.), *thaesu, thaïssaṁ, thaïuṁ* (H.), *thaïa* (H. R.), *utthaïa, samutthaïuṁ* (H.), *ŏtthaïa, samŏtthaïa* (R.), in JM. a cerebral : *ṭhaïya, ṭhāiūṇa* (Āv. 30, 4). The parallel root **sthak* forms in Pāli *thaketi*, in M. JM. Ś. Mg. *ḍhakkaï*, °*di* (§ 221). Yet there occurs also JM. *thakkissaï* (T. 5, 19).

1. Jenaer Literaturzeitung 1878, p. 486.

§ 310. In Mg. *sta* is retained (Hc. 4, 289) and *stha* becomes *sta* (Hc. 4, 291; Namisādhu on Rudraṭa, Kāvyālaṁkāra. 2, 12) : *hasti-* = *hastin*; *uvastida* = *upasthita*; *śamuvastida* = *samupasthita*; *śustida* = *susthita*. According to Namisādhu *sta* becomes *śta*. The Lalitav. has : *tatthastehiṁ* = *tatrasthaiḥ* (565, 20); *uvastidāṇaṁ* = *upasthitānām*; *kaḍastalāṇaṁ* = *kaṭasthalānām*, *pāśastide* = *pārśvasthitaḥ* *ṇiastāṇādo* = *nijasthānāt* (566,3.9,12.15); *stidā* = *stitāḥ*, *astāṇastide asthānasthitāḥ* (567, 1.2). In the Mṛcch. STENZLER and GODABOLE, who here, as often elsewhere, follows STENZLER, mostly write *śta* for *sta*, but *ttha* for *stha*. Thus *haśta* = *hasta* (12, 14; 14, 1; 16, 23; 21, 12; 22, 4; 121, 25; 122, 20; 126, 24), but *hattha* (32, 18; 39, 20; 134, 1, 2, 3; 135, 1. 2; 160, 3; 171, 3) and *hatthi-* = *hastin* (40, 9; 168, 4); as also in Śak. 117, 4; Veṇīs. 34, 14 it stands. In the Mṛcch. the MSS mostly have °*ttha*°, only at 16, 25; 21, 12 one of the MSS has °*śta*°, at 21, 22 one of the MSS has also *hacche*, and once *haśce*, against this one of them has at 14, 1 *hastādo*, at 22, 4 five of the MSS have *haste*, at 126, 24 two of them have *haste*, so that °*sta*° is better attested than °*śta*°. Further pro ex. *thuṇu* = *stuhi* (113, 12; 115, 9), the MSS, however, *stuṇu, stuṇa* (or *śuṇu, suṇu* and so on = *śṛṇu*); *maśta* and *maśtaka* = *masta* and *mastaka* (12, 17; 20, 17; 21, 22; 149, 25; 151, 24) but *mattha* (161, 7) : the MSS mostly have °*sta*°, rarely °*ttha*°

and only at 161, 7 one of them has °*śta*°; A points to °*śtha*° at 12, 17; 149, 25, as STENZLER writes in *iśthiā* = *itthiā* = *strīkā* (12, 3. 5; 119, 23; 136, 13; 140, 10; 145, 3. 4; 146, 4; 164, 20), against *itthiā* (112, 6; 134, 1. 25). The MSS again have mostly °*tthi*°; only at 112, 6 B, 140, 10E and 145, 4 D they have °*śti*°; on the other hand 112, 6 H. has *isthiaṁ*, C °*stri*°, 136, 13 DE, 140, 10 D °*sti*°; to which also points °*sni*° 136, 13 of B, to °*śthi*° at the most A 119, 23; 140, 10. One should read *istiā*. In Prab. at 62, 7, there stands *itthiā* and so also in other places here and always in Veṇīs., Mudrār. in other words, and often in Mṛcch. °*ttha*° stands for °*sta*°. For *stha* stands *ttha* in Mṛcch. pro ex. in *thāvalaa*, °*laka* = *sthāvaraka* (96, 17; 116, 4; 118, 10; 119, 11; 121, 9; 122, 9 etc.) and so the MSS, except at 96, 17, where BCDF have *sthā*°; *thoaṁ* = *stokam* (157, 6); *avatthide* = *avasthitaḥ* (99, 3); *uvatthida* = *upasthita* (118, 23; 138, 13; 175, 17), and *ṭṭha*, pro ex. *paṭṭhāvia* = *prasthāpya* (21, 12); *śaṁṭhāvehi* = *saṁsthāpaya* (130, 11); *śaṁṭhida* (v.l. °*thi*°) = *saṁsthita* (159, 15); *āhalaṇaṭṭhāṇehiṁ* (v.l. °*tthā*°) = *ābharaṇasthānaiḥ* (141, 2). So also in the other dramas with a few exceptions, as °*mastie* = °*mastike*, *vastie* = **vastrike* beside °*hatthie* = °*hastike* (Caṇḍak. 68, 16; 69, 1), *astaṁ* (Caṇḍak. 70, 14), beside *samutthide* (72, 1); *pastide* = *prasthitaḥ*, *ṇivastide* = *nivastritaḥ* (Mallikām. 114, 4. 11). The vv. ll. furnish more information. We should, with Hc., everywhere write *st*.

§ 311. *spa* and *spha* become *ppha* (Vr. 3, 36. 51; Hc. 2, 53. 90; Kī. 2, 100. 49; Mk. fol. 25. 19). *spa* = *ppha*: M. Ś. *phaṁsa* = *sparśa*, Ś. *pariphaṁsa* (§ 74), M. AMg. *pharisa*, AMg. *pharisaga* (§ 135), AMg. JM. JŚ. *phāsa* (§ 62); *phandaṇa* = *spandana* (Hc. 2, 53); *paḍipphaddhi-* = *pratispardhin* (§ 77). The aspiration does not take place in AMg. *puṭṭha* = *spṛṣṭa* (Āyār. 1, 1, 4, 6, 7, 4; 1, 6, 2, 3; 1, 8, 3, 6. 4, 1; Sūyag. 65. 111. 122. 144. 170. 350; Uttar. 48. 51. 61. 106. 126; Vivāhap. 97f. 116. 145; Paṇṇav. 134; Ovav.), *apuṭṭha* (Āyār. 1, 8, 4,1; Vivāhap. 97f.), *apuṭṭhaya* (Sūyag. 104), very often immediately beside *pharisa* or *phāsa* and *phusaï* = *spṛśati* (§ 486). In Āyār. 1, 6, 5, 1 there stands *phuṭṭho*. So also *phusaï* and *pusaï* (wipes; § 486). In compounds the aspiration does not take place as a rule (§ 301): M.A. *avarŏppara* = *aparaspara* (G.; Hc. 4, 409); M. AMg. JM. Ś. *parŏppara* = *paraspara* (Hc. 1, 62; 2, 53; G.; Karp. 77, 10; 101, 1; Paṇhāv. 68; Paṇṇav. 646; Vivāhap. 1099; Āv. 7, 11; Erz.; Prab. 9, 16; Bālar. 218, 11; Mallikām. 124, 8; 158, 19; 160, 8; 223, 12), Ś. also, probably falsely, *parappara* (Mālatīm. 119, 6; 358, 1; Uttarar. 108, 1; Mallikām. 184, 20). Cf. § 195. — AMg. *dupparisa* = *duḥsparśa* (Paṇhāv. 508). — *nippiha* = *niḥspṛha* (Hc. 2, 23). From *bṛhaspati* there occurs, beside *bihapphadi* and *bahapphadi* also AMg. *bahassaï*, *bihassaï* (§ 53), and numerous other forms in grammarians (§ 212). Likewise stands in AMg. beside *vaṇapphaï* = *vanaspati* (Hc. 2, 69; Paṇhāv. 341; Paṇṇav. 35; Jīv. 213. 316; Vivāhap. 93. 144), JŚ. *vaṇapphadi* (Kattig. 401, 346), also AMg. *vaṇassaï* (Hc. 2, 69; Mk. fol. 25; Āyār. 1, 1, 5, 4; 2, 1, 7, 3. 6; 2, 2, 2, 13; Sūyag. 792. 857; Paṇhāv. 29; Jīv. 13. 316 (beside °*ppha*°). 969f.; Paṇṇav. 44. 742; Uttar. 1039. 1048; Vivāhap. 30, 430. 465f.; Ṭhāṇ. 25. 26. 52). The forms with *ssa* presuppose that *pati*, as after vowels, at the beginning of the second member of a compound, has become *vaï*, so that *ssa* is =*sva*. Cf. § 195. 407. The similar phonetic transformation occurs in *sihaï*=**spṛhati* (Hc. 4, 34. 192; Mk. fol. 25) for **svihaï*. AMg. has *pihĕjjā*=*spṛhayet* (Ṭhāṇ. 158). *chihā* is not=*spṛhā* (Hc. 1, 128; 2, 23; Mk. fol. 25), but belongs like *chihaï* (touches: Hc. 4, 182), to a root **kṣibh*, which is a parallel root to *kṣubh* (§ 66). — *spha*=*ppha* : M. AMg. Ś. *phaḷiha*=*sphaṭika* (§ 206), M. *phuḍa*=*sphuṭa* (G. H. R.); *phuliṅga*=*sphuliṅga* (G.R.); *apphodaṇa*=*āsphoṭana* (G.), *apphālia*=*āsphālita* (G.R.); *papphuraï*=*prasphurati* (G.H.). *khoḍaa* is not=*sphoṭaka* (Vr. 3, 16; Hc. 2, 6; Kī. 2, 76; Mk. fol. 21) and *kheḍaa* is not=*spheṭaka*, *kheḍia* is not=*spheṭika* (Hc. 2, 6), but the words presuppose side-forms with an initial *skha*. Cf. § 90. 120. 306. 306. According to Mk. fol. 67 in Ś. *phoḍaa* alone is permitted; thus *vipphoḍaa*=*visphoṭaka* (Śak. 30, 1). — In Mg., according to Hc. 4, 289, *spa* and *spha* are retained: *buhaspadi*=*bṛhaspati*; according to Namisādhu on Rudraṭa, Kāvyālaṁkāra 2, 12 they become *śpa*, *śpha* : *bihaśpadi*.[1] In Mṛcch. 133, 24; Śak. 115, 11 stands *phulanti*=*sphuranti*, Prab. 58, 1, *phalasa*, 58, 8 *phaṁsa*; ed. Bomb. P. have twice *phalasa*, M. more correctly *phaliśa*. We should read *sphulanti*, *spaliśa* and so in all similar cases.

1. The actual form in the printed edition is *vihaspadī*.

§ 312. If the consonant following a sibilant is a nasal, the sibilant becomes *h* (§ 262-264) and the order of sounds is reversed. Thus *śna*, *ṣṇa* and *sna*, when not separated by a separation vowel (§131 ff.), they uniformly become *ṇha*; *śma*, *ṣma*, *sma* become *mha* (Vr. 3, 32. 33; C. 3, 6; Hc. 2, 74, 75; Kī. 2, 90. 94; Mk. fol. 25. 26). — *śna*=*ṇha*: *aṇhaï*, AMg. *aṇhāi*=*aśnāti* (§ 512); AMg. JŚ. *paṇha*=*praśna* (Sūyag. 523; Kattig. 399, 311); *siṇ!.a*=*śiśna* (Bh. 3, 33; Hc. 3, 75). — *śma* becomes *mha*: *kamhāra*, Ś. *kamhīra*=*kāśmīra* (§120); *kumhāṇa*=*kuśmāna* (Hc. 2, 74). *raśmi* always becomes *rassi* (Bh. 3, 2; Hc. 1, 35; 2, 74. 78; Pāiyal. 47); AMg. Ś. *sahassarassi*=*sahasraraśmi* (Vivāhap. 169; Rāyap. 238; Nāyādh.; Ovav.; Kappas.; Ratn. 311, 8; Prab. 14, 17; Priyad. 18, 15). In the anlaut *ś* is assimilated to *m* : AMg. *maṁsu*=*śmaśru*, *nimmaṁsu*=*niḥśmaśru*, JŚ. *maṁsuga*==*śmaśruka* (§ 74), also *massu* (Bh. 3, 6; Hc. 2, 86; Kī. 2, 53) and *māsu* (Hc. 2, 86); M. Ś. *masāṇa*, Mg. *maśāṇa*=*śmaśāna*, whilst in AMg. JM. *susāṇa* *m* has been assimilated to *s* (§ 104). — *ṣṇa*=*ṇha* : M. AMg. JM. Ś. *uṇha*=*uṣṇa* (G. H. R.; Karp. 45, 5; Āyār. 1, 5, 6, 4; Uttar. 58; Kappas.; Erz.; Ṛṣabhap.; Śak. 29, 5. 6; 74, 9; Vikr. 48, 11); Ś. *aṇuṇhadā*=*anuṣṇatā* (Mālav. 30, 6), *uṇhaa*=*uṣṇaka*, *uṇhattaṇa*=**uṣṇatvana* (Hc. 4, 343, 1). AMg. *siuṇha* =*śitoṣṇa*, in AMg., however, usually *usiṇa* (§ 133). — *uṇhisa*=*uṣṇīṣa* (Hc. 2, 75); M. AMg. Ś. *kaṇha*, AMg. *kiṇha*, beside M. Ś. *kasaṇa*, AMg. JM. *kasiṇa*=*kṛṣṇa*, M. AMg. JM. Ś. *kaṇha*=*kṛṣṇa* (§52); JM. D. *viṇhu*=*viṣṇu* (§72. 119). — *ṣma*=*mha*: M. *umhā*=*ūṣman* (Grr.; G.), *umhavia*, *umhāla* (G.); M. AMg. Ś. Mg. A. *gimha*=*grīṣma* (§ 83); M. JM. Ś. *tumhārisa*=*yuṣmādṛśa* (§ 245); M. JM. Ś. A. *tumhe*=*yuṣme* (§ 422). — *mahiṣmati* becomes in Ś. *mahissadi* (Bālar. 67, 14). — *bhīṣma*, according to Hc. 2, 54, becomes *bhippha*, *śleṣman*, according to Hc. 2, 55, Mk. fol. 25, becomes *sepha-* beside *silimha* and AMg. JM. A. *simbha-*, AMg. *sĕmbha-* (§267). The forms presuppose the line of transformation **bhīṣva*, **bhīṣpa*, *śleṣman*,

**śleṣpan* (§ 251. 277). On *kohaṇḍī = kūṣmāṇḍī*, AMg. *kohaṇḍa, kūhaṇḍa, kūhaṇḍa = kūṣmāṇḍa* see § 127, on A *gimbha = grīṣma* § 267. — In the pronominal ending of the loc. sing. *-ṣmin*, which dialectically has been extended also to nouns in *-i* and *-u*, *ṣ* is assimilated to *m* : M. *uahimmi*, JM. *uẏahimmi = udadhau*; AMg. *sahassarassimmi = sahasraraśmau*; AMg. *uummi = ṛtau*; M. *pahummi = prabhau* (§ 366ᵃ. 379). In AMg *-ṣmin* mostly becomes *-ṁsi* : *kucchiṁsi = kukṣau*; *pāṇiṁsi = pāṇau*; *leluṁsi = leṣṭau* (§ 74. 379), in A. it becomes *-hĩ* from *-ssiṁ* (§ 263. 313) : *akkhihĩ = akṣṇi*; *kalihĩ = kalau* (§ 379). — *kṣṇa, kṣma* too are treated like *ṣṇa, ṣma*: M. AMg. *saṇha = ślakṣṇa* (§ 315); M. AMg. *pamha = pakṣman* (Vr. 3, 32; Hc. 2, 74; Kī. 2, 94; G.H.R.; Uvās. ; Ovav.); M. AMg. Ś. *pamhala = pakṣmala* (Hc. 2, 74; Mk. fol. 25; G.H.R.; Vivāhap. 822; Nāẏādh.; Ovav.; Kappas.; Mālatīm. 217, 4; Mallikām. 249, 10 [text *vahmala*]; Caṇḍak. 87, 8); Ś. *pamhalida* (Mahāv. 101, 17). Beside *tiṇha = tīkṣṇa* (Bh. 3, 33; C. 3, 6 p. 54; Hc. 2, 75, 82; Kī. 2. 90) the forms found in the text are M. AMg. JM. Ś. Mg. A. *tikkha* (C. 2, 3; 3, 6 p. 48; Hc. 2. 82; H.; Karp. 28, 7; 38, 11; 39, 7; 65, 2; Sūẏag. 280. 289; Uttar. 338; Dasav. 625, 36; Kappas.; Erz.; Śak. 135, 14; Prab. 4, 4 [so correctly the ed. Bomb. M. P.]; Veṇīs. 61, 14; Mahāv. 101. 16; Bālar. 289, 13; Mallikām. 82, 14; Hāsy. 32, 4; Mg. Mṛcch. 164, 15; A. Hc. 4, 395, 1); AMg. *sutikkha* (Vivāhap. 424); Ś. *tikkhattaṇa* (Viddhaś. 99, 9); A. *tikkhei* (Hc. 3, 344); *tikkhālia* (sharpened; Deśīn. 5, 13; Pāiẏal. 200) only. According to Mk. fol. 26 one says *tikkha* in a literary sense, and *tiṇha* in a secondary sense, as *tiṇho raïaro* "the sharp sun". In Karp., however, *tikkha* is used also in a secondary sense. — *lakṣmī* always becomes, also as a proper noun, M. AMg. JM. JŚ. Ś. D. A. *lacchī* (Bh. 3, 30; C. 3, 6. 36; Hc. 2, 17; Kī. 2, 82; Mk. fol. 24; Pāiẏal. 96; G.H.R.; Karp. 31, 2; 49, 2; Nāẏādh.; Ovav.; Kappas.; Erz.; Kk.; Ṛṣabhap. 12; Kattig. 399, 319. 320; 401, 344; Śak. 81, 11; Vikr. 35. 6. 11; 52, 5; Mālav. 33, 17; Prab. 4, 8; Mālatīm. 218, 2; Karp. 22, 5; 35, 3; 110, 8; Anarghar. 277, 1; Mallikām. 73, 6; D. Mṛcch. 99, 25; A. Hc. 4, 436); on the other hand, *lakṣmaṇa* always becomes M. JM. Ś. *lakkhaṇa* (C. 3, 6; Mk. fol. 24; R.; KI. 2; Uttarar. 32, 5; 127, 5; 190. 1; 204. 11; Mahāv. 52, 14; Anarghar. 115, 12; 317, 16; Unmattar. 6, 2; Pras. 88, 6).

§ 313. *sna = ṇha*, always also in the anlaut in AMg. JM. JŚ., which otherwise mostly retain *n* (§ 224) : *ṇhāi = snāti* (Hc. 4, 14); JM. *ṇhāmo = snāmaḥ* (Āv. 17, 7), *ṇhāittā* (Āv. 38, 2); *ṇhaviūṇa* (Erz.), *ṇhāvesu, ṇhāvinti* (T. 6, 5); AMg. *ṇhāṇei, ṇhāṇittā* (Jīv. 610), *ṇhāṇĕnti* (Vivāhap. 1265), *ṇhāvei* (Niraẏāv. 17), *ṇhāvĕnti* (Vivāhap. 822), *ṇhāveha* (Vivāhap. 1261); Ś. *ṇhāissaṁ* (Mṛcch. 27, 14), *ṇhāduṁ* (Mallikām. 128, 11), *ṇhāia* (Nāgān. 51, 6; Priyad. 8, 13; 12, 11); M. *ṇhāa*, AMg. JM. *ṇhāia*, Ś. *ṇhāda = snāta* (Pāiẏal. 238; H.; Sūẏag. 730; Vivāhap. 187. 790 f.; Uvās.; Nāẏādh.; Ovav.; Kappas.; Nirayāv.; Āv. 17, 8; Erz.; Mṛcch. 27, 12); *ṇhāvaanto* [text °*vaẏando*] = *snāpayan* (Mallikām. 239, 3); AMg. JM. *ṇhāviẏa = snāpita* (Uvās.; Erz.); AMg. JM. JŚ. Ś. A. *ṇhāṇa = snāna* (Vr. 3, 33; Kī. 2, 90; Rāẏap. 56; Nāẏādh. ; Ovav.; Erz.; Kattig. 402, 358; Mṛcch. 90, 14; Vikr. 34, 6; Mallikām. 190, 16; Hc. 4, 399); AMg. *aṇhāṇa = asnāna* (Paṇhāv.

452), *aṇhāṇaya* (Ṭhāṇ. 531; Vivāhap. 135); JM. *ṇhavaṇa* = *snapana* (T. 6, 1. 3. 6 [text *nha°*]; Kk.); Ś. *ṇhavaṇaa* = *snapanaka* (Nāgān. 39. 4. 13); AMg. *ṇhāviyā* = *snāpikā* (Vivāhap. 964). So also *ṇhāvia* = **snāpita*; however, Ś. Mg. *ṇāvida* (§ 210). Ś. *paṇhuda* = *prasnuta* (Mahāv. 65, 4; Uttarar. 73, 10). In *sneha* and *snigdha* in M. AMg. JM. A. *s* is assimilated to *n* as a rule (Vr. 3, 64; Bh. 3, 1; Hc. 2, 77. 102. 109; Kī. 2, 58; Mk. fol. 26). Thus M. Ś. *ṇeha* (G.H.R.; Hc. 4, 332, 1. 406, 2. 422, 6. 8. 426, 1; Piṅgala 2, 118), AMg. JM. *ṇeha* (C. 2, 27; Pāiyal. 120; Nāyādh.; Nirayāv.; Erz.; Kk.), in verses *ṇeha* also in Mg. (Mṛcch. 157, 6) and D. (Mṛcch. 105, 16); M. *ṇiddha*, AMg. JM. *niddha*, *ṇiddha* (H.R.; Āyār. 1, 5, 6, 4; 2, 1, 5, 5; Sūyag. 590; Jīv. 224. 351; Paṇhāv. 285; Uttar. 1022; Ovav.; Kappas.; Erz.); *ṇehālu* = *snehavat* (C. 2, 20 p. 45; Hc. 2, 59 [*ṇe°*]); A. *niṇṇeha*, JM. *ninneha* = *niḥsneha* (Hc. 4, 367, 5; Erz.); Beside there occur *saṇeha*, A. *sasaṇehi*, *saṇiddha*, M. JM. Ś. *siṇiddha*, the forms which alone can be used in Ś. (§140). In *susā* = *snuṣā* (Hc. 1, 261) beside AMg. *ṇhusā*, M. AMg. JM. Ś. *suṇhā*, M. *sŏṇhā* (§ 148), P. *sunusā* (§ 139. 148), *n* has been assimilated. — *sma* = *mha*: PG. M. AMg. JM. Ś. A. *amhe* = *asme* (§ 419); M. JM. Ś. *amhārisa* = *asmādṛśa* (§ 245); M. Ś. A. *vimhaa*, JM. *vimhaya* = *vismaya* (G. R.; Erz.; Śak. 38, 8; Hc. 4, 420, 4). — *bhasman*, according to Hc. 2, 51, becomes also *bhappa*, which points to the intermediate steps **bhasvan*, **bhaspan* (§ 251. 277. 312), by the side of AMg. JM. *bhāsa*, Ś. *bhassa* (§ 65), JM. *bhasama* (§ 132). The pronominal ending *-smin*, that dialectically has been extended also to nouns in *-a*, becomes either *-ssiṁ*, Mg. *śśiṁ*, as in Ś. *tassiṁ*, Mg. *taśśiṁ* = *tasmin* (§ 425). *eassiṁ*, Ś. *edassiṁ*, Mg. *edaśśiṁ* = *etasmin* (§ 426); PG. *casi* = *cāsmin*, AMg. Ś. *assiṁ* = *asmin* (§ 429), or M. AMg. JM. JŚ. *-mmi*, as *tammi*, *eammi*, *eyammi* (§ 425. 426), M. *jŏvvaṇammi* = *yauvane*, AMg. *bambhammi kappammi* = *brāhme kalpe*, JM. *pāḍaliputtammi* = *pāṭaliputre* (§ 366[a]), or AMg. mostly *-ṁsi*, as *taṁsi*, *imaṁsi* (§ 425. 430). *logaṁsi* = *loke*, *dāragaṁsi* = *dārake* (§ 366[a]), as AMg. *aṁsi* = *asmi* also supports (§ 74. 498). *-ssiṁ*, through **-siṁ*., in all the dialects in the pronominal declension, and in Mg. A. also in the nominal declension, has become *-hiṁ*, as in *tahiṁ*, *jahiṁ*, *kahiṁ* = *tasmin*, *yasmin*, *kasmin*; Mg. *kulāhiṁ* = *kule*; *gharahī* = *ghare* (§ 264. 366[a]. 425. 427. 428). Instead of *-mmi* Hc. 1, 23 permits also *-ṁmi*: *vaṇammi* and *vaṇaṁmi* = *vane*. This spelling is very frequent in AMg. in MSS, and has often been retained in many editions, perhaps correctly. — *s* has been assimilated with *m* in AMg. *mi* = **smi* = *asmi*, AMg. JM. *mo* = *smaḥ*, beside the usual *mhi*, *mha*, *mho* (§ 498), on the other hand *m* has been assimilated to *s* in JM. *sarāmī*, *saraï*, AMg. *saraï*, JM. *sarasu* = *smarāmi*, *smarati*, *smara*, M. *visaria*, *visaria*, JŚ. *visarida* = *vismṛta*, beside JM. *vissariya*, dialectical *vimharaï* = *vismarati*, usual *sumaraï*, Ś. *sumaredi*, *visumarāmi*, Mg. *śumaledi*, *visumaledi* (§ 478); *seram* = *smeram* (Hc. 2, 78). M. *bharaï* (Vr. 8, 18; Hc. 4, 74; Kī. 4, 49; Mk. fol. 53; G. s.v. *smṛ*; H. R. s. v. *smar*), JM. *bhariya* = *smṛta* (Pāiyal. 194; Erz.), also *bhalaï* (Hc. 4, 74), M. *saṁbharaṇa* (G.) will stand for **mharaï*, **mbharaï* (§ 267). According to Mk. fol. 54 some taught also *maraï*, *vibharaï* (MS *viṁbharaï*).

§ 314. In Mg. according to Hc. 4, 289 *ṣṇa*, *sna* become *sṇa* and *ṣma*, *sma* become *sma*; only in *griṣma, ṣma* becomes *mha*: *viṣṇu* = *viṣṇu*; *usma-* = *ūṣman*; *vismaa* = *vismaya*; but *gimha* = *griṣma*. For *sma*, Śīlāṁka too attests this; while commenting on the readings of the text *akasmāt* (Āẏār. 1, 7, 1, 3), *akasmāddaṇḍa* (Sūẏag. 682) and *asmākam* (Sūẏag. 983); he notes that these words were spoken by all in the land of Magadha, even down to the wives of herdsmen, as Skt. So here too they should be pronounced. Similarly Abhayadeva on Ṭhāṇ. 372 *akasmāddaṇḍa*. For AMg. the only correct forms are the forms, such as *akamhābhaẏa* (Samav. 19; Ṭhāṇ. 455); the forms with *sma* have been adopted from Skt. Namisādhu on Rudraṭa, Kāvyālaṁkāra 2, 12 teaches *viśṇu* = *viṣṇu* and indirectly also *ś* for *ṣ*, *s* in other sound-groups. For *śna, śma* the rules are wanting in Hc.; hence it remains uncertain, whether they become *śṇa, śma* or *sṇa, sma* or *ṇha, mha*. The manuscripts of the dramas do not have merely *gimha* (Mṛcch. 10, 4), but also *paṇha* = *praśna* (Mṛcch. 80, 18; 81, 5); *uṇha* = *uṣṇa* (Mṛcch. 116, 17; Veṇīs. 33, 12); *viṇhu* = *viṣṇu* (Prab. 63, 15); *tuṇhīa* = *tūṣṇika* (Mṛcch. 164, 14); always *amhāṇam, amhe, tumha, tumhāṇam, tumhe* (pro ex. Mṛcch. 31, 15; 158, 23; Prab. 53, 15. 16; Mṛcch. 139, 13; 16, 19); *amhāliśa* = *asmādṛśa* (Mṛcch. 164, 5); *ṇhāāmi* = *snāmi, ṇhāde* = *snātaḥ* (Mṛcch. 113, 21; 136, 11) etc. The ending *-smin* in the MSS always becomes *-śśiṁ*, and *-sma* always becomes *-mha*. So has also the Lalitav.: *edaśśim* = *etasmin* (565, 6), *yāṇiśśamha* = *jnāsyāmaḥ* (565, 9), *amhadeśiya, amhāṇaṁ, tumhāṇaṁ* (565, 12. 14; 566, 9), *payāsĕmha* [sic] = *prakāśāyāma* (567, 1).

§ 315. So long as a separation-vowel does not appear, a semi-vowel following a sibilant is assimilated (§ 131-140), according to the principal rules (§ 279. 287. 296. 297). — *śya* = *ssa*; Mg. *śśa*: JM. Ś. *avassaṁ* = *avaśyam* (Erz.; Lalitav. 555, 5; Śak. 44. 6; 128, 9; Vikr. 53. 12; Mudrār. 264, 5; Karp. 103, 6; M. *ṇāsaï*, AMg. *nassaï*, JM. *nāsaï*. Ś. *ṇassadi* = *naśyati*; JM. *nassāmo* = *naśyāmaḥ* Mg., *viṇaśśadu* (§ 63); Ś. *rāasāla* = *rajaśyāla* (Mṛcch. 23, 19; 58, 7; 151, 16; 173, 1); M. *vesā* = *veśyā* (H.), Ś. *veśājaṇa* (Mṛcch. 57, 15) and *vĕssājaṇa* (Mṛcch. 53, 20); AMg. *vĕssa, vaïssa* = *vaiśya* (§ 61). — *śra* = *ssa*, Mg. *śśa*: M. AMg. *mīsa*. Ś. *missa*, Mg. *miśśa* = *miśra* (§ 64); M. JM. Ś. *visamaï* = *viśrāmyati*, Ś. *vissamiadu* (§ 64. 489); Ś. *sussūsidupuruvvo sussūsidavvo* = *śuśrūṣitapūrvaḥ śuśrūṣitavyaḥ* (Mṛcch. 39, 23); Mg. *śuśśūśide* = *śuśrūṣitaḥ* (Mṛcch. 37, 1); AMg. JM. Ś. *sĕṭṭhi-* = *śreṣṭhin* (Uvās.; Nāẏādh.; Niraẏāv.; Ovav. ; Erz.; Mṛcch. 28, 20; 142, 12; Śak. 139, 5, Mudrār. 41, 8; 43, 1; 243, 2; 248, 7; 252, 1; 254, 4). On *aṁsu* = *aśru, maṁsu* = *śamśru* see § 74. — *śla* becomes *ssa*, Mg. *śśa*: M. AMg. *saṇha* = *ślokṣṇa*[1] (Bh. 3, 33; Hc. 1, 118; 2, 75. 79; Mk. fol. 21. 26; H.R.; Vivāhap. 424; Uttar. 1040; Nāẏādh.; Ovav.; Kappas.); M. *parisaṇha* = *pariślakṣṇa* (R.); but also with assimilation of *s* M. *laṇha* (Hc. 2, 77; Mk. fol. 21; Karp. 88, 2; 96, 2), *laṇhaa* (Karp. 49, 11). In AMg. both the forms sometimes stand immediately beside one another *saṇha laṇha* (Savav. 211. 214; Paṇṇav. 96; Ovav. § 166). AMg. *saggha* = *ślāghya* (Sūẏag. 182); Ś. *sāhaṇia* = *ślāghaniya* (Mālav. 32, 5), but also *lāhaï* = *ślāghate* (Hc. 1, 187); AMg. *sĕmbha*; AMg. JM. A. *simbha-*, dialectical *sepha* = *śleṣman* (§ 267. 312), but also AMg. *lissanti* = *śliṣyante* (Sūẏag. 218). — AMg. *lesaṇaẏā* (Ovav.) is not, with

LEUMANN, to be equated as = (*saṁ*) *śleṣaṇatā*, but it is = *reṣaṇatā* (damage). Generally the group is separated either by *a* or *i*. — *śva* = *ssa*, Mg. *śśa*: M. AMg. JM. *āsa*, AMg. JM. Ś. *assa* = *aśva* (§ 64); M. AMg. JM. Ś. *pāsa* = *pārśva* (§ 87), falsely Ś. *passa* (Priyad. 23, 16); JŚ. *viṇassara* = *vinaśvara* (Kattig. 401, 339); Ś. *vissāvasu* = *viśvāvasu* (Mallikām. 57, 1); Mg. *viśśāvaśu* (Mṛcch. 11, 9); M. *sasaï*, *āsasaï* = *śvasiti*, *āśvasiti*; M. *ūsasaï*, AMg. *ussasaï* = *ucchvasiti*; M. *ṇisasaï*, AMg. *nissasaï*, Ś. *ṇisasadi* = *niḥśvasiti*; Mg. *śaśadi*, *ūśaśadu*, *ṇiśaśadu*, *śamaśśasadu* (§ 496); M. *sāvaa*, JM. *sāvaẏa*, Ś.Ā. *sāvada* = *śvāpada* (G.R.; Erz.; Śak. 32, 7; Mṛcch. 148, 22). — *ṣya* = *ssa*, Mg. *śśa*: Ś. *abhujissā* = *abhujiṣyā* (Mṛcch. 59, 25; 60, 11; 65, 1); AMg. *ārussa* = *āruṣya* (Sūẏag. 293), beside *ārusiẏāṇaṁ* (Āẏār. 1, 8, 1, 2); Ś. *pussarāa* = *puṣyarāga* (Mṛcch. 70, 25; so we should read)[3]; AMg. JM. *maṇūsa*, M. AMg. Ś. *maṇussa*, Mg. *maṇuśśa* = *manuṣya* (§ 63); AMg. JM. *sisa*, JM. Ś. *sissa* = *śiṣya* (§63); in future, as A. *karisu* = *kariṣyāmi* (Hc. 4, 396, 4). *phuṭṭisu* = *sphuṭiṣyāmi* (Hc. 4,422, 12), JM. *bhavissaï*, Ś. *bhavissadi*, Mg. *bhaviśśadi*, M. *hŏssaṁ*, A. *hosaï* (§ 521). In M. AMg. JM. A. this *ssa*, after a long vowel, and often also after a short vowel, has become *ha* through *sa*, as *kāhimi*, *kāhāmi*, *kāhaṁ* = **kārṣyāmi* = *kariṣyāmi*; *hohāmi*, *hohimi* = **bhoṣyāmi*; *kittaïhimi* = *kirtayiṣyāmi*; A *pĕkkhīhimi* = **prekṣiṣyāmi* (§263. 520 ff.). — *ṣva* = *ssa*, Mg. *śśa*; AMg. *osakkaï*, *paccosakkaï* = **apaṣvaṣkati*, **pratyapaṣvaṣkati*; M. *parisakkaï* = **pariṣvaṣkati* (§ 302); Ś. *parissaadi* = *pariṣvajate* (Mālatīm. 108, 3; Mṛcch. 327, 10 = 484, 12 ed. GOḌABOLE), *parissaadha* = *pariṣvajadhvam* (Śak. 90, 8; Vikr. 11, 2; Uttarar. 204, 5), *parissaïa* = *pariṣvajya* (Śak. 77, 9; Mālatīm. 210, 7). — On AMg. *piusiẏā*, M. *piussiā*, AMg. *piussiẏā*, M. AMg. *piucchā* = *pitṛṣvasā*, AMg. *māusiẏā*, M. *māussiā*, *māucchā* = *mātṛṣvasā*, dialectical *pupphā*, *pupphiā* see § 148. — *sya* = *ssa*, Mg. *śśa* : M. JM. Ś. *rahassa* = *rahasya* (G.H.; Karp. 66, 11; Erz.; Mṛcch. 60, 7; Vikr. 15, 3. 12; 16, 1. 11. 18; 79, 9; Karp. 67, 1); M.Ś. *vaassa*, M. *vaaṁsa*, JM. *vaẏaṁsa* = *vayasya* (§ 74); Ś. *hassa* = *hāsya* (Mṛcch. 44, 1) ; in the genitive sing. in *-sya*, as M. Ś. *kāmassa* = *kāmasya* (H. 2, 148, 326. 586; Śak. 120, 6; Prab. 38, 12; Karp. 93, 1). Dialectically there occurs also *ha* from *sa* (§ 264), as Mg. *kāmāha* (Mṛcch. 10, 24), A. *kāmahŏ* (Hc. 4, 446); beside M. AMg. JM. JŚ. Ś. Ḍh. *tassa*, Mg. *taśśa*, A. *tassu*, *tasu*, *tāsu*, M. *tāsa*, also Mg. *tāha*, A. *tahŏ* = *tasya* (§ 425). Likewise in future as AMg. *dāhāmo* beside *dāsāmo* = *dāsyāmaḥ* (§ 530); JM. *pāhāmi*, AMg. *pāhaṁ* = *pāsyāmi*, AMg. *pāhāmo* = *pāsyāmaḥ* (§ 524). — *sra* = *ssa*, Mg. *śśa* : M. *ūsā* = *usrā* (Lalitav. 555, 1); JM. *tamissā* = *tamisrā* (Kk.); M. *visambha*, Ś. *vissambha* = *visrambha* (§ 64); M. AMg. JM. JŚ. Ś. *sahassa*, Mg. *śahaśśa* = *sahasra* (§ 448). — *sva* = *ssa*, Mg. *śśa* : *bappasāmihi* = *bappasvāmibhiḥ* (6, 11), *sakakāle* = *svakakāle* (7, 44) *sahattha* = *svahasta* (7, 51); JM. Ś. *tavassi-*, Mg. *tavaśśi-* = *tapasvin* (Erz.; Kk.; Śak. 22,7; 76,8), JM. Ś. *tavassiṇi*, Mg. *tavaśśiṇi* = *tapasvini* (Kk.; Śak. 39, 4; 78, 11; 123. 12; 129, 16; Mg. Mṛcch. 152, 6); M. JM. *sarassai*, Ś. *sarassadi* = *sarasvatī* (G.; Erz.; Vikr. 35, 5); M. *siṇṇa* = *svinna* (G. H.); Ś. *sāadaṁ*, Mg. *śāadaṁ* = *svāgatam* (§ 203). On M. *maṇaṁsi-* = *manasvin*, AMg. *oẏaṁsi-* = *ojasvin* and similar other forms see § 74; on *haṁsa* = *hrasva*, beside *hassa*, *rahassa* see § 354.

1. Hc. and with him JACOBI, KZ. 23, 598 wrongly derive *saṇha* from *sūkṣma* and Hc. at 2, 75 expressedly differentiates between *saṇha*=*sūkṣma* and *saṇha*=*ślakṣṇa*. Correctly WEBER, ZDMG, 28, 402; P. GOLDSCHMIDT, Specimen p. 68; CHILDERS. s v. *saṇho*. — 2. Aup. S. s. v. — 3. PISCHEL, Rudraṭa's Śṛṅgāratilaka p. 102 f.; Mahāvyutpatti 235, 28.

§ 316. In the conjunction tenuis+sibilant, according to the grammarians the aspirate was dialectically pronounced in place of the tenuis in Skt. : *khṣira* beside *kṣira*; *vathsa* beside *vatsa*; *aphsaras* beside *apsaras*[1]. Pkt. presupposes this pronunciation universally in the case of *tsa* and *psa*, in the case of original *kṣa* only when it goes back to *śṣa*[2]. The aspiration passed to the sibilant, which according to § 211 became *cha*. The phonetic groups thus originating, i.e. *ścha* (*kcha*), *tcha*, *pcha* regularly became *ccha*. In the case of original *kṣa*, on the other hand, the aspiration did not take place, the sounds were transposed as Mg. *ska*, *ẖka* (§ 324) points, and *ṣka* for *kṣa* became *kkha* (§ 302). The assumption of ASCOLI[3] that *ṣa* possibly became *kha* has no support in Pkt. (§ 265), just as little as the theory of JOHANSSON[4] that the different phonetic changes rest on pronunciation, division of syllables and the accent.[5]

1. Literature in JOHANSSON, Shāhbāzgarhi 2, 21 f.; WACKERNAGEL, Altind. Gr. §113. — 2. WACKERNAGEL, Altind. Gr. §116. — 3. Kritische Studien p. 236ff. — 4. Shāhbāzgarhi 2, 22. — 5. Cf. PISCHEL, GGA. 1881, p. 1322f.

§ 317. The grammarians regard the change of *kṣa* to *kha* as regular (Vr. 3, 29; Hc. 2, 3; Kī. 2, 88; Mk. fol. 24), and they have grouped the words that show *cha* under the *ākṛtigaṇa akṣyādi* (Vr. 3, 30; Hc. 2, 17; Kī. 2, 82; Pkt. p. 60). Mk. fol. 24 groups the words that always have *cha* for *kṣa* in the gaṇa *kṣurādi*, and includes in it the words *kṣura, akṣi, makṣikā kṣira, sadṛkṣa, kṣetra, kukṣi, ikṣu, kṣudhā*, and *kṣudh*. The words which have *cha* and *kha*, he gives in the *ākṛtigaṇa kṣamādi*. The verdict of the grammarians, however, holds good only for M. In other dialects the sound varies so much so that in one and the same dialect we find not seldom the words with *kha* beside those with *cha*, without ourselves being able to blame tradition in every case (§ 321). The Avestā preserves best the original condition.

§ 318. If Skt. *kṣa* goes back to *śṣa*, so in the Avestā it becomes *ša*, in Pkt., originally through **śṣha*, **scha* (§ 316) it becomes *ccha* : *chaa*=Av. *šata* in *hušata*=*kṣata* from *kṣan* (Hc. 2, 17); in addition to AMg. *chaṇa* (murder)=*kṣaṇa* (Āyār. 1, 2, 6, 5; 1, 3, 1, 4; 1, 5, 3, 5); *chaṇe*=**kṣaṇet* (Āyār. 1, 3, 2, 3; 1, 7, 8, 9), *chaṇāvae, chaṇantaṁ*=**kṣaṇāpayet*, **kṣaṇantaṁ* (Āyār. 1, 3, 2, 3); but M. *khaa*=*kṣata* (G.H.R.), *parikkhaa* (R.); AMg. *khaṇaha*=**kṣaṇata* (Āyār. 1, 7, 2 , 4); AMg. *akkhaya*, JŚ. °*da* (Sūyag. 307; Pav. 385, 69); Ś. *parikkhada* (Mṛcch. 53, 25; 61, 24; Śak. 27, 9), *aparikkhada* (Vikr. 10, 4), *avarikkhada* (Mṛcch. 53, 18. 24). — M. AMg. JM. *chuhā*=Av. *šuδa*=*kṣudhā* (Grr.; H.; Ṭhāṇ. 328; Vivāhap. 40, 647; Rāyap. 258; Nāyādh. 348; Ovav.; Dvār. 500, 7; Erz.), *chuhāiya* (hungry; Pāiyal. 183); but also AMg. JM. Ś. *khuhā* (Ṭhāṇ. 572; Vivāhap 162, 493, 816; Paṇhāv. 200; Nāyādh.; Ovav.; Dasav. 635, 16 [*khuppivāsā:*]; Dasav. N. 662, 1. 2; Erz.; Karp. 76, 9 ed. Bomb. whilst KONOW 75, 6 reads *chuhā*); AMg. *khuhiya*=*kṣudhita* (Paṇhāv. 340). — M. *chetta*, AMg. *chitta*=Av. *šoiθra* =*kṣetra*, but also AMg. JM. JŚ. Ś. *khĕtta*, AMg. *khitta* (§84). M. AMg.

JM. JM. Ś. *acchi* = Av. *aši* = *akṣi* (Grr.; G.H.R.; Āyār. 1, 1, 2, 5; 1, 8, 1, 19; 2, 2, 1, 7; 2, 3, 2, 5; Vivāgas. 11; Vivāhap. 1152; Āv. 8, 20; 30, 4; Śak. 30, 5; 31, 13; Vikr. 43, 15; 48, 15; Ratn. 319, 18; Karp. 11, 2; Nāgān. 11, 9; Jīvān. 89, 3); but also AMg. JM. Ś.A. *akkhi* (Sūyag. 383; Erz.; Vikr. 34, 1; Anarghar. 305, 13; Hc. 4, 357, 2). —AMg. *accha* (§57), M. AMg. Ś. *riccha* (§ 56) = Av. *arĕša* = *ṛkṣa*; but also M. AMg. JM. Ś. *rikkha* (§56). — M. *kaccha* = Av. *kaša* = *kakṣa* (H.); but also AMg. JM. *kakkha* (G.R.; Nāyādh. 434). — *tacchaï* (Hc. 4, 194), AMg. *tacchiya* (Uttar. 596 [text °*tthi*°]) = Av. *taša-* = *takṣatī*, **taṣkita* , but also *takkhaï* (Hc. 4, 194); *takkhāṇa* = *tatkṣan* (§ 403).

§ 319. Original *kṣa* becomes *hša* in the Avestā, *kkha* in Pkt.; AMg. *khattiya*, Ś. *khattia* = *kṣatriya* (Sūyag. 182. 373. 495. 585; Samav. 232; Uttar. 155 f. 506. 754; Vivāgas. 152f.; Vivāhap. 135; Ovav.; Kappas.; Mahāv. 28, 14; 29, 22; 64. 21; Uttarar. 167. 10; Anarghar. 58, 8; 70, 1; 155, 5; 157, 10; Hāsy. 32, 1; Pras. 47, 7; 48, 4.5); JM. *khattiā* (sic.; KI. 3); AMg. *khattiyāṇi* = *kṣatriyāṇi* (Kappas.), *khatti-* = *kṣatrin* (Sūyag. 317); Ś. *ṇikkhatti-kada* = *niḥkṣatrikṛta* (Mahāv. 27, 6), to Av. *hšaθra*. — AMg. JM. *khīra* = Av. *hšira* = *kṣīra* (Hc. 2, 17; Sūyag. 817, 822; Vivāhap. 660, 942; Paṇṇav. 522; Uttar. 895; Uvās.; Ovav.; Kappas.; Nāyādh.; Āv. 28, 23; 42, 2); *khīri* = *kṣīri* (Pāiyal. 240); M. *khīroa*, JM. *khīroya* = *kṣīroda* (G.H.; Erz.); AMg. *khīrodaya* (Ovav.); Ś. *khīrasamudda* = *kṣīrasamudra* (Prab. 4, 7); but also M. *chīra* (Grr.; Pāiyal. 123; G. H.); AMg. *chīrabirālī* = *kṣīrabiḍāli* (Vivāhap. 1532; [text °*vi*°]). For Ś. Mk. fol. 67 expressly prescribes *khīra*.— *khivaï* = *kṣipati* goes back to Av. *hšviw* (Hc. 4, 143); M. *akkhivaï* = *ākṣipati* (R.); *ukkhivaï* = *utkṣipati* (H.); *samukkhivaï* (G.); JM. *khivasi* (Erz. 83, 18), *khivei* (Erz.); AMg. *khivāhi* (Āyār. 2, 3, 1, 16), *pakkhivaha* (Āyār. 2, 3, 2, 3), *pakkhivĕjjā* (Āyār. 2, 3, 2, 3; Vivāhap. 270), *nikkhiyavva* (Paṇhāv. 373); *pakkhippa* (Sūyag. 280, 282. 288. 378); Ś. *khividuṁ* = *kṣeptum* (Vikr. 25, 16), *khitta* = *kṣipta* (Mṛcch. 41, 6.22) *akkhitta* = *ākṣipta* (Vikr. 75, 12 so we should read); *uvakkhiva* = *upakṣipa* (Mṛcch. 72, 14), *ukkhivia* = *utkṣipya* (Mṛcch. 3, 17), *ṇikkhividuṁ* = *nikṣeptum* (Mṛcch. 24, 22), *ṇikkhitta* (Mṛcch. 29, 13; 145, 11; Śak. 78, 13; Vikr. 84, 8), *ṇikkhivia* (Vikr. 75, 10), *parik-khiviāmo* = *parikṣipyāmahe* (Caṇḍak. 28, 11) etc.; but also *ucchitta* = *utkṣipta* (Bh. 3, 30; Deśīn. 1, 124; Pāiyal. 84) and M. *chivaï* (touches; Hc. 4, 182; G.H.R.); *chitta* (touched; Hc. 4, 258; Pāiyal. 85; H.). — AMg. JM. *khuḍḍa* = *kṣudra*, *khuḍḍaya*, AMg. *khuḍḍaga* = *kṣudraka* (§ 294) = Av. *hšudra* (semen). — M. *khuṇṇa* = *kṣuṇṇa* (Deśīn. 2, 75; Pāiyal. 222; H.) from Av. *hšusta*; but also *ucchuṇṇa* = *utkṣuṇṇa* (Pāiyal. 201). — M. *khubbhaï* = *kṣubhyati* (Hc. 1, 154; R.); *saṁkhuhia* (G.), AMg. *khobhaïuṁ* = *kṣobhayitum* (Uttar. 921), *khobhittae* (Uvās.), *khubhiya* (Ovav.), *kokhubbhamāṇa* (§ 556); Ś. *saṁkhohida* = *saṁkṣobhita* (Śak. 32, 8); A. *khuhia* (Vikr. 67, 11); M. *khoha* = *kṣobha* (R.); JM. *mohakkhoha* (Pav. 380, 7), but also PG. °*cchobhaṁ* = °*kṣobham* (6, 32); *vicchuhire* = *vikṣubhyanti* (Hc. 3, 142); AMg. *chubhanti ucchubhaï*, *nicchubhaï*, JM. *chubhaï*, *chuhaï*, M. *vicchuhaï* etc. (§66). — M. *sikkhaï* = *śikṣati* (H.); M. A. *sikkhia*, JM. *sikkhiya*, Ś. *sikkhida* = *śikṣita* (G. H.; Erz.; Mṛcch. 37, 5; Vikr. 62, 11), JM. Ś. *sikkhanta-* (Erz.; Mṛcch. 71,

21), Ś. *sikkhīadi*, *sikkhidukāma* (Mṛcch. 39, 22; 51, 24); *sikkhāvemi* (Priẏad. 40, 4) connected with Av. *asihšant*.

§ 320. Sometimes Pkt. and Av. go asunder *uccha-* = *ukṣan* (Bh. 3.30; Hc. 2, 17; 3, 56); *ucchāṇa-* (Hc. 3, 65), but Av. *uhšān*. Mk. fol. 24 permits, however, also *ukkha-*, beside *uccha-*. — PG. M. AMg. JM. Ś. Ā. *dakkhiṇa* = *dakṣiṇa* (§65). Ś. *dakkhiṇā* = *dakṣiṇā* (Mṛcch. 5, 1; Karp. 103, 6), but Av. *dašiṇa*. However, AMg. has *daccha* (Uvās.), beside AMg. JM. *dakkha* (Nāẏādh.; Ovav.; Erz.). — M. *macchiā* (Grr.; H.); AMg. JM. *macchiẏā* (Vivāgas. 12; Uttar. 245. 1036. 1064; Ovav.; Dvār. 503, 6), AMg. *macchigā* (Paṇhāv. 72) = *mahši* = *makṣikā*; but also Ś. *ṇimmakkhia* = *nirmakṣika* (Śak. 36, 16; 124, 7; Viddhaś. 62, 2). M. AMg. JM. Ś. *rakkhasa* = *rākṣasa* (R.; Sūẏag. 105, 339. 468; Uttar. 996, 1084; Ṭhāṇ. 90; Ovav.; Erz.; Mṛcch. 68, 8; Śak. 43, 6; 45, 1; Mahāv. 96, 12; 97. 7. 15; 99, 2; Bālar. 221, 5), AMg. *rakkhasi* = *rākṣasi* (Uttar. 252) related with Av. *raš*, *rašaṅh*. — M. JM. *vaccha* = *vṛkṣa* (Grr.; Pāiẏal. 54; G.; Karp. 64, 2; Erz.; Dasav. N. 645, 5 in an enumeration, of words which mean "tree") related with Av. *urvāhš* (to grow). Besides *vaccha*, according to Vr. 3, 31; Hc. 2, 127; Kī. 2, 83; Mk. fol. 24 *vṛkṣa* can form also *rukkha*, and according to Rāmatarkavāgīśa and Mārkaṇḍeya fol. 66 only *rukkha* is used in Ś. (Pischel on Hc. 1, 153; 2, 17). AMg. Ś. employ only *rukkha* (Āẏār. 1, 7, 2, 1; 1, 8, 2, 3; 2, 1, 2, 3; 2, 3, 2, 15, 2, 3, 3, 13; 2, 4, 2, 11. 12.; Sūẏag. 179. 314. 325 425. 613; Vivāhap. 275. 445; Samav. 233; Paṇṇav. 30; Rāẏap. 154; Jīv. 548. 550 f.; Dasav. N. 645, 5; Nāẏādh.; Ovav.; Kappas.; Mṛcch. 40, 24; 72. 8; 73, 6. 7; 77, 16; 87, 11. 12; Śak. 9, 10; 10, 2; 12, 2. 6; Mālav. 72, 3); AMg. Ś. *kapparukkha* = *kalpavṛkṣa* (Āẏār. 2, 15, 20; Mallikām. 291, 2); M. JM. have *rukkha* (H.R.; Āv. 47, 11 ff.; Ṛṣabhap. 29; Erz.), JM. *kapparukkha* (Erz.) beside *vaccha*. The word *rukkha* has nothing to do with *vṛkṣa*, but is = *rukṣa*, for which Roth (Über gewisse Kürzungen des Wortendes im Veda p. 3) has shown the meaning "tree" in the Veda.

§ 321. Variation between *kkha* and *ccha* is found also in the words, other than those already mentioned. The M. AMg. JM. *ucchu* beside AMg. Ś. *ikkhu* = *ikṣu*, AMg. JM. *ikkhāga* = *aikṣvāka* (§ 117. 84). — M. AMg. JM. *kucchi* = *kukṣi* (G.; Āẏār. 2, 15, 2. 4. 10. 12; Paṇhāv. 281; Vivāhap. 295. 1035. 1274; Uvās.; Kappas.; Erz.); *kucchimaī* = *kukṣimatī* (pregnant; Ḍeśīn. 2, 41), beside AMg. Ś. *kukkhi* (Nāẏādh. 308; Paṇhāv. 217; Mālav. 65, 16), which Hc. Deśīn. 2, 34 declares as provincial. — *chura* = *kṣura* (Grr.), *churamaḍḍi-*, *churahattha* = *kṣuramardin*, *kṣurahasta* (barber; Deśīn. 3, 31), beside M. AMg. *khura* (Karp. 94, 4; Sūẏag. 546; Vivāhap. 353. 1042; Nāẏādh.; Uvās.; Kappas.), *khurapatta* = *kṣurapattra* (Ṭhāṇ. 321). — AMg. A. *chāra* = *kṣāra* (saltpetre; potash; Grr.; Uvās.; Hc. 4, 365, 3), *chāribhūẏa* = *kṣāribhūta* (Vivāhap. 237), *chāriẏa* = *kṣārita* (Vivāhap. 322 f. 348), beside AMg. JM. *khāra* (Sūẏag. 520. 281; Ovav.; Kk.). — Cf. § 326. — M. AMg. JM. *pĕcchaī*, but Ś. *pĕkkhadi* = *prekṣate* (§84). — M. AMg. JM. *vaccha* = *vakṣas* (Grr.; G.H.R.; Karp. 84, 4; Uvās.; Nāẏādh.; Ovav.; Kappas.; Erz.), but Ś. *vakkhatthala* = *vakṣaḥsthala* (Mṛcch. 68,19); Dhanaṁjayav. 11, 9; Hāsy. 40, 22), against the dialect *vacchatthala* (Bālar. 238, 9;

Mallikām. 156, 10 [text °ṭṭha°]; 201, 13 [text °ṭṭa°]; Cait. 38, 11; 44, 9). — M. JM. JŚ. *sāriccha*, but AMg. Ś. A. *sārikkha* = **sādṛkṣya* (§ 78. 245). The variation shows that on the Indian soil, even in the same dialect, without regard to the different origin of *kṣa*, both the pronunciations went side by side.[1] One said for example *akhṣi* and *akṣi*, and their contaminations in Pkt. are *acchi* and *akkhi*.

1. So correctly ASCOLI, Kritische Studien p. 238f.; JOHANSSON, Shāhbāzgarhi 2, 20. Cf. PISCHEL, GGA. 1881, p. 1322 f.

§ 322. With the different treatments of *kṣa* in *kṣaṇa* and *kṣamā* is connected the difference in meaning. *kṣaṇa* becomes, according to Bh. 3, 31; Hc. 2, 20; Mk. fol. 24, *chaṇa* in the meaning "festival", on the other hand it becomes *khaṇa* in the meaning "moment". Thus M. AMg. JM. *chaṇa* "festival" (Pāiyal. 284; G. H.; Śak. 119, 7; Nāyādh. 266; Vivāhap. 822; Kk. 271, 24), but M. AMg. JM. Ś. *khaṇa* "moment" (G.H.R.; Nāyādh. § 135. 137; p. 300; Dasav. 613, 39; Kappas.; Erz.; Kk.; Ṛṣabhap.; Śak. 2, 14; 126, 6; Viddhaś. 99, 1; Karp. 58, 3; 59, 6; 105, 4). According to Mk. fol. 67 *cha* never occurs into Ś. Hence in Śak. 118, 13, with three MSS we should read *uvatthidakkhaṇe*. Kī. 2, 83 teaches *khaṇa* and *chaṇa* with a difference of meaning. — *kṣamā* becomes, according to Hc. 2, 18, *chamā* in the meaning "earth", but *khamā* in the meaning "patience". Vr. 3, 31; Kī. 2, 83; Mk. fol. 24 place *khamā* and *chamā* beside one-another without distinguishing between their meaning; C. 3, 4 has only *khamā*. In AMg. *chamā* = "earth" (Dasav. 641, 13), in M. AMg. JM. *khamā* = "patience" (H. ; Vivāhap. 162; Dvār. 502, 19), AMg. *khamāsamaṇa* = *kṣamāśramaṇa* (Kappas.).

§ 323. In AMg. JM. sometimes a long vowel is retained before *kṣa*. Then *kkha* becomes *ha* (§ 188) through *kha* (§ 87). Especially frequent it is in the case of the root *ikṣ* and its derivatives: AMg. *īhā* = *ikṣā*[1] (Nāyādh.; Ovav.; Kappas.); AMg. *aṇuppehanti* = *anuprekṣante* (Ovav. § 31), *aṇupehāe* (Āyār. 2, 1, 4, 2), *aṇuppehā* = *anuprekṣā* (Ṭhāṇ. 211. 213; Uttar. 899; Ovav.), *uvehĕjjā* (Āyār. 2, 1, 5, 5, 9, 2; 2, 3, 1, 16. 18; 2, 3, 2, 1. 3, 8), *uvehamāṇa* = *upekṣamāṇa* (Āyār. 1, 3, 1, 3; 1, 4, 4, 4; 2, 16, 5), *pehe* = *prekṣeta* (Uttar. 726), *peha* = *prekṣasva* (Sūyag. 139), *pehamāṇa* (Āyār. 1, 8, 2, 11; 1, 8, 4, 7; 2, 3, 1, 6); JM. *pehamāṇio* (Āv. 17, 10); AMg. *pehāe* (Āyār. 1, 2, 5, 5; 1, 8, 1, 20; 1, 8, 4, 10; 2, 1, 1, 3; 2, 1, 4, 1. 4ff.; 2, 1, 9, 2; 2, 4, 2, 6; Uttar. 33), *pehiya* (Uttar. 919), *pehiyā* (Sūyag. 104), *pehiyaṁ* (Dasav. 633, 3). *pehā* = *prekṣā* (Dasav. 613, 21), *pehi* = *prekṣin* (Āyār. 1, 8, 1, 20; Uttar. 30), *pehiṇi* (Uttar. 663), *samuppehamāṇa* (Āyār. 1, 4, 4, 4), *samupehamāṇa* (Sūyag. 506), *samupehiyā* (Dasav. 629, 39), *saṁpehei* (Vivāhap. 152. 248. 841. 916; Uvās.; Nāyādh.; Nirayāv.; Kappas.), *saṁpehaī* (Dasav. 643, 10). *saṁpehāe* (Āyār. 1, 2, 4, 4; 1, 5, 3, 2; 1, 6, 1, 3 [*sā*°]; Sūyag. 669), *sāpehiyā* (Āyār. 1, 7, 8, 23), *saṁpehittā* (Vivāhap. 152, 248). Further AMg. *lūha*, beside *lukkha* = *rūkṣa*, *lūhei*, *lūhiya* = *rūkṣayati*, *rūkṣita*[2] (§ 87. 257); AMg. JM. *seha* = Pāli *sekha* = Skt. *śaikṣa* (Āyār. 2, 2, 3, 24; Sūyag. 165. 511. 520; Ovav.; Kappas.; Kk.); AMg. *sehanti* = **śaikṣanti* (Sūyag. 115), *sehāvei* = **śaikṣāpayati*[3] (Vivāhap. 797; Ovav.; Nāyādh.) *sehāviya* (Vivāhap. 1246). — The same phonetic change has taken place in secondarily shortened vowels in AMg. *suhuma, suhama* = *sūkṣma* (§ 82. 131. 140), and in secondarily lengthened vowels in M. AMg. JM. Ś. *dāhiṇa* = *dakṣiṇa*; AMg. *dāhiṇilla, āyāhiṇa, payāhiṇa, pāyāhiṇa* (§ 65) and AMg. *dehaï, dehae* = **dṛkṣati*, **dṛkṣate*, A. *drehi* (§66.554).

1. So correctly LEUMANN, Aup. S. s. v.; falsely equated as = *ihā* by JACOBI, Kalpas. s. v. and STEINTHAL, Specimen s. v. — 2. So rightly LEUMANN, Aup. S. s. v.; falsely equated as = *lūṣita* by JACOBI and STEINTHAL l. c. — 3. So rightly LEUMANN, Aup. S. s. v.; falsely STEINTHAL l. c. = *sedhayati*.

§ 324. In Mg., according to Vr. 11, 8 *kṣa* becomes *ska* : *laskaśe* = *rākṣasaḥ*; *daske* = *dakṣaḥ*. Hc. 4, 297 and Namisādhu on Rudraṭa, Kāvyālaṁkāra 2, 12 teach this phonetic change only for *prekṣ* (that is to say *iṣ* with *pra*) and *ācakṣ* (i.e. *cakṣ* with *ā*) : *pěskadi* = *prekṣate*; *āc̆askadi* = *ācaṣṭe*. In all other words, according to them (Hc. 4, 296) *kṣa* becomes *ḫka*[1] in the inlaut; *yaḫke* = *yakṣaḥ*; *laḫkaśe* = *rākṣasaḥ*; *paḫka* = *pakṣa* (Hc. 4, 302). In the anlaut *kṣa* is treated according to the rules that hold good for the other dialects: *khaayalahalā* = *kṣayajaladharāḥ*. Kṛṣṇapaṇḍita in PETERSON, Third Report p. 344 teaches *śka* : *paśka* = *pakṣa*; *laśkā* = *lākṣā*; *paśkāladu* = *prakṣālayatu*, for which C. 3, 39 p. 52 and Hc. 4, 228 have *pakkhāladu* in the same verse with *kṣa* treated as in the anlaut. Lalitav. has throughout *śka*: *alaśkiyyamāṇa* = *alakṣyamāṇa* (565, 7); *laśkidaṁ* = *lakṣitaṁ* (566, 4); *bhiśkaṁ* = *bhikṣām* (566, 8); *yujjhaśkamāṇaṁ* = *yuddhakṣamāṇām* (566, 11); *laśkaṁ, laśkāiṁ* = *lakṣam, lakṣāṇi* (566, 11). Likewise also *pěśkiyyaṁdi, pěśkiyyaśi* [so to be read], *pěśkiduṁ* = *prekṣyante, prekṣyase, prekṣituṁ* (569, 13. 15. 19, 566, 7). Against the dialects offends *pac* [*c*] *akkhikadaṁ* = *pratyakṣikṛtam* (566, 1). The MSS of the dramas and the editions based on them treat *kṣa* in Mg. exactly in the same way as in the rest of the dialects, not merely in the anlaut, as *khaṇa* = *kṣaṇa* (Mṛcch. 136, 15. 16; 160, 11; Prab. 50, 9), but also throughout in the inlaut. From quite sporadic variants of some of the MSS, like that of Mṛcch. 13, 6 *peṣa, pěttha*, 21, 15, *pěścha*, 132, 20. *laścide, laśchide*, 132, 21 *pěścāmi, pecchāmi*, the rules of the grammarians cannot be established. Nevertheless they are to be framed out. For *jeṇa attaṇo pakkhaṁ ujjhia parapakkho pamāṇikariadi* (Mudrār. 178, 6)[3] Hc. 4, 302 reads *ye appaṇo pahkaṁ ujjhia palaśśa paḫkhaṁ pamāṇikaleśi*[4] and for *amaccarakkhasaṁ pěkkhiduṁ ido eva āacchadi* (Mudrār, 154, 3)[5] he reads *amaccalaḫkaśaṁ pěśkiduṁ idǒyyeva āaścadi*. Hence, for example in Mṛcch. 120, 3 instead of *akkhihiṁ bhakkhiadi dantehiṁ pěkkhiadi* = *akṣibhyāṁ bhakṣyate dantaiḥ prekṣyate* we should read *aḫkihiṁ bhahkiadi dantehiṁ pěskiadi*. The MSS give no variant.

1. In the edition at p. 14, 2 is printed *kṣasya śko 'nādau yathā yaśke laśkase yakṣo rākṣasa iti*. The best MS (KIELHORN, Report, Bombay 1881, p. 34 Nr. 53), however, reads *ḫko, yaḫke laḫkase* [sic.] — 2. From the words of Kṛṣṇapaṇḍita : *jihvāmūlīyaśca kvacicchaurasenyādau vakṣyate takṣaḥ taḫko śakāraśca māgadhyāṁ vakṣyate pakṣaḥ paśko* [sic] *lākṣā lāśkā* [sic] indeed it does not necessarily follow that he supported *taḫka* for Ś.; at times the manuscript gives *o* in the nom. sing. in Mg. too; however, the following words make it apparent that *taḫka* cannot be Mg. Triv. and Sr. agree with Hc. here also. — 3. So TELANG. From the manuscripts it is not possible to ascertain whether *pala* or *palaśśa*, and *kalīadi* or *kaleśi* are to be inserted here rightly. — 4. Correctly there would be *uyyhia* (§ 236). — 5. So TELANG. The MS E correctly has *yyeva*, elsewhere quite false *eva* or *jjevva* and *rakkhasaṁ*, as also the edd. Calc.

§ 325. As in Pāli, in AMg. JM. also *kṣulla*, with loss of aspiration, becomes *culla* (Deśīn. 3, 22; Pāiyal. 58); JM. *cullatāya* = *kṣullatāta* (uncle; Erz.); AMg. JM. *cullapiu* = *kṣullapitṛ* (uncle; Dasav. 628, 5; Erz.); AMg. *cullamāuyā* (aunt.; Antag. 70; Nāyādh. § 84-87. 95, 96; Nirayāv.); AMg. *culla sayaya*, °*ga* = *kṣullaśataka* (Uvās.), *cullahimavanta-* = *kṣullahimavat* (Ṭhāṇ. 72. 74. 176. 177); *cullodaa* (the eldest brother; Deśīn. 3, 17). *cullaka* has been taken also into Skt. by the Jainas (BÜHLER, Pāiyal. s. v. *cullo*).

§ 326. If *kṣa* goes back to early *ẓaẓ*, through *ẓzha*, *ẓjha*, it becomes *jjha*[1] in Pkt. : *jharaī* = *kṣarati* (Hc. 4, 173), JM. *jharei* (Erz.); *ṇijjharaï* = *niḥkṣarati* (Hc. 4, 20); M. *ŏjjhara* = **avakṣara* (Hc. 1, 98; Deśīn. 1, 160; Pāiyal. 216; H. R.), equated by Hc. as = *nirjhara*, that itself originates from Pkt.[2], and becomes M. Ś. *ṇijjhara* (G. H.; Pras. 124, 7; Ś. Mallikām. 134, 7; Bālar. 241, 6; 263, 22 [text °*jja*°], AMg. JM. *nijjhara* (Pāiyal. 216). Beside one another stand *ŏjjhara* and *nijjhara* in AMg. (Paṇṇav. 80. 84 ff. 94 [text *ujjhara* and several times *nijjara*]) A. *pajjharaï* = *prakṣarati* (Hc. 4, 173; Piṅgala 1, 102); *pajjharia* (Kī 2, 84); Ś. *pajjharāvedi* (Karp. 105, 8). To it probably belongs also *jharaa* (goldsmith; Deśīn. 3, 54). — AMg. *jhiyāi* for **jhāi* = **kṣāti* = *kṣāyati*[3] (burns [intransitive]; Sūyag. 273; Nāyādh. 1117; Ṭhāṇ. 478), *jhiyāyanti* (Ṭhāṇ. 478); M. *vijjhāi* (Hc. 2, 28; H), *vijjhāanta-* (H.); M. *vijjhāa* (G.H.R.), AMg. JM. *vijjhāya* (Nāyādh. 1113; Dasav. 641, 29; Āv. 25, 3); M. *vijjhavaï* (G.), *vijjhavei* (H. R.), *vijjhavia* (H. R.); AMg. *vijjhavĕjja*, *vijjhavĕntu* (Āyār. 2, 2, 1, 10), *vijjhāviya* (Uttar. 709). *samijjhāi* (Hc. 2, 28) is an analogical formation in connection with $\sqrt{}$*indh.*[4] — AMg. *jhāma* = *kṣāma* (scorched; ashes) Āyār. 2, 1, 10, 6; 2, 10, 22), *jhāmei* (Sūyag. 722; Vivāhap. 1257), *jhāmāvei*, *jhāmanta-* (Sūyag. 722); AMg. JM. *jhāmiya* (Deśīn. 3, 56; Vivāhap. 1251), *jhāmāvei*, *jhāmanta-* (Sūyag. 722); AMg. JM. *jhāmiya* (Deśīn. 3, 56; Vivāhap. 321, 1251; Āv. 25, 1; 26, 17); JM. *nijjhāmemo* (Dvār. 505, 9), beside M. Ś. *khāma* (meagre; G.; Karp. 41, 1). — M. AMg. *jhijjaī* = *kṣiyate* (Vr. 8, 37; Hc. 2, 3; 4, 20; H. R.; Lalitav. 562, 21; Uttar. 633); M. *jhijjae*, *jhijjāmo* [so to be read], *jhijjihisi* (H.), *jhijjanti* (G. H.); JM. *jhijjāmi* (Ṛṣabhap. 35 [so to be read with ed. Bomb.]); A. *jhijjaū̃* (Hc. 4, 425, 1); M. JM. *jhijjanta-* (G.H.R.; Kk. III, 68); Ś. *jhijjanti* (Viddhaś. 99, 2); M.Ś.A. *jhīṇa* = *kṣiṇa* (Hc. 2, 3; Kī. 2, 84; Pāiyal. 181; G.H.R.; Mṛcch. 29, 5; 69, 23; 74, 20; A. Vikr. 56, 21), beside M. AMg. Ś. *khīṇa* (Hc. 2, 3; H.; Aṇuog. 282 ff.; Sūyag. 212; Samav. 88; Kappas.; Anarghar. 293, 10, where, however, the ed. Calc. 216, 6 has *jhīṇa*), and *chiṇa* (Hc. 2, 3). — *jhoḍaī* = *kṣoṭayati* (throws; hurls; Dhātupāṭha 35, 23) in *jhoḍia* (hunter; Deśīn. 3, 60); *ṇijjhoḍaī* = **niḥkṣoṭayati* (tears asunder; splits; Hc. 4, 124), perhaps also in *jhŏṇḍaliā* (a game analogous to the shepherd's dance; Deśīn. 3, 60). — Apparently *jhampaï* (to wander about; Hc. 4, 161) also belongs to it: however, it might have developed from *kṣap* (to send off; Dhātupāṭha 35, 84c), a root that occurs also in AMg. *jhampittā* = *aniṣṭavacanāvakāśaṁ kṛtvā* (to blame; Samav. 83) and *jhampia*, JM. *jhampiya* (torn; shaken; Deśīn. 3, 61; Erz. 85, 28) and *jhampaṇi* (eye-brow; Deśīn. 3, 54; Pāiyal. 250)[5]. — *jharua* (midge; Deśīn. 3, 54), will be derived from the root *kṣar* with the suffix *-uka* (§ 118. 596), to which belongs *kṣāra* (sharp; pricking biting) that forms AMg. A. *chāra*, AMg. JM. *khāra* in the meaning "saltpetre", "potash" (§ 321) — Hc. 4, 181 mentions also *avaajjhaī* beside *avacchaī* = **avacakṣati* (§ 499).

1. WACKERNAGEL, Literatur-Blatt für orientalische Philologie 3, 54; Altind. Gr. § 209. — 2. JACOBI in ZACHARIAE Beiträge zur indischen Lexicographie p. 59. — 3. Not to be confused with AMg. *jhiyāi* = *dhyāti* (§131.280.479). — 4. WEBER, ZDMG. 28, 376. 428; on H. 109. 333. 407; S. GOLDSCHMIDT, Prākṛtica p. 16 f. *vijjhāi* as *vidhyā* has entered also into Skt. of the Jainas (ZACHARIAE, Epilegomena zu der Ausgabe des Anekārthasaṁgraha, Wien, 1893 p. 1 ff. — 5. BÜHLER, Pāiẏal, s. v. *jhaṁpaṇīu*.

§ 327. *tsa* becomes *ccha* (Vr. 3, 40; C. 3, 4; Hc. 2, 21; Kī. 2. 92; Mk. fol. 25), Mg. *śca* (§ 233), through *thsa*, *tsha*, *tcha* (§ 316) : AMg. *kucchaṇijja* = *kutsanīya* (Paṇhāv. 218); *kucchia* = *kutsita* (Kī. 2, 92); *ciicchaī* = *cikitsati*, Ś. *cikicchidavva*, AMg. *tigicchaī*, *vitigicchāmi* (§ 215. 555); AMg. *teicchā*, *tigicchā* = *cikitsā*, *vitigicchā* = *vicikitsā*, *tigicchaga* = *cikitsaka* (§ 215), Ś. *ciicchaa* (Mālav. 27, 12; so to be read with the Bengal MSS and with the Telugu manuscript of BOLLENSEN for *cikissaa*, *ciissaa* ed. PAṆḌIT 52, 2); AMg. JM. Ś. *bibhaccha* (Uvās. § 94; Āv. 8, 19; Dvār. 506, 21; Kk. 264, 26; Mālatīm. 215, 1), Ś. *bīhaccha* (Prab. 45, 11; so to be read), Mg. *bīhaśca* (Mṛcch. 40, 5; so to be read) = *bibhatsa* M. JM. Ś. A. *macchara* = *matsara* (C. 3, 4; Hc. 2, 21; G.H.R.; Erz.; Śak. 161, 12; Mālav. 64, 20; Hc. 4, 444, 5); JM. Ś. *vaccha* = *vatsa* (Bh. 3, 40; Erz.; Kk.; Mṛcch. 94, 15; 150, 12; Vikr. 82, 6. 8. 13; 87, 17), Mg. *vaśca* (Hc. 4, 302); AMg. JM. *sirivaccha* = *śrīvatsa* (Paṇhāv. 259; Samav. 237; Ovav.; Erz.); M. JM. Ś. *vacchala* = *vatsala* (G. H.; Dvār. 501, 3; 503, 38; 507, 30; Erz.; Śak. 158, 12), Mg. *vaścalaẏ* (Mṛcch. 37, 13; so to be read). — Beside AMg. *charu* = *tsaru* (Pāiẏal. 121, Deśīn. 5, 24; Paṇhāv. 266; Samav. 131; Ovav.; Nāẏādh.), dialectically was used also *tharu* = **staru* (Deśīn. 5, 24). In Paṇhāv. 322, the text has *ccharu* and the commentary has *ttharu*—.

§ 327ª. In compounds, in which *t* stands at the end of a syllable and the following syllable originally begins with *śa* or *sa*, the sound-groups **tśa*, *tsa* become *ssa*, or with lengthening of the vowel standing before they become *sa*. *t*+*śa*: AMg. *ūsaveha* = *ucchrapayata* from **utśrapayata*, *ūsaviẏa* = *ucchrapita*; AMg. JM. *ūsiẏa* = *ucchrita*, AMg. also *ussiẏa*, *samussiẏa*, *ussaviẏa*; Ś. *ussāvedi* (§ 64); M. *ussūṇa* = *ucchūna* (G.); AMg. *ussuṁka* = *ucchulka* (§74); M. *ūsasaï* = *ucchvasiti*, AMg. *ūsasanti*; Mg. *ūśaśadu*; AMg. also *ussasaï* (§ 64. 496); AMg. *ussāsa* = *ucchvāsa* (Nāẏādh.; Bhag.; Ovav.), M. A. *ūsāsa* (G. R.; Hc. 4, 431, 2); *ūsasira* = **ucchvasira* (Hc. 2, 145); M. *ūsasia*, JM. *ūsasiẏa*, Ś. *ūsasida* = *ucchvasita* (G. H. R.; Śak. 119, 6; Kk. III, 513, 1; Śak. 132, 13; Vikr. 7, 12); *sūsāsa* = *socchvāsa* (Hc. 1, 157); *ūsīsa* (Pāiẏal. 118, JM. *ūsisaa* (Āv. 16, 8) = *ucchirṣaka*; the synonymous *ūsaa* (Deśīn. 1, 140) is = **ucchaya* from *ud*+*śaya*; *ūsua* = **ucchuka* from *ud*+*śuka* (Hc. 1, 114); AMg. *tassaṅkiṇo* = *tacchaṅkinaḥ* from *tad*+*śaṅkinaḥ* (Sūyag. 936). — *t*+*sa* : AMg. *ussagga* = *utsarga* (Bhag.; Kappas.); AMg. JM. *ussappiṇī* = *utsarpiṇī* (Kappas.; Ṛṣabhap.); AMg. *usseha* = *utsedha* Pāiẏal. 168; Bhag.; Uvās.; Ovav.); AMg. *tassanni-* = *tatsaṁjñin* (Āẏār. 1, 5, 4, 2), *tassaṁdhicāri-* = *tatsaṁdhicārin* (Āẏār. 2, 2, 2, 4); *ūsaraï* = *utsarati* (Hc. 1, 114), *ūsāria* = *utsārita* (Hc. 2, 21), JM. *ussārittā* (Erz. 37, 28; v.l. *ūsā°*);

AMg. *ūsatta* = *utsakta* (Kappas.); *ūsitta* = *utsikta* (Hc. 1, 114; Pāiẏal. 187), but also *ussikkaī* = **utsiknati* (to let loose; to throw up; Hc. 4, 91. 144). — According to Hc. 1, 114 *tsa* in *utsāha* and *utsanna* becomes *ccha* only : M.Ś. A. *ucchāha* (G. R.; Śak. 36. 12; Mālav. 8, 19 [to be so read with the v.l.]; Piṅgala 1, 96a); *ucchanna* (Hc. 1, 114); Ḍh. *ucchādida* = *utsādita* (Mṛcch. 38, 18; 39, 1). In *utsuka* and *utsava*, according to Vr. 3, 42; Kī. 2, 93; Mk. fol. 25 *ccha* never appears : Hc. 2, 22 permits it beside *s*. So M. *ucchua* (Hc.; on H. 984), but mostly M. Ś. *ūsua* (Grr.; G.H.R.[1]; Śak. 87, 14; Karp. 58, 2), Ś. also *ussua*, AMg. JM. *ussuẏa* (Śak. 84, 13; Mālav. 35, 1; 37, 20; Ovav.; Erz.); Ś. *pajjussua* = *paryutsuka* (Śak. 19, 6; 57, 11) and *pajjūsua* (Vikr. 21. 19); Ś. *samūsua* = *samutsuka* (Śak. 142, 4; Vikr. 67, 12), M. *ūsuia* = *utsukita* (H.); AMg. *osuẏa* = *autsuka* (Ovav.). — M. Ś. *ūsava* = *utsava* (G. H. R.; Śak. 121, 12; Cait. 244, 18); AMg. *ussava* (Vivāhap. 822) and *ūsaa* (Niraẏāv.); M. *gāmūsava* = *grāmotsava* (G.); M. JM. Ś. *mahūsava* = *mahotsava*; Ś. *vasantūsava* = *vasantotsava* (§ 158), beside M. Ś. *uccchava* = (H. 369; Mallikām. 209, 18), Ś. *ṇirucchava* (Śak. 118, 13)[2]. — *utsaṅga* always becomes M. AMg. JM. A. *ucchaṅga* (G.H. [read 422]. R.; Ovav.; Erz.; Hc. 4, 336; Vikr. 51, 2). — I would rather prefer, with Indians, to derive M. CP. *ucchallaï* (G.H.R.; Hc. 4, 326)), JM. *ucchalliẏa* (Erz.) beside *ūsalaï* (Hc. 4, 202), *ūsalia* (Deśīn. 1, 141), *ūsaliẏa* (Pāiẏal. 79) from *śal* with *ud* than to derive it, with ZACHARIAE[3] from **sal* with *ud*. — *utthallaï* (Hc. 4, 174; cf. Kī. 4, 46), *utthalliẏa* (Pāiẏal. 179), *utthalia* (Deśīn. 1, 107) is with BÜHLER[4] to be derived from *sthala*+*ud*. Like *t*+*śa* is treated *ṭ*+*śa* too in AMg. *chassaẏa* = *ṣaṭśata* (Kappas.).

1. The v. l. to H. 479 points, as that on Vr. 3, 42, rather to *ūsua* than to *ussua*. — 2. Wrongly doubled by LASSEN, Inst. p. 151 and rejected by BÖHTLINGK on Śak. 77, 6. — 3. KZ. 33, 444 ff. — 4. Pāiẏal s. v. *utthalliẏaṁ*.

§ 328. *psa* through *phsa*, *psha*, *pcha* becomes *ccha* (§ 316; Vr. 3, 40; C. 3, 4; Hc. 2, 21; Kī. 2, 92; Mk. fol. 25)[1]: *chāa* = Pāli *chāta* = *psāta* (hungry; Deśīn. 3, 33; Pāiẏal. 183). In the meaning "meagre" (Deśīn. 3, 33; Pāiẏal. 87), *chāa* is = **kṣāta*[2]. — *accharā*, *accharasā* = Old Hindī *apchar*, Sindhī *apcharā*[3] = *apsarā*, *apsarāḥ* (§ 410), from *chara* = *psaras* (form) in M. *samaccharehiṁ* = *samarūpaiḥ* (R. 7, 62) and AMg. *uttarakurumāṇusaccharāo* = *uttarakurumānuṣar* = *ūpāḥ* (Paṇhāv. 288)[4]. — *jugucchā* = *jugupsā*; M. *juucchaï*, AMg. *dugucchaï*, Ś. *jugucchedi* = *jugupsati* (§ 215. 515). — JM. *ghĕcchāmo* = **ghṛpsyāmaḥ* (Āv. 23, 6). — *licchaï* = *lipsati* (Hc. 2, 21); *licchā* = *lipsā* (Bh. 3, 40; Mk. fol. 25); AMg. *licchu* = *lipsu* (Uttar. 961).

1. Wrongly the change to *ppa* too has been assumed by WEBER, Bhag. 1, 414 and to *ppha* by PISCHEL, Ved. Studien 1, 79. — 2. BÜHLER, Pāiẏal, s. v. *chāẏaṁ*, PISCHEL, ZDMG. 52, 96. As *chāta* the word has entered into Skt. too (ZACHARIAE, Epilegomena to his edition of the Anekārthasaṁgraha, Wien 1893, p 15 note 2). — BEAMES, Comp. Gr. 1, 309. The form *abbharā*, which LASSEN, Inst. p. 267 mentions, and of which the etymology has been given by ASCOLI, Kritische Studien p. 262, and BARTHOLOMAE, ZDMG. 50, 722, is a wrong reading, as shown by PISCHEL, ZDMG. 51, 589 ff. — 4. PISCHEL, ZDMG. 52, 93 ff.

§ 329. *ḥka*, *ḥkha*, *ḥpa*, *ḥpha*, according to Hc. 2, 77 more correctly *ḫka*, *ḫkha*, *ḫpa*, *ḫpha*, are treated like the corresponding sound-groups with a sibilant (§ 301 ff.), therefore, become *kha* (in conjunctions), *kkha*, *ppa* (in conjunctions), *ppha*, Ś. *antakkaraṇa* = *antaḥkaroṇa* (Vikr. 72, 12); Ś. *ṇikkhattikada* = *niḥkṣatrikṛta* (Mahāv. 27, 6); M. AMg. JM. JŚ. Ś. Mg. D.A. *dukkha* = *duḥkha* (G.H.R.; Āẏār. 1, 1, 1, 7. 2, 3, 3, 5. 6, 2 etc.; Uvās.; Kappas.; Niraẏāv.; Nāẏādh.; Āv. 9, 6; 10, 20; Erz.; Kk.; Ṛṣabhap.; Pav. 380, 12; 381, 14. 20; 383, 75; 385, 67, 69; Mṛcch. 28, 11; 78, 12; Śak. 51, 14; 84, 14; 136, 13; Vikr. 9, 19; 51, 12; 53, 11; Mg. Mṛcch. 159, 12; Prab. 28, 17; 29, 7; D. Mṛcch. 101, 12; A. Hc. 4, 357, 4; Vikr. 59, 6; 60, 18); Ś. *ṇiddukkha* = *nirduḥkha* (Śak. 76, 8). Ś. *dukkhida* = *duḥkhita* (Vikr. 16, 6; 34, 1). — In AMg. JM. JŚ. is found beside *dukkha* also *duha* (Sūẏag. 126. 156. 259. 406; Uttar. 505. 574. 599. 626; Paṇhāv. 504; Dasav. N. 646, 6. 14; Nāẏādh. 478; Erz.; Kk.; Kattig. 401, 349). Likewise M. *duhia* (Hc. 1, 13 [so to be read]; Kī. 2, 113 [so to be read]; H. R.), AMg. JM. *duhiya* (Uttar. 599; Vivāhap. 116; T. 6. 10; Dvār. 501, 10; Kk.), JŚ. *duhida* (Pav. 383, 75) = *duḥkhita*; M. *duhāvia* (G.); AMg. *duhi-* = *duḥkhin* (Sūẏag. 71; Uttar. 577). The forms with *h* are found almost exclusively in verses, and *duha* often stands directly beside or in parallel with *suha* = *sukha*, which has influenced its form[1]. Reversely *sugga* (comfort; well-being; Deśīn. 8, 56) is formed according to *dugga* = *durga* (pain.; Deśīn. 5, 53; Triv. 1, 3, 105)[2]. — *puṇapuṇakkaraṇa* = *punaḥpunaḥkaraṇa* (Deśīn. 1, 32); *antappāa* = *antaḥpāta* (Hc. 2, 77). Whether in Mg. the sound-groups have been rightly treated in the MSS is doubtful. Cf. also § 342. 347. *ḥśa*, *ḥṣa*, *ḥsa* become *ssa*, Mg. *śśa*, or with lengthening of the preceding vowel *sa*, Mg. *śa* (§64): Ś. *cadussāla catuḥśāla* (Mallikām. 209, 19; 215, 5; text *caü°*), *cadussālaa* = *catuḥśālaka* (Mṛcch. 6, 6; 16, 11; 45, 25; 93, 16, 18; Dhūrtas. 6, 5); Ś. *cadussamudda* = *catuḥsamudra* (Mṛcch. 55, 16; 78, 3; 147, 17); Mg. *ṇiśśalida* = *niḥsṛta* (Lalitav. 566, 15); M. *ṇisaṅka* = *niḥśaṅka*, JM. *nissaṅka* (§ 64); M. Ś. *ṇisaha* = *niḥsaha*, beside *nissaha* (§ 64); JM. *ṇisesa* = *niḥśeṣa* (KI. 1); Ś. *dussanta* = *duḥṣanta* (Śak. 16, 12; 76, 10), Mg. *duśśanta* (Śak. 160, 10); *dussaṁcara* and *dūsaṁcara* = *duḥsaṁcara* (Kī. 2, 113); Ś. *dussiliṭṭha* = *duḥśliṣṭa* (Mahāv. 23, 19); M. JM. Ś. A. *dūsaha* beside Ś. *dussaha* = *duḥsaha* (§ 64); Ś. *suṇasseha* = *śunaḥśepha* (Anarghar. 58, 5; 59, 12); *dussila—duḥśila* (Deśīn. 6, 67). Cf. § 340.

1. Cf. Jacobi, KZ. 25, 438 ff.; where, however, there are many errors. — 2. Pischel, BB. 6, 95.

§ 330. The sound-combinations *hṇa*, *hna*, *hma*, *hla* become *ṇha*, *mha*, *lha* (Vr. 3, 8; Hc. 2, 74. 75. 76; Kī. 2, 95. 96. 99; Mk. fol. 21) through metathesis of the consonants. M. AMg. JM. JŚ. Ś. *avaraṇha* = *aparāhṇa* (Bh. 3, 8; Hc. 2, 75; G. H.; Aṇuog. 74; Bhag.; Erz.; Kattig. 402, 354; 403, 373; Vṛṣabh. 41, 2); AMg. JŚ. *puvvaṇha* = *pūrvāhṇa* (Bh. 3, 8; Hc. 2, 75; Mk. fol. 21; Ṭhāṇ. 244; Aṇuog. 74; Bhag.; Kattig. 402, 354); AMg. *puvvāvaraṇha* (Nāẏādh. 332.481; Ṭhāṇ. 244; Kappas. § 212. 227; Niraẏāv. 53. 55; Vivāgas. 124 [text *paccā°*]); M. AMg. JM. JŚ. Ś. *majjhaṇha* = *madhyāhna* (Hc. 2, 84; H. 494; Karp. 94, 6; 96, 2; Ṭhāṇ. 243; Āv. 46, 6; Erz.; Kattig. 402, 354; Ratn. 321, 32; Dhūrtas. 7, 20; Karp. 59, 4; Viddhaś. 40, 5; Cait. 92, 13; Jīvān. 46, 10. 17). On *majjhaṇṇa* = *madhyaṁdina* see § 148. 214. — M. AMg. JM. A. *gĕṇhaï*, JŚ. *giṇhadi*, Ś. Mg. *gĕṇhadi* =

gṛhṇāti (§ 512). — M.Ś. Mg. A. *ciṇha*=*cihna*, beside M. AMg. JM. *cindha* (§ 267). —*jaṇhu*=*jahnu* (Bh. 3, 33; Hc. 2, 75). — *niṇhavaï*=*nihnute*, AMg. *niṇhavĕjja*, *niṇhave*, *aṇiṇhavamāṇa*, M. *ṇiṇhuvijjanti*, Ś. *ṇiṇhuvīadi*, *ṇiṇhuvida* (§ 473). — AMg. JM. Ś. *vaṇhi*=*vahni* (Bh. 3, 33; Hc. 2, 75; Kī. 2, 99; Vivâhap. 417; Erz.; Mudrār. 253, 8). — M. D. *bamha-*=*brahman* (Hc. 2, 74; H.; Mṛcch. 105, 21; PG. Ś. Mg. *bamhaṇa*=*brāhmaṇa* (§ 287); Ś. *bamhaṇṇa*=*brāhmaṇya* (§ 282); *bamhacera*=*brahmacarya* (§ 176); beside dialectical *bambha-*, *bambhaṇa*, *bambhacera* (§ 250. 267). — *sumhā*=*suhmāḥ* (Hc. 2, 74). — *alhāda*=*āhlāda* (Bh. 3, 8); AMg. *kalhāra*=*kahlāra* (Bh. 3, 8; Hc. 2, 76; Kī. 2, 95; Mk. fol. 21; Paṇṇav. 35; Sūyag. 813); *palhāa*=*prahlāda* (Hc. 2, 76); AMg. *palhāyaṇijja*=*prahlādanīya* (Jīv. 821; Nāyādh. § 23), AMg. *palhāyaṇa*=*prahlādana* (Uttar. 838); M. AMg. Ś. *palhattha* =**prahlasta*, M. *palhatthaï*, AMg. *palhatthiya* (§ 285); AMg. JM. *palhava* =*pahlava* (Paṇhāv. 42 [text °*hla*°]; Dvār. 498, 17), AMg. *pahlavī* (Nāyādh. § 117), *palhaviyā* (Vivāhap. 792; Ovav. § 55); *lhasaï*, *parilhasaï*=*hlasati parihlasati* (Hc. 4, 197), A. *lhasiũ* (Hc. 4, 445, 3).

§ 331. Through metathesis, according to Hc. 2, 124, *hya* may become *yha*: *guyha*=*guhya*; *sayha*=*sahya*. The grammarians teach the same for the stem of the pronoun of the second person : *tuyha*, *uyha* (§ 420ff). This phonetic change that is common in Pāli, has not as yet been attested in Pkt. It is apparently to be assumed for Mg. P. CP. in agreement with the phonetic rules otherwise valid for these dialects (§ 236. 252. 280. 287). The editions write *jjha* in Mg.; yet in Mṛcch. 170, 18=463, 8 ed. GODABOLE, the MSS have *sahya*, *sattha*, *śattha*, *ssattha* for *sajjha* of the text, so that *śayha* will have to written. So in spite of § 252, in all other dialects *ya* after its transposition has become *ja*, so that *hya* appears as *jha*, and in the inlaut, as *jjha* (Vr. 3, 28; C. 3, 20; Hc. 2, 26. 124; Kī. 2, 87; Mk. fol. 23). Ś. *aṇugĕjjhā*=*anugrāhyā* (Mṛcch. 24, 11); AMg. *abhirujjha*=*abhiruhya* (§ 590), *abhiṇigijjha*=*abhinigṛhya*, *parigijjha*=*parigṛhya* (§ 591); *najjhaï*=*nahyate* (Hc. 2, 26), M. *saṁṇajjhaï* (R.); JM. *gujjha*=*guhya* (Hc. 2, 26. 124; Erz.); *gujjhaa*=*guhyaka* (Bh. 3, 28); *dujjha*=*dohya* (Deśīn. 1, 7); *vajjha*=*vāhya* (C. 3, 20; Kī. 2, 87), *vajjhaa*=*vāhyaka* (Bh. 3, 28); Ś. *sajjha*=*sahya* (Hc. 2, 26, 124; Śak. 51, 15); M. *sajjha*=*sahya* (R.). On *hijjo*, Ś. *hio*=*hyas* see § 134.

§ 332. *hra* and *rha* are mostly separated by a partition-vowel (§ 132-140). *daśārha* becomes AMg. *dasāra* (Hc. 2, 85; Antag. 3; Ṭhāṇ. 80. 133; Nāyādh. 528. 537. 1235. 1262. 1277; Nirayāv. 78 ff.; Samav. 235; Uttar. 665. 671). *hrada* becomes AMg. *haraya* (§ 132), or with transposition of the consonants AMg. A. *draha*, AMg. *daha* (§ 268. 354). — *hva*, as in Pāli, is firstly transposed as *vha*, which becomes *bha*, in the inlaut *-bbha-* (C. 3, 1. 21. 26; Hc. 2, 57; Kī. 2, 97; Mk. fol. 26). *gabbhara*=*gahvara* (Kī. 2, 97). — AMg. JM. *jibbhā*=*jihvā* (C. 3, 1. 21. 26; Hc. 2, 57; Mk. fol. 26; Āyār. 1, 1, 2, 5; p. 137, 1; Sūyag. 280. 639; Uttar. 943. 986; Uvās.; Ovav.; Āv. 42, 3); AMg. *jibbhindiya* (Vivāhap. 32. 531; Ṭhāṇ. 300; Paṇhāv. 529), A. *jibhindiu* (Hc. 4, 427, 1; so to be read), beside M. AMg. JM. JŚ. Ś. *jihā*, Mg. *yihā* (§ 65). — *vibbhala*=*vihvala* (C. 3, 1; Hc. 2, 58; Kī. 2, 72),

AMg. *vĕbbhala* (Bh. 3, 47; Paṇhāv. 165), beside M. JM. *vihala* (Grr.; G. H. R.; Kk.), JM. *vihaliya* = *vihvalita* (Erz.). On *bhibbhala, biṁbhala,* M. *bhĕṁbhala,* Ś. *bhĕṁbhaladā* see § 209.

§ 333. As in the case of simple consonants (§ 218 ff.), so also in the case of conjunct mutes of the same class, we find here and there cerebrals in place of dentals of Skt. — *tta* = *ṭṭa* : Ś. *maṭṭiā,* AMg. JM. *maṭṭiyā* = *mṛttikā* (§ 49). — AMg. *vaṭṭa* = *vṛtta* (round; § 49); AMg. *oṇiyaṭṭa* = *avanivṛtta* (Kappas.), *viyaṭṭa* = *vivṛtta* (Ovav., beside AMg. *vatta* (Ovav.), *nivvatta* (Ovav.); JM. *jahāvatta* = *yathāvṛtta* (Erz.), and throughout *tt* in the rest of the dialects — From both *pattana* and *paṭṭana,* the words that occur side by side in Skt. AMg. JM. A. have only *paṭṭaṇa* (Vr. 3, 23; Hc. 2, 29; Mk. fol. 23; Āyār. 1, 7, 6, 4; 2, 11, 7; Ṭhāṇ. 347; Paṇhāv. 175-246. 406. 486; Uttar. 891; Vivāhap. 40. 295; Uvās.; Ovav.; Nāyādh.; Kappas.; Erz.; Hc. 4, 407). — *ttha* = *ṭṭha*: AMg. JM. *uṭṭhei,* A. *uṭṭhaï*- **utthāti,* M. *uṭṭhia,* AMg. JM. *uṭṭhiya,* beside Ś. *utthehi, utthedu, utthida*; AMg. *kaviṭṭha* beside AMg. Mg. *kavittha* = *kapittha* (§ 309). — *ddha* = *ḍḍha*: AMg. JM. *iḍḍhi* beside usual *riddhi* (§ 57). — AMg. *vaḍḍhi, vuḍḍhi* = *vṛddhi,* M. *parivaḍḍhi* = *parivṛddhi*; M. AMg. JM. Ś. Mg. *vuḍḍha* = *vṛddha* (§ 53). — AMg. *saḍḍhā* *śraddhā* (Hc. 2, 41; Sūyag. 603. 611. 620; Nāyādh.; Bhag.; Ovav.; Kappas.), *jāyasaḍḍha* (Vivāhap. 11. 101. 115. 191), *uppaṇṇasaḍḍha, saṁjāyasaḍḍha* (Vivāhap. 11. 12); AMg. JM. *saḍḍha* = *śrāddha* (Āyār. 2, 1, 11, 5; 2, 2, 2, 8. 10: Erz.); AMg. *saḍḍhi-* = *śraddhin* (Āyār. 1, 3, 4, 3; 1, 5, 3; Sūyag. 71; Kappas.); AMg. *mahāsaḍḍhi-* (Āyār. 1, 2, 5, 5), *saḍḍhiya* = *śrāddhika* (Ṭhāṇ. 152), *saḍḍhaï-* = *śrāddhakin* (Ovav.), beside M. AMg. JM. Ś. *saddhā* (Hc. 1, 12; 2. 41; H.; Āyār. 1, 1, 3, 2; Uvās.; Erz.; Śak. 38, 5; Prab. 42, 2. 8; 44, 11; 46, 8; 48, 1. 2 etc.), Mg. *śaddhā* (Prab. 47, 2; 63, 4), M. *saddhālua* (H.) and always AMg. *saddahaï* (Vr. 8, 33; Hc. 4, 9; Kī. 4, 46; Mk. fol. 54; Vivāhap. 845. 1215; Uttar. 805), *saddhāi* (Uttar. 804), JŚ. *saddahadi* (Kattig. 399, 311); AMg. *saddahāmi* (Vivāhap. 134; Nāyādh. § 133); M. *saddahimo* (G. 990); AMg. *saddahanti* (Vivāhap. 841 f.), *saddahe* (Āyār. 1, 7, 8, 24; Uttar. 170), *saddahasu* (Sūyag. 151), *saddahāhi* (Vivâhap. 134); JM. *asaddahanta* (Āv. 35, 4); AMg. *saddahāṇa* (Hc. 4, 238; Sūyag. 322), *asaddahāṇa* (Sūyag. 504); AMg. JŚ. *saddahamāṇa* (Hc. 4, 9; Sūyag. 596. 625; Pav. 388, 6); AMg. *asaddahamāṇa* (Vivāhap. 1215); M. *saddahia* (Bh. 8, 33; R. 1, 38); JŚ. *saddahaṇa* (Pav. 388. 6). — *nta* = *ṇṭa*: AMg. *viṇṭa, tālaviṇṭa,* M. *vĕṇṭa,* M. AMg. Ś. *tālavĕṇṭa,* AMg. *tāliyaṇṭa* = *vṛnta tālavṛnta* (§ 53). — *ntha* = *ṇṭha* : *gaṇṭhaï* = *grathnāti* (Hc. 4, 120), beside *ganthaï* (Mk. fol. 54); M. AMg. JM. JŚ. D. *gaṇṭhi* = *granthi* (Hc. 4, 120; G.H.; Karp. 10, 2; 76, 4; Sūyag. 719; Vivāhap. 104; Uttar. 877; Ovav.; Erz.; Pav. 385, 69; Śak. 144, 12; Prab. 18, 1; Bālar. 36, 3; 130, 6; 148, 16; 297, 16; 299, 1; Viddhaś. 71, 1; 83, 1; Karp. 23, 2; 76, 10; 112, 5; Karṇas. 11, 1; D. Mṛcch. 104, 7); AMg. *gaṇṭhilla* (Vivāhap. 1308); AMg. *gaṇṭhiga* = *granthika* (Sūyag. 869); AMg. *gaṇṭhibheya* (Vivāgas. 100; Uttar. 289; Paṇhāv. 151 [°*da*]); but *ganthibheya* (Paṇhāv. 121); *gaṇṭhicchea* = *granthiccheda* (Deśīn. 2, 86; 3, 9); AMg. *gaṇṭhicchedaya* (Sūyag. 714), *gaṇṭhiccheda* (Sūyag. 719); Mg. *gaṇṭhiśchedaa* (Śak. 115, 4. 12; so to be read); Ś. *ṇiggaṇ*-

ṭhidagaṇṭhira (Bālar. 131, 14); JŚ. *dugganṭhi* (Pav. 385, 68); AMg. *niyaṇṭha* =*nirgrantha* (Sūyag. 962. 986. 989. 992; Vivāhap. 149 ff.), *mahāniyaṇṭha* (Uttar. 635), but AMg. *ganthima* (Āyār. 2. 12, 1; 2, 15, 20; Paṇhāv. 519; Vivāhap. 823; Jīv. 348; Dasav. N. 561, 10; Aṇuog. 29, Nandis. 507; Ovav. § 79 XI [so to be read]), seldom *gaṇṭhima* (Nāyādh. 269); AMg. JŚ. *gantha*=*grantha* (Āyār. 1, 7, 8, 11; Paṇhāv. 506; Kappas.; Kattig. 399, 317. 318; 404, 386. 387); AMg. *saṁgantha* (Āyār. 1, 2, 1, 1); AMg. JŚ. *niggantha*=*nirgrantha* (Āyār. 2, 5, 1, 1; 2, 6, 1, 1; 2, 15, 29; p. 132, 4 ff.; Sūyag. 938. 958. 964. 992; Vivāhap. 381; Uvās.; Ovav.; Kappas. etc.; Kattig. 404, 386); AMg. *nigganthī* (Āyār. 2, 5, 1, 1). — *nda*=*ṇḍa* : *kaṇḍaliā* =*kandarikā* (Hc. 2, 38), of uncertain meaning. Cf. *kaṇḍali vva* as v.l. for *visalaa vva*=*viṣalateva* at H. 410. — AMg. *bhiṇḍimāla* beside usual *bhiṇḍivāla*=*bhindipāla* (§ 248.) — In the case of consonants of different classes, in cases other than those mentioned in § 289 ff. 308 f., cerebralization occurs in the sound-group *gdha* in *thaḍḍha* (Pāiyal. 75), M. *ṭhaḍḍha* (Hc. 2, 39; H. 537)=**stagdha* from *√*stagh*, to which belong Pāli *ṭhahati* (stands), Pkt. *thāha* (ground; bottom), *thaha* (residence), *thaggha* (deep), *atthāha*, *atthaggha* (bottomless, deep; § 88), and *utthaṅghaī* (throws up), M. *utthaṅghia* (§ 505), *utthaṅghaṇa*, *utthaṅghi-* (G.). — *chūḍha* with its compounds=*kṣubdha*, is an analogical formation (§ 66).

§ 334. The rules given in the preceding paragraphs hold good for conjuncts of more than two consonants: pro ex. *uppāveī*=*utplāvayati* (Hc. 2, 106); M. *uppua*=*utpluta* (H.); *utthala*=*utsthala* (R.); M. *ucchevaṇa*= *utkṣepaṇa* (R.); AMg. *ṇiṭṭhāṇa*=*niḥsthāna* (Vivāgas. 102); AMg. *kayasāvattā*=*kṛtasāpatnyā* (Deśīn. 1, 25); M. *māhappa*=*māhātmya* (G. R.); M. AMg. Ś. *maccha*=*matsya* (R.; Sūyag. 71. 166. 274; Uttar. 442. 595. 944; Vivāgas. 136; Vivāhap. 248. 483); Mg. *maśca* (§ 233); AMg. *macchattāe* (Vivāgas. 148); *macchabandha* (Erz.); M. *ujjoa*=*uddyota* (G.H.R.); M.Ś. *aggha*=*arghya* (H.; Śak. 18, 3; 72, 3); M. *sāmaggaa*=*sāmagryaka* (R.); M. AMg. *taṁsa*=*tryasra* (§ 74); JM. *vaṭṭā*=*vartman* (path; Deśīn. 7, 31; Erz.); M. AMg. JM. Ś. A. *paṁti*=*paṅkti* (§ 269); M. AMg. JM. Ś. *viṁjha* =*vindhya* (§ 269); M. *attha*=*astra* (R.) etc. Very many examples have been furnished in appropriate places. *jyotsnā* forms M. AMg. JM. Ś. D. A. *jŏṇhā* (Hc. 2, 75; G. H. R.; Karp. 1, 4; 2, 5; 29, 1; 88, 2; Mallikām. 29, 3; Jīv. 787; Kk.; Śak. 55, 2; Mālav. 28, 10; Bālar. 292, 15; Anarghar. 277, 3; Mallikām. 124, 7; 243, 15; 252, 3; Karṇas. 16, 8; D. Mṛcch. 101. 9; A. Hc. 4, 376, 1), *jŏṇhāla*=**jyotsnāla* (Hc. 2, 159), Ś. *jŏṇhiā*=*jyautsnikā* (Mallikām. 238, 9), or AMg. *dosiṇā* (§ 215), Ś. *dosiṇī*=*jyoutsnī* (§ 215). M. JM. *sāmattha* (Hc. 2, 22; G. H. R.; Erz.; Kk.); presupposes one **sāmartha* (§ 281); *sāmarthya* regularly becomes *sāmaccha* (Hc. 2, 22). — Pāli *disvā* makes it probable that in AMg. *dissā* (Sūyag. 728; Vivāhap. 1414), *padissā*=**pradiṣṭvā* (Vivāhap. 1415) too the long vowel is original and the short one is metrical. Thereto points also AMg. *dissam āgayaṁ* =*dṛṣṭvāgatam* (Uttar. 695), where *dissam* stands, according to § 349 for *dissaṁ*, and this again stands for *dissā* according to § 114. The regular form from *dṛṣṭvā* would be **diṭṭhā*. On the loss of aspiration in conjunct consonants see § 213.

III. DROPPING OFF AND ENTRY OF CONSONANTS IN THE ANLAUT.

§ 335. The consonants may drop off when they begin the second member of a compound and stand between vowels. It so takes place also in the case of consonants standing in the anlaut of enclitics and sometimes also after proclitics, whilst associated words are deemed to be compounds (184). Otherwise dropping off of initial consonants is merely sporadic and dialectical: *ūā* = Pāli *ūkā* = *yūkā* (Deśīn. 1, 139; Triv. 1, 3, 105) beside *jūā* (Deśīn. 1, 159), AMg. *jūẏā* (Āẏār. 2, 13, 18; Aṇuog. in Weber, Bhag. 2, 265 note), *jūva* (§ 230)[1]; *ŏkkaṇi* = **yūkani* (louse; Deśīn. 1, 159). — AMg. *ahā°* = *yathā°* (Hc. 1, 245); e.g. *ahāsuẏaṁ* = *yathāśrutam* (Āẏār. 1, 8, 1, 1; p. 137, 26); *ahāsuttaṁ ahākappaṁ ahāmaggaṁ* = *yathāśrutaṁ yathākalpaṁ yathāmārgam* (Āẏār. p. 137, 26 [°*suẏaṁ*]; Nāẏādh. 369; Vivāhap. 165; Uvās.; Kappas.); *ahārāiṇiẏāe* = **yathāratnikāya* (Āẏār. 2, 3, 3, 5; Ṭhāṇ. 355 f.); *ahāṇupuvvie* = *yathānupūrvyā* (Āẏār. 2, 15, 13; Ovav.); *ahāriham* = *yathārtham* (Āẏār. 2, 15, 16; Sūẏag. 695; Uvās.); *ahāsaṁthaḍaṁ* = = *yathāsaṁstṛtam* (Āẏār. 2, 7, 2, 14); *ahāsuhuma* = *yathāsūkṣma* (Āẏār. 2, 15, 18; Vivāhap. 213); *āhattahiẏaṁ* = **yāthātathiyam* (Sūẏag. 484, 506) *āhākaḍaṁ* = **yāthākṛtam* (Āẏār. 1, 8, 1, 17; Sūẏag. 405. 408); *āhāpariggahiẏa* = **yāthāparigṛhita* (Ovav.). — AMg. *āva-* = *yāvat* in *āvakahā°* = **yāvatkathā°* (Sūẏag. 120); *āvakahāe* = **yāvatkathāyai* (Āẏār. 1, 8, 1, 1; Ṭhāṇ. 274); *āvakahaṁ* = **yāvatkathām* (Āẏār. 1, 8, 4, 16); *āvakahiẏa* = **yāvatkathika*, all in the meaning "continuously", "for life". — AMg. *āvanti* = *yāvanti* (Āẏār. 1, 4, 2, 3; 1, 5, 1, 1 ff.). Dropping off of initial *t* or *y* takes place also in *uyha, ujjha, ubbha, umha* (§ 420 ff.). Cf. *ẏāiṁ* § 427.

1. Pischel, BB. 3, 241.

§ 336. *y*, as in Pāli, is put before *eva* in Mg. P. *yeva*, behind short or shortened vowels *yyeva*. Mg. *idŏ yyeva, mama yyeva* (Hc. 4, 302), falsely *eva* (Lalitav. 567, 1); P. *savvassa yyeva* = *sarvasyaiva*; *tūrātŏ yyeva* = *durād eva* (Hc. 4, 316. 323). As in the case of original *y* (§ 252), here also the MSS of the dramas do not conform to the rule, but they write *jeva, jjeva, jĕvva, jjĕvva*, that is to say, the forms of the words that can be used in Ś. (§ 95). Vr. 12, 23 teaches for Ś. *jĕvva*, Hc. 4, 280 *yyeva*, which is found in only one part of the South Indian manuscripts[1]. In A. *jeva* with the dropping off of the syllable *va* (§ 150) and change of *e* into *i* (§ 85) becomes *ji* (C. 2, 27[b]; Hc. 4, 420 with Word-Index). The older form *jẹ* is found in M. (H. 524 v.l. = Hc. 2, 217; R. 4, 36), AMg. (Uttar 669) and JM. (Āv. 12, 24) and is considered by the grammarians (Hc. 2, 217; cf. C. 2, 27[a] p. 46; Kī. 4, 83) as an expletive. The v.l. *cia.* in H. 524 points to the correct reading. *ya* enters in A. before *iva* also, which becomes *jiŭa, jeŭa* = **yiva* (§261). A. *jiŭa* seems to support the usual derivation of Pāli *viya* from **yiva* by metaphesis[2]. But Pāli *viya* cannot be separated from M.Ś. Mg. *via*, AMg. JM. *viẏa*, and these from AMg. JM. *viva, piva* and dialectical *miva*. Hence Pāli *viya*, M. Ś. Mg. *via*, AMg. JM. *viẏa* are to be derived from *viva*, which is to be equated as = *v*+*iva* according to § 337. *via* is the single prevailing form in Ś. Mg. (Vr. 12, 24; Mṛcch. 2, 16. 19. 21. 22. 25;

3, 17. 20; 8, 3 etc. Mg. Mṛcch. 10, 1; 133, 12. 24; 134, 2; 136, 14 etc.), more rarely in M. (Vr. 9, 16; Hc. 2, 182; H. R.; Karp. 1, 4; 16, 4; 64, 8), yet more rarely *viẏa* in AMg. JM. (C. 2, 22; Bhag.; Erz.), since these dialects use *va, vva, iva* (§ 92. 143). *viva* is found in AMg. JM. behind vowels (Hc. 2, 182; Kī. 4, 83; Paṇhāv. 505, 6. 7. 10; Nāẏādh. § 35.92; p. 349. 1450; Uttar. 593. 596. 634; Vivāgas. 83. 239; Vivāhap. 171; Niraẏāv.; Kappas.; Erz.; Kk.), as v.l. also in M. (H. R.). After anusvāra *viva* becomes in M. AMg. JM. *piva* (C. 2, 22; Hc. 2, 182; Kī. 4, 83), where on the analogy of *vi*, *pi* = *api* might have had a hand. The derivation of *piva* from *pi* = *api* + *iva*[3] makes the meaning improbable. So *piva* M. (G. s. v. *iva*; H.; Weber on H. 1); AMg. (Sūẏag. 758; Paṇhāv. 231. 340. 508; Nāẏādh. § 23. 122; p. 269. 271. 289. 354. 439. 740. 1045. 1433; Vivāgas. 112; Rāẏap. 255; Vivāhap. 794. 807. 823. 943; Niraẏāv.; Kappas.; Āv. 7, 29; Dvār. 497, 37; Erz.; Ṛṣabhap.). Vr. 10, 4, hence wrongly, restricts *piva* to P. — *miva* (Vr. 9, 16; C. 2, 27[1] ; p. 47; Hc. 2, 182; Kī. 4, 83), which is found after anusvāra in M. (H.; Weber on H. 1; R.); and is not with Bloch[4] to be doubted,[5] probably originated either from *viva* or *piva*, through assimilation with the preceding *ṁ*[6], as we find also *mi* for *vi*, *pi* = *api*[7]. Cf. *heṁ meva, hevaṁ meva* in the inscription of Aśoka in Senart s. v.

1. Pischel on Hc. 4. 280. — 2. Childers s. v. *iva*; E. Kuhn, Beiträge p. 64; E. Müller, Simplified Grammar p. 62; Windisch, BKSGW. p. 232; doubtingly Weber on H. 1, note 2. — 3. Jacobi, Kalpasūtra p. 100; cf. also Goldschmidt, Prākṛtica p. 30; Weber on H. 1; Bloch, Vr. und Hc. p. 34. — 4. Vr. und Hc. p. 34 ff.— 5. Correctly against him Windisch, l. c. p. 234 f.; Konow, GGA. 1894, p. 478—6. Other explanations in Weber H.[1] p. 47; P. Goldschmidt, Specimen, p. 69; S. Goldschmidt, R. s. v.; Windisch, l. c. p. 234. In Vr. 9, 16 we should probably read *piva* for *mmiva*. — 7. S. Goldschmidt, Prākṛtica p. 31; Klatt; ZDMG. 33. 459; Weber, H. s. v. *mi*. Also inscriptionally in JM. (KI. 10; beside *vi* and *pi*).

§ 337. *v* is thrust forward in M. Ś. Mg. *via*, AMg. JM. *viẏa*, AMg. JM. *viva* = *iva* (§ 336); AMg. *vuccaï*, Ś. Mg. *vuccadi* = *ucyate* (§ 544); AMg. JM. *vutta* = *ukta* (Sūẏag. 74. 844. 921. 974. 986. 993; Uttar. 717; Uvās.; Niraẏāv.; Ovav.; Kappas.; T. 4, 19; 5, 2; Āv. 11, 22; Erz.); M. AMg. JM. *vubbhaï* = *uhyate* (§ 266. 541). *vuccaï, vutta, vubbhaï* may be derived also from the present stem[1] = **vacyate*, **vakta*, **vabhyate* with change of *a* into *u* according to § 104, as it is certain for M. *vuttha* = **vasta* = *uṣita*, from √*vas* (to live; § 303. 564)[2], and for AMg. *parivusiẏa* from √*vas* (to put on; Āẏār. 1, 6, 2, 2. 3, 1; 1, 7, 4, 1. 5, 1). JŚ. Ś. Mg. have *utta* (Pav. 382, 42; Cait. 41, 10; 72, 5; 127, 17; Kāleẏak. 23, 11; Mg. Mṛcch. 37, 12), and so throughout in compounds, as M. *paccutta* = *pratyukta* (H. 918); AMg. *nirutta* = *nirukta* (Paṇhāv. 406); M. Ś. *puṇarutta* (G.H.R.; Mṛcch. 72, 3; Śak. 56, 16; Mālav. 86, 4; Bālar. 120, 6; Vṛṣabh. 15, 16; Mallikām. 73, 3), AMg. *apuṇarutta* (Jīv. 612; Kappas.). — A. *vuṭṭhae* = *uttiṣṭhanti* (Piṅgala 1, 125[a]); M. JM. *vūḍha* = *ūḍha* (R.; Erz.), beside M. *ūḍha* (G.)[3]; JM. *vuppanta-* = *upyamāna* (Āv. 25, 29); *vŏccattha* (perverse cohabitation; Deśīn. 7, 58) = **uccastha* from *ucca*, as AMg. *vuccattha* (= *paryasta*; *bhraṣṭa*; Uttar. 245) points.

1. WINDISCH, BKSGW. 1893, 230, note 1. — 2. Cf. E. KUHN, Beiträge p. 37. — 3. Sometimes it cannot be said with certainty whether or not *vūḍha* in R., as elsewhere often, is = *vyūḍha, vu, vŏ* often is = *vi*+*ud*.

§ 338. Prothesis of *h* is found in *hare* (Hc. 2, 202; Kī. 4, 83), *hire* (Vr. 9, 15), beside *are*[1]; *hira* (Hc. 2, 186; § 259) beside M. *ira* = *kira* (§ 184); AMg. *huṭṭha* = *oṣṭha* (Āẏār. 1, 1, 2, 5); AMg. *havvāe*, dative from **arvāka* = *arvāñc* (Āẏār. 1, 2, 2, 1; Sūẏag. 565. 575. 578. 601. 609. 616. 625 f.). The adverb AMg. *havvaṁ* "quickly", which the commentators explain with *śighram* or *arvāk* and with WARREN[2] and LEUMANN[3] they trace back to *arvāk*, also supports this. JACOBI[4] doubtingly equates it as = *bhavyam*, WEBER[5] earlier, likewise doubtingly = *savvaṁ* = *sarvam*, later[6] = *havyam* = "at call" (Ṭhāṇ. 124. 125. 127. 155 ff. 207. 208. 285 ff. 539. 585; Antag. 14. 18 f. 30. 32; Samav. 89. 95. 110; Vivāgas. 18 ff. 130; Nāẏādh. § 94; p. 306. 378. 565. 620. 624 f. 737. 792. 819 etc.; Vivāhap. 96 f. 125 f. 146 f. 154 f. 170. 181 f. 334 etc.; Rāẏap. 248 ff.; Jīv. 260. 356. 411; Aṇuog. 394. 436. 454. 455; Paṇṇav. 838; Niraẏāv.; Uvās.; Ovav.; Kappas.).

1. PISCHEL, KB. 7, 462; P. GOLDSCHMIDT, GN. 1874, p. 474. — 2. Over de godsdienstige en wijsgeerige Begrippen der Jaina's p. 52 ff. — 3. Aup. S. s. v. — 4. Kalpas, s. v. — 5. Bhag. 1, 416, note 1. — 6. Verzeichniss 2, 2, 423, note 3.

IV. FINAL CONSONANTS

§ 339. Finally only a simple or nasalized vowel can stand in Pkt. Hence final consonants, excepting the nasals, are dropped : *maṇā* = *manāk* (Hc. 2. 169); M. AMg. JM. Ś. Mg. *tāva* = *tāvat* (§ 185); M. AMg. JM. Ś. *pacchā* = *paścāt* (§ 301); AMg. *abhū* = *abhūt*; *akāsi* = *akārṣit* (§ 516); AMg. *akariṁsu* = *akārṣuḥ* (§ 516). Cf. § 395. The vowels standing in the auslaut are sometimes nasalized (§ 75. 114. 181), and short vowels are also lengthened (§ 75. 181).

§ 340. The final consonant of the first member of a compound is assimilated with the initial consonant of the following member, as a rule (§ 335ff.), so much so that the stems ending in consonants go over to the *a*-declension (§ 355 ff,). Sometimes, mostly in verses, the first member before consonants is treated as absolutely in the auslaut. So M. *uamahihara* = = *udak*+*mahīdhara* (G. 631); *uasindhu* = *udak*+*sindhu* (395); M. *eaguṇā* = *etadguṇaḥ* (Hc. 1, 11); *jaarakkhaṇa* = *jagadrakṣaṇa* (G. 50), and several times in *jagat* in G. R.; AMg. *taḍitaḍiẏa* = *taḍittaḍita* (Ovav. § 16, p. 31, 13); M. *taḍibhāva* = *taḍidbhāva* (G. 316); M. *viasia* = *viyat*+*śrita* in rhyme with *viasia* = *vikasita* (R. 6, 48); M. *vijjuvilasia* = *vidyudvilasita* (4, 40), and more often in *vidyut* in G. R.; M. *sarisaṁkula* = *saritsaṁkula* in rhyme with *sarisaṁ kulaṁ* = *sadṛśaṁ kulam* (R. 2, 46); M. *saürisa* = *satpuruṣa* (G. 992), beside frequent *sappurisa*; *sabhikkhu* = *sadbhikṣu* (Hc. 1, 11). Particularly frequent is the dropping off of *s* of *dus*, in association with the compounds with *su*, that often stand directly by its side : M. AMg. JM. *dulaha* = *durlabha* (Kī. 2, 114; Mk. fol. 32; G. 1133; H. 844; Karp. 92, 4; Dasav. 618, 12 parallelly with *sulaha* 14; Kk. 271, 33). M. *dulahattaṇa* = *durlabhatva* (G. 503); AMg. *duciṇṇa* = *duścirṇa* (Ovav. § 56 p. 62, 14), according to *suciṇṇa* = *sucirṇa* standing before it; AMg. *dumuha* = *durmukha* (Paṇhāv. 244), beside *sumuha*: AMg. *durūva* = *dūrūpa* (Sūyag. 585. 603. 628. 669. 738, Vivāhap. 117. 480; Ṭhāṇ. 20), mostly beside *surūva* = *surūpa*; AMg. *duvanna* = *durvarṇa* (Sūyag. 628. 669. 738; Vivāhap. 480 [°*ṇṇa*]), beside *suvaṇṇa*; M. *dusaha* = *duḥsaha* (Hc. 1, 115; G. 158. 511; H. 486); *duhava* = *durbhaga* (Hc. 1, 115; cf. §231); M. *dohagga* = *daurbhāgya* (H.).

§ 341. Reversely the final consonant is sometimes retained, especially before vowels, in addition to in compounds, particularly before enclitics. AMg. *chac ca* = *ṣaṭ ca*, *chac ceva* = *ṣaḍ eva*, *chap pi* = *ṣaḍ api* (§ 441); AMg. *asiṇād i vā avahārād i vā* = *aśanād iti vā apahārād iti vā* (Āyār. 2, 1, 5, 1); AMg. *sucirād avi* = *sucirād api* (Uttar. 235); AMg. *tamhād avi ikkha* = *tasmād apikṣasva* (Sūyag. 117); AMg. *jad atthi* = *yad asti* (Ṭhāṇ. 33); AMg. *aṇusaraṇād uvatthāṇā* = *anusmaraṇād upasthānāt* (Dasav. N. 656, 1); Mg. *yad iścaśe* = *yad icchase*; *mahad antalaṁ* = *mahad antaraṁ* (Mṛcch. 123, 5; 136, 18). In compounds : AMg. *tadāvaraṇijja* = *tadāvaraṇīya* (Uvās. § 74); AMg. *tadajjhavasiyā*, *tadappiyakaraṇā*, *tadaṭṭhovaüttā* = *tadadhyavasitāḥ*, *tadarpitakaraṇāḥ*, *tadarthopayuktāḥ* (Ovav. § 38, p. 50, 31 ff.); AMg. *tadubhaya* (Ovav. § 117. 122); JM. *taduvikkhākāriṇo* = *tadupekṣākāriṇaḥ* (Kk. 261, 27), beside the cases like M. *eāvatthā* = *etadavasthā* (R. 11, 132), AMg. *eyāṇurūva* = *etadanurūpa* (Kappas. § 91, 107). In AMg *tārūvattāe tāvannattāe tāphāsattāe* = *tadrūpatvāya tadvarṇatvāya tatsparśatvāya* (Paṇṇav. 523 ff. 540), *tāgandhattāe tārasattāe* = *tadgandhatvāya tadrasatvāya* (Paṇṇav. 540), and in the frequent AMg. JM. *eyārūva* = *etadrūpa* (Āyār. 2, 15, 23, 24; Sūyag. 992; Vivāgas. 116; Vivāhap. 151. 170. 171; Uvās.; Kappas.; Erz.), *ā* is to be explained either according to § 65 or § 70. AMg. *sadaṅgavī* = *ṣaḍaṅgavid* (Ovav.; Kappas.). *r*, originating from *s* in *dus* and *nis*, is always retained before vowels (Hc. 1, 14; Kī. 2, 124) : *duravagāha* (Hc. 1, 14); AMg. *duraïkkama* = *duratikrama* (Āyār. 1, 2, 5, 4); M. *durāroha* (H.); JM. *duraṇucara*, *duranta*, *durappa-* = *durātman* (Erz.); AMg. *durahiyāsa* = *duradhivāsa* (Uvās.); Ś. *durāgada* = *durāgata* (Vikr. 32, 11); M. JM. *duria* = *durita* (G.; KI. 1, 22); *duruttara* (Hc. 1, 14); M. Ś. *ṇirantara*, JM. *nirantara* (Hc. 1, 14; G. H.; Erz.; Mṛcch. 68, 19; 73, 8; Prab. 4, 4,); M. *ṇiravĕkkha* = *nirapekṣa* (R.); M. *ṇirālamba* (H.); M. *ṇirikkhaṇa* = *nirikṣaṇa* (H.); A. *ṇiruvama*, JM. *niruvama* = *nirupama* (Hc. 4, 401, 3; Erz.); *ṇirūsua* = *nirutsuka* (G.). The rule holds good also for *prādus*: AMg. *pāduresae* = *prādureṣayet* (Āyār. 1, 7, 8, 17), *pādurakāsi* = *prādurakārṣit* (Sūyag. 123), beside AMg. *pāubbhūya* = *prādurbhūta* (Vivāgas. 4, 38; Vivāhap. 190; Kappas.), *pāubbhavitthā* (Vivāhap. 1201) and *pāukujjā* = *prāduṣkuryāt* (Sūyag. 474), *pāukarissāmi* = *prāduṣkariṣyāmi* (Uttar. 1), against *karissāmi pāuṁ* (Sūyag. 484), *karĕnti pāuṁ* [text *pāu*], *karemi pāuṁ* (Sūyag. 912. 914). Cf. § 181. So also M. *bāhir uṇhāiṁ* = *bāhir uṣṇāṇi* (H. 186). On original *r* see § 342 ff., on *m* § 348 ff.

§ 342. In all the dialects *aḥ*, arising from the original *ar*, mostly becomes *o* : M. AMg. *anto* = *antaḥ* from *antar* (G.H.R.; Āyār. 1. 2, 5, 5; 2, 1, 2, 7, 3, 10; 2, 7, 2, 1; Sūyag. 753; Uvās.); AMg. *aho* = *ahaḥ* from *ahar* (§ 386); AMg. *pāo* = *prātaḥ* from *prātar* (Kappas.). *punaḥ* from *punar* becomes M. AMg. JM. JŚ. Mg. Ḍh. Ā. *puṇo* in the meaning "again", "afresh" (G.H.R.; Āyār. 1, 1, 5, 3; 1, 2, 1, 1. 2, 2; 1, 4. 1, 3. 2, 2; 1,

6, 4, 2; Sūyag. 45. 151. 178. 277. 433. 468. 497. Uttar. 202; Āv. 28, 14; Erz.; Kk.; Pav. 383, 24; 384, 49; 386, 10; 388, 8; Kattig. 403, 375; Mṛcch. 29, 11; 58, 8, 13); Mg. Mṛcch. 176, 5. 9; Prab. 58, 8; Ḍh. Mṛcch. 39, 17; Ā. Mṛcch. 103, 3), especially, in combinations M. JM. JŚ. Ś. Mg. D. *puṇo vi* (Kī. 2, 126; G.H.; Āv. 8, 34. 52; 12, 35; Erz. 27, 6; 33, 37; Kattig. 402, 367; Mṛcch. 20, 24; 21, 7; 41, 6; 45, 16; 81, 9; 94, 19; Śak. 22, 2; 68, 2; Vikr. 11, 2; 13, 18; 28, 1; 82, 17; Mahāv. 65, 2; Caṇḍak. 93, 14; Mg. Mṛcch. 80, 5; 115, 9; 117, 3; 132, 22; 148, 14; 162, 9; D. Mṛcch. 103, 17), for which AMg. prefers *puṇar avi* (Kī. 2, 126; Āyār. 1, 8, 2, 6; 2, 1, 7, 3; Sūyag. 100, 643. 842; Vivāhap. 1038. 1496; Jīv. 287. 288. 296; Paṇṇav. 848; Nāyādh.; Ovav.; Kappas.), that is known also to JM. (Āv. 11, 24; Dvār. 497, 26; 498, 14; Erz.); according to Kī. 2, 126 one says also *puṇa vi*. For *puṇo* M. has after vowels and anusvāra also *uṇo*, with dropping off of *p* according to § 184 (G.H.R.). In the meaning "but", "now" *punaḥ* becomes in AMg.JM.JŚ. *puṇa* (Āyār. 1, 4, 2, 5; 2, 1, 1. 3. 4. 14; 2, 2, 3, 10; Sūyag. 46, 292; Vivāhap. 139; Dasav. 642, 2; Dasav. N. 648; 33; 652, 11; Nāyādh.; Ovav.; Kappas.; Āv. 8, 50; 12, 2; Erz.; Kk.; Kattig. 404, 387. 389). There is found in M. too sometimes *puṇa* after anusvāra (G. H.), but mostly *uṇa*, as in Ś. Mg. (§ 184). For Mg. *kiṁ puṇa* (Mṛcch. 169, 4) we should read with GOḌABOLE (458, 9), *kiṁ uṇa*. In M. are found in the meaning "but", "now" also *puṇo*, *uṇo*. In A. *puṇaḥ*, in both the meanings, becomes *puṇu* (Hc. 4, 426 and Word-Index; Piṅgala 1, 33, 34. 37. 42 ff. 77. 84. 90. 95. 100; Vikr. 71, 10). After dropping off of the final *r* the words sometimes go over to the *a*-stem and are inflected. So AMg. *antaṁ* (Āyār. 2, 10, 6), *anteṇa* in the combination *anto anteṇa* (Āyār. 2, 5, 1, 14; 2, 6, 1, 11), *antāo* (Āyār. 2, 10, 6); AMg. *pāyaṁ* = *prātar* (Sūyag. 337. 341); *na uṇā* = *na *punāt* (Hc. 1, 65); AMg. *puṇāiṁ* (Paṇhāv. 389; Uvās. § 119. 174), *puṇāi* (Hc. 1, 65; Paṇhāv. 414), *na uṇāi* (Hc. 1, 65), that are to be considered as in the acc. plur. Cf. § 345. From *anto* AMg. forms also *antohiṁto*, that is to say, an ablative = "from within" (Āyār. 2, 7, 2, 1; Ṭhāṇ. 408; Rāyap. 254f.). Cf. § 343. 365.

§ 343. Original *r*, like the secondary one (§ 341), is mostly retained before the vocalic initial of the second member in a compound; *antarappa-* = *antarātman* (Hc. 1, 14); M. *antaria*, AMg. JM. *antariya*, Ś. *antarida* = *antarita* (G. H. R.; Nāyādh.; Ovav.; Kappas.; Erz.; Śak. 67, 2; 73, 10; Vikr. 31, 1; 41, 17; 43, 7); M. Ś. *puṇarutta* = *punarukta*, AMg. *apuṇarutta* (§ 337); AMg. *apuṇarāvatti-* = *apunarāvartin* (Uttar. 859; Kappas.), *apuṇarāvattaga* (Ovav.). So also AMg. JM. *puṇar avi* (§ 342), and cases, like AMg. *puṇar ei*, *puṇar ĕnti* = *punareti*, *punar yanti* (Āyār. 1, 3, 1, 3. 2, 1). Before a consonantal initial of the second member, as a rule, comes in the form of the absolute final : M. *antomuha* = *antarmukha* (G. 94); *antovisambha* = *antarvisrambha* (Hc. 1, 60); M. *antohutta* (Deśīn. 1, 21; H. 373), *antosindūria* (H. 300); AMg. *antojala* (Nāyādh. 764), *antŏjjhusira* = *antaḥsuṣira* (Nāyādh. 397; cf. § 211), *antoduṭṭha* = *antarduṣṭa* (Ṭhāṇ. 314), *antomāsa* (Ṭhāṇ. 364); AMg. JM. *antomuhutta* (Vivāhap. 180. 273; Samav. 215; Jīv. 49. 322; Uttar. 977 f. 997. 1003. 1047 ff.; Kappas.; Ṛṣabhap. 43); AMg. *anto-*

muhuttiẏa (Vivāhap. 30), *antomhuttūṇa* (Samav. 215), *antosālā* = *antaḥśālā* (Uvās.), *antosalla* = *antaḥśalya* (Sūẏag. 695; Ṭhāṇ. 314; Samav. 51; Vivāhap. 159; Ovav.); JM. *antonikkhanta* = *antarniṣkrānta* (Ṛṣabhap. 45); AMg. *pāosiṇāṇa* = *prātaḥsnāna* (Sūẏag. 337). The same form is found sometimes also before vowels : M. *antouvariṁ* = *antarupari* (Hc. 1, 14), for which in G. 1056 (the passage meant by Hc.) stands *antovariṁ*, which with P (cf. J) is to be read as *anto avariṁ ca pariṭṭhieṇa*; AMg. *antoanteura* (§344). To M. *antovāsa* = *antaravakāśa* we should add *anta* (§ 342), that occurs also before consonants, as AMg. *antabhamara* = *antarbhramara* (Kappas.), *antarāẏalehā* = **antarrājallekhā* (Kappas.); *puṇapuṇakkaraṇa* = *punaḥpunaḥkaraṇa* (Deśīn. 1, 32); AMg. *puṇapāsaṇaẏāe* = **punaḥpaśyanatāyai* (Vivāhap. 1128). Before consonants there takes place also assimilation : Ś. *antakkaraṇa* = = *antaḥkaraṇa* (Vikr. 72, 12); *antaggaa* = *antargala* (Hc. 2, 60); *antappāa* = *antaḥpāta* (Hc. 2, 77); JM. Ś. *puṇaṇṇava* = *punarnava* (Dvār. 504, 5; Karp. 83, 3); JŚ. *apuṇabbhava* = *apunarbhava* (Pav. 386, 5); *puṇapuṇakkaraṇa* (Deśīn. 1, 32). The ablative *puṇā* = **punāt* (§ 342) is to be assumed in M. *apuṇāgamaṇāa* (G. 1183); AMg. *apuṇāgama* (Dasav. 640, 22); likewise *antā* should be viewed in *antāvei* = *antarvedi* (Hc. 1, 14). The lengthening in *ā* can be explained also according to § 70.

§ 344. In *antaḥpura* and its derivatives *aḥ* becomes *e* in lieu of *o* in all the dialects, as in Pāli : M. AMg. JM. Ś. *anteura* (Hc. 1, 60; G. R.; Sūẏag. 771; Paṇhāv. 262; Nāẏādh. § 19. 102; p. 1079 ff. 1273. 1290. 1327. 1460. 1465; Vivāgas. 156. 159. 172 ff.; Vivāhap. 792. 1278; Niraẏāv.; Ovav.; Kappas.; Āv. 15, 13; Erz.; Śak. 38, 5; 57, 11; 70, 7; 137, 8; 138, 1; Mālav. 33, 1; 38, 3; 74, 7; 84, 16; 85, 6; Bālar. 243. 12; Viddhaś. 83, 7; Karp. 35, 3; 45, 10; 99, 4; Pras. 45, 4. 13; Jīvān. 42, 16; Kaṁsav. 55, 11; Karṇas. 18, 22; 37, 16 etc.); M. *anteuraa* (at H. 980); AMg. JM. *anteuriẏā*, Ś. *anteuriā* = *antaḥpurikā* (Nāẏādh. 1229; Erz.; Kk.; Viddhaś. 11, 1). Against it there appears *anto* in AMg. *antoanteura* (Nāẏādh. 723. 1301; Vivāhap. 791; Ovav.), *antoantepuriẏa* (Ovav.). In Vivāgas. 145 *antapuriẏaṁsi* is edited. *e* appears for *aḥ* also in *anteāri-* = *antaścārin* (Hc. 1, 60).

§ 345. In all the dialects, except in the nom. sing. of the *a*-stem in AMg. Mg. and in certain adverbs in AMg., where it becomes *e*, *aḥ* arising from *as* becomes *o*. AMg. JM. *aggao*, Ś. Mg. *aggado* = *agrataḥ* (§69); AMg. *piṭṭhāo* = *pṛṣṭhāt*, AMg. JM. *piṭṭhao*, Ś. D. *piṭṭhado* = *pṛṣṭhataḥ* (§ 69); in the nom. sing. PG. *patibhāgo* = *pratibhāgaḥ* (§ 363); M. *rāo* = *rāgaḥ* (H. 12); JM. *putto* = *putraḥ* (Erz. 1, 2); JŚ. *dhammo* = *dharmaḥ* (Pav. 380, 7); Ś. *ṇioo* = *niyogaḥ* (Mṛcch. 3, 7); Ḍh. *puliso* = *puruṣaḥ* (Mṛcch. 34, 12); Ā. D. *govāladārao* = *gopāladārakaḥ* (Mṛcch. 99, 16; 102, 15); P. *tāmotaro* = *dāmodaraḥ* (Hc. 4, 307); CP. *mekho* = *meghaḥ* (Hc. 4, 325); A. *kāmo* = *kāmaḥ* (Piṅgala 2, 4); but AMg. *purise*, Mg. *puliśe* = *puruṣaḥ* (Āẏār. 1, 1, 1, 6; Mṛcch. 113, 21). Likewise *maṇo* = *manaḥ*, *saro* = *saraḥ*, *jaso* = *yaśaḥ* (§ 356). In AMg. there is found *-o* also, instead of *-e*, for *-aḥ* of the nominative in verses (§ 17). and before *iva* in prose : *khuro iva* = *kṣura iva*, *vāluẏākavalo iva* = *vālukākabala iva* = *vālukākabala iva*, *mahāsamuddo iva* = *mahāsamudra iva* (Nāẏādh. § 144);

kummo iva=kūrma iva, kuñjaro iva=kuñjara iva, vasabho iva=vṛṣabha iva, sīho iva=siṁha iva, mandaro iva, sāgaro iva, cando iva, sūro iva (Sūẏag. 758; Kappas. § 118). Beside Kappas. *saṅkho iva* in the quoted passage, Sūẏag. has *saṅkha* [sic] *iva*; Kappas. has *jīve* [sic] *iva*, Sūẏag. *jīva* [sic] *iva*; both of them have *vihaga* [sic] *iva*, and the adjectives always end in *-e* beside them. All this makes it probable that these are cases of Sanskritism and that *-e* has to be written throughout and that probably *va* is to be written for *iva*, that in AMg. is found in the text just feebly and is uncertain (§ 143). The same sound-change occurs in all other cases, in which Skt. *-aḥ* goes back to *as*, as in the ablative singular in *-tas*: M. *koḍarāo*, JM. *kŏṭṭarāo=*koṭarātaḥ=*koṭarāt* (H. 563; Erz. 1, 10); AMg. *āgārāo=āgārāt* (Uvās. § 12); JŚ. *carittādo=caritrāt* (Pav. 380, 6); Ś. *mūlādo=mūlāt* (Śak. 14, 6); Mg. *haḍakkādo=hṛdakāt* (Mṛcch. 115, 23); in the first pers. plur. indicative in *-maḥ=mas*: M. *lajjāmo*; AMg. *vaḍḍhāmo*; JM. *tāḷemo*; Ś. *pavisāmo* (§ 455); AMg. *bhavissāmo*; JM. *pĕcchissāmo*; AMg. Ś. *jāṇissāmo* (§ 521. 525. 534) etc. In AMg. one always says *bahave=bahavaḥ* and *bahūn* (§ 380 ff.), in M. AMg. *ṇe=naḥ* (§ 419). In adverbs the sound sometimes varies in AMg. in the texts. *adhaḥ* becomes M. JM. *aho* (G.; Erz. 50, 30 [so with A to be read]; Ṛṣabhap. 30), AMg., however, mostly *ahe* (Āẏār. 1, 5, 6, 2; 1, 6, 4, 2; 1, 8, 4, 14; 2, 1, 1, 2. 3, 2. 10, 6; 2, 15, 8; Sūẏag. 52. 215. 222. 271. 273. 304. 397. 428. 520. 590; Uttar. 1031. 1033; Vivāhap. 105 f. 260. 410. 753; Uvās.; Ovav.; Kappas.), *ahedisāo=adhodiśaḥ* (Āẏār. 1, 1, 1, 2); *ahebhāga* (Āẏār. 1, 2, 5, 4), *ahebhāgi-=adhobhāgin* (Sūẏag. 829), *ahecara* (Āẏār. 1, 7, 8, 9), *ahegāmiṇī* (Āẏār. 2, 3, 1, 13), *ahevāẏa=adhovāta* (Sūẏag. 829), *ahesiraṁ=adhaḥśiraḥ* (Sūẏag. 288), but *ahosiraṁ* (Sūẏag. 268; Ovav.; Nāẏādh.), *aheloga* beside *adhologa* (Ṭhāṇ. 61 f.) and *ahe ahologe* (Ṭhāṇ. 189), also independently standing probably falsely, *aho* (Sūẏag. 476; Uttar. 513); *pure=puraḥ* (Āẏār. 2, 1, 4, 5, 9, 2), *purekamma-=*puraskarman* (Hc. 1, 57; Āẏār. 2, 1, 6, 4. 5; Paṇhāv. 492); *purekaḍa*, *purĕkkhaḍa* and *purakkaḍa=puraskṛta* (§49. 306), *porekacca=*paurahkṛtya*, (Ovav.; Kappas.), *porevacca=*paurovṛttya* Paṇṇav. 98. 100. 103; Vivāgas. 28. 57; Samav. 134; Ovav.; Kappas.), everywhere beside *āhevacca=ādhipatya* (§ 77); *rahe=rahaḥ* (Uttar. 331. 333), but *rahokamma-* (Ovav.); Ś. *suvo=śvaḥ*, but AMg. *suve, sue* (§ 139). beside AMg. *suẏarāe =śvorātre* (Āẏār 2, 5, 1, 10). As in *suẏarāe* so in AMg. *adhaṁ=adhaḥ* (Āẏār. 1, 1, 5, 2. 3), *ahaṁ* (Āẏār. 1, 2, 6, 5; 1, 4, 2, 3. 4 1, 7, 1, 5) and *puraṁ=puraḥ* (Nāẏādh.) there has occurred transition to the *a*-stem. Cf. § 342. It still remains uncertain whether in compounds as well we should throughout read or not read *ahe°*, *rahe°*. On AMg. JM. *hĕṭṭhā* and derivatives see § 107.

§ 346. In A. *o* from *aḥ* mostly becomes *u* (Hc. 4, 331; Kī. 5, 22); *jaṇu=janaḥ* (Hc. 4, 336); *lou=lokaḥ* (Hc. 4, 366. 420, 4), *sīhu=siṁhaḥ* (Hc. 4, 418, 3); *bhamaru=bhramaraḥ, makkaḍu=markaṭah, vāṇaru=vānaraḥ* (Piṅgala 1, 67); *ṇisiaru=*niśicaraḥ, dhārāharu=dhārādharaḥ* beside *sāmalo=śyāmalaḥ* (Vikr. 55, 1. 2); *tavu=tapaḥ, siru=śiraḥ* (Hc. 4, 441, 2, 445, 3); *aṅguliu jajjariāu=aṅgulyo jarjaritāḥ* (Hc. 4, 333); *vilāsiṇiu=vilāsinīḥ* (Hc.

4, 348); *sallaü* = *sallakiḥ* (Hc. 4, 387, 1). The same sound-change is common in Ḍh. : *luddhu jūḍialu papaliṇu* = *ruddho dyūtakaraḥ prapalāyitaḥ* (Mṛcch. 30, 1); *vippadīvu pādu* = *vipratipaḥ pādaḥ* (Mṛcch. 30, 11); *esu vihavu* = *eṣa vibhavaḥ* (Mṛcch. 34, 17), beside nominatives in *o* (§ 25. 345). Further in the abl. sing. in P. *tūrātu, tumātu, mamātu,* beside *tūrāto, tumāto, mamāto* = *dūrāt, tvat, mat* (Hc. 4, 321); M. *ṇahaalāu* = *nabhastalāt, raṇṇāu* = *araṇyāt* (§ 365); JŚ *udaẏādu* (Pav. 383. 27), according to which Hc. permits this form also in Ś. Mg. (365). In the first pers. plur. indicative: AMg. *icchāmu, accemu, dāhāmu, vuchāmu,* A. *lahimu* (§ 455). Cf. § 85.

§ 347. At the end of the first member of a compound *o* may enter for Skt. *as, aḥ* before consonants, as in the auslaut. Commonly there appears sometimes, however, assimilation in M. AMg. JM. in the stem in *-a* (§ 407); M. *jasavamma* = *yaśovarman* (G.), JM. *jasavaddhaṇa* = *yaśovardhana* (Kī. 4), beside *jasoā* = *yaśodā* (G.H.); AMg. JM., *namŏkkāra,* beside *namoẏāra, navaẏāra,* M. *ṇamakkāra* (§ 306); *ṇahaara* = *nabhaścara* (§ 301); M. *ṇahaala* = *nabhastala* (G. H. R.); *ṇahavaṭṭha* = *nabhaḥpṛṣṭha* (G.), *tamaraaṇiara* = *tamorajonikara* (R. 3, 34); AMg. *tavalova* = *tapolopa* (Ovav.), beside AMg. JM. *tavokamma-* = *tapaḥkarman* (Uvās.; Ovav.; Kappas.; Erz.), Ś. *tavovaṇa* = *tapovana* (Śak. 16, 13; 18, 10; 19, 7; 90, 14; Vikr. 84, 20); JM. Ś. *tavaccaraṇa* = *tapaścaraṇa* (§301); M. A. *avarŏppara* = *aparaspara*; M. AMg. JM. Ś. *parŏppara* = *paraspara* (§ 195. 311); M. AMg. JM. *maṇahara* = *manohara* (Hc. 1, 156; G. H.; Rāẏap. 114; Ovav.; Kappas.; Erz.), beside AMg. JM. A. *maṇohara* (Hc. 1, 156; Kappas.; Erz.; Vikr. 66, 15); M. *maṇaharaṇa* (Karp. 51, 6; 55, 4); AMg. *maṇapaoga* = *manaḥprayoga, maṇakaraṇa* (Ṭhāṇ. 114) beside *maṇojoga* (Ṭhāṇ. 113); *uraaḍa* = *urastaṭa* (Kī. 2, 110); AMg. *uraparisappa* = *uraḥparisarpa* (Ṭhāṇ. 121); AMg. *mihokahā* = *mithaḥkathā* (Āẏār. 1, 8, 1, 9); AMg. *maṇosilā* (Hc. 1, 26; Kī. 2. 153; Āẏār. 2, 1, 6, 6; Sūẏag. 834; Jīv. 519; Rāẏap. 123; Paṇṇav. 25; Uttar. 1041), beside *maṇasilā* (Hc. 1, 26; 4, 286; Kī. 2, 153), *maṇāsilā* (Hc. 1, 26, 43; f. § 64) and *maṇaṁsilā* (Hc. 1, 26: cf. § 74); M. *siravihatta* = *śirovibhakta* (G. 51), beside *siracchea* = *śiraścheda* (G. 322), *sirakamala* = *śiraḥkamala* (G. 342), *siralagga* = *śirolagna* (H. 529); but Ś. *sirodhara* (Śak. 144, 12), Mg. *śiloluha* = *śiroruha* (Mṛcch. 17, 2). The stem *accharā* (§97. 410) is from *apsaras* (§ 97. 410). On AMg. *ahe°, pure°* see § 345. If the second member of a compound begins with a vowel, the *a*-stem tends to enter into the first member. The vowels in such cases follow the rules of the vocalic saṁdhi (§ 156 ff.): M. *mahiraantaria* = *mahīrajontarita* (R. 13, 52), *mahiraüṭṭhāṇa* = *mahīrajaütthāna, mahiraügghāa* = *mahīrajaüdghāta* (R. 13, 37. 49), *asuroraṭṭhi* = *asurorosthi* = *asura+uras+asthi* (G. 7), *ṇahaṅgaṇa* = *nabhoṅgaṇa* (G. 139. 231. 235 etc.), *ṇahāhoa* = *nabhaābhoga* (G. 416), *ṇahuddeso* = *nabhaüddeśa* (G. 558), *tamāṇubandha* = *tamonubandha* (G. 506), *tamugghāa* = *tamaüdghāta* (G. 1179) etc.

§ 348. Final *n* and *m* become anusvāra (Vr. 4, 12; C. 2, 11; Hc. 1, 23; Mk. fol. 34); Ś. *tassiṁ,* Mg. *taśśiṁ* = *tasmin*; *eassiṁ,* Ś. *edassiṁ* = *etasmin*; Ś. *jassiṁ,* Mg. *yaśśiṁ* = *yasmin*; Ś. *kassiṁ,* Mg. *kaśśiṁ* = *kasmin*; AMg. Ś. *assiṁ* = *asmin*; Ś. *imassiṁ,* Mg. *imaśśiṁ* = **imasmin* (§ 425 ff.); AMg. P.

bhagavaṁ, Ś. Mg. *bhaavaṁ* = *bhagavān*; Ś. Mg. *bhavaṁ* = *bhavān*; AMg. *āyavaṁ* = *ātmavān*, *nāṇavaṁ* = *jñānavān*, *bambhavaṁ* = *brahmavān*; AMg. *ciṭṭhaṁ* = *tiṣṭhan*, *payaṁ* = *pacan*, *kuvvaṁ* = *kurvan*, *haṇaṁ* = *ghnan* (§396); AMg. *rāyaṁ*, Ś. *rāaṁ*, P. *rājaṁ*, Mg. *lāaṁ* = *rājan* (§ 399); A. *vāeṁ* = *vātena*, *koheṁ* = *krodhena*, *daïveṁ* = *daivena*, after dropping off of the final *a* (§ 146). — *ahaṁ* = *aham*; *tumaṁ* = *tvam*; M. Ś. *aaṁ*, AMg. JM. *ayaṁ* = *ayam*; Ś. *iaṁ* = *iyam* (§ 417 ff.); AMg. JM. JŚ. *iyāṇiṁ*, *idāṇiṁ*, Ś. Mg. *dāṇiṁ* = *idānīm* (§ 144); Ś. *sāadaṁ*, Mg. *śāadaṁ* = *svāgatam* (§203); M. *jalaṁ*, *jalahiṁ*, *vahuṁ* = *jalam*, *jaladhim*, *vadhūm* (H. 161; G. 147; Hc. 3, 124); Ś. *aṅgāṇaṁ* = *aṅgānām*, *devīṇaṁ* = *devīnām*, *vadhūṇaṁ* = *vadhūnām* (Śak. 32, 8; 43, 11; 89, 6); Mg. *devadāṇaṁ bamhaṇāṇaṁ ca* = *devatānāṁ brāhmaṇānāṁ ca* (Mṛcch. 121, 10); M. AMg. JM. *kāuṁ*, Ś. Mg. *kāduṁ* = *kartum* (§ 574). Cf. also § 75. 83. 181. A vowel with bindu (§179, note 3) is equivalent to a long vowel (§ 74. 75. 83. 86. 114). If, therefore, in verses, the metre requires a short syllable, the old *m* remains unaltered before the following vowel (Vr. 4, 13; Hc. 1, 24; Mk. fol. 34)[1]: M. *surahim iha gandham āsisirabālamaüluggamāṇa jambūṇa maarandam āravindaṁ ca* = *surabhim iha gandham āśiśirabālamukulodgamānāṁ jambūnāṁ makarandam āravindaṁ ca* (§ G. 516); M. *tam aṅgam ĕṇhiṁ* = *tad aṅgam idānīm* (H. 67); AMg. *aṇiccam āvāsam uvĕnti jantuṇo* = *anityam āvāsam upayanti jantavaḥ* (Āyār. 2, 16, 1); AMg. *cittamantam acittaṁ vā* (Sūyag. 1); JM. *kāraviaṁ acalam imaṁ bhavaṇaṁ* (KI. 22); *appiam eaṁ bhavaṇaṁ* (KI. 23); *vissariyaṁ tuham egam akkharaṁ* = *vismṛtaṁ tvayaikam akṣaram* (Āv. 7. 33); JM. *tavassiṇīm eyaṁ* = *tapasvinīm etām* (Kk. 262, 19); JŚ. *adisayam ādasamutthaṁ visayādīdaṁ aṇovaman aṇantam* = *atiśayam ātmasamutthaṁ viṣayātītam-anupamam anantam* (Pav. 380, 13); Mg. *maaṇam aṇaṅgam* = *madanam anaṅgam*, *śaṁkalam iśalaṁ vā* = *śaṁkaram īśvaraṁ vā* (Mṛcch. 10, 13; 17,4)[2].

1. WEBER, H[1]. p. 47. — 2. The MSS and, with them, the Indian editions write, often wrongly, the nasal instead of the vowel with bindu. So also in the inscriptions (KI. 10. 11. 12; PG. 7, 45. 49). Wrong is also *vanso* (KI. 2), *rohinsakūa* (KI. 20, 21). Cf. § 10.

§ 349. In AMg. JM. JŚ. *m* remains, instead of being transformed into anusvāra, when the word ending in *m* is to be strongly emphasized, especially before *eva*, before which in this case a small vowel is often lengthened, and against § 83, a long one is retained (§ 68) : AMg. *evam eyaṁ bhante taham eyaṁ bhante avitaham eyaṁ bhante icchiyaṁ eyaṁ bhante paḍicchiyaṁ eyaṁ bhante icchiyapaḍicchiyam eyaṁ bhante* (Uvās. § 12; cf. Vivāhap. 946; Ovav. § 54; Kappas. § 13. 83, and above § 114); AMg. *evaṁ akkhāyaṁ* = *evam ākhyātam* (Āyār. 1, 1, 1, 1); AMg. *evam egesiṁ no nāyaṁ bhavaī* = *evam ekeṣām no jñātaṁ bhavati* (Āyār. 1, 1, 1, 2); AMg. *jam eyaṁ bhagavayā paveiyaṁ tam eva abhisamĕccā* = *yad etad bhagavatā praveditaṁ tad evābhisametya* (Āyār. 1, 7, 5, 1); AMg. *ayaṁ teṇe ayaṁ uvacarae ayaṁ hantā ayaṁ ĕttham akāsi* = *ayaṁ steno 'yam upacarako 'yaṃ hantāyam ittham akārṣit* (Āyār. 2, 2, 2, 4); AMg. *aham avi* = *aham api* (Āyār. 2, 5, 2, 4); JM. *amhāṇam eva kule samuppannā paramabandhavā* = *asmākam eva kule samutpannāḥ paramabāndavāḥ* (Dvār. 500, 1); JM. *evam imaṁ kajjaṁ* = *evam idaṁ kāryam* (Erz. 5, 35); JM. *evam avi bhaṇie* = *evam api bhaṇite* (Āv. 16, 24); JŚ. *pattegam eva pattegaṁ* = *pratyekam* *eva pratyekam* (Pav. 379, 3); *sayam evādā* = *svayam evātmā* (Pav. 381 15). Sometimes secondary anusvāra (§ 181) too is transformed into *m* under this condition : AMg. *iham egesim āhiyaṁ* = *ihaikeṣām āhitam* (Sūyag. 18); *sŏccam idaṁ* = *śrutvedam* (Āyār. 2, 16, 1; cf. § 587), *dissam āgayāṁ* = *dṛṣṭvāgatam* (Uttar. 695; cf. § 334), under the pressure of metre; AMg. *iham āgae* = *ihāgataḥ* (Ovav. § 38), *iham āgacchĕjjā* = *ihāgacchet* (Ovav. § 21), where, as the context shows, the accent lies on *iha*. The MSS even in cases other than those cited above very often write *m* instead of *ṁ*, which is considered as correct by JACOBI[1] and has been included in the text by all the editors without any consequence and rule. Even the MSS other than those of the Jainas, in Pkt. very often write *m* for *ṁ*, as stands very often in earlier European and many recent Indian editions. Thus pro ex. the ed. Bomb. (Karp. 6, 4) writes *dhuāgidam ālaviadi*, KONOW 3, 3, however, correctly has *dhuvāgidaṁ ālaviadi*; ed. Bomb. 20, 8 has *cāruttaṇam avalaṁbedi*, but KONOW 17, 7 *caṅgattaṇaṁ avalambedi*; ed. Bomb. 25, 2 *āsaṇam āsaṇaṁ*, but KONOW 23, 9 *āsaṇaṁ āsaṇaṁ* etc. As here, so in AMg. JM. too, we should revise the writing *m* for *ṁ*, i.e. the MSS are to be corrected. However, it only remains doubtful whether *m* is correct or not, as particularly in strictly homogeneous words as admitted by JACOBI. The MSS are not clear on this point. Sanskritism has its play also in *uparilikhitam ajātāye* = *uparilikhitam *adyatvāya* (PG. 7. 45) and in *sayam āṇataṁ* = *svayam ājñaptam* (PG. 7, 49), whilst *evamādikehi* = *evamādikaiḥ* (PG. 6, 34) may be interpreted as a compound. On *m* for *ṁ* HOFFER's[2] opinion was more correct than that of LASSEN[3].

1. ZDMG. 35, 677; Erz. §24, xxx. Among the examples quoted by JACOBI, good many are from verses, hence not capable of verification, as *muhuttam avi* (Āyār. 1, 2, 1, 3); *iṇam eva* (Āyār. 1, 2, 3,4); *attāṇam eva* (Āyār. 1, 3. 3. 4), where *eva* should be deleted, as also after *saccam*, so that the verse reads : *saccaṁ samabhiyāṇāhi mehāvī māraṁ taraï*; *satthāram evaṁ* (Āyār. 1, 6, 4, 1) etc. A wholly doubtless Sanskritism is *teṇam iti* (Āyār. 2, 2, 2, 4). The same holds goods for *m* as for *t* (§203). — 2. De Prakrita dialecto § 66. — 3. Inst. § 53.

§ 350. An anusvāra, that originated from original *n*, *m*, disappears often before vowels and consonants in M. AMg. JM. JŚ. M.AMg. JM. JŚ. *tammi*, *jammi*, *kammi*, AMg. *taṁsi*, *jaṁsi*, *kaṁsi* = *tasmin*, *yasmin*, *kasmin* (§425 ff.) M. *jŏvvaṇammi* = **yauvanasmin* = *yauvane*; AMg. *logaṁsi* = *loke*; JM. *tihuyaṇammi* = *tribhuvane*; JŚ. *ṇāṇammi* = *jñāne* (§ 366a); in the first person singular optative : M. *kuppĕjja* = *kupyeyam*, in AMg. with lengthening of the final *haṇĕjjā* = *hanyām*; Ś. *kuppe*, from **kupyem* = *kupyeyam* too has the dropping off, (§ 460); in the absolutive in **tvānam* : AMg. *ciṭṭhittāṇa* (§ 583), *kāuāṇa* (§ 584); M. AMg. JM. *gantūṇa* (§ 586); JŚ. *kādūṇa* (§ 21. 584); likewise the forms in AMg. in *-ccāṇa*, *-yāṇa* beside those in *-ccāṇaṁ*, *-yāṇaṁ* (§ 587. 592). In the genitive plural the forms without anusvāra are dominant in M. (§ 370). They are found also in AMg. (§370), especially before enclitics, as *duhāṇa ya suhāṇa ya* = *duḥkhānāṁ ca sukhānāṁ ca* (Uttar. 626); *subhaddappamuhāṇa ya deviṇaṁ* = *subhadrāpramukhāṇāṁ ca devinām* (Ovav. § 40. 47. 56) against *subhaddappamuhāṇaṁ deviṇaṁ* = (Ovav. § 43); *dasaṇha vi vaṭṭamāṇāṇaṁ* = *daśānām api vartamānānām* (Uvās. § 275). Further in

JM., as °*purisāṇa aṭṭhārasapagaībbhantarāṇa* = °*puruṣāṇām aṣṭādaśaprakṛtyabhyantarāṇāṁ* (Āv. 12, 44. 45); *dŏṇha* °*viruddhāṇa naravarindāṇa* = *dvayor* °*viruddhayor naravarendrayoḥ* (Āv. 26, 7); *savaṇāṇa* = *śravaṇayoḥ* (Erz. 2, 13); *puttāṇa* = *putrāṇām* (Erz. 29, 8), and in JŚ., as *saṅgāsattāṇa tadha* [text *taha*] *asaṅgāṇaṁ* = *saṅgāsaktānāṁ tathāsaṅgānām* (Kattig. 398, 304), *radaṇāṇa* [text *raẏa*°], *savvajoẏāṇa riddhiṇa* = *ratnānām, sarvadyotānām, ṛddhīnām* (Kattig. 400, 325); *disāṇa savvāṇa suppasiddhāṇaṁ* = *diśāṁ sarvāsāṁ suprasiddhānām* (Kattig. 401, 342). In the last example and similar ones, where the forms with and without anusvāra stand beside one another (§370), as in other analogous cases (§ 180), the forms will have to be written with ardhacandra in place where there has been denasalization. To me it appears necessary, especially where in the texts at present there stands a denasalized form in the nominative and accusative singular on account of metre. Thus M. *ṇisasia varāia* = *niḥśvasitaṁ varākyā* (H. 141) which is to be read as *ṇisasiã varāiã*, since the ardhacandra does not make position; AMg. *taẏã saṁ ca jahāi seraẏaṁ* = *tvacaṁ svāṁ ca jahāti svairakaṁ* (Sūẏag. 118); *pāṇehi ṇaṁ pāvã viojayanti* = *prāṇair nūnaṁ pāpaṁ viyojayanti* (Sūẏag. 278); *appege vaĩ juñjanti* = **apyeke* **vācīṁ* [= *vācaṁ*] *yuñjanti* (Sūẏag. 169); *vāsaṁ vayaṁ vittĩ pakappayāmo* = *varṣaṁ vayaṁ vṛttiṁ prakalpayāmah* (Sūyag. 948); *taṁ isĩ tāḷaẏanti* = *tam ṛṣiṁ tāḍayanti* (Uttar. 360); *taṁ jaṇã tāḷaẏanti* (Uttar. 365); *aṇṇaṁ vā pupphã saccittaṁ* = *anyad vā puṣpaṁ sacitram* (Dasav. 622, 39); *tilapiṭṭhã pūipinnāgaṁ* = *tilapiṣṭaṁ pūtipiṇyākam* (Dasav. 623. 7); Mg. *gaaṇã gaścante* = *gaganaṁ gacchan* (Mṛcch. 113, 11); *khaṇã ẏūḷake* = *kṣaṇaṁ jūṭakaḥ* (Mṛcch. 136. 15); *khanã uddhacūḍe* = *kṣaṇam ūrdhvacūḍaḥ* (Mṛcch. 136. 16); A. *maĩṁ jāṇiã mialoaṇi* = *mayā jñātāṁ mṛgalocanīm*; *ṅavataḷĩ* = *navataḍitam*; *puhavĩ, piã* = *pṛthivīṁ, priyām* (Vikr. 55, 1. 2. 18). Likewise in all cases, where at present *ṁ* is printed although the metre requires a short syllable, so AMg. *abhirujjha kāyã vihariṁsu ārusiẏāṇã tattha hiṁsiṁsu* = *abhiruhya kāyaṁ vyahārṣur āruṣya tatrāhiṁsiṣuḥ* (Āẏār. 1, 8, 1, 2); AMg. *saṁvaccharã sāhiẏaṁ māsaṁ* = *saṁvatsaraṁ sādhikaṁ māsam* (Āẏār. 1, 8, 1, 3); AMg. *na vijjai bandhanã jassa kiṁci vi* = *na vidyate bandhanaṁ yasya kiñcid api* (Āẏār. 2, 16, 12). The same rules hold good also for the nasal vowel marked with bindu. So in M. AMg. JM. JŚ. A. in the instrumental plural occurs the forms in *-hiṁ, -hĩ, -hi* beside one another (§ 180. 368), and in AMg. JM. the denasalized form is used before enclitics. Thus AMg. *kāmehi* [text °*hiṁ*] *ẏa saṁthavehi ẏa* = *kāmaiś ca saṁstavaiś ca* (Sūẏag. 105); AMg. *hatthehiṁ pāehi ẏa* = *hastābhyāṁ pādābhyāṁ ca* (Sūẏag. 292); AMg. *bahūhiṁ ḍimbhaehi ẏa ḍimbhiẏāhi ẏa dāraehi ẏa dāriẏāhi ẏa kumārehi ẏa kumāriẏāhi ẏa saddhiṁ* (Nāẏādh. 431. 1407); AMg. *pariẏaṇaṇaẏaramahiliẏāhiṁ saddhiṁ* = *parijananagaramahilikābhiḥ sadhrīm* (Nāẏādh. 449), but *pariẏaṇamahilāhi ẏa saddhiṁ* (Nāẏādh. 426); AMg. *bahūhiṁ āghavaṇāhi ẏa paṇṇavaṇāhi ẏa viṇṇavaṇāhi ẏa saṇṇavaṇāhi ẏa* = *bahvībhir ākhyāpanābhiś ca prajñāpanābhiś ca vijñāpanābhiś ca saṁjñāpanābhiś ca* (Nāẏādh. 539; cf. Nāẏādh. § 143; Uvās. § 222).

§ 351. A final *-am* = Pkt. *-aṁ* becomes *u* in A. So in the accusative singular of the masculine and the nominative accusative singular of the neuter of *a*- stems, in the genitive singular of the pronouns of the first and second persons, in the first person singular of the future of Parasmaipada, in the absolutive in original *-tvīnam* and in sporadic adverbs: *vāasu* = *vāyasam* (Hc. 4, 352); *bharu* = *bharam* (Hc. 4, 340, 2); *hatthu* = *hastam* (Hc. 4, 422, 9); *vaṇavāsu* = *vanavāsam* (Erz. 3, 22); *aṅgu* = *aṅgam* (Hc. 4, 332,2); *dhaṇu* = *dhanam* (Kk. 272, 35); *phalu* = *phalam* (Hc. 4, 341, 2); *mahu, majjhu* = *mahyam* (Hc. s.v. *ma*; *mahu* pro ex. also Vikr. 58, 9; 59, 13. 14) *tujjhu* = **tuhyam* (Hc. s.v. *tu*); *pāvisu, karisu, païsisu* = Pkt. *pāvissaṁ, karissaṁ, pavisissaṁ* = *prāpsyāmi, kariṣyāmi, pravekṣyāmi* (Hc. 4, 396, 4); *gampiṇu, gamĕppiṇu* = **gantvinam, gamitvinam*; *karĕppiṇu* = **karitvinam*; *brŏppiṇu* = **brūtvinam* (§ 588); *ṇiccu* = *nityam* (Erz. 3, 23); *ṇisaṅku* = *niḥśaṁkam* (Hc. 4, 396. 1) *paramatthu* = *paramārtham* (Hc. 4, 422, 9); *samāṇu* = *samānam* (Hc. 4, 418, 3). So also *viṇu* (Hc. 426 and s.v.; Vikr. 71, 7) from **viṇaṁ* = *vinā* (§ 114). Also in Ḍh. *-aṁ* becomes *u* : *paḍimāśuṇṇu deulu* = *pratimāśūnyaṁ devakulam*; *ganthu* = *grantham*; *daśasuvaṇṇu kallavattu* = *daśasuvarṇaṁ kalyavartam* (Mṛcch. 30, 11; 31, 16; 34, 17); but very often beside it stands the accusative in *-aṁ* : *samavisamaṁ* = *samaviṣamam*; *kulaṁ*; *deulaṁ*; *jūdaṁ*; *savvaṁ suvaṇṇaṁ*; *daśasuvaṇṇaṁ kallavattaṁ* etc. (Mṛcch. 30, 8. 9. 12. 18; 32, 8; 34, 12). Also in A. of Piṅgala and Kālidāsa the form in *-aṁ* and *-ā* is dominant.

§ 352. Final *-kam* of Skt. becomes *-uṁ*, *-ũ* in A. So in the nom. acc. sing. neuter of the *a*-stem, in the nomin. sing. of the pronouns of the first and second persons, in the first pers. sing. of the indic. pres. and in certain adverbs : *hiaḍaũ* = *hṛdayakam* (Hc. 4, 350, 2 and s. v.); *rūaḍaũ* = *rūpakam*; *kuḍambaũ* = *kuṭumbakam* (Hc. 4, 419, 1. 422, 14); *haũ* = **ahakam* (Hc. 4, 375 and s. v.); *tuhũ* = *tvakam* (§ 206); *jāṇau* = **jānakam* = *jānāmi*; *jivaũ* = *jivāmi*; *cajaũ* = *tyajāmi* (§ 454); *maṇāũ* = JM. *maṇāgaṁ* (§ 114) = Skt. **manākam* = *manāk* (Hc. 4, 418. 426); *sahuṁ* = *sahũ* = *sākáṁ* (§ 206). Further in the infinitively used nouns in original *-kam*, as *akkhaṇaũ* = *ākhyānakam* (§ 579) and in *ehaũ* = **eṣakam* in the meaning of *etad* (Hc. 4, 362).

V. SAṀDHI CONSONANTS.

§ 353. The consonants, that were originally permitted to stand in the final position Skt. as saṁdhi-consonants for the purpose of avoiding hiatus are employed dialectically in Pkt. too, as in Pāli[1], whereby the cases mentioned in § 341. 343. 348. 349. result. Especially frequently *m* is so employed : AMg. *anna-m-anna°*, *aṇṇa-m-aṇṇa°*[2] = *anyonya°* (Āyār. 2, 14, 1; Uttar. 402; Vivāhap. 105, 106), *anna-m-anno* (Āyār. 2, 14, 1) *anna-m-annaṁ* (Āyār. 2, 7, 1, 11; Sūyag. 630; Paṇhāv. 231; Vivāhap. 180; Uttar. 402; Kappas. 46). *aṇṇa-m-aṇṇeṇaṁ* (Vivāhap. 123; Kappas. § 72; Nirayāv. § 11), *aṇṇa-m-aṇṇāe* (Vivāhap. 931), *anna-m-annassa* (Āyār. 2, 5, 2, 2. 3. 5; 2, 8, 6, 2; Vivāhap. 187. 508. 928; Uvās. § 79; Ṭhāṇ. 287; Nirayāv. §18; Ovav. §38.89), *anna-m-annehiṁ* (Sūyag. 633.635; Nirayāv. § 27), *aṇṇa-m-aṇṇāṇaṁ* (Vivāgas. 74); JŚ. *aṇṇa-m-aṇṇehiṁ* (Pav. 384, 47). Whilst in Vedic *anyānya*, M. *aṇṇaṇṇa*, JM. *annanna* (§ 130) the stem stands in the first member, in Skt. *anyonya*, M. AMg. JM. Ś. *aṇṇŏṇṇa* (§ 84) the nominative is benumbed; it is the case in AMg. JŚ. with the accus., so that *m* is here originally authorized. The same holds good for

M. AMg. A. *ĕkka-m-ĕkka*, AMg. *ega-m-ega* = *ekaika*, M. *ĕkka-m-ĕkka*° (R. 5, 85, 87; 13, 87); M. *ĕkka-m-ĕkkaṁ* (Hc. 3, 1; R. 5, 48; 8, 32); AMg. *ega-m-egaṁ* (Sūẏag. 948. 950; Nāẏādh. § 125); A. *ĕkka-m-ĕkkaũ* (Hc. 4, 422. 6); *ĕkka-m-ĕkkeṇa* (Hc. 3, 1); AMg. *ega-m-egāe* (Vivāhap. 224; Nāẏādh. § 125); M. AMg. *ĕkka-m-ĕkkassu* (H. 416. 517; Śak. 101, 14; Uttar. 401); AMg. *ega-m-egassa* (Ṭhāṇ. 456; Vivāhap. 215. 222); M. *ĕkka-m-ĕkke* (R. 3, 56); AMg. *ega-m-egaṁsi* (Vivāgas. 50; Vivāhap. 1043 ff. 1191); AMg. *ega-m-ege* (Vivāhap. 214); M. *ĕkka-m-ĕkkā* (R. 7, 59; 10, 41). — Saṁdhi-consonant is *m* in : *aṅga-m-aṅgammi* = *aṅge'ṅge* (Hc. 3, 1); AMg. *virāiẏaṅga-m-aṅge* = *virājitāṅgāṅgāḥ*, *ujjoiẏaṅga-m-aṅge* = *uddyotitāṅgāṅgāḥ* (Ovav. § 11. 16), *haṭṭhatuṭṭhacitta-m-āṇandiẏa* = *hṛṣṭatuṣṭacittānandita* (Nāẏādh. § 23; Ovav. § 17; Kappas. § 5. 15; Bhag. 2, 260), beside °*citte āṇandiẏe* (Kappas. 50). Often before *ādi* : AMg. *haẏa-m-āi goṇa-m-āi gaẏa-m-āi sīha-m-āiṇo* = *hayādayo gavādayo gajādayaḥ siṁhādayaḥ* (Uttar. 1075); AMg. *sugandhatĕlla-m-āiehiṁ* = *sugandhatailādikaiḥ* (Kappas. § 60); AMg. °*candaṇa-m-ādiehiṁ* (Uvās. § 29); AMg. °*raẏaṇa-m-āieṇaṁ* = °*ratnādikena* (Kappas. § 90; cf. § 112; Ovav. § 23); AMg. *āhāra-m-āiṇi* (Dasav. 626, 6); JM. *palaṇḍulasuṇa-m-āihiṁ* (Āv. 40, 18); JM. *kāmadheṇu-m-āiṇa*, *logapāla-m-āiṇaṁ* (Kk. 270, 29; 275, 37); JŚ. *rūva-m-ādiṇi* = *rūpādini* (Pav. 384, 48). Other examples are : AMg. *āriẏa-m-aṇāriẏāṇaṁ* (Samav. 98; Ovav. § 56); AMg. *sārassaẏa-m-āiccā* = *sārasvatādityau* (Ṭhāṇ. 516); AMg. *esa-m-aṭṭhe* = *eṣo'rthaḥ* (Vivāhap. 193; Nāẏādh. § 29; Ovav. § 90; Kappas. § 13), *esa-m-āghāo* = *eṣa āghātaḥ* (Dasav. 625, 39), *esa-m-aggī* = *eṣo'gniḥ* (Uttar. 282), *eẏa-m-aṭṭhassa* (Niraẏāv. § 8), *āẏāra-m-aṭṭhā* = *ācārārthāt* (Dasav. 636, 9), *lābha-m-aṭṭhio* = *lābhārthikaḥ* (Dasav. 641,42); AMg. *savvajiṇa-m-aṇuṇṇāa* = *sarvajinānujñāta* (Paṇhāv. 469. 539); AMg. *vatthagandha-m-alaṁkāraṁ* (Sūẏag. 183; Ṭhāṇ. 450; Dasav. 613, 17); AMg. *atīẏaüppanna-m-aṇāgaẏāiṁ* = *atītotpannānāgatāni* (Sūẏag. 470; cf. Vivāhap. 155; Dasav. 627, 27); AMg. *dīha-m-addha-* = *dīrghādhvan* (Ṭhāṇ. 41. 129. 370. 570; Sūẏag. 787. 789; Vivāhap. 38. 39. 848. 1128. 1225 f. 1290; Paṇhāv. 302. 326; Ovav. § 83; Nāẏādh. 464. 1137); AMg. *atthāha-m-atāra-m-aporisiẏaṁsi udaẏaṁsi* = **astāghātārāpauruṣīya udake* (Nāẏādh. 1113); AMg. *āukkhemassa-m-appaṇo* = *āyuḥkṣemasyātmanaḥ* (Āẏār. 1, 7, 8, 6); JM. *aṭṭhārasa-m-aggalesu* = *aṣṭādaśārgaleṣu* (Kl. 19), *ūru-m-antare* (Āv. 15, 18); AMg. *purao-m-aggao ẏa* = *purato'grataśca* (Vivāhap. 830). *y* and *r* are employed more rarely as saṁdhi-consonants. In AMg. *egāheṇa vā duẏāheṇa vā tiẏāheṇa vā caüẏāheṇa vā* (Āẏār. 2, 3, 1, 11; 2, 5, 2, 3. 4) —cf. *egāhaṁ vā duẏāhaṁ vā tiẏāhaṁ vā* (Jīv. 261. 286. 295). — *caüẏāheṇa* = *caturaheṇa* might have been influenced by *duẏāheṇa* = *dvyahena* and *tiẏāheṇa* = *tryaheṇa*, as the lengthening of the vowel is explained on the analogy of *egāheṇa*, *egāhaṁ*. AMg. *kiṁ aṇeṇa bho-ẏ-aṇeṇa* (Āẏār. 1, 6, 4, 3); AMg. *su-ẏ-akkhāẏa* = *svākhyāta* (Sūẏag. 590. 594), beside *suakkhāẏa* (Sūẏag. 603. 620); AMg. *veẏavi-ẏ-āẏarakkhie* = *vedavid ātmarakṣitaḥ* (Uttar. 453); *bahu-ẏ-aṭṭhiẏa* = *bahvasthika* (Āẏār. 2, 1, 10, 5; cf. however, § 6, where without *ẏ*); AMg. *mahu-ẏ-āsava* = *madhvāsrava* (Ovav. § 24); JM. *rāẏā-ẏ-u* = *rājā*+*u* (Āv. 8, 1); JM. *du-ẏ-aṅgula* = *dvyaṅgula* (Erz. 59, 13). *r* is established etymologically in AMg. *vāhi-r-ivosahehiṁ* = *vyādhirivauṣadhaiḥ* (Uttar. 918), *sihi-r-iva* (Dasav. 633,

34), *vāẏu-r-iva* (Sūẏag. 758; Kappas. § 118), where *r* is an old ending of the nominative, therefore, *vahir ivo°*, *sihir iva* (so LEUMANN), *vāẏur iva* (so JACOBI) may be written. *r* is the saṁdhi-consonant by analogy with such cases, as AMg. *aṇu-r-āgaẏaṁ* = *anvāgatam* (Vivāhap. 154)[3]; AMg. *du-r-aṅgula* = *dvyaṅgula* (Uttar. 767; commentary *duaṅgula*; cf. above JM. *duẏaṅgula*); AMg. JM. *dhi-r-atthu* = *dhigastu* (Hc. 2, 174; Triv. 1, 3. 105; Nāẏādh. 1152 1170 ff.; Uttar. 672. 677; Dasav. 613, 31; Dvār. 507, 21). AMg. *su-r-aṇucara* = *svanucara* (Ṭhāṇ. 350) is built according to *duraṇucara*, already cited above[4], and reversely *duāikkhaṁ* (Ṭhāṇ. 349) probably had been formed according to the analogy of *suāikkhaṁ*, if the reading is correct.

1. E. KUHN, Beiträge p. 61 ff.; E. MÜLLER, Simplified Grammar p. 63; WINDISCH, BKSGW. 1893, 228, ff. — 2. The texts vary also in the following examples from AMg. between *nna*, and *ṇṇa*. — 3. Abhayadeva says : *rephasyāgamikatvād anvāgatam anurūpam āgamanaṁ he skandaka taveti dṛśyaṁ*. — 4. Abhayadeva : *rephaḥ prākṛtatvāt*. Cf. BEZZENBERGER, BB. 4, 340, note 2.

VI. TRANSPOSITION OF SYLLABLES.

§ 354. In some cases, sometimes two syllables standing side by side are transposed and that without existence of any phonetic ground : *aïrāhā* = *acirābhā* and *aïhārā* (lightening; Deśīn. 1, 34). — *alacapura* = *acalapura* (Hc. 2, 118). — *āṇāla* = *ālāna* (Vr. 4, 29; Hc. 2, 117; Kī. 2, 117), *āṇālakhambha*, *āṇālakkhambha* = *ālānastambha* (Hc. 2, 97). — *kaṇeru* = *kareṇu* (Vr. 4, 28; Hc. 2, 116; Kī. 2, 119; Mk. fol. 38). The grammarians restrict this transposition to the feminine, a thing that corresponds with Pāli[1]. In AMg. *kareṇu* is used in the feminine (Nāẏādh. 327. 328. 337. 338; Uttar. 337 954), and in Ś. in the masculine (Pāiẏal. 9; Mālatīm. 203, 4). So also JM. *kareṇuẏā* = *kareṇukā* (Pāiẏal. 9; Erz.). According to Mk. fol. 68 transposition never takes place in Ś. — M. *ṇaḍāla*, M. AMg. JM. *ṇiḍāla* = *lalāṭa*, beside *ṇalāḍa*, M. AMg. *ṇilāḍa*, Ś. *lalāḍa* (§ 260) .—JM. A. *draha* = *hrada* (Hc. 2, 80; Deśīn. 8, 14; Āv. 42, 27; Hc. 4, 423, 1), AMg. *daha* (Hc. 2, 80. 120; Āẏār. 2, 1, 2, 3; 2, 3, 3, 2; Aṇuog. 386; Paṇṇav. 80; Nāẏādh. 508 ff.; Vivāhap. 119. 361. 659; Ṭhāṇ. 94), frequently also in compounds, as *kesariddaha*, *tigicchaddaha* (Ṭhāṇ. 75. 76), *paümaddaha*, *puṇḍariẏaddaha* (Ṭhāṇ. 75 ff.; Jīv. 582 f.); M. AMg. *mahaddaha* (H. 186 Ṭhāṇ. 75. 382); AMg. A. *mahādaha* (Ṭhāṇ. 176; Hc. 4, 444, 3), beside AMg. *haraẏa* with a separation vowel (132). — M. AMg. JM. Ś. A. *dihara* for **diraha* (§ 132)[2] = *dirgha* (Hc. 2, 171; G. H. R.; Karp. 43, 11; Nandīs. 377; Erz.; Uttarar. 125, 6; Bālar. 235, 15; Mallikām. 81, 9; 123, 15; 161, 8; 198, 17; 223, 9; Hc. 4, 414, 4). — AMg. *pāhaṇāo* = *upānahau aṇovāhaṇaga*, *°ẏa*, AMg. *chattovāhaṇa*, beside Ś. *uvāṇaha* (§ 141).—JM. Ś. A. *marahaṭṭha* = *mahārāṣṭra* (Hc. 1, 69; 2, 119; Kk. 44; Bālar. 72, 19; Piṅg. 1, 91, 116a. 140a), M. *marahaṭṭhī* (Viddhaś. 25, 2), beside *maraḍhī* (§ 67). — AMg. *rahassa* for **harassa* = *hrasva* (Ṭhāṇ. 20. 40. 445. 452), beside *hassa* (Āẏār. 1, 5, 6, 4; 2, 4, 2, 10; Vivāhap. 38. 39), *hassikarĕnti* (Vivāhap. 126). The MSS and texts more often have *hrassa* (Ṭhāṇ. 119; Nandīs. 377; WEBER, Bhag. 1, 415). According to Bh. 4, 15 one says *haṁsa* too (§ 74). — AMg. JM. A. *vāṇārasi* = *vārāṇasi* (Hc. 2, 116; Antag. 63;

Nāyādh. 508. 787. 791. 1516. 1528 [text *vārāṇasie*]; Nirayāv. 43 ff. Paṇṇav. 60; Ṭhāṇ. 544; Uttar. 742; Vivāgas. 136. 148 f.; Vivāhap. 284 ff. Erz.; Piṅgala 1, 73 [*vaṇarasi*; GOLDSCHMIDT *varaṇasi*]; Hc. 4, 442 1). In Ś. stands *vārāṇasī* (Bālar. 307, 13; Mallikām. 156, 24; 161, 17; 224, 10), likewise in Mg. (Prab. 32, 9), for which the ed. Bomb. 78, 11 rightly reads *vālāṇasī*, which is to be corrected as *vālānaśī*. — *haliāra* beside *hariāla* = *haritāla* (Hc. 2, 121). — *halua* beside *lahua* = *laghuka* (Hc. 2, 122). — *hulaï* beside *luhaï* (wipes of, Hc. 4, 105). For *luhaï* Vr. 8, 67; Kī. 4, 53 have *lubhaï*. Through this it becomes probable that *hulaï* may be equated as = **bhulaï*, and that it is identical with *hulaï* (throws; Hc. 4, 143), to which might be connected *bhullaï* (falls down; Hc. 4, 177), the passive, and JM. Ś. *bhulla* (forgotten; forgetfully; bewildered; Āv. 46, 5; Karp. 113. 1) the past passive participle[3]. — It is phonetically impossible to equate M. *iharā* (Pāiyal. 241; G.), with the grammarians (Hc. 2, 212; Mk. fol. 38) as = *itarathā*, and to explain it through transposition from **iarahā* with Mk. and WEBER[4], since in M. the MSS mostly have *iarā* (H. 711; R. 11, 26), *iharā*, as stated in § 212, have originated from **itharatā*. According to Mk. fol. 68 Ś. has only *idaradhā*.

1. PISCHEL on Hc. 2, 116. — 2. S. GOLDSCHMIDT, R. s. v.— 3. PISCHEL on Hc. 4, 177. — 4. On Hāla 711.

III. MORPHOLOGY.

A. THE NOUN

§ 355. Following the rule, that in Pkt. the consonants in the final position fall off (§ 339), the consonantal declension is almost completely lost. A large number of its remnants are found only in the case of the stems in *t*, *n*, *ś*, *s*, otherwise almost sporadically in verses. So M. *vivaā* = *vipadā* (Śukas. 33, 7); AMg. *dhammavio* = *dharmavidaḥ* (nom. plur.; Sūyag. 43); AMg. *vāyā* = *vācā* (Dasav. 630. 32; Uttar. 28); AMg. *veyavido* = *vedavidaḥ* (nom. plur. Uttar. 425). *āo* (water) = *āpaḥ* (Triv. in BB. 3, 239) too is to be considered as a remnant of the consonantal declension. The neuter *āpas*, which is quoted by Ujjvaladatta on Uṇādisūtra 2, 58 and is found many a time in the texts, is traced back to the nom. plural[2]. In AMg. *āo* has become one masculine *āu* (Hc. 2, 174; Deśīn. 1, 61), likewise *teo* = *tejaḥ* has become *teu*, however, in the formular phrase *āū teū vāū* = *āpas tejo vāyuḥ* the vowel has been set on the pattern of *u* of *vāu* = *vāyu*. Likewise *kāyasā* is said for *kāyeṇa*, beside *maṇasā vayasā*, and *balasā* for *baleṇa* beside *sahasā* (§ 364) and others in enumerations (§ 358, 364. 367. 375. 379. 386). So *āū teū vāū* (Sūyag. 606; Samav. 228 [text *teo*]; Dasav. 614, 40 [text *u*] Āyār. 2, 2, 2, 13 [text *āo teo vāu*]); also *vāū teū āū* (Vivāgas. 50); *āu teū vā vāu* (Sūyag. 19); *āu teū ya tahā vāū ya* (Sūyag. 37); *āū agaṇi ya vāū* (Sūyag. 325); *puḍhavi āu gaṇi vāū* (Sūyag. 378); *āuteuvāuvaṇassaïsarira* (Sūyag. 803); *āuteuvāuvaṇassaïṇāṇavihāṇaṁ* (Sūyag. 806); *āusarira teusarira vāusarira* (Sūyag. 792); *āūteuvaṇassaï°* (Vivāhap. 430); *teuvāuvaṇassaï* (Āyār. 2, 1, 7, 3); *āukāya teukāya vāukāya* (Āyār. 1, 8, 1, 11; Samav.

17); *āukāẏa* (Vivāhap. 1439); *āukāiẏa teukāiẏa vāukāiẏa* (Vivāhap. 1438 f. [text mostly °*ū*°]; Aṇuog. 260; Dasav. 614, 38), *āukkāiẏa* (Jīv. 41); *āulĕsse* (Vivāhap. 10); *āubahula* (Jīv. 226); *āujivā tahāgaṇi vāujivā* (Sūẏag. 425; cf. Uttar. 1045. 1047); *teuphāsa* = *tejaḥsparśa* (Āẏār. 1, 7, 7, 1; 1, 8, 3, 1); *teujiva* (Uttar. 1053); *teū vāū ẏa* (Uttar. 1052). The two words are used as wholly independent *u*-stems as well: nom. sing. *āū* (Sūẏag. 332; Paṇṇav. 369[3]); nom. plur. *āū* (Ṭhāṇ. 82); gen. plur. *āūṇaṁ* (Uttar. 1047), *teūṇaṁ* (Uttar. 1055). In a non-technical sense *tejas* is treated in AMg. as the remnant of a neuter noun in *-as*. — From the nom. plur. *sarao* = *śaradaḥ* of *śarad* (autumn), in M. AMg. JM. Ś. A., a masc. sing. *saraa*, AMg. JM. *saraẏa* = Pāli *sarada*[4] has been inferred (Vr. 4, 10. 18; Hc. 1, 18. 31; Kī. 2, 133; Mk. fol. 34; G.H.R.; Ṭhāṇ. 238. 527; Nāẏādh. 916; Kk. 264, 6; Bālar. 127, 14; Hc. 4, 357, 2); likewise *diso* from *diśaḥ* (Kī. 2, 131; in case the word is not to be read as *disā*). In other respects the treatment of the consonantal stem is a twofold one. In a small number of cases the word after loss of the final consonant is made end in the vowel preceding it and crosses over the vocalic declension corresponding to the gender, and in majority of words the stem is augmented by insertion of *-a* in the masculine and neuter, and of *-ā* or *-ī* in the feminine. See § 395 ff.

1. STENZLER, BB. 6, 84. — 2. So in WEBER, Bhag. 1, 397, note 2 and E. KUHN, Beiträge p. 67, more correctly than BB. 3, 240. — 3. Malayagiri on Paṇṇav. 369 remarks: *āū iti puṁliṅgatā prākṛtalakṣṇavaśāt saṁskṛte tu strītvam eva.* — 4. So in CHILDERS, Dictionary s. v. more correctly than BB. 3, 240.

§ 356. The gender of Skt. has not always been preserved in Pkt. The variation has been brought about partly by the rule of the final syllable. Thus in M. JM. the neuter in *-as*, in pursuance of the nomin. in *-o* (§ 345), is used in the masculine (Vr. 4, 18; Hc. 1, 32; Kī. 2, 133; Mk. fol. 35) : M. *tuṅgŏ ccia hoi maṇo* = *tuṅgam eva bhavati manaḥ* (Hc. 284); *esa saro* = *etat saraḥ* (G. 513); *khuḍio mahĕndassa jaso* = **kṣuditaṁ mahendrasya yaśaḥ* (R. 1, 4); *aṇṇo aṇṇassa maṇo* = *anyad anyasya manaḥ* (R. 3, 44); *māruaIaddhathāmo mahīrao* = *mārutalabdhasthāma mahirajaḥ* (R. 4, 25); *tamālakasaṇo tamo* = *tamāla-kṛṣṇaṁ tamaḥ* (R. 10, 25); *tāriso a uro* = *tādṛśaṁ coraḥ* (Subhadrāh. 8, 3); JM. *bārasāiccodaẏāhio teo* = *dvādaśādityodayāhitaṁ tejaḥ* (Erz. 26, 33); *tavo kao* = *tapaḥ kṛtam* (Erz. 26, 35). *nabhas* and *śiras*, according to the grammarians (Vr. 4, 19; Hc. 1, 32; Kī. 2, 134; Mk. fol. 35), only as neuter, are used according to the *a*-declension : M. *ṇahaṁ* (G. 451. 495. 1036; R. 4, 54; 5, 2. 6. 35. 43. 74 etc.); M. *siraṁ* (R. 4, 56; 11, 36. 56. 132 etc.). In AMg. too the neuter nouns in *-as*, not rarely, are used as masculine, and then form the nomin. sing. in *-e* (§ 345) : *māuoẏe* = *mātrojaḥ* (Ṭhāṇ. 159); *tame* = *tamaḥ* (Ṭhāṇ. 248); *tave* = *tapaḥ* (Samav. 26); *maṇe* = *manaḥ* (Vivāhap. 1135 f.); *pĕjje* = *preyaḥ* (Ovav. § 56); *vacche* = *vakṣaḥ* (Uvās. § 94); *ee soẏā* = *etāni srotāṁsi* (Āẏār. 1, 5, 6, 2). AMg. *aẏaṁ* = *ayas* (Sūẏag. 286); AMg. *seẏaṁ* = *śreyas* (Hc. 1, 32; § 409); *vaẏaṁ* = *vayas* (Hc. 1, 32), beside AMg. *vao* (Āẏār. 1, 2, 1, 3 in the verse); *sumaṇaṁ* = *sumanaḥ* (Hc. 1, 32). Ś. Mg. so form almost exclusively (§ 407). In A. *maṇu* (Hc. 4,350. 422, 9) and *siru* (Hc. 4, 445. 3), phonetically rather = *manaḥ*, *śiraḥ* (§ 346), may be equated as = **nanam*, **śiram* (§ 351). The voc. *ceu* = *cetaḥ* (Piṅgala 1, 4[b]; text *ceja*; v. l. *ceḍa*; cf. BOLLENSEN, Vikr. p. 528) speaks in support of *-aḥ*.

§ 357. Like the neuter nouns in *-as*, many neuter nouns in *-a* have dialectically become masculine in Pkt. This change has probably been produced from the nomin. accus. plur., which beside the endings *-āṇi*, *-āiṁ*, as in the Veda, has also the ending *-ā*, which is like that of the masculine (§ 367). So one says AMg. *tao ṭhāṇāṇi* (Ṭhāṇ. 143), *tao ṭhāṇāiṁ* (Ṭhāṇ. 158) and *tao ṭhāṇā* (Ṭhāṇ. 163. 165) = *triṇi sthānāni*. The nomin. sing. *ṭhāṇe* may be deduced from the last form : AMg. *esa ṭhāṇe aṇārie* = *etat sthānam anāryam* (Sūẏag. 736). Examples in AMg. are numerous beyond measure; *esa udagaraẏaṇe* = *etad udakaratnam* (Nāẏādh. 1011); *uṭṭhāṇe kamme bale vīrie* = *utthānaṁ karma balaṁ vīryam* (Vivāhap. 171; Nāẏādh. 374; Uvās. §73); *duvihe daṁsaṇe pannatte* = *dvividhaṁ darśanaṁ prajñaptam* (Ṭhāṇ. 44); *maraṇe* = *maraṇam* (Samav. 51. 52), *mattae* = *mātrakam*, beside the plural *mattagāiṁ* (Kappas. S. § 56), and several others[1]. In Āẏār. at 1, 2, 1, 3 stand in the verse beside one another : *vao accei jŏvvaṇaṁ ca jīvie* = *vayo'tyeti yauvanaṁ ca jīvitam*. In AMg. sometimes the pronouns too are moved into the neuter masculine: AMg. *eẏāvanti savvā kammasamārambhā* = *etāvantaḥ sarve karma-samārambhāḥ* (Āẏār. 1, 1, 1, 5, 7); *āvantike ẏāvanti logaṁsi samaṇā ẏa māhaṇā ẏa* = *āvantike ca yāvanto loke śramaṇāś ca brāhmaṇāś ca* (Āẏār. 1,4, 2, 3; cf. 1, 5, 2, 1. 4); *ẏāiṁ tumāiṁ ẏāiṁ*, *te jaṇagā* = *yas tvaṁ yau te janakau* (Āẏār. 2, 4. 1, 8); *ẏāim* [§ 335. 353] *bhikkhū* = *ye bhikṣavaḥ* (Āẏār. 2, 7, 1, 1); *jāvanti 'vijjāpurisā savve te dukkhasaṁbhavā* = *yāvanto 'vidyā puruṣāḥ sarve te duḥkhasaṁbhavāḥ* (Uttar. 215); *je garahiẏā saṇiẏāṇappaogā ṇa tāṇi sevanti sudhīradhammā* = *ye garhitāḥ sanidānaprayogā na tān sevante sudhīra-dharmāḥ* (Sūẏag. 504). So is explained *ṇo in' aṭṭhe*, *ṇo iṇaṁ aṭṭhe* (§ 173) too; cf. also *se*, Mg. *śe* = *tad* § 423. In JM. the predicate is generally of the neuter when it refers to persons of different genders : *tao sāgaracando kamalāmeḷā ẏa......gahiẏāṇuvvaẏāṇi sāvagāṇi saṁvuttāṇi* = *tataḥ sāgaracandraḥ kamalāpiḍā ca. . . .gṛhitānuvratau śrāvakau saṁvṛttau* (Āv. 31, 22), and previously (31, 21) it is said about the same : *pacchā imāṇi bhoge bhuñjamāṇāṇi viharanti* = *paścād imau bhogān bhuñjānau viharataḥ* ; *tāni* is used (Āv. 38, 1) with reference to *māẏāpiiṇaṁ* = *mātāpitroḥ*; *tāṇi ammāpiẏaro pucchiẏāṇi* = *tau ambāpitarau pṛṣṭau* (Erz. 37, 29); *tāhe rāẏā sā ẏa jaẏahatthimmi ārūḍhāiṁ* = *tadā rājā sā ca jayahastiny ārūḍhau* (Erz. 34, 29); [*maẏaṇamañjariẏā kumāro ca*] *niẏaẏabhavaṇe gaẏāī sānandahiẏaẏāiṁ* = [*madanamañjarikā kumāraś ca*] *nijaka-bhavane gatau sānandahṛdayau* (Erz. 84, 6). More examples in JACOBI, Erz. p. LVI, § 80. Transition of the neuter *a*-stems to the masculine is frequent in Mg. too; in other dialects it is almost only sporadic. So Mg. *eśe śe daśa-ṇāmake maï kaḷe* = *etat tad daśanāmakaṁ mayā kṛtam* (Mṛcch. 11, 1); *āmala-ṇantike vele* = *āmaraṇātikaṁ vairam* (Mṛcch. 21, 14); *duālae* = *dvārakam* (Mṛcch. 79, 17); *pavahaṇe* = *pravahaṇam* (Mṛcch. 96, 22; 97, 19. 20; 99. 2; 100, 20 etc.); *eśe civale* = *etac civaram* (Mṛcch. 112, 10); *śohide* = *sauhṛdam* (Śak. 118, 6); *bhoaṇe śaṁcide* = *bhojanaṁ saṁcitam* (Veṇīs. 33, 3); *usṇe luhile* = *uṣṇaṁ rudhiram* (Veṇīs. 33, 12); *bhatte* = *bhaktam*, *eśe śe śuvaṇṇake* = *etat tat* *suvarṇakam* (Mṛcch. 163 19; 165, 7). In Ś. D. we find the following used in the masculine : *pavahaṇo* (Mṛcch. 97, 7; D. 110, 15) beside the more frequent *pavahaṇaṁ*; in Ś. *pabhādo* (Mṛcch. 93, 7) beside *pabhādaṁ* = *prabhātam* (Mṛcch. 93. 5. 6); more often Ś. *hiao* = *hṛdayam*, particularly, when the heart is spoken of (Vikr. 22, 21 [so with A. to be read]; 23, 10; cf. 46, 17. 19; Ratn. 298, 11. 12; Mālatīm. 348, 6 [so with v. l. to be read; Viddhaś. 97, 10; Priyad. 20, 2; Nāgān. 20, 13. 15)[2]. The dialect is not definite in *catto* = *cattram* (spindel; Deśīn. 3, 1). Cf. also § 360.

1. Hoernle, Uvās., Translation, note 55. — 2. Pischel, De gr. Pr. p. 5.

§ 358. According to the grammarians (Vr. 4. 18; Hc. 1, 32; Kī. 2, 133; Mk. fol. 35) the neuter in *-an* becomes masculine in *-a* : *kammo* = *karma*; *jammo* = *janma*; *ṇammo* = *narma*; *mammo* = *marma*; *vammo* = *varma*. Thus we have found PG *sammo* = *śarma* (7, 46); AMg. *kamme* = *karma* (Sūyag. 838. 841 f. 844. 848. 854. Nāyādh. 374; Uvās. § 51. 73. 166); Mg. *camme* = *carma* (Mṛcch. 79, 9). In all the dialects, however, they, more frequently become neuter of *a*-stems[1], what is prescribed by Mk. for *preman* and by Hc. for *dāman*. So M. *kammaṁ* (R. 14, 46); M. Ś. *ṇāmaṁ* (H. 452. 905; Vikr. 30, 9) ; M. *dāmaṁ* (H. 172); M. *pĕmmaṁ* (R. 11, 88; Ratn. 299, 18); M. *romaṁ* (R. 9, 87); *cammaṁ sammaṁ* (Hc. 1, 32). The masculine in *-iman* may become feminine, to which the nomin. in *-ā* gave rise : *esā garimā*, *mahimā*, *nillajjimā*, *dhuttimā* (Hc. 1, 35; cf. Mk. fol. 35). So M. A. *candimā* = **candriman* (§ 103); AMg. *mahimāsu* (Ṭhāṇ. 288). In the same way AMg. *addhā* = *adhvā* from *adhvan* (Ovav.); M. *umhā* = *ūṣmā* from *ūṣman* (Bh. 3, 32; Hc. 2, 74; G. R.); JM. *vaṭṭā* = *vartmā* from *vartman* (Deśīn. 7, 31; Erz. 60, 30. 34. 35; cf. § 334); *sĕmbhā* = *śleṣmā* from *śleṣman* (Mk. fol. 25; cf. § 267) have become feminine. AMg. *sakahāo* = *sakthīni* (Samav. 102; Jīv. 621) is derived from the stem *sakthan* with a separation-vowel according to § 132, therefore, from **sakathan*, nomin. sing. **sakahā*. The Jainas divide the year according to the old custom into the three seasons *grīṣma*, *varṣāḥ* and *hemanta*[2]. As in other cases (§ 355. 364. 367. 375. 379. 386), the gender and the number of *grīṣma* and *hemanta* have in AMg. been regulated, when the season is to be indicated as such, according to the feminine plural *varṣāḥ* as a sequence to the formular combination. One says : *gimhāhi* = **grīṣmābhiḥ* (Sūyag. 166); *gimhāsu* = **grīṣmāsu* (Vivāhap. 465): *hemantagimhāsu . . vāsāsu* (Kappas. S § 55); *gimhāṇaṁ* (Āyār. 2, 15, 2. 6. 25; Nāyādh. 880; Kappas. § 2. 96. 120. 150. 159 etc.); *hemantāṇaṁ* (Āyār. 2, 15, 22; Kappas. § 113. 157. 212. 227). From the masculine in *-a* not seldom are found the neutral forms dialectically in the nomin.-accus. plur. a thing that might have been the result of the ending in *-ā* here as well (cf. § 357). So M. AMg. Ś. *guṇāiṁ* = *guṇān* (Hc. 1, 34; Mk. fol. 35; G. 866; Sūyag. 157; Vivāhap. 508; Mṛcch. 37, 14); M. *kaṇṇāiṁ* = *karṇau* (H. 805); M. *pavaāi*, *gaāiṁ*, *turaāi*, *rakkhasāi* = *plavagān*, *gajān*, *turagān*, *rākṣasān* (R. 15, 17)[3]; AMg. *pasiṇāṇi* = *praśnān* (Āyār. 2, 3, 2, 17), *pasiṇāiṁ* (Nāyādh. 301. 577; Vivāhap. 151. 973. 978; Nandīs. 417; Uvās. § 58. 121. 176), as already in Skt. *praśna* is neuter (Maitryupaniṣad. 1, 2); AMg. *māsāiṁ* = *māsān* (Kappas. § 114); AMg. *pāṇāiṁ* (Āyār. 1, 6, 5, 4; 1, 7, 2,

1 ff.; 2, 1, 1, 11; p. 132, 6. 22), *pāṇāṇi* (Āyār. 2, 2, 3, 2; p. 132. 28) beside the usual *pāṇe* (e.g. Āyār. 1, 1, 6, 3; 1, 3, 1, 3; ,1, 6, 1, 4) = *prāṇān*; AMg. *phāsāiṁ* (Āyār. 1, 4, 3, 2; 1, 8, 2, 10, 3, 1; Sūyag. 297) beside *phāse* (Āyār. 1, 6, 2, 3. 3, 2. 5, 1; 1, 7, 8, 18) = *sparśān*. AMg. *rukkhāiṁ* (Hc. 1, 34), AMg. *rukkhāṇi* = *rukṣān* (trees; Āyār. 2, 3, 2, 15; cf. § 320); *devāiṁ* (Hc. 1, 34), *devāṇi* (C. 1, 4) = *devāḥ*; JŚ. *ṇibandhāṇi* = *nibandhān* (Pav. 387, 12); Mg. *dantāiṁ* = *dantān* (Śak. 154, 6), *goṇāiṁ* = *gāḥ* (Mṛcch. 122, 15; 132, 16) beside the usual mascul. (§ 393). Hc. 1, 34 mentions in the singular too *khaggaṁ* beside *khaggo* = *khaḍgaḥ*; *maṇḍalaggaṁ* beside *maṇḍalaggo* = *maṇḍalāgraḥ*; *kararuhaṁ* beside *kararuho* = *kararuhaḥ*. and reversely Mk. fol. 35 has *vaaṇo* beside *vaaṇaṁ* = *vadanam*; *ṇaaṇo* beside *ṇaaṇaṁ* = *nayanam*. Neutral plural forms of the masculine are found from *i*- and *u*-stems too : AMg. *sāliṇi vā vihiṇi vā* = *śālīn vā vrīhīn vā* (Āyār. 2, 10, 10; Sūyag. 682), in association with the following neuter : AMg. *uūiṁ* = *ṛtūn* (Kappas. § 114); *bindūiṁ* (Hc. 1, 34; Mk. fol. 35); AMg. *heūiṁ* = *hetūn* beside *pasiṇāiṁ* (Vivāhap. 151). Neuter forms from the feminine are more seldom. So AMg. *tayāṇi* (Āyār. 2, 13, 22; Nāyādh. 1137; Vivāhap. 908) from the singular *tayā* (Paṇṇav. 32; Vivāhap. 1308. 1529); cf. *tayāpāṇae* (Vivāhap. 1255) and *tayāsuhāe* (Kappas. § 60) = **tvacā* = *tvak*; AMg. *pāuyāiṁ* = *pādukāḥ* (Nāyādh. 1484); Ś. *ricāiṁ* from **ricā* = *ṛk* (Ratn. 302, 11); AMg. *paṁtiyāṇi* (Āyār. 2, 3, 3, 2; 2, 11, 5) beside *paṁtiyāo* (Vivāhap. 361; Aṇuog. 386) = **paṅktikāḥ*; AMg. *bhamuhāiṁ* (Āyār. 2, 13, 17) beside *bhamuhāu* (Jīv. 563) = **bhruvuke* (§ 124. 206); AMg. *itthiṇi vā purisāṇi vā* = *striyo vā puruṣā vā* (Āyār. 2, 11, 18) too probably is to be understood in the meaning "something womanish", "something manly". *akṣi* may be used as feminine (Vr. 4, 20; Hc. 1, 33. 35; Kī. 2, 132; Mk. fol. 35), according to Hc. 1, 33 also as masc. Hc. 1, 35 teaches that the masculine nouns *añjali, kukṣi, granthi, nidhi, raśmi, vali, vidhi*, that have been classed by him under the *gaṇa añjalyādi*, may become feminine. So is explained AMg. *ayaṁ aṭṭhi, ayaṁ dahī* = *idam asthi, idaṁ dadhi* (Sūyag. 594), the dative *aṭṭhie* (§ 361), and so the nomin. *sappī* = *sarpiḥ* (Sūyag. 291) and the nomin. *havī* = *haviḥ* (Dasav. N. 648, 9) too must be understood in which the *s*- stems, after dropping off of *s*, have gone over to the *i*-declension. Cf. § 411, note. Beside *paṇho* = *praśnaḥ* Pkt. has *paṇhā* too (Vr. 4, 20; Hc. 1, 35; Kī. 2, 132; Mk. fol. 35; Sr. fol. 14), that occurs in AMg. *paṇhāvāgaraṇāiṁ* (Nandīs. 471; Samav.), the name of the tenth aṅga. In the v.l. to C. 3, 6 *paṇhaṁ* too occurs; the plural. AMg. *pasiṇāiṁ, pasiṇāṇi* have been mentioned above. In the sense of *arśāṁsi* AMg. has *aṁsiyāo* = **arśikāḥ* (Vivāhap. 1306). Beside *paṭṭha, piṭṭha, puṭṭha* = *pṛṣṭha* frequent are *paṭṭhī, piṭṭhī, puṭṭhī* (§ 53). The feminine *āśaṁsā* becomes M.Ś. *āsaṁgho* (§ 267); *prāvṛṣ* becomes in M. AMg. JM. Ś. a masculine *pāusa* = Pāli *pāvusa* (Vr. 4, 18; Hc. 1, 31; Kī. 2, 131; Mk. fol. 35; G. H.; Nāyādh. 81. 638 f. 644. 192; Vivāhap. 798; Erz.; Vikr. 33, 14); *taraṇi*, according to Hc. 1, 31, 2, is used only as masculine[4]. On *diso* = *dik*, *sarao* = *śarad* see § 355, on the numerals 2—4 see § 436. 438. 439.

1. S. GOLDSCHMIDT, R. p. 151, note 2. — 2. JACOBI on Kalpas. § 2 p. 99. — 3. It is

not quite certain whether these forms constitute a proof rather of the spurious nature of R. 15. 16. 17, as presumed by S. GOLDSCHMIDT R. p. 318, note 9. — 4. Cf. in general already PISCHEL, De gr. Pr. p. 5 f.

§ 359. In A. the gender is more flexible than in the rest of the dialects, if not almost wholly irregular, as meant by Hc. 4, 445. In verses very often the gender is determined by the metre and rhyme: *jo pāhasi so lehi*=*yat prārthayase tal labhasva* (Piṅgala 1, 5[a]; cf. Vikr. p. 530 f.); *mattāiṁ* =*mātrāḥ* (P. 1, 51. 60. 83. 127); *rehāiṁ*=*rekhāḥ* (P. 1, 52); *vikkanam*= *vikramaḥ* (P. 1, 56); *bhuaṇe*=*bhuvanāni* (accus.; P. 1, 62[b]); *gāhassa*= *gāthāyāḥ* (P. 1, 128); *sagaṇāi*=*sagaṇān* (P. 1, 152); *kumbhaī̃*=*kumbhān* (Hc. 4, 345); *antraḍi*=*antram* (Hc. 4, 445, 3); *ḍālaī̃* (Hc. 4, 445, 4), plural of *ḍālā* (branch; Pāiyal. 136; Deśīn. 4, 9, where *ḍāli*); however, AMg. too has *ḍāla* in *egaṁsi rukkhaḍālayaṁsi ṭhiccā* (Nāyādh. 492), and *ḍālaga* (Āyār. 2, 7, 2, 5); *khalāiṁ*=*khalān* in rhyme with *raaṇāiṁ* (Hc. 4, 334); *viguttāiṁ*=**viguptāḥ*=*vigopitāḥ* (Hc. 4, 421, 1); *ṇiccintāī̃ hariṇaī̃*=*niścintā hariṇāḥ* (Hc. 4, 422, 20); *amhaīṁ* beside *amhe*=*asme* (Hc. 4, 376).

§ 360. The dual with the exception of the numerals *do*=*dvau* and *duve*, *be*=*dve* is completely lost. In its place the plural has entered both in the case of noun and verb (Vr. 6, 63; C. 2, 12; Hc. 3, 130; Kī. 3, 5; Āv. 6, 12), that also is associated with the numeral for 2 (§ 436. 437). M. *balakeśavāṇaṁ*=*balakeśavayoḥ* (G. 26), *hatthā tharatharanti*=*hastau tharatharāyete* (H. 165), *kaṇṇesu*=*karṇayoḥ* (R. 5, 65), *achaiṁ*=*akṣiṇi* (G. 44); AMg. *jaṇagā*=*janakau* (Āyār. 1, 6, 1, 6), *pāhaṇāo*=*upānahau* (Ṭhāṇ. 359), *bhumagāo acchiṇi, kaṇṇā, uṭṭhā, aggahatthā, hatthesu, ṭhaṇayā, jāṇūiṁ, jaṅghāo, pāyā, pāesu*=*bhruvau, akṣiṇi, karṇau, oṣṭhau, agrahastau, hastayoḥ, stanakau, jānunī, jaṅghe, pādau, pādayoḥ* (Uvās. § 94); JM. *hatthā, payā*=*hastau, pādau* (Āv. 6, 14), *taṇhāchuhāo*=*tṛṣṇākṣudhau* (Dvār. 500, 7), *do vi puttā jamalagā*=*dvāv api putrau yamalakau* (Erz. 1, 8) *cittasaṁbhūehiṁ*=*citrasaṁbhūtābhyām* (Erz. 1, 26); Ś. *māhavamaarandā āacchanti*=*mādhavamakarandāv āgacchataḥ* (Mālatīm. 293, 4), *rāmarāvaṇāṇaṁ*=*rāmarāvaṇayoḥ* (Bālar. 260, 21), *sidārāmehiṁ* =*sitārāmābhyām* (Pras. 64, 5), *sirisarassadiṇaṁ*=*śrīsarasvatyoḥ* (Viddhaś. 108, 5); Mg. *lāmakaṇhāṇaṁ*=*rāmakṛṣṇayoḥ* (Kaṁsav. 48, 20), *amhe vi … luhilaṁ pivamha*=*āvām api rudhiraṁ pibāva* (Veṇīs. 35, 21), *kalĕmha*=*karavāva* (Caṇḍak. 68, 15; 71, 10); D. *candaṇaaviraehiṁ*=*candanakavirakābhyām* (Mṛcch. 105, 8), *sumbhaṇisumbhe*=*śumbhaniśumbhau* (Mṛcch. 105, 22); A. *rāvaṇarāmahā̃, paṭṭaṇagāmahā̃*=*rāvaṇarāmayoḥ, paṭṭanagrāmayoḥ* (Hc. 4, 407). In cases like Ś. *duve rukkhaseaṇake*=*dve rukṣascanake* (Śak. 24, 1) there is no dual, but the accus. plur. (§ 367[a]) with a change of gender according to § 357[1].

1. HOEFER, De Prakrita dialecto. p. 136 f.; LASSEN, Inst. p. 309; BOLLENSEN on. Vikr. 347; WEBER, IS. 14, 280 f.

§ 361. According to Vr. 6, 64; C. 2, 13; Kī. 3, 14; Sr. fol. 7; in a quotation in Āv. 6, 12 in Pkt. the genitive occurs in the place of the dative. Hc. 3, 132 teaches that dative may stand when it expresses a purpose. The texts are in accord with him. A dative of the singular is found almost only in PG. M. AMg. JM., mostly in the case of the *a*-stems, as the dative of goal and purpose. PG. *ajātāe*=**adyatvāyo* (7, 45); *vāsasata-*

sahassāya = *varṣaśatasahasrāya* (7, 48); M. *ṇivāraṇāa* = *nivāraṇāya*, *āāsāa* = *āyāsāya*, *maraṇāa* = *maraṇāya*, *harārāhaṇāa* = *harārādhanāya*, *hāsāa* = *hāsāya*, *gāravāa* = *gauravāya*, *mohāa* = *mohāya*, *apuṇāgamaṇāa* = *apuṇargamanāya* (G. 15. 90. 324. 325. 340. 869. 946.1183); M. *vaṇāa* = *vanāya* (Bālar. 156, 14), *tāvaparikkhaṇāa* = *tāpaparikṣaṇāya* (Karp. 52, 3). H. and R. do not have the dative. AMg. *ahiẏāẏa* = *ahitāya* (Āẏār. 1, 3, 1, 1); *gabbhāẏa* = *garbhāya* (Sūẏag. 108), *aïvāẏaẏa* = *atipātāya* (Sūẏag. 356); *tāṇāẏa* = *trāṇāya* (Sūẏag. 377); *kūḍāẏa* = *kūṭāya* (Uttar. 201), all in verses. Generally the dative ends in AMg. JM. in *-āe* (§ 364) and it is so extraordinarily frequent in AMg. AMg. *parivandaṇamāṇaṇapūẏaṇāe jāimaraṇamoẏaṇāḍe* = *parivandanamānanapūjanāya jātimaraṇamocanāya* (Āẏār. 1, 1, 1, 7); beside *tāṇāẏa* in verse, there stands in prose *tāṇāe* (Āẏār. 1, 2, 1, 2. 3. 4), and likewise in the verse (Uttar. 217); *mūlattāe kandattāe kandhattāe taẏattāe sālattāe pavālattāe pattattāe pupphattāe phalattāe biẏattāe viuṭṭanti* = *mūlatvāya kandatvāya skandhatvāya tvaktvāya śālatvāya pravālatvāya pattratvāya puṣpatvāya phalatvāya bijatvāya vivartante* (Sūẏag. 806); *eẏaṁ ṇe pĕccabhave ihabhave ẏa hiẏāe suhāe khamāe nisseẏasāe āṇugāmiẏattāe bhavissaï* = *etan naḥ pretyabhava ihabhave ca hitāya sukhāya kṣamāyai niḥśreyasāyānugāmikatvāya bhaviṣyati* (Ovav. 38, p. 49; Vivāhap. 162) etc.; AMg JM. *vahāe* = *vadhāya* (Āẏār. 1, 3, 2, 2; Vivāhap. 1254; Āv. 14, 16; so to be read); *vahaṭṭhaẏāe* = *vadhārthakāya* (Erz. 1, 21); *hiẏaṭṭhāe* = *hitārthāya* (Āv. 25, 26); *mam' atthāe* = *mamārthāya* (Erz. 63, 12). The dative is correct in Ś. Mg. in verses only, since these dialects otherwise have lost the dative of the *a*-stems also : Mg. *cāludattaviṇāsāa* = *cārudattavināśāya* (Mṛcch. 133, 4). Hc. 4, 302 read with the Devanāgarī, Draviḍian and Kashmirian recensions the dative also in Śak. 115, 7; *śāmipaśādāa* = *svāmiprasādāya*, where the Bengal recension has *śāmippaśādatthaṁ*. In Ś. Mg. all the good texts in prose always have the paraphrasing with *atthaṁ* = *artham* and *ṇimittaṁ* = *nimittam*[1]. The dative stands in Ś. in prose wrongly : *ṇivvudilāhāa* = *nirvṛtilābhāya* (Mālav. 33, 14); *āsisāa* (!) = *āśiṣe* (Mālav. 70, 13); *suhāa* = *sukhāya* (Karp. 9, 5; 35, 6; 115, 1); *asusaṁrakkhaṇāa* = *asusaṁrakṣaṇāya* (Vṛṣabh. 51, 11); *vibudhavijaāa* = *vibudhavijayāya* (Vikr. 6, 20); *tilodaadāṇāa* = *tilodakadānāya* (Mṛcch. 327, 4); *ceḍiāaccaṇāa* [text °*āẏa* = *ceṭikārcanāya* (Mukund. 17, 12). Other examples from bad texts have been collected by BÖHTLINGK[2] and BOLLENSEN[3]. In Rājaśekhara the scribe is not responsible for this (§ 22). Datives of even stems other than *a*- are found. So AMg. *appege accāe haṇanti appege ajiṇāe vahanti appege maṁsāe vahanti appege soṇiẏāe vahanti evaṁ hidaẏāe pittāe vasāe picchāe pucchāe vālāe siṅgāe visāṇāe dantāe dāḍhāe nahāe ṇhāruṇie aṭṭhie aṭṭhimiṁjāe aṭṭhāe aṇaṭṭhāe* (Āẏār. 1, 1, 6, 5; Sūẏag. 676), where *accāe* from *accā* (body; physique; commentary = *śarīram*), *vasāe* = *vasāyai*, *dāḍhāe* = *daṁṣṭrāyai*, *aṭṭhimiṁjāe* = *asthimajjāyai* are dative from the feminine in *-ā*; *ṇhāruṇie* is from a feminine **snāyuni* (§ 255), and *aṭṭhie* is from the neuter *asthi*, used as a feminine (§ 358), the rest are from the masculine and neuter : *se na hassāe na kiḍḍāe na raẏie na vibhūsāe* = *sa na hāsyāya na krīḍāyai na ratyai na vibhūṣāyai* (Āẏār. 1, 2, 1, 3); JM. *kittividdhie* = *kīrtivṛddhaye* (KI. 20). So also wrongly in Ś. *kajjasiddhie* = *kāryasiddhaye* (Mālav. 56, 13; Jīvān. 21, 7); *jadhāsamihidasiddhie* = *yathāsa-*

mihitasiddhaye (Viddhaś. 44, 7). From consonantal stems sometimes in Ś. is found the dative *bhavade* in the "solemn greeting formula"[4] *sŏtthi bhavade* = *svasti bhavate* (Mṛcch. 6, 23; 77, 17; Vikr. 81, 15). But here we have a case of Sanskritization. It is to be written as *bhavado*, as CAPPELLER Ratn. 319, 17 has done; cf. *sŏtthi savvāṇaṁ* (Vikr. 83, 8) and the v.l. to Vikr. 81, 15. The Infinitives in *-ttae*, *-ittae* (§ 578) too are old dative.

1. LASSEN, Inst. p. 299; PISCHEL, BB. 1, 111 ff.; on Hc. 3, 132. Wrongly HOEFER, De Prakrita dialecto p. 126 f.; BOLLENSEN on Vikr. p. 168 and Mālav. p. 233; WEBER, IS. 14, 290 ff.; BB. 1, 343 f. — 2. On Śak. 40, 18, p. 203. — 3. On Mālav. p. 233. — 4. WEBER, BB. 1, 343.

§ 362. In the following paragraphs a paradigma has been provided for the purpose of better lucidity of all the forms, that are found in the grammarians; but the cases, that have hitherto not been found in the texts, have been put inside angular brackets. For P. CP. material is mostly wanting, as our all knowledge exclusively rests upon the grammarians. Cf. further KIELHORN, EI. 3, 313, note 10. PG. VG. are especially built up. Unusual constructions like AMg. °*saṁdhivālasaddhiṁ saṁparivuḍe* (Ovav. § 48, p. 55, 11; Kappas. § 61), which, along with *saddhiṁ*, is found more often in AMg. (Nāyādh. 574. 724. 1068. 1074. 1273. 1290. 1327; Ovav. § 55) do not come into consideration for the purpose of morphology. The forms, which are common to all or most of the dialects have not been specifically indicated, and less important dialects, like Ā. D. Ḍh., are not mentioned in the paradigma.

(1) STEMS IN -a.

(a) MASCULINE AND NEUTER.

§ 363. Mascul. *putta* = *putra*.

Singular.

N. *putto*; AMg. Mg. *putte*; AMg. in verses also *putto*; A. mostly *puttu*.

Acc. *puttaṁ*; A. *puttu*.

I. M. AMg. JM. *putteṇa*, *putteṇaṁ*; JŚ. Ś. Mg. P. CP. *putteṇa*; A. *putteṇa*, *puttiṇa*, *putteṁ*, *puttĕ*.

Dat. M. *puttāa*; AMg. *puttāya* in verses, otherwise AMg. JM. *puttāe*; Mg. *puttāa* in verses.

Abl. M. *puttāo*, *puttāu*, *puttā*, *puttāhi*, *puttāhiṁto*, [*puttatto*]; AMg. JM. *puttāo*, *puttāu*, *puttā*; JŚ. *puttādo*, *puttādu*, *puttā*, Ś. Mg. *puttādo*; P. CP. *puttāto*, *puttātu*; A. *puttahĕ puttahu*.

G. *puttassa*; Mg. *puttaśśa*, *puttāha*; A. *puttassu*, [*puttasu*], *puttahŏ*, °*ho*, *puttaha*.

L. M. JM. JŚ. *puttammi*, *putte*; AMg. *puttaṁsi*, *puttammi*, *puttaṁmi*, *putte*; Ś. P. CP. *putte*; Mg. *putte*, *puttāhiṁ*; A. *putte*, *puttĕ*, *putti*, *puttahĩ*.

V. *putta*; M. also *puttā*; AMg. *putta*, *puttā*, *putto*; Mg. *putta*, *putte*.

Plural

N. *puttā*; AMg. also *puttāo*; A. also *putta*.

Acc. *putte*; M. AMg. A. also *puttā*; A. also *putta*.
I. M. AMg. JM. JŚ. *puttehi*, °*hiṁ*, °*hĩ*; Ś. Mg. *puttehiṁ*; A. *puttahiṁ*, °*hĩ*, °*hi*, *puttehiṁ*, °*hĩ*, °*hi*.
Abl. [*puttāsuṁto*, *puttesuṁto*, *puttāhiṁto*, *puttāhi*, *puttehi*, *puttāo*, *puttāu*, *puttatto*]; AMg. *puttehiṁto*, *puttehiṁ*; JM. *puttehiṁ*; A. *puttahũ*.
G. M. AMg. JM. JŚ. *puttāṇa*, °*ṇaṁ*, °*ṇā̃*; Ś. Mg. *puttāṇaṁ*; Mg. also [*puttāhā̃*]; A. *puttāhā̃*, *puttahā̃*, *puttāṇaṁ*.
L. M. AMg. JM. JŚ. *puttesu*, °*suṁ*, °*sũ*; Ś. Mg. *puttesuṁ*, (*puttesu*); A. *puttahĩ* (*puttehĩ*, *puttihĩ*).
V. *puttā*; Mg. also *puttāho*; A. *puttahŏ*, °*ho*.

The neuter nouns are declined in the same manner, as *phala*, only nom. acc. sing. *phalaṁ*, A. *phalu*;

Nom. acc. voc. plur. M. AMg. JM. *phalāiṁ*, °*ĩ*, °*i*; AMg. JM. also *phalāṇi*, *phalā*; JŚ. *phalāṇi*; Ś. Mg. *phalāiṁ*; A. as M., however, also *phalaĩ*.

In PG. there are found the following forms, to which are added the few sure ones from VG. with the courtesy of EI. 1, p. 2, note 2.

Singular.

N. *mahārājādhirājo* 5, 1; *bhāraddāyo* 5, 2; *patibhāgo* 6, 12; and so still nom. in *-o*; 6, 14. 19-26. 29. 40; 7, 44. 47.
Acc. *parihāraṁ* 5, 7; *vāṭaka*[*ṁ*] *puvvadattaṁ* 6, 12. 28. 30—34. 36. 37 [may be also neuter].
I. *madena* 6, 40; *likhiteṇa* 7, 51.
D. *ajātāye* 7, 45; *vāsasatasahassāya* 7, 48.
Abl. *kāṁcipurā* 5, 1.
G. *kulagŏttassa* 6, 9; *sāsaṇassa* 6, 10; and so also G. in *-sa*, *-ssa*; 6, 12—26. 38. 50; VG. 101, 1. 2. 7 [*devakulassa*]. 8.
L. *visaye* 5, 3; *cillarekakoḍuṁke* 6, 12; and so also : 7, 42. 44.
Neuter : Acc. *nivataṇaṁ* 6, 38; *vāraṇa*[*ṁ*] 7, 41; *uparilikhitaṁ* 7, 44; *āṇataṁ* 7, 49.

Plural.

N. *patibhāgā* 6, 13-18. 20-22 : *addhikā*, *kolikā* 6, 39; *gāmeyikā āyuttā* VG. 101, 10.
Acc. °*desādhikatādike*, *bhojake* 5, 4; *vallave govallave amacce ārakhādhikate gumike tūthike* 5, 5; and so also 5, 6; 6, 9; 7, 43. 46.
I. *evamādikehi* 6, 34; *parihārehi* 6, 35; VG. 101, 11; apparently °*hiṁ* is meant.
G. *pallavāṇaṁ* VG. 101, 2; *pallavāṇa* 5, 2; *maṇusāṇa* 5, 7; *vatthavāṇa* °*bamhaṇāṇaṁ* 6, 8; *bhātukāṇa* 6, 18; *bamhaṇāṇaṁ* 6, 27. 30. 38; *pamukhāṇaṁ* 6, 27. 38 (where °*ṇa*). Perhaps everywhere °*ṇaṁ* is meant.

§ 364. On the declension of *a*-stems see Vr. 5, 1-13; 11, 10. 12. 13. C. 1, 3. 5. 7. 8. 13-16; 2, 10; Hc. 3, 2-15; 4, 263. 287. 299. 300. 321; 330-339. 342. 344-347; Kī. 3, 1-16; 5, 17. 21-25. 28-34. Mk. fol. 41. 42. 68. 69. 75; Sr. fol. 5-9. In A. the bare stem is often used as the nom. acc. gen. sing. and plur., and in others too as *a*-stems (Hc. 4, 344. 345; Kī. 5, 21). Since the final vowel is lengthened and shortened according to metre and rhyme (§ 100), the form of the nom. plur. often appears in the singular and vice-versa. So *phaṇihārā, visā, kandā, candā, kantā* = *phaṇihāraḥ, viṣaḥ, kandaḥ, candraḥ, kāntaḥ* (Piṅgala 1, 81[a]); *sialā* = *śitalaḥ, daḍḍhā* = *dagdhaḥ* in relation with *gharu* = *gṛhaḥ* (Hc. 4, 343); *gaa* = *gajāḥ, gajān, gajānām* (Hc. 4, 335. 418. 3. 345); *supurisa* = *supuruṣāḥ* (Hc. 4, 367). In other dialects too, in verses, the stem is occasionally used in lieu of a case-form. So AMg. *buddhaputta* = *buddhaputra* for *buddhaputto* (Uttar. 13); *pāṇajāi* = *prāṇajātayaḥ* for *pāṇajāio* (Āyār. 1, 8, 1, 2); *pāvaya* = *pāvaka* for *pāvao* (Dasav. 634, 5); Mg. *pañcayyaṇa* = *pañcajanāḥ, gāma* = *grāmaḥ; caṇḍāla* = *caṇḍālaḥ; ṇala* = *naraḥ; śila* = *śiraḥ* (Mṛcch. 112, 6—9). In place of *śila* Mk. fol. 75 reads *śili* and he teaches thence, that in Mg. the nom. ends in *-e* and *-i*. Likewise Vr. 11, 9, who too recognizes the stems as nominative. *śili* stands for *śile* according to § 85; likewise *śakki* for *śakke* = *śakyaḥ* (Mṛcch. 43, 6—9). On the ending *-o, -e* = *-aḥ* see § 345, on *-u* = *-aḥ* § 346, on A. *-u* = *-am* § 351. According to Bhāgīrathīvardhamāna, in Cāṇḍālī, the nom. sing. may end in *-o* too, beside in *-e, -i*: *eśo puliśo* (Mk. fol. 82). — In Nāgarāpabhraṁśa he teaches nom. sing. in *-o* too, beside that in *-u* (Mk. fol. 79). In the instrumental singular, in AMg. several forms in *-sā* are found on account of assonance with the former I. of the *s*-stems. Thus particularly *kāyasā* from *kāya* in the combination *maṇasā vayasā kāyasā* = *manasā vacasā kāyena* (Āyār. p. 132, 1; 133, 5; Sūyag. 358. 428. 456; Vivāhap. 603 ff.; Ṭhāṇ. 118. 119. 187; Uttar. 248; Uvās. § 13-15; Dasav. 625, 30), *kāyasā vayasā* (Uttar. 204); comparatively rare is *maṇasā vayasā kāeṇa* (Sūyag. 257) and *maṇasā kāyavakkeṇaṁ* (Sūyag. 380; Uttar. 222. 752). Further *sahasā balasā* = *sahasā balena* (Āyār. 2, 3, 2, 3; Ṭhāṇ. 368); *paogasā* = *prayogeṇa*, parallel with *visrasā* from *visras* (Vivāhap. 64. 65). According to such cases are formed in verses: *ṇiyamasā* = *niyamena* (Ovav. § 177); *jogasā* = *yogena* (Dasav. 631, 1; Sūriyapannatti in the Verzeichniss 5, 2, 2, 575, 4); *bhayasā* = *bhayena* (Dasav. 629, 37), except that a *s*-stem stands beside it. Cf. § 355. 358. 367. 375. 379. 386. On M. AMg. JM. *putteṇaṁ* see § 182, on A. *puttĕṇa* § 128, *putteṁ* § 146. The dative in *-āe* in PG. AMg. JM. (§ 361) cannot be traced back to Skt. *-āya*, which remains in PG. and becomes *āya* in AMg. and *-āa* in M. (§ 361). AMg. *sāgapāgāe* (Sūyag. 247. 249) phonetically corresponds to one **śākapākāyai*, that is to say to the dative of a feminine. In AMg. this dative is especially frequent from the abstract neuter in *-tta* = *-tva*, as *itthittāe purisattāe ṇapuṁsagattāe* (Sūyag. 817); *devattāe* = *devatvāya* (Āyār. 2, 15, 16; Samav. 8. 10. 16; Uvās.; Ovav.); *rukkhattāe* = *rukṣatvāya* (Sūyag. 792. 803); *goṇattāe* = *gotvāya* (Vivāgas. 51); *haṁsattāe* = *haṁsatvāya* (Vivāgas. 241); *ṇeraïyattāe, dāriyattāe, mayūrattāe* = *nairayikatvāya, dārikātvāya, mayūratvāya* (Vivāgas. 244); *aṭṭhicammacchirattāe* = *asthicarmaśirātvāya* (Aṇutt. 12) etc.; cf. § 361. Beside these stand the datives of abstract feminine in *-tā*, like *paḍibūhaṇayāe* = *pratibṛṁhaṇatāyai, posaṇayāe* = *poṣaṇatāyai* (Sūyag. 676); *karaṇayāe* = *karaṇatāyai* (Vivāhap. 817. 1254; Uvās. § 113); *savaṇayāe* = *śravaṇatāyai* (Nāyādh. § 77. 137. Ovav. § 18. 38). *puṇapāsaṇayāe* = **punaḥpaśyantāyai* (Vivāhap. 1228; Nāyādh. § 137) etc. That the datives from femin. nouns, otherwise, frequently stand between the datives of the masc. and neut. nouns is shown by § 361. An influence therefore, through the feminine may be possible, and the AMg. *devattāe* may have its *tt* of the neuter *devatva* and the ending of the feminine *devatā* wrongly used with it. But the datives in *-āe*, even otherwise, from mascul. and neut. are so numerous that this explanation is impossible. It must be admitted that dialectically *-āi* too could be used as the ending of the mascul. and neut. *vahāi* = *vadhāya* (Hc. 3, 132) should either be traced back to AMg. JM. *vahāe* (§ 361) according to § 85 in case the verb would be found in verses, or it is to be derived from the Avestā *yasnāi*, Greek ἵππωι = ἵππῳ-.

§ 365. Hc. 3, 8 and Mk. fol. 41 show that for the abl. sing. in M. the forms in *-ādo*, *-ādu*, like *vacchādo*, *vacchādu*, as Kī. 3, 8, too has, are not to be deduced with Bhāmaha from Vr. 5, 6. The author of R. who at R. 8, 87 writes *rāmādo*, openly follows Bhāmaha, as in *udu* = *ṛtu* (§ 204). The usual form of the abl. sing. in M. AMg. JM. is in *-āo* = **ātaḥ* (§ 69. 345). Beside it is found metri causa *-āu* too: M. *sisāu* = *śirṣāt* (G. 37); *ṇahaalāu* = *nabhastalāt* (H. 75); *raṇṇāu* = *araṇyāt* (H. 287); AMg. *pāvāu* = *pāpāt* (Sūyag. 415) beside *pāvāo* (Sūyag. 110. 117); *dukkhāu* = *duḥkhāt* (Uttar. 218). The abl. in *-du*, taught by Hc. 4, 276 for Ś. belongs to JŚ. (§ 21), where *udayādu* = *udayāt* (Pav. 383, 27), beside *aṇaüdayādo* (Kattig. 399, 309) and forms like *carittādo* = *caritrāt* (Pav. 380, 6), *ṇāṇādo* = *jñānāt* (Pav. 382, 5), *visayādo* = *viṣayāt* (Pav. 382, 6), *vasādo* = *vaśāt* (Kattig. 399, 311) are found. In Ś. Mg. the abl. always ends in *-do* (Kī. 5, 79; Mk. fol. 68; § 69. 345). On forms with short *a*, like AMg. *ṭhāṇao* see § 99. Not seldom in M. AMg. JM. is also the abl. in *-ā* = Skt. *-āt*. So M. : *vasā* = *vaśāt*, *bhaā* = *bhayāt*, *guṇā* = *guṇāt*, *veā* = *vegāt*, *bhavaṇā* = *bhavanāt*, *dehattaṇā* = **dehatvanāt*, *bhāruvahaṇāarā* = *bhārodvahanādarāt* (G. 24. 42. 84. 125. 242. 390. 716. 848. 854. 924); *gharā* = *gṛhāt*, *balā* = *balāt* (H. 497. 498); *aïrā* = *acirāt* (R. 3, 15); *ṇacirā* (Bālar. 179, 2); *misā* = *miṣāt*, *ṇivesā* = *niveśāt* (Karp. 12, 8; 75, 2); AMg. *maraṇā* (Āyār. 1, 3, 1, 3, 2, 1); *dukkhā* (Āyār. 1, 3, 1 2; Uttar. 220); *kohā*, *māṇā*, *lobhā* = *krodhāt*, *manāt*, *lobhāt* (Āyār. 2, 4, 1, 1); *balā* (Sūyag. 287, 293; Uttar. 593); *ārambhā* (Sūyag. 104); *nāyaputtā* (Sūyag. 318); *bhayā* = *bhayāt*, *lābhā*, *mohā*, *pamāyā* = *pramādāt* (Uttar. 207. 251. 434. 627); *kohā*, *hāsā*, *lobhā*, *bhayā* (Uttar. 751; cf. Dasav. 615, 28), mostly in verses; JM. *niyamā* (Kk. 259, 6, 18); AMg. JM. *aṭṭhā* (Dasav. 620, 20; Erz.); JŚ. *ṇiyamā* (Kattig. 400, 328; 401, 341). I have located only *balā* in Ś. (Mṛcch. 68, 22), only *kālaṇā* in Mg. (Mṛcch. 152, 7; cf. 145, 17) in the critical texts. The MSS, however, have *kālaṇāe* for *kālaṇā*; the ed. Cal. Śak. 1792 p. 324, 11 and GOḌABOLE, 413, 1 correctly have *kālaṇado*, as STENZLER too elsewhere reads (133, 1; 140, 14; 158, 21; 165, 7). Mk. fol. 69 permits *-ā* too in Ś., in addition, and quotes *kāraṇā* as an example. Frequent in M. is the abl. sing. in *-hi*: *mūlāhi*. *kusumāhi*, *gaaṇāhi*, *varāhi*, *biāhi* = *bijāt* (G. 13. 69. 193. 426. 722; cf. further 1094. 1131. 1164); *dūrāhi*, *hiaāhi* = *hṛdayāt*, *aṅgaṇāhi*, *ṇikkammāhi vi chĕttāhi* = *niṣkarmaṇo 'pi kṣetrāt* (H. 50, 95. 120. 169; cf. further 179. 429. 594. 665. 877. 934. 998); *ravāhi*, *dhirāhi* = *dhairyāt*, *dantujjoāhi* = *dantoddyotāt*, *paccakkhāhi* = *pratyakṣāt*, *ghaḍiāhi* = *ghaṭitāt*, *aṇuhūāhi* = *anubhūtāt* (R. 3, 2: 4, 27; cf. also 4, 45. 56; 6, 14. 77; 7, 57; 8, 18; 11, 88; 12, 8. 11; 14,

20. 29; 15, 50); *hiaāhi* (Karp. 79, 12; v. l. *hiaāu*); *daṇḍāhi* = *daṇḍāt* (Bālar. 178, 20; text against the metre °*hiṁ*). In AMg. is found *piṭṭhāhi* = *pṛṣṭhāt* (Nāyādh. 958f), beside *piṭṭhāo* (938. 964). Seldom is the abl. in -*hiṁto*: *kandalāhiṁto* = *kandalāt* (G. 5); *chĕppāhiṁto* = *śepāt*; *hiaāhiṁto* = *hṛdayāt*, *raïharāhiṁto* = *ratigṛhāt* (H. 240. 451. 553); *mūlāhiṁto* = *mūlāt* (Karp. 38, 3); *rūāhiṁto* = *rūpāt* (Mudrār. 37, 4). Rājaśekhara employs the abl. in -*hi* and -*hiṁto* wrongly in Ś. too : *candaseharāhi* = *candraśekharāt* (Bālar. 289, 1; text °*hiṁ*); *pāmarāhiṁto* = *pāmarāt*, *candāhiṁto* = *candrāt*, *jalāhiṁto* = *jalāt*, *tumhārisāhiṁto* = *yuṣmādṛśāt* (Karp. 20, 6; 53, 6; 72, 2; 93, 9) ; *pādāhiṁto* = *pādāt*, *gamāgāmāhiṁto* = *gamāgamāt*, *thaṇaharāhiṁto* = *stanabharāt* (Viddhaś. 79, 2; 82, 4; 117, 4). On the corresponding forms of pronouns see § 415ff. The ending -*hi* is present in adverbs in M. AMg. JM. in *alāhi* = *alam*[1] (Vr. 9, 11; Hc. 2, 189; Kī. 4, 83 [text *aṇāhi*]; H. 127; Vivāhap. 813. 965. 1229. 1254; T. 5, 6 [text °*hiṁ*]), °*hiṁto* in AMg. *antohiṁto* = *antarāt* (§ 342) and *bāhiṁhiṁto* = *bāhiṣṭāt* (Ṭhāṇ. 408). *uttarāhi* and *dakṣiṇāhi* (WHITNEY §1100 c), the forms in -*hi* serve, as noted by E. MÜLLER[2], as adverbs. Hence one may in -*hi*, neither with LASSEN[3], search for an old ending -*bhi*, nor with WEBER[4], a plural ending, above all -*hiṁ* is never found beside it. The ending -*hiṁto* is, with LASSEN[6], to be considered as having originated from -*bhis*, or more correctly from -*bhyas*, the ending of the abl. plur. + *tas*, the ending of the abl. sing.; and therefore, -*hiṁto*, (Sr. fol. 7) not *hinto* is to be written. The *a* of the stem has its lengthening according to § 69. The abl. *vacchatto* (Hc. 3, 8; Sr. fol. 7), *rukkhatto* corresponding to the form [*puttatto*] are double formations = *vṛkṣāt* + *tas*, *rukṣāt* + *tas*. — For A. the forms found in the text are *vacchahĕ*, *vacchahu* = *vṛkṣāt* (Hc. 4, 336); *jalahu* = *jalāt* (Hc. 4, 415). Kī. 5, 30 has beside *rucchahĕ* also *rucchādu* [text °*dū*] = *vṛkṣkāt*. With LASSEN[7] it is to be read as *vacchahĕ*, *vacchādu*. The origin of the forms in -*hĕ*, -*hu* is obscure.

1. So rightly WEBER H¹. p. 40, note 1. — 2. Beiträge p. 22. — 3. Inst. p. 303. — 4. H¹. p. 49. — 5. In Bālar. 178, 20 °*hiṁ*, as mentioned, is against the metre, 289, 1 too a wrong reading. — 6. Inst. p. 310. — 7. Inst. p. 451.

§ 366. Corresponding to the rules of the grammarians (Vr. 11, 12; Hc. 4, 299) we find in Mg. in the gen. sing. the ending, beside -*śśa* = -*sya*, also -*ha* from -*sa* with lengthening of *a* of the stem (§ 63. 264). In the examples with -*āha* quoted by Hc. from Śak. and Veṇīs, the printed editions and manuscripts have -*aśśa* or variant readings[1]. The genitive forms in -*āha* are : *kāmāha* = *kāmasya* (Mṛcch. 10, 24); *cāludattāha* = *cārudattasya* (Mṛcch. 13, 25; 100, 20; 154, 10; 164, 2. 4), beside *cāludattaśśa* (Mṛcch. 79, 15; 100, 22); *ṇiyyādamāṇāha*, *aṇiyyādamāṇāha* = *niryātayamānasya*, *a*°; *ĕkkāha* = *ekasya*; *avalāha* = *aparasya*; *ayyamitteāha* = *āryamaitreyasya*; *śālakāha* = *śyālakasya*, *śalilāha* = *śarirasya*; *cālittāha* = *cāritrasya* etc. (Mṛcch. 21, 13. 14; 24, 3; 32, 4. 5; 45, 1; 112. 10; 124, 21). To it corresponds the genitive in -*ha* in A., as *kaṇaaha* = *kanakasya*; *caṇḍālaha* = *caṇḍālasya*; *kavvaha* = *kāvyasya*; *phaṇindaha* = *phaṇindrasya*; *kaṇṭhaha* = *kaṇṭhasya*; *paaha* = *padasya* (Piṅgala, 1, 62. 70. 88ᵇ. 104. 109. 117). The common form of the genitive singular in A. is that in -*ho*, mostly in -*hŏ* (Hc. 4, 338; Kī. 5, 31); *dullahahŏ* = *durlabha*-

sya; *sāmiahŏ* = *svāmikasya*, *kṛdantahŏ* = *kṛtāntasya*; *kantahŏ* = *kāntasya*; *sāarahŏ* = *sāgarasya*; *tahŏ virahahŏ ṇāsantaahŏ* = *tasya virahasya naśyataḥ* (Hc. 4, 338. 340. 370. 379. 395, 7. 419, 6. 432). One *kantahŏ* phonetically corresponds to one **kāntasyaḥ*, that is to say a mixture of *a*- and consonantal declensions like the nom. plur. in *āo* (§ 367). Beside the genitive in *-ssu* from *-ssa* = = *-sya* (§ 106), as *parassu* = *parasya*; *suaṇassu* = *sujanasya*; *khandhassu* = *skandhasya*; *tattassu* = *tattvasya*; *kantassu* = *kāntasya* (Hc. 4, 338. 440. 445, 3), according to Hc. 4, 338; Kī. 5, 31 even the genitive in *-su* is used, as *rukkhasu* (Kī. 3, 31; in LASSEN, Inst. p. 451 *vacchasu*) in A. I may perhaps accidentally, attest the form only in the pronouns (§ 425. 427).

1. PISCHEL on Hc. 4,299.

§ 366[a]. In the locative singular the forms in *-e* and those in *-mmi* = *-smin* (§ 313. 350), quoted above from pronominal declensions (§ 313. 350), often stand directly beside one another. So M. *mukke vi ṇaramaïndattaṇammi* = *mukte'pi naramṛgendratve* (G. 10); *diṭṭhe sarisammi guṇe* = *dṛṣṭe sadṛśe guṇe* (H. 44); *ṇaïpūrasaricchahe jŏvvaṇammi* = *nadipūrasadṛśe yauvane* (H. 45); *suṇahapaŭrammi gāme* = *śunakapracure grāme* (H. 138); *devāattammi phale* = *daivāyatte phale* (H. 279); *hantavvammi dahamuhe* = *hantavye daśamukhe* (R. 3, 3); *apūramāṇammi bhare* = *apūryamāṇe bhare* (R. 6, 67); *gaammi paose* = *gate pradoṣe* (R. 11, 1); *ṇihaammi pahatthe* = *nihate prahaste* (R. 15, 1); JM. *pāḍaliputtammi puravare* (Āv. 8, 1) and *pāḍaliputte nagarammi* (Āv. 12, 40); *dullahalambhammi māṇuse jamme* = *durlabhalambhe mānuṣe janmani* (Āv. 12, 13); *kae'kae vā vi kajjammi* = *kṛte'kṛte vāpi kārye* (Āv. 12, 18); *cĕttammi ṇakkhatte vihuhatthe* = *caitre nakṣatre vidhuhaste* (KI. 19); JŚ. *tivihe pattammi* = *trividhe prāpte* (Kattig. 402, 360; text °*mhi*; *accudammi sagge* = *acyute svarge* (Kattig. 404, 391; text °*mhi*). All the examples occur in verses. In prose in JM. the locative in *-e* is mostly used, as *girinagare nagare* (Āv. 9, 12); *matthae* = *mastake* (Āv. 11, 1); *puratthime disibhāe ārāmamajjhe* = **purastime digbhāga ārāmamadhye* (Āv. 13, 24); more seldom that in *-mmi*, *-ṁmi* as *raïgharammi* = *ratigṛhe* (Āv. 11, 13); *komuimahūsavaṁmi* = *kaumudimahotsave* (Erz. 2, 7); *majjhaṁmi* (Erz. 9, 1); forms of both the types sometimes stand in prose beside one another, as *vijjānimmiẏaṁmi siẏarattapaḍāẏāhūsie pāsāe* = *vidẏānirmite śitaraktapatākābhūṣite prāsāde* (Erz. 8, 24). In verses both the forms are usable according to the metre, as *bharahammi* = *bharate*, *tihuẏaṇammi* = *tribhuvane*, *sisammi* = *śirṣe* (Āv. 7,22; 8, 17; 12, 24), and *guṇasilujjāṇe* = *guṇaśilodyāne*, *avasāṇe*, *sihare* = *śikhare* (Āv. 7, 24. 26. 36). In JŚ. too both the locatives are current. In Kattig. several times the MS writes *-mhi* instead of *-mmi*: *kālamhi* (399, 321) against *kālammi* (400, 322); *pattamhi* (402, 360); *accudamhi* (404, 391); also in pronouns : *tamhi* = *tasmin* (400, 322) beside *tammi* in the same line and *jammi* (399, 322). This may simply be an error of handwriting. Pav. has only *-mmi* : *dāṇammi* (383, 69); *suhammi*, *asuhammi* (385, 61); *kāẏacĕṭṭhammi* (386, 10; 387, 18); *jiṇamadammi* (386, 11), etc. The same error occurs in Kattig. in *savvaṇhū* for the correct *savvaṇṇū* (Pav. 381, 161) = *sarvajñaḥ* (398. 302. 303). Cf. § 436. — In AMg. the most usual form is that in *-ṁsi* = *-smin* (§ 74. 313); *logaṁsi* = *loke* (Āẏār. 1, 1, 1, 5. 7; 1, 3, 1, 1, 2, 1; 1, 4, 2, 3; 1, 5, 4, 4; 1, 6, 2, 3; 1, 7, 3, 1; Sūẏag. 213.

380. 381. 463. 465 etc.); *susāṇaṁsi vā sunnāgāraṁsi vā giriguhaṁsi vā rukkhamūlaṁsi vā kumbhārāyaṇaṁsi vā* = *śmaśāne vā śūnyāgāre vā giriguhāyāṁ vā rukṣamūle vā kumbhakārāyatane vā* (Āyār. 1, 7, 2, 1); *imaṁsi dāragaṁsi jāyaṁsi samāṇaṁsi* = *asmin dārake jāte sati* (Ṭhāṇ. 525; Vivāhap. 1275; cf. Vivāgas. 116). Forms in *-mmi*, *-ṁmi* are not rare; in verses: *samayaṁmi* (Āyār. 1, 8, 1, 9; 2, 16, 9); *bambhammi ya kappammi ya* = *brāhme ca kalpe ca* (Āyār. p. 125, 34); *dāhiṇaṁmi pāsammi* [sic] = *dakṣiṇe pārśve* (Āyār. p. 128, 20); *logaṁmi* = *loke* (Sūyag. 136. 410); *saṁgāmaṁmi* = *saṁgrāme* (Sūyag. 161); *āuyāṁmi* = *āyūṁṣi* (Uttar. 196); *maraṇantammi* = *maraṇānte* (Uttar. 207); *jalaṇammi* = *jvalane* (Nāyādh. 1394). Later such forms stand even in prose, beside the loc. in *-e*, hardly rightly, as *dāruṇammi gimhe* (Nāyādh. 340); *uṭṭhiyaṁmi sūre sahassarassiṁmi diṇayare teyasā jalante* = *utthite sūrye sahasraraśmau dinakare tejasā jvalati* (Vivāhap. 169; Aṇuog. 60; Nāyādh. § 34; Kappas. § 59), and beside the loc. in *-ṁsi*, as *gimhakālasamayaṁsi jĕṭṭhāmūlamāsammi* = *grīṣmakālasamaye jyeṣṭhāmūlamāse* (Ovav. § 82). The loc. in *-e* in early prose, in comparison with that in *-ṁsi*, is a little more numerous: *harae* = = *hrade* (Āyār. 1, 6, 1, 2); *viyāle* = *vikāle* (Āyār. 2, 1, 3, 2); *lābhe santelābhe sati* (Āyār. 2, 1, 1, 1ff); *paḍipahe* = *pratipathe*, *parakkame* = *parākrame* (Āyār. 2, 1, 5, 3), *sapaḍiduvāre* = *svapratidvāre* (Āyār. 2, 1, 5, 5), more frequently in verses, as *loe* = *loke* (Āyār. 1, 8, 4, 14; 2, 16, 9; Uttar. 22. 109); *laddhe piṇḍe* = *labdhe piṇḍe* (Āyār. 1, 8, 4, 13); *ārāmāgāre, nagare, susāṇe, rukkhamūle* (Āyār. 1, 8, 2, 3); *maraṇante* (Uttar. 213); *dharaṇitale* (Sūyag. 296), also beside the loc. in *-ṁsi* and *-mmi*, as *sisiraṁsi addhapaḍivanne* = *śiśire ardhapratipanne* (Āyār. 1, 8, 1, 21); *saṁsāraṁmi aṇantage* (Uttar. 215. 222); *pattammi āese* = *prāpta ādeśe* (Uttar. 227). In later day prose there stand also beside the loc. in *-ṁsi*, as *taṁsi tārisagaṁsi vāsagharaṁsi abbhintarao sacittakamme bāhirao dūmiyaghaṭṭhamaṭṭhe* is followed still by seven loc. in *-e* — *taṁsi tārisagaṁsi sayaṇijjaṁsi sāliṅgaṇavaṭṭie* is followed by eight loc. in *-e* — *puvvarattāvarattakālasamayaṁsi* (Kappas. § 32). Dialectically the loc. in *-hiṁ* from *-ssiṁ* are also found (§ 65. 264); Mg. *evaṁvaḍḍakāhiṁ gallakkappamāṇāhiṁ kulāhiṁ*[1] = *evaṁvaḍrake galvarkapramāṇe kule* (Mṛcch. 126, 9); Mg. *pavahaṇāhiṁ*[2] = *pravahaṇe* (Mṛcch. 119, 23), are also found. In addition, the loc. is put also in *-hĩ* in A. *desahĩ* = *deśe*; *gharahĩ* = *gṛhe* (Hc. 4, 386, 422, 15); *hradahĩ* = *hrade*; *paḍhamahĩ* = *prathame*, beside *tie pāe* = *tṛtīye pāde*; *samapāahĩ* = *samapāde*; *sisahĩ* = *śirṣe*; *antahĩ* = *ante*; *cittahĩ* = *citte*; *vaṁsahĩ* = *vaṁśe* (Piṅgala 1, 4[b]. 70. 71. 81[a]. 120. 155[a]; 2, 102). The loc. in prose ends in *-e* in Ś. and mostly in Mg. too; as for Ś. Mk. fol. 69 expressly remarks : Ś. *gehe*, *āvaṇe* = *āpaṇe* (Mṛcch. 3, 9. 14. 15), *muhe* = *mukhe* (Śak. 35, 10), Mg. *haste*; *vihave vihaḍide* = *vibhave vighaṭite* (Mṛcch. 21, 12; 32, 21); *śamale* = *samare* (Veṇis. 33, 8). In verses in Mg. the loc. in *-mmi* too is found, sometimes beside that in *-e*; *caṇḍālaülammi* = *caṇḍālakule*; *kūvammi* = *kūpe* (Mṛcch. 161, 14; 162, 7); *śomammi gahammi* = *saumye grahe*; *śevide apaścammi* = *sevite 'pathye* (Mudrār. 177, 5; 257, 2; cf. ZDMG. 39, 125. 128). Rājaśekhara errs here too against the dialect, since he uses the loc. in *-mmi* in prose also : *majjhammi* (Karp. 6, 1), beside *majjhe* (Karp. 12, 10; 22, 9); *kavvammi* = *kāvye* (Karp. 16, 8); *rāmammi* = *rāme*; *sedusimantammi* =

setusimante (Bālar. 96, 3; 194, 14). In Indian editions the loc. in *-mmi* is often found in Ś., which perhaps is not a fault of the MSS, but of the authors, who did not know to write Ś. correctly, Cf. e. g. Pras. 35, 3; 39, 2; 44, 8. 9; 45, 5; 47, 6; 113, 8. 12; 119. 14. 15; Karṇas. 25, 3; 37, 6; Kaṁsav. 50, 2. 14; Mallikām. 87, 4; 88, 23. Naturally the writings, such as *cāṇakkammi akaruṇe* (Mudrār. 53, 8); *hiaaṇivvisesammi jaṇe* = *hṛdayanirviśeṣe jane* (Viddhaś. 42, 3), *gacchatammi deve* (Cait. 134, 10) too are wholly wrong. In A. the loc. usually ends in *-i* from *-e*: *tali* = *tale*, *patthari* = *prastare*; *andhāri* = *andhakāre*; *kari* = *kare*; *mūli viṇaṭṭhaī* = *mūle vinaṣṭe*; *bāri* = *dvāre* (Hc. 4, 334. 344. 349. 354. 427. 436); sometimes it ends in *-ĕ* too: *appiĕ diṭṭhaī*, *piĕ diṭṭhaī* = *apriye* **dṛṣṭake*, *priye* **dṛṣṭake*; *pie diṭṭhĕ* = *priye dṛṣṭe*; *sughĕ* = *sukhe* (Hc. 4, 365, 1. 396, 2).

1. So it is to be read; cf. Mṛcch. 139, 23, the v. l. in GODABOLE 348, 2 and in LASSEN, Inst. p. 430. — 2. So to be read with the ed. Calc. 1829 p. 227, 6 and ed. GODABOLE p. 331, 8 according to the v. l.

§ 366b. In the voc. sing. of the *a*-stem pluti is found frequently (§ 71). According to Hc. 3, 38; Sr. fol. 5 the vocative of the masculine may end in *-e* too, beside in *-a*, *-ā*: *ajjo* = *ārya*; *devo* = *deva*; *khamāsamaṇo* = *kṣamāśramaṇa* (Hc.); *rukkho* = *rukṣa*; *vaccho* = *vṛkṣa* (Sr.). Such vocatives are found in AMg., and there they are used not only for the vocative singular, but also for the vocative plural of the masculine, so that probably they may not be considered as the nom. sing. of the masc. used as the vocative, especially when in AMg. in prose they always end in *-e*. The examples are : AMg. *ajjo* = *ārya* (Sūyag. 1016; Uttar. 415; Vivāhap. 132. 134; Kappas. Th. § 1. S. § 18. 52); as plur. = *āryāḥ* (Ṭhāṇ. 146. 147; Vivāhap. 132. 188 f. 193. 332; Uvās. § 119. 174); *tāo* = *tāta* (Nāyādh. § 83. 85. 98); *devo* = *deva* (Nāyādh. § 38); *puriso* = *puruṣa* (Sūyag. 108); *ammayāo* = *ambātātau*, therefore, plur. (Antag. 61. 62; Vivāhap. 804. 805. 808 ff. [more often *ammatāo*]; Nāyādh. § 134. 138. 145; p. 260. 862. 887 etc.). Likewise one says in the feminine AMg. JM. *ammo* = *amba* (Hc. 3, 41; Uvās. § 140; Āv. 13, 33; 14, 27); also used as the plur. of parents (Nāyādh. § 138; Uttar. 574). The example given by Hc., *ammo bhaṇāmi bhaṇie* is H. 676, where WEBER and the Bombay edition read *bhaṇie bhaṇāmi attā*; T. reads *attā bhaṇāmi bhaṇie*; in Bhuvanapāla the stanza is wanting. Thus Hc. found *ammo* in M. too Perhaps in *o*, is stuck to the particle *u*, that is employed, according to the lexicographers, in addressing (*āmantraṇe*) and in calling from off (*saṁbodhane*). Against this, in AMg. *bhante* = *bhadanta*[1] (§ 165); Mg. *bhāve* = *bhāva* (Mṛcch. 10, 22; 11, 24; 12, 3; 13, 6. 24; 14, 10 etc.); *ceḍe* = *ceṭa* (Mṛcch. 21, 25) beside *ceḍā* (Mṛcch. 118, 1; 119, 11. 21; 121, 9; 122, 9 etc.); *uvāśake* = *upāsaka* (Mṛcch. 114, 7) *bhaṭṭake* = *bhaṭṭaka* (Śak. 114, 5; 116, 11); *lāutte* = *rājaputra* (Śak. 117, 5); *puttake* = *putraka* (Śak. 167, 7)[2], the nomin. must be considered to have been used vocatively. Whether even in A. *bhamaru* = *bhramara* (Hc. 4, 368); *mahiharu* = *mahidhara* (Vikr. 66, 16) are to be taken as in the nomin. is doubtful, since in A. the final *a*, also elsewhere, becomes *u* (§ 106). The form in *-e* is used in Mg. as acc. sing. in *mama śile śadakhaṇḍe kaleśi* = *mama śiraḥ śata-*

khaṇḍaṁ karoṣi (Mṛcch. 151, 25). Other examples quoted by LASSEN[3] have disappeared from the new edition. Cf. § 367b. In Veṇīs. at 33, 12 according to the ed. Calc., we should read *labbhadi* instead of *lambhaï* in GRILL, so that *maṁśae*, *uṇhe* (read *usṇe*), *luhile* are nom. according to § 357.

1. This is the correct explanation. Cf. WEBER, Bhag. 2, 155, note 3; PISCHEL on Hc. 4, 257. Wrongly E. MÜLLER, Beiträge p. 50, where further literature. — 2. Misunderstood by S. GOLDSCHMIDT Prākṛtica p. 28. See PISCHEL, GGA, 1880, p. 326. — 3. Inst. p. 429.

§ 367. The masculine nom. plur. ends in all the dialects in *-ā*=*āḥ*: M. AMg. JM. Ś. *devā*=*devāḥ* (H. 355; Ovav. § 33; Erz. 4, 31; Mṛcch. 3, 13); JŚ. *aṭṭhā*=*arthāḥ* (Pav. 382, 26); Mg. *puliśā*=*puruṣāḥ* (Lalitav. 565, 13); CP. *samuddā*, *saïlā*=*samudrāḥ*, *śailāḥ* (Hc. 4, 326); D. *dakkhiṇattā* =*dākṣiṇātyāḥ* (Mṛcch. 103, 5); Ā. *visaddhā*=*visrabdhāḥ* (Mṛcch. 99, 16); A. *ghoḍā*=*ghoṭāḥ* (Hc. 4, 330, 4). In AMg. in verses the masc. nom. plur. is found in *-āo* too; *māṇavāo*=*mānavāḥ* (Āyār. 1, 3, 3, 3; Sūyag. 412); *tahāgayāo*=*tathāgatāḥ* (Āyār. 1, 3, 3, 3); *hayāo*=*hatāḥ* (Sūyag. 295); *samatthāo* =*samarthāḥ*; *omarattāo*=*avamarātrāḥ*; *sisāo*=*śiṣyāḥ*; *āujivāo*=*abjivāḥ* (Uttar. 755. 768. 794. 1045); *virattāu* [so the commentary; text °*āo*]=*viraktāḥ* ; *sāgarāu*=*sāgarāḥ* (Uttar. 758. 1000). Other cases further Uttar. 698. 895. 1048. 1049. 1053. 1059. 1061. 1062. 1064. 1066. 1071. 1084. So also in M. or JM. *vaṇṇāo* beside *vaṇṇā*=*varṇāḥ* in a grammatical citation in Lakṣmīnāthabhaṭṭa on Piṅgala. 1, 2 (p. 3, 5). Indian editions have these plural forms wrongly in Ś. too, e.g. Dhanaṁjayav. 11, 7 ff.; 14, 9 f.; Cait. 43, 18 ff. Tracing of the plur. in *-āo*, which is the usual in the case of the feminine in *ā* (§ 376), back to Vedic. *-āsas*, hence the derivation of Pkt. *jaṇāo* from Vedic *janāsas* is linguistically impossible. V. Mg. *bhasṭālakāho*, A. *loahŏ* are the direct continuation (§ 372). Pkt. shows that *-āsas* is to be explained from *ās*+*as*, that is to say, the ending *-as* of the consonant stem has supplemented the plur. of the *a*-stem. Pkt. *māṇavāo* is, therefore, a double formation,[1] like the abl. sing. *vacchatto* (§ 365). In A. the ending *-ā* appears often shortened (§ 364) : *gaa*=*gajāḥ*; *supurisa*=*supuruṣāḥ*; *bahua*=*bahukāḥ*; *kāara*=*kātarāḥ*; *meha*=*meghāḥ* (Hc. 4, 335. 367. 376. 395, 5; 419, 6). — In the nom. acc. plur. of the neuter the most usual form is in *-iṁ*, before which *a* is lengthened; beside it, in verses *-ī* and *-i* are used (§ 180. 182). On the forms *dhaṇāṁiṁ*, *vaṇāṁiṁ* taught by Kī. 3, 28 see § 182. Vr. 5, 26 teaches for M. *-i* only, C. 1, 3 only *-ṇi*; Hc. 3, 26 and Sr. fol. 17 teach *-ī*, *-iṁ*, *-ṇi*, Kī. 3, 28, Mk. fol. 43 *-iṁ* only. M. has *-iṁ*, *-ī*, *-i* : *ṇaaṇāiṁ*=*nayanāni* (H. 5); *aṅgāī vi piāiṁ* (H. 40); *raaṇāi va garuaguṇasaāi* =*ratnāniva gurukaguṇaśatāni* (R. 2, 14). In AMg., already in the oldest texts, *-ṇi* too, beside *-iṁ*, is quite usual; *pāṇāiṁ bhūyāiṁ jivāiṁ sattāiṁ*=*prāṇān bhūtāni jivāni sattvāni* (Āyār. 1, 6, 5, 4; 1, 7, 2, 1; 2, 1, 1, 11), beside *pāṇāṇi vā bhūyāṇi vā jivāṇi vā sattāṇi vā* (Āyār. p. 132, 28); *udagapasūyāṇi kandāṇi vā mūlāṇi vā pattāṇi vā pupphāṇi vā phalāṇi vā biyāṇi vā hariyāṇi vā* (Āyār. 2, 2, 1, 5). Often both the forms stand beside one another: *sĕ jjāiṁ puṇa kulāiṁ jāṇĕjjā taṁ jahā uggakulāṇi vā bhogakulāṇi vā rāinnakulāṇi vā* ... still follow nine compounds with *kulāṇi* (Āyār 2, 1, 2, 2); *agārāiṁ ceyiāiṁ taṁ* *jahā āesaṇāṇi vā āyoyaṇāṇi vā devakulāṇi vā*—yet follow eleven forms in *āṇi*—*tahappagārāiṁ āesaṇāṇi vā. . . bhavaṇagihāṇi vā* (Āyār. 2, 2, 2, 8); *aṇṇāṇi ya bahūṇi gabbhādāṇajammaṇa-m-āiyāiṁ kouyāiṁ* (Ovav. [§ 105]); *khettāiṁ* in the same verse with *khĕttāṇi*=*kṣetrāṇi* (Uttar. 356). The form in *-ṇi*, as in JM.[2], especially before enclitics is selected. In verses the metre decides in AMg. too the choice between *-iṁ, -ĩ, -i.* So in Uttar. 357 we should read *tāiṁ tu kkĕttāĩ supāvayāiṁ*=*tāni tu kṣetrāṇi supāpakāni*; Dasav. 619, 17 stands *pupphāi biyāiṁ vippaïṇṇāi*; in 621, 1 we should read *sattucuṇṇāiṁ kolacuṇṇāĩ āvaṇe.* In JM. the position is the same, as in AMg. : *pañca egūṇāiṁ addāgasāyāiṁ. . . pakkhittāiṁ*=*pañcaikonāny *ādarpakaśatāni. . . prakṣiptāni*; *nicchiddāiṁ dārāiṁ*=*niśchidrāṇi dvārāṇi* (Āv. 17, 15. 19); *tāṇi vi pañca corasayāṇi. . . saṁbohiyāṇi pavvaïyāṇi*=*tāny api pañca coraśatāni. . . saṁbodhitāni pravrajitāni* (Āv. 19, 2); *bahūṇi vāsāṇi* (Erz. 34, 3), beside *bahūiṁ vāsāiṁ*=*bahūni varṣāṇi* (Erz. 34, 17). Writings like *vatthābharaṇāṇi rāyasantiyāiṁ* (Erz. 52, 8) in prose are probably not correct, even when both the forms often stand closely beside one another, as in *pŏṭṭāiṁ āṇehi tie rattagāṇi āṇiyāṇi* (Erz. 31, 8). In Ś., according to Vr. 12, 11; Kī. 5, 78; Mk. fol. 69, *-ṇi* too may be used beside *-iṁ.* So stands *suhāṇi*=*sukhāni* (Śak., 99, 4) and *apaccaṇivvisesāṇi sattāṇi* (Śak. 154, 7) in most of the MSS; for *vaaṇāṇi*=*vacanāni* (Vikr. 87, 22) the best MSS have *vaaṇāiṁ*, and so all the critical texts give in Ś. Mg., elsewhere, *-iṁ*[3] only. Dialectically nom. acc. plur. in *-ā* are often found beside those in *-iṁ* or in *-ṇi*: AMg. *udagapasūyāṇi kandāṇi vā mūlāṇi vā tayā pattā pupphā phalā biyā* (Āyār. 2, 3, 3, 9); *bahusaṁbhūyā vaṇaphalā* (Āyār. 2, 4, 2, 13. 14); *pāṇā ya taṇā ya biyā ya paṇagā ya hariyāṇi ya* (Kappas. S. § 55). The form of the following words might have influenced *tayā*= **tvacāḥ*=*tvacaḥ* in the second example (cf. however, *tayāṇi* too § 358), and *pāṇā*=*prāṇāḥ* in the third example. In other cases, however, such a hypothesis is out of question : *māuyaṅgā*=*mātraṅgāni* (Ṭhāṇ. 187); *ṭhāṇā*=*sthānāni* (Ṭhāṇ. 163, 165); *pañca kumbhakārāvaṇasayā*=*pañca kumbhakārāpaṇaśatāni* (Uvās. § 184); *nahā*=*nakhāni, aharŏṭṭhā uttarŏṭṭhā*=*adharŏṣṭhe uttaroṣṭhe* (Kappas. S. § 43); *cattāri lakkhaṇā, ālambaṇā*=*catvāri lakṣaṇāni, ālambanāni* (Ovav. p. 42 f.). JM. *pañca sayā piṇḍiyā* (Āv. 17, 1), beside *pañca pañca suvaṇṇasayāṇi* (Āv. 16, 30); Ś. *midhuṇā* (Mṛcch. 71, 22), beside *midhuṇāiṁ* (Mṛcch. 71, 14); *jāṇavattā*=*yānapātrāṇi* (Mṛcch. 72, 23; 73, 1); *viraïdā mae āsaṇā*=*viracitāni mayāsanāni* (Mṛcch. 136, 6), beside *āsaṇāiṁ* (Mṛcch. 136,), and in Mg. (Mṛcch. 137, 3); *duve piā uaṇadā*=*dve priye upanate* (Vikr. 10, 3); *aṇurāasūaā akkharā*=*anurāgasūcakānyakṣarāṇi* (Vikr. 26, 2). Hc. 1, 33 mentions *naaṇā*=*nayanāni*; *loaṇā*=*locanāni*; *vaaṇā*=*vacanāni*; *dukkhā*=*duḥkhāni*; *bhāaṇā*=*bhājanāni.* He sees in them the masculine that is definitely possible. The numerous neuter that have become masculine appear to me to suggest that the form in *-ā* is to be equated with the corresponding Vedic one, and that it has given cause for change of the gender. Before the endings *-iṁ, -i,* a short vowel often appears in A. : *ahiulaĩ*=*ahikulāni*; *loaṇaĩ jāisaraĩ*=*locanāni jātismaraṇāni*; *maṇorahaĩ*=*manorathāḥ*; *ṇiccintaĩ hariṇāĩ*=*niścintā hariṇāḥ* (Hc. 4, 353. 365, 1. 414, 4. 422, 20).

1. That is probably already meant by LASSEN. Inst. p. 307. — 2. JACOBI, Erz.

p. xxxvi, § 39. In AMg. the examples are frequent: I cannot formulate the rule from JM., so I too have listed a large number of forms in *-ṇi*. — 3. Pischel, De Kālidāsae Çākuntali recensionibus p. 29 f.; KB. 8, 142. Wrongly Bollensen, Mālavikā. p. 113 and Preface p. ix.

§ 367ᵃ. In the acc. plur. of the masculine usual in all the dialects is the ending *-e*, that has been extended from the pronominal declension[1]. M. *calaṇe* = *caraṇau*; *ṇiaame*, *garuaare* = *nicatamān*, *gurukatarān*; *dose* = *doṣān* (G. 24. 82. 887); *dosaguṇe* = *doṣaguṇau*; *pāe* = *pādau*; *sahatthe* = *svahastau* (H. 48. 130. 680); *dharaṇihare* = *dharaṇidharān*; *mahihare* = *mahidharān*; *bhiṇṇaaḍe a garue taraṅgappahāre* = *bhinnataṭāṁś ca gurukāṁs taraṅgaprahārān* (R. 6, 85.90; 9,53); AMg. *samaṇamāhaṇaaïhikivaṇavaṇimage* = *śramaṇabrāhmaṇātithikṛpaṇavanipakān* (Āyār. 2, 2, 2, 8. 9); *sāhie māse* = *sādhikān māsān* (Āyār. 1, 8, 1, 2. 4, 6); *ime eyārūve urāle kallāṇe sive dhanne maṅgalle sassirie cŏddasa mahāsumiṇe* = *imān etadrūpān udārān kalyāṇāñśivān dhanyān māṅgalyān saśrikāṁś caturdaśa mahāsvapnān* (Kappas. § 3); JM. *bhoe* = *bhogān* (Āv. 8, 24; 12, 14. 20; Dvār. 495, 7); *te nagaraloe jalaṇasaṁbhamubbhantaloyaṇe palāyamāṇe* = *tān nagaralokāñ jvalanasaṁbhramodbhrāntalocanān palāyamānān* (Āv. 19, 10); *te ya samāgae* = *tāṁś ca samāgatān* (Kk. 263, 22); JŚ. *sese puṇa titthayare sasavvasiddhe visuddhasabbhāve samaṇe ya °viriyāyāre* = *śeṣān punas tīrthakarān sasarvasiddhān viśuddhasadbhāvāñ śramaṇāṁś ca °viryācārān* (Pav. 379, 2); *vividhe visae* = *vividhān viṣayān* (Pav. 384, 49); Ś. *adikkantakusumasamae vi rukkhae* = *atikrāntakusumasamayān api rukṣakān* (Śak. 10, 2); *purā paḍiṇṇāde duve vare* = *purā pratijñātau dvau varau* (Mahāv. 65, 5); *dārake* = *dārakau* (Uttarar. 191, 5); Mg. *avale* = *aparān* (Mṛcch. 118, 14); *ṇiapāṇe vihave kule kalatte a* = *nijaprāṇān vibhavān kulāni kalatrāṇi ca* (Mudrār. 256, 5)[2]; D. *sumbhaṇisumbhe* = *śumbhaniśumbhau* (Mṛcch. 105, 22). That the same ending is found in neuter too, as in AMg. *bahave jīve* = *bahūni jīvāni* (Uvās. § 218); Ś. *duve rukkhaseaṇake* = *dve rukṣasecanake* (Śak. 24, 1); A. *bhuaṇe* = *bhuvanāni* (Piṅgala 1, 62ᵇ), is explained from the change of gender described in § 356 ff. Dialectically we find also the acc. plur. of the masc. in *-ā* = *ān* (§ 89; Sr. fol. 6); M. *guṇā* = *guṇān*, *ṇiddhaṇā* = *nirdhanān* (Śukas. 57, 5. 6; Siṁhāsanadv. in IS, 15, 355 [so to be read]; Vetālap. p. 219, No. 17 ed. Uhle; on Hc. 2, 72); *dosā* = *doṣān* (Śukas. 57, 5. 6); AMg. *rukkhā mahallā* = *rukṣān mahataḥ* (Āyār. 2, 4, 2, 11. 12)[3]; *purisā*, *āsā* = *puruṣān*, *aśvān* (Nāyādh. 1378. 1388 f.); *bandhavā* = *bāndhavān* (Uttar. 576); *saṁphāsā* = *saṁsparśān* (Āyār. 1, 8, 2, 14); *uvassayā* = *upāśrayān* (Kappas. S. § 60); metri causa *guṇa* = *guṇān* (Dasav. 637, 4) too. The form in *-ā*, *-a* is usual in A.; *saralā sāsa* = *saralāñ śvāsān*; *ṇirakkhaa gaa* = *nirakṣakān gajān*; *desaḍā* = *deśān*; *siddhatthā* = *siddhārthān* (Hc. 4, 387, 1. 418, 3. 6, 423, 3); *maṇḍā maṇḍakān*; *vipakkhā* = *vipakṣān*; *kuñjarā* = *kuñjarān*; *kavandhā* = *kabandhān* (Piṅgala 1, 104ᵃ. 117ᵃ. 120ᵃ 2, 230). The single remnant of an acc. with a nasal vowel would be *dālaṁ* = *dārān* (Prab. 47. 1 = 55ᵃ, 5 P. = 58, 16 M.), if the reading is correct. The ed. Bomb. 102, 3 reads *lisiṇaṁ dālāṇaṁ* against grammar and prosody.

1. Weber, Hl p. 51; S. Goldschmidt, KZ. 25, 438. — 2. The verse is to be read: *yaś mahadha lahkiduṁ ṇiapāṇe vihave kule kalatte a* (Hillebrandt, ZDMG, 39, 121). *kule* and *kalatte* may be construed also as the acc. sing. according to § 366ᵇ.— 3. It might be considered also as the acc. plur. of the neut. according to § 358. 367.

§ 368. The ins. plur. ends in all the dialects in *-ehiṁ* = Vedic *-ebhis* (§ 72), that alternates with *-ehi*, *-ehĩ* in verses (§ 178) and with *-ehi* before enclitics in prose too in AMg. JM. (§ 350) : M. *amūlalahuehi sāsehiṁ* = *amūlalaghukaiḥ śvāsaiḥ* (G. 23); *avahatthiasabhāvehi dakkhiṇṇabhaṇiehiṁ* = *apahastitasadbhāvair dākṣiṇyabhaṇitaih* (H. 353); *kañcaṇasilalehiṁ chiṇṇāavamaṇḍalehi* = *kāñcanaśilātalaiś chinnātapamaṇḍalaiḥ* (R. 9, 55). Obviously in such cases we should read *-hĩ* for *-hi* (§ 178; cf. § 370). AMg. *tilaehiṁ laüehiṁ chattovehiṁ sirisehiṁ sattavaṇṇehiṁ* = further 19 instr. follow— = *tilakair lakucaiś *chattropaiḥ śiriṣaiḥ saptaparṇaiḥ* (Ovav. § 6); *santehiṁ taccehiṁ tahiehiṁ sabbhūehiṁ aṇiṭṭhehiṁ akantehiṁ appiehiṁ amaṇuṇṇehiṁ amaṇāmehiṁ vāgaraṇehiṁ* = *sadbhis *tāttvais* (§ 281) *tathyaiḥ sadbhūtair aniṣṭair akāntair apriyair amanojñair *amanāpair vyākaraṇaiḥ* (Uvās. § 259); JM. *māyandamahuavindehiṁ* = *mākandamadhukavṛndaiḥ* (KI. 18); *vatthābharaṇehiṁ* = *vastrābharaṇaiḥ* (Āv. 26, 27); *tehiṁ kumārehiṁ* = *taiḥ kumāraiḥ* (Āv. 30, 9); JŚ. *vihavehiṁ* = *vibhavaiḥ*; *sahassehiṁ* = *sahasraiḥ* (Pav. 380, 6. 12); *maṇavayakāehiṁ* = *manovacaḥkāyaiḥ* (Kattig. 400, 332); Ś. *jaṇehiṁ* = *janaiḥ* (Lalitav. 568, 6; Mṛcch. 25, 14); *jādasaṅkehiṁ devehiṁ* = *jātaśaṅkair devaiḥ* (Śak. 21, 5); *bhamarasaṅghavihaḍidehiṁ kusumehiṁ* = *bhramarasaṅghavighaṭitaiḥ kusumaiḥ* (Vikr. 21, 9); Mg. *tattastehiṁ* = *tatrasthaiḥ* (Lalitav. 565, 20); *attaṇakelakehiṁ pādehiṁ* = *ātmiyābhyām pādābhyām* (Mṛcch. 13, 9); *maścabandhaṇovāehiṁ* = *matsyabandhanopāyaiḥ* (Śak. 114, 2); Ḍh. *vippadivehiṁ pādehiṁ* = *vipratipābhyāṁ pādābhyām*; A. *lakkhehĩ* = *lakṣaiḥ*; *sarehiṁ, saravarehiṁ, ujjāṇavaṇehiṁ, ṇivasantehiṁ, suaṇehiṁ* = *śaraiḥ, sarovaraiḥ, udyānavanaiḥ, nivasadbhiḥ, sujanaiḥ* (Hc. 4, 335. 422, 11). The inst. in *-ahiṁ* is frequent in A. : *guṇahĩ* = *guṇaiḥ*, *paārahĩ* = *prakāraiḥ*; *savvahĩ pānthiahĩ* = *sarvaiḥ pathikaiḥ* (Hc. 4, 335. 367, 5. 429, 1); *khaggahĩ* = *khaḍgaiḥ*; *gaahĩ, turaahĩ, rahahĩ* = *gajaiḥ, turagaiḥ, rathaiḥ* (Piṅgala 1, 7. 145a). On this, as well on the instr. in *-ĕhiṁ*, *-ihiṁ* see § 128.

§ 369. Of the large number of forms, that grammarians permit for the abl. plur., we have hitherto been able to attest only the abl. in *-ehiṁto*, that is very frequent in AMg. and is shown to have clearly originated from the ins. plur. + suffix *-tas*, while those in *-suṁto* are shown to have arisen from the loc. plur. + suffix *-tas*: *tilehiṁto* = *tilebhyaḥ* (Sūyag. 594); *maṇussehiṁto vā pañcindiyatirikkhajoṇiehiṁto vā puḍhavikāiehiṁto vā* = *manuṣyebhyo vā pañcendriyatiryagyonikebheyo vā pṛthivikāyikebhyo vā* (Ṭhāṇ. 58); *ṇeraïehiṁto vā tirikkhajoṇiehiṁto vā maṇussehiṁto vā devehiṁto vā* (Ṭhāṇ. § 336; cf. Vivāhap. 1534 and elsewhere often); *sarisaehiṁto rāyakulehiṁto* = *sadṛśakebhyo rājakulebhyaḥ* (Nāyādh. § 123); *kolaghariehiṁto vaehiṁto* = *kaulagṛhikebhyo vrajebhyaḥ* (Uvās. § 342. 343). Cases like *therehiṁto ṇaṁ godāsehiṁto kāsavagŏttehiṁto. . . . chaluehiṁto rohaguttehiṁto kosiyagŏttehiṁto* etc. (Kappas. Th. § 5 ff.), are to be considered as those of the plur. majestatis. Beside it AMg. JM. have also an abl. in *-ehiṁ* = Skt. *-ebhyaḥ*, so that the ins. and the abl. have become identical. AMg. *°nāmadhĕjjhehiṁ vimāṇehiṁ oiṇṇā* = *°nāmadheyebhyo vimānebhyo 'vatīrṇāḥ* (Ovav. § 37); *saehiṁ saehiṁ gehehiṁto niggacchanti* = *svakebhyaḥ svakebhyo gṛhebhyo nirgacchanti* (Kappas. § 66; cf. Nāyādh. 1048; Vivāhap. 187. 950. 943); *saehiṁ saehiṁ ṇagarehiṁto ṇiggacchanti* = *svakebhyaḥ svakebhyo nagarebhyo nirgacchanti* (Nāyādh. 826); *gāratthehi ya* *savvehiṁ sāhavo saṁjamuttarā*=*gṛhasthebhyaś ca sarvebhyaḥ sādhavaḥ saṁyamottarāḥ* (Uttar. 208); JM. *jharei romakūvehiṁ seo*=*kṣarati romakūpebhyaḥ svedaḥ* (Erz. 4, 23; cf. JACOBI § 95). Cf. § 376. In A. the abl. ends in *-ahũ* : *girisiṅgahũ*=*giriśṛṅgebhyaḥ*; *muhahũ*=*mukhebhyaḥ* (Hc. 4, 337. 422, 20); *rukkhahuṁ*=*rukṣebhyaḥ* (Kī. 5, 29). *-huṁ*, *-hũ* corresponds phonetically exactly to the ending *-bhyām* of the abl. dual. That it may be an abridgement of *-suṁto* (LASSEN, Inst. p. 463) is wrong.

§ 370. The gen. plur. ends in all the dialects in *-āṇaṁ*=Skt. *-ānām*. In M., however, occurs the denasalised form in *-āṇa*, that is found in AMg. JM. JŚ. too, in AMg. particularly before enclitics (§ 350), and elsewhere too, as *gaṇāṇa majjhe*=*gaṇānāṁ madhye* (Kappas. § 61=Ovav. 48, p. 55, 13=Nāẏādh. § 35), is almost the prevalent one. In places, where in M., both the forms stand beside one other, as *kuḍilāṇa pĕmmāṇaṁ*=*kuṭilānāṁ premṇām* (H. 10), *maāṇa oṇimillacchāṇaṁ*=*mṛgāṇāṁ avanimilitākṣāṇam* (R. 9, 87), *sajjaṇāṇaṁ pamhusiadasāṇa*=*sajjanānāṁ vismṛtadaśānām* (G. 971), as in the analogous cases in the nom. acc. neut.; inst. loc. plur., we should for *-āṇa* read *-āṇã* (§ 178), that is pointed to by the metre as well in the example frcm R. Ś.Mg., except in verses, have only the form in *-āṇaṁ*. For Mg. Hc. 4, 300 teaches also a gen. in *-ahã*. None of the MSS writes this at the places referred to by him in Śak. (§ 178); the Lalitav. too, which mostly conforms to Hc.'s rules, has the gen. in *-āṇaṁ* only (565, 14; 566, 3. 10. 11). Against this *-āhã* and shortened *-ahã*, are the most usual endings in A., which go back to the pronominal ending *-sām* : *ṇivaṭṭāhã* =*nivṛttānām*; *sŏkkhahã*=*saukhyānām*; *taṇahã*=*tṛṇānām*; *mukkāhã*=*muktānām*; *mattahã maagalahã*=*mattānāṁ madakalānām*; *saüṇāhã*=*śakunānām* (Hc. 4, 332. 339. 370. 406. 445, 4); *vaṅkakaḍakkhahã loaṇahã*=*vakrakaṭākṣayor locanayoḥ* (Vetālap. p. 217, Nr. 13); *mahabbhaḍahã*=*mahābhaṭānām* (Kk. 261, 5). According to C. 1, 5, elsewhere the ending *-haṁ* too is found beside *-ṇaṁ* : *devāhaṁ* beside *devāṇaṁ*; *tāhaṁ* beside *tāṇaṁ*. Hc. 4, 300, who assigns them to M., too has the rest of the examples in C. from *-ā*, *-n* and pronominal declension.

§ 371. In the loc., in M. AMg. JM. the principal form is in *-esu* =*-eṣu*, beside which sometimes *-esuṁ* is found, as M. *sacandaṇesuṁ āroviaroaṇesu* [read °*sũ*; § 370)=*sacandaneṣv āropitarocaneṣu* (G. 211); *vaṇesuṁ*=*vaneṣu* (H. 77); in AMg., more often in Nāẏādh. § 61-63, beside the more frequent forms in *-su*; notwithstanding the *MSS and the ed. Calc. p. 106 ff.* always being in accord, we should throughout read °*su*. In Ś. the texts partly have *-su* (Lalitav. 555, 11. 12; Mṛcch. 9, 2; 24, 25; 25, 1; 37, 23; 70, 3; 71, 17; 97, 22; 100, 2; etc.; Mālav. 19, 12; 30, 6; 611, 19. 20; 67, 10; 75, 1; Vikr. 35, 6; 75, 3, 6), and partly *-suṁ* (Vikr. 23, 13; 52, 1. 5. 7[1]; Śak. 9, 12; 30, 2; 50, 11; 51, 5; 53, 9; 60, 8; 64, 2; 72, 12 etc. in the Bengali recension, whilst the Kashmirian, Draviḍian and Devanāgarī recensions have *-su*). The Indian editions mostly have *-su*. In Mg. stands *pāeśu* (Mṛcch. 19, 6), but *pādeśuṁ* (121, 20. 22), beside *calaṇeśu* (121, 24) and *keśeśu* (122, 22) in verses; Veṇīs. has *keśeśu* (35, 19), Mudrār. has *kammeśu* =*karmasu* (191, 9), and Prab. has *puliśeśu* (62, 7). On the analogy of the ins. and gen., which always end in *-ṁ*, for prose *-suṁ*, Mg. *-śuṁ* will be more correct. In A. the loc. and the ins. have become identical : *saahĩ = śateṣu*; *maggahĩ = mārgeṣu*; *gaahĩ = gateṣu*; *kesahĩ = keśeṣu*; *aṇṇahĩ taruarahĩ = anyeṣu taruvareṣu* (Hc. 4, 345. 347. 370, 3. 422, 9). In Hc. 4, 423, 4 for *gavakkhehiṁ* we should read *gavakkhahĩ* and in 445, 2 probably *ḍuṅgarahĩ*. The instrumental stands in the sense of the loc. too in AMg. *jaganissiehĩ bhūehiṁ tasanāmehĩ thāvarehiṁ ca no tesim ārabhe daṇḍaṁ* (Uttar. 248). Cf. § 376.

1. Cf. Pischel, De Kālidāsae Çākuntali recensionibus p. 31.

§ 372. The vocative is like the nominative. In AMg. *ajjo* and *ammayāo* are used as the voc. plur. too (§ 366b). For the voc. plur. of Mg. Kī. 5, 94 (cf. Lassen, Inst. p. 393) permits the ending *-hu* too, Mk. fol. 75 *-ho* with *a* of the stem lengthened before it : *bamhaṇāhu = brāhmaṇāḥ* (Kī. 5, 97). This voc. occurs in *bhasṭālakāho*, as in Mṛcch. 165, l. 5 instead of *bhaśṭālakā ho* we should read. It is usual in A., where the ending mostly is *-hõ*, without lengthening of *a* of the stem : *taruṇahõ = taruṇāḥ*; *loahõ = lokāḥ* (Hc. 4, 346. 350, 2. 365, 1). In A. the ending *-hõ* comes after all the stems: *taruṇihõ = taruṇyaḥ* (Hc. 4, 346); *aggihõ = agnayaḥ*; *mahilāhõ = mahilāḥ* (Kī. 5, 20); *cadummuhahõ = caturmukhāḥ*, *harihõ = harayaḥ*, *taruhõ = taravaḥ* (Sr. fol. 60 ff.). Lassen, Inst. p. 399 has already rightly noticed that in Mg. *-āhu* (*-āho*) the Vedic. ending *-āsas* has continued. Since he wrongly referred the rule of Kī. on Mg., to the nom. plur., he separated, the A. form from that of Mg. at p. 463 and sought in *ho* the particle *ho*, as they had done till then also in Mṛcch. 165, l. 5. In A. the endings of the *a*-stems have been extended to the rest of the vocalic stems too. — See § 105 on AMg. *ghiṁsu-*, *pāṇu-*, *pilaṁkhu-*, *manthumilakkhu-*, the nouns that have become *u*-stems.

§ 373. The declension of the *a*-stems in PG. VG. (§ 363) agrees most faithfully with that of Ś. The dat. sing., which is not usual in Ś., alone is deviating; in PG. however, it appears in two forms, of which that in *-āye* is put in the dative in AMg. JM. (§ 361. 364), and the abl. sing., which ends in *-ā* here, but in Ś., almost always ends in *-ādo* (§ 365).

b) Feminine in -ā.

§ 374. *mālā* (garland).

Singular

Nom. *mālā*.
Acc. *mālaṁ*.
Ins. M. *mālāe*, *mālāi*, *mālāa*, the remaining dialects only *mālāe*, A. *mālaĕ*.
Dat. *mālāe*; only in AMg.
Abl. M. AMg. JM. *mālāo*, *mālāu*, [*mālāhiṁto*, *mālāi*, *mālāa*, *mālatto*]; Ś. Mg. *mālādo* and *mālāe*; A. *mālahĕ*.
Gen. Loc. M. *mālāe*, *mālāi*. *mālāa*, the rest of the dialects only *mālāe*; A. : gen. *mālahĕ*.
Loc. [*mālahĩ*].
Voc. *māle*, *mālā*.

Plural

Nom. Acc. Voc. M. AMg. JM, *mālāo*, *mālāu*, *mālā*; Ś. Mg. *mālāo*, *mālā*.

Ins. M. AMg. JM. *mālāhi, mālāhĩ, mālāhiṁ*; Ś. Mg. *mālāhiṁ*.
Abl. M. AMg. *mālāhiṁto*, [*mālāsuṁto, mālāo, mālāu*); A. *mālahu*.
Gen. M. AMg. JM. *mālāṇa, mālāṇă, mālāṇaṁ*; Ś. Mg. *mālāṇaṁ*; A.: [*mālahu*].
Loc. M. AMg. JM. *mālāsu, mālāsũ, mālāsuṁ*, Ś. Mg. *mālāsu, mālāsuṁ*.
In PG. are found the nom. sing. *paṭṭikā* (7, 48. 51), *kaḍa tti = kṛteti* (7, 51), and the acc. sing. (or plur.) *pilā bādhā = piḍāṁ bādhām* (or *piḍā bādhāḥ*) (6, 40), as well as the acc. sing. *simaṁ = simām* (6, 28).

§ 375. On the declension of the *ā*-stems cf. Vr. 5, 19-23; C. 1, 3. 9. 10; Hc. 3, 27. 29. 30. 4, 348, 352; Kī. 3, 7. 23. 25. 27; Mk. fol. 43; Sr. fol. 14 f. On the shortening of *ā* in the nom. sing. in A. see § 100. So also Mg. *śevida = sevitā* (Mṛcch. 117, 1). The instrumental, the genitive, the locative, and according to the grammarians partly the ablative too, have become identical. The common form is *mālāe* = Skt. *mālāyai*, that is to say = the usual form of the gen. abl. in the Yajurveda and the Brāhmaṇas and known to the Avestā too[1]. Sometimes in verses the forms in *-āe* and *-āi* stand side by side, as *pucchiāi muddhāe = pṛṣṭāyā mugdhāyāḥ* (H. 15). On metrical grounds, in M. the form in *-āi*, that is to be brought in throughout, where in the texts *-aĕ* may have to be read, dominates. The v. l. mostly has the correct reading *-āi*, as G. 44. 46. 56. 65. 71. 212. 222. 243. 290. 453. 474. 684. 870. 931. 954. Some grammarians (Hc. 3, 29; Kī. 3, 27; Sr. fol. 14) teach a form in *āa* too, which is forbidden by others (Vr. 5, 23; Mk. fol. 43). Such forms are found in M. as v.l. So.: *jŏṇhāa = jyotsnayā*; *ṇevacchakalāa = nepathyakalayā*; *helāa = helayā*; *hariddāa = haridrāyāḥ*; *caṅgimāa = caṅgimatvena* (Karp. ed. Bomb. 31, 1, 86, 4; 53, 9; 55, 2; 71, 4; 79, 12). Konow reads for them *jŏṇhāi, ṇevacchakalāi, helāi, haliddai, caṅgimāi* (29, 1; 86, 9; 51, 2; 52, 4; 69, 3; 78, 9). Some MSS sometimes have *-āa*. Since G.H.R. do not know *-āa* except in *tiaḍāa = trijaṭāyāḥ* (R. 11,100) and *ṇisaṇṇāa = niṇaṇṇāyāḥ* (R. 10, 101), they are not to be accepted as doctior lectio, with S. Goldschmidt, but as errors for °*āi*, as C. has. This *-āa* goes back to the abl. gen. Skt. *-āyāḥ*, so that *jŏṇhāa = jyotsnāyāḥ*, of which the strictly corresponding form **jŏṇhāā* is forbidden by Vr. 5, 23; Hc. 3, 30; Sr. fol. 14. In A. *-āe* has been shortened to *-aĕ* : *ṇiddaĕ = nirdayā*; *candimaĕ = candrimayā*; *uḍḍāvantiaĕ = uḍḍāpayantyā*; *mañjiṭṭhaĕ = mañjiṣṭhayā* (Hc. 4, 330, 2. 349. 352, 438, 2). — On the dative in *-āe* in AMg. see § 361.364. —Of the forms of the abl. sing. mentioned by the grammarians I can locate in the texts only those in *-āo*, Ś. Mg. *-ādo* more often : AMg. *paratthimāo vā disāo āgao ahaṁ aṁsi dāhiṇāo vā disāo. . paccatthimāo. . . uttarāo. . . uḍḍhāo = *purastimāto vā diśa āgato 'ham asmi dakṣiṇāto vā diśaḥ. . . *pratyastimātaḥ . . . uttarātaḥ. . . ūrdhvātaḥ* (Āyār. 1, 1, 1, 2); *jibbhāo = jihvātaḥ* (Āyār. p. 137, 1); *siyāo = śibikātaḥ* (Nāyādh. 870, 1097. 1189. 1354. 1497); *chāyāo = chāyātaḥ* (Sūyag. 639); *aṭṭaṇasālāo = aṭṭanaśālātaḥ* (Kappas. § 60; Ovav. § 48); *māyāo = māyātaḥ* (Sūyag. 654; Ovav. § 123); *sūṇāo = sūnātaḥ* (Nirayāv. § 10); Ś. *bubhukkhādo = bubhukṣātaḥ, dakkhiṇādo, vāmādo = dakṣiṇātaḥ, vāmātaḥ*; *padolikādo = pratolikātaḥ* (Mṛcch. 2, 33; 9, 9; 162, 23); Mg. *lac-*

chādo = *rathyātaḥ* (Mṛcch. 158, 13). Ablative in *-āe* (C. 1, 19; Hc. 3, 29; Sr. fol. 14) occurs in Ś. and Mg. : Ś. *imāe maataṇhiāe* = *asyā mṛgatṛṣṇikāyāḥ* (Vikr. 17, 1), which with BOLLENSEN cannot be considered to be instr.; Mg. *śĕyyāe* (text *sĕjjāe*) = *śayyāyāḥ* (Cait. 149, 19). — The form *mālatto* follows from Hc. 3, 124, and is taught explicitly by Triv. 2, 2, 34. It is an analogical formation from the masc. and neut. (§ 365). In A. the abl. sing. has become identical with the genitive. The ending *-hĕ* corresponds to the pronominal ending *-syāḥ*, so that *tahĕ dhaṇahĕ* (Hc. 4, 350) strictly is = *tasyā* **dhanyasyāḥ* = *tasyā dhanyāyāḥ*[2]. Hc. 4, 350 takes *bālāhĕ* as abl., so that *visamatthaṇa* to be taken as bahuvrīhi, is = "before the young woman with uneven breasts". Genitive are : *tucchamajjhahĕ*, *jampirahĕ*, *tucchaarahāsahĕ*, *alahantiahĕ*, *vammahaṇivāsahĕ*, *muddhaḍahĕ* = *tucchamadhyāyāḥ*, *jalpanaśīlāyāḥ*, *tucchatarahāsyāyāḥ*, *alabhamānāyāḥ*, *manmathanivāsāyāḥ*, *mugdhāyāḥ* (Hc. 4, 350); *tisahĕ* = *tṛṣāyāḥ*: *muṇāliahĕ* = *mṛṇālikāyāḥ* (Hc. 4, 395, 7. 444). — Examples for the loc. are: M. *dukkhuttarāi paavie* = *duḥkhottarāyāṁ padavyām*: *gāmaracchāe* = *grāmarathyāyām* (H. 107. 419); AMg. *suhammāe sabhāe* = *sudharmāyāṁ sabhāyām* (Kappas. §14 and often): AMg. JM. *campāe* = *campāyām* (Ovav. § 2. 11: Erz. 34, 25); JM. *saẏalāe naẏarie* = *sakalāyāṁ nagaryām* (Dvār. 497, 21); *ikkikkāe mehalāe* = *ekaikasyāṁ mekhalāyām* (T. 5, 11); Ś. *susamiddhāe* = *susamṛddhāyām*; *edāe padosavelāe* = *etasyāṁ pradoṣavelāyām*; *rukkhavāḍiāe* = *rukṣavāṭikāyāṁ* (Mṛcch. 4, 20: 9, 10; 73, 6. 7); Mg. *andhaālapūlidāe ṇāśiāe* = *andhakārapūritāyāṁ nāsikāyām*; *padoliāe* = *pratolikāyām*: *śuvaṇṇacoliāe* = *suvarṇacorikāyām* (Mṛcch. 14, 22: 163, 16; 165, 2). AMg. *giriguhaṁsi* for *giriguhāe* = *giriguhāyām* (Āẏar. 1, 7, 2, 1) has been formed according to the loc. in *-ṁsi* of the mascul. and neut. standing beside it. Cf. similar cases in § 355. 358. 364. 367. 379. 386. As a rule the vocative, as in Skt., ends in *-e*, a form that is known to Vr. 5, 28 alone; whilst Hc. 3, 41: Mk. fol. 44: Sr. fol. 14 permit even the nom. form in *-ā* as the vocative. Such vocatives in *-ā* are : M. *attā* (mother-in-law; Mk. fol. 44; H. 8, 469. 543. 553. 653. 676. 811); M. AMg. *piucchā* = *pitṛṣvasaḥ* (Hc.; Mk.: H.; Nāẏādh. 1299; 1348). M. *māuā* = *mātṛke* (H.); *māucchā* = *mātṛṣvasaḥ* (Hc.; Mk.; H.); AMg. *jāẏā* (Uttar. 442), *puttā* = *putri* (Nāẏādh. 633 f. 648 f. 655. 658), and the frequent M. Ś. *halā* (Hc. 2, 195; H.), in Ś., mostly joined with the vocative in *-e* of a proper noun, as *halā saüntale* (Śak. 9, 10); *halā aṇusūe* (Śak. 10, 12): *halā ṇomālie* (Lalitav. 560, 9; text *no*); *halā cittalehe* (Vikr. 9. 3); *halā maaṇie* (Ratn. 293, 29); *halā ṇiuṇie* (Ratn. 297, 28) etc., or with proper nouns ending in an other vowel, as *halā uvvasi* (Vikr. 7, 17), or with adjectives, used substantively, as *halā apaṇḍide* (Priyad. 22, 7), in M. Ś. used as plur. too (H. 893. 901; Śak. 16, 10; 58, 9; Vikr. 6, 13; 7, 1: 11, 1; Karp. 108, 5). JM. has *hale* too (Hc. 2, 195 Erz.), that Kī 5, 19 mentions as A., and what is found in A. as *hali* (Hc. 4, 332, 2; 358, 1). Ś. *amba* (mother; Śak. ed. BURKHARD 201, 19; 202, 20; Ratn. 315, 26; 327, 6; Mahāv. 56, 3; Mālatīm. 179, 6; 225, 4; Nāgān. 84, 15: Anarghar. 310, 1 etc. is by origin a particle according to LANMAN[3] and BECHTEL[4]. In A. the final *-e* is shortened, as *sahiĕ* = **sakhike*; *ammiĕ*; *bahiṇuĕ* = *bhaginike* (Hc. 4, 358, 1. 367, 1. 396, 2. 422, 14), or it becomes *-i*, as in *hali*, mentioned above, and in *ammi*, *muddhi* = *mugdhe* (Hc. 4, 395, 5. 376, 1). On AMg. JM. *ammo* see § 366*b*.

1. PISCHEL, BB. 6, 281, note 3. — 2. With LASSEN, Inst. p. 462. we may also consider it to be a case of transfer from the *a*-stems. — 3. Noun-Inflection p. 360. — 4. Hauptprobleme p. 265 f.

§ 376. In all the dialects the usual form in the nom. acc. plur. is that in *-o* (§ 367); nom. M. *mahilāo* = *mahilāḥ* (H. 397); AMg. JM. *devayāo*, Ś. *devadāo* = *devatāḥ* (Ṭhāṇ. 76; Erz. 29, 3; Śak. 71, 8); acc. AMg. *kalāo* = *kalāḥ* (Uttar. 642; Nāyādh. § 119; Ovav. § 107; Kappas. § 211); JM. *caüvvihāo vaggaṇāo* = *caturvidhā vargaṇāḥ* (Āv. 7, 4); Ś. *paḍiviāo* = *pradīpikāḥ* (Mṛcch. 25, 18); A. *savvaṅgāo* = *sarvāṅgāḥ* (Hc. 4, 348). In verses *-o* interchanges with *-u*, that is widely prevalent there : M. nom. *dhaṇṇāu tāu* = *dhanyās tāḥ* (H. 147) against Ś. *dhaṇṇāŏ kkhu tāo kaṇṇaāo* [so to be read] *jāo* (Mālatīm. 80, 1); AMg. *thiyāu* = *strikāḥ* (Sūyag. 225); acc. A. *aṇurattāu bhattāu* = *anuraktā bhaktāḥ* (Hc. 4, 422, 10). Sometimes both the forms stand beside one another on account of metre, as M. *dāraggalāu jāāo* = *dvārārgalā jātāḥ* (H. 322); *raïviramalajjiāo apattaṇiaṁsaṇāu* = *rativirāmalajjitā aprāptanivasanāḥ* (H. 459); *paḍigaāu disāo* = *pratigatā diśaḥ* (R. 1, 19). More seldom is the nom. acc. in *-ā*: M. *rehā* = *rekhāḥ* (G. 22; H. 206), beside *rehāu* (Hc. 474) and *rehāo* (G. 509. 682); *sariā sarantapavahā. . . vūḍhā* = *saritaḥ saratpravāhāḥ. . . ūḍhāḥ* (R. 6, 50); *mehalā* = *mekhalāḥ* (Mṛcch. 41, 2); AMg. *dŏjjhā* = *dohyāḥ*; *dammā* = *damyāḥ*; *rahajŏggā* = *rathayogyāḥ* (Āyār. 2, 4, 2, 9); *pakkā* = *pakvāḥ*; *rūḍhā* = *rūḍhāḥ* (Āyār. 2, 4, 2, 15. 16); *bhajjā* = *bhāryāḥ* (Uttar. 660; *nāvāhi tārimāŏ tti pāṇipĕjja tti no vae* = *naubhis *tārimā iti pāṇipeyā iti no vadet* (Dasav. 629, 1); Ś. *pūijjantā devadā* = *pūjyamānā devatāḥ*; *gaṇiā* = *gaṇikāḥ* (Mṛcch. 9, 1. 10); *agahidatthā* = *agṛhitārthāḥ* (Śak. 120, 11); *adiṭṭhasujjapāā. . . ṇāgakaṇṇā via* = *adṛṣṭasūryapādāḥ . . . nāgakanyā iva* (Mālav. 51, 21; cf., however, the v. l.). Mk. fol. 69 permits in Ś. *-āo* only, and so we should probably correct throughout. In Mṛcch. 25, 20 stand beside one another : *tāo. . . padīviāo avamāṇidaṇiddhaṇakāmuā via gaṇiā ṇissiṇehāo dāṇiṁ saṁvuttā* = *tāḥ. . . pradīpikā avamānitanirdhanakāmukā iva gaṇikā niḥsnehā idānīṁ saṁvṛttāḥ*. STENZLER has, with AB, already corrected *saṁvuttā* as *saṁvuttāo*; DH, in GODABOLE p. 72, have *gaṇiāo* for *gaṇiā*, so that °*kāmuāo* is to be read. Sometimes in AMg. too, both the forms stand side by side : *indabhūipamŏkkhāo cŏddasasamaṇasāhassīo ukkosiyā samaṇasaṁpayā* = *indrabhūtipramukhyāś caturdaśaśramaṇasāhasrya *utkośitāḥ śramaṇasaṁpadaḥ* (Kappas. § 134; cf. 135 ff.). Cf. Āyār. 2, 4, 2, 9. 15. 16. — For the endings of the ins. gen. loc. § 178. 350 hold good; cf. § 368. 370. 371 too. — In Mg. the ins. is in *-ehiṁ* instead of that in *-āhiṁ* in *ambikamādukehiṁ* = *ambikāmātṛkābhiḥ* (Mṛcch. 122, 5) is not to be objected to in the mouth of the Śakāra, since the writer has openly and intentionally changed the gender. Against this R. 7, 62 does not have the ins. *accharehiṁ* = *apsarobhiḥ* from the stem *accharā* (§ 410)[1], that was earlier read also in Vikr. 40, 11[2], but the first *samaccharehiṁ* is to be analysed, as *sama*+*ccharehiṁ* = *sama*+*psarobhiḥ* (§ 328)[3]. — As in the masc. and neutr. (§ 369), in the fem. too, the form in *-hiṁ* is used for the abl., what is forbidden by Hc. 3. 127; M. *dhārāhiṁ*

= *dhārābhyaḥ* (H. 170) and for the loc. (§ 371) : M. *mehalâhi* (Karp. 16, 1), in the sense of *mehalāsu*, as Kāvyaprakāśa 74, 1 has in the v. l.,—*mekhalāsu*; AMg. *hatthuttarāhiṁ* = *hastottarāsu* (Āyār. 2, 15, 1. 2. 5. 6. 17. 22. 25; Kappas.); *gimhāhi* (Sūyag. 166), in the sense of *gimhāsu* (Vivāhap. 465) = **griṣmāsu* (§ 358); *aṇantāhiṁ osappiṇiussappiṇihiṁ viikkantāhiṁ* = *anantāsu avasarpiṇyutsarpaṇiṣu vyatikrāntāsu* (Kappas. § 19); *visāhāhiṁ* = *viśākhāsu* (Kappas. § 149); *cittāhiṁ* = *citrāsu* (Ṭhāṇ. 363; Kappas. § 171. 174); *uttarāsāḍhāhiṁ āsāḍhāhiṁ* (Kappas. § 205. 211); *chinnāhi sāhāhi* = *chinnāsu śākhāsu* (Uttar. 439; text °*hiṁ*)[4]. — Abl. in *-hiṁto* are AMg. *antosālāhiṁto* = *antaḥśālābhyaḥ* (Uvās. § 195); *itthiyāhiṁto* = *strikābhyaḥ* (Jīv. 263. 265). In A. the abl. has the ending *-hu* = *-bhyaḥ*: *vayaṁsiahu* = *vayasyābhyaḥ* (Hc. 4, 351). According to Hc. the same form is used for the gen. plur. too. Cf. § 381. In the loc. the form in *-su* prevails here too (cf. § 371). In Ś. Śak. 29, 4, there stands *viralapādavacchāāsuṁ vaṇarāisuṁ* = *viralapādapacchāyāsu vanarājiṣu* in the Bengal recension, and *-āsu*, *-isu* in the rest. — In the voc. the form in *-o* is prevalent : Ś. *devadāo* (Bālar. 168, 7; Anarghar. 300, 1); *dāriāo* = *dārikāḥ* (Vikr. 45, 6); *avaloidā buddharakkhidāo* = *avalokitābuddharakṣite* (Mālatīm. 284, 11). On *halā* see § 375. — On *ajjū* = *āryā* see § 105.

1. The question, raised by S. GOLDSCHMIDT, R. p. 247, note 8, whether we should recognize a neuter *acchara* is naturally to be answered in the negative. — 2. BOLLENSEN on Vikr. p. 326; cf. HOEFER De Pr. dialecto p. 150 f.; LASSEN, Inst. p. 316f. and § 410. — 3. PISCHEL, ZDMG, 52, 93 ff. — 4. That here we have a case of the instr. is proved by instances like *hatthuttarāhiṁ nakkhatteṇaṁ jogovagaeṇaṁ* (Āyār. 2, 15, 6, 17; cf. Kappas. § 2). Cf. Kappas. § 157. 174. 211, and SPEYER, Vedische und Sanskrit Syntax (Strassburg 1896; Grundriss 1, 6) § 42.

(2) STEMS IN *-i*, *ī* AND *-u*, *-ū*

(a) MASCULINE AND NEUTER

§ 377. Masculine *aggi* = *agni*.

Singular

N.	*aggi* [*aggiṁ*].
Acc.	*aggiṁ*.
I.	*aggiṇā*, A. also *aggiṇa*, *aggiṁ*.
Abl.	M. AMg. JM. *aggio*, *aggiu*, *aggiṇo*, *aggihiṁto*, [*aggihi*, *aggitto*]; JŚ. [Ś. Mg.] *aggido*; A. *aggihĕ*.
G.	M. AMg. JM. *aggiṇo*, *aggissa*, [*aggio*]; Ś. Mg. *aggiṇo*; A. [*aggihĕ*].
L.	*aggimmi*, AMg. mostly *aggiṁsi*, AMg. JM. *aggiṁmi* too; A. *aggihĩ*.
V.	*aggi*, *aggī*.

Plural.

N.	M. AMg. JM. *aggiṇo*, *aggī*, *aggīo*, *aggao*, *aggaü*; Ś. *aggīo*, *aggiṇo*.
Acc.	M. AMg. JM. *aggiṇo*, *aggī*, *aggao*.
I.	M. AMg. JM. *aggīhĩ*, *aggīhĩ*, *aggīhiṁ*; Ś. Mg, *aggīhiṁ*.
Abl.	M. AMg. JM. *aggīhiṁto*, [*aggīsuṁto*, *aggitto*, *aggio*]; A. *aggihũ*.
G.	M. AMg. JM. *aggiṇa*, *aggiṇã*, *aggiṇaṁ*; Ś. Mg. *aggiṇaṁ*; A. *aggihã*, *aggihũ*.

L. M. AMg. JM. *aggisu, aggisũ, aggisuṁ*; Ś. Mg. *aggisu, aggisuṁ*; A. *aggihĩ*.
V. M. AMg. JM. *aggiṇo, aggĩ*; A. *aggihõ*.

Likewise go the neuter, as *dahi* = *dadhi*; only nom. acc. sing. M. AMg. JM. *dahiṁ, dahĩ, dahi*, Ś. Mg. *dahiṁ, dahi*; V. *dahi*; nom. acc. voc. plur. *dahiiṁ, dahiĩ* (not Ś. Mg.), *dahiṇi* (not Ś. Mg.), *dahi* (not Ś. Mg.). — In PG. is found the acc. sing. neutr. *udakādiṁ* 6, 29, the gen. sing. masc. *sattissa* = *śakteḥ* 6, 17, *bhaṭisa* = *bhaṭṭeḥ* 6, 19, and the acc. plur. masc. *vasudhādhipataye* = *vasudhādhipatin* 7, 44 (cf. LEUMANN, EI. 2, 484).

§ 378. Masc. *vāu* = *vāyu*.

Singular.

N. *vāū* [*vāuṁ*].
Acc. *vāuṁ*.
I. *vāuṇā*; A. also *vāuṇa, vāuṁ*.
Abl. M. AMg. JM. *vāūo, vāūu* [*vāuṇo, vāūhiṁto, vāutto*]; A. *vāuṇĕ*.
G. M. AMg. JM. *vāuṇo, vāussa* [*vāuo*]; Ś. Mg. *vāūṇo*, Mg. in verses *vāuśśa* too; [A. *vāuhĕ*].
L. *vāummi*, AMg. *vāuṁsi* too, AMg. JM. *vāuṁmi*.
V. *vāu, vāū*.

Plural.

N. M. AMg. JM. *vāuṇo, vāū, vāūo, vāavo, vāao, vāaü*; Ś. *vāuṇo, vāao*.
Acc. M. AMg. JM. *vāuṇo, vāū*, AMg. also *vāavo*.
I. M. AMg. JM. *vāūhi, °hĩ, °hiṁ*; Ś. Mg. *vāūhiṁ*.
Abl. [*vāūhiṁto, vāūsuṁto, vāutto, vāūo*]; AMg. *vāūhiṁ* also, A. *vāuhũ*.
G. M. AMg. JM. *vāūṇa, °ṇā̃, °ṇaṁ*; Ś. Mg. *vāūṇaṁ*, A. *vāuhā̃*; *vāuhũ*.
L. M. AMg. JM. *vāūsu, °sũ, °suṁ*; Ś. Mg. *vāūsu, vāūsuṁ*; A. *vāuhĩ*.
V. AMg. *vāavo*; A. *vāuhõ*.

Likewise go the neuter, as *mahu* = *madhu*; only nom. acc. sing. *mahuṁ, mahũ, mahu*; Ś. Mg. *mahuṁ, mahu*; voc. *mahu*; nom. acc. voc. plur. *mahūiṁ, mahūĩ* (not Ś. Mg.), *mahūṇi* (not Ś. Mg.), *mahū* (not Ś. Mg.). — In PG. *u*-stem is not found.

§ 379. On the declension of *i*- and *u*- stems see Vr. 5, 14-18. 25-27. 30; C. 1, 3. 11-14; Hc. 3, 16 — 26; 4, 340. 341. 343 — 347; Ki. 3, 8. 11, 13. 15. 17 — 22. 24. 28. 29; 5, 20, 25 — 27. 33 — 35. 37; Mk. fol. 42 — 44; Sr. fol. 9 = 12. In the nom. sing., according to Hc. 3, 19, some taught beside the lengthening also the equivalent (§ 74) nasalization : *aggiṁ, ṇihiṁ, vāuṁ, vihuṁ*. Triv. and Sr. do not mention this form; in Paṇhāv. 448 *susāhuṁ*, as the nom., is edited, probably wrongly for *susāhū*, since beside it stand *suisī, sumuṇī* = *svṛṣiḥ, sumuniḥ*. On the nom. in -*ī*, -*ū* see § 72. From *sakhi* the nom. sing. is JM. *sahī* (KI. 14). In the neuter prevails in the nom. the denasalized form and the nasalized form, in the acc.; however, AMg. *taū* = *trapu* (Sūyag. 282) is made certain on account of the metre; probably it is to be read as *taũ*. In the nom. stands AMg. Ś. *dahiṁ* (Ṭhāṇ. 230; Mṛcch. 3, 12 [to be read so for *dahīṁ*]), but AMg. *dahi* (Ṭhāṇ. 514); AMg. Ś. *vatthu* = *vastu* (Uttar. 172; Lalitav. 516, 12); Ś. *ṇaaṇamahu* = *naya-*

namadhu (Mālav. 22, 3). On AMg. *aṭṭhi, dahi* see § 358. Acc. are AMg. Ś. *acchiṁ* (Āyār. 1, 1, 2, 5; Śak. 31, 13); *aṭṭhiṁ*=*asthi* (Sūyag. 594); AMg. *dahiṁ* (Āyār. 2, 1, 4, 5; Ovav. § 73; Kappas. S. § 17); AMg. Ś. *mahuṁ* (Āyār. 2, 1, 4. 5. 8, 8; Ovav. § 73; Kappas. S. § 17; Śak. 81, 8); JŚ. *vatthuṁ* (Kattig. 400. 335). The very frequent Skt. *svasti* always becomes *sŏtthi* in Ś. (e.g. Mṛcch. 6,23; 25, 4; 54, 11. 19; Vikr. 15, 16; 29, 1; 44, 5; Ratn. 296, 32; 319, 17 etc.), and therefore, it is to be considered as a nom. in the same manner as *sāhu* (e. g. Mṛcch. 28, 24; 37, 16; 41, 19; Vikr. 26, 6; Ratn. 300, 13; 309, 1) and *suṭṭhu* (e. g. Mṛcch. 27, 21; 28, 24; 29, 14; 41, 18; Prab. 18, 3), Mg. *śāhu* (Veṇīs. 34, 3. 23; 35, 14; Mṛcch. 38, 7; 112, 9, 161, 15 etc.). Against this we should read *lahuṁ*, with edns. Calc. and GOḌABOLE for *lahu* (Mṛcch. 75, 8; Vikr. 28, 10) as stands in Śak. 39, 3; 76, 1; Mṛcch. 21, 13; 59, 8; 107, 11; 112, 11; 116, 5; 166, 16; 169. 24; Ratn. 300, 5; 302, 25; 303, 20; 312, 8; 320, 32 etc.; in the verse *lahu* is correct (Mṛcch. 99, 24; Veṇīs. 33, 13). — With regard to the ins. it is to be noted that M. *païṇā*=*patyā*, forms as one says M. *gahavaïṇā* (H. 172), AMg. *gāhāvaïṇā* (Uvās. § 6)=*gṛhapatinā*, Mg. *bahiṇipadiṇā*=*bhaginipatinā* (Mṛcch. 113, 19). From *akṣi* the ins. is M. *acchiṇā*=*akṣṇā* (G. 32); from *dadhi* is found Ś. *sadahiṇā*=*sadadhnā* (Mṛcch. 69, 3). For the expected *aṭṭhiṇā*=*asthnā, muṭṭhiṇā*=*muṣṭinā, laluṇā*=*leṣṭuna* AMg. has *aṭṭhiṇa, muṭṭhiṇa, leḷūṇa*, with shortening of *ā* before the enclitic *vā* and lengthening of the final vowel of the stem on the analogy of the preceding and following ins. in *-ena* in the combination *daṇḍeṇa vā aṭṭhiṇa vā muṭṭhiṇa vā leḷūṇa vā kavāleṇa vā* (Āyār. 2, 1, 3, 4; Sūyag. 647. 692. 863). On similar cases of assimilation see § 355. 358. 364. 367. 375. 386, on the instr. *aggiṇa, aggiṁ, vāuṁ* in A. see § 146. — For the abl. the following have been located in the texts: M. *uahiu*=*udadheḥ* (G. 56, 470); AMg. *kucchio*=*kukṣeḥ* (Kappas. § 21.32); *dahia*=*dadhnaḥ* (Sūyag. 594; text °*hi*°); JŚ. *hiṁsāido*=*hiṁsādeḥ* (Pav. 386, 4; text °*ātido*); JM. *kammaggiṇo*=*karmāgneḥ* (Āv. 19, 16); AMg. *ikkhūo*=*ikṣoḥ* (Sūyag. 594; text °*to*); JM. *sūrihiṁto* (Kk. II, 509, 4); A. *girihĕ* (Hc. 4, 341, 1). — In the gen. in M. JM. AMg. the forms *aggiṇo*, therefore, the form of the neut. transported into Skt., but evidently from the *n*-stems, which often become identical with the *i*-stems (§ 405), and *aggissa*, therefore, the form built on the analogy of the *a*-stem, are current side by side; likewise in the case of the *u*-stems, in JŚ. too: M. *giriṇo* (G. 141) and M. AMg. *girissa* (G. 510; Sūyag. 312); M. *uahiṇo* (R. 5, 10) and *uahissa* (R. 4, 43. 60)=*udadheḥ*; M. *raviṇo* (G. 50. 272; H. 284) and *ravissa, raïssa* (R. 4, 30; Karp. 25, 13)=*raveḥ*; M. *païṇo* (H. 54. 55. 297) and *païssa* (H. 38. 200)=*patyuḥ*; M. *pasuvaïṇo*=*paśupateḥ* (H. 1), *paävaïṇo*=*prajāpateḥ* (H. 969), *bhuaṁgavaïṇo*=*bhujaṁgapateḥ* (G. 155); *ṇaravaïṇo*=*narapateḥ* (G. 413), but AMg. JM. *gāhāvaïssa*=*gṛhapateḥ* (Sūyag. 846; Vivāhap. 435 f.; 1207 ff.; Uvās. § 4. 6. 8. 11; Kappas. § 120; Āv. 7, 7); AMg. *muṇissa*=*muneḥ* (Āyār. 2, 16, 5; Sūyag. 132); *isissa*=*ṛṣeḥ* (Uttar. 363; Nirayāv. 51); *rāyarisissa*=*rājarṣeḥ* (Vivāhap. 915 f.; Nāyādh. 600. 605. 611. 613); *sārahissa*=*sāratheḥ* (Uttar. 668); *andhagavaṇhissa* (Antag. 3), and *andhagavaṇhiṇo* (Uttar. 678=Dasav. 613, 33)=*andhrakavṛṣṇeḥ*; *aggissa*

(Vivāhap. 909; Dasav. N., 654, 6; Nirayāv. 50); JM. *pañcālāhivaīṇo pañcālādhipateḥ* (Erz. 8, 8); *hariṇo* = *hareḥ* (Āv. 36, 30; 37, 49); *nābhissa* = *nābheḥ* (Āv. 48, 13.33). — M. *pahuṇo* (G. 847. 1006, 1065) and *pahussa* (H. 243) = *prabhoḥ*; AMg. *bhikkhuṇo* (Āyār. 1, 5, 4, 1; 2, 16, 8; Sūyag. 133. 144; Uttar. 284) and more frequently AMg. JŚ. *bhikkhussa* (Āyār. 1, 7, 5, 1 ff.; Pav. 387, 19); AMg. *usussa* = *iṣoḥ* (Vivāhap. 1388); *maccussa* = *mṛtyoḥ* (Paṇhāv. 401); *sāhussa* = *sādhoḥ* (Uttar. 418. 571); *vatthussa* = *vastunaḥ* (Paṇhāv. 398); JM. *bandhussa* = *bandhoḥ* (Sagara 8, 5); M. *viṇhuṇo* = *viṣṇoḥ* (G. 16); *caṇḍaṁsuṇo* = *caṇḍāṁśoḥ* (Karp. 35, 7); *ambuṇo* = *ambunaḥ* (G. 1196). In Ś. Mg. the form in -*ssa* is not used in prose : Ś. *rāesiṇo* = *rājarṣeḥ* (Śak. 21, 4; 50, 1; 130, 1; Vikr. 7, 2; 22, 16; 23, 14; 36, 8; 80, 4; Uttarar. 106, 10; 113, 1; Pras. 46, 9; Anarghar. 111. 13), *vihiṇo* = *vidheḥ* (Vikr. 52, 18; Mālatīm. 361, 10); *sahassarassiṇo* = *sahasraraśmeḥ* (Prab. 14, 17; Veṇīs. 25, 6); *paāvadiṇo* = *prajāpateḥ* (Ratn. 306, 2; Mālatīm. 65, 6); *udaraṁbhariṇo* = *udaraṁbhareḥ* (Jīvān. 43, 15); *dāsarahiṇo* = *dāśaratheḥ* (Mahāv. 52, 18; Anarghar. 157, 10); *guruṇo* = *guroḥ* (Śak. 22, 13; 158, 3; Vikr. 83, 1; Anarghar. 267, 12); *muhamahuṇo* = *mukhamadhoḥ* (Śak. 108, 1); *adhammabhīruṇo* = *adharmabhīroḥ* (Śak. 129, 10); *vikkamabāhuṇo* = *vikramabāhoḥ* (Ratn. 322, 33); *sattuṇo* = *śatroḥ* (Veṇīs. 62, 3; 95, 15; Jīvān. 19, 9); *pahuṇo* = *prabhoḥ* (Prab. 18, 1; Jīvān. 9, 1); *induṇo* = *indoḥ* (Jīvān. 19, 10); *mahuṇo* = *madhunaḥ* (Hāsy. 43, 23); Mg. *lāeśiṇo* = *rājarṣeh* (Veṇīs. 34, 1); *śattuṇo* = *śatroḥ* (Śak. 118, 2). In the verse stands Mg. *viśśāvaśuśśa* = *viśvāvasoḥ* (Mṛcch. 11, 9). The gen. M. *dahiṇo* (Karp. 15, 1) is from *dadhi*. On PG. see § 377. — In A. for the gen. we have to assume the same ending, as in the case of the *a*-stems, as for the abl., therefore *girihĕ*, *taruhĕ*. In the loc. in M. JM. JŚ. the ending is -*mmi*, in JM. -*ṁmi* too : M. *païmmi* = *patyau* (H. 324. 849); *jalahimmi* = *jaladhau*; *girimmi* = *girau*; *asimmi* = *asau* (G. 146. 153. 222); *uahimmi* = *udadhau*, *jalaṇihimmi* = *jalanidhau* (R. 2, 39; 7, 2. 7. 12; 5, 1); JM. *girimmi* = *girau* (KI. 17); *vihimmi* = *vidhau*, *uyahimmi* = *udadhau* (Sagara 7, 1; 9, 3). In AMg. the common form is that in -*ṁsi* : *kucchiṁsi* = *kukṣau* (Āyār. 2, 15, 2 ff.; Vivāhap. 1274; Kappas.); *pāṇiṁsi* = *pāṇau* (Āyār. 2, 1, 11, 5; 2, 7, 1, 5; Vivāhap. 1271; Kappas. S. 29); *rāsiṁsi* = *rāśau* (Āyār. 2, 1, 1, 2). Beside them are found in AMg. *taṁmi rāyarisiṁmi namiṁmi abhinikkhamantaṁmi* = *tasmin rājarṣau namāv abhiniṣkrāmati* (Uttar. 279); *acciṁmi*, *accimāliṁmi* (Vivāhap. 417); *agiṇimmi* (Dasav. 620, 24); more often *sahassarassiṁmi* (366a). Likewise with the *u*-stems : M. *pahummi* = *prabhau* (G. 210); *seummi* = *setau* (R. 8, 93); JM. *meruṁmi* = (T. 5, 3); JŚ. *sāhummi* = *sādhau* (Kattig. 399, 315; MS °*ha*°); AMg. *leluṁsi* = *leṣṭau* (Āyār. 2, 5, 1, 21); *bāhuṁsi*, *ūruṁsi* = *bāhau*, *ūrau* (Dasav. 617, 12); *uuṁmi* = *ṛtau* (Ṭhāṇ. 527; text *udu*°). Corresponding to *rāo* = *rātrau* (§ 386) AMg. has also *ghiṁsu* for **ghiṁso* = *ghraṁse* (§ 105; Sūyag. 249; Uttar. 58. 109) in verse. Mg. has in verse *kedummi* = *ketau* (Mudrār. 176, 4). Ś. has *vatthuṇi* = *vastuni* (Bālar. 122, 11; Dhūrtas. 9, 10). According to Mk. fol. 69 in Ś. the correct forms are *aggimmi* and *vāummi*. — In A. the ending of loc. is -*hĩ* = -*ṣmin* : *kalihĩ* = *kalau*; *akkhihĩ* = *akṣṇi*; *saṁdhihĩ* = *saṁdhau* (Hc. 4, 341, 3. 357, 2. 430, 3), *āihĩ* = *ādau* (Piṅgala 1, 85. 142).

For the *u*-stems the examples are wanting; Hc. 4, 341 teaches *-hi* for *i*- and *u*-stems. — In the voc. beside a short vowel is found a long vowel too (§ 71); M. *gahavaï* (H. 297), but AMg. *gāhāvaī* (Āyār. 1, 7, 2, 2. 3, 3. 5, 2; 2, 3. 3, 16) = *gṛhapate*; AMg. *muṇī* = *mune* (Āyār. 1, 6, 1, 4; Uttar. 713. 714. 719); AMg. JM. *mahāmuṇī* (Sūyag. 419; Kk. II, 505, 25); AMg. *maharisī* = *maharṣe* (Sūyag. 182); AMg. *subuddhī* = *subuddhe* (Nāyādh. 997, 998. 1003); AMg. *jambū* = *jambo* (Uvās.; Nāyādh. and often). Vr. 5, 27 forbids the long, and so mostly even the short vowel only is found : M. *khavia-sarvvari* = *kṣapitaśarvarika*, *diṇavaï* = *īdinapate* (H. 655); M. *pavaṁgavaī* = *plavaṅgapate* (R. 8, 19); JM. *pāvavihi* = *pāpavidhe* (Sagara 7, 15); JM. *suravaï* = *surapate* (Kk. 276, 19); AMg. *muṇi* (Sūyag. 259); AMg. *bhikkhu* = *bhikṣo* (Sūyag. 245. 301); M. JM. *pahu* = *prabho* (G. 717. 719. 736; R. 15, 90; Kk. 269, 35); Ś. *rāesi* = *rājarṣe* (Uttarar. 125, 8). Ś. *jaḍāo* = *jaṭāyo* (Uttarar. 70, 5) is probably a wrong reading.

§ 380. In the nom. plur. the forms *aggiṇo* and *aggī*, *vāuṇo* and *vāū* go side by side in M. JM. AMg. : M. *kaïṇo* = *kavayaḥ* (G. 62) and *kaī* = *kapayaḥ* (R. 6, 59. 83); *giriṇo* (G. 114) and *girī* (G. 450; R. 6, 34. 60) = *girayaḥ*; *riuṇo* (G. 1195) and *riū* (G. 245. 721) = *ripavaḥ*; *pahuṇo* (G. 858. 861. 873. 880. 894) and *pahū* (G. 868) = *prabhavaḥ*; AMg. *amuṇī* beside *muṇiṇo* = *amunayaḥ*, *munayaḥ* (Āyār. 1, 3, 1, 1); *giyaraïṇo* = *gitaratayaḥ* beside *giyanaccaṇaraï* = *gitanṛtyaratayaḥ* (Ovav. § 35); *ṇāṇārui* = *nānārucayaḥ* (Sūyag. 781); *isiṇo* = *ṛṣayaḥ* beside *muṇī* = *munayaḥ* (Uttar. 367); *haya-m-āi goṇa-m-āi gaya-m-āi siha-m-āiṇo* (§ 353; Uttar. 1075); *vinnū* = *vijñāḥ* (§ 105; Āyār. 1, 4, 3, 1); *gurū* = *guravaḥ* (Āyār. 1, 5, 1, 1); *pasū* = *paśavaḥ* (Āyār. 2, 3, 3, 3); *apasū* (Sūyag. 601); *uū* = *ṛtavaḥ* (Samav. 97; Vivāhap. 798; Aṇuog. 432); *dhāuṇo* = *dhātavaḥ* (Sūyag. 37); JM. *sūriṇo* = *sūrayaḥ* (Kk. 264, 41; 267, 41; 270, 6. 36. 42 etc.); *sāhuṇo* = *sādhavaḥ* (Āv. 9, 22; 26, 36; 27, 7; 46, 3. 9; Kk. 274, 36) and *sāhū* (T. 4, 20); *guruṇo* = *guravaḥ* (Kk. 271, 6; 274, 28. 36). In AMg. prevalent is the form in *-ī*, *-ū*, which is found perhaps exclusively in certain words, such as *ūrū* (Uvās. § 94; Sūyag. 639 and often; also in M. G. 489), provided that one could see in them something like the old dual, likewise, a few cases as in AMg. *pāṇī* (Kappas. S. § 43), AMg. *indaggī* = *indrāgnī* (Ṭhāṇ. 82), AMg. *do vāū* = *dvau vāyū* (Ṭhāṇ. 82), M. *bāhū* = *bāhū* (G. 428). The forms other than those quoted are found just sporadically in the three dialects. Thus : AMg. *nāyao* = *jñātayaḥ* (Sūyag. 174. 179. 628. 635), *anāyao* (Sūyag. 628); AMg. *rāgaddesādayo* = *rāgadveṣādayaḥ* (Uttar. 707); JM. *bhavadattādayo* (Erz. 17, 28); AMg. *risao* = *ṛṣayaḥ* (Ovav. § 56, p. 61, 29); JM. *maharisao* (Erz. 3, 14); AMg. °*ppabhiyao* = *-prabhṛtayaḥ* (Ovav. § 38, p. 49, 32; 73 so to be read; cf. v. l.); AMg. *jantavo* (verse ! Āyār. 1, 6, 1, 4; Uttar. 712. 798. 799; Sūyag. 105) beside *jantuṇo* (Āyār. 2, 16, 1); AMg. *sāhavo* = *sādhavaḥ* (Uttar. 208). From *bahu* (many) the nom. in AMg. is always formed as *bahave* (§ 345; Āyār. 1, 8, 3, 3. 5. 10; 2, 1, 4, 1. 2; 2, 5, 2, 7, 2, 15, 8; Sūyag. 852 916; Uttar. 158. 169; Uvās.; Nāyādh.; Kappas. etc.). So also in JM. (Erz. 17, 28), probably wrongly for *bahavo* (Erz. 38, 24) or *bahū* (Erz. 38, 21). In Ś. the forms in *-i*, *-ū*, that are formed according to the nom. of the *a*-stems, are not used. The *i*-stems, like the feminine, partly have the nom. in *-io*, as *isio* = *ṛṣayaḥ*, *gírio* = *girayaḥ* (Śak. 61, 11; 98, 8; 99, 12; 126, 15); *risio* = *ṛṣayaḥ* (Mṛcch. 326, 14), partly in *-ṇo*, as *kaïṇo* = *kapayaḥ* (Bālar. 238, 5); *mahesiṇo* = *maharṣayaḥ* (Bālar. 268. 1); *isiṇo* = *ṛṣayaḥ* (Unmattar. 3, 7); *cintāmaṇipahudiṇo* = *cintāmaṇiprabhṛtayaḥ* (Jīvān. 95, 1). In the case of the *u*-stems in Ś., beside the forms in *-ṇo*, as *paṅguṇo* = *paṅgavaḥ* (Jīvān. 87, 13); *bālataruṇo* = *bālataravaḥ* (Karp. 62, 3); *taruṇo* (Karp. 67, 1); *binduṇo* (Mallikām. 83, 15) occurs also the form *bindao* = *bindavaḥ* (Mṛcch. 74, 21). *bandhū* = *bandhavaḥ* (Śak. 101, 13) is not Ś., but M. only *dihagomāo* from **dihagomāao* (§ 165) = *dīrghagomāyavaḥ* can be located in a verse in Mg. (Mṛcch. 168, 20); otherwise examples for *i*- and *u*- are almost wanting.

§ 381. According to Vr. 5, 14, in the acc. only the forms *aggiṇo* and *vāuṇo* are permissible. But dialectically almost all the forms of the nom. are found in the acc. too : M. *païṇo* = *patin* (H. 705); JM. *sūriṇo* = *sūrin* (Kk. 267, 38; 270, 2); AMg. *mahesiṇo* = *maharṣin* (Āyār. 1, 5, 5, 1); but also AMg. *mittanāī* = *mitrajñātin* (Uvās. § 69. 92; so to be read for °*ṇāiṁ*) ; *mallaī*, *lĕcchaī* = *mallakin*, *licchavīn* (Vivāhap. 499 f.; Nirayāv. § 25); *nāyao* = *jñātīn* (Āyār. 1, 6, 4, 3; Sūyag. 378 [text *ṇāio*]); AMg. *pasavo* = *paśūn* (Sūyag. 414); JM. *guruṇo* = *gurūn* (Kk. 269, 35); JM. *sāhuṇo* = *sādhūn* (Kk. 271, 15); AMg. *bāhū* = *bāhū* (Sūyag. 222. 286); AMg. *sattū* = *śatrūn* (Kappas. § 114); AMg. *bahū* = *bahūn* (Āyār. 1, 6, 1, 4; Uttar. 216), beside *bahave*, as in the nom. (Āyār. 2, 2, 2, 8. 9; Uvās. § 119, 184), in addition to *vasudhādhipataye* of PG. — Examples of the neuter, of which the nom. and acc. are identical are : M. *acchīiṁ* = *akṣiṇi* (Hc. 1, 33; 2, 217; G. 44; H. 40, 54), *acchīĩ* (H. 314); M. AMg. JM. *acchiṇi* (H. 314 in Mk. fol. 44; cf. v. l. ; Āyār. 2, 2, 1, 7; Uvās. § 94; Āv. 8, 20; 30, 4); AMg. *acchi* (Vivāgas. 11), falsely in Ś. too (Jīvān 89, 3) AMg. *aṭṭhiṇi* = *asthīni* (Sūyag. 590); AMg. *sāliṇi* = *śālīn* (Āyār. 2, 10, 10); *vihiṇi* = *vrihīn* (Āyār. 2, 10, 10; Sūyag. 682); *dariṇi* = *dariḥ* (Āyār. 2, 10, 11); JM. *āiṇi* = *ādini* (Kk. 274, 4); JŚ. *ādiṇi* (Pav. 384, 48); M. *aṁsūiṁ* = *aśrūṇi* (G. 130. 1208); *paṇḍūĩ* = *paṇḍūni* (G. 384. 577) and *paṇḍūiṁ* (G. 462); *bindūiṁ* = *bindūn* (G. 223); AMg. *maṁsūiṁ* = *śmaśrūṇi* (Uvās. § 94); *maṁsūṇi* (Āyār. 1, 8, 3, 11); *dārūṇi* (Sūyag. 247); *pāṇūṇi* = *prāṇān* (Aṇuog. 432; Vivāhap. 423); *kaṅgūṇi* = *kaṅgavaḥ* (Sūyag. 682); *milakkhūṇi* = **mlaicchānı* (Āyār. 2, 3, 1, 8); A. *aṁsū* (Piṅgala 1, 61). According to Vr. 5, 26 only the forms like *dahīi*, *mahūi* would be usable; Kī. 3, 28 teaches *dahīiṁ*. — For the endings of the ins. gen. loc. § 178. 350 hold good; cf. § 368. 370. 371 also. Examples for the ins. are : M. *haīhĩ*, °*hi* = *kavibhiḥ* (G. 84. 88) and = *kapibhiḥ* (R. 6, 64. 78. 94); AMg. *kimīhiṁ* = *kṛmıbhiḥ* (Sūyag. 278); JM. *āihiṁ* = *ādibhiḥ* (Āv. 7, 12); Ś. *isihiṁ* = *ṛṣibhiḥ* (Śak. 70, 6); Mg. °*ppahudihiṁ* = °*prabhṛtibhiḥ* (Śak. 114,2); M. *acchihiṁ*, °*hĩ*, °*hi* (H. 338.341.457. 502); Ś. *acchihiṁ* (Vikr. 48,15; Ratn. 319,18) ; Mg. *akkhihiṁ* (Mṛcch. 120, 13; 152,22) = *akṣibhyām* M. *riūhiṁ* = *ripubhiḥ* (H. 471; G. 718); M. *sisūhĩ* = *śiśubhiḥ* (G. 1046); AMg. *vaggūhiṁ* = *vagnubhiḥ* (Vivāhap. 946; Nāyādh. § 25. 79; p. 302. 736.757. 1107; Rāyap. 266 f.; Uttar. 300; Ṭhāṇ. 527; Ovav. § 53. 181; Kappas.) ; AMg. *ūrūhiṁ* = *ūrubhyām* (Ṭhāṇ. 401); Ś. *gurūhiṁ* = *gurubhiḥ*

(Hāsy. 40,17); Ś. *bindūhiṁ* = *bindubhiḥ* (Veṇīs. 66,21; Nāgān. 24,13; Karp. 72,1). — The abl. occurs in M. *acchihiṁto* = *akṣibhyām* (G. 223); JM. *ujjāṇāiṁto* = *udyānādibhyaḥ* (Dvār. 498.20); AMg. *kāmiḍḍhihiṁto* = *kāmarddheḥ* (honorific plural; Kappas.; Ṭh. § 11). As in the case of the *a*-stems (§ 369), so in the case of *i*- and *u*- stems too, the ins. is used as the abl. : *santi egehiṁ bhikkūhiṁ gāratthā saṁjamuttarā* = *santy ekebhyo bhikṣubhyo gṛhasthāḥ saṁyamottarāḥ* (Uttar. 208). — A. *taruhũ* = *tarubhyaḥ* (Hc. 4,341) is properly = *taruṣu*, that is to say = the loc., with which the ablative has become identical, according to Hc 4,340 the gen. too; yet it will be better to consider *taruhũ* as in the loc., whilst *bihũ* = *dvayoḥ* (Hc. 4,383,1), by all means, stands in the sense of the gen. — Examples for the genitive are : M. *kaiṇaṁ* = *kavinām* (H. 86); *kaiṇa* = *kapinām* (R. 6,84); *giriṇa* (G. 137. 449; R. 6,81); AMg. *dhammasārahiṇaṁ* = *dharmasārathinām* (Ovav. § 20; Kappas. § 16); metrically *isiṇa* = *ṛṣiṇām* (Sūyag. 317) and *isiṇaṁ* (Uttar. 375. 377); *udahiṇa* = *udadhinām* (Sūyag. 316); *vihiṇaṁ* = *vrihiṇām* (Vivāhap. 421); JŚ. *jadiṇaṁ* = *yatinām* (Pav. 385,63); *āiṇaṁ* = *ādinām* (Kattig. 401,340); Ś. *mahivadiṇaṁ* = *mahipatinām* (Lalitav. 555,14); Ś. *acchiṇaṁ* = *akṣṇoḥ* (Vikr. 43,15; Nāgān. 11.9); M. *icchūṇaṁ* = *ikṣūṇām* (H. 740); *riūṇa* = *ripūṇām* (G. 106. 166.237); *tarūṇa* = *tarūṇām* (G. 140); AMg. *bhikkhūṇaṁ* = *bhikṣūṇām* (Āyār. 1,7,7, 2); *savvaṇṇūṇaṁ* = *sarvajñānām* (Ovav. § 20); *milakkhūṇaṁ* = *mlecchānām* (Suyag. 817); Mg. *bāhūṇa* = *bāhvoḥ* (in the verse; Mṛcch. 129,2); *pahūṇaṁ* = *prabhūṇām* (Kaṁsav. 50,4); JŚ. *sāhūṇaṁ* = *sādhūnām* (Pav. 379,4). A. has the ending -*hã* = -*sām* of the pronoun : *saüṇihã* = *śakuninām* (Hc. 4,340); on -*hũ* see above. — The loc., for example is found as M. *girisu* (G. 138); M. AMg. *acchisu* (H, 132; Āyār. 2, 3,2,5); Ś. *acchisuṁ* (Śak. 30,5); M. *riūsu* = *ripuṣu* (G. 241); JŚ. metrically *ādisu* = *ādiṣu* (Pav. 383,69); AMg. *uūsu* = *ṛtuṣu* (Nāyādh. 344); Ś. *ūrūsu* = *ūrvoḥ* (Bālar. 238,7; text °*ru*°). In A. the form *duhũ* corresponds to one **duṣu* (femin.; Hc. 4,340), whilst *tihĩ* (Hc. 4,347), properly is = *tribhiḥ*, therefore = the instr., as in the case of the *a*- stems (§ 371). — The voc. occurs in JM. *sayalaguṇanihiṇo* = *sakalaguṇanidhayaḥ* (Sagara 7,12); AMg. *jantavo* (Sūyag. 335.424), *bhikkhavo* (Sūyag. 157; text °*kkhu*°). For JM. *guruo* (Kk. III, 513,22) should be read *gurūo*. On A. see § 372.

§ 382. In AMg. the forms of the plur. of *bahu* (much) that are valid for the masculine are mostly used for the feminine too : *bahave pāṇajāi* = *bahvyaḥ prāṇajātayaḥ* (Āyār. 1,8,1,2); *bahave sāhammiṇio* = *bahviḥ* **sādharmiṇiḥ* (Āyār. 2,1,1,11; 2,2,1,2, 2,5,1,2; 2,10,2); *bahave devā ya devio ya* (Āyār. 2,15,8); *bahave khuḍḍākhuḍḍiyāo vāvio* = *bahvyaḥ kṣudrākṣudrikā vāpyaḥ* (Jīv. 476); *bahūṇaṁ samaṇāṇaṁ bahūṇaṁ samaṇiṇaṁ bahūṇaṁ sāvayāṇaṁ bahūṇaṁ sāviyāṇaṁ bahūṇaṁ devāṇaṁ bahūṇaṁ devīṇaṁ* (Kappas. S. § 64; Nāyādh. 498.518, 615.654; Vivāhap. 242); *bahūhiṁ āghavaṇāhi ya paṇṇāvaṇāhi ya viṇṇavaṇāhi ya saṇṇavaṇāhi ya* = *bahvibhir* **ākhyāpanābhiś ca* **prajñāpanābhiś ca* **vijñāpanābhiś ca* **saṁjñāpanābhiś ca* (Nāyādh. § 143; p. 539.889; Uvās. § 222; Vivāhap. 814); *bahūhiṁ khujjāhiṁ* = *bahvibhiḥ kubjābhiḥ* (Nirayāv. § 4; Vivāhap. 791; Nāyādh. § 117; p. 832.837; Vivāgas. 226; *bahūsu vāvisu* = *bahviṣu vāpiṣu* (Nāyādh. 915); *bahūsu vijjāharisu* = *bahviṣu vidyā*-

dhariṣu (Nāyādh. 1275; so the commentary; text *bahusu vijjāsu*). Cf. also Ovav. § 8. On the available Skt. forms like *girisu*, *vagguhiṁ* see § 99; on the going of the *a*-stems over into the *u*-declension in M. AMg. see § 105, on AMg. *sakahāo* = *sakthini* § 358.

§ 383. The masculine in -*ī* and -*ū* shorten their *ī* and *ū* according to Hc. 3,43; Mk. fol. 42. 43; Sr. fol. 12 and are declined wholly like the nouns in -*i*, -*u*. So nom. *gāmaṇi* = *grāmaṇīḥ*; acc. *gāmaṇiṁ*; ins. *gāmaṇiṇā* gen. *gāmaṇiṇo* and *gāmaṇissa*; voc. *gāmaṇi*; nom. *khalapū* = *khalapūḥ*; acc. *khalapuṁ*; ins. *khalapuṇā*; *gen. khalapuṇo*; voc. *khalapu* (Hc. 3,24. 42. 43. 124). Sr. adds the nom. plur.: *khaḷavaü*, *khalavao*, *khaḷavuṇo*, *khaḷavū*. Examples are : M. *gāmaṇi gāmaṇiṇo* = *grāmaṇīḥ*, *grāmaṇyaḥ* (H. 449.633); *gāmaṇiṇaṁ* (R. 7,60); JM. *asogasiri*, *asogasiriṇo* = *aśokaśrīḥ aśokaśriyaḥ* (Āv. 8,2. 32); S. *candasiriṇo*, *candasiriṇā* = *candraśriyaḥ candraśriyā* (Mudrār. 39, 3; 56,8; 227,2.7); Ś. *māhavasiriṇo* = *mādhavaśriyaḥ* (Mālatīm. 211,1); S. *aggaṇi* = *agraṇīḥ*. (Mṛcch 4,23; 327,1). The forms *saaṁbhuṁ*, *saaṁbhuṇo* = *svayaṁbhuvam*, *svayaṁbhuvaḥ* (G. 1.813), *saaṁbhuṇo*, *saaṁbhussa*, *saaṁbhuṇā* (Mk. fol. 42 f.) may be derived from *svayaṁbhū* or from °*bhu*.

b) FEMININE

§ 384. In Pkt, the feminine forms in -*i*, -*u*, as *bhūmisu*, *suttisu*, (§ 99) are retained only in some passages in verses. Otherwise the feminine in -*i*, -*u*, with which those in -*ī* and -*ū* have become identical, without any differentiation between words of one and more syllables. The declension exactly corresponds to that of the feminine in -*ā* in § 374ff., and this thing holds good for all the endings, as already noted there. In isolated cases we have to keep in view what follows.

§ 385. The grammarians give, for the ins. abl. gen. loc. sing. the forms : *ṇaï*, *ṇaie*, *ṇaia*, *ṇaiā* from *ṇai* = *nadī* (Bh. 5,22; Kī. 3,26; Mk. fol. 43); *ruia*, *ruiā*, *ruii*, *ruie* from *rui* = *ruci* (Sr. fol. 15); *buddhia*, *buddhiā*, *buddhii*, *buddhie* from *buddhi*; *sahia*, *sahiā*, *sahii*, *sahie* from *sahi* = *sakhi*; *dheṇūa*, *dheṇūā*, *dheṇūi*, *dheṇūe* from *dheṇu* = *dhenu*; *vahūa*, *vahūā*, *vahūi*, *vahūe* from *vahū* = *vadhū* (Hc. 3, 29). Of these, the forms in -*iā*, -*ūā* are not available, and those in -*ii* -*ūi* are rare in the texts : M. *ṇaii* = *natyāḥ* (G. 1000); AMg. *mahii* = *mahyāḥ* (Sūyag. 312), more often correctly in the v. l. for -*iĕ* of the texts, as G. 139.860. 922. For *gabbhiṇii* = *garbhiṇyāḥ*, now WEBER H. 166 correctly reads *gabhiṇia*. In all cases, where the forms in -*ie*, -*ūe* stand in the text, and the metre requires a short, as *mahiĕ*, *siriĕ*, *tajjaṇiĕ*, *pavittharaṇiĕ*, *ṇaariĕ*, *ṇivasiriĕ*, *lacchiĕ* etc. (G. 122.212. 247.268. 501.928); *vahūĕ* (H. 874.981), the forms in -*ia* or in -*ii*, *ūa* or in -*ūi* are to be put, as WEBER H. 69 has corrected -*ia*, which is attested for all the examples collected by him at p. 40 in Hāla[1] by the manuscripts. At H. 86, there is found the v. l. *hasaṁtii* beside *hasaṁtia*, *hasaṁtie* (cf. IS. 16,53 too). For *vahūĕ* (H. 874, 981) the old Śāradā manuscripts of Kāvyaprakāśa give the v. l. at 874 *vahūo*, *vahūa*, at 981 *bahūi*, *bahūi*. We have, therefore, to write *vahūa* or *vahūi*, as also H. 786. 840.874; *vahūa* stands in H. 457. 608.635.648, everywhere with the v. l *vahūe* or *bahūe*. Cf. § 375.

The forms in *-ia*, *-ūa* are, likewise those in *-ii*, *-ūi*, confined to verses, but with the stems in *-i*, *-ī* in M. very frequently : ins. *bandīa* = *bandyā*; *vāhia* = *vyādhyā*; *laliaṅgulia* = *lalitāṅgulyā* (H. 118. 121. 458); *āhiāiā* = *abhijātyā*; *rāasiria* = *rājaśriyā*; *diṭṭhia* = *dṛṣṭyā*; *ṭhiia* = *sthityā*; *jāṇaia* = *jānakyā* (R. 1,11.13. 45; 4,43; 6,6); *sippia* = *śuktyā*; *muṭṭhia* = *muṣṭyā*; *devīa* = *devyā* (Karp. 2,4; 29,4; 48,14); gen. *koḍia* = *koṭeḥ*; *ghariṇia* = *gṛhiṇyāḥ*; *giriṇaia* = *girinadyāḥ* (H. 3,11. 14.37); *dhaṇariddhia siria a saliluppaṇṇāi vāruṇia a* = *dhanarddhyāḥ śriyaś ca salilotpannāyā vāruṇyāś ca* (R. 2, 17); *dharaṇia* = *dharaṇyāḥ* (R. 2,2; 7,28); *sarassaia* = *sarasvatyāḥ*; *rūḍhia* = *rūḍheḥ* (Karp. 1,1; 51,3); L. *pāṇaüḍia* = *prāṇakuṭyām* (H. 227; on the meaning cf. Pāiyal. 105 with Deśīn. 6,38); D. *ṇaaria* = *nagaryām* (Mṛcch. 100,2). For the ablative examples are wanting. The usual forms in all the dialects, except A., that C. 1,9 alone knows, are those in *-ie*, *-ūe*, which, however, are not found in the abl. So ins. M. *bhaṇantie* = *bhaṇantyā* (H. 123); AMg. *gaie*, Ś. *gadie* = *gatyā* (Kappas. § 5; Śak. 72,11); Mg. *śattie* = *śaktyā* (Mṛcch. 29,20); P. *bhagavatie* = *bhagavatyā* (Hc. 4,323); gen. *lacchie* = *lakṣmyāḥ* (G. 68); AMg. *nāgasirie māhaṇie* = *nāgaśriyā brāhmaṇyāḥ* (Nāyādh. 1151); Ś. *radaṇāvalie* = *ratnāvalyāḥ* (Mṛcch. 88,21); Mg. *majjālie* = *mārjāryāḥ* (Mṛcch. 17,7); loc. *paavie* = *padavyām* (H. 107); AMg. *vāṇārasie ṇayarie* = *vārāṇasyāṁ nagaryām* (Antag. 63; Nirayāv. 43. 45; Vivāgas. 136. 148. 149; Vivāhap. 284 ff.; Nāyādh. 1516. 1528). AMg. JM. *aḍavie* = *aṭavyām* (Nāyādh. 1137; Erz. 1,4; 13,30; 21,21); S. *masāṇavidhie* = *śmaśānavithyām* (Mṛcch. 72,8); Mg. *dhalaṇie* = *dharaṇyām* (Mṛcch. 173,16). The form is found to have been shortened to *-iĕ* in A. too : ins. *maragaakantiĕ* = *marakatakāntyā*; gen. *gaṇantiĕ* = *gaṇantyāḥ*; *radiĕ* = *ratyāḥ* (Hc. 4,349. 333. 446).

§ 386. In the ins., *diṭṭhiā* = *diṣṭyā* (e.g. Mṛcch. 68,2; 74,11; Vikr. 10,20; 26,15; 49,4 etc.) used adverbially, Ś. has retained an old ins. in *-ā*. In the A. of Piṅgala, more than once, we find an ins. in *-i* ; *kitti* = *kīrtyā* (1,65ᵃ;2,66); *bhatti* = *bhaktyā* (2,67), and so is also *eavisattii* for °*ttā* (S. GOLDSCHMIDT, °*tti*) = *ekaviṁśatyā* to be read at 1,142. — On the dative in *-ie* in AMg. JM.Ś. see § 361. — The abl., except in A., where, according to Hc. 4,350, like the gen., it ends in *-hĕ*, has the endings *-io*, *-ūo*, JŚ.S.Mg. *-ido*, *-ūdo* : AMg. *araïraio* = *aratirateḥ* (Sūyag. 654; Ovav. § 123); *kosio* = *kośyāḥ* (Sūyag. 593); *nayario* = *nagaryāḥ* (Nirayāv. § 19; p. 44.45; Nāyādh. 1135); *pŏkkhariṇio* = *puṣkariṇyāḥ*; *corapallio* = *corapallyāḥ* (Nāyādh. 1060.1427.1429); *gaṅgāsindhūo* = *gaṅgāsindhoḥ* (Ṭhāṇ. 544; Vivāhap. 482 f.) Ś. : *aḍaido* = *aṭavyāḥ* (Śak.35.8); *ujjaiṇido* = *ujjayinyāḥ* (Ratn. 321,22;, 322,9); *sacido* = *śacyāḥ* (Vikr. 44,8); Mg. *ṇaalido* = *nagaryāḥ* (Mṛcch. 159, 13) — The gen. has in A., as in the case of *a*-stems (§ 375), the ending *-hĕ*, before which the vowel is shortened : *joantihĕ* = *paśyantyāḥ*; *mĕllantihĕ* = *muñcantyāḥ*; *gorihĕ* = *gauryāḥ*; *tumbiṇihĕ* = *tumbinyāḥ* (Hc. 4,332,2. 370,4. 395,1. 427,1); *kaṅguhĕ* = *kaṅgoḥ* (Hc, 4,367,4). — In the loc. in AMg. we find frequently *rāo* = *rātrau* likewise alone (Āyār. 1,8,2,6; Sūyag. 247.255. 519; Nāyādh. 302.374), and in the combination *aho ya rāo* (Āyār. 1,1,2,1. 2,2; 1,4,1,3; Sūyag. 295. 412. 485; Uttar. 430), or in *aho ya rāo ya* = *ahaś ca* *rātrau ca* (Paṇhāv. 373), *rāo vā viẏāle vā* (Āẏār. 2,1,3,2; 2,2,3,2.23 [so correctly ed. Calc. p. 126], *diẏā ẏa rāo ẏa* = *divā ca rātrau ca* (Āẏār. 1,6,3,3. 4,1; Uttar. 847), *diẏā vā rāo vā* (Sūẏag. 846; Dasav. 616,13). Sometimes in AMg. the ending of the masc. and neutr. is extended over to to the feminine : *piṭṭhiṁsi* becomes *piṭṭhi* (§ 53; Nāẏādh. 940); *bhittiṁsi* = *bhittau* (Āẏār. 2,5,1,21); *rāẏahāṇiṁsi* = *rājadhānyām* (Āẏār. 2,1,2,6; 2,1,3,4: 2,3,1,2) between pure loc. in -*ṁsi* of the masc. and the neutr. Cf. § 355.358. 364. 367. 375.379. Ś. has *rattimmi* = *rātrau* (Jīvān. 9,23; 17,23; Mallikām. 226,4); *bhūmimmi* = *bhūmau* (Mallikām. 337,21). In A. the loc. ends in -*hĩ* = -*ṣyām*; *mahihĩ* = *mahyām*; *riddhihĩ* = *ṛddhau*; *sallaïhĩ* = *śallakyām*; *vāṇārasihĩ* = *vārāṇasyām*; *ujjeṇihĩ* = *ujjayinyām* (Hc. 4,352.418,8.422,9.442,1); *ṇadihĩ* = *nadyām* (Piṅgala 1,5[a]), in the A. of Piṅgala, in the case of the *i*- stems, also in -*ĩ* : -*i* and shortened -*i* : of stems in *puhavī* = *pṛthivyām* (1,121; text °*ni*) *dharaṇi* = *dharaṇyām* (1,137[a]); *puhavi* = *pṛthivyām* (1, 132[a]); *mahi* = *mahyām*; (1, 143[a]). — The vocative ends in -*i*, -*u* : M. *māhavi* = *mādhavi*; *bhaïravi* = *bhiravi*; *devi* = *devi* (G. 285. 287. 290. 331); *thorattaṇi* = *sthūlastani* (H. 925); Ś. *bhaavadi bhāiradhi* = *bhagavati bhāgirathi* (Bālar. 163,10; Pras. 83,4); JM. Ś. *putti* = *putri* (Āv. 12,11. 17; Bālar. 165,3; 174,8); Ś. *sahi māladi*) = *sakhi mālati* (Mālatīm. 94,2); Mg. *vuḍḍhakusṭaṇi* = *vṛddhakuṭṭani* (Mṛcch. 141,25; 152,22); *kaccāiṇi* = *kātyāyani* (Caṇḍak. 69, 1); M. *vevantoru* = *vepamānoru* (H. 52); *suaṇu* = *sutanu* (G. 186; H.); *kariaroru* = *karikaroru* (H. 925); in Mg. with pluti *vāśū* (Mṛcch. 127,1).

§ 387. The nom. acc. voc. plur. end in -*io*, -*īo*, that alternate with -*iu*, -*īu* in verses : nom. M. *kattio* = *kṛttayaḥ* (H. 951); *riddhio* = *ṛddhayaḥ* (G. 92); *lumbio* = **lumbyaḥ* (H. 322); *ṇaio* = *nadyaḥ*; *ṇaario* = *nagaryaḥ* (G. 360. 403); AMg. *mahāṇaio* = *mahānadyaḥ* (Ṭhāṇ. 76. 77.79); *hiraṇṇa-koḍīo* = *hiraṇyakoṭyaḥ* (Uvās. § 4), *itthio* = *striyaḥ* (Ṭhāṇ. 121); M. *taruṇiu* = *taruṇyaḥ* (G. 113; H. 546); JM. *palavantio*. . *avarohajuvaio* = *pralapantyaḥ*. . . *avarodhayuvata-yaḥ* (Sagara 4,13); *vasahio* = *vasatayaḥ* (T. 4, 22); Ś. *gidio* = *gītayaḥ* (Mahāv. 121,7)); *mahuario* = *madhukaryaḥ* (Mṛcch. 29,5. 7; 70,2); *āidio* = *ākṛtayaḥ* (Śak. 132,6); . *païdio* = *prakṛtayaḥ* (Vikr. 73,12; Mudrār. 39,1; 56,8); A. *aṅguliu* = *aṅgulyaḥ* (Hc. 4,333), with a short vowel, as on metrical grounds in other dialects too (§ 99); M. *kulavahūo* = *kulavadhvaḥ* (H. 459); AMg. *suravadhūo* (Ovav. § [38]); *rajjūo* = *rajjavaḥ* (Jīv. 503). — Acc. M. *sahirio* = *sahanaśilāḥ* (H. 47); AMg. *vallio* = *vallīḥ* (Āẏār. 2,3,2,15); *osahio* = *oṣadhiḥ* (Āẏār. 2,4,2,16; Sūẏag. 727; Dasav. 628,33); *savattio* = *sapatnīḥ* (Uvās. § 239); *saẏagghio* = *śataghnīḥ* (Uttar. 285); JM. *goṇio* (Āv. 7,10); Ś. *bhaavadio* = *bhagavatīḥ* (Śak. 79,13); A. *vilāsiṇiu* = *vilāsinīḥ* (Hc. 4,348), and with *ī sallaīu* = *śallakīḥ* (Hc. 4,387,1), AMg. *bahūo coravijjāo* = *bahvīś coravidyāḥ* (Nāẏādh. 1421), but also *bahave sāhammiṇio* = *bahvīḥ* **sādhar-miṇīḥ* (§ 382). — Voc. JM. *bhaẏavaio devaẏāo* = *bhagavatyo devatāḥ* (Dvār. 503,25); M. Ś. *sahio* = *sakhyaḥ* (H. 131.619; Śak. 12,1; 90,8; Cait. 73,7; 83,12 etc.); Ś. *bhodio* = *bhavatyaḥ* (Viddhaś. 121,1); *bhaavadio* = *bhagavatyaḥ* (Uttarar. 197,10; Anarghar. 300,1); M. *sahiu* (H. 412. 743). In A. the voc. has the ending -*hõ* : *taruṇihõ* = *taruṇyaḥ* (Hc. 4,346). The forms in -*i*,

-ū, taught by Hc. 3,27, 124, are likewise found in the texts : nom. M. *asaï mha* = *asatyaḥ smaḥ* (H. 417); voc. M. *piasahī* = *priyasakhyaḥ* (H. 903); acc. AMg. *itthī* = *strīḥ* (Verse 1; Uttar. 253). For the remaining cases of the plur. a few examples will suffice. Ins. M. Ś. *sahīhiṁ* = *sakhībhiḥ* (H. 144; Śak. 167,9); M. *diṭṭhīhiṁ* (G. 752), *sahīhĩ*, *sahīhi* (H. 15. 60. 69. 810.840); JŚ. *dhūlīhiṁ* (Pav. 384,60); AMg. *cilāīhiṁ vāmaṇīhiṁ vaḍabhīhiṁ babbarīhiṁ. .damiḷīhiṁ siṁhalīhiṁ. .* = *kirātībhirvāmanībhir vaḍabhībhir barbarībhir draviḍībhiḥ siṁhalībhiḥ* (Ovav. § 55); Ś. *aṅgulīhiṁ* = *aṅgulībhiḥ* (Mṛcch. 6,7; Śak. 12,1). Āẏār. 1,2,4,3, without a v.l., has *thībhi* = *strībhiḥ*; A. *pupphavaīhi* = *puṣpavatībhiḥ* (Hc. 4,438,3) and with a shortened vowel : *asaïhĩ* = *asatībhiḥ*, *dĕntihĩ* = *dadatībhiḥ* (Hc. 4,396,1. 419,5). — Gen. M. *sahīṇa* = *sakhīnām* (H. 482); *thuīṇa* = *stutīnām* (G. 82); *taruṇīṇaṁ* (H. 545); cf. H. 174; AMg. *savattīṇaṁ* = *sapatnīnām* (Uvās. § 238. 239); M. Ś. *kāmiṇīṇaṁ* (H. 559; Mṛcch. 71,22); M. *vahūṇam* = *vadhūnām* (G. 1158; H. 526; R. 9, 71.93) and *vahūṇa* (R. 9,40. 96; 15,78). Loc. M. *rāīsu* = *rātriṣu* (H. 45); *giriaḍīsu* = *giritaṭīṣu* (G. 374); AMg. *itthīsu* = *strīṣu* (Āẏār. 2,16,7; Sūẏag. 405. 409); JM. *kujoṇīsu* = *kuyoniṣu* (Sagara 11, 4); M. AMg. *vāvīsu* = *vāpīṣu* (G. 166; Nāẏādh. 915); M. °*tthalīsuṁ* (G. 256) and °*tthalīsu* (G. 350. 421) = °*sthalīṣu*; Ś. *vaṇarāīsuṁ* = *vanarājiṣu* (Śak. 29.4; Uttarar. 22,13; text °*isu*); *devīsuṁ* (Śak. 141,9). In A. the loc. has become identical with the ins.: *disihĩ* = **diśīṣu*, *dikṣu*, but also *duhũ* = *dvayoḥ* (Hc. 4,340; cf. § 381).

§ 388. In PG. is found only the loc. sing. *āpiṭṭiyaṁ* (6,37) that is to say *āpiṭṭiyaṁ* = *āpiṭṭyām*, therefore, the form of Pāli. — If the feminine forms in *-i*, *-u*, *-ī*, *-ū* occur at the end of a compound, they naturally, as in Skt., take the endings of the masc. or those of the neuter, when they relate to a masc. or neuter. So M. *kareṇa va pañcaṅguliṇā* (G. 17); M. *sasialāsuttiṇā. . kavāleṇa* = *śaśikalāśuktinā. .kapālena* (G. 40); Ś. *mae mandabuddhiṇā* = *mayā mandabuddhinā* (Śak. 126, 10); Ś. *mohidamadiṇā* = *mohitamatinā*, *ṇidiṇiuṇabuddhiṇā* = *nītinipuṇabuddhinā* (Mudrār. 228,1; 269,3); Ś. *ujjumadiṇo* = *ṛjumateḥ* (Pras. 46,9). Mg. *musṭie* = *muṣṭinā* = *muṣṭāmuṣṭi*, really = *muṣṭyā muṣṭinā* (Mṛcch. 170,15) is also noticed.

3) Stems in *-ṛ*.

§ 389. The distinction, that Skt. makes between nomina agentis and words of relationship, has been maintained in Pkt. In the nom, acc. sing. and nom. plur., the forms identical with those of Skt. are retained. Otherwise, corresponding to the change of *ṛ* to *i* or *u* (§ 50ff), the stems in *-ṛ* have become *i-* or usually *u*-stems, or the stem of the acc. sing. is employed as new thema, according to the *a*-declension : *pii-*, *piu-*, *piara* = *pitṛ-*; *bhaṭṭi-*, *bhattu-*, *bhattāra-*. The feminina of the words of relationship too are declined as the *ā*-stems, to which the nom. sing. gave the impulse : *māā-*, *māi-*, *māū-*, *māarā-*. Hence the grammarians (Vr. 5,31 — 35; Hc. 3,44 — 48; Kī. 3,30 — 34; Mk. fol. 44; Sr. fol. 13.16.18) teach for the *ṛ*-stems, all the forms that are valid for the *a-*, circumstantial *ā-*, and *u*-stems, and it has not as yet been possible to get all of them authenticated. The forms that have been found in the texts provide with the following paradigms.

§ 390. Nomina agentis. — *bhattu* = *bhartṛ* (husband).

Singular.

Nom. *bhattā*; AMg. *bhattāre*, also JM. *bhattāro*.
Acc. *bhattāraṁ*; Mg. *bhattālaṁ*.
Gen. *bhattuṇo*, AMg. also *bhattārassa*.
Loc. JM. Ś. *bhattāre*.
Voc. *bhattā*.

Plural.

Nom. M. AMg. *bhattāro*; AMg. also *bhattā*.
Ins. AMg. *bhattārehiṁ*.
Loc. AMg. *bhattāresu*.
Voc. AMg. *bhattāro*.

In the meaning "master" *bhartṛ* has become an *i*-stem in Ś. (§ 55.289) and as such is declined in the oblique cases: Ś. nom. *bhaṭṭā* (Lalitav. 563, 23; Ratn. 293,32; 294,11 etc.); acc. *bhaṭṭāraṁ* (Mālav. 45.16; 59.3; 60,10); ins. *bhaṭṭiṇā* (Śak. 116, 12; 117, 11; Mālav. 6, 2.9; 8, 7); gen. *bhaṭṭiṇo* (Śak. 43,10; 117,7; Mālav. 6,22; 40,18; 41,9. 17; Mudrār. 54,2; 149,2); voc. *bhaṭṭā* (Ratn. 305,17. 23; Śak. 144,14), also in Ḍh. (Mṛcch. 34,11. 17). — Examples for individual cases are : nom. AMg. *ṇeẏā* = *netā* (Sūẏag. 519; text *ṇetā*); *kaṇṭhacchĕttā* (Uttar. 633); JM. *dāẏā* = *dātā* (Erz. 58,30); M. JM. Ś. *bhattā* (Karp. 43,4; Āv. 11,2; Erz.; Mṛcch. 4,4.5); JŚ. *ṇādā* = *jñātā*, *jhādā* = *dhyātā* (Pav. 382, 42; 386, 70), *kattā* = *kartā* (Pav. 384,36. 58.60); Ś. *sāsidā* = *śāsitā*, *dādā* = *dātā* (Kāleyak. 24,16; 25,22); Ś. *rakkhidā* = *rakṣitā* (Śak. 52,5; Mukund. 15,5); AMg. *udagadāẏāre* [text °*dātāro*] = *udakadātā* (Ovav. § 86); AMg. *bhattāre* (Nāẏādh. 1230); AMg. *uvadaṁsĕttāre* [text °*ro*] = *upadarśayitā* (Sūẏag. 593); JM. *bhattāro* = *bhattā* (Āv. 12,5. 12. 16. 17; Erz. 6,36; 85,22). — Acc. M. AMg. JM. Ś. *bhattāraṁ* (H. 390; Samav. 84; Erz.; Mālatīm. 240.2); Mg. *bhattālaṁ* (Veṇīs. 33,8); AMg. *udagadāẏāraṁ* = *udakadātāram* (Ovav. § 85); *pasatthāraṁ neẏāraṁ* = *praśāstāraṁ netāram* (Samav. 84); *satthāraṁ* = *śāstāram* (Āẏār. 1,6,4,1); AMg. JŚ. *kattāraṁ* = *kartāram* (Uttar. 412; Pav. 379,1). — Gen. M. JM.Ś. *bhattuṇo* (Karp. 7,1; Erz. 41,23; Śak. 81, 70; Vikr. 52,14; 82,6. 16; 88,14 etc.); AMg. *udagadāẏārassa* = *udakadātuḥ* (Ovav. § 85). — For the loc. Ś. *bhattari* (Śak. 109,10) we should, with the v. l. read *bhattāre*, that Hc. 3,45 teaches and JM. too has (Āv. 23,5). False are also the readings *bhaṭṭari* of the Kashmirian- (105,15), *bhattuṇi* of the Devanāgarī- and *bhattummi* of the Drāviḍian recensions (70,12 ed. Böhtl.; 248,6 ed. Madras). The mansuscripts of the Drāviḍian recension waver between *bhattummi*, *bhaṭṭari bhattari*, *bhattaṁmi*. — Voc. *bhattā*, see above. — Plural : nom. M. *soāro* = *śrotāraḥ*, (Vajjālagga 325,17); AMg. *pasatthāro* = *praśāstāraḥ* (Sūẏag. 585; Ovav. § 23.38); *uvavattāro* = *upapattāraḥ* (Sūẏag. 699. 766.771; Vivāhap. 179. 508.610; Ovav. § 56.69. ff.); *akkhāẏāro*, *āgantāro*, *ṇeẏāro* [text *ṇetāro*], *pannattāro* = *ākhyātāraḥ*, *āgantāraḥ*, *netāraḥ*, **prajñaptāraḥ* (Sūẏag. 81. 439. 470.603); AMg. *gantā* = *gantāraḥ* (Sūẏag. 150); *saviẏā* = *savitārau*, *taṭṭhā* = *tvaṣṭārau* (Ṭhāṇ. 82). To it belongs also AMg. *bhaẏantāro*, which, in Ovav. § 56 appears as *bhavantāro*[1], and is used as the nom. of the sing. too, (Āẏār. 2,1,11,11; 2,2,2,6 — 14; 2,5,2,3; Sūẏag. 562.766; Ovav. § 56.129) and the voc. (Āẏār. 2,1,4,5; Sūẏag. 239. 585.603. 630.635). Its meaning is = *bhavantaḥ* or *bhagavantaḥ*, by which the scholiasts inter alia reconstruct it, and it is derived directly from *bhavant*, the participle used as a pronoun, like the voc. *āusantāro* = *āyuṣmantaḥ* (Āẏār. 2,4,1,9; used as a sing.) from *āyuṣmant*. There is found also the gen. *bhaẏantārāṇaṁ* (Āẏār. 2,2,2,10; Sūẏag. 635). Ins. *dāẏārehiṁ* = *dātṛbhiḥ* (Kappas. § 112) — Loc. *āgantāresu* = *āgantṛṣu* (Āẏār. 2,7,1,2. 4. 5; 2,7,2,1. 7.8), *dāẏāresu* = *dātṛṣu* (Āẏār. 2,15,11.17). — The neutra are inflected, according to Sr. fol. 18 either on the pattern of the *a*-declension of the stem, e. g. *kattāra-*, or on the model of the *u*-declension of the stem, e.g. *kattu-*.

1. LEUMANN, Aup. S. s. v. considers the word as a contamination of the pres. part *bhavant* and the fut. part. *bhavitṛ*. — 2. The hypothesis of STEINTHAL (Specimen der Nāyādhammakahā p. 40), that the nomina agentis are wanting in Jaina-Prākṛt (i.e. AMg.), is wrong. AMg., on the contrary, is the single dialect, in which they are frequent.

§ 391. Words of relationship. — *piu* = *pitṛ*.

Singular.

Nom. *piā* [*piaro*]; Ś. Mg. *pidā*.
Acc. *piaraṁ*; AMg. JM. *piẏaraṁ*; Ś. *pidaram*; Mg. *pidalaṁ*.
Ins. *piuṇā* [*piareṇa*]; Ś. Mg. *piduṇā*; A. *piara*.
Gen. *piuṇo*; AMg. *piuṇo*, *piussa*; JM. *piuṇo*, *piẏarassa*; Ś. Mg. *piduṇo*; A. *piaraha*.
Voc. [*pia*, *piā*, *piaraṁ*, *piaro*, *piara*].

Plural.

Nom. [*piaro*], [*piuṇo*]; AMg. JM. *piẏaro*; AMg. also *pii*; Ś. *pidaro*.
Acc. [*piare*, *piuṇo*]; AMg. *piẏaro*; Ś. *pidaro*, *pidare*.
Ins. [AMg. *piūhiṁ*, also *piihiṁ*; [*piarehim*].
Gen. AMg. *piūṇaṁ*, also *piiṇaṁ*.
Loc. [*piūsuṁ*].

Sing. : nom. is very frequent : M. *piā* (R. 15,26); AMg. JM. *piẏā* (Sūẏag. 377. 635. 750.; Jīv. 355; Nāẏādh. 1110; Erz. 14,13); Ś. *pidā* (Śak. 21,2; Uttarar. 113,6; Kāleyak. 24,18); Ā. *pidā* (Mṛcch. 104,17); Mg. *pidā* (Mṛcch. 32,11); AMg. JM. *bhāẏā* = *bhrātā* (Āẏār. 2,15,15; Sūẏag. 377. 635. 750; Uttar. 217; Erz. 14,13); Ś. Ā. *bhādā* (Uttarar. 128,10; Pras. 83,6; Veṇīs. 102,4; 103,22; Ā. Mṛcch. 104, 18); Ś. *jāmādā* = *jāmātā* (Mālatīm. 235,4; Mallikām. 210,23; Priẏad. 27, 4 [text °*do*]; Mg. *yāmādā* (Mṛcch. 139,25). Acc. Mg. *piẏaraṁ* (Āẏār. 1,6,4,3; Sūẏag 176. 217.330.345); *ammāpiẏaraṁ* (Ṭhāṇ. 126; Uttar. 573); Ś. *pidaraṁ* (Vikr. 81,10; 82,8; Mālav. 84,5; Veṇīs. 61,4; Kāleyak. 18,22; Kaṁsav. 50,12 etc.), in Ā. too (Mṛcch. 101.17) and Ḍh. (Mṛcch. 32,10); JM. *bhāẏaraṁ* Ś. *bhādaraṁ* = *bhrātaram* (Erz. 85,4; Veṇīs. 95,14; 104,12; Mālatīm. 240,

2). — Ins. M. AMg. *piuṇā* (G. 1197; Vivāhap. 820.827), Mg. *piduṇā* (Mṛcch. 167,24), A. *piara* (Śukas. 32,3); JM. *bhāuṇā* (Erz. 45,28), Ś. *bhāduṇā* (Mālav. 71,2; Mālatīm. 244,2); Ś. *jāmāduṇā* (Ratn. 291,2). — Gen. M. AMg. *piuṇo* (R. 8,28; Kk. 262,28; Nāyādh. 784; Kappas. Th. § 3); AMg. *ammāpiuṇo* (Ṭhāṇ. 125) beside *ammāpiussa* (Ṭhāṇ. 126); JM. *piuṇo* (Erz. 9,19; 17,17) and *ammāpiyarassa* (Erz. 77,30); Ś. *piduṇo* (Mṛcch. 95,2. 15; Uttarar. 73,10; Mudrār. 262,6; Pārvatīp. 11,4; 28,6; Mukund. 34,3); Ś. *bhāduṇo* (Mālatīm 242,1; 245,5; 249,4; Bālar. 113,7; 144,10; Veṇīs. 60,21; 64,7; Mudrār. 35,9); Ś. *jāmāduṇo* (Veṇīs. 29,12; Mallikām. 21,4; 212,17; Viddhaś. 48,9); A. *piaraha* (Piṅgala, 1,116, in the meaning of the acc.). — Plural: nom. AMg. *piyaro* (Ṭhāṇ. 511. 512). frequently in the compound *ammāpiyaro* (Āyār. 2,15,11. 16; Vivāhap. 809. 926; Ṭhāṇ. 524.525; Antag. 61; Nāyādh. § 114. 116; p. 292. 887. 965 and often); AMg. JM. *bhāyaro* (Sūyag. 176; Samav. 238; Kk. 267,36; Erz.); also AMg. *bhāyarā* (Uttar. 402.622) and AMg. *do pii* = *dvau pitarau* [as the names of stars; Ṭhāṇ. 82), Ś. *bhādaro* (Uttarar. 12,7; Veṇīs 13,9). False are Ś. *mādarapiarā* (sic; Kaṁsav. 50,14) and *bhāarā* (sic; Kaṁsav. 50,10). We should read *mādāpidaro* and *bhādaro*. — Acc. AMg. JM. *ammāpiyaro* (Antag. 4, 23.61. Nāyādh. § 134.138; p. 260.887; Vivāhap. 808; Erz. 37,29); Ś. *pidaro* (Vikr. 87,17); AMg. also *ammāpiyare* (Uttar. 643; commentary °*raṁ*); Ś. *mādāpidare* = *mātāpitarau* (Śak. 159,12). — Ins. AMg. *ammāpiūhiṁ* (Āyar. 2,15,17; Nāyādh. § 138; p. 889) and AMg. JM. *ammāpiihiṁ* (Kappas. § 94; v. l. °*piū*°; Ṭhaṇ. 527; Vivāhap. 1206; Āv. 37,2; 38,2) JM. *māyāpiihiṁ* (Āv. 17,31); AMg. *piihiṁ*, *bhāihiṁ* (Sūyag. 694; text °*ihiṁ*), false *piyāhiṁ* (104) and *pitāhiṁ* (692); Ś. *bhādarehiṁ* (Mṛcch. 106,1) is merely conjectural. — Gen. AMg. *ammāpiūṇaṁ* (Kappas. § 90; Nāyādh. § 120; p. 905.965) and *ammāpiiṇaṁ* (Ovav. § 72; v. l. °*piū*°; 103. 107); JM. *māyāpiiṇaṁ* (Āv. 37,21). The proper noun AMg. *culaṇipiya* = *culaṇipitṛ* is declined as : nom. *culaṇipiyā*, acc. °*piyaṁ*, gen. °*piyassa*, voc. °*piyā* (Uvās. s.v.).

§ 392. *mātṛ* (mother) forms the nom. M. *māā* (H. 400.508); AMg. JM. *māyā* (Āyār. 1,2,1,1; Sūyag. 115.161.377.635.750; Nāyādh. 1110; Jīv. 355 Kappas. § 46. 109; Erz. 5,19; 10,4. 7); Ś. Ā. Mg. *mādā* (Uttarar. 126,6; Veṇīs. 29,12; Ā Mṛcch. 104,17; Mg. Mṛcch. 129.6). In the meaning 'divine mother', the stem *māarā*, which is declined like the feminine in *-ā*, makes its appearance according to Hc. 3,46.—Acc. M. *māaraṁ* (Hc. 3,46), AMg. JM. *māyaraṁ*, Ḍh. Ś. *mādaraṁ* (Āyār. 1, 6, 4, 3; Sūyag. 176.217. 330. 345; Erz.; Ḍh.; Mṛcch. 32,12; Ś. Mṛcch. 141.11; Śak. 59,7; Vikr. 82, 3; 88, 16 etc.) in M. also *māaṁ* (H. 741), and so the word may generally be declined as an *ā*-stem : sing. ins. JM. *māyāe* (Āv. 11,3.9); gen. Ś. *mādāe* (Karp. 19, 5); voc. M. *māe* (H. s.v. *māā*), Ś. *māde* (Veṇīs. 58,17; Viddhaś. 112,8); plur. : ins. AMg. *māyāhiṁ* (Sūyag. 104); gen. A. *māahā̃* (Hc. 4,399). The nom. plur. is AMg. *māyaro* (Ṭhāṇ 512; Samav. 230; Kappas. § 74. 77); besides AMg. JM. have *i-* and *ū-* stems (Hc. 3,46); gen. loc. sing. *māūe* (Kappas. § 93; Āv. 12,9; loc. Vivāhap. 116) : ins. plur. *māihiṁ* (Sūyag. 692 [°*i*°]. 694); gen. plur. *māiṇaṁ*, *māiṇa* (Hc. 1,135;

3,46) which appears more frequently in compounds (§ 55). Voc. sing. *māi* in A. Piṅgala 1,2. — From *duhitṛ* the nom. Ś. is *duhidā* (Mālav. 37,8; Ratn. 291,1; Viddhaś. 47,6. 10; Priyad. 52,6), the acc. Ś. *duhidaraṁ* (Śak. 128,2), the voc. Ś. *duhide* (Viddhaś. 38,3 ed. Calc.). JM. *dhiyā*, Ś. Mg. *dhidā* and M. *dhūā*, AMg. JM. *dhūyā*, Ś. Mg. *dhūdā* are mostly used (§ 65.148), which are inflected as *ā*-stems, JM. *dhiyā*, Ś. Mg. *dhidā* especially in the combinations JM. *dāsiedhiyā*, Ś. *dāsiedhidā*, Mg. *dāśiedhidā*, taken as compounds (cf. *dāsieutta*). In Ś. Mg. manuscripts and texts write *dhtā* mostly falsely. Nom. Ś. *dāsiedhidā* (Ratn. 302,8); AMg. JM. *dhūyā* (Āyār. 1,2, 1,1; 2,15,15; Sūyag 635, 657; Vivāgas. 105. 214. 228; Antag. 55; Nāyādh. 586.781.1068.1070.1228; Vivāhap. 602.987; Jīv. 355; Āv. 10,23; 11,10; 12,3; 29, 14; 37,26ff.; Erz. 5,38); Ś. *ajjādhūdā* = *āryāduhitā* (Mṛcch. 53,23; 54,7; 94,11; 325,14); acc. M. *dhūaṁ* (H. 388), AMg. *dhūyaṁ* (Vivāgas. 228.229; Nāyādh. 820); ins. M. *dhūāi* (H. 370); *dhūāe* (H. 864); Ś. *dāsiedhidāe* (Nāgān. 57,4). Mg. *dāśiedhidāe* (Mṛcch. 17,8); gen. Ś. *dāsiedhidāe* (Mṛcch. 77,12; Nāgān. 47,10); Ś. *ajjādhūdāe* (Mṛcch. 53,15; 94,4); loc. AMg. *dhūyāe* (Nāyādh. 727); voc. JM. *dāsiedhie* (Erz. 68,20); Ś. *dāsiedhide* (Mṛcch. 51,7. 10; 72,19; Karp. 13,2 [Konow °*dhūde*]; Viddhaś 85,11; Ratn. 294,3; 301,18; Nāgān. 57,3; Caṇḍak. 9,16); Mg. *dāśiedhide* (Mṛcch. 127,23). Plural : nom. acc. AMg. JM. *dhūyāo* (Āyār. 2,1,4,5; 2,2,1,12; Vivāgas. 217; Āv. 10,23; 12,1; Erz. 14,12) ins. JM. *dhūyāhi* (Erz. 14,16); gen. AMg. *dhūyāṇaṁ* (Āyār. 1,2,5,1); Ś. *dhidāṇaṁ* (Mālatīm. 288,5); voc. Ś. *dāsiedhidāo* (Cait. 84,7). From the stem *dhūyarā* is found the acc. sing. AMg. *dhūyaraṁ* (Uttar. 641), ins. plur. *dhūyarāhi* (Sūyag. 229). — From *svasṛ* the nom. sing. is AMg. *sasā* (Hc. 3,35; Pāiyal. 252; Sūyag. 176).

4) Stems in *o* and *au*.

§ 393. Of the old flexion of *go* only a few remnants are traceable in AMg.: nom. *suyago* = *abhinavaprasūtā gauḥ* (Sūyag. 180). nom. plur. *gāo* = *gāvaḥ* (Dasav. 628, 15); acc. plur. *gāo* **gāvaḥ* = *gāḥ* = (Āyār. 2,4,2,9.10); ins. plur. *gohiṁ* = *gobhiḥ* (Aṇuog. 351); gen. plur. *gavaṁ* = *gavām* (Samav. 83; Uttar. 293). The nom. sing. in AMg. is *gave* = **gavaḥ* (Āyār. 2,4,2,10; Dasav. 628,17), as also in Sūyag. 147 we have to read for *gavaṁ* of the text; the nom. plur. is AMg. *gavā* in *jaraggavā* = *jaradgāvaḥ* (Sūyag. 185). For the mascul. *goṇo* is mostly used in AMg. Mg. (Hc. 2,174; Deśīn. 2,104; Triv. 1,3,105; Āyār. 2,1,5,3; 2,3,3,8. 13; 2,4,2,7; Sūyag. 708. 720. 724 f. 727; Jīv. 356; Paṇhāv. 19; Samav. 131; Nāyādh; Ovav.; Uvās.; Mṛcch. 97,21; 98,20; 99,12; 100,13; 107,18; 112,17; 117,15; 118,5. 12-14. 24; 122,15; 132,16; in the last two places *goṇāiṁ* with a change of gender according to § 358); AMg. *goṇattāe* = *gotvāya* (Vivāgas. 51). The fem. is JM. *goṇi* (Āv. 7, 10. 12; 43,10), or M. *gāī* (Hc. 1,158; H.), AMg. JM. *gāvī* (C. 2,16; Hc. 2,174; Āyār. 2,1,4,3. 4; Vivāgas. 67; Jīv. 356; Dasav. 618,39; Dasav. N. 658,7; Āv. 43,11.20; Dvār. 504,12. 14; Erz.). For the masc. Hc. 1,158 mentions *gaüo*, *gāo*, for the femin. *gaüā*, *gāī*. Of them *gaüo* = *gavayaḥ*, *goṇo* is either = **gŏṇṇo* for **guṇṇo* =

**gūrṇáḥ* from √*gur* according to § 66[1], or = **gavana*. Cf. also § 8. 152.

1. So more correctly than BB. 3,237.

§ 394. *nau* (ship) always forms, from the strong stem, a femin. *ṇāvā*, which is as a rule inflected according to the *ā*-declension (Hc. 1,164; Sr. fol. 16); sing. nom. AMg. *nāvā*, Ś. *ṇāvā* (Nāẏādh. 741. 1339; Vivāhap. 105; Uttar. 716; Mṛcch. 41,20), A *ṇāva* (Hc. 4,423,1); acc. M. *ṇāvaṁ* (G. 812) AMg. *nāvaṁ*, *ṇāvaṁ* (Āẏār. 2,3,1,13 ff.; Sūẏag. 68.271.438; Vivāhap. 105; Nāẏādh. 741); ins. gen. AMg. *nāvāe* (Āẏār. 2,3,1,15 ff.; Nāẏādh. 1339 f.; Uvās. § 218); abl. AMg. *nāvāo* (Āẏār. 2,3,2,2. 3); plur. ins. AMg. *nāvāhi* (Dasav. 629,1).

5) Stems in *-t*.

§ 395. The nouns in *-t*, having a single stem, of which *t* is preceded by a vowel, cross over to the corresponding vocalic declension after dropping off of the final *t* : M. *indaïṇā* = *indrajitā* (R. 14,16), gen. *indaïṇo* (R. 12,58.84) and *indaïssa* (R. 15,61), loc. *indaïmmi* (R. 13,99); *taḍi* = *taḍit* (Hc. 1,202), A. *taḷi* = *taḍitam* (Vikr. 55,2); *marū* = *marut* (Kī. 2,123; M. *vijjū* = *vidyut* (Vr. 4,9; Bh. 4, 26; Hc. 1,15; Kī. 2, 129; H. 585). From *jagat*, the nom. sing. is M. *jaaṁ* (R. 5, 20; 9, 73), AMg. *jage* (Sūẏag. 74), A. *jagu* (Hc. 4,343,1); the acc. AMg. *jagaṁ* (Sūẏag. 405.537); the gen. A. *jaassu* (Hc. 4,440); the loc. M. *jaammi* (H. 364; R. 3,12; Karp. 78,4; 80,4) and *jae* (G. 239; H. 303), AMg. *jagai* (Sūẏag. 104; text °*ti*) and *jagaṁsi* (Sūẏag. 306), JŚ. *jagadi* (Pav. 382, 26; text °*ti*), A. *jagi* (Hc. 4,404; Kk. 261,1). The feminine nouns mostly take the ending *-ā* : *sarit* becomes Pāli *saritā*, M. *sariā* (G. H. R.), JM. *sariẏā* (Erz.), A *saria* (Vikr. 72,9); M. gen. plur. *sariāhã* (Hc. 4,300); A, also ins. plur. *sarihĩ* = **saribhiḥ* = *saridbhiḥ* (Hc. 4,422,11). The passing over to the *ā*-declension is prohibited by the grammarians for *vidyut*. Cf. § 244. According to Hc. 1,33 there is found *vijjuṇā* too beside *vijjūe*, according to C. 1,4 nom. plur. *vijjuṇo* too.

§ 396. The stems in *-at*, *-mat*, *-vat* behave partly according to the mode of Skt., especially in AMg., and partly according to that of the *a*-declension of the strong stems in *-anta*, *-manta*, *-vanta*. Thus with the flexion of Skt. : sing. nom. AMg. *jāṇaṁ* = *jānan* (Sūẏag. 1,322); *vijjaṁ* = *vidvān* (Sūẏag. 126.306. 380 ff.); *cakkhumaṁ* = *cakṣuṣmān* (Sūẏag. 546); *diṭṭhimaṁ* = *dṛṣṭimān* (Sūẏag. 200.531); *āẏavaṁ ṇāṇavaṁ dhammavaṁ bambhavaṁ* = *ātmavān jñānavān dharmavān brahmavān* (Āẏār. 1,3,1,2), *puṭṭhavaṁ* = *spṛṣṭavān* (Āẏār. 1,7,8,8; in the passive sense), *thāmavaṁ* = *sthāmavān* (Uttar. 50. 90), *ciṭṭhaṁ*, *aciṭṭhaṁ* = *tiṣṭhan*, *atiṣṭhan* (Āẏār. 1,4,2,2,), *kuvvaṁ* = *kurvan* (Sūẏag. 31,863), *kiṇaṁ*, *haṇaṁ*, *paẏaṁ* = *kriṇan*, *ghnan*, *pacan* (Sūẏag. 609); AMg. JM. *mahaṁ* (Āẏār. 1,7,1.4; Sūẏag. 582; Ovav. § 5; Kk. 271. 11); JM. *arahaṁ* = *arhan* (Dvār. 495,9). In M. I have not been able to locate this form. In Ś. Mg. it is confined to *bhagavat* and *bhavat* (pronoun) (Hc. 4,265). So Ś. *bhaavaṁ* (Mṛcch. 28,1; 44,19; Mudrār. 20,7; 179,3; Ratn. 296,5. 23; Vikr. 10,2; 23, 19; 43,11 etc); likewise Mg. (Mudrār. 178.6; Caṇḍak, 43,7); Ś. *bhavaṁ* (Mṛcch. 4,24; 6,23; 7,3; 18,25; Śak. 37,

1 etc.), *atthabhavaṁ* = *atrabhavān* (Śak. 33,3; 35,7), *tatthabhavaṁ* = *tatrabhavān* (Vikr. 46,5; 47,2; 75,3. 15); likewise P. *bhagavaṁ* (Hc. 4,323), as in AMg. (Āẏār. 1,8,1,1, ff.; Uvās. and very often). — Ins. AMg. *maïmaẏā* = *matimatā* (Āẏār. 1,7,1,4. 2,5), *maimaẏā* (Āẏār. 1,8,1,22.2, 16. 3,14.4,17; Sūẏag. 373); AMg. *jāṇaẏā pāsaẏā* = *jānatā paśyatā* (Āẏār. 1,7,1,3); AMg. JM. *mahaẏā* = *mahatā* (Āẏār. 1,2,1,1; Sūẏag. 718; Vivāgas. 239; Nāẏādh. § 15.135 etc.; Kk. 259,37), used also for the femin. in consonance with the following masculine and neuter (§ 355) : *mahaẏā iḍḍhie mahaẏā juie mahaẏā baleṇaṁ*... = *mahatyṛddhyā mahatyā dyutyā mahatā balena*... (Jīv. 588 [text *juttie*]; Kappas. 102; Ovav. § 52); M. *bhaavaā* (G. 896), AMg. JM. *bhagavaẏā* (Āẏār. 1,1,1,1,7. 3,5 etc.; Uvās; and very often; Kk. 268, 17), Ś. *bhaavadā* = *bhagavatā* (Lalitav. 265,18; Śak. 57,17; Vikr. 23,6; 72, 14; 81,2); likewise in Ś. *bhavadā* = *bhavatā* (Śak. 36,16; Vikr. 19,15), *atthabhavadā*, *tatthabhavadā* (Vikr. 16,11; 30,9; 80,14; 84,19; Śak. 30,2), as also in the gen. : Ś. *bhaavado* (Śak. 120,5; Ratn. 294,5; 295,6), likewise Mg. (Prab. 52,6; Caṇḍak. 43,6); Ś. *bhavado* (Śak. 38,6. 8; 39,12; Mṛcch. 52,12; Vikr. 18,10,20,19; 21,19 etc.), *atthabhavado* (Vikr. 21,10), *tatthabhavado* (Mṛcch. 6,4; 22,12; Vikr. 38, 18; 51, 13; 79.16). So also in the proper noun Ś. gen. *rumaṇṇado* = *rumaṇvataḥ* (Ratn. 320,16), of which the nom. is *rumaṇṇo*, as that of an *n*-stem (Priyad. 5,5). In the case of adjectives and participles only the forms of the *a*-stems are elsewhere usable in Ś. Mg. Hence false is Ś. *guṇavado* (Śak. 84,8 ed. BURKHARD), for which ed. BÖHTLINGK 43,14, ed. Madras. 186,11 and the Kashmir recension 72,15 have likewise the false dative *guṇavade*. On the dative *bhavade* see § 361. — Gen. AMg. *mahao* = *mahataḥ* (Sūẏag. 312), *bhagavao* = *bhagavataḥ* (Āẏār. 1,1,2,4; 2,15,9 ff.; Kappas. § 16.28; Vivāhap. 1271; Uvās.; and very often), *paḍivajjao* = **pratipadyataḥ*, *viharao* = *viharataḥ* (Uttar. 116), *aviẏāṇao* = *avijānataḥ* (Āẏār. 1,1,6,2; 1,4,4,2; 1,5,1,1), *akuvvao* = *akurvataḥ* (Sūẏag. 540), *pakuvvao* = *prakurvataḥ* (Sūẏag. 340), *karao* = *kurvataḥ* (Āẏār. 1,1,1,5), *haṇao* = *ghnataḥ* (Āẏār 1,6,4,2; 1,7,1,3), *kittaẏao* = *kīrtayataḥ* (Uttar. 726), *dhiimao* = *dhṛtimataḥ* (Āẏār. 2,16,8). On Ś. Mg. see above. — Loc. Ś. *sadi* = *sati* (Śak. 141.7); M. *himavaï* = *himavati* (Mudrār. 60,9). — Voc. AMg. JM. *bhagavaṁ*, *bhaẏavaṁ* (Vivāhap. 205; Kappas. § 111; Erz. 2,32; 44,18; Dvār. 495,13); Ś. *bhaavaṁ* (Ratn. 296,24; 298,14; 300,33; Prab. 59,4; Śak. 73,5; Vikr. 86,10; Uttarar. 204,8 etc.); P. *bhagavaṁ* (Hc. 4,323). Beside AMg. *āusaṁ* = *āyuṣman* (Āẏar. 1,1,1,1; Sūẏag. 792; Samav. 1) AMg. very frequently has *āuso* (Āẏār. 1,7.2.2; 2,2,2, 6-14; 2, 5,1,7.13; 2,6,1,5. 10.11; 2,7,1,2; 2,7,2,1. 2; Sūẏag. 594; Uvās.; Ovav.; Kappas. etc.); further *samaṇāuso* (Samav. 31; Ovav. § 140; Nāẏādh. 518.614.617.652 ff.), that is used for the plural too (Sūẏag. 579,582; Nāẏādh. 497.504). *āuso* is rightly equated by LEUMANN (Aup. S. s. v.) as = **āyuṣmas*, hence it is to be connected with the Vedic vocatives in *-as* (WHITNEY § 454). — In the plur. the nom. and the voc. only are formed dialectically according to the old flexion too. Nom.: AMg. *sīlamanto guṇamanto vaïmanto* (Āẏār. 2,1,9,1); *mūlamanto kandamanto*

khandhamanto tayāmanto sālamanto pavālamanto etc. (Ovav. § 4), *bhagavanto* (Āyār. 1,4,1,1,; 2,1,9,1; Vivāhap. 1235; Kappas. Ś. § 61), and so also Ś. nom. *bhaavanto* (Mudrār. 20,5). For Ś. *kidavanto = kṛtavantaḥ* (Jīvān. 40,26) we have to read *kidavantā*, on the other hand for the voc. *bhavantā* (Śak. 27, 16 ed. Böhtlingk) we should with the ed. Madras. 135,7 read *bhaavanto*, as stands in Veṇīs.102,2. — Nom. plur. neut. are AMg. *pariggahāvanti* (Āyār. 1,5,2,4; cf. 1,5,3,1); *balavanti* (Uttar. 753); *eyāvanti savvāvanti = etāvanti *sarvāvanti* (Āyār. 1,1,1,5. 7); *āvanti = yāvaanti* (Āyār. 1,4,2,3; 1,5,2,1, 4; cf. § 357); *jāvanti* (Uttar. 215). The sing. *abhiddavaṁ = abhidravan* metrically stands for the plural (Āyār. 2,16,2). Cf. Pischel, Ved. Stud. 2.227. So also in prose the voc. JM. *bhayavaṁ* (T. 4,14,20) in addressing several individuals. — As AMg. *samaṇāuso* is used for the plur. too, so is used very frequently the plural *āusanto* for the singular; hence it is to be taken as pluralis majestatis, since the nom. sing. in prose would be *āusante* : *āusanto samaṇā = āyuṣmañ śramaṇa, āusanto gāhāvai = āyuṣman gṛhapate* (Āyār. 1,7,2,2; 5,2; 2,1,3,2; 2,3,1,16 ff.; 2,3,2,1.2. 16; 2,3,3,5 ff. etc.); *āusanto goyamā = āyuṣman gotama* (Sūyag. 962. 972.981) beside *āyuso goyamā* (Sūyag. 964); *āusanto udagā = āyuṣmann udaka* (Sūyag. 969.972. 1012.1014). A doubtless plural is for example *āusanto niyaṇṭhā = āyuṣmanto nirgranthāḥ* (Sūyag. 989.992). From the weak stem are formed *jāṇao, ajāṇao* (Āyār. 2,4,1,1), in case one, with the commentary and Jacobi (SBE. XII, 149), will like to take it as the nom. plur. However it is not possible for the prose, so that the forms are to be explained as the gen. sing., which gives also a better sense.

§ 397. With the exception of the cases noted under § 396 the formation in *-anta, -manta, -vanta* prevails in all the dialects : sing. nom. M. *pianto = piban*; *calanto = calan*; *bahuguṇavanto = bahuguṇavān*; *kuṇanto = kṛṇvan* (H. 13. 25. 203. 265); AMg. *sāsanto* beside *sāsaṁ = śāsat* (Uttar. 38); *aṇusāsanto* (Uttar. 39); *kiṇanto, vikkiṇanto = kriṇan, vikriṇan* (Uttar. 1010); *mūlamante, kandamante = mūlavān kandavān*, (Ovav. § 5); *vaṇṇamante, gandhamante = varṇavān, gandhavān* (Bhag. 1,420); *virāyante = virājan* (Ovav. § 48); *visiyanto = viṣīdan, ramanto = ramamāṇaḥ* (Dasav. 613, 16; 641,21); *cullahimavante = cullahimavān* (Ṭhāṇ. 176); JM. *saṁthuvvanto = saṁstūyamānaḥ*; *gāyanto = *gāyan*; *dĕnto = *dayan*; *agūhanto = agūhan*; *paloĕnto = pralokayan* (Āv. 7,25; 8,26; 9,5. 6; 15,21); *kandanto = krandan* (Erz. 42,12); JM. Ś. *mahanto* (Erz. 8,5; 50,5; 63,28; Kk. 274,4; Vikr. 45,1; Mallikām. 245,5; Mudrār. 43,8); Ś. *karĕnto = kurvan* (Mṛcch. 6,13; 40,23), *jāṇanto* (Mṛcch. 18,23; 104,1); *puloanto = pralokayan* (Mahāv. 99,3), *cittavanto = cittavān* (Śak. 87,13); Mg. *puścaṁde = pṛcchan* (Lalitav. 565,20); *mahante = mahān* (Mṛcch. 132,11; 169,18; Prab. 58,9; Veṇīs. 35,17; 36,3); *colaante = corayan* (Mṛcch. 165.9); *daṁśaante = darśayan* (Śak. 114,11); *mantaante = mantrayan* (Prab. 32,10; so to be read; ed. Bomb. 78,12 °*to*); Ḍh. *ācakkhantŏ = *ācakṣat* (§ 88; Mṛcch. 34,24); P. *cintayanto = cintayan, paribbhamanto = paribhraman* (Hc. 4,323); A. *hasantu = hasan, daṁsijjantu = darśyamāna* (Hc. 4,383.3,418,6), *jagganto = jāgrat* (Piṅgala 1,62a), *valanta = valan*; *ulhasanta = ullasan*; *guṇavanta = guṇavān* (Piṅgala 1,4b; 2,45);

nom. neut. *bhaṇantaṁ* = *bhaṇat* (H.218); *kirantaṁ* = *kirat* (G. 1182); Ś. *dīsantaṁ* = *dṛśyamānam* (Uttarar. 77,6); A. *dhaṇamanta* = *dhanavat* (Piṅgala 2,45). Mg. *dahante* (more correctly *ḍahaḍahante* with the v. l.; Veṇīs. 35,23) is in apposition with the neut. *śoṇidaṁ* = *śoṇitam*. In the acc. masc. the Skt. form becomes identical with the later formation of Pkt. : AMg. Ś. *mahantaṁ* (Āyār. 1,3,2,3; Sūyag. 944; Mṛcch. 40,22); M. *pijjantaṁ*, *aṇuṇijjantaṁ*, *avalambijjantaṁ*, *paāsantaṁ* = *pīyamānam*, *anunīyamānam*, *avalambyamānam*, *prakāśayantam* (G. 466-469); AMg. *samārambhantaṁ* = *samārabhamāṇam*, *kiṇantaṁ* = *kriṇantam*, *giṇhantaṁ* = *gṛhṇantam* (Āyār. 1,2,2,3; 1,2,5,3; 2,7,1,1); JM. *jampantaṁ* = *jalpantam* (Kk. 262,5)); Ś. *jāṇantaṁ*, *santaṁ*, *asantaṁ* (Mudrār. 38,2; 63,9.10), *kappijjantaṁ* = *kalpyamānam* (Mṛcch. 4,10), *uvvahantaṁ* = *udvahantam* (Mṛcch. 41,10). False is Ś. *bhaavadaṁ* for *bhaavantaṁ* (Vikr. 87,17). Mg. *mālantaṁ* = *mārayantam*, *yiantaṁ* = *jīvantam* (Mṛcch. 123,22; 170,5); *alihantaṁ* = *arhantam* (Laṭakam. 14,19); A. *dārantu* = *dārayantam* (Hc. 4,345); neuter: M. *santam asantaṁ* (H. 513); Ś. *mahantaṁ* (Mṛcch. 28,11). — Ins. M. *pianteṇa* = *pibatā*, *paḍanteṇa* = *patatā* (H. 246. 264); AMg. *viṇimuyanteṇaṁ* = *vinimuñcatā* (Ovav. § 48); *aṇukampanteṇaṁ* = *anukampatā* (Āyār. 2,15,4); JM. *jampanteṇa* = *jalpatā* (KI. 15; Erz. 10,26); *kuṇanteṇa* = Vedic *kṛṇvatā* (KI. 15); *vaccanteṇaṁ* = *vrajatā* (Āv. 11,19); JŚ. *arahanteṇa* = *arhatā* (Pav. 385,63); Ś. *calaṁteṇa* = *calatā* (Lalitav. 568,5); *gāanteṇa* = *gāyatā*, *karĕnteṇa* = *kurvatā* (Mṛcch. 44,2; 60,25; 61,24); *haranteṇa* (Uttarar. 92,9) *bhuttavanteṇa* = *bhuktavatā* (Jīvān. 53,11); Mg. *gaścanteṇa* = *gacchatā* (Mṛcch. 167,24); *āhiṇḍanteṇa* = *āhiṇḍamānena* (Caṇḍak. 71,12); A. *pavasanteṇa* = *pravasatā* (Hc. 4,333), *bhamantĕ* = *bhramatā* (Vikr. 55,18; 58,9; 69,1; 72,10); *roanteṁ* = *rudatā* (Vikr. 72,11). — Abl. AMg. *cullahimavantāo* = *cullahimavataḥ* (Ṭhāṇ. 177). — Gen. M. *ārambhantassa* = *ārabhamāṇasya*, *ramantassa* = *ramamāṇasya*, *jāṇantassa* = *jānataḥ* (H. 42,44. 243), *visahantassa* = **viṣahataḥ*, *vŏcchindantassa* = *vyavacchindataḥ* (R. 12,23; 15,62); AMg. *āusantassa* = *āyuṣmataḥ* (Āyār. 2, 7, 1, 2; 2, 7, 2, 1); *bhagavantassa* = *bhagavataḥ* (Kappas. § 118); *vasantassa* = *vasataḥ* (Uvās. § 83), *cayantassa* = *tyajataḥ* (Ovav. §170); *cullahimavantassa* (Jīv. 388 f.); *kahantassa* = *kathayataḥ* (Sūyag. 907); *jiṇantassa* = *jayataḥ* (Dasav. 618,14); JM. *acchantassa* = *ṛcchataḥ*, *dhūvĕntassa* = *dhūpayataḥ*, *sārakkhantassa* = *saṁrakṣataḥ* (Āv. 14, 25; 25, 4; 28, 16); *karĕntassa*, *kuṇantassa* = *kurvataḥ* (Erz. 1,24; 18,10); JM. *cintantassa*, Ś. *cintaantassa* = *cintayataḥ* (Erz. 11,8; 18,16; Śak. 30,5); Ś. *mahantassa* = *mahataḥ* (Uttarar. 105,5); *maggantassa* = *mārgamāṇasya*, *ṇikkamantassa* = *niṣkrāmataḥ* (Mṛcch. 95,7; 105,24); *haṇumantassa* = *hanumataḥ* (Mahāv. 125.14); Mg. *vaññaṁdaśśa* = *vrajataḥ* (Lalitav. 566,7), *alihantaśśa* = *arhataḥ* (Prab. 52,7); CP. *naccantassa* = *nṛtyataḥ* (Hc. 4,326); A. *mĕllantahŏ* = *tyajataḥ*, *dĕntahŏ* = = **dayataḥ*, *jujjhantahŏ* = *yudhyataḥ*, *karantahŏ* = *kurvataḥ* (Hc. 4,370,4.379,1. 400). — Loc. M. *samāruhantammi* = *samārohati*, *hŏntammi* = *bhavati*, *ruantammi* = *rudati* (H. 11. 124. 596; *haṇūmante* and *haṇumantammi* = *hanumati* (R. 1,35; 2,43); AMg. *jalante* = *jvalati* (Kappas. § 59; Nāyādh § 34; Uvās § 66; Vivāhap. 169); *sante* = *sati* (Āyār. 2,5,1,5; 2,8,1, 2,9,1), *himavante* = *himavati* (Uvās. § 277); *arahantaṁsi* = *arhati* (Kappas. § 74; Nāyādh. § 46), *abhinikkhamantammi* = *abhiniṣkrāmati* (Uttar. 279); Ś: *mahante* = *mahati* (Śak. 29,7); D. *jiante* = *jīvati* (Mṛcch. 100,9); A. *pavasantĕ* = *pravasati* (Hc. 4,422,12). — Voc. M. *āloanta sasanta jambhanta ganta roanta mucchanta paḍanta khalanta* = *ālokayan śvasan jṛmbhamāṇa gacchan rudan mūrchan patan skhalan* (H. 547); *mahanta* (desirous), *muanta* = *muñcan* (H. 510,643), Mg. *alihanta* = *arhan* (Prab. 54,6; 58,7; Laṭakam. 12,13). — Plural: nom. M. *paḍantā*, *ṇivaḍantā* = *patantaḥ*, *nipatantaḥ* (G. 122. 129.442); *bhindantā* = *bhindantaḥ*, *jāṇantā* = *jānataḥ* (H. 326. 821); AMg. *silamantā* = *śilamantaḥ* (Āẏār. 1,6,4.1); *jampantā* = *jalpantaḥ* (Sūẏag. 50); *vāẏantā ẏa gāẏantā ẏa naccantā ẏa bhāsantā ẏa sāsantā ẏa sāvĕntā ẏa rakkhantā ẏa* = *vādayantaś ca gāyantaś ca nṛtyantaś ca bhāṣamāṇaś ca śāsataś ca śrāvayantaś ca rakṣantaś ca* (Ovav. § 49, V); *pūrayantā*, *pĕcchantā*, *ujjoĕntā*, *karĕntā* = *pūrayantaḥ*, *prekṣamāṇāḥ*, *uddyotayantaḥ*, *kurvantaḥ* (Ovav. [§ 37]); *buddhimantā* = *buddhimantaḥ* (Sūẏag. 916); *arahantā* = *arhantaḥ* (Kappas. § 17. 18), also in the combination *arahantā bhagavanto* (Āẏār. 1, 4, 1, 1,; 2, 4, 1, 4 [so to be read]; Vivāhap. 1235), likewise *samaṇā bhagavanto silamantā* (Āẏār, 2,2,2,10); JM. *kiḍḍantā* = *krīḍantaḥ* (Āv. 30,15); *gavesantā* = *gaveṣayantaḥ*, *coijjantā* = *codyamānāḥ* (Kk. 273, 42; 274, 3); *santā* = *santaḥ*, *carantā* = *carantaḥ* (Erz. 1.12.13.); Ś *pūijjantā* = *pūjyamānāḥ*, *sikkhantā* = *śikṣantaḥ* (Mṛcc.h 9, 1; 71,21), *khelantā* = *khelantaḥ* (Uttarar, 108, 2); Mg. *śaśantā* = *śvasantaḥ*, *paḍivaśantā* = *prativasantaḥ* (Mṛcch. 116,17; 169,3); A. *phukkijjanta* = *phūtkriyamāṇāḥ* (Hc. 4,422,3); *guṇamanta* = *guṇavantaḥ* (Piṅgala 2,118); neuter: AMg. *vaṇṇamantāiṁ gandhamantāiṁ rasamantāiṁ phāsamantāiṁ* = *varṇavanti gandhavanti rasavanti sparśavanti* (Āẏār. 2,4,1,4; Vivāhap. 144; Jīv. 26); acc. M. *uṇṇamante* = *unnamataḥ* (H. 539); AMg. *arahante bhagavante* = *arhato bhagavataḥ* (Vivāhap. 1235; Kappas. § 21), *samārambhante* = *samārabhamāṇān* (Āẏār. 1, 1, 3, 5); JŚ. *arahante* (Pav. 379,3); neutrum : AMg. *mahantāiṁ* (Vivāhap. 1308 f.). — Ins. M. *visaṁghaḍantehiṁ* = *visaṁghaṭadbhiḥ*, (H. 115), *viṇintehiṁ* = *vinirgacchadbhiḥ* (G. 138); AMg. *jivantehiṁ* = *jīvadbhiḥ*, *ovaẏantehi ẏa uppaẏantehi ẏa* = *apapatadbhiś cotpatadbhiś ca* (Kappas. § 97); *pannāṇamantehiṁ* = **prajñānamadbhiḥ* (Āẏār. 1,6,4,1); *āvasantehiṁ* = *āvasadbhiḥ* (Āẏār. 1,5,3,4); *bhagavantehiṁ* = *bhagavadbhiḥ* (Aṇuog. 95); *arahantehiṁ* = *arhadbhiḥ* (Ṭhāṇ. 288; Aṇuog. 518 [°*ri*°]; *santehiṁ* = *sadbhiḥ* (Uvās. § 220. 259. 262); JM. *āpucchantehiṁ* = *āpṛcchadbhiḥ* (Āv. 27,11); *maggantehiṁ* = *mārgamāṇaiḥ* (Āv. 30, 17); *gāẏantehiṁ* = *gāyadbhiḥ*, *bhaṇantehiṁ* = *bhaṇadbhiḥ*, *āruhantehiṁ* = *ārohadbhiḥ* (Erz. 1,29; 2,15, 21); Ś. *gacchantehiṁ* = *gacchadbhiḥ* (Mudrār. 254,3); *aṇicchantehiṁ* = *anicchadbhiḥ* (Bālar. 144,9); *gāantehiṁ* = *gāẏadbhiḥ* (Cait. 42,2); Mg. *paviśantehiṁ* = *praviśadbhiḥ* (Caṇḍak. 42,11); A. *ṇivasantahĩ* = *nivasadbhiḥ*, *valantahĩ* = *valadbhiḥ* (Hc. 4,422,11. 18). — Gen. M. *ĕntāṇaṁ* = *āyatām*, *cintatāṇa* = *cintayatām* (H. 38,83); AMg. *arahantāṇaṁ bhagavantāṇaṁ* (Vivāhap. 1235; Kappas. § 16; Ovav. § 20.38); *santāṇaṁ* = *satām* (Uvās § 85); *pannāṇamantāṇaṁ* = **prajñānamatām* (Āẏār 1, 6,1,1,); JM. *āẏarantāṇaṁ* = *ācaratām* (Dvār. 502,28), *carantāṇaṁ* = *caratām* (Āv. 7,9), *kuṇantāṇaṁ* = *kurvatām* (Kk. 270,40), *joẏantāṇaṁ* = *paśyatām* (Erz. 73,18); JŚ *arihantāṇaṁ* (Pav. 379,4; 383,44 [°*ra*°]; Ś. *pĕkkhantāṇaṁ* = *prekṣamāṇānām* (Veṇīs. 64,16; Nāgān. 95,13); Mg. *alihantāṇaṁ* = *arhatām*, *ṇamantāṇaṁ* = *namatām* (Prab.

46,11; 47,1); *ṇiskamantāṇaṁ* = *niṣkrāmatām* (Caṇḍak. 42,12); A. *pĕcchantāṇa* = *prekṣamāṇānām*, *cintantāhã* = *cintayatām*, *ṇavantāhã* = *namatām*, *joantāhã* = *paśyatām* (Hc. 4,348. 362. 399. 409). — Loc. M. *dhavalāantesu* = **dhavalāyatsu* (H. 9); JM. *naccantesu* = *nṛtyatsu* (Erz. 2,2), *gacchantesu* = *gacchatsu* (Āv. 7,26; Erz. 7,19), *kiḷantesu* = *krīḍatsu* (Erz. 16,16); Ś. *parihariantesu* = *parihriyamāṇeṣu* (Mudrār. 38,10), *vaṭṭantesu* = *vartamāneṣu* (Pārvatīp. 2,5; text *vaṭṭadesu*). — Voc. AMg. *āusantā* = *āyuṣmantaḥ* (Āẏār. 2,3,2,17).

§ 398. In the case of the stems in *-at*, *-mat*, *-vat* we find sporadically forms that are built on the model of monostemic type of nouns, that is to say, from the weak stem: nom. JM. *bhagavo* (Erz. 25,19); Mg. *haṇūme* = *hanūmān* (Mṛcch. 11,8); cf. Mg. *haṇūmaśihale* (Mṛcch. 133,12) and M. °*variahaṇumaṁ* (R. 12,88); AMg. *asaṁ* = *asat* (Sūẏag. 35); acc. AMg. frequently *mahaṁ* = *mahantam* and *mahat* (Āẏār. 2,15,8; Uttar. 325; Vivāgas. 221; Vivāhap. 1325; Uvās. s. v. *maha*; Nāẏādh. § 22. 122), femin. too (Vivāhap. 105), and *bhagavaṁ* = *bhagavantam* (Uvās. s. v.; Kappas. § 15. 16. 21; Bhag. 1,420; Ovav. § 33. 38. 40 etc.). — Forms from the weak stem in *-ta*, carried over to the *a*-declension are also found. So nom. sing. AMg. *ajāṇao* = **ajānataḥ* = *ajānan* (Sūẏag. 273; text *avijāṇao*), *viẏāṇao* = *vijānan* (Nandīs. 1); nom. plur. femin. *amaïmaẏā* = **amatimatāḥ* = *amatimatyaḥ* (Sūẏag. 213); gen. plur. mascul. *bhavaẏāṇaṁ* = **bhavatānām* = *bhavatām* (Uttar. 354). For Ś. *himavadassa* (Pārvatīp. 27,13; 32,19; 35,1) we should read *himavantassa*, as in the last place Glaser (31,15) has. — From *arhat* are always formed the nom. *arahā*, *arihā*, as from the stem *arhan* (e. g. Uvās. § 187; Kappas.; Ovav.); likewise is found M. *haṇumā* (Hc. 2,159; Mk. fol. 37; R. 8,43). Cf. also § 601. — On AMg. *āusantāro*, *bhaẏantāro* see § 390.

6) Stems in *-n*

§ 399. 1) Stems in *-an*, *-man*, *-van*. *-rāa-*, AMg. JM. *rāẏa-*, Mg. *lāa*; = *rājan*. In the declension of *rājan*, the old *n*-stem and the *a*-stem, appearing in the beginning of a compound, come beside one another. Besides an *i*-stem should be deduced from the original separation-vowel *i* (§ 133).

Singular.

Nom. *rāā*, [*rāo*]; AMg. JM. *rāẏā*; Mg. *lāā*; P. *rājā*; CP. *rācā*.
Acc. *rāāṇaṁ*; [*rāiṇam rāaṁ*]; AMg. JM. *rāẏāṇaṁ*, *rāẏaṁ*; Mg. *lāāṇaṁ*.
Ins. *raṇṇā*, *rāiṇā*; JM. also *rāeṇa*; [*rāaṇā*, *rāṇā*]; Mg. *laññā*; P. *raññā*, *rāciñā*.
Abl. [*raṇṇo*, *rāiṇo*, *rāāo*, *rāādo*, *rāāu*, *rāādu*, *rāāhi*, *rāāhiṁto*, *rāā*, *rāāṇo*].
Gen. *raṇṇo*, *rāiṇo*; AMg. JM. also *rāẏassa*; [*rāāṇo*, *rāaṇo*]; Mg. *laññō*, *lāiṇo*, P. *raññō*, *rāciño*.
Loc. [*rāimmi*, *rāammi*, *rāe*].
Voc. [*rāa*, *rāā*, *rāo*]; AMg. JM. *rāẏa*, *rāẏā*, AMg. also *rāẏaṁ*, Ś. *rāaṁ*; Mg. (*lāaṁ*]; P. *rājaṁ*.

Plural.

Nom. *rāāṇo*; AMg. JM. *rāẏāṇo*, *rāiṇo*; [*rāā*]; Mg. *lāāṇo*.

Acc. *rāāṇo*, AMg. JM. *rāẏāṇo*; [*rāiṇo, rāe, rāā*].
Ins. *rāihiṁ*; [*rāehiṁ*].
Abl. [*rāihiṁ, rāihiṁto, rāāhiṁto, rāisuṁto, rāāsuṁto*].
Gen. *rāiṇaṁ*, [*rāiṇaṁ, rāāṇaṁ*]; JM. *rāiṇam, rāẏāṇaṁ*.
Loc. [*rāisuṁ, rāesuṁ*].
Voc. = nom.

On the declension of *rājan* see Vr. 5,36 — 44; Hc. 3,49 — 55; 4,304; Kī. 3, 35 — 40; Mk. fol. 44. 45; Sr. fol. 20. Cf. § 133. 191. 237. 276. Most of the cases are found in the texts often in AMg. JM. Ś. : sing. : nom.: Ś. *rāā* (Mṛcch. 28,2. 12; 68.8; Śak. 40,7; Vikr. 15,4; 39,13; 75,3; 79,7 etc.); AMg. JM. *rāẏā* (Sūẏag. 105; Ovav. § 11. 15; Uvās,; Kappas.; Āv. 8,37; 21,1 ff.; Erz.); Mg. *lāā* (Mṛcch. 128,10; 139,25; 140,1; Caṇḍak. 43,5); P. *rājā*, CP. *rācā* (Hc. 4,304. 323. 325). — Acc. JM. *rāẏāṇaṁ* (Erz. 2,5; 24,26; Kk. III, 510,32) and *rāẏaṁ* (Uttar. 443; Ovav. § 55; Nāẏādh. § 78; Niraẏāv. § 8.22; Erz. 33,23); Mg. *lāāṇaṁ* (Mṛcch. 138,25). — Ins. AMg. JM. *raṇṇā, rannā* (Nāẏādh. § 23; Ovav. § 41; Kappas.; Āv. 8,23. 30. 33. 40. 53; Erz. 24,23; 25,11) and JM. *rāiṇā* (Āv. 8,35. 38; 9,17; Erz. 1,22; 18,19; 24, 28; 25,6; Kk. 260,30; 261,7; 270, 42; III, 510,6); JM. *rāeṇa* (Āv. 8,6); Ś. *raṇṇā* (Mṛcch. 4,10; 102,1; 103,15; Śak. 57,4); Mg. *laññā* (Śak. 113,7; 117,3) in concord with Hc. 4,302; whilst in Mṛcch. 158,23. 25 *laṇṇā* stands; P. *raññā, rāciñā* (Hc. 4,304. 320). — Gen. AMg. JM. *raṇṇo, ranno* (Uvās. § 113; Ovav. § 12. 13.47. 49; Kappas.; Āv. 8,12.27. 29. 54; Erz. 1,2; 32,13; 33,25); JM. also *rāiṇo* (Erz. 46,24; 47,3; 4; 49,1) and *rāẏassa* (Kk. II,505,17; III, 512,34); Ś. *raṇṇo* (Mṛcch. 99,25; 101,21. 23; Śak. 29,3; 54,2; Vikr. 28,19) and *rāiṇo* (Mālatīm. 90,6; 99,4; Kaṁsav. 49,10); Mg. *lañño*, written as *laṇṇo* (Mṛcch. 168,3) and *lāiṇo* (Mṛcch. 171,11); P. *rañño, rāciño* (Hc. 4,304). — Voc. AMg. *rāẏā* (Niraẏāv. § 22); mostly *rāẏaṁ* (Uttar. 409.414.417.418.444.503 etc.); JM. *rāẏa* (Kk. 261,12); Ś. *rāaṁ* (Hc. 4,264; Śak. 31,10); Mg. *lāaṁ* (Hc. 4,302); P. *rājaṁ* (Hc. 4,323); A. *rāa* (Hc. 4,402). — The nom. voc. *rāo*, ins. *rāaṇā*, abl. gen. *rāāṇo* are mentioned only by Sr., and the abl. *rāādo, rāādu* by Bh. Kī. 3,40 mentions also the ins. *rāṇā*, which is meant by C. 3,19, p. 49 too, where we should read *rājñā* in place of *rājā*. — Plural : nom. AMg. JM. *rāẏāṇo* (Āẏār. 1,2,3,5; Sūẏag. 182; Nāẏādh. 828. 830; Jīv. 311; Erz. 17,29; 32,24. 32; Kk. 263; 16), JM. also *rāiṇo* (Erz. 9,20; Kk. III, 512,13 [so to be read for *rāyaṇo*]); Ś. *rāāṇo* (Śak. 58,1; 121,12; Mudrār. 204,1); Mg. *lāāṇo* (Śak. 115,10). — Acc. AMg. JM. *rāẏāṇo* (Nāẏādh. 838; Kk. 263,16). — Ins. AMg. JM. *rāihiṁ* (Nāẏādh. 829. 833; Erz. 33,12). — Gen. AMg. JM. *rāiṇaṁ* (Āẏār. 1,2,5,1; Nāẏādh. 822 ff. 832 ff.; Āv. 15,10; Kk. 263,11), JM. also *rāẏāṇaṁ* (Erz. 28,22).

§ 400. At the end of compounds, the *a*-stem does not prevail, as in Skt., but all the stems appear dialectically as unconnected words : sing. nom. AMg. *ikkhāgarāẏā* = *aikṣvākarājaḥ* (Ṭhāṇ. 458; Nāẏādh. 692. 729); *devarāẏā* = *devarājaḥ* (Āẏār. 2,15,18; Uvās. § 113; Kappas.); JM. *vikkamarāo* = *vikramarājaḥ* (Kk. II, 507,12), also *dīharāẏā* = *dīrgharājaḥ* (Erz. 6,2); Ś. *mahārāo* = *mahārājaḥ* (Śak. 36,12; 56,11; 58,13; Vikr. 5,9;

9,4; 10,20); *juarāo* = *yuvarājaḥ* (Śak. 45,6); *aṅgarāo* (Veṇīs. 66,3); *vaccharāo* = *vatsarājaḥ* (Priyad. 32,2; 33,7); *vallaharāo ṇāma rāā* (Karp. 32,4). — Acc. JM. *gaddabhillarāyāṇaṁ* (Kk. 261,29); Ś. *mahārāaṁ* (Vikr. 27,17). — Ins. AMg. *devarannā* (Kappas.); Ś. *aṅgarāeṇa* (Veṇīs. 60,5); *ṇāarāeṇa* = *nāgarājena* (Nāgān. 69,18); *mahārāeṇa* (Vikr. 8,9; 29,13). Nāyādh. 852 has the mixed form AMg. *devaraṇṇeṇaṁ*. — Gen. AMg. *asurakumāraraṇṇo*, *asuraraṇṇo* (Vivāhap. 198); *devaraṇṇo* (Vivāhap. 220 ff.), *devaranno* (Kappas.); JM. *sagaranno* = **śakarājñaḥ* (Kk. 268,15); *vaïrasiṁharāyassa* (Kk. II,505, 17); Ś. *vaccharāassa* (Priyad. 33,9); *kaliṅgaraṇṇo* (Priyad.: 4,15); *riurāiṇo* = *ripurājasya* (Lalitav. 567.24); *mahārāassa* (Vikr. 12, 14 28,1); *aṅgarāassa* (Veṇīs. 62,13); Mg. *mahālāaśśa* (Prab. 63,4). — Voc. AMg. *pañcālarāyā* (Uttar. 414); *asurarāyā* (Vivāhap. 254), both with pluti; Ś. *aṅgarāa* (Veṇīs. 66, 14); *mahārāa* (Vikr. 12, 13). — Plural nom. AMg. *gaṇarāyāṇo* (Kappas. § 128); — M. *lāḍayavisayarāyāṇo* = *lāṭakaviṣayarājāḥ* (Kk. 264, 18); Ś. *bhimaseṇaṅgarāā* = *bhimasenāṅgarājau* (Veṇīs, 64,9).— Acc. AMg. *gaṇarāyāṇo* (Nirayāv. § 25). — Ins. AMg. *devarāihiṁ* (Vivāhap. 241). — Gen. AMg. *devarāiṇaṁ* (Vivāhap. 240 f.; Kappas.); JM. *sagarāiṇaṁ* (Kk. 266,41). For Ś. Mg. only the forms of the *a*-stems will be correct.

§ 401. *ātman* forms : sing. nom. AMg. *āyā* (Āyār. 1,1,1,3. 4; Sūyag. 28.35.81.838; Uttar. 251; Vivāhap. 132.1059 ff.; Dasav. N. 646,13); JŚ. *ādā* (Pav. 380,8 etc.; § 88); M. AMg. JM. JŚ *appā* (G. 333.798.887.899. 952.956. 1120; H. 39. 193.361. 672.754.880; R.; Uttar. 19; Dasav. N. 646,5; Nāyādh.; Bhag. 1,420; Erz.; Kk.; Pav. 380,11; 382,27; 385,61; Mṛcch. 12,7; 78,11; Śak. 19,7; 137,6; 140,7; Ratn. 291,2; 295,9; 299,17; 307,31 etc.); Ś. Mg. *attā* (Śak. 104,4; Mg. Mṛcch. 140,21)[1]. — Acc. M. AMg. JM. JŚ. Ḍh. *appāṇaṁ* (G. 240,860. 898.953. 1070. 1201; H. 516. 730. 756. 902. 953; R.; Āyār. 1,3,3,2; 2,3,1,21; Sūyag. 415 [°*ṇā*]; Vivāhap. 178; Kappas. § 120; Nāyādh.; Nirayāv.; Āv. 17,9. 10; Erz.; Kk.; Pav. 382, 27; 385, 65; 386, 70; Kattig. 399, 313; Mṛcch. 32, 14); AMg. also *attāṇaṁ* (Āyār. 1,1,3,3; 1,3,3,4; 1,6,5,4; 2,5,2,2 [so to be read for *attā ṇaṁ*]; Sūyag. 474 [°*ṇā*] and *āyāṇaṁ* (Sūyag. 367); Ś. Mg. only *attāṇaaṁ* = **ātmānakam* (Mṛcch. 90,21; 95,4; 96,7. 10. 14; 141,17; Śak. 14,3 [so to be read]; 24,1; 60,8; 63,9; 64,2; 74,5; 124,8; 137,12; 159,12; Vikr. 7,17; 23,13 etc.; Mg. Mṛcch. 37,13; 133,21; 162,21. 24; 169,7); false *attāṇaṁ* (Mṛcch. 327,3; Priyad. 41,14); *appāṇaṁ* (Priyad. 12,9; 23,10; 28,1. 5) and *appāṇaaṁ* (Cait. 75,16)[2]. — Ins. M. AMg. JM. Ś. *appaṇā* (G. 78. 83. 910; H. 159; R.; Āyār. 2,5,2,2.3; Sūyag. 170; Vivāhap. 67. 178; Kappas. S. § 59; Erz.; Vikr. 84,7). — Abl. AMg. *āyao* = **ātmataḥ* (Sūyag. 474), and so, or we have to read *attao* for *āttao* of the text in Sūyag. 472 too; JM. *appappaṇo* (T. 5,18). — Gen. M. AMg. JM. JŚ. D. Ā. *appaṇo* (H. 6.281.285; R.; Āyār. 1,2,5,1,1. 5; 1,3,2,1; Sūyag. 16; Kappas. § 8. 50.63. 112: p. 2; Nāyādh.; Erz.; Pav. 380,7; D. Mṛcch. 103,20; Ā. Mṛcch. 104,9); M. *attaṇo* (G. 63. 90 [v. l. °*ppa*°]. 96; H. 201 [v. l. °*ppa*°]), and so always in Ś. Mg. (Mṛcch. 141,15; 150,13; 166,15; Śak. 13,10; 25, 1; 32,1.8; 51,4; 54,7 etc.; Vikr. 13,4; 15,3; 32,17; 46,7; Ratn. 297,32; 303,32; 304,11 etc.; Mg. Mṛcch. 114,14; 116,19; 154,20; 164,4). — Voc. *appaṁ*

(Hc. 3,49). — Plur. nom. *appāṇo* = *ātmānaḥ* (Bh. 5,46; Hc. 3,56; Kī. 3,41; Mk. fol. 45). — From *appa-* = *ātma-*, that appears in the beginning of a compound, has been deduced a substantive *appa-*, that is declined according to the *a*-declension (Hc. 3,56; Mk. fol. 45): nom. *appo*; abl. *appão, appāu, appāhi, appāhiṁto, appā*; loc. *appe*; voc. *appa, appā*; Plur. ins. *appehi*; abl. *appāsuṁto*; gen. *appāṇaṁ*; loc. *appesu*. Found in the texts are: acc. AMg. *appaṁ* (Sūyag. 282); ins. AMg. *appeṇa* (Sūyag. 282), *appeṇaṁ* (Sūyag. 207); gen. A. *appahŏ* = **ātmasyaḥ* (Hc. 4,346); loc. AMg. *appe* (Uttar. 293); plur. *appā* in M. *suhaṁbharappa ccia* = *sukhaṁbharātmāna eva* (G. 993). With *kaḥ svārthe*, this stem occurs in JM. *appayaṁ* (Erz. 52,10) and A. *appaũ* (Hc. 4,422,3) = *ātmakam*. Further new *a*-stems are built from the old strong and weak stems. Thus from the strong stem : sing. nom. M. JM. *appāṇo* = **ātmānaḥ* = *ātmā* (Vr. 5,45; Hc. 3,56; Mk. fol. 45; G. 882; H. 133; R.; Sagara 10,1); *attāṇo* (Mk. fol. 45); AMg. *āyāṇe* (Vivāhap. 132). — Ins. AMg. *appāṇeṇaṁ* (Āyār. 1,1,7,6; 1,5,5,2; 2,1,3,3. 5; 2,15, 2,24; Vivāhap. 178). — Gen. JM. *appāṇassa* (Erz.). — Loc. M. *appāṇe* (R.). — Plur. nom. AMg. *āyāṇā* (Sūyag. 65); *appāṇā* (Hc. 3,56). With *kaḥ svārthe* : acc. JM. *attāṇayaṁ* (Erz.); Ś. Mg. *attāṇaaṁ* (see above). — Gen. M. *appāṇaassa* (G. 955). In the first member of a compound there appears the strong stem in AMg. *appāṇarakkhi* = *ātmarakṣi* (Uttar. 197); JŚ. *appāṇasamaṁ* (Kattig. 400,331). From the weak stem : sing. nom. *appaṇo* (Kī. 3,41). — Acc. A. *appaṇu* (Hc. 4,337). — Ins. M. *appaṇeṇa* (Kī. 3,41; H. 827); A. *appaṇeṁ* (Hc. 4,416). With *kaḥ svārthe* : acc. *appaṇaaṁ* (Hc. 2.153); A. *appaṇaũ* (Hc. 4,350,2); gen. Mg. *attaṇaaśśa* (Mṛcch. 163,20). — In the first member of a compound the weak stem appears in Ś. *attaṇakeraka* (Mṛcch. 74, 8; 88,24), Mg. *attaṇakelaka* (Mṛcch. 13, 9; 21, 20; 118,17 ; 130,10; 139,16 : 164,3; 167,2) ; A. *appaṇachandaũ* = *ātmacchandakam* (Hc. 4,422,14). It occurs also in the ins. *appaniā appanaïā*, (Hc. 3,14.57) of which the explanation is uncertain and in JM. *savvaappaṇayāe* = **sarvātmanatayā* (Erz. 58,31). Whilst the nom. sing. AMg. *āyā* would be taken as in the femin. (§ 358), they built as ins. sing. AMg. *āyāe* = *ātmanā* (Vivāhap. 76.845), *aṇāyāe* = *anātmanā* (Vivāhap. 76).

1. In Śak. 104,4 we should probably read with I *appā*. — 2. PISCHEL on Hc 3,56. Wrongly WEBER, IŚ, 14,235.

§ 402. The stems, appearing in Skt. in compounds and as the strong-stems, also of other masculine nouns ending in *-an*, are used, as independent *a*-stems, beside the old flexion of Skt. as in the case of *ātman* (§ 401); So sing. nom. *addhā* and *addhāṇo* = *adhvā* (Bh. 5,47; Hc. 3,56; Mk. fol. 45); acc. AMg. *addh'* for *addhaṁ* (§ 173; Sūyag. 59) and in the bahuvrīhi *dihamaddhaṁ* = *dirghādhvānam* (§ 353); loc. AMg. *addhāṇe* (Uttar. 712). In the first member of a compound stands the strong *a*-stem in AMg. *addhāṇapaḍivaṇṇa* = *adhvapratipanna* (Vivāhap. 153). Since *addhā* elsewhere in AMg. is used as feminine (§ 358), the acc. *addhaṁ* too may be derived from it. — Sing. nom. D. *bamhā* (Vr. 5,47; Hc. 3,56; Mṛcch. 105,21), JM. *baṁbho* (Erz. 30,20), AMg. *bambhe* (Kappas. Th. § 6) = *brahmā*; acc. M. *bamhaṁ* (H. 816); gen. AMg. *bambhassa* (Jīv. 912); plur. nom. AMg. *bambhā*, as *ajjamā* = *aryamaṇau* (Ṭhāṇ. 82). — Sing. nom. *muddhā* and *muddhāṇo* = *mūrdhā* (Hc. 3,56; Mk. fol. 45); acc. AMg. *muddhāṇaṁ* (Ovav. § 19; Kappas. § 15); ins. AMg. *muddheṇa* (Uttar. 788) and *muddhāṇeṇaṁ* (Uvās. § 81.83); loc. AMg.; *muddhi* = *mūrdhni* (Sūyag. 243) and *muddhāṇaṁsi* (Vivāhap. 1442); plur. nom. AMg. °*kayamuddhāṇā* = °*kṛtamūrdhānaḥ* (Nāyādh. § 40). — M. *mahimaṁ* = *mahimānam* (G. 885).—M. *savvatthāmeṇa* = *sarvasthāmnā* (H. 567). — Ś. *vijaavammā* = *vijayavarmā* (Ratn. 320,16), voc. *vijaavammaṁ* (Ratn. 320,19.32); Ś. *diḍhavammā* = *dṛḍhavarmā* (Priyad. 4,15); but PG. *sivakhandavamo* = *śivaskandavarmā* (5,2), *bhaṭṭisammasa* = *bhaṭṭiśarmaṇaḥ* (7,50), VG. *sirivijayabuddhavammassa* (101,3); Ś. *cittavammo* = *citravarmā* (Mudrār. 204,2); Ś. *miaṅkavammo* (Viddhaś. 73,2), *miaṅkavammassa* (Viddhaś. 43,7; 47,6; 113,2); A. *vaṁkima* = *vakrimāṇam* (Hc. 4,344); *ucchā* and *ucchāṇo* = *ukṣā* (Hc. 3.56; Mk. fol. 45); also *ukkhāṇo* (Mk. fol. 45); *gāvā* and *gāvāṇo* = *grāvā*; *pūsā* and *pūsāṇo* = *pūṣā* (Hc. 3,56; Mk. fol. 45); *takkhā* and *takkhāṇo* = *takṣā* (Hc. 3,56). So is explained also AMg. *siṁghāṇa* = *śleṣman* (§ 267). At the end of bahuvrīhi the words mostly go over to the *a*-declension from the stem of the composita, particularly when the last member is a neuter (cf. § 404) : M. *thirapĕmmo* = *sthirapremā* (H. 131; so to be read with H.[1] 134, as also Bhuvanapāla (IS. 16,117) has °*pimmo*; M. *aṇṇŏṇṇapparūḍhapĕmmāṇaṁ* (Pārvatīp. 45.13); AMg. *akamme* = *akarmā* (Āyār. 1,2,3,1); AMg. *kayabalikamme* = *kṛtabalikarmā* (Ovav. § 17), femin. °*kammā* (Kappas. § 95); JŚ. *rahidaparikammo* = *rahitaparikarmā* (Pav. 388,27); AMg. *saṁvuḍakammassa* = *saṁvṛtakarmaṇaḥ* (Sūyag. 144); AMg. *bahukūrakammā* = *bahukrūrakarmāṇaḥ* (Sūyag. 282); JM. *kayāyamaṇakammā* = *kṛtācamanakarmāṇaḥ* (Dvār. 500,39); AMg. *jāyathāme* = *jātasthāmā* (Kappas. § 118); AMg. *itthiyāo...parūḍhanahakesakakkharomāo* = *striyaḥ...prarūḍhanakhakeśakakṣaromṇyaḥ* (Ovav. § 72); JM. *namuināmo* = *namucināmā* (Erz. 1,20), but also *cittasaṁbhūyanāmāṇo* = *citrasaṁbhūtanāmānau* (Erz. 1,19); Ś. *laddhaṇāmassa* = *labdhanāmnaḥ* (Ratn. 321.29); Ś. *kidāāraparikammaṁ* = *kṛtācāraparikarmāṇaṁ* (Śak. 30,6); Ś. *aṇṇasaṁkantappĕmmā* = *anyasaṁkrāntapremāṇaḥ* (Vikr. 45,2); Mg. *diṇṇakalaviladāme* = *dattakaravīradāmā* (Mṛcch. 157,5), *uddāme* = *uddāmā* (Mṛcch. 175,14). For Mg. *uddāmĕvva kiśolī* (Mṛcch. 161,5) we should read *uddāma vva kiśolī*.

§ 403. From *maghavan* the nom. sing. is *maghoṇo* (Hc. 2,174) from the extended weak stem of acc. AMg. *maghavaṁ* (Vivāhap. 249). — *yuvan* is inflected as : sing. nom. M. JM. Ś. *juvā*, *juā* (Bh. 5,47; Hc. 3, 56; H.; Dvār. 501,15; Mṛcch. 28,5. 9; Pārvatīp 31,8); beside M. JM. *juvāṇo* (Bh. 5,47; Hc. 3,56; Kī. 3,41; Mk. fol. 45; H.; Prab. 38,10; Dvār. 506,31 also at the end of compounds), AMg. *juvāṇe* (Vivāhap. 212.214. 218.222.280. 287. 349) and *juvaṁ*, as from a *t*-stem (§ 396; Āyār. 2,4,2, 10; 2,5,1,1); with *kaḥ svārthe* : M. *haṁsajuāṇao* (Vikr. 64,5; 74,4); femin. M. °*juāṇā* (H.); ins. M. *juāṇeṇa* (H.), JM. °*juvāṇeṇa* (Erz. 43,18); voc. M. *juāṇa* (H.); plur. nom. M. *juāṇā*, AMg. *juvāṇā* (H., also at the end of compounds; Ṭhāṇ. 371; Antag. 55); ins. M. °*juāṇehi* (H.); gen. AMg. *juvāṇāṇaṁ* (Aṇuog. 328); voc. AMg. *juvāṇā* in *he juvāṇa tti* (Ṭhāṇ. 488;

Aṇuog. 324). — From *śvan* are found; sing. nom. *sāṇo* (Bh. 5,47; Hc. 3,56), AMg. *sāṇe* (Āyār. 2,4,1,8), A. *sāṇa* (Piṅgala 1,99), therefore, the stem, which likewise occurs in AMg. (Paṇhāv. 20); gen. AMg. *sāṇassa* (Uttar. 12). — From the different stems, which one tends to put together under *panthan* or *pathin* or *pathi* or *path*, are found inclusive of *patha* : sing. nom. *pantho* (Hc. 1,30) and *paho* (Vr. 1,13; Hc. 1,88; Kī. 1,18; Mk. fol. 7); acc. AMg. JM. *panthaṁ* (Hc. 1,88; Āyār. 1,7,1,2; Ṭhāṇ. 248; Āv. 22,26; 46,5. 11. 15), AMg. *panth'*=*pantham* (§ 173; Sūyag. 59), AMg. *pahaṁ* (Sūyag. 59; Uttar. 324); ins. M. JM. *paheṇa* (G. 423; Kk. 269,29; Āv. 36,33), AMg. *paheṇaṁ* (Uttar. 635); abl. JM. *panthāo* (Kk. 264,4); loc. JM. *panthe* (Erz. 36,28); A. *panthi* (Hc. 4,429,1), AMg. *pahe* (Uttar. 324), JM. *pahammi* (Dvār. 504,1); plur. nom. M. *panthāṇo* (H. 729), AMg. JM. *panthā* (Sūyag. 110; Erz. 7,3); gen. AMg. *panthāṇaṁ* (Sūyag. 189): loc. AMg. *panthesu* (Uttar. 53). — In compounds appear the stems M. JM. *pantha*, °*vantha* (H.; R.; Āv. 46,6) and *paha*, °*vaha* (G.H.R.; Kk.; Erz.).

§ 404. The neutra in *-an* sometimes become masculine (§ 358); but they are inflected mostly like the neutra in *-a*. Thus e.g. *pĕmma-*=*preman* : sing. nom. M. Ś. *pĕmmaṁ* (H. 81.95.124. 126. 232; Ratn. 299,18; Karp. 78,3. 6); acc. M. Ś. *pĕmmaṁ* (H. 522; Vikr. 51,16; Karp. 76,8. 10); ins. *pĕmmeṇa* (H. 423. 746.966); gen. M. Ś. *pĕmmassa* (H. 53, 390. 511. 910.940; Karp. 75,9); loc. M. *pĕmmammi* (Karp. 79,5), M. Ś. *pĕmme* (H. 304; Karp. 75,10); plur. nom. M. *pĕmmāiṁ* (H. 127. 236.287); gen. M. *pĕmmāṇaṁ* (H. 10). — Sing. nom. M. Ś. Mg. *ṇāmaṁ*, AMg. J.M. *nāmaṁ* (H. 452; Kappas. § 108; Āv. 13,29; 14,19; Erz. 4,34; Vikr. 30,9; Mg. Mudrār. 191,5; 194,7); acc. Ś. Mg. *ṇāmaṁ* (Mṛcch. 28,21; 37,25); ins. Ś. Mg. *ṇāmeṇa* (Vikr. 16,9; Mṛcch. 161,2), AMg. JM. *nāmeṇa* (Āv. 8,5), AMg. *ṇāmeṇaṁ* (Ovav. § 105), *nāmeṇaṁ* (Kappas. § 107); loc. M. *ṇāme* (G. 89); plur. nom. JM. *nāmāṇi* (Āv. 13,28) and AMg. JM. *nāmāiṁ* (Uvās. § 277; Āv. 14,18). Skt. *nāma* (by name; namely) becomes M. Ś. Mg. *ṇāma* (G. H. R; Mṛcch. 23,22; 28,23; 40,22; 94,25; 142,12 etc.; Mg. Mṛcch. 21, 10; 38, 2; 40, 9), JM. *nāma* (Āv. 15, 8; 16, 29; 39, 2; Erz. 1,1.20; 11,17 etc.), but AMg. *nāmaṁ* (Ovav. § 11; Kappas. § 124; Uvās.; Bhag.; Nāyādh.; Nirayāv.) and *nāma* (Ovav. § 1. 12; Kappas. § 42. 129). — Sing. nom. AMg. JŚ. *jammaṁ*=*janma* (Uttar. 636; Kattig. 399,321); acc. M. AMg. *jammaṁ* (H. 844; Āyār. 1,3,4. 4; Sūyag. 689); ins. Ś. *jammeṇa* (Śak. 141,10); abl. AMg. *jammāo* (Sūyag. 689. 756); gen. AMg. *jammassa* (Sūyag.); loc. JM. Ś. *jamme* (Āv. 12,13; 25,37; Nāgān. 35,5), A. *jami* (Hc. 4,383, 3; so to be read). — Sing. nom. M. AMg. *kammaṁ*=*karma* (R. 14,46; Uttar. 247.413.505); acc.; AMg. JŚ. *kammaṁ* (Sūyag. 381. 382. 456. 496; Kattig. 399,319; 400, 327; 403,373. 374. 377); ins. AMg. *kammeṇaṁ* (Vivāhap. 168. 190; Uvās. § 72. 76); gen. M. AMg. JŚ. *kammassa* (H. 614; Uttar. 178; Paṇṇav. 665. 671 f.; Kappas. § 19; Pav. 383,27), Mg. *kammāha* (Hc. 4,299, with note; the Kashmir recension of Śak. reads 108,13 *kammaṇo*); loc. AMg. *kammaṁsi* (Ṭhāṇ. 208; Rāyap. 249), JM. *kamme* (Erz. 38,31); against the dialect is Ś. *kammammi* (Kaṁsav.

50,2) for the correct *kamme* (Kāleyak. 25,8); plur. nom. AMg. *kammā* (Uttar. 113); acc. AMg. *kammāiṁ* (Sūẏag. 284; Uvās. § 138; Ovav. § 153) and *kammā* (Uttar. 155), *ahākammāṇi* (Sūẏag. 873), JŚ. *kammāṇi* (Pav. 384,59); ins. AMg. *kammehiṁ* (Āẏār. 1,4, 2,2.3,3; 1,5,2,3; Sūẏag. 716.718. 719. 721. 771; Uttar. 155. 175. 205. 218. 221. 593; Vivāhap. 147. 168. 185), *ahākammehiṁ* (Uttar. 155. 205); gen. AMg. *kammāṇaṁ* (Sūẏag. 1012; Uttar. 156. 205; Samav. 112; Uvās. § 74), *kammāṇa* (Uttar. 177); M. according to Hc. 4,300 also *kammāhã*; loc. Ś. *kammesu* (Viddhaś. 28,6), Mg. *kammeśu* (Mudrār. 191,9). On the nom. Ś. *kamme* see § 358. Of the sporadic forms may further be mentioned; sing. loc. AMg. *cammaṁsi* = *carmaṇi* (Kappas. § 60), *romaṁsi* = *romṇi* (Uvās. § 219), *ahaṁsi* = *ahani* (Āẏār. 2.15, 11); Ś. *pavve pavve* = *parvaṇi parvaṇi* (Kāleyak. 13,20); plur. acc. M. *cammāiṁ* (H. 631); ins. AMg. *lomehiṁ* = *lomabhiḥ* (Uvās. § 94.95); AMg. Ś. *dāmehiṁ* = *dāmabhiḥ* (Jīv. 348; Rāẏap. 63; Mṛcch. 69,1); loc. M. *dāmesu* (G. 784); JŚ. *pavvesu* = *parvasu* (Kattig. 402,359). Dialectically the old Skt. forms have sometimes been retained : sing. nom. M. *camma* = *carma* (H. 955); nom. acc. AMg. JŚ. Ś. Mg. *kamma* = *karma* (Āẏār. 1,4,3,2; 2,2,2, 13. 14; Sūẏag. 282; Uttar. 113. 178; Pav. 386,4; Veṇis. 62,5; Uttarar. 197,10; Mg. Śak 114,6 [verse]; Veṇīs. 33,5). For Ś. Mg,, except in verses, the form will be false for *kammaṁ*. In Mṛcch. 70,24 we should read *amūiṁ...kammatoraṇāiṁ*, which is pointed to by the v. l. in GOḌABOLE p. 201; for Ś. *pema* (Prab. 41,6) the ed. Bomb. 91,6 reads *ppemā* for *pĕmma* (Karp. 77,10 ed. Bomb.) KONOW 76,8 rightly has *pĕmmaṁ*. Ins. AMg. *kammaṇā* (Āẏār. 1,3,1,4); probably an error for *kammuṇā*, as AMg. JM. elsewhere have (§ 104; Āẏār. 1,4,4,3[1]; 1,8,1,13. 17; Sūẏag. 108. 151. 377. 542. 873. 978; Uttar. 28. 43. 177. 217. 505. 592. 573 f.; Jīv. 796; Paṇhāv. 134. 391; Vivāhap. 283. 1808; Erz. 25,20; Sagara. 2,9). Likewise there appears *u* for *a* in the gen. sing. AMg. *kammuṇo* (Uttar. 170.223. 312), in the gen. plur. AMg. *kammuṇaṁ* (Sūẏag. 542) and in the ins. sing. AMg. *dhammuṇā* from *dharman* in the compound *kāladhammuṇā saṁjjutta* = *kāladharmaṇā saṁyukta* (Ṭhāṇ. 157; Vivāgas. 82 ff. 117. 155. 207. 217. 225. 238; Nāẏādh. 329. 1099. 1421). Corresponding to Skt. *karmataḥ* AMg. has *kammao* (Uvās. § 51), and Ś. *jammado* (Ratn. 298,11) is = Skt. *janmataḥ*. The loc. Ś. *kammaṇi* (Bālar. 251,8) will be false. A loc. plur. AMg. *kammasu* = *karmasu* stands at Sūẏag. 403 in the verse. — As the masculine forms a new stem in *-āṇa* (§ 401. 402), so the neutra dialectically forms a stem in *-aṇa* : AMg. *jammaṇaṁ* = *janma* (Hc. 2,174; Jīv. 122. 123. 136 ff.); AMg. JM. *jammaṇa°* (Uttar. 1105; Paṇhāv. 72 ff.; Nāẏādh. 290; Vivāhap. 1159. 1738. 1741 f. 1773; Sagara 6,10; Erz.); JM. *kammaṇaṁ* = *karma* (Erz. 52,17; 56,31), *kammaṇa°* (Erz. 29,23). The same stem with *u*, as in the ins. gen sing., gen. plur. of *karman*, occurs in the abl. sing. AMg. *kammuṇāu* (Aẏār. 1,7,8,2; Sūẏag. 17).[2] *bamhaṇa* = *brahman* (Kī. 3,41) too is to be taken as included in the neuter.

1. JACOBI reads with the ed. Calc. against the MSS *kammāṇi*, to accept which he is constrained to refer to this acc. plur. by *saphalaṁ* (SBE. XXII, p. 4). We should with the MSS read *kammuṇā*, and *saphalaṁ* is to be assumed as = *svaphalam*.—2. *kammuṇā·u* can also be separated. However, perhaps the interpretation given above is better.

§ 405. 2) Stems in *-in, -min, -vin.* The stems in *-in, -min, -vin,* partly according to the mode of Skt., and partly on the basis of the stem in *-i,* that appears in the beginning of the composita, are declined according to the *i*- dectension. Sing. nom. M. AMg. JM Ś., *hatthi,* Mg. *hasti,* A. *hatthi = hasti* (R. 8,36; Ovav. § 11; Erz. 16,18; Mṛcch. 40,22.25; Mg. Hc. 4,289; Mṛcch. 40,9; 168,4; A. Hc, 4,443) ; M. *sihi = śikhi* (H. 13) ; AMg. JM. Ś. *tavassi,* Mg. *tavaśśi = tapasvi* (Kappas. S. § 61; Āv. 32, 18; Erz. 25,6; Śak. 132,8; Mg. Mṛcch. 97.3) ; AMg. *mehāvi = medhāvi* (Āẏār. 1,2,2,3; 1,2,6,2.5; 1,6,4,2.3), metrically also *mehāvi* (Sūẏag. 414); JŚ. *ṇāṇi,* AMg. *ṇāṇi = jñāni* (Kattig. 402. 358. 360; 403, 377. 379. 282. 384; 404, 386; Sūẏag. 318) ; neuter M. *viāsi* (Mukund. 14, 10) ; Ś. *kāri* (Bālar. 56, 14). The acc., in majority of cases, is formed according to the *i*-declension: M. AMg. JM. *hatthiṁ = hastinam* (Mṛcch. 41, 16; Āẏār. 2,1,5,3; Vivāhap. 850; Niraẏāv. § 18; Erz. 72,21) ; AMg. *tavassiṁ* (Āẏār. 2,2,2,4; Vivāhap. 232), *bambhaẏāriṁ = brahmacāriṇam* (Uttar. 487), *oẏassiṁ teẏassiṁ vaccassiṁ jasassiṁ = ojasvinaṁ tejasvinaṁ varcasvinaṁ yaśasvinam* (Āẏār. 2,2, 1,12), *pakkhiṁ = pakṣiṇam* (Āẏār. 2,3,3,8; 2,4,2,7), *sĕṭṭhiṁ = śreṣṭhinam* (Samav. 84); JM. *sāmiṁ = svāminam* (Āv. 32, 14. 32; 33, 6) ; Ś. *kañcuiṁ = kañcukinam* (Vikr. 45,10; Priyad. 48,21), but elsewhere Ś. *piaāriṇaṁ* (Vikr. 10,14), *uaāriṇaṁ* (Vikr. 12,11; 13,18), *jālovajiviṇaṁ = jālopajivinam* (Śak. 116,7), *vāliṇaṁ* (Mahāv. 55,12).—Ins. M. *sasiṇā* (R. 2,3; 10,29. 42), *avalambiṇā* (G. 301); AMg. *gandhahatthiṇā* (Niraẏāv. § 18), *nihāriṇā = nirhāriṇā* (Ovav. § 56), *tāmaliṇā bālatavassiṇā* (Vivāhap. 235) ; JM. Ś. *sāmiṇā,* Mg. *śāmiṇā = svāminā* (Āv. 32,24; Kk. 260,29; Śak. 116,8; Mahāv. 120,12; Veṇīs. 62,23; 64,5; 66,8; Mg. Mṛcch. 118,21; 162,17. 19; Veṇīs. 35,12); JM. *visambhaghāiṇā = visrambhaghātiṇā* (Erz. 68,4), metrically also *mantiṇa* for *mantiṇā = mantriṇā* (Āv. 13,13) ; Ś. *kaṇṇovaghādiṇā = karṇopaghātinā* (Śak. 29,8) ; Mg. *kāliṇā = kāriṇā* (Mṛcch. 158,21; Prab. 54,6).—Abl. AMg. *sihario = śikhariṇaḥ* (Ṭhāṇ. 177).—Gen. M. *piṇāiṇo = pinākinaḥ* (G. 41), *sasiṇo* (G. 60. 953. 1108. 1132; H. 319; R. 10,46), *guṇasāliṇo vi kariṇo = guṇaśālino'pi kariṇaḥ* (H. 788); AMg. *jasassiṇo = yaśasvinaḥ* (Sūẏag. 304), *gihiṇo = gṛhiṇaḥ* (Uvās. § 83. 84); JM. *sāmiṇo* (T. 5,12) and AMg. JM. *sāmissa* (Vivāhap. 188; Āv. 32,27) ; JM. *egāgiṇo = ekākinaḥ* (Erz. 9,16). In AMg. JM. more frequent is the ending *-issa,* that is further traceable elsewhere in JŚ. only: AMg. *māẏissa, amāẏissa = māyinaḥ, amāyinaḥ* (Ṭhāṇ. 150), *bambhaẏārissa = brahmacāriṇaḥ* (Nāẏādh. § 87; Uttar. 917 f.), *vatthadhārissa = vastradhāriṇaḥ* (Āẏār. 2,5,2,1) ; *abhikaṅkhissa = abhikāṅkṣiṇaḥ* (Uttar. 921), *tavassissa* (Vivāhap. 231. 233. 236), *hatthissa* (Rāẏap. 270; Vivāhap. 491, 493) ; both forms stand beside one another in AMg. *egantacārissa tavassiṇo* (Sūẏag. 909); JM. *paṇaīssa = praṇayinaḥ, virahissa = virahiṇaḥ* (Kk. 270,23; 274,4) *kāmissa = kāminaḥ* (Erz. 71, 4), *sĕṭṭhissa = śreṣṭhinaḥ* (Āv. 37.26) ; JŚ. *kevalaṇāṇissa = kevalajñāninaḥ* (Pav. 381,20) ; Ś. *virohiṇo = virodhinaḥ, vāsiṇo, paribhoiṇo = paribhogiṇaḥ* (Śak. 18,11; 23,8; 38,5), *ahiṇivesiṇo = abhiniveśinaḥ* (Mālav. 41,17), *sohiṇo = śobhinaḥ* (Ratn. 292, 12) ; Mg. *śāmiṇo = svāminaḥ* (Śak. 117,6), *aṇumaggagāmiṇo = anumārgagāmiṇaḥ* (Veṇīs. 35,6).—Loc. AMg. *ruppimmi = rukmiṇi siharammi = śikhariṇi* (Ṭhāṇ. 75)), *cakkavaṭṭiṁsi = cakravartini* (Nāẏādh.

§ 46).—Voc. AMg. JM. *sāmi* (Kappas. § 49; Nāẏādh. § 46. 73; Āv. 32, 26); JM. *sāmi* (Āv. 15,24; Erz. 6,34; 8, 19); Ś. *kañcui* (Vikr. 45,15; Ratn. 327,7; Priyad. 50,8 [text °*i*].—Plural: nom. M. *phaṇiṇo, virāviṇo, saṅkiṇo* (G. 390. 611. 863. 880), *guṇiṇo* = *guṇinaḥ*, *cāiṇo* = *tyāginaḥ* (H. 673), also *sāmī* = *svāminaḥ* in *sāmi ccia* (H. 91), *vaṇahatthī* = *vanahastinaḥ* (R. 8,36); AMg. *duvālasaṅgiṇo* = *dvādaśāṅginaḥ* (Ovav. § 26), *daṇḍiṇo muṇḍiṇo sihaṇḍiṇo jaḍiṇo picchiṇo* beside *daṇḍī muṇḍisihaṇḍī picchī* in immediately following verses (Ovav. § 49, V), *agāriṇo, daṁsiṇo* = *darśinaḥ* (Sūẏag. 301. 368. 370), *tassaṅkiṇo* = *tacchaṅkinaḥ* (Sūẏag. 936), *abambhacāriṇo* = *abrahmacāriṇaḥ* (Uttar. 351), *pāragāmiṇo, dhuvacāriṇo, sammattadaṁsiṇo* = *samyaktvadarśinaḥ* (Āẏār. 1,2,2,1; 1,2,3,4; 1,2,6,3), beside the more frequent nom. in *-ī*, as *nāṇī* = *jñāninaḥ*, *akkandakārī* = *ākrandakāriṇaḥ*, *pakkhī* = *pakṣiṇaḥ* (Āẏār. 1,4,2,3; 1,6,1,6; 2,3,3,3), *hatthī* = *hastinaḥ* (Āẏār. 2,3,2,17; Sūẏag. 172; Nāẏādh. 348), *oẏaṁsī teẏaṁsī vaccaṁsī jasaṁsī* = *ojasvinas tejasvino varcasvino yaśasvinaḥ* (Vivāhap. 185), *rūvī ẏa arūvī ẏa* = *rūpiṇaś ca cārūpiṇaś ca* (Vivāhap. 207), *cakkavaṭṭī* = *cakravartinaḥ*, *cakkajohī* = *cakrayodhinaḥ* (Ṭhāṇ. 197. 512). JM. too has both the forms beside one another: *mantiṇo* = *mantriṇaḥ* (Kk. 262,30), *dariddiṇo* = *daridriṇaḥ* (Erz. 50,2), beside *mahātavassī* = *mahātapasvinaḥ* (Kk. 269,24), *hatthī* = *hastinaḥ* (Erz. 32,6). In Ś. and probably in Mg. too the form in *-ī* is not used so little, as in the case of the *i*-stems (§ 380): Ś. *pakkhiṇo* = *pakṣiṇaḥ*, *sippiṇo* = *śilpinaḥ*, *avvattabhāsiṇo* = *avyaktabhāṣiṇaḥ* (Mṛcch. 38,21; 71,2; 103,6), *kusumadāiṇo* = *kusumadāyinaḥ*, *dhammaāriṇo* = *dharmacāriṇaḥ* (Śak. 10,2; 20,1), *parivanthiṇo* = *paripanthinaḥ* (Vikr. 8, 9), *kañcuiṇo* = *kañcukinaḥ* (Mallikām. 186, 16). Very seldom and probably a wrong reading is the ending *-īo* in Ś.: *sāmīo* = *svāminaḥ* (Kaṁsav. 48,19; 50,1). Neuter: AMg. *akālapaḍibahiṇi akālapaḍibhoiṇi* = *akālapratibodhiny akālapratibhogīni* (Āẏār. 2,3,1,8), *rāẏakulagāmiṇi* (Niraẏāv. § 21).—Acc. AMg. *pāṇiṇo* = *prāṇinaḥ* (Sūẏag. 266), *maüli* = *mukulinaḥ* (Paṇhāv. 119), *ṭhāṇi* = *sthāninaḥ* (Sūẏag.); JM. *bharahaṇivāsiṇo* (Sagara 9, 8).—Ins. AMg. *pakkhihiṁ* = *pakṣibhiḥ* (Sūẏag. 289), *savvadarisihiṁ* = *sarvadarśibhiḥ* (Nandīs. 388), *paravāihiṁ* = *paravādibhiḥ* (Ovav. § 26), *mehāvihiṁ* = *medhāvibhiḥ* (Ovav. § 48; Kappas. § 60), *hatthihi* (Nāẏādh. 330. 344); JM. *mantihi* = *mantribhiḥ* (Āv. 8,36; Kk. 262,17); Mg. *vaṁdihiṁ* = *vandibhiḥ* (Lalitav. 565, 13).—Abl. AMg. *asaṇṇihiṁto* = *asaṁjñibhyaḥ*, *pakkhihiṁto* = *pakṣibhyaḥ* (Jīv. 263. 265); A. *sāmihũ* = *svāmibhyaḥ* (Hc. 4,341,2).—Gen. M. *barahiṇa* = *barhiṇām* (G. 349); AMg. *mahāhimavantaruppiṇaṁ* = *mahāhimavadrukmiṇoḥ* (Samav. 114. 117), *pakkhiṇaṁ* = *pakṣiṇām* (Jīv. 325), *gandhahatthīṇaṁ, cakkavaṭṭiṇaṁ, savvadarisiṇaṁ* (Ovav. § 20; Kappas. § 16); JM. *kāmatthiṇaṁ* = *kāmārthinām*, *vāiṇaṁ* = *vādinām* (Erz. 29,31; 69,20), *paṇaiṇa* = *praṇayinām*, (KI. 15); JŚ *dehiṇaṁ* (Kattig. 402, 363); Mg. *śāmiṇaṁ* = *svāminām* (Kaṁsav. 48, 17; 49,12; so to be read for °*mi*°).—Loc. M. *paṇaisu* = *praṇayiṣu* (G. 728); AMg. *hatthisu* = *hastiṣu*, *pakkhisu* = *pakṣiṣu* (Sūẏag. 317), *tavassisu* = *tapasviṣu* (Paṇhāv. 430); Ś. *sāmisu* (Mahāv. 119,14; so to be read).—Voc. S. *saṁkaragharādhivāsiṇo* (Mālatīm. 128,7); Mg. *vaṁdiṇo* (Lalitav. 565, 17; 566, 5. 15). A large number of forms built according to Skt. flexion are retained in verses, especially in AMg. (§ 99).

§ 406. Sometimes also in the case of nouns in *-in*, we find the stem extended by *a* : *sakkhiṇo* = *sākṣi* (Hc. 2,174), but JM. Ś. *sakkhi*, Mg. *śaḥki* (Āv. 38,5; Mṛcch. 53,11; 164,25), Ś. *sakkhikadua* = **sākṣikṛtvā* (Vikr. 45,20), plur. nom. M. Ś. *sakkhiṇo* (Karp. 86,5; Ś. Uttarar. 77,4; Karp. 14,2); M. *sihiṇaṁ* = *śikhi*, plural nom. *sihiṇā*, ins. *sihiṇehī̃* (bosom; Deśīn. 8,31; Triv. 1,4,121; Karp. 31,7; 79,10; 95,10); AMg. *kimiṇa* = *kṛmin*, *sakimiṇa* = *sakṛmi* (Nāyādh. 995; Paṇhāv. 525. 529); AMg. Ś. *barahiṇa*, A. *baṁhiṇa* = *barhin* (Paṇṇav. 54; Ovav. § 4; Nāyādh. § 61. 62; p. 914; Uttarar. 21, 9; A Vikr. 58, 8), A. *barihiṇa* (Hc. 4, 422, 8), beside M. Ś. *barahi-* (G. ; Viddhaś. 51, 7); M. JM. *gabbhiṇa* = *garbhin* (Vr. 2,10; Hc. 1, 208; Kī.2,31; Mk. fol. 15; G. R.; Sagara 4,11; cf. § 246). —In PG. the following forms are found: *°yāji* (5,1), gen. *°ppadāyino* = *pradāyinaḥ* (6,11), but also *khaṁdakŏṁḍisa* = *skandakuṇḍinaḥ* (6, 19), *nāganaṁdisa* = *nāganandinaḥ* (6, 25), *golisa* = *goḍinaḥ* (6, 25) from *goḍa* = *goṇḍa* 2) in B.-R. appropriately; ins. plur. *°sāmīhi* = *°svāmibhiḥ* (6, 11). *°vāsihi* = *°vāsibhiḥ* (6,35. 36).

(7) Stems in *-s*.

§ 407. Like nouns in *-t* and *-n*, those in *-s* too have three stems: 1) the old stem in *-s*, 2) after dropping off of *s*, a stem in *-a*, *-i*, *-u*, i.e. in the vowel that was immediately before the *s*, and 3) a stem in *-sa*, formed by extension with *a*. So : M. *siroampa* = *śiraḥkampa* (R. 12, 31), *sirakavalaṇa* = *śiraḥkavalana* (G. 351); AMg. *devīo*...*°raïyasirasāo* = *devyaḥ*... *°racitaśiraskāḥ* (Ovav. § 55); Mg. *śilaścālaṇa* (Mṛcch. 126, 7). Cf. § 347. AMg. *joiṭhāṇa* = *jyotiḥsthāna*, *joisama* = *jyotiḥsama* (Uttar. 375. 1009); PG. *dhamāyubalayasovadhanike* = *dharmāyurbalayaśovardhanakān* (6, 9; cf. VG. 101, 8); M. JM. *āukkhae* = *āyuḥkṣaye* (H. 321; Erz. 24, 36), JM. *āudalāṇi* = *āyurdalāni* (Kk. 268, 22). In M. JM. AMg. the neuter nouns in *-as* are used as masculine as a rule (§ 356).

§ 408. Nouns in *-as*.—The forms built from the old *s*-stem are : sing. masc. nom. AMg. *dummaṇā*, *sumaṇā* (Sūyag. 692), Ś. *duvvāsā* = *durvāsāḥ* (Śak. 72, 10), the stem also in compounds *duvvāsāsāvo* = *durvāsaḥśāpaḥ* (76, 5), with a long vowel according to § 64; Ś. *purūravā* = *purūravāḥ* (Vikr. 40, 21), Mg. *śamaśśaśidamaṇā* = *samāśvastamanāḥ* (Mṛcch. 134, 23). One must consider, M. JŚ. Ś. Mg. *ṇamo*, AMg. JM. *namo* = *namas*, as neuter, since Ś. Mg. do not turn the neuter in *-as* into masc. (e.g. M. : G. H.; AMg.; Vivāhap. 172; Ovav.; Kappas.; JM.: Kk.; Ṛṣabhap.; JŚ. : Pav. 379,4; 389, 4; Ś.: Mṛcch. 128, 18.21; Śak. 120,5; Mg.: Mṛcch. 114,10. 22; 133, 17; Prab. 46, 11). Cf. § 175. 498. Neuter is also JŚ. *tao* = *tapaḥ* (Pav. 387,26). Acc. Ś. *purūravasaṁ* (Vikr. 36,9); neut. AMg. JŚ. *maṇo* = *manas* (Kappas. § 121; Pav. 386, 70). The old forms in the ins. are frequent in AMg. JM. : AMg. *maṇasā vayasā* = *manasā vacasā* (Ṭhāṇ. 40), more often *maṇasā vayasā kāyasā* (§ 364), *na cakkhusā na maṇasā na vayasā* (Paṇhāv. 461); AMg. JM. *teyasā* = *tejasā* (Āyār. 2, 16, 5; Paṇhāv. 507;

Ṭhāṇ. 568; Ovav. § 22; Vivāhap. 169; Rāẏap. 238; Kappas. § 39.59. 118; Erz. 39, 8); AMg. JŚ. *tavasā* = *tapasā* (Sūẏag. 348; Uttar. 174; Uvās. § 76. 264; Ovav. § 21. 24. 38. 62; Pav. 388, 27); AMg. *raẏasā* = *rajasā* (Āẏār. 2,1,1,1. 3,4; Sūẏag. 551), *sahasā* (Ṭhāṇ. 368), *ceẏasā*, *jasasā* (Samav. 81. 83. 85), *sirasā* (Kappas.; Ovav.), also in Ś. (Vikr. 27, 17). On the ins. in *-sā* of *a-* stems see § 364.—Loc. *urasi*, *sirasi*, *sarasi* (Hc. 4, 448); AMg. *tamasi* (Āẏār. 1, 6, 1, 3); Ś. *purūravasi* (Vikr. 35, 15), *tavasi* (Śak. 21, 5); Mg. *śilaśi* (Mṛcch. 17, 1; 116, 15).

§ 409. The usual flexion is with the *a*-stem: sing. nom. M. *vimaṇo* (R. 5, 16); AMg. *uggatavo* = *ugratapāḥ* (Uttar. 362), *tammaṇe* = *tanmanāḥ* (Vivāhap. 114), *piimaṇe* = *prītimanāḥ* (Kappas. § 15, 50; Ovav. § 17), *uggatave dittatave tattatave mahātave ghoratave* (Ovav. § 62); °*raïẏavacche* = °*racitavakṣāḥ* (Ovav. § 19); JM. *tammaṇo* = *tanmanāḥ*, *bhāsurasiro* = *bhāsuraśirāḥ* (Erz. 12,6; 69, 6); JŚ. *adhikatejo* = *adhikatejāḥ* (Pav. 381, 19); fem. M. *vimaṇa vva* (R. 4,31), AMg. *piimaṇā* (Kappas. § 5); Ś. °*saṁkantamaṇā* = °*saṁkrāntamanāḥ* (Mṛcch. 29, 3); *pajjassuamaṇā* = *pratyutsukamanāḥ* (Śak. 50, 2); neut. M. *dummaṇaṁ* (R. 11, 14); AMg. JM. *seẏaṁ* = *śreyaḥ* (Uttar. 204. 672. 678; Vivāgas. 218; Vivāhap. 232; Nāẏādh. 333. 482. 574. 609. 616; Uvās.; Ovav.; Kappas.; Erz.). Mg. *śila* (Mṛcch. 112, 8. 9) stands on account of metre for *śile* = *śiraḥ*. Cf. § 364. In the masc. the comparative in *-yas* in AMg. JM. partly has extended its strong stem with *a*, as *seẏaṁse* = *śreyān*, *pāvīẏaṁse* (text *pāvaṁse*) = *pāpiyān* (Ṭhāṇ. 314. 315), and partly have weakened them, as AMg. *kaṇiẏase* = *kanīyān* (Kappas. Th. § 1; Antag. 32), JM. *kaṇiẏaso* (Dvār. 501, 29), which, however, as the acc. AMg. JM. *kaṇiẏasaṁ* (Uvās.; Dvār. 495, 30) too can be equated as = Skt. *kanīyasa*, which, however, is probably itself in the first place secondary. From the old comparative *báliyas* has developed an adjective **balīya*, nom. Ś. *balio* (Śak. 50, 5; 51, 2), which has regularly shortened its *ī* under the influence of the old accent: *balia* (strong, thick, dense; Deśīn. 6,88; Mg. Mṛcch. 14,10; JM. Āv. 35,17; Erz. 9,17; Kk. 261,42) and of which the neuter *baliaṁ* is used adverbially in the meaning "very" (Pāiẏal. 90; M. Śak. 55,16; Ś. Vikr. 27,21; 51,15; Mālav. 68,11; Mg. Śak. 154, 13; Veṇīs. 34,3).—Acc. AMg. masc. *dummaṇaṁ* (Kappas. § 38), *jāẏaveaẏaṁ* = *jātavedasam* (Uttar. 365), *jāẏateẏaṁ* = *jātatejasam* (Samav. 81); femin. M. *vimaṇaṁ* (R. 11,49); very frequently in the neuter: M. AMg. *uraṁ* (R. 1, 48; 4,20. 47; Āẏār. 1,1,1,5; Vivāgas. 127); M. AMg. *jasaṁ* = *yaśas* (R. 2, 5; 4,47; Uttar. 170), Ḍh. *jaśaṁ* (Mṛcch. 30, 9); M. *ṇahaṁ*, AMg. *nahaṁ* (R. 1,7; 5,2. 64; Ovav.); AMg. *tamaṁ* (Sūẏag. 31. 170); M. *siraṁ* (R. 11,35. 64. 73. 90. 94); AMg. Mg. *maṇaṁ* (Uttar. 198; Mṛcch. 30, 24); AMg. *vaẏaṁ* = *vayas* (Āẏār. 1, 2, 1, 2. 5 beside nom. *vao* in 1, 2, 1, 3); JM. *teẏaṁ* = *tejas* (Erz. 3, 10; 8, 24); AMg. JŚ. *raẏaṁ* = *rajas* (Sūẏag. 113; Pav. 385, 61); A. *taü*, *tavu* = *tapas* (Hc. 4, 441, 1. 2).—Ins. M. *vaccheṇa* = *vakṣasā* (G. 301); *sireṇa* = *śirasā* (Hc. 916), also in A. (Hc. 4, 367, 4) and Ś. (Bālar. 246, 6), AMg. *sireṇaṁ* (Ṭhāṇ. 401); M. *tameṇa* = *tamasā* (R. 2, 33); AMg. *teeṇa* (Uttar. 363), *teeṇaṁ* = *tejasā* (Uttar. 341; Vivāhap. 1250; Uvās. § 94); M. AMg. *raeṇa*, AMg. *raeṇaṁ* = *rajasā* (H. 176; Uttar. 109;

Ovav. § 112); M. *maṇeṇa*, AMg. *maṇeṇaṁ* = *manasā* (G. 347; Sūyag. 841 f. 844; Paṇhāv. 134); JM. *parituṭṭhamaṇeṇaṁ* = *parituṣṭamanasā* (masc.; Erz. 39, 9); Ś. *purūraveṇa* (Vikr. 8, 14); A. *chandeṇa* = *chandasā* (Piṅgala 1, 15); femin. M. *vimaṇāi* (H. 118); Ś. *taggadamaṇāe* = *tadgatamanaskayā* (Viddhaś. 43, 8).—Abl. M. *sirāhi* (G. 58), *ṇahāhi* (G. 1164; R. 13, 51); AMg. *tamāo* and metrical *tamao* = *tamasaḥ* (Sūyag. 31. 170), *pĕjjāo* = *preyasaḥ* (Ovav. § 123).—Gen. M. *asuddhamaṇassa* = *aśuddhamanasaḥ* (masc.; H. 35); Ś *purūravassa* (Vikr. 22, 16), *tamassa*, *rajassa* (Prab. 48, 1; 56, 14); JM. *jasassa* (KI. 21). A. *jasaha* = *yaśasaḥ* (Erz. 86, 19).—Loc. M. AMg. *ure* (G. 773; H. 31.276.299. 671; R. 11,76; 12,56. 62; 15, 50. 53. 64; Vivāgas. 168), M. also *urammi* (G. 1022; R. 11, 100; 15, 46) and AMg. *uraṁsi* (Kappas. S. § 29; Uvās.); M. *ṇahammi* (G. 135. 476. 819. 829; R. 13, 53; 14, 23. 83), *ṇahe* (R. 13, 58), AMg. *ṇabhe* (Sūyag. 310); A Mg. *tamaṁsi* (Āyār. 1, 4, 4, 2); Ś. *sŏtte* = *srotasi* (Karp. 71, 1); AMg. *tave* = *tapasi* (Vivâhap. 194); AMg. M. *sire* (R. 4, 4; Uttar. 664); JM. *sirammi* (Erz. 58, 1; Kk. 268, 39); M. *sarammi* = *sarasi* (H. 491. 624); M. JM. D. *maṇe* = *manasi* (R. 5, 20; Erz. 79,34; Mṛcch. 104, 2); AMg. A *chande* = *chandasi* (Vivâhap. 149; Piṅgala 1,93); A *maṇi*, *siri* (Hc. 4,422, 15. 423,4).—Plural: nom. M. *sarā* = *sarāṁsi* (masc.; G. 524); AMg. *ahosirā* = *adhaḥśiraḥ*, *mahāyasā* = *mahāyaśasaḥ*, *hāravirāiyavacchā* = *hāravirājitavakṣasaḥ* (Ovav. § 31. 33), *thūlavayā* = *sthūlavacasaḥ* (Uttar. 15), *pāvaceyā* = *pāpacetasaḥ* (Sūyag. 289); A. *āsattamaṇa* = *āsaktamanasaḥ* (Kk. 261, 4); femin. M. *gaavaāo* = *gatavayaskāḥ* (H. 232); AMg. °*raïyasirasāo* = °*racitaśiraskāḥ* (Ovav. § 55), *miyasirāo* = *mṛgaśirasi* (Ṭhāṇ. 81).—Acc. femin. Ś. *sumaṇāo* = *sumanasaḥ* (Mṛcch. 3, 1. 21); neut. AMg. *sarāṇi* (Āyār. 2, 3, 3, 2). —Ins. M. *sarehi* (H. 953), *sirehi*, *sirehiṁ* (H. 682; R. 6,60), °*maṇehĩ* (masc.; G. 88), *urehi* (R. 6, 60); femin. M. *vimaṇāhiṁ* (R. 11, 17), *maṅgalamaṇāhi* (R. 15,43).—Gen. M. *sarāṇa* (H. 953); JM. *gayavayāṇa* (KI. 14), femin. M. *gaavaāṇa* (H. 233).—Loc. AMg. *tavesu* (Sūyag. 318), *saresu* (Nāyādh. 412). Like *āpas* becoming *āū* and *tejas* becoming *teū* (§ 355), *vacas* too becomes AMg. *vaū* (femin.): *itthivaū* = *strīvacaḥ* (Paṇṇav. 363. 368. 369); *puṁvaū* (Paṇṇav. 363), *pumavaū* (Paṇṇav. 363. 368. 369), *napuṁsagavaū* (Paṇṇav. 363. 369), *egavaū*, *bahuvaū* (Paṇṇav. 367).—In the case of words in *-as* the stem *-sa* is rare: AMg. *adiṇamaṇaso* = *adinamanāḥ* (Uttar. 51); JM. *viuso* = **viduṣaḥ* = Vedic *viduḥ* = *vidvān* (Erz. 69, 18).

§ 410. *apsaras* is declined in all the dialects as an **ā*-stem, that is found is Skt. too: sing. nom. AMg. JM. Ś. *accharā* (Paṇhāv. 229; Ṭhāṇ. 269. 489; Nāyādh. 1525; Erz. 64, 26; Śak. 21,6; Vikr. 16,15; Karṇas. 15,2); Ś. *aṇaccharā* = *anapsarāḥ* (Vikr. 7,18); plur. nom. AMg. Ś. *accharāo* (Ovav. [§ 38], Paṇhāv. 218; Vivāhap. 245. 254; Bālar. 218, 11); ins. AMg. Ś. *accharāhiṁ* (Vivāhap. 245; Ratn. 322,30; Bālar. 202, 13), and so to be read also in Vikr. 40,11 for *accharohiṁ*. On the ostensible form *accharehiṁ*, that is correct in R. 7,45, at the end of a bahuvrīhi related with *dharāharehiṁ*, see § 328. 376; on the stem *accharā*°, AMg;. *acchara*° see § 97.347. According to Hc. 1,20; Sr. fol. 25 the stem *accharasā* is also formed: nom. sing. *accharasā*, nom. plur. *accharasāo*. To it belongs the acc. M. *accharasaṁ* R. 13,47.

§ 411. 2) Nouns in *-is* and *-us*. The old forms are : sing. ins. AMg. *cakkhusā* = *cakṣuṣā* (Paṇhāv. 461; Uttar. 726. 734. 779); AMg. *viusā* = *viduṣā* (Hc. 2,174 p. 68).—Gen. Ś. *āuso* = *āyuṣaḥ* (Vikr. 80,4), *dhaṇuho* = *dhanuṣaḥ* (§ 263; Bālar. 113, 17; rightly ?).—Plur. gen. AMg. *joisaṁ* = *jyotiṣam* (Ovav. § 36 ; so to be read with the MSS ABβD), also *joisām* in the combination *joisām ayaṇe* (Vivāhap. 149; Kappas. § 10; Ovav. § 77). The nominative sing. in *-ū* may be tugged either with it or with the *ū*-stem : AMg. *viū* = Vedic *viduḥ*[1] (Sūyag. 89. 147. 342. 560. 665; Uttar. 644. 691; Āyār. 2, 16, 5[2]), *dhammaviū* = *dharmaviduḥ* (Āyār. 1, 3, 1, 2,) *egaviū* = *ekaviduḥ*, *dhammaviū* = *dharmaviduḥ*, *maggaviū* = *mārgaviduḥ*, *pāraviū* = *pāraviduḥ* (Sūyag. 560. 565. 665), *ĕkkārasaṅgaviū* = *ekādaśāṅgaviduḥ*, (Nāyādh. 967), *bārasaṅgaviū* = *dvādaśāṅgaviduḥ* (Uttar. 691), *cakkhū*, *ega°*, *bi°*, *ti°* = *cakṣuḥ*, *eka°*, *dvi°*, *tri°* (Ṭhāṇ. 188); *dhaṇū* = *dhanuḥ* (Hc. 1,22); Ś. *āū* = *āyuḥ* (Vikr. 81, 20; cf. *āuo* = **āyukaḥ* 82, 13); Ś. *dihāū* = *dīrghāyuḥ* (Hc. 1, 20; Mṛcch. 141, 16; 154, 15; Śak. 165, 12; Vikr. 80,12; 84,9; Uttarar. 71,8 ete.).—From the *i*- or *u*-stem are derived: sing. nom. AMg. *sappī* = *sarpiḥ* (Sūyag. 291; neuter), *joī* = *jyotiḥ* (Uttar. 374 f.; mascul.); cf. 358[3]; M. *haviṁ* = *haviḥ* (Bh. 5, 25) M. *dhaṇuṁ* = *dhanuḥ* (H. 603. 620; R. 1, 18. 24. 45); AMg. *āuṁ* = *āyuḥ* (Āyār. 1, 2, 1, 2).—Acc. AMg. *joiṁ* = *jyotiḥ* (Uttar. 375. 677. 1009; Nandīs. 146), *sajoī* = *sajyotiṣam* (Sūyag. 270), *sappiṁ* = *sarpiḥ* (Āyār. 2, 1, 8, 8: Kappas. S. § 17; Ovav. § 73), *cakkhuṁ* = *cakṣuḥ* (Āyār. 1,8,1,4), also *cakkhu* (Sūyag. 223), as in the nom. (Uvās. § 5; so to be read). *paramāuṁ* (Ovav. § 53; Samav. 112); M. AMg. Ś. *dhaṇuṁ* = *dhanuḥ* (H. 177. 631; Nirayāv. § 5; Veṇīs. 62,17); Ś. *dihāuṁ* = *dīrghāyuṣaṁ* (Uttarar. 132, 9).—Ins. AMg. *joiṇā* = *jyotiṣā* (Āyār. 2, 16, 8; Sūyag. 460. 7,31), *accie* = *arciṣā* from *arcis* has become feminine (Ovav. § 33. 56); Ś. *dihāuṇā* (Śak. 44, 6; so to be read).—Abl. AMg. *cakkhūo* (Āyār. 2, 15, 5, 2).—Gen. AMg. *āussa* (Sūyag. 504), *cakkhussa* (Uttar. 924 f.).—Loc. AMg. *āummi* (Sūyag. 212); JM. *cakkhummi* (Āv. 15, 17).—Plur. nom. masc. AMg. *ueyaviū joisaṅgaviū*, *viū* (Uttar. 743. 756), *dhammavidū* (Āyār. 1,4,3,1), *aṇāū* = *anāyuṣaḥ* (Sūyag. 322); neuter *cakkhūiṁ* (Hc. 1, 33); AMg. *cakkhū* (Sūyag. 549. 639).—Ins. *dhaṇūhiṁ* (Nirayāv. § 27).—The stem in *-sa* occurs : nom. Ś. *dihāuso* = *dīrghāyuḥ* (Hc. 1, 20; Mālav. 55, 13); M. *adiharāuso* (H. 950); *dhaṇuhaṁ* = *dhanuḥ* for **dhanuṣam* (§ 263; Hc. 1, 22), from which the loc. M. *dhaṇuhe* (Karp. 38, 11), the stem M. *dhaṇuha°* (Prab. 65,5); JM. *cirāusā* (T. 7,8; femin.). *āśis* forms, according to Triv. 1,1,3,3, the nom. *āsī* = *āśiḥ*, or the form *āsisā*, derived from it, that Hc. 2, 174 too teaches. There are found in JM. the acc. *āsisaṁ* (Erz. 80, 11) and *laddhāsiso* = *labdhāśiḥ* (Erz. 84,25); Ś. ins. *āsisāe* (Veṇīs. 23, 17), ins. plur. *āsisāhiṁ* (Mallikām. 79, 3). Beside them is assured the extended form *āsisā* built from the weak stem : Ś. nom. (Śak. 83, 1); acc. *āsisaṁ* (Mālatīm. 351, 7); gen. *āsisāe* (Nāgān. 84, 15; so to be read with the v. l. for *āsisāṁ* of the text); gen. plur. *āsisāṇaṁ* (Mālatīm. ed. Bomb. 107, 12; cf. v. l. ed. BHĀṆḌĀRKAR p. 363; Mahāv. 133, 5).

1. PISCHEL, Ved. Stud. 2,236.—2. The words *viū* [text *vidū*] *nae dhammapaẏaṁ aṇuttaraṁ* belong to verse 4. The hypothesis of JACOBI with regard to the use of *vidūṇate* in the meaning of *vidunvataḥ* (SBE. XII. 212, note 2) is linguistically impossible. *nate* is a wrong form used for *nae* (§ 203)=*nayet* (§ 493, note 4).—3. Where *sappī* is to be deleted.

§ 412. From *puṁs* are found four stems: 1) *puṁ-* from *puṁs-* in M. AMg. JM. *puṁgava* (G. 87; Uttar. 666; Nāẏādh. 1262. 1272; Erz. 4,25); AMg. *puṁveẏa* (Samav. 62 [text °*veda*]; Bhag.), *puṁvaū*=**puṁvacaḥ* (Paṇṇav. 363), *pumāṁs-*, which occurs in the nom. sing. AMg. *pumaṁ*= *pumān* (Dasav. 628, 9); 3) the stem *puma-* deduced from it, AMg. nom. sing. *pume* (Ṭhāṇ 479. 482), AMg. acc. sing. *pumaṁ* (Āẏār. 2, 4, 1, 8. 9; Dasav. 637, 8), and in the derivatives and compounds like AMg. *pumavaū* =**puṁvacaḥ* (Paṇṇav. 363 [text °*veū*]. 368. 369), *pumaāṇamaṇi*=**pumājñāpani* (Paṇṇav. 363 ff. 369), *pumapannavaṇi*=**puṁprajñāpani* (Paṇṇav. 364), *pumitthiveẏa*=*puṁstriveda* (Uttar. 960), *pumattaṁ*=*puṁstvam* (Uttar. 421), *pumattāe*=*puṁstvāya* (Ovav. § 102; Ṭhāṇ. 479. 482. 523), *pumavaẏaṇa*=*puṁvacana* (Paṇṇav. 370. 388; Ṭhāṇ. 174 [text *pumma*°]), 4) the stem *puṁsa-* extended from *puṁs-* in AMg. *puṁsakoilaga*=*puṁsaskokilaka* (Ṭhāṇ. 568), *napuṁsaveẏa* (Uttar. 960). In PG., from the *s*-stem, is found only *bhūyo* (7,41).

(8) THE REMAINING CONSONANTAL STEMS.

§ 413. In addition to the *t*-, *n*-, and *s*-stems, numerous forms are built according to the old flexion from the *ś*-stems only, particularly from *diś*, and that mostly in formular phrases, like AMg. *diso disaṁ* (Āẏār 2, 16, 6); AMg. JM. *diso disiṁ* (Paṇhāv. 197; Uttar. 793; Nāẏādh. 348; Erz. 13, 6. 38,26; 63,25). M. JM. *disi disi* (Viddhaś. 90, 5; Erz. 7, 29); AMg. *padiso disāsu* (Āẏār. 1, 1, 6, 2); elsewhere seldom, as gen. M. *puvvādiso* =*pūrvadiśaḥ* (Bālar. 179, 2); Mg. *ṇiśi* (Mṛcch. 10, 14; Verse) only sporadic forms are found (§ 355), as ins. sing. AMg. *vāẏā*= *vācā* (Uttar. 28; Dasav. 630, 32), *kāẏaggirā*=*kāyagirā* (§ 196; Dasav. 634, 24). All the remaining consonantal stems almost always are taken over to the *a*-, and the feminine ones to the *ā*- or *i*- declension. Thus *vāc*, through **vācā* becomes M. *vāā* (Bh. 4, 7; G. 69), AMg. *vāẏā* (Sūẏag. 931. 936); acc. *vāaṁ*, AMg. *vāẏaṁ* (G. 67; Sūẏag. 932), ins. M. Ś. Mg. *vāāe* (G. 63; Pras. 46, 14; 47, 1; Mg. Mṛcch. 152, 22), M. *vāāi* (H. 572), AMg. *vāẏāe* (Dasav. 631,34; Paṇhāv. 134); gen. Mg. *vāāe* (Mṛcch. 163, 21); loc. M. *vāāi* (H. 32); plur. nom. M. *vāā* and *vāāo* (G. 93); acc. AMg. *vāẏāo* (Āẏār. 1, 7, 1, 3); ins. AMg. *vāẏāhi* (Āẏār. 2, 16, 2); loc. M. *vāāsu* (G. 62). Beside them AMg. frequently has *vaī*=**vaci* from **vaci'* with *a* according to § 81[1]: sing. nom. *vaī* (Āẏār. p. 132, 16. 17; Vivāhap. 70), acc. *vaīṁ* (Āẏār. 1,5,3,1 [so to be read]; 2,3,1,21; 2,3,3,16; p. 132, 15. 17; Sūẏag. 169 [read *vaī*]. 866), *vaī*° (Āẏār. 1,5,5,4; 1,7,2,4; 2,13,22; p. 133, 2; Sūẏag. 128; Uttar. 646; Jīv. 25. 276; Vivāhap. 1431. 1453. 1462; Kappas. § 118 [so to be read]).—*tvac* forms sing. nom. AMg. *taẏā*=**tvacā* (Sūẏag. 639; Vivāhap. 1308. 1529); abl. AMg. *taẏāo* (Sūẏag. 639);

plur. gen. AMg. *taẏāṇaṁ* (Sūẏag. 806); nom. plur. AMg. *taẏāṇi* (§ 358). The stem often appears in compounds, as AMg. *taẏappavāla°* = *tvakprabāla* (Paṇhāv. 408), *taẏāsuha* = *tvaksukha*(Nāẏādh. § 34; Ovav. § 48; Kappas. § 60), *taẏāmanta* (Ovav. § 4,15), *sarittaẏā* = *sadṛktvacaḥ* (Vivāhap. 123; nom. plur.). From *ṛc* is found the acc. plur. Ś. *ricāiṁ* (§ 358). From *bhiṣaj* is formed the nom. sing. *bhisao* (Hc. 1,18), from *yakṛt*, the gen. sing. AMg. *jagaẏassa* = **yakṛtasya* (Vivāhap. 869), from *śarad* the nom. sing. *sarao* (§ 355).—From *vid* AMg. forms nom. sing. *saḍaṅgavi* (Vivāhap. 149; Kappas. § 10; Ovav. § 77), *veẏavi* = *vedavit* (Āẏār. 1,4,4,3; 1,5,4,3; 1,5,5,2; Uttar. 742), from *pariṣad*, sing. nom. is AMg. *parisā* from **pariṣadā* (Vivāgas. 4. 13. 15. 58. 138. 242; Ovav.; Uvās.; and very often, also in JM. Erz. 33,10), ins. gen. loc. is AMg. *parisāe* (Kappas. § 113; Ovav. § 56); plur. nom. AMg. *parisāo* (Vivāhap. 303), ins. *parisāhiṁ* (Nāẏādh. 1026), gen. *parisāṇaṁ* (Vivāgas. 201). From *saṁpad* the nom. is *saṁpaā*, from *pratipad*, nom. *paḍivaā* (Hc. 1,15), JM. *saṁpaẏā*, *āvaẏā* (Erz. 81,35); A. *saṁpaï* = **saṁpadi*, likewise *āvaï* = *āpad*, *vivaï* = *vipad* (Hc. 4,335, 372. 400); cf. AMg. *āvaīkālaṁ* = *āpatkālam* (Ovav. § 86); acc. A. *saṁpaa* (Piṅgala 1,81[a];) GOLDSCHMIDT *maṅgala*), plur. nom. M. *saṁpaā*, AMg. *saṁpaẏā* (H. 518; Kappas. § 134 ff.), *āvaïo* (G, 988). From *hṛd* the acc. is AMg. *hiẏaṁ* (Āẏār. 1,1,2,5,).—*kṣudh* forms nom. *chuhā*, *khuhā* (§ 318)—On *āū* see § 355.—*kakubh* builds nom. *kaühā* (Hc. 1,21), *gir* forms nom. *girā*, likewise *dhur*, nom. *dhurā*, *pur*, nom. *purā* (Hc. 1, 16); acc. D. *dhuraṁ* (Mṛcch. 102, 2); plur. nom. AMg. *girāo* (Paṇhāv. 287), ins. *girāhiṁ* (Vivāhap. 944; Kappas. § 47; Nāẏādh. § 23), gen. *girāṇaṁ* (Uttar. 358). —In AMg. *aho* is the acc. from *ahar* (day; § 342), frequently in the combination *aho ẏa rāo* or *aho ẏa rāo ẏa* (§ 386).—The very frequent *diś* forms mostly in all the dialects *disā*, Mg. *diśā* in compounds as in flexion : nom. *disā*, acc. *disaṁ*, ins. gen. loc. *disāe*, abl. *disāo*, AMg. also *ahedisāo*, *aṇudisāo* (Āẏār 1,1,1,2; Sūẏag. 574), Ś. *puvvadisādo* (Ratn. 313,7); plur. nom. acc. *disāo*' ins. *disāhiṁ*, gen. *disāṇaṁ*, loc. *disāsu*, AMg. also *vidisāsu* (Ṭhāṇ. 259 ff.). From **diśi*, we frequently have in AMg. JM. the acc. *disiṁ*, particularly in the combination *diso disiṁ* (see above), but elsewhere too (Vivāgas. 4. 38; Kappas. § 28. S. § 61 [v. l. *disaṁ*], *aṇudisiṁ* (Kappas. S. § 61), *chaddisiṁ* (Vivāhap. 145), *paḍidisiṁ* (Ṭhāṇ. 135; commentary : *ikāras tu prākṛtatvāt*), and in the composition *disi°* (Vivāhap, 161; Ovav. § 2; Kappas. § 27. 63; Uvās. § 3. 7; Āv. 14,10) and *disī°* (Uvās. § 50) : so also gen. plur. JŚ *disiṇaṁ* (Kattig. 402,367) beside *disāṇa* (401, 342), loc. JŚ *disisu* (Kattig. 401,341), A. *disihĩ* (Hc. 4,340,9)—*prāvṛṣ* becomes *pāuso* (§ 358); from *upānah* the stem is Ś. *uvāṇaha* (Mṛcch. 72,9), nom. acc. plur. in AMg. *pāhaṇāo*, *vāhaṇāo* (§ 141).

1. WEBER, (Bhag. 1,404) wrongly traces *vaï°* back to *vacas*.

B. COMPARISON.

§ 414. Pkt. employs *-tara*, *-tama*, *-īyas*, *-iṣṭha*, as suffixes of the comparative and the superlative exactly like Skt. : M. *tikkhaara* = *tikṣṇatara*

(H. 505) ; JM. *ujjalatara* = *ujjvalatara* (Āv. 40,6), *daḍhayara* = *dṛḍhatara* (Erz. 9,35) ; AMg. *paggahiyatara* = *pragṛhitatara* (Āyār. 1,7,8,11), *thovatara* = *stokatara* (Jīyak. 92); Ś. *adhiadara* = *adhikatara* (Mṛcch. 72,3;79,1; Mālatīm. 214,1; Vṛṣabh. 10,21; Nāgān. 24,5), *ṇihudadara* = *nibhṛtatara* (Vikr. 28,8), femin. *diuṇadarā* = *dviguṇatarā* (Mṛcch. 22,13), °*rī* (Priyad. 25,7); JM. Ś. *mahattara* (Erz.; Uttarar. 118,5) Mg. *mahattala* (Śak. 118, 5) ; *piaama* (H. R.), JM, *piyayama* (Dvār. 498,26; Erz.) Ś. *piadama* (Vikr. 28,9; 52,20;58,5; Prab. 39,2), A. *piaama* (Vikr. 66,16) = *priyatama*; AMg. *taratama* (Kappas.); AMg. JM. *kaṇiyasa* (§ 409), Ś. *kaṇiasī* (femin.; Mālav. 78,9) Ś. *kaṇiṭṭha* = *kaniṣṭha* (Mahāv. 3, 14; Kāleyak. 26, 20; Subhadr. 3,18), AMg. *kaṇiṭṭhaga* (Uttar. 622) ; AMg. *seyaṁ* = *śreyas* (§ 94), *seyaṁsa* (§ 409) ; PG. *bhūyo* (7,41), AMg. JM. *bhujjo* (§ 91; Āyār. 1,5, 4,2; 1,6,3,2; 2,2,2,7; Sūyag. 361. 579. 787. 789, 979; Uttar. 212.232.238. 239. 365. 434. 842; Vivāhap. 18. 27. 30. ff. 145. 233 f. 387 etc.; Uvās.; Nāyādh.; Ovav.; Kappas.; Erz.), Ś. *bhūo* (Śak. 27.6; 90,14; 123, 13; Mālav. 48,7), Ś *bhūiṭṭha* (Śak. 27,5; Mālav. 71, 3) = *bhūyas*, *bhūyiṣṭha*, beside Ś. *bahudara* (Mṛcch. 37,23; Śak. 73,3; Uttarar. 66,1; Cait. 42,2; 43,5; 45,11); AMg. *pĕjja-* = *preyas* (§ 91; Āyār. 1,3,4,4; Sūyag. 885; Paṇṇav. 638; Vivāhap. 125. 1026; Uttar. 199; Uvās.), also *pijja-* (Uttar. 822. 876) ; AMg. *pāviyaṁse* = *pāpīyān* (§ 409), JM. *pāviṭṭha* = *pāpiṣṭha* (Kk.); AMg. JM. Ś. *jĕṭṭha* = *jyeṣṭha* (Āyār. 2,25,15; Vivāhap. 333. 511; Uttar. 622 [*ji*]; Uvās.; Kappas.; Nāyādh.; Dvār. 495,26; Erz.; Vikr. 88,16; Uttarar. 128,12; Anarghar. 297,13); AMg. *dhammiṭṭha* = *dharmiṣṭha* (Sūyag. 757) ; JM. *dappiṭṭha* = *darpiṣṭha* (Kk. 270,9) ; Ś. *adibaliṭṭha* (Pras. 83,10). On AMg. *hĕṭṭhima* see § 107. Double formations are : AMg. *uttaratara* (Ovav.), *baliyataraṁ* (Vivāhap. 839); *jĕṭṭhayara kaṇiṭṭhayara*, (Hc. 2, 172). Noteworthy hybrid formations are the adverbs AMg. *bhujjataro* and *bhujjayaro*, in which the comparative suffix *-tara* has been added to the comparative stem *bhujja* = *bhūyas*, and they have retained the ending *-o* of *bhujjo* = *bhūyas*. On their pattern[1], as also in a large number of other cases,[2] are regulated *appataro*, *oppayaro* = *alpataram* in the combination *appataro vā bhujjataro vā* or *appayaro vā bhujjayaro vā* (Āyār. 2,3,1,13; Sūyag. 628. 699. 751. 986; Vivāhap. 40; Ovav. § 69).—Sometimes the positive is used in the sense of the comparative : M. *ovaaṇāhi vi lahuaṁ* "quicker than downward rush" (R. 6,77), *seubandhalahuaṁ* "smaller than a bridge" (R. 8, 15) ; Ś. *tatto vi...pia tti* "dearer than thou" (Śak. 9,10), *paḍhuma-daṁsaṇādo vi savisesaṁ piadaṁsaṇo* "more charming than at the first view (Vikr. 24,1).

1. LEUMANN, Aup. S. s. v. *appataro*.—2. § 355 on *āū*.

C. THE PRONOUN.

§ 415. The Pronoun of the first person.

Singular.

Nom. *ahaṁ*, *ahaaṁ*, JM. *ahayaṁ*, *haṁ*, [*amhi*, *ammi*, *mmi*, *ahammi*]; Mg. *hage*, *hagge*, [*hake*, *ahake*]; A *haũ*.

Acc. *maṁ, mamaṁ, mahaṁ, me*, [*mi, mimaṁ, ammi, amhaṁ, amha, mamha, ahaṁ, ahammi, ṇe, ṇaṁ*] ; A. *maĩ*.

Ins. *mae, maï*, [*mamae, mamāi, maāi*], *me*, [*mi; mamaṁ, ṇe*]; A. *maĩ*.

Abl. [*matto, mamatto, mahatto, majjhatto, maïtto*], *mamāo*, [*mamāu, mamāhi*] *mamāhiṁto* etc. (§ 416); P. [*mamāto, mamātu*]; A. [*mahu, majjhu*).

Gen. *mama, maha, majjha, mamaṁ, mahaṁ, majjhaṁ, me, mi* [*maï, amha, amhaṁ*] ; A. *mahu, majjhu*.

Loc. [*mae*] , *maï*, [*me, mi, mamāi*] , *mamammi*, [*mahammi majjhammi, amhammi*] ; A. *maĩ*.

Plural.

Nom. *amhe*, [*amha, amho, mo, bhe*] ; D. *vaaṁ*; AMg. JM. *vayaṁ* too; Mg. [*hage*] too; P. *vayaṁ, ampha, amhe*; A. *amhe, amhaĩ*.

Acc. *amhe, amha*, [*amho*], *ṇo, ṇe*; A. *amhe*, [*amhaĩ*].

Ins. *amhehiṁ*, [*amhāhiṁ, amhe, amha*], *ṇe*; A. *amhehĩ*.

Abl. [*amhatto, amhāhiṁto, amhāsuṁto, amhesuṁto, mamatto, mamāhiṁto, mamāsuṁto, mamesuṁto*; A. *amhahã*]; JM. *amhehiṁto*.

Gen. *amhāṇaṁ, °ṇa, amhaṁ, amha, mha*, [*amhāhã*] , *amhe*, [*amho, mamāṇaṁ, °ṇa, mahāṇaṁ, °ṇa, majjhāṇaṁ, °ṇa, majjha, ṇe*], *ṇo, ṇe*; A. *amhahã*.

Loc. *amhesu, amhāsu*, [*amhasu, mamesu, mamasu, mahesu, mahasu, majjhesu, majjhasu*]; A. *amhāsu*.

Cf. Vr. 6,40—53; 11,9; 12,25; C. 1,26—31; 2,27; 3,105—117; 4,301. 375—381; Kī. 3,72—83; 5, 40—48.97.114; Mk. fol. 49.70; Sr. fol. 30—32.

§ 416. A very large number of forms taught by grammarians have not as yet been attested in the texts, and therefore, their correctness still remains doubtful[1]. From amongst the forms, which perhaps are inferred only according to the schema given by Sr., one can be in doubt about only some of them. Sr. teaches, of course not merely, as Hc., in the abl. sing. of all the stems given above the forms : *mamatto, mamāo*; *mamāu, mamāhi, mamāhiṁto*; *mahatto, mahāo, mahāu, mahāhi, mahāhiṁto, majjhatto, majjhāo, majjhāu, majjhāhi, majjhāhiṁto*; *maïtto, maio, maiu, maihi. maihiṁto*; *mamā, mahā, majjhā*; but also the special feminine forms *mamāa, mamāā, mamāi, mamāe*, likewise from the stems *maha, majjha, maï*, so that he mentions 39 forms for the abl. In the loc. sing. he teaches in addition *amhattha, amhassiṁ, amhammi, amhahiṁ, amhe*, further the feminine forms *amhāa, amhāā, amhāi, amhāe*, and all these forms also from the stems *mama, maha, majjha*, altogether 41 forms. Likewise in the case of the pronoun of the second person from the stems *tuma, tuva, tuha, tumha, tubbha, tujjha, tui, taï*. How far such forms could be used in literature, only the future can tell.

1. Bloch goes too far, Vr. und Hc. 36. Cf. Konow, GGA. 1894. 478.

§ 417. Singular. In the nom. all the dialects, including Ḍh. (Mṛcch. 32, 7; 34, 25; 35, 1), Ā. (Mṛcch. 101,17; 103,10; 105, 1) and D. Mṛcch. 102, 23; 104, 19; 106, 1) employ *ahaṁ* = *aham*, Mg. *hage* (e.g. Mṛcch. 12, 14; 136,16; 175, 15; Lalitav. 565, 17; 566, 6. 16; Śak. 113,5.9; 114,2; Mudrār. 193, 8; 194, 2 etc.). So teach also Vr. 11, 9 (who has also *hake* and *ahake*), Hc. 4, 301; Sr. fol. 63; Kī. 5, 97 (who has *hake* too), Mk. fol, 55 (who has also *hakke, hake, hagge*). In Mṛcch., with the exception of the three particular places, which are all in verse, STENZLER has *hagge* elsewhere throughout (12, 5; 13, 4.8; 16, 18; 20, 14; 21, 20; 37, 4 etc.), as also in Hāsy. 31, 3; Prab. 32, 6. 14 stands, and in Prab. 55, 15; 58, 17 (K. *hakke*) is to be read for *haggo*; so has the ed. P. 58, 17; whilst at 55, 15 it has *haṁ*; the ed. Bomb. has *ahaṁ* (55, 15) and *hagge* (58, 17); the ed. M. has *ahaṁ* in both the places, as also Mudrār. 178,2 (v. l. *hage*); 187,1; 193, 1 (v. l. *hage*), 267, 2; Veṇīs. 35. 4 and elsewhere stands in uncritical editions. The MSS of Mṛcch. in GOḌABOLE almost all have *hage*, as is to be read there. Both the forms are correct, since they go back to one **ahakáh* (§ 142. 194) i.e. *ahakám* (Vyākaraṇamahābhāṣya I, 91, 11), Aśoka *hakaṁ* with so frequent change of gender in Mg. (§ 357). A. *haũ* (Hc. s.v. *haüṁ*; Piṅgala 1, 104a; 2, 121; Vikr. 65, 3 [so to be read for *haï*, *haṁiṁ*; cf. v. l. A] and M. *ahaaṁ* (H. R.), JM. *ahayaṁ* (Āv. 7, 34; 36, 49; Erz.) go back to *ahakáṁ*. Sometimes after vowels (§ 175) appears M. AMg. JM. Mg. *haṁ* (R. 15, 18; Karp. 75, 2; Uttar. 575. 623; Samav. 83; Erz. 12, 22; 53, 34; Mṛcch. 136, 11). Of the remaining four forms Vr. and Mk. have *ahammi* only, Kī. has *amhi*, Hc. alone has *mmi* too. All the four forms are rejected by BLOCH[1] as errors committed by the grammarians. However, it is certain that already in Skt. *asmi* was used in the sense of "I"[2], a meaning, that has developed from the original parenthetical *asmi* "I am", as is shown appropriately by the much quoted *rāmo'smi sarvaṁ sahe*. We may compare this with the use of *asti* in B-R. s.v.1 *as* p. 535, which is found in Pkt. too : AMg. *atthi ṇaṁ bhante gihiṇo...ohināṇe ṇaṁ samuppajjaï* (Uvās. § 83); *atthi ṇaṁ bhante jiṇavaẏaṇe...āloijjaï* (Uvās. § 85); *atthi ṇaṁ bhante...siddhā parivasanti* (Ovav. § 162); *taṁ atthi ẏāiṁ te kahiṁ pi* [ed. *vi*] *devāṇuppiẏā erisae orohe diṭṭhapuvve* (Nāẏādh. 1284); *taṁ atthi ẏāiṁ* [ed. *ẏā*] *ittha kei bhe* [ed. *te*] *kahiṁ pi* [ed. *vi*] *accherae diṭṭhapuvve* (Nāẏādh. 1376); Ś. *atthi ĕttha ṇaare...tiṇṇi purisā...siriṁ ṇa sahanti* (Mudrār. 39, 2). Likewise *santi* (Āẏār. 2, 1, 4, 5; Sūẏag. 585) and more often *siẏā* = *syāt* (as in Pāli *siyā* and *assa*) are used (Āẏār. 1,1,2,1; 1,1,6,3; 1,2,6,1; 1,5,5,2; 2,5,1,11; 2,6,2,2; Dasav. 613,22), and so certainly *amhi* = *asmi* too is to be used. *ammi* and *mmi* are not cooked up forms, as AMg. *mi, mo, mu* (§ 468) show, when even the examples given by Hc. 3, 105 rest on false readings.[3] *ahammi* should be = *ahaṁ mi*.

1. Vr. und Hc. p. 37.—2. KONOW, GGA. 1894, 478; JACOBI, Compositum und Nebensatz. (Bonn 1897), p. 62, note 2.—3. BLOCH, Vr. und Hc. p. 37. In Hc. 3, 105 we should with ed. Bomb. read *jeṇa haṁ viddhā* for *teṇa haṁ diṭṭhā* (WEBER on H. 441). Correct, however, is the partition *jeṇ' ahaṁ* (§ 173). Cf. § 34.

§ 418. Except in A., the form that can be used in all the dialects in the acc. is *maṁ* = *māṁ* (H. R.; Uvās. s. v. *ma*-; Erz. Kk. s. v. *ahaṁ*; Ṛṣabhap. s. v. *ma*[1]; Ś. e.g. Mṛcch. 2,22. 25; Śak. 16. 10; Vikr. 16,6; Mg. Mṛcch. 11,1; 29,23; 32,5.15). A. has *maĩ* (Hcī. 4, 377. 414, 4; Vikr. 69, 2). In M. AMg. JM. is found also *mamaṁ* (H. 16; R. 11,84; Ṭhāṇ. 477;

Nāẏādh. s. v.; p. 932; Uttar. 791; Vivāhap. 257. 1215; Uvās. § 68 [so to be read with the MSS for *mama*]. 140. 219; Dvār. 500,8; Erz. 43, 29). For Mg. *mama* (Mṛcch. 129, 4) we should, in the verse, read *mamā̃*. After *mamaṁ*, AMg. has formed also a feminine *mamiṁ*; *mamaṁ vā mamiṁ vā* (Sūẏag. 680). We should read *amhi ahammi* for *asmi asammi* in Kī. 3, 73. Rare is M. AMg. *mahaṁ* (R. 15.90; Vivāgas. 221), which escaped notice of the grammarians, more often *me* in AMg., as in the Veda[2], (Āẏār. 1,1,6,5; Uttar. 362. 710; Ṭhāṇ. 158. 360. 361; Kappas. § 16).—The ins. is *mae* in all the dialects, except in A., which has *maĩ* (Hc. 4,330, 2.346.356 etc.; Vikr. 55, 1). *me* stands in the sense of the ins. in JM. (Erz. 72, 12; 83,32); Mg. Mṛcch. 40, 5; *maī* in Mg. (Mṛcch. 11, 1) in a verse.—In the abl. *mamāhiṁto* alone can be located in AMg. JM. (Vivāhap. 1245; Nāẏādh. 1329; Erz. 54, 20) and *mamāo* in JM. (Āv. 27, 25; Dvār. 495, 23).—In the gen. *mama* is rare in M. At. H. 123 we should read *mamaṁ ti* with the v. l. (§ 182), so that G. H. R. do not have *mama*, except in H. 617; it stands in M. (Śak. 55, 15). M. uses *maha, mahaṁ, majjha, majjhaṁ, me*, JM. AMg. often in addition to *mama* also *mamaṁ* (Vivāgas. 121 f.; Uvās.; Bhag.; Āv. 12, 28), Ś. *mama* (Mṛcch. 9, 7; Śak. 9, 13; Vikr. 16, 5), *maha* (Lalitav. 554,7; Pras. 83,6; 123,3; Veṇīs. 11,25), *me* (Mṛcch. 15,25; Śak. 27,9.10; Vikr. 8, 15); *majjha*, that is forbidden by Mk. fol. 70 for Ś., stands at Karp. 10,10; 58,1 against the dialect for *mama* or *maha*; Mg. *mama* (Mṛcch. 14,1; 21,8.12; 30,25), *maha* (Mṛcch. 114,18; Veṇīs. 33,13), *me* (Mṛcch. 9,25; 10,3.5; Veṇīs. 34,22; 35,2.8.14); Ḍh. *mama* (Mṛcch. 31,1; 34,17); Ā. *maha* (Mṛcch. 102, 25; 103, 22), likewise D. (Mṛcch. 104,2.11); A. *mahu* (Hc. 4,333. 370,2. 379,1; Vikr. 59, 13.14), *majjhu* (Hc. 4,367,8.379,2); under the pressure of the rhyme with *paĩ* also *maĩ* at Vikr. 63, 4.—*maha* goes back likewise as *majjha*, to *mahyam*. For *me* stands *mi* metri causa in AMg. Uttar. 489. False readings are JM. *mujjha, muha* (Erz.). We should read *yad imaṁ* in the place of P. *yati maṁ* (Hc. 4,323).—Loc. M. JM. *mamammi* (R.; Erz.); Ś. *maï* (Mālav. 41,18); [JM. *maï* (Vasudevahiṇḍi, p. 331)] A. *maĩ* (Hc. 4,377).

1. These references hold good also for the rest of the cases in the sing.; besides one should also see Nāyādh. ed. STEINTHAL s.v. s.v. In places, where nothing has been noted, the old texts, like Āyār., Sūyag., Uttar., Āv., have the same forms. Only a few examples have been given from Ś. Mg., as most of the forms are very frequent. This holds good also for the rest of the pronouns.—2. PISCHEL, ZDMG. 35,714.

§ 419. Plural. Nom. The form that can be used in all the dialects, including PG. (6,41), is *amhe*, for which in Mg. *asme* is to be written (§ 314) = Vedic *asme*[1]: M. (G. 1072; H. s. v. *amha*); AMg. (Āẏār. 2,6,1,10; Nāẏādh. § 137; Vivāgas. 229; Sūẏag. 1016; Vivāhap. 134); JM. (Erz. 3,28; 12,13. 19; Kk. 271,7); Ś. (Mṛcch. 20,18; Śak. 16,12; Vikr. 6,13); Mg. (Mṛcch. 158,23; 161, 14,17; 168,11; Veṇīs. 35,21); A. (Hc. 4,376,1). In AMg. *vaẏaṁ* = *vayam* too is frequent (Āẏār. 1,4,2,5; 1,7,1,5; 2,1,9,11; 2,2,2,10; 2,3,1,17; 2,5,1,10; 2,6,1,10; Sūẏag. 585. 603. 633. 935. 948. 972; Uttar. 432. 446. 748; Vivāhap. 1180; Dasav. 613,11), that occurs in JM. too (Kk. 270,1). In Ś. too Vr. 12,25 and Mk. fol. 70 permit *vaaṁ*.

It stands in Mṛcch. 103,5 in D., in Ś. only in bad texts (also Mālav. 46,12; 48,18)[2]. For Mg. Hc. 4,301 teaches in the plural as well *hage*, what is confirmed by 4,302 (p. 148) in a passage from Vikrāntabhīma; A. has also *amhaĩ* (Hc. 4,376). For P. Kī. 5,114 teaches *vayaṁ*, *ampha* and *amhe*. —According to C. 2,27 *bhe* may be used in the plural in all the cases.— Acc. M, AMg. *ṇe*=*nas* with the ending *-e* of the noun in *-a* (§ 367*a*) (R. 3,16; 5,4; Āẏār. 1,6,1,5 [*ne*]; Sūẏag. 174. 176. 239), but Ś. *ṇo* (Śak. 26,12); JM. Ś. also *amhe* (T. 5.3; Mālatīm. 361,2; Uttarar. 7,5; Veṇīs. 70,5), Mg. *asme* (Veṇīs. 36,5), M. *amha* (H. 356), A. *amhe* (Hc. 4,422,10), according to Hc. 4,376 also *amhaĩ*.—Ins. M. AMg. JM. Ś. *amhehiṁ* (H. 509; Nāẏādh. § 137; Āv. 16,6; Erz. 5,10; Mṛcch. 23,23; Viddhaś. 27,4; Mālatīm. 283,2), M. also *amhehi* (H.R.), as also PG. has (6,29); Mg. *asmehiṁ* (Mṛcch. 11,19; 21,11); in AMg. also *ṇe* (Āẏār. 1,4,2,3); A *amhehĩ* (Hc. 4,371).—Abl. JM. *amhehiṁto* (Āv. 47,20).—Gen. M. JM. Ś. *amhāṇaṁ* (H. 951 [°*ṇa*]; Erz. 2,17; Kk.; Mṛcch. 2,18. 19,24), Mg. *asmāṇaṁ* ([text *amhāṇaṁ*]; Lalitav. 565,14; Mṛcch. 31,15; 139,13; Śak. 116,2); M. AMg. JM. *amhaṁ* (H.; Uttar. 356. 358; Vivāgas. 217. 218; Nāẏādh. § 26. 116; p. 482. 609. 616; Vivāhap. 233. 511; Āv. 8,17; 14,16; 17,17; Erz. 6,35; 12,34), M. JM. also *amha* (H.; Āv. 11,9; 17.7; Erz.; Kk.), that wrongly occurs in Ś. in Vikr. 73,12, for which with P should be read either *amhe* which is to be considered as in the acc. (cf. *maṁ* of the Dvāviḍ. recen.), or with the ed. Bomb. 119,7 *amhāṇaṁ*. In M. '*mha* too (H.). *amhaṁ* is in AMg. JM. the prevalent form, which PG. too has (5,3; 7,42). It corresponds to one Skt. **asmām*, i.e. a gen. built from the stem *asma-* with the ending of the consonantal declension, whilst *amhāṇaṁ* presupposes one **asmānām*, and M. *amhāhã*, A. *amhahã* (Hc. 4,379. 380. 439) mentioned by Hc. 4,300 presuppose one **asmāsām*, therefore, with the ending of the pronominal declension. On AMg. *asmākaṁ* see § 314. AMg. JM. have also *amhe* (Sūẏag. 969; T. 5,6); Ś. very frequently has *ṇo*=*naḥ* (Śak. 17,11; 18,8; 26,12; Vikr. 5,11; 6,16; 10,3), and AMg. *ṇe* (Vivāhap. 132 f.).— Loc. Ś. *amhesu* (Śak. 30,1; Mālav. 75,1; Veṇīs. 70,2), *amhāsu*, quoted from an unnamed author in Hc. 3,117, mentioned in Sr. fol. 32, and taught by Hc. 4,381 himself for A., stands in M. R. 3,32.

1. PISCHEL, ZDMG. 35,716—2. PISCHEL, KB. 8,142 f.

§ 420. The Pronoun of the Second Person.

Singular

Nom. *tumaṁ, tuṁ, taṁ,* [*tuha, tuvaṁ*]; Ḍh. *tuhaṁ*; A. *tuhũ*.

Acc. *tumaṁ,* [*tuṁ, taṁ*], *te,* [*tuha, tuvaṁ, tume, tue*]; Ś. Mg. *de* too; Ḍh. *tuhaṁ*; A. *taĩ, paĩ*.

Ins. *tae, taï, tue, tui,* [*tumaṁ*], *tumae,* [*tumaï*] [*tumāi, tume, te, de,* [*di, bhe*]; A. *taĩ, paĩ*.

Abl. *tatto, tumāhi. tumāhiṁto, tumāo,* [*tumāu, tumā, tumatto, taïtto, tuitto*], *tuvatto,* [*tuhatto, tubbhatto, tumhatto, tujjhatto,* further from all these stems with the endings *-o, -u,* (Ś. Mg. *-do, -du*), *-hi, -hiṁto,* then *tumā, tuvā, tuhā, tubbhā, tumhā, tujjhā, tumha, tuyha, tubbha, tujjha, tahiṁto*]; P. [*tumāto, tumātu*]; A. *tujjhu, taü, tudhra*].

Gen. *tava, tujjha, tuha, tuhaṁ, tubbha, tubbhaṁ, tumha, tumhaṁ, te, de,* [*taï*], *tu,* [*tuva, tuma*], *tumaṁ, tumma,* [*tume, tumo, tumāi, di, i, e, ubbha, uyha, umha, ujjha*]; Ś. *tuha, de*; Mg. *tava, tuha, de*; A. *taü, tujjhu, tujjhaha, tudhra, tuha.*

Loc. *taï, tumammi, tume, tuvi, tui,* [*tue, tae, tumae, tumāi, tummi, tuvammi, tuhammi, tubbhammi, tumhammi, tujjhammi*]; AMg. *tumaṁsi*; Ś. *taï, tui*; A. *taĩ, paĩ.*

Plural.

Nom. *tumhe, tubbhe,* [*tubbha, tumha, tujjhe, tujjha, tuyhe, uyhe, bhe*]; AMg. *tubbhe*; JM. *tumhe, tubbhe*; Ś. Mg. (?) *tumhe*; A. [*tumhe, tumhaï*].

Acc. as the nom., and *vo,* AMg. *bhe.*

Ins. *tumhehiṁ, tubbhehiṁ,* [*tujjhehiṁ, tuyhehiṁ, tummehiṁ, umhehiṁ, ubbhehiṁ, ujjhehiṁ, uyhehiṁ*], *bhe*; AMg. *tubbhehiṁ, tumehiṁ, tubbhe, bhe*; JM. *tumhehiṁ, tubbhehiṁ*; Ś. *tumhehiṁ*; A. *tumhehĩ.*

Abl. [*tumhatto, tubbhatto, tujjhatto, tuyhatto, umhatto, ubbhatto, ujjhatto, uyhatto*; from the same stems with the endings *-e, -u* (Ś. Mg. *-do -du*), *-hi, -hiṁto, -suṁto*]; A. *tumhahã.*

Gen. *tumhāṇaṁ, °ṇa,* [*tubbhāṇaṁ, °ṇa, tujjhāṇaṁ, °ṇa, tuhāṇaṁ, °ṇa, tuvāṇaṁ, °ṇa, tumāṇaṁ, °ṇa*], *tumhaṁ, tumha, tubbhaṁ,* [*tubbha, tujjhaṁ, tujjha, tu*], *bhe, vo*; AMg. *tubbhaṁ, tumhāṇaṁ, tubbhe, bhe*; JM. *tumhāṇaṁ, tubbhaṁ, tumha, tumhaṁ*; Ś. Mg. *tumhāṇaṁ*; A. *tumhahã.*

Loc. [*tumhesu, tubbhesu, tujjhesu, tuhesu, tuvesu, tumesu, tusu, tumhusu* etc., *tumhāsu* etc., *tujjhisuṁ, tumbhisuṁ*; A. *tumhāsã*].

Cf. Vr. 6,26—39; C. 1,18—25; 3,26; Hc. 3,90—104; 4,368—374; Kī. 3,59—71; 5,113; Mk. fol. 47—49. 70. 75; Sr. fol. 26—30 and take notice of § 416.

§ 421. Singular. Nom. The prevalent form is *tumaṁ* from the stem *tuma* in all the dialects, except Ḍh. A. : (M. G. H. R.; AMg. e.g. Āyār. 1,5,5,4 [read *tumaṁ si*]; Uvās.; Kappas.; JM. e.g. Āv. 8,33; 14,29; Erz.; Kk.; Ś. e.g. Lalitav. 561, 5. 11. 15; Mṛcch. 4. 5; Śak. 12, 8; Mg. e.g. Lalitav. 565, 15; Mṛcch. 19, 8; Prab. 58, 1; Mudrār. 267, 1; Ā. Mṛcch. 99, 18. 19; 101, 23; 103, 2; D. Mṛcch. 101, 10. 21; 103, 17. 18)[1]. In AMg. the nom. *tume* too appears to occur (Nāyādh. § 68 against *tumaṁ* § 70; p. 448. 450), which was related to *tumaṁ,* like Mg. *hage* to *ahakám* (§ 417). In M. *taṁ* too (G.H.R.), which AMg. (Uttar. 637. 670. 678. 712) and JM. (Ṛṣabhap.; Erz.) too have in verses, is very frequent; beside it seldom appears *tuṁ* (H.; Śak. 78,11 ed. Böhtl.). Ḍh. *tuhaṁ* (Mṛcch. 34,24; 35,1. 3; 39,8), A. *tuhũ* (Hc. s.v. *tu*; Piṅgala 1,4b) go back to *tvakám* (§ 206)[2]. In Piṅgala 1,5b *taĩ* (Goldschmidt *taïṁ,* text *taï*; cf. Bollensen on Vikr. p. 530) has been used as nom.—Acc. *tumaṁ* as in the nom. in the same dialects (Ś. Mṛcch. 4,9; Śak. 51,6; Vikr. 23,1; Mg. Mṛcch. 12,10; Mudrār. 183,6); Ḍh. *tuhaṁ* (Mṛcch.

31, 12); A. *taĩ* (Hc. 4, 370) and *paĩ* (Hc. 4, 370; Vikr. 58,8; 65, 3). On *pa* see § 300. *te* is acc. in AMg. (Uvās. § 95. 102; Uttar. 368.677.696), likewise in Ś. (Mṛcch. 3,13) and *de* in Ś. (Mṛcch. 54,8) and Mg. (Mṛcch. 128, 12. 14)[3].—Ins. M. *taï, tae, tui, tue, tumae, tumāe tumāi, tume* (G. H. R.); JM. *tae, tumae, tume*; AMg. *tume* (so also Uvās, § 139. 167 to be read with the v. l.); Ś. *tae* (Lalitav. 554,6; 555,5; Śak. 12, 12; Ratn. 299, 1.2), *tue* (Mṛcch. 7,5; Vikr. 25,5; Mahāv. 56, 3); Mg. *tae* (Lalitav. 566, 4), *tue* (Mṛcch. 31,23. 25; Veṇīs. 34,3; Prab. 50,9). The dramas waver; Mṛcch. Vikr. Veṇīs., and most others have *tue* (Vikr. 42,6 is to be corrected as *tue* with A); Śak. Ratn. have *tae*. Often the MSS waver at the same place in M. too. Ā. has *tue* (Mṛcch. 102,1; 103,2; 105,1), D. *tue* (Mṛcch. 101,25) and *tae* (105,4), where, however, GOḌABOLE p. 299,5 reads more correctly *tue*.—*te, de*, even where they stand with a past passive participle form, may be considered as gen. But the interpretation as the ins. is sometimes necessary, as Ś. Mṛcch. 60,24 *ṇa hu ḍe...sāhasaṁ karĕnteṇa...ācaridaṁ = na khalu tvayā...sāhasaṁ kurvatā...ācaritam*, or very probably, as Ś. Mṛcch. 29,14 *suṭṭhu de jāṇidaṁ = suṣṭhu tvayā jñātam*, compare with 27,21; 28, 24 *suṭṭhu tue jāṇidaṁ*. A *taĩ, paĩ*, (Hc. 4,370; 422,18; Vikr. 55,18; 58,9), as in the acc.—Abl. M. *tumāhi, tumāhiṁto, tumāo* (G. H.); Ś. *tatto = tvattaḥ* (Śak. 9,10), *tuvatto* (Mallikām. 219, 8) and undoubtedly in the meaning of the sing., but against the dialect, *tumhāhiṁto* (Karp. 53,6; Viddhaś. 71,6; 113,6) P. *tumāto, °tu* (Hc. 4,307. 321).—Gen. M. *tuha, tuhaṁ, tujjha, tujjhaṁ, tumhaṁ, tumma, tu, te, de* (G. H. R.); AMg. *tava, te, tubbhaṁ*[4], *tuhaṁ* (Uttar. 444. 597 f.), *tumaṁ* (Āyār. 1,3,3,4; Uttar. 358); JM. *tuha, tumha, tujjha, tava, tujjhaṁ*, (Āv. 7,11; 22,5), *tuhaṁ* (Āv. 7,33; 12, 14); Ś. *tuha* (Lalitav. 554,5; Mṛcch. 22,25; Śak. 15,1; Vikr. 26,9); *te* in Ś. only Mṛcch. 3,16 (v. l. *de*); 80,20; Vikr. 24,7, elsewhere always *de* (§ 185); hence *te* is obviously false.[5] Against the dialect are also *tava* and *tujjha*. In Vikr, *tava* stands at 27,21 only, where the MSS BP have *tuha*, as also the ed. Bomb. 48,5 reads; in Mṛcch. only in 17,21; 24,3 in the repetition of words of the Śakāra and in 138,23 in reproduction of Skt. words; 151,21. In Ratn., in places where *tava* or *tua* stood earlier, CAPPELLER reads *tuha*, so that Ratn. has only *tuha* (294,21; 299,3; 305,8; 309, 6; 313,12. 27; 318,26) and *de*. We should read *tuha*, as we have in 39,5 of the ed. Bomb. for *tuva, tua* in Prab. 37,14:39,5 of the editions. *tujjha* correctly stands in the dramas, Mṛcch. 100,11 (Ā.); 104,1 (D). 17 (Ā.); Śak. 55,15 (M.), Nāgān. 45,7 (M.); in Ś. it occurs only in Śak. 43,9, and is, therefore, false, since Lalitav. 554,4; Karp. 10,9; 17,5; Nāgān. 71,11; Karṇas. 52, 13 and other Indian editions do not come into consideration. Against this Mg., like AMg. JM., has *tava* (Mṛcch. 12,19; 13,9; 14,1; 21,3; 22,4 etc.; Śak. 116,11), *te* (Mṛcch. 31,17; 113,1), about which the observation made above holds good; elsewhere very often *de* (e.g. Mṛcch 21,22; Śak. 113, 7; Mudrār. 184,2), wrong *tujjha* (Mṛcch. 176,6, for which we should read *tue* with GOḌABOLE 478, 1; Nāgān. 67, 1 for which we should read *te* [*de*] with the ed. Calc. 63,1; Prab. 58, 17 where BROCKHAUS in fact has *ujjha*, and for which, with the v. l., we should read *tuha*; Ḍh. *tuha* (Mṛcch.

39,5); A. *taü*, *tujjhu* (Hc. 4,367,1. 370,4. 372. 425), the remarkable *tudhra* (Hc. 4,372), *tujjhaha* (Vikr. 72,10; on this BOLLENSEN), *tuha* (Hc. 4,361. 370,1. 383,1; Piṅgala 1,123[a]), *tumha* (Piṅgala 1,60*a*), *tujjhe* in rhyme with *jujjhe*=*yudhi* (Piṅgala 2, 5). AMg. *tubbhaṁ* is=*tubhyam*; *tuha*, *tujjha*, *tuyha* presuppose one **tuhyam* (cf. *mahyam*). From this are deduced the stems *tubbha*, *tuyha*, *uyha*, that appear in the plural.[6] The stems *tuyha*, *uyha* must have originated either from Mg. or from a dialect related to Mg. (§ 236. 331).—Loc. M. *taï*, *tuvi*, *tumammi*, *tume* (G. H. R.); AMg. *tumaṁsi* (Nirayāv. § 15); JM. *taï*, *tumammi*; Ś. *taï* (Vikr. 30,3; 84,4), *tui* (Mālav. 41,19; Veṇīs. 13,8 [so to be read with the ed. Calc. 1870, p.26,5]); A. *taĩ*, *paĩ*, as in the acc. ins. (Hc. 4,370). In JM. too *paĩ* and *païṁ* have been used by Dhanapāla[7] in the Ṛṣabhap.

1. See note 1 to § 418.—2. BOLLENSEN on Vikr. p. 528 reads *tũhũ* and wants to derive it from *tumhaṁ* at p. 529.—3. PISCHEL, GGA. 1877, 1066; BB. 3,250 note; ZDMG, 35. 714.—4. HOERNLE on Uvās. Transl., note 262.—5. Certainly wrong is *de* in the beginning of the sentence in Śak. ed. BÖHTL. 107,13, as already noted by BOLLENSEN on Vikr. 176.—6. Differently KERN Jaartelling 102, MÜLLER, Beiträge 55, note 1.—7. KLATT, ZDMG. 33,448.

§ 422. Plural. Nom. Except in AMg. the usual form, in all the dialects, is *tumhe*=**tuṣme*: M. (H. R.); JM. (Erz.); Ś. (Mṛcch. 24,15; 70,15; Śak. 106,2; 109,7); Mg. (Mṛcch, 16,19; 149,17); A. (Hc. 4,369). For Mg. the correct form will be **tusme* or even *tuyhe*; cf. *tusmā°*, EI. 3,313,4, that KIELHORN has correctly equated as=*yuṣmat*. The same stems are to be presupposed also for the plural forms in other cases for this dialect, in which now °*mh*° stands in the editions. AMg. has throughout *tubbhe*=Aśoka *tuphe* (Āyār. 1,4,2,4; 2,3,3,5. 7; Sūyag. 192. 194. 783. 972; Vivāhap. 132. 332; Nāyādh. [also § 138 to be read so with the v. l. for *tumhe*]; Uvās.; Kappas.; Nirayāv.). In a contemptuous sense is used *tumāiṁ* (Āyār. 2,4,1,8). JM. has, beside *tumhe*, also *tubbhe* (Āv. 14,28. 30; 41,22; Erz.; Kk.); according to Hc. 4,369 A. has also *tumhaĩ*; according to Kī. 5,113; P. has *tumpha*, *tuppha*, *tumhe*.—Acc. *tumhe* : M. (R. 3,27); Ś. (Mṛcch. 24,17; Nāgān. 48,13); JM. *tubbhe* (Dvār. 497,18; 468,38) and *tumhe* (T. 5,3); AMg. *tubbhe* (Uvās. and *bhe*[1], which originated from it under the influence of loss of accent (Nāyādh. 938. 939; Uttar. 363); A. has *tumhe*, *tumhaĩ* according to Hc. 4,369.—Ins. M. *tumhehi* (H. 420); AMg. *tubbhehiṁ* (Vivāgas. 17; Uttar. 579 [°*bhbhe*°]; Uvās.; Kappas.; Nāyādh. s.v. p. 359. 361. 363. 419 etc.), also *tumehiṁ* (Nāyādh. 454, if the reading is correct), *tubbhe* (Sūyag. 932) and *bhe* (Āyār. 1,4,2,4; Nāyādh. 1284. 1376 [text *te*]); JM. *tumhehiṁ* (Erz.), *tubbhehiṁ* (Āv. 11,26; 18,27; Erz.); Ś. *tumhehiṁ* (Mahāv. 29,4; Viddhaś. 48,5); *tumhehĩ* (Hc. 4,371).—Gen. in all the dialects *tumhāṇaṁ* : M. (H. 676, °*ṇa*); AMg. (Sūyag. 964); JM. (Erz.; Kk.); Ś. (Lalitav. 568,5; Mṛcch. 17,22; Vikr. 48,4; Mālatīm. 285, 2); Mg. (Lalitav. 566,9; Śak. 118,4; Mudrār. 178,4; 258,4). In M. more frequent is *tumha* (R.), in AMg. the prevalent form is *tubbhaṁ* (Sūyag. 967. 1017; Nāyādh, § 79; p. 452. 590; Uttar. 355; Vivāhap. 1214; Vivāgas 20. 21; Uvās.; so to be read with the v. l. for *tumhaṁ* in also Kappas. § 79). Besides there is found in AMg. *tubbhe* (Uvās. § 68, 153 [so to be read]) and often *bhe* (Āẏār. 1,4,2,6; 2,1,5,5. 9,6; Sūẏag. 284. 734. 972; Nāẏādh. 907; Uttar. 50; Vivāhap. 132), which JM. too has (Āv. 24,8. 12). M. Ś. frequently have also *vo = vaḥ* (G. H. R.; Śak. 20,7; 52,15; Vikr. 51,16), likewise PG. (7,46), that I cannot locate in other dialects and in Mṛcch. In Āv. 41,18 we should read *keṇa bhe kiṁ gahiẏaṁ*. A. has *tumhahã*. (Hc. 4,373). According to Hc. 4,300 there is found in M. *tumhāhã* too. I cannot quote any form of the loc. Śākalya,[2] according to Mk. fol. 48 f., taught, without any strong justification, the forms *tujjhisuṁ, tumbhisuṁ*; A. has *tumhāsu* according to Hc. 4,374. According to C. 2,26 *bhe* is used in all the cases in the plural. It is found in the texts in the acc., the ins. and the gen. On the ecriture *hha* for *bbha* (*bhbha*) in the MSS of Sr. see PISCHEL, De gr. Pr. p. 3.

1. E. MÜLLER (Beiträge p. 55) has already noted that *bhe* is not = Skt. *bho* (WEBER, Bhag. 1,404, note 4; LEUMANN, Aup. S. s. v.).—2. PISCHEL, De gr. Pr. p. 2f.

§ 423. Not only are the nom. singular masculine and the fem. of the stem *sa-*, as in Classical Skt., been retained, but dialectically also in other cases, partly in concord with the Iranian dialects.[1] Sing. : nom masc. M. JM. JŚ. S. Ā. D. P. *so* (H. s. v. *sa-*; G. R. Erz. Ṛṣabhap. s. v. *ta-*; Kk. s. v. *tad*; JŚ. Pav. 380,7; 381,16. 21; Kattig. 398, 302; 399, 312; Ś. Lalitav. 555. 1; 560, 19; Mṛcch. 6,8; Śak. 52,5; Vikr. 10,2; Ā. Mṛcch. 99, 16; 101,6; D. Mṛcch. 100,5. 9; P. Hc. 4,322. 323), seldom *sa* (Hc. 3,3; PG. 7,47; M. R. 11, 21 [where, however, with C. we should read *a = ca*]); AMg. (Āẏār. 1,5,5,4 [where *sa cceva* is to read]; Uttar. 361 [*sa eso* beside *eso hu so* 362] ; JM. (Erz. 6, 36; Kk. 258, 4); Ś. Mṛcch. 42,11 [in A. only]; 63,18) ; AMg. *se* (Āẏār. 1,1,1,4 ff. ; Uvās. ; Nāẏādh.; Kappas. s. v. *ta*[2]); Mg. *śe* (Lalitav. 565,6; Mṛcch. 19, 17; Śak. 114,2; A. *su* and *so* (Hc. s. v. s. v.). Wrongly stands *so* in AMg. in Āẏār. 1,1,1,4 and elsewhere in prose (cf. § 17). In accord with alteration in gender (§ 356 ff.) one says AMg. *se diṭṭhaṁ ca ṇe = tad dṛṣṭaṁ ca naḥ*; *se duddiṭṭhaṁ ca bhe = tad durdṛṣṭaṁ ca vaḥ* (Āẏār. 1,4,2,3.4); Mg. *eśe śe daśaṇāmake = etad tad daśanāmakam* (Mṛcch. 11,1), *śe muṇḍe = tan muṇḍam* (Mṛcch. 122,7) *eśe śe śuvaṇṇake = etat tat suvarṇakaṁ* (Mṛcch 165,7), *śe kamma = tat karma* (Śak. 114.6); A. *so sukkhu = tat saukhyam* (Hc. 4,340, 1).—Acc. AMg. *se* corresponding to *me* (§ 418) and *te* (§ 421) in *se s' evaṁ vaẏantaṁ = sa tam evaṁ vadantam* (Āẏār. 2,1,7,8,9,6), whilst in *se s' evaṁ vaẏantassa* (Āẏār. 2,1,2,4,6,4. 7,5. 9,2;2,5,1,11;2,6,1,10) the second gen. *se* is = *sa tasyaivaṁ vadataḥ*; A. *su* (Hc. 4,383,3; masc.), *so* (Piṅgala 1,5[a]; neuter.). —Inst. AMg. *se* (Sūẏag. 838. 848 854. 860).—Gen. M. AMg. JM. Ś *se*, Mg. *śe* very frequently as masc. and fem., corresponding to *me* and *te* (Vr. 6,11; C. 1,17; Hc. 3,81; Kī. 3,48; Sr. fol. 22; Ś. masc. Mṛcch. 12,24; Śak. 37,10; Vikr. 15,10; femin. Lalitav. 561,9; Mṛcch. 25, 8; Śak. 21, 2; Vikr. 46, 1; Mg. masc. Mṛcch. 36, 10; 161, 7; femin. Mṛcch 134,8; Veṇīs. 34,12); AMg. JM. metri causa also *sĕ* (Dasav. 633,17; 635,4; Āv. 8,2.16) and AMg. *si* (Sūẏag. 282)[3].—Plural. nom. AMg. *se* (Āẏār. 1,4,2,1 [ed. Calc. *te*]; Sūẏag. 859); Mg. *śe* (Mṛcch. 167,1)[4].—Acc. JŚ. *se* (Pav. 388,4; beside nom. *te*).—Gen. JM. *se* (C.1,17;

Hc. 3,81; Sr. fol. 22; Kk. 273,29; cf. § 34) and *siṁ* (Vr. 6,12; Hc. 3,81; Sr. fol. 22).—Voc. AMg. *se* (Āẏār. 1,7,2,1). As in the Atharvaveda 17, 1,20 f.[5], in the Śatapathabrāhmaṇa (B.-R. s. v. *sa* p. 452), in Pāli *sace* (when) *sa*, in Pāli *sĕyyathā se*, so in AMg. *se* is placed before pronouns and pronominal adverbs without any influence on the meaning. Initial *t* of the pronoun *ta-* and *j* of the pronoun *ya-* are in most cases reduplicated after it. So AMg. *sĕ ttaṁ* (Āẏār. 2,1,1,2. 4,4. 5,2. 5;2,3,1,14; 2,4,2,7. 8; Jīv. 36ff. 316f.; Vivāhap. 160. 596; Paṇṇav. 7 ff. 63.480); *se taṁ* (Āẏār. 1,2, 5,5; Kappas. Th. § 7—9); *se teṇ' aṭṭheṇaṁ* (Vivāhap. 34 ff. 46 ff.); *sĕ jjaṁ* (Āẏār. 1,2,6,5; 2,1,1,1. 4. 11; 2,1,2,3. 3,4 ff.; 2,3,1,2 ff.; 2,7,2,2 ff.); *sĕ jjāiṁ* (Āẏār. 2,1, 1,14. 2,2. 3,10; 2,5,1,4); *sĕ jjāṇ' imāṇi* (Āẏār. 2,2,2,10); *sĕ jje ime* (Ovav. § 70. 71. 73 ff.); *sĕ jjāo* (Āẏār. 2,1,1,3; Ovav § 72); *se jaṁ* (Āẏār. 1,1,1,4); *se kiṁ taṁ* (Aṇuog. 356; Nandīs. 471; Paṇṇav. 62. 480; Ovav. § 30; Kappas. Th. § 7—9); *se ke ṇaṁ* (Nāẏādh. § 138); *se kahaṁ eẏaṁ* (Vivāhap. 142); *se kei* (Sūẏag. 301); *se kiṁ tu hu* (Sūẏag. 846). In contrast to Pāli *sĕyyathā* in AMg. *j* of *jahā* is never reduplicated after *se* : *se jahā* (Āẏār. 1,6,1,2; Sūẏag. 593 f. 613. 747; Vivāhap. 134. 161 f. 270. 929; Uvās. § 12. 210; Ovav. § 54; Nāẏādh. § 133). The scholiasts explain *se* as *tad*; e. g. Śīlāṅka on Āẏār. 230 *sĕ tti tacchabdārthe*; p. 300 *seśabdas tacchabdārthe sa ca vākyopanyāsārthaḥ*, an explanation, that is more correct than that by CHILDERS[6] and WEBER[7]. The reduplication of *t* and *j* in Pkt. and *y* in Pāli *sĕyyathā* shows that *se* should not be taken as nom. *se* AMg. of, that Pāli too makes improbable, if not impossible[8]. *se* is rather = Vedic *sĕ'd* i.e. *śa* = *id*, that is used exactly as *sá*. It is proved through the RV. 4,37,6 : *séd ṛbhavo yám dvatha yūyám indraśca mártyam* 1 *sá dhībhir astu sánitā medhāṣātā so' árvatā*, where *se' d yám...sa'*[5] wholly is = AMg. *sĕ jjaṁ se*. Hence one writes in a better way *sĕttaṁ*, *sĕjjaṁ*, etc., like Pāli *sĕyyathā* and *sace*[9].

1. WACKERNAGEL, KZ. 24, 600 ff. In the Veda there occurs also the loc. *sasmin*. —2. The remark made under § 418, note 1 holds good.—3. *se* is merely an enclitic, hence a wrong reading in Śak. ed BÖHTLINGK 25,6, as also *de* (§ 421, note 5).—4. *śe* cannot be gen, sing., since after p. 166, 24 both the Cāṇḍālas speak. The Calc. editions (316,10 ed. Calc. 1829, 357,1 ed. Calc. Śak. 1792) and GODABOLE p. 452,6 read *eśe* that is translated in the old Calc. edition and in GODABOLE as *ete*, rightly with the scholiasts.—5. Hitherto overlooked, even by DELBRÜCK, Altind, Syntax § 140.— 6. Dictionary s. v. *sa*.—7. Bhag. 1. 421 f., where also additional examples from Vivāhap. are given.—8. E. KUHN, Beiträge p. 9.—9. The Vedic accent prohibits assumption of proclisis of *se* and reduplication according to § 196.

§ 424. The impersonal pronouns partly have the special endings of the pronouns as in Skt, and partly they are inflected like nouns. Only the loc. sing. masc. and neut. and nom. plur. masc. have the pronominal endings. In the abl. sing masc. and neut., abl. gen. loc. sing. fem. and gen. plur. masc. fem. neut., both the endings are found to be used, partly for the sake of dialectical distinction. The stem of the fem. ends in the case of *tad*, *etad*, *yad*, *kim*, *idam* in *-ā* or *-i* (Hc. 3,32; Kī. 3,45) : *tā-*, *ti-*; *eā-*, *ei-*; *jā-*, *ji-*; *kā-*, *kī-*; *imā-*, *imā-*. *yad*, *tad*, and *kim*, however, have only *ā* in the nom. acc. sing. and gen. plur. (Hc. 3,33),

Ś. Mg. in the case of all the pronouns have only *ā*. Cf. Vr. 6,1 ff.; Hc. 3,58 ff.; Kī. 3,42 ff.; Mk. fol. 45 ff.; Sr. fol. 19 ff.

§ 425. The pronoun *ta-*. Sing. nom. acc. neutr. M. AMg. JM. JŚ. Ś. Mg. Ḍh. Ā. D. A. *taṁ* (JŚ. Pav. 381,20; 385,61; Ś. Lalitav. 561, 13; 562,23; Mṛcch. 2,18; Śak. 27,6; Mg. Lalitav. 565,19 Mṛcch. 40,5; Ḍh. Mṛcch. 31,4; 32,3. 8; 35,7; Ā. Mṛcch. 102,1; D. Mṛcch. 102,19; A. Hc. 4,360); A. in the sense of "therefore" also *traṁ* (Hc. 4,360; see § 268 and cf. § 427) and *tu* in the combination *taṁ tu* (Vikr. 55,19) in correlation with *ju* (§ 427).—Acc. masc. and fem. in all dialects *taṁ*.—Ins. *teṇa*, AMg. *teṇaṁ*, A. *teṁ* (Hc. s. v. *ta-*); according to Hc. 3,69 also *tiṇā*; femin. M. *tie*, *tia*; AMg. JM. *tie*, *tāe*; Ś *tāe* (Lalitav. 555,1; Mṛcch. 79,3; Śak. 40,4 [so to be read for *tae*, as also Mṛcch. 77,10 with D]; Vikr. 45,21); Mg. *tāe* (Mṛcch 133,21); P. *tie* (Hc. 4,323); A. *tāĕ* (Hc. 4,370,2).—As pure abl. AMg. JM. have *tāo* (e.g. Ovav. § 101; Uvās. § 90. 125; Āv. 8,48; Sagara 6,4), AMg. also as femin. (Dasav. 613,24). The forms *tatto*, *tao*, Ś Mg. *tado* (Kī. 3,50; where also *tadao*), *to*, *tamhā*, taught by grammarians (Vr. 6,9.10; Hc. 2,160; 3,66.67; Mk. fol. 46), are adverbially used, *tamhā* in AMg. and JŚ. only (Pav. 380,8; 381, 20; 382,23. 27; 384,36); *to*, that occurs, in addition to in M. AMg. JM. A. (Hc. s. v.), in verses in Mg. (Mṛcch. 11, 11), is obvious = *átas* (§ 142). In addition there comes AMg. *taohiṁto* (Vivāhap. 1047. 1189. 1240 f. 1283. 1288 f.; Nāẏādh. 1178) and *tā* M. JM. JŚ. (Pav. 398,303); Ś (Lalitav. 555,2; 561,15; Mṛcch. 2,16. 18. 22; 3,20); Mg. (Lalitav. 565,8. 15; 567,1; Mṛcch. 20,21; 21,12); Ḍh. (Mṛcch. 29,15; 30,13; 32,8); Ā. (Mṛcch. 101,23; 105,2); D. Mṛcch. 101,1.9; 102,18; 103,16; 104,19); A. (Hc. 4,370,1). *tā* = Vedic *tāt*[1] is wrongly equated as = *tāvat*. From A. Hc. 4,355. gives also *tahāṁ*.—Gen. masc. neut. M. AMg. JM. JŚ. Ś. Ḍh. *tassa*, also PG. *tasa* (7,41.45); Mg. *taśśa* (Mṛcch. 14,1. 7; 19,10; 37,25) and *tāha*, (Mṛcch. 13,25; 36,13; 112 9; 164,2); M. also *tāsa* (Vr. 6, 5.11; Hc. 3,63; Vetālap. p. 218 Nr. 15); A. *tassu*, *tasu*, *tāsu*, *tahŏ* (Hc. s. v. *ta-*); femin. M. *tissā*, *tie*, *tia*, according to Vr. 6,6; Hc. 3,64 also *tiā*, *tii*; AMg. JM. *tise* (also in Vr. Hc.), *tāe*, *tie*: Ś. *tāe* (Mṛcch. 79,3; 88,20; Śak. 21,8; Vikr. 16,9 15); Mg. *tāe* (Mṛcch. 133,19; 152,5); P. *tie* (Hc. 4,323); A. *tahĕ* (Hc. s. v. *ta*), *tāsu* (acc. in rhyme with *jāsu*; Piṅgala 1,109. 115). —Loc. masc. neut. M. JM. *tammi*; AMg. *taṁsi*, *tammi* *taṁmi* (also Āẏār. 1,2,3,6); Ś. *tassiṁ* (Mṛcch. 61,24; Śak. 73,3; 74,1; Vikr. 15, 12); Mg. *taśśiṁ* (Mṛcch. 38,16; 121, 19; Prab. 32, 7), according to Hc. 3, 11 also *taṁ*. Wrong is JŚ. *tamhi* (Kattig. 400,322) by the side of the correct *tammi*. A. has, according to Kī. 5, 50, also *tadru*, as in relation with *yadru* (§ 427). In the sense of "there", "thither" very frequent is *tahiṁ* (Vr.6,7; Hc. 3,60) in all dialects. As *tatra* in Skt., so *tattha* in Pkt. is used in the sense of the loc. too (Vr. 6,7; Hc. 2, 161, who has also *taha*, *tahi*). Femin. *tie*, *tia*, according to 3, 60 also *tāhiṁ*, *tāe*; AMg. *tise* (Ovav. § 83; Nāẏādh. 1148). As loc. feminine, we should probably consider also M. AMg. JM. *tāhe* for **tāse* (corresponding to *tise*, that mostly stands in correlation with *jāhe* and has the meaning "then" = *tadā* (Vr. 6,8; Hc. 3, 65; G. R., Erz.;

s. v. *tāhe* and *jāhe*; Uvās. s. v. *ta-* and *ja-*; Nāẏādh. § 143; p. 768. 944. 1052.1420.1435 etc.).—Plural. Nom. *te*, femin, *tāo*, neuter. *tāiṁ*, in all dialects, AMg. JM. also *tāṇi*. Ś. Mg. have, beside *te*, also *de* after other pronouns[2]: Ś. *ede de* (Mṛcch. 39, 3; Uttarar. 68, 8; Mālatīm. 243, 3 [*edĕ kkhu de*]; 273, 4); Mg. *ede de* (Mṛcch. 38, 19), *ye de* (Mudrār. 183, 2), elsewhere also Ś. *te* (Uttarar.77,4.5; Mudrār.260,1), as *tāo* (Mṛcch. 25,20;29, 7; Mālatīm. 80,1; Prab. 17,8) and *tāiṁ* (Uttarar. 60, 5).—Acc. *te*, also JŚ. (Pav. 379,3; 381,21) and A. (Hc. 4, 336); wrong Ś. *de* in the beginning of a sentence (Uttarar. 72, 5); femin. AMg. *tāo* (Niraẏāv.59).—Ins. *tehiṁ*, femin. *tāhiṁ*, in M. AMg. JM. also *tehi*, *tāhi* (Ś. masc. Mṛcch. 25, 14; Prab. 10,9; 12,11).—Abl. AMg. *tĕbbho* (Sūẏag. 19; correct ?); AMg. JM. *tehiṁto* (Paṇṇav. 308 f.; Āv. 48, 14) and JM. *tehiṁ* (Erz. 22, 5).—Gen. M. *tāṇaṁ*, *tāṇa*; Ś. *tāṇaṁ* (Uttarar. 73, 10), also femin. (Prab. 39,1); AMg. *tesiṁ*, *tesi*, femin. *tāsiṁ*, *tāsi*; JM. *tesiṁ*; femin. *tāsiṁ* and *tāṇaṁ* for masc. and femin.; JŚ. masc. *tesiṁ* (Pav. 379,5; 383,44); A *tāṇa*, *tāhã*, *tahã* (Hc. s. v. *ta-*); according to Hc. 4,300 *tāhã* in M. too, according to 3,62 *tāsa* in the plural too.—Loc. *tesu* (Hc. 3,135; M. R. 14,13; JM. Erz. 4,3); Ś. *tesu* (Vikr. 35,6; Mudrār. 38,10; 160,2) and *tesuṁ* (Śak. 162,13); femin. JM. Ś. *tāsu* (Erz. 15,14; Mālatīm. 105, 1); A. *tahĩ* (Hc. 4,422,18). On AMg. *tāṁ*, *teṇāṁ* see § 68, on AMg. *sĕ ttaṁ* § 423.

1. HOEFER, De Prakrita dialecto p. 171; PISCHEL, BB. 16, 171 ff.—2. BOLLENSEN on Vikr. 1.176 too strictly limits *de*, when he permits it to stand only after *je*; it is not used even as a correlative. The form makes it certain that *de* was an enclitic in such cases.

426. The pronoun *eta-* is inflected essentially like *ta-* (G. s. v. *etat*; H. R. s. v. *ea-*; Uvās.; Kappas.; Nāẏādh.; Erz.; Kk. s. v. *eya-*). The nom. sing. Masc. is M. JM. JŚ. Ś. Ā. D. *eso* (JŚ. Kattig. 398, 314; Ś. Mṛcch. 6,10; Śak. 17,4; Vikr. 7,2; Ā. Mṛcch. 99,19; 100,23; D. Mṛcch. 102,16), AMg. *ese*, in verses also *eso* (Uttar. 361 f.) Mg. *eśe* (Lalitav. 565, 6.8; 567, 2; Mṛcch. 11, 1; Prab. 32, 10; Śak. 113, 3; Veṇīs. 33, 15), Ḍh. *esu* (Mṛcch. 31,12; 34,17; 35,15). A. *ehŏ* (Hc. s.v. *eha*). Differently from *sa* (§ 423), beside it there occurs very frequently, however, *esa* (Hc. 3,3), which, according to Hc. 3,85 is used also for the femin. and neut. : *esa*, *mahī*, *esa siraṁ*. *esa* does not stand merely as an adjective before substantives, but also as a substantive, in verse, as in prose, e.g. JŚ. Pav. 379,1; Ś. Mṛcch. 54,13; Vikr. 82,14. In Mg. *eśa* is seldom (Mṛcch. 139,17); in Ḍh. stands *esa* (Mṛcch. 36,23). The femin. is *esā* (Ś. Lalitav. 555,2; Mṛcch. 15,24; Vikr. 7,13; Śak. 14,6; also P.Hc. 4,320 and D. (Mṛcch. 102,23), Mg. *eśā* 10,23.25; 13,7,24; Prab. 32,9), A. *eha* (Hc. s.v.: Piṅgala, 2,64), the neut. PG. *etaṁ* (6,30), M. *eaṁ*, AMg. JM. *eyaṁ*, Ś. Mg. Ā. D. *edaṁ* Ś. (Lalitav. 555,18; Mṛcch. 2, 18; Vikr. 6, 1; also acc. Mṛcch. 49,8.14; Śak. 25, 1; Vikr. 13,4; Mg. nom. Mṛcch. 45,21; 168,18; 169,7; acc. Mṛcch. 29,24; 132,21; Ā. nom. Mṛcch. 100,18; D. acc. Mṛcch. 100,16); A *ehu* = **eṣam* (Hc. s. v. *eha*), also acc. *ehaũ* = **eṣakam* (Hc. 4,362).—Acc. masc. femin. neut. M. *eaṁ*, AMg. JM. *eyaṁ*. Ś. Mg. *edaṁ*; A. masc. *ehu* (Piṅgala 1,81).—In the ins. M. has *eeṇa* (H. R.), AMg. *eeṇaṁ*, JM. beside *eeṇa* also *eiṇā*, Ś. Mg. beside *edeṇa* (Ś. Mṛcch. 42,12; Vikr. 31,14; Uttarar. 78,3; 163,3; Mg.

Mṛcch. 118,11; 133,19; 154,9) much more frequently *ediṇā* (Ś. Mṛcch. 5,5; 18,3; Śak. 10,12; Vikr. 53,1; Uttarar. 13,11; Mālatīm. 31,4; 73,3; 100,3; Ratn. 293,21; Mg. Mṛcch. 39,25; 40,11; Veṇīs. 36,1). See § 128. In the femin. beside *eẏāye* JM. has also the form *eie*, from the femin. stem *ei* = **eti-*, mentioned by Hc. 3, 32; both the forms are valid for the abl. gen. loc. too. In Ś. Mg. the ins. gen. loc. is pronounced as *edāe*: ins. (Ś. Mṛcch. 94,16; 95,8; Vikr. 27,15; 41,7; Ratn. 299,8; Mg. Mṛcch. 173,8; Prab. 61,7); gen. (Mg. Mṛcch. 123,3); loc. (Ś. Mṛcch. 9,9; 42,11).—For the abl. Vr. 6,20 gives *ĕtto, edādo, edādu, edāhi*; Hc. 3, 82: *ĕtto, ĕttāhe, eāo, eāu, eāhi, eāhiṁto, eā*; Kī, 3,51: *etto. edo* [sic.], *edādu, edāhi, ĕttha*. From it is *ĕtto* = **etataḥ* (§ 197); it is used in AMg. M. JM. in the sense of "hence", "thence", "now", in AMg. as pure abl. too: *ĕtto uvasaggāo* = *etasmād upasargāt* (Nāẏādh. 761); *ĕtto annaẏaraṁ* = *etasmād anyataram* (Āẏār. 2,1,2,4. 6,4. 7,8; 2,2,3,18; 2,6,1,5). This use is wrong in Ś. In Indian editions in places where it occurs, such as in Mālatīm, ed. Bomb. 69,9; 255,1, we should read *imādo*, as in the first place, the ed. Calc. 1866 p. 37, 13 and the ed. BHAṆḌĀRKAR 92, 3 have. In AMg. *itto* too (Sūẏag. 360; Uttar 599). *ĕttāhe*, however, is derived from the stem *ĕttā* = *etá-*[1], and like *tāhe* (§ 425), is to be taken as the loc. sing. of the feminine. It is used in M. adverbially in the sense of "now" (Hc. 2, 134; G. H. R.), in A. as *ĕttahĕ* in the meaning "hence" (Hc. 4, 419, 6. 420, 6) and of "hither." (Hc. 4, 436). According to it is built A. *téttahĕ* "thither" (Hc. 4, 436). JM. *eẏāo* (Dvār. 495, 27).—Gen. M *eassa*; AMg. JM. *eẏassa*; Ś. *edassa* (Śak. 29,2; Vikr. 32,3; Uttarar. 67.6); Mg. *edaśśa* (Lalitav. 565, 8; Mṛcch. 19,5; 79, 19) and *edāha* (Mṛcch. 145,4; 164, 4).—Loc. according to Hc. 3, 60 *eassiṁ*, according to 3, 84 *eammi*; AMg. JM. *eẏammi, eẏaṁmi*; in AMg. also *eẏaṁsi* (Sūẏag. 790; Vivāhap. 116. 513 [text *eesi*, correctly in the commentary], 1119); Ś. *edassiṁ* (Śak. 78,12; Vikr. 6,3; 23, 17; Ratn. 301,5; Priyad. 13,16; Prab. 36,1); Mg. *edaśśiṁ* (Lalitav. 565,6; Mṛcch. 134, 22; 137, 4; Mudrār. 185, 1). On *aammi, iammi* see § 429.—Plural. Nom. M. AMg. JM. *ee* : JŚ. Ś. *ede* (Pav. 386, 8; 389, 1; Mṛcch. 8,2; Śak. 41,1; Mālatīm. 243, 3; 284, 10); Mg. *ede* (Mṛcch 29, 23; 38, 19; 71, 22); striking *ede akkhalu* Mṛcch. 40, 2 (all editions) = *etāni akṣarāṇi*; A *ei* (Hc. 4,330.363); femin. M. *eāo*; AMg. JM. *eẏāo*, Ś. *edāo* (Caṇḍak. 28,10; Mallikām. 336, 8.13), JM. also *eẏā*; neut. M. *eāi*; AMg. JM. *eẏāiṁ*, AMg. JM. also *eẏāṇi* (Sūẏag. 321; Erz.), Ś. *edāiṁ* (Mṛcch. 128, 4; 153, 9. 13); Mg. *edāiṁ* (Mṛcch. 132, 16; 169,6).—Acc. masc. AMg. JM. *ee*, A. *ei* (Hc. 4,363).—Ins. masc. neuter. M. JM. *eehiṁ, eehi*; Ś. Mg. *edehiṁ* (Ś. Mṛcch. 24, 1; Prab. 12, 10; 14, 10; Mg. Lalitav. 565, 13; Mṛcch. 11, 12; 122, 19; 132, 15); femin. AMg. JM. *eẏāhiṁ*.—Gen. masc. neutr. M. *eāṇa* (Hc. 3,61; G.H.); PG. *etesi* (6, 27); AMg. JM. *eesiṁ, eesi*, JM. also *eẏāṇaṁ*; Ś. *edāṇaṁ* (Mṛcch. 38, 22; Uttarar. 11,4; 165,3; 197,10); femin. M. *eāṇa* (H. 89), according to Hc. 3,32 also *eiṇaṁ, eāṇaṁ*; AMg. JM. *eẏāsiṁ*, JM. also *eẏāṇaṁ*; Ś. *edāṇaṁ* (Ratn. 293, 13; Karp. 34,3,4).—Loc. M. AMg. (e.g. Āẏār 1,2,5,3); JM. *eesu, eesuṁ*; Ś. *edesuṁ* (Śak. 9,12.14) and *edesu* (Mudrār. 72,3).

1. S. GOLDSCHMIDT, Prākṛtica p. 22.

§ 427. The relative pronoun *ja-*, Mg. *ya-* is inflected almost wholly like the demonstrative *ta-*. In the nom. acc. sing. neut. A has *ju* too (Hc. 4,350,1; 418,2), beside the frequent *jaṁ* (Hc. s. v. *jo*); both the forms stand beside one another in *jaṁ ju* (Vikr. 55,19; cf. *taṁ tu* § 425). Besides A. uses *dhruṁ* too (Hc. 4,360; cf. *traṁ* § 425). According to Kī. 5, 49 *jruṁ* is used in the acc. sing. for the demonstrative *druṁ*. The example is: *jruṁ eintesi druṁ pāvasi=yac cintayasi tat prāpnoṣi.* The old form *yad* has been retained in AMg. *jad atthi* and Mg. *yad iścáśe* (§ 341).—In the ins. sing. is found, according to Hc. 3,69 also *jiṇā*; A. has *jeṁ* (Hc. 4,350,1) beside *jeṇa* (Hc. s. v. *jo*); in Piṅgala 2,272. 280 stands *jiṇi*, for which probably we have to read *jiṇa=jiṇā.*—In the abl. is found also *jā*=Vedic *yāt* (BB. 16,172), in A. also *jahāṁ* according to Hc. 4,355, beside *jāo, jao, jado, jatto, jamhā* (Vr. 6,9; Hc. 2,160; 3,66), about which the remark made in § 425 holds good.—In the gen. Mg. has also *yāha* (Mṛcch. 112,9), beside *yaśśa* (Mṛcch. 19,10; 165,7); A. *jāsu, jasu* (Hc. s. v. *jo*; Piṅgala 1, 68. 81a. 89a, 135 etc.), also in the fem. Hc. 4,368; Piṅgala 1,109.111 ff.), for which in M. are used *jia, jie* (G.H. s.v. *ja-*), *jissā* (Vr. 6,6; Hc. 3,64; Karp. 49,4.7; 84,11), according to Vr. Hc. also *jiā, jii, jise*; A. has *jahĕ* for **jāse* (Hc.4,359); Ś. *jāe* (Mṛcch.170,25; 172,5; Prab.39,6).—In the loc. is used in AMg. *jaṁsi=yasmin*, in verses also *jaṁsī* (§ 75), sometimes for the femin. too: *jaṁsī guhāe* (Sūẏag. 273) and in relation to *naī=nadī* (Sūẏag. 297), in relation to *nāvā=nauḥ* (Uttar. 716); in A. stands *jassammi=yasyām* (Piṅgala 1,52), in AMg. *jassaṁmi* in the sense of the gen. (Vivāhap. 264). According to Hc. 3,60 beside *jāe, jie, jāhiṁ* too is used in the femin., as *jahiṁ* in the masc. neut., which is frequent in all dialects in the sense of "where", "whither". A. has also *jahī, jahi* (§ 75), according to Kī. 5,50 also *yadru*, as *tadru* in the demonstrative (§ 425). Presumably *jadru* is to be written. On *jāhi* see § 425. According to Vr. 6,7 even *jattha* is used in the sense of the locative; beside it, Hc. 2,161 teaches also *jahi, jaha* in the sense of *yatra.* In the nom. plur. beside the usual *je* (Hc. s. v. *jo*) A. has also *ji* (Hc. 4,387,1), in the neut. AMg. has *ẏāiṁ* too (Āẏār. 2,1,3,4. 5,5. 9,1; 2,2,2,10; 2,3,3,8; 2,4,1,8; 2,5,1,10. 2,4; 2,7,1,1; Nāẏādh. 450. 1248; cf. 1376), beside *jāiṁ*, the adverbial *yāiṁ=yad* stands, which may be equated with *āiṁ* with the scholiasts on Nāẏādh. 450, since it appears only after *i* (*pi, avi, ii, atthi*), and *ẏ* would be explained as that in *ẏāvi* (§ 335).—In the abl. plur. AMg. has *jehiṁto* (Paṇṇav. 308 f.), in the gen. plur. M. JM. *jāṇa, jāṇaṁ*, JM. also, as always AMg. *jesiṁ, jesi*, Ś. *jāṇaṁ* (Uttarar. 68,9), A. *jāhā̃* (Hc. 4,353. 409); in the fem. AMg. has *jāsiṁ* (Vivāgas. 189). On AMg. *jāṁ, jeṇām* see § 68, on AMg. *sĕ jjaṁ, se jahā* §423. In PG. we find only the nom. sing. *jo* (7,44).

§ 428. In the interrogative as in Skt. there are found two stems: *ka-* and *ki-*.—The stem *ka-* is inflected like the stems *ta-* and *ja-* (§ 425. 427). The abl. *kāo, kao, kado, katto, kamhā* (Vr. 6,9; Hc. 2,160; 3,71; Kī. 3,49) are analysed in the same way as in the case of *ta-* and *ja-*. A. has also *kaü* (Hc. 4,416—418) and *kahāṁ* (Hc. 4,355), AMg. also *kaohiṁto* (Jīv. 34. 263; Paṇṇav. 304; Vivāhap. 1050ff. 1340. 1433. 1522. 1526. 1528.1603ff.) In the gen. Vr.6,5; Hc.3,63; Kī.3,47; Mk. fol. 46 give, beside *kassa*, also *kāsa* (Kī. ed. *kāso*), that occurs as *kāsu* in A. (Hc. 4,358,2) and as *kāha* in Mg. (Mṛcch. 38,12), and according to Hc. 3,63 that is also feminine. The loc. is M. *kammi*, AMg. *kaṁsi* (Āyār. 1,2,3,1), and *kamhi* (Uttar. 454; Paṇṇav. 637), Ś. *kassiṁ* (Mṛcch. 81,2; Mahāv. 98,14), Mg. *kaśśiṁ* (Mṛcch. 80,21; Prab.50,13); in all dialects frequent are *kahiṁ, kattha* (§293) in the sense of "whither?", "where?", beside which Hc. 2,161 mentions also *kahi, kaha,* as *kāe kāhiṁ* for the femin. 3,60. AMg. *kāhe* "when?" (Vr. 6,8; Hc. 3,65; Kī. 3,44; Mk. fol. 46; Vivāhap. 153) is to be considered as *tāhe jāhe* (§ 425.427). As the gen. there occurs in A. *kahě* (Hc. 4,359). In the nom. femin. plur. is found many times in Ś. *kā* instead of *kāo* in the phrase *kā amhe* [*kā vaaṁ*] with the gen. loc. or ins. (Śak. 16,12; Mālav. 46,12; 65,3). Probably it is to be corrected as *kāo* (§ 376)[1]. The neuter A. *kāĩ* (Hc. s.v.) (Prabandhac. 109,5) is used like *kiṁ*, also adverbially in the sense of "why', "on what reason?"; likewise *kaĩ* (Hc. 4,426; Vikr. 62,11). The gen. are M. *kāṇaṁ, kāṇa* (G. s. v. *kim*); AMg. JM. *kesiṁ*. In PG. is found only the nom. sing. *ko* in *ko ci* (6,40).—In all the dialects is formed the nom. acc. sing. neut. *kiṁ* = *kim* from the stem *ki*-. Ś. *kitti* (Lalitav. 555,4), that occurs as a v. l. also in Śak. 15,4 and elsewhere, is not with Johansson[2] and Konow[3] to be taken as **kidti*, but as an erroneous ecriture for *kiṁ ti*[4]. The ins. *kiṇā* (Hc. 3,69; Kī. 3,55; Mk. fol. 45) occurs in M, *kiṇā vi* (G. 413), and as adverb "in which manner?", "by what means?" in AMg. (Uvās. § 167). *tiṇā, jiṇā* might be formed according to it.—*kiṇo* and *kisa* are mentioned as abl. by Hc. 3,68; *kiṇo* as an interrogative particle also by Hc. 2,216; Kī. 4,83, as it used in M. (G.182; H. s. v.), is used[5]. *kisa*, (Mg. *kiśa*) occur in M. (H.R, but not G.), JM. (Āv. 18,14; Erz.), AMg. (Nirayāv. § 13; Dasav. N. 648,23.33), especially frequently in Ś. and Mg. (Ś. Mṛcch. 29,8; 95,18; 151, 12; 152, 12; 161,16; Ratn. 290,30; 295,19; 299,1.15; 301,25; 302,5; 303,23.30; 305,24; 310,29; 314,32; 316,23; 317,33; Mallikām. 253,5; 266,6 etc.; Mg. Mṛcch. 113,17; 114,8; 121,2; 151,24; 170,16; Veṇīs. 33,16), but not in Kālidāsa (Pischel on Hc. 3,68). Although it is undoubtedly used later as abl., as Mg. *kiśa kālaṇādo* = *kasmāt kāraṇāt* (Kaṁsav. 49,6), nevertheless according to its origin it is gen., corresponding to Pāli *kissa*, as also Kī. 3, 46 mentions, and it has, like the latter, almost always the adverbial meaning "why?", as Kī. 4,83 mentions. Striking is the meaning "what?" in Mg. In Mṛcch. 112, 8 *kiṇo* too is to be interpreted accordingly. For the gen. sing. femin. Vr. 6,6; Hc. 3,64; Kī. 3,46; Mk. fol. 46 give the forms *kissā, kise, kia, kiā, kii, kie*, Hc. 3,60 the last one also for the loc. *kia* stands at H. 604 and so we have to read for *kie* in G. 1123. 1152, also, that is correct at G. 1145.—A. has as interrogative also *kavaṇa*, from which are found the nom. sing. masc. *kavaṇu*, feminine *kavaṇa*, ins. sing. neut. *kavaṇeṇa*, gen. sing. masc. *kavaṇahě* (H. s v. *kavaṇa*), acc. sing. neutr. *kavaṇu* (Prabandhac. 70,11.13). Cf. therewith also Skt. *kavapatha, kavāgni, kavoṣṇa* and Pkt. *kavaṭṭia* § 246).

1. So rightly Lassen, Inst. p. 326; wrongly Bollensen on Mālav. p. 191.—Weber, IS. 14,262 ff. has overlooked that in the Devanāgari-recension of Śakuntalā

too, in all the places referred to by him at p. 263, the MSS have only *-ā*, and that *-āo* is just a conjecture of Böhtlingk.—2, Shāhbāzgarhi 1,176.—3. GGA. 1894, 480.—4. So rightly Bloch, Vr. und Hc. 35.—5. Cf. also Haripāla on G. 182 : *kiṇo iti kasmādarthe deśinipātaḥ*.

§ 429. The stems combined together under the pronoun *idam* in Skt. have been retained as a whole in Pkt. The *a*-stem is very much restricted in its use; the stem *ima-*, except in A., where it is almost completely wanting, became prevalent. From the *a-* and *i-* stems are found to have been formed : nom. sing. masc. AMg. JM. *ayaṁ* (Uvās. Nāyādh. Nirayāv. s. v.; Kappas. Kk. s. v. *ima*); Ś. Ḍh. *aaṁ* (Ś. Mṛcch. 3,24; Śak. 13,3; Vikr. 29,12; Ḍh. Mṛcch. 34,9.12). Whilst *aaṁ* is very frequent in Ś., it has almost entirely vanished from M. It stands only in R. 14, 44 *ahavāaṁ kaakajjo* = *athavāyaṁ kṛtakāryaḥ*, a passage, that is cited as an example by Hc. 3,73 too: elsewhere *imo* occurs for it. It is completely wanting in Mg., where *eśe* is used. In fact Hc. 4, 302 cites *ayaṁ dāva śe āgame* = Śak. 114.11; but here only the Dravidian and Devanāgarī recensions read *aaṁ*, as throughout, offending against the dialect. The Bengali recension has *ĕttake*, the Kashmirian *ittake*. In AMg. *ayaṁ* in the combination *ayam eyārūve* = *ayam etadrūpaḥ* has become completely indeclinable, so that one says also *ayameyārūvaṁ*, *ayameyārūvassa*, *ayameyārūvaṁsi* too.[1] As in Pāli, so in AMg. too, *ayaṁ* is used as femin. at the same time: *ayaṁ kosī* = *iyaṁ kośī*, *ayaṁ araṇī* = *iyam araniḥ* (Sūyag. 593. 594), and so on, or it is to be taken as the masc. (§ 358), also *ayaṁ aṭṭhi* = *idam asthi*; *ayaṁ dahī* = *idaṁ dadhi* (Sūyag. 594). As neuter it stands in AMg. *ayaṁ tĕllaṁ* = *idaṁ tailam* (Sūyag. 594), therefore, formed from the *aya-* stem. The femin. *iyaṁ* has been attested in Ś. only : *iaṁ* (Mṛcch. 3,5,21; Śak. 14,1; Vikr. 48,12). Since Mg. employs elsewhere only *eśā*, *iaṁ* is a false reading in Mṛcch. 39,20 (all editions), brought in through the immediately following Ś. *iaṁ* in the same combination with *kalā*. The neut. *idaṁ* has been retained in AMg. M. and Ś. only, and that in fact as nom. only (Karp. 92,6 [rightly?]; Sūyag. 847 [rightly?]; Mṛcch. 3,20 [so to be read with C for *imaṁ*]; 7,8;42,8; Śak 15,1; Vikr. 19,15; 45.15; 86,6); as acc. is used *imaṁ* (Mṛcch.24,21; 38.23; 39,14; 42,3; 61,24; 105,9; 147,18; Śak. 57,8; 58,13). For *idaṁ* (Vikr. 40,20) we should read, with A *edaṁ*, and for *idaṁ* in Vikr. 47,10, where it would have been used as masc., we should, with ed. Bomb. 79,3 and ed. Sh. P. Pandit 94,7, read *imaṁ*. In Mg. *idaṁ* appears in *taṁ ṇidaṁ* at Lalitav. 566,20, falsely for *taṁ ṇedaṁ*; Mg. has as nom. and acc. neut. only *imaṁ* (Mṛcch. 108.11; 166,24; 169.22), as also P. as acc. (Hc. 4, 323).—Ins. M. *eṇa* (R. 14,47); A. *eṁ* (Vikr. 58,11).—Abl. M. *ā* = Vedic *āt* in the sense of *tāvat*[2].—Gen. M. JM. *assa* = *asya* (Hc. 3,74; Kī. 3,56; Mk, fol. 47; Karp. 6,5; Pārvatīp. 30,15; KI. 4.5), falsely given for *jassa* of the editions and best MSS by Weber on H. 979; falsely in Ś. too in Vikr. 21,1, where we have to read °*sūidassa* for °*sūidaṁ assa* with the MSS BP and the ed. Calc. 1833, and at Prab. 8,7, where we should read *jado se* for *jado ssa* (so all the four editions).—Loc. *assiṁ* = *asmin* (Vr. 6,15; Hc. 3,74; Kī. 3,56; Mk. fol. 47), in AMg. in verses (Āyār. 1,4,1,2; Sūyag, 328. 537. 938. 941. 950; Uttar. 22), and in prose (Āyār. 1,1,2,1;

1,5,3,3; 2,2,1,2; 2,2,9; Sūy̆ag. 695; Vivāhap. 163; Jīv. 797,801), as already *casi* = *cāsmin* in PG. 7,46[3]. For Ś. *kaṇiṭṭhamādāmaha assiṁ* (Mahāv. 98,4) we should, with the ed. Bomb. 219,8, read °*mādāmahassa*. It stands in Ś. in the text in Pārvatīp. 5,10; Mallikām. 219, 23.—Ins. plur. *ehi* AMg. Ḍh. *ehiṁ* (Rāy̆ap. 249; Mṛcch. 32,7), femin. *āhi*, loc. JM. *esu* (Hc. 3,74; T.7,16), gen. M. *esiṁ* (H.771).—Probably *aammi* and *iammi* are the loc. from it, and with the grammarians (Hc. 3,48; Sr. fol. 22), are not to be derived from *etad*. For *iammi* Triv. 2,2,87 and Sr. fol. give, probably more correctly, *iammi*, as likewise Hc. 3,89, gives from *adas* both *aammi* and *iammi*. Therefore *aammi* permits us to derive it from *ada-* = *adas*, but also from *aa-* = *aya-* (§ 121), as undoubtedly the loc. sing, AMg. *ay̆aṁsi* (Uttar. 498), the nom. sing. neut. AMg. *ay̆aṁ* (Sūy̆ag. 594; see above), and at least according to the meaning A. *āa-*, whereof have been found in the text, the ins. *āeṇa* = *anena*, *āahŏ* = *asya*, *āahiṁ* = *asmin*, *āaï* = *imāni* (Hc. 4, 365. 383, 3). *iammi*, however, belongs to *idam*, hence to the stem *ia-* = *ida-*. Loc. from one *i*-stem are *iha* "here", "*hither*" = **itha* (§ 266; Vr. 6,17; Hc. 3,75. 76), A. as masc. and femin. = *asmin* and *asyām*, *ithī*, in all dialects *ĕttha* = Vedic *itthā* (§ 107), and M. AMg. JM. *ĕṇhiṁ* "now" (Bh. 4,33; Hc. 2,134), for which the MSS. give more often as v. l. *iṇhiṁ* (G. H. R. s. v.), likewise wrong is *ittha*, which Vr. 6, 17 and Hc. 3,76 expressly forbid, so that in Ś. too in Prab. 46,8 and in P. with v. l. and Hc. 4,323 too we have to read *ĕttha*. In Mg. is used *ĕṇhiṁ* in verses only (Mṛcch. 29, 22;40,6), in Ś. not absolutely, but *idāṇiṁ*, *dāṇiṁ* (Hc. 4,277; § 144). Hence wrong in Hāsy. 36,11; Karp. 62,10 and more often in Indian editions. Likewise the word has not been as yet located in A., where *eväahī* stands in the sense of "now" (Hc. 4,420). Deśīn. 1,50 mentions the pronoun *ajjho* (according to Droṇa), femin. *ajjhā*, by which the audience is to be pointed to, can be derived from the gen. *asya* through **ahya*.

1. STEINTHAL, Specimen Anm. 77—2. PISCHEL, BB. 16,172.—3. PISCHEL, GN. 1895,211 ff.

§ 430. The stem *ana* has been retained in the ins. *aṇeṇa* only and indeed only in prose of AMg. (Āy̆ār. 1,6,4,3), JM. (Erz. 30,14), in Ś. (Mṛcch. 95,2; Śak. 163,8; Vikr. 41,11) and in Mg. (Mṛcch. 149,24, Mudrār. 192,3); AMg. also *aṇeṇaṁ* (Uttar. 487).—The most usual stem is *ima-*, femin. *imā-* or *imi-* (Hc. 3,32), in Ś. Mg. only *imā-*, as in all dialects in the nom. acc. sing. and plur. It is used in all the cases of the sing. and plur. (G. s. v. *idam*; H. R.; Erz.; Kk.; Uvās.; Kappas.; Nāy̆ādh. s. v. *ima-*; Hc. s. v. *imaṁ*). Sing. : nom. *imo*, AMg. *ime*, in verses also *imo* (Uttar. 247; Dasav. N. 654, 26; Nandīs. 84), femin. *imā*, also *imiā* = **imikā* (Hc. 3,73), neut. *imaṁ*. In Ś. Mg. these forms, even in the neuter (§ 429), are not used by good writers. In many of the later-day dramas *imo* is found in Ś. so frequently, that it can hardly be considered to be a contribution of the edition, as Pras. 11, 12. 18; 12,5.9. 13; 14,9; 17,9; 34,6; 35,1; 45,1. 12. 14; 46, 1. 2 etc.; Mukund. 14,15. 17; 19,14; 70,15; Unmattar. 4,12; Vṛṣabh. 23,9; 26,5;48,3 etc. Here we have cases of error against the dialect. A. has only the neut. *imu*. In AMg. *ime*, like *ay̆am* (§ 429), in the combination *im' eẏārūva*, has wholly weakened, so that one says also *im' eẏārūvā* (nom. sing. fem.; Uvās § 113. 167 [so to be read; see v. l.]. 168), *im' eẏārūveṇaṁ* (v. l. to Uvās. § 72). In addition, the usage described in § 173 has indeed made its contribution after the weakening of the nasal sound—Acc. masc. fem. neut. *imaṁ* (masc. Ś. Mṛcch. 24,21; Śak. 18,10; Vikr. 72,18; Mg. Mṛcch. 169,17; Śak. 115,11; femin. Ś. Mṛcch. 54,18; Śak. 14,2; Ratn. 297,23; neut. § 429); A. neut. *imu* (Hc.; Kī. 5,10).—Ins. masc. fem. neut. M. *imeṇa*; AMg. *imeṇaṁ*, *imeṇa*; JM. *imeṇa*, *imiṇā*; Ś. Mg. only *imiṇā* (Ś. Mṛcch. 24,16; Śak. 16,10; Vikr. 24,10; Mg. Veṇīs. 35,1); femin. M. *imīe*, *imīa* (also Śak. 101,13), Ś. *imāe* (Mṛcch. 90,15; Śak. 81,10; Ratn. 291,2). In Viddhaś. 96,8, where *imiā* stands wrongly, we should with the v. l. read *iaṁ*, as *ṇijjhāadi* = *nirdhyāyati* shows.—Abl. AMg. (Sūẏag. 630. 635), JM. *imāo*, Ś. Mg. *imādo* (Ś. Mṛcch. 12,25; 74,25; Mudrār. 57,3; Ratn. 299,11; Mg. Lalitav. 565,8), also femin. (AMg. Āẏār. 1,1,1,4; Ś. Ratn. 315,12; Mg. Mṛcch. 162,23).—The remark made under § 375 on Ś. *imāe* (Vikr. 17,1) holds good in this place too.—Gen. *imassa* (Ś. Mṛcch. 148,12; Śak. 108,1; Vikr. 45,4); Mg. *imaśśa* (Mṛcch. 32,17; 152, 6; Śak. 118,2); femin. M. *imīe*, *imīa* (Karp. 27,12); AMg. *imīse*; JM. *imīe*, *imāe*; Ś. *imāe* (Śak. 168,14).—Loc. masc. neutr. M. *imammi*, AMg. *imammi* (in verses; Uttar. 180; Āẏār. 2,16,12), *imaṁsi* (prose; Āẏār. 2,3,1,2; 2,5, 2,7; Vivāhap. 1275; Ovav. § 105); Ś. *imassiṁ* (Mṛcch. 65,5; Śak. 36,16; 53,8; Vikr. 15,4); Mg. *imaśśiṁ* (Veṇīs. 33,7); femin. AMg. *imīse* (Vivāhap. 81 ff.; Uvās. § 74. 253. 255. 257; Ṭhāṇ. 31. 79; Samav. 66); JM. *imāi* (Ṛṣabhap. 7; so to be read with ed. Bomb. for *imāiṁ*, as in Erz. 35,18 for *imāe*); Ś. *imassiṁ* (Śak. 18,5), for which *imāe* would be expected.—Plural nom. masc. *ime* (Ś. Mṛcch. 69,18; Vikr. 41,19; Mālatīm. 125,5; Mg. Mṛcch. 99,8); femin. *imāo* (Ś. Mṛcch. 70,1 and also at 71,8 so to be read for *imā*); M. also *imā* (Karp. 101,4) and *imīu* (Karp. 100,6); neut. *imāiṁ* (Ś. Mṛcch. 69,16; Mālatīm. 125,3); AMg. JM. also *imāṇi* (Āẏār. 2,2,2,10; Āv. 31,21).—Acc. masc. *ime*; femin. JM. *imīo*; ins. masc. neutr. M. *imehi*; AMg. Ś. *imehiṁ* (Sūẏag. 778; Śak. 62,6; Vikr. 45,9; Ratn. 296, 23), fem. AMg. *imāhiṁ* (Āẏār. 2,2,3,18; 2,7,2,7).— Gen. masc. neutr. *imāṇa*; AMg. *imesiṁ* (Hc. 3,61); femin. M. *imāṇaṁ*, *imiṇaṁ* (Hc. 3,32); AMg. *imāsiṁ* (Uvās. § 238); Ś. *imāṇaṁ* (Śak. 119,3; Vṛṣabh. 15, 8).—Loc. M. *imesu*; Ś. *imesuṁ* (Śak. 53, 9; Vikr. 52, 1) and *imesu* Mālatīm. 125, 1).

§ 431. The stem *ena-* exists in the acc. sing. only, and indeed only in M. Ś. Mg., but even here it is seldom : masc. M. *eṇaṁ* (R. 5, 6); Ś. (Mṛcch. 51,9); Mg. (Mudrār. 265,1); femin. *eṇaṁ* Ś. (Mṛcch. 24,2, in repetition of the word of Śakāra in Mg.); Mg. (Mṛcch. 21,12; 124, 17), Mk. fol. 47 teaches them also in the ins. sing., but both the forms he restricts to the neuter. In M. AMg. JM. either under the influence of accent (*ená-*) or that of the early loss of accent *ena-* has become *iṇa-*, from which frequently is formed the nom. acc. sing. neut. *iṇaṁ* (Vr. 6,18; Hc. 3,79; Kī. 3,57), especially in AMg. (G. s. v. *idam*; H. Erz.; Kk. s. v. *iṇaṁ*; Āẏār. 1,1,2,2. 4; 1,1,3,4. 5,4. 6,3.7,2; 1,2,4,3; 1,2,5,5; 1,3,3,1; 1,4,2,2 etc.; Uttar. 281. ff. 351. 355;

Ovav. § 94). Cf. § 81. 173. In AMg. *iṇaṁ* is also acc. masc (Sūẏag. 142. 307) is frequent. Perhaps *imaṁ* is to be read. In M. AMg. JM. *iṇamo* too is used as the nom. acc. neut.(Vr. 6,18;Hc. 3,79; Kī. 3,57; Mk. fol. 47; G. s. v. *idam* and *etat*; Sūẏag. 259; Dasav. N. 658,30; 661,27; Ovav § 124; Āv. 7,21. 29; 13,11). In Dasav. N. 647,12 it is used as plural too : *iṇamo udāharaṇā*. LEUMANN writes in Āv. *iṇam-o*, hardly rightly. The interpretation of the form is uncertain. Through *iṇa-* the stem has been weakened further to *ṇa-*, P. *na*, which is used in the acc. sing. masc. fem. neut., acc. plur. masc., ins. sing. and plur. masc. fem. neut. (Hc. 3,70. 77). Sing. acc. masc. *ṇaṁ* (M. G. 1071; H. 131; R. s. v. *ṇa*; AMg. Uttar. 601. 670; Ś. Mṛcch. 68,5; Śak. 12,2; Vikr. 15,13; Mg. Mṛcch. 164,11; Prab. 32,11; 53,12; A. Hc. 4,396) ; femin. *ṇaṁ* (M. H. R. s. v. *ṇa*; Ś. Śak 77,9; Vikr. 12,19; Mg. Mṛcch. 123,4; 132,23) ; neut. *ṇaṁ* (M. R. s. v.; Ś. Mṛcch. 45, 25; Śak. 11,1; Vikr. 31,9; Mg. 96,12; Ḍh. Mṛcch. 31.9)—Ins. masc. neut. M. JM. A. *ṇeṇa* (R. Erz. s. v. *ṇa*; Āv. 11,21; 15,31; 16,15; 28,10; Dvār. 501,3; Piṅgala. 1,17) ; P. *nena* (Hc. 4,322)[1]; fem. *ṇāe* (Hc. 3,70; Erz. s.v. *ṇa*) ; P. *nāe* (Hc. 4,322). — Plur. acc. *ṇe* (Hc. 3, 77). —Ins. masc. neut. JM. *ṇehiṁ* (Āv. 18,4; Erz. 3,28; Dvār. 500,31. 35; 505, 27) ; femin. *ṇāhiṁ* (Hc. 3,70). In P. Hc. 4,322 restricts the stem to the ins. sing. In Ś. Mg. it is noticeable in acc. sing. only in critical texts; false reading is *ṇeṇa* Śak. BÖHTL. 68,10; 108,8.

1. For *tattha ca nenal katasinā nena* we should read *tattha ca nena katasinānena* = *tatra ca tena kṛtasnānena* Cf. § 133.

§ 432. The pronoun *adas* according to Vr. 6,23; Hc. 3,88; Kī. 3, 58; Mk. fol. 47 is inflected : sing. nom. masc. femin. *amū*, neut. *amuṁ*; acc. *amuṁ*; ins. *amuṇā*; abl. *amūo, amūu, amūhiṁto*; gen. *amuṇo amussa*; loc. *amummi* plur. : nom. *amuṇo*, as also Vr. 6,23 we should read for *amūo* (cf. v. l.) ; femin. *amūu, amūo*; neutr. *amūṇi, amūiṁ*; ins. *amūhi*; abl. *amūhiṁto, amūsuṁto*, gen. *amūṇa*; loc. *amūsu*. A few forms only have as yet been located in the text. Sing. nom. AMg. *aso* = *asau* (Sūẏag. 74) and *amuge* = **amukaḥ* (Āẏār. 2,4,1,9; Nandīs. 361. 363. 364), JM. *amugo* (Āv. 34,30); acc. masc. A. *amuṁ* (Hc. 4,439,3); neutr. Ś. *amuṁ* (Mṛcch. 70,24); ins. M. *amuṇā* (Karp. 27,4) ; loc. AMg. *amugammi* = **amukasmin* (Paṇhāv 130) ; plur. nom. masc. M. *ami* (G. 246). According to Vr. 6,24; Hc. 3,87 the nom. sing. in all the three genders would be *aha* : *aha puriso, aha mahilā, aha vaṇaṁ*. In the first two examples from the literature, which Hc. quotes as proof and which can be attested (= G. 892 and R. 3,16) *aha* is = *atha*, likewise in all the passages in G. (s. v. *etat*) and H. (s. v. *aha*), where the scholiasts assume it as = *ayam, iyam, eṣaḥ, eṣā, asau*, so that upto the present day the assumption of a pronoun *aha* is nowhere necessary. Kī. 3,58 has the nom. sing. *aho*, which may be = *asau* according to § 264. In A. the nom. acc. plur. is spelt as *oi* (Hc. 4,364); it is = **ave* from the stem *ava-*, which is current in the Iranian dialect.—On loc. sing. *aammi, iammi* see § 429.

§ 433. All the remaining pronouns are inflected according to § 424, 425. One says, therefore, for example in the sing. abl. *parāhiṁto* =

parasmāt (G. 973), AMg. *savvāo*=*sarvasmāt* (Sūyag. 743), and also in the femin. (Āyār. 1,1.1,4); femin. AMg. *annayarīo* (Āyār. 1,1,1,2. 4); in the loc. JM. *annammi* (Āv. 25,5; Sagara 10,15). *aṇṇassiṁ*=*anyasmin* (Mahāv. 98, 14; Mālatīm. 111, 7; Ratn. 298,24); JŚ. *kadarassiṁ*=*katarasmin* (Anarghar. 271,9), but AMg. *kayaraṁsi* (Vivāhap. 227) and *kayarammi* (Ovav. § 156 ff.); Ś. *kadamassiṁ*=*katamasmin* (Vikr. 35,13); Ś. *avarassiṁ* =*aparasmin* (Cait. 40,10); Ś, *parassiṁ*=*parasmin* (Lalitav. 567,18), but AMg. *paraṁsi* (Sūyag. 750), JŚ. *parammi* (Pav. 387,25); AMg. *saṁsi*= *svasmin* (Vivāhap. 1257) beside abl. *sāo*=*svāt* (Vivāgas. 84); AMg. also *annayare*=*anyatarasmin* (Ovav. § 157). Plural : acc. PG. AMg. *anne*, JŚ. Ś. *aṇṇe*=*anyān* (PG. 5,6; 7,43; Āyār. 1,1,6,3; 1,1,7,2; Pav. 383,24; Bālar. 229,9); abl. AMg. *kayarehiṁto*=*katarebhyaḥ* (Paṇṇav. 160 ff.; Vivāhap. 260. 262. 460. 1057 f.), *saehiṁ*=*svakebhyaḥ*, *savvehiṁ*=*sarvebhyaḥ* (§ 369); gen. AMg. JM. *annesiṁ*=*anyeṣām* (Āyār. 1,1,4. 7,1; 1,5,6,1; 1,7,2,3; 1,8,1,16; Sūyag. 387. 663; Nāyādh. 1138. 1140; Kappas. § 14; Āv. 14,7); AMg. JM. *savvesiṁ*=*sarveṣām* (Āyār. 1,1,6,2; 1,2,3,4; 1.4,2,6; 1,6,5,3; Uttar. 625. 797; Āv. 14,18); AMg. JŚ. *paresiṁ*=*pareṣām* (Uttar. 625. 797; Pav. 385, 65), but M. *aṇṇāṇam* (Mudrār. 83,3; Karp. 1,2), also femin. Ś. (Priyad. 24,8); Ś. *savvāṇaṁ* (Vikr. 83,8); *avarāṇaṁ*=*apareṣām* Mṛcch. 69,10). According to Hc. 3,61 *aṇṇesiṁ* and *savvesiṁ* are used for the femin. too, and so JŚ. has *savvesiṁ itthiṇam*=*sarvāsām strīṇām* (Kattig. 408, 384). The regular forms in AMg. JM. are *aṇṇāsiṁ*, *savvāsiṁ*. Loc. plur. in A. is *aṇṇahī̃* (Hc. 4,422,9). On *kati* see § 449.

§ 434. Of the nouns, *ātman* (§ 401) and *bhavat-* (§ 396) are used as in Skt. Of the pronominal derivatives in *-iya*, Hc. 2,147 mentions *maia madiya*. Besides, for it are used *kera*, *keraa keraka* (§ 176). Without epenthesis *kārya* would become **kara*, and from it have originated in A. *mahāra*, *mahāraü*=**mahakāra* from the gen. *maha* (§ 418) +*kāra* (Hc. 4,351. 358,1. 434) in the sense of *madiya*, likewise *tuhāra*=*tvadiya* (Hc. 4.434), *amhāra*=*asmadiya* (Hc. 4,345. 434). A. *hamāra* (Piṅgala. 2,121), metri causa also *hammāra* (Piṅgala 2,43) has originated through the line of development **mhāra* (§ 141), **mahāra* (§ 132), *hamāra* (§ 354), A. *tohāra* =*yuṣmākam* (Piṅgala 2,25 stands metrically for **tohāra*, and has arisen from *tumhāra*, **tŏmhāra* (§ 125), **tŏhāra*, *tohāra* (§ 76. 89. 127), exactly as *kohaṇḍī* from *kūṣmāṇḍī* (§ 127). On the derivatives in *-dṛś*, *-dṛśa*, *dṛkṣa* see § 121. 122. 245. 262; on *ĕttia*, *ittia*, *ĕttila*, *ĕitula tĕttia*, *tittia*, *ettila tĕttula*, *jĕttia*, *jittia*, *jĕttila*, *jĕttila*, *jĕttula*, *kĕttia*, *kittia*, *kĕttila*. *kĕttula* see § 153, on A. *sāha*=*śaśvat* § 64. 262. on AMg. *evaïya*, *kevaïya* § 149. A. *evaḍu* in the sense of *iyat* (Hc. 4,408) is=**ayavaḍra*=JM. *evaḍḍa* (§ 149), as *kevaḍu* (Hc. 4,408) =**kayavaḍra*. Analogical formations are *jevaḍu*, *tevaḍu* (Hc. 4,395,7. 407). In Mṛcch. 164,5 we should read *evaḍḍe* for Mg. *evaḍḍhe*.

D. THE NUMERALS.

435. **1**, in all the dialects is *ĕkka*=*eka* (§ 91), femin. *ĕkkā*. in AMg. JM. more frequently *ega*. It is inflected according to the pronominal in-

flection. So sing. loc. M. *ĕkkammi* (G. 153. 441; H. 827), very seldom *ĕkke* according to the nominal declension (H. 846), AMg. *egaṁsi*(Vivāhap. 1394ff.); AMg. JM. *egaṁmi*(Paṇṇav. 521; Erz. 2,21), AMg. JM. *egammi*(Vivāhap. 922f. 928. 931. 1658f. 1736. 1752; Āv. 10,22; 11,12. 18; 17,22; 19,9. 18; 22,10; etc.); JM. *ĕkkammi* (Āv. 27,19); Ś. *ĕkkassiṁ* (Karp. 19,7); Mg. *ĕkkaśśiṁ* (Mṛcch. 81,13); A. *ĕkkahĩ* (Hc. 4,357,2), also as femin. (Hc. 4,422,9); plur. nom. masc. M. JM. *ĕkke* (G. 721. 866. 909; Kk. 273,23); AMg. *ege* (Āẏār. 1,1,2,2. 3,4. 4,6; Sūẏag. 74. 204. 240. 438. 597; Uttar. 219; cf. § 174); gen. masc. AMg. *egesiṁ* (Āẏār. 1,1,1,1. 2; 1,1.2,4; 1,2,1,2,4; 1,2, 3,3 etc.; Sūẏag 46. 81) and *egesi* (Sūẏag. 19. 35. 74). Of the less frequent forms mention should be made of sing. ins. AMg. *ĕkkeṇaṁ*(Vivāhap. 258 ff.), JM. *egeṇaṁ* (Āv. 33,24); gen. Mg. *ĕkkāha* (Mṛcch. 32,4). In JŚ. Ḍh. the following has been found in the text: *ĕkkaṁ* (Kattig. 403, 370. 377; Mṛcch. 30,5). Before other numerals appears as stem *ĕkka*°, AMg. JM. also *ega*° but *ĕkkā*°, AMg. JM. also *egā*°; A. *eā*°, *eggā*° in *ĕkkārasa*, AMg. JM. *egārasa* A. *eāraha*, *ĕggāraha* (11), *ĕkkārasama* (the eleventh) (§ 443. 449); AMg. *ĕkkāṇaüiṁ* (91) (§ 446). The *ā* is to be explained according to § 70. In PG. is found *aneka* (6,10), in which *k* is never doubled. M. Ś. *aṇea* (G. H.; Mṛcch. 23,8; 71,16; 73,8). AMg. JM. *aṇega* (Vivāhap. 145. 1285; Nāẏādh.; Kappas.; Erz.; Kk.); JM. *aṇeẏa* (Erz.); AMg. *'ṇega* (§ 171); Ś. *aṇeaso* = *anekaśaḥ* (Śak. 160,3); AMg. *'ṇegaso* (§ 171).

436. **2** in the nominative and accusative is *do*, *duve*, *be*, neuter *dŏṇṇi duṇṇi*, *bĕṇṇi biṇṇi* (Vr. 6,57, where *doṇi*; C. 1,10ᵃ p. 41; Hc. 3,119. 120; Kī. 3,85. 86; Mk. fol. 49).[1] *do* = *dvau* and *duve*, *be* = *dve* (neuter) are old duals and are declined and used as plurals. Nom. acc. *do* is frequent in M. (G. H. R.) AMg. Uvās. s. v. *du*; Kappas. s. v.; Weber, Bhag. 1,424), JM. (Erz.)[1]; traceable in A. too (Piṅgala 1,5), and in D. (Mṛcch. 101,13), and it has as yet not been located in the text in Ś. Mg. Ś. *do vi* (Pras. 84, 4; Bālar. 216,20; 246,5) is an error for *duve vi*, as stands in Śak. 106,1. *do* is used in all the genders. As femin., it stands e. g. in M. *do tiṇṇi* [*mahilāo*] (H. 587), *do tiṇṇi rehā* = *dvitrā rekhāḥ* (H. 206); AMg. *do guhāo* = *dve guhe*, *do devaẏāo* = *dve devate*, *do mahāṇaio* = *dve mahānadyau*, *do kattiẏāo*, *do rohīṇio*, *do migasirāo*, *do addāo* = *dve kārttikyau*, *dve rohiṇyau*, *dve mṛgaśirasī dve ārdre* (Ṭhāṇ 73. 75. 76. 77. 79. 81); *do disāo* = *dve diśau* (acc.; Ṭhāṇ. 55); as neuter. : M. *do vi dukkhāi* = *dve api duḥkhe* (H. 24); AMg. *do do payāṇi* = *dve dve pade* (Ṭhāṇ. 27), *do sayāiṁ* = *dve śate* (Samav. 157), *do khuḍḍāiṁ bhavaggahaṇāiṁ samaẏūṇāiṁ* = *dve kṣudre bhavagrahaṇe samayoni* (Jiv. 1027. 1110), *do nāmadhejjā* = *dve nāmadheye* (Āẏār. 2,15. 15). It appears also in the beginning of compounds : M. *doaṅgulaa* = *dvyaṅgulaka* (H. 622); AMg. JM. *domāsiya* = *dvimāsika* (Āẏār. 2,1 2,1; Sūẏag. 758; Vivāhap. 166; T. 4,6); AMg. *dokiriẏā* = *dvikriyā* (Vivāhap. 52; Ovav. § 122); M. JM. *dojīha* = *dvijihva* (Prabandhac. 289,1; Erz. 82,17), *domuha* = *dvimukha* (Erz. 39,21), *dovaẏaṇa* = *dvivadana* (Hc. 1,94; Erz. 39,13). So also *doghaṭṭa* (elephant; Pāiẏal. 9; Prākṛtamañjarī on Vr. 4,33; Erz. 35,28; Bālar. 50,1; 86,12), that is read as *dŏgghaṭṭa* in Mallikām. at 55,7 in Ś. and in 144,10 in Mg. as *dŏgghuṭṭa* in Deśīn. 5,44 as *dugghuṭṭa*

and in Triv. 2,1,30 *dughoṭṭa* from *ghaṭṭa-*, *ghuṭṭa-* *ghŏṭṭa-* (to drink)[2]; *dohada, dohala* (§ 222. 244) = **dvihṛd*[3]. Beside *do*, there occurs frequently in this case *du*, which has gone off the compounds in which the accent did not fall on the first syllable. So M. *duuṇa* = *dviguṇá* (R. 11,47); AMg. *duguṇa* (Āẏār. 2,2,2,7; Sūẏag. 241; Vivāhap. 969); *duāi* = *dvijātiḥ* (Hc. 1,94; 2,79); AMg. JM. *dupaẏa* = *dvipada* (Āẏār. 2,1,11 9; Uvās. § 49; Kk. 265,4. 5; III, 511,32); AMg. *duviha* = *dvividha* (Ṭhāṇ. 44; Āẏār. 1,7,8,2; 1,8,1,15; Uvās.), *dukhura* = *dvikhura* (Uttar. 1075; see commentary; Jīv. 75), *dupakkha* = *dvipakṣa* (Sūẏag. 456), *du-ẏ-āheṇa* = *dvyahena* (Āẏār. 2,5, 2,3. 4), *du-ẏ-āhaṁ* = *dvyaham* (Jīv. 261. 286. 295), *duhattha* = *dvihasta* (Ṭhāṇ 208); JM. *dugāuẏa* = *dvigavyūta, du-y-aṅgula* = *dvyaṅgula* (Erz. s.v. *du*). Beside M. *dohāia, dohāijjaī* = *dvidhākṛta, dvidhākriyate* (R. s. v. *duhā*), AMg. *dodhāra* = *dvidhākāra* (Ṭhāṇ. 401) stands AMg. *duhā* = *dvidhā* (Sūẏag. 351. 358); M. *duhāia* (R. 8,106); AMg. *duhākijjamāṇa* (Vivāhap. 137); AMg. *duhao* = **dvighātaḥ* (twice; twofold; in two parts; Āẏār. 1,3,3,5; 1,7,8,4; Uttar. 234; Sūẏag. 35,640; Ṭhāṇ. 186; Vivāhap. 181. 282) etc. The regular continuations of *dvi* are *bi* (§ 300) and *di*, which always occurs in certain words, as *dia*, JM. *diẏa* = *dvija* *diraa* = *dvirada* (§ 298), and always in Ś. Mg. except in the ordinals (§ 449). Ś. *dudhā* (Śak. ed. Böhtlingk 78,8) is wrong, in the same way *duuṇia* (Mallikām. 224,5) for *duuṇida*.—The neut. *dŏṇṇi*, sometimes also *duṇṇi*, is formed according to *tiṇṇi*[4]. It is combined with the masculine and feminine too, as masc. M. *dŏṇṇi vi bhiṇṇasarūā* = *dvāvapi bhinnasvarūpau* (G. 450), *dŏṇṇi vi bāhū* = *dvāv api bāhū* (Hc. 3,142); AMg. *dŏṇṇi vi rāẏāṇo* = *dvāvapi rājānau, doṇṇi vi rāiṇaṁ aṇiẏā* = *dvāv api rājñām anīkau* (Niraẏāv. § 26. 27), *dŏṇṇi purisajāe* = *dvau* **puruṣajātau* (Sūẏag. 575); JM. *dunni muṇisihā* = *dvau munisiṁhau* (T. 4,4), *te dŏnni vi* (Erz. 78,35); Ś. *dŏṇṇi khattiakumārā* = *dvau kṣatriya-kumārau* (Pras. 47,7; cf. 48,4); femin. AMg. *dŏṇṇi saṁgahaṇagāhāo* = *dve saṁgrahaṇagāthe* (Kappas. § 118); Ś. *dŏṇṇi kumārio* = *dve kumāryau* (Pras. 48,5).—From *do*, the ins. is *dohiṁ, dohi* (in C. 1,7 p. 40), in the fem. too, as in M. *paṁtihĩ dohiṁ* = *paṅktibhyāṁ dvābhyāṁ* (Karp. 101,1); AMg. *dohiṁ ukkhāhiṁ* = *dvābhyām ukhābhyām* (Āẏār. 2,1,2,1); JM. *dohi vi bāhā-hiṁ* = *dvābhyām bāhābhyām* (Dvār. 507,33).—The abl. is, according to Hc. 3,119. 130, *dohiṁto, dosuṁto*, according to C. 1,3 p.39 *dohiṁto*, according to Mk. fol. 49 *dosuṁto*.—In the gen. the numerals for 2-19 according to Vr. 6,59; Hc. 3,123, according to Hc. also *kati*, according to C. 1,6 the numerals generally and according to Kī. 3,89 the numerals 2—4 have the endings *-ṇha, -ṇhaṁ*. So M. AMg. JM. *dŏṇha, dŏṇhaṁ* (also Āẏār. 2,7,2,12; Ṭhāṇ. 47. 67. 68; KI. 10), also in the fem. AMg. *tāsiṁ dŏṇhaṁ* (so rightly in the commentary; text *duṇhiṁ*) = *tayor dvayoḥ* (Uttar. 661). In Ś. and apparently in Mg. too, on the contrary, the ending is *-ṇṇaṁ* corresponding to the Lena-dialect and Pāli[5]: *dŏṇṇaṁ* (Śak. 56,15; 74,7 [femin.]; 85,15 [fem.]; Veṇīs. 60,16 [so to be read with v. l. for *dohiṇaṁ*]; 62,8; Mālav. v. l. to 77,20 [fem.], as also in M. is found more often as v.l. (H. s.v. *do*), and in Mk. fol. 49 the MSS give. Whilst *dŏṇṇaṁ* has followed the analogy of *tiṇṇaṁ* = *triṇām*, the ending *-ṇhaṁ* seems to have originated from an intermixture of the nominal and the pronominal forms **doṇaṁ* and **dosaṁ* respectively, since it presupposes one **dvauṣṇām.*—The loc. is *dosuṁ, dosu* (in C. 1,3 p. 39), also JŚ. (Kattig. 402, 359), and in the femin., as M. *dosuṁ dokandalisuṁ* = *dvayor doḥkandalyoh* (Karp. 95, 12), A. *duhũ* (Hc. 4,340,2).

1. These quotations hold good for all cases, although not noted. In the text of Ki. there stands *doṇhi* (3,85); *doni* (3,86); *be* is wanting.—2. PISCHEL on Hc. 4, 10; also Ki. 4.46—3. LÜDERS, GN. 1898,2 ff.—4. PISCHEL, KZ. 35,144.—5. PISCHEL KZ. 35,144 f.

§ 437. *duve* = *dve* is used as the nom. and the acc. for all the three genders in all the dialects: M. (H. 846; neut.); AMg. (Āẏār. 1,8,4,6 (acc.); Sūẏag. 293 (acc.) 620. 853. 972; Uttar. 200; Samav. 238; Kappas. Th. § 4; Uvās. s. v. *du*), as femin. *bhajjā duve* = *bhārye dve* (Uttar. 660); JM. *due vi* (Āv. 8,49); *duve vi* (Erz. 21,6); *duve jaṇā* (Āv. 19, 10); *duve corasenāvaïṇo* = *dvau 'corasenāpati* (Erz. 13,4); A. *dui* (Piṅgala 1,31. 42). Whilst in comparison with *do*, it is not frequent in these dialects, particularly in M. and A., it is the only form in Ś. Mg. So Ś. masc. (Mṛcch. 24.15; Śak. 24,1; 41,1; Vikr. 21,19: Mālav. 17,8; 18,22; 30,1; Mālatīm. 358,1; Viddhaś. 66,1; Mallikām. 223,5; 227,12; 250,1; Kāleyak. 25,20), femin. (Viddhaś. 44,7), neut. (Mṛcch. 61, 10; Mālav. 54,7). masc. or neut. (Mṛcch. 153,18; Vikr. 10,3), Mg. (Mṛcch. 81,13; acc., neut.). From it builds Ś. also the ins. *duvehiṁ* (Mṛcch 44,1; 51,23; 327,3; Mudrār. 232, 7) = **dvebhiḥ* the gen. *duveṇaṁ* (Śak. ed. BÖHTLINGK 38,5; 45.23; 53,19 [the Kashmiri rec., however, has *dŏṇhaṁ*, the Bengali recension has *doṇṇaṁ*]; Mallikām. 102, 6; Kāleyak. 21,1; 23,11), the loc. *duvesu* (Mallikām. 335, 10).—*be* is found in PG. 6.14.20.31.39, seldom in M. (H. 752), in AMg. in the beginning of compounds as *beindiẏa, bĕndiẏa* = *dvīndriya* (§ 162), *bedoṇiẏa* = *dvidroṇika* (Uvās. § 235); in JŚ. (Kattig. 399,310; acc.); in A. (Hc. 4,439; Piṅgala 1,9.68); in A. shortened as *bi* (Piṅgala 1,153). From it, the neuter is *biṇṇi* (C. 1,10[a] p. 41; Hc. 3,120; A. Hc. 4,418,1; Piṅgala 1,95). According to C. 1,3 p. 39; 1,6 p. 40; 1,7 p. 40; Hc. 3,119 *be* is inflected as: ins. *behi*, abl. *behiṁto*, gen. *bĕṇhaṁ*, loc. *besu, besuṁ*. A. has ins. *behĩ* (Hc. 4,367,5), gen. *bihũ* (Hc. 4,383,1), loc. *behĩ* (Hc. 4,370,3). Corresponding to Skt. *dvā*° stands *bā*° before other numerals, e.g. in AMg. *bārasa* (12), *bāvisaṁ* (22), *bāẏālisaṁ* (42), *bāvattariṁ* (72). Cf. § 443 ff.

§ 438. **3** in the nom. and the acc. masc. and femin. is *tao* = *trayaḥ*, neut. *tiṇṇi* = *triṇi*, with *ṇṇ* according to the gen. *tiṇṇaṁ*. The forms are used in all the three genders without distinction; *tao* is not mentioned by the grammarians (Vr. 6,56; Hc. 3,121; Kī. 3,85 [text *tiṇhi*]; Mk. fol. 49) and is seen in AMg. only: AMg. masc. (Ṭhāṇ. 110.112.118.197; Kappas. s. v. *ti*; Sūẏag. 293 [acc.] and often); metrically *taü* too in *taü āẏāṇā* = *triṇy ādānāni* (Sūẏag. 65); femin. *tao parisāo* = *tisraḥ pariṣadaḥ* (Ṭhāṇ. 138; Jīv. 905. 912. 914. 917); *tao kammabhūmio* = *tisraḥ karmabhūmayaḥ* (Ṭhāṇ. 165; cf. 176); *tao antaraṇaïo* = *tisro 'ntaranadyaḥ* (Ṭhāṇ. 177); *tao uccārapāsavaṇabhūmio* (Kappas. S. § 55; acc.); neut. *tao ṭhāṇāṇi* = *triṇi sthānāni* (Ṭhāṇ. 143), beside *tao ṭhāṇāiṁ* (158) and *tao ṭhāṇā* (163. 165);

tao pāṇagāiṁ = *triṇi pānakāni* (Ṭhāṇ. 161.162; Kappas. S. § 25); *tao vatthāiṁ* = *triṇi vastrāṇi*, *tao pāyāiṁ* = *triṇi pātrāṇi* (Ṭhāṇ. 162). Likewise *tiṇṇi* is used in all the dialects: M. *tiṇṇi rehā* = *tisro rekhāḥ*, *tiṇṇi* [*mahilāo*] H. 206. 587); neut. (R. 9,91); AMg. masc. *tiṇṇi purisajāe* = *trīn *puruṣajātān* (Sūyag. 575); *jāmā tinni* = *yāmās trayaḥ* (Āyār. 1,7,1,4); *tinni ālāvagā* = *traya ālāpakāḥ* (Sūyag. 814. 815 [°*ṇṇ*°]; *ime tinni nāmadhĕjjā* = *imāni triṇi nāmadheyāni* (Āyār. 2,15,15); *tiṇṇi vi uvasaggā* = *trayo 'py upasargāḥ* (Uvās. § 118); *tiṇṇi vaṇiyā* = *trayo vaṇijaḥ* (Uttar. 233); femin. *eyāo tinni payaḍio* = *etās tisraḥ prakṛtayaḥ* (Uttar. 970); *tinni lĕssāo* = *tisro leśyāḥ* (Ṭhāṇ. 26), *tinni sāgarovamakoḍākoḍio* = *tisraḥ sāgaropamakoṭākoṭyaḥ* (Ṭhāṇ. 133); neut. (Āyār. 1,8,4,5; p. 125,26; Sūyag. 778; Samav. 157; Vivāhap. 90; Kappas. § 138. Th. § 1); JM. femin. *tinni dhūyāo* = *tisro duhitaraḥ* (Āv. 12,1); *tinni bherio* = *tisro bheryaḥ*, *tinni vi gosīsacandaṇamaio devayāpariggahiyāo* = *tisro 'pi gośīrṣacandanamayyo devatāparigṛhītāḥ* (Āv. 34,7.8); neut. *tāṇi tiṇṇi vi* = *tāni triṇy api* (Erz. 37,11); Ś. masc. *tiṇṇi purisā* = *trayaḥ puruṣāḥ*, *ede tiṇṇi vi* = *ete trayo 'pi*, *edĕ kkhu tiṇṇi alaṁkārasaṁjoā* = *ete khalu trayo 'laṁkārasaṁyogāḥ*, *tiṇṇi rāāṇo* = *trayo rājānaḥ* (Mudrār. 39,3; 72,1; 108,9; 204,4), *ime tiṇṇi miaṅgā* = *ete trayo mṛdaṅgāḥ*, *bālataruṇo tiṇṇi* = *bālataravas trayaḥ* (Karp. 3,2; 62,3); femin. *tiṇṇi āidio* = *tisra ākṛtayaḥ* (Śak. 132,6); JŚ. neut. (Kattig. 402,363); A. *do tiṇṇi vi* = *dvau trayo 'pi*, *tiṇṇi rehāiṁ* = *tisro rekhāḥ* (Piṅgala 1,5.52).—The ins. is *tīhiṁ* (Vr. 6,55; C. 1, 7 p. 40; Hc. 3,118; Kī. 3,84; Mk. fol. 49; G. 265; Kappas. § 227; Nāyādh. 1026; Uttar. 987), more often in AMg. JM. printed as *tihiṁ* (Sūyag. 97; Āyār. 2,1,2,1; Ṭhāṇ. 114. 116. 117; Samav. 232; Ovav. § 136; Erz. 49, 22), a form that probably is correct in verses only on account of prosodical requirement, as in A. (Hc. 4,347); cf., however, *caühiṁ* § 439.—Ablative *tihiṁto* (C. 1,3 p. 39; Hc. 3,118; Mk. fol. 49); according to Kī. 3,84; Mk. fol. 49 also *tīsuṁto*.—For the genitive Vr. 6,59; C. 1,6 p. 40; Hc. 3,118. 123 teach *tiṇhaṁ*, *tiṇha*, and so *tiṇhaṁ* in AMg. JM. (Ṭhāṇ. 125; Āyār. 2,7,2,12; Vivāhap. 53. 140; Kappas. § 114 : Erz. 28,21); also as femin. AMg. *pasatthalesāṇa tiṇhaṁ pi* = *praśastaleśyānāṁ tisṝṇām api* (Uttar. 986 f.); JM. *tiṇhaṁ parisāṇa* = *tisṝṇāṁ pariṣadām* (Kk. 275, 31). Mk. fol. 49 teaches, as it appears *tiṇṇam* = *trīṇām*, a form that is to be expected Ś. Mg. (§ 436).—Loc. M. *tīsu* (Vr. 6,55; C. 1,3 p. 39; Hc. 3, 118; R. 8,58), also *tīsuṁ* (C. 1,3 p. 39), and metri causa *tisu* (Hc. 3,135).—At the beginning of compounds there appears in all the dialects *ti*°, in AMg. also *te*° = *traya-* in *teindiya*, *tĕndiya* = *trīndriya* (§ 162), and before other numerals, as *teraha* = *trayodaśa*, *tevīsaṁ* = *trayoviṁśati*, *tĕttisa* = *trayastriṁśat*, *teālīsā* = *trayaścatvāriṁśat* etc. (§ 153). AMg. has also *tāyattisā* (33; Kappas.; Ṭhāṇ. 125) and *tāvattisā* (Vivāhap. 218), and the thirty three gods in AMg. JM. are called *tāyattisagā*, *tāvattisayā*, *tāvattisagā* = *trayastriṁśakāḥ* (Kappas. § 14; Vivāhap. 215.218.223; Kk. 275,34). See § 254.

§ 439. **4** has the nom. masc. *cattāro* = *catvāraḥ* (Vr. 6,58; C. 1,3 p. 39; Hc. 3,122; Kī. 3,87; Mk. fol. 49; Ś. Uttarar. 12,7). The same form is valid for the acc. too according to the grammarians. Likewise the acc. *caüro* = *caturaḥ* (C. 1,3 p. 39; Hc. 3,122; AMg. Uttar. 768) in

AMg. is used in verses also as the nom. (Hc. 3,122; Uttar. 1033; Vivāhap. 82). Hc. 3,17 mentions as nom. acc. also *caūo*, *caüo* from the stem *caü-*. In Ś. at Prab. 68, 7 there is a nom. femin. *catasso* (all editions) edited, for which at least *cadasso* = *catasraḥ* is to be written. As in the case of 2 and 3 (§ 436. 438), in the case of 4 too, almost always the neutr. *cattāri* = *catvāri* (Vr. 6,58; C. 1,3 p.39; Hc.3,122; Kī. 3,87; Mk.fol.49) is used in connection with all the genders : masc. PG. *cattāri pattibhāgā* = *catvāraḥ pratibhāgāḥ* (6,18); *addhikā cattāri* = *ārdhikāś catvāraḥ* (6,39); M. *cattāri pakkalabaīllā* (H. 812); AMg. *cattāri ālāvagā* = *catvāraḥ ālāpakaḥ* (Āyār. 2,1, 1,11; Sūyag. 812); *cattāri ṭhāṇā* = *catvāri sthānāni* (Sūyag. 688); *cattāri purisajāyā* = *catvāraḥ *puruṣajātāḥ* (Sūyag. 626); *ime cattāri therā* = *ime catvāraḥ sthavirāḥ* (Kappas. Th. § 5.11), *cattāri hatthī* = *catvāro hastinaḥ* (Ṭhāṇ. 236); acc. *cattāri agaṇio* = *caturo'gnīn* (Sūyag. 274); *cattāri māse* = *caturo māsān* (Āyār. 1,8,1,2); *cattāri mahāsumiṇe* = *caturo mahāsvapnān* (Kappas. § 77; Nāyādh. § 49); JM. *mahārāyāṇo cattāri* = *mahārājāś catvāraḥ* (Erz. 4,36); Mg. *cattāli ime* (Mṛcch. 158, 4); femin. : AMg. *imāo cattāri sāhāo* = *imāś catasraḥ śākhāḥ* (Kappas. Th. § 5); *cattāri kiriyāo* = *catasraḥ kriyāḥ* (Vivāhap. 47); *cattāri aggamahisīo* = *catasro' gramahiṣyaḥ* (Ṭhāṇ. 228 ff.); acc. *cattāri saṁghāḍīo* = *catasraḥ saṁghāṭīḥ* (Āyār. 2,5,1,1); *cattāri bhāsāo* = *catasro bhāṣāḥ* (Ṭhāṇ. 203); neutr. AMg. *cattāri samosaraṇāṇi* = *catvāri samavasaraṇāni* (Sūyag. 445); *cattāri sayāiṁ* = *catvāri śatāni* (Samav. 158); JM. *cattāri aṅgulāṇi* (Erz. 37,2).—Ins. *caūhiṁ* throughout in AMg. (Hc. 3,17; Kī. 3,88; Mk. fol. 49; Vivāhap. 437; Ṭhāṇ. 207; Samav. 14; Uvās. § 18. 21; Ovav. § 56; also femin. : *caühiṁ paḍimāhiṁ* (Āyār. 2,2,3,18; 2,6,1,4; 2,8,2); *caūhiṁ kiriyāhiṁ* = *catasṛbhiḥ kriyābhiḥ* (Vivāhap. 120 ff.); *caühiṁ ukkhāhiṁ* = *catasṛbhir ukhābhiḥ* (Āyār. 2,1,2,1); *caühiṁ hiraṇṇakoḍīhiṁ °paüttāhiṁ* = *catasṛbhir hiranyakoṭibhiḥ °prayuktābhiḥ* (Uvās. § 17). In prose *caūhiṁ*, which Sr. fol. 18 quotes beside *caūhi*, *caühi*, *caühiṁ*, would be expected. Hc. 3,17 too mentions *caūhi* beside *caühi*. Cf. *tihiṁ* § 438.—Abl. *caühiṁto* (Mk. fol. 49), *caüsuṁto* (Kī. 3,88; Mk. fol. 49; Sr. fol. 18), *caūsuṁto* (Sr. fol. 18).—Gen. PG. *catuṇhaṁ* (6,18), M. AMg. JM. *caüṇhaṁ* (Vr. 6,59; C. 1,6 p. 40; Hc. 3,123 [also °*ṇha*]: Kī. 3,89; Āyār. 2,7,2,12; Kappas. § 10.14; Vivāhap. 149. 787; Erz. 9,18], also feminine *eyāṇaṁ* (*eyāsiṁ*) *caüṇhaṁ paḍimāṇaṁ* = *etāsāṁ catasṝṇāṁ pratimānām* (Āyār. 2,2,3,21; 2,5,1,9; 2,6,1,7; 2,8,6), *porisiṇaṁ caüṇhaṁ* = *pauruṣiṇāṁ catasṛṇām* (Uttar. 893). According to the analogy of *dŏṇṇaṁ*, *tiṇṇaṁ*, expected is in Ś. Mg. *caduṇṇaṁ*, as Mk. fol. 49 appears to teach. Examples are wanting.—Loc. AMg. JM. *caüsu* (Uttar.769; Vivāhap. 82; Erz. 41,35); *caüsum* (Erz. 44, 8), also as femin. *caüsu vidisāsu* = *catasṛṣu vidikṣu* (Ṭhāṇ. 259; Jīv. 228; Vivāhap. 925.927); *caüsu vi gaïsu* = *catasṛṣv api gatiṣu* (Uttar.996). The expected *caūsu* is mentioned by Hc.3,17 beside *caüsu* and by Sr. fol.18 beside *caūsuṁ*, *caüsuṁ*, *caüsu*.—In compounds, before vowels, there appears *caür°*, as AMg. *caüraṁsa* = *caturaśra* (Ṭhāṇ. 20.493; Uvās. § 76), *caüraṅguli* (Ṭhāṇ. 270), *caürindiya* (Ṭhāṇ. 25.122.275.322; Samav. 40. 228; Vivāgas. 50 etc.) M. *caürāṇaṇa* (G.); also before other numerals, as AMg. *caürāsiiṁ* (84; Kappas.). Before consonants partly appears *caüra°* with regular assimilation, as M. *caüddisaṁ* = *caturdiśam* (R.), AMg. JM. *caümmuha* = *caturmukha* (Ovav.; Erz.), Ṣ. *cadussālaa* = *catuḥśālaka* (Mṛcch.

6,6;16,11 [°*sāla*]; 45,25), *cadussamudda*=*catuḥsamudra* (Mṛcch. 55,16; 78,3; 147,17), partly *caü*°, as M. *caüjāma*=*caturyāma* (H. R.), *caümuha*=*caturmukha* (G.), AMg. *caüpaẏa*=*catuṣpada* (Āẏār.2,1,11,9) beside *caüppaẏa* (Uttar. 1074; Uvās.), A. *caümuha* (Hc. 4,331), *caüppaa* (Piṅgala 1,118), D. *caüsāara* (verse; Mṛcch. 101,12) =*catuḥsāgara*. Cf. § 340 ff. Both appear also before other numerals: AMg. *caüddasa*=*caturdaśan* (Kappas. § 74), beside *caüdasa* in verse (Kappas. § 46b) and with contraction, *cŏddasa* (Kappas; Nāẏādh.). M. *cŏddaha*, *cŏddasi*, as also *cŏgguṇa* beside *caügguṇa*=*caturguṇa*, *cŏvvāra* beside *caüvvāra*=*caturvāra* etc. (§ 166.443 ff.). In A. *co* appears not only in the beginning of compounds, but also independently (Piṅgala 1,65; cf. § 166). The neuter is in A. *cāri* (Piṅgala 1,68. 87. 102) from *catvāri*, **cātvāri* (§ 65), **cātāri* (§ 87), **cāāri* (§ 186), *cāri* (§ 165). It is employed as the first member of compounds: *cāripāa*=*catuṣpāda*, *cāridahā*=*caturdaśa* (Piṅgala 1,102. 105. 118), as also *caüro* in AMg. *caüropañcindiẏa*=*catuṣpañcendriya* (Uttar. 1059), A stem *caüra*- occurs in AMg. *caürāsiiṁ*, *corāsiiṁ*=*caturaśiti*, *caürāsiima*, *caturaśita* (Kappas.; Samav. 139—142). On *cāur*° see § 78.

§ 440. **5** is inflected: nom. acc. AMg. JM. Ś. *pañca* (Vivāhap. 138. 141; Ṭhāṇ. 361; Kappas.; Uvās.; Erz.; Mudrār. 204,1); ins. AMg. *pañcahiṁ* (Uttar. 374; Vivāhap. 120 ff.; Ṭhāṇ. 353; Nāẏādh.; Uvās.; etc.) A. *pañcahĩ* (Hc. 4,422,14); gen. AMg. *pañcaṇhaṁ* (Hc. 3,123; Āẏār. 2,7, 2,12; Samav. 16), A *pañcahã* (Hc. 4,422,14); loc. JM. *pañcasu* (Erz. p. XLI), in verses also AMg. *pañce* (Uttar. 704). Rāmatarkavāgīśa in Lassen, Inst. p. 319 note ** mentions also the abl. *pañcahiṁto*, *pañcasuṁto*, gen. *pañcaṇṇaṁ*, loc. *pañcasuṁ*, and a loc. femin. *pañcāsuṁ*, Rishikesh p. 128 also femin. nom. *pañcā*, ins. *pañcāhiṁ*. In the beginning of compounds mostly appears *pañca*°, in AMg. JM. also *pañcā*° in *pañcāṇaüiṁ* (95), Ṭhāṇ. 261: Samav. 150. 151; Kk. 263, 11. 16. 17; many times false °*ṇaüyaṁ*); likewise in *pañcāvaṇṇā* (55; Hc. 2,174; Deśīn. 6,27; Triv. 1,3,105=BB. 3,245). The *ā* is to be explained according to § 70. In combination with other numerals there appears *pañca* in AMg. JM. A. also as *paṇṇa* (*panna*), *paṇa*, *paṇu* (§ 273).

§ 441. **6** *ṣaṣ* becomes *cha* according to § 211. It is inflected: nom. acc. AMg. *cha* (Kappas. § 122; Vivāhap. 54: Samav. 156. 163; Uvās.); ins. AMg. *chahiṁ* (Sūẏag. 380. 844; Samav. 232; Ṭhāṇ. 194; Bhag. 1,425; Nāẏādh. 833; Uttar. 768. 778); gen. AMg. JŚ. *chaṇhaṁ* (Hc. 3,123; Āẏār. 2,15. 16; Vivāhap. 82. 89. 123; Uttar. 776. 979; Jīv. 271; Nāẏādh. 832. 834. 844; Kattig. 399, 309), also *chaṇha* (Hc. 3,123): loc. *chasu* (Ṭhāṇ. 27; Uttar. 987). The old nom. *ṣaṭ* has been retained before enclitics: AMg. *chap pi*=*ṣaḍ api* (Āẏār. 1,8,4,6; Niraẏāv. 81; Vivāhap. 798; Dasav. 639,2; Nāẏādh. 828. 830. 836. 845 ff.), *chac ceva* (Uttar. 1065), *chac ca* (Aṇuog. 399; Jīv. 914; Jīẏak. 61; Vivāhap. 82. 1237; Kappas. Th. § 7). Rāmatarkavāgīśa, according to Lassen, Inst. p. 320, knows: nom. *chā*, femin. *chāo*; ins. *chaehiṁ*; *chaāhiṁ*; abl. *chaāhiṁto* (so to be read); gen. *chaaṇṇaṁ* (read *chaṇṇaṁ*); loc. *chasu* (*chāsu*), *chisu*. As the first member of compounds seldom there appears *cha*°, as JM. *ckakhaṇḍa* (Erz. 18,8;

probably a wrong reading for *chakkhaṇḍa*), mostly *ṣaṭ°*, before vowels as *chaḍ°* as *chaḍakkhara* = *ṣaḍakṣara* (Skanda; Deśīn. 3,26), AMg. also *saḍ°* in *saḍaṅgavi* = *ṣaḍaṅgavid* (Vivāhap. 149; Kappas.; Ovav.), or *chaḷ°*, as *chaḷaṁsa* = *ṣaḍaśra* (Ṭhāṇ. 493; see § 240), before consonants with regular assimilation (§ 270), as M. Ś. *chagguṇa*, *chagguṇaa* = *ṣaḍguṇa*, *°guṇaka* (Mudrār. 233,9; Anarghar. 67,11); AMg. *chaddisiṁ* (Vivāhap. 97 ff. 145); AMg. *chabbhāya* = *ṣaḍbhāga* (Uttar. 1036; Ovav. [*°ga*]; M. *chappaa*, JM. *chappaya* (C. 3,3; Hc. 1,265; 2,77; G. H. Kk.), AMg. *chattala* = *ṣaṭtala* (Ṭhāṇ. 495); M. A. *chaṁmuha* = *ṣaṇmukha* (Bh. 2,41; C. 3,3.14; Hc. 1, 25. 265; Karp. 1,10; Hc. 4,331); M. JM. *chaṁmāsa* = *ṣaṇmāsa* (H.; Erz.); AMg. *chaṁmāsiya* = *ṣaṇmāsika* (Āyār. 2,1,2,1); M. Ś. *chaṁmāsia* = *ṣaṇmāsika* (Karp. 47,10; 82,8); Ś. *chaccaraṇa* (Bālar. 66,7). Likewise before other numerals: AMg. *chaḷasii* (86; Samav. 143; Vivāhap. 199); AMg. JM. A. *chavvisaṁ* (26; Uttar. 1092; Erz.; Piṅgala 1,68); AMg. *chattisaṁ*, *°sā* (36; Kappas.; Ovav.; Uttar. 1043), *chappaṇṇaṁ* (56; § 273); AMg. *chaṇṇaüiṁ* (Samav. 151), JM. *channavai* (Kk. III, 514,24). Before 40,60,70 there enters in AMg. *chā°*, with *ā* according to § 70; *chāyālisaṁ* (46; Kappas.), *chāvaṭṭhiṁ* (66; Samav. 123), *chāvattariṁ* (76; Samav. 133). A. has *chaha* = **ṣaṣa* (§ 263) in *chahavisa* (26; Piṅgala 1,95 [GOLDSCHMIDT *chavvisa*]. 97 [GOLDSCHMIDT] *caüvvisa*]) and *chaha* (6; Piṅgala 1,96). In agreement with Skt. *ṣoḍaśa* Pkt. has *soḷasa*, A. *soḷaha* (§ 443).

§ 442. **7** is inflected: nom. acc. M. AMg. JM. *satta* (H. 3; R. 15,29; Āyār. 2,1,11,3.10; Ṭhāṇ. 445; Erz. 14,4); ins. AMg. *sattahiṁ* (Ṭhāṇ. 446); gen. AMg. JM. JŚ. *sattaṇhaṁ* (Hc. 3,123; Āyār. 2,1,11,11; Kappas. § 14; Vivāhap. 26. 222; Ṭhāṇ. 445; Kk. 275, 33; Kattig. 399.308), also *sattaṇha* (Hc. 3,123); loc. *sattasu* (Ṭhāṇ. 44; Uttar. 904). In compounds there appear *satta°*, *sattā°*, Mg. *śatta°* (Mṛcch. 79,13; Prab. 51,8). On *chattavaṇṇa*, *chattivaṇṇa* = *saptaparṇa* see § 103.—**8** is inflected: nom. acc. AMg. *aṭṭha* (Ovav.; Kappas.; Uvās.), also *aḍha* (Vivāhap. 82; verse; text *aṭha*; see § 67); A. also *aṭṭhāĩ* (Piṅgala 1,9. 83) and *aṭṭhāā* (1,116); ins. AMg. *aṭṭhahiṁ* (Uvās. § 27; Vivāhap. 447; Uttar. 768; Ṭhāṇ. 475); gen. AMg. JM. *aṭṭhaṇhaṁ* (Hc. 3,123; Kappas. § 14; Vivāhap. 416. 417; Erz. 12,21), also *aṭṭhaṇha* (Hc. 3,123); loc. AMg. *aṭṭhasu* (Vivāhap. 416. 417). In compounds there appears *aṭṭha°*: AMg. *aṭṭhaviha* = *aṣṭavidha* (Uttar. 895); Ś. *aṭṭhapaŏṭṭha* = *aṣṭaprakoṣṭha* (Mṛcch. 73,2) and *aṭṭhā°*: AMg. JM. *aṭṭhāvaya* = *aṣṭāpada* (Ovav.; Erz.). Before other numerals *aṭṭha°* stands in AMg. *aṭṭhahattariṁ* (78; Samav. 134.135); JM. *aṭṭhatisaṁ* (38), *aṭṭhasaṭṭhi* (68); Erz. p. XLI), against this *aṭṭhā°* in *aṭṭhārasa*, A. *aṭṭhāraha* (18; § 443); AMg. JM. *aṭṭhāvisaṁ* (28), *aṭṭhāvaṇṇaṁ* (58), *aṭṭhāṇaüiṁ* (98; Samav. 78. 79. 117. 152. 153; Erz. XLI), and *aḍha°* in AMg. *aḍhāyālisaṁ* (48; Samav. 111), AMg. also *aḍhayāla* (Samav. 210), *aḍhasaṭṭhiṁ* (68; Samav. 126; text. mostly *aḍa°*). So also A. *aḍhāisa* (Piṅgala 1,127 [text, BOLLENSEN, Vikr. 549, GOLDSCHMIDT *aṭhāisa*]. 144[text *aṭhaīsa*, GOLDSCHMIDT *aṭṭhāisao* for *aṭhaīsa pāa bho* of the text]), *aḍhaālisa* (text *aṭhalā°*; 48; Piṅgala 1,95) beside *aṭṭhāisa* (28; Piṅgala 1,64.86) and *aṭṭhāsaṭṭhā* (68; Piṅgala 1,106). See § 67.—**9** is inflected: nom. acc. AMg. JM. *nava* (Kappas. § 128; Erz. 4,

14); inst. *navahiṁ* (Uttar. 998); gen. AMg. *navaṇhaṁ* (Hc. 3,123; Āyār. 2, 15,6; Ovav. § 104; Kappas.; Nāyādh.), also *navaṇha* (Hc. 3,123). In compounds *ṇava°* enters: *ṇavaṇavāṇaṇa* (G. 426), likewise before other numerals: A. *ṇavadaha* (19; Piṅgala 1,111); AMg. *ṇavaṇaüiṁ* (99; Samav. 154).—**10** M. *dasa* or *daha*, AMg. JM. Ś. *dasa*, Mg. Ḍh. *daśa* (§ 262) is inflected: nom. acc. M. AMg. Ś. *dasa* (Karp. 12,7; Uvās.; Samav. 162. 165. 166; Pras. 19,5); false Mg. *daha* for *daśa* (Lalitav. 566,11); ins. AMg. JM. *dasahiṁ* (Kappas. § 227; Erz. 32,12), M. also *dasahi* (R. 11,31; 15.81). Mg. *daśehiṁ* (Mṛcch. 32,18); gen. AMg. JM. *dasaṇhaṁ* and *dasaṇha* (Hc. 3,123; Uvās. § 275; Erz. 28,22), Mg. *daśāṇaṁ* (Mṛcch. 133,20). In AMg. *uvāsagadasāṇaṁ* (Uvās. § 2. 91), the gen. in the femin. *dasā* = **daśā* occurs. Loc. M. AMg. *dasasu* (R. 4,58; Uvās. p. 168,7), CP. *tasasu* (Hc. 4,326). In compounds appear M. A. *dasa°* and *daha*, AMg, JM. Ś. *dasa°*, Mg. *daśa* (§ 262); A. *daha°* is found also in combination with other numerals: *ĕkkadaha* (11; Piṅgala 1, 114), *cāridahā* and *dahacāri* (14; Piṅgala 1, 105. 110), *dahapañca* and *dahapañcāī̃* (15; Piṅgala 1,49. 106. 113), *dahasatta* (17; Piṅgala 1,79. 123), *ṇavadaha* (19; Piṅgala 1,111).

§ 443. The numerals from **11** to **18** are: **11** AMg. *ĕkkārasa*, *ikkārasa* (Vivāhap. 82. 165; Kappas.; Uvās,), M. A. *eāraha* (Bh. 2,44; Mk. fol. 19; Piṅgala 1,66. 109—112) and *ĕggāraha* (Piṅgala 1,77.78. 106. 134), also *gārahāī̃* (2,111) and *ĕkkādaha* (§ 442); CP. *ekātasa* (Hc. 4,326). —**12** AMg. JM. JŚ. *bārasa* (Āyār. 2,15,23.25; Paṇṇav. 52; Vivāhap. 82; Uttar. 691; Uvās.; Kappas.; Erz.; Kattig. 402, 369; 403,371 [text *vā°*]), femin. JM. *bārasī* (T. 6,7), and AMg. JM. *duvālasa* (§ 244); M. A. *bāraha* (Bh. 2,44; Mk. fol. 19; Piṅgala 1,49. 69 etc.).—**13** AMg. *terasa* (Sūyag. 669; Uvās.; Kappas.), femin. *terasī* (Āyār. 2,15,4; Kappas.), M. A. *teraha* (Bh. 2,44; Mk. fol. 19; Piṅgala 1,9. 11. 58.66).—**14** *cŏddaha* (Hc. 1,171), AMg. JM. *cŏddasa* (Uvās.; Kappas.; Erz.,[1] and *caüddasa* (Kappas.), metri causa also *caüdasa* (Kappas. § 46b), A. *caüddaha* (Piṅgala 1, 133. 134), also *cāuddāhā* (2,65) and *cāridahā*, *dahacāri* (§ 442).—**15** AMg. JM. *paṇṇarasa* (§ 273), A. *paṇṇaraha*, as Vr. Hc. generally teach (§ 273), A. also *dahapañca*, *dahapañcāī̃* (§ 442).—**16** AMg. JM. *soḷasa*, also AMg. *solasaya* (Jīv. 228), A. *soḷaha* (Piṅgala 1,103. 104. 105), also *soḷā* (2,67. 97).—**17** AMg. JM. *sattarasa* (Vivāhap. 198; Erz.), A. *dahosatta* (§ 442).—**18** AMg. JM. *aṭṭhārasa*, as also PG. 6,34, A. *aṭṭhāraha* (Piṅgala 1,79). On *ra* for *da* see § 245, on *la* for *da* § 244. Therefore, the flexion is that of *daśan* (§ 442), e.g. ins. A *eārahahī̃* (Piṅgala 1,66 [°*hi*], 109 ff.; BOLLENSEN, Vikr. p. 538 *eggārahahi*), AMg. *bārasahiṁ* (Sūyag. 790; Uttar. 1034); A. *bārahahī̃* (Piṅgala 1,113); AMg. *cŏddasahiṁ* (Jīv. 228; Ovav. § 16, p. 31, 21); AMg. *paṇṇarasahiṁ* (Jīv. 228); gen. AMg. *duvālasaṇhaṁ* (Uvās.); AMg. *caüddasaṇhaṁ* (Vivāhap..952), *cŏddasaṇhaṁ* (Kappas.); *paṇṇarasaṇhaṁ* (Hc. 3,123); AMg. JM. *soḷasaṇhaṁ* (Vivāhap. 222; Erz. 28,20), *aṭṭhārasaṇhaṁ* (Hc. 3,123) and °*ṇha* (Erz. 42,28); loc. *paṇṇarasasu* (Āyār. p. 125,33); Vivāhap. 734).

1. These citations are valid also for the following numerals, when other works are not quoted. The numerals for 11-100 are frequently found mostly in Mg.,

particularly in compounds, in addition partly in JM. A. For the rest of the dialects examples are wanting.

§ 444. **19** is AMg. *egūṇavisaṁ* = *ekonaviṁśati* (cf. § 445; Vivāhap. 1243; Nāyādh. § 12), A. *egūṇaviṁsā* (Piṅgala 2,238) and *ṇavadaha* (§ 442). Beside it AMg. JM. have also *aüṇavisai* and *aüṇavisaṁ* (Uttar. 1091; Erz. XLI). The same forms occur in AMg. JM. in other tens too beside one another. So: *egūṇapannāsaïma* (the 49th; Samav. 153) and *aüṇāpaṇṇa* (49; Ovav. § 163; Vivāhap. 158); *egūṇasaṭṭhiṁ* (59; Samav. 118 and *aüṇaṭṭhiṁ* Kappas. § 163; cf. v. l.); *egūṇasattariṁ* (69; Samav. 126) and *aüṇattariṁ* (Kappas. § 178). Further one says AMg. JM. *aüṇatisaṁ*, *aüṇatisaṁ* (29; Uttar. 1093; Erz. p. XLI) and AMg. *egūṇāsiiṁ* (79; Samav. 136), *egūṇaṇa-üiṁ* (89; Samav. 146).—*aüṇa*°, *aüṇā*° (§ 70) cannot be derived with E. MÜLLER[1] and LEUMANN[2] from *ekona*, but is = *aguṇa*, corresponding to *dviguṇa*, *triguṇa* etc., M. *duvṇa*; AMg. *duguṇa* (§ 436), AMg. *aṇantaguṇa* (Vivāhap. 1039). Cf. old Hindī. *agunis*, *gunīs* (19), Gujarātī *ogaṇis*,[3] which is = **apaguṇaviṁśati*.

1. Beiträge p. 17.—2. Aup. S. s. v. *aüṇāpanna*.—3. HOERNLE, Comp. Gr. p. 257.

§ 445. The numerals for **19—58** form in AMg. JM. the nom. as neut. in *-aṁ* or as fem. in *-ā*, in A. in *-a*, and those for **59—99** as neuter in *-iṁ* or femin. in *-ī*. In the rest of the cases they are mostly inflected as femin. sing., and have, as in Skt., the numbered object either in the gen. plur. or in the corresponding case of the plur. beside them.—**20** forms also *visaī* = *viṁśati* (Kappas.; Uvās.), nom. *visai* and *visaïṁ* (Erz. XLI[1]). AMg. *aüṇavisai* (19), *visai* (20), *ĕkkavisai* (21), *paṇavisai* (25), it *sattavisaī* (27), Uttar. 1091-1093),A. *caüvisaī*(24; Piṅgala 1,87). However, *visaṁ* (Kappas.; Erz.) or *visā* (Hc. 1,28.92; Frz.), A. *visa* (Piṅgala 1,95; Hc. 4,423,4), have been mostly regulated according to the following tens and been formed, as reversely also *tīsaī* = *triṁśat* in AMg. is found (Uttar. 1093), in correspondence with *visaī* = *viṁśatiḥ*. If another number enters before it, one says: AMg, JM. *ĕkkavisaṁ*, *egavisā*, *igavisaṁ* (21; Uttar. 1092; Vivāhap. 198; Erz.); *bāvisaṁ* (22; Uttar. 1070. 1091. 1092; Vivāhap. 198; Erz.), A. *bāisa* (Piṅgala 1,68); *tevisaṁ* (23; Uttar. 1092; Samav. 66; Erz.), A. *teisa* Piṅgala 1,150); *caüvisaṁ* (24; Hc. 3,137; Vivāhap. 180; Uttar. 1092; Ṭhāṇ. 22), *caüvvisaṁ* (Vivāhap. 198; Erz.), A. *caüvisaha* (Piṅgala 1,87 [so GOLDSCHMIDT]), *covisa* (2,291) and *covisa* (2,279); *paṇavisaṁ*, *paṇuvi-saṁ* and *paṇuvisā* in *paṇuvisāhi* (25; § 273), A. *pacisa* (Piṅgala 1,120); *chavvisaṁ* (26; Uttar. 1092; Erz.), A. *chavvisa* and *chahavisa* (§ 441); AMg. *sattavisaṁ* (27; Uttar. 1093), and *sattāvisaṁ* (Vivāhap. 85 ff.); *sattāvisā* (Hc. 1,4); A. *sattāisā* (Piṅgala 1,51. 52. 58); *aṭṭhāvisaṁ*, °*visā* (Vivāhap. 82), A. *aṭṭhāisa*, *aḍhāisa* (28; § 442); *aüṇatisaṁ*, *aüṇattisaṁ* (29; § 444).—**30** is *tisaṁ* (Kappas.; Nāyādh.; Erz.) and *tisā* (Hc. 1,28. 92), A. *tisā* (Piṅgala 1,51.60), also in *tisakkharā* = *triṁśadakṣarā* (1,52), *tisaṁ* (1,61). The numerals, that enter before it, as in all the following tens, are the same as in the case of **20**, with the alterations required by the phonetic law. So *battisaṁ* (32; Vivāhap. 82; Erz.), *battisā* (Kappas. (A. *battisa* (Piṅgala 1,62.69), for which in M. also *dosoḷaha* = *dviṣoḍaśa* is said (Karp.

100,8) ; *tĕttisaṁ*, *tittisaṁ* (33, Kappas., Vivāhap. 18. 33. 391; Uttar. 909. 994. 1001. 1094; Erz.), AMg. also *tāyattisā*, AMg. *tāvattisaga*, JM. °*ya* (§ 438) ; *cŏttisaṁ* (34; Ovav.; Samav. 100) ; *paṇatisaṁ* (35; Vivāhap. 200); *chattisaṁ*, °*sā* (36; Kappas.; Ovav.), *aṭṭhattisaṁ* (Kappas.) and *aṭṭhatisaṁ* (Erz.)—**40** *cattālisaṁ* (Kappas.; Vivāhap. 199; Erz.) and *cattālisā* (Vivāhap. 82), *cāyālisaṁ* (Erz.) and contracted *cālisa* in JM. *cālisasāhassa* = *catvāriṁśatsāhasrya* (Erz. 10,35) and independently in A. (Piṅgala 1,153. 155), a form, which in AMg. JM. A. appears almost always, when other numerals enter before it, as A. *iālisa* (41; Piṅgala 1,125), AMg. JM. *bāyālīsaṁ* (42; Vivāhap. 158; Kappas.; Ovav.; Nāyādh.; Ṭhāṇ. § 262; Erz.); *teālisā* (43; Hc. 2,174) ; JM, *teyālisaṁ* (Erz.) ; AMg. *caüyālisaṁ* and *coyālisaṁ*, *coyālisā* (44; Samav. 108, 109; Vivāhap. 218; Paṇṇav. 105 f.). A. *caüālisa* (Piṅgala 1,90 [GOLDSCHMIDT *pa* [*ñcatālisā*]]. 97) and *coālisaha* (2, 238) ; AMg. *paṇayālisā* (Paṇṇav, 55), *paṇayālisaṁ* (45; Vivāhap. 158; Samav. 109; Ovav.); for A. *pacatālisaha* (Piṅgala 1,93.95) we should read *pacaālisahī*; AMg. *chāyālisaṁ* (46; Kappas.); AMg. *siyālisaṁ* (47; Vivāhap. 653)[2]; AMg. JM. *aḍhayālisaṁ*, A. *aḍhaālisa* (48; § 442), but AMg. also *aṭṭhacattālisaṁ* (Vivāhap. 372); AMg. *ĕkkūṇapaṇṇa* (49; Jīv. 62). There appears in verses in AMg. even the abridged form *cāli* (Uvās. § 277,6), and in AMg. JM. *cattā* (Uvās. § 277,6; Erz.), also in compounds with other numerals, as JM. *bicatta* (Erz.) and as *cāla* in AMg. *igayāla* (text *igu*°; Vivāhap. 199) ; JM. *bāyāla* (42; Erz.); A. *beāla* (Piṅgala 1,95) ; AMg. *paṇayāla* (45; Samav. 109) ; *paṇayālasayasahassā* (4,500,000; Uttar. 1034) AMg. *aḍhayāla* (48; Samav. 210; Paṇṇav. 99 [*aḍa*°]; Vivāhap. 290 [*aḍa*°]).—**50** *paṇṇāsaṁ*, *paṇṇāsā*, *paṇṇā* in the rest of fifties °*paṇṇaṁ*, °*vaṇṇaṁ* (§ 273). The shortened forms are derived probably from **pañcāśat*, **pañcaśat*, **pañcśat*, **pañcat* (§ 81. 148).

1. This citation is valid for the entire paragraph, as well as for the following ones. The assumptions of JACOBI are based partly on not printed sources, and hence they could not generally be checked by me.—2. Cf. *sayārī* § 446.

§ 446. **60** AMg. *saṭṭhiṁ* (Samav. 118. 119), in compound *saṭṭhi*: *saṭṭhitanta* (Vivāhap. 149; Ovav.) ; JM. *saṭṭhiṁ*, *saṭṭhi* (Erz.) ; Ś. *chaṭṭhiṁ* (acc.; Mṛcch. 54,16), probably with the majority of MSS and editions to be read as *saṭṭhiṁ*; A. *saṭṭhi* (Piṅgala 1,105; in composition 1,61). In compounds with other numerals in AMg. JM. °*saṭṭhiṁ* alternates with °*vaṭṭhiṁ* and °*aṭṭhiṁ* (§ 265): *egūṇasaṭṭhiṁ* and *aüṇaṭṭhiṁ* (59), *igasaṭṭhiṁ* and *egaṭṭhi*°; *bāsaṭṭhiṁ* and *bāvaṭṭhiṁ*; *tesaṭṭhiṁ* and *tevaṭṭhiṁ*; *caüsaṭṭhiṁ* and *cosaṭṭhi* (Vivāhap. 82) and *caüvaṭṭhi*°; *paṇasaṭṭhiṁ* and *paṇṇaṭṭhiṁ* (Kappas.); *chāvaṭṭhiṁ*, *sattasaṭṭhiṁ*, *aḍhasaṭṭhiṁ*, *aṭṭhasaṭṭhi*° (WEBER, Bhag. 1,426; Samav. 118—126; Erz.).—**70** AMg. JM. *sattariṁ* and *sattari*°, JM. also °*sayari*°, *sayari*° (Samav. 127. 128; Prabandhac. 279,12; Erz.). On the *r* see § 245. In combination with other numerals °*sattariṁ* alternates with °*hattariṁ*, °*vattariṁ* with °*attari*°; AMg. *egūṇasattariṁ* with *aüṇattariṁ* (69; § 444), *ĕkkasattariṁ* (Samav.; text *eka*°); *bāvattariṁ*, JM. also *bisattari*°; *tevattariṁ*, *covattariṁ*, JM. *caühattari*; AMg. *pañcahattarie* (instr.: Kappas. § 2), *pannattari* (so Samav. thrice; read°*riṁ*), JM. *paṇa*-

saÿari (Prabandhac. 279, 12); *chāvattariṁ*; *sattahattariṁ aṭṭahattariṁ*, JM. *aṭhattari°* (WEBER, Bhag. 1,426; 2,248; Samav. 126—135; Erz.). In A. is found *ehattari* (71; Piṅgala 1,95. 97. 100) and *chāhattarı* (76; text *che°*; 2, 238).—**80** AMg. *asiiṁ*, JM, *asii*, *asii°* (Samav. 137; Vivāhap. 94. 95; Erz.). In combination with other numerals: AMg. *egūṇāsiiṁ* (79); JM. *ĕkkāsii*; AMg. *bāsiiṁ*; AMg. *tesiiṁ* ins. also *teÿāsie* (Samav.), JM. *tesii*; AMg. *caürāsiiṁ*, *corāsiiṁ*, *corāsi*, JM. *caürāsii°*, *culāsii°*; AMg. *pañcāsiiṁ*, *chaḷasiim*, *sattāsiim*, *aṭṭhāsiim*(Samav. 136 —145; Kappas.; Erz.). In A. are found *asi* (80), *beāsi* (82), *aṭṭhāsi* (88)(Piṅgala 1,81.98;2,238).—90 AMg. *naüiṁ*, JM. *naüi* (Samav. 147; Erz). In combination with other numerals: AMg. *egūṇaṇaüiṁ* (89); *ĕkkāṇaüiṁ* (Samav.; text *ekā°*), *bā°*, *te°*, *caü°*, *pañcā°*, *chaṇṇaüiṁ* and *chhṇṇaüi* (Vivāhap. 82), *sattāṇaüiṁ*, *aṭṭhā°*; JM. *bāṇaüi*, *te°*, *pañcā°* and *paṇa°*, *channaüi* (Samav. 146—153; Erz.). In A. is found *chaṇṇavaī* (96; Piṅgala 1,95).

§ 447. The following examples show flexion and construction of the numerals for 19—99: AMg.: nom. *tevisaṁ titthakarā* = *trayoviṁśatis tīrthakarāḥ* (Samav. 66); *bāÿālisaṁ sumiṇā tisaṁ mahāsumiṇā bāvattariṁ savvasumiṇā* = *dvācatvāriṁśat svapnās triṁśan mahāsvapnā dvāsaptatiḥ sarvasvapnāḥ* (Vivāhap. 951 [where *°vi°*]; Nāÿādh. § 46; Kappas. § 74); *tāÿattisā logapālā* = *trayastriṁśat lokapālāḥ* (Ṭhāṇ. 125).—Acc. *visaṁ vāsāiṁ* = *viṁśatiṁ varṣāṇi* (Uvās. § 89. 124. 266); *paṇṇāsaṁ joÿaṇasahassāiṁ* = *pañcaśataṁ yajanasahasrāṇi* (Ṭhāṇ. 266); *pañcāṇaüiṁ* (text *°yaṁ*) *joÿaṇasahassāiṁ* = *pañcanavatiṁ yojanasahasrāṇi* (Ṭhāṇ. 261).—Ins. *pañcahattarie vāsehiṁ...ĕkkavisāe titthaÿarehiṁ . . . tevisāe titthaÿarehiṁ* = *pañcasaptatyā varṣaiḥ...ekaviṁśatyā tīrthakaraiḥ*; *tĕttisāe sattāvannāe dantisahassehiṁ* = *trayastriṁśatā saptapañcaśatā dantisahasraiḥ* (Niraÿāv. § 24. 26).—Gen. *eesiṁ tisāe mahāsumiṇāṇaṁ* = *eteṣāṁ triṁśato mahāsvapnānām* (Vivāhap. 951; Nāÿādh. §46; Kappas. §74); *battisāe °saÿasāhassiṇaṁ caürāsiie* [so to be read] *sāmāṇiÿasāhassiṇaṁ tāÿattisāe tāÿattisagāṇaṁ caüṇhaṁ logapālāṇaṁ* = *dvātriṁśataḥ °śatasāhasriṇāṁ caturaśityāḥ sāmānikasāhasriṇāṁ trayastriṁśatas trayastriṁśakānāṁ caturṇāṁ lokapālānām* (Kappas. § 14; cf. Vivāhap. 211).—Loc. *tisāe niraÿāvāsasaÿasahassesu* = *triṁśati niryāvāsaśatasahasreṣu* (Vivāhap. 83 ff.); *egavisāe savalesu bāvisāe parisahe* (metrically for *°hesu*) = *ekaviṁśatyāṁ śabaleṣu dvāviṁśatyāṁ* **pariṣaheṣu* (Uttar. 907).—JM. *pañcanaüi rāiṇaṁ* and *rāÿāṇo* (Kk. 263,11. 17). More seldom these numerals are inflected in the plural. According to C.1,6, as in the case of numerals for 2—19 (§436), the gen. is formed in -*ṇhaṃ*: *visaṇhaṁ*, *tisaṇhaṁ*, AMg. *tinni tevaṭṭhāiṁ pāvāduÿasaÿāiṁ* = *triṇi trayaḥṣaṣṭāni prāvādukaśatāni* (Sūÿag. 778); *paṇuvisāhi ya bhāvaṇāhiṁ* = *pañcaviṁśatyā ca bhāvanābhiḥ* (Āÿār. p. 137,25); *pañcahiṁ chattisehiṁ aṇagārasaehiṁ* = *pañcabhiḥ ṣaṭtriṁśair anagāraśataiḥ* (Kappas. § 182); JM. *tiṇhaṁ tevaṭṭhāṇaṁ naÿarasaÿāṇaṁ* = *trayāṇāṁ trayaḥṣaṣṭānāṁ nagaraśatānām* (Erz. 28,21);[1] M. *caüssaṭṭhisu suttisu* = *catuḥṣaṣṭyāṁ śūktiṣu* (Karp. 72,6). This flexion is usual in A.: *eāisehī bāisehī* (Piṅgala 1,58. 69); *chahavisaü* (P. 1,97); *sattāisāī* (P. 1,60); *paeaālisahī* (P. 1,93. 95; see § 445); *ehattariu* (acc.), *ehattarihiṁ* (P. 1,95. 100). Cf. also § 448.

1. The three examples *tinni tevāṭṭhāiṁ pā°* *pañcahiṁ chattīsehiṁ aṇa* *tiṇhaṁ tevaṭṭhāṇaṁ*

na° might have formed a single paragraph. They correspond to the "wholly illogical construction" of the numerals in the Vedic language in WHITNEY[1] § 480, note; KIELHORN § 203. I owe the correct explanation to KIELHORN, who alos is of the opinion, that at Erz. 28,21 with the v. l. we should read *°ṭṭhā* instead of *°ṭṭhī°*

§ 448. **100** is M. *saa* (H. R.), AMg. JM. *saẏa* (Kappas.; Ovav.; Uvās.; Erz.), Ś *sada* (Mṛcch. 6,6; 151,22; Vikr. 11,4), Mg. *śada* (Mṛcch. 12,5; 116,8; 122,20; Veṇīs. 33,4). It is inflected as neuter according to the *a*-declension. The remaining hundreds are formed by making the units enter before the plural of 100: AMg. *do saẏāiṁ* (200), *tiṇṇi saẏāiṁ* (300), *cattāri saẏāiṁ* (400), (Samav. 157. 158); *pañca saẏā* (500; Kappas. §142), *cha saẏāiṁ*(600), also *cha saẏā* (Samav. 159) and *chassaẏā* (Kappas. § 166); A. *caüsaa* (400; Piṅgala. 1,81). Substantive neuter is *sattasaa* (H.).—**1000** is M. AMg. JM. JŚ. Ś. *sahassa* (G. H. R.; Kappas.; Uvās.; Erz.; Pav. 380,12; Mṛcch. 72,22; Prab. 4,4.5), Mg. *śahaśśa* (Lalitav. 566,10; Veṇīs. 33,3;34,21; 35;8). It is inflected as neuter according to the *a*-declension. In AMg. one says also *dasa saẏāiṁ* (Samav. 162) or *dasa saẏā* (Kappas. § 166), as for 1100 *ĕkkārasa saẏāiṁ* (Samav. 163) or *ĕkkārasa saẏā* (Kappas. § 166), for 1200 *bārasa saẏā*, for 1400 *caüddasa saẏā* (Kappas. § 166), for 1721 *sattarasa ĕkkavise joẏaṇasae* (1721 yojanas; acc.; Vivāhap. 198). The remaining thousands are formed like the corresponding hundreds: AMg. *do sahassāiṁ* (Samav. 163), acc. *duve sahasse* (Sūẏag 940); *tiṇṇi, cattāri, cha, dasa sahassāiṁ* (Samav. 163-165); *aüṇaṭṭhiṁ sahassā* (59000; Kappas. §136); JM. *puttāṇaṁ saṭṭhī sahassā* (60000; Sagara 1,13) and *saṭṭhiṁ pi tuha suẏasahassā* (7,7; cf. 10,4; 11,5), gen. *saṭṭhie puttasahassāṇaṁ* (8,5); also with *sāhassi* = *sāhasri*, as AMg. *coddasa samaṇasāhassio, chattisaṁ ajjiẏāsāhassio, tiṇṇi saẏasāhassio* etc. (Kappas. § 134—137; cf. §161 ff.; Vivāhap. 287). In the combination of hundreds and thousands with units the units are placed first, and are combined in a compound: *aṭṭhasaẏaṁ* = 108 (Vivāhap. 831; Kappas.; Ovav.); *aṭṭhasahassaṁ* = 1008 (Ovav.). The tens are expressed thereafter in the following manner: *tisaṁ ca sahassāiṁ dŏṇṇiẏaaüṇāpaṇṇe joẏaṇasae* = 30249 yojanas (Vivāhap. 158); *sattarasa ĕkkavise jo ẏaṇasae* = 1721 y.; *cattāri tise joyaṇasae* = 430y.; *dasa bāvise jo°* = 1022y.; *cattāri caüvvise jo°* = 424y., *satta tevise jo°* = 723 y., *tiṇṇi igaẏāle jo°* = 1341 y., *dŏṇṇi joẏaṇasahassāiṁ dŏṇṇi ẏa chaḷasie jo°* = 2286 y. (Vivāhap. 198, 199), *siẏālisaṁ joẏaṇasahassāiṁ dŏṇṇi ẏa tevaṭṭhe joẏaṇasae* = 47 263 y. (Vivāhap. 653), also with *uttara*, as *tiṇṇi joẏaṇasahassāiṁ dŏṇṇi ẏa battisuttare jo°* = 3232 y° (Vivāhap. 198); *bāvaṇṇuttaraṁ aḍhaẏālisuttaraṁ, cattālisuttaraṁ, aṭṭhalisuttaraṁ, chattisuttaraṁ, aṭṭhāvisuttaraṁ joyaṇasaẏasahassaṁ* = 100052, 100048, 100044, 100038, 100036, 100028 y. (Jīv. 243), and with *ca*, as *chakkoḍisae paṇavaṇṇaṁ ca koḍio* = 655 **koṭi** (Vivāhap. 200). Here the acc. occurs throughout. **100,000** is PG. *satasahassa* (6, 11;7,42. 48). AMg. *egaṁ saẏasahassaṁ* (Samav. 165) or *egā saẏasāhassī* (Kappas. § 136); cf. Ś. *suvaṇṇasadasāhassio* = *suvarṇaśatasāhasrikaḥ* (Mṛcch. 58,4); AMg. JM. also *lakkhaṁ* = *lakṣam* (Kappas. § 187; KI. 12; Erz.), Mg. *laśkaṁ* (Lalitav. 566,11).—**1,000,000** = AMg. *dasasaẏasahassāiṁ* (Samav. 166), Mg. *daha* (wrongly for *daśa*) *laśkāiṁ* (Lalitav. 566, 11).—**10,000,000** *koḍi* = *koṭiḥ* (Samav. 167; Erz.). In AMg. *koḍākoḍi*, *paliovamā, sāgarovamā sāgarovamākoḍākoḍi* etc. designate still higher numbers (Kappas.; Ovav.; Uvās. etc.).

§ 449. The ordinals, of which the feminine ends in *-ā*, when not noted below, are : **1** *paḍhama, puḍhama, paḍhuma, puḍhuma* (§ 104. 221). AMg. also *paḍhamilla* (Vivāhap. 108. 177. 380) and *paḍhamillaga* (Nāẏādh. 624), with the suffix *-illa* (§ 595), A. also *pahilla*, femin. *pahilī* (Kī. 5,99; Prabandhac. 62,5; 157,3 [text here *païlī*]), as in new Indian dialects (BEAMES, Comp. Gr. 2,142; HOERNLE, Comp. Gr. § 118. 400. 401). The word can be derived from **prathara* neither with BEAMES, nor from AMg. *paḍhamilla*, **paḍhaïlla* with HOERNLE, but it presupposes one **prathila*.—**2**. M. *duia, biia bia, bii* (Rv.1,6) *biijja*; JM. *duiẏa*, AMg. JM. *biiẏa, biẏa*; A. *bia*; AMg. also *ducca,dŏcca*; Ś Mg. *dudia*, in verses also *dudia* (§ 82.91.165.300).—**3**. M. *taïa*, AMg. JM. *taïẏa*; Ś. *tadia*; AMg. also *tacca*; A. *tia, taïjjī* (fem.), (§ 82. 91. 165. 300). Kī. 2,36 knows also *tiijja*, which occurs in AMg. *aḍḍhāijja* (§ 450).—**4**. M. AMg. JM. A. *caüttha* (Hc. 1,171; 2,33; H. R.; Sūẏag. 606; Āẏār. p. 132 ff.; Uvās.; Kappas.; Erz.; Kk.; Piṅgala 1,105), according to Hc. 2,33 also *caüṭṭha*; M. also *cŏttha* (§ 166; Hc. 1,171; H.); Ś. Mg. *caduttha* (Mṛcch. 69, 21. 22 [cf. v. l.]; Mg. 169,7; text everywhere *caü°*). D. *caüttha* (Mṛcch. 100,6), Ś also *caduṭṭha* (Śak. 44,5). The femin. is M. JM. *caütthī, cŏtthī* (Hc. 1,171; Erz. p. XLII), AMg. *caütthā* (Āẏār. p. 132 ff.). In *addhuṭṭha* (3½; § 450) there is one **tuṭṭha* = **turtha* (cf. *turya, turiya*).—**5**. *pañcama* occurs in all the dialects (H.; Kappas.; Uvās.; Erz.; Ś. Mṛcch. 70,5.6; D. Mṛcch. 100,7; A. Piṅgala 1, 59). The feminine ends in *-ī*, in AMg. in *-ā* too (Āẏār. p. 132 ff.).—**6**. in all the dialects *chaṭṭha*, femin. *-°ī* (Vr. 2,41; Hc. 1,265; 2,77; Kī. 2,46; H.; Sūẏag. 606,686; Vivāhap. 167; Kappas.; Uvās.; Ovav.; Erz.; Ś. Mṛcch. 70, 22. 23; Śak. 40,9; D. Mṛcch. 100,7. 8; A. Piṅgala 1,50), in AMg. femin. also *chaṭṭhā* (Āẏār 2,1,11,9) by form-association with the preceding numbers. For Mg. *saṭhṭha* [sic!] Prab. 28,16, as also the ed. P. 31,4 has, and for which at 73,1 in the ed. Bomb. stands *saṭṭha* and at 36,13 the ed. M. reads *saṭṭa*, is to be corrected as *chaṭṭha*. By *pañcabbhahia* = *pañcābhyadhika* the numeral is expressed in M. in Śak. 120,7.—**7**. M. AMg. JM. Ś. A. *sattama* (H.; Uvās.; Kappas Erz.; Mṛcch. 71,11. 12; Piṅgala 1,59).—**8**. AMg. JM. Ś. D. *aṭṭhama* (Vivāhap. 167; Uvās.; Ovav.; Kappas.; Erz.; Mṛcch. 72,1; D. Mṛcch. 100,6).—**9**. AMg. JM. *navama* (Uvāss; Kappas.; Erz.), D. *ṇavama* (Mṛcch. 100,8).—**10**. M. AMg. JM. *dasama* (R.; Vivāhap. 167; Uvās.; Erz.), femin. AMg. *dasamī* (Kappas).—The ordinals **11**.—**19**. are derived from the corresponding cardinals with the ending *-ma*, feminine *-mī*. Hitherto they have been found in the texts in AMg. JM. only. Thus : **11**. AMg. *ĕkkārasama* (Sūẏag. 695; Vivāhap. 167; Uvās.; Kappas.).—**12**. AMg. JM. *bārasama* (Sūẏag. 699; Vivāhap. 167; Erz.), AMg. also *duvālasama* (Āẏār. 1,8,4,7; Sūẏag. 699. 758).—**13**. AMg. *terasama* (Āẏār. 2,15,22; Vivāhap. 167; Sūẏag. 695; Kappas.).—**14**. *caüdasama* (Sūẏag. 758) and *cŏddasama* (Vivāhap. 167).—**15**. *pannarasama* (Vivāhap. 168).—**16**. *soḷasama* (Vivāhap. 167).—**18**. AMg. *aṭṭhārasama* (Vivāhap. 167; Nāẏādh. 1450. 1451) and *aḍhārasama* (Vivāhap. 1429; Nāẏādh. 1404).—**19**. *egūṇavisama* (Nāẏādh.

§ 11), and *a egūṇavisaïma* (Vivāhap. 1606). On *khoḍasama* (16.)see § 265.—**20**. *visaïma* or *visa*; **30**. *tisaïma* or *tisa*; **40**. *cattālisaïma*; **49**. *auṇāpanna*; **55**. *pannapannaïma* (Kappas.) ; **72**. *bāvattara*; **80**. *asiima*; **97**. *sattānaüya*. In the case of other numbers sometimes the long forms and sometimes the short forms are used, as **23**. JM. *tevisaïma* (T. 4,2) ; **24**. AMg. *caüvisaïma* (Vivāhap. 167) and *caüvisa* (Ṭhāṇ. 31); **84**. *caurāsiiṁ*, **85**. *pañcāsiima* (Kappas.). Cf. WEBER, Bhag. 1,426.—*kati* is inflected : AMg. JM. A. *kaï* (Vivāhap. 289. 301.413f. 416.855.878 ff.; Erz. 17,21; Hc. 4,376,1.420,3); ins. AMg. *kaïhiṁ* Paṇṇav. 662; Vivāhap. 74. 332); gen. *kaïṇhaṁ* (Hc. 3, 123) ; loc. AMg. JM. *kaïsu* (Paṇṇav. 521. 530; Vivāhap. 736 f. 1536; Erz. 66,16).

§ 450. To express ½ is added in AMg. *addha* or *aḍḍha* = *ardha* as in Skt., before the next higher ordinal (§ 291): *aḍḍhāijja* from *aḍḍha* + **tiijja*, **tijja* = **tijja* = *ardhatṛtiya* (§ 449) (2½;) Samav. 157; Jīv. 268 270. 660. 917. 982; Nāyādh. 347; Paṇṇav. 51. 55. 81. 611 f.; Vivāhap. 199. 202. 734. 1786; Nandīs, 198. 200; Kappas.); *addhuṭṭha* from *ardha* + **turtha* = *ardhacaturtha* (3½; Kappas.); *addhaṭṭhama* = *ardhāṣṭama* (7½; (Āyār. 2,15,6 [so to be read]; Kappas.: Ovav.); *addhanavama* (8½; Kappas.) ; *addhachaṭṭhehiṁ bhikkhāsaehiṁ* (550) ; *aḍḍhāijjāiṁ °sayāiṁ* (250), *aḍḍhuṭṭhāiṁ °sayāiṁ* (350), *addhapañcamāiṁ °sayāiṁ* (450) (Samav. 156—158) ; *addha-ohaṭṭhāiṁ joyaṇāiṁ* (5½ yojanas; Jīv. 231). —1½, on the contrary, is expressed by *divaḍḍha* (Vivāhap. 137. 1123; Samav. 157; Jīv. 149; Paṇṇav. 685 f. 692. 698), that is neither = *adhyardha*,[1] nor, as the position of the members of the compound shows, *dvitiya* + *ardha*,[2] but is = *dvikārdha* (§ 230). So also : *divaḍḍhaṁ °sayaṁ* (150; Samav. 157).

1. WEBER Bhag. 1,398. 409. 411; ERNST KUHN, Beiträge p. 41.—2. CHILDERS s.v.; BEAMES, Comp. Gr. 1237 f,; E. MÜLLER Beiträge p. 34.

§ 451. IX is in AMg. *saïṁ* = *sakṛt* (§ 181), in JM. *ĕkkavāraṁ* = *ekavāram* (Kk. 266, 25; 274, 21) and *ĕkkasiṁ* (Sagara 4,4), which in Hc. 2, 162 is spelt as *ĕkkasi* and *ĕkkasiaṁ* and is equated as = *ekadā*. For the purpose of enumeration AMg. uses *khutto* = *kṛtvaḥ* (§ 206) ; *dukkhutto*, *dukhutto* = *dvikṛtvaḥ* (Ṭhāṇ. 364; Āyār. 2,1,1,6) ; *tikhutto*, *tikkhutto* = *trikṛtvaḥ* (Ṭhāṇ. 5. 11. 17. 41. 60. 364; Āyār 2,1,1,6; 2,15,20; Antag. 5. 11. 17. 41. 60; Vivāhap 12. 156. 161. etc.; Uvās.; Kappas.); *sattakkhutto*, *°kh°* (Nāyādh. 910. 925. 941; Jīv. 260. 621), *tisattakkhutto* = *trisaptakṛtvaḥ* (Ovav. § 136; Vivāhap. 230 [*°khu°*]. 411); *aṇegasayasahassakkhutto* = *aneka-śatasahasrakṛtvaḥ* (Vivāhap. 145. 1285); *aṇantakhutto* (Jīv. 308; Vivāhap. 177. 414. 416. 418) ; *evaïkhutto* = **evatikṛtvaḥ* (Kappas.). In M. the word is spelt as *huttaṁ* : *saahuttaṁ*, *sahassahuttaṁ* (Hc. 2, 158: Dhvanyāloka 52,6). For 'for the second time' AMg. uses *dŏccam*, *duccaṁ* (Āyār. 2,15,21; Vivāhap. 166. 234. 235; Ovav. § 85; Uvās.; Kappas.); 'for the third time' is *taccaṁ* (Vivāhap. 166. 234. 235; Uvās.).—As the expression of times Pkt., like Skt., uses *°viha* = *°vidha*, in the case of adjectives and *°hā* = *°dhā* in the case of adverbs : AMg. *duviha*, *tiviha*, *caüvviha*, *pañcaviha*, *chavviha*. *satta-viha*, *aṭṭhaviha*, *navaviha*, *dasaviha* (Uttar. 885—990), *duvālasaviha* (Jīv. 44; Vivāhap. 159.), *solasaviha* (Uttar. 971; Ṭhāṇ. 593 [*°dhā*]), *aṭṭhāvi-saïviha* (Uttar. 877), *battisaïviha* (Vivāhap. 234); JŚ. *tiviha* (Kattig. 402,

360) etc.; AMg. *duhā, pañcahā, dasahā* (Uttar. 1046. 889. 704). *duhā, tihā, caühā, pañcahā, chahā, sattahā, aṭṭhahā ṇavahā, dasahā, saṁkhĕjjahā asaṁkhĕjjahā, aṇantahā* (Vivāhap. 997—1012).—AMg. JM. *egao* (Vivāhap. 277. 282. 950; Āv. 46, 24) is = *ekataḥ*; the more frequent *egaẏ ao* (Vivāhap. 137 —141. 187. 510. 513. 970. 983. 996 ff. 1430. 1434)) = **ekakataḥ*; *duhao* see § 436.—As in Skt., in AMg. JM. JŚ, too, one says *duga* (Ṭhāṇ. 568. 569; Erz.; Kattig. 403, 371), *duẏa* (Uttar. 903) = *dvika*; AMg. JM. *tiẏa* = *trika* (Uttar 902; Erz.); *chakka* = *ṣaṭka* (Uttar. 904) etc.; likewise JM. *sahassaso* = *sahasraśaḥ* (Sagar. 6,5); Ś. *aṇeaso*, AMg.'*ṇegaso* = *anekaśaḥ* (§ 435).

E. The Verb.

§ 452. In Pkt. the verb has undergone far greater loss than the noun has. As in the case of nouns (§ 355), the *a*-stems prevail on phonetic grounds, so that the second conjugation, with comparatively a fewer exceptions, has followed the analogy of the first one. Thereby the character of the class has almost been effaced. The ātmanepada is frequent in all the dialects in participles only; elsewhere it is somewhat usable only in M. AMg. JM. JŚ., but it is limited completely to the sing. and the third person plural of the present indicative in Ś., in Mg. almost exclusively to the first person sing. ind. present. The cases found in Ś. mostly are formular expressions (§ 457). Many verbs, that in Sanskrit are conjugated in ātmanepada only, have in Pkt. the endings of the parasmaipda, as mostly in the passive too. Further *āsi, āsi* = *āsit*, that are used as the sing. of the first, second and third persons and the plur. of the third person of the imperfect, have been retained in M. AMg. JM. Ś, in addition to *abhavi* in AMg. (§ 515). Remnant of the strong and *s*-aorists, includingsporadic ātmanepada forms in frequent use (§ 517), are found in AMg. and ingrammarians (§ 516), from the perfect in AMg. only (§ 518); the conditional has completely disappeared. All these tenses are expressed by means of participles with the auxiliary verb *as* or *bhū* or only by the past passive participle. The pluperfect too is formed in the same manner (519). Besides we find simple future in parasmaip., ātmanep. and passive of the verbal nouns of the infinitive, in the passive too (§ 580), the absolutive, the present participle of the parasmaipada, the ātmanepada and passive, the past passive participle and the particip. necessitatis, of the moods, the indicative, the optative, (the precative too) and the imperative. Of the secondary verbal forms, like Skt., Pkt. has the causative, the desiderative of the intensive and a large number of denominatives. The dual is completely lost. Except in A., the endings generally correspond to those of Skt. Deviations are shown in the following paragraphs. Characteristic is the extension of the present stem, from which all the tenses, the verbal nouns and the passive can be formed. It serves also for nominal derivation.

(a) Present.

1. Indicative of the Parasmaipada.

453. The flexion shows the paradigma of the first conjugation *vaṭṭa* = *varta-*, in Skt. in ātmanepada only.

	Sing.	Plur.
1.	*vaṭṭāmi*	*vaṭṭāmo*
2.	*vaṭṭasi*	*vaṭṭaha*, JŚ. Ś. Mg. Ḍh. *vaṭṭadha*, P. CP. *vaṭṭatha*
3.	*vaṭṭaī*, JŚ. Ś. Mg. Ḍh. *vaṭṭadi*, P. CP. *vaṭṭati*	*vaṭṭanti*

In A. the usual flexion is :—

1.	*vaṭṭaü̃*	*vaṭṭahũ*
2.	*vaṭṭasi*, *vaṭṭahi*	*vaṭṭahu*
3.	*vaṭṭaï*	*vaṭṭahĩ*

§ 454. The grammarians (Vr. 7,30; Hc. 3,154; Mk. fol. 51; Sr. fol. 47) mention also *-ami*, beside also the usual ending *āmi* in all the dialects, excluding A. : *jāṇami* = *jānāmi*; *lihami* = *likhāmi*; *sahami* = *sahe*; *hasami* = *hasāmi*. It occurs in A. too : *kaḍḍhami* = *karṣāmi* (Hc. 4, 385); *pāvami* = **prāpāmi* = *prāpnomi*; *bhāmami* = *bhramāmi* (Vikr. 71,7.8), *bhaṇami* = *bhaṇāmi* (Piṅgala 1, 153). The vowel has been regulated according to that of the second and third persons. In some cases, as in the first person plur. (§ 455), *i* has entered for *a* : M. *jāṇimi* = *jānāmi* (H. 902), *aṇuṇijjimi* = *anuniye* (H. 930); A. *pucchimi* = *pṛcchāmi*, *karimi* = **karāmi* = *karomi* (Vikr. 65,3; 71,9). Forms in *-mhi* and *-mmi* sometimes found in MSS and editions[1] are wrong,[2] as *ṇivedĕmhi* for *ṇivedemi* (Nāg. 20,3; cf. 20,10), *pasādĕmhi* for *pasādemi* (Nāg. 44,8), *gacchamhi*, *gacchahmi* for *gacchāmi* (Mālav. 5,5; Vṛṣabh. 20,17).—In A. the usual ending is *-aü̃*: *kaḍḍhaü̃* = *karṣāmi* (Hc. 4,385), *kijjaü̃* = *kriye* in the sense of *kariṣyāmi* (Hc. 4,385; 445,3); *jāṇaü̃* = *jānāmi* (Hc. 4,391. 439,4), *joijjaü̃* = *vilokye*, *dĕkkhaü̃* = *drakṣyāmi*, *jhijjaü̃* = *kṣiye* (Hc. 4,356.357,4.425); *pāvaü̃* = *prāpnomi*, *pakāvaü̃* = **pakvāpayāmi* = *pacāmi*, *jivaü̃* = *jivāmi*, *cajaü̃* (text *tajaü̃*) = *tyajāmi* (Piṅgala 1,104a; 2,64); *piāvaü̃* (text *piyāvaü*) = **pibāpayāmi* = *pāyayāmi* (Prabandhac. 70,11.13). According to the phonetic laws of A., *jāṇaü̃* can be derived from **jānakam* only (§ 352). The verbal forms with infixed *ak*, such as *pacataki*, *jalpataki*, *svapitaki*, *paṭhataki*, *addhaki*, *ehaki*, mentioned by the grammarians, in addition to the first pers. sing. *yāmaki* = *yāmi*, located by Aufrecht in Kauṣītakībrāhmaṇa 27,1,[3] are to be compared with **jānakam*. It is to be admitted that, as in the future (§ 520), the ending of the subsidiary tenses has taken the place of that of the principal tenses.[4]

1. Bollensen on Mālav. p. 123; Weber on Hāla 417.—2. Bloch, Vr. und Hc. p. 47. AMg. *aṇusāsaṁmī* for **aṇusāsāmi* = *anuśāsmi* Uttar. 790 is hardly correct.—3. ZDMG. 34,175f.—4. Hoernle, Comp. Gr. § 497 finds in it the ending of the imperative.

§ 455. In the 2. sing. indic. A has beside the ending *-si* also *-hi* (§ 264) : *marahi* = **marasi* = *mriyase*, *ruahi* = Vedic *ruvasi* = *rodiṣi*, *lahahi* = *labhase*, *visūrahi* = *khidyase*, *ṇisarahi* = *niḥsarasi* (Hc. 4,368. 383,1. 422, 2.439,4). In Mg. the ending is naturally *-śi* : *yāśi*, *dhāvaśi*, *palāaśi*, *mali-*

hiśi, gaścaśí (Mṛcch. 9,23,24;10,3).—In the 3. sing. indic. in verses AMg. and A. do not seldom contract the ending *-aï* to *-e* (§ 166); in Ś. Mg. Ḍh. the ending is *-di*, in P. CP. *-ti* : M. AMg. JM *vaṭṭaï*, but JŚ, Ś. *vaṭṭadi* (§ 289); M. *vaḍḍhaï* = *vardhate*, but Ś. *vaḍḍhadi* (§ 291); Mg. *cilāadi* = *cirāyati* (Śak. 115,9); Ḍh. *vajjadi* = *vrajati* (Mṛcch. 30,10); P. *lapati*, *gacchati* (Hc. 4, 319).—The 1. plur. indic., in all the dialects, except in A., ends in *-mo*, in verses in *-mu* and *-ma* too, the ending of the subsidiary tenses (Vr. 7,4; Hc. 3,144. 167; Kī. 4,7; Mk. fol. 51); *hasāmo, hasāmu hasāma*. Except in PG. *vitarāma* (5,7), M. future *dacchāma* = *drakṣyāmaḥ* (R. 3,50) and in *-mha* = *smaḥ* (§ 498), *-ma* has, up to this time, been seen merely as v.l.[1] and for prose it is not correct. M. *tajjāmo, vaccāmo, ramāmo* (H. 267. 590. 888), *kāmemo* = *kāmayāmaḥ* (H. 417), in the passive *musijjāmo* = *muṣyāmahe* (H. 335); AMg. *vaḍḍhāmo* = *vardhāmahe* (Kappas. § 91. 106), *jivāmo* (Nāyādh. § 137), *āciṭṭhāmo* = *ātiṣṭhāmaḥ* (Sūyag. 734), *uvaṇemo* = *upanayāmaḥ, āhāremo* = *āhārayāmaḥ* (Sūyag. 734), *icchāmu* (Uttar. 376), *accemu* beside *accimo* = *arcayāmaḥ, arcāmaḥ* (Uttar. 368.369), in future *dāhāmu* = *dāsyāmaḥ* (Uttar. 355.358), also in aor. *vucchāmu* = *avātsma* (Uttar. 410); JM. *tāḷemo* = *tāḍayāmaḥ* (Dvār. 497,1), *pĕcchāmo* = *prekṣāmahe* (Āv. 33,15), *vaccāmo* = *vrajāmaḥ* (Kk. 263,16; 272, 18), *pajjosavemo* (Kk. 271,7); Ś. *pavisāmo* = *praviśāmaḥ* (Śak. 92,1), *jāṇāmo* = *jānimaḥ* (§ 510), *sumarāmo* = *smarāmaḥ* (Mālatīm. 113,9), *uvacarāmo* = *upacarāmaḥ* (Mālatīm. 232,2; text *tuvarāma*; cf. v. l. and ed. Calc. 1866 p. 91,17), *vaḍḍhāmo* = *vardhāmahe* (Mallikām. 153,10; Mahāv. 17,11; [so to be read; cf. ed. Bomb. 38,3]), *cintemo* = *cintayāmaḥ* (Mahāv. 134,11), *vandāmo* = *vandāmahe, uvaharāmo* = *upaharāmaḥ* (Pārvatīp. 27,11; 29,13); D. *bŏllāmo* (Mṛcch. 105,16). The forms in *-mha*, that are sometimes found in the text, as *ciṭṭhamha* (Ratn. 315,1), *viṇṇavĕmha, saṁpādĕmha, pārĕmha, karĕmha* (Śak 27,7; 53,5; 76,60; 80,5) are wrong. They belong to the imperative (§ 470). In M. JM. and in verses in AMg. the post tonic syllable *ā* often becomes *i*, so that the ending then is *-imo* (§ 108); M. *jampimo* = *jálpāmaḥ* (H. 651); M. JM. *ṇamimo* = *ṇámāmaḥ* (G. 35. 969; Kk. 277,30); M. JM. *bhaṇimo* = *bháṇāmaḥ* (Hc. 3,155; H.; Prabandhac. 100,8; Kk. 266,14) beside *bhaṇāmo* (H.); M. AMg. *vandimo* = *vándāmahe* (H. 659; Nandīs. 81); *pacimo* = *pácāmaḥ* (Mk. fol. 51); M. *savimo* = *śápāmaḥ* (G. 240); M. *sahimo* = *sáhāmahe* in *visahimo* (H. 376); *hasimo* = *hásāmaḥ* (Bh. 7,31). Likewise M. *gamimo* = **gámāmaḥ* (H. 892), *jāṇimo, ṇa āṇimo* = **jánāmaḥ na* **jānāmaḥ* (H.), *bharimo* = **bhárāmaḥ* and *saṁbharimo* (we remember; H. s. v. *smar*; G. 219), *ālakkhimo* = *ālakṣāmahe* (G. 188), and on its analogy : *pucchimo* = *pṛcchámaḥ* (H. 453), *lihimo* = *likhámaḥ* (H. 244), *suṇimo* = **śruṇámaḥ* (H. 518, wrongly also in Ś. Bālar. 101,5). The grammarians (Vr. 7,4. 31; Hc. 3,155; Mk. fol. 51; Sr. fol. 47) know also the forms in *-amu, -ama, -imu, -ima* : *paḍhamu, paḍhama, pacimu, bhaṇamu bhaṇama, bhaṇimu, bhaṇima, sahamu, sahima, sahimu, hasamu, hasama, hasimu, hasimo.*—In A. the usual ending is *-hũ* : *lahahũ* = *labhāmahe caḍāhũ* = *ārohāmaḥ, marāhũ* = *mriyāmahe* (Hc. 4,386. 439,1). The abl. plur. of the *a*-stems has the same ending where it would be derived from *-bhyām* (§ 369). Here the origin is completely obscure.[2] Beside this there is found *lahimu* too (Hc. 4,386).

1. Particularly in Ś., as *vaṭṭāma* (Prab. 68,8) for which the ed. P. p. 69[a] reads *vasaṁma*, the ed. M. p. 84, 15 *vasamha*, the ed. Bomb. 137,7, *ahivaṭṭahmo*. One emends it as *vaṭṭāmo* or *vasāmo*; *viraema* = *viracayāmaḥ* (Śak. ed. BÖHTLINGK 49,17; *tuvarāma* (Mālatim. 232,2 etc.).—2. Improbable is the explanation of HOERNLE, Comp, Gr. § 497 p. 335.

§ 456. The ending of the 2. plur. in M. JM. AMg. is *-ha*, in Ś. Mg. Ā. *-dha*, in A. *-hu* or *-ha* : *ramaha*, *paḍhaha*, *hasaha* (Vr. 7,4); *hasaha*, *vevaha*, (Hc. 3,143) ; *pacaha*, *saṅkaha* (Kī. 4,6) ; *hoha* (Mk. fol. 51); M. *ṇa āṇaha* = *na jānitha*, *dĕcchiha* = *drakṣyatha* (R. 3,13. 23), *taraha* (you know; H. 897) ; JM. *jāṇaha* (Kk. 273,44); *kuppaha* = *kupyatha*, *paẏacchaha* (Erz. 10, 20; 15,36); AMg. *āikkhaha*, *bhāsaha*, *pannaveha* (Āẏār. 1.4,2,4); *bhuñjaha* (Sūẏag. 194); *vaẏaha* = *vadatha* (Kappas.; Ovav.; Uvās.; Nāẏādh.), *āḍhāha*, *pariẏāṇaha*, *agghāẏaha*, *uvaṇimanteha* (Nāẏādh. § 83); Ś. *pĕkkhadha* = *prekṣadhve* (Mṛcch. 40,25; Śak. 14,8), *ṇedha* = *nayatha* (Mṛcch. 161,9);[1] Mg. *pĕskadha* (Mṛcch. 157,13; 158,2; 162,6), *pattiāadha* = *pratyayadhve* (Mṛcch. 165,9) ; Ā. *acchadha* (Mṛcch. 99,16); A. *pucchaha* and *pucchahu* (Hc. 4,364. 422,9), *icchahu* and *icchaha* (Hc. 4,384), *puampaha* = *prajalpatha* (Hc. 4,422,9). Probably °*hu* should be read in all such cases. On the ending *-itthā* see § 517.—The 3. plur. ends in all the dialects in *-nti*: M. *muanti* = **mucanti*, *ruanti* = *rudanti*, *hŏnti* = *bhavanti*, *dĕnti* = *dayante* (Erz. 3,14. 15); AMg. *caẏanti* = *tyajanti*, *thananti* = *stananti*, *labhanti* = *labhante* (Āẏār. 1,6,1,2) ; Ś. *gacchanti*, *pasidanti saṁcaranti* (Mṛcch. 8,4; 9,1. 11); Mg. *aṇṇeśanti* = *anveṣanti*, *pianti* = *pibanti* (Mṛcch 29,23; 113,21); CP. *ucchallanti*, *nipatanti* (Hc. 4,326); A. *vihasanti* = *vikasanti*, *karanti* = *kurvanti* (Hc. 4,365; 445,4). In A., however, the common ending is *-hĩ*, of which the origin is obscure[2] : *maüliahĩ* = *mukulayanti*, *aṇuharahĩ* = *anuharanti*, *lahahĩ* = *labhante*, *ṇavahĩ* = *namanti*, *gajjahĩ* = *garjante*, *dharahĩ* = *dharanti*, *karahĩ* = *kurvanti*, *sohahĩ* = *śobhante* etc. (Hc. 4,365,1. 367,4. 5.382). In the passive *ghĕppahĩ* = *gṛhyante* (Erz. 158,14). The same ending is found in AMg. *accahaiṁ* = *tiṣṭhanti* (Uttar. 667)[3] in verses and in *āḍhāhiṁ*, *parijāṇāhiṁ* (Vivāgas. 217; cf. § 223. 500. 510) in prose.

1. According to Hc. 4,268. 302 *-ha* too would be permissible in Ś. Mg. Cf. also PISCHEL., KB. 8,134 ff.—2. Improbable is the explanation of HOERNLE, Comp. Gr. § 497 p. 337.—3. So to be read with JACOBI, SBE. 45,114, note 2. The edition in the text and in the commentary has *atthihiṁ*; the commentary explains *atthahi* (sic ?) as *iti tiṣṭhanti*. Cf. *assāsi* § 461.

2. INDICATIVE OF THE ĀTMANEPADA.

§ 457. The flexion is :

	Sing.	Plur.
1.	*vaṭṭe*	is wanting
2.	*vaṭṭase*	is wanting
3.	*vaṭṭae*, JŚ. *vaṭṭade*	*vaṭṭante*

Cf. Vr. 7,1.2.5; Hc. 3,139. 140. 145; 4,274. 302. 319; Kī. 4,2.3; Mk. fol. 50. Vr. and Hc. limit the use of the endings *-se*, *-e* explicitly to the *a*-stems, a thing that is mentioned by Mk. too. According to Hc. 4, 274, in Ś. and according to 4,302 in Mg. too, the ending *-de* — *-te* would be permissible in the case of the *a*-stems. The best texts do not confirm these. All MSS in the example quoted by Hc. of Mg. from Veṇīs. 35,17;36,3 read *śuṇiad* = *śrūyate* and the text has *śuṇiadi*. Without doubt by Ś. here, as in other cases(§ 21), is meant JŚ. Vr. 12, 17 and Mk. fol. 70 forbid ātmanepada for Ś. Mg. completely. It is found in sporadic forms in verses and in prevalently standing expressions. Examples from different dialects are : 1. M. *jāṇe* (H. 902), *ṇa āṇe* (R. 3,44; Śak. 55,15); frequently in Ś. : *jāṇe* (Śak. 131,9; Mālav. 66,8; Lalitav. 564,4; Anarghar. 66,5; Uttarar. 22,13; 64,7; Viddhaś. 67,1; 96,1) and *ṇa āṇe*, as we should read all through with the v. l. in places where sometimes even now there stands in the text *ṇa jāṇe* (Śak. 70,11; 123,14; Vikr. 35,5; Mālav. 30,8; 34,9; Veṇīs 59,5); in AMg. too (Uttar. 512); M. *maṇṇe* = *manye* (G. H. [delete 546] ; R.), in Ś too (Mṛcch. 22,13; Mallikām. 56,1; 60,7; 74,22; 80,15; 83,5; Anarghar. 61,3; 66,10; Viddhaś. 20,6), and *aṇumaṇṇe*(Śak. 59,11), and in AMg. *manne* (Uttar. 571), in M. also according to the 1. class *maṇe* (H.R.; Hc. 2,207), and so is probably also the adverbially used *vaṇe* (Hc. 2,206), originally a 1. sing. ātmanep., if it be = *maṇe* (§ 251) or = *vaṇe* (cf. Dhātupāṭha in B-R. s. v. *van*). S. GOLDSCHMIDT has reconstructed the word in R. 14,43 (ZDMG. 32,103) according to Hc. In Vr. 9,12 *vale* stands. AMg. *rame* (Uttar. 445) ; Ś. *lahe* = *labhe* (Vikr. 42,7), *icche* (Mṛcch. 24,21; 25,10) ; Mg. *vāe* = *vāmi* and *vādayāmi*, *gāe* = *gāyāmi* (Mṛcch. 79, 12. 13).—2. M. *maggase*, *jāṇase*, *vijjhase*, *lajjase*, *jampase* (H. 6.181. 441.634. 943), *sohase* (G. 316); AMg. *pabhāsase* = *prabhāṣase*, *avabujjhase* = *avabudhyase* (Uttar. 358. 503) ; AMg. *iścaśe* = *icchase* (Mṛcch. 123,5; P. *payacchase* = *prayacchase* (Hc. 4,323),—3. M. *taṇuāae*, *paḍicchae*, *vaccae*, *pĕcchae*, *dāvae*, *ṇiacchae*, *palambae*, *andolae*, *laggae*, *parisakkae*, *vikuppae* (H. 59.701; 140. 169. 397. 489. 507. 582. 855. 951. 967), in the passive *tirae* = *tiryate* (H. 195. 801. 932), *jujjae* = *yujyate*, *jhijjae* = *kṣiyate*, *ṇivvarijjae* = *nirvriyate*, *khijjae* = *kṣiyate* (H. 12. 141. 204. 362) ; JM. *bhuñjae* = *bhuṅkte*, *nirikkhae* = *nirikṣate* (Erz. 25,30; 70,7); *cintae* (Āv. 36,25; Erz. 70,35; 74,17); *ciṭṭhae* = *tiṣṭhate*, °*viuvvae* = **vikurvate* = *vikurute* (Āv. 36,26. 27) ; passive *muccae* = *mucyate* (Erz. 71,7) ; *tirae* = *tiryate*, *ḍajjhae* = *dahyate* (Dvār. 498,21. 22); AMg. *lahae*, *kilae*, *bhañjae* (Uttar. 438. 570. 789) ; *titikkhae* = *titikṣate*, *saṁpavevae* = *saṁpravepate* (Āyār. 2,16,3) ; JŚ. *maṇṇade* = *manyate*, *bandhade* = *bandhnīte*, *jāyade* = *jāyate*, *bhāsade* = *bhāṣate*, *bhuñjade* = *bhuṅkte*, *kuvvade* = **kurvate* = *kurute* (Kattig. 399, 314; 400, 327. 332. 333; 403, 382. 384; 404, 309); passive *ādiyade* (Pav. 384,60); *thuvvade* = *stūyate*, *jujjade* = *yujyate*, *sakkade* = *śakyate* (Kattig. 401,351; 403,380; 404,387); D. *jāae* = *jāyate*, *vaṭṭae* = *vartate* (Mṛcch. 100,3.6). For Ś. Hc. 4,274 mentions *acchade*, *gacchade*, *ramade*, for P. 4,319 *lapate*, *acchate*, *gacchate*, *ramate*, for the passive Ś. *kijjade* = *kriyate* (4,274), P. *giyyate*, *tiyyate* (so to be read), *ramiyyate*, *paḍhiyyate* (4,315) ; at 4,316 stands *kirate* = *kriyate*.—In the 1. plur. sometimes the forms, such as *kāmamhe* = *kāmayāmahe*, that, however, are not authenticated by good manuscripts, are also found (WEBER on H. 417).—3. plur. M.

gajjante = *garjante* (Hc. 1,187 [see the translation]; 3,142), *bihante* = **bhīṣante*, *uppajjante* = *utpadyante* (Hc. 3,142), *ucchāhante* = *utsāhayante* (H. 638); AMg. *uvalabhante* (Sūyag. 755), *riyante* (Āyār. 1,8,2,16; Dasav. 613, 12), *ciṭṭhante* = *tiṣṭhante* (Āyār. 1,8,4.10). The examples from AMg. on the whole and from JM. in the largest measure are from verses.

§ 458. Beside the ending *-nte*, Pkt. has also the ending *-ire*, corresponding to Vedic Skt. and Pāli:[1] *pahuppire* = **prabhutvire* (§ 286) in *dŏṇṇi vi na pahuppire bāhū* = *dvāvapi na prabhavato bāhū*; *vicchuhire* = **vikṣubhire* (Hc. 3, 142); *haseire*, *hasaïre*, *hasire* = *hasante*; *saheire*, *sahaïre*, *sahire* = *sahante*; *hueire*, *huaïre*, *huire*, *hoeire*, *hoaïre*, *hoire* = *bhavante* (Sr. fol. 46. 47). Sr. fol. 49 teaches this ending for the optative too: *hujjaïre*, *hujjāire*, *huĕjjaïre*, *huĕjjāire* = *bhaveran* and the fol. 51 for the future: *hasehiire*, *hasihiire* = *hasiṣyante*. According to Hc. 3,142 *-ire* is used in the 3. sing. too: *sūsaïre gāmacikkhallo* = *śuṣyati grāmacikhallaḥ*. Triv. 2, 2, 4, who gives as examples *sūsaïre tāṇa tāriso kaṇṭho* = *śuṣyati tāsāṁ tādṛśaḥ kaṇṭhaḥ*, teaches the same thing.

1. E. KUHN, Beiträge p. 94; E. MÜLLER, Simplified Grammar p. 97; WINDISCH, Über die Verbalformen mit dem Charakter *r* im Arischen, Italischen und Celtischen, Leipzig, 1887 (AKSGW. X. No. VI), where further literature is also mentioned. Cf. particularly p. 32 f. of the SA. 478 f.

3. OPTATIVE.

§ 459. The optative is extraordinarily frequent in AMg. and JM., more seldom in M. and just sporadically in the other dialects. Its manner of formation is two-fold. In M. AMg. JM. the flexion is usual, that P. too has, but in Mg. A. it is sporadic.

	Sing.	Plur.
1.	*vaṭṭĕjjā, vaṭṭĕjja, vaṭṭĕjjāmi*	*vaṭṭĕjjāma*
2.	*vaṭṭĕjjāsi, vaṭṭĕjjasi, vaṭṭĕjjāhi, vaṭṭĕjjahi, vaṭṭĕjjāsu, vaṭṭĕjjasu, vaṭṭĕjjā.*	*vaṭṭĕjjāha, vaṭṭĕjjaha*
3.	*vaṭṭĕjjā, vaṭṭĕjja,* [*vaṭṭĕjjaï*]	*vaṭṭĕjjā, vaṭṭĕjja*

These dialects, AMg. JM. especially in verses, JŚ. almost always, Ś. exclusively, Mg. A. sporadically, have beside these the flexion:

	Sing.	Plur.
1.	Ś. *vaṭṭeaṁ, vaṭṭe*	is wanting
2.	AMg. A. *vaṭṭe*, A. *vaṭṭi*	is wanting
3.	AMg. JM. JŚ. Ś. Mg. *vaṭṭe*	AMg. Ś. *vaṭṭe*

That the two kinds of formation go back to the optative of the first conjugation in *-eyam*, as assumed by JACOBI,[1] is phonetically impossible. It follows clearly that the 1. sing. in *-e* has followed the analogy of the 2. and 3. sing., a form, that is used as 3. plur. too. The forms in *-ĕjjā* and *-ĕjja* are hence quite appropriate. The lengthening of the final vowel is original. The shortening is found in prose only before enclitics, as: *āgacchĕjja vā ciṭṭhĕjja vā nisiĕjja vā tuyaṭṭĕjja vā ullaṅghĕjja vā palaṅghĕjja vā* = *āgacched vā tiṣṭhed vā niṣīded vā śayita vā ullaṅghed vā pralaṅghed vā* (Ovav. § 150; cf.

Vivāhap. 116; Āẏār. 1,7,2,1; other examples Āẏār. 2,2,1,8; 2,3,2,7 etc.), beside in the lengthening, as *avaharĕjjā vā vikkhirĕjjā vā bhindhĕjjā vā acchindĕjjā vā pariṭṭhavĕjjā vā = apahared vā viṣkired vā bhindyād vā acchindyād vā pariṣṭhāpayed vā* (Uvās. § 200), elsewhere in verses only, as always in M. We may compare AMg. *kujjā = kuryắt* (§ 464), *dĕjjā = deyắt, hŏjjā = bhūyắt* (§ 466), thus it is clear that even *kuvvĕjjā* presupposes one **kurvyắt, karĕjjā* one **karyắt* and *havĕjjā* one **bhavyắt*; that is to say the optative in *-ĕjjā* goes back to the optative formed with *-yā-* of the second conjugation.[2] For *ĕ*, very often MSS give *i*, that is not possible to explain according to § 84, since the development has resulted from the 1. sing.; hence *-eye-* by no means originally existed in the form. Rather *ĕ*, according to § 119, has originated from *i*, that is a separation-vowel: AMg. *bhuñjĕjjā = *bhuñjiyắt, bhuñjyắt, karejjā = *karyắt = *karyắt*, likewise *jāṇijjā jāṇĕjja = jāniyắt.* The first conjugation too may have exercised its influence in the prevalent *e*-colouring. It is only in this manner that *ā* and the reduplication of *j* are explained.[3] On the remnant of the old flexion of the second conjugation and the precative see § 464. 465. 466.

1. KZ. 36,577.—2. Whether one derive *karyā't* from the present stem *kar* with JACOBI, or take it as = precative *kriyā't* with PISCHEL, KZ. 35,143, it is equally valid for the explanation. That I exactly meant, as JACOBI, is shown by the affix of the passive **karya'te* KZ. 35,141, what JACOBI has overlooked. The question is only about the equation *karjjaī: kriya'te = karĕjjā: kriyắt* (KZ. 35,143).—3. PISCHEL, KZ. 35,142 ff.

§ 460. Singular: 1. AMg. *āosĕjjā vā haṇĕjjā vā bandhĕjjā vā mahĕjjā vā tajjĕjjā vā tāḷĕjjā vā nicchoḍĕjjā vā nibbhacchĕjjā vā...varovĕjjā = ākrośeyaṁ vā hanyāṁ vā badhniyāṁ vā mathniyāṁ vā tarjayeyaṁ vā tāḍayeyaṁ vā niśchoṭayeyaṁ vā nirbhartsayeyaṁ vā...vyaparopeyam* (Uvās. § 200), *pāssijjā = paśyeyam* (Niraẏāv. § 3), *muccĕjjā = mucyeya*(passive, Uttar. 624), *aïvāĕjjā, aïvāẏāvĕjjā = atipātayeyaṁ, samaṇujāṇĕjjā = samanujāniyām* (Hc. 3,177); JM. *laṅghĕjja* (Āv. 8,18); M. *kuppĕjja = kupyeyaṁ* (H. 17); Ś. *bhaveyaṁ* (Vikr. 40.21; Pārvatīp. 29,9) and *bhave* (Śak. 65,10; Mālav. 67,10) = *bhaveyam, pahave = prabhaveyam* (Śak. 25,1), *laheaṁ* (Śak. 13,9; 30,9; Pārvatīp. 27,16; 29,8) and *lahe* (Mudrār. 38,2; cf. Vikr. 42,7?) = *labheya, jīveaṁ = jīveyam* (Mālav. 55,11), *kuppe = kupyeyam* (Mālav. 67,10).[1] Seldom *-mi* is the ending of the primary tense: M. *ṇĕjjāmi = nayeyam* (R. 3,55); AMg. *karĕjjāmi = kuryām* (Vivāhap. 1281).—2. In the 2. sing. the form ends in *-ijjā*, seldom in *-ĕjjā*; AMg. *udāharijjā = udāhareḥ* (Sūẏag. 932); *uvadaṁsĕjjā = upadarśayeḥ* (Āẏār. 1,5,5,4); *viṇaĕjja = vinayeḥ* (Dasav. 613,27). In AMg. the ending *-si* comes in usually: *paẏāĕjjāsi = prajāyethāḥ* (Nāẏādh. 420); *nivedijjāsi = nivedayeḥ* (Ovav. § 21); *samaṇuvāsĕjjāsi = samanuvāsayeḥ, uvalimpijjāsi = upalimpeḥ, parakkamĕjjāsi = parākrāmeḥ* (Āẏār. 1,2,1,5; 4,4; 5,3; 6,2 etc.); *vattĕjjāsi = vartethāḥ* (Uvāv. § 200).—Beside that stands the form in *-e*: *dāve = dāpayeḥ, paḍigāhe = pratigrāhayeḥ* (Kapas. S. § 14—16), almost always in verses only: *gaccha = gaccheḥ* (Sūẏag. 178); *pamāẏae = pramādayeḥ, āie = *ādriyeḥ = ādriyethāḥ, saṁbhare = saṁsmareḥ* (cf. § 267. 113), *care = careḥ* (Uttar. 310 ff. 332. 440. 504). Sometimes the form in *-ĕjjāsi* is used in the place of that in *-e* or in *-ĕjjā* at the end of verses corresponding to the paragraph in prose against the metre.[2] Thus *āmŏkkhāe*, *parivvaĕjjāsi* metrically false for *parivvae* (Sūẏag. 99.200.216); *ārambhaṁ ca susaṁvude carĕjjāsi*, metrically wrong for *care* (Sūẏag. 117); *no pāṇiṇaṁ paṇe samārabhĕjjāsi*, metrically wrong for *samārabhĕjjāsi* (Āẏār. 1, 3,2,3). Cf. besides in prose: Āẏār. 1,2,1,5; 4,4; 5,3; 6,2; 1,3; 1,4; 1,4,1,3; 3,3;1,5,2,5; 4,5; 6,1 etc. The 2. sing. in- *ĕjjāsi* occurs in JM. too: *uilagĕjjāsi* = **vilagyeḥ* (Erz. 29,12), *āhaṇĕjjāsi* (Āv. 11,1), *vaṭṭĕjjāsi* (Āv. 11,11), *pĕcchĕjjāsi* (Āv. 23,18).

1. PISCHEL, Die Recensionen der Cakuntalā p. 22 f.; BOLLENSEN on Mālav. p. 228. —2. JACOBI, who has not admitted the forms in *ĕjjāsi* in his edition of Āyār., thinks that *si* is to be separated and may stand for *se* = *asau* (SBE. 22,17, note 1). The scholiasts give the correct direction.

§ 461. Beṣides -*ĕjjāsi* there occurs in AMg. also -*ĕjjasi*: -*āosĕjjasi* = *ākrośeḥ*, *haṇĕjjasi* = *hanyāḥ*, *vavarovĕjjasi* = *vyaparopayeḥ* (Uvās. § 200). Moreover, the 2. sing. has the endings of the imperative -*hi* and in M. JM. A. especially -*su* (§ 467), before which the vowel is short or long: M. *hasĕjjahi* = *haseḥ* (Hc. 3, 175; Sr. fol. 50); AMg. *vandĕjjāhi* = *vandethāḥ*, *pajjuvāsĕjjāhi* = *paryupāsithāḥ*, *uvaṇimantĕjjāhi* = *upanimantrayeḥ* (Uvās. 187); JM. *vaccĕjjasu* = *vrajeḥ* (Āv. 25,20). *bhaṇĕjjasu* = *bhaṇeḥ* (Āv. 25, 31. 43); M. JM. *karĕjjāsu* (H. 154. 181. 634; Erz. 81, 10), JM. *karĕjjasu* (Sagara 7.5), M. *kuṇijjāsu* (Śukasaptati 48,4) = *kuryāḥ*, A. *karijjasu* (Piṅgala 1,39. 41. 95. 144 etc.); JM. *sāhijjasu* = *sādhaya* in the sense of *kathaya* (Kk. 272,19); M. *galijjāsu* = *galeḥ*, *pamhasijjāsu* = *prasmareḥ*, *pariharijjāsu* = *parihareḥ* (H. 103. 348. 521); A. *salahijjasu* = *ślāghasva*, *bhaṇijjasu* = *bhaṇa*, *ṭhavijjasu* = *sthāpaya* (Piṅgala 1,95. 109. 144), since in A. the passive is used in the sense of the active as well, many of these forms may be taken also as the imperative of the passive, as *muṇijjasu* beside *muṇiāsu* (§ 467), *dijjasu*(§ 466) on account of *i* by the side of *dĕjjahi*. A critical edition of the Piṅgala may some day reveal whether *i* or *ĕ* is to be read. The forms in -*ĕ*, -*i* in A., mentioned by Hc. 4,387 as of the imperative, likewise are of the old optative: *karĕ* = *kare* = **kareḥ* = *kuryāḥ* (Hc. 4,387) and thence *kari* (Prabandhac. 63,7; Śukasaptati 49,4) according to § 85. So: A. *viāri* = *vicārayeḥ*, *ṭhavi* = *sthāpayeḥ*, *dhari* = *dhārayeḥ*, really = **vicāreḥ*, **sthāpeḥ*, **dhāreḥ*, (Piṅgala 1, 68. 71. 72); *joi* = **dyoteḥ* = *paśya* (Hc. 4, 364. 368), *ruṇujhuṇi*, *roi* = **rodeḥ* = *rudyāḥ*, *cari* = *careḥ*, *mĕlli* in the sense of *tyajeḥ*, *kari* = **kaseḥ* = *kuryāḥ*, *kahi* = **katheḥ* = *kathayeḥ* (Hc. 4,368. 387, 1. 3. 422,14). The same formation is found in AMg. in a verse in *assāsi* (text *asāsi*, correctly in the commentary): *evam assāsi appāṇaṁ* (Uttar. 113), explained by the commentator as *evam ātmānam āśvāsaya*. Cf. *acchahiṁ*, *āḍhāhiṁ*, *parijāṇāhiṁ* (§ 456). Thus is explained also *puṇḍe* = *vraja* (Deśīn. 6,52) as optative. Cf. also *puḍa utsarge* Dhātupāṭha 28,90. *hassĕjje* = *haseḥ*, that is taught by Hc. 3,175; and Sr. fol. 50 as the imperative, is a double formation with the optative character of both the conjugations. Sr. teaches also *haseijjahi*, *haseijjasu*, *haseijje*.

§ 462. 3. sing. PG. *karĕyya*, *kāravĕjjā* (6,40); M. *jivĕjjā* = *jivet* (H. 588), *paavĕjja* = *pratapet*, *dharĕjja* = *dhriyeta*, *viharĕjja* = *viharet*, *ṇamĕjja* =

namet (R. 4, 28; 5, 4; 8, 4); JM. *vivajjĕjjā* = *vipadyeta*, *nirakkhijjā* = *nirikṣeta*, *sakkĕjja* = *śakyet* (Erz. 43, 22; 49, 35; 79, 1), *aïkkamijjā* = *atikrāmet* (Kk. 271,7); AMg. *kuppĕjjā* = *kupyet*, *parihareĕjjā* = *pariharet* (Āyār. 1,2, 4,4; 5,3), *karĕjjā* = **karyāt* = *kuryāt* (Āyār. 2,5,2, 2, 4. 5; Paṇṇav. 573; Vivāhap. 57. 1524. 1549 ff.), *karĕjja* (Āyār. 2,2,2,1), *labhĕjjā* = *labheta* (Kappas. S. § 18), passive: *ghĕppĕjjā* = *gṛhyeta* (Paṇhāv. 400); in verses often with a short final vowel: *rakkhĕjja* = *rakṣet*, *viṇaĕjja* = *vinayet*, *sevĕjja* = *seveta*; passive: *muccĕjja* = *mucyeta* (Uttar. 198. 199. 247); P. *huvĕyya* = *bhavet* (Hc. 4,320. 323); A. *caĕjja* = *tyajet*, *bhamĕjja* = *bhramet* (Hc. 4,418,6). Sr. fol. 51 gives also *hasĕjjaï*. Beside *-ĕjjā*, *-ĕjja* AMg. JM. often have forms in *-e* = *-et*: *gijjhe* = *gṛdhyet*, *harise* = *harṣet*, *kujjhe* = *krudhyet* (Āyār. 1,2,3,1.2), *kiṇe*, *kiṇāvae* = **krīṇet*, **krīṇāpayet* (Āyār. 1,2,5,3), especially in verses: *care* = *caret* (Āyār. 1,2,3,4; Uttar. 190. 567), *ciṭṭhe* = *tiṣṭhet*, *uvaciṭṭhe* = *upatiṣṭhet* (Uttar. 29. 30) beside *uvaciṭṭhĕjjā*, *ciṭṭhĕjjā* (Uttar. 34. 35), *labhe* = *labheta* (Uttar. 180); sometimes both the forms occur in the same verse: *acchiṁ pi no pamajjiẏā no vi ẏa kaṇḍuẏae muṇi gāẏaṁ* = *akṣy api no pramārjayen napi ca kaṇḍūyayen munir gātram* (Āyār. 1,8,1,19); JM. *parikkhae* = *parikṣeta*, *ḍahe* = *dahet*, *vināsae* = *vināśayet* (Erz. 31,21; 38,18). In Ś. Mg. is found only *-e*: Ś. very frequently *bhave* = *bhavet* (Mṛcch. 2,23; 51,23; 52,13; Śak. 20,3; 50,3.4;53,4; Vikr. 9,3;23, 5,16 etc.) *pūrae* = *pūrayet* (Mālav. 73, 18), *uddhare* = *uddharet* (Vikr. 6, 16)[1]; Mg. *bhave* = *bhavet* (Mṛcch. 164,6; 170,18. 19), *mūśe* = *mūṣet*, *khayye* = **khādyet* = *khāḍet* (Mṛcch. 119,16. 17)[2]. With the exception of *hŏjjā* (§ 466) JM. too hitherto has the opt. only in *-e*: *have* = *bhavet* (Pav. 387, 25; Kattig. 398,302. 309. 312. 315; 400,336; 401,338. 343. 345 ff. etc.), *ṇāsae* = *nāśayet* (Kattig. 401,341).

1. So we should read for *uddharedi* with the v. l., ed. Calc. 1830, Lenz, Sh. P. Pandit (6,7 *sam vdhdhare*), since *avi ṇāma* is joined with the optative only (Śak. 13,9; Vikr. 13, 18;40,21; Mālav, 44,1; Mahāv. 17,9; Mālatim. 56,2; 28,1,4; Mg. Mṛcch. 170,18) or future (Mālatim. 74,3; 100,1; 284,9) when a wish is intended to be expressed. The indicative (Veṇīs. 58,7) and the imperative (Mg.; Mṛcch. 114,16) denote an interrogation.— 2. Cf. Mṛcch. 121,3. where for *khajje* we should read *khayyedi* beside *mūśedi*.

§ 463. The 1. plur. occurs only in PG. *karĕyyāma* (7,41). For JM. Jacobi (Erz. xlvii) suggests (*pucchĕjjāmo*) and (*kahĕjjāmo*). Forms such as *rakkhemo* (Erz. 52,15) are not optative (Jacobi, Erz. s. v. *rakkhaï*), but indicative (§ 472). In the 2. plur. as in the 2. sing. the ending of the imp. enters: AMg. *bhavĕjjāha* = *bhaveta* (Nāẏādh. 912.915.918.920), *viharĕjjāha* = *vihareta* (915. 918), *gacchĕjjāha* = *gaccheta* (916. 918), *ciṭṭhĕjjāha* = *tiṣṭheta*, *uvāgacchĕjjāha* = *upāgaccheta* (921); JM. *pāĕjjāha* = *pāyayeta* (Erz. 38,1), and with *ă*: *khamĕjjaha* = *kṣamedhvam*, *ḍhoĕjjaha* = *ḍhaukedhvam*, *duhĕjjaha* = = *duhyāta* (Erz. 25,26; 26,16; 37,37), *kahĕjjaha* = *kathayeta* (Āv. 47,23), *bharijjaha* = **bhareta* (may you fill; Kk. 265,10); D *karĕjjāha* (Mṛcch. 99,24); A. *rakkhĕjjahu* (Hc. 4,350,2).—3. plur. AMg. *āgacchĕjjā* (Ṭhāṇ. 125: *logantiẏadevā.....ā°*); Ś. *bhave* = *bhaveyuḥ* (Vikr. 26,2; *akkharā.....visajjidā bhave*; Raṅganātha: *bhave ity atra bahuvacana ekavacanaṁ ca*); AMg. *manne* = *manyeran* (Sūẏag. 575. 576. 578.); *jaha ṇaṁ ee purisā* [text *purisā*] *manne*;

uncertain, since beforehand 575 *jahā ṇaṁ esa purise manne*), *samabhiloe* = *samabhilokayeyuḥ* (Vivāhap. 929; *te pĕcchāgā taṁ naṭṭiyaṁ... samabhiloĕ ttil hanta bhante samabhiloe*).

§ 464. The old formation of the optative of the 2. conjugation has been retained in a few verbs in AMg. JM. So particularly the very frequent AMg. *siyā* = *syāt* (e. g. Āyār. 1,1,2,2; 6,3; Vivāhap. 39,40. 146f. etc.; Kappas.), also *asiyā* = *na syāt* (Āyār. 1,5, 5, 2); AMg *kujjā* = *kuryāt* (e. g. Āyār. 1,2,6,1; Uttar. 28. 29. 198; Dasav. 613, 15; Kappas. etc.), also in *pāukujjā* = *prāduṣkuryāt* (Suyag. 474); AMg. *būyā* = *brūyāt* (e. g. Āyār. 1,4,2,6; 1,5,5,3), especially frequent in the combination *kevalī būyā* (Āyār. p. 72. 77 f. 132ff.); besides AMg. *haṇiyā* = *hanyāt* (Āyār. 1,3,2,3), found sporadically in verses, beside *haṇijjā* (Jīv. 295; Uttar. 198), *haṇĕjjā* (Paṇhāv. 396. 397), JM. *āhaṇĕjjāsi* (Āv. 11, 1) and AMg. *haṇe* (Āyār. 1,2, 6,5; 1,3,2,3). A 2. sing with the ending *-hi* of the imperative is AMg. *ĕjjāhi* = *eyāḥ* (Āyār. 2,5,1,10; Erz. 29,5).

§ 465. An old optative is the hitherto obscure Pāli, AMg. JM. *sakkā*. CHILDERS[1] wished to take it as a past passive participle = *śakta*, which became an indeclinable, PISCHEL[2] considered it as a shortened dative sing., and FRANKE[3], with whom JOHANSSON agrees, takes it as the nom. sing. fem., which has become the nom. plur. neut. It is accurately = Vedic *śakyāt* and is appropriately used as the opt. in earliest writings. So: AMg. *na sakkā na souṁ saddā soyavisayaṁ āgayā* "the sounds, that have come within the reach of hearing cannot be not-heard" (Āyār. p. 136,14); *na sakkā rūvam adaṭṭhuṁ cakkhuvisayam āgayam* "one cannot not see a form that has come within the range of eye-sight" (Āyār. p. 136, 22; cf. p. 136,31; 137,7. 18); *egassa dŏṇha tiṇha va saṁkhĕjjāṇa va pāisuṁ sakkā disanti sarirāiṁ ṇioyajivāṇ' aṇantāṇaṁ* "one can see one, two or three or numerable (ṇioya- beings), they see bodies of unending number of many ṇioya- being.[1]; *kiṁ sakkā kāuṁ je jaṁ nĕcchaha osahaṁ muhā pāuṁ* "what can one do there, when you do not like to drink medicine in vain" (Paṇhāv. 329; cf. Dasav. N. 644,28). Cf. also Nāyādh. § 87. JM. *kiṁ sakkā kāuṁ* "what can one do" (Āv. 30,10); *na sakkā eeṇa uvāeṇaṁ* "it cannot be done by this means" (Āv. 35,11); *na yā sakkā pāuṁ so vā anne vā* "and neither he nor others can drink" (Āv. 42,8; cf. 42, 28 *na vi appaṇo pivaï na vi annaṁ sakkei jūhaṁ pāuṁ*). In consequence of the phonetic resemblance with *sakkaï* = *śakyate* the infinitive is later used in the passive sense. So: *ṇo khalu se sakkā keṇaī subāhueṇa vi uraṁ ureṇaṁ giṇhittae* "he could not be caught breast to breast even by a very strong person" (Vivāgas. 127); *no khalu se sakkā keṇaī...nigganthāo pāvayaṇāo cālittae vā khobhittae vā vipariṇāmittae vā* "he could not by anybody be staggered or made waver from or made disloyal to his faith in Jainism (Uvās. § 113), and the same change in the first pers. sing., as in the other opt. in *ā*, in *ṇo khalu ahaṁ sakkā...cālittae...* (Nāyādh. 765. 770). Cf. further Uvās. § 119. 174; Dasav. 636,25. Manifestly an exactly similar development takes place in the case of AMg. *cakkiyā*, about whose optative character there cannot be any doubt. So: *eyaṁsi ṇaṁ bhante dhammatthikāyaṁsi...cakkiyā kei āsittae vā ciṭṭhittae vā*..."can, O Lord, anybody sit or stand in this religious organisation?" (Vivāhap. 513;cf. 1119.1120.1346.1389); *erāvai kuṇālāe jattha cakkiyā siyā egaṁ pāyaṁ jale kiccā egaṁ pāyaṁ thale kiccā evaṁ cakkiā* "when there (is a stream) like the Airāvatī in Kuṇālā, where he (can go across), he should go across it with one foot in the water and one foot on the dry land" (Kappas. S. § 12; cf. §13). *cakkiyā* stands for **cakiyā* = **cakyāt* according to § 195, belongs to M. *caaï* (can; is capable; Vr. 8,70 [so to read for *vaaï*] Hc. 4,86; Kī. 4,60; R.) = **cakati*, from which Aśoka has *caghati* for **cakhati* with aspiration according to § 206[5]. I derive *caaï* = **takati* from *taki sahane* (Dhātupāṭha 5,2; cf. Patañjali on Pāṇini 3,1,97, ed. KIELHORN 2,82) with palatal for dental according to § 216.—Accordingly Pāli, AMg., *labbhā* = **labhyāt* too is opt., like AMg. *savve pāṇā...na bhayadukkhaṃ ca kiṁci labbhā pāveuṁ*, "may no creature experience the least fear and grief" (Paṇhāv. 363; Abhayadeva: *labhyā yogyo* [sic; read *yogyāḥ*]); *na tāiṁ samaṇeṇa labbhā daṭṭhuṁ na kaheuṁ na vi ya sumareuṁ* "a mendicant should not see it, should not talk about it and should not even think about it" (Paṇhāv.466; Abhayadeva—*labbha tti labhyāni ucitāni*); *dugaṁchāvattiyā vi labbhā uppāeuṁ* (ed. *uppāteu*; Paṇhāv. 526; Abhayadeva : *labhyā ucitā yogyetyarthaḥ*), for which at 537 f. stands : *na duguṁchāvattiy avvaṁ labbhā uppāeuṁ* "he should not excite the feeling of abhorrence".

1. Dictionary s. v. *sakko* p. 420.—2 Ved. Stud. 1,328—3. BB, 17,256.—4. BB. 20,91.—5. MORRIS, Journal of the Pāli Text Society 1891—3, p. 28 ff., who at p. 30 wrongly maintains that I had erroneously equated, under Hc. 4,86, *caaï*=*tyajati*. where I have just translated Hc. and have expressly separated *caaï* from its other synonyms. Cf. also KERN, Jaartelling p. 96. Wrong GRIERSON, Academy 1890, No. 964, p. 369. WACKERNAGEL, Altind. Gr. p. xx, note 9 compares Greek τέχνη.

§ 466. Of the precative too, which is used in the sense of the optative, only a few remnants have survived mostly in AMg. and JM. So PG. *hoja* (7,48); M. *hŏjja* (R. 3,32; 11,27 28.120); AMg. JM. *hŏjjā*, *hŏjja* = *bhūyāt* (Ṭhān. 98; Vivāhap. 729 ff.; Dasav. 620,27. 28; 621,36; Erz. 35,81; 37,37; 70,14). The same form is in JM. also 1. sing. : *cakkavaṭṭi hŏjjāhaṁ* (Erz. 4,28) and in AMg. JM. 3. plur. : *savve vi tāva hŏjjā kohovaüttā, lobhovaüttā* = *sarve 'pi tāvad bhūyāsuḥ krodhopayuktāḥ lobhopayuktāḥ* (Vivāhap. 84 [where text *hŏjja*; cf. WEBER, Bhag. 1,430]. 92. 109); *kevaïyā hŏjjā* = *kiyanto bhūyāsuḥ* (Vivāhap. 734. 738; cf. 753 ff.); JM. *kiha dhūyāo suhiyāo hŏjja* = *kathaṁ duhitaraḥ sukhitā bhūyāsuḥ* (Āv. 10, 23; cf. 12,2). AMg. JM., however, form the 1. sing. also *hŏjjāmi* (Dasav. 621,43; Erz. 29,19), JM. the 2. sing *hŏjjāsi* (Erz. 29,14; 37,9), *hŏjjāhi* (Āv. 10,42) and *hŏjjasu* (Erz. 23,4), as in the optative of the present. AMg. has also *hŏjjāi* (Vivāhap. 1042) and a participle *hŏjjamāṇa* in the sense of the present (Vivāhap. 733 ff.; 1736 ff.; Paṇṇav. 521). JŚ. *hŏjjā* (Pav. 385,69; text *hŏjjaṁ*). In places where *hŏjja* is found in Ś. (Mallikām. 84,1; 87,5;109,4;114,14;156,20) it is against the dialect. AMg. *dĕjjā* = *deyāt* (Āyār. 2,1,2,4; 11,5), in addition to which JM. has the 2. sing. *dĕjja* (Āv. 12,6), *dĕjjāsi* (Erz. 37,9), A. has *dĕjjahi* (Hc. 4,383,3), *dijjasu* (Piṅgala 1,36. 121; 2,119; cf. § 461), JM. has the 2. plur. *dĕjjaha* (Erz. 61,27). AMg. *saṁdhĕjjā* = *saṁdheyāt* (Sūyag. 223), *ahiṭṭĕjjā* = *adhiṣṭheyāt* (Ṭhāṇ. 368), *pahĕjja* = *praheyāt* (Uttar. 199). Perhaps also A. *kijjasu* = *kriyāḥ*, in case it is not taken rather as an imperative of the passive (§ 461. 467. 547. 550). The grammarians (Vr. 7,21; Hc. 3,165. 178; Kī 4,29. 30; Sr. fol. 48) teach, besides *hŏjjā* and *hŏjja* also the forms *hŏjjaï*, *hŏjjāi*, *hŏjjaü*, *hŏjjāu hŏjjasi*, *hŏjjāsī*, Kī. 4,29 also *hŏjjaia*, *hŏjjāia*, Sr. also *hoĕjja*, *hoĕjjā*, *huejja*, *huĕjjā*, *hujja*, *hujjā*, *hujjaïre*, *hujjāire huejjaīre*, *huĕjjāire* (§ 458), the forms that are found partly in the text only and according to Hc. 3,177; Sr. fol. 49 there stand *hŏjjā* and *hŏjja* in the sense of the ind., opt., imp. and imperf. pres., of the aor., perf. prec., future I and II, and of the conditionalis. Cf. with this KIELHORN, IA. XVII, p. 135; Inscriptiones Sanskrites du Combodge, Index, p.[625] 445, column 2.I owe this reference to KIELHORN. Thus in fact there stands AMg. *dĕjjā* in the sense of *adāt* (Uttar. 621), and *būẏā* in the combination *kevali būẏā* (§ 464) in the sense of *braviti* or *abravit*, and through this it appears so inexplicable, that even AMg. *care* (Uttar. 532. 549. 552), *pahaṇe* (Uttar. 561), *udāhare* (Uttar. 674) and *pucche* (Vivāhap. 149. 150; Rāmacandra = *pṛṣṭavān*, the forms that undoubtably stand in the preterite, in addition to *acchia*, *gĕṇhia*, *daliddāia*, *maria*, *hasia*, *huvia*, *dehia* mentioned by grammarians in the sense of the imperf., aorist and perfect (Vr. 7,23; Hc. 3,163 Kī. 4,22. 23. 25; Mk. fol. 52) are optative of the present, *kāhia*, *ṭhāhia*, *hohia* (Vr. 7,24; Hc. 3,162; Kī. 4,23. 24; Mk. fol. 51) are optative of the aorist. What is right has already been substantially noticed by LASSEN (Instit. p. 353 ff.) who wanted to explain the forms in *-ia* as in the precative. AMg. *acche*, *abbhe* (Āẏār. 1,1,2,5), which stand in the sense of the optative = *ācchindyāt*, *abhindyāt*, reversely may be old aorist, which are regulated by Vedic *chedma* and *abhet*. The explanation as the 3. sing. imperf. or aorist[1] leaves the form as obscure as the explanation as the optative the meaning[2].

1. WEBER, Bhag. 1.430, and according to him E. MÜLLER, Beiträge p. 60; JACOBI, Āẏār. p. xii, both of whom, according to WEBER, give *kare*, although, according to Bhag. 2,301, it is clearly an error for *karenti* (MS *kareti*); the edition reads at p. 173 *kerei*.—2. In the sense of preterite stands *prabrūẏāt* (Hastyāyurveda 2,60, 2) ; at parallel places stands *provāca* or *abravīt*.

4. IMPERATIVE.

§ 467. The paradigm is :

	Sing.	Plur.
1.	[*vaṭṭāmu*, *vaṭṭamu*]	AMg. JM. *vaṭṭāmo*; M. Ś. Mg. Ḍh., also JM. *vaṭṭamha*, *vaṭṭĕmha*
2.	*vaṭṭa*, *vaṭṭasu*, *vaṭṭesu*, *vaṭṭehi*, AMg. also *vaṭṭāhi*, A. *vaṭṭu*, *vaṭṭahi*	*vaṭṭaha*; Ś. Mg. [Ḍh] *vaṭṭadha*, *vaṭṭedha*; A. *vaṭṭahu*, *vaṭṭehu*; CP. *vaṭṭatha*
3.	*vaṭṭaü*, Ś. Mg. Ḍh. *vaṭṭadu*	*vaṭṭantu*, A. also *vaṭṭahĩ*

The 1. sing. can be located only in the grammarians who mention *hasāmu*, *pĕcchāmu* (Hc. 3,173), *hasamu* (Bh. 7,18; Kī. 4,26; Sr. fol. 51) as

examples. As regards correctness of this form, there is less to be doubted, than the 2. sing. in *-su* used all the dialects, especially in M., as also in the optative (§ 461). This form has hitherto been considered to be in the ātmanepada and the ending *-su*, we have been equating as = Skt. *-sva*, hence *rakkhasu* = *rakṣasva*[1]. The circumstance, that this ending is found also with the verbs, that are never conjugated in the ātmanepada in Skt. and further that it frequently occurs in Ś. Mg., that otherwise use little of ātmanepadam, shows that this is wrong. The endings *-mu*, *-su -u* correspond to the endings *-mi*, *-si*, *-i* of the indicative. M. *viramasu* = *virama*, *rajjasu* = *rajyasva* (H. 149), *rakkhasu* = *rakṣa* (H. 297), *parirakkhasu* = *parirakṣa* (R. 6,15), *osarasu* = *apasara* (H. 451); M. JM. Ś. *karesu* = *kuru* (H. 48; Sagara 3,12; Kk. 273, 41; Ratn. 299,5; 316,6; 328,24; Karṇas. 21,7; 30,5;37,20; Veṇīs. 98,15; Pras. 84,9 etc.); M. *aṇuṇesu* = *anunaya* (H. 152. 946); Ś. *āṇesu* = *ānaya* (Śak. 125,8[2]; Karṇas. 51,17), *avaṇesu* = *apanaya* (Viddhaś. 48,10); M. AMg. JM. Ś. *bhuñjasu* = *bhuṅgdhi* (H. 316; Uttar. 369; Āv. 12,14; Mṛcch. 70,12); AMg. *jāsu* = *yāhi* (Sūyag. 177); AMg. *kahasu* (Uttar. 700. 703), Ś. *kadhesu* (Bālar. 53,12; 164,17; 218,16; Karṇas. 37,7. 12) = *kathaya*, AMg. *saddahasu* = *śraddhehi* (Sūyag. 151); JM. *khamasu* = *kṣamasva* (Sagara 3,12; Dvār. 497,13), *uarasu* = *vṛṇīṣva* (Sagara 1,15), *sarasu* = *smara* (Āv. 7,34); M. JM. *kuṇasu* = *kuru* (H. 607. 771; Sagara 6,2. 11. 12; Kk. 266, 16; 274,27); Mg. *lahkaśu* = *rakṣa* (Caṇḍak. 69,1), *āgaśceśu* (Mṛcch. 116,5) = *āgaccha*, *deśu* Prab. 58,8; B. *dessu*, P. M. Bb. *dehi*), *dihkaśu* (Prab. 58, 18: B. *dikkhassu*, P. *dikkhassa*, M. *dikkhehi*, Bb. *dikkhaya*) = *dikṣaya*, *dhāleśu* (Prab. 60, 10; B. *dhālĕssu*, P. Bb. *dhālesu*, M. *dāvaa*) = *dhāraya*; A. *kijjasu* = *kuru* (passive in the sense of the active § 550; Piṅgala 1,39; 2,119. 120), *muṇiāsu*, metrically for *muṇiasu*, passive of *muṇ* (§ 489) in the sense of the active (Piṅgala 1,111,112) beside *muṇijjasu* (2,119), *bujjhasu* = *budhyasva* (Piṅgala 2,120). In Ś. in the texts we find, more than once, ātmanepada forms in *-ssa*, as *uvālahassa* (Śak. 11,4), *avalambassa* (Śak. 119,13; 133,8), *pĕkkhassa* (Prab. 56,14), *paḍivajjassa* (Veṇīs. 72,19), also *parirambhassu* (Viddhaś. 128,6), and many others in Indian editions. We should see in them examples of Sanskritisms, that should be removed from the texts. The v. l. has mostly the correct reading. In AMg. the imp. in *-su* is seen only in verses.

1. LASSEN, Inst. P. 179. 338; WEBER, Hāla[1] p. 61; JACOBI, Erz. § 54; BLOCH, Vr. und Hc. p. 43—2. So to be read with R; cf. BLOCH l. c. p. 43.

§ 468. If the stem ends in a short vowel, as a rule, as in Śak., it is used as the 2. sing. imp.; if it ends in a long vowel, the ending *-hi* comes in. In AMg. mostly and in M. JM. Mg. sometimes, the *a*-stems take the ending *-hi*, before which *a* is lengthened. A. too has this formation frequently; here, however, *ā* is again shortened. In Ś. Mg. the ending *-āhi* appears beside *-a* in the case of the roots of the ninth conjugation and those formed on their analogy, in connection with the 3. sing. in *-ādu*. In Ḍh. and A. final *a* becomes *u* (§ 106): M. AMg. JM. Ś. Mg. *bhaṇa*, A. *bhaṇu* (H. 163. 400; Nāyādh. 260; Āv. 15,3; Śak. 50,9; 114,5; Piṅgala 1,62; Hc. 4,401,4), but D. Ś. Mg. also *bhaṇāhi* (D. Mṛcch. 100,4; on Ś. Mg. see § 514). A. *bhaṇahī* (Vikr. 63,4); Ā. *ciṭṭha* = *tiṣṭha*, *ehi*, *vāhehi* (Mṛcch. 99,18. 20;100, 18); AMg. Ś. *gaccha*, (Uvās. § 58. 259; Lalitav. 561,15; Śak. 18,2; Mṛcch. 38,22; 58,2), Mg. *gaśca* (Mṛcch. 38, 22; 79,14), but AMg. also *gacchāhi* (Uvās. § 204) ; M. JM. *pĕccha* (H. 725; Āv. 18,12); Ś. D. *pĕkkha* (Śak. 58,7; Mṛcch. 17,20; 42,2; D. 100,14), Mg. *pĕska* (Mṛcch. 12,16,13,6;21, 15), A. *pĕkkhu* (Hc. 4,419,6) and *pĕkkhahi* (Piṅgala 1,61); M. Ś. *hasa* (H. 818; Nāgān. 33,5), Mg. *haśa* (Mṛcch. 21,4) ; Mg. *piva* = *piba* (Prab. 60,9) and *pivāhi* (Veṇīs. 34,2. 15), *palittāāhi* = *paritrāyasva* (Mṛcch. 175, 22; 176,5. 10); M. *rua* (H. 895) beside *ruehi* (784) and *ruasu* (143. 885. 909), Ś. *roda* Mṛcch. 95,15; Nāgān. 24,8. 12) = *rudihi*; AMg. *vigiñca* = **vikṛntya* = *vikṛnta* (Āyār. 1,2.4,3; Uttar. 170), *jāṇāhi* = *jānīhi* (Āyār. 1,2,1,5), *bujjhāhi* = *budhyasva*, *vasāhi* = *vasa*, *harāhi* = *hara*, *vandāhi* = *vandasva*, *akkamāhi* = *ākrāma* (Kappas. § 111. 114; Ovav. § 53; Uvās § 58. 204; Nīrayāv. § 22) ; JM. *viharāhi* = *vihara* (Āv. 11,6) : M. JM. AMg. Ś. *karehi* (H. 225, 900; Āv. 11,4; Kk. s. v. *kar*; Ovav. § 40; Mṛcch. 66,14; 325,18; 326,10; Śak. 78, 14,153,13), Mg. *kalehi* (Mṛcch. 31,8;123,10; 176,5) ; A. *karāhi*, *karahi* (Piṅgala 1,149; Hc. 4,385) and *karu* (Hc. 4,330, 2); D. *oṇāmehi* = *avanāmaya* (Mṛcch. 102,2) ; AMg. *paḍikappehi* = *pratikalpaya*, *saṁṇāhehi* = *saṁnāhaya*, *uvaṭṭhāvehi* = *upasthāpaya*, *kāravehi* = *kāraya* (Ovav. § 40), *roehi* = *rocaya* (Vivāhap. 134); JM. *pucchehi* = *pṛccha* (Kk. 272,31), *maggehi* = *mārgaya*, *viyāṇehi* = *vijānīhi* (Erz. 59,6; 71,12); Ś. *mantehi* = *mantraya*, *kadhehi* = *kathaya* (Lalitav. 554,8; 565,15), *siḍhilehi* = *śithilaya* (Śak. 11,1; Veṇīs. 76,4), *jālehi* = *jvālaya* (Mṛcch. 25,18); Mg. *mālehi* = *māraya* (Mṛcch. 123,15; 165,24), *ghośehi* = *ghoṣaya* (Mṛcch. 162, 9) ; Ḍh. *pasalu* = *prasara* (text °*ru*; Mṛcch. 32,16), whilst elsewhere the MSS wrongly give -*a* in the final syllable : *gĕṇha* (29,16,30,2), *paaccha* (31,4. 7, 9; 32,3. 8. 12.14; 34,24; 35,7), *āaccha* (39,17); *dehi* (32,23; 36,15); A. *suṇehi* = *śṛṇu* (Piṅgala 1,62) ; M. JM. Ś. *hohi* = **bhodhi* = Vedic *bodhi* = *bhava* (H. 259. 372; Erz. 11,31; 39,24; Mṛcch. 54,12. Śak. 67,2; 70,9; Vikr. 8,8; 12,12; 23,6 etc). On the ostensible imp. in -*e*, -*i* in A. see § 461.

§ 469. The 3 sing. ends in -*u*, in Ś. Mg. D. Ḍh. in -*du* = -*tu* : M. *maraü* = *mriyatām* (H. s. v. *mar*), *paaṭṭaü* = *pravartatām* (R. 3,58), *deu* = **dayatu* (G. 58); AMg. *pāsaü* = *paśyatu* (Kappas. § 16), *āpucchaü* = *āpṛcchatu* (Uvās. § 68), *viṇeu* = *vinayatu* (Nāyādh. § 97. 98) ; JM. *kiraü* = *kriyatām*, *suvvaü* = *śrūyatām* (Erz. 15,9; 17,14); *deu* = **dayatu* (Kk. II, 508,29), *suyaü* = *svapitu* (Dvār. 503,3); Ś. *pasīdadu* = *prasīdatu* (Lalitav. 561,9; Śak. 120,11), *āruhadu* = *ārohatu* (Uttarar. 32,6.7), *kadhedu* = *kathayatu* (Śak. 121,10), *suṇādu* = *śṛṇotu* (Vikr. 5,9;72,14; 80,12; Veṇīs. 12,5; 59,23 etc.); D. *gacchadu* (Mṛcch. 101,1); Mg. *muñcadu* = *muñcatu*, *śuṇādu* = *śṛṇotu*, *ṇisīdadu* = *niṣīdatu* (Mṛcch. 31,18. 21;27,3; 38,9) ; A. *ṇandaü* = *nandatu* (Hc. 4,422,14), *dijjaü* = *dīyatām*, *kijjaü* = *kriyatām* (Piṅgala 1, 81[a]); M. JM. AMg. A. *hou*, Ś. Mg. Ḍh. *bhodu* = *bhavatu* (M. H. R.; Hc. s. v. *bhū*; JM. Erz. 18, 12; Kk. s. v. *ho*; AMg. Kappas. Nāyādh. s. v. *ho*;

Ś. Mṛcch. 4,23; Śak. 24,13; Vikr. 6,17; Mg. Mṛcch. 38,8; 79,18; 80,4; Ḍh. Mṛcch. 30,14. 18;31, 19.22; 34,20).

§ 470. As 1. plur. imp. in AMg. and partly in JM. is used the 1. plur. indicative: AMg. *gacchāmo...vandāmo namaṁsāmo sakkāremo saṁmāṇemo...pajjuvāsāmo* = *gacchāma...vandāmahai namasyāma satkārayāma saṁmānayāma...paryupāsāmahai* (Vivāhap. 187.263; Ovav. § 38), *giṇhāmo* = *gṛhṇāma*, *sājjāmo* = **svādyāmahai* = *svādāmahai* (Ovav. § 86), *jujjhāmo* = *yudhyāmahai* (Nirayāv. § 25); JM. *harāmo* = *harāma* (Erz. 37,11), *gacchāmo* = *gacchāma*, *pavisāmo* = *praviśāma* (Sagara 5,1.6). Vr. 7. 19 and Hc. 3,176 know only the ending *-āmo*: *hasāmo*, *tuvarāmo*; Sr. fol. 51 also *hasimo*, *hasemo*, *hasamo*, as in the indicative. Thus we find AMg. *bhuñjimo* = *bhuñjāma* (verse; Uttar. 675); JM. *nijjhāmemo* = *niḥkṣāmayāma* (Dvār.505, 9), *karemo* (Erz. 2.27; 5,35), *pūremo* = *pūrayāma* (Sagara 3,17); AMg. *homo* (Uttar. 678 = Dasav. 613,34). The proper ending of the imp. is *-mha*, that has not been attested in AMg,; in M. JM. it is found very seldom; therefore, it has not been mentioned by Vr. Hc. Sr.[1]: on the other hand, the only form occurring in Ś. Mg. Ḍh. is prescribed by Mk. fol. 70 for Ś. A rich collection from Mṛcch., Śak., Vikr., Mālav., Ratn. has been given by BLOCH.[2] M. *abbhatthěmha* = *abhyarthayāma* (R. 4,48); JM. *ciṭṭhamha* = *tiṣṭhāma*, *gacchamha* = *gacchāma* (Erz. 14,33; 60,21);[3] Ś. *gacchamha* (Mṛcch. 75,3; Śak. 67,10; 79,8; 115,3; Vikr. 6,14; 18,13; Mālav. 30,12; 32,13; Ratn. 294,8; 295,11; 303,20; 312,24 etc.), *uvavisamha* = *upaviśāma* (Śak. 18,9), *uvasappamha* = *upasarpāma* (Śak. 79,11; Vikr. 24, 3; 41,14: Nāgān. 13,8; Bālar. 216,1), *pěkkhamha* = *prekṣāmahai* (Mṛcch. 42,14; Vikr. 31,14; 32,5; Ratn. 303,25 etc.), *karěmha* = *karavāma* (Śak. 81,16; Vikr. 6,15; 10,15; 53,14; Ratn. 303,21; Prab. 63,11; Veṇīs. 9,23 etc.), *ṇiveděmha* = *nivedayāma* (Śak. 160,7 [so to be read]; Mālav. 45,15; 293,29; 309,26), *adivāhěmha* = *ativāhayāma* (Ratn. 299,32), *hŏmha* = *bhavāma* (Śak. 26,14; Vikr. 36,12); Mg. *aṇṇeśamha*[4] = *anveṣayāma* (Mṛcch. 171,18), *pivamha* = *pibāma* (Veṇīs. 35,22), *palāamha* = *palāyāmahai* (Caṇḍak. 72,2), *kalěmha* (Mṛcch. 167,19; 168,7; 170,21, Caṇḍak. 68,15; Veṇīs. 36, 6); Ḍh. *aṇusalěmha* = *anusarāma* (Mṛcch. 30,13; 36,19), Ḍh. Mg. Ś. *kiḷěmha* = *krīḍāma* (Mṛcch. 30,18; 94,15; 131,18), Ḍh. Mg. *ṇiveděmha* (Mṛcch. 36,22; 171,11). Forms in *-mo* and *-ma* that are found in manuscripts and editions sporadically, as *pěkkhāmo* (Mālav. 15,17), Mg. *pěskāmo* (Mṛcch. 119,1), *pavisāmo* (Mālav. 39,19; v.l. *pavissamha*; Sh. P. PANḌIT 75, 2 correctly *pavisamha*; cf. Ratn. 294,17; 302,29; Nāgān. 27,7; Mahāv. 35, 17), *avakkamāma* (Mālav. 48,18; correctly *avakkamamha* (Mṛcch. 22,2), *ṇivārema* (Mālav. 62,13; v.l. *ṇivārěhmi*), Mg. *ṇaccāmo* (Prab. 61,7; ed. M. 72,22 correctly *ṇaccamha*)[5] are likewise wrong in the imp., like the forms in *-mha* for the ind. (§ 455). If, therefore *-mha* is related to the imperative only, its derivation from *smaḥ* (we are)[6] is wrong. *-mha* is = *-sma* of the aorist and one *ṇěmha* = **neṣma* (§ 474) is regulated exactly in the same manner as Vedic *jeṣma*, *geṣma deṣma*, used only imperatively and according to the 2. sing. *neṣa*, *parṣa* (WHITNEY § 894c. 896: cf. also NEISSER, BB.20,70 ff.). A. uses the 1. plur. of the ind. : *jāhũ* = *yāma* (Hc. 4,386).

1. Ś. Mg., in which the imp. in *-mha* is everywhere frequent, are treated by these grammarians very little. It is, therefore, not astonishing that this form is not mentioned by them, a thing that BLOCH, Vr. und Hc. p.43 has severely criticised.—2. l.c.p.44 unfortunately with many wrong quotations and without distinguishing between the three dialects. The examples given above have been selected in view of this.—3. Overlooked by JACOBI, Erz. p. XLVII.—4. For Mg., according to Hc. 4,289, *aṇṇeśasma, pivasma, kaleśma* etc. would be expected. Cf., however, § 314.—5. More in BLOCH, l.c. p. 45.—6. BOPP, Vgl. Grammatik II,120; BURNOUF and LASSEN, Essai sur le Pali (Paris 1826) p. 180 f.; HOEFER, De Prakrita dialecto § 187 nota III; LASSEN, Inst. § 117,2; BRUGMANN, Grundriss II,[1] 1354, note 1; BLOCH. l. c. p. 46 f.

§ 471. As 2. plur. the 2nd plur. of the ind. (§ 456) is used M. *ṇamaha* (G. H. R.; Karp. 1,7), A. *namahu* (Hc. 4,446), CP. *namatha* (Hc. 4,326); M. *rañjeha* = *rañjayata*, *raeha* = *racayata*, *deha* = **dayata* (H. 780); M. *uaha* = **upata*[1] = *paśyata* (Bh. 1,14; Deśīn. 1,98; Triv. 2,1,75; G. H.; Śak. 2,14); also *uvaha* (Sr. fol. 45; Karp. 67,8; Pratāp. 205,9; 212,10; v. l. to H.); AMg. *haṇaha khaṇaha chaṇaha ḍahaha paẏaha ālumpaha vilumpaha sahasakkāreha viparāmusaha* = *hata khanata kṣaṇuta dahata pacata ālumpata vilumpata sahasātkārayata viparāmṛśata* (Sūyag. 596; cf. Āẏār. 1,7,2,4), *khamāha* = *kṣamadhvam* (Uttar. 366. 367), *tāḷeha* = *tāḍayata* (Nāẏādh. 1305); JM. *acchaha* = *ṛcchata* (Āv. 14,30), *kaṇḍūẏaha* (Erz. 36,21), *ciṭṭhaha, āisaha, giṇhaha* = *tiṣṭhata, ādiśata, gṛhṇita* (Kk. 264,11.12), *ṭhaveha, daṁseha* = *sthāpayata, darśayata* (Kk. 265,7; 274,21); Ś. *parittāadha* = *paritrāyadhvam* (Śak. 16,10; 17,6; Vikr. 3,17; 5,2; Mālatīm. 130,3), Mg. *palittāadha* (Mṛcch. 32,25); AMg. JM. *kareha* (Kappas.; Uvās.; Nāẏādh.; Kk. 270, 45), AMg. also *kuvvahā* (Āẏār. 1,3,2,1), A. *karehu* (Piṅgala 1,122), *karahu* (Hc. 4,346; Piṅgala 1,102. 107), *kuṇehu* (Piṅgala 1,90. 118), *kuṇahu* (text °*ha*; Piṅgala 1,16. 53. 79), Mg. *kaledha* (Mṛcch. 32,15; 112,2; 140,23); Ś. *paattadha* = *prayatadhvam* (Śak. 52,15), *samassasadha* = *samāśvasita* (Vikr. 7,1), *avaṇedha* = *apanayata*, *hodha* = *bhavata*, *māredha* = *mārayata* (Mṛcch. 40,24; 97,23; 161,16); Mg. *ośaladha* = *apasarata* (Mṛcch. 96,21. 23; 97, 1; 134,24. 25; 157,4. 12 etc.; Mudrār. 153,5; 256,4 [so to be read]; Caṇḍak. 64,5), *śuṇādha* = *śṛṇuta* (Lalitav. 565,17; 566,5; Mṛcch. 158,19; Prab. 46, 14. 16), *māledha* = *mārayata* (Mṛcch. 165, 123; 166, 1)[2]. Ḍh. *ramaha* (Mṛcch. 39,17) is with BLOCH[3]; to be emended as *ramamha* A. *piahu* = *pibata* (Hc. 4, 422, 20), *ṭhavahu* = *sthāpayata*, *kaheḥu* = *kathayata* (Piṅgala 1,119. 122). D. has *āacchadha* = *āgacchata* beside *jatteha* = *yatadhvam*, *karĕjjāha* = *kuruta*, *johaha* (Mṛcch. 99, 24; 100,3).—The 3. plur. ends in all dialects in *-ntu*: M. *dĕntu* = **dayantu* (G. 44), *ṇandantu, vilihantu* (Karp. 1,1. 4); AMg. *bhavantu* (Vivāhap. 508), *ṇijjantu* = *niryāntu*, *phusantu* = *spṛśantu* (Ovav. § 47. 87), *suṇantu* = *śṛṇvantu* (Nāẏādh. 1134); Ś. *pasīdantu* = *prasīdantu* (Mudrār. 253,4), *pĕkkhantu* = *prekṣantām* (Mṛcch. 4,3), *hŏntu* = *bhavantu* (Vikr. 87,21); Mg. *paśīdantu* = *prasīdantu* (Śak. 113,5); A. *pīḍantu* (Hc. 4,385), and the ind. *lehĩ* Hc. 4,387,3)[4].

1. PISCHEL on Hc. 2,211. Wrong WEBER, Hāla[1] p. 29, note 4 and on Hāla 4.—2. On Ś. cf. PISCHEL, KB. 8,134 ff.—3. Vr. und Hc. p. 45.—4. In case one reads *jaṁ* for *je* here we have a case of the indicative.

§ 472. As remarked in § 452, the *a*-stems have become prevalent through coalescence of the 1. and 2. conjugations. Beside them, except in A., the *e*-stems have undergone wide extension. Vr. 7,34 and Kī. 4,37—39 permit *e* in all the tenses and moods; Hc. 3,158, with whom Mk. fol. 51 seems to be in accord, limits its occurrence to the indic., imp. and the parasmaipada pres. participle. Bh. gives as examples *haseï, hasaï, paḍheï, paḍhaï, hasĕnti, hasanti, haseu, hasaü*; Hc. has *hasei, hasaï, hasema, hasemu, hasemo*; *haseu, hasaü, suṇeu, suṇaü, hasĕnto, hasanto*; Kī. *hasaï, hasei, caaï, caei*, Mk. *bhaṇaï, bhaṇei, bhaṇasi, bhaṇesi*. These forms in *-e* are found in a large number in all classes, beside those *-a*, and this can be confirmed with certainty, in spite of the great fluctuation in MSS. Its entire mode of formation forbids it directly to be put in a series with the causatives and denominatives.[1] From *kṛ* one forms *karaï* and *karei*, JŚ. Ś. Mg. *karedi*, the causative, however, *kārei*, Ś. Mg. *kāredi*, JŚ. *kārayadi* (Kattig. 403, 385). One says *hasaï* and *hasei*, but in the caus. *hāsei*, Ś. *muñcadi, muñcedi*; but in the caus. *moāvedi* etc. Hence it is more correct to say that the character *-e* from *-aya* of the derived verbs can plainly enter into Pkt.[2] too. I do not consider it correct to say that the forms such as Ś. *gacchĕmha* (Mṛcch. 43. 20; 44,18), Ḍh. *gĕṇhĕmha* (Mṛcch. 36,24), *aṇusalĕmha* (Mṛcch. 30,13; 36, 19), Ḍh. Ś Mg. *kilĕmha* (Mṛcch. 30,18;94,15;131,18), Ś. *suvĕmha* (Mṛcch. 46,9) are to be explained with BLOCH[3] as false.

1. JACOBI, Erz. § 53, II. where *nemi, demi* are to deleted completely (§ 474).—2. LASSEN, Inst. § 120,3.—3. Vr. und Hc. p. 45.

§ 473. The verbs of the first conjugation, of which the roots end in *-i, -u* are conjugated mostly as in Skt. : *ji* forms *jaaï* (Hc. 4,241; G. H. s. v. *ji*; Karp. 2,6), AMg. JM. *jay̆aī* (Nandīs. 1,22; Erz.), Ś. *jaadi* (Vikr. 44,4; Mudrār. 224,4. 5. 6), imperative Ś. *jaadu* (Śak. 41,1; 44,3; 138,6; 162,1; Vikr. 27,8; 28,14; 44,3; 47,20; 82,8. 9; Ratn. 296,1; 305,15;320,16; 321,28 etc.). The form *jedu*, that is often found beside *jaadu*, pro-ex. Veṇīs. 59,13 beside *jaadu* 29,11, further in Prab. 32,12, Mg. *yedu* beside Ś. *jaadu* 40,8 and occurring only in the Devanāgarī recension of Śak. (ed. BÖHTLINGK 27,12; 29,17; 89,15; 90,9; 107,8) is badly accredited[1]. In M. JM. AMg. Ḍh. A. *ji* is conjugated also according to the 9. conjugation; in M. JM. AMg. A. it goes over to the 1. conjugation at the same time : Ḍh. *jiṇādi* (Mṛcch. 34,22) ; AMg. *jiṇāmi* (Uttar. 704); M. *jiṇaï* (Vr. 8,56; Hc. 4,241; Sr. fol. 49), AMg. *parāiṇaï* (Vivāhap. 123.124); A. *jiṇaï* (Piṅgala 1,123[a]); M. *jiṇanti* (R. 3,40); AMg. *jiṇĕjja* (Uttar. 291), *jiṇāhi* (Jīv. 602; Kappas. § 114; Ovav. § 53), *jiṇantassa* = *jayataḥ* (Dasav. 618, 14) ; JM. *jiniuṁ* (absol.; Āv. 36,42) ; A. *jiṇia* (Piṅgala 1,102[a]). On the passive *jiṇijjaï, jivvaï* see § 536. For Ś Mk. fol. 71 appears to prescribe or to forbid *jiṇadi*. From the absolutive Ś. *samassaïa*(Śak. 2,8) follows a present **samassaaï* = *samāśrayati*. In AMg. *śri* too is conjugated according to the 9. conjugation like *ji* : *samussiṇāmi, samussiṇāsi* (Āy̆ar. 1,7,2,1. 2).—Of *ci* an) *mi* are found also the contracted forms (§ 502). For the roots in *-u, -ū* Hc. 4,233 teaches, without distinguishing between the classes, a similar conjugation: *niṇhavaï, nihavaï* = *nihnute, cavaï* = *cyavate, ravaï* = *rauti, kavaï* = *kavate, savaï* = *sūte, pasavaï* = *prasūte*. So AMg. *pasavaï* (Uttar. 641), *niṇhavĕjja* (Āy̆ār. 1,5,3,1), *niṇhave* (Dasav. 631,31), *aṇiṇhavāmāṇa*

(Nāyādh. § 83); whilst the passive M. *ṇiṇhuvijjanti* (H. 657), Ś. *ṇiṇhuviadi* (Ratn. 303,9) and the past participle Ś. *ṇiṇhuvido* (Śak. 137,6) = **ṇiṇhuvaï* presuppose the flexion according to the 6. conjugation; M. *paṇhaaï* = *prasna-uti* (H. 409. 462 v. l. *paṇhuaï*) ; AMg. A. *ravaï* (Ṭhāṇ. 450; Piṅgala 2,146). Beside *ravaï*, *ru* too is conjugated according to the 6. conjugation too: *ruvaï* (Hc. 4,238); M. *ruvaï*, *ruvanti*, *ruvasu* (H. s. v *rud*), *paḍiruanti* (R.), passive *ruvvaï* and *ruvijjaï* (Hc. 4,249), M. *ruvvasu* in the middle sense (H. 10). Thence is deduced a root *ruv*, that like *dhau*, *svap* (§ 482,497), secondarily is conjugated according to the first class : *rovaï* (Hc. 4, 238); M. *rovanti* (H. 494); JM. *rovāmi* (Dvār. 503.17), inf. *roviuṁ* (Dvār. 503,15; 504,6), past passive participle *roviya* (Dvār. 504,7). The grammarians derive the forms from *rud*(Vr. 8,42; Hc. 4,226)occasioned through similarity in flexion (§ 495) and similarity in meaning. Cf. Gypsy *ruvāva*, *rovāva* "to weep"and English "*to cry*", "to weep" and "to shout"[2].—AMg. *luĕjjā* = **luvĕjjā* = *luniyāt* (Vivāhap. 1186), *puvanti* = *plavante* (Vivāhap. 1232) according to the 6. conjugation. Cf. also § 494. 503. 511.

1. CAPPELLER on Ratn. p. 369; almost everywhere is found in the text the v. l. *jaadu*, beside *jedu*, in the best MSS; cf. pro ex. Mudrār. 38,4; 46,4 : 54,6; 84,7 etc.— 2. WEBER on Hāla 141; PISCHEL on Hc. 4,226.

§ 474. The roots of the 1. conjugation in -*i* tend to change -*aya* into -*e* by saṁprasāraṇa : M. *ṇesi*, *ṇei* = *nayasi*, *nayati* (H. 553. 939. 647), *āṇ ei* (R. 8,43); AMg. JM. *niṇei* = *nirṇayati* (Uttar. 578; Erz. 29,6); JM. *nei* (Erz. 11,11), M. *pariṇei* (Karp. 7,4), Ś. *pariṇedi* (Viddhaś. 50,1), *āṇedi* (Karp. 109,8). According to these also the 1. sing. JM. *nemi* (Sagara 9,6), M. *āṇemi* (Karp. 26,1), Ś. *avaṇemi* = *apanayāmi*, *aṇuṇemi*, *parāṇemi* (Mṛcch. 6,7; 18,23; 166,16); 3. plur. M. *ṇĕnti* (R. 3,14; 5,2; 6,92). Imp. JM. Ś. *ṇehi* (Erz. 43,24; Vikr. 41,2), AMg. Ś. *uvaṇehi* = *upanaya* (Vivāgas. 121. 122; Mṛcch. 61,10; 64,20. 25; 96,14; Vikr. 45.9), Ś. *āṇehi* (Vikr. 41, 1) and *āṇesu* (Śak. 125,8 [so to be read] ; Karṇas. 51,17), *avaṇesu* = *apanaya* (Viddhaś. 48,10), Ś. *ṇedu* (Mṛcch 65,19; 67 7); Ś. Mg. *ṇĕmha* (Mudrār. 233,5 [so to be read; cf. v. l. and the Calcutta editions, that have *ṇĕhma*] ; Mg. Mṛcch. 170, 12) JM. *niṇeha* (Dvār. 496,5); Mg. Ś. *ṇedha* (Mṛcch. 32, 15; 161,9). In verses are found JM. *āṇasu* (Erz. 78,9) and A. *āṇahi* (Hc. 4,343,2). They are to be explained from **āṇaasu*, **āṇāsu* **āṇaahi*, **āṇāhi*. The flexion of Skt. occurs in M. *ṇaaï* (Viddhaś. 7,2) *ṇaanti* (G. 803), Ś. *pariṇaadu* (Śak. 39,3), *ṇaïa* = **nayiya* = *nītvā* (Mṛcch. 155,4) and in the parasmaipada pres. participle Mg. *ṇaante* = *nayan* (Mṛcch. 169,12).—*ḍi* with *ud* forms *uḍḍei*, 3, plur. *uḍḍĕnti* (Hc. 4,237; H. 218; G. 232 [to be read *uḍḍinti* with J] . 770; Mg. Mṛcch. 120,12), particip. parasmaip. *uḍḍĕnta* (G. 543; so to be read with P). —*lei* = *layati* from *lī* (Hc. 4,238);M. *ahilei*(G.R.), *ahilĕnti*(H.) *parilĕnta* (R.), whilst M. *alliaï* (G.H.R.), JM. *alliyaï* (Āv.47,16), AMg. *uvalliyaï* (Āyār.2,2,2,4), M. *samalliaï* (R.) JM. *samalliyaï* (Āv. 47,17) presuppose a flexion **liyáte*, the participia M. *āḷiamāṇa* (G.) Ś. *ṇiliamāṇa* (Vikr. 80,20), the flexion of Skt. (§ 196). Likewise is inflected *daya-* (to give; Hc. s. v. *dā*; Kī. 4,34) : M. JM. *dei*, *dĕnti*, *dehi*, *desu*, *deu*, *deha*, particip. *dĕnta-* (G. H. R.; Erz.; Kk.); AMg. *dei* (Nirayāv. § 21. 22), *demo* (Vivāhap. 819); JŚ. *dedi* (Kattig. 399,319. 320; 402, 360. 365. 366); Ś. *demi* (Ratn. 312,30; Mṛcch. 105,9), *desi* (Mālav. 5,8), *dedi* (Mṛcch.66,2; 147,17; Vikr. 43,14; Viddhaś. 29,7) *dehi* (as in Skt.) very frequently (pro ex. Mṛcch. 38,4. 23;44, 24;94, 17; Śak. 95,11; 111,6 etc.), *dedu* (Karp. 38,1); D. *deu* (Mṛcch. 105,21); particip. Ś. *ḍěnta-* (Mṛcch. 44,19); Mg. *demi* (Mṛcch. 31,17; 45,2; 79,18; 127,12; 131,9. 10. 13), *dehi* (Mṛcch. 45, 12;97,2; 132,4), *deśu* (Prab. 58,8), *dedha* (Mṛcch, 160,11; 164,14. 16; 170,6); Ḍh. *dehi* (Mṛcch. 32,23; 36,15); P. *teti* (Hc. 4,318), *tiyyate* (to be read so; Hc. 4,315); A. *desi dei, děnti, dehu, děntahŏ* = *dadataḥ, děntihiṁ* = *dadatibhiḥ* (Hc. s. v. *dā*), absol. *děppiṇu* (Hc. 4,440) and *devaṁ*(Hc. 4,441). The flexion **daaï* = **dáyati* presupposes the future Ś. *daïssaṁ* = *dayiṣye* (Mṛcch. 80,20), false *dāissaṁ* (Śak. ed. BÖHTLINGK 25,6; Karp. 112,5), *daïssāmo* (Viddhaś. 121,3; s. v. l.); cf. Vr. 12,14; Mg. *daïśśaṁ* (Mṛcch. 31, 6. 8. 15; 32,9. 24; 33,22; 35,8; 80,19; 81,5; 97,3; 123,21; 124,5. 9), and the absol. Ś. Mg. *daïa* = **dayiya* = *dayitvā* (Mṛcch. 32,19 [*a*°]; 37,12; 51,12; 168,2). The root *dā* is preserved only in M. JM. *dāūṇa dāuṁ, dijjaï* (G. H. R.; Erz.), AMg. inf. *dāuṁ* (Uvās.; Nāyādh.), Ś. *diadi* (Mṛcch. 55, 16;71,6; so to be read also in(Mṛcch. 49,7 for *dijjadi*), *diadu* (Karp.103,7), *dādavva* (Mṛcch. 66,2; 150,14; Karp. 103,6; Jīvān. 43,12. 15); Mg. *diadi, diadu* (Mṛcch. 145,4); in the fut. M. JM. AMg. *dāhaṁ, dāsaṁ* (§ 530), past participle *diṇṇa datta* (§ 566). AMg. uses mostly *dalayaï* (§ 490), for which we often find *dalaï* as v. l. (HOERNLE, Uvās.; Translation, note 287).

§ 475. Hc. 4,60 teaches the forms *hoi, huvaï, havaï, bhavaï*, in combinations *pabhavaï, paribhavaï, saṁbhavaï* and *ubbhuaï*, which presupposes a simplex **bhuvaï* from *bhū*. This occurs in *bhuvadi*, that is taught by Hc. 4, 269 beside *huvadi, bhavadi, havadi, bhodi, hodi* as Ś.; further in the aorist AMg. *bhuvi* (§ 516) and in P. *phuvati* (Kī. 5,115). Vr. 8,1; Kī. 4,56; Mk. fol.53 teach *hoi. huvaï* and Vr. 8,3; Mk. fol. 53 in compounds *bhavaï* as *pabhavaï, ubbhavaï, saṁbhavaï, paribhavaï*, Kī. 4,58, *havaï* as *pahavaï*. Vr.'s rule 12,12 is not clear on Ś., for which Kī. 5,81 and Mk. fol. 71 prescribe *bhodi* whilst Śākalya, according to Mk. authenticates *hodi* too and Sr. fol. 71 teaches *bhodi hodi, bhuvadi, huvadi* etc. (*ityādi*). —*bhavaï*, the form that exactly corresponds to Skt. *bhavati* is frequent in AMg. (Āyār. 1,1,1,1 ff; Ṭhāṇ. 156; Vivāhap. 116. 137. 917. 926. 935 ff. ; Nandīs. 501 f. ; Paṇṇav. 666. 667 ; Kappas. S. § 14—16), *bhavasi* (Vivāhap. 1245. 1406), *bhavanti* (Vivāhap. 926. 1309; Ovav. § 70 ff. ; Kappas.), *bhavaü* (Kappas.) ; also in JM. it is not seldom: *bhavaï* (Āv. 10, 20; 13. 37; 20, 11 ff.), *bhavanti* (Erz. 3,14), *bhavasu* (Erz. 11, 10). Beside them AMg. JM. have also the forms with initial *ha*: JM. *havāmi* (Erz. 35,15), AMg. JM. *havaï* (Paṇṇav. 32. 115: Nandīs. 329. 361 ff.; Uttar. 342. 344. 754 (beside *hoi*); Āv. 36,44) ; AMg. *havanti* (Sūyag. 253. 255; Vivāhap. 138; Paṇṇav. 40. 42. 91. 94. 102. 106. 115 etc ; Nandīs. 461 ; Jīv. 219; Ovav. § 130) ; likewise in the optative beside *bhavějjā* (Ovav. § 182), 2. plur. *bhavějjāha* (Nāyādh. 912. 915. 918. 920) in verses also *havějja* (Sūyag. 341 ; Vivāhap. 426 ; Ovav. § 171), *havějjā* (Uttar. 459), JM. *havijja* (Erz. 74, 11). In prose in Āv. 29,19 we should with the v. l.

read *hǒjjā*, for *havějjā*. AMg. JM. have also the opt. *bhave* (Vivāhap. 459; Uttar. 678; Nandīs. 117 ; Erz.). In Ś. Mg. 1. sing. is *bhaveaṁ*, 1.2. 3. sing. 3. plur. *bhave* are the only forms that can be used (§ 460—462). In compositum occurs also Ś. *pahave* (Śak. 25,1); false is Ś. *have* (Mālav. 44,1.3)[1]. In JŚ, the form that is very usual is *havadi* (Pav. 380,9; 381, 16;382,24; 384, 54. 58; 385,65; 386,70.4; 387, 18. 19 ; 388,5; Kattig. 398. 303; 400, 334), also *havedi* (Kattig. 401, 341 ; MS *havei*), beside *hodi* (Pav. 381, 18; 385, 64; 386,6; Kattig 399,308; 400,326. 328. 329. 330; 402, 368; 403,372. 376. 381; 404,391), *homi* (Pav. 385. 65), *hunti* (Kattig. 401, 352), *hǒnti* (Kattig. 402, 363. 364; 404, 387), inf. *hoduṁ* (Kattig. 402, 357); MS *houṁ*). The opt. is *have* (Pav. 387,25; Kattig. 398, 302; 399, 309. 312. 315; 400,336; 401,338. 345 etc.). Therefore, Hc. should have Ś. *havadi, hodi* (§ 21.22). Of the stem *bhava-*, the forms, excluding the mentioned ones, are only sporadic : Mg. *bhavāmi* (Mṛcch. 117,6) ; Ś. *bhavidavvaṁ* (Śak. 32, 6 ; Karp 61, 11), that is supported by JŚ. *bhavidavvaṁ* (Kattig. 404, 388; MS °*viya*°) and Ś. *bhavidavvadā* (Śak. 126,10; Vikr. 52, 13) ; inf. *bhaviuṁ* (Hc. 4,60), Ś. Mg. *bhaviduṁ* (Śak. 73,8; 116,1 [so to be read] ; in Mālav. 47,7 false reading[1]). Very frequent is the absolutive *bhavia* in Ś. (Mṛcch. 27,12;45,8; 64,19; 78,10; Śak. 30,9; 119,3, 13; 160, 1; Vikr. 24,5; 25,15 etc.) and Mg. Mṛcch. 16,16; 124,23; 134,23; 170,11), JŚ. *bhaviya* (Pav. 380,12; 387,12), AMg. *bhavittā* (Ovav. ; Kappas.), *pāubbhavittāṇaṁ* (Uvās.). On the future see § 521. The passive Mg. *bhaviadi* (Mṛcch. 164,10) stands in the sense of the fut. parasmaip. (§550). M. *aggabhavantiǒ* in G. 588 is a false reading for *aggabharantiu* (see v. 1. p. 376). In addition to in the forms mentioned in AMg. JM. JŚ. the stem *hava* is found also in M. *havanti* (G. 901. 936. 976). The stem *bhava-* is prevalent in formations with addition of prefixes. I have only to add BLOCH's examples from Ś. Mg.: Ś. *aṇubhavanto* = *anubhavan* (Vikr. 41,9), *aṇubhavida* (Karp. 33,6). The stem *hava-* is usual only after the prefix *pra-*, further in the substantive *vihava*[3]; elsewhere it occurs just sporadically after *anu-* in M. *aṇuhavaï* (H. 211), Ś. *aṇuhavanti* (Mālav. 51,22; Prab. 44,13); yet Mālav. has the v. 1. *aṇuhǒnti*, in Prab. *aṇubhavanti*, as it should be read; similarly in Śak. 74,6 we should, with the v. 1., read *vibhāvedi* for *vihāvedi*. Vr. is substantially correct when he requires *bhava-* for the composita.

1. BLOCH, Vr. und Hc. p. 41, who has compiled plentiful collections for S. Mg. from Mṛcch., Śak. Vikr., Mālav., Ratn. on *bhū* should be supplemented for completing the list.—2. I. c. p. 39.40.—3. BLOCH, I. c. p. 40.

§ 476. *huva-*, that is to say the flexion according to the sixth conjugation occurs in M. *huvanti* (G. 988; H.285), in the opt. *huvia* (§ 466) and P. *huvěyya* (Hc.4,320.323), ind. pass. Mg. *huviadi* (Veṇīs. 33,6.7;35,8; in the sense of the fut. parasmaip.; cf. *bhaviadi* § 475) and especially in the future in Ś. and Mg. (§ 521). Offending against the dialect, a false form is Ś. fem. parasmaip. pres. part. *huvanti* and probably also Mg. particip. necessitatis *huvidavvaṁ* (Lalitav. 555,5; 565, 13).—In M. JM. A. in the simplex, the dominating stem is *ho-* from *hava-*, which AMg. too more seldom and JŚ. frequently have *homi, hosi, hoi hǒnti* and *hunti*; imp. *hohi, hosu, hou, homo, hŏntu*; indic. pres. pass. *hoiaï*, *hoijjaï*; parasmaip. pres. particip. *hŏnto*, *hunto*, âtmanep. *hamāṇo*; inf. *houṁ*, JŚ. *hoduṁ*; absol. *haūṇa*; particip. nec. AMg. JM. *hoẏavva*[1]. On *hŏjja*, *hŏjja* see § 466. In addition to this, the precative in AMg. is *hoi*, *hou* only, especially in the combination *hoū ṇaṁ*, and the preterite *hŏtthā* in frequent use. In Ś. one says *homi*, *hosi*, *hŏnti*, imp. *hohi*, *hŏmha*, *hodha*, *hŏntu*, Mg. imp. *hodha*[2], but Ś. Mg. Dh. only *bhodi*, *bhodu*[3]. False forms in the texts are *bhomi*, *hodi*, *bhohi hodu*, *bhŏntu*[4]. P. has *photi* (Ki. 5.115). The particip. nec. is Ś. Mg. *hodavva*[5]; on Ś. JŚ. *bhavidavva* see § 475, on Mg. *huvidavva* see above. The particip. pret. is M. *hūa* (Hc. 4,64; Kī 4,57; Mk. fol. 53) in *maṇḍaṇihūaṁ* (H. 8), *aṇuhūa* (Hc.4,64; H. 29), *parihūeṇa* (H. 134; so to be read with the v. l. and ed. Bomb.), *pahūa* (Hc. 4,64), A. *hūā* (Hc. 4,384), and *huā* (Hc. 4,351), Ś. Dh. D. *bhūda* (Ś. e.g. Mṛcch. 55,16; 78,3; Śak. 43,9; 80,2; Vikr. 23,14; 51,21; 53,12 [read °*bhūdo*]; Ḍh. Mṛcch. 36,21; 39,16; D. Mṛcch. 101,13), Mg. *kiappahūda* = *kiẏatprabhūta* (Veṇīs. 34,16).—Sr. fol. 47 knows also the flexion *hoaï*, *hoei*, *huaï*, *huei*, exactly according to the type of the a-stem.

1. References under the instances quoted in §469 on *hou* and in the relevant paragraphs. on JŚ. in § 475. Cf. also WEBER, Sitzungsberichte der Kgl. Preuss. Ak. der Wissenschaften zu Berlin 1882,811 f.; IS. 16,393.—2. References in BLOCH, l. c. p. 41.—3. PISCHEL, KB. 8,141 and above § 469; Mg. *bhodi* e.g. Mṛcch. 121,6; 168,3.4.5, false *hodi* 168,6.—4. BLOCH, l. c. p. 41; collection also in BURKHARD, Flexiones Pracriticae p. 20 f.—5. BLOCH, l.c.p. 42. On the flexion of *bhū* cf. also DELIUS, Radices Pracriticae s.v.

§ 477. The roots in -*ṛ* and -*ṝ* form the stem in -*ara*: *dharai*, *varaï*, *saraï*, *haraï*, *jaraï*, *taraï* (Vr. 8, 12; Hc 4,234; Kī 4,32). In OIA this flexion has been carried over to a few roots found in the Vedas, or seldom or merely mentioned by the grammarians, such as in the case of *jṝ*, *dhṛ*, *mṛ*, *vṛ*, *stṝ* in Pkt. this is the rule. Beside it the flexion with the *e*-stem is frequent. So: M. JM. *dharaï* and *dharemi*, *dharei*, *dharĕnti*, particip. pres. *dharanta* and *dharĕnta* (G. H. R.; Erz.); Ś. *dharāmi* = *dhriye* (Uttarar. 83,9); A. *dharaï* (Hc. 4,334; 438,3) and *dharei* (Hc. 4,336), *dharahĩ* (Hc. 4,382), imp. *dharahi* (Hc. 4,421; Piṅgala 1,149).—M. *osaraï* = *apasarati*, *osaranta-* = *apasarat-*, *osaria* = *apasṛta* (G. H. R.), imp. *osara*, *osarasu* (H.); JM. *osaraï* (Erz. 37,30); Mg. *ośaladi* (Mṛcch. 115,23), *ośalia* = *apasṛtya* (Mṛcch. 129, 8); imp. JM. Ś. *osara* = *apasara* (Erz. 71,31; Vikr. 10,12), Mg. *osala* (Prab. 58.2; so rightly ed. M. 73,6), Ś. *osaramha* (Uttarar. 66,7), JM. *osaraha* = *apasarata* (Kk. 265,6; II, 507,1), Mg. *ośaladha* (§ 471); M. *samosaraï*, *samosaranta-* etc. (G. H. R.), AMg. imp. *samosaraha* (Nāẏādh. 1233. 1235); Ś. *ṇisaradi* (Dhūrtas. 8,6); M. AMg. *pasaraï* (R.; Vivāhap. 908), Ś. *pasaradi* (Śak. 31,10), Mg. *paśalaśi* (Mṛcch. 10,15), Ḍh. imp. *pasalu* (Mṛcch. 32,16), also Ḍh. *aṇusalĕmha* (§ 472) beside Ś. *aṇusaramha* Viddhaś. 105,5). Cf. § 235.—M. JM. *marāmi* = *mriye*, *maraï*, *maranti*, imp. *mara*, *marasu*, *maraü*, particip. pres. *maranta-* (H.; Erz.); AMg. *maraï* (Sūẏag. 635; Uttar. 214; Vivāhap. 363 f.), *maranti* (Uttar. 1099 ff.; Vivāhap. 1434), *maramāṇa* (Vivāhap. 1385); Ś. *maradi* (Mṛcch. 72,22; so to be read); Mg; *malāmi* (Mṛcch. 118,13), but also *maledu*, *malĕnti* (Mṛcch. 114,21; 118,12); A. *marahi*, *maraï* (Hc. 4,368. 420,5). M *marijjaü* = *mriyatām* (H. 950) stands in the sense of the passive, AMg. inf. *marijjiuṁ*

(Dasav. 624,40; cf. § 580) in the sense of the active. AMg. *mijjaï*, *mijjanti* (Sūyag. 275. 328. 333. 540. 944) are correctly equated by the scholiasts as = *miyate*, *miyante*.—JM. *varasu* = *vṛṇuṣva* (Sagara 1, 15).—M. JM. *haraï* (G. H. R.; Erz.)., JŚ. *haradi* (Kattig. 400, 336), M. also *haremi* (H. 705), AMg. opt. *harĕjjāha* (Nāyādh. 915. 918), Mg. *halāmi*, *haladi* (Mṛcch. 11,8; 30,21. 24); very frequently in composita in all dialects, as M. *ahiharaï*, *paharaï* (G.), JM. *pariharāmi* (Kk. 272,16), AMg. *sāharanti* = *saṁharanti* (Ṭhāṇ. 155), *paḍisāharaï* = *pratisaṁharati* (Vivāhap. 239), *viharaï* (Kappas.; Uvās. etc.), Ś. *uvahara*, *uvaharantu* (Śak. 18,3; 40,9); *avaharadi* = *apaharati* (Mṛcch. 45,24), Mg. *palihalāmi* = *pariharāmi* (Mṛcch. 125,10), *śamudāhalāmi* (Mṛcch. 129,2), also *vihaledi* = *viharati* (Mṛcch. 40.9), A. *aṇuharahĩ*, *aṇuharaï* (Hc. 4,367,4; 418,8).—M. *taraï* (G. H.); AMg. *taranti* (Uttar. 567), *uttaraï* (Nāyādha. 1060), *paccuttaraï* (Vivāhap. 909); Ś. *odaradi* = *avatarati* (Mṛcch. 44,19; 108,21; Mālatīm. 265,6), imp. *odaramha* = *avatarāma* (Mālatīm. 100,3; Priyad. 12,4); Mg. imp. *odala* = *avatara* (Mṛcch. 122,14. 15. 16), absol. *odalia* (Mṛcch. 122,11) = Ś. *odaria* (Vikr. 23,17); A. *uttaraï* (Hc. 4,339).—*kṛ* forms, corresponding to Skt. *kiráti*, M. *ukkiraï* (H 119), *kiranta-* (G. R.).

§ 478. According to Hc. 4,74 *smṛ* may form *saraï*, so stands JM. *sarāmi* (Āv. 41,20), AMg. *saraï* (Uttar, 277) in a verse, JM. *saraï* (Āv. 47, 27), *sarasu* (Āv. 7,34) in prose. The usual form in all the dialects, that Vr. 12,17; Mk. fol. 72 particularly prescribe for Ś. in addition is *sumara-* for *smara-* with a separation-vowel (Vr. 8,18; Hc. 4,74; Kī. 4,49 Mk. fol. 53). Beside it the prose very frequently has the *e*-stem *sumare-*. So M. *sumarāmi* (R. 4,20 [so to be read]. 22); JM. absol. *sumariūṇa* and *sumariya*, past passive particip. *sumariya* (Erz.); AMg. imp. *sumaraha* (Vivāhap. 234); Ś *sumarāmi* (Mṛcch. 134,15; Uttarar. 118,1). *sumarasi* (Uttarar. 126,6), better authenticated *sumaresi* (Mṛcch. 66,15. 18; 103,20; 104,10; 105,15; Vikr. 23,9), as *sumaredi* (Śak. 70,7; 167,8; Mālatīm. 184, 4; Viddhaś. 125,11) and in the imp. *sumarehi* (Ratn. 317,17), *sumaresu* (Vikr. 13,4), *sumaredha* (Śak. 52,16), further *sumara* (Mālatīm. 251, 2; all texts) and A. *suvarahi* (Hc. 4,387), opt. *sumari* = *smareḥ* (Hc. 4,387,1); Ś. *sumarāmo* (Mālatīm. 113.9); Mg. *śumalāmi*, *śumaleśi*, *śumaledi* (Mṛcch. 115, 23; 127,25; 134,13), imp. *śumala* and *śumalehi* (Mṛcch. 128,20; 168,11; 170,8); particip. praet. pass. Ś. *sumarida* (Mālatīm. 249,6; Prab. 41,7) Mg. *śumalida* (Mṛcch. 136, 19); particip. nec. Ś. *sumaridavva* (Vikr. 48,14; Mālatīm. 184,3), Mg. *śumalidavva* (Mṛcch. 170,9). In conjunction with *vi* Hc. 4,75 teaches *vimharaï*, and *visaraï*, whence M. *vīsaria* = *vismṛta* (H. 361; Śak. 96,2), JM. *vissariya* (Āv. 7,34); JŚ. *vīsarida* (Kattig. 400,335; text° *ya*). Mk. fol. 54 teaches *visaraï*, *visuraï* and *visaraï* that occurs in M. *visaria* (R. 11,58) and in the modern Indian languages.[1] In Ś. and Mg. the stem is strictly the same as in the simplex; pro ex. Ś. *visumarāmi* (Śak. 126,8), *visumaresi* (Vikr. 49,1); Mg. *viśumaledi* (Mṛcch. 37,12). Ś. *vimharida mhi* of Vikr. 83,20 has been wrongly equated in the text against all the MSS by BOLLENSEN; the ed. Bomb. p. 133,9 correctly has *visumarida mhi*[2], as *visumarida* stands also in Śak. 14,2; Vṛṣabh. 14,6. On *bharaï* see § 313.

1. PISCHEL on Hc. 4,75.—2. Wrongly BOHTLINGK on Śak. 59,10, where we should at least read *vimhario* with the ed. Bomb. 1883, p. 64,11.

§ 479. The roots in *-ai* are conjugated as a rule as in Skt. (Vr. 8,21. 25. 26), Hc. 4,6; Kī. 4,65. 75); M. *gāanti* (Kāleyak. 3,8; Bālar. 181, 6), *uggāanti*=*udgāyanti* (Dhūrtas. 4,14), *gāanta-* Karp. 23,4); JM. *gāẏaï* (Āv. 8, 29), *gāẏanti* (Dvār. 496,36) *gāẏantehiṁ* gāīuṁ Erz. 1, 29; 2, 10); AMg. *gāẏauti* (Jīv. 593; Rāẏap. 96. 181), *gāẏantā* (Ovav. § 49 V), *gāẏamāṇe* (Vivāhap. 1253); Ś. *gāāmi* (Mudrār. 35,1), *gāadi* (Nāgān. 9,6), *gāadha* (Viddhaś. 12,4), imp. also of the *e*-stem *gāedha* (Viddhaś. 122,10; 128,4), *gāanteṇa*, *gāanto* (Mṛcch. 44,2. 4); Mg. *gāe*, *gāidaṁ* (Mṛcch. 79,14; 117,4).—Ś. *parittāadi*=*parirāyate* (Mṛcch. 128,7), *parittāasu* (Mahāv. 30,19, Bālar. 173,10; Viddhaś. 85,5), *parittāāhi* (Uttarar. 63,13), *parittāadu* (Ratn. 325,9. 32), *parittāadha* (Śak. 16,10; 17,6; Vikr. 3,17; 5,2; Mālatīm. 130,3); Mg. *palittāadha*, *palittāadu* (Mṛcch. 32,25; 128,6).—JM. *jhāẏasi*=*dhyāyasi* (Erz. 85,23), *jhāẏamāṇi* (Erz. 11,19); AMg. *jhiẏāẏāmi*, *jhiẏāẏasi*, *jhiẏāẏaï*, *jhiẏāẏaha*, *jhiẏāẏamāṇa* (Nāẏādh.); M. *ṇijjhāaï*=*nirdhyāyati* (H. 73. 413); Ś. *ṇijjhāadi*, (Mṛcch. 59,24; 89,4; Mālatīm. 258, 4), *ṇijjhāanti* (Mṛcch. 69,2), *ṇijjhāido* (Mṛcch. 93,15), *ṇijjhāidā* (Vikr. 52,11), *saṁjhāadi* (Mṛcch. 73,12).—S. *ṇiddāadi*=*nidrāyati* (Mṛcch. 46,5; 69,2; Mālav. 65, 8).—Ś. *parimilāadi*=*parimlāyati* (Mālatīm. 120,2; so to be read with ed. Bomb. 92,2 and ed. Madras 105,3).—Since in Pkt. the roots ending in *-ā* may be a inflected according to the fourth conjugation (§ 487), so reversely the roots in *-ai* follow sometimes in M. JM. AMg. the analogy of the roots in *ā*: M. *gāi* (Vr 8,26; Hc. 4,6; H. 128. 691), *gāu* (Bh. 8,26), *ganta-* (H. 547); JM. *uggāi* (Āv. 8,28); M. *jhāi*=Epical *dhyāti* (Vr. 8,26; Hc. 4,6; R. 6,61), JŚ. *jhādi* (Pav. 385,68) beside *jhāẏadi* (Pav. 385,65; 403,372); *jhāu* (Bh. 8,26), *ṇijjhāi* (Hc. 4,6); AMg. *jhiẏāi* (Vivāgas. 219; Uvās. § 280; Nāẏādh.; Kappas.), *jhiẏāmi* (Vivāgas. 114. 220; Nāẏādh.), *jhiẏāsi* (Vivāgas. 114), *jhāijja* (verse; Uttar. 14). Likewise AMg. *jhiẏāi*=*kṣāẏāti* beside *jhiẏāẏanti* (§ 326); AMg. *gilāi*=Epical *glāti* (Āẏār. 2,1,11,1, 2), beside *vigilāĕjjā* (Āẏār. 2,2,3,28); M. *niddāi*, *milāi* (Hc. 4,12.18), in addition to which Epical *mlāhti*.—In Ś. is found several times *parittāhi* (Śak. 145,8; Prab. 11, 13); Uttarar. 60,4.5; Mālatīm. 357,11), in Mg. *palittāhi* (Mṛcch. 175,19). The v. l. almost everywhere has in Ś. the correct *parittāāhi*. On *palāẏa-* see § 567.

§ 480. The verbs *iṣ*, *gam*, *ẏam*, of the old *-ska-* class are conjugated in all the dialects as in Skt.: *icchaï*, *gacchaï*, *jacchaï*. Isolated are Mg. *śāṁyammadha* (§ 488) and AMg. *uggamamāṇa* (Paṇṇav. 41). Hc. 4,215, besides derives *acchaï* from *ās*, Kī. 4,10 from *as* (to be), the scholiasts mostly equate it with *tiṣṭhati*. ASCOLI tries to trace the corresponding Pāli *acchati*, from a hypothetical future **ātsyati* or **ātsyate*[1] of *ās*, CHILDERS[2] and PISCHEL[3] from **āssakadi* from *ās*, as Hc., E. MÜLLER from *gam* with dropping out of *g*[4], later with TRENCKNER and TORP from an aorist **ātsīt* from *ās*[5]; E. KUHN considers it to be an inchoative formation from *ās*[6], JOHANSSON thinks it to be a future **assyati*, **atsyati* from **as*[7]. However, it strictly corresponds Skt. fourth to *ṛcchati* from *ṛ* "to come into", "to knock at", of the *-ska-* conjugation, and which the Indian grammarians post as *ṛch* and B.-R. as *arch.* The meaning "to remain", "to stand" comes from the statement, that it is used in the sense of *indriyapralaya* as well as of *mūrtibhāva*, given in the Dhātupāṭha 28,15. The use of *ṛcchati*, *ārchat* in the Brāhmaṇa[8] may also be compared. Examples are : M. *acchasi*. *acchanti*, *acchaï*, *acchijjaï* (G. H.); JM. *acchaï*, *acchae*, *acchāmo*, *acchasu*, *acchaha*, *acchantassa*. *acchiuṁ*, *acchiya*, *acchiyavvaṁ* (Erz.; Dvār. 498,12; 500,9; 501,9; Āv. 14,25. 30; 24,17; 26,28 : 29,22); AMg. *acchaï* (Āyār. 1,8,4,4; Uttar. 902 ff.), *acchāhi* (Āyār. 2,6,1,10; Vivāhap. 807.817), *acchĕjja* (Hc. 3,160; Vivāhap. 116; Ovav. § 185), Ā. *acchadha* (Mṛcch. 99,16)[9]; P *acchati*, *acchate* (Hc. 4,319); A. *acchaü* (Hc. 4,406,3). On *acchia* see § 466.

1. Kritische Studien zur Sprachwissenschaft p. 265, note 49.—2. Dictionary s. v *acchati*—3. GGA. 1875, 627 f.; BB. 3,155 f.; on Hc. 4,215—4. Beiträge p. 36.—5. Simplified Grammar. p. 100—6. In E. MULLER, Beiträge p, 66.—7. Shāhbāzgarhi II, 23; KZ. 32,460, note 2.—8. B.-R. s. v. *arch*; PISCHEL, GGA, 1890, 532. JOHANSSON l. c. note 3 wrongly rejects this derivation. since he thinks Ἔρχονται.—19. On Vr. 12, 19 see PISCHEL, KB. 8.143 f.

§ 481. Deviating from Classical Skt. *kram* retains, as not seldom in the Epic in Skt., the short vowel in the parasmaip : M. *kamanta*., *akkamasi*, *akkamanta-*, *ṇikkamaï*, *ṇikkhamaï*, *viṇikkamaï*, *viṇikkhamaï*, *saṁkamaï* (G. H.); JM. *kamaï* (Ṛṣabhap. 38), *akkamāmo* (Erz. 35,36), *aïkkamaï*, *aïkkamĕjja* (Āv. 47,23; Kk. 271,2.7); AMg. *kamaï* (Vivāhap. 1249); *aïkkamaï* (Vivāhap. 136. 137), *aïkkamanti* (Kappas. S. 63), *avakkamaï*, *avakkamanti* (Vivāhap. 845. 1252), *avakkamĕjjā* (Āyār. 2,1,10,6), *mikkhamaï*, *nikkhamanti* (Vivāhap. 146; Nirayāv. § 23; Kappas. § 19), *nikkhamĕjja* (Āyār. 2,1,1,7; 2,1,9,2), *nikkhamamāṇa* (Āyār. 2,2,3,2), *paḍiṇikkhamaï* °*anti* (Vivāhap. 187,916; Nāyādh. § 34; p. 1427; Ovav.; Kappas.), *pakkamaï* (Vivahap. 1249), *vakkamaï* °*anti* (Vivāhap 111. 465; Paṇṇav. 28. 29. 41. 43; Kappas. § 19.46b), *viukkamanti* (Vivāhap. 465), metrically also *kammaï* = *krāmyati* (Uttar. 209); Ś *adikkamasi* (Ratn. 297,29); Ś. D. *avakkamadi* Mṛcch. 97,24; 103,15); *ṇikkamāmi* (Śak. 115,6), *ṇikkamadi* (Mṛcch. 51,4; Vikr. 16,1), *ṇikkama* (Mṛcch 16,10; Śak. 36,12), *ṇikkamamha* (Priyad. 17,16; Nāgān. 18,3; Ratn. 306,30; Karp. 85,7). In Mālatīm. 188,2 *parikkāmadi* is a false reading for *paribbhamadi* or *paribbhamanti*, as the ed. Bomb. 1892 and the ed. Madras (both °*mandi*) have; in 285,2 stands *parikkamedha*; Mg. *adikkamadi* (Mṛcch. 43,10), *avakkamamha*, *ṇiskamadi*, *ṇiskama* (Mṛcch. 22,2; 134,1; 165,22; 166,22). Cf. § 302.

§ 482. Several verbs, that in Sanskrit are of the first conjugation, presuppose in Pkt., as the vowel shows to be of the sixth conjugation. M. *jiaï* = **jiváti* for *jī'vati*, *jianti*, *jiaü*, *jianta-*, but also *jīasi*, *jivĕjja*, *jīanta-*, (Hc. 1,101; G. H. R.), Ś. Mg. have only a long vowel. So Ś. *jiāmi* (Uttarar. 132, 7; so to be read with ed. Calc. 1831, p. 89,10), *jīvadi* (Mṛcch. 172,6; 325,18), *jiāmo* (Mudrār. 34,10), *jiveaṁ* (Mālav. 55,11), *jiva* (Mṛcch. 145,11; Śak. 33,7; 67,7), *jiadu* (Mṛcch. 154,15); Mg. *yiadi*, *yiuaśi*, *yiva*, *yianta-* (Mṛcch. 12,20; 38,7; 161,19; 170,5; 171,8.9), also *yīveśi* (Mṛcch. 119,21).—*ghisaï* = **ghasáti* for *ghásati* = *ghasti* (Vr. 8,28 [so to be read]; Hc. 4,204; Kī. 4,46 [text *ghạ*°] ; Mk. fol. 55).—*jimaï* beside *jemaï jimmaï* (§ 488).—AMg. *bhisanta-* (Ovav.), *bhisamiṇa* (Nāẏādh.), *bhisamāṇa* (Rāẏap. 47. 105), intensive *bhibbhisamiṇa*, °*māṇa* (§ 556) from *bhisaï* = **bhāsáti* for *bhásati* (§ 109; Hc. 4,203).—*uvvivaï* = **udvipáte* for *udvépate* (§ 236).—The doubling of *l* in M. *alliaï uvalliaï samalliaï* = *āliyate, upā*° *samā*° (§ 196. 474), and AMg. causative *alliẏāvei* (§ 551) too may point to the same flexion. Cf. § 194. $\sqrt{}$*ruh* tends to be inflected according to the 6th conjugation when it is combined with a prefix : M. JM. *āruhaï*, *samāruhaï samāruhasu* (G. H. R.; Erz.); AMg. *duruhaï* = *udrohati* (§ 118; Ovav.; Uvās.; Nāẏādh. and often) in Vivāhap. throughout (pro ex. 124, 534, 506. 824 f. 980. 1128. 1231,1301.1311.1317.1325ff.) and elsewhere often as v. l. *durūhaï*, hardly correct, *duruhĕjja* (Āẏār. 2,3, 1,13. 14), JM. *duruhĕttā* (Erz.) AMg. *paccoruhaï*, *paccoruhanti* (Ovav.; Kappas.; Nāẏādh. also 870. 1354. 1456); Vivāhap. 173. 948), *viruhanti* (Uttar. 356), *āruhaï* (Vivāhap. 1273); Ś. *āruhadha*, *āruha* (Mṛcch. 40,24; 66,14, 17), *āruhadi* (Pras. 35,8), *āruhadu* (Uttarar. 32,6. 7); Mg. *āluha* Nāgān. 68,3), *āluhadu, ahiluha, ahiluhāmi, ahiluhadu* (Mṛcch. 99,8; 119,3. 6,9. 11. 13). The simplex is inflected : M. JM. *rohanti* (G. 727; Dvār. 503,7) and so also *ārohadu* (Śak. 39,12; 97,18; Vikr. 39,2).—*dhau* (to wash) may, according to Hc. 4,238, form *dhāvaï* = Skt. *dhāvati*. In M. however, it behaves as one of the 6. conjugation: *dhuvasi* (Hc. 2,216 = H. 369), *dhuasi* (H.), *dhuvaï* (Hc. 4,238), *dhuaï* (H.), *dhuvanta-* (R.). Thence a root *dhuv* is deduced, that secondarily is inflected according to the 1. conjugation, as *ru*, *svap* (§ 473. 497) : AMg. *dhovasi dhovaï* (Niraẏāv. 77; Sūẏag. 344) ; also according to the *e*-conjugation *dhovei* (Niraẏāv. 76. 77; Nāẏādh. 1219. 1220. 1501), *padhovĕnti* (Āẏār. 2,2,3,10); JM. *dhovanti* (Āv. 25,22); Ś. *dhoadi* (Mṛcch. 70,10), inf. *dhoiduṁ* (Mṛcch. 45,5); Mg. *dhovehi*, fut. *dhoiśśaṁ* (Mṛcch. 45,7. 20). So Pāli *dhovati*.—*hivaï*, which Hc. 4,238 mentions beside *havaï*, is derived from *bhū* by Sr. fol. 47.—Beside the usual *siaï*, JM. AMg. *siẏaï*, Ś. *sīdadi*, Mg. *śīdadi* = *sīdati*, according to Hc. 4,219, *saḍaï* too is in use (Pischel on Hc. 4,219). On *pasia* see § 80, on *bhaṇ* § 514.

§ 483. *ghrā*, *pā*, *sthā* build the present stem, as in Skt. by reduplication : *āigghaï* = *ājighrati* (Hc. 4,13), *jigghia* = *ghrāta* (Deśīn. 3,46).—M. *piaï*, *pianti*, *piaū*, *piantu* (G. H. R.), *pivaï* (Nāgān. 41,5), *piāmo* (Karp. 24,9 = Kāleyak. 16,17, where *pibāmo*) ; JM. *pivaï* (Āv. 30,36; 42,12. 18.20. 28.37), *piẏaha* = *pibata* (Dvār. 496,35), also *piei* (Erz. 69,1); AMg. *pivaï* Vivāhap. 1256), *piva* (Nāẏādh. 1332), *pie* (Dasav. 638,26), *piĕjja* (Āẏār. 2,1,1,2), *piẏamāṇe* (Vivāhap. 1253) ; Ś. *pivadi* (Viddhaś. 124,4), *pianti* (Mṛcch. 71,10), *pivadu* (Śak. 105,13), *āpivanti* (Mṛcch. 59,24); Mg. *pivāmi, pivāhi, pivamha* (Veṇīs. 33,4; 34,2. 15; 35,22), *pianti* (Mṛcch. 113, 21), *piva* (Prab. 60,9); A. *piaï*, *pianti*, *piahu* (Hc. 4,419,1. 6; 422,20). On *pijjaï* see § 539.—*sthā* forms M. AMg. JM. *ciṭṭhaï* (Hc. 4,16; H.; Āẏār. 1,2,3,5. 6; 1,5,5,1; Sūẏag. 310.613; Nāẏādh.; Kappas. Erz.; Kk.);

JM. *ciṭṭhae* (Āv. 36,26; Kk.); AMg. *ciṭṭhanti* (Sūyag. 274. 283.291. 612 f.; Kappas.), *ciṭṭhante* (Āyār. 1,8,4,10), *ciṭṭhĕjjā* (Āyār.2,1,4,3 [text false *cĕ°*]; 2,1,5,6. 6,2; 2,3,2,6; Vivāhap. 116. 925), *ciṭṭhe* (Āyār. 1,7,8,16), *ciṭṭhaṁ*, *aciṭṭhaṁ* (Āyār. 1,4,2,2); M. *ciṭṭhaü* (H.); JM. *ciṭṭhaha* (Kk.); AMg. inf. *ciṭṭhittae* (Vivāhap. 513. 1119) · beside *ṭhāittae* (Āyār 2,8,1. 2), particip. nec. *ciṭṭhiyavva* (Vivāhap. 163); AMg. *āciṭṭhāmo* (Sūyag. 734), *pariviciṭṭhaï* (Āyār. 1,4,2,2), also in the noun *saṁciṭṭhaṇa* = *avasthāna* (Vivāhap. 55 ff.). Whilst *ciṭṭhaï* is seldom in M., so much that Vr. Kī. Mk. do not at all mention it for M., *ciṭṭhadi* is the exceptional form in Ś. (Vr. 12,16. Kī. 5,81 [text *ṭhiṭṭhadi*]; Mk. fol. 71; Mṛcch. 27, 4; 45,23 54,4. 10; 57,3; 59,23; 72,10 etc.; Śak. 34,3; 79,11; 155,10 Vikr. 15,12. 14; 24,6; 41,9 and very often), *ciṭṭhāmi* (Mṛcch. 6,8; Vikr. 33,4), *ciṭṭha* (Mṛcch. 65,5; Śak. 12,4; Vikr. 32,5), *ciṭṭhamha* (Priyad. 17,4; Mālatīm. 255,5), *ciṭṭhadha* (Mālatīm. 247,4) and very often, also in composita, as *aṇuciṭṭhadi* (Mṛcch. 151,16; 155,5; Vikr. 41,6), *aṇuciṭṭhāmi* (Prab. 69,3) *aṇuciṭṭha* (Vikr. 83,1), *aṇuciṭṭhida* (Mṛcch. 54,2; 63,25; Vikr. 80,15), *aṇuciṭṭhiadu* (Mṛcch. 3,7; Śak. 1,9; Prab. 3,5) etc. So also Ā. *ciṭṭha* (Mṛcch. 99,18); D. *ciṭṭhaü* (Mṛcch. 104,2), *aṇuciṭṭhiduṁ* (Mṛcch. 102,19); A. *ciṭṭhadi* (Hc. 4,360). Mg. has *ciṣṭhadi*, that is pointed to by the manuscripts (§ 303), according to Vr. 11,14; Hc. 4,298; Kī. 5,95 [text *ciṭṭaḥ*] ; Mk. fol. 75 [MS *ciṭṭīrā*].According to Kī. 5,96 P. too has the same form as Mg. Cf. also § 216. 217. Like all roots in *-ā* (§ 487), *ghrā* and *sthā* too behave according to the 2. and 4. conjugations: M. AMg. *agghāi* = Epic *āghrāti* (H. 641; Nāyādh. §82; Paṇṇav. 429. 430); M. *agghāanta-* = *ājighrat-* (H. 566; R. 13. 82); AMg. *agghāyaï* (Āyār. p. 136,27. 33); opt. *agghāijja* (Nandīs. 363); AMg. *agghāyaha*, *agghāyamāṇa* (Nāyādh. § 83. 104); M. JM. *ṭhāi* = **sthāti* (Vr. 8,26; Hc. 4,16; Kī. 4,76; H. R.; Erz.; Āv. 41,8), M. *ṇiṭṭhāi* (H.), *saṁṭhāi* (H. R.); JM. *ṭhāha* (Āv. 27,27); A. *ṭhanti* (Hc. 4,395,5); AMg. *ṭhāĕjjā* (Āyār. 1,5,4,5,) *abbhuṭṭhanti* = *abhyuttiṣṭhanti* (Sūyag. 734); JM. *ṭhāyanti* (Ṛṣabhap. 27) corresponding to *ṭhāanti ṭhāaï ṭhāaü*, in Vr. 8,25. 26; Kī.4, 75. 76 (§ 487) .After *ud*, the vowel, according to the analogy of the *a*-declension, is also shortened: *uṭṭhaï* (Hc. 4,17); so JM. *uṭṭhaha* (Erz. 59,30); A. *uṭṭhaï* (Piṅgala 1,137a). Usually the flexion with the *e*-stem is selected: AMg. *uṭṭhei*(Vivāhap. 161. 1246; Uvās. § 193), *abbhuṭṭhei* (Kappas.); JM. *uṭṭhemi* (Āv. 41,19), *uṭṭhei* (Dvār. 503,32), *uṭṭhehi* (Erz. 42,3), *samuṭṭhehi* (Dvār. 503,27.31); Ś. *uṭṭhehi* (Mṛcch. 4,14; 18,22;51,5.11; Nāgān. 86,10; 95,18; Priyad. 26,6; 37,9; 46,24;53,6.9), *utthehi* (Vikr. 33,15), *utthedu* (Mṛcch. 93,5; Śak. 162,12), *uṭṭhedha* (Mṛcch. 24,17); Mg. *uṭṭhehi*, *uṭṭhedu*, *uṭṭhedi*, also *uṭṭhanta-* (Mṛcch. 20,21; 134,19; 169,5). Cf. § 309.

§ 484. *daṁś* forms according to Hc. 1,218 *ḍasaï* (§ 222) corresponding to Skt. *daśati*. So J.M. *ḍasaï* (Āv. 42,13); AMg. *dasamāṇe*, *dasantu* (Āyār. 1,8,3,4). Ś. forms, with retention of the nasal *daṁsadi* (Śak. 160, 1), past passive participle from the present stem: *daṁsido* (Mālav. 54,6).—*labh* shows nasal in the stem in AMg. *lambhāmi* (Uttar 103) and in the fut. and passive in Ś. Mg. (§ 525. 541). On *khāi* = *khadati* (also Kī. 4, 77) and *dhāi* = *dhāvati* see § 165.

§ 485. Of the verbs of the 6th conjugation, those which insert a nasal in the present stem, *lip*, *lup*, *vid* and *sic* are treated as in Skt. From *lip* is found also *allivaï* = *ālimpati* (§ 196; Hc. 4,39). Beside the *a*-stem the *e*-stem too may be used, as Ś. *siñcedi* (Śak. 74,9) beside *siñcamha*, *siñcadi* (Śak. 10,3; 15,3). *sic* forms also *seaï* = **secati* (Hc. 4,96).— *muc* does not usually insert a nasal in M. JM. AMg. (Hc. 4,91): M. *muasi*, *muaï*, *muanti*, *mua*, *muasu*, *muanta-* (G. H. R.; Śak. 85,3), *āmuaï* (G.); JM. *muẏaï* (Āv. 17,4; Erz. 52,8), *muẏasu* (Kk. 262,19), *muẏanto* (Erz. 23,34; so to be read); AMg. *muẏaï* (Vivāhap. 104. 508), *omuẏaï* (Āẏār. 2,15.22; Vivāhap. 796. 835. 1208. 1317; Kappas.), *muẏantesuṁ* = *muñcatsu* (Nāẏādh. § 62. 63), *viṇimmuẏamāṇa*, *muẏamāṇa* (Vivāhap. 254), *viṇimmuẏamāṇi* = *vinirmuñcamānā* (Vivāhap. 822). So also JŚ. *muẏadi* (Kattig. 403,383). The nasalized stem too is not rare in M. JM: M. *muñcaï* (H. 614; R. 3,30; 4,9; 7,49; 12,14), *muñcanti* (G. 258), *muñcaha* (R. 15,8; Karp. 12,6), *muñcanto* (Karp. 67,6; 86, 10); JM. *muñca*. *muñcasu*, *muñcaha* (Erz.), *muñca*, *muñcanti* (Kk. 261,12;272,7); in Ś. Mg. it alone can be used: Ś. *muñcadi* (Mudrār. 149.6), *muñca* (Mṛcch. 175,21; Śak. 60,14; Ratn. 316,4; Nāgān. 36,4;38, 8), *muñcadu* (Vikr. 30,2), *muñcadha* (Mṛcch. 154,16;161,18); Mg. *muñcadu*, *muñcanti* (Mṛcch. 31,18.21; 168,19), *muñca* (Prab. 50,6). Not rare is also the *e*-stem: M. *muñcesi* (H. 928); Ś. *muñcedi*, *muñcesi* (Śak. 51,6;154,12). *muñcedha* (Mṛcch. 161,25; Śak. 116,7), *muñcehi* (Mṛcch. 326,10; Vṛṣabh. 20,15;59,12).—*kṛt* (to chop) forms AMg. *kantaï* (Sūẏag. 360), dialectically *oandaï* = *apakṛntati* (Hc. 4,125 = *ācchinatti*; cf. § 275). In AMg. the root in conjunction with *vi* with retention of the nasalization goes over to the 4. conjugation: *vigiñcaï* = **vikṛntyati*, *vigiñcamāṇe* (Āẏār. 1,3,4,3; 1,6,2,4); *vigiñca* (Āẏār. 1,3,2,1; Uttar. 170), *vigiñcĕjja* (Āẏār. 2,3.2,6); absol. *vigiñca* (Sūẏag. 500. 506). Cf. *kicci* § 271 and *ṇiruñjhaï* § 507.

§ 486. *spṛś* forms in AMg. regularly *phusaï* = *spṛśati*, *phusanti* = *spṛśanti*, *phusantu* = *spṛśantu*, *phusmāṇe* = *spṛśamānaḥ* (Āẏār. 1,6,1,3.3,2. 5,1; 1,7,7, 1; Vivāhap. 97.98. 354.355. 1288; Ovav.). Identical with it are *phusaï* *pusaï* (polishes; Hc. 4,105; G. H. R.) and *phusaï* (roams about; Hc. 4, 161)[1]. Hc. 4,182 mentions also *phāsaï*, *phaṁsaï*, *pharisaï*, that presuppose one * *sparśati*.—*phāsaï* occurs in AMg. *saṁphāse* = *saṁspṛśet* = **saṁsparśet* (Āẏār. 2,1,3,3.5,5.9,2. 4.5.6. 10,2. 3; 2,3,2,13). *pharisaï* is formed like *karisaï* = *karṣati*, *marisaï* = *marṣati*, *varisaï* = *varṣati*, *harisaï* = *harṣati* (Vr. 8,11; Hc. 4,235; Kī 4,72)[2]. The same type of conjugation is presupposed by *puṁsaï* (polishes; Hc. 4, 105), *uppuṁsia*, *ŏppuṁsia* (G. 57. 778 beside *ŏppusia* 723) which has been forced into Skt. as *utpuṁsaya*.[3]— *truṭ* forms also *toḍaï* = *trŏṭati* (Hc. 4,116), beside *tuḍaï* = *truṭáti* and *tuṭṭaï* = *trúṭyati*, as *mil* forms *melaï* in M. *meliṇa* (§ 562). AMg. *melanti* (Vivāhap. 950), A. *melavi* (Hc. 4,429,1).—On *kṛ*, *mṛ* see § 477, on *sṛ* § 235, on *phuṭṭaï* § 488, note 1.

1. The usual basic meaning is "to slip over something, to go away", that easily yields "to rest". The derivation from *proñch* (WEBER. Hāla s. v. *pus*: S. GOLDSCHMIDT, ZDMG. 32, 99) is linguistically impossible.—2. Reference in PISCHEL on Hc. 4.235 and above under § 135.—3. ZACHARIAE, Beiträge zur indischen Lexicographie p.58. The

nasal in *puṁsaï* is not original as S. GOLDSCHMIDT, ZDMG. 32,99 note 2 means, but it is to be explained, as in *phaṁsaï*, according to § 74. In H. 706 Dhvanyāloka 155,11 reads *mā puṁsa* for *mā pusasu*.

§ 487. The 4. conjugation has in Pkt. undergone a wider extension than in Skt. The number of roots conjugated according to this class that were either never or only seldom so conjugated in Skt. is larger.[1] All the roots and stems ending in a vowel, other than *a*, may according to Hc. 4,240 (cf. Vr. 8,21. 25. 26; Kī. 4,65. 75. 76; Mk. fol. 54), follow this conjugation: *pāaï* = **pāyati* beside *pāi* = *pāti* (protects); *dhāaï*, *dhāi* = *dadhāti*; *ṭhāaï*, *ṭhāi*, 3. plur. *ṭhāanti*, JM. *ṭhāyanti*, A. *thanti* (§ 483); *vikkeaï* beside *vikkei* = **vikrayati*[2]; *hoaūṇa* beside *hoūṇa* from the stem *ho* = *bhava*, which according to Sr. fol. 47 is inflected also as *hoāmi*, *hoasi*, *hoaï* (§ 476). The duplicity of flexion is sometimes found already in Vedic, as *uvvāaï* = Vedic *udvāyati*, *uvvāi* = Skt. *udvāti*.—*jambhāaï*, *jambhāi* are denominatives from *jṛmbhā*. AMg. *jāi* (Sūẏag. 540; Uttar. 170), beside the usual M. *jāaï* = *jāyate*, too is formed from *jan* according to such an analogy. Examples from literature are M. *māasi*, *māaï*, *māanti*, *amāanta-* (H.), JM. *māẏanti* (Erz.), Ś. *ṇimmāanta-* (Mālatīm. 121,1) from *mā*, which forms also *māyate*; according to Dhātupāṭha 26,33. A. *māi* (Hc. 4,351,1) in addition to *māti*, *mimite*.—M. *vāaï* (Ratn. 293,3), *vāanti*, *vāanta-* (G. R.), *ṇivvāanti*, *ṇivvāanta-* (R.), *parivāaï* (G.), *pavvāaï* (R.), Ś. *vāadi* (Śak 115,2 v. l.), beside M. *vāi*, *āvāi*, *ṇivvāi* (G. H.), JŚ. *ṇivvādi* (Pav. 388,6), M *vanti* (Karp. 10,2 v. l.; Dhūrtas. 4,20 v. l.), further *vāanti* (Karp. 12.4).—JM. *paḍihāẏaï* (Āv. 33, 28); Ś. *paḍihāadi* = **pratibhāyati* = *pratibhāti* (Bālar. 135,11) beside *paḍihāsi* (Vikr. 7,18), *paḍihādi* (Mṛcch. 71,25 [°*bhā*°]; Śak. 12,7; Vikr. 13,2;24,2; Nāgān. 5,9), often with the v. l. *paḍihāadi*; M.A. *paḍihāi* (Hc. 3,80; G.H.; Hc. 4,441,1); Ś. *bhādi* (Mṛcch. 73,14), *vihādi* (Prab. 57,2).—Ś. *pattiāasi* = *pratiyāsi* (§ 281; Mṛcch. 82,3; Ratn. 301,7;317,9; Nāgān. 37,7 [so correctly the v. l]), *pattiāadi* (Nāgān. 30,3 [so correctly ed. Calc. 29,8]; Pras. 46,14; Ratn. 309,24; Vikr. 41,10 [so to be read with v. l.]; Mg. *pattiāaśi* (Mṛcch. 130,13), *pattiāadi* (Mṛcch. 167,2), *pattiāadha* (Mṛcch. 165,9; Mudrār. 257,4 (so rightly v. l. and ed. Calc. 212,9]), *pattiāanti* (Mṛcch 167,1), passive *pattiāiadi* (Mṛcch. 165,13).[3]. Against this are inflected in AMg. JM. M. completely according to the analogy of the first conjugation AMg. *pattiẏāmi* (Sūẏag. 1015; Uvās. § 12; Nāẏādh. § 133; Vivāhap. 134. 161. 803), *pattiẏaï* (Vivāhap 845), *pattiẏanti* (Vivāhap. 841 f.), opt. *pattiĕjjā* (Paṇṇav. 577; Rāẏap. 250), imperative *pattiẏāhi* (Sūẏag. 1016; Vivāhap. 134); JM. *pattiẏasi* (Erz. 52,20), *apattianteṇa* (T. 6,18); M *pattiasi*, *pattiaï* (R. 11,90; 13,44), from which the imperative is M. *pattia* (H.), falsely M. *pattihi* (R. 11. 94; the v. l. rightly *pattia*; Kāvyaprakāśa 195,2; v. l. rightly *pattia*) and M. *pattisu* (H. v. l.), in dependence upon the false etymology = *pratihi*. Ś. *pattijjāmi* (Karp. ed. Bomb. 42,12), *pattijjasi* (Karṇas. 31,11) are false; for the first one KONOW 40,9 reads *pattiāmi*.—*ṇhāi* = *snāti* (Hc. 4,14); AMg. *siṇāi* (Sūẏag. 344); JM. *ṇhāmo* = *snāmaḥ* (Āv. 17,7); Mg. *sṇāāmi* = *snāmi* (Mṛcch. 113,21).—Cf. § 313. 314.—AMg. *paccāẏanti* (Ovav. § 56) belongs to *jan* (LEUMANN s. v,), likewise *āyanti*, as Kappas. § 17 is to be read according to the v. l.; opt. l. sing. *payāĕjjā* (Nirayâv. 59), 2. sing. *payāĕjjāsi* (Nāyādh. 420). On AMg. *jāi* = *jāyate* see above. Cf. also § 479.

1. LASSEN, Inst. p. 343; PISCHEL, BB. 13,9.—2. *vikkeaī* is more correctly taken as the denominative from *vikreya* (§ 511).—3. There with the help of the v. l. it is to be read: *yaṁ śaccakaṁ pi ṇa pattiāīadi*. The form *pattiāedi* is likewise false like Ś. *pattiyāedi* in Mṛcch. 325,19.

§ 488. The auslaut of the roots ending in a consonant in conjunction with *ya* undergoes the alteration described in the section on Phonetics (§ 279—286): *ṇaccaï* = *nṛtyati*; *jujjhaï* = *yudhyate*; *tuṭṭaï* = *truṭyati* *maṇṇaï* = *manyate*; *kuppaï* = *kupyati*; *lubbhaï* = *lubhyati*; *uttammaï* = *uttāmyati*; *ṇassaï*, AMg. JM. *nāsaï*, M. *ṇāsaï* = *naśyati* (§ 63): *rūsaï*, *tūsaï*, *sūsaï*, *dūsaï*, *pūsaï*, *sisaï* (Bh. 8,46: Hc. 4,236; Kī. 4.68), AMg. JM. *pāsāï* = *paśyati* (§ 63).—According to the *e*-conjugation is formed JM. *tūsedi* (Kattig. 400,335), Deviating from Skt. are conjugated according to the 4. class pro ex. *kukkaï*, *kŏkkaï* = **krukyati* = **kruśati* = *krośati* (Hc. 4, 76)[2]; *callaï* = **calyati* = *calati* (Vr. 8,53; Hc. 4,231) beside the usual *calaï*, also in composita as *oallanti* = *avacalanti*, *oallanta-* (R.), *paallaï* (Hc. 4,77), *pariallaï* (Hc. 4,162); *jimmaï* = **jimyati* beside *jimaï*, *jemaï* = *jemati* (Hc. 4,230; cf. 4,110); *thakkaï* = **sthakyati* (Hc. 4,16)[3]; **millaï* = **milyati* = *mīlati* in composita: *ummillaï*, *ṇimillaï*, *pamillaï*, *saṁmillaï* (Vr. 8,54; Hc. 4,232; G. R.; in A. *ummillaï* (Hc. 4,354); Mg. *śaṁyammadha* = **saṁyamyata* = *saṁyacchata* (Mṛcch. 11, 3); Ś. *ruccadi* = **rucyate* = *rocate* (Vikr. 31,3; 40,18; Mālav. 15,14; 77, 21), A. *ruccaï* (Hc. 4,341,1), beside *roadi* (Mṛcch. 7,14; 44,5; 58,14; Śak. 54,4; Vikr. 24,7; 41,18), Mg. *loadi* (Mṛcch. 139,16; Śak. 159,3); *laggaï* = **lagyati* = *lagati* (Vr. 8,52; Hc. 4,230); Ś. *olagganti* (Mālav. 39,14), *vilaggantaṁ* (Mṛcch. 325,14); Mg. *laggadi* (Mṛcch. 79,10); A. *laggaï* (Hc. 4,420,5; 422,7), *laggivi* (Hc. 4,339): Ḍh. *vajjasi*, *vajjadi*, *vajja* from *vraja* (Mṛcch. 30,4. 10; 39,10), Ś. *vajjamha* (Pras. 35,17), false *vaccasi* (Cait. 57, 2)[4], Mg. *vayyĕnti*, *pavayyāmi* (Mṛcch. 120,12; 175,18). In Mg. A. *vraj* may be conjugated also according to the 9. class: Mg. *vaññāmi*, *vaññandaśśa* (Lalitav. 566,7. 17). *vaññadi* = **vrajñāti* (Hc. 4,294; Sr. fol. 63)[5]; A. *vuñaï*, absol. *vuñĕppi*, *vuñĕppiṇu* (Hc. 4,392). AMg. has also *vayāmo* (Sūyag. 268), *vayanti* (Sūyag. 277).

1. PISCHEL, BB. 13,18 f. In many cases one could think of flexion according to the 6. class, as it certainly is in *phuṭṭai* = *sphuṭáti* (Vr. 8,53; Hc. 4,231).—2. PISCHEL, BB. 3,256.—3. PISCHEL, BB. 3,258 f.—4. Cf. § 202. In Mṛcch. 109,19 we should for *vajjissāmo* read *bajjhissāmo*, fut. pass. from *bandh*; cf. v. l.—5. In the verse in Mudrār. 250,5 it is closer to read *vayyedha* instead of the transmitted *vajjeha*, with HILLEBRANDT, ZDMG. 39,109 *vaññedha*. Cf. also *vaññāe* (Mallikām. 144,7).

§ 489. Some roots that follow the 4. conjugation in Sanskrit go over to the first class or to the sixth class, partly compulsorily and partly optionally in Pkt.—*man* may form as well *maṇaï* = **manate* (Hc. 4,7), beside the usual *maṇṇaï* = *manyate*. Thereof the l. sing. pres. ātm. *maṇe* is frequent in M. (§ 457). M. AMg, JM. A. *muṇaï*, JŚ. *muṇadi* (Vr. 8,23; Hc. 4,7; Mk. fol. 53; G.H.R.; Acyutaś. 82; Pratāp. 202,15; 204,10; Vikr. 26,8;

Āẏār. 1,7,8,13; Ovav.; Kappas.; Erz ; Kk.; Hc. 4,346; Piṅgala 1,85. 86. 90. 95 etc.; Kattig. 398, 303; 399, 313. 316; 400,337) and according to the *e*-conjugation AMg. *muṇeẏavva* (Paṇṇav. 33), JŚ. *muṇedavva* (Pav. 380,8; text °*ẏa*°) too are traced back to *man*. Against this derivation stands the meaning "to know" as well as Pāli *munāti*. I derive *muṇaï* from Vedic *mūta* in *kāmamūta* and Skt. *muni*. Cf. *animo movere*. —As sometimes already in Epic Skt., *śam* in Pkt. may form its stem according to the 1. class: *samaï* (Hc. 4,167), *uvasaṁaï* (H. 4,239). So M. *paḍisamaï* (R. 6,44) ; AMg. *uvasamaï* (Kappas. S. § 59); JM. *uvasamasu* (Erz. 3,13), *pasamanti* (Āv. 16,20) ; Mg. *uvaśamadi* (Hc. 4,299 = Veṇīs. 34,11, where GRILL reads *uvaśammadi*; cf. however, the v. l. and ed. Calc. 71,7). But more frequent is the conjugation according to the 4. class, as in Skt. : M. *ṇisammaï*, *ṇisammanti*; *ṇisammasu*, *ṇisammanta-* (G.), *pasammaï*, *pasammanta-* (G.R.) ; *parisāmaï* (Hc. 4,167).—*śram* is conjugated according only to the 1. class: AMg. *samaï* (Uttar. 38); JM. *uvasamanti* (Āv. 35,29); M. JM. *visamāmi*, *visamasi*, *visamaï*, *visamāmo*, *visamau*, *visamaü* (G.H.R.; Erz.; Hc. 1,43;4,159) ; JM. *visamamāṇa* (Dvār. 501,5) ; Ś. *visama* (Mṛcch. 97,12), *visamamha* (Ratn. 302, 32), passive *vīsamīadu* (Mṛcch. 77,11), *vissamīadu* (Śak. 32,9; Vikr. 77,15).—*vidh* (*vyadh*) behaves in M. AMg. JM according to the 6. class with an inserted nasal: M. *vindhanti* (Karp. 30,6) ; AMg. *vindhaï* (Uttar. 788), opt. *vindhĕjja* (Vivāhap. 122), *āvindhĕjja vā pivindhĕjja vā* (Āẏār. 2,13,20), also in the causative *āvindhāvei* (Āẏār. 2,15,20) ; JM. *āvindha* (Āv. 38,7, 10. 35), *āvindhāmo*, *āvindhasu* (Āv. 17,8; 38,33), *vindhaï* (Āv. 38. 36). In AMg. *vehaï* = *vedhati* (Sūẏag 186) behaves according to the 1. class, and with *ud* according to the 6. class without a nasal : *uvvihaï* = **udvidháti* = *udvidhyati* (Nāẏādh. 958. 959; Vīvāhap. 1388).—*śliṣ* forms *silesaï* = **śleṣati* = *śliṣyati* (Hc. 4,190) according to the first class.

§ 490. The verbs of the 10. conjugations and the denominatives and causatives, so far they are formed similarly, tend to contract *-aya-* to *-e-*: PG. *abhatthemi* = *abhyarthayāmi* (7,44); M. *kahei* = *kathayati* (H.), *kahĕnti* (G.); JM. *kahemi*, *kaheha* (Erz.); AMg. *kahei* (Uvās.), *parikahemo* (Niraẏāv. 60); Ś. *kadhehi* = *kathaya* (Mṛcch. 4,14; 60,2; 80,17; 142,9; 146, 4; 152,24; Śak. 37.16; 50,12; Vikr. 51,11 etc.), *kadhesu* (Bālar. 53,12; 164,17; 218,16), *kadhedu* = *kathayatu* (Mṛcch. 28,2; Śak. 52,7; 113,12); Mg. *kadhedi* (Śak. 117,5).—M. *gaṇei* = *gaṇayati*, *gaṇĕnta* (R.); *gaṇesi* (Śak. 156,5).—M. *cintesi*, *cintei*, *cintĕnti*,, *cinteuṁ* (G. H. R.); AMg. *cintei* (Uvās.); JM. *cintesi* (Erz.), *cintĕnti* (Āv. 43,21) ; Ś. *cintemi* (Vikr. 40,20), *cintehi* (Śak. 54,7; Vikr. 46,8; Ratn. 309,13), *cintemo* (Mahāv. 134,11).—Ś. *takkemi* (Mṛcch. 39,3; 59,25; 79,1. 4; 95,3; Śak. 9,11; 98,8; 117,10; 132,11 and very often), likewise Mg. (Mṛcch. 99,11; 122,12; 141,2; 163,22; 170,17); A. *takkei* (Hc. 4,370, 3).— AMg. *pariẏāvĕnti* = *paritāpayanti* (Āẏār. 1,1,6,2) : Ś. *saṁtāvedi* Śak. 127,7).—AMg. *veḍhei* = *veṣṭayati* (Vivāhap. 447; Nāẏādh. 621; Niraẏāv. § 11), *varemo* = *varayāmaḥ* (Vivāgas. 229), *vedemo* = *vedayāmaḥ* (Vivāhap. 70). Uncontracted forms are more frequent only before the following double consonants, especially *nt*, as AMg. *tāḷaẏanti* = *tāḍayanti* (verse; Uttar. 360,365) beside *tāḷěnti* (Vivāhap. 236), *tāḷei* (Nāẏādh. 1236. 1305), *tāḷeha* (Nāẏādh. 1305), *sobhoẏantā* (Jīv. 886), *paḍisaṁveẏaẏanti* (Āẏār. 1,4,2,2); M. *avaaṁsaanti* = *avataṁsayanti* (Śak. 2,15); JM. *cintayanto, cintayantāṇaṁ* (Erz.); Ś. *cintaanto* (Vikr. 42,8), *cintaantassa* (Śak. 30,5); P. *cintayamāṇī, cintayanto* (Hc. 4,310. 322); Ś. *daṁsaantie* = *darśayantyā, daṁsaamha, daṁsaïssaṁ, daṁsaïssasi °di*; Mg. *daṁśaante* beside Ś. *daṁsemi, daṁsesi, daṁsehi, daṁseduṁ* (§ 554); Ś. *paāsaanto* = *prakāśayan* (Ratn. 313,33) beside M. *paāsei, paāsěnti, paāsěntiṁ* (G.); Mg. *paẏāśěmha* (text °*sě*°) = *prakāśayāma* (Lalitav. 567,1); Ś. *pesaanteṇa* = *preṣayatā* (Śak. 140,13); Ś. *āāsaanti* = *āyāsayanti* (Vṛṣabh. 50,10). More seldom in other cases, as Ś. *pavesaāmi* (Mṛcch. 45,25) beside Ś. *pavesehi* (Mṛcch. 68,5); Mg. *paveśehi* (Mṛcch. 118, 9. 19); Ś. *viraaāmi* = *viracayāmi* (Śak. 79,1), Ś. *assāsaadi* = *āśvāsayati* (Veṇīs. 10,4); Ś. *ciraadi* = *cirayati* (Mṛcch. 59,22); Ś. *jaṇaadi* = *janayati* (Śak. 131,8), where, however, we should with the v. l., read *jaṇedi*, as M. *jaṇei* (H.), *jaṇěnti* (H. R.); M. *vaṇṇaāmo* = *varṇayāmaḥ* (Bālar. 182,10). Always in AMg. JM. and in AMg. very frequently is used *dalaya-* "to give"; *dalaẏāmi* (Nāẏādh. § 94; Niraẏāv. § 19; p. 62; Erz. 97,27), *dalaẏaï* (Vivāgas. 35. 132. 211. 223; Nāẏādh. § 55. 125; p. 265. 432. 439. 442. 449; Rāẏap. 191 ff.; Āẏār. 2,1,10,1; Uvās.; Kappas.; Ovav. etc.), *dalaẏāmo* (Vivāgas. 230; Nāẏādh. 291), *dalaẏanti* (Vivāgas. 84,209; Nāẏādh. § 120), *dalaẏějjā dalaẏāhi* (Āẏār. 1,7,5,2;2,1, 10,6.7; 2,6,1,10), *dalaẏaha* (Niraẏāv. § 19), *dalaẏamāṇe* (Nāẏādh. § 113; Kappas. § 103 [so to be read, as § 28 *dalaẏaï* with A]). Cf. § 474.

§ 491. In Skt. denominatives may be derived from nominal stems without a particular suffix, as *aṅkurati* from *aṅkura, kṛṣṇati* from *kṛṣṇa, darpaṇati* from *darpaṇa* (Kielhorn § 476; Whitney § 1054). This sort of formation, that is not frequent in Skt., is very usual in Pkt., especially in M. and A. The denominatives derived from the feminine forms ending in *-ā* shorten it, as in all similar cases (§ 487. 500. 510f.) and are conjugated according to the 1. conjugation. Thus from M. *kahā* = *kathā* are derived *kahāmi kahasi, kahaï kahāmo, kahaha, kahanti*. From this it results that beside the forms ending in *-e-* = *-aya-*, mentioned in § 490, those in *-a-* are found not seldom. So: M. *kahaï* (Hc. 1,187; 4,2; H. 59); AMg. *kahāhi* (Sūẏag. 423), *kahasu* (Uttar. 700, 703); A. *kahi* = **katheḥ* = *kathayeḥ* (Hc. 4,422, 14).—M. *gaṇaï, gaṇanti, gaṇantīe* (H.); A *gaṇaï. gaṇanti gaṇantiě* (Hc.; also 4,353). – M. *cintaï, cintanta-* (H.), *viintantā* = *vicintayantaḥ* (G.); A. *cintaï, cintantāhã* = *cintayatām* (Hc.).—M. *ummūlanti* = *unmūlayanti* (H.), *ummūlanta-* (R.) beside *ummūlěnti* (R.), *kāmantao* = *kāmayamānaḥ* (H.) beside *kāmei* (Hc. 4,44), *kāmemo* (H.), *kāměnti* (G.), *pasāanti* = *prasādayanti* beside *pasāesi, pasāamāṇassa* (H.), *papphoḍaï, papphoḍantī* = *prasphoṭayanti*, °*yantī* (H.), *maülanti* = *mukulayanti* (H.), *maülaü* (G). *maülanta-* (R.) beside *maülei, maülěnti* (R.), *maülintā* (G.); A. *pāhasi* = *prārthayasi* (Piṅgala 1,5a; cf. Bollensen, Vikr. p. 530). *a* is found preponderantly, as the uncontracted forms before *nt.* (§ 490). Thence it is possible that the entire formation of these forms has developed. A *gaṇaanti* = Skt. *gaṇayanti* must have through **gaṇānti* become *gaṇanti*, whence are deduced *gaṇāmi, gaṇasi*, *gaṇaï*. In Ś. Mg. the forms with *a*, except in verses, are never found. In no case we can assume transition of *e* into *a*[1]. On the causatives see also § 551 ff., on the denominatives § 557 ff.

1. WEBER, Hāla[1] p. 60; cf., however, there the note 4.

§ 492. The roots in -*ā* of the 2. conjugation are conjugated as in Skt. or according to the 4. conjugation (§ 487). *khyā* in conjunction with prefixes may in AMg. be conjugated according to the 2. conjugation : *akkhāi* = *ākhyāti* (Vivāhap. 966) ; *akkhanti* = *ākhyānti* (Sūyag. 456. 465. 522) ; = *āghaṁ* = *ākhyān* (Sūyag. 397, *paccakkhāmi* (Uvās.), *paccakkhāi* (Ṭhāṇ. 119; Vivāhap. 119. 607; Uvās.) ; *paccakkhāmo* (Ovav.). Ḍh. *akkhanto* (Mṛcch. 34,24) is a false reading for *ācakkhanto* (§ 499). However, in AMg., as in Pāli, the roots are mostly reduplicated (and inflected according to the *a*-conjugation as *ghrā*, *pā*, *sthā* (§ 483)[1]: *āikkhāmi* = **ācikhyāmi* (Sūyag. 579; Ṭhāṇ. 149; Jīv. 343; Vivāhap. 130 139. 142. 325. 341. 1033), *āikkhaï* (Sūyag. 620; Āyār. 2,15,28,29; Vivāhap. 915. 1032; Uvās.; Ovav.; Kappas.) = Pāli *ācikkhati*; *saṁcikkhaï* (Āyār. 1,6,2,2), *āikkhāmo* (Āyār. 1,4,2,5,), *āikkhanti* (Āyār. 1,4, 1,1; 1,6,4,1; Sūyag. 647. 969; Vivāhap. 139. 341; Jīv. 343), *abbhāikkhaï*, *abbhāikkhĕjjā* (Āyār. 1,1 3,3), *abbhāikkhanti* (Sūyag. 969); *paccāikkhāmi* (Āyār. 2,15,5,1), *āikkhe*, *āikkhĕjjā* (Āyār. 1,6,5,1; 2,3,3,8; Sūyag. 661.663), *paḍiyāikkhe* (Āyār. 1,7,2,2), *paḍisaṁcikkhe*, *saṁcikkhe* (Uttar. 103. 106), *āikkhāhi* (Vivāhap. 150), *āikkhaha* (Āyār. 2,3,3,8 ff.; Nāyādh. § 83), *āikkhamāṇa* (Ovav. 59), *paccāikkhamāṇa* (Vivāhap. 607), *saṁcikkhamāṇa* (Uttar. 440).

1. PISCHEL, BB. 15,126. The usual derivation from *cakṣ* (§ 499) is erroneous.

§ 493. *i* is inflected mostly as in Skt. The 3. plur. parasmaipada nevertheless is M. AMg *ĕnti* (G.R.; Kāleyak. 3,8; Āyār. p. 15,6), likewise in composita: M. *aṇṇĕnti* = *anuyanti* (R.) ; M. *ĕnti* = *āyanti* (R.; Dhūrtas. 4,20 Karp. 10,2) ; M. AMg. *uvĕnti* = *upayanti* (G.; Āyār. 2,16,1; Sūyag. 468; Dasav. 627, 12), AMg. *samuvĕnti* (Dasav. 635,2). AMg. has for it also *inti* (Paṇṇav. 43), *niinti* = *niyanti* in the sense of *niryanti* (Paṇhāv. 381. 382), *palinti* = *pariyanti* (Sūyag. 95.134), *saṁpalinti* (Sūyag. 52), *uvinti* (Sūyag. 259) and *uvinte* (Sūyag 271), *samanninti* = *samanuyanti* (Ovav.[§37]) It is convenient to consider *e* as the original that developed on the analogy of the sing. *emi*, *esi*, *ei* and to derive *i* from it according to § 84. If, however, AMg. *niinti* is the correct reading, it cannot be separated from M. *ṇinti* (G.; H. v. l. ; R.), *viṇinti* (Dhvanyāloka 237,2 = H. 954), *aïnti* (G.), *parinti* (R.), which then must be explained as having arisen from *ṇiinti*, **ṇinti*, **viṇiinti*, **viṇinti*, **aiinti*, **aïnti*, **pariinti*, **parinti*. *inti*, as Pāli too has, is formed according to **imo*, **iha* = Skt. *imáh*, *itha*. The participle is JM. *into* (Dvār. 499,27) ; it occurs in M. *ṇinta*- (G.H.R.), *viṇinta*- (G.), *aïnta*-, *parinta*-, (R.), *pariṇinta*- (Sarasvatīk. 9,21)[2] = *niyant*-, *viniyant*-, *atiyant*-, *pariyant*-, **pariniyant*- too. *e* found in the v. l. *ṇĕnti* (G.H.R.), *viṇĕnti* (Sarasvatīk 206,25)[3] must be explained as having arisen from *i* according to § 119, in the same way as in the forms *ĕnti*, *aṇṇĕnti*, *uvĕnti*, cited above. From the plural-forms **aimo*, **aiha* = *atimaḥ*, *atitha*, *ṇimo, *ṇiha = nīmaḥ, nītha, *parimo, *pariha = parimaḥ, paritha and others a singular is deduced: M aii = *atiti (Hc. 4, 162; R.) ṇisi = *niṣi (R.); M. JM. ṇii = *niti (G. H. R.; Āv. 41, 13.22), M. parii = *pariti (Hc. 4,162; R.)[4]. AMg. gives the regular forms ei (Āyār. 1,3,1,3; 1,5,1,1.4,3; Sūyag. 328. 460), accei (Āyār. 1,2,1,3. 6,4; 1,5,6,3; Sūyag. 540), uei = udeti (Sūyag. 460), ueu (Āyār, 2, 4, 1, 12; text udeu), uvei = upaiti (Āyār. 1,2,6,1; 1,5,1,1; Sūyag. 268. 523) etc. AMg. ĕjjāsi (Āyār. 2,6,1,8) is = eyāḥ; imp. is ĕjjāhi (Āyār. 2,5,1,10). On i with palā see § 567.—śi forms in AMg. sayaï, āsayaï (Kappas. § 95); opt. sae (Āyār. 1,7,8,13) and saĕjjā (Āyār. 2,2,3,25. 26), particip. pres. sayamāṇa (Āyār. 2,2,3,26). Monstrous is Ś. serade (Mallikām. 291,3).

1. E. Kuhn, Beiträge p. 96.—2. So correctly Zachariae, KZ. 28,414.—3. So correctly Zachariae, KZ. 28,415—4. On these forms treated collectively by S. Goldschmidt, ZDMG. 32,110 ff. and Zachariae, KG. 28,411 ff., where is given further literature. The setting up of a root nī "to go away" is impossible. From the Śatapathabrāhmaṇa upanayati (Oldenberg, KZ. 27.281) and Pkt. ṇiṇaï + *nirṇayati (Hc. 4,162) is deduced a root nī "to go", which occurs in AMg. nae = nayet (§ 411; note 2; Āyār. 2,16,5), but that has nothing to do with ṇii, as the flexion and parallel forms aii, parii show. The hypothesis that ni stands in the sense of niḥ simply creates difficulty. Further instances on this are wanting. It is impossible to derive ni, with Weber, ZDMG. 26,741, from nis "weakened".

§ 494. The roots ending in -u, -ū of the second conjugation mostly go over to the first conjugation: paṇhaaï = prasnauti, ravaï = rauti, savaï = sūte, pasavaï = prasūte, aṇiṇhavamāṇa = aninhuvāna; hnu goes over to the 6th conjugation too (§ 473). stu is conjugated in M. JM. AMg. as a verb of the 9. conjugation in Pkt.: thuṇaï (Hc. 4,241; Sr. fol. 49), thuṇimo (Bālar. 122, 13); AMg. saṁthuṇaï, absol. saṁthuṇittā (Jīv.612), abhitthuṇanti (Vivāhap. 833) abhitthuṇamāṇā, abhisaṁthuṇamāṇā (Kappas. § 110. 113); JM. thuṇei according to the e-conjugation (Kk. II, 508,23), absol. thuṇiya (Kk. II.508,26). In Ś. Mg. it follows the 5. conjugation: Ś. uvatthuṇṇanti = *upastunvanti (Uttarar. 10,9; 27,3; so to be read; cf. Lassen; Inst. p. 268 note); Mg. thuṇu (Mṛcch. 113,12; 115,9). The passive thuvvaï (§ 536) presupposes a flexion also according to the 6. conjugation = *thuvaï = Skt. *stuváti, the absol. JM. thoūṇa (Kk. 277,31; II, 507, 25; III, 513,3) one *stotvāna.—brū has retained its old flexion of Skt. in the frequent AMg. bemi = bravīmi (§ 166; Hc. 4,238; Āyār. p. 2 ff; 8 ff.; Sūyag. 45. 84. 99. 117. 159. 200. 322. 627. 646f. 863. 950; Dasav. p. 613 f.; 618, 16; 622 ff.). From it is built a 3. plur. AMg. JM. bĕnti (Dasav. N. 651,5. 16. 20; 658,25; 661,8; Erz. 4,5), binti (Sūyag. 236); the 1. plur. is AMg. būma (Uttar. 784; verse), the imp. būhi (Sūyag. 259.301.553). On the optative būyā see § 464. In A. it behaves according to the 6. conjugation: bruvaha = brūta (Hc. 4,391); AMg. buiya presupposes the same flexion (§ 565).

§ 495. The roots rud, śvas and svap have completely gone over to the a-conjugation. rud is conjugated according to the 6. conjugation in M. and mostly in JM. A. too: M. ruāmi, ruasi, ruaï, ruanti, rua, ruehi, ruasu (H.R.; Dhvanyāloka 173,3 = H. 966); JM. ruyasi (Āv. 13,33; 14,27), ruyaï (Āv. 14,26), ruyasu (Sagar. 6,11), ruyaha (Āv.14.28), ruyanti (Āv. 13,33; Erz. 15,24), ruyantie (Erz. 22,36), ruyamāṇi (Erz. 43,19), ruyāmāṇiṁ (Āv. 14,

26); A. *ruahi* = *rodiṣi* (Hc. 4,383,1), *ruaī* (Piṅgala 1,137a). More seldom is the flexion according to the 1. conjugation in AMg. JM. A: AMg. *royanti* (Sūyag. 114); JM. *royaï* (Āv. 17,27), particip. fem. *royantī* (Āv. 12,34); JM. AMg. *royamāṇa* (Erz. 66,24; Uttar. 169; Vivāhap. 807; Vivāgas. 77. 118. 155. 225. 239. 240); A. *roi* = **rodeḥ* = *rudyāḥ* (Hc. 4,368), *roantĕ* = *rudatā* (Vikr. 72,11). This alone is prevalent in Ś. Mg., as Ś. *radasi* (Mṛcch. 95,22), *roadi* (Mṛcch. 95,5; Veṇīs. 58,20 [so to be read for *roidi* with v. l. as also Uttarar. 84,2]), *roanti* (Veṇīs. 58,15), *roda* (Mṛcch. 95,12; Nāgān. 24,8.12;86,10 [*roa*]), *rodiduṁ* (Śak. 80,8; Ratn. 318,27), also according to the *e*-conjugation *rodesi* (Mālatīm. 278,7), as with the v. l. for *rodisi* of the text we should read, if one will not like to read with the ed. Bomb. 1892 p. 207,3 and the ed. Madras. II, 65,4 *rodiadi* [both] the texts have *rodiadi*], as stands also at Ratn. 318,9 and Mudrār. 263,6; Mg. *loda*, *lodamāṇaśśa* (Mṛcch. 20,25;158,12). The flexion according to the 6. conjugation occurs in Mg. only in Mṛcch, 158,7.9 *luadi* in verses; in Ś stands *rudatu* [sic] Viddhaś. 87,9 in both the editions, certainly falsely. Cf. § 473.

§ 496. *śvas* is inflected : M. *sasaï*, particip. pres. parasmaip. *sasanta*- (H. R.), *āsasaï* (G.), *āsasu* for *āsasasu* (H.), *ūsasaï*, *ūsasanta*- (Hc. 1,114; G. R.), *samūsasanti*, *samūsasanta*- (G. H.), *ṇisasaï*, *ṇisasanta*- (Hc. 4,201; G.H.), *visasaï* (Hc. 4,43; H. 511 v. l.); AMg. *ussasaï* (Vivāhap. 112), *ūsasanti* (Vivāhap. 26. 852; Paṇṇav. 320 ff. 485), *ūsasĕjja*, *ūsasamāṇe* (Āyār. 2,2,3,27), *nissasaï*, *nisasanti* (Vivāhap. 112.852; Paṇṇav. 320 ff. 485), *nisasamāṇa* (Vivāhap. 1253; Āyār. 2,2,3, 27), *visase* (Uttar. 181); Ś. *ṇisasanti*, *ṇisasadi* (Mṛcch. 39,2;69,8;70,8;79,1), *visasāmi*, *visasadi* (Śak. 65,10;106,1), *samassasa* = *samāśvasihi* (Vikr. 7, 6;24,20; Ratn. 327,9; Veṇīs. 75,2; Nāgān. 95,18), *samassasadu* (Mṛcch. 53,2.23; Śak. 127,14;142,1; Vikr. 71,19;84, 11; Ratn. 319,28 and often, also Veṇīs. at 93, 16 with the ed. Calc. 220,1 to be read), *samassasadha* (Vikr. 7,1); Mg. *śaśadi*, *śaśantā* (Mṛcch. 38,8; 116,17), *ūśaśadu* (Mṛcch. 114,20), *śamuśśaśadi* (Mṛcch. 133,22), *ṇiśaśadu* (Mṛcch. 114,21), *śamaśśaśadu* (Mṛcch. 130.17).

§ 497. *svap* as a rule follows the 6. conjugation: M. *suasi*, *suvasi* = **supási* (H.), *suaï* (Hc. 4,146; H.), *suvaï* (Hc.1,64), *suanti* (G.), *suvasu*, *suaha* (H.); JM. *suvāmi* (Erz. 65,7), *suyaï* (76,32), *suyaü* (Erz. 50,13; Dvār. 503,3), *suyantassa* (Erz. 37,12), *suyamāṇo* (Dvār. 503,4); Ś *suvāmi* (Karṇas. 18,19); *suvĕmha* (Mṛcch. 46,9), particip. nec. *suvidavvaṁ* (Mṛcch. 90,20); A. *suahĩ* = *svapanti* (Hc. 4,376,2). The secondary root *suv* = *sup* is sometimes conjugated according to the 1. conjugation just as *rovaï* beside *ruvaï* and *dhovaï* beside *dhuvaï* (§ 473.482); *sovaï* (Hc. 1,64); JM. *sovĕnti* (Dvār. 503, 28), inf. *souṁ* (Dvār. 501,7); A. particip. nec. *soevā* (Hc. 4,438,3).

§ 498. With the exception of AMg., in all the dialects the 1. and 2. sing. and plur. of *as* are used only as enclitics, in which the sing. forms lose the initial *a* (§ 145). Sing. M. JM. Ś. *mhi*, *si*, Mg. *smi* (text *mhi*) *śi*. The 1. plur. according to Vr. 7,7 is *mha*, *mho*, *mhu*, according to Hc. 3,147; Kī. 4,9; Sr. fol. 50 only *mha*, *mho*. We have found in the text M. *mha* and *mho* (H.), Ś. *mha* (Śak. 26,11; 27,6; 55,13; 58, 6; Vikr. 23,8. 14 etc.) corresponding to the Epical *sma*. The very seldom 2. plural is M. *ttha*

(R.3,3). In AMg. the 1. sing. is *aṁsi* (§ 74.313; Āyār. 1,1,1,2.4;1,6,2,2;1,6, 4,2;1,7,4,2;1,7,5,1; Sūyag. 239. 565 ff. 689), enclitic *mi* (Uttar. 113. 116. 406. 439.574. 590. 597. 598. 615.625. 708; Kappas. § 3.29), as also in JM. (Āv. 28,14. 15; Erz. 65.10; 68,21) the 1. plur. *mo* (Āyār. 1,1,2,2. 3,4 [so to be read according to § 85]), as also JM. has (Āv. 27,4). The 3. sing. in all the dialects is *atthi*, that in Mg. is to be equated as *asti*. *atthi* is used for all persons of the sing. and plur. as a non-enclitic form (Hc.3, 148; Sr. fol. 50). Thus Ś. *atthi dāva ahaṁ* (Mudrār. 42,10;159,12); Mg. *asti dāva hage* (Mudrār. 193,1; cf. v. 1); 3. plur. AMg. *natthi sattovavāiyā* = *na santi sattvā upapāditāḥ* (Sūyag. 28), *ṇatthi ṇaṁ tassa dāragassa hatthā vā pāyā vā kaṇṇā vā* = *na sto nūnaṁ tasya dārakasya hastau vā pādau vā karṇau vā* (Vivāgas. 11); JM. *jassa oṭṭhā natthi* = *yasyauṣṭhau na staḥ* (Āv. 41,6); Ś. *atthi aṇṇāiṁ pi candaüttassa kovakāraṇāiṁ cāṇakke* = *santyanyāny api candraguptasya kopakāraṇāṇi cāṇakye* (Mudrār. 164,3; so to be read; cfr. v. 1 and ed. Calc. Saṁvat 1926 p. 141,14). The 3. plur. *santi* is seldom : M. (g.) AMg. (Uttar. 200; Āyār. 1,1,2,2;2,1,4,5; Sūyag. 585); JŚ. (Pav. 383,74; 385, 65); Mg. *śanti* (Veṇīs. 34,21; cf., however, v. 1.). From the imp. is found in AMg. *tthu* in the combination *namo tthu ṇaṁ* (Hc. 4,283;380.760; Ovav. § 20,87; Kappas. § 16). The optative is AMg. *siyā* (§ 464). On the use of *atthi*, *santi*, *siyā* in the beginning of a sentence, as also on the pronominal use of *amhi*, *ammi*, *mmi*, see § 417. Accordingly we have the following flexion of *as* :

Sing.	Plur.
1. AMg. *aṁsi*, *mi*; M. JM. JŚ. Ś. *mhi*, JM. also *mi*; Mg. *smi*.	1. M. *mho*, *mha*; Ś. *mha*; Mg. *sma*; AMg. *mo*, *mu*; JM. *mo*.
2. M. JM. Ś. *si*; Mg. *śi*.	2. M. *ttha*.
3. M. JM. AMg. JŚ. Ś. *atthi*; Mg. *asti*.	3. M. AMg. JŚ. *santi*; Mg. *śanti*.
Opt. AMg. *siyā*; imp. AMg. *tthu*.	On the imperf. *āsi* see § 515.

§ 499. The rest of the roots in Skt. behaving as of the 2. conjugation go over to the *a*-conjugation and are conjugated according to the 1. conjugation. So one says: AMg. *ahiyāsae* = *adhyāste* (Āyār. 1,8,2,15) and = *adhyāsīta* (Āyār. 1,7,8,8 ff.); AMg. *pajjuvāsāmi* = *paryupāse* (Vivāhap. 916; Nirayāv. § 3; Uvās.), *pajjuvāsaï* (Vivāhap. 917; Nirayāv. § 4; Uvās.), *pajjuvāsāhi*, *pajjuvāsĕjjāhi* (Uvās.); *pajjuvāsanti* (Ovav.).—M. *ṇiacchaï* = **nicakṣati* = *niścaṣṭe* (Hc. 4,181; R. 15,48), *ṇiacchāmi* (Śak. 119.7), *ṇiacchae*, *ṇiacchaha*, *ṇiacchanta-*, *ṇiacchamāṇa*, also according to the *e*-conjugation, *ṇiacchesi* (H.), *avaacchaï*, *avaakkhaï*, *avakkhaï*, *oakkhaï* = *avacaṣṭe* (Hc. 4, 181; *avakkhaï* also Vr. 8,69); AMg. *avayakkhaï* (Nāyādh. 958); Ś. *ācakkha* (Ratn. 320,32), past pass. part. of the pres. stem *ācakkhida* = **ācakṣita* (Śak. 63,15 [so to be read]; 77, 14; 160,15), *aṇāakkhida* (Vikr. 80,4): Mg. *ācaskadi* (Hc. 4, 297), *aṇācaskida* (Mṛcch. 37,21); Ḍh. *ācakkhanto* (Mṛcch. 34,24; so to be read; cf. v. 1. in Godabole p. 101,4); A. *āakkhahi* (Vikr. 58,8; 59, 14; 65,3), *āakkhiu* (Vikr. 58,11); Ś. inf. *paccācakkhidum* (Śak. 104,8). Cf. § 324.—JŚ. *padussedi* (Pav. 384,49) is not = *pradveṣṭi*, as the translation suggests, but = *praduṣyati* and is used for the explanation of AMg. JM. JŚ. *dosa* (§ 129). *sāhaï* = *śāste* (Hc. 4,2); M. JM. *sāhāmi*, *sāhaï*, *sāhāmo*, *sāhanti*, *sāhasu* (H. R.; Erz.; Kk.), also according to *e*-conjugation : *sāhemi*, *sāhĕnti*, *sāhesu*, *sāhehi*, *sāheu*, *sāhĕnti* (H. R.; Erz.; Kk.) ; of the weak root *śiṣ* according to the 4. conjugation *sīsaï* (Hc. 4,2), seen up till now only as passive = *śiṣyate* (G. R.); AMg. *aṇusāsammi* = **anuśāsāmi* = *anuśāsmi* (Uttar. 790)[1], *aṇusāsanti* (Sūyag. 517; Uttar. 33); passive D. *sāsijjaï* (Mṛcch. 103,16), Ś. *sāsīadi* (Mṛcch. 155,6) ; Mg. *śāśadi* (Mṛcch. 158,25).—M. *haṇaï* = *hanti* (H. 214), *ṇihaṇanti*, and according to the *e*-conjugation *ṇihaṇemi* (R.) ; AMg. *haṇāmi* (Vivāhap. 254. 850 f.), *haṇaï* (Vivāhap. 849 f.), in verse also *haṇāi* (Uttar. 630), *abhihaṇaï* (Vivāhap. 348), *samohaṇaï* (Vivāhap. 114. 212 ff. 420; Nāyādh.§ 91. 96; p. 1325; Kappas.); JŚ. *ṇihaṇadi* (Kattig. 401, 339) ; AMg. *haṇaha* (Uttar. 365), *haṇanti* (Sūyag 110), *samohaṇanti* (Rāyap. 32. 45). *sāhaṇanti* = *saṁghnanti* (Vivāhap. 137.138.141), in verse also *viṇihanti* (Sūyag. 339), opt. *haṇiyā haṇijjā*, *haṇĕjjā haṇe* (§ 464), imp. *haṇaha* (Sūyag. 596; Āyār. 1,7,2,4); JM. *āhaṇāmi* (Āv. 28,2), *haṇaï* (Erz. 5,32), imp. *haṇa* = *jahi* (Erz. 2,15), opt. *āhaṇĕjjāsi* (Āv. 11,1) ; Ś. *paḍihaṇāmi* = *pratihanmi* (Mudrār. 182,7 v. l.), *vihaṇanti* (Prab. 17,10); Mg. *āhaṇedha* (Mṛcch. 158,18); A. *haṇaï* (Hc. 4,418,3).

1. JACOBI SBE. 45,151, note 1 wrongly likes to read *aṇusasammi*. Cf. § 74.182.

§ 500. The 3. conjugation of Skt. has been preserved in Pkt. only in a few remnants. For *dā* in the present is used *de-* = *daya-* (§ 474), mostly in AMg., sometimes *dalaya-* in JM. (§ 490).—Of *dhā*, the old stem *dahā* = *dadhā-* has generally been preserved only in composita with *sad* = *śrad*, which behaves almost exclusively according to the *a*-conjugation, as sometimes also in Vedic and Epic Skt. and in Pāli *dahati*[1]. So *saddahaï* = *śraddadhāti* (Vr. 8, 33; Hc. 4,9; Kī. 4,46; Sr. fol. 57) ; M. *saddahimo* = *śraddadhāmaḥ* (H. 23), past passive participle of the present stem *saddahia* (Bh. 8,33; Hc. 1,12; Acyutaś. 8) ; AMg. *saddahāmi* (Vivāhap. 134. 1316; Nirayāv. 60; Uvās. § 12.210; Nāyādh. § 132), *saddahaï* (Vivāhap. 845; Paṇṇav. 64; Uttar. 805), in the verse also with the old flexion *saddahāi* (Uttar. 804) ; JŚ. *saddahadi* (Kattig. 399, 311); opt. *saddahe* (Uttar. 170), *saddahĕjjā* (Rāyap. 250; Paṇṇav. 577. 583), imp. *saddahasu* (Sūyag. 151) and *saddahāhi* (Vivāhap. 134; Rāyap. 249.258); JM. *asaddahanto* (Āv. 35,4); AMg. *saddahamāṇa* (Hc. 4,9; Āyār. 2,2,2,8). In AMg., in addition, is found also *āḍahaï* (Ovav. § 44), *āḍahanti* (Sūyag. 286). Cf. § 222. Elsewhere *dhā*, and other roots in *-ā* (§ 483. 487), are conjugated according to the 2. or 4. conjugation: *dhāi*, *dhāaï* (Hc. 4,240); M. *saṁdhanteṇa* = *saṁdadhatā* (R. 5,24); AMg. JM. with cerebralization (§ 223) very frequently : *āḍhāmi* (Āyār. 1,72,2; Vivāhap. 1210), *āḍhāi* (Ṭhāṇ. 156. 285.479 ff.; Vivāgas. 460. 575; Nirayāv.§ 8. 18;.19. p. 61 ff.; Rāyap. 78.227.252; Uvās.§ 215. 247; Nāyādh. § 69; p. 460.575; Vivāhap. 228. 234; Āv. 27,3), AMg. *āḍhanti* (Vivāgas. 458; Vivāhap. 239), *āḍhāyanti* (Vivāhap. 245; Nāyādh. 301.302.305), *āḍhāhiṁ* (Vivāgas. 217; cf. § 456), *āḍhāha* (Nāyādh. 938) and *āḍhaha* (Vivāhap. 234), *āḍhāmāṇa* (Vivāhap. 240), *āḍhāyamiṇa* (Āyār. 1,7,1,1; 1,7,2,4.5), *aṇāḍhāya-*

miṇa (Āyār. 1,7,1,2) and *aṇāḍhāyamāṇa* (Uvās. [so to be read; see v. l.; Vivāgas. 217; Rāyap. 282), passive *aṇāḍhāijjamāṇa* (Vivâhap. 235; Uvās.). Like *sthā* (§ 483), also *dhā* with prefixes usually goes ever to the *e*-conjugation: M. *saṁdhei* (H. 733; R. 15,76), *saṁdhĕnti* (R. 5,56), *saṁdhiṇti* (G. 1041; so to be read; see v.l.); *vihesi* (G. 332; read *khambhehi va vihesi* and cf. v.l); AMg. *saṁdhei* (Āyār. 1,1,1,6), *saṁdhemāṇa* (Āyār. 1,6,3,3), opt. *nihe* (Āyār. 1,2, 5,3; 1,4,1,3), *pihe* (Sūyag. 129); JM. *aïsaṁdhei* (Āv. 46,25); Ś. *aṇusaṁdhemi* (Karp. 70,3), *aṇusaṁdhedha* (Karp. 23,1). AMg. *saṁdhaï* (Sūyag. 527), **nihaï*, **pihaï* is the connecting link.—*hā*- forms AMg. *jahāsi* (Sūyag. 174. 176), *jahāi* (Sūyag. 118), *jahaï* (Ṭhāṇ. 281), *pajahāmi* (Uttar. 377), *vippajahāmi* (Vivāhap. 1237. 1242), *vippajahaï* (Vivāhap.; Ovav.), *vippajahanti* (Sūyag. 633. 635. 978), opt. *jahe* (Āyār. 2,16,9), *payahijja* and *payahĕjja* Sūyag. 128. 147), *payahe* (Sūyag. 410), *pajahe* (Uttar. 456), *vippajahe* (Uttar. 244), imp. *jahāhi* (Sūyag. 414), particip. *vippajahamāṇa* (Vivāhap. 1385); JŚ. *jahādi* and *jahadi* (Pav. 383,24; 385,64). According to the 4. conjugation: AMg. *hāyaï* (Ṭhāṇ. 294 f.); future Ś. *parihāissadi* = *parihāsyate* (Śak. 2,1).—*mā* see § 487.

1. Pischel, BB. 15,121.

§ 501. *bhī* shows the old flexion in *bihemi* = *bibhemi*, *bihei* = *bibheti* (Hc. 1,169; 4,238). M. JM. *bihaï* (Vr. 8,19; Hc. 3,134. 136; 4,53), *bīhante* (Hc. 3,142), JM. *bīhasu* (Erz. 81,34), dragged to *bhī*, and M. *bihei* (H. 311. 778), JM. *bīhehi* (Erz. 35,33; 83,7), *bīhesu* (Erz. 82,20), formed according to the *e*-conjugation, do not belong to *bhī*, but they are = **bhīṣati* from √*bhīṣ*, of which only the causative is used in Skt. AMg. *bīhaṇa* and *bīhaṇaga* (§ 213. 263) prove it. Generally *bhī* is conjugated as *ai*-roots (§ 479) always in Ś. Mg. So JM. *bhāyasu* (Erz. 31,18); Ś. *bhāāmi* (Vikr. 24,13; 33,11), *bhāādi* (Ratn. 301,18; Mālav. 63.12), *bhāāhi* (Śak. 90,12; Mālav. 78,20; Ratn. 300,10; Priyad. 16,18; 21,5; Mallikām. 293,15); Mg. *bhāāmi*, *bhāāśi* (Mṛcch. 124,22.23; 125,21). In M. according to the analogy of the *a*-roots as well (§ 479); *bhāi* (Vr. 8,19; Hc.4,53); *bhāsu*, v. l. *bhāhi* (H. 583).—*hu* (to offer) goes over to the 9. conjugation in AMg.: *huṇāmi*, *huṇāsi* (Uttar. 375), *huṇaï* (Vivâhap. 910); also with retention of the reduplication: AMg. *juhuṇāmi* (Ṭhāṇ. 436. 437). Cf. Skt. *hunet* in Böhtlingk s. v. *hun* (!).

§ 502. Remnants of the 5. conjugation of Skt. are found almost only in Ś. and even there they are not definite. Most of the roots of the 5. conjugation have gone over to the 9. conjugation but mostly they behave according to the *a*- and *e*-conjugations: AMg. *saṁciṇu* (Uttar. 170); Ś. *avaciṇomi* (Mālatīm. 72,5 [ed. Bomb. 1892 p. 53,1 and ed. Madras. 61,3 *avaïṇummi*]; Unmattar. 6,19), *avaciṇumo* (Pārvatīp. 27,14), *ucciṇosi* (Viddhaś. 81,9; both the editions; nevertheless indefinite); false forms also Priyad. 11,4; 13,15.17. Against that *ciṇaï* (Vr. 8,29; Hc. 4,238.241), fut. *ciṇihii* (Hc. 4,243), passive *ciṇijjaï* (Hc. 4,242.243); *ucciṇaï* (Hc. 4,241); M. *ucciṇasu*, *samucciṇaï* (H.), *viciṇanti* (G.); AMg. *ciṇāi* (Uttar. 931. 937. 942. 948, 952 etc.; Vivāhap. 112. 113. 136. 137), *uvaciṇai* (Uttar. 842; Vivāhap. 113. 136. 137) and *saṁciṇaï* (Uttar. 205), *uvaciṇaï* (Vivāhap. 38.39), *ciṇanti* (Ṭhāṇ.

107; Vivāhap. 62. 182), *uvaciṇanti* (Ṭhāṇ. 108; Vivāhap. 62); Ś. imp. *avaciṇamha* (Śak. 71,9; Mālatīm. 111,2.7 [so to be read; cf. v.l.; Cait. 73, 11; 75,12 [°*ṇu*]), past passive participle *viciṇida* (Mālatīm. 297,5), also according to the *e*-conjugation: Ś. *ucciṇedi* (Karp. 2,8), inf. *ávaciṇeduṁ* (Lalitav. 561,8). In M. Mg. A. *ci* is conjugated according to the 1. conjugation too: *uccei* (Hc. 4,241, H. 159), *uccĕnti* (G. 536), imp. *ucceu* (Sr. fol. 49), inf. *ucceuṁ* (H. 159); Mg. *śaṁcehi* (Veṇīs. 35,9), A. opt. *saṁci* (Hc. 4,422,4); likewise *mi* in M. *ṇimesi* (G. 296). Cf. 473.

§ 503. *dhu* (*dhū*) forms AMg. *dhuṇāi* (verse; Āẏār. 1,4,4,2), usually M. AMg. *dhuṇaï* (Vr. 8,56; Hc, 4,59; 241; Kī. 4,73; G. 437; H. 532; R. 15,23; Viddhaś. 7,2; Sūẏag. 321), opt. AMg. *dhuṇe* (Āẏār. 1,2,6,3; 1,4,3,2; 1,5,3,5; Sūẏag. 408. 550); AMg. *vihuṇāmi* (Nāẏādh. 938); M. *vihuṇaï* (R. 7,17; 12,66); M. AMg. *vihuṇanti* (G. 552; R. 6,35; 13,5; Ṭhāṇ. 155); AMg. *vihuṇe* (Sūẏag. 921), *vihuṇāhi* (Uttar. 311), *niddhuṇe* (Uttar. 170), absol. *dhuṇiẏa*, *vihuṇiẏa* (Sūẏag. 111.113), *vihūṇiẏā* (Āẏār. 1,7,8,24), *saṁvidhuṇiẏa* (Āẏār. 1,7,6,5), *niddhuṇittāṇa* (Uttar. 605), particip. pres. ātmanep. *viṇiddhuṇamāṇa* (Vivāhap. 1253); passive *dhuṇijjaï* (Hc. 4,242); Ś. absol. *avadhuṇia* (Mālatīm. 351,6). It may be conjugated according to the 6. conjugation as well: *dhuvaï* (Hc. 4,59), from which the passive *dhuvvaï* (§ 536); further according to the *e*-conjugation M. *vihuṇĕnti* (R. 8,35); Ś. *vidhuvedi* (Mṛcch. 71,20). On the past passive participle *hūṇa*, *vihūṇa*, *vippahūṇa* see § 120.—Of *śru* is found the flexion according to the 5. conjugation only in the 2. sing. imp. in Ś. Mg. So Ś. *suṇu* (Śak. 78,4; Vikr. 42,12); Mg. *śuṇu* (Mṛcch. 121,23; Veṇīs.34,19, [Grill false *śiṇu*], in the 2. plur. too *śuṇudha* (Śak. 113,9). But in Ś in both the places stand; the v. l. *suṇa*, as in Ratn. 304,9;309,9; Viddhaś. 63,2 against *suṇu* 72,5 stands, and since beside it is found *suṇāhi* too (Mṛcch. 104,16; Śak. 77,6; Mālav. 6,5; 45,19; Vṛṣabh. 42,7), the 1. plur. *suṇamha* (Vikr. 41,17; Ratn. 302.7; 316,25), or, according to the *e*-conjugation *suṇĕmha* (Nāgān. 28,9; 29,7), the 2. plur. is *suṇadha* (Śak. 55,12), so *suṇa* will have to be read throughout in Ś. In Mg. too *śuṇu* for *śuṇa* may be a Sanskritism. The 2. plur. in Mg. is *śuṇādha* (Lalitav. 565,17; 566,5; Mṛcch. 158,19; 162, 17; Prab. 46,14. 17) or *śuṇedha* (Mṛcch. 154,9), and so in Śak. 133.9 with the v. l. and in Hc. 4,302 we should read either *śuṇadha* or (cf. Z) *śuṇādha*. In any case, in Ś. Mg. the conjugation according to the model of the 9 conjugation is usual: Ś. *suṇāmi* (Mālatīm. 288,1); Mg. *śuṇāmi* (Mṛcch. 14,22); wrongly Ś. *suṇomi* (Veṇīs. 10,5; Mudrār. 249,4.6), for which with the v. l *suṇāmi* or *suṇemi* is to be read. Ś. *suṇādi* (Mālav. 71,3; Mukund. 13,17; Mallikām. 244,2), also *suṇedi* (Mṛcch. 325,19); Mg. *śuṇādi* (Mṛcch. 162,21). Against the dialect is Ś. *suṇimo* (Bālar. 101,5), for which *suṇāmo* is correct. Very frequent is the 3. sing. imp. Ś. *suṇādu* (Mṛcch. 40.21; 74,5; Śak. 20,12; 21,4; 57, 2; 159,10; Vikr. 5,9; 72,14; 80,12; 83,19; 84,1; Mālav. 78,7; Mudrār. 159,12 etc.), Mg. *śuṇādu* (Mṛcch. 37,3); 3. plur. imp. Ś. *suṇantu* (Mṛcch. 142,10), Mg. *śuṇantu* (Mṛcch. 151,23). In M. the stem is carried over to the *a*-conjugation: *suṇaï*, *suṇimo*, *suṇanti*, *suṇasu*, *suṇaha* (G. H. R.), likewise in A. 2. plur. imp. *ṇisuṇahu* (Kk. 272,37), JM. *suṇai*, *suṇanti*, (Kk.), *suṇa* (Dvār. 495,15), *suṇasu* (Kk.; Erz.); AMg. JM. *suṇaha* (Ovav. § 184; Āv. 33,19); AMg. *suṇantu* (Nāyādh. 1134), *suṇamāṇa* (Āyār. 1,1,5,2), *apaḍisuṇamāṇa* (Nirayāv. § 25). In JM. AMg., however, the flexion according to the *e*-conjugation prevails: JM. *suṇei* (Āv. 35,30; 42,41; 43,2; Kk.; Erz.); AMg. *suṇemi* (Ṭhāṇ. 143), *suṇei* (Vivāhap. 327; Nandīs. 371. 373. 504; Āyār. 1,1,5,2; p. 136,8. 16; Paṇṇav. 428 ff.), *paḍisuṇei* (Uvās.; Nirayāv.; Kappas.), *paḍisuṇĕnti* (Vivāhap. 1227; Nirayāv.; Uvās.; Kappas. [so or °*ṇi*° so to be read also in § 58] etc.). AMg. *paḍisuṇĕjjā* (Rāyap. 251), *paḍisuṇijjā* (Kappas.), *paḍissuṇe* (Uttar. 31,33) are opt. For the 3. sing. imp. Hc, 3,158 suggests *suṇaü, suṇeu, suṇāu*. AMg. has *suṇeu* (Sūyag. 363), 2. plur. *suṇeha* (Sūyag, 243. 373. 397. 423 f.; Uttar. 1). The passive M. JM. *suvvaï* (§ 536) presupposes a conjugation according to the 6. conjugation **suvaï* = **śruvátí*.

§ 504. AMg. *pappoi* [text *pappŏtti*; commentary *papputti*] = *prāpnoti* (Uttar. 430), JŚ. *pappodi* (Pav. 389,5) found in verses are formed according to the 5. conjugation from *āp* with *pra*. Elsewhere *āp* in AMg. with the stem of the 9. conjugation is inflected according to the *a*-conjugation: *pāuṇaï* = **prāpuṇāti*, **prāpuṇati* (Vivāhap. 845; Ovav. § 153; Paṇṇav. 846), *pāüṇanti* (Sūyag. 433. 759. 771; Ovav. § 74. 75. 81. 117); *saṁpāuṇanti* (Vivāhap. 926), opt. *pāuṇĕjjā* (Āyār. 2,3,1, 11. 2,6; Ṭhāṇ. 165. 416), *saṁpāuṇĕjjāsi* (text °*se*; Uttar. 345); inf. *pāuṇittae* (Āyār. 2,3,2,11). In M. JM. JŚ., in verses in AMg., Ś. A. the usual flexion is according to the 1. conjugation: *pāvaï* = **prāpati* (Hc. 4,239). So M. *pāvasi*, *pāvaï*, *pāvanti*, *pāva*, *pāvaü* (G. H. R.), also according to the *e*-conjugation *pāvĕnti* (G.); AMg. *pāvaï* (Uttar. 933. 939. 944. 954 etc.; Paṇṇav. 135); opt. *pāvijjā* Nandīs. 404); JM. *pāvaï* (Kk. 272,5), *pāvanti* (Ṛsabhap. 41), and according to the *e*-conjugation *pāvei* (Erz. 50,34), *pāvĕnti* (Kk. 266,4; Erz. 46,1 [so to be read]); JŚ. *pāvadi* (Pav. 380, 11; Kattig. 400,326; 403, 370); Ś. *pāvanti* (Viddhaś. 63,2); absol. JŚ. *pāviya* (Kattig. 402, 369), and according to the *e*-conjugation JŚ Ś. *pāvedi* (Kattig. 399, 307; Ratn. 316,5), *pāvehi* (Mālav. 30,11; so to be read); A. *pāvami* (Vikr. 71,8). From the same stem is formed also the future Ś. *pāvaïssaṁ* (Śak. 54,3). Hc. 4,302 reads Mudrār. 187,2 in AMg. *pāvemi*; the MSS and editions have *ācemi*, *jācemi*, *paḍicchemi*. (Hc. 4, 141. 142 mentions also *vāvei* = *vyāpnoti* and *samāvei* = *samāpnoti*.

§ 505. *takṣ*, as already in Skt. too, behaves according to the 1. conjugation: AMg. *tacchanti* (Sūyag. 274), *tacchiya* (Uttar. 596).—From *śak* very frequent ins. is *sakkaṇomi* = *śaknomi* (§ 140. 195; Śak. 51,2; Ratn. 305, 33; 327, 17; Uttarar. 112,8) or *sakkuṇomi* (Mṛcch. 166,13; Vikr. 12,12; 15,3; 46,18; Mudrār. 242,3; 246,1 : 252,2 [everywhere to be so read]: Nāgān. 14,8 11; 27, 15 etc.). In other dialects it behaves according to the 4. conjugation: *sakkaï* = **śakyati* (Vr. 8,52; Hc. 4,230; Kī. 4,60). So JM. A. *sakkaï* (Erz.; Hc. 4,422,6.441,2), JM. opt. *sakkĕjja* (Erz. 79.1), and according to the *e*-conjugation JM. *sakkei* (Āv. 42,28). *sakkĕnti* (Erz. 65,19), *sakkeha* (Sagara 10,13 [so to be read]). On the opt. *sakkā* see § 465.—*stṛ*, that in Śkt. follows the 5. or 9. conjugation, is inflected in Pkt. according to the analogy of roots in *ṛ* (§ 477): M. *ŏttharaï* = *avastṛṇoti*, *ŏtthariа* = *avastṛta*, *vittharaï*, *vittharanta-*, *vitthariuṁ*, *vittharia* (R.) ; JM. *vitthariya* = *vistṛta* (Erz.) ; Ś. *vittharanta-* (Mālatīm. 76,4;258,3) ; A. *ŏttharaï* (Vikr. 67,20). To it belongs also *utthaṅghaï* (to raise up; to throw up; Hc. 4,36. 144), past passive participle *utthaṅgia* (R. s.v. *stambh*) = **utstaghnoti* (PISCHEL, BB. 15,122 f.) Cf. § 333.

§ 506. The tottering flexion of the 7. conjugation in Pkt. has completely disappeared. The nasal has been carried from the weak forms to the strong ones and the stem is inflected according to the *a-* or *e-* conjugation : *chindaï* = *chinatti* (Vr. 8, 38; Hc. 4,124. 216; Kī. 4,46; Mk. fol. 56) ; *acchindaï* (Hc. 4,125) ; M. *achindaï* (G.), *vŏcchindanta-* (R.) ; JM, *chindāmi* and *chindei* (Erz.) abs. *chindittu* (Kk.) ; AMg. *chindāmi* (Aṇuog. 528; Nirayāv. § 16) ; *chindasi* (Aṇuog. 528), *chindaï* (Sūyag. 332; Vivāhap. 123.1306; Nāyādh. 1436; Uttar 789), *acchindaï vicchindaï* (Ṭhāṇ. 360), *vŏcchindasi vŏcchindaï* (Uttar. 321. 824), opt. *chindĕjjā* (Vivāhap. 123. 1306) ; *chinde* (Uttar. 217), *acchindĕjja* (Āyār. 2.3,1,9; 2,9,2; 2,13,13), *vicchindĕjja* (Āyār. 2,13,13), *chindāhi* (Dasav. 613,27), *chindaha* (Āyār. 1,7,2,4), present participle *chindamāṇa* (Aṇuog. 528), absol. *palicchindiyāṇaṁ* (Āyār. 1,3,2,4) ; Ś. absol. *paricchindia* (Vikr. 47,1). On AMg. *acche* see § 466. 516.—*pīsaï* for **piṁsaï* (§ 76) = *pinaṣṭi* (Hc. 4,185) ; Ś. *pīsedi* (Mṛcch. 3,1.21) ;—*bhañjaï* = *bhanakti* (Hc. 4,106) ; M. *bhañjaï*, *bhañjanta-* (H.R.) ; JM. *bhañjiūṇa*, °*je*° (Erz.) ; AMg. *bhañjaï*, *bhañjae* (Uttar. 788. 789) ; Ś. future *bhañjaïssasi* (Vikr. 22,2). absol. *bhañjia* (Mṛcch. 40,22; 97,23). Mg. *bhayyadi* [text *bhajjadi*; ed. Calc. *bhajjedi*] (Mṛcch. 118,12) must be considered as passive and *vibhayya* (text *bibhajja*, (Mṛcch. 118,21) as its imperative; against it stands Ś. imp. *bhajjedha* (Mṛcch. 155,4) in the active sense, with which may be compared *jujjaï* (§ 507).—*bhindaï* = *bhinatti* (Vr. 8,38; Hc. 4,216; Kī. 4,46; Mk. fol. 56) ; M. *bhindaï*, *bhindanta-* (G. H. R.) ; JM. *bhindaï* (Erz.) ; AMg. *bhindaï* (Ṭhāṇ. 360; Vivāhap. 1327), *bhindĕnti*, *bhindamāṇe* (Vivāhap. 1227. 1327), opt. *bhindĕjja* (Āyār. 2,2,2,3; 2,3,1,9) ; Ś. Mg. absol. *bhindia* (Vikr. 16,1; Mṛcch. 112,17). On AMg. *abbhe* see § 466. 516.

§ 507. *bhuj* forms *bhuñjaï* (Hc. 4,110; Mk. fol. 56), *uvahuñjaï* (Hc. 4, 111) ; M. *bhuñjasu* (H.) ; JM. *bhuñjaï* (Erz.), *bhuñjai* (Āv. 8,4,24), *bhuñjanti* (Erz.; Kk.), *bhuñjae* (Ātmanep.; Erz) *bhuñjāhi* (Āv. 10,40), *bhuñjasu* (Āv. 12,20), *bhuñjaha*, *bhuñjamāṇa*, *bhuñjiya bhuñjjittā* (Erz.) ; AMg. *bhuñjaï* (Uttar. 12; Vivāhap. 163), *bhuñjai* (Sūyag. 209) ; *bhuñjāmo* (Vivāhap. 624), *bhuñjaha* (Sūyag. 194; Vivāhap. 623), *bhuñjanti* (Dasav. 613,18), *bhuñjĕjjā* (Āyār. 2,1,10,7; Vivāhap. 515,516), *bhuñje* (Uttar. 37; Sūyag. 344), imp. *bhuñja* (Sūyag. 182) ; *bhuñjasu*, *bhuñjimo* (Uttar. 369.675), *bhuñjaha* (Āyār. 2,1,10,7), *bhuñjamāṇa* (Paṇṇav. 101. 102 [°*je*°]. 103 [°*je*°] ; Kappas.) ; JŚ. *bhuñjade* (Kattig. 403. 382; 404,390) ; Ś. *bhuñjasu* (Mṛcch. 70,12), inf. *bhuñjiduṁ* (Dhūrtas. 6,21) ; A. *bhuñjanti* inf. *bhuñjaṇahã*, *bhuñjaṇahĩ* (Hc. 4,335,444,1).—From *yuj* the present are *juñjaï*, *jujjaï* (Hc. 4,109), that may be compared with *bhajjedha* § 506 and under *rudh*. M. *paüñjaïuṁ* (Karp. 7,1). M. *jujjae*, *jujjaï* (H.), *jujjanta-* (R.) are passive forms. AMg. *juñjaï* (Paṇṇav. 842 ff.; Ovav. § 145.146), *paüñjaï* (Vivāhap. 1312; Nāyādh. § 89), opt. *juñje* (Uttar. 29), *paüñje* (Samav. 86), *juñjamāṇa* (Paṇṇav. 842 ff.), absol. *uvaüñjiūṇa* (Vivāhap. 1591) ; absol. M. *niuñjiya* (Erz.) ; Ś. *paüñjadha* (Karp.

6,7), imp. passive from the present stem *paüñjiadu* (Mṛcch. 9,7), whilst the very frequent Ś. *jujjadi* (Mṛcch. 61,10; 65,12; 141,3 155,21; Śak. 71, 10; 122,11; 129,15; Vikr. 24,3; 32,17; 82,17 etc.) = *yujyate* is, like the future Ś. *ahiujjissadi* = *abhiyokṣyate* (Uttarar. 69, 6).—*rudh* forms *rundhaï* (Vr. 8,49; Hc. 4,133.218.239; Kī. 4,52; Mk. Sr. fol. 56). So M. *rundhasu* (H.); AMg. *rundhaï* (Ṭhāṇ. 360); Ś. *rundhedi* (Mallikām. 126,3; text. °*ei*); A. absol. *rundheviṇu* (Vikr. 67,20) and *rujjhaï* = **rudhyati* (Hc. 4,218), also with the inserted nasal M. *ṇiruñjhaï* (H. 618), JŚ. absol. *niruñjhittā* (Pav. 386,70), with which is compared AMg. *vigiñcaï* = *vikṛntyati* (§ 485). M. AMg. *rumbhaï* (Vr. 8,49; Hc. 4,218; Kī. 4,52; Mk. Sr. fol. 56; H.R.; Uttar. 902), AMg. *nirumbhaï* (Uttar. 834), passive M. JM. *rubbhaï* (§ 546) belong to a root **rubh*, that is an analogical formation on the roots in gutturals (§ 266).—*hiṁs* forms in AMg. *hiṁsaï* = *hinasti* (Uttar. 927. 935. 940. 945. 950 etc.), *vihiṁsaï* (Āyār. 1,1,1,4.5,5. 6,3), *hiṁsanti* (Āyār. 1,1,6,5).

§ 508. The forms of *kṛ*, built according to the 8. conjugation, are further found in AMg. JM. JŚ. only, notwithstanding the weak stem *kuru-* having been taken to the *a*-conjugation as *kurva-*: AMg. *kuvvaï* = **kurvati* (Sūyag. 321. 328[°*aï*]. 359 [°*ai*]. 550. 551; Uttar. 43; Dasav. 613,19 [°*ai*]), *pakuvvaï* (Āyār. 1.2,6,2), *viuvvaï* (Vivāhap. 114; Rāyap. 60 ff. 79. 82; Uvās.; Nāyādh.; Kappas. etc.), *kuvvanti* = *kurvanti* (Sūyag. 231. 240. 359. 472. 646; Vivāhap. 409), *vikuvvanti* (Vivāhap. 214. 215), opt. *kuvvĕjjā*, °*jja* (Uttar. 19.289), usually, however, *kujjā* (§ 464), imp. *kuvvahā* (Āyār. 1,3,2,1), pres. part. ātmanep. *kuvvamāṇa* (Āyār. 1,1,3,1; Paṇṇav. 104; Nāyādh. 930), *viuvvamāṇa* (Vivāhap. 1033 f. 1054), *pakuvvamāṇa* (Āyār. 1,2,3,5; 1,5,1,1); JM. *kuvvai* (Kk.), *kuvvanti* (Āv. 7,11), *viuvvaï* (Āv. 35,6), *viuvvae* (Āv.36,27), absol. *viuvviūṇa*, past passive particip. *viuvviya* (Erz.); JŚ. *kuvvadi* (Kattig. 399,313; 400,329; 401,340; 402,357), *kuvvaṁ* (Pav. 384,58), *kuvvantaṁ* (Kattig. 400,332), *kuvvanto* (Kattig. 403,378), also ātmanep. *kuvvade* (Kattig. 403,384). The Vedic flexion according to the 5. conjugation has been retained in M. JM. JŚ. Ś. A. Vedic. *kṛṇoti* becomes, according to § 502, *kuṇaï* (Vr. 8,13; Hc. 4,65; Kī. 4,54; Mk. 59). So M. *kuṇasi*, *kuṇaï*, *kuṇanti*, *kuṇa*, *kuṇasu kuṇaü*, *kuṇanta-* (G.H.R.); JM. *kuṇaï* (Kk.; Ṛṣabhap.), *kuṇanti*, *kuṇaha* (Kk.), *kuṇasu* (Kk.; Erz.; Sagara 6,2. 11.12), *kuṇanta-*, *kuṇamāṇa-* (Kk.; Erz.), *kuṇanteṇa* (KI. 15), also wholly sporadic *kuṇaï* in AMg. in verse (Samav. 85); JŚ. *kuṇadi* (Kattig. 399, 310. 319; 402, 359. 367; 403,370. 371. 385; 404, 388. 389. 391); A. *kuṇahu* (Piṅgala 1, 16. 53. 79 [text °*ha*] and *kuṇehu* (Piṅgala 1,90. 118). In Ś. Mg. *kuṇa-* is never used (Vr. 12,15; Mk. fol. 72). It is correct, therefore, in dramas only in gāthās composed in M., as in Ratn. 293,6; Mudrār. 83,3; Dhūrtas. 4,19; Nāgān. 25,4; 41,5; Bālar. 120,6; Viddhaś. 92,8; Karp. 8,9; 10,1; 55,3; 67,5, etc. Pratāp. 218,17;220,15;389,14 etc. Rājaśekhara wrongly uses *kuṇa* in Ś. too, as in Bālar. 69,13;168,7;195,13;200,12; Viddhaś. 36,2; 48,9.11; 80,14; 83,3; 123,14. For *kuṇomi* (Karp. 107,6 ed. Bomb.) KONOW reads 115,6 correctly *kadiadu*, and so perhaps in Bālar. and Viddhaś. too in the critical editions. *kuṇa-* is removed from Ś. It is found, however, elsewhere in later days dramas too, as in Hāsy. 32,12; 39,14; Cait. 36,11; 37,5;

39,1.10;44,12;47,7;80,14;92,14; Karṇas. 22,8; Jīvān. 39,15;41,7;81,14; 95,2; Mallikām. 69,1; 336,3 etc. is perhaps a smaller contribution of the publishers than that of the authors. Out and out monstrous is Ś. *kummo* = *kurmaḥ* (Jīvān. 13,6), against this correctly Ḍh. *kulu* = *kuru* (Mṛcch. 31,16).

§ 509. *kṛ* is conjugated mostly on the analogy of the roots in *ṛ* of the first conjugation (§ 477): *karaï* (Vr. 8,13; Hc. 4,65.234.239; Mk. fol. 59); however, in M. JM. AMg. JŚ. almost, in Ś. Mg. all exclusively according to the *e*-conjugation. *a*- forms are: PG. opt. *karĕyya*, *karĕyyāma* (6,40;7,41); M. *karanta-c*(R.); JM. *karae* = *kurute* (Kk. II, 506,5), *karanti* (Ṛṣabhap. 39. 40); AMg. *karaï* (not definite; Rāẏap. 233), *karanti* (Sūẏag. 297; Uttar. 1101; Vivāhap. 62; Jīv. 102; Paṇṇav. 56.574), *pakaranti* (Uttar. 15; Paṇṇav. 575), *viẏāgaranti*, *vāgaranti* (Sūẏag. 523.695); JŚ. *karadi* (Kattig. 400,332); opt. AMg. *kare* (Sūẏag. 348,385 393), *nirākare* (Sūẏag. 442), *karĕjjā* (§ 462), *viẏāgarĕjjā* (Sūẏag. 525.527), *vāgarĕjjā* (Āẏār. 2,3,2,17); frequently in A. *karimi* (Vikr. 71,9), *karaũ* (Hc. 4,370,2), *karaï*, *karadi*, *karanti*, *karahĩ* (Hc. s. v. √*kar*), opt. *kari* (Hc. 4,387,3; Śukasaptati 49,4; Prabandhac. 63,7), imp. *karahi* (Hc. 4,385; Piṅgala 1,149), *karu* (Hc. 4,330,3), *karahu* (Hc. 4,346; Piṅgala 1,102.107.121 [text °*ha*]), inf. *karaṇa*, absol. *karevi*, *karĕppiṇu* (Hc. s.v. √*kar*). —*e*-forms are very frequent: M. *karemi*, *karesi*, *karei*, *karĕnti*, *karehi*, *karesu*, *karĕnta*- (H.R.); JM. *karei* (Erz.; Kk.; Āv. 9,17; 14,14), *karemo* (Erz. 2,27;5,35; Kk. 264,11. 14; Āv. 17,14; Sagara 2,14), *karĕnti* (Erz.; Kk.), *karehi*, *karesu*, *kareha* (Kk.), *karĕnta*-, *karemāṇa* (Erz.); AMg. *karemi* (Ṭhāṇ. 149.476; Nāẏādh. § 94; Uvās.), *karei* (Āẏār. 1,2,5,6; 1.3,2,1; Sūẏag. 403.406.853; Vivāhap. 915-917.931. 945; Niraẏāv. 49; Uvās.; Kappas.), *karemo* (Sūẏag. 734), *karĕnti* (Āẏār. 1,3,2,1; Rāẏap. 183; Jīv. 577.597; Uvās.; Kappas.), imp. *viẏāgarehi* (Sūẏag. 962), *kareha* (Uvās.; Nāẏādh.; Kappas.), *karemāṇa* (Uvās.), *viẏāgaremāṇe*, *viẏāgarei* (Āẏār. 2,2, 3,1). Sporadic is AMg. *kajjanti* (Uvās. § 197.198) in the active sense; at the parallel place § 184 stands *karĕnti*, JŚ. *karedi* (Pav. 384,59; Kattig. 400,324; 402,369; 403,377.383); Ś. *karemi* (Lalitav. 561,15; Mṛcch. 16,4; 103,17; 151,22; Śak. 165,8 [to be taken from the v.l. over to the text]; Vikr. 82,5; 83,5. 6 etc.), *karesi* (Ratn. 303,29; Mālatīm. 265,2; Prab. 44,2 [so to be read with P. M. Bomb.]), *karedi* (Lalitav. 560,9; Mṛcch. 73,11; 147,18; 151,19.20; Śak. 20.5; 56,16; Vikr. 75,5), *karemo* (Śak. 80,5 [so to be read]), *alaṁkarĕnti* (Mālatīm. 273,5 [so to be read; cf. v.l.]), *karehi* (Mṛcch. 66,14; 325,18;326,10), *karesu* (Ratn. 299,5; 316,6; 328,24; Veṇīs. 98,15; Pras. 84,9; Karṇas. 21,7;30,5; 37,20), *karedu* (Mālatīm. 351,7), *karĕmha* (Śak. 81,16; Vikr. 6,15;10,15; 53,14; Prab. 63,11; Ratn. 303,21; Uttarar. 101,8), *karedha* (Mālatīm. 246,5), *karĕnta*- (Mṛcch. 6,13;40,23; 60,25; 61,24; 105,1; 148,8).—Mg. *kalemi* (Mṛcch. 12,15; 31,17. 20; 97,4; 113,23 etc.; Śak. 114,3), *kaleśi* (Mṛcch. 151,25; 160,3), *kaledi* (Mṛcch. 81,6; 127,6; 135,2; 158,25; Nāgān. 68,5 [so to be read]), *kalehi* (Mṛcch. 31,8; 123,10; 176,5), *kalĕmha* (Mṛcch. 167,19; 168,7; 170,21; Veṇīs. 36,6; Caṇḍak. 71,10), *kaledha* (Mṛcch. 32,15; 112,2; 140,23), *kalĕntaā* (voc.; Mṛcch. 30,9;108,17).

§ 510. The forms built according to the 9. conjugation are found in most of the dialects more frequently of only *jñā*, which behind *na*, according to § 170, loses its initial *j*: M. *jāṇāi* (Karp. 35,8); JM. *jāṇāsi* (Erz. 57,8); AMg. *jāṇāsi* (Vivāhap. 1271; Rāẏap. 267; Uttar. 745), *aṇujāṇāi* (Sūẏag. 1.16), *na ẏāṇāi, jāṇāi* (Sūẏag. 161.520), *pariẏāṇāi* (Vivāhap. 228; Rāẏap. 252 [°*jā*°]); *viẏāṇāsi, viẏāṇāi* (Uttar. 745.791); JŚ. *jāṇādi* (Pav. 382,25; 348,48), *viẏāṇādi* (Pav. 388,2); Ś. *jāṇāsi* (Mṛcch. 57,9; 65,10; 82, 12; Śak. 13,5: Mālatīm. 102,3; Mudrār. 37,2); D. *āṇāsi* (Mṛcch. 101,8,9. 10); Ś. *jāṇādi* (Vikr. 9,4; Mālatīm. 264,5; Mahāv. 34,1; Mudrār. 36,3.4.6; 55,1 etc.); Mg. Ś. D. *āṇādi* (Mṛcch. 37,25; 51,25;101,11); Ś. *viāṇādi* (Prab. 13,19), *jāṇādu* (Mṛcch. 94,13; Mudrār. 36,7); Mg. *ẏāṇāśi* (Veṇīs. 34,18), *yāṇādi* (Mṛcch. 114,1), *āṇādi* (Mṛcch. 37,25), *viāṇādi, paccabhiāṇādi* (Mṛcch. 38,13; 173,7). Except in Ś. Mg. *jñā* mostly goes according to the *a-* conjugation : *jāṇaï* (Vr. 8,23; Hc. 4,7; Kī. 4,47). So : M. *jāṇimi, jāṇasi, jāṇase, jāṇaï, jāṇimo* and *jāṇāmo, jāṇa, jāṇasu* (H.), after *ṇa*: *āṇasi, āṇaï āṇimo āṇaha* (H.R); JM. *jāṇasi* (Dvār. 502,21), *na ẏāṇasi* (Erz. 52,17), *jāṇaï* (Erz. 11,2; Kk. 277,10), *na ẏāṇaï* (Āv. 21,18; 38,8; Erz. 30,3; 37,25); AMg. *jāṇasi* (Uttar. 745), *jāṇaï* (Vivāhap. 284. 363. 911. 1194. 1198 etc.; Sūẏag. 476, 540; Uttar 202; Āẏār. 1,2,5,4; Paṇṇav. 366. 432. 518 ff. 666; Jīv. 339 ff.), *parijāṇaï* (Āẏār. p. 132,9 ff.), *aṇujāṇaï* (Vivāhap. 603 ff.), *samaṇujāṇaï* (Āẏār. 1,1,3,6; 1,2,5,2.3), *jāṇāmo* (Vivāhap. 131. 144. 1180. 1406; Ṭhāṇ. 147; Sūẏag. 578), *jāṇaha, pariẏāṇaha* (Vivāhap. 132,234), opt. *jāṇe* (Sūẏag. 364), imp. *jāṇa* (Āẏār. 1,3,1,1) and *jāṇāhi* (Sūẏag. 249. 304; Kappas. S. § 52), *viẏāṇāhi* (Paṇṇav. 39), *samaṇujāṇāhi* (Sūẏag 247), *aṇujāṇaü* (Kappas. § 28), *jāṇaha* (Āẏār. 1,4,2,5), *jāṇamāṇa* (Samav. 82); JŚ *jāṇadi* (Kattig. 398, 302), *viẏāṇadi* (Pav. 381,21), *jāṇa* (Kattig. 401, 342); Ś. *jāṇāmo* [text false °*ṇi*°; cf. v. 1.] (Mālatīm. 82,9; 94,3; 246,1; 248,1; 255,4; Viddhaś. 101,1), *ṇa āṇadha* (Mālatīm. 245,8), imp. *jāṇa* (Karp. 63,8) and *jāṇāhi* (Mṛcch. 41,24 [so to be read]; 169,20; Vikr. 15,10 41,5; Mālatīm. 239,1 [so to be read]), *aṇujāṇāhi* (Śak. 26,12; Vikr. 29,9); Mg. *yāṇāhi* (Mṛcch. 80,21); A. *jāṇaũ* (Hc. 4,391. 439,4), *jāṇaï* (Hc. 4,401, 4.419,1), *jāṇu* (Piṅgala 1,26 [text *jāṇa*]), *jāṇahu* (Piṅgala 1,105. 106. 144). In Ś. Mg. the flexion according to the *a-* conjugationis restricted to *jāṇāmo, jāṇa, jāṇāhi*, which should not be considered to have been built from the strong stem of the 9. conjugation and to *jāṇadha*. Against the dialect is Ś. *jāṇasi* (Lalitav. 560,18), wrongly also *jāṇedi* (Nāgān. 67,3), for which we should, with the v. 1., read *jāṇādi*, as also for Mg. *yāṇadi* (Hc. 4,292), *paccahijāṇedi*(Mṛcch. 132,24)is to be read °*ṇādi*. On the other hand, correct is the *e-* form in JM. *jāṇei* (Kk. III, 512,4), JŚ. *viẏāṇedi* (Kattig. 399,316; text °*ei*) and A. *jāṇehu* (Piṅgala 1,5. 14). JŚ. has *ṇādi* = **jñāti*(Pav. 382,25) too; M. has *aṇāa* = *ajñāta* (RBI).

§ 511. *krī* forms *kiṇaï* (Vr. 8,30; Hc. 4,52), with prefix *vi vikkiṇaï* (Vr. 8,31; Hc. 4,52; Kī. 4,70; Mk. fol. 54). So: M. *vikkiṇaï* (H. 238); JM, *kiṇāmi* (Āv. 31,9), *kiṇaï* (Erz. 29,28), absol. *kiṇiẏa*, future *kiṇīhāmo* (Āv. 33,15), *vikkiṇāmi, vikkiṇaï* (Āv. 23,23,26), *vikkiṇanti* (Āv. 31,7), *paḍivikkiṇaï* (Āv. 33,15); AMg. *kiṇaï* (Ṭhāṇ. 516), opt. *kiṇe*, particip. pres.

kiṇanta- (Āyār. 1,2,5.3); Ś. imp. *kiṇadha* (Caṇḍak. 51,10. 11. 12; 53,7), future *kiṇissadi* (Caṇḍak. 52,4.7), past passive particip. *kiṇida* (Karp. 32, 9;73,2), *ṇikkiṇasi* (Mṛcch. 61,16), *vikkiṇida* (Mṛcch. 50,4; Karp. 74,3; Laṭakam. 13,15; 18,10); Mg. *kiṇadha* and with *i* fut. *kiṇiśśaṁ* (Mṛcch. 32, 17; 118,14; 125,10); Ḍh.. *vikkiṇia* (Mṛcch. 32,10. 12. 14). With the prefix *vi krī* is inflected also on the analogy of the roots in- *i* of the 1. conjugation : *vikkei* (Vr. 8,31; Hc. 4,52. 240; Kī. 4,71; Mk. fol. 54). So M. v. l. to H. 238. *vikkeaï* (Hc. 4,240) is a denominative from *vikreya*, therefore = **vikreyati*.—*pū* forms *puṇaï* (Hc. 4,241), *lū* likewise *luṇaï* (Vr. 8,56; Hc. 4,241; Kī. 4,73; Mk. fol. 57). Besides both the roots may be conjugated on the analogy of the roots in *-u*, *-ū* of the 6. conjugation: AMg. opt. *luĕjjā* (Vivāhap. 1186), passive *puvvaï*, *luvvaï* beside *puṇijjaï luṇijjaï* (§ 536). The shortening of *ī*, in *kiṇaï* is explained from the old accent *krīṇắti* and it corresponds to the shortening of *ū* in *punaï* = *punắti*, *junaï* = *lunắti*. On M. JM. AMG. A. *jiṇaï*, Ḍh. *jiṇādi*, AMg. *samussiṇāi* see § 473, on *muṇaï* § 489.

§ 512. The old flexion of the roots ending in a consonant occurs in AMg. *aṇhāi* = *aśnāti* (Ovav. § 64. 65). The usual formation, however, is *aṇhaï* (Hc. 4,110). The roots are inflected on the analogy of the roots of 7. conjugation with the weak stem formed according to either *a*- or *e*-conjugation (§ 506 f.). Of influence in this case was that a part of the roots, such as *granth*, *bandh*, *manth*, already had the nasal and another part as *aṇhaï* = *aśnāti*, *gĕṇhaï* = *gṛhṇati* was forced to take it inside the stem according to the phonetic rules of Prâkrit. So : *gaṇṭhaï* = *grathnāti* (§ 333; Hc. 4,120; Mk. fol. 54); Ś. *ṇiggaṇṭhida* (Bālar. 131,14).—*gĕṇhaï* = *gṛhṇāti* (Vr. 8,15; Hc. 4,209; Kī. 4,63); M. *gĕṇhaï*, *gĕṇhanti*, *gĕṇha*, *gĕṇhaü*, *gĕṇhanta*- (G. H. R.); JM. *gĕṇhasi* (Āv. 44,6), *gĕṇhaï*, *giṇhaï*, *giṇhae* (Kk.); *gĕṇhanti* (Āv. 35,3), *gĕṇha* (Erz.; Kk.); *gĕṇhāhi* (Āv. 31,11) and *gĕṇhesu* (Erz.), *gĕṇhaha*, *giṇhaha* (Āv. 33,17; Kk.); AMg. *gĕṇhaï* (Vivāhap. 916. 1032. 1659; Uvās.), *gĕṇhĕjjā* (Vivāhap. 212. 214), *giṇhaï* (Vivāhap. 1035; Paṇṇav. 377 ff.; Nāyādh. 449; Uvās.; Kappas.; Nirayāv. etc.), also *giṇhei* (Uvās.), *abhigiṇhaï* (Uvās.), *ogiṇhaï* (Vivāhap. 838), *giṇhaha* (Vivāhap. 623), *giṇhanti* (Vivāhap, 24; Nirayāv.), *giṇhāhi* (Nāyādh. 633), *giṇhaha*, *uvagiṇhaha* (Vivāhap. 332); JŚ. *giṇhadi* (Pav. 384,59 [text *giṇṇadi*], Kattig. 399, 310; 400, 335), *giṇhedi* (Kattig. 400,335); Ś. *gĕṇhasi* (Mṛcch. 49,15), *gĕṇhadi* (Mṛcch. 45,9; 74,18; Śak. 73,3;159,13), *gĕṇhanti* (Mṛcch. 70,3), *gĕṇha* (Mṛcch. 16,3; 38,4; 55,1; 75,2 etc.; Ratn. 305,7), *gĕṇhadu* (Mṛcch. 49,8; 74,14), *aṇugĕṇhadu* (Śak. 56,11; Mudrār. 19,4), *gĕṇhadha* (Mṛcch. 97,24), *aṇugĕṇhantu* (Mudrār. 262,5 [so to be read]), absol. *gĕṇhia* (Mṛcch. 41,12; 59,8; 75,8; 105,2; 107,10; Vikr. 10,2; 52,5; 72,15; 84,20), inf. *gĕṇhiduṁ* (Mṛcch. 94,12) particip. nec. *gĕṇhidavva* (Mṛcch. 150,14; Vikr. 30,9); Mg. *gĕṇhadi* (Mṛcch. 128,19; 145,17), *gĕṇha* (Mṛcch. 45,21; 132,13; Mudrār. 264,1; 265,1), *gĕṇhadu* (Mṛcch. 22,3.5), *gĕṇhia* (Mṛcch. 12, 14; 96,12. 18; 116,5; 126,16; 132,16; Caṇḍak. 64,8); Ḍh. *gĕṇha* (Mṛcch. 29,16; 30,2); A. *gṛṇhaï* (Hc. 4,336), *gĕṇhaï* (Piṅgala 1,60), absol. *gṛṇhĕppiṇu* (Hc. 4,394. 438,1). In A. *grah* is conjugated according to the 6th conjugation too : *gṛhanti* (Hc. 4,341,2).

§ 513. *bandh* is conjugated M. *bhandhaï* (Hc. 1,187; H. R.; Pracaṇḍap. 47,6); *ṇibandhaï* (R.), *bandhanti* (G. R.), *aṇubandhanti* (R.), *bandhasu* (R.), *ābandhantīa* (Hc. 1,7), future *bandhihii*, passive *bandhijjaï* (Hc. 4,247), also according to the *e*-conjugation : *bandhĕnti* (R.), inf. *bandheuṁ* (Hc. 1,181), JM. *bandhaha, bandhiūṇa, bandhiya*, (Erz.), *bandhiuṁ, bandhittu* (Kk.); AMg. *bandhaï* (Ṭhāṇ. 360; Vivāhap. 104. 136. 137. 331. 391 ff. 635 ff. 1810 ff.; Ovav. § 66; Paṇṇav. 638. 653. 657. 663 etc.), *paḍibandhaï* (Sūyag. 179), *bandhanti* (Ṭhāṇ. 108; Vivāhap. 66. 1435; Paṇṇav. 638. 657. 663 etc.), *bandhĕjjā* (Vivāhap. 420. 421; Uvās. § 200), *bandhaha* (Vivāhap. 234, 1263), inf. *bandhiu°* (Nirayāv. § 15); JŚ. *bandhade* (Kattig. 400,327); Ś. *bandhāmi* (Laṭakam. 18,12), *aṇubandhasi* (Śak. 86,14), *aṇubandhanti* (Uttarar. 60.7), absol. *bandhia* (Mṛcch. 155,3; Prab. 14,10 [so to be read] ; Ratn. 317,11), *ubbandhia* (Ratn. 315,28; Nāgān. 34,15;35,9), also according to the *e*-conjugation : *bandhesi* (Priyad. 4,16); *obandhedi* = *avabadhnāti* (Mṛcch. 89,5; 152,25); Mg. absol. *bandhia* (Mṛcch. 163,16), past passive participle *bandhida* (Mṛcch. 162,17), according to the *e*-conjugation imp. *paḍibandhedha* (Śak. 113,12).—*manth* forms *manthaï* (Hc. 4,121). To the flexion of Skt. *mathati* corresponds AMg. opt. *mahĕjjā* (Uvās. § 200), where, however, the v. l. points to *manthĕjjā*.

§ 514. In Ś. Mg. Ḍh. *bhaṇ* follows the analogy of the roots of the 9. conjugation, because *bhaṇāmi* was construed as **bha-ṇā-mi*. In the 2. 3. sing. indic., 3. sing. imp., 2. plur. indic. and imp. the length is retained as in the 1. sing. plur. Examples are extraordinarily numerous : Ś. *bhaṇāsi* (Mṛcch. 51, 7. 10; 52, 11; 53,54; 57,11; Vikr. 10,5; 22,14; Mālav. 27,13; Mudrār. 71,1.2. 4; 72,2. 4; 73,2 etc.), *bhaṇādi* (Mṛcch. 23,19; 67,14; 74,13; 94,11; Śak. 51,4; 158,2; Vikr. 16,5; 46,5; Mālav. 16, 18; 64,20 etc.), *bhaṇādu* (Mṛcch. 18,25); Mg. *bhaṇādi* (Mṛcch. 13,7), *bhaṇādha* (Mṛcch. 32,18; 96,21; 97,1; Prab. 46,16; Caṇḍak. 64,6; Mudrār. 154,1; 257,6; 258,2 [so to be read throughout, as also in Ś. Uttarar. 123,7]; Ḍh. *bhaṇādi* (Mṛcch. 34,12). The 2. sing. imp. is Ś. D. *bhaṇa* (Mṛcch. 88,19; Śak. 50,9; Vikr. 47,1; Nāgān. 30,1; D. Mṛcch. 100,8) or Ś. *bhaṇāhi* (Vikr. 27,7; Mālav. 39,9; Veṇīs. 10,12; 100,14; Nāgān. 44,13; Jīvān. 10,4); Mg. *bhaṇa* (Śak. 114,5) and *bhaṇāhi* (Mṛcch. 81,13. 15; 165,4). Beside them these dialects have also the *e*-conjugation : D. Ś. *bhaṇesi* (Mṛcch. 105,8; Śak. 137,12 [so to be read]); Mg. *bhaṇeśi* (Mṛcch. 21,8. 20.22); Ḍh. *bhaṇesi* (Mṛcch. 39,16); Ś. *bhaṇehi* (Mṛcch. 61,13; 79, 3). In the rest of the dialects *bhaṇ* behaves regularly according to the *a*-conjugation: further *bhaṇāi* in JM. Āv. 22,41.42 beside the usual *bhaṇaï*.

IMPERFECT

§ 515. The single imperfect, that has been retained in more than one dialects, is the imperfect of *as* (to be). However, only the 3. sing. *āsi* or *āsi* = *āsit*, which is used for all the persons in the sing. and plur., is found (Vr. 7,25; Hc. 3,164; Kī. 4,11; Sr. fol. 54). So 1. sing. AMg. *ke ahaṁ āsi* (Āyār. 1,1,1,3); Ś. *ahaṁ khu...āsi* (Mṛcch. 54,16)[1]; 2. sing Ś. *tumaṁ...gadā āsi* (Mṛcch. 28,14) *tumaṁ kiṁ mantaanti āsī* (Māḷatīm. 71,4), *tumaṁ khu...me piasahi āsi* (Mālatīm. 141,11 f.), *kilinto āsi* (Uttarar. 18,12), *kisa tumaṁ*, ed. *tuaṁ*] *mantaanti āsi* (Karṇas. 37,7f.)[2]; 3. sing. M. *āsi* (G.H.); JM. *āsi, āsi* (KI. 2; Dvār. 495,19;499,20;504,19; Erz.); AMg. *āsi* (Sūẏag. 896; Uvās. § 197; Ovav. § 170), *āsi* (Uttar. 660; Jīv. 239.452); Ś. very frequently; e.g. *āsi* (Lalitav. 560,14; 568,1; Mṛcch. 41,21; Śak. 43,6;105, 10;117,12;129.13;162, 13; Vikr. 11,2; 27,21; 35,7.9), *āsi* (Uttarar. 20,12; 78,4; Veṇīs. 12,1,6); Ḍh. *āsi* (Mṛcch. 36,18); 1. plur. AMg. *āsi mo, āsi mo*[3] (Uttar. 402), *āsi amhe* (Uttar. 403); 3. plur. M. *je āsi...mahāṇaipavahā* (G. 449), *āsi rahā* (R. 14,33), *je°gŏcchaā āsi...vañjulā* (H.422); JM. *mahārāẏāṇo cattāri mittā āsi* (Erz. 4,36); AMg. *uvasaggā bhīmāsi* (Āẏār. 1,8,2,7), *tassa bhajjā duve āsi* (Uttar. 660); Ś. *pasaṁsantio āsi* (Bālar. 289,2).—Besides we find only AMg. *abbavi = abravit* (Hc. 3,162; Uttar. 279. 281; Sūẏag. 259), used also as 3. plur. too : *abambhacāriṇo bālā imaṁ vaẏaṇam abbavi* (Uttar. 351).—On the hypothetical preterite *udāhare, care, pahaṇe, pucche, acchia, gĕṇhia* etc. see § 466. The preterite postulated by BOLLENSEN[4] rests on false readings and misunderstood forms[5]. See also § 517.

1. Notwithstanding Pāli *āsim*, we should not with the v.l. read here *āsiṁ*, as BLOCH, Vr. and Hc., presumes.—2. In H. 805, *āsi* should not be considered, with WEBER, as=*āsīḥ*, but as=*āśīḥ* with the scholiasts.—3. *āsi* of the text should be so corrected. As the immediately following *āsi amhe* and the exceptional use of *āsi, āsī* point, it is not to be read with LEUMANN, WZKM. 5,134., *āsīmo* or *āsīmu*, but *mo* should, with scholiasts, be considered as a pronoun.—4. Mālavikā. p. 188.230.—5. BLOCH, Vr. und Hc. p. 46.

AORIST

§ 516. Of the strong aorist only AMg. *acche = *ācchet* from *chid*, *abbhe* = Vedic. *ābhet* from *bhid* (Āẏār. 1,1,2,5), that are used in the sense of the opt. (§ 466), are noticeable, in addition to *abhū = abhūt* in verse in AMg. (Uttar. 116), which has been used there in the 3. plur.: *abhū jiṇā atthi jiṇā aduvā vi bhavissai*. Very numerous, on the other hand, in AMg. are the many forms of the *s*- aorist in the parasmaip., frequently derived from the present stem. The very seldom 1. sing. parasmaip. shows, as in Pāli[1], a doubled *s* : *akarissaṁ c' ahaṁ* (Āẏār. 1,1, 1,5); *pucchiss' ahaṁ* (verse; Sūẏag. 259). The 2. sing. occurs in *akāsi = akārṣiḥ* (Samav. 82); *kāsi* (Uttar. 415) and in *vaẏāsi = avādiḥ* (Sūẏag. 924), a form, that is connected with Pāli forms like *agamāsi*[2]. Both the forms are more frequent than the 3. sing. So *akāsi* (Āẏār. 1,8,4,8; 2,2,2,4; Sūẏag. 74; Kappas. § 146), *akāsi* (Sūẏag. 120.123. 298), behind *mā* also *kāsi* (Hc, 3,162; Sūẏag. 234; Uttar. 14), according to Hc. 3,162; Sr. fol. 54 also *kāhi* and according to Deśīn. 1,8 *akāsi* in the sense of *paryāptam*. The same forms are used also as 1. sing. *jaṁ ahaṁ puvvaṁ akāsi = yad aham pūrvam akārṣam* (Āẏār. 1,1,4,3); *aham eẏam akāsi = aham etad akārṣam* (Sūẏag. 621) and used also as 1. plur.: *jahā vaẏaṁ dhammam aẏāṇa-māṇā pāvaṁ purā kammam akāsi mohā* (Uttar. 433 f.). This corresponds to the use of the imperf. *āsi* (§ 515). As 3. sing.: *vaẏāsi* (Sūẏag. 578; Vivāhap. 165.1260.1262.1268; Ovav.; Uvās.; Kappas.), very frequently in the meaning of the 3. plur. (Āẏār. 1,4,2,4; Sūẏag. 783; Vivāhap. 131.186.236.238.332.

809.951; Antag. 61; Nāẏādh. § 68 ff. u.s.w.) etc., also *vaẏāsi* (Sūẏag. 565. 841; Ovav. §53.84ff.). Other examples for the 3. sing. are: *ṭhāsi, ṭhāhī* from *sthā* (Hc. 3.162); *paccāsi* from *aś* with *parti* (Āẏār.1,2,5,5); *acārī* (Āẏār. 1,8,3,2); *kahesi* from *kathaya-* (Paṇhāv. 303. 327). From *bhū* the 3. sing. is *bhuvi* = **abhuvit* (Vivāhap. 78.844 [text here °*iṁ*]; Nandīs. 501. 502 [text *bhuviṁ ca*]; Jīv. 239.452 [text here °*iṁ*]), or from the present stem *bhava-*: *ahesi* from **abhaviṣit*, **abhaïṣit*, **abhaiṣīt* (§ 166; Hc. 3,164), according to Hc. used also as 1. 2. sing., and found in the text as 3. plur.: *samaṇā...tattha viharantā puṭṭhapuvvā ahesi suṇaehiṁ* (Āẏār. 1,8,3,6). Likewise is explained AMg. *annesi* = **ājñāyiṣit* (cf. § 487; Āẏār. 1,2,6,5; 1,5, 2,1. 3,4; 1,8,1,14). That the form is not = *anveṣi*, but is the aorist of *jñā*, has already been assumed by JACOBI[3]. One 1. plur. occurs in *vucchāmu* = *avātsma* from *vas* "to live" (Uttar. 410), formed from an aorist stem **vatsa-*. The 3. plur. ends in *-iṁsu* = Skt. *iṣuḥ*. So: *parivicittthiṁsu* (Āẏār. 1,4,4,4); *pucchiṁsu* (Āẏār. 1,8,2,11; Sūẏag. 301 [text °*issu*]); *ciṇiṁsu, uvaciṇiṁsu* (Vivāhap. 62; Ṭhāṇ. 107. 108 [text °*ṇa*°]); *bandhiṁsu, udīriṁsu, vediṁsu nijjariṁsu* (Ṭhāṇ. 108; Vivāhap. 62 [text °*ĕṁsu*]); *sijjhiṁsu, bujjhiṁsu* (Sūẏag. 790; Vivāhap. 79); *āẏāiṁsu* from *jan* with *ā* (Kappas. § 17—19; cf. § 487); *pariṇivvāiṁsu* (Sūẏag. 790); *bhāsiṁsu, seviṁsu* (Sūẏag. 704); *atariṁsu* (Sūẏag. 424; Uttar. 567); *hiṁsiṁsu* (Āẏār. 1,1,6,5; 1,8,1,2; 1,8,3,3); *vihariṁsu* (Āẏār. 1,8,1,2;1,8,3,5); *luñciṁsu, nihaṇiṁsu* (Āẏār. (1,8, 3,11.12); *kandiṁsu* from *krand* (Āẏār. 1,8,1,4; 1,8,3 10); *viṇaīṁsu* = *vyanaiṣuḥ* (Sūẏag. 454); *abhaviṁsu* (Sūẏag. 157.551) and *bhaviṁsu* (Vivāhap. 157). Beside the usual *akariṁsu* (Ṭhāṇ. 149); *kariṁsu* (Vivāhap. 62.79; Nāẏādh. § 118; Sūẏag. 790 [text *karesu*], *uvakariṁsu* (Āẏār. 1,8, 3,11), is found also *vikuvviṁsu* (Vivāhap. 214.215) from the present stem *kuvva-* (§ 508). Aorists of the causative are *giṇhāviṁsu* (Nāẏādh. § 123); *paṭṭhāvaïṁsu* from *sthā* with *pra* (Kappas. § 128); *saṁpahāriṁsu* from *dhar* with *sam* and *pra* (Sūẏag. 585.620); aor. of a denominative is *rikkāsi* (Āẏār. 1,8,1,3) from one **riknaya-*. The 3. plur. is used also for other persons. Thus for the 1. sing.: *kariṁsu vāhaṁ* (Ṭhāṇ. 476); for the 3. sing. *āhiṁsiṁsu* [text °*sa*°] *vā hiṁsaï vā hiṁsissaï vā* (Sūẏag. 680); *puṭṭho vi nābhibhāsiṁsu* (Āẏār. 1,8,1,6); *āsiṁsu* [text °*sa*°] *bhagavaṁ* (Āẏār. 1,8,2,6); *seviṁsu* (Āẏār. 1 8,3,2). An old Skt. form is *addakkhu* (Vivāhap. 332), *addakkhū* (Āẏār. 1,5,1,3; may be sing. too) = *adrākṣuḥ*, frequently used as 3. singular: *adakkhu* (Āẏār. 1,2,5,2: Vivāhap. 1306), *addakkhu* (Āẏār. 1,8,1, 9), *addakkhū* (Āẏār. 1,5,2,1.6,1; 1,8,1,16.17)[4]. In Kappas. S. 19 *adakkhu* is a wrong reading for *adaṭṭhu*, as the v. l. has. Accordingly is formed *niṇṇakkhu* (Āẏār. 2,2,1,4,5.6) *niḥ* used as 3. singular from *naks* with *niḥ*.

1. E. KUHN, Beiträge p. 111; E. MÜLLER, Simplified Grammar p. 114.—2. E. KUHN, l. c. p. 114; E. MÜLLER, l. c. p. 116.—3. SBE. XXII, p. 44, note 2—4. In certain places one may be in doubt, whether or not there is an adjective **ādrākṣu*, as it certainly appears for *dakkhu, adakkhu* = **drākṣu* or *adrākṣu* **dṛkṣu*, **adṛkṣu* in Sūyag. 151.

§ 517. In AMg. we frequently find one 3. sing. ātmanep. in *-itthā ittha*. The form is built exclusively from the present stem, and this as well as the unusual dental, which Pāli too has, for the expected cerebral

(§ 303), makes it doubtful, as to whether it is derived correctly from the *s*-aorist[1]. Examples are *samuppajjitthā* from *pad* with *sam* and *ud* (Vivāhap. 151. 170; Nāẏādh. § 81. 87; p. 771; Uvās.; Kappas. etc.); *roitthā* from *ruc* (Hc. 3,143); *vaḍḍhitthā, abhivaḍḍhitthā* from *vṛdh* (Kappas.); *riitthā* from *riẏate* (Āẏār. 1,8,1,1; 1,8,3,13); *esitthā* (Āẏār. 1,8,4,12); *viharitthā* (Āẏār. 1,8,1,12); *bhuñjitthā* (Āẏār. 1,8,1,17. 18), *sevittha, sevitthā* (Āẏār. 1,8,2,1; 1,8,4,9); *apiittha, apivitthā* [so to be read] from *pā* (to drink) with privative *a* (Āẏār. 1,8,4,5. 6); *aṇujāṇitthā* (Āẏār. 1,8,4,8); *kuvvitthā* from the present stem *kuvvaï* (§ 508) (Āẏār. 1,8,4,15); *udāharitthā* (Uttar. 353. 408), *jaẏitthā, parājaẏitthā* (Vivāhap. 500); *dalaẏitthā* (Vivāhap. 502). From *bhū* is derived the form *hotthā* from the present stem *ho-* = *bhava-* (§ 476) (Vivāhap. 5. 168.182; Ṭhāṇ. 79; Uvās.; Kappas.; Nāẏādh.; Ovav. etc.); also with augment in the verse *ahŏtthā* (Uttar. 619); with *prāduḥ* on the other hand, from the stem *bhava-*: *pāubbhavitthā* (Vivāhap. 1201). Of the causative the form ends in *-ĕtthā, -ĕttha*: *kārĕtthā-* from *kāre-* = *kāraya-* (Āẏār. 1,8,4,8); *pahārĕtthā*, mostly °*ttha* from *pahāre-* = *pradhāraya-* (Sūẏag. 1012; Vivāhap. 153. 831; Vivāgas. 123; Ovav. § 50; Nāẏādh. § 81 etc.); but also *jāvaïttha* from *yāpaya-* (Āẏār. 1,8.4,4). The same form is used also for persons other than the 3. sing. Thus for the 2. plur. in *labhittha* [so the commentary; text °*bhĕ*°]: *jaï me ṇa dāhittha ih'* [so the commentary; text *ah'*] *esaṇijjaṁ kim ajja jannāṇa labhittha lābhaṁ* (Uttar. 359); for the 3. plur.: *vippasaritthā* (Nāẏādh. 348): *bahave hatthī...diso disiṁ vippasaritthā, kasāitthā*, denominative from *kaśā* (Āẏār. 1,8,2, 11); *pāubbhavitthā* (Nāẏādh. § 59; Ovav. § 33 ff.); *bahave...devā antiẏaṁ pāubbhavitthā*; more often *hŏtthā* (Āẏār. 2,15,16; Ṭhāṇ. 197; Nāẏādh. 628; Samav. 66.229; Uvās. § 4. 184. 233. 234; Kappas. Th. § 5. 6; Ovav. § 77.—Cf. § 520. On the precative see § 466.

1. Hypotheses on the origin of the form in JOHANSSON, KZ. 32,450 ff.

PERFECT

§ 518. Of the perfect, only the 3. plur. parasmaip. *āhu* = *āhuḥ* is preserved in AMg. (Āẏār. 1,4,3,1; Sūẏag. 74 [text *āha*]. 132. 134. 150.316. 468. 500); *udāhu* (Uttar. 424); also *āhū* (Āẏār. 1,5,1,3) and *udāhū* (Sūẏag. 454). More frequent, as in Pāli, is the recent formation *āhaṁsu* (Āẏār. 2,1,4,5; Sūẏag. 37. 166. 202, 241. 356. 445. 456. 463. 465. 778. 842; Vivāhap. 130. 139. 142. 179 438. 1033. 1402; Ṭhāṇ. 148. 438 ff.; Paṇhāv. 95. 106; Jīv. 12. 13; Kappas. S. § 27). Both the forms are employed for other persons as well. So *āhaṁsu* for the 1. sing.: *tao 'haṁ evam āhaṁsu* (Uttar. 623); for the 3. sing.: *evam āhaṁsu nāẏakulanandaṇo mahappā jiṇo varavīraṇāmadhĕjjo kahesi ẏa* (Paṇhāv. 303. 327); likewise for the 3. sing. *āhu* (Sūẏag. 257. 308; Uttar. 365. 646; Kappas. and *udāhu* (Āẏār. 1,2,4,4; Sūẏag. 159. 304. 387. 518. 974. 989. 992 ff.; Uttar. 756).

PLUPERFECT

§ 519. With the exception of the cases mentioned in § 515—518, in Pkt. the past tense is expressed either by the present, particularly in narration, or generally by paraphrasis with the past passive participle, by which the person or thing spoken of, that in the case of transitive verbs goes over to the instrumental: *abalāṇa tāṇa...vasio aṅgesu...seo* "sweat clung to the limbs of these women" (G. 210); *kiṁ ṇa bhaṇio si bālaa gamaṇidhūāi* "have you, O boy, not been told by the daughter of the village chief? (H. 370); *siāparimaṭṭheṇa va vūḍho teṇa vi ṇirantaraṁ romañco* "he exhibited uninterrupted thrill of hair, as if touched by Sītā" (R. 1,42); JM. *pacchā rannā cintiyaṁ* "later the king thought, (Āv. 32,19); *annayā bhūyadinneṇa vinnāyaṁ* "once Bhūtadinna learnt" (Erz. 1, 24); AMg. *suyaṁ me āusaṁ teṇa bhagavayā evam akkhāyam* "I have heard that the long-lived Lord had spoken thus" (Āyār. 1,1,1,1); *urālā ṇaṁ tume devāṇuppie sumiṇā diṭṭhā* "O beloved of gods, you have seen an excellent dream" (Kappas. § 9); Ś. *tā aāṇanteṇa ediṇā ĕvvaṁ aṇuciṭṭhidaṁ* "so he has done thus unknowingly" (Mṛcch. 63,24); *sudaṁ khu mae tādakaṇṇassa muhādo* "I have heard from the mouth of the father Kaṇva (Śak. 14,12); Mg. *śūdaṁ tue yaṁ mae gāidaṁ* "did you hear what I sang?" (Mṛcch. 116, 20); *adha ĕkkadiaśaṁ mae lohidamaścake khaṇḍaśo kappide°* "one day I cut the *rohita*-fish into pieces" (Śak. 114,9); A. *tumhĕhĩ amhĕhĩ jaṁ kiaũ diṭṭhaũ bahuajaṇeṇa* "many people have seen what was done by you and by us (Hc. 4,371); *sabadhu karĕppiṇu kadhidu maĩ* "I have said on oath" (Hc. 4,396,3). Pkt. may form in this manner by addition of *āsi* (was) the pluperfect from a past passive participle.[1] So: M. *jo sisammi viiṇṇo majjhajuāṇehi gaṇavai āsi* "he, whom the young men had put over my head, was Gaṇapati" (H. 372); JM. *tayā ya so kumbhayāro...gāmaṁ annaṁ gao āsi* "and at that time the potter had gone to another village" (Sagara 10, 18); *jaṁ te sukkhiyaṁ āsi buddhileṇa addhalakkhaṁ* "that half lac, that Buddhila had spoken to thee" (Erz. 10,34); Ś. *ahaṁ khu radaṇachaṭṭhiṁ uvavasidā āsi* "I had brought the (prescribed) fast to end on the *ratnaṣaṣṭhi* (for the vow)" (Mṛcch. 54, 16); Ś. *tumaṁ mae saha...gadā āsi* "you had gone with me" (Mṛcch. 28,14); *ajja devi ajjagandhālie pādavandaṇaṁ kāduṁ gadā āsi* "today the queen had gone to adore the feet of Her Majesty Gāndhārī" (Veṇīs. 12,6); *puṇo mandassa vi me tattha paccuppaṇṇaṁ uttaraṁ āsi*, "although dull, I had prepared the answer" (Mālav. 57,16); *taĕkkhu cittaphalaaṁ pabhāde hatthikidaṁ āsi* "I had taken the picture into my hand in the morning" (Mālatīm. 78,3); Ḍh. *tassa jūḍialassa muṭṭhippahāleṇa ṇāsikā bhaggā āsi* "the nose of the gambler was broken with a stroke of the fist (Mṛcch. 36,18). In many cases they may be taken as adjectival participle.

1. FICK, Sagara p. 26.

FUTURE

§ 520. By far the most usual, in Ś. Mg. exclusively attestable formation of the future of the roots ending in a consonant, is that of the stem in *-i*. But Pkt. does not employ merely the crude stem, but more frequently the present stem, as well as the stem in *-e*. The 1. sing. has in AMg. JM. often, in other dialects almost sporadically, the ending *-mi*, mostly *-m*. the ending of the secondary tense, which in A. with *a* of the stem becomes *u* (351). In the 2. sing. *-issasi*, Mg. *-iśśaśi*, in the 3. sing. *-issaï*, Ś. Ḍh. *-issadi*, Mg. *-iśśadi* the regular, in Ś. Mg. Ḍh., except rarely in verses, is only the usual ending. In M. JM. AMg., in lieu of it, mostly enters 2. sing. *-ihisi*, 3. *-ihii*, also the contracted *-ihī* and prosodically shortened *-ihi*, a phonetic transformation that has disappeared from the roots and stems ending in long vowels and diphthongs. The grammarians mention for the 1. sing. too the ending *-ihāmi*, *-ihimi*: *kittaïhimi* beside *kittaïssaṁ* = *kīrtayiṣyāmi* (Hc. 3,169); *sŏcchihimi*, *sŏcchihāmi* from *śru*; *gacchihimi*, *gacchihāmi* beside *gacchissaṁ* from *gaṁ* (Hc. 3,172); *hasihimi* beside *hasissaṁ*, *hasissāmi* (Sr. fol. 52). For the roots and stems ending in long vowels *-himi* too is prescribed: *kāhimi* from *kṛ*, *dāhimi* from *dā* (Hc. 3,170; Sr. fol. 52), *hohimi* from *bhū* (Bh. 7,14; Hc. 3,167. 169; Kī. 4,16), *hasehimi* beside *hasehāmi*, *hasĕssāmi* from the *e*-stem of *has* (Sr. fol. 52), to which *hasehii* (Bh. 7,33; Hc. 3,157) too belongs. We find in the texts such forms with *-i* upto the present day only in A. : *pĕkkhihimi* = *prekṣiṣye*, *sahihimi* = *sahiṣye* (Vikr. 55,18.19). According to Hc. 4,275 Ś. has in the 3. sing. *-issidi* : *bhavissidi*, *karissidi*, *gacchissidi*, according to 4,302 in Mg. *-iśśidi* : *bhaviśśidi*. In South Indian manuscripts, in several places the future forms in *-issidi* are found; they are unknown in the texts. Probably in Hc. by Ś. is again meant JŚ., in which the examples for the future are hitherto wanting. The 1. plur. mostly ends in *-issāmo*, in verses seldom in *-issāma* too, as M. *karissāma* (H. 897), after long vowels in *-hāmo*, metrically in *-hāmu* too. The grammarians admit beside the forms like *hasissāmo* also *hasihimo* (Bh. 7, 15; Hc. 3,167; Sr. fol. 52), *hasihissā*, *hasihitthā* (Bh. 7,15; Hc. 3, 168; Sr. fol. 52), Bh. 7,15 also *hasihāmo*. Sr. fol. 52, *hasehissā*, *hasehitthā*, *hasĕssāmo*, *hasĕssāmu*, *hasissāmu*, *hasĕssāma*, *hasehāma*, *hasihāma*, *hasehimo*, *hasehimu*, *hasihimu*; further *sŏcchimo*, *sŏcchimu*, *sŏcchima*, *sŏcchihimo*, *sŏcchihimu*, *sŏcchihima* *sŏcchissāmo*, °*mu*, °*ma*, *sŏcchihāmo*, *sŏcchihissā*, *sŏcchihitthā* (Bh. 7,17; Hc. 3, 172), *gacchimo*, *gacchihimo*, *gacchissāmo*, *gacchihāmo*, *gacchihissā*. *gacchihitthā* (Hc. 3,172); *hohimo*, *hŏssāmo*, *hohāmo*, *hohissā*, *hohitthā* (Bh. 7,13. 15; Hc. 3, 168; Kī. 4,18), *hohissāmo*, *hohitthāmo* (Kī. 4,18). Cf. further § 521. 523. 531. The ending *-ihissā* for the 1. plur. is completely obscure[1]. The ending *-hitthā*, *-ihitthā* is prescribed for the 2. plural too : *hohitthā* (Hc. 3,166); *sŏcchitthā*, *sŏcchihitthā* (Bh. 7,17; Hc. 3,172) beside *sŏcchiha*, *sŏcchihiha*, *gacchitthā*, *gacchihitthā* (Hc. 3,172) beside *gacchiha*, *gacchihiha*, *hasehitthā*, *hasihitthā* (Sr. fol. 52) beside *hasehiha*, *hasihiha*. The one found in the text in AMg. is *dāhittha* = *dāsyatha* (Uttar. 359). Accordingly this might have belonged to the 2. plur. and thence taken over to the 1. plur. It still remains undecided if it is connected with the ending *-itthā*, which is assigned to the aorist. The usual ending of the 2. plur. is *-issaha*, Ś. Mg. *-issadha*. The 3. plur. ends in *-issanti*, in JM. AMg. very frequently in *-ihinti*, *-hinti* too. Sr. fol. 51 teaches *-ire* : *hasehiire*, *hasihiire*.

1. According to Kī.'s *hohitthāmo* LASSEN, Inst. p. 353 tries to explain *hohissā*, *hohitthā* as abridgment of *hohissāmo*, *hohitthāmo*. But since *hohitthā* is also the 2. plural, the explanation is not plausible. The free use of *āsi*, *ahesi*, *āhu*, *udāhu* and the 3. sing. preterite in *-itthā* may be compared. For the sake of brevity *i* is always pushed over the ending.

§ 521. The examples for the future are regulated according to the present stem (§ 473 ff.) for the sake of simplication of the survey. Thc future of *ji* is JM. *jiṇissaī* (Erz. 22,29), AMg. *parājiṇissaī* (Niraẏāv. § 3); from *nī*, M. *ṇehii* = *neṣyati* (G. 223), JM. *niṇehii* = *nirṇeṣyati* (Erz. 52,13), *nehinti* (Erz. 29,15), AMg. *uvaṇehii* (Ovav. § 197), *viṇehii* (Nāẏādh. § 87); *uvaṇehinti* (Ovav. §106), but from the present stem Ś. *aṇuṇaïssaṁ* (Ratn. 316,15), *avaṇaīssaṁ* (Śak. 102,14; 104,13), *uvaṇaïssaṁ* (Śak. 137,3), *ṇaīssadi* (Mṛcch. 58,3), *āṇaïssadi* (Mālatīm. 104,1), *ṇaïssadha* (Karp. 33,8); Mg. *ṇaïśśaṁ* (Mṛcch. 169,13). On Ś. *daīssaṁ* Mg. *daīśśaṁ* from *daya-* (to give) see § 474.—In the future of *bhū* all the present stems are to be found, however, the dialects maintain distinction in their employment. M. A. use only *ho-*, that Ś. Mg. do not know. JM. *bhavissāmi* (Dvār. 501,38); Ś. *bhavissaṁ* (Mṛcch. 9, 12; Śak. 51, 13; 85,7; Mālav. 52,19; Ratn. 315,16; 318,31; Karp. 8,7; 52,2), *aṇubhavissaṁ* (Mālatīm. 278,9); Mg. *bhaviśśaṁ* (Mṛcch. 116,23); Ś. *bhavissasi* (Mṛcch, 4,6; Ratn. 296,25); Mg. *bhaviśśaśi* (Śak. 116,4); AMg. JM. *bhavissaï* (Vivāhap. 844 Jīv. 239. 452; Uttar. 116; Ovav. § 103. 109. 114. [115]; Kappas.; Dvār. 495,27; 504,5; Erz. 11,35; Kk. 268,33; 271,13.15); Ś. *bhavissadi* (Mṛcch. 5,2; 20,24; Śak. 10,3; 18,3; Vikr. 20,20; Mālav. 35,20; 37,5; Ratn. 291,2; 294,9; Mālatīm. 78,9; 89,8; 125,2 etc.); Mg. *bhaviśśadi* (Prab. 50,14); AMg. *bhavissāmo* (Āẏār. 1,2,2,1; Sūẏag. 601); AMg. *bhavissaha* (Vivāhap. 234); JM. *bhavihinti* (Āv. 47,20); Ś. *bhavissanti* (Mālatīm. 126,3). False is *havissadi, havissaṁ* (Mālav. 37,19; 40,22)[1], since the stem *hava* is used only after the prefix *pra*, as in Ś. *pahavissaṁ* (Uttarar. 32,4). Ś. Mg. use also the stem *huva-*: Mg. *huviśśaṁ* (Mṛcch. 29,24; 32,19; 40,1; 118; 17; 124,12); Ś. *huvissasi* (Veṇīs. 58,18); Ś. *huvissadi* (Mṛcch. 22 14; 24,4; 64,18; Vikr. 36,6; 46,4. 6; 53,2. 13; 72,19; Mālav. 70,6; Veṇīs. 9,21; Vṛṣabh. 47,11 etc.); Mg. *huviśśadi* (Mṛcch. 21,14. 15; 117,15; 118,16. 17; Veṇīs. 33,3); Ś. *huvissanti* (Mṛcch. 39,4; Caṇḍak. 86, 14). From the stem *ho-* are derived: *hŏssāmi* (Bh. 7,14; Hc. 3,167. 169; Kī. 4,16); M. *hŏssaṁ* (Vr. 7,14; Hc. 3,169; Kī. 4,17; H. 743); A. *hosaï* (Hc. 4,388; 418,4), and *hose* (Prabandhac. 56,6; cf. § 166); *hŏssāmo, hŏssāmu, hossāma* (Bh. 7,13. 15; Hc. 3,167. 168; Kī. 4,18), mostly with *h* from *ṣ* (§ 263): JM. *hohāmi* (Bh. 7,14; Hc. 3,167; Kī. 4,16; Āv. 26,36); *hohimi* (Bh. 7,14; Hc. 3,167; Kī. 4,16); *hohissaṁ* (Kī. 4,17); JM. *hohisi* (Hc. 3,166. 178.; Erz. 62,31); M. JM. *hohii* (Hc. 3,166. 178; Kī. 4,15; G.H.R.; Āv. 43,13; Erz. 37,1), *hohī* (Erz. 6,36; Dvār. 495,15; T. 7,10; Kk. 265,41; 270,43); before double consonants *hohi*: *hohi tti* (Dvār. 495,24); 1. plur. *hohāmo, hohāmu, hohāma, hohimo, hohimu, hohima, hohissā, hohitthā* (Bh. 7,13,15; Hc. 3,167.168), *hohissāmo, hohitthāmo* (Kī. 4,18); 2. plur. *hohitthā* (Hc. 3,166; Kī. 4,15); 3. plur. M. JM. *hohinti* (Bh. 7,12; Hc. 3,166; Kī. 4,15; H. 675; Sagara 2,15). In AMg. sometimes the stem *hŏkkha-* is met: *hŏkkhāmi* (Uttar. 63. 202), *hŏkkhaṁ*) (Uttar. 63), *hŏkkhaï, hŏkkhanti* (Samav. 240 ff.) It is probably merely a false reading deduced from **bhoṣya-* (§ 265). Cf. also § 520. According to Hc. 3,178 from the precative too a future is derived: *hojjahimi, hŏjjāhimi, hŏjjassāmi, hŏjjahāmi hŏjjassaṁ; hŏjjahisi, hŏjjāhisi; hŏjjahii, hŏjjāhii*. Sr. fol. 53 teaches *hŏjjehii, hŏjjihii, hŏjjāhii*.

1. More examples in BLOCH, Vr. und Hc. 42,—2. The forms, that are hitherto incapable of verification, have been quoted here without mentioning the dialects.

§ 522. The roots in *ṛ*, *ṝ* according to the 1. and 6. conjugations form in all the dialects the future, as in Skt. : Ś. *aṇusarissaṁ* (Viddhaś. 115,6), *visumarissaṁ* = *vismariṣyāmi* (Śak. 14,3), *visumarissasi* (Śak. 89,7), *visumarissadha* (Śak. 86,6); Ś. *sumarissasi* (Ratn. 313,6); Ś. *pariharissaṁ* (Śak. 25,1), *pariharissadi* (Vikr. 79,7); Mg. *palihaliśśadi* (Prab. 42,5;47,7); *vihaliśśaṁ* (Mṛcch. 40,6); AMg. *viharissaï* (Ovav. § 114. [§ 115]), *viharissāmo* (Āẏār. 2,2,3,3; 2,7,1,2; Vivāhap. 979), *viharissaha* (Vivāhap. 234); JM. *viharissanti* (Kk. 269,38); *marissasi* (Mṛcch. 72,18); Mg. *malīhiśi* (verse; Mṛcch. 9,24); M. *aṇumarihii* (R. 14,55); M. *harihii* (H. 143); AMg. *tarihinti* (Uttar. 253) and *tarissanti* (Uttar. 567; Sūẏag. 424), *nijjarissanti* (Ṭhāṇ. 108).—Of the roots in *-ai gai* forms : AMg. *gāhii* = *gāsyati* (Ṭhāṇ. 451); M. *uggāhii* (R. 11,84); against that Ś. *gāissaṁ* (Śak. 2,8; Viddhaś. 122,11; 128,4; Kaṁsav. 8,16), Mg. *gāiśśaṁ* (Mṛcch. 116,20;117, 3); from *trai* the fut. is Mg. *palittāiśśadi* (Mṛcch. 12,10).

§ 523. Of the roots of the old *ska-* class *ṛ* forms in JM. *acchihisi* (Āv. 11,11), *yam* JM. *paẏacchissāmo* (Dvār. 503,4). In the case of *gam* the formation from the stem *gami-* prevails that is exclusively dominant in Ś. Mg. The form *gacchissidi* taught by Hc. 4,275 for Ś. is not attested by the texts. So : JM. *gamissāmi* (Erz. 60, 19); Ś. *gamissaṁ* (Mṛcch. 8,24; 9,7; 15,10; 54,19; Śak. 17,4; Ratn. 293,24; 296,26; 297,12; 314,26; Karp. 35,3; 108,4; 109,2; Nāgān. 42,7. 15; 43,10; Jīvān. 42,17.23; 43,17 etc.), *āgamissaṁ* (Karp. 22,7; 107,4); Mg. *gamiśśaṁ* (Mṛcch. 20,10.14;32,2; 97,1; 98,2; 112,18); Ś. *gamissasi* (Mṛcch. 3,17; Śak. 24,15); AMg. *gamihii* (Uvās. § 125; Vivāhap. 175; Niraẏāv. § 27); A. *gamihī* (Hc. 4,330,2); M. *samāgamissaī* (H. 962); Ś. *gamissadi* (Mṛcch. 94,2; Śak. 56,14; Mālatīm. 103,7), *āgamissadi* (Uttarar. 123,7; Karp. 105,3); Ḍh. *gamissadi* (Mṛcch. 36, 23); AMg. Ś. *gamissāmo* (Ovav. § 78; Karp. 36,6); AMg. *uvāgamissanti* (Āẏār. 2,3,1,2 ff.). From the stem *gaccha-* are built : *gacchissāmi* (JM. Āv. 21,10), *gacchissaṁ*, *gacchihāmi*, *gacchihimi*; *gacchihisi* (Hc. 3,172); AMg. *gacchihii* (Hc. 3,172; Sr. fol. 52; Ovav. § 100.101; Uvās. § 90); *āgacchissaī* (Uvās. § 188); according to Sr. also *gacchehii*; *gacchissāmo*, *gacchihāmo*, *gacchihimo*, *gacchihissā*, *gacchihitthā*, *gacchihiha* (AMg. Āẏār, 2.3,3,5), *gacchihitthā*; *gacchihinti* (Hc. 3,172). Beside them is found a future AMg. *gacchaṁ* (Vr. 7,16; Hc. 3,171; Kī. 4,19; Sr. fol. 53; Ṭhāṇ. 156.285), according to Hc. also *gacchimi*, that according to the grammarians is inflected : *gacchisi*, *gacchii*, *gacchimo*, *gacchiha*, *gacchinti*, according to Sr. also *gacchei*. The hypothesis that *gacchaṁ* may have been formed on the analogy of *daccham*, *mŏcchaṁ*, *vicchaṁ*, *rŏcchaṁ*, *vĕcchaṁ*, *vŏcchaṁ* (§ 525.526. 529) is convenient, but wholly improbable. We should assume a root *gacch*, deduced from *gacchaï*, and derive *gacchaṁ* from **gacchsyāmi*, **gakṣyāmi*. Cf. *sŏcchaṁ* § 531.

§ 524. Of the reduplicated roots of the first conjugation *pā* forms JM. *pāhāmi* = *pāsyāmi* (Āv. 42,27); AMg. *pāhaṁ* (Uttar. 593 [text *pāhiṁ*]), *pāhisi* (Kappas. S. § 18), *pāhāmo* (Āẏār. 2,1,5,5; 2,1,9,6); M. *pāhinti*

(R. 3,21; text false °*hĕ*). The future of *sthā* is M. *thāhii* (Pracaṇḍap. 47,4), Ś. *ciṭṭhissaṁ* (Śak. 30,9; Vikr. 15,5; Nāgān. 69,14; Karp. 22,2); Mg. *ciṣṭhiśśaṁ* (Caṇḍak. 42,11), *aṇuciṣṭhiśśaṁ* (Mṛcch. 40,11; cf. v.l. and § 303); Ś. *ciṭṭhissadi* (Vikr. 43,8); AMg. Ś. *ciṭṭhissāmo* (Nāyādh. 908.939; Viddhaś. 61,8).—Ś. *uṭṭhissāmo* (Mṛcch. 20,22) goes back to *uṭṭhaï*, AMg. *uṭṭhehinti* (Vivāhap. 1280) to *uṭṭhei* (§ 483).

§ 525. The future from *dṛś* in M. JM. AMg. is *dacchaṁ* = *drakṣyāmi* (Vr. 7,16; Hc. 3,171; Sr. fol. 52). The rules for *gam* (§ 523) hold good in this case too. One says: M. *dacchāmi* (R. 11,77), *dacchimi* (R. 11,85); M. *dacchihisi* (H. 819; R. 11,93 [to be read so with C; false S. GOLDSCHMIDT p. 286 note 1]); AMg. *dacchisi* (Uttar. 679 = Dasav. 613,35, where correct is the text); JM. *dacchihī* (Erz. 24,12); M. *dacchihi* (R. 14,55), *dacchāma* (R. 3,50), *dacchiha* (R. 3,23 [so to be read]). Beside them one says also AMg. *pāsihii* from *pāsaï* = *paśyati* (Ovav. [§ 115]). To Ś. Mg. Ḍh. both the verbs are unknown in fut.: they use *ikṣ* with ***pra***, that is known also to the rest of the dialects: M. *pĕcchissaṁ* (M. 743), *pĕcchihisi* (H. 566); JM. *pĕcchissāmo* (Dvār. 505,28); Ś. *pekkhissaṁ* (Mṛcch. 4,11; 77,12; 93,16; Śak. 90,15;125,15; Vikr. 11,2; 13,19; Prab. 37,13; 38,1 etc.), *pĕkkhissadi* (Ratn. 300,1; Uttarar. 66,7); Mg. *pĕkkhiśśaṁ* (Mṛcch. 40,10), *pĕkkhiśśadi* (Mṛcch. 123,22); Ḍh. *pĕkkhissaṁ* (Mṛcch. 35,15.17); A. *pĕkkhīhimi* (Vikr. 55,18).—As in the present (§ 484), so in the fut. too *labh* may take a nasal in the root: Ś. *lambhissaṁ* = *lapsye* (Cait. 83,2); Ś. *uvālambhissaṁ* = *upālapsye* (Priyad. 19,15); but also Ś. *lahissaṁ* (Mṛcch. 70,12); Ś. *uvālahissaṁ* (Śak. 61,2;130,4); AMg. *labhissāmi* (Āyār. 2,1,4,5); JM. *lahissāmo* (Erz. 13,30). From *sah* we find in AMg. the fut. *sakkhāmo* = Epic *śakṣyāmaḥ* (Āyār. 1,8,2,14).—From the stems *khā-* and *dhā* contracted from *khāda-* and *dhāva-* (§ 165) are formed the fut. *khāhii* and *dhāhii* (Bh. 8,27; Hc. 4,228). So Mg. *khāhiśi* (Mṛcch. 11,11) in verse, against *khāiśśaṁ* (Mṛcch. 124,10) in prose.

§ 526. Of the roots of the 6. conjugation *pracch*, corresponding to the present *pucchaï* = *pṛcchati*, forms the fut. Ś. *pucchissaṁ* (Mṛcch. 4,22; 81,1.2.10; Śak. 19,3;50,4; Mālatīm. 103,10; Veṇīs. 59,1; Karp. 3,4); Mg. *puściśśaṁ* (Prab. 50,46;53,12); AMg. *pucchissāmo* (Āyār. 1,4,2,6; Ovav. § 38).—*sphuṭ* forms according to the present *phuṭṭaï* (§ 488, note 1), A. *phuṭṭisu* (Hc. 4,422,12); M. *phuṭṭihisi*, *phuṭṭihii* (H. 768.281 [so to be read]). *muc* forms *mŏcchaṁ* = *mokṣyāmi* (Hc. 3,172; Kī. 4,19; Sr. fol. 53). The rules for *gam* (§ 523) hold good in this case. So M. *mŏcchihii* (R. 4,49) and *mocchihi* (R. 3,30; 11,126). JM. says also *muñcihii* (Dvār. 504,11), Ś. *muñcissadi* (Vikr. 72,20), as from *sic* Ś. *siñcissaṁ* (Śak. 15.4). On *mṛ* see § 522.—From *viś* Kī. 4,19 teaches *vicchaṁ*, for which, as already LASSEN (Inst. p. 351) has noted, *vĕcchaṁ* would be expected, that the rest of the grammarians derive from *vid*. We find in the texts the forms of the *i*-stem only, as AMg. *aṇupavisissāmi*, *pavisissāmi* (Āyār. 2,1,4,5), *pavisissāmo* (Āyār. 1,8,2,14); JM. *pavisihii* (Erz. 29,16); Mg. *paviśiśśaṁ*, *uvaviśiśśaṁ* (Mṛcch. 36,1;124,8).

§ 527. The roots of the 4. conjugation mostly use the present stem: M. *kilammihisi* (G. 954), *kilammihii* (H. 196) from *kilammaï* = *klāmyati* (§ 136); AMg. *sivvissāmi* from *sivyati* (Āyār. 1,6,3,1); M. *kuppissaṁ* (H. 898); Ś. *kuppissadi* (Mṛcch. 94,7.8; Uttarar. 66,9); but also Ś. *kuvissaṁ* (Uttarar. 32,3; Viddhaś. 71,3); Ś. *ṇaccissaṁ* (Viddhaś. 122,11; 128,5), *ṇaccissadi* (Cait. 57,12) from *nṛt*; AMg. *sajjihii, rajjihii, gijjhihii, mujjhihii, ajjhovavajjihii* from *saj, raj, gṛdh, muh, pad* (Ovav. § 111); AMg. *bujjhihii* from *budh* (Ovav. § 116), *sijjhihii* from *sidh* (Vivāhap. 175; Nirayāv. §27; Ovav. § 116), *sijjhihinti* (Ovav. § 128), *sijjhissanti* (Āyār. 2,15,16); JM. *sijjhihī* (Erz. 28,16;34,20; Dvār. 508,8); M. Ś. *vivajjissaṁ* from *pad* with *vi* (H. 865; Mṛcch. 25,15); AMg. *paḍivajjissāmi* (Uvās. § 12,210), Ś. *paḍivajjissaṁ* (Mālatīm. 117,5), Ś. *paḍivajjissadi* (Śak. 70,12; Nāgān. 22,7), AMg. *paḍivajjissāmo* (Ovav. § 38); M. *pavajjihisi* (H. 661); AMg. *uvavajjihii* (Vivāhap. 175; Nirayāv. § 27; Ovav. § 100.101), *uvavajjissaha* (Vivāhap. 234), *samuppajjihii* (Ovav. § 115), *uppajjissanti* (Ṭhāṇ. 80.133); Ś. *saṁpajjissadi* (Vikr. 43,12); JM. *vaccihisi* (Erz. 77,33), M. *vaccihii* (H.918) from *vaccaï* (§ 202), but JM. *pavvaïssāmi* (Āv. 32,27), AMg. *pavvaïhii* (Ovav. § 115) from *vrāj*; M. *maṇṇihisi* (G. 954; H. 663), JM. *mannissaï* (Erz. 12,35), Ś. *maṇṇissadi* (Uttarar. 95,2 [so to be read]); JM. *viṇassihisi* (Erz. 29,16), *viṇāsihī* (Dvār. 495,17); M. *laggissaṁ, laggihisi* (H. 375.21), *laggihii* (G. 70), Mg. *aṇulaggiśśaṁ* (Caṇḍak. 42,12); A. *rūsesu* from the *e*-stem of *ruṣ* (Hc. 4,414,4), like JM. *mannehi* (Āv. 12,12) from the *e*-stem of *man*. Deviating from the present (§ 489) *śram* forms the future in M. *visammihii* (H. 576 [so to be read]).—Corresponding to the present *jāi*, AMg. *āyanti, paccāyanti* (§487) the future of *jan* are AMg. *payāhisi* (Vivāhap. 946; Kappas. §9; Nāyādh. § 26), *payāhii* (Ovav. § 104; Kappas. § 79; Nāyādh. § 51), *paccāyāhii* (Vivāhap. 1190; Ṭhāṇ. 523; Ovav. § 102), *āyāissanti* (Kappas. § 17). On *śak* see § 531.

§ 528. The verbs of the 10. conjugation and similarly built causatives and denominatives form the future as in Skt. with regular elision of the *y*: *kittaïssam, kittaïhimi* = *kīrtayiṣyāmi* (Hc. 3,169); AMg. *dalaïssaï* (Vivāhap. 1288), *dalaïssanti* (Ovav. § 108); Ś. *kuṭṭaïssaṁ* (Mṛcch. 18,5), *aṇuūlaïssaṁ* = *anukūlayiṣyāmi* (Mālatīm. 267,8), *cūraïssaṁ* (Karp. 21,2), *vāraïssadi, cintaïssadi, ṇiattaïssadi* = *nivartayiṣyati* (Śak. 55,2;87,1; 91,6), *puloaïssadi* (Vṛṣabh.22,9), *viṇodaïssāmo* (Śak. 78,10), *visajjaïssadha* (Śak. 86.5), *saddāvaïssaṁ* = **śabdāpayiṣyāmi* (Mṛcch. 60,1), *moāvaïssasi* = **mocāpayiṣyasi* (Mṛcch. 60,13); Mg. *gaṇaïśśaṁ* (Śak. 154,6), *maḍamaḍaïśśaṁ, tāḍaïśśaṁ, lihāvaïśśaṁ, dūśaïśśaṁ* (Mṛcch. 21,22;80,5;136,21;176,6), *vāvādaïśśadi* = *vyāpādayiṣyati* (Veṇīs. 36,5). In Mṛcch. 128,14 Mg. *moḍaïśśāmi* with the ending *-mi* as against *moḍaïśśaṁ* in Mṛcch. 113,1, is prosodically attested. As against this Ś. *ṇikkāmaïssāmi* at Mṛcch. 52,9 is to be corrected as °*aïssaṁ*. In M. AMg. JM. we find the future also from the contracted form in *-e*: M. *mārehisi* (H. 567); JM. *vattehāmi* = *vartayiṣyāmi* (Āv. 47, 26); *viṇāsehāmi* = *vināśayiṣyāmi* (Dvār. 495,31); *nāsehii* (T. 5,20); *melavehisi* = *melayiṣyasi* (Āv. 30,8); *jaṇehī* (Erz. 12,28); *nivārehī* (Erz. 8,21); *kahehinti* (Āv. 26,36); AMg. *sehāvehii* = **śaikṣāpayiṣyati*, *sikkhāvehii* =

śikṣāpayiṣyati (Ovav. § 107), *ceyĕssāmo* = *cetayiṣyāmaḥ* (Āyār. 2,1,9,1; 2.2, 2,10), *sakkārehinti*, *saṁmāṇehinti*, *paḍivisajjehinti* (Ovav. § 108), *uvaṇimantehinti* (Ovav. § 110), *saddavehinti* (Vivāhap. 1276), *ṇŏllavehinti* (Vivāhap. 1280). Not seldom are also the future of the denominatives formed without a suffix (§ 491), to which are attached the causative (§ 533): Ś. *kadhissaṁ* (Mṛcch. 80,25), M. *kahissaṁ* (H. 157), beside the usual Ś. *kadhaïssaṁ* (Mṛcch. 19,2; Śak. 51,12; 105,7), Mg. *kadhaïśśaṁ kadhaïśśaśi* (Mṛcch. 139,23; 165, 15); AMg. **kārāvissaṁ* = *kārāpayiṣyāmi* = *kārayiṣyāmi* (Āyār. 1,1,1,5); Ś. *khaṇḍissaṁ* = *khaṇḍayiṣyāmi* (Karp. 18,7); M. *puloissaṁ* = *pralokayiṣyāmi* (H. 743), A. *paloissaṁ* (Mṛcch. 104,21); Ś. *vaḍḍhāissaṁ* = **vardhāpayiṣyāmi* (Śak. 37,10), *viṇṇavissaṁ* = *vijñāpayiṣyāmi*, *sussūissaṁ* = *śuśrūṣayiṣyāmi* (Mṛcch. 58,11; 88,11); Mg. *mālīśśaśi* = *mārayiṣyasi* (Mṛcch. 125,7); Ś. *takkissadi* = *tarkayiṣyati* (Vikr. 79,9; v. l. *cintissadi*), *mantissadi* (Ratn. 299, 9) beside *mantaïssadi* (Mṛcch. 54,1).

§ 529. Of the verbs of the 2. conjugation ending in *-ā*, *khyā* forms AMg. *paccāikkhissāmi* = **pratyācikhyiṣyāmi* (Āyār. 2,1,9,2), *yā* AMg. *nijjāissāmi* according to § 487 (Ovav. § 40 [so to be read with Q for *nijjāhissāmi* of the text]), JM. *jāhii* (Erz. 29,12; 35,5), *vā* AMg. *pariṇivvāhii* (Vivāhap. 175; Nāyādh. 390 [so to be read]), *parinivvāissanti* (Āyār. 2,15,16), *snā* Ś. *ṇhāissaṁ* (Mṛcch. 27,14) according to § 487.—From *i* the fut. is AMg. *ĕssāmi* (Ṭhāṇ. 142), *ĕssanti* (Sūyag. 45. 56. 71); with the prefix *ā* M. *ehisi* (H. 385), M. AMg. *ehii* (H. 137. 784 [so to be read]. 855. 918; R. 10,79; Āyār. 2,4,1,2, [so to be read]; Uvās. § 187), JM. *ehī* (Erz. 24,11), *ehinti* (Erz. 29,13), A. *esī* (Hc. 4, 414, 4). From this is found also a wholly isolated optative M. *ehijja* (H. 17) standing there.—*rud* forms *rŏcchaṁ* = **rotsyāmi* (Vr. 7,16; Hc. 3,171; Sr. fol. 53), in Kī. 4,19 *rucchaṁ*, but M. *roissaṁ* (H. 503), Ś. *rodissaṁ* (Mṛcch. 95,23; Nāgān. 3,1), also *rudissāmo* (Mallikām. 154,23).—From *svap* the fut. is Ś. *suvissaṁ* (Mṛcch. 50,4; Priyad. 34,3), Mg. *śuviśśaṁ* (Mṛcch. 43,12; Prab. 60,15).—*vid* has the fut. *vĕcchaṁ* = **vetsyāmi* (Vr. 7,16; Hc. 3,171; Sr. fol. 53), but Ś. *vedissadi* (Prab. 37,15), AMg. *vedissanti* (Ṭhāṇ. 108).—*vac* forms *vŏcchaṁ* (§ 104; Vr. 7,16; Hc. 3,171; Sr. fol. 53). So M. AMg. *vŏcchaṁ* (Vajjālaga 324,10; Paṇhāv. 331; Ovav. 184 [text *bŏ°*]; Nandīs. 92 [text *bŏ°*]; Jīyak. 1. 60) and *vŏcchāmi* (Vivāhap. 59; Paṇhāv. 330; Uttar. 737. 897); but AMg. also *vakkhāmo* = *vakṣyāmaḥ* (Dasav. 627,23), *pavakkhāmi* (Sūyag. 278. 284). In Kī. 4,21 *vacchihimi*, *vacchimi*, *vacchi* are published. Cf. 4,20. The forms *rŏcchaṁ*, *vĕcchaṁ*, *vŏcchaṁ* and all similarly built ones are not used in Ś. Mg., as Mk. fol. 70 expressly mentions and the texts attest. For their flexion the rules for *gacchaṁ* (§ 523) hold good.—From *duh* the fut. is *duhihii* (Hc. 4,245).

§ 530. From *dā* the future is AMg. JM. *dāhāmi* (Āyār. 2,1,10, 1; Uttar. 743; Erz. 59,23. 34)[1] and *dāhaṁ* (Vr. 7,16; Hc. 3, 170; Kī. 4,19; Erz. 10,24), according to Hc. also *dāhimi*; AMg. *dāhisi* (Āyār. 2,1,2,4; 2,2, 3,18; 2,5,1,7; 2,6,1,5); JM. *dāhī* (Āv. 43,22; Erz.); AMg. *dāhāmo* (Āyār. 2,5,1,10), *dāhāmu* (Sūyag. 178; Uttar. 355. 358), *dāhittha* (Uttar. 359); JM. *dāhinti* (Erz. 80, 22). In Ś. Mg. the fut. Ś. *daïssaṁ* (Mṛcch. 80,20), Mg.

daïśśaṁ = **dayiṣyāmi* (Mṛcch. 31,6.8.15;32,9. 24;33,22;35,8;80,19 etc;§474); are formed from the stem *daya-*, corresponding to the present *dedi* = **dayati*. We should read *daïssaṁ* for Ś. *dāissaṁ* (Karp. 112,5; Śak. ed. Böhtlingk 25,6; Priyad. 23,4) and *daïssanti* for *deissanti* (Kāleyak. 2,13).—*dhā has* attested the old reduplicated stem also in future (cf. § 500) in combination with *śrad* : AMg. *saddahissaï* (Nāyādh. 1114—1116). Elsewhere in combination with prefixes, in future in AMg. the flexion points to °*dhaï*° °*haï* (§ 500); AMg. *pehissāmi*, metrically for *pi*°, as the ed. Calc. has (Āyār. 1,8,1,1), but Ś. according to the 4. conjugation; *pihāissaṁ* (Viddhaś. 70,8); AMg. *saṁdhissāmi*, *parihissāmi* (Āyār. 1,6,3,1); also in Ś. *saṁdhihisi* (Bālar. 22,18), certainly against the dialect, in which **saṁdhāissasi* is to be expected.—From *hā* AMg. has the fut. *vippajahissāmo* (Sūyag. 633. 635), from *bhī* Ś. has *bhāissaṁ*, *bhāissadi* (Śak. 140,11; 135,14).

1. In Āyār. 1,7,7,2 Jacobi twice reads *dāsāmi*, 2,5,1,11. 23 *dāsāmo* beside *dāhāmo*. In the first place the ed. Calc. reads *dalaïssami*, as also the v. l. has; in the second one *dāssāmo*, and in the third *dāsāmo*.

§ 531. Of the verbs of the 5. conjugation *ci* forms the fut. Ś. *avaciṇissaṁ* (Ratn. 295,25; Vṛṣabh. 58,20; Cait. 73,10), AMg. *ciṇissanti*, *uvaciṇissanti* (Ṭhāṇ. 107. 108; Vivāhap. 62). According to Hc. 4,243 *ciṇihii* would be passive; according to the form it is parasmaip.—*śru* forms according to the grammarians *sŏcchaṁ* (V. 7,16; Hc. 3,171. 172; Kī. 4, 19; Sr. fol. 53) with the flexion according to *gacchaṁ* (§523). This *sŏcchaṁ* does not belong to *śru*, but to Vedic *śruṣ*, and, therefore, stands regularly for **śrokṣyāmi*. The fut. from *śru* are Ś. *suṇissaṁ* (Mṛcch. 60,7.9; Śak. 20,7; Vikr. 24,5; 31,1.9; Mālav. 83,3 etc.), *suṇissāmo* (Mallikām. 129,3; 132,9), Mg. *śuṇiśśaṁ* (Mṛcch. 21,21), JM. *suṇissaï* (Kk. 265,4), in AMg. also from the *e-* stem; *suṇĕssāmi* (Ṭhāṇ. 143), *suṇĕssāmo* (Ovav. § 38).—From *āp* AMg. forms the fut. *pāuṇissāmi* (Āyār. 1,6,3,1), *pāuṇihii* (Uvās. § 62; Ovav. § 100. 116)[1] corresponding to the present *pāuṇaï* (§ 504). The rest of the dialects derive it from the present stem *pāva-*: A. *pāvisu* (Hc. 4,396,4); Ś. *pāvissasi* (Kāleyak. 7,6); M. *pāvihisi* (H. 462. 510), and so also against the dialect in Ś. (Vikr. 42,10); Mg. *pāvihiśi* (Mudrār. 177,6; [so to be read for *vahesi*; cf. v. l. and ZDMG. 39,125]); M. *pāvihii* (H. 918).—*śak* forms the future according to the 4. conjugation (§ 505); M. *sakkihisi* (Viddhaś. 64,1 [so to be read]); Ś. *sakkissāmo* (Cait. 75,15; text *sakkissamha*); JM. *sakkissaha* (Kk. 265,11); also with the *e-* stem; JM. *sakkehii* (Āv. 45,8), *sakkehi* (Dvār. 501,39).

1. So correctly Leumann, Aup. S, s. v. *pāuṇ*; wrongly Hoernle, Uvās., translation, note 108 on *vṛ*.

§ 532. The future of *chid*, *bhid*, *bhuj* according to the grammarians are formed; *chĕcchaṁ*, *bhĕcchaṁ*, *bhŏcchaṁ* corresponding to Skt. *chetsyāmi*, *bhetsyāmi*, *bhokṣyāmi* (Hc. 3,171; Sr. fol. 53). Their flexion is like that of *gacchaṁ* (§ 523). From *chid* are found : AMg. *acchindihinti vicchindihinti*, *vŏcchindihinti* (Vivāhap. 1277), from *bhid* ; AMg. *bhidissanti* (Āyār. 2,1,6,9) for which one could expect *bhindissanti*, as for *bhidanti*, rather for, *bhindanti*, from *bhuj* : AMg. *bhŏkkhāmi* (Āyār. 2,1, 11,1), *bhŏkkhasi* (Kappas. S. § 18), *bhŏkhhāmo* (Āyār. 2,1,5,5; 2,1,9,6). JM. has *bhuñjihī* (Erz. 6,36), likewise *bhuñjissaī* (T. 5,18). According to Hc. 4,248 *saṁrundhihii* would be fut. of the passive; according to the form it belongs to the parasmaipada.

§ 533. In all the dialects the fut. of *kr̥* is formed as in Skt.; AMg. JM. *karissāmi* (Āyār. 1,2,5,6; Ṭhāṇ 149. 476; Dasav. 627,24: Nandīs. 354; Uttar. 1; Erz. 46,7); M. JM. Ś. *karissaṁ* (H. 743.882; Erz. 11,31; Mudrār. 103,6; Nāgān. 43,7); Mg. *kaliśśaṁ* (Mr̥cch. 96,13); A. *karisu* (Hc. 4,396, 4); M. *karihisi* (H. 844); Ś. *karissasi* (Mr̥cch. 9,12; Śak. 58,2); A. *karihisi* (Vikr. 55,19); AMg. *karihii* (Vivāhap. 175); JM. *karissaï* (Āv. 32,19; Erz. 5,22); AMg. *karissai* (Dasav. 627,24); Ś. *karissadi* (Prab. 39,9; 42,2; Uttarar. 197,11); Mg. *kaliśśadi* (Prab. 51,1; 58,15 [so to be read; see v.1]); AMg. JM. *karissāmo* (Kappas. § 91. 128; Ovav. § 38; Erz. 3,11); M. *karissāma* (H. 897); AMg. Ś. *karissanti* (Vivāhap. 62; Ovav. [§ 105]; Nāgān. 43,11). Corresponding to the use of the *e*-stem in the present (§ 509), the same is used in fut. too, in Ś. Mg., however, always in the uncontracted form: AMg. *karĕssaṁ* (Vivāhap. 1255), but Ś. *karaïssaṁ* (Mr̥cch. 60,11; 120,8; Śak. 59,10; 60,15; 76,2; 142,2), Mg. *kalaïśśaṁ* (Mr̥cch. 96,20; 124,11. 14; 125,5. 8; 127,6; 134,8; 165,1; Caṇḍak. 42,10), *kalaïśśaśi* (Mr̥cch. 32,19); M. JM. AMg. *karehii* (H. 724; Kk. 265,3 [so to be read]; Ovav. § 116 [the commentator has *kāhii*]), but Ś. *karaïssadi* (Prab. 42,8), Mg. *kalaïśśadi* (Mr̥cch. 140,6); JM. *karĕssāmo* (Kk. 274,26) and *karehāmo* (Erz. 25,25); AMg. JM. *karehinti* (Ovav. § 105. 128; Āv. 43,18), AMg. *karĕssanti* (Āyār. 2,15,16), but Ś. *karaïssanti* (Śak. 142,4). In AMg. the fut. is formed from the stem *kuvva-* (§ 508) too; *viuvvissāmi* (Vivāhap. 1397 f.), *vikuvvissanti* (Vivāhap. 214. 215). M. JM. AMg. have, besides, frequently the future *kāhaṁ* = **karṣyāmi*, that is inflected as *gaccaṁ* (§ 523; Vr. 7,16; Hc. 3,170; Kī. 4,19; Sr. fol. 52). So: M. JM. *kāhaṁ* (H. 187; Erz. 80,18); JM. *kāhāmi* (Erz. 5,23; 83,8); according to Hc. and Sr. also *kāhimi*; M. AMg. *kāhisi* (H. 80. 90. 683; Uttar. 679 = Dasav. 613,35); M. AMg. JM. *kāhii* (Hc. 3,166; H. 410. 683; R. 5.4; Nirayāv. § 27; Āv. 32,7); JM. AMg. *kāhi* (Erz. 8,21; 71,8; Dvār. 495,18 [*kāhi tti*]; Dasav. 617,28); JM. *kāhāmo* (Erz. 15.13; 80,18; Sagara 3,15), *kāhiha* (Āv. 33,27), AMg. JM. *kāhinti* (Ovav. § 105; Uttar. 253; Āv. 43,36). A. *kīsu* (Hc. 4,389) presupposes one **krīṣyāmi*.

§ 534. From *jñā*, corresponding to Skt., AMg. forms *ṇāhisi* = *jñāsyasi* (Sūyag. 106); *ṇāhii* (Ṭhāṇ. 451), *nāhii* (Dasav. 617,28), *nāhi* (Dasav. 617,32.34) = *jñāsyati*. In all the dialects the formation from the present stem *jāṇa-* is usual. So: M. Ś. *jāṇissaṁ* (H. 749; Mr̥cch. 3,2; Ratn. 307, 26); M. *jāṇihisi* (H. 528. 643), likewise A. (Vikr. 58,11); AMg. *jāṇihii* (Ovav. § 115); Ś. *jāṇissadi* (Mālav. 87,9; Ratn. 299,5. 7; Viddhaś. 114,5); Laṭakam. 6,6), *abbhaṇujāṇissadi* (Mālav. 40,7), *ahijāṇissadi* (Śak. 102,15); AMg. Ś. *jāṇissāmo* (Sūyag. 962; Vikr. 23,18; 28,12); Mg. *yāṇiśśamha*, false for *yāṇiśśāmo* (Lalitav. 565,9).—From *krī* the fut. is Ś. *kiṇissadi* (Caṇḍak. 52,4.7), Mg. *kiṇiśśaṁ* (Mr̥cch. 32,17; 118,14; 125,10); JM. *kiṇihāmo* (Āv. 15); from *grah* Ś. *gĕṇhissaṁ* (Mr̥cch. 74,19; 95,22; Ratn. 316,

22; Mudrār. 103,9), *gĕṇhissadi* (Mṛcch. 54,5; 74,24; Kāleyak. 7,6), *aṇuginhissadi* (Pārvatīp. 30,18); AMg. *giṇhissāmo* (Āyār. 2,2 3,2). JM. *ghĕcchāmo* (Āv. 23,6) belongs, like *ghĕppaï* (§ 548), to a root **ghṛp*, present **ghivaï* (§ 212), is therefore = **ghṛpsyāmaḥ*.—*bandh* forms AMg. *bandhissaï* (Vivāhap. 1810 ff.), *bandhissanti* (Ṭhāṇ. 108); Ś. *aṇubandhissaṁ* (Viddhaś. 14,13). According to Hc. 4,247 *bandhihii* would be the future of the passive : according to the form it is in parasmaipada.—*bhaṇ* regularly forms AMg. *bhaṇihāmi* (Jīyak. C. 11); M. Ś. *bhaṇissaṁ* (H. 12.604; Mṛcch. 21,24; 24,20; Viddhaś. 72, 2; Mallikām. 83,4 [text *pha°*]; Mālatīm. 265,1; 276,7); Ś. *bhaṇissasi* (Mṛcch. 58,8); M. *bhaṇihii* (H. 858.918); Ś. *bhaṇissadi* (Ratn. 304,1); JM. *bhaṇissaha* (Kk. 274,19); Ś. *bhaṇissadha* (Mālatīm. 246, 7,); M. *bhaṇihinti* (G. 965). From the *e*-stem is built Mg. *bhaṇaïśśaṁ* (Mṛcch. 32,20).

PASSIVE

§ 535. In Pkt. the passive is formed in a three-fold manner. Either 1) the Skt. form with *ya* is used after undergoing the alterations as required by the phonetic laws of Pkt.; since after vowels, *-ya* becomes *-jja* in M. JM. JŚ. AMg. A. and *-yya* in P., in Ś. Mg. it drops; after consonants it is assimilated with the consonant; or *-iẏa*, that in M. JM. JŚ. AMg. A. becomes *-ijja*, in Ś. Mg. *-ia*, in P. *-iyya*, enters 2) into the root, or more frequently 3) into the present stem. Thence from *dā* one says M. JM. AMg. A. *dijjaï*, JŚ. *dijjadi*, P. *tiyyate*, Ś. Mg. *diadi*; from *gam* M. JM. AMg. *gammaï*, *gamijjaï*, P. **gamiyyate*, Ś. *gamiadi*, *gacchiadi*, Mg. **gaściadi*. Forms in Ś. *-ijja*, Mg. *-iyya* (mostly printed *-ijja*) are very often found in the texts; they are, however, exceptionally perhaps in verses, for Ś, Mg. false[1]. In D. *kahijjadi* (§ 103,15) for *kadhiadi* and *sāsijjaï* (103,16) for *sāsiadi* (155,6) are not to be objected to (§ 26). The "characterless" passive[2] in R. as *ārambhante* (8,82; particip.), *rumbhaï*, *rumbhanta* (s. v. *rudh*). *osumbhanta*, *ṇisumbhanta* (s.v. *sudh*) are wrong readings for *ārabbhante*, *rubbhaï*, *rubbhanta*, *osubbhanta*, *ṇisubbhanta*, as the similar ones are more often found in the manuscripts. Likewise false is the reading *uvabhuñjanto* (IS. 15,429) for *uvabhujjanto*; *ŏcchundaï* (R. 10,55), for which the manuscript C has *apphundaï*, is not clear. The optative *vĕjja*, *lahĕjja*, *acchĕjja* for *vijjĕjja*, *lahijjĕjja*, *acchijjĕjja* (Hc. 3,160) are presumably purely metrical shortenings, as the fut. pass. AMg. *samucchihinti* for *samucchijjihinti* from *chid* (§ 549). Vr. 7,8; Hc. 3,160; Kī. 4,12; Mk. fol. 51 teach *-ia* and *-ijja* without distinguishing between the dialects; Mk. fol. 71 mentions in Ś. *-ia* only and forbids forms like *dubbhaï*, *libbhaï*, *gammaï* for Ś., a thing with which the texts are in accord, taught by Vr. 7,9; 8,57—59; Hc. 4,242—249; Mk. fol. 62. The derivation of the "irregular passive" like *sippaï*, *juppaï*, *āḍhappaï*, *dubbhaï*, *rubbhaï* etc. from the past passive participles according to false analogy, which JACOBI[3] has given with the approbation of JOHANSSON[4], is wholly wrong. See § 266. 286. To the passive belong an indicative, an optative and an imperative; moreover, aor., fut., inf., pres. participle and preterite are formed from the passive. The endings as a rule are those of the parasmaip.; however, M. JM. JŚ. AMg. frequently, and P. according to the grammarians always, have the endings of the ātmanep., especially in the participle.

1. Bollensen on Mālav. p. 223. The following paragraphs give examples of false forms.—2. S. Goldschmidt on R. 8,82 note 4 p. 256.—3. KZ. 28,249 ff.—4. KZ. 32,446 ff., where further literature.

§ 536. As in the case of the future (§ 521), so also in the case of the passive, the examples are arranged according to the present stem § 473 ff. The roots in *-u*, *-ū*, without distinction of the class, may be conjugated according to the 6. conjugation of Skt. (§ 473) and build their passive accordingly; M. *ṇiṇhuvijjanti.* (H. 657), Ś. *ṇiṇhuviadi* (Ratn. 303,9) from *hnu*; *ruvvaï*, *ruvijjaī*, (Hc. 2,249), M. *ruvvasu* in the sense of the middle (H. 10) from *ru*; M. *thuvvasi stūyase* (G. 298), *thuvvaï* = *stūyate* (Hc. 4,242; Sr. fol. 54; G. 253); JŚ. *thuvvade* (Kattig. 401,351), AMg. *thuvvanti* (text *thuva°*) = *stūyante* (Vivāhap. 1232), JM. *thuvvanta-* (Erz. 24,2), *saṁthuvvanta-* (Āv. 7,26); beside *thuṇijjaï* (Hc. 4,242) from *stu*; *dhuvvaï*, *dhuṇijjaï*, M. *vihuvvaï*, *vihuvvanta-*, *odhuvvanti* (R.), AMg. *uddhuvvamāṇihiṁ* (Ovav.; Kappas.) from *dhū*, *puvvaï*, *puṇijjaï*, A. *puṇijje* (Piṅgala 2,107) from *pū*, *luvvaï*, *luṇijjaï* from *lū*, *huvvaï*, *huṇijjaï* from *hu* (Vr. 8,57; Hc. 4,242; Kī. 4,74; Mk. fol. 58; Sr. fol. 54); from *śru*: M. JM. *suvvaï*, *suvvanti*, *suvvamāṇa* (G. H. R.; Āv. 37,44; Erz.; Kk.), M. *suvvanta-* (Karp. 51,3); AMg. *suvvae* (Sūyag. 154), *suvvai* (Sūyag. 277; text *°cca°*), *suvvanti* (Uttar. 280; text *°cca°*); beside *suṇijjaï* (Vr. 8,57; Hc. 4,242; Sr. fol. 54), *suṇijjae*, *suṇiaï*, *suṇiae* (Sr. fol. 54); Ś. *suṇiadi* (Mṛcch. 29,2; 64,6; 97,7; Śak. 50,12; 139,6; Ratn. 315,21; Prab. 14,9; Karp. 3,3; 24,3; 45,3; Vṛṣabh. 47,14; 51,7 etc), *suṇiyaṁti* (sic; Lalitav. 555,2), *suṇianti* (Śak. 58,1; Uttarar. 127,6; Prab. 8,8), *suṇiadu* (Vikr. 48, 9); Mg. *śuṇiadi* (Mṛcch. 45,1; 163,22; 169,18; Mudrār. 191,5; Veṇīs. 35, 18; 36,3); A. *suṇijje* (Piṅgala 2,107). JM. has also *summaü* (Erz. 11,16), what **sumaï* beside **suvaï* one presupposes in accordance with § 261. According to the grammarians (Vr. 8,57; Hc. 4,242; Kī. 4,73; Mk. fol. 58) *ji* too, according to Hc. 4,243 *ci* too, has the same formation of the passive: *civvaï*, *ciṇijjaï*, fut. *civvihii*, *jivvaï*, *jiṇijjaï*, according to Hc. also *cimmaī* fut. *cimmihii*, which also is to be explained as JM. *summaü*. It is not correct to assume an analogical formation according to the roots in *-u*, *-ū* with Jacobi, whose entire hypothesis is wrong[1], and Johansson[2]. *civvaï* is a regular passive from *civ* (Dhātupāṭha 21,15 *civṛ ādānasaṁvaraṇayoḥ*), *jivvaï*, apparently from *jiv* (Dhātupāṭha 15,85 *jivi prīṇanārthaḥ*) that is equated with *jinv*. The case will be decided only when the meaning will be settled with certainty. AMg. has *cijjanti*, *uvacijjanti*, *avacijjanti* (Paṇṇav. 628. 629), Ś. *viciadu* (Vikr. 30,15). According to Hc. 3,160 the passive from *bhū* is *hoïaï*, *hoijjaï*. In Ś. it is *bhaviadi* in *aṇubhaviadi* (Ratn. 317,5), *aṇuhaviadu* (Nāgān. 4,5), and *aṇuhuviadi* (Kāleyak. 9,22), *abhibhaviadi* (Mālatīm. 130,5), particip. *ahibhūamāṇa* (Śak. 16,10), in Mg. *bhaviadi* (Mṛcch. 164,10 and *huviadi* (Veṇīs. 33,6. 7; 35,8), both in the sense of the fut. parasmaip. (§ 550). On *pahuppaï* see 286.—From *ni* the passive is M. *ṇijjaï* (G. H. R. JM. *ninijjanta-* (Āv. 24,4), Ś. *ṇiadi* (Śak. 78,8), *āṇiadi* (Vikr. 31,5; Karp.

26,8), *āṇiadu* (Karp. 26,7), *ahiṇiadu* (Śak. 3,5); *aṇuṇiamāṇā* (Mṛcch. 23,23. 25); Mg. *ṇiadi* (Mṛcch. 100,22).

1. KZ. 28,255.—2. KZ.32,449. Falsely also P. GOLDSCHMIDT, Specimen p. 71; GN, 1874, p 513; S. GOLDSCHMIDT, ZDMG. 29,494.

§ 537. The roots in *-ṛ* form the passive mostly from the present stem: M. *dharijjaï* (R.), fut. *dharijjihii* (H. 778; so to be read); Mg. *dhaliadi* (Prab. 50,10); M. *aṇusarijjanti* (G. 627); M. *ṇivvarijjae* (H. 204); M.A., *sumarijjaï* = *smaryate* (R. 13,16; Hc. 4,426). JM. *sumarijjaü* (Erz. 15,3), Ś. *sumariadi* (Mṛcch. 128,1). The roots in *-ṝ* form the passive as in Skt. or according to the analogy of the roots in *-ṛ*: Ś. *kīranta-* from *kṝ* (Bālar. 199,10) against the dialect, in which *kirianta-* would be expected. : *jīraï* (also = *jiryati*) and *jarijjaï* (Hc. 4,250), AMg *nijjarijjaï* (Uttar; 885; so correctly in the commentary); M. JM. *tīraï* (Hc. 4,250; G. H. R.; Erz.), *tīrae* (H.; Erz.; Dvār. 498,21) and M. *tarijjaï* (Hc. 4,250; G.), AMg. *viyarijjaï* (Uttar. 354). Conversely *hṛ* follows the roots in *-ṝ*: M. AMg. *hīrasi* (G. 726; Uttar. 711); M. JM. *hīraï* (Vr. 8,60; Hc. 4,250; Kī. 4,79. 80; Mk. fol. 62; H. R.; Āv. 35,13), M. *hīranti* (G.), *hīranta-* (H.), AMg. *avahīranti* (Vivāhap. 890; Paṇṇav. 398 ff.), *avahīramāṇa* (Vivāhap. 890; Paṇṇav. 404); but Ś. *avahariāmi* (Uttarar. 97,1; text °*ri*°), *avahariasi* (Nāgān. 95,14), *avahariadi* (Dhūrtas. 13,5), *avahariadu* (Mṛcch. 25,6), *uddhariadi* (Mālatīm. 246,5); Mg. *āhalīadu* (Prab. 63,4). Cf. Kī. 4.79.80. Hence false in Ś. *hīrasi* (Bālar. 174,9). From *pṝ* are found M. *pūrijjanta-* (H. 116), *ahiūrijjanti* = *abhipūryante* (G. 872); JM. *āūrijjamāṇa* (Erz. 24,5) and M. *pūraï*, *āūramāṇa*, *paripūranta-* (R.). On *vāhippaï* beside *vāharijjaï* see § 286, on *kṛ* § 547.

§ 538. From the *ai-* roots the passive are : M. JM. *gijjanta-* (H. 644; Kk. 264,2); JM. *gijjanti* (Erz. 40,19); AMg. *parigijjamāṇa* (Nāyādh. § 117); P. *giyyate* (Hc. 4,315); Ś. *ṇijjhāiadi* (Mālav. 60,6); from the verbs of the old *-ska-* conjugation: M. *acchijjaï* (H. 83); Ś. *icchīadi* (Mudrār. 57,4), Mg. *iściadi* (Śak. 118,6). Like *rammaï*, *ramijjaï* (Vr. 8,58), P. *ramiyyate* (Hc. 4, 315) formed from *ram* are formed from *gam* M. JM. *gammaï* = *gamyate* (Vr. 8,58; Hc. 4,249; Kī. 4,13; Sr. fol. 54; H. R.; Erz.), AMg. *gammanti* (Ovav. 56, p. 63,13), *samaṇugammanta-* (Ovav. [§ 37]) and °*gammamāṇa* (Nāyādh. § 103.105); M. *gammaü* (H. 715), fut. *gammihii* (Hc. 4,249; H. 609) partly with an active meaning; M. *gamijjanti* (G. 846; so to be read); Ś. *gamiadu* (Mālatīm. 285,5; printed °*mi*°), *gacchiadi* (Śak. 25,2; Vikr. 22, 10.15), *avagacchiadi* (Mudrār. 58,4), *āacchiadi* (Nāgān. 19,11). For *aṇugacchijjanti* in Mṛcch. 25,10 we have in Ś. correctly *aṇugacchianti*; M. *saṁjamijjanti* (G. 289).—From *dhau* (to wash), corresponding to the flexion according to the 6. conjugation (§ 482) is formed the passive M. particip. *dhuvvanta-* (H. R.), *dhuvvamāṇa*.

§ 539. From *pā* (to drink) the passive forms are M. *pijjaï* (H.), *pijjae* (Karp. 24,12), *pijjanti* (G.), *pijjanta-* (Karp. 10,8), Ś. *piviadi* (Mṛcch. 71,7; Vikr. 9,19), as we should read in Mṛcch. 87,13 too for *piiadi* and in Vikr. 48,15 with the v. l. for *piadi*, imp. Ś *piviadu* (Mṛcch. 77,11). Against the dialect is Ś. *pijjanti* Śak. 29,5, for which we should read *pivianti* in all cases with the remaining recensions *pianti* (Kashmīr recension *piante*). False is Mg. *pijjae* (Prab. 28,15) too, as Bb. M. P. too have; *piviadi* would be correct.—*sthā* forms Ś. *aṇuciṭṭhiadi* (Mṛcch. 4,13). imp. *aṇuciṭṭhiadu* (Mṛcch. 3,7; Śak. 1,9; Ratn. 290,28; Prab. 3,5; Nāgān. 2,17). Kī. 4,14 teaches *ṭhiaï*, *thijjaï*.

§ 540. Besides the usual formations *khaṇijjaï* (Hc. 4,244), JM. participle *khannamāṇa* (Erz. 39,7), from *khan* is mentioned as passive *khammaï* too (Hc. 4,244; Sr. fol. 56). So M. *ukkhammanti*, *ukkhammanta-*, *ukkhammiavva* (R.). The form is not to be separated from *jammaï* from *jan* (Hc. 4,136) and *hammaï* from *han* (Vr. 8,45; Hc. 4,244; Sr. fol. 56) beside *haṇijjaï*. So M. *āhammiuṁ* *ṇihammaï*, *ṇihammanti*, *pahammanta-* (R.); AMg. *hammaï* (Āyār. 1,3,3,2; Sūyag. 289), *hammanti* (Uttar. 668. 1008; Paṇhāv. 289 [commentary correctly]; Sūyag. 294.431), *hammantu* (Paṇhāv. 129), *paḍihammĕjjā* (Ṭhāṇ. 188), *viṇihammanti* (Uttar. 156); AMg. JM. *hammamāṇa* (Sūyag. 278. 297. 393. 647. 863; Paṇhāv. 202; Vivāgas. 63; Nirayāv. 67; Erz.); AMg. *vihammamāṇa* (Sūyag. 350), *suhammamāṇa* (Sūyag. 270). It is wholly improbable to assume a formation on the analogy of *gammaï* from *gam* with JACOBI[1] and JOHANSSON[2]. *jammaï* points to the fact that there occurred denominatives from *janman*, Pkt. *jamma-*, *hanman*, Pkt. *hamma-*, **khanman*, Pkt. *khamma-*[3]. Cf. § 550. 557. On *khuppaï* see § 286.

1. KZ. 28,254.—2. KZ. 32,449.—3. Mk. fol. 57 teaches *khammaï* like *hammaï* (§ 550) as active.

§ 541. From *dṛś*, corresponding to Skt. *dṛśyate*, is regularly formed M. JM. *dīsaï* (Hc. 3,161; Sr. fol. 56; G. H. R.; Erz.; Kk.); M. *dīsae* (Karp. 54,10), *dīsanta-* (H. R.); M. AMg. *dīsanti* (Karp. 4,10; Dasav. 635,12); AMg. *dissaï* (Āyār. 1,2,3,3), *adissamāṇa* (Āyār. 1,2,5,3; Sūyag. 646); Ś. *dīsadi* (Mṛcch. 50,24; 138,23; 139,8; Vikr. 7,3; 10,4; 39,6; 40,6; Ratn. 295,10; Nāgān. 52,8 etc.), *dīsadha* (Karp. 3,8), *dīsanti* (Śak. 99,12; Viddhaś. 71,9; 119,13; Mālatīm. 201,2), *dīsadu* (Karp. 54,4), Mg. *dīśadi* (Lalitav. 565,8; Mṛcch. 138,24; 139,10. 11; 147,4. 15; 168,18), *dīśanti* (Mṛcch. 14, 11).—*labh* forms M. *labbhaï* = *labhyate* (Hc. 4,249; H. R.; Mṛcch. 153,17), as we should read in JM. too for *lajjhaï* (Erz. 60,16), that is a wrong reading; AMg. fut. *lubbhihī* in the active sense (Dasav. 624,14); Ś. *labbhadi* (Śak. 23,14); beside it *lahijjaï* (Hc. 4,249), as in A. (Piṅgala 1,117), and in Ś. Mg. from the nasalised present stem (§ 484. 525); Ś. *lambhīadi* (Mālatīm. 217,3), *lambhīāmo* (Mālatīm. 240,4), *uvālambhīadı* (text °*bhijjaï*, Mallikām. 218,8); Mg. *ālambhīadi* (Mudrār. 194,2; to be so read; cf. v. l. and ed. Calc. saṁvat 1926 p. 162,8).—*vah* has the passive M. AMg. JM. *vubbhaï* (Hc. 4,245; Kī. 4,79 [text *va*°]; Mk. fol. 62; G. H.; (Erz.), M. *ṇivvubbhaï* (R.). So also we should in H. 275 read *vubbhasi* for *ujjhasi* (cf. WEBER on it) and Dasav. 635,8 *vubbhaī* for misread *vujjhaī*. Cf. § 266. Hc. 4, 245 teaches *vahijjaï* too. According to Mk. fol. 72 in Ś. only *vahīadi* is used.

§ 542. Of the roots of the 6. conjugation *pracch* forms the passive M. JM. AMg. *pucchijjaï*: M. *pucchijjantī* (particip.; H.); JM. *pucchijjāmi* (Erz.); AMg. *pucchijjanti* (Paṇṇav. 388); Ś. *pucchiasi* (Viddhaś. 118,8), *pucchīadi*

(Mṛcch. 57,18; 72,25).—*kṛt* has in AMg. *kiccaï* (Uttar. 177).—*muc* forms in M. JM. AMg. *muccaï* = *mucyate*; M. *muccaï*, *muccanti* (G.), *muccanta-* (R.); JM. *muccāmi*, *muccae* (Erz.); AMg. *muccaï* (Vivāhap. 37), *muccae* (Uttar. 243), *muccanti* (Kappas.; Ovav.), *muccĕjjā* (1. sing.; Uttar. 624), *muccĕjja* (3. sing.; Sūyag. 104; Uttar. 247), *pamuccaï*, *vimuccaï* (Āyār. 1,3, 3,5; 2,16,12); JŚ. *vimuccadi* (Pav. 384,60); but Ś. *muñcīadu* (Mudrār. 247,7; [so to be read for *muñcijjadu*, *muñcadu* of the editions]) in the face of the fut. *muccissadi* (Śak. 138,1; Vikr. 77,16 [so to be read]).—From *lup* is found M. *luppanta-* (G. 384), AMg. *luppaï*, *luppanti* (Sūyag. 104), from *sic* JM. *siccanto* (Dvār. 504,10), AMg. *abhisiccamāṇī*, *parisiccamāṇa* (Kappas.), *saṁsiccamāṇa* (Āyār. 1,3,2,2); Ś. *siccanti* (Mudrār. 182,1); so to be read with the Calc. editions]), *siccamāṇā* (Mālatīm. 121,2). On *sippaï* see § 286, on *mṛ* § 477. *chippaï* and *chivijjaï*, that Hc. 4,257 derives from *spṛś*, belong to *kṣip* (§ 319).

§ 543. For verbs of the 4. conjugation the characteristic examples are: M. *paḍibujjhijjaï* = *pratibudhyate* (G. 1172); A. *rūsijjaï* = *ruṣyate* (Hc. 4,418,4). The verbs of the 10. conjugation, the causatives and the similarly formed denominatives mostly built the passive as in Skt. through the insertion of the passive element within either the root or the stem, without *-ya*, *-aya*, Pkt. *-a*, *-e*: *kārīaï*, *kārijjaï*, *karāvīaï*, *karāvijjaï*, *hāsīaï*, *hāsijjaï*, *hasāvīaï*, *hasāvijjaï* (Vr. 7,28. 29; Hc. 3,152. 153; Sr. fol. 55.56). M. *cheijjanti* (G. 1198), Ś. *chedīanti* (Mṛcch. 71,4) = *chedyante*; M. *tosijjaï* = *toṣyate* (H. 508), *samatthijjaï* = *samarthyate* (H. 730), *kavalijjaï* = *kavalīkriyate* (G. 172), *pahāmijjanta-* = *prabhrāmyamāṇa* (R. 7,69); JM. *mārijjaï* = *māryate* (Erz. 5,34), *mārijjaü*, *mārijjāmi* (Erz. 5,26; 32,26); AMg. *āghavijjanti* = *ākhyāpyante* (Nandīs. 398. 427. 428. 451. 454. 456. 465 ff.), *piḍḍaï* = *pīḍyate* (Āyār. 1,2,5,4); Ś. *pabodhīāmi* = *prabodhye* (Śak. 29,9), *vāvādīadi* = *vyāpādyate* (Mṛcch. 41,7; Uttarar. 97,1; Mudrār. 250,2; Veṇīs. 35,20), *saṁpadhārīadu* = *saṁpradhāryatām* (Vikr. 22,19), *viṇṇavīadi* = *vijñāpyate* (Vikr. 30,21), *jīvāvīadi* = *jīvyate* (Mṛcch. 176,7), *avadārīadu* = *avatāryatām* (Karp. 26,9), *sukkhavīanti* = *śoṣyante* (characteristically **śuṣkāpyante*; Mṛcch. 71,4); A. *ṭhavije* = *sthāpyate* (Piṅgala 2,93. 101). Exceptions are found in the case of the denominatives in M.: *kajjalaïjjaï* (R. 5,50); *valaïjjaï* (G. 1028), *kaṇḍaïjjanta-* (H. 67), *maṇḍalaïjjanta-* (S. 1034). From *kathaya-* the regular passive are: M. *kahijjaï* (Hc. 4,249), *kahijjanti*, *kahijjaü* *kahijjanta.* (H.); AMg. *parikahijjaï*. (Āyār. 1,2,5,5; 1,4,1,3); D. *kahijjadi* (Mṛcch. 103,15); Mg. *kadhīyadu* (sic; Lalitav. 566,9); A. *kahijjaï* (Piṅgala 1,117), *kahije* (Piṅgala 2,93.101). Besides Hc. 4,249 teaches also *katthaï*, that is found in AMg. (Āyār. 1,2,6,5) and phonetically must have been **kacchaï* (§ 280). Perhaps it belongs to *katth*. AMg. *pakatthaï* (Sūyag. 234) is = **prakatthate*. On *āḍhappaï*, *āḍhavīaï*, *viḍhappaï*, *viḍhavijjaï*, *viḍhappīadi* see § 286.

§ 544. Of the verbs of the 2. conjugation *yā* has the passive A. *jāijjaï* (Hc. 4,419,3); in AMg. is found *pattiāïadi* (§ 487). On the roots in *-u*, *-ū*, see § 356. *rud* has Ś. *rodīadi* (§ 495), *svap* in M. *suppaü* = *supyatām* (H.), in Ś. *suvīadi* (Karṇas. 18,20). *vac* forms *vuccaï* (Hc. 3,161; § 337); AMg.

vuccaï (Uttar. 3; Vivāhap. 34. 35. 102. 928; Kappas.; Ovav.; Uvās. etc.), *vuccaī* (Uttar. 2) *pavuccaï* (Āẏār. 1,1,4,3.5,1,1.1.6,1; 1,2,2,1. 6,2. 4; 1,4 1,2; 1,5,3,3; Vivāhap. 202. 374 f. 409. 444; Rāẏap. 144 ff.), *pavuccaī* (Sūẏag. 351); *vuccanti* (Sūẏag 978. 979. 994 ff.; Dasav, 629,22). *vuccamāṇa* (Sūẏag. 393; Vivāhap. 149); Ś. *vuccāmi* (Karp. 32,9), *vuccasi* (Śak. 12,8), *vuccadi* (Mṛcch. 77,12; 79,2; 87,12; 138,2. 3; Viddhaś. 128,1 [text *uccadi*]; Bālar. 96,12 [text *uccadi*]), *vuccanti* (Mṛcch. 29,7); Mg. *vuccadi* (Mṛcch. 36, 11).—From *duh*, besides *duhijjaï*, is taught *dubbhaï*; from *lih*, besides *lihijjaï*, also *libbhaï* (Hc. 4,245; Kī. 4,79; Mk. fol. 62; so also in Vr. 8,59 we should read *libbhaï*; cf. v. l.). On this see § 266. JM. has *dujjhaü* (Āv. 43. 11), fut. *dujjhihii* (Āv. 43,20), probably a false reading for *dubbhaü*, *dubbhihii*. Cf. *lajjhaï*, *vujjhaī* § 541. On *sisaï*, D. *sāsijjaī* from *śās* see § 499, on *hammaï*, *haṇijjaï* from *han* § 540.

§ 545. From *dā*, corresponding to Skt. *dīyate*, the passive is M. JM. A. *dijjaï* (H. R.; Erz.; Hc. 4,438,1; Piṅgala 1,121), M. also *dijjae* (H.; Karp. 76,7; 89,9), A. also *dije* (Piṅgala 2,102. 105). *dijjaü* (Piṅgala 2,106) in the active sense, 3. plur. *dijjahĩ* (Hc. 4,428; Piṅgala 2,59 [so to be read]) JŚ. *dijjadi* (Kattig. 401,345); Ś. *dīadi* (Mṛcch. 55,16; 71,6), false *dijjadi* (Mṛcch. 49,7; Karp. 61,9), *dijjantu* (Karp. 113,8). *dijjandu* (Viddhaś. 124, 14), beside the correct *dīadu* (Karp. 103,7); Mg. *dīadi*, *dīadu* (Mṛcch. 145, 5); P. *tiyyate* (Hc. 4,315).—To *dhā* belongs AMg. *āhijjaï* = *ādhīyate* (Sūẏag. 603. 674 ff.), *āhijjanti* (Āẏār. 2,15,15; Jīv. 12; Kappas.), explained by commentators as *ākhyāyate*, *ākhyāyante*. From *hā* the passive forms are Ś. *parihīasi* (Śak. 51,5), *parihīadi* (Mālatīm. 212,4), *parihīamāṇa* (Karp. 76,1). On *huvvaï*, *huṇijjaï* from *hu* see § 536. Of the roots of the 5. conjugation the following form the passive : *ci* : *ciṇijjaï*, *civvaï*, AMg. *cijjanti*, Ś. *viciadu* (§ 536), *dhu* : *dhuṇijjaï*, *dhuvvaï* (§ 536), *śru* : *suṇijjaï*, *suvvaï*, JM. *summaü*, Ś. *suṇiadi*, Mg. *śuṇiadi* (§ 536), *āp* : Ś. *pāviadi* (Viddhaś. 43,2), A. *pāviaï* (Hc. 4,366), *śak.* : Ś. *sakkiadi* (Viddhaś. 87,2; Cait. 84,5; 85,13; 258,16), Mg. *śakkiadi* (Mṛcch. 116,6).

§ 546. The roots of the 7. conjugation form the passive mostly as in Skt., more rarely from the present stem : M. *chijjaï*, *chijjanti*, *vŏcchijjaï* R.); JM. A. *chijjaï* (Erz.; Hc. 4,357,1; 434,1); Ś. *chijjanti* (Mṛcch. 41,2), fut. *chijjissadi* (Mṛcch. 3,16).—M. JM. *bhajjaï bhajjanti*, *bhajjanta-* (G. R.; Erz.), M. fut. *bhajjihisi* (H. 202); Mg. *bhayyadi*, imp. *vibhayyā* (Mṛcch. 118, 12. 21; see § 506).—M. *bhijjaï*, *bhijjanti*, *bhijjanta-* (G. H. R.); AMg. *bhijjaï* (Āẏār. 1,3,3,2), *bhijjaü* (Vivāhap. 1230), *bhijjamāṇa* (Uvās. § 218); Ś. *ubbhijjadu* (Karp. 83,1), *ubbhijjanti* (Viddhaś. 72,3; text °*ndi*).—M. *bhujjanta-*, *uvahujjanta-* (G.); JM. *bhujjaï* (Erz.); AMg. *bhujjaī* (Uttar. 354); but also *bhuñjijjaï* (H. 4,249); JM. *paribhuñjijjaï* (Dvār. 500,36); Ś. *bhuñjiadi* (Śak. 29,6).—M. *jujjanta-* (R.), and in the meanings "it is proper", "it is in accord with" = Skt. *yujyate* always M. *jujjaï* (H. 924), *jujjae* (H. 12), JŚ. *jujjade* (Kattig. 403, 380), Ś. *jujjadi* (Mṛcch. 61, 10; 65, 12; 141, 3; 155, 21; Śak. 71,10; 122,11; 129,15; Vikr. 24,3; 32,17; 82,17 etc.), in the usual meaning, on the contrary : Ś. *ṇiuñjiāmi*, *ṇiuñjiasi* (Karp. 18,3.2), *ṇiuñjiadi* (Mālatīm. 22,5 [so to be read; see p. 372]); *paüñjiadi*

(Karp. 19,8), *paüñjiadu* (Mṛcch. 9,7). On *juppaï* see § 286. For *rudh* Hc. 4,245 teaches *rundhijjaï* and *rubbhaï*, in combination with the prefixes *anu*, *upa*, *sam* 4,248; *aṇu-*, *uva-*, *saṁ-* °*rujjhaï*, °*rundhijjaï*. In the texts are found M. *parirujjhaï* (G. 434); Ś *uvarujjhadi* (Vikr. 82,15 v. l.; cf. 131,10 ed. Bombay). M. *rubbhaï*, *rubbhanta-*, *rubbhamāṇa* (R.), JM. *rubbhaï* (Āv. 41,9) are passive from *rubh* (§ 507).

§ 547. *kṛ* forms the passive in M. JM. usually *kīraï* (Vr. 8,60; Hc. 4,250; Kī. 4,79; Mk. fol. 62; Sr. fol. 54), therefore, like *hṛ*, on the analogy of the roots in *-ṝ* (§ 537). So M. *kīraï*, *kīrae*, *kīranti*, *kīraü*, *kīranta-* (G. H. R.); JM. *kīraï* (Erz.; Āv. 9,23; 13,26; Dvār. 497,7), *kīraü* (Kk. 269,37; so to be read); JŚ. *kīradi* (Kattig. 399, 320; 401, 350). Sometimes AMg. has the same form (Vivāhap. 135. 796; Ovav. § 116. 127.128). *kīramāṇa* (Dasav. 629,5), *kīranta-* (verse; Āẏār. 1,8,4,8); it is mentioned as *kīrate* for P. by Hc. 4,316 and by Rājaśekhara (pro ex. Bālar. 176.16 [*kīradi*]; 224,17 [*kīraü*]; 228,8 [*kīraï*]; Karp. ed. Bomb. 22,4 [*kīradi*]) and used by later writers, such as Bilhaṇa, Karṇas. 53,16 (*kīradi*) in Ś. too, that perhaps is simply a contribution of the edition, as Karp. 22,4 Konow (p. 19,7) correctly has *kariadi*. Hc. 4,250 mentions also *karijjaï*, and so A. has *karīje* (Piṅgala 2,93. 101. 102. 105) and *karijjasu* (Piṅgala 1,39. 41. 95. 144; 2,119). Hc. 1,97 further has *kijjaï* =*kriyate* in *duhākijjaï*, *dohākijjaï*, and according to Hc. 4,274 *kijjadi* and *kijjade* are be used in Ś. So stands *kijjadu* in Ś. (Lalitav. 562,24), elsewhere, however, in none of the texts. *kijjaï* is found in M. at R. 13,16, and it is the usual form in A. : *kijjaü̃* (Hc. 4,338; 445,3) in the sense of the fut. active (§ 550), *kijjaü* (Piṅgala 1,81a) in the active sense, *kijjahĩ* (so to be read; text °*hi*) =*kriyante* (Piṅgala 2,59). On A. *kijjasu*, *karijjasu* see § 461. 466. In AMg. almost the only prevalent form in prose is *kajjaï* = **karyate* (Āẏār. 1,2,1,4; 1,2,2,3. 5,1; Sūẏag. 656. 704. 838 ff.; Ṭhāṇ. 291; Vivāhap. 52. 99. 136. 137. 182. 346. 444. 1406; Paṇṇav. 636 ff.), *kajjanti* (Āẏār. 1,2,5,1; Vivāhap. 47. 50. 52. 1302; Ovav. § 123. 125), *kajjamāṇa* (Sūẏag. 368; Vivāhap. 840), *duhā*°, *tihā*° (Vivāhap. 141). In Ś. are used exclusively *kariadi* (Mṛcch. 18,11; 69,10; Śak. 19,6), *alaṁkariadi* (Śak. 19,5), *karīanti* (Śak. 77,4; Ratn. 293,21), *kariadu* (Śak. 54,1; 168,15; Karp. 22,9; 26,3; 63,6; 68,2; 113,8; Viddhaś. 99,5), in Mg. *kaliadi* (Mudrār. 154,4; 178,7), *kaliadu* (Mṛcch. 39,21; 160,6).

§ 548. *jñā* forms, according to Hc. 4,252, *ṇajjaï*, *ṇāijjaï*, *jāṇijjaï*, *ṇavvaï*, according to Kī. 4,81 *jāṇiaï*, *āṇiaï*, *ṇajjiaï*, *ṇavviaï*, *ṇajjaï*, *ṇavvaï*. Of them *ṇajjaï*=*jñāyate* is the current form in M. (G. H. R.), JM. (Erz.), AMg. (Uvās.; Niraẏāv. [in JM. AMg. *najjaï*]). Ś. has *jāṇiadi* (Ratn. 300,8; 318,12; Vṛṣabh. 45,10; 47,10; Karp. 28,2; Viddhaś. 119,4), *jāṇiadu* (Nāgān. 84.5), behind *ṇa* (not) *āṇiadi* (§ 170; Mṛcch. 74,9; 88,25; Mālatīm. 285,5; Nāgān. 38,3 [so to be read]) corresponding to A. *jāṇiaï* (Hc. 4,330,4). In lieu of *ṇavvaï* Triv. 2,4,84 and Sr. fol. 56 have *ṇappaï*, that stands in place of *āḍhappaï*, *viḍhappaï*, i.e. =*jñāpyate*. Accordingly one **ṇavaï*, of which the regular passive is *ṇavvaï*[1], is to be deduced from the causatives such as Ś. *āṇavedi*, *viṇṇavedi*.—*kri* forms Ś. *vikkiṇiadi* (Karp. 14,5), *vikkiṇia-*

anti (Mudrār. 108,9; [so to be read]); *pū* has *puvvaï*, *puṇijjaï*, A. *puṇijje*; *lū* has *luvvaï*, *luṇijjaï* (§ 536), *granth* has Ś. *ganthīanti* (Mṛcch. 71,3 [text *gatthī°*]). From *grah* the passive forms are *gĕṇhijjaï* (Hc. 4,256; Kī. 4,82) and *gahijjaï* (Sr. fol. 56), S. *aṇuggahīadu* (Vikr. 21,10). M. JM. AMg. A. use for it *ghĕppaï* = Pāli *ghĕppati*, which the Indian grammarians (Hc. 4,256; Kī. 4,82; Mk. fol. 62; Sr. fol. 56) and the European scholars drag to *grabh*, though it belongs to the parallel root **ghṛp* (§ 212). So M. *ghĕppaï*, *ghĕppae*, *ghĕppanti*, *ghĕppanta-* (G. H. R.; Ānandavardhana in Dhvanyāloka 62,4; Viśvanātha, Sāhityadarpaṇa 178,3); JM. *ghĕppaï* (Kk. 273,37), *ghĕppanti* (Erz. 67,12; Āv. 36,42); AMg. *ghĕppĕjjā* (Paṇhāv. 400); A. *ghĕppaī* (Hc. 4,341,1), *ghĕppanti* (Hc. 4,335). Falsely in Ś. (Mallikām. 101,6; 144,8). In verse stands *gĕjjhaī* = *gṛhyate* in AMg. Dasav. N. 655,5.6. Kī. 4, 82 teaches also *ghĕppijjaï*. —*bandh* forms *bajjhaï* = *badhyate* (Hc. 4,247); AMg. *bajjhaī* (Uttar. 245); JŚ. *bajjhadi* (Pav. 384,47); Ś. *bajjhanti* (Mṛcch. 71,2); according to Hc. 4,247 also *bandhijjaï* (Pav. 384,47); Ś. *bajjhanti* (Mṛcch. 71,2); according to Hc. 4,247 also *bandhijjaï*.—From *bhaṇ*, which in the present behaves according to the 9. conjugation (§ 514), the passive is M. *bhaṇṇaï* = *bhaṇyate* (Hc. 4,249 [so to be read]; Kī. 4,13; H. R.), *bhaṇṇaü* (G. R.; Śak. 101,16), *bhaṇṇamāṇa* (H.), *bhaṇṇanta* (R.), and *bhaṇijjaï* (Hc. 4,249), *bhaṇijjaü* (H.); A. *bhaṇije* (Piṅgala 2,101), perhaps also *bhaṇijjasu* (Piṅgala 1,109; cf. § 461); JM. *bhaṇṇaï* (Erz.; Kk.); Ś. *bhaṇīadi* (Mṛcch. 151,12; Prab. 39,3). False is Ś. *bhaṇijjandi* (Prab. 42,5; P. *°jjanti*, M. *°jjamāṇā*) for *bhaṇīanti*, as Bb. 93,4 reads (only wrongly *°ṇi°*).

1, Wholly wrong is S. GOLDSCHMIDT, ZDMG. 29,494; JACOBI, KZ, 28,255, JOHANSSON, KZ. 32,449f.

§ 549. In the passive is found in AMg. an aorist: *muccimsu* (Sūyag. 790), and in almost all the dialects a future, which too is wholly likewise formed, like the fut. Parasmaip. from the present stem of the parasmaip. So: 1. M. *kalijjihisi* from *kal* (H. 225. 313). *khajjihii* from *khād* (H. 138), *ḍajjhihisi* (H. 105), *ḍajjhihii* (Hc. 4,246) from *dah*, *disihii* (H. 619; R. 3,33 [so to be read]), *dharijjihii* (H. 778); JM. *ḍajjhihii* (Āv. 32,25); *khammihii* from *khan* (Hc. 4,244).—6. AMg. *muccihii* (Ovav. § 116; Nāyādh. 390 [text *°himti*]; Vivāhap. 175), *muccissanti* (Āyār. 2,15.16), but also *pamŏkkhasi* = *pramokṣyase* (Āyār. 1,3,1,2; 1,3,3,4); Ś. *muccissadi* (Śak. 138,1; Vikr. 77,16 [so to be read]); AMg. *uvalippihii* (Ovav. § 112).—4. JM. *khŏṭṭijjihii* (Āv. 32,2) from *khuṭṭaï* (Hc. 4,116).—10. Causatives and denominatives: AMg. *mārijjissāmi* (Uvās. § 256); JM. *chiḍḍijjihii* (Āv. 33.2) from *chidraya-*, *vāvāijjissaï* (Erz. 43,22).—2. *hammihii* from *han* (Hc. 4,244; cf. § 540. 550. 557); AMg. *paḍihammihii* (Nāyādh. § 30); *dubbhihii* (Hc. 4, 245), JM. *dujjhihii* (Āv. 43,20; cf.; however § 544).—5. *civvihii*, *cimmihii* from *ci* (Hc. 4,242. 243; cf. § 536); M. *jhijjihisi* from *kṣi* (H. 152. 628); M. *samappihii* (H. 734. 806; R. 5,4).—7. M. *bhajjihisi* from *bhañj* (H. 202); AMg. *vŏcchijjihinti* from *chid* with *vyud* (Sūyag. 1011), *samucchihinti*, metrically for *samucchijjihinti* (Sūyag. 869), Ś. *chijjissadi* (Mṛcch. 3,16); Ś. *ahiujjissadi* from *yuj* with *abhi* (Uttarar. 69,6); *samrujjhihii* (Hc. 4,248).—8. AMg. *kajjissaï* (Vivāhap. 492); JM. *kīrihii* (Āv. 16,9).—9. *bajjhihii*

(Hc. 4,247). Ś. *bajjhissāmo* (Mṛcch. 109,19; see § 488, note 4) from *bandh*; JM. *ghĕppihii* from **ghṛp* (Āv. 7,5).

§ 550. The passive is sometimes used in the sense of parasmaipadam. WEBER has rightly compared such forms with the deponentia of Latin[1]. So : M. *gammihisi* (H. 609)[2], doubtful *gammasu* (H. 819) in the sense of the causative : M. *gasijjihii* (H. 804) ; M. *dīsihisi* (R. 15,86), where, however, C has *dakṣihisi* i.e. *dacchihisi* (§ 525); M. *pijjaï* (Hc. 4,10; H. 678)[2]; M. *bhaṇṇihisi* (H. 906)[3]; *hammaï* = *hanti* (Vr. 8,45; Hc. 4,244; Kī. 4,46; Mk. fol. 57; Sr. fol. 56; cf. § 540), particip. pres. ātmanep. AMg. *vihammāṇa* Uttar. 787) ; fut. AMg. *hammihanti* (Ṭhāṇ. 512); AMg *labbhihi* (Dasav. 624,14) ; A. *dijjaü*, *kijjaü* (§ 545. 547; cf. § 461. 466). The future too is used prevalently in the active sense in which the metre might have often associated. Very interesting is that the present passive in Mg. A. is sometimes used in the sense of the fut. parasmaip., therefore, "I am made" is used in lieu of "I shall make". For Mg. Mk. fol. 75 teaches in the Parasmaip. *bhavissadi* and *bhuviadi*. So Mg. *bhaviadi* (Mṛcch. 164,10) and *huviadi* (Veṇīs. 33,6.7; 35,8) "he will be", *vāvādiaśi* "thou wilt kill" (Mṛcch. 167,25), *pivāśiaśi* (so to be read; Veṇīs. 34,6) "that thou wilt be thirsty"; A. *kijjaũ* (Hc. 4,338. 445,3) "I shall make".

1. WEBER, Hāla[1] p. 64, where, however, all the examples are false, likewise, excluding *samappihii* and *dīsihisi*, the examples in S. GOLDSCHMIDT, ZDMG. 29,492 and on R. 15,86 p. 325 note 10.—2. WEBER on Hāla 609.

CAUSATIVE

§ 551. As in Skt. the causative is formed by insertion of *-e-* = Skt. *-aya* into the strengthened root : *kārei* = *kārayati*, *pāḍhei* = *pāṭhayati*, *uvasāmei* = *upaśāmyati*, *hāsei* = *hāsayati* (Vr. 7,26; Hc. 3,149; Kī. 4,44; Śr. fol. 55). Cf. § 490. The roots in *-ā* add *-ve-* = Skt. *-paya-* : M. *ṇivvāvĕnti* = *nirvāpayanti* (G. 524) ; Ś. *ṇivvāvedi* (Mālatīm. 217,5), fut. *ṇivvāvaïssaṁ* (Mālatīm. 266,1), past passive participle *ṇivvāvida* (Mṛcch. 16,9); AMg. *āghāvei* = *ākhyāpayati* (Ṭhāṇ. 569) ; Mg. *pattiāvaïśśaṁ* (Mṛcch. 139,12) from *yā* with *prati* (§ 281. 487) ; PG. *aṇuvaṭṭhāveti* = *ānuprasthāpayati* (7,45) ; AMg. *ṭhāvei* = *sthāpayati* (Nirayāv. § 4; Kappas. § 116) ; AMg. *ṭhāvemi* (Erz. 43,32); Ś. *samavatthāvemi* = *samavasthāpayāmi* (Vikr. 27,6); *pajjavatthāvehi* = *paryavasthāpaya* (Vikr. 7,17), *paṭṭhāvia* (absol.; Mṛcch. 24,2), *paḍiṭṭhāvehi* (Ratn. 295,26) ; Mg. *stāvemi*, *stāvia* (absol.), *stāvaïśśaṁ* (Mṛcch. 97, 5;122,11; 132,20; 139,2), *pasṭāvia* (absol. Mṛcch. 21,12) ; A. *paṭhāviaï* (passive; Hc. 4,422,7); AMg. *ṇhāveha* = *snāpayata* (Vivāhap. 1261). *jñā* forms the caus. from the present stem : JM. *jāṇāvei* (Hc. 3,149; Erz), *jāṇāviyaṁ*, *jāṇāviuṁ* (Kk.); M. *jāṇāveuṁ* (H.). With prefixes it is formed with shortening of the root-vowel, as in Skt. too : AMg. JM. *āṇavei* (Niryāv.; Kappas.; Erz.) ; AMg. *āṇavemāṇa* (Sūyag 734), *paṇṇavemāṇa* (Ovav. § 78); Ś. *āṇavesi* (Mṛcch. 94,9), *āṇavedi* (Lalitav. 563,21. 29; 564,23; 568, 11; Mṛcch. 4,19; 7,3; 16,2 and very frequently), *āṇavedu* (Mṛcch. 3,7; Śak. 1,8; Nāgān. 2,16 etc.), but *āṇāvidavvaṁ* (Mṛcch. 58,13) beside *viṇṇaï*-

davvā (58,12), hence with GODABOLE 167,8 to be read *āṇa°*; *viṇṇavemi* (Mṛcch. 78,10). *viṇṇavedi* (Mṛcch. 74,6; 96,5; Śak. 138,10; Vikr. 12.13 etc.), *viṇṇavemo* (so to be read according to § 455; Śak. 27,7), *viṇṇavehi* (Mṛcch. 27,14; 74, 21; Vikr. 16,20; Mālatīm. 218,1), *viṇṇavissaṁ*, *viṇṇaïdavvā* (Mṛcch. 58,11. 12), *viṇṇavidaṁ* (so to be read; Vikr. 48,8), *viṇṇaviadi* (Vikr. 30,21); Mg. *āṇavedi* (Śak. 114,1), *viṇṇavia* (absol.; Mṛcch. 138, 25; 139,1). Like *jñā*, the other roots ending in *-ā* also shorten the vowel in M. JM. AMg. So particularly often *sthā* : M. JM. AMg. *ṭhavei* (G. H. R.; Erz.; Kk.; Uvâs.; Kappas. etc.; cf. Hc. 1,67); M. *ṭhavijjanti* (G. 995), *uṭṭhavesi* (H. 390), *saṁṭhavehi* (G. 997); AMg. *uvaṭṭhaveha* (Nāẏādh. § 130); A. *ṭhavehu* (Piṅgala 1,87. 125. 145).—M. *ṇimmavesi* = *nirmāpayasi* (G. 297); AMg. *āghavemāṇa* = *ākhyāpayamāna* (Ovav. § 78), *āghaviya* = *ākhyāpita* (Paṇhāv. 376. 431. 469), *āghavijjanti* = *ākhyāpyante* (Nandīs. 398. 427. 428. 451, 454. 456. 465 ff.), inf. *āghavittae* (Nāẏādh. § 143). As in Skt., certain roots in *-i*, *-ī* too have the same formation : Ś. passive *jaāviasi* = *jāpyase* (Śak. 31,11); AMg. *ūsaveha* (Vivāhap. 957), *ussaveha* (Kappas. § 100) = *ucchrāpayata*; Ś. *bhāāvesi* from *bhī* (§ 501; Mṛcch. 91,19). From the present stem is built *kiṇāvei* (Ṭhāṇ. 516), *kiṇāvae* (Āẏār. 1,2,5,3), *kiṇāvemāṇa* (Sūẏag. 609) from *krī*; Ś. *viciṇāvedi* (so to be read; Mudrār. 54,1) from *ci*; AMg. *alliẏāvei* (Nāẏādh. 434) from *lī*.

§ 552. The element *-ve-* = Skt. *-paya-* is employed in Pkt. for formation of the causative also from the roots in vowels other than *-ā*, *-i*, *-ī*, and in diphthongs and consonants. As a rule it is added to the present stem in *-a*, that is mostly lengthened, wherein the analogy of the *ā-* roots might have taken a hand. This formation is seldomer than the causative in *-e-* = *-aya-*. So : *hasāvei* (Vr. 7,26; Hc. 3, 149; Sr. fol. 55), *hasāvia* (Hc. 3,152), also M. *hāsāvia* (Hc. 3,153 = H. 123); AMg. *paẏāvemāṇa* from *pac* (Sūẏag. 609); M. *ramāvĕnti*, *sahāvĕnti* (H. 325. 327); Ā *kappāvemi* from *kḷp* (Mṛcch. 105,3); Ś. *ghaḍāvehi* (Mṛcch. 95,21), M. *vihaḍāvia* (G. 8) from *ghaṭ*; Ś. *jīvāvehi* (Uttarar. 63,14), *jiāvesu* (Viddhaś. 84,4), *jīvāvedu* (Mṛcch. 326,3), *jīvāviadi* (Mṛcch. 176,6), *jīvāvia* (absol.; Mālatīm. 215,1), *jīvāvidā* (Mṛcch. 173,4; 177,16); Mg. *yīvāvidā* (Mṛcch. 171,14); AMg. *dalāvei* (Vivāgas. 168); AMg. *samārambhāvei* (Āẏār. 1,1,2,3; 1,1,3,5), *samārambhāvĕjjā* (Āẏār. 1,1,2,6; 1,1,3,8); Ś. *ṇivattāvĕmi* (Mṛcch. 77,15): Mg. *palivattāvehi* (Mṛcch. 81,17. 19); Ś. *vaḍḍhāvemi* (Karṇas. 21,8); Ś. *dhovāvedi* (Mṛcch. 45,9); JM. *abbhuvagacchāvia* from *gam* with *abhi* and *upa* (Āv. 30,9); AMg. *piẏāvae* from *pā* (to drink; Dasav. 638,26). —AMg. *nicchubhāvei* (Nāẏādh. 823, 824. 1313) from *nicchubhaï* from *kṣubh* with *ni* (Nāẏādh. 1411; Vivāhap. 114; Paṇṇav. 827.832.834); Ś. *paḍicchāviadi* (Mṛcch. 69,12) from *iṣ* with *prati*; Ś. *pucchāvedi* from *pracch* (Viddhaś. 42, 4); JM. *melavehisi* (Āv. 30,8); Ś. *moāvemi*, *moāvehi* (Śak. 27,11; 24,2), M. *moāvia* (Mṛcch. 41,17) from *muc*; Mg. *lihāvemi* (Mṛcch. 133,1) from *likh*.—*uvasamāvei* (Hc. 3,149) from *śam*; *tosavia* from *tuṣ*, *sosavia* from *śuṣ* (Hc. 3,150); Ś. *lohāvedi* (Śak. 61,3).—AMg. *vaḍhāvei* (Vivāgas. 170) from *veḍhei* (§ 304. 490).—M. *ruāvei*, *ruāvia*, *roāvia* (H.), Ś. *rodāvida* (Mṛcch. 21,1) from *rud*.—From *dā* (to give) is built in JM. a double form *davāvei* in the meaning "to cause to give" (Erz.).—Ś. *suṇāvidā* (Mālav. 31,8).—AMg. *chindāvae* (Dasav. 638,30).—*karāvei, karāvia, kārāvei* (Vr. 7,27; Hc. 3, 149. 152. 153; Kī. 4,44); AMg, *kāravemi* (Uvās. § 13. 14. 15). *kāraveha* (Kappas. § 57. 100); JM. *kāravei* (Erz. 30,7), *kārāviya* (Erz.).—JM. *gĕṇhāvemi* (Āv. 34,19).

§ 553. For *-e, -ve-* are found dialectically, particularly in A., not seldom *-a-, -va-*, it may be that here we have formations according to the model of the denominatives or a flexion, which might have arisen from originally contracted forms and regularly shortened before doubled consonants (§ 491). So: *hasāvaï* (Hc. 3,149; Sr. fol. 55); *ghaḍāvaï* (Hc. 4, 340), *ugghāḍaï* (Hc. 4,33) beside Ś. *ghaḍāvehi* (Mṛcch. 95,21); *vippagālaï*=*vipragālayati* (Hc. 4,31); *uddālaï*=*uddālayati* (Hc. 4,125); *pāḍaï*=*pātayati* (Hc. 3,153) beside M. *pāḍei* (R, 4,50), Mg. *pāḍemi* (Mṛcch. 162,22); *bhamāvaï* (Hc. 3,151) from *bhram*; A. *uttārahi* (Vikr. 69,2) beside Ś. *odāredi* (Uttarar. 165,3), *padāredi* (so to be read; Prab. 15,10); JM. A. *māraï* (Hc. 3,153; Erz. 5,32; Hc. 4,330,3) beside M. *māresi, mārehisi* (H.). *mārei* (Mudrār. 34,10), Ś. *māredha* (Mṛcch. 161,16; 165,25), Mg *mālemi* (Mṛcch. 12,5; 123,3), *mālehi* (Mṛcch. 123,5; 124,2. 17; 165,24), *māledu* (Mṛcch. 125,8), *māledha* (Mṛcch. 165,23; 166,1; 168,8; 171,18); for Mg. *mālantaṁ* (Mṛcch.12 3,22) is to be read *mālĕntaṁ*; A. *mārei* (Hc. 4,337); *hāravaï* (Hc. 4,31); A. *vāhahi* (Piṅgala 1,5a) beside Ā. *vāhehi* (Mṛcch. 100,18), Mg. *vāheśi* (Mṛcch. 122,15); *melavaï* (Hc. 4,28) from *mil* (§ 486) beside JM. *melavehisi* (§ 528); *nāsavaï, nāsaï* (Hc. 4,31) from *naś*; AMg. *vedanti* (Paṇṇav. 786 ff.), *veyanti* (Jīv. 281 ff.)=*vedayanti*; *nimmavaï*=*nirmāpayati* (Hc. 4,19) beside M. *ṇimmavesi* (G. 297); *āḍhavaï, viḍhavaï* from *dhā* (§ 286. 500); M. *ṭhavaï* (G. 980), *saṁṭhavanti* (H. 39); *paṭṭhavaï, paṭṭhāvaï* (Hc. 4,37); A. *pariṭhavahu, saṁṭhavahu* (Piṅgala 1,10.85) beside *ṭhāvei, ṭhavei* (§ 551); *karāvaï* (Hc. 3,149); *viṇṇavaï* (Hc. 4,38) beside Ś. *viṇṇavedi* (§ 551); *palāvaï* from *lū* with *pra* (Hc. 4,31).

§ 554. From *dṛś* Hc. 4,32 teaches the causative *dāvaï, daṁsaï, dakkhavaï, darisaï*. Of them *dāvaï* is found (also in Sr. fol. 57) in M. *dāvanteṇa* (H.); more often forms with *-e-*: M. *dāvemi* (Ratn. 322,5; *taṁ te dāvemi* according to Dhanika on Daśarūpa 42,6 for *taṁ taṁ daṁsemi* of the editions), *dāvei, dāvĕnti, dāvae, dāveha, dāvĕnti, dāvia* (H. R.), *dāvijjaü* (Ratn. 321, 32), *dāviāï* (Karp. 56,7); JM. *dāviya* (Erz.), *dāvia, dāvijjasu* (Ṛṣabhap. 10. 49); Ś. *dāvida* (Mudrār. 44,1). The word is=Marāṭhī *dāvṇeṁ*[1]. The derivation from *di*[2] is false. *dāvei, dāvaï* stands for *darpayati, darpati* from *dṛpa saṁdipane* (Dhātupāṭha 34,14) according to § 62. To the same root belong Skt. *darpaṇa* (mirror) and M. *addāa*, AMg. JM. *addāga, addāya* (mirror; § 196, where we should read=**ādāpaka*=**ādarpaka*[2]). *daṁsaï* occurs in AMg. *daṁsanti*=*darśayanti* (Sūyag. 222), M. *daṁsantiṁ*=*darśayantīm* (G. 1055; without v. l.); more frequently with *-e-*; M. *daṁsintiṁ* (G. 1054); JM. *daṁsei, daṁseha* (Erz.; Kk.); Ś. *daṁsemi* (Mṛcch. 74,16; Mālatim. 38,9), *daṁsesi* (Mṛcch. 90,21; Śak. 167,10), *daṁsehi* (Ratn. 321, 20), *daṁseduṁ* (Mudrār. 81,4); before doubled consonants (§ 490): *daṁsaantie, daṁsaamha* (Prab. 42,7; Uttarar. 77,3; 113,2); fut. *daṁsaïssaṁ* (Śak.

63,9; Ratn. 311,4), *daṁsaïssasi* (Śak. 90,10), *daṁśaïssadi* (Mālatīm. 74,3; 78,7); Mg. *daṁśaante* (Śak. 114,11).—*darisaï* (also Hc. 3,149) occurs in JM. as *darisei* (Erz.). According to Mk. fol. 74 it occurs in the form *darisedi* in Āvantī. In the Mṛcch., that plays in Āvantī, at 70,5 the Vidūṣaka uses it : *darisaanti*; at 100,4 stands in D. : *darisesi*.—*dakkhavaï*, in Sr. fol. 57 *dakkhāvaï* is a causative form *dakkhaï* and = Marāṭhī *dākhaviṇeṁ*, Gujarātī *dākhavavuṁ*[3]; A. *dĕkkhāvahi* (Vikr. 66,16) is a causative from *dĕkkhaï* The South Indian manuscripts of the drama write *dakkhaï*, whilst the Nāgarī MSS, partly the South Indian too, write *dĕkkhaï*[4], which Hc. 4, 181 teaches and what is frequent in A. (Hc. s. v. *dĕkkhaï*, Piṅgala 1,87a), on the other hand, it is false, for Ś which requires *pĕkkhadi*[5]. *dakkhaï* and *dĕkkhaï*, the inscriptions of Aśoka too have, *dakkhaï*, is attested by Singhalese in *dakinawa*, *dĕkkhaï*, in all the modern Indian languages, including Gypsy,[6] both go back to one **dṛkṣati*, that occurs in *amūdṛkṣa*, *idṛkṣa*, *etādṛkṣa*, *kidṛkṣa*, *tādṛkṣa*, *sadṛkṣā*[7]. The derivation from the future[8] is miscarried to *ĕ*, which goes back to *i*; it is possible to explain[9] the forms differently likewise to assume an analogy according to *pĕkkhaï* for *dekkhaï*[10] is unlikely. On AMg. *dehaï* see § 66.—From *bhram* the causative are also *bhamāḍai*, *bhamāḍei* according to Hc. 3,151; 4,30, for which the synonymous form *tamāḍai* (Hc. 4,30) stands, beside *bhāmei bhamāvaï*, *bhamāvei*. Gujarātī has the same causative formation[11]. Hc. 4,161 teaches *bhammaḍaï*, *bhamaḍaï*, *bhamāḍaï* also as a substitute for the simplex *bhram*.—On the fut. of the caus. see especially § 528 too, on the passive § 543.

1. GARREZ, JA. 1872,20,204.—2. WEBER, ZDMG. 26,741, 28,424; on H. 315.—3. PISCHEL on Hc. 4,32.—4. PISCHEL, GGA. 1873,46 f; Vikramorvaśīya p. 616 f.; Die Recensionen der Śākuntalā p. 11 f.—5. PISCHEL, De Kālidāse Śākuntali recensionibus p. 32f.; KB. 7.453 ff.; 8,144 ff.—6. PISCHEL, KB. 7,458; 8,146; JOHANSSON KZ. 32, 463; BEAMES, Comp. Gr. 1,161; POTT, Zigeuner 2,304; MIKLOSICH. Über die Mundarten und die Wanderungen der Zigeuner Europas 7,43.—7. WEBER, KB. 7,764 who, however, wrongly sees therein at Bhag. 1,414,3; IStr. 3,150; H.1 p. 260; KB. 7,486; IS. 14,69ff. "an old reduplication of a hitherto wanting desiderative formation".—8. CHILDERS in MUIR, OST. 2,23 note 40; KB. 7,450 f.; Dictionary s. v. *passati*; PISCHEL, KB. 7,459; 8, 147.—9, P. GOLDSCHMIDT, GN. 1874.509 ff.; JOHANSSON, KZ. 32,463 f.; Shāhbāzgarhī 2,24.—10. BEAMES, Comp. Gr. 1,162; cf., however, 3,45 f.—11. BEAMES, Comp. Gr. 3,81; HOERNLE, Comp. Gr. p. 318 f.

DESIDERATIVE

§ 555. The desiderative is formed as in Skt. : AMg. *digicchanta-* = *jighatsat-* (Āyār. 1,8,4,10); *jugucchaï*, *juucchaï* (Hc. 2,21; 4,4) = *jugupsate*; M. *juucchaï*, *juucchasu* (R.); AMg. *dugucchaï*, *duguṁchaï*, *duucchaï*, *duuṁchaï* (Hc. 4,4; cf. § 74. 215), *duguṁchamāṇa* (Āyār. 1,2,2,1; Sūyag. 472. 525), *dugaṁchamāṇa*, *dugaṁchaṇijja* (Uttar. 199.410), *adugucchiya* (Āyār. 2,1,2,2); Ś. *jugucchedi*, *jugucchanti* (Mālatīm. 90,5; 243,5), *juucchida* (Anarghar. 149, 10; Bālar. 202,13), *adijuucchida* (Mallikām. 218,7. 12); *jugucchaṇia* (Viddhaś. 121,10; so to be read); Mg. *adiyuuścida* (Mallikām. 143,4. 15; so to be read); *ciicchaï* (Hc. 2,21; 4,240) = *cikitsati*; AMg. *tigicchaï* (Uttar. 601), *tigicchiya* (Uttar. 458), *vitigicchiya* (Ṭhāṇ. 194), *vitigicchāmi* (Ṭhāṇ. 245), *vitigiṁchaï* (Sūyag. 727 f.), *vitigiṁchiya* (Vivāhap. 150); Ś. *cikicchidavva* (Śak. 123,14). Cf. § 74. 215.—Mg. *pivāśiaśi* (Veṇīs. 34,6; cf. § 550); Ś. *bubhukkhida* = *bubhukṣita* (Vṛṣabh. 19,5); *licchaï* = *lipsate* (Hc. 2,21); AMg. JM. *sussūsaï* (Dasav. 637,30, 32; Erz. 31,13) = *śuśrūṣate*; AMg. *sussūsamāṇa* (Dassav. 636,6. 10; Ovav.); Ś. *sussūsaïssaṁ* (Mṛcch. 88,11), *sussūsaïduṁ* (Mālav. 29,12), *sussūsidavva* (Mṛcch. 39,23); Mg. *śuśśūśida* (Mṛcch. 37,11).

INTENSIVE

§ 556. The intensive is formed as in classical Skt. The vowel undergoes *vṛddhi* in the reduplication : *cakkammaï* for **cākammaï* = **cākramyate* (Hc. 4,161).—AMg. *khokhubbhamāṇa* (Paṇhāv. 169. 210; Ovav.; Kappas.) from *kṣubh*.—AMg. *jāgaraï* = *jāgarti*, *jāgaramāṇie* (Vivāhap. 116), *jāgaranti* (Āyār. 1,3,1,1), *jāgaramāṇassa* (Vivāhap. 173), *paḍijāgarĕjjā* (Dasav. 636,6), *paḍijāgaramāṇi* (Uvās.; Kappas.); M. *jagganti* (Dūt. 5,12), *jaggesu* (H. 335), *paḍiaggia* = **pratijagrita* (G.); Ś. *jaggedha* (Mṛcch. 112,3); A. *jaggevā* (Hc. 4,438,3); causative AMg. *jaggāvaï* (Āyār. 1,8,2,5): M. *jaggāvia* (R. 10,56); AMg. *bhibbhisamiṇa* for **bhebhisamiṇa*, **bhĕbbhisamiṇa* from *bhisaï* = *bhāsati* (§ 482; Nāyādh. § 122; Jīv. 481 [°*bhijjha*°]. 493 [*mijhjhi*°]. 541 [*mijhjhisamāṇi*], *bhibbhisamāṇa* (Jīv, 105; cf. v. l. on Nāyādh. § 122); AMg. *lālappaï* (Sūyag. 414), *lālappamāṇa* (Āyār. 1,2,3,3; 1,2,6,1). In the reduplication the nasal vowel stands M. *caṁkammanta*- (H.), *caṁkammia* (R.), *caṁkamia* (Karp. 47,6), JM. *caṁkamiyavva* (Āv. 23,12) = *caṁkramyate*; *ḍhuṁḍhullaï* (Hc. 4,161. 189), *ḍhaṁḍhallaï* (Hc. 4,161), *ḍhaṁḍholai* (Hc. 4,189) have a nasal vowel. For *ṭuṇṭuṇṇanto* (Kāvyaprakāśa 271,5 = H. 985) we should, according to the best manuscripts or the text and the commentary read with Abhinavagupta on Dhvanyāloka 116,7 *ḍhuṁḍhullanto*. This reading is proved also by the quotations of the stanza in other unpublished rhetoricians.

DENOMINATIVE

§ 557. The denominatives are formed, as in Skt., either by 1) addition of the verbal endings directly to the stem of the noun, 2) or to the stem in -*a*- = Skt. -*ya*-, before which the final vowel of the noun is lengthened or 3) to the stem of the causative Pkt. -*e*-, -*ve*-, -*va*-. The first type of denominative is more frequent in Pkt. than in Skt. : AMg. *appiṇāmi* = **arpaṇāmi* (Nirayāv. § 23; Nāyādh. 1313; text °*ppa*°), JM. *appiṇaï* (Āv. 44,3) from *arpaṇa*; AMg. *paccappiṇāmi* = **pratyarpaṇāmi* from *pratyarpaṇa*[1] (Nirayāv. § 20), *paccappiṇaï* (Vivāgas. 222; Rāyap. 231; Kappas. § 29; Ovav. § 42. 44. 46 [so to be read here throughout]), *paccappiṇāmo* (Nirayāv. § 25), *paccappiṇanti* (Vivāhap. 503. 948; Jīv. 625. 626; Uvās. § 207; Kappas. § 58. 101; Nāyādh. § 33. 100. p. 610; Nirayāv. § 4.24), *paccappiṇĕjjā* (Paṇṇav. 844; Ovav. § 150), *paccappiṇāhi* (Ovav. § 40. 41. 43. 45; Nirayāv. § 22; Kappas. § 26), *paccappiṇaha* (Vivāgas. 222; Vivāhap. 503. 948; Jīv. 625. 626; Kappas. § 57. 100; Nirayāv. § 20. 21. 24; Uvās. § 206), *paccappiṇijjaï* (Nirayāv. § 25), *paccappiṇittā* (Nāyādh. 607. 610. 614); *kham-*

maï=**khanmati*, *jammaï*=**janmati*, **hammaï*=*hanmati* (§ 540); M. *dukkhāmi* (R. 11, 127) from *duḥkha*, like *suhāmi* (H. 617) from *sukha*[2]; *dhavalaï* (Hc. 4,24); *nimmāṇaï* (Hc. 4,19; Kī. 4,46; Mk. fol. 54) from *nirmāṇa*; A. *paḍibimbi* (Hc. 4,439,3); A. *pamāṇahu*=*pramāṇayata* (Piṅgala 1,105); *pahuppaï*=**prabhutvati* (§ 286); M. *maṇḍanti* (G. 67); *missaï* (Hc. 4,28) from *miśra*; *vikkeaï* (Hc. 4,240) from *vikreya*; A. *sukkahī* (Hc. 4,427,1) from *śuṣka*. More examples see under § 491 and cf. § 553.

1. LEUMANN, Aup. S. s. v. seeks in *paccappiṇ* the present stem of *praty-arp*. According to JACOBI, KZ. 35,573, note 2 *iṇaī* is the derivative syllable, by which probably the same is meant as in LEUMANN. That a noun *paccappiṇa* is not found is naturally no ground against the aforesaid explanation.—2. These and similar forms may be considered as contracted from *dukkhaāmi*, *suhaāmi* (§ 558).

§ 558. As in Skt., so in Pkt. too, the usual formation of the denominative is that with *-a-*=Skt. *-ya-*. The syllables *-āa-* in M. JM. AMg. are not seldom contracted: M. *atthāaï*, *atthāanti*=**astāyate*, **astāyante* from *asta* (G. R.); from the frequent *atthamia* (G. R.)=*astamita* have been deduced *atthamaï* (R.) and a substantive *atthamaṇa* (H. R.); AMg. *amarāẏaï* (Āẏār. 1,2,5,5); M. *alasāaï*, *alasāanti* (H.); M. *umhāi*, *umhāanta*, *umhāamāṇa* (G.) from *ūṣmāya-*; Ś. *kuravaāadi*=*kurabakāyate* (Mṛcch. 73,10); *garuāi*, *garuāaï* (to become a teacher; to behave like a teacher; Hc. 3,138); Mg. *cilāadi*=*cirāyati* (Śak. 115,9); M. *taṇuāi*, *taṇuāaï*, *taṇuāae*=**tanukāyati* (to become thin; H.); M. *dhūmāi* (H.); AMg. *mamāẏamāṇa*, *amamāẏamāṇa* from *mama* (Āẏār. 1,2,3,3; 1,2,5,3); *lohiāi*, *lahiāaï* (Hc. 3,138); M. *saṁjhāaï* (G. 632). Ś. *saṁjhāadi* (Mṛcch. 73,12)=*saṁdhyāyate*; Ś. *sidalāadi*=*śitalāyati* (Mālatīm. 121,2); M. *suhāaï* (H.), Ś. *suhāadi* (Śak. 49,8)=*sukhāyati*. Worthy of being particularly mentioned are the large number of denominativa that express onomatopoetically, a sound, a strong physical or mental movement, etc. They are found mostly also in the modern Indian dialects, many in Skt. too, here partly only in the basic form, to which they are traced back[1]. The examples *damadamāi*, *damadamāaï* (Hc. 3,138) "does *damadama*", used for the sound of a drum,=Marāṭhī *damadamṇeṁ*[2], indicate the type. More seldom they are formed like the causativa. So: Ś. *kaḍakaḍāanta-* (Mālatīm. 129,4).—Ś. *kurukurāasi* (so to be read; cf. v. l.; Hāsy. 25,7), *kurukurāadi* (Mṛcch. 71,16; Ratn. 302,8), *kurukurāanta-* (Karp. 14,3;70,1); *kurukuria* (ardently desired; Deśīn. 2,42), whence *kurukura* in Hc., Uṇādigaṇasūtra 17); AMg. *kiḍikiḍiẏābhūẏa* (Vivāgas. 201. 242 [text here °*ḍibhū*°)]. —AMg. *kuukūvamāṇa* (Vivāgas. 201); JM. *khalakkhalei* (Erz.); AMg. *gumagumāẏanta-* (Kappas. § 37), also *gumagumanta-* (Ovav. § 4). *gumagumāiẏa* (Ovav. § 5); Ś. *ghumaghumāadi* (Jīvān. 43,3)[3]; AMg. *guluguleṅta-* (for the trumpet of the elephant; Ovav. § 42), *gulaguleṅta-* (Uvās. § 102); AMg. JM. *gulugulāiẏa* (Paṅhāv. 161 [°*la*°]; Vivāhap. 253; Ovav. § 54 p. 59,7; Erz.; JM. *ghurughuranti* (for the grunting of the wild boar; Erz. 43,10); Mg. *ghulaghulāamāṇa* (Mṛcch. 117.23), from which Skt. *ghurughura* in Hc. l. c. and others; *ṭiriṭillaï* with dissimilation (Hc. 4,161); M. *tharatharei* (H. 187 [so to be read with v. l.]. 858), *tharatharĕnti* (H. 165 [so to be read with R]); JM. *tharatharantī* (Āv. 12,25; text °*ha*°); Ś. *tharatharedi* (Mṛcch. 141,17; so to be read with GOḌABOLE 388,4), *tharatharāanta-* (Mālatīm. 124,1) = Skt. *tharatharāyate*, Marāṭhī (*tharatharṇeṁ*, Urdū *tharatharānā*[4], Gujarātī *tharatharvuṁ* "to tremble"; AMg. *dhagadhaganta-* (Nāyādh. 340), explained as *jājvalyamāna*, *dhagadhagāiya* (Kappas. § 46); Ś. *dhagadhaggaamāṇa* (Jīvān. 89,2); JM. AMg. *dhamadhamĕnta-* (Erz.; Uvās.), Ś. *dhamadhamāadi* (Nāgān. 18,3); JM. *phuraphuranta-* (Erz. 85,5); Ś. *phuraphurāadi* (Mṛcch. 17,15); AMg. *maghamaghĕnta-* (Ovav. § 2; Nāyādh. § 21 [°*ghi*°]; Rāyap. 28. 111; Jīv. 543; Samav. 210), *maghamaghanta-* (Kappas. [also °*ghi*°]; Rāyap. 60. 190; Jīv. 499; Vivāhap. 941); M. *mahamahaï* (Hc. 4,78; H.), JM. *mahamahiya* (Pāiyal. 197) = Marāṭhī *maghamaghṇeṁ*, Gujarātī *maghamaghvuṁ*[5]; AMg. *masamasāvijjaï* (Vivāhap. 270.383); AMg. JM. *misimisanta-*, *misimisĕnta-*, *misimisinta-* (Ovav.; Nāyādh.; Kappas.; Rāyap. 44; Āv. 40,6), usually *misimisimāṇa* or °*semāṇa* (Vivāgas. 121. 144; Nāyādh. 324. 456. 612. 651. 1172; Vivāhap. 236. 237. 251. 254. 505. 1217 etc.; Nirayāv.; Uvās.) is explained as *dedipyamāna* and taken into Skt. as *miṣamiṣāyate*; Ś. *silasilāadi* (Jīvān. 43,3); M. *simisimanta-* (H. 561), Ś. *simisimāanta-* (Bālar. 264, 2); M. *surasuranta-* (H. 74) = Marāṭhī; *surasurneṁ*[6]; JM. *sulusulĕnta-* (Erz. 24,29).—M. *dhukkādhukkaï* (H. 584) = Marāṭhī *dhukadhukṇeṁ*[7]; AMg. *harāharāiya* (Paṇhāv. 161) have a strengthened vowel. Cf. also Ś. *susuāadi* (Mṛcch. 44,3) "does *su- su*" and Ś. *sāsāasi*, Mg. *kākāaśi* (Mṛcch. 80, 14. 15) derived from *sā* and *kā* respectively.

1. BEAMES, Comp. Gr. 3,89 ff.; ZACHARIAE, GGA. 1898,465 ff, who has collected together the Pkt. examples, particularly from H. and Erz.—2. PISCHEL on Hc. 3,138.—3. JACOBI on Kappas. § 36 p. 105; cf. ZACHARIAE, l. c. p. 466 note 2.—4. STENZLER on Mṛcch. 141, 17 p. 309.—5. PISCHEL on Hc. 4,78; cf. JACOBI on Kappas. § 32 p. 104.—6. WEBER on H. 74.—7. WEBER on H. 584.

§ 559. Built according to the pattern of the causativa the denominativa are : AMg. *uccārei* (caus.) *vā pāsavaṇei vā khelei vā siṅghāṇei vā vantei vā pittei vā* (Vivāhap. 112); AMg. *uvakkhaḍei* = **upaskṛtayati* (Nāyādh. 425. 448), °*ḍinti* (Nāyādh. 856), °*ḍĕjja*, °*ḍie* (Āyār. 2,2,2.2), °*ḍeu* (Uvās. § 68), °*ḍeha* (Nāyādh. 483), more frequently *uvakkhaḍāvei* (Vivāgas. 124. 133. 195. 204. 205. 231. 233; Nāyādh. 430. 632. 734. 736. 1423. 1496), °*ḍāvinti*, *ḍāvĕnti* (Kappas. § 104; Nāyādh. § 114), °*ḍāvĕttā* (Nāyādh. § 114; p. 425. 448. 482; Vivāhap. 228); AMg. *ṇhāṇei* = **snānayati* (Jīv. 610), *ṇhāṇĕnti* (Vivāhap. 1265); *teavaï* = **tejapayati* from *tea-* = *tejaḥ* (Hc. 4,152); JM. *dukkhāvei* (Āv. 42,14. 18), caus. from *dukkhāmi* (§ 557); *duhāvaï* = **dvidhāpayati* (splits; Hc. 4,124); JM. *dhirāvia* (Sagara 8,14); AMg. *piṇaddhei* (Nāyādh. 775 [text °*ddhaï*]. 779); Ś. *piṇaddhāvida* (Śak. 74,1); M. *biuṇei* (text *vi*°; H. 685) = *dviguṇayati*; M. *bhasaṇemi* (so to be read; H. 312) from *bhasman* (ashes); AMg. *maïlinti* (Paṇhāv. 111), *maïliya* (Vivāhap. 387), M. *maïlei*, *maïlĕnti*, *maïlanta*, *maïlijjaï* from *maïla* (dirt; black)[1]; M. *lahuei* = *laghayati* (G. 1148); M. *saccavaï* = *satyāpayati* (Hc. 4,181; Kī. 14 in DELIUS, Radices p. 11; the edition has at 4,66 false *sacchara*), *saccavia* (Pāiyal. 78; G. H. R; Śak. 120,7); Ś. *saddāvemi* = *śabdāpayāmi* (Mṛcch. 50,24), *saddāvesi* (Śak. 138,2); AMg. *saddāvei* (Kappas.; Ovav.; Nāyādh.; Nirayāv. etc.); Ś. *saddāvedi* (Mṛcch. 54,8; 141,16), *saddāvehi* (Mṛcch. 54,5), *saddāvaïssaṁ*

(Mṛcch. 60,1), *saddāviadi* (Mṛcch. 150,17); JM. AMg. *saddāvěttā*, °*vittā*, *saddāviỳa* (Erz.; Kappas. etc.), causative from *saddei* = *śabdayati*; AMg. *sikkhāvei* (Nāỳādh. 1421 f.). Ś. *sikkhāvehi* (Ratn. 293,17) from *śikṣā*; Ś. *sidalāvedi* (Uttarar. 121,7) from *śitala*; Ś, *sukkhavianti* (Mṛcch. 71,4.) Mg. *śuskāvaïśśaṁ* (Mṛcch. 133,15) from *śuṣka*; M. *suhāvesi*, °*vei*, °*věnti* (G. H.), Ś. *suhāvedi* (Mallikām. 201,17) from *sukha*.

1. Cf. ZACHARIAE, GN. 1896, 265 ff., who derives *maïla* from **mṛdilá*. See also § 595, note 5.

VERBAL NOUNS

a) PARTICIPLES

§ 560. The present participle of the parasmaipada is formed from the present stem with the ending *-anta*, extended from the strong ending *-ant*, that is inflected according to the *a*-declension (§397. 473—514). Dialectically, especially, in AMg., we find in a large number of forms that sporadically show the flexion of Skt. (§ 396), formed also according to the pattern of the monostemic nouns (§ 398). In all classes the feminine ends in *-anti* : AMg. *asantie* = *asatyām* (Ovav. § 183), JM. *santī* (Erz. 8,22), but in the meaning "chaste" M. *saī*, (H.) = *satī* "not chaste" *asaī* (H.) = *asatī*; AMg. *ĕjjantiṁ* = **eyantīm* (cf. § 561; Dasav. 635,10), *viṇimuỳantiṁ* = *vinimuñcantīm* (*Jīv. 542*) *aṇuhŏntī* = *anubhavantī* (*Paṇṇav. 137*); M. *apāvantī* = *aprāpnuvatī* (H. 483); Ś. *huvaṁtī*, *pĕkkhaṁtī*, *gacchaṁtī* (Lalitav. 555,5; 560,11; 561,14), *pasaṁsantīo* = *praśaṁsantyaḥ* (Bālar. 289,2), *uddīvantī*, *bhaṇantī*, *paḍhantīe* (Mṛcch. 2,22; 41,20; 44,2) etc. According to Vr. 7,11; Hc. 3,182 the feminine may be formed also from the weak stem of the verbs of the first conjugation : *hasaī* = **hasatī* = *hasantī*; *vevaī* = **vepatī* = *vepamānā*.—Particip. fut. parasmaip. are : AMg, *āgamissaṁ* (nom. neuter, and accus. masc.; Āỳār. 1,3,3,3), *bhavissaṁ* = *bhaviṣyat* (Kappas. § 17), that may be derived also from *bhaviṣya*, as in JM. *bhavissacakkavaṭṭi* (Erz. 12,25) and Ś. *bhavissakuṭṭaṇi* (Viddhaś. 51,11; Karp. 13,2). The participle in the parasmaipada of the causative (§ 551-554), the desiderative (§ 555), the intensive (§ 556) and the denominatives have the same ending.

§ 561. The parasmaipada present participle, without distinction of conjugation, is built from the present stem (§ 473-514) mostly in *-māṇa* = Skt. *māna* (Vr. 7,10; Hc. 3,181). It is particularly frequent in AMg. in which the parasmaipada present participle has, on the other hand, entirely receded back[1]. It often stands in AMg. beside the finite verb in the parasmaipada. So e.g. *aḍamāṇe aḍaï* (Vivāhap. 191); *phusamāṇe phusaï* (Vivāhap. 354. 355); *paccakkhāi paccakkhamāṇe* (Vivāhap. 607); *haṇamāṇe haṇaï*, *saddahaï asaddahamāṇe*, *saṁvĕllamāṇe saṁvĕllei* (Vivāhap. 849 f. 1215. 1325); *pehaï*, *pehamāṇe* (Paṇṇav. 435); *vigiñcamāṇe vigiñcaï* (Āỳār. 1,3,4,3); *pāsamāṇe pāsaï*, *suṇamāṇe suṇei*, *mucchamāṇe mucchaï* (Āỳār. 1,1,5,2.3), *āikkhamāṇā āikkhaha* (Ovav. § 59). As in Pāli, so in AMg. JM. too, from *as* (to be) is formed an ātmanepada present participle *samāṇa* (Āỳār. 2,1,1,1 ff.; Ṭhāṇ. 525. 526; Vivāgas. 13. 116. 239; Paṇhāv. 67; Vivāhap. 263. 271. 1275. 1388; Paṇṇav.

436; Uvās.; Kappas.; Niraẏāv.; Erz.; Sagara 4,9; Āv. 29, 16; 35,25 etc.).—*emāṇa* = *praviśan* (Deśīn. 1,144) is = *ayamāna*, AMg. *ĕjjamāṇa* (Uvās § 81.215. 261; Vivāgas. 229; Nāẏādh. 487. 491. 514. 575. 758. 760 etc.; Vivāhap. 1207) = *eyamāna*; cf. *ĕjjantiṁ* § 560.—To the precative belongs *hŏjjamāṇa* (§ 466).

1. WEBER, Bhag. 1,432.

§ 562. The ātmanepada participle has the same ending in the future: AMg. *esamāṇa* (Ṭhāṇ. 178), in the causative (§ 551-554), the desiderative (§ 555), intensive (§ 556), the denominatives (§ 557-559). In the passive partly the ending of the parasmaipada is used, particularly in Ś. Mg., and partly that of the ātmanepada, especially in AMg. (§535-548).—In place of *-māṇa*, sometimes in AMg. is found *-miṇa* : *āgamamiṇa* (Āẏār. 1,6, 3,2; 1,7,4,1; 1,7,6,2; 1,7,7,1); *samaṇujāṇamiṇa* (Āẏār. 1,6,4,2; 1,7,1,3); *āḍhāẏamiṇa* (Āẏar. 1,7,1,1; 1,7,2,4.5); *aṇāḍhāẏamiṇa* (Āẏār. 1,7,1,2); *apariggahamiṇa* (Āẏār. 1,7,3,1); *amamāẏamiṇa* (Āẏār. 1,7,3,2); *āsāemiṇa* = *āsvādayamāna* (Āẏār. 1,7,6,2); *aṇāsāẏamiṇa* (Āẏār. 2,3,2,4); *nikāmamiṇa* (Sūẏag. 405); *bhisamiṇa* (Nāẏādh. § 122; Jīv. 481. 493 [commentary °*mā*°; cf. 541 *bhisamāṇi*]), *bhibbhisamiṇa* (§ 556). The form that is found also in the inscriptions of Aśoka[1] is almost restricted to Āẏār., and in many cases has the v. l. *-māṇa*. Cf. § 110.—Very seldom is the ending *-āṇa* = Skt. *-āna* : AMg. *buẏābuẏāṇā* = *bruvanto 'bruvantaś ca* (Sūẏag. 334). *vihammāṇa* stands for *vihammamāṇa* = *vighnan* (Uttar. 787), in case one does not like to equate it as = **vihanmāna* (cf. § 540. 550), *vakkamāṇa* (Nāẏādh. § 46-50) for *vakkamamāṇa*, as e.g. at Kappas. § 74. 76. 77 stands; the v. l., however, has there also under § 74.76 *vakkamāṇa*. For *-aṇa* M. has *-iṇa* in *meliṇa* (H. 702) from *melaī* from *mil* (§ 486). Cf. Skt. *āsina*, as also Pkt. has.

1. BÜHLER, ZDMG. 46,72, whose explanation, however is incorrect. See § 110.

§ 563. The feminine has the ending *-māṇā* according to Vr. 7,11, but according to Hc. 3,182 *-māṇī*. In AMg. the ending throughout is *-māṇī* : *samāṇī*, *saṁlavamāṇī*, *āhāremāṇī*, *abhisiccamāṇī*, *uddhuvvamāṇīhiṁ* (Kappas.); *bhuñjamāṇī*, *āsāemāṇī*, *uvadaṁsemāṇī*, (Uvās.); *paccaṇubhavamāṇī*, *parihāẏamāṇī*, *uddhuvvamāṇīhiṁ* (Ovav.); *visaṭṭamāṇiṁ* (Ṭhāṇ. 312); *roẏamāṇī* (Vivāgas. 84; Vivāhap. 807); *suẏamāṇie* (Vivāhap. 116), *dehamāṇī* (Vivāhap. 794. 795); *viṇimmuẏamāṇī* (Vivāhap. 822); *ĕjjamāṇio* (Niraẏāv. 59); *duruhamāṇī* (Dasav. 620,33); *jāgaramāṇie* (Vivāhap. 116); *paḍijāgaramāṇī* (Kappas.; Uvās.); *ḍajjhamāṇie*, *dijjamāṇiṁ* (Uttar. 284. 362); *dhikkārijjamāṇī*, *dhikkārijjamāṇī*, *thukkārijjamāṇī* (Nāẏādh. 1175). Likewise in JM. : *samāṇī* (Kk. 260,29; Erz. 36,14; false °*ṇā* 53,5); *karemāṇio*, *pehamāṇio* (Āv. 11,14; 17,10); *paḍicchamāṇī*, *jhāẏamāṇī*, *paloemāṇī*, *kuṇamāṇī*, *khannamāṇie*, *nivaḍamāṇī*, *ruẏamāṇī* (Erz. 8,14; 11, 19; 17,8; 23,13; 39,7; 43,19), *karemāṇī* (Dvār. 503,30). From M. WEBER has in H. : *pasūamāṇāe* (123), *bhaṇṇamāṇā* (145), *jampamāṇā* (198), *majjamāṇāe* (246), *veamāṇāe* (312), but *jampamāṇie* (389). The recension R has only at 198 °*ṇā*, elsewhere althrough °*ṇie*, also at 145, where it reads *bhaṇamāṇie*, the recension of Bhuvanapāla (IS. 16,1 ff.), throughout has °*ṇī*, °*ṇie*, as also mostly S and T. *ī* is not merely a characteristic for R[1] and Bhuvanapāla, that is to say both Jaina recensions. On the basis of the usual agreement of M. with JM. AMg. for M. too *i*, not *ā*, will be correct. In other texts in M. examples are wanting. In Ś. the femin. always ends in *-ā*: *ṇivattamāṇā*, *vaṭṭamāṇā*, °*ṇāe* (Vikr. 5,11; 35,11. 12); *apaḍivajjamāṇā* (Vikr. 52,14); *ahibhūaamāṇa*, *āuliamāṇā*, *ahiṇandiamāṇā* (Śak. 16,10; 17,12; 79,10); *bādhiamāṇā* (Vikr. 28,1); *aṇuniamāṇā* (Mṛcch. 23,23. 25); *siccamāṇā* (Mālatīm. 121,2).—P: has *cintayamāṇi* (Hc. 4,310).

1. WEBER, Hāla[2] p. xxix; cf. on. H. 123.

§ 564. The past passive participle, as in Skt., is formed with the suffixes *-ta* and *-na*. Deviating from Skt. *-ta* in certain cases is added directly to the roots, where Skt. adds it after the *i*-stem: *ohaṭṭha* (ridiculed; Deśīn. 1,153) = **apahasta* = *apahasita* = (§ 155); *khuṭṭa* (torn; Deśīn. 2,74; cf. § 568); *laṭṭha* (attracted towards another; lively; friendly; Deśīn. 7,26) = **laṣṭa* = *laṣita*. In AMg. the word is *lāḍha* according to § 66. 304 (Āẏār. 2, 3,1, 8; Sūẏag. 401; Uttar. 76. 453. 454), explained by the commentators as *sādhu*, *sādhvanuṣṭhāne tatpara*, *sudanuṣṭhānatayā pradhāna*, etc. Cf. also Skt. *rāḍhā* M. *vuttha* (Pāiẏal. 225; R. 11,88. 90), *uvvuttha* (G. 538), *paüttha* (H. R.); JM. *pavuttha* (Āv. 23,7; 25,7), *paüttha* (Erz.); M. *paḍiuttha* (R. 4,50), for which according to C we should read *pariuttha* (Deśīn. 6,13) or *parivuttha* (G. 540) from *vas* (to live) = **vasta* with secondary change of *a* to *u* (§ 104. 303). Beside them is found the regular M. *usia* = *uṣita* (G. 484. 933) and from the present stem M. *vasia* (Pāiẏal. 225; G. H.), *uvvasia*, *pavasia* (H.), Ś. *uvavasida* (Mṛcch. 54,16).—M. *ṇiattha* = **nivasta* (Karp. 46,12) from *vas* (to dress), AMg. *paṇiẏattha* = **pranivasta* (Ovav. [§ 38]). JM. *niẏatthiẏa* (Erz. 59,31) is *nivastrita*. Cf. § 337.—JM. *tuṭṭa* = *truṭita* (Erz. 71,28), A. *tuṭṭaü* (Hc. 4,356).—AMg. *aṇālatta* = **anālapta* (Uvās. § 58); JM. *saṁlatta* (Erz.).—A. *tinta* = *timita* (Hc. 4,431,1).—M. *guttha* = **guphta* = *guphita* (H. 63; Karp. 69.8; 73,10)[1]. *grah* adds, as in the infinitive (§ 574) and the absol. (§ 586), the ending to the *-i-* and not to the *-ī-* stem (Hc. 1,101); M. *gahia* (G. H. R.; Śak. 120,6) JM. *gahiẏa* (Erz.; Āv. 17,11; 18,4; Dvār. 500,20; 501,2; Kk.); AMg. *gahiẏa* (Uvās.; Ovav.; Kappas.; Nāẏādh.); JŚ. Ś. *gahida* (Pav. 389,1; Mṛcch. 3,23; 15,5; 50,2; 53,10; Śak. 33,14; 40,4; 96,9; Vikr. 19,16; 31,13; 80,15,20); Mg. *gahida* (Mṛcch. 16,14. 17.21; 133,7; 157,5) and *gihida* (Mṛcch. 112,10). The texts of the dramas very often have *gahīda* and *gihīda*, the forms, that are correct in verses only, as Mg. *gahiḍa* (Mṛcch. 17,1; 170,15).

1. Differently WEBER on H. 63.

§ 565. Very frequently in all the dialects the past passive participle is formed from the present stem. Examples in order of sequence of the present stem are: *tavia* (Hc. 2,105) beside Ś. *saṁtappida* (Mṛcch. 7,18; 8,16) according to the 4th conjugation and the common *tatta* = *tapta*; AMg. *tasiẏa* beside *tattha* = *trasta* (Vivāhap. 1291); Ś. *jaṇida* = *jāta* (Lalitav. 561,3; Mṛcch. 28,8); M. *asahia* = *asoḍha* (G.); AMg. *jaṭṭha* = *iṣṭa* (offered; Uttar. 753); A. *jiṇia* (§ 473); Ś. *aṇubhavida* (Karp. 33,6) = *anubhūta*; M. *vāharia* = *vyāhṛta* (Śak. 88,1); M. *osaria* = *avasṛta* (G. H. R.), *samosaria* (G. H.); AMg. JM. *samosariẏa* = *samavasṛta* (H.; Vivāgas. 151; Uvās.; Niraẏāv.; Āv. 31,22; cf. § 235); Mg. *niśśalidaśśa* = *niḥsṛtasya* (Lalitav. 566,15); Ś.

sumarida, Mg. *śumalida* = *smṛta*, M. *visaria*, *visaria*, JM. *vissariya*, JŚ. *visarida*, Ś. *visumarida* = *vismṛta* (§ 478); Mg. *gāida* (Mṛcch. 117,4); Ś. *ṇijjhāida* (Mṛcch. 93,15; Vikr. 52,11); JM. *acchiya* from *ṛ* (Āv. 26,28; Erz. 33,30): M. *icchia* (H.R.), AMg. JM. *icchiya* (Uttar. 702; Vivāhap. 161. 946; Ovav. § 54; Uvās.; Kappas.; Āv. 39,6; Kk. 274,26; Erz.); S. *icchida* (Vikr. 20, 19), AMg. JM. *paḍicchiya* (Ovav. § 54; Vivāhap. 161. 946; Āv. 39,6); Ś. *paḍicchida* (Mṛcch. 77,25; 161,5; Śak. 79,9; Mālatīm. 140,9; 250,5), both of them belong to *iṣ*, not to *ips* (§ 328); *jigghia* = *ghrāta* (Deśīn. 3,46); Ś. *aṇuciṭṭhida* (Mṛcch. 54,2; 63,25; Vikr. 80,15; Mālav. 45,14; 70,3; Mudrār. 266,3); M. *pucchia* (H.), JM. *pucchiya* (Erz.; Sagar. 2,8). Ś. *pucchida* (Mṛcch. 28,21; Mālav. 6,10), beside AMg, *puṭṭha* (Uttar. 31. 113); Ś. *ṇiṇhuvida* (Śak. 137,6); M. *ṇaccia*, *paṇaccia* from *nṛt* (H.); AMg. *paḍiyāikkhiya* (Kappas.; Ovav. § 86) beside *paccakkhāa* = *pratyākhyāta* (Ovav. § 87); AMg. *buiya* (Āyār. 1,8,1,20; 1,8,2,1; Uttar. 509) = **bruvita*, *ahābuiya* = **yathābruvita* (Sūyag. 531) from the present stem *bruva*-(§ 494); *duhia* = *dugdha* (Deśīn. 1,7); A. *haṇia* = *hata* (Piṅgala 1,85. 146a) beside *hatta* (§ 194); Ś. *ācakkhida* (§ 499); M. AMg. JM. Ś. *āḍhatta* (Pāiyal. 240; Hc. 2, 138; G. H.; R. s.v. *rabh*; Ṭhāṇ. 511; Vivāhap. 34,433; Paṇṇav. 540; Rāyap. 78; Erz.; Dvār. 496,13; 498,14.37; Sagara 4,5; 7,11; T. 6,20; 7,3. 15; Āv. 12,24; 44,2; Mallikām. 223,12; 252,13); M. *samāḍhatta* (H.); M. JM. Ś. *viḍhatta* (Hc. 4,258; G. R.; Erz.; Mṛcch. 2,23; Anarghar. 275,7; 290,2), A. *viḍhattũ* (Hc. 4,422,4) from the stem *dadh*- from *dhā* = **dhatta* for *hita*, in case one does not like to derive it from the causative (§ 286). Cf. § 223. **dhatta* perhaps in AMg. sticks to *nidhatta* (v. l. *nihatta*; Ṭhāṇ. 496, explained by the commentator as *nikācita* [sic], *miścita*; *jaḍha* (relinquished; Hc. 4,258), AMg. *vijaḍha* (Uttar. 1045. 1047. 1052. 1055. 1058. 1066. 1071. 1074. 1077. 1095. Jīv. 236 f.), *vippajaḍha* (Āyār. 1,6,6,6; Nirayāv. § 16; Vivāgas. 239; Nāyādh. 435, 442. 1167. 1444; Vivāhap. 454; Aṇuog. 50. 596 [text here °*ḍḍha*]) from a root *jah* for **jāḍha*, with a short vowel according to § 67, deduced from the present *jahaï* (§ 500); AMg. also *vippajahiya* (Nāyādh. 1448); AMg. *tacchiya* (Uttar. 596); JM. *vitthariya* = *vistṛta* (Erz.); Ś. *viciṇida* = *vicita* (Mālatīm. 297,5); A. *pāvia* (Hc. 4,387,1); A. *bhañjia* (Piṅgala 1,120a); AMg. JM. *viuvviya* (Ovav.; Nāyādh.; Av. 30,18) and *veuvviya* (Āyār. p. 127,14; Dvār. 507,28) from *viuvvaï* (§ 508); cf. *vikurvita*; M. *jāṇia* (Hc. 4,7), *jāṇida* (Mṛcch. 27,21; 28, 17. 24; 29,14; 82,15; 148,23; 166, 9; Mudrār. 184,4; Viddhaś. 29,2), *aṇabhijāṇida* (Mṛcch. 153,2), *paccabhiāṇida* (Uttarar. 61,7; 62,7); Mg. *yāṇida* (Lalitav. 566,8); A. *jāṇiu* (Hc. 4,377, 423,1; Vikr. 55,1 [so to be read]). M. has *ṇāa* (R.), JM. *nāya* (Erz.; Kk.), Ś. in composita usually *ṇāda* = Skt. *jñāta*, as *abbhaṇuṇṇāda* (Śak. 84,11; Vikr. 12,14; 29,13; 39,20; 46,3; 84,2; Mudrār. 46,8), *viṇṇāda* (Mṛcch. 37,21; Śak. 73,5; 168,15; Vikr. 29.21; 80,4; Mālav. 46,16; 47,3), *aviṇṇāda* (Mālav. 34,7), *paḍiṇṇāda* (Mālav. 13,9; 85,2); Ś. *kiṇida*, *vikkiṇida* from *krī* (§ 511).—On *ṇia* = *nīta* and composita see § 81, on *khāa*, *dhāa* § 165, on *āa* § 167, on *chūḍha* and composita § 166, on *uvviḍha* § 126, on **vutta*, **vūḍha* and composita § 337, on the participle AMg. Mg. in -*ḍa* § 219, on *ūsaḍha*, *nisaḍha*, *visaḍha*, *samosaḍha* § 67; on causative, desiderative, intensive, denominative § 551-559. The feminine ends in *-ā*, only in A. Sometimes also in *-i*, as *ruddhi* = *ruddhā*, *diṭṭhi* = *dṛṣṭā* (Hc. 4,422,14; 431,1).

§ 566. The suffix *-na* is used not only in the same cases as in Skt., but has undergone a very wide extension[1] : *khaṇṇa* (cavity; Deśīn. 2,66), beside AMg. JM. *khatta* (Deśīn. 2,66; Vivāgas. 102; Erz.)[2], AMg. *ukkhatta* (Vivāgas. 114). M. *ukkhāa* (H.), *ukkhaa* (G. R.), *samukkhaa* (H.); cf. Vr. 1,10; Hc. 1,67; JM. *khaẏa* (Erz.) and *khaṇiẏa* (Erz.), *ukkhaẏa* (Erz.); Ś. *ukkhaṇida* (Uttarar. 100,7; so to be read).—M. Ś. *cukka* from **cukna* (Pāiẏal. 191; H. R.; Viddhaś. 63,1) from *cukkaï* (Hc. 4,177), Ś. *cukkadi* (Viddhaś. 93,2), which is common in the new Indian languages[3] and stands as *cukk* in Dhātupāṭha too[4].—M. *chikka* (touched; Pāiẏal. 85; Hc. 2, 138; H. 481 [so to be read with R]) = **chikna* from **chik*, a guttural sideform from **chip*, *chivaï*[5].—M. JM. AMg. *ḍakka* (bitten; Hc. 2,2; H. s. v. *daś*; Erz.; Paṇhāv. 65.537; Ṭhāṇ. 431) = **dakna*, also in the sense of "seized with the teeth" Deśīn. 4,6).—*diṇṇa*, JM. AMg. also *dinna*, from **didna* with the old reduplication vowel *i*[6], very frequent in all the dialects (Vr. 8,62; Hc. 1,46; 2,43; Pāiẏal. 184) : M. (G. H. R.) ; JM. (Kī. 11. 15; Āv. 17,20; 27,13; Erz.; Kk.; Ṛṣabhap.) ; AMg. (Uvās.; Kappas.; Ovav. etc.) ; JŚ. (Kattig. 402. 363. 364. 366) ; Ś. (e.g. Mṛcch. 37,8; 44,3; 51,23; Śak. 59,7; 159, 12; Vikr. 48,2; Ratn. 291,1) ; Mg. (Mṛcch. 113,20; 117,7;126,7; Śak. 113,8) ; A. (Vikr. 67,19; Hc. s. v. *dā*). Hc. 1,46 teaches also *datta*, that stands in PG. 7,48 as *datā* = *dattā*, but elsewhere found only in proper nouns, as *dattajasa* (PG. 6,21), *devadatto* (Hc. 1,46), Ś. *somadatto* (Vikr. 7,2)[7].—M. *buḍḍa*, *ābuḍḍa*, *ṇibuḍḍa* (H. 37; so to be read). *viṇibuḍḍa* (G. 490) from *bruḍ*, *vruḍ*, with the denominatives *buḍḍaï*, *āuḍḍaï*, *ṇiuddaï* (Hc. 4,101; cf. Vr. 8,68).—Ś. *bhulla* for **bhulna* (Karp. 113,1) from which *bhullaï*, occurring in the new Indian languages[8] (Hc. 4,177).—M. *ummilla* (G. H. R.), *ṇimilla* (G. R.), *oṇimilla* (R.) = **mīlna* from *mil*.—*mukka* from **mukna* from *muc*, very frequent in the main dialects (Hc. 2,2); M. *mukka*, *ava*°, *ā*°, *ummukka*, *pa*°, *paḍi*°, *pari*° (G. H. R.); JM. *mukka* (Āv. 23,21; Erz.; Ṛṣabhap.; Kk.). *āmukka* (Āv. 38,12), *pa*°, *pari*°, (Erz.) *vi*° (Erz.; Ṛṣabhap.); AMg. *mukka* (Uttar. 706. 708; Uvās.; Kappas.), *ummukka* (Paṇṇav. 136; Uttar. 1037), *viṇimukka* (Uttar. 755), *vippamukka* (Vivāhap. 186. 263. 455. 1351 [*a*°]; Uttar. 1; Paṇṇav. 134. 483), *vimukka* (Paṇṇav. 134. 136. 137. 848) ; Ś. *mukka* (Mṛcch. 71,9; 109,19; Vikr. 43,15; 47,2; Prab. 45,11; Bālar. 24,9; 195,9;202,16; 204,19 etc.), *pamukka* (Bālar. 246,13; Uttarar. 84,2), *vimukka* (Bālar. 170,14; 203,14; 210,2; Pras. 35,2; Veṇīs. 62,7; 63,11. 12;65,8;66,9); Mg. *mukka* (Mṛcch. 29,19. 20; 31,23. 25; 32,5; 136,16;168,4; Prab. 50,14; 56,10); Ḍh. *mukka* (Mṛcch. 31,24;32,1); A. *mukkāhã* (Hc. 4,370,1). Hc. 2,12 mentions also *mutta*, that falsely occurs in Ś. *pamutta* (Uttarar. 20,12). *muktā* (pearl) always becomes *muttā* and *mauktika* always *mŏttia*[9]; cf. Ś. *mukka-mŏttia* (Bālar. 195,9).—*ragga* (Hc. 2,10) = **ragṇa* = Skt. *rakta*; in addition to *raggaa* (dress coloured in saffron; Pāiẏal. 261; Deśīn. 7,3); found in the text is only *ratta* : M. JM. Ś. (H.; Erz.; Mṛcch. 71,3; 73,12; Śak. 134,13; Mālav. 28,17; 45,11); M. *latta* (Mṛcch. 129,1; Nāgān. 67,6).—M. *rikka* =

**rikṇa* from *ric* (Pāiyal. 218; Deśīn. 7,6) = "a little" (H.), *aïrikka*, (H.), *païrikka*, *pavirikka* = *pravirikṇa* (G. H. R.); M. JM. *virikka* (G.; Āv. 47,21; Erz.), according to Deśīn. 6,71 also in the meanings "wide", "exclusive"; *aṇarikka*, *avarikka* (deprived of favourable opportunity; Deśīn. 1,20); beside it M. *ritta* = *rikta* (Pāiyal. 218; H.), *aïritta* (R. 14,51; v. l. °*rikka*).—M. *ruṇṇa* (Vr. 8,62; Hc. 1,209; G. H. R.), *oruṇṇa*, *paruṇṇa* (R.), but Ś. *rudida* (Śak. 33,4; Ratn. 314,32; Uttarar. 20,12; Caṇḍak. 95,10; Vṛṣabh. 50,5; Dhūrtas. 11,12).—M. JM. AMg. Ś. *lukka* (torn; separated by violence; with standing hairs; extracted; concealed) = **lukna*, from *luñc*[10] (Hc. 2,2; H. R.; Erz.; Kappas.; Viddhaś. 27,4); *ullukka* (Deśīn. 1,92); M. Ś. *ṇilukka* (H. R.; Viddhaś. 51,7). JM. *nilukka* (Āv. 23,14) with the denominatives *lukkaï*, *ullukkaï*, *nilukkaï* (Hc. 4,55. 116), JM. *nilukkantehiṁ*, *nilukkanto*, (Āv. 23,17. 19).—M. *lhikka* (concealed; abolished; Hc. 4,258; G.) beside **likka* = **ślikna* (§ 210), form which the denominatives *lhikkaï*, *likkaï* (Hc. 4,55). —M. *sikka* = **sikna* from *sic* (Karṇas. 14,4) beside the usual *sitta* = *sikta*. —*sakka* = **ṣvaṣkṇa*[11] "in *osakka* (gone away; Pāiyal. 178; Deśīn. 1,149) beside M. *pariṣakkia* (H. 608).—AMg. *sŏlla* = *sūd*+*na* = *sūdita*, *sŏllaya* (§ 244).—On *juṇṇa* and composita see § 58, on *ṇumaṇṇa* § 118, on *uvvĕlla* § 107, on *hūṇa* and composita § 120. The femin. ends in *-ā*, A. only sometimes in *-ī*, as *diṇṇī* (Hc. 4,401,3).

1. On further extension of the suffix *-na* in Pkt. S. GOLDSCHMIDT, Prākṛtica p. 8, note 2; JOHANSSON, Shāhbāzgarhi, 1. 185 have expressed the correct opinions. Elsewhere, as already remarked by JOHANSSON, all the etymologies of S. GOLDSCHMIDT, that come here into consideration, are wrong, likewise those of P. GOLDSCHMIDT, GN. 1874,520 ff. Cf. also PISCHEL, BB. 6, 85f.—2. Falsely equated as = *khātra* by JACOBI, Erz. s.v.; see 90.—3. PISCHEL on Hc. 4,177.—4. WEBER on Hāla 465.—5. Not correct—WEBER, on Hāla 481.—6. PISCHEL, BB. 15,126—7. PISCHEL on Hc. 1,46.—8. PISCHEL on Hc. 4,177.—9. STENZLER on Mṛcch. 29,20; PISCHEL on Hc. 2,2. Cf. § 61*a*,—10. False WEBER on Hāla 49.—11. WEBER on Hāla 608.

§ 567. *i* with *palā* is conjugated, as in Skt., according to the 1. conjugation: M. *palāaha* (R. 15,8; so to be read with C), *palāanta-* (G.H.), *palāiavva* (R. 14,12; so to be read with the v.l.), *vivalāaï*, *vivalāanti*, *vivalāanta-*, *vivalāamāṇa* (G.H.R.); JM. *palāyaï* (Āv. 19,22; Erz.), *palāyamāṇa* (Āv. 18,1; Erz.), *palāyasu* (Erz. 9,37), *palāiuṁ* (Āv. 19,16); Ś. *palāidukāma* (Mallikām. 225,11); Mg. *palāaśi* (Mṛcch. 9,23; 11,7; 132,3), imp. *palāamha* (Caṇḍak. 73,2), particip. pres. *palāantī* (Mṛcch. 16,22), absolutive *paalāia*, fut. *palāiśśaṁ* (Mṛcch. 120,13; 171,15). Contraction has occurred on the analogy of the roots in *-ai* and *-ā* (§ 479. 487): Mg. *palāmi* (Mṛcch. 22,10), *palāśi* (Mṛcch. 11,21); Ḍh. *palāsi* (Mṛcch. 30,7); M. *vivalāi* (G. 934). Accordingly beside the usual M. *palāia* (H. R.), Ś. *palāida* (Vikr. 46,5), Mg. *palāida* (Mṛcch. 12,19) = Skt. *palāyita* is formed also from the contracted stem *palā* a present past passive participle M. *palāa* = **palāta*, *vivalāa* = **vipalāta* (R.), JM. *palāya* (Āv. 23,15; 32,5; Erz.), to which belongs also *palāa* (thief; Deśīn. 6,8). Cf. § 129. 243. In JM. the participle has also the suffix *-na*: *palāṇa* (Erz.), for *ā* of which there appears *ī* in Ḍh. in *papaliṇu* = *prapalāyita* (Mṛcch. 29,15; 30,1), as in the pres. participle in *-miṇa*, *-iṇa* (§ 562).

§ 568. Deviating from Skt. in Pkt. the past passive participle from a number of roots is formed also with *-ta*, which in Skt. have only *-na*: M. *khuḍia* (Hc. 1,53; G.H.R,), Ś. *khuḍida* (Mṛcch. 162,7; Anarghar. 157,9; Uttarar. 11,10 [so to be read]) = **kṣudita* = Skt. *kṣuṇṇa*[1]; M. *ukkhuḍia* (H.R.); also *khuṭṭa* (broken into pieces; Deśīn. 2,74), beside JM. *khunna*, M. *khuṇṇa* (Pāiyal. 222; H. 445). To other roots belong *khuṇṇa* (wrapped about; Deśīn. 2,75) and Ā. *khuḍida* (run away; Mṛcch. 100,12).[2]—*chaïa* (covered; Hc. 2,17; Triv. 1,4,22) = **chadita*, equated by grammarians as = *sthagita*[3], beside the usual *chaṇṇa* = Skt. *channa*.—*viddāa* (Hc. 1, 107), JM. *viddāya* (Āv. 17,32) = **vidrāta* = Skt. *vidrāṇa*.—AMg. *amilāya* (Kappas. § 102) = **amlāta* = Skt. *amlāna*.—M. *lua* (Hc. 4,258; Deśīn. 7,23; R.) = **lūta* = Skt. *lūna*.

1. Pischel, BB. 15,125 f.—2. Stenzler on Mṛcch. 100,12 p. 288.—3. Pischel, BB. 15,125.

§ 569. A parasmaipada past participle is found in AMg. *puṭṭhavaṁ* = *spṛṣṭavān* (Āyār. 1,7,8,8), but it has a passive sense. Elsewhere only in later day writers and uncritical editions: Ś. *kidavanto* [sic], *sudavandeṇa* [sic], *bhuttavanteṇa*, *uttavanto* (Jīvān. 40,26; 42,15;53,11;87,3); *bhaṇidavanto*, *gadidavanto*, *calidavanto* (Cait. 38,13; 128,5; 130,18); *pĕkkhidavanto*. [text *pĕssi°*] *āadavanto*, *adivāhidavando* [sic], *aṇubhūdavando* [sic] (Mallikām. 155, 18; 209,1 222,12), *saṁpādiavando* [sic], *pesidavanto* (Adbhutad. 58,10;119, 25); Mg. *gadidavanto* [sic], *giliavante* (Cait. 150,5. 6); femin. Ś. *paḍicchidavadī* (Viddhaś. 43,6); *ṇidavadī* (Mallikām. 259,3).

§ 570. The particip. necessitatis in *-tavya* is not seldom built from the present stem: *haseavva*, *hasiavva* = *hasitavya* (Hc. 3,157; Kī. 4,39); AMg. JM. *hoyavva* = *bhavitavya* (Kappas.; Erz.), Ś. Mg. *hodavva*, JŚ. Ś. also *bhavidavva*, Mg. also *huvidavva* (§ 475.476); JM. *acchiyavva* (Dvār. 500,9; 501,8); Ś. *avagacchidavva* (Mṛcch. 66,3); AMg. *ciṭṭhiyavva* (Vivāhap. 163), Ś. *avagacchidavva* (Mṛcch. 66,3); AMg. *ciṭṭhiyavva* (Vivāhap. 163), Ś. *aṇuciṭṭhidavva* (Mudrār. 50,4); AMg. *pucchiyavva* = *praṣṭavya* (Sūyag. 986. 989. 992), *puccheyavva* (Kappas.), Ś. *pucchidavva* (Śak. 50,5; Hāsy. 27,13); AMg. *vigiñciyavva* from *vikṛt* (§ 485; Dasav. N. 646,3); M. *rūsiavva* (H.); AMg. *pāsiyavva* from *paś* (Paṇṇav. 667; Kappas.); Ś. *saṁtappidavva* (Mṛcch. 94,3), *ṇaccidavva* (Priyad. 19,11.12;26,6;27,5; Karp. 4,1); AMg. *paritāveyavva* = *paritāpayitavya*, *uddaveyavva* = *uddrāvayitavya* (Āyār. 1,4,1,1), *dameyavva* = *damayitavya* (Uttar. 19); Ś. *sumarāidavva* (Priyad. 14,7); Ś. *āsidavva* (Priyad. 14,3); JM. *soyavva* = *svaptavya* (Āv. 39,16), Ś. *suvidavva*, *suidavva* (Mṛcch. 90,20; Śak. 29,7); Ś. *dādavva* (Cait. 84,6. 13; Jīvān. 43,12. 15; Priyad. 10,23), *suṇidavva* (Mudrār. 227,6) beside *sodavva* (Śak. 121,10), M. *soavva* (R. 2,10), JM. *soyavva* (Āv. 33,19) from *śru*; AMg. *bhindiyavva* (Paṇhāv. 363.537); AMg. *bhuñjiyavva* (Vivāhap. 163), beside *bhŏttavva* (Hc. 4,212; Kī. 4,78); AMg. *jāṇiyavva* (Paṇṇav. 666; Kappas.). *parijāṇiyavva* (Āyār. 1,1,1,5.7); Ś. *jāṇidavva* (Priyad. 24,16); Mg. *yāṇidavva* (Lalitav. 565,7); JŚ. *ṇādavva* (Kattig. 401,352; text *°ya°*); JŚ. *muṇedavva* (Pav. 380,8; text *°ya°*); Ś. *gĕṇhidavva* (Mṛcch. 150,14; Vikr. 30,9), whilst *ghĕttavva* (Vr. 8,16; Hc. 4,210), AMg. *parighĕttavva* (Āyār. 1,4,1,1; 1,5,5,5,4;

Sūẏag. 647 f. 699.783,789), *oghĕttavva* (Kappas.) belong to **ghṛp* (§ 212). According to Hc. 4,211 *vac* forms the particip. nec. *vŏttavva*, and so it stands in Ś. in Vikr. 23,15. But since in Ś. the infinitive is never *vŏttuṁ*, but always *vattuṁ* (§ 574) we should read, with the ed. Bomb. 40,9 and the Drāviḍ. recension 630,14 ed. PISCHEL = 39,4 ed. PAṆḌIT, *vattavva*, as stands also in Mṛcch. 153,15 and JM. AMg. have (Erz.; Sūẏag. 994.996; Vivāhap. 139.204; Kappas.; Ovav.). *vŏttavva* is to be assigned to M.—From *rud* is built *rŏttavva* according to Vr. 8,55; Hc. 4,212. M. *roiavva* is found in the text (H.). From *kṛ* are built the forms M. *kāavva* (Vr. 8,17; Hc. 4,214; H. R.), AMg. JM. *kāẏavva* (Āẏār. 2,1,10,7; Dasav. 630,11; Erz.), JŚ. Ś. *kādavva* (Pav. 386,11 [text °*ẏa*°]; Lalitav. 554,6; Mṛcch. 166,4; 327,1; Vikr. 48,13; Prab. 11,7; Priyad. 11,10). Mg. *kādavva* (Mṛcch. 161,7) = *kartavya* (§ 62). From *muc* Hc. 4,212 teaches *mŏttavva* = *moktavya*.—In A. the endings are *-iĕvvaũ, -ĕvvaũ,-evā*; *kariĕvvaũ* = *kartavyam*; *mariĕvvaũ* = *martavyam*; *sahĕvvaũ* = *soḍhavyam*; *soevā* = *svaptavyam*; *jaggevā* = *jāgartavyam* (Hc. 4,438; cf. Kī. 5,52). *-ĕvva* is to be considered as the basic form to which goes back *-evā* from which an extended formation is *-ĕvvaũ*, with the suffix *-ka*, nom. acc. neut. *-kam*. *-ĕvva* is = Skt. *-eyya*, with change of *ya* into *va* certainly visible elsewhere in A too (§ 254). The participial meaning occurs in Vedic *stuṣéyya*, perhaps also in *śapatheyyà*; cf. *didṛkṣeya*. According to Kī. 5,55 *-ĕvvaüṁ* is used also in the sense of the infinitive.

571. *-anīya* appears in M. JM. AMg. as *-aṇijja*, in Ś. Mg. as *-aṇia*, corresponding to the formation of the passive (§ 535; cf. 91); AMg. *pūẏaṇijja* (Kappas.; Ovav.), Ś. D. *pūaṇia* (Mṛcch. 28,7; 101,13); AMg. *vandaṇijja* (Uvās.; Kappas.), Ś. *vandaṇia* (Mṛcch. 66,17); M. AMg. JM. *karaṇijja* (H.; Āẏār. 2,3,3,16;2,4,2,5; Erz.), Ś. *karaṇia* (Vikr. 36,8; Nāgān. 4,15), false *karaṇijja* (Śak. 2,5; Vikr. 43,6), where the v. l. has the correct *karaṇia* JM. *sārakkhaṇijja* (Āv. 28,16.17) = *saṁrakṣaṇīya* Ś. *rakkhaṇia* (Śak. 74,8); AMg. *darisaṇijja* (Āẏār. 2,4,2,2; Ovav.), *daṁsaṇijja* (Uvās.; Ovav.), Ś. *daṁsaṇia* (Śak. 132,6; Nāgān. 52,11). Further stands in AMg. in Āẏār. 2,4, 2,2 *darisaṇijjaṁ*, immediately beside *darisiṇie* (sic; ed. Calc. correct °*sa*°) and in § 4 *darisaṇiẏaṁ*, Sūẏag. 565 *darisaṇiẏa* [sic], JM. *daṁsaṇio* (Erz. 60,17), M. *dūsahaṇio* (H. 363). On the other hand in Ś. Mg. very often the forms in *-ijja*, such as Mg. *palihalaṇijja* (Prab. 29,8), but ed. Bomb. 74,2; ed. P. p. 32 and ed. M. p. 37 rightly *palihalaṇia*, as in Ś. *pariharaṇia* (Śak. 52,15) are found. In Mālav. 32,5 all the manuscripts have Ś. *sāhaṇijje*, at all other places in Mālav. the manuscripts waver (BOLLENSEN on Mālav. p. 223). Deviations from the rule, therefore, are simply errors of manuscripts, as in the case of the passive, and are to be corrected. From the present stem are built AMg. *vippajahaṇijja* (Nāẏādh. § 138) and Ś. *pucchaṇia* (Mṛcch. 142,6).

§ 572. *-ya is* employed substantially as in Skt. : *kajja*, Mg. *kayya* = *kārya* in all the dialects very frequently; JM. *dullaṅgha* = *durlaṅghya* (Sagara 3,16); *dujjha* = *dohya* (Deśīn. 1,7); JŚ. *ṇeya*, JM. *neẏa* = *jñeya* (Pav. 381, 20; Erz.); AMg. *pĕjja* = *peya* (Uvās.; Dasav.; 629,1), *kāẏapijja* = *kākapeya*

(Dasav. 628,41; so to be read), whilst *pibba* (water; Deśīn. 6,46; cf. Introduction p. 7; Triv. 2,1,30) = **pibya* is derived from the present stem *piba*-; AMg. *bhavva* = *bhāvya* (Kappas. § 17.22); AMg. *āṇappa*, *vinnappa* = *ājñāpya*, *vijñāpya* (Sūyag. 253. 256); AMg. *vacca* = *vācya* (Sūyag. 553 ff.); AMg. *vŏjjha* from **vahya* = *vāhya* (§ 104; Nāyādh. § 65), therefore, from the present stem, as M. AMg. Ś. *gĕjjha* (Hc. 1,78; Karp. 29,4; 81,4; Jīv. 500; Bālar. 75,19), M. *hatthaggĕjjha* = *hastagrāhya* (R. 10,43), M. *dugghĕjjha* (R. 1,3; Sāhityadarpaṇa 332,13 = Kāvyaprakāśa 330,8 [so according to the best manuscripts instead of *duḥkhaṁ jaṁ* of the edition] and often cited; Sarasvatīk. 155,3 [text °*jjaṁ*]; Acyutaś. 62 [text °*gga*]), Ś. *aṇugĕjjha* (Mṛcch. 24,21), Mg. *duggĕyha* (Caṇḍak. 42,8; text *duggĕjja*, v. l. *duggea*), A. *duggĕjjha* (Erz. 76,19) = **gṛhya* from the present stem *gṛha*- (§ 512).

b) INFINITIVE.

§ 573. The formation of the inf. in *-tum* is distinguished from that of Skt. chiefly by the fact that in Pkt. the ending is added to the bare stem or to the present stem in *i*. So to the present stem: JM. *gāiuṁ* (Erz.), Ś. *gāiduṁ* = *gātum* (Mūdrār. 43,2); Ś. *gacchiduṁ* (Śak. 62,11), *aṇugacchiduṁ* (Mudrār. 261,2) beside *gamiduṁ* (Vṛṣabh. 19,11) and *gantuṁ*, that is usual in all the dialects; JM. *piviuṁ* (Āv. 42,8) beside *pāuṁ* (Āv. 42,8; 45,6), as also AMg. (Āyār. 1,1,3,7), M. (H. R.) and Ś. *pāduṁ* (Śak. 105, 14) have; Ś. *aṇuciṭṭhiduṁ* (Mṛcch. 102,19) beside *ṭhāduṁ* (Nāgān. 14,9) and JM. *uṭṭhiuṁ* (Āv. 33,14); Mg. *khāduṁ* (Mṛcch. 123,7) from **khādi* from **khāadi* = *khādati* beside JM. *khāiuṁ* (Erz.), Ś. *khādiduṁ* (Vikr. 25,19); JM. *ṇihaṇiuṁ* = *nikhātum* from *khan* (Erz. 66,2); *haseuṁ* (Hc. 3,157) from the *e*-stem beside *hasiuṁ*; M. *pucchiuṁ* (Sarasvatīk. 14,17), Ś. *pucchiduṁ* (Mṛcch. 88,20; Mālav. 5,4. 17), Mg. *puścidum* (Caṇḍak. 42,9) = *praṣṭum*; M. *paḍimuñciuṁ* (R. 14,2) beside *mŏttuṁ* = *moktum* (Hc. 4,212); M. *ṇacciuṁ* (H.); M. *rūseuṁ* (H.), at the same time according to the *e*-conjugation. On the inf. of *bhū* see § 401. 402. The verbs of the 10. conjugation and the similarly built causatives and denominatives generally add *-tum* to the present stem in *-e*, *-ve*: M. *jāṇāveuṁ*, *ṇivvāheuṁ* = *nirvāhayitum*, *pasāeuṁ* = *prasādayitum*, *laṅgheuṁ* = *laṅghayitum* (H.); AMg. *vāreuṁ* = *vārayitum* (Sūyag. 178): *parikaheuṁ* = *parikathayitum* (Ovav. § 183); *paribhāeuṁ* = *paribhājayitum* (Nāyādh. § 124); JŚ. *cāleduṁ* = *cālayitum* (Kattig. 400,322); Ś. *kāmeduṁ* = *kāmayitum* (Mālatīm. 235,3), *kāreduṁ* (Mudrār. 46,9), *dhāreduṁ* (Mṛcch. 166,14; 326,12), *daṁseduṁ* = *darśayitum* (Mudrār. 81,4); Mg. *aṅgikalāveduṁ*, *śośāvedūṁ*, *śodhāveduṁ*, *pŏsṭāveduṁ*, *luṇāveduṁ* (Mṛcch. 126,10; 140,9). More seldom is the uncontracted form: Ś. *ṇiattāiduṁ* = *nivartayitum* (Vikr. 46,17), *tāḍaïduṁ* (Mālav. 44,16), *sabhājaïduṁ* (Śak. 98,8), *sussūsaïduṁ* (Mālav. 29,12); Mg. *mālaïduṁ* (Mṛcch. 164,19). On the other hand, from the *a*-stem (§ 491) are frequently derived: M. *dhāriuṁ* (H.), Ś. *dhāriduṁ* (Vikr. 15,3; 40,7); Ś. *māriduṁ* (Mṛcch. 160,14; Śak. 146,8), Mg. *māliduṁ* (Mṛcch. 170,2) beside *māleduṁ* (Mṛcch. 158,24), JM. *māreuṁ* (Erz. 1,25); M. *vaṇṇiuṁ* = *varṇayitum*, *veāriuṁ* = *vitārayitum* (H.); AMg. *saṁvediuṁ* (Āyār.

p. 137,18); JM. *cintiuṁ, paḍibohiuṁ, vāhiuṁ* (Erz.); Ś. *kadhiduṁ* (Śak. 101, 9; 144,12), *avatthāviduṁ* = *avasthāpayitum* (Uttarar. 112,9), *ṇivediduṁ* (Śak. 51,3); Mg. *paśtiduṁ* = *prārthayitum* (Lalitav. 566,8).

§ 574. Examples of the 2. conjugation are : *paccācakkhiduṁ* = **pratyācaṣṭum* (Śak. 104,8); Ś. *avaciṇeduṁ* (Lalitav. 561,8) beside M. *ucceuṁ* (H.); JM. *pāveuṁ* = *prāptum* (Erz.); Ś. *suṇiduṁ* (Vikr. 26,5; Mudrār. 38,2; Veṇīs. 99,6; Anarghar. 61,6; 110,4), beside M. AMg. JM. *souṁ* (H.; Āyār. p. 136,14; Erz. as absol. § 576); Ś. *bhuñjiduṁ* (Dhūrtas. 6,21) beside M. AMg. *bhŏttuṁ* = *bhoktum* (Vr. 8,55; Hc. 4,212; cf. Kī. 4,78; Nāyādh. § 124; Dasav. N. 649,16); AMg. *ubbhindiuṁ* (Dasav. 620,15) beside *bhĕttuṁ* (Dasav. 634,9); Ś. *jāṇiduṁ* (Lalitav. 567,18; Śak. 119,2; Ratn. 309,22) beside JM. *nāuṁ* (Erz.; as absol. § 576), Ś. *viṇṇāduṁ* (Vikr. 24,13); AMg. *giṇhiuṁ* (Nirayāv. § 20; as absol. § 576), JM. *gĕṇhiuṁ* (Erz.), Ś. *gĕṇhiduṁ* (Mṛcch. 94,12) beside M. *gahiuṁ* (H.), whilst M. *ghĕttuṁ* (Vr. 8,16; Hc. 4,210; R.) belongs to **ghṛp* (§ 212); Ś. *aṇubandhiduṁ* (Mālav. 6,18) beside M. *bandheuṁ* (citation under Hc. 1,181).—From *rud* the inf. is M. *rŏttuṁ* (Vr. 8,55; Hc. 4,212; cf. Kī. 4,78; H.), but Ś. *rodidum* (Śak. 80,8); from *vid* according to Vr. 8,55 *vĕttuṁ*; from *vac* in M. JM. AMg. *vŏttuṁ* (Hc. 4, 211; H.; Erz.; Dasav. N. 646,21), but in Ś. *vattuṁ* (Śak. 22,2; 50,9; Vikr. 30, 2;47,1); *svap* forms in M. *sŏttuṁ* = *svaptum* (H.), in JM. *souṁ* (Dvār. 501,7) from **sotuṁ* of *sovaï* (§ 497); *kṛ* has in M. JM. AMg. *kāuṁ* = *kartum* (§ 62; Vr. 8,17; Hc. 4,214; G. H. R.; Erz.; Āv. 30,10; Dasav. N. 644,28), M. *paḍikāuṁ* (H.); Ś. *kāduṁ* (Lalitav. 561,13; Mṛcch. 59,25; Śak. 24,12; Vikr. 29,14; Karp. 41,6; Veṇīs. 12,6) and *kariduṁ* (Śak. 144,12); Mg. *kāduṁ* (Mṛcch. 123,7).

§ 575. Deviating from Skt., from the *i*-stem are formed : M. JM. *mariuṁ* = *martum* (H.; Erz.), Ś. *mariduṁ* (Ratn. 316,5; 317,15; Caṇḍak. 93,9); JM. *parihariuṁ* (Erz. 58,24), Ś. *vihariduṁ* (Vikr. 52,6), beside M. *vāhattuṁ* = *vyāhartum* (R. 11,116); JM. *samākarisiuṁ* = *samākraṣṭum* (Dvār. 498,31); M. *ukkhiviuṁ* = *utkṣeptum* (H.), Ś. *khividuṁ* (Vikr. 25,16), *ṇikkhividuṁ* (Mṛcch. 24,22); M. JM. *dahiuṁ* (R.; Erz.), Ś. *dahiduṁ* (Śak. 72,12) = *dagdhum*; JM. *saṁdhiuṁ* = *saṁdhātuṁ* from the present **saṁdhaï* (§ 500), Ś. *aṇusaṁdhiduṁ* (Mṛcch. 5,4); Ś. *ramiduṁ* = *rantum*, *ahiramiduṁ* = *abhirantum* (Mṛcch. 28,4; 75,2).

§ 576. In AMg. the form in *-tum* as inf. is considerably seldom. In addition to the forms referred to in the foregoing paragraphs may be mentioned : *jiviuṁ* (Āyār. 1,1,7,1); *adaṭṭhuṁ, agghāuṁ, aṇāsāuṁ* (Āyār. p. 136, 22. 31; p. 137,7); *aṇusāsiuṁ* (Sūyag. 59); *dāuṁ* = *dātum* (Āyār. 2,1,10,6; 2,5,1,10; Uvās. § 58; Nāyādh. § 124); *aṇuppadāuṁ* = *anupradātum* (Uvās. § 58) = JŚ. *dāduṁ* (Kattig. 403,380; text *dāuṁ*); *bhāsiuṁ* = *bhāṣitum, paviuṁ* = *plavitum* (Sūyag. 476. 531. 508). Most of these inf. occur in verses. More frequently the form is used as absolutive : *ujjhiuṁ* in the sense of *ujjhitvā* (Sūyag. 676); *tariuṁ* (Sūyag. 950); *gantuṁ* (Sūyag. 178; Āyār. 2,4,2,11.12; Kappas. S. § 10); *daṭṭhuṁ* = *draṣṭum* (Āyār. 1,4,4,3; Sūyag. 150); *niddĕṭṭhuṁ* = *nirdeṣṭum* (Dasav. N. 643,38): *laddhuṁ* = *labdhum* (Āyār. 1,2,4,4; 1,2,5,3; p. 15,32; Sūyag. 289. 550; Uttar. 157. 158. 169. 170; Dasav. 631,26,636,

20); *bhittuṁ* = *bhĕttum* (Kappas. § 40); *kāuṁ* = *kartum* (Sūẏag. 84; Dasav. N. 643.34), *puraokāuṁ* (Nandīs. 146; Kappas. S. § 46. 48; Ovav. § 25.126); *āhantuṁ* (Āẏār. 1,8,3,4); *parighĕttuṁ* (Paṇhāv. 489. 495), *gaheuṁ* (Sūẏag. 296). Prevalently is used the form in this meaning too in verses, but it is not restricted to AMg. and occurs frequently in JM. too, more seldom in M. as absol.[1]. Hc. teaches thus *daṭṭhuṁ*, *mŏttuṁ* (2,146), *ramiuṁ* (3,136), *ghĕttuṁ* (4,210). Examples from JM. are : *gantuṁ* (Āv. 7,31; Erz. 522; Kk. II, 508,18); *daṭṭhuṁ* (Āv. 24,4; Kk. III. 510,31.38); *jiṇiuṁ* = *jetum* (Āv. 36,42); *kahiuṁ* = *kathayitum* (Erz. 7,11); *kaḍḍheuṁ* (Erz. 74,30); *ṭhaviuṁ* = *sthāpayitum* (Erz. 7,5); *viheuṁ* = *vidhātum* (Kk. s. v.); *souṁ* = *śrotum* (Erz. 2,9; 11,34; 12,5; Kk. s.v.); *kāuṁ* (Āv. 7,17); *nāuṁ* = *jñātum* (Erz. 12,11); *ghĕttuṁ* = **ghṛptum* (Āv. 22,29; 23,7; 31,7). M. has *palīviuṁ* = *pradīpayitum*; *bhaṇiuṁ*; *bhariuṁ*; *mŏttuṁ*; *voliuṁ*; *lahiuṁ*; *pāviuṁ* (H. 33, 298. 307. 334. 360. 364. 484. 490. 516. 595); *jāṇiuṁ* = *jñātum* (R. 14, 48). The form can be derived from the absol. in -*ūṇa* (§ 586), therefore, *kāuṁ* can be traced back to *kāūṇa*, with dropping off of the *n*, as in A. *putteṁ* = *putreṇa*. The similar change of meaning in A. (§ 579), however, makes it probable that in fact dialectically the inf. has been used as the absolutive, as reversely the absol. too is employed as the infinitive (§ 585. 588.590).

1. Weber, Bhag. 1,433; H.[1] p. 66.

§ 577. As in Skt., in Pkt. too, the inf. in -*tu* stands before *kāma* and *manas*: AMg. *akkhiviukāma* = *ākṣeptukāma*, *giṇhiukāma* = *grahitukāma*, *uddāleukāma* = *uddālayitukāma* (Niraẏāv. § 19), *jiviukāma* (Āẏār. 1,2, 3,3), *vāsiukāma* = *varṣitukāma* (Ṭhāṇ. 155), *pāukāma* (from *pā* "to drink"; Nāẏādh. 1430), *jāṇiukāma*, *pāsiukāma* (Paṇṇav. 666. 667), *saṁpāviukāma* (Kappas. § 16; Ovav. § 20; Dasav. 634,39); JM. *paḍibohiukāma* = *pratibodhayitukāma* (Erz. 3,37), *kaḍḍhiukāma* (Dvār. 506,36); Ś. *jividukāma* (Mudrār. 233,3), *vattukāma*, *ālihidukāma* (Śak. 130,11; 133,11), *viṇṇavidukāma* (Mahāv. 103,9), *sikkhidukāma* (Mṛcch. 51,24), *pamajjidukāma* = *pramārṣṭukāma* (Vikr. 38,18), *daṭṭhukāma* (Mālatīm. 72,2; 85,3); *tāḍiumaṇā* = *tāḍayitumanāḥ* (Karp. 70,7). It is used independently too with the entry of the suffix -*ka*: *ālĕddhuaṁ* = **ālegdhukam* = *āleḍhum* (§ 303; Hc. 1,24; 2,164); AMg. *aladdhuẏaṁ* = **alabdhukam*, in the sense of the absol. (Dasav. 636,19). This last form makes it probable that the forms in -*ṭṭu*, -*ittu*, used as the absol. as well in AMg. JM., are originally infinitive, therefore, do not go back to Skt. -*tvā*, that regularly appears as -*ttā* (§ 582). So AMg.: *kaṭṭu* = *kartu*° in the sense of *kṛtvā* (Hc. 2,146; Āẏār. 1,6,3,2; 2,1,3,2. 11,1; 2,2,2,3; 2,3,1,9. 2,21. 3,15. 16; Sūẏag. 288. 358; Bhag.[1]; Uvās.; Kappas.; Ovav.; Dasav. 631,29; 641,37 etc.); *puraokaṭṭu* (Ovav.); *avahaṭṭu* = *apahartu*° (Āẏār. 2,6, 2,1; Sūẏag. 233; Ovav.; Bhag.); *abhihaṭṭu* (Āẏār. 2,6,2,2), *āhaṭṭu* (Āẏār. 1,2,4,3; 1,7,2,1. 2.3; 1,7,7,2; 1,8,2,12; 2,1,1,11; 2,1,2,4; 2,1,5,5. 6,4), *samāhaṭṭu* (Sūẏag. 410), *appāhaṭṭu* (Sūẏag. 582), *nihaṭṭu* (Āẏār. 2,1,10,6; 2,6,2,2), *uddhaṭṭu* (Āẏār. 2,3,1,6; Sūẏag. 222.243), *sāhaṭṭu* = *saṁhartu*° (Āẏār. 2,3,1,6; Vivāhap. 237. 254; Vivāgas. 90. 121. 144. 157; Uvās.; Kappas.; Ovav.; Niraẏāv. etc.); *adaṭṭhu* = *adraṣṭu*° (Kappas. S. § 19; so to be read); *vandittu* (Kappas.); *caïttu* = *tyaktu°* (Uttar. 45. 411); *sahĕttu* (Dasav. 614,27); *pavisittu* = *pravesṭu°* (Dasav. 631,5); *āittu* from *ādriyate* (Āẏār. 1,4,1,3; commentary = *ādāya, gṛhitvā*); *tarittu* = *tarītu°*, *khavittu* = *kṣapayitu°* (Dasav. 636,3.4); *pamajjittu* = *pramārṣṭu°* (Dasav. 630,20); *viṇaĕttu* (Āẏār. 1,5,6,2); *uvasaṁkamittu* (Āẏār. 1,7,2,1.3; 1,7,3,3); *viẏahittu* from *vijahaï* from *hā* (§ 500; Āẏār. 1,1,3,2); *suṇittu* = *śrotu°* (Dasav. 642, 16); *durūhittu* (Sūẏāg. 293)); *chindittu, bhuñjittu* (Dasav. 640,21; 641,36); *jāṇittu* (Āẏār. 1,2,1,5; 1,2,4,2; 1,4,1,3; 1,5,2,2; 1,6,2,1; Dasav. 630,34).—JM. *gantu* (Kk. II, 506,34); *kaḍḍhittu* (Erz. 10,38); *paṇamittu, ṭhavittu* = *sthāpayitu°*, *vandittu* (Kk. 260,11;268,4;276,7); *uttarittu* (Kk. 506,25; 511,7); *jāṇittu, paẏaḍittu* = *prakaṭayitu°*, *thuṇittu* = *stotu°* (Kk. III, 514,16. 17.20), *viṇihittu* = *vinidhātu°* (Erz. 72,23), almost exclusively in verses. The reduplication of *t*, since in the inf. it goes back to AMg. *-ttae* = *-tave* (§ 478), can hardly be explained from dependence upon the absol. in *-ttā* = *-tvā*, rather the forms, in which reduplication might occur on phonetic grounds, such as *kaṭṭu, sāhaṭṭu*, had been of influence or there occurred a shifting of the accent. Cf. § 578.

1. Weber, Bhag. 1,433 f.

§ 578. In AMg. the most usual form of the inf. is that in *-ttae*, *-ittae*. Infinitive like *pāẏae* (Āẏār. 2,1,1,2; 2,1,9,1. 2; 2,1,10,7; 2,2,2,2; 2,6,1,10; 2,7,2,4. 5. 6; Nāẏādh. § 144; Ovav. § 96) = Vedic *pátave* beside *pivittae* (Ovav. § 80.98), *bhŏttae* (Āẏār.; Nāẏādh. l.c,; Ovav. § 96; Sūẏag. 430) = Vedic **bhóktave* beside *bhuñjittae* (Ovav. § 86), *vatthae* (Āẏār. 2,2, 2,10; Kappas. S. § 62) = Vedic *vástave* [in AMg., however, from *vas* "to live"] make it certain that one has not to think with Weber[1] about the Vedic absolutive in *-tvā́ya*, but rather with E. Müller[2] about the Vedic inf. in *-tave* that occurs in Pāli and in the Leṇa-dialect, in which the ending is added also to the *i*- and *i*- stems: *ávitave, cáritave, srávitave, hávitave.*[3] The reduplication of *t* points to the accent on the final (§ 194). Consequently one may more correctly base the infinitive on *-tavai*, that in the Veda has a double accent. AMg. *ittae* (Kappas. S. § 27) is hence to be equated as = Vedic *étavaí*, likewise *pāẏave* = *pátavai*; with *gamittae* is compared Vedic *yámitavaí*, with *piṇidhattae* (Ovav. § 79) Vedic *dátavaí*. This inf. is prevalently formed from the present stem: *hŏttae* (Kappas. S. §53) beside *pāubbhavittae* (Vivāhap.; Nāẏādh.) from *bhū*; *viharittae* (Bhag.; Uvās.; Nāẏādh.; Kappas. etc.); *sumarittae sarittae* (Āẏār. p. 135,17.20); *tarittae* (Āẏār. 1,2,3,6); *uttarittae* (Nāẏādh. 1339; Ovav. § 96; *pariccaïttae* (Uvās. § 95); *gacchittae* (Ovav. § 79), *āgacchittae* (Ṭhāṇ. 155), *uvāgacchittae* (Kappas.), beside *gamittae* (Āẏār, 1,2,3,6; Bhag.); *ciṭṭhittae* (Vivāhap. 513; Kappas.); beside *ṭhāittae* (Āẏār. 2,8,1 ff.; Kappas.); *nisiittae* from *sad* with *ni* (Vivāhap. 513); *aṇulimpittae* (Ovav. § 79); *pucchittae* (Bhag.; Nāẏādh.); *pāsittae* (Nāẏādh.); *kāhaïttae* (Āẏār. p. 135,6); *dūijjittae* from *dūtaya-* (Kappas.; Ṭhāṇ. 365); *pariṭṭhāvittae* (Kappas.); *abhisiñcāvittae* (Niraẏāv.); *pūraïttae* (Āẏār. 1,3,2,2); *āghāvittae* from *ākhyāpaya-* (Nāẏādh.); *dhārittae* (Āẏār. 1,7,7,1; 2,5,2,5); *dhārĕttae* (Āẏār. 2,5,2,3); *esittae* (Āẏār. 2,2,3,14. 18); *āsaïttae, saïttae* from *śi* (Vivāhap. 513); *paḍisuṇĕttae* (Āẏār.

2,5,1,10), *dhuṇitta* (Sūẏag. 139); *bhañjittae* (Uvās.); *bhindittae* (Vivāhap. 1228); *viuvvittae* from *kṛ* with *vi* (Bhag.), beside *karittae, karĕttae* (Ovav. § 79.85; Nāẏādh.; Bhag.; Kappas.); *giṇhittae, ge°* (Bhag.; Niraẏāv.; Ovav. § 86); *jāgarittae* (Kappas.).

1. Bhag. 1,434; *pavvāittāe* is a false reading.—2. Beiträge p. 61.—3. Delbrück, Altind. Verbum § 203.

§ 579. In A according to Hc. 4,441, the inf. has the endings *-aṇa, -aṇahã, -aṇahĩ, -evã*. Kī. 5,55 teaches *-evi, -ĕppi, -ĕppiṇu, -aṇaṁ, -aüṁ, -ĕvvaüṁ*. Cf. § 570.588. The infinitive in *-aṇa* are clearly infinitively used nouns in *-ana*, of which *-aṇahã*, according to the form, is the genitive plural, and *-aṇahĩ* the loc. sing. plur. or the ins. plur. So: *ĕcchaṇa* = *eṣṭum* from *iṣ* (to wish; Hc. 4,353); *karaṇa* = *kartum* (Hc. 4,441,1); also with the suffix *-ka* in *akkhaṇaü̃* = *ākhyātum*, properly = *ākhyānakam* (Hc. 4,350,1); *bhuñjaṇahã* and *bhuñjaṇahĩ* (Hc. 4,441,1); *lahaṇaṁ* (Kī. 5,55).—*evaṁ* is found in *devaṁ* = *dātum* (Hc, 4,441,1). It is clearly derived from the present stem *de-* = *daya*. (§ 474) with the ending *-vaṁ*, that goes back to *-vana* = Vedic *-vane*, so that *devaṁ* may correspond to Vedic *dāváne*. Some day when more examples will be available we may become certain about this form. An inf. in *-tu* is *bhajjiu* (Hc. 4,395,5), that is derived from the passive stem of *bhañj* in the active sense, as also elsewhere in A. (§ 550), in case *bhaṁjiu* = *bhañjiu* is not read with one of the Pūṇā manuscripts. The inf. stands in the sense of the absol. (Hc. 4,439), as reversely many forms of the absol. are used in the sense of the inf. (§ 588). Kī. 5,55 has *lahaüṁ* [text *lahatuṁ*].

§ 580. Pkt. has a real infinitive of the passive[1]: M. *disiuṁ* from *disaï* = *dṛśyate* (R. 4,51; 8,30), *ghĕppiuṁ* from *ghĕppaï* = **ghṛpyate* (R. 7, 71), *āhammiuṁ* from *hammaï* from *han* (§ 540; R. 12,45); JM. *dijjiuṁ* from *dijjaï* = *dīyate* (Erz. 6,7). Beside there stands AMg. *marijjiuṁ* from *mriyate* (Dasav. 624,40) beside the usual *mariuṁ*, Ś. *mariduṁ* (§ 575). On A *bhajjiu* see § 579.

1. Goldschmidt, ZDMG. 28,491 ff.

ABSOLUTIVE

§ 581. The distinction, that Skt. makes in the use of the absolutiva in *-tvā*, and *-ya*, is not maintained in Pkt. The suffixes enter likewise into the verbs with and without prefixes. *-tvā* is, however, not used in M., and in Ś. Mg. Ḍh it is limited to the two absolutives *kadua* from *kṛ* and *gadua* from *gam*, which according to Vr. 12,10; Kī. 5,74. 75; Mk. fol. 68 must always be used in Ś., with which the texts are in accord[1]. So Ś. *kadua* (Mṛcch. 72,6; 74,6. 9; 77,25; 78,9; 95,8; Śak. 20,6; 33,3; 54,2; 77,13; 140,6; Vikr. 15,8; 44,10; 45,20; 52,11. 21; 84,2 etc.); Ś. *gadua* (Mṛcch. 2,17; 51,4; 53,15; 74,24 etc.; Śak. 23,7; Vikr. 16,18; 30,3). Hc. 4,272 and Sr. fol. 61 permit in Ś. too *karia* and *karidūṇa, gacchia* and *gacchidūṇa* for which *karia* and *gacchia* are found in bad texts[2], and *karidūṇa*, which will belong to JŚ. (§ 21). It is doubtful whether *gacchia* and *karia* are not emended in composita: *āacchia* (Ratn. 308,30); *āgacchia* (Veṇīs. 35,21); *samāgacchia* (Mudrār. 44,5); *alaṁkaria* (Mṛcch, 150,13). However, we find also *āadua* (Cait. 128,13; Mallikām. 225,1); *āgadua* (Mallikām. 153,24; 177,21); *ṇiggadua* (Mallikām. 215,5; 226,10; 229,15. 20), all admittedly in later day bad texts. The two forms are proper to Mg. too. So *kadua* (Mṛcch. 19,6; 81,13; 108,17; 115,2 etc.; Śak. 133,7; Mudrār. 193,8 etc.); Mg. *gadua* (Mṛcch. 40,10 [so to be read with GOḌABOLE]; 43,12; 118,22; 136,21; 164,10; Śak. 116,9 etc.), likewise in Ḍh. (Mṛcch. 36,22). In Mṛcch. 132,25 stands in Mg. *gacchia*, for which we should in any case read *gaścia* with the v. l.; in 127,5 all the MSS have Mg. *gaḍia*, which is to be equated as = °*gatya*. All the MSS of Hc. too have cerebralisation in 4,272. 302, according to which *kaḍua*, *gaḍua* would be established. Since, however, Triv. and Sr. teach *kadua* and *gadua*, it is a pure case of error of manuscripts. The forms are traced back to **káduvā*, **gáduvā* with a separation vowel and weakening of the final *ā* (§ 113. 139). On *kāūṇa*, *āacchiūṇa āgantūṇa* and others see § 584.

1. PISCHEL, KB. 6,140.—2. PISCHEL, l. c.—In Mālav. at 67,15 E rightly has *gadua*.

§ 582. The suffix *-tvā*, Pkt. *-ttā*, after nasals *-tā*, forms the most usual absol. in AMg.; in JŚ. too this form is frequent and in JM. not seldom[1]. Generally the ending is added to the present stem: all that has been said about the infinitive holds good in individual cases. So: AMg *vandittā* (Hc. 2.146; Ovav. § 20; Nāẏādh.; Uvās.; Bhag. etc.); *vasittā* (Āẏār. 1,4,4,2); *caïttā* = **tyajitvā* (Āẏār. 1,4,4,1: 1,6,2,1; Ovav. § 23; Uttar. 450. 517. 541); *avakkamittā* (Āẏār, 2,1,1,2); *gantā* = Pāli *gantvā* (Ovav. § 153) beside *āgamĕttā* (Āẏār. 1,5,1,1; 1,7,2,3), *aṇugacchittā* (Kappas.), *uvāgacchittā* (Vivāhap. 236[2]; Ovav.; Kappas.; Niraẏāv.), *niggacchittā*, *paḍiniggacchittā* (Niraẏāv.); *vantā* = *vāntvā* (Āẏār. 1,3,1,4; 1,6,5,5; 2,4,2,19; Sūẏag. 321); *bhavittā* (Vivāhap. 844; Ovav.; Kappas.; Uvās. etc.); *jiṇiṭṭā* (Sūẏag. 929); *uvaṇĕttā* = **upanitvā* (Suẏag. 896); *pivittā* (Āẏār. 2,1,3,1); *uṭṭhittā* (Niraẏāv.), *abbhuṭṭhittā* (Kappas.); *pāsittā* (Rāẏap. 21; Sūẏag. 734; Ovav. § 54, p. 59, 15; Uvās.; Nāẏādh.; Niraẏāv. Kappas.); *nijjhāittā* = **nidhyātvā* (Āẏār. 1,1,6,2); *muẏittā* (Vivāhap. 508), *omuẏittā* (Kappas.) from *muc*; *āpucchittā* (Uvās.), *aṇāpucchittā* (Kappas.) from *pracch*; *lumpittā*, *vilumpittā*[3] (Āẏār. 1,2,1,3; 1,2,5,6; cf. Sūẏag. 676. 716 ff.); *aṇulimpittā* (Jīv. 610); *mantā* = *matvā* (Āẏār. 1,1,5,1; 1,3,1,3; Sūẏag. 403. 493 [so to be read throughout]); *uttāsaïttā* = **uttrāsayitvā* (Āẏār. 1.2,1,3); *vicchaḍḍaïttā*, *vigovaïttā*, *jaṇaïttā* (Ovav.); *āmantĕttā* (Sūẏag. 578); *āphālittā* = **āsphālayitvā* (Sūẏag. 728); *pagappaĕttā* = **prakalpayitvā* (Sūẏag. 935); *ṭhavĕttā* = *sthāpayitvā* (Āẏār. 2,7,1,5; p. 129,16; Uvās.); *sikkhāvĕttā*, *sehāvĕtta* = **śikṣāpayitvā*, **śaikṣā*°; *saddāvittā* = *śabdāpayitvā* (Kappas.; Niraẏāv.), *aṇupālittā*, *nivesittā* (Kappas.); *ahittā* = **adhitvā* = *ādhitya* (Sūẏāg. 463); *viditttā* (Āẏār. 1,1,5,1; 1,2,6,2); *saṁṭhuṇittā* from *stu* (Jīv. 612); *hantā* (Āẏār. 1,2; 1,3. 5,6; Sūẏāg. 358. 676. 716 ff.; Kappas.); *parihittā* (Sūẏāg. 239), *paripihĕttā* (Āẏār. 2,2,3,27), °*hittā* (Kappas.), *paḍipihittā* (Sūẏag. 728; text; °*pe*°) from *dhā* with *pari*, and *pari*, *prati*+*pi*; *jahittā* (Uttar. 753); *vippajahittā* (Āẏār. p. 125,1; Uttar. 881) from *hā*; *huṇittā* (Vivāhap. 910) from *hu* (to offer); *pāuṇittā* from *āp* with *pra* (Sūẏag. 771; Vivāhap. 135. 235. 968. 969; Paṇṇav. 846; Nāẏādh. 1225; Ovav.; Kappas.; Uvās. etc.); *suṇittā* (Uvās.), *paḍisuṇittā* (Kappas.; Niraẏāv.); *avidhūṇittā* (Sūẏag. 859); *chĕttā*, *bhĕttā* (Āẏār. 1,2,1,3; 1,2,5,6; Sūẏag. 676. 716 ff.); *viuvvittā* (Bhag.; Kappas.) beside *karĕttā*, *karittā* (Āẏār. 2,15,5; Ovav.; Kappas.; Niraẏāv.); *jāṇittā* (Āẏār. 1,3,1,1. 3,1. 4,2; 1,6,5,2; Dasav. 630,40), *apariẏāṇittā* (Ṭhāṇ. 42), *viẏāṇittā* (Dasav. N. 653,14; Ovav.; Kappas.) from *jñā*; *kiṇittā* (Sūẏag. 609) from *krī*; *abhigiṇhittā* (Āẏār. 2,15,24). *ogiṇhittā* (Ovav.), *pagiṇhittā* (Nāẏādh.) from *grah*. Examples from JM. are: *gantā* (Āv. 42,7); *caḍittā* (Āv. 29,1); *karisittā* = *kṛṣṭvā* (Āv. 28,2); *laṅghittā* (Erz.); *vandittā* (Kk.; Erz.); *melittā* (Kk.); *uṭṭhĕttā* (Āv. 10,41); *ṇhāittā* (Āv. 38,2); *ussārittā*, *ullĕttā* = *ārdrayitvā*, *ṭhavittā*, *bhuñjāvittā*, *mārĕttā*, *veḍhĕttā* (Erz.); *paḍigāhĕttā*, *pāĕttā* = *pāyayitvā*, *vāhittā* (Āv. 9,3; 30,9; 38,6); *vinnavittā* (Kk.); *nevacchĕttā* = **nepathyayitvā* (Āv. 26,27); *āhaṇittā* (Āv. 29,5); *paccakkhāittā* = **pratyākhyāyitvā* (Erz.); *suṇĕttā* (Āv. 7,33; Erz.); *bhuñjittā* (Erz.); *jāṇittā* (Kk.); *giṇhittā* (Sagara 2,17; Kk).—According to Hc. 4,271 in Ś. too the forms in *-ttā* would be permissible, as *bhŏttā* = *bhuktvā*, *hŏttā* = *bhūtvā*, *paḍhittā* = *paṭhitvā*, *rantā* = *ratvā*. But they are altogether foreign to the common Ś[4]. On the other hand they are frequent in JŚ.; to them the rule of Hc. may be related (§ 21). So: *cattā* = *tyaktvā* (Pav. 385,64; Kattig. 403,374); *ṇamaṁasittā* = *namasyitvā* (Pav. 386,6); **ālocittā* = *ālocayitvā* (Pav. 386,11); *niruñjhittā* = *nirudhya* (Pav. 386,70); *ṇihaṇittā* = *nihatya* (Kattig. 401,339); *jāṇittā* = *jñātvā* (Pav. 385,68; Kattig. 401, 340. 342. 350); *viyāṇittā* = *vijñāya* (Pav. 387,21); *bandhittā* = *baddhvā* (Kattig. 402, 355). On AMg. *dissā*, *dissaṁ*, *dissa* = *dṛṣṭvā*, *padissā* = **pradṛṣṭvā* see § 334.

1. The statement of Jacobi (Erz. § 61) that this absol. has rare use in JM. is wrong. Some of the forms in Erz. stand, of course, in places that are written in AMg.; but yet there remain sufficiently others, as the above list shows, that can be multiplied easily.—2. The manuscripts indicate the absolutive very frequently only through ˀttā behind the verbum finitum (Weber, Bhag. 1,382). So here *uvāgacchanti ˀttā*, which is to be read as *uvāgacchittā*. The editor of Vivāhap. has misunderstood this and he gives the forms as *uvāgacchantittā*, *nigacchantittā*, *bandhantittā eḍantittā* (236), *saṁpeheittā* (152), *pasaïttā* (156), *duruheitta* (172), yet *vippajahāmittā* behind *vippajahāmi* (1231, 1242 ff.), *aṇuppavisāmittā* behind *aṇupovisāmi* (1242 ff.) etc. So also *pāuṇantittā* (Sūẏag. 771). Such forms are silently emended above.—3. The commentators see in these and analogous forms in Āẏār. and Sūẏag. often nomina agentis in *-tṛ*. In some places one may be in doubt whether they are correct or not, although phonetics might not present any difficulty.—4. Pischel on Hc. 4,271.

§ 583. In addition to the absolutive in *-ttā* AMg. has an absol. in *-ttāṇaṁ* that presupposes one Vedic **-tvānam*[1]: *bhavittāṇaṁ* (Nāẏādh.; Bhag.), *pāubbhavittāṇaṁ* (Uvās.); *vasittāṇaṁ* (Kappas. § 227); *aṇupariẏaṭṭittāṇaṁ* = **anuparivartitvānam* (Ovav. § 136; Bhag.), *abhinivaṭṭittāṇaṁ* (Sūẏag. 593 ff.); *duruhittāṇaṁ* (Ovav. § 79, II. III); *caïttāṇam* = **tyajitvānam* (Ovav. § 169. Uttar. 12.217. 294. 539.576); *pāsittāṇaṁ* from *paśya-* (Vivāhap. 942. 1322; Niraẏāv. § 7; Nāẏādh. § 22. 23. 24. 44. 46 ff.; Kappas. § 3. 5. 6. 31. 32. 47. 70. 74 ff. 87. p. 96; Nandīs. 169); *ciṭṭhittāṇa* metrically for °*ṇaṁ* (Dasav. 622,28); *āpucchittāṇaṁ* (Kappas. S. §48); *phusittāṇaṁ* from *spṛś* (Ovav. § 131. 140; Bhag.); *saṁpajjittāṇaṁ* (Bhag.), *uvasaṁpajjittā-*

ṇaṁ (Kappas. S. § 50, Ovav. § 30, VI; Bhag.; Uvās.); *jhūsittāṇaṁ* (Ṭhāṇ. 56); *paḍivajjittāṇaṁ* (Āyār. 2,1.11,11); *āyāmĕttāṇaṁ* (Sūyag. 681); *vidittāṇaṁ* (Āyār. 1,7,8,2); *saṁpihittāṇaṁ* = **saṁpidhitvānam* = *saṁpidhāya* (Samav. 81; text °*pa*°); *saṁvidhuṇittāṇaṁ* (Ovav. § 23); *karĕttāṇaṁ* (Dasav. 614,27); *ogiṇhittāṇaṁ* (Kappas. S. § 9; Uvās.), *pagiṇhittāṇaṁ*, *saṁgiṇhittāṇaṁ* (Nāyādh.). *caïttāṇaṁ* in JM. (Kk. 272,11) stands clearly in a metrical quotation in AMg.

1. The form *pītvānam* referred to by the European grammarians (Benfey, Vollst. Gr. § 914, VI, 3; Weber, Bhag. 1,423; Whitney[1], § 993c) rests, as already noted by Wackernagel, Altind. Gr. p. xxiv, note 3, on a printing error in the annotation of the Calcutta edition of Pāṇini 7,1,48. The Kāśikā rightly has *pītvīnaṁ*. That *ṇaṁ* is not an appended particle, as meant by Weber l.c.. Hāla[1] p. 66 f., today no more needs to be pressed forward. In the AMg. texts published by Jacobi, and partly in those published by Leumann too, therefore, the *ṇaṁ* printed separately is to be combined with the preceding absol. That has righty already been observed by Stevenson, Kalpa Sūtra p. 143).

§ 584. Instead of *-ttāṇaṁ* is found according to the grammarians also *-tuāṇaṁ* from -**tuvāṇaṁ* = -**tvānam* (§ 139) and with loss of the nasal *-tuāṇa*: *kāuāṇaṁ* (Hc. 1,27): *haseuāṇaṁ*, *hasiuāṇaṁ*, *ghĕttuāṇaṁ* (Sr. fol. 58. 59); *kāuāṇa* (Hc. 1,27; Sr. fol. 59); *souāṇa*, *bhĕttuāṇa* (Hc. 2,146); *haseuāṇa*, *hasiuāṇa*, *vŏttuāṇa*, *mŏttuāṇa*, *rŏttuāṇa*, *bhŏttuāṇa*, *daṭṭhuāṇa* (Sr. fol. 58. 59); *ghĕttuāṇa* (Hc. 4,210; Sr. fol. 59). Such forms have not yet been located in the texts. On the other hand, the suffix in the form *-tūṇaṁ*, *-ūṇaṁ* and particularly in *-tūṇa*,*-ūṇa* JŚ. *-dūṇa*, P. *-tūna* builds the most usual absol. in M. JM. JŚ. P., that is found in AMg. too, particularly in verses (§ 585. 586). According to Hc. 4,271.272 *-dūṇa* would occur in Ś. too, *bhodūṇa*, *hodūṇa*, *paḍhidūṇa*, *randūṇa*, *karidūṇa*, *gacchidūṇa*. In fact in Ś. and Mg. we find in many dramas the forms in *-tūṇa*, *-ūṇa* (seldom in *-dūṇa*, as would be expected for *-ūṇa*). So Ś. *āaccahiūṇa*, *pĕkkhiūṇa*, *kāriūṇa* (Lalitav. 568,1.2. 5), *kāūṇa* (Vikr. 41,11; 84,8; Mālatīm. 236,2 [°*u*°]; ed. Madras *kādūṇa*), *āgantūṇa* (Mālatīm. 363,7; text °*attū*° ed. Madras. °*ndū*°), *ghĕttūṇa* (Karp. 7,6; Mallikām. 57.19; 159,9 [text *ghakkūṇa*]; 177,21; 191,16 [text *ghĕkkūṇa*]; 219,13 [text *ghakkūṇa*]; 229,8 [text *ghĕkkuṇa*]) and *gheūṇa* (Mālatīm. 149,4; v.l. *ghĕttūṇa*; ed. Madras *ghattūṇa*), *daṭṭhūṇa* (Cait. 38,7), *dāūṇa* (Jīvān. 18,2) etc.; Mg. *paviśiūṇa* (Lalitav. 566,7). AMg. *dāūṇa dattvā* = (NPK 47). In several Indian editions of dramas, as in Cait.; Mallikām.; Kāleyak.; Jīvān., such forms are met with at every step. In verses probably they are correct, as in Mg. *ghĕttūṇa* (Mṛcch. 22,8) and certainly in Ā. D. *bhĕttūṇa* (Mṛcch. 99,17; 100,5), D. *hantūṇa* (Mṛcch. 105,22; so to be read). Elsewhere according to the testimony of the best texts and MSS they are false in Ś. Mg., as also in Mālatīm. 236,2 B rightly has *kadua*. Somadeva and Rājaśekhara mix up the dialects with one another (§ 11.22). JŚ. has the absol. in *-dūṇa*: *kādūṇa*, *ṇedūṇa*, *jāidūṇa*, *gamidūṇa*, *gahidūṇa*, *bhuñjāvidūṇa*, for which the texts mostly wrongly have *-ūṇa* instead of *-dūṇa* (§ 21). The statement of Hc. on Ś. refers to JŚ. here as well.

§ 585 The ending *-tūṇaṁ* = *ūṇaṁ* is found pro ex in PG. *kātūṇaṁ* = **kartvānam* (6,10.29) = AMg. JM. *kāūṇaṁ* (Dasav. N. 645.25; Āv. 9,18; 27,18; 31,14,15; Erz. 72,4; 78,3) beside JM. *viuvviūṇaṁ* (Āv. 31,13); PG.

nātūṇaṁ = **jñātvānam* (6,39) = AMg. JM. *nāūṇaṁ* (Ovav. § 23; Erz. 85, 12); M. *uccariūṇaṁ* (G. 260), *rŏttūṇaṁ* (H. 869); *ghĕttūṇaṁ* (Vajjālagga 324,25); AMg. *uvaüñjiūṇaṁ*, *hoūṇaṁ* (Vivāhap. 550. 1281); *namiūṇaṁ*, *pannaveūṇaṁ* (Dasav. N. 643,33.35), *bandhiūṇaṁ* (Sūẏag. 274.292); JM. *gantūṇaṁ* (Erz. 69,24;75,31; 76,10;77,32;78,9.11; Dvār. 506,16); *bhareūṇaṁ* (Āv. 9,13), *hoūṇaṁ* (Erz. 77,14), *ṇhaviūṇaṁ*, *dāūṇaṁ* (Erz. 69,30), *daṭṭhūṇaṁ* (Āv. 9,11;13,3; 25,17.39; Erz. 79,6.21; 82,18), *paribhamiūṇaṁ* (Erz. 74,34), *jampiūṇaṁ*, *paẏampiūṇam* = **prajalpitvānam* (Erz. 83,2;79,15; 85,28), *viheūṇaṁ* = **vidhayitvānam* = *vidhāya* (Kk. 267,16), *nisuṇiūṇaṁ* (Erz. 77,18) beside *soūṇaṁ* (Kk. 260,17), *chindiūṇaṁ* (Āv. 37,40), *bhuñjiūṇaṁ* (Dvār. 500,36). The form in *-ūṇaṁ*, which is considered as the older one, stands sometimes immediately beside that in *-ūṇa*, in prose before *ca*, as JM. *bhaṇiūṇa āpucchiūṇa...gantūṇaṁ ca* (Dvār. 496,18), *bhañjiūṇaṁ ca.... giṇhiūṇa* (Dvār. 500,29), in verses on metrical grounds, as JM. *nimantiūṇaṁ gantūṇa* (Erz. 80,23), *pĕcchiūṇa kumaro hasiūṇaṁ* (Erz. 82,8). In the sense of the inf. stands *maḷiūṇaṁ* = **mraditvānam* (Āv. 12,8); the prose version at 11,2 for it has *maddiuṁ* = *marditum*.

§ 586. The most usual form of the absol. in M. JM. is that in *-ūṇa*. It is found in AMg. and JŚ. too, where it is pronounced *-dūṇa* (§584). The rules of the infinitive hold good for it. So M. *jeūṇa* Hc. 4,241; G. 1197; R. 8,74) beside JM. *jiṇiūṇa* (Hc. 4,241; Erz. 22,16), *nijjiṇiūṇa* (Erz. 82,13); M. JM. *hoūṇa* (G. H.; Erz.; Dvār. 495,30), according to Hc. 4,240 also *hoaūṇa*; AMg. JM. *caïūṇa* = **tyajitvāna* (Uttar. 30.277.303.552; Erz.); *haseūṇa* (Hc. 3,157; Kī. 4,39) beside M. JM. *hasiūṇa* (Kī. 4,39; H. R.; Sarasvatīk. 135,12; Erz.), M. *vihasiūṇa* (G.); M. JM. AMg. *gantūṇa* (G. R.; Erz.; Āv. 19,3; Ovav. § 168.169); M. AMg. JM. *daṭṭhūṇa* (Hc. 4,213; G. H. R.; Karp. 74,7; Āẏār. 2,3,1,6; Āv. 24,11; Dvār. 498,28; Erz.; Kk.); AMg. *vajjiūṇa* (Paṇṇav. 104); M. JM. *pāūṇa* from *pā* (to drink; G.; Mudrār. 83,2; Dvār. 496,28); M. *voḍhūṇa* (R.); AMg. JM. *vandiūṇa* (Kappas. Th. 13,9; Sagara 2,8;11,12; Kk.); AMg. *laddhūṇa* = **labdhvāna* (Sūẏag. 846. 848); JM, *āpucchiūṇa* (Erz.; Dvār. 496,18); M. JM. *mŏttūṇa* = **muktvāna* (Hc. 4,212.237; G. H. R.; Viddhaś. 11,8; Erz.; Kk.; Dvār. 497,18; 498, 38; Sagara 7,13; JM. *mariūṇa* (Sagara 11,7.9); AMg. *viddhūṇa* = **viddhvāna* (Sūẏag. 928); M. *paḍivajjiūṇa* = **pratipadyitvāna* = *pratipadya* (H.); M. *uḍḍeūṇa* (G.); *avahatthiūṇa*, *pajjāliūṇa*, *āphāliūṇa* (H.), *uaūheūṇa* = *upagūhya*, *ṇiameūṇa* = *niyamya* (R.); JM. *sammāṇeūṇa* (Erz.); *ḍhakkeūṇa* (Dvār. 499, 8), *rañjiūṇa* (KI. 11); *bheseūṇa* = **bheṣayitvāna* (Kk.), *ṭhaviūṇa* (Sagara 1, 10; Erz.), *thāiūṇa* = **sthāgayitvāna* (Āv. 30,4); M. D. JM. *hantūṇa* (Hc. 4,244; R.; Mṛcch. 105,22 [so to be read]; Erz.) beside M. *ahaṇiūṇa* (Mṛcch. 41,16), JM. *haṇiūṇa* (Āv. 17,31); M. *rŏttūṇa* (Bh. 8,55; Hc.4,212; R.), M. also *roūṇa* (H.), whilst JM. *roviūṇa* (Sagara 7,11) belongs to *ru* (§ 473); *vĕttūṇa* (Bh. 8,55); M. *vŏttūṇa* from *vac* (Hc. 4,211; R.); JM. *piheūṇa* (Sagara 10,17); M. JM. AMg. *dāūṇa* (Bh. 4,23; G.; Kāvyaprakāśa 343, 3; Dvār. 500,19; Erz. 78,1; Paṇhāv. 367); M. *dhuṇiūṇa* (R. 6,20); JM. *pāviūṇa* (Erz.); M. JM. *soūṇa* (Bh. 4,23; Hc. 3,157; 4,237; G. H. R.; Erz.; Kk.; Sagara 7,.; 11,12; Āv. 18,20; 31,23) beside *suṇiūṇa* (Hc. 3,157);

JM. *chĕttūṇa* (Erz.) and *chediūṇa* (Kk.) II, 507,11); JM. *bhañjiūṇa* and °*je*° (Erz.); Ā. D. JM. *bhĕttūṇa* (Mṛcch. 99,17;100,5; Erz.), JM. also *bhindiūṇa* (Sagara 3,1.6.18); AMg. *bhŏttūṇa* (Vr. 8,55; Hc. 4,212; Ovav. § 185), JM. also *uvabhuñjiūṇa* (Erz.); VG. *kātūṇa* (101,9), JŚ. *kādūṇa* (§ 21.584), M. JM. *kāūṇa* (Bh. 4,23; 8,17; Hc. 2,146; 4,214; G. H. R.; Erz.; Kk.; Dvār. 499,39 etc.), wrongly also in Ś. (§ 584), JM. also *viuvviūṇa* (Dvār. 507,40; Erz.); M. JM. *gahiūṇa* (G. 282; Vajjālagga 326,9; Erz.; Dvār. 503,1; KI. 17; Kk. II, 505,29) beside JM. *gĕṇhiūṇa* (Āv. 43,7; Erz.); M. JM. AMg. *ghĕttūṇa* (Vr. 8,16; Hc. 2,146; 4,210; G. H. R.; Erz.; Kk.; Sagara 5,14; Nāẏādh. 960; Paṇhāv. 367), which is found in verse in Mg. too (Mṛcch. 22,8) and falsely in Ś. too (§ 584), AMg. *parighĕttūṇa* (Paṇhāv. 487) and M. *gheūṇa* (Bh. 4,23; Sarasvatīk. 180,4 as v.l. to H. 130 but *ghĕttūṇa* 347,9; Priyad. 33,15: falsely in Ś. § 584) belong to **ghṛp*; M. *ṇāūṇa*, JM. *nāūṇa* (Hc. 4,7; R. 11,21; Dvār. 496,16; Erz.; Kk.) beside M. JM. AMg. *jāṇiūṇa* (H.; Kk.; Āv. 8,23; Paṇhāv. 394), JM. *viẏāṇiūṇa* (Erz.); M. *ābandhiūṇa* (R. 12.60); AMg. *bandhiūṇa* (Sūẏag. 285).—In P. the absol. ends, according to Hc., in *-tūna*; *samappetūna* = **samarpayitvāna* (2,164), *gantūna*, *rantūna*, *hasitūna*, *paḍhitūna*, *kadhitūna* (4,312), *naṭṭhūna*, *natthūna*, *daṭṭhūna* from *naś* and *dṛś* (4,313), according to Vr. 10,13; Mk. fol. 87 in *-tūnaṁ* : *dātūnaṁ*, *kātūnaṁ*, *ghĕttūnaṁ*, *hasitūnaṁ*, *patitūnaṁ*; Sr. fol. 64,65 permits both the forms : *hasitūnaṁ*, *hasitūna*, *daṭṭhūna*, *datthūna*; Namisādhu on Rudraṭa, Kāvyālaṁkāra 2,12 p. 14,11 has *āgantūna*, Amaracandra in Kāvyakalpalatāvṛtti p. 9 *gantūna*.

§ 587. Beside *-ttā* = *-tvā* is found in AMg. JŚ., very seldom in JM. too, also *-ccā*, beside *-ttāṇaṁ* in AMg. also *-ccāṇaṁ*, *-ccāṇa*. Since Vedic *-tyā* stands just metrically for *-tya*, which is added to compound roots ending in a short vowel and a nasal showing suffix, whilst *-ccā* always has *-ā* in prose, that is seldom shortened in verses, and enters also after every kind of root ending in a consonant, it is not correct to trace *-ccā* back directly to Vedic *-tyā*. There occurs the change of *-tvā* into -**tyā*, of -**tvānam* into -**tyānam*, that is found elsewhere too in AMg. (§ 281.299). Thus : AMg. *hŏccā* = **bhūtyā* = *bhūtvā* (Sūẏag. 859); AMg. JŚ. *ṭhiccā* = **sthityā* (Sūẏag. 565; Vivāhap. 739.927; Kattig. 402,355); AMg. *suṭhiccā* (Sūẏag. 938.941.950); AMg. *ciccā* (Sūẏag. 117.378; Uttar. 515; Kappas. § 112) and *cĕccā* (Āẏār. 1,6,2,2;2,15,17; Ovav. § 23 from **tiyaktyā* (§ 280) = *tyaktvā*, *pĕccā* = *pitvā* (Āẏār. 2,1,4,5), *apiccā* = *apitvā* (Sūẏag. 994).—AMg. *pĕccā* (Āẏār. 1,1,1,3), *piccā* (Sūẏag. 28) is also = **pretyā* = *pretya*.—AMg. *abhisamĕccā* = **abhisametyā* = *abhisametya* (Āẏār. 1,1,3,2 [so to be read]; 1,7,6,2.7,1); *vaccā* (Sūẏag. 565 ff.), probably more correctly *vuccā* (Sūẏag. 783) = **vaktyā* = *uktvā*; *daccā* from *dā* (Vivāhap. 227); *hiccā* from *hā* (to lose; Sūẏag. 330.345; Āẏār. 1,4,4,1; 1,6,2,1.4,1); *hiccā* from *hā* (to leave; Sūyag. 330. 345; Āẏār. 1.4.4.1; 1.6.2, 1.4,1) also *hĕccā* (Āẏār. 1,6,4,3) and metrical *hĕcca* (Sūẏag. 144); *sŏccā* from *śru* (Hc. 2,15; Āẏār. 1,1,1,4.2,4;1,5,3,1;1,6,4,1;1,7,2,3;2,4, 1,1; Sūẏag. 154.181.298.322 etc.; Dasav. 631,18; Ovav.; Kappas.; Uvās.), these also in JŚ. (Pav. 386,6) and JM. (Kk.; where also *succā*), also *sŏccaṁ* in AMg. *sŏccam idaṁ* (§ 349; Āẏār. 2,16,1); *bhŏccā* from *bhuj* (Hc. 2,15;

Āyār. 2,1,4,5. 9,4.10,3; Sūyag. 194.202.203.226; Vivâhap. 227; Kappas.); *abhŏccā* (Sūyag. 994), metrically also *abhŏcca* (Āyār. 1,8,1,10); AMg. JŚ. *kiccā* from *kṛ* (Āyār. 2,3,1,14.2,9; Sūyag. 26; Bhag.; Uvās,; Ovav.; Kappas.; Pav. 379,4; Kattig. 402,356 ff. 375 f.; AMg. *ṇaccā, naccā* from *jñā* (Hc. 2,15; Āyār. 1,3,2,1.3; 1,6,1,3.4; 1,7,8,1.25; 1,8,1,11.14.15; 2,1,2,5 ff.; Sūyag. 155.228.237; Dasav. 629,5; 631,35; 633,35). The ending *-ccāṇa, -ccāṇaṁ* occurs in AMg. *hiccāṇaṁ* (Sūyag. 86), *hĕccāṇaṁ* (Sūyag. 433), *ṇaccāṇaṁ* (Sūyag. 43); metrically also *hĕccāṇa* (Sūyag. 551), *naccāṇa* (Sūyag. 188), *sŏccāṇa* (Dasav. 634,41; 637,16), *ciccāṇa* (Sūyag. 378. 408). In prose *cĕccāṇa* (Āyār. 1,7,6,5) is hardly correct. The ed. Calc. has *cĕccā*.—On AMg. *bujjhā* = *buddhvā* see § 299.

§ 588. The Vedic absol. in *-tvī* (DELBRÜCK, Altind. Verbum. § 221) and *-tvīnam*, as *iṣṭvīnam, pītvīnam* (Pāṇini 7,1,48 and Kāśikā thereupon; cf. above § 583 note) have been retained in A. *-tvī* became *-ppi*, after nasals *-pi* (§ 300), which after long vowels, later after short vowels too became *-vi* : *-tvīnam*, corresponding to it, has become *-ppiṇu, -piṇu, -viṇu* (Hc. 4, 439.440; Kī. 5,53). The endings are mostly added to the present stem. So: *jiṇĕppi* (Hc. 4,442,2) and *jĕppi* (Hc. 4,440) from *ji*; *jhāivi* from *dhyai* (Hc. 4,331); *dĕppiṇu* = **detvīnam* from *daya-* (Hc. 4,440); *gampi* = **gantvī* = Vedic *gatvī́*, *gamĕppi, gampiṇu, gamĕppiṇu* (Hc. 4,442; Kī. 5,59); *pĕkkhevi* (Hc. 4,340,2), *pĕkkhivi* (Hc. 4,430,3; so to be read), *pĕkkheviṇu* (Hc. 4, 444,4); *dĕkkhivi* (Hc. 4,354); *chaḍḍeviṇu* from *chard* (Hc. 4,422,3); *mĕllavi* (Hc. 4,353), *mĕllĕppiṇu* (Hc. 4,341,1) from *mĕllaï* (gives up; Hc. 4,91. 430,3); *melavi* from *mil* (Hc. 4,429,1); *cumbivi, vichoḍavi* (Hc. 4,439,3.4); *bhaṇivi* (Hc. 4,383.1; so to be read); *piavi* from **pibatvī* = Vedic *pītvī́* (Hc. 4,401,3); *marĕppi* (Kī. 5,60); *laggivi* (Hc. 4,339); *buḍḍavi* (Hc.4,415); *lāivi* = **lāgayitvī* (Hc. 4,331.376,2); *levi* (Hc. 4,395,1.440), *lĕppiṇu* (Hc. 4,370,3. 404), *leviṇu* (Hc. 4,441,2) from *lā*; *brŏppi, brŏppiṇu* from *brū* (Hc. 4,391; Kī. 5,58); *rundheviṇu* (Vikr. 67,20); *karĕppi, kṛppi* (Kī. 5,59), *karevi* (Hc. 4,340,2), *karĕppiṇu* (Hc. 4,396,3); *ramevi, remĕppi, ramĕppiṇu* from *ram* (Kī. 5,53); *luṇĕppi* (Kī. 5,57); *vuñĕppi, vuñĕppiṇu* from *vraj* (§ 488; Hc. 4,392); *gṛṇhĕppiṇu* (Hc. 4,394.438,1), *gĕṇhĕppi, gĕṇhĕppiṇu* (Kī. 5,62). Forms in *-ūṇa*, as *soūṇa, hasiūṇa* (Piṅgala 1,61[a], 62[a]) are not A., but M., and reversely the forms like *laṅghevi, pĕcchavi, nisuṇevi, vajjevi, jālevi*, that are found in JM. (Erz. 78,21; 81,19.24; 84,5), do not belong to this dialect, but to A. In A. these absolutives are used in the sense of the infinitive too : *saṁvarevi* (Hc. 4,422,6); *jĕppi, caĕppiṇu* = **tyajitvīnam, leviṇu, pālevi* (Hc. 4,441,2); *lahevi, lahĕppi, lahĕppiṇu* (Kī. 5,55), as on the other hand, the inf. *bhajjiu* stands in the sense of the absol. (§ 579). On the absolutively used inf. in *-tum, -tu* see § 576.577.

§ 589. The absolutiva in *-ia* = *-ya* are very rare in M., since M. employs the ending *-ūṇa*. In G. R. no example is found. In H. a single example probably is *saṁmilia* (137); hence we should write *saṁmiliadāhiṇa-aṁ* = *saṁmilitadakṣiṇakam* and take it as an adverb, parallel to *suiraṁ* and *aviaṇhaṁ*, standing beside it. *pāḍia* (880) should not, with WEBER, be taken as a "ger•ndium", but as a past passive participle with the scholiasts, likewise *aṇuṇia* (129) against WEBER and the scholiasts, to be read, therefore, *aṇuṇiapio*. In Kāvyaprakāśa 72,10 = H. 977, instead of *balāmoḍia*, with the best manuscripts we should read *balāmoḍii* (§ 238), as also Rājānakānanda has in his Kāvyaprakāśanidarśana; the second best manuscript of Kāvyapr. reads *balāmoḍheṇa*. H. 879, where WEBER, earlier (H.[1] Supplement No. 44) read *pĕkkhia uṇa* with Kāvyapr. 68,5 and Sāhityad. 102,20, now correctly he has *pĕkkhiūṇa*, as also the best manuscripts of Kāvyapr. have and stands in Sarasvatīk. 48.21. In the verse of Dhanika, Daśarūpa 91,9 we should read *ṇijjhāaṇehamuddhaṁ*, therefore, *ṇijjhāa* = *nirdhyāta*. Of the examples collected by WEBER, H.[1] p. 67, according to him *gahia* (Kāvyapr. 82,9) alone stands the test, for which we should read *lahia* according to the best manuscripts. Besides there comes *viṇijjia* = *vinirjitya* (Karp. 8,6) and *vajjia* = °*varjya* (Bālar. 157,4), whilst at 10, 10 *ŏtthariа*, which the editor translates as *avatīrya*, is = *avastṛta*, whilst *ŏtthariarāhu*° stands for *rāhuŏtthаria*°, as elsewhere too (§ 603). Nothing can be said with regard to the dialect whence originate *bhamia*, *ramia* in Hc. 2,146 and *gĕṇhia* at 4,210. Vr. 4,23; 8,16 does not mention for M. the ending *-ya*. Therefore, here too particularly Rājaśekhara has again erred against the dialect.

§ 590. The absol. in *-ya* is rare in the old Āv. -texts in JM. too; on the other hand, it is frequent in later day passages in Erz. But here too it enters again the endings *-ūṇa* and *-ttā*, as in AMg. against *-ttā*, *-ttāṇaṁ*. In AMg. a number of absol. in *-ya*, that are formed, as in Skt. directly from the root, are current. Excepting verses (§ 584) and excluding the absol. *kadua* and *gadua* (§ 581) *-ya* is the only prevalent ending in Ś. Mg. Ḍh. (Vr. 12,9; cf. § 581), in which it enters almost always into the crude form or into the present stem in *-i*. In AMg. JM. in verses the ending is often *-ẏā* (§ 73). In JŚ. too- *ẏa* is not seldom. Examples for individual classes are: Ś. *ṇaïa* = **ṇayiya* = *nitvā* (Mṛcch. 155,4), but *āṇia* (Mālatīm. 236,3; Pras. 41,2), *avaṇia* = *apaniya* (Veṇīs. 66,21); Ś. *samassaïa* = **samāśrayiya* = *samāśritya* (Śak. 2,8); Ś. *daïa* from *daya-* (Mṛcch. 51,12), and *deia* from *de-* (Mudrār. 203,7); Ś. Mg. *bhavia*, JŚ. *bhaviẏa* (§ 475); AMg. *viṇikkassa* = *vinikṛṣya* (Sūẏag. 280); Ś. *odaria* = *avatīrya* (Vikr. 23,17), Mg. *odalia* (Mṛcch. 122, 11); Mg. *aṇuśalia* = *anusṛtya-* (Prab. 51,12), *ośalia* = *apasṛtya* (Mṛcch. 129, 8); Ś. *pariharia* (Mṛcch. 136,8), Mg. *palihalia* (Prab. 28,16; 51,12) = *parihṛtya*; JM. *sumariẏa* (Erz.), Ś. *sumaria* (Mṛcch. 8,15; Śak. 63,14); JM. *pĕcchiẏa* (Sagara 4,2. 11; Erz.), *pikkhiẏa* (Kk.), Ś. *pĕkkhia* (Mṛcch. 41,6.10.22; 73,2; 78,25; Śak. 18,10; Vikr. 15,16), Mg. *pĕskia* (Mṛcch. 96,23), AMg. *pehiẏā*, *sāpehiẏā*, *samupehiẏā* (§323); AMg. *uvalabbha* (Āẏār. 1,6,4,1), *labhiẏa* (Āẏār. 1,7,1,2; 2,4,1,2), but Ś. *lambhia* (§ 484. 525.541; Cait. 125,10; 132,17; 134,9), AMg. *nikkhamma* = *niṣkramya* (Āẏār. 1,6,4,1), but Ś. *ṇikkamia* (Priyad. 34,3); AMg. *viukkamma* = *vyutkramya* (Āẏār. 1,7,1,2), but Ś. *adikkamia* = *atikramya* (Ratn., 295,9); AMg. *pakkhippa* = *prakṣipya* (Sūẏag. 280.282); AMg. *pāsiẏa* (Āẏār. 1,3,2,3); metrically (§ 73) also AMg. JM. *pāsiẏā* (Uttar. 361; Erz. 38,36), and AMg. *passa* (Uttar. 222. 239. 240), *aṇupassiẏā* (Sūẏag. 122), *saṁpassiẏa* (Dasav. 642,11); AMg. JM. *pariccajja* (Āẏār. 1,3,3,3; Uttar. 561; Erz.), JM. also *pariccaïẏa* (Erz.), Ś. *pariccaïa*

(Mṛcch. 28,10; Ratn. 298,12) = *parityajya*[1]; AMg. *samārabbha* (Samav. 81), JM. *ārabbha* (Erz.), but Ś. *ārambhia* (Śak. 50,2); AMg. *abhikaṅkha* = *abhikāṅkṣya* (Āyār. 2,4,1,6, ff.); AMg. *abhirujjha* = *abhiruhya* (Āyār. 1,8,1,2), but A. D. Ś. *ahiruhia* (Mṛcch. 99,19; 103,15; Vikr. 15,5), Mg. *ahiluhia* (Mṛcch. 99,4; 121,11; 164,3); AMg. *pavissa* = *praviśya* (Āyār. 1,8,4,9), but Ś. *pavisia* (Mṛcch. 18,10; 27,3; 93,2; Śak. 70,7; 115,6; 125,13; Vikr. 75,4), Mg. *paviśia* (Mṛcch. 19,10; 29,24; 37,10; 112,11; 125,22; 131,18); JŚ. *āpiccha* (Pav. 386,1), JM. *āpucchiẏa* (Dvār. 495,31 between *cintiūṇa* and *paṇamiūṇaṁ*), *aṇāpucchiẏa* (Āv. 11,23); Ś. *siñcia* (Mṛcch. 41,6); AMg. *nisamma* from *śam* (Āyār. 1,6,4,1; Kappas.); *vissamia* from *śram* (Mālatīm. 34,1); JM. *paḍivajjiẏa* = *pratipadya* (Erz.); AMg. *paḍucca* for **paḍiucca* from *paḍivaccaï* (§ 163. 202; Vivāhap. 29. 35. 99. 111. 127. 128. 136. 272 etc.; Ṭhāṇ. 185. 186; Āyār. 1,5,5,5; Sūyag. 332. 776; Uttar. 1019. 1044. 1047. 1051 ff.; Nandīs. 395 ff.; Jīv. 33. 118 ff.; Aṇuog. 14. 15. 154 ff.; 235 ff.; Dasav. N. 644,17; 649,9 etc.), in verses also *paḍuccā* (Sūyag. 266; Dasav. N. 644,13); Ś. *paṭṭhāvia*, *ṭhāvia* (Mṛcch. 24,2; 59,7); JM. *āroviẏa* (Erz.), *samāroviẏa* (Dvār. 503,33); Ś. *vajjia* = *varjayitvā* (Śak. 52,11 [so to be read]; Mālatīm. 98,6; Ratn. 316,16; Nāgān. 24,4), also in Ḍh. (Mṛcch. 30,5); Ś. *coria*, *vāvādia* (Mṛcch. 37,14; 40,22); Mg. *paveśia* (Mṛcch. 140,14 [so to be read with GODABOLE]; 158,22), *ohālia* = *apahārya* (Mṛcch. 96,24). In the sense of the inf. is used AMg. *aṇupāliẏā* = *anupālya* (Uttar. 583).

1. Accordingly from *tyaj* the attested absol. are : JŚ. *cattā* (§ 582, AMg. *caïttā* (§ 582), AMg. *caïttāṇaṁ* (§ 583), AMg. JM. *caïūṇa* (§ 586), AMg. *ciccā*, *cĕccā*, *ciccāṇa*, *cĕccāṇa*. (§ 587); A. *caĕppiṇu* (§ 588), AMg. JM. °*cajja*, JM. *caïẏa* Ś. *caïa* (a 590). Besides the absolutively used inf. AMg. *caïttu*.

§ 591. Examples of the 2. conjugation are : AMg. *samĕcca* = *sametya* (Āyār. 1,8,15); JM. *thuṇiya* (Kk. II. 508,26) from *stu*; Ś. *ṇisasia* from *śvas* with *nis* (Mṛcch. 41,22); AMg. *āhacca* = *āhatya* (Āyār. 1,1,4,6. 7,4; 1,7,2,4; 2,6,2,3), but Ś. *āhaṇia* (Ratn. ed. Calc. 1871 p. 46,10); JŚ. *ādāya* (Pav. 386,6), AMg. *samādāya* (Āyār. 1,2,6,3), *paḍisaṁdhāya* (Sūyag. 720), *paṇihāya* = *praṇidhāya* (Uvās. § 192); AMg. *jahāya* (Uttar. 635. 914), *vippajahāya* from *hā* with *vi* and *pra* (Sūyag. 217. 628; Vivāhap. 146); falsely Ś. *ṇimmāya* (Lalitav. 554,13), for which **ṇimmāia* would be correct; AMg. *dhuṇiẏa* (Sūyag. 111; Dasav. 637,21), *vihūṇiyā* (Āyār. 1,7,8,24; Sūyag. 54), *vihuṇiya* (Sūyag. 113), *saṁvidhuṇiya* (Āyār. 1,7,6,5); Ś. *odhuṇia* (Adbhutad. 52,12; so to be read), *avadhuṇia* (Mālatīm. 351,6; Veṇīs. 61,5 [so to be read]; 63,9); JM. *suṇiẏa* (Erz.; Kk.), Ś. *suṇia* (Mṛcch. 148,10; Śak. 62,11; 70,11; Vikr. 26,1; Ratn. 302,7; Priyad. 29,17), Mg. *śuṇia* (Mṛcch. 37,10; 38,20). Ḍh. *paḍissudia* = *pratiśrutya* (Mṛcch. 35,5) must in any case be pronounced as *paḍiśudia* (cf. v. l.); it is wanting in most of the MSS/, in GODABOLE too. AMg. JŚ. *pappa* = *prāpya* (Āyār. 1,2,3,6; Ṭhāṇ. 188; Uttar. 1017. 1019; Paṇṇav. 523. 540. 541. 665. 667. 712. 781; Dasav. N. 649,5. 8. 11 [°*ā*]; 653,1; Pav. 384,49), but JŚ. also *pāviẏa* (Kattig. 402, 369) like Ś. *samāvia* (Ratn. 323,2); Ś, *bhañjia* (Mṛcch. 40,22; 97,23; Śak. 31,13; Cait. 134,12);

AMg. *chindiẏa* (Āẏār. 2,1,2,7), *chindiẏachindiẏā*, *bhindiẏabhindiẏā* (Vivāhap. 1192); Ś. *paricchindia* (Vikr. 47,1); AMg. *palicchindiẏa* (§ 257); Ś. *bhindia* (Vikr. 16,1) and *bhedia* (Mṛcch. 97,24; cf. § 586), Mg. *bhindia* (Mṛcch. 112 17); AMg. *bhuñjiẏa* (Āẏār. 1,7,1,2; 2.4,1,2; Sūẏag. 108), Ś. *bhuñjia* (Cait. 126,10; 129,10); AMg. *abhijuñjiẏa* (Sūẏag. 293 [°*ẏa*]; Ṭhāṇ. 111. 112. 194; Vivāhap. 178); JM. *niuñjiẏa* (Erz.); AMg. *parinnāẏa* (Āẏār. 1,1,2,6 ff.; 1,2,6,2. 5; Sūẏag. 214) [°*ṇṇā*°], and *parijāṇiyā* (Sūẏag. 380. 381), *jāṇiẏa* (Dasav. 641,24), *viẏāṇiẏā* (Dasav. 631,35; 637,5; 642,12); Ś. *jāṇia* (Ratn. 314,25; Priyad. 15,15; Vṛṣabh. 46,7), *aāṇia* (Śak. 50,13; Mudrār. 226,7 v. l.), Mg. *yāṇia* (Mṛcch. 36,12); Ś. *bandhia* (Mṛcch. 155,3; Prab. 14,10 [so to be read with P. M.]; Ratn. 317,11), *ubbandhia* (Ratn. 315,28; Caṇḍak. 92,11; Nāgān. 34,15), Mg. *bāndhia* (Mṛcch. 163,16); JM. *gĕṇhiẏa* (Dvār. 507,4), Ś. Ā. *gĕṇhia* (Mṛcch. 41,12; 59,8; 75,8; 105,2 [Ā.]; 107,10; Śak. 136,15; Vikr. 10,2; 52,5; 72,15; 84,20; Mālatīm. 72,7; Ratn. 303,20), Mg. *gĕṇhia* (Mṛcch. 12,14; 20,3. 10; 96,12. 18; 116,5; 126,16; 132,16; Śak. 116;2; Caṇḍak. 64,8), JŚ. JM. *gahiẏa* (Kattig. 403,373; Erz.), but in AMg. JM. mostly *gahāẏa* (Āẏār. 1,8,3,5; 2,3,1,16. 17. 2,2. 3. 16; 2,10,22; Sūẏag. 136. 491. 783. 1017; Vivāhap. 229. 825. 826; Uvās.; Niraẏāv.; Āv. 17,10; 35,12; 37,31; 46,2; Erz) = Skt. *grahāya* (BÖHTLINGK s. v.), a retranslation into Skt., since *gahāẏa* is an absol. from a denominative **gahāaï*, **gahāi* (§ 558) = **grahāyati*; in compounds also AMg. *abhiṇigijjha* = *abhinigṛhya* (Āẏār. 1,3,3,4), *parigijjha* = *parigṛhya* (Āẏār. 1,2,3, 3.5) and the double forms AMg. *avagijjhiẏa*, *nigijjhiẏa* (Kappas.), *pagijjhiẏa* (Āẏār. 2,1,6,2; 2,3, 1,15; 2,3,3,1—3; Ovav.).

§ 592. Corresponding to the absol. in *-ttāṇaṁ*, *-ttāṇa* beside *-ttā* and *-ccāṇaṁ*, *-ccāṇa* beside *-ccā* AMg. has an absol. in *-ẏāṇaṁ*, *-ẏāṇa* too, beside that in *-ẏa*, metrically *-ẏā*[1]: *āviḷiẏāṇa*, *paripiliẏāṇa*, *parissāviẏāṇa* from *piḍ* and *sru* (Āẏār. 2,1,8,1); *ussiñciẏāṇaṁ* from *sic* with *ud* (Āẏār. 2,1,7,8); *saṁsiñciẏāṇaṁ* from *sic* with *sam*[2] (Āẏār. 1,2,3,5); *samupehiẏāṇaṁ* metrically for °*ppe*° from *ikṣ* with *samutpra* like *samupehiẏā* (§ 323. 590; Erz. 38,36 in a citation from Āvaśyakaniryukti 17,41)[3]; *lahiẏāṇa* = *labdhvā* (Uttar. 627); *ārusiẏāṇaṁ* = *āruśya* (Āẏār. 1,8,1,2); *takkiẏāṇaṁ* = *tarkayitvā* (Āẏār. 1,7.2, 4); *parivajjiẏāṇa* = *parivarjya* (Āẏār. 1,8,1,12. 18); *oattiẏāṇaṁ* = *apavartya* (Āẏār. 2,1,7,8); *palicchindiẏāṇaṁ* = *paricchidya* (Āẏār. 1,3,2,1); *palibhindiẏāṇaṁ* = *paribhidya* (Sūẏag. 243); *abhijuñjiẏāṇaṁ* = *abhiyujya* (Āẏār. 1,2,3,5); *akiẏāṇaṁ* = *akṛtvā* (Ovav. § 142).

1. There are insurmountable phonetic difficulties against the derivation of *-yāṇaṁ* from *-ttāṇaṁ*. JACOBI, in his edition of the Āẏār. throughout separates *ṇaṁ* here too wrongly as is proved by the form in *-āẏṇa*.—2. So to be read with B, which is pointed to also by the explanation as *saṁsicya* by the scholiasts. Cf. *saṁsiccamāṇā* 1.3,2,1—3. JACOBI, Erz. p. 158.

§ 593. In AMg. a number of forms are found in *-āe*, that are used absolutively: *āyāe* (Āẏār. 1,6,2,1 2; 2,1,3,6 ff.; 2,1,9,2; Vivāhap. 136; Niraẏāv. § 17. 19) = *ādāya*; *samāẏāe* (Āẏār. 1,5,3,5); *nisāe* (Bhag.; Kappas.), *nissāe* (Bhag.) = Pāli *nissāya* = Skt. **niśrāya* from *śri* (cf. *gahāẏa* § 591); *saṁkhāe*

= *saṁkhyāya* beside *uṭṭhāya* (Āyār. 1,8,1,1); *samuṭṭhāe* (Āyār. 1,2,2,1.6,1); *pehāe* from *ikṣ* with *pra* (§ 323); *aṇupehāe* (§ 323); *uvehāe* (Āyār. 1,3,3,1), *saṁpehāe* (§ 323)[1]. Since these forms are connected with the accusative, as in *egaṁ appāṇaṁ saṁpehāe* (Āyār. 1,4,3,2), *āuraṁ logaṁ āyāe* (Āyār. 1,6,2,1), it cannot be doubted that they have a verbal meaning. In very many cases, however, they certainly are nominal forms, as in the frequent *uṭṭhāe, uṭṭhei, uṭṭhāe uṭṭhittā* (Uvās. § 193; Nirayāv. § 5; Ovav. § 58.60; Vivāhap. 161. 1246), *uṭṭhāe uṭṭhĕnti* (Ovav. § 61). The scholiasts see in *uṭṭhāe* an ins. sing. of a fem. **uṭṭhā*[2], what and what only the form can be according to meaning and order of words[3]. Likewise e.g. in *aṇāṇāe puṭṭhā* = *anājñayā* (in the sense of *anājñānena*) *spṛṣṭāḥ* (Āyār. 1,2,2 1), and in cases like *aṭṭam eyaṁ tu pehāe aparinnāe kandaï* (Āyār 1,2,5,5), it can hardly be doubted that *aparinnāe* is = *aparijñayā*, and not *aparijñāya*, as the scholiasts like[4]; whilst *pehāe*, standing beside it, undoubtedly has the sense of the absol., but according to the form is = *prekṣayā*. Consequently I believe that all these forms are originally in the instr. of the fem. in *-ā*, that would be used also as verbal forms. In support of this speak the cases like *annamannavitigiṁchāe paḍilehāe* too (Āyār. 1,3,3,1), where the compositum *annam°* points to the nominal nature of *vitigiṁchāe*, whilst a verbal meaning to *paḍilehāe*, standing by it, can be deduced from examples like *nigganthā paḍilehāe buddhavuttam ahiṭṭhagā* (Dasav. 626,23) although it is often elsewhere certainly substantival (e. g. Āyār. 1,2,6,2; 1,5,1,1; 1,7,2,3), whilst sometimes (Āyār. 1,2,5,5; 1,5, 6,2) one may be in doubt. In the literal sense "to cleanse", "to wipe off" the absolutive is *paḍilehittā* (Āyār. 2,2,1,2 ff.) or *paḍilehiyā* (Āyār. 1,7,8,7; 2,1,1,2 [°*ya*°]; but *paḍilehittā* also in the transferred sense "to discuss", "to consider" (Āyār. 1,1,6,2; 1,7,8,20). *pehāe, saṁpehāe* are hardly to be explained otherwise. Forms like *āyāe, nisāe* may be built on such a pattern. In no case can *-e* be equated as = *-ya*[5]. AMg. *aṇuvii* (Āyār. 1,1,3,7; 1,4,3,1; 1,6,5,3; 2,2,3,3; 2,4,1,3. 2,19; 2,7,1,2. 2,1. 8; p. 133,8.10; 134,5 ff.; Sūyag. 474. 531; Dasav. 629,15; 630,1; Dasav. N. 661,3 [*aṇuvii*]), with privative *a aṇaṇuvii* (Āyār. p. 133,9. 10; 134,6 ff.) is explained as *anucintya, anuvicintya, vicārya* by the scholiasts. The frequent vv. ll. *aṇuviyi, aṇuviyi, aṇuvīti, aṇuvitiya* show that in this case we have nothing to do with an absol. *aṇuvii* is an adverb = **aṇuviti* "deeply" "attentively" and belongs to Vedic *viti*[6].

1. JACOBI writes sometimes *saṁpehāe*, sometimes *sapehāe*, sometimes *sa pehāe*, even in the same paragraphs, as 1,4,3,2, where stands in line 10 *saṁpehāe*, in line 14 *sa pehāe*. The manuscripts are not consistent; cf. pro ex. 1,2,2,4. Throughout it is to be read *saṁpehāe*, in verses, where a short syllable is required, probably *sāpehāe*.—2. WEBER, Bhag. 1,435, note.—3. HOERNLE on Uvās. Transl. note 286 wants to see in it the dat. sing. of a masc. *uṭṭha*.—4. The ed. Calc. reads *aparinnāya*, but the scholiasts, like JACOBI, *aparinnāe*. —5. E. MÜLLER, Beiträge p. 63.—6. Cf. PISCHEL, Ved. Stud. 1,295 ff.; GELDNER. 2,156 ff. *viti* requires a fresh research.

§ 594. In A: *-ya* becomes *-i* (Hc. 4,439), that has originated from Pkt.-*ia*, through the dropping off of *a*: *daï* = Ś. *daïa* from *daya-* (Piṅgala 1,5*a* [cf. BOLLENSEN, Vikr. p. 530]. 38. 39. 86*a* 122), also contracted (§ 166) *de*

(Piṅgala 1,33); *parihari*, *pasari* (P. 1,120a. 143a); *gaï* from *gā* (to go; P. 2, 64); *bhaï* = **bhavi* = Ś. Mg. *bhavia* from *bhū* (P. 2,243); *cali* (P. 2,88); *vali* (IS. 15,394; Prabandhac. 159,1); *kŏppi* = °*kupya* (P. 1,123a) from the present stem; *māri* = °*mārya* = *mārayitvā* (Hc. 4,439,1); *saṁcāri*, *vicāri* (P. 1,43.107); *laï* from *lā* (to take; P. 1,37. 86. 107.121); *kari* (Hc. 4, 357,4; P. 1,81.82.86); *jāni* from *jñā* (P. 1,119). Beside *ṭhavi* (P. 1,102. 107) = Ś. *ṭhavia* = °*sthāpya* is found *thappi* (P. 1,123a,137a), that may be considered as a case of double formation. The reduplication may be purely metrical too, as probably this is the case in *jiṇṇi* = **jiṇia* from *ji* (§ 473) and *suṇṇi* = Ś. *suṇia* from *śru* (P. 2,112.242). Whether forms in *-ia* such as *kaḍḍhia*, *laïa* (P. 1,107. 121), *ṇisuṇia*, *suṇia* (Sarasvatīk. 140,1;216,9) are regular, may be ascertained only by critical texts. *mutti* (P. 1,116a) presupposes one **muktya*, hence a hybrid formation from *muktvā* and °*mucya*.

IV. TOWARDS FORMATION OF WORDS AND COMPOSITION.

§ 595. In addition to the suffixes of Skt. Pkt. possesses a number of suffixes, particularly Taddhita suffixes, that are wanting in Skt. Besides there are many suffixes that in Skt. are little employed, but are frequently used in Pkt. To them particularly belong the *l*-suffixes. The grammarians (Vr. 4, 25; C. 2,20 and p. 45; Hc. 2,159; Kī. 2,140; Mk. fol. 36) teach that *-āla*, *-ālu*, *-illa*, *-ulla* stand in the sense of *-mat* and *-vat*. So M. *sihāla* = *śikhāvat* (G.); AMg. *saddāla* = *śabdavat* (Bh. 4,25; Hc. 2,159; Ovav.); *dhaṇāla* = *dhanavat* (Bh. 4,25); *jaḍāla* = *jaṭāvat* (C.; Hc.), *jŏṇhāla* = *jyotsnāvat* (Hc.), *phaḍāla* = **phaṭāvat* (C.; Hc.), *rasāla* = *rasavat* (Hc.); *ṇiḍḍāla* = **nidrāvat* (Kī.); *saddhāla* = *śraddhāvat* (C.); *harisāla* = *harṣavat* (Mk.).—Without alteration of meaning *āla*+*ka* occurs in AMg. *mahālaẏa* = *mahat* (Āẏār. 2,1,4,5; Uvās.; Ovav.; Bhag.), femin. *mahāliẏā* (Uvās.; Ovav.); *emahālaya*, femin. *emahāliẏā* (§ 149), femin. *kemahāliẏā* (§ 149; also Jīv.), 216.220 ff.; AMg. JM. *mahaïmahālaẏa* (Āẏār. 2,3,2,11. 3,13; Uvās., Nāẏādh.; Erz.), femin. AMg. *mahaïmahāliẏā* (Uvās.; Ovav.; Niraẏāv.). The form is an intensive formation. To see a double femininum in it (LEUMANN, Aup. S.), as already remarked by LEUMANN himself, is not possible, since the word is used as masc. and neuter. *-mīsālia* (Hc. 2,170) is past passive participle of a denominative from **mīsāla* = *miśra*.—*ālu*, which Skt. too has (WHITNEY[1] (§ 1192. 1227), occurs in *ṇiddālu* = *nidrālu* (Bh.; Kī.); *isālu* = *irṣyālu* (Hc.; Mk.); *ṇehālu* = *snehala* (C.; Hc.); *daālu* = *dayālu* (Hc.); with *kaḥ svārthe* in M. *lajjāluā* (Hc.; H.), *saṅkālua* (G.), *saddhālua* (H.).—Dialectically throughout frequent is *-illa*, that stands for *-ilá* (§ 194). So *viārilla* (Bh.), *sohilla* (C.; Hc.), *dhaṇaïlla* (Kī.), *guṇilla* (Mk.), *chāilla*, *jamaïlla* (Hc.); *phaḍilla* (C.); M. *kiḍaïlla*, *kesarilli*, *tulilla*, *thalaïlla*, *ṇeurilla* (G.), *māṇaïlla*, *rāilla*, *lohilla*, *sohilla*, *harilli* (H.); M. AMg. *taṇaïlla* (grassy; G.; Jīv. 355); AMg. *kaṇṭaïlla* (Paṇhāv. 61; Dasav. N. 660,14), metri causa also *kaṇṭaïla* (Sūẏag. 293), *tūṇaïlla* (Aṇuog. 118; Paṇhāv. 465. 513. 522; Ovav.; (Kappas.), *niẏaḍilla* = *nikṛtimat* (Uttar. 990), *māilla* = *māẏāvin* (Sūẏag.

233; Ṭhāṇ. 582), *amāilla* (Āẏār. 1,8,4,16), also in the substantives *niẏaḍillaẏā, māillaẏā* occurring with the suffix *-tā* (Ṭhāṇ. 338; Vivāhap. 687; Ovav.; cf. § 219), *arisilla = arśasa, kasilla = kāsavat, sāsilla = śvāsin* (Vivāgas. 177), *ganṭhilla = granthila* (Vivāhap. 1308), *bhāsilla = bhāṣin* (Uttar. 791). *bhāillaga = bhāgin* (Ṭhāṇ. 120); JM. *kalaṅkilla = kalaṅkin* (Kk.), *satthillaẏa* from *sārtha* (Erz.), *gŏṭṭhillaẏa = gauṣṭhika* (Āv. 26,37). Rājaśekhara and later day writers use *-illa* not in M. only, as in *muttāhalilla* (Karp. 2,5; 100,5), *thoratthaṇilla, kandalilla* (Karp. 81,4; 88,3), particularly against the dialect in Ś. too, as *kodūhalilla* (Bālar. 168,3); *lacchiilla, kivāilla* (Kāleẏak. 2,8;9,7); *tattilla* (Mallikām. 77,12), as in M. (Hc. 2, 203; H.) and D. (Mṛcch. 101,21). As in *tattilla* (Deśīn. 5,3), *-illa* occurs also in other provincialisms like *kaṇaïlla* (parrot; Pāiẏal. 125; Deśīn. 2,21) from *kaṇa*; *goilla = gomat* (Deśīn. 2,98); M. Ś. *chaïlla* (clever; cunning; Pāiẏal. 101; Deśīn. 3,24; H.; Karp. 1,2; 4,8 [Ś.]; 76,10 [Ś.]; Kāleẏak. (3,7), which is probably rightly connected to √*chad* by WEBER[1], and is to be completely separated from A. *chaïlla* (beautiful; Hc. 4,412), since this, as the NIA, languages show[2], stands for **chavilla*, therefore, belongs to *chavi* (beauty; Pāiẏal. 113) = Skt. *chavi, chavī*, whilst *chaïlla* (lamp; similar; trifling; beautiful; Hc. 2,159; Deśīn. 3,35) is to be derived from *chāyā*, as Triv. 2,1,30 teaches falsely from *chaïlla*. *-illa* stands also in the sense of "there-existing" (*tatrabhave*; *bhave*; C. 2,20 p. 45; Hc. 2,163; Mk. fol. 37); *gāmilla* (a villager; C.), *gāmilliā* (a village woman; Hc.), AMg. *gāmĕllaga* (Vivāgas. 31); M. *gharillaa* (master of the house; H.); *gharillī* (mistress of the house; Deśīn. 2,106), and in M. JM. and particularly in AMg. it does not change the meaning of the word, to which it is added (*svārthe*; Hc. 2,164). So M. *mūillaa = mūka* (H.); AMg. *bāhirilla = bāhira* (Jīv. 879; Vivāhap. 198.1876 ff.; Ṭhāṇ, 261 f.), M. *abāhirilla* (H.); AMg. *andhillaga = andha* (Paṇhāv. 79): *pallavilla = pallava* (Hc. 2,164). So chiefly are built adjectives, that express number, time or place, partly from adverbs. So AMg. *ādilla = ādi* (Vivāhap. 463. 858. 923. 1118. 1330; Jīv. 788. 1042; Paṇṇav. 642. 646), *ādillaga* (Vivāhap. 1547); AMg. *paḍhamilla = prathama* (Vivāhap. 108.177), *paḍhamillaga* (Nāẏādh. 624); AMg. *uvarilla* (Ṭhāṇ. 341; Aṇuog. 427 ff.; Jīv. 240 ff. 710; Nāẏādh. 867; Paṇṇav, 478; Samav. 24.36.144; Vivāhap. 102. 198. 224. 392. 437. 1240.1331 ff. 1777; Ovav.), in the meaning "upper garment" M. *avarilla, varilla* (§ 123), *savvaüvarilla* (Jīv. 878f.), *savvupparilla* (Jīv. 879), AMg. *uttarilla* (Ṭhāṇ. 264ff. 358; Jīv. 227 ff.; Nāẏādh. 1452.1518.1521; Paṇṇav. 103 ff. 478; Rāẏap. 68. 71; Vivāhap. 1331 ff.), *dāhiṇilla* and *dakkhiṇilla = dakṣiṇa* (§ 65), *puratthimilla*[3] from *purastāt* (Ṭhāṇ. 264ff. 493; Jīv. 227ff. 345; Paṇṇav. 478; Rāẏap. 67.72 f.; Samav. 106.108,113 ff.; Vivāgas. 181; Vivāhap. 1331 ff.), *paccatthimilla*[4] from **pratyastam* (Ṭhāṇ. 264 ff.; Jīv. 227 ff.; Paṇṇav. 478; Samav. 106,113 ff.; Vivāgas. 181; Vivāhap. 1331 ff. 1869), *uttarapaccatthimilla* (Ṭhāṇ. 268); AMg. JM. *majjhilla = madhya* (Ṭhāṇ. 341; Jīv. 710; Vivāhap. 104.922.1240 f.; Āv. 46, 29; Erz.); AMg. *majjhimilla = madhyama* (Aṇuog. 383); AMg. *hĕṭṭhilla* (§ 107); AMg. JM. *puvvilla* (Uttar. 764.770; Āv.8,46); *purilla* (on Vr. 4,25; C. 2,20 p. 45; Hc. 2,163.164; Mk. fol. 37; Deśīn.6,53) from *purā* and *puras*, *purilladeva* (Asura; Deśīn. 6,55; Triv. in BB.13,12), *purillapahāṇā* (fang of a serpant; Deśīn. 6,56), whereof the ultimate constituent probably is *praghāṇa*; AMg. *pacchilla* (Vivāhap. 1118.1520), *pacchillaẏa* (Vivāhap. 1593f.). In AMg. *raïlliẏa* = *rajoyukta* (Vivāhap. 387)[5], dialectical *theṇilla* (taken; fearful; Deśīn.5,32; cf § 307) occur the past passive participle from the denominative of *rajas*, *stena*[6]. AMg. *āṇilliẏa* = *ānīta* (Vivāhap. 961) is explained from the fact that *āṇia* = *ānīta* is used adjectively and perhaps also substantively (Deśīn. 1,74). As the examples show, the final vowel of the stem falls off before *-illa*, partly it is retained.— *-ulla* stands in the same meaning as *-illa*, but is much more seldom : *viārulla* = *vikāravat* (Bh. 4, 25; C. 2,20 p. 45; Hc. 2,159); *maṁsulla* = *māṁsavat*, *dappulla* = *darpin* (Hc. 2, 159); *uvahārulla* from *upahāra* (Kī. 2,140; text *uvahāruṇṇaṁ*); *appulla* from *ātman* (Bh. 4,25; C. 2,20 p. 45; Hc. 2,163; Mk. fol. 36 [MS *aṇullo*]); *piulla* = *priya*, *muhulla* = *mukha*, *hatthullā* = *hastau* (Hc. 2,164); M. *chaülla* (H.) beside *chaïlla*, *thaṇullaa* = *stana* (G.); AMg. *pāullāiṁ* = *pāduke* (Sūẏag. 253); AMg. JM. *kacchulla* = *kacchura* (Vivāgas. 177; Erz.); *cūḍullaa* = *cūḍaka* (Hc. 4,395,2.430,2), *kuḍullī* = *kuṭī* (Hc. 4,422,14.429,3. 431,2); *vāulla* = *vācāla* (Deśīn. 7,56).— *-alla* occurs for *-ala* in M. *ĕkkalla* = *eka* (Hc. 2,165; H.), JM. *ĕkkallaẏa* (Erz.), also *ekalla* (Hc.); cf. Mālatīm. 348,1; A. also *ekala* (Prabandhac. 121,10); M. AMg. *mahalla* = *mahat* (G.; Prabandhac. 113,3; Āẏār. 2,4,3,11.12), AMg. *mahallaẏa* (Āẏār. 2,4, 2,10), femin. *mahalliẏā* (Āẏār. 2,1,2,7), *sumahalla* (Vivāhap. 246); AMg. *andhalla* = *andha* (Paṇhāv. 523), beside *andhala* (Hc. 2,173); M. *pāsalla*, *pāsallia* from *pārśva* (G.); *navalla* = *nava* (Hc. 2,165); *mūalla* beside *mūala* = *mūka* (Deśīn. 6,137), from which M. *mūalliaa* (R. 5,41; so to be read), is a denominative. Also M. *pisalla* = *piśāca* is perhaps explained more correctly from **pisāalla* = *piśāca* + *alla* than from *piśācālaya* (§ 232). On *suhalli*, *suhĕlli* see § 107. In Mg. *gāmelua* (Mṛcch. 97,1) = *grāmya*, *grāmiṇa* occurs the suffix *-elua*, that is to say *-elu* + *ka*.

1. On H. 720. Beside it is found also *chaülla* mentioned below.—2. Pischel, on Hc. 4,412.—3. The texts often have false *puracchimilla*, as also *puratthima*, and *puracchima* based on it.—4. The texts often have *pavvatthimilla* and *paccacchimilla*. The word perhaps does not belong to *paścāt*, from which originates *pacchilla*. Cf. § 149 and Hoernle, Uvās. s.v. *paccatthima*.—5. *maïliya* = *kaṭhinamalayukta*, that stands beside it, will be correct, since it belongs to AMg. *maïlinti*, M. *maïlei* (§ 559).—6. Cf. e.g. Skt. *tundilita* with *tundila* and AMg. *tundilla* (Uttar. 229). That the reduplication of *l* is associated with accent makes the cases like *kuḍilla* = *kuṭila* (Pāiẏal. 155), *kuḍillaa*, *koḍilla* (Deśīn. 2,40), *tundilla* = *tundilla*, *gaṇṭhilla* = *granṭhila* (Uttar. 229; Vivāhap. 1308) certain.

§ 596. As a kṛt- suffix dialectically very frequent is *-ira* (Vr. 4,24; Hc. 2,145; Kī. 2,138; Mk. fol. 36), which expresses the notion of the root as a "characteristicum" a "duty" or "noble" execution. So M. *agghāiri* (femin.) from *ghrā* with *ā* (H.), *andolira* (G.), femin. *andoliri* (H.), *alajjira* (H.), *avalambiri* (femin.), *ullaviri*, *ullāviri* (femin.; H.); *ūsasira* from *śvas* with *ud* (Hc.); *gamira* (Hc.; Kī.); M. *gholira* (G.H.R.), in later-day writers also in Ś. (Mallikām. 109,9;122,12), M. *parigholira* (G.); M. A. *jampira*, AMg. *aẏampira* from *jalp* (§ 296); AMg. *jhusira*, *ajhusira* (§ 211); M. *ṇacciri* (femin.) from *ṇaccaï* – *nṛtyati* (H.); *namira* (Hc.); AMg. *parisakkira* from *ṣvaṣk* with *pari* (Nāẏādh.; cf. § 302), M. *pĕcchira* from *ikṣ* with *pra*, femin. *pĕcchirī* (H.; so to be read throughout); M. A. *bhamira* from *bhram* (Bh.; Hc.; Mk.; G. H. R.; Hc. 4,422,15); *rovira* (Hc.), M. *roiri*, *ruiri* from *ru* (H.) M. *lambira* (G.), *lasira* (R.); *lajjira* (Hc.), M. femin. *lajjirī* (H.); M. A., in Rājaśekhara also in Ś. *vĕlira*, *uvvĕllira* (§ 107); M. JM. *vevira* from *vepate* (Hc.; G. H. R.; Erz.), in later day writers in Ś. too (Mallikām. 119, 2;123,15); *sahira* (Mk.), M. femin. *sahirī* (H.); *hasira* (Bh.; Hc.); M. femin. *hasirī* (G. H.); *apaḍicchira* (stupid; Deśīn. 1,43) from *iṣ* with *prati*. Seldom is *-ira* used as a taddhita- suffix too, as in M. *gavvira*, femin. °*ri* from *garva* (H.). On *-uka* for *-ika* see § 118.162 [*ūsuga*]. 326 [*jharua*].

1. Pischel, on Hc. 2,145. Cf. Weber, H[1]. p. 68.

§ 597. *-tva* = Pkt. *-tta* (§ 298) can be used in AMg. JM. only, in AMg. often in the dative *-ttāe* (§ 361.364); *pīṇatta*, *pupphatta* = *puṣpatva* (Hc. 2, 154); AMg. *mūlatta*, *kandatta*, *khandatta*, *taẏatta*, *sālatta*, *pavālatta*, *pattatta*, *pupphatta*, *phalatta*, *biẏatta* (Sūẏag. 806); *āṇugāmiẏatta* (Ovav. § 38, p. 49; Vivāhap. 162); *devatta* (Uttar. 235; Bhag.; Uvās.; Ovav.; Kappas.); *neraïyatta* = *nairayikatva* (Vivāgas. 244; Uvās.; Ovav.); *māṇusatta* (Uttar. 234 f.); *pumatta* = *puṁstva* (§ 412); *rukkhatta* = **rukṣatva* (Sūẏag. 812; cf. 811); *sāmitta*, *bhaṭṭitta*, *mahattaragatta* = *svāmitva*, *bhartṛtva*, *mahattarakatva* (Paṇṇav. 98. 100. 102. 112); JM. *ujjugatta*, *vaṅkatta* = *ṛjukatva*, *vakratva* (Āv. 46,31. 32), **maṇuyatta* = *manujatva*, *micchatta* = *mithyātva*, *siẏatta* = *śitatva* (Kk.), *asoẏatta* = *aśaucatva* (Erz.). To *-tva* has further been added the suffix *-tā* in *māuttaẏā* = **mṛdukatvatā* (Hc. 2,172). Very frequent, particularly in M.Ś. is Vedic *-tvana* = Pkt. *-ttaṇa*, A. also *-ppaṇa* (§ 298. 300; Vr. 4,22; Hc. 2,154; Kī. 2,139; Mk. fol. 45). So M. *amarattaṇa* (R.), *alasattaṇa*, *asahattaṇa*, *āulattaṇa*, *garuattaṇa*, *cirajīvittaṇa*, *ṇiuṇattaṇa* (H.); *ṇiddattaṇa*, *tucchattaṇa*, *dāruṇattaṇa dīhattaṇa* (G.); *piattaṇa* (H.); *pīṇattaṇa* (Bh.; Hc.; G. R.); *mahurattaṇa* (G. H.); from *ā*-stems: *mahilattaṇa* (G. H.); *vesattaṇa* = **veśyātvana* (H.); from *i*-, *ī*-, stems: *asaïttaṇa* (H.); *juaïttaṇa* (G); *maïttaṇa* = **matitvana* (G.); *dūittaṇa* = **dūtītvana* (H.); from *u*-stems: *taruttaṇa* (G.); AMg. *takkarattaṇa* = **taskaratvana* (Paṇhāv. 147); *tirikkhattaṇa* = **tirakṣatvana* (Uttar. 234); *āẏariẏattaṇa* = **ācāryatvana* beside *āẏariẏatta* (Uttar. 316); JM. *pāḍiherattaṇa* = **prātihāryatvana* (Āv. 13,25), *dhammattaṇa* = **dharmatvana* (Kk. 259,12), *sāvaẏattaṇa* = **śrāvakatvana* (Dvār. 506,28), *turiẏattaṇa* = **tvaritatvana* (Āv. 42,21; 43,3), *paravasattaṇa* (Erz.); Ś. *aṇṇahiaattaṇa* = **anyahṛdayatvana* (Viddhaś. 41,8.9; Nāgān. 33,6), *pajjāulahiaattaṇa* = **paryākula*° (Karṇas. 19,10), *suṇṇahiaattaṇa* = **śūnya*° (Mṛcch. 27,19; Priyad. 20,4; Nāgān. 21,6); *ahirāmattaṇa* (Vikr. 21,1); *ṇisaṁsattaṇa* = **nṛśaṁsatvana* (Ratn. 327,18); *ṇiuṇattaṇa* = **nipuṇatvana* (Lalitav. 561,1); *dūdattaṇa* = **dūtatvana* (Jīvān. 87,13); *bālattaṇa* (Lalitav. 561,2 [*vā*°]; Uttarar. 121,4; Mudrār. 43,5); *bamhattaṇa* (Ratn. 308,5), *bamhaṇattaṇa* (Pras. 46,12); *sahāattaṇa* = **sahāyatvana* (Śak. 59,10; Jīvān. 39,15; 78,2); *aṇujīvittaṇa* (Mahāv. 54,19); *ucidakārittaṇa* (Bālar. 54,17), *gharaṇittaṇa* (Anarghar. 315,10); *bhaavadittaṇa* (Mālatīm. 74,3); *medhāvittaṇa* (Ratn. 303,32); *lajjāuittaṇa* (Mahāv. 29,6 [Pischel °*lui*]); *sarasakaïttaṇa* (Karṇas. 31,1); *pahuttaṇa* = **prabhutvana* (Mālav. 14,3; 30,5); *bhīruttaṇa*

(Pras. 45,5); Mg. *aṇiccattaṇa* = **anityatvana* (Mṛcch. 177,10); *mahulattaṇa śulahittaṇa* = **madhuratvana*, **surabhitvana* (Prab. 60,12.13); *śavvaṇṇattaṇa* = **sarvajñatvana* (Prab. 51,6; 52,6); *śughaliṇittaṇa* = **sugṛhiṇitvana* (Veṇīs. 35,1); *pattattaṇa* = **pattratvana* (Hc. 4,370,1); *vaḍḍattaṇa* and *vaḍḍappaṇa* = **vaḍratvana* (Hc. 4,366); *suhaḍattaṇa* = **subhaṭatvana* (Kk. 260,44); *gahilattaṇa* = **grahilatvana* (Piṅgala 1,2[a]).

§ 598. Without effecting alteration in the meaning of the word *-ka* enters into Pkt. more frequently than into Skt. (Hc. 2,164; Mk. fol. 37). In PG. P. CP., sometimes in Ś. Mg. too, it remains *-ka*, in AMg. JM. JŚ. it becomes *-ga, -ẏa*, in the other dialects *-a*. Numerous examples for all the dialects have been included in different paragraphs. Sometimes it is set in doubly, as *bahuaẏa* (Hc. 2,164), also behind other suffixes (§ 595), further it is added to adverbs, as *ihaẏaṁ* (Hc. 2,164) and to the infinitive, as *ālĕddhuaṁ* (§ 303. 577), AMg. *aladdhuẏaṁ* (§ 577). The vowel of the stem is sometimes lengthened dialectically (§ 70). Beside *-ka*, we find dialectically also *-kha, -ha* (§ 206) and *-ika*, AMg.*-iẏa*, as in PG. *vadhanika* = *vardhanaka* (6,9); AMg. *macciẏa* = **martyika* = *martyaka* (Āẏār. 1,2,5,4; 1,3,2,1: Sūẏag. 351); AMg. *tumba-viṇiẏa* = *tumbaviṇaka* (Ovav.); Mg. *bhālika* = **bhārika* = *bhāravat* (Mṛcch. 97,19. 20); M. *savvaṅgia* = *sarvāṅgiṇa* (Hc. 2,152; R.).— *-kya* occurs in *pārakka* (Hc. 2,148), *-ikya* in *rāikka* = *rājakiya* (Hc. 2,148); *goṇikka* (herd of cattle; Deśīn. 2,97; Triv. 1,3,105)[1]; *caccikka* from *carcā* (besmearing the body with fragrant paste; Hc. 2,174; Triv. 1,4,121), according to Deśīn. 3,4 also adjective in the meaning "decorated"[2]; *mahisikka* (herd of buffaloes; Deśīn. 6,124)[3].

1. Pischel, BB. 3,243.—2. Pischel, BB. 13,12.—3. Pischel, GGA 1881, p. 1320 f.

§ 599. Like *-ka*, in A. *-ḍa* = Skt. *-ṭa* too is added, without change in the meaning of the word. Very often, *-a* = *-ka* enters behind it, in addition (Hc. 4,429. 430). So: *kaṇṇaḍaa* = *karṇa* (Hc. 4,432); *davvaḍaa* = *dravya* (Śukas. 32,3); *diahaḍa* = *divasa* (Hc. 4,333. 387,2); *dūaḍaa* = *dūta* (Hc. 4,419,1); *desaḍa* (Hc. 4,418,6) *desaḍaa* 4,419,3) = *deśa*; *dosaḍa* = *doṣa* (Hc. 4,379,1); *māṇusaḍa* = *mānuṣa* (Prabandhac. 112,8); *māriaḍa* = *mārita* (Hc. 4,379,2); *mittaḍa* = *mitra* (Hc. 4,422,1); *rāṇṇaḍaa* = *araṇya* (Hc. 4,368); *rūaḍaa* = *rūpaka* (Hc. 4,419,1); *hatthaḍa, hatthaḍaa* = *hasta* (Hc. 4,439,1. 445,3); *hiaḍa* = **hṛda* = *hṛd* (Kī. 5,15. 17; Hc. 4,422.12), *hiaḍaa* (Hc. 4,350,2). In *maṇiaḍa* = *maṇi* (Hc. 4,414,2) probably *ka*+*ṭa* = **maṇikaṭa* is to be assumed, that is pointed to by the hiatus, and not the suffix *-aḍa*. The femin. ends in *-ḍi* (Hc. 4,431) : *ṇiddaḍi* = *nidrā* (Hc. 4, 418,1); *suavattaḍi* = *śrutavārttā* (Hc. 4,432). The ending *-aḍi* is pointed to also by the femin. in Skt. *-i, -ī,* : *goraḍi* = *gauri* (Hc. s. v. and s. v. *gori*); *buddhaḍi* = *buddhi* (Hc. 4,424); *bhumhaḍi* = *bhūmi* (§ 210); *mabbhīsaḍi* from *mā bhaiṣiḥ* (Hc. 4,422,22); *rattaḍi* = *rātri* (Hc. 4,330,2); *vibhantaḍi* = *vibhrānti* (Hc. 4,414,2); with *-ka* : *dhūlaḍiā* = **dhūlaṭikā* = *dhūli* (Hc. 4,432). Here in relation to Skt. the infix *-aḍ-* makes its appearance, and not the suffix. *-ḍa*, that is dialectical in A., and is combined also with other suffixes like *-ka*. So with *-ulla* (§ 595) in *bāhabalullaḍa* = *bāhābala* and *bāhabalullaḍaa* (Hc. 4,430,3), also in the last example *-ulla*+ = *ḍa*+ = *ka*.

§ 600. According to the grammarians, in Pkt. *-itta* too is used in the sense of the taddhita-suffixes *-mat*, *-vat* (Vr. 4,25 [so to be read for *-inta*]; C. 2,20 p. 45; Hc. 2,159; Kī. 2,140; Mk. fol. 36); *kavvaïtta*, *māṇaïtta* from *kāvya*, *māna* (C.; Hc.;); *rosaïtta* from *roṣa* (Bh. 4,25 [so to be read]; Kī.); *pāṇaïtta* (Bh. 4,25 [so to be read]) from *prāṇa*. With insertion of *kaḥ svārthe* (Kālidāsa used this suffix in Ś. *-ittaa*, femin. *-ittā*: *paoharavitthāraïttaa* = *payodharavistārayukta* (cf. Candraśekhara); *ummādaïttaa* = *unmādin*, *unmādakārin* (*ittakaśabdo matubarthaḥ*; Candraś.); *ucchāhaïttaka* = *utsāhaśālin* (*matubartha ittakaśabdaḥ*; Candraś.); *āāsaïttiā* = *āyāsakāriṇi* (Candraś.); (*saṁtāvaṇivvāṇaittiā* = *saṁtāpanirvāṇakāriṇi* (Candraś); *bahumāṇasuhaïttaa bahumānasukhayukta* (cf. Candraś.); *piaṇiveaṇaïttaa* = *priyanivedaka* (Candraś.); *saṁtāvaṇivvāvaïttaa* = *saṁtapanirvāpaka* (Candraś.) (Śak. 11,3; 21,8; 35,7; 36,12; 51,12; 55,1; 79,14; 86,5; 140,14); *icchidasaṁpādaittaa* = *iṣṭasaṁpādayitā* (Raṅganātha; Vikr. 20,19); *juvadivesalajjāvaïttaa* = *yuvativeṣalajjayitṛka* (Kāṭayavema; Mālav. 33,17); *ahilāsapūraïttaa* = *abhilāṣapūrayitṛka* (Kāṭ.; Mālav. 34,14), *asoaviāsaïttaa* = *aśokavikāśayitṛka* (Kāṭ. Mālav. 43,3). The suffix is to be derived with Böhtlingk[1] from *-yitra*, *-yitraka*, and not with the Indians and Benfey[2] from *-yitṛ*, *-yitṛka*. It forms, therefore, the derivatives from denominatives and causatives. One *vitthāraïttāa* is = **vistārayitraka* from *vistāraya-*.

1. On Śak. 9,20 p. 161. Cf. Bollensen on Vikr. 20,19, p. 244; Pischel, De Kālidāsae Śāk. rec. p. 33 f.—2. GGA. 1856 p. 1226. Lassen, Inst. p. 134, note has already assumed that the explanation with the help of, *hetuka* that rests on the wrong reading *-itua*, is wrong. Cf. Chandraśekhara on Śak. 36,12 (p. 180) *utsāhahetav iti śaṁskarasyājñanam*.

§ 601. According to § 397 *-mat* and *-vat* become *-manta*, *-vanta* from the strong stems *-mant*, *-vant* (Vr. 425; C. 2,20 p. 45; Hc. 2,159; Kī. 2, 140; Mk. fol. 37). In the matter of the suffix Śkt. and Pkt. do not always agree closely. So AMg. *āyāramanta-* (Dasav. 633,33), but Śkt. *ācāravant-*; AMg. *cittamanta-* (Āyār. 2,1,5,2; p. 133,33; 136,3) = Skt. *cittavant-*; AMg. *vaṇṇamanta-*, *gandhamanta-*, *rasamanta-* = *phāsamanta-* = *varṇavant-*, *gandhavant-*, *rasavant-*, *sparśavant-* (Āyār. 2,4,1,4; Sūyag. 565; Jīv. 26; Paṇṇav. 379; Vivāhap. 144); AMg. *vijjāmanta-* = *vidyāvant-* (Uttar. 620); *sīlamanta-*, *guṇamanta-*, *vaïmanta-* = *śīlavant-*, *guṇavant-*, *vāgvant-* (Āyār. 2,1,9,1); *pupphamanta-* = *puṣpavant-*, *bīyamanta-* = *bījavant-*, *mūlamanta-* = *mūlavant-*, *sālamanta-* = *śālavant-* (Ovav.); A. *guṇamanta-* (Piṅgala 1, 132a; 2,118), *dhaṇamanta-* (Piṅgala 2,45. 118), *puṇamanta-* (Piṅgala 2,94), metrically for *puṇṇamanta-* (C.; Hc.) = *puṇyavant-*. As regards others, the corresponding formations have not hitherto been found in the text, as AMg. *pannāṇamanta* = **prajñānamant* (Āyār. 1,4,4,3; 1,6,4,1), *pattamanta-* = **pattramant-*, *hariyamanta-* = **haritamant-* (Ovav.). According to § 398 also the suffix *-maṇa* in *dhaṇamaṇa* (C. 2,20 p. 45; Hc. 2,159) = *dhaṇamant*, **dhaṇaman* goes back to *-mant*.—*bhattivanta-* = *bhaktimant-* (Hc. 2,159).

§ 602. In AMg. many adjectives are formed with the *kṛt*-suffix *ima*[1], partly from the present stems, which express that something connected with the root has happened, may or must happen. They often correspond to the German adjective in *-bar*. So : *ganthima, veḍhima, pūrima, saṁghāima* from *granth, veṣṭ, pūraya-, saṁghātaya-* (Āyār. 2,12,1;2,15,20; Nāyādh. 269; Vivāhap. 823; Jīv. 348; Nandīs. 507 etc.; cf. 304. 333); *ubbheima*=*udbhida* (Dasav. 625,13) ; *khāima, sāima* from *khād, svādaya-* (Sūyag. 596; Vivāhap. 184; Dasav. 639,14; Uvās.; Nāyādh.; Ovav.; Kappas.) ; *pāima* from *pācaya-* (Āyār. 2,4,2,7) ; *pūima, apūima, māṇima, amāṇima* from *pūjaya-, mānaya-* (Dasav. 641,14. 15) ; *bahukhajjima* from *kkādya-* from *khād* (Āyār. 2,4,2,15) *bahunivvaṭṭima* from *vartaya-* with *nis* (Āyār. 2,4,2,14 [so to be read]; Dasav. 628,31); *lāima, bhajjima* (Āyār. 2,4,2,15; Dasav. 628,34); *vandima, avandima* (Dasav. 641,12) ; *vāhima* (Āyār. 2,4,2,9) ; *vusima* from *vaśaya-* (Sūyag. 511) ; *vehima* (Dasav. 628,30); *saṁtārima, saṁpaima,* (Āyār. 2,3,1,13. 14). From the adverbs *purastāt* and **pratyastam* are derived AMg. *puratthima*= **purastima* (Bhag.; Kappas.; Nāyādh.; Uvās.; Ovav.), and *paccatthima*= **pratyastima* (Bhag.; Uvās.). *puratthima* also in JM. *uttarapuratthima* (Āv. 14, 10). From it is again derived *puratthimilla, paccatthimilla* (§ 595).—In A., according to Hc. 4,443, there enters the suffix *-aṇaa* for expressing a characteristical peculiarity : *māraṇaa, bŏllaṇaa, vajjaṇaa, bhasaṇaa*=*māraṇaśila, bhāsaṇaśila, vādanaśila* [*vajja*=*vādya-*], *bhāṣaṇaśila*[2]. They correspond to the adjectives in *-ana* in Skt. (WHITNEY § 1150) +*kaḥ svārthe*.

1. HOERNLE, JACOBI, LEUMANN and STEINTHAL posit wrongly the substantive in *-īman*. Many of these adjectives in the neuter are substantively used.—2. Cf. PISCHEL on Hc. 4,443.

§ 603. In the matter of compounds Pkt. is distinguished from Skt. only to the extent that individual members do not follow one another in a strictly logical sequence (Mk. fol. 65)[1]. They enter particularly into M., where the requirement of the metre is often the cause. So M. *dhavalakaovavia* for *kaadhavalovavia*=*kṛtadhavalopavita* (G. 1); *kāsāraviralakumuā*=*viralakumudakāsārāḥ* (G. 271); *virahakaravattadūsahaphālijjantammi* = *duḥsahavirahakarapattrasphālyamāne* (H. 153) ; *daralambigŏcchakaīkacchusacchahaṁ*=*daralambikapikacchugucchasadṛśam* (H. 533); *kañcuābharaṇamĕttāo*=*kañcukamātrābharaṇāḥ* (H. 546) ; *muhalaghaṇapaavijjantaaṁ*=*mukharaghanapiyamānapayasam* (R. 2,24) ; *saṁkhohuvvattaṇintaraaṇamaūhaṁ*=*saṁkṣobhodvṛttaratnaniryanmayūkham* (R. 5,40); *kaaṇibbharadasadisaṁ*=*nirbharikṛtadaśadiśam* (R. 8,27)[2]; AMg. *pacchannapalāsa*=*palāśapracchanna* (Āyār. 1,6,1,2); AMg. *lohāgaradhammamāṇadhamadhamĕntaghosaṁ*=*dhmāyamānalohakaradhamadhamāyamānaghoṣam* (Uvās. § 108)[3]; AMg. *taḍivimalasarisa*=*vimalataḍitsadṛśa* (Kappas. § 35); AMg. *uḍuvaïpaḍipuṇṇasomavaÿaṇe*=*pratipūrṇoḍupatisaumyavadanaḥ* (Ovav. p. 29,13).

1. JACOBI on Kalpas. § 35, p. 104; BHĀNDĀRKAR, Transactions of the Second Session of the International Congress of Orientalists, London 1876. p. 313, note 6; S. GOLDSCHMIDT, R. p. 206, note 7. Cf. HOERNLE, Uvās., Translation, note 201. The scholiasts explain this with *prākṛte pūrvanipātāniyamaḥ*, a rule that is wrongly attributed to Vr. by a scholion on H. 546, and which is referred to by scholiasts, often without necessity, as can be proved by the collection of instances in S. GOLDSCHMIDT, R. p. 329 s.v. *pūrva*[*ni*]*pātāniyama*.—2. So rightly S. GOLDSCHMIDT, R. p. 251, note 3.—3. Cf. Abhayadeva thereupon p. 40.

ABBREVIATIONS AND LIST OF THE EDITIONS USED

A. = Apabhraṁśa.
Ā. = Āvantī (§ 26).
Acyutaś. = Acyutaśataka. Madras 1872.
Adbhutad. = Adbhutadarpaṇa ed. PARAB. Bombay 1896 = Kāvyamālā. 55.
AMg. = Ardhamāgadhī.
Amṛtodaya ed. ŚIVADATTA and PARAB. Bombay 1897 = Kāvyamālā. 59.
Anarghar. = Anargharāghava ed. DURGĀPRASĀD and PARAB. Bombay 1887 = Kāvyamālā. 3.
Antag. = Antagaḍadasāo. Calcutta saṁvat 1931.
Aṇuog. = Aṇuogadārasutta. Calcutta saṁvat 1936.
Aṇuttar. = Aṇuttarovavāiẏasutta. Calcutta saṁvat 1931.
Arch. S. of W. I. = Archeological Survey of Western India.
Aup. S. = Aupapātika Sūtra. By ERNST LEUMANN. Leipzig 1883.
Āv. = Āvaśyaka-Erzählungen ed. LEUMANN. Leipzig. 1897.
Āẏār. = Āẏāraṅgasutta ed. JACOBI. London 1812. The Calcutta edition of saṁvat 1936 too has been used.

Bālar. = Bālarāmāyaṇa ed. GOVINDA DEVA ŚĀSTRI, Benares 1869.
BB. = BEZZENBERGER's Beiträge zur Kunde der Indogermanischen Sprachen.
Bh. = Bhāmaha.
Bhag. = WEBER, Über ein Fragment der Bhagavatī. Berlin 1866. 1867.
Bhartṛharinirveda ed. DURGĀPRASĀD and PARAB. Bombay 1892 = Kāvyamālā. 29.
BKSGW. = Berichte der Kgl. Sächsischen Gesellschaft der Wissenschaften.
B.-R. = BÖHTLINGK und ROTH, Sanskrit Wörterbuch.
BSOS. = Bulletin of the School of Oriental Studies.
Bü. = BÜHLER, HEMACHANDRA.
BVV. = Bhāratīya Vidyā Bhavan Siṅghī Jaina Grantha Mālā.
BW = BÖHTLINGK, Sanskrit-Wörterbuch in kürzerer Fassung.

C. = Caṇḍa.
Cait. = Caitanyacandrodaya ed. RĀJENDRALĀL MITTRA. Calcutta 1854.
Caṇḍak = Caṇḍakauśikam ed. JAGANMOHANAŚARMAN. Calcutta Saṁvat 1924.
Candral. = Candralekhā, ed A. N. Upadhye, Bharatīya Vidyabhavana, Bombay 1945.
Cat. Cat. = Catalogus Catalogarum.
CP. = Cūlikāpaiśācī.

D. = Dākṣiṇātyā.
Dasav. = Dasaveẏāliẏasutta ed. LEUMANN, ZDMG. 46,581 ff.

Dasav. N. = Dasaveẏāliẏanijjutti see Dasav.

De gr. Pr. = De grammaticis Prācriticis. Vratislaviae 1874.

Deśīn. = Hemacandra, Deśīnāmamālā ed. PISCHEL. Bombay 1880.

Ḍh. = Ḍhakkī.

Dhanaṁjav. = Dhanaṁjayavijaya ed. ŚIVADATTA and PARAB. Bombay 1895 = Kāvyamālā. 54.

Dhūrtas. = Dhūrtasamāgama ed. CAPPELLER o. O. u. J.

Dhvanyāloka ed. DURGĀPRASĀD and PARAB. Bombay 1891 = Kāvyamālā. 25.

Dūtāṅgada ed. DURGĀPRASĀD and PARAB. Bombay 1891 = Kāvyamālā. 28.

Dvār. = Die Jaina Legende von dem Untergange Dvāravatīs vol. II of H. JACOBI. ZDMG. 42,493 ff.

EI. = Epigraphia Indica.

Erz. = Ausgewählte Erzāhlungen in Māhārāṣṭrī by H. JACOBI, Leipzig. 1886.

G. = Gaüḍavaho ed. Sh. P. PAṆḌIT. Bombay 1887.

GGA. = Göttingische gelehrte Anzeigen.

GM. = Gommaṭasāra, Secret Books of the Jainas. X, 1937.

GN. = Nachrichten von der Königl. Gesellschaft der Wissenschaften zu Göttingen.

Grr. = Grammarians.

H. = Hāla, The Saptaśatakam of—. Published by A. WEBER. Leipzig 1881. Cf. § 13. The edition of DURGĀPRASĀD and PARAB, Bombay 1889 = Kāvyamālā. 2, too has been used.

Hāsy. = Hāsyārṇava ed. CAPPELLER o. O. u. J.

Hc. = Hemacandra.

IA. = Indian Antiquary.

IAlt. = Indische Alterthumskunde.

IF. = Indogermanische Forschungen.

Inst. = Institutiones lingue Pracriticae.

IS. = Indische Studien.

IStr. = Indische Streifen.

JA. = Journal Asiatique.

JASB. = Journal of the Asiatic Society of Bengal.

JBoAS. = Journal of the Bombay Branch of the Royal Asiatic Society.

Jīv. = Jīvābhigamasutta, Ahmedābād saṁvat 1939.

Jīvān. = Jīvānandana ed. DURGĀPRASĀD and PARAB. Bombay 1891 = Kāvyamālā. 27.

JM. = Jaina-Māhārāṣṭrī.

JRAS. = Journal of the Royal Asiatic Society.

JŚ. = Jaina-Śaurasenī.

Kā = Kāvyānuśāsana. Published in Kāvyamālā 71, 1901.
Kāleyak. = Kāleyakutūhalam. o. O. 1882.
Kalpal. = Pkl.
Kalpasūtra ed. JACOBI. Leipzig 1879; see Kappas.
Kalpat. = Prākrit Kalpataru of Rāmaśarman Tarkavāgīśa, ed. M. GHOSH. Calcutta.
Kaṁsav. = Kaṁsavadha ed. DURGĀPRASĀD and PARAB. Bombay 1888 = Kāvyamālā. 6.
Kappas. = Kappasutta; see Kalpasūtra.
Karṇas. = Karṇasundarī ed. DURGĀPRASĀD and PARAB. Bombay 1888 = Kāvyamālā. 7.
Karp. = Karpūramañjarī ed. KONOW (cf. § 22, note 7). The edition of DURGĀPRASĀD and PARAB. Bombay 1887 = Kāvyamālā. 4 too has been used.
Kattig. = Kattigeyāṇupĕkkhā (§ 21).
KB. = KUHN's Beiträge.
KI. = Kakkuka Inscription (§ 10).
Kī. = Kramadīśvara, Saṁkṣiptasāra, ed. by ŚYĀMĀCARAṆA KAVIRATNA. Calcutta 1316, Bengali year.
Kk. = Kālakācāryakathānakam. By H. JACOBI ZDMG. 34,247 ff. Kk. II. III. By E. LEUMANN. ZDMG. 37. 493 ff.
KZ. = KUHN's Zeitschrift für vergleichende Sprachforschung.

Lalitav. = Lalitavigraharājanāṭikā ed. KIELHORN, GN. 1893, p. 552 ff.
Laṭakam. = Laṭakamelaka ed. DURGĀPRASĀD and PARAB. Bombay 1889 = Kāvyamālā. 20.

M. = Māhārāṣṭrī.
Mahāv. = Mahāvīracarita ed. TRITHEN. London 1848. Beside it has been used the edition of AIYAR, RANGACHARIAR and PARAB. Bombay 1892.
Mālatīm. = Mālatīmādhava ed. BHAṆḌĀRKAR. Bombay 1876. Beside it have been used the editions of KAILASH CHANDRA DUTT, Calcutta 1866, of MANGESH RĀMAKRISHNA TELANG, Bombay 1892 and an edition in Telugu script, of which the title page is wanting in my copy.
Mālav. = Mālavikāgnimitra ed. BOLLENSEN. Leipzig. 1879. Besides the editions of TULLBERG, Bonnae ad Rhenum 1840 and of SH. P. PAṆḌIT, Second edition, Bombay 1889 have been used.
Mallikām. = Mallikāmārutam ed. JIBANANDA VIDYASAGAR. Calcutta 1878.
Mg. = Māgadhī.
Mk. = Mārkaṇḍeya.
Mṛcch. = Mṛcchakaṭikā ed. STENZLER. Bonnae 1847. The editions Calcutta 1829, of Rāmamayaśarmatarkaratna, Calcutta śakābdāḥ 1792, and particularly the valuable edition of NĀRĀYAṆA BĀLAKRISHNA GOḌABOLE, Bombay 1884 too have been used.

Mudrār. = Mudrārākṣasa ed. KĀSHĪNATH TRIMBAK TELANG. Bombay 1884. Beside it the edition Calcutta 1831 and that of TĀRANĀTHA-TARKAVĀCASPATI, Calcutta saṁvat 1926 have been used.

Mukund. = Mukundānanda Bhāṇa ed. DURGĀPRASĀD and PARAB. Bombay 1889 = Kāvyamālā. 16.

Nāgān. = Nāgānanda ed. GOVIND BHAIRAV BRAHME and SHIVARAM MAHADEO PARANJAPE. Poona 1893. Beside it the edition of JIBANANDA VIDYASAGAR, Calcutta 1873.

Nandīs. = Nandīsutta. Calcutta saṁvat 1936.

Nāẏādh. = Nāẏādhammakahā. Calcutta saṁvat 1933. In places where the quotations are given according to paragraphs and not according to page or without mention of details they refer to : Specimen der Nāẏādhammakahā. Inaugural Dissertation...of P. STEINTHAL Leipzig 1881.

NPK. = Nāṇapaṁcamīkahāo SJG. 25.

Niraẏāv. = Niraẏāvaliẏāo. Benares saṁvat 1941. Citations according to paragraphs or without mention of details relate to Niraẏāvalisuttam...by S. WARREN. Amsterdam 1879.

OST. = Original Sanskrit Texts.

Ovav. = Ovavāiẏasutta. Calcutta saṁvat 1936. The citation is according to the edition : Das Aupapātika Sūtra...by ERNST LEUMANN. Leipzig 1883.

P. = Paiśācī.

Pāiẏal. = Pāiẏalacchī ed. BÜHLER. Göttingen 1878.

Paṇhāv. = Paṇhāvāgaraṇāiṁ. Calcutta saṁvat 1933.

Paṇṇav. = Paṇṇavaṇā. Benares saṁvat 1940.

Pārvatīp. = Pārvatīpariṇaya ed. MANGESH RĀMAKRISHNA TELANG. Bombay 1892. Beside it the edition of GLASER, Wien 1883.

Pav. = Pavaẏaṇasāra (§ 21).

PG. = Pallava Grant (§ 10).

Piṅgala = The Prākṛita-Piṅgala-Sūtras...ed. ŚIVADATTA and PARAB. Bombay 1884 = Kāvyamālā. 41.

Pkl. = Prākṛtakalpalatikā. Cited according to the sketch in RISHIKESH SASTRI, A Prakrita Grammar. Calcutta 1883, a book to which the references are to pages.

Pkt. = Prākrit.

Prab. = Prabodhacandrodaya ed. BROCKHAUS. Lipsiae 1835. 1845. Beside it the editions Pūṇā 1851 (P.), those of VĀSUDEVAŚARMAN, Bombay 1898 (B.), and SARASVATĪ TIRUVEṀKAṬĀCĀRYA, Madras 1884 (M.) in Telugu characters have been used.

Pracaṇḍap = Pracaṇḍapāṇḍava...published by CARL CAPPELLER. Strassburg 1885. Beside it has been used the edition : The Bālabhārata... ed. DURGĀPRASĀD and PARAB. Bombay 1887. = Kāvyamālā 4.

Prākṛitamaṇidīpa—Published by SRINIVASA GOPACHARY, Mysore 1954.

Pras. = Prasannarāghava ed. GOVINDADEVA ŚĀSTRI. Benares 1868.

Pratāp. = Pratāparudrīya. Madras 1868. Telugu print.

Priyad. = Priyadarśikā ed. VISHNU DĀJĪ GADRE. Bombay 1884. The edition of JIBANANDA VIDYASAGARA, Calcutta saṁvat 1931 too has been used.

Proc. ASB. = Proceedings of the Asiatic Society of Bengal.

RB. = Rāvaṇavaha or Setubandha...published by SIEGFRIED GOLDSCHMIDT, Strassburg 1880. The edition of ŚIVADATTA and PARAB, Bombay 1895 = Kāvyamālā. 47 too has been used.
[RB = Rāvaṇavadha-Mahākāvyam, edited by RADHAGOVINDA BASAK Calcutta 1959.]

Ratn. = Ratnāvalī ed. CAPPELLER in : Sanskrit-Chrestomathie published by OTTO BÖHTLINGK. Second edition. St. Petersburg 1877, p. 290ff.

Rāẏap. = Rāẏapaṣenaïẏasutta [Calcutta saṁvat 1936].

Ṛṣabhap. = Ṛishabhapañcāçikā. By JOH. KLATT in ZDMG. 33,445 ff. Beside it the edition of DURGĀPRASĀD and PARAB, Bombay 1890 = Kāvyamālā. Part VII, p. 124 ff.

Rukmiṇīp. = Rukmiṇīpariṇaya ed. ŚIVADATTA and PARAB. Bombay 1894 Kāvyamālā. 40.

Rv. = Rāmatarkavāgīśa.

Ś. = Śaurasenī.

Sagara = A jainistische Bearbeitung der Sagara-sage. Inaugural-Dissertation ...of RICHARD FICK. Kiel 1888.

Sāhityad. = Sāhityadarpaṇa ed. RÖER. Calcutta 1853.

Śak. = Śakuntalā ed. PISCHEL. Kiel 1877.

Samav. = Samavāẏaṅgasutta. Benares 1880.

Sarasvatīk. = Sarasvatīkaṇṭhābharaṇa ed. BOROOAH. Calcutta 1883.

SAW. = Sitzungsberichte der Kais. Akademie der Wissenschaften in Wien.

SBE. = Sacred Books of East.

Skt. = Sanskrit.

Sr. = Siṁharāja.

Śr. = Śṛṅgāraprakāśa of Bhojadeva. (First eight chapters). ed. by G. R. JOSYER, Mysore 1955.

Subhadr. = Subhadrāharaṇa ed. DURGĀPRASĀD and PARAB. Bombay 1888 = Kāvyamālā. 9.

Śukas. = Śukasaptati. Textus simplicior. Published by RICHARD SCHMIDT. Leipzig. 1893.

Sūẏag. = Sūẏagaḍaṅgasutta. Bombay saṁvat 1936.

T. = Tīrthakalpa = BÜHLER, A Legend of the Jaina Stūpa at Mathurā. Wien 1897 = SAW. Vol. CXXXVII.

Ṭhāṇ. = Ṭhāṇaṅgasutta. Benares saṁvat 1937.
Triv. = Trivikrama.

Unmattar. = Unmattarāghava ed. DURGĀPRASĀD and PARAB. Bombay 1889 = Kāvyamālā. 17.
Uttar = Uttarajjhayaṇasutta. Calcutta saṁvat 1936.
Uttarar. = Uttararāmacarita ed. TĀRĀ KUMĀRA CHAKRAVARTI. Calcutta 1870. The edition Calcutta 1831 and that of PREMACHANDRA TARKABĀGĪŚA [sic], Calcutta 1862 too have been used.
Uvās. = Uvāsagadasāo ed. HOERNLE. Calcutta 1890.

Ved. Stud. = PISCHEL und GELDNER, Vedische Studien.
Veṇīs. = Veṇīsaṁhāra. Published by JULIUS GRILL, Leipzig 1871. Beside it the edition of KEDARA NATHA TARKARATNA, Calcutta 1870.
VG. = Vijayabuddhavarman Grant (§ 10).
Vh. = Vasudevahiṇḍi, edited by MUNIMAHĀRĀJA CATURAVIJAYA and PUṆYAVIJAYA in the Ātmānanda Jaina Granṭha Ratnamālā.
Viddhaś. = Viddhaśālabhañjikā ed. BHĀSKAR RĀMACHANDRA ĀTRE. Poona 1886. Beside it the edition of JIBANANDA VIDYASAGAR, Calcutta 1873.
Vidyāp. = Vidyāpariṇaya ed. ŚIVADATTA and PARAB. Bombay 1893 = Kāvyamālā. 39.
Vikr. = Vikramorvaśīyam...published by F. BOLLENSEN, St. Petersburg 1846.
Vivāgas. = Vivāgasuya. Calcutta saṁvat 1933.
Vivāhap. = Vivāhapannatti. Benares saṁvat 1938.
Vr. = Vararuci.
Vṛṣabh. = Vṛṣabhānujā ed. ŚIVADATTA and PARAB. Bombay 1895 = Kāvyamālā. 46.

WZKM. = Wiener Zeitschrift für die Kunde des Morgenlandes.

ZDMG. = Zeitschrift für Deutschen Morgenländischen Gesellschaft.
ZWS. = Zeitschrift für die Wissenschaft der Sprache.

APPENDIX I

GENERAL INDEX

The references are to paragraphs

B.

APPENDIX II

GLOSSARY OF SELECTED WORDS—PISCHEL

The references are to paragraphs

a 184.
aïmuṁka 246.
aïmuṁtaa 246.
aïrāhā 354.
aïi 493.
aüṇa, °ā 128, 444.
akarissaṁ 516.
akasmāt 314.
akasmāddaṇḍa 314.
akāsi, akāsī 516.
akkhanto 88, 491, 499.
agaḍa 231.
aggiṁ 146.
aṅgālia 102.
aṅgua 102.
acchaī 57,480.
accharā 328, 410.
acchaia, °riya °rïa 138.
accharehiṃ328,376,410.
acchiya 565.
acchivaḍaṇa 9.
acche 516.
acchera 138.
ajjama 261.
ajjuā 105.
ajjū 105.
aṭaï 198.
aṭṭha 290.
aṭṭhi 308.
aḍa 149.
aḍha 67,442,449.
aṇa- 77.
aṇaṇuvīi 593.
aṇamilia 77.
aṇarāmaa 77.
aṇavadagga 251.
aṇavayagga 251.
aṇālatta 564.
aṇiuṁtaa 246,251.
aṇiṭṭhubhaya 120.
aṇuvīi 593.
aṇuvvasa 196.
aṇusedhi 66.
aṇelisa 121.
aṇṇaütthiya 58.
aṇṇaṇṇa 130.
aṇṇatta 293.
aṇṇatto 197.
aṇhaga 231.
ateṇa 307.
atta- =ātman 277,401.
atto 197.
attha=atra 293.
attha=artha 290.
atthaggha 88.
atthabhavaṁ 293.
atthamaï 558.
atthamaṇa 149,558.
atthāha 88.
atthi=asti 145; used pleonastically 417.
adakkhu 516.
adas 432.
adimŏttaa 246.
adu 155.
addakkhu 516.
addāa, °ga °ya 196,554.
adduṭṭha 290,450.
adhaṁ 345.
ana- 430.
anamatagga 251.
anta° 343.
antaṁ 342.
antāo 342.
antāvei 343.
anteura 344.
anteuriā 344.
anteṇa 342.
antoanteura 344.
antouvariṁ 343.
antovāsa 230.
antohiṁto 342, 365.
antohutta 343.
andhāra 167.
annesī 516.
apuṇā° 343.
app 174.
appa- =ātman 277,401.
appataro 414.
appayaro. 414.
appāhaï 286.
appiṇaï 557.
appulla 595.
appegaïya 174.
appege 174.
apsaras, declension of 410.
abbavī 515.
abbhaṅga 234.
abbhaṅgiya °da 234.
abbhaṅgei 234.
abbhe 516.
abhū 516.
abhŏcca 587.
amilāya 568.
amba = amla 295; = āmra 295.
ambaṇu 295.
ambira 137,295.
ambila 137,295.
ammayāo 366*b*.
ammo 366*b*.
amhāra 434.
Ayyuā 105.
Alacapura 354.
aladdhuyaṁ 577.
alasī 244.
alāhi 365.
alla 111,294.
avaajjhaï 326.
avajjhāa 28, 123.
avariṁ 123.
avarilla 123.
avarŏppara 195, 311.
avaha 212.
avahoāsa 123.
avahovāsa 123.
avi 143.
as (to be) 145, 498.
asmākam 314.
ahaṁ=adhaḥ 345.
ahā° 335.
ahittā 582.
Ahimajju 283.
Ahimañju 283.
Ahimaṇṇu 283.
Ahivaṇṇu 251.
ahe=adhaḥ 345.

ahesi 516.
aho = adhaḥ 345.
aho ẏa rāo 386, 413.

āa = āgata 167.
āamba 295.
āambira 137.
āikkhaï 492.
āittu 577.
āiriẏa 151.
āu = āpas 355.
āuṇṭaṇa 232.
āusantāro 390.
āusanto 396.
āū teū vāū 355.
āo = āpas 355.
ācaskadi 324.
āḍahaï 222.
āḍhatta 223, 286, 565.
āḍhappaï 223, 286.
āḍhavaï 223, 286.
āḍhavīaï 286.
āḍhāi 223,500.
āḍhia 223.
āṇamaṇī 248.
āṇāḷa 354.
āṇilliẏa 595.
ātman, declension of— 401.
āda- 88,277,401.
ādu 155.
āp, flexion of 504.
ābuḍḍa 566.
āmela 122.
āmoda 238.
āẏa- 88,277,401.
āẏambila 137.
āra 165.
°āra 167.
āliddha 303.
ālĕddhuaṁ 303, 577.
ālĕddhuṁ 303.
āva° 335.
āvaï 254.
āvajja 130,246.
āvantī 335.
āveḍa 122.
āveḍha 304.
āveḍhaṇa 304.
āsaṁgha 267.
āsaṁghaï 267.
asaṁghā 261.
āsi, āsī = āsīt, used for all persons of the sing. and plur. 515.

āsiao 28.
āhaṁsu 518.
āhittha 308.
āhu 518.
āhevacca 77.

i, flexion of 493.
i = iti 93.
ia, iẏa 116.
ii 116.
iṁ 184.
-iṁsu 516.
iṅgāla 102.
iṅgālī 102.
iccee 174.
iṭṭagā 304.
iṭṭā 304.
iṇ' 173.
itto 197.
itthiẏā 147.
itthī 147.
idam 429.
idāṇiṁ 144.
idha 266.
indova 168.
indovatta 168.
iẏāṇiṁ 144.
ira 184.
iva 143.
isi 102.
iharā 212, 354.

īsa 102.
īsattha 117, 148.
īsāsaṭṭhāṇa 117.
īsi 102
īsiṁ 102.
isiẏa 102.
īsīsa 102.
īsīsi 102.

uaha 471.
ukkera 107.
ukkosaï 112.
ukkoseṇaṁ 112.
ukkhala 66, 148.
ukkhā 294.
ukkhuḍia 568.
ucchilla 294.
ucchu 117.
ucchūḍha 66.
ujjovemāṇa 246.
ujjha 335, 420.
ujjhāa 155.
uṭṭa 304.

uṭṭhāe 593.
uṭṭhubhaha, °bhanti 120.
uḍḍasa 222.
uḍḍāsa 222.
uḍḍha 330.
uṇa 184,342.
uṇā 342.
uṇāi 342.
uṇo 342.
uttūha 58.
utthalaï 327[a].
utthalia 327[a].
udāhu 518.
udīṇa 165.
uddha 83,300.
uppiṁ 123, 148.
ubbha = ūrdhva 300.
ubbha = *tubhya 335, 420.
ubhao 123.
ubhaopāsaṁ, °siṁ 123.
umbara 165.
ummilla 566.
ummuggā 104.
umha 335,420.
uyha 335, 420.
uraaḍa 307.
urāla 245.
ulla 111.
uvakkhaḍāvei 559.
uvakkhaḍei 559.
uvaha 471.
uvviṇṇa 276.
uvvivaï 236.
uvvīdha 126.
uvvuṇṇa 276.
uvvuttha 564.
uvvĕllira 107.
usu 117.

ūā 335.
ūsaḍha 67.
ūsalaï 327[a].
ūsalia 327[a].
ūsava 327[a].
ūsāra 111.
ūsua 327[a]
ūhaṭṭha 155.
ūhasia 155.

eā° 435.
ekala 595.
ekalla 595.
ĕkka 435.
ĕkkalla, °ẏa 595.

kerisa 121, 245.
kela 166.
kelaa, °ka 176.
keliśa 121.
kelī 166.
kevaïẏa 149.
kevaciraṁ, °cci° 149.
kesua 76.
keha 166, 262.
kŏjja 206.
koḍilla 232, 595, note 6.
koḍha 66.
koḍhi- 66.
koḍhiẏa 66.
kŏppi 594.
kŏḷhāhala 242, 304.
kŏḷhua 242, 304.
kohaṇḍī 127.
kohala 123.
kohaḷī 127.
kkhu 94.
kram, flexion of 481.
krī, flexion of 51.

khaṇa 322.
khaṇṇa 566.
khaṇṇu 90, 309.
khaḷlihaḍaü 110, 207, 242.
khallīḍa 110.
khatta 566.
khamā 322.
khambha 306.
khammaï 540.
khasia 232.
khahaẏara, °cara 206.
khāi 165.
khāṇu 309.
khiṅkhiṇī 206.
khīla 206.
khu 94, 148.
khujja 206.
khuṭṭa 564, 568.
khuḍia, °da 222, 568.
khuḍḍia 206.
khuṇṇa 568.
khutto 206.
khuppaï 286.
khuluha 139, 206.
kheḍaa 311.
kheḍia 311.
khĕḍḍa 90, 206.
khĕḍḍaï 90, 206.
khĕḍḍā 122.
kheḷadi 206.
khĕḷḷaï 206.
khokhubbhamāṇa 556.
khodaa 311.
khyā, flexion of 492.

gaï 594.
gaüa 152, 393.
gacchaṁ 523.
gaḍa 219.
gaḍhaï 212.
gaḍhiẏa 221.
gaṇṭhaï 333.
gaṇṭhi 333.
gaṇṭhilla 595, note 6.
gadua 113, 139, 581.
ganthaï 333.
ganthima 333.
gabbhiṇa 246, 406.
gamĕppi, gamĕppiṇu 588.
gamesaï 261.
gampi 588.
garua, °ẏa 123.
garukka 299.
garuḷa 240.
gaḷoī 127.
gavāṇī 165.
gahara 9, 132.
gahāẏa 591.
gahia, gahiẏa, gahida 564.
gāī 393.
gāuẏa 65, 80.
gāṇa 165.
gāṇī 165.
gāmilla 595.
gāmilliā 595.
gāmeṇī 161.
gāmelua 595.
gāmĕllaga 595.
gāẏarī 62.
gāra 142.

gārava 61ᵃ.
gāva = gāyanti 254.
gāvī 393.
gindu 107.
gimbha 267.
gimha 314.
gihida 564.
guṁcha 74.
guḍāha 206.
guttha 564.
gr̥ṇhĕppiṇu 588.
gĕjjha 109, 572.
gĕjjhaï 548.
gĕndua 107.
geruẏa 60, 118.
gehi 66.
go, declension of 393.
goilla 595.
goṇa 393.
goṇikka 598.
goṇī 393.
Gothubha 208.
Goḷā 244.
gŏlhā 242.
goḷhāphala 242.
grah, flexion of 512.

Ghaḍukka 150.
ghatta 281.
gharillaa, °llī 595.
gharola 168.
gharoliẏā 168.
gharolī 168.
ghāaṇa 209.
ghiṁsu 101, 105.
ghisaï 103, 209, 482.
gheūṇa 586.
ghĕcchāmo 212, 534.
ghettavva 212, 570.
ghĕttuāṇa, °aṁ 212, 584.
ghĕttuṁ 212, 574.
ghĕttūṇa 584, 586.
ghĕttūṇaṁ 586.
ghĕppaï 107, 212, 286, 548.
ghĕppiuṁ 580.
ghĕppijjaï 548.
ghrā, flexion of 483.

caïūṇa 586.
caïtta 281.
caïttā 582.
caïttu 577.
caükka 302.
cakkāa 167.
cakkiẏā 465.
cakkhaï 202.
cakṣ, flexion of 499.
caccara 299.
caccikka 508.
cacchaï 216.
cattāri for all genders 439.
candimā 103.
caraṇa 257.
calaṇa 257.
caviḍā 80, 238.

ṭhera 166,308.

ḍakka 222,566.
ḍaḍḍhāḍi 222.
ḍaṇḍa 222.
ḍambhia 222.
ḍara 222.
ḍaraï 222.
ḍasaï 222.
ḍahaï 222.
ḍola 222.
ḍolā 222.
ḍolia 222.
ḍohaḷa 222,224.
ḍhakka 221.
ḍhakkaï, °ei 221.
ḍhaṅka 213,223.
ḍhaṅkaṇī 221.
ḍhaṅkiśśaṁ 221.
ḍhaṁkuṇa 107,212,267.
ḍhajjaï, °ḍi 212.
ḍhaṁḍhallaï 556.
ḍhayyadi 212.
ḍhiṅka 213.
ḍhiṁkuṇa 267.
ḍhilla 556.
ḍhuṁḍhullaï 556.
ḍhĕṅkī 213, 223.
ḍhĕṁkuṇa 107,212,267.
ḍhĕlla 150.

ṇaïa 590.
nae 411, note 2, 493. note 4.
nakka 306.
nagiṇa 133.
ṇaṅgala 260.
ṇaṅgaliẏa 260.
ṇaṅgula 260.
ṇaṅgūla 260.
ṇaṅgola 127,260.
ṇaccā, naccā 587.
naccāṇa 587.
ṇaccāṇaṁ 587.
ṇajjaï 548.
ṇaḍāla 260, 354.
ṇappaï 548.
ṇaṁ 150
namŏkkāra 195,306.
ṇamoẏāra 306.
ṇalāḍa 260,354.
ṇavaï 251.
ṇavakāra 251.
ṇavaẏāra 306.
ṇavara, °raṁ 184.
ṇavari 184.
ṇavvaï 548.
ṇavvīaï 548.
ṇahaara 301.
ṇāijjaï 548.
ṇāū 152.
ṇāūna 586.
ṇakkha 194.
ṇāliara 129.
Ṇāhala 260.
ṇāhii, nāhī 534.
ṇiattha 564.
ṇiandhaṇa 201.
ṇiura 126.
ṇikkamaï. °adi 302.
ṇikkha 306.
ṇikkhamaï, ni °302,481.
ṇigiṇa 101,133.
ṇighasa 202, 206.
ṇijjūḍha 221.
ṇijjharaï 326.
nijjhoḍaï 326.
ṇiṭṭhuhia 120.
ṇiḍāla 260, 354.
niṇṇakkhu 516.
ṇiṇṇāra 167.
ṇiṇhaga 231.
ṇiddha, ni° 313.
ṇibuḍḍa 566.
nibhelaṇa, 206, 266.
ṇimaï 118,261.
ṇimilla 566.
ṇimeḷa 122.
nimboliẏā 167,247.
ṇimma 149.
niẏatthiẏa 564.
ṇiẏamasā 364.
niẏāga 254.
niraṅgaṇa 234.
ṇilāḍa 260,354.
ṇisaḍha 67.
Ṇisaḍha 223.
nisiraï 235.
nisīḍha 221.
nissāe 593.
nisseṇī 149.
ṇihasa 206.
ṇihāa 206.
ṇihitta, ni° 286.
ṇihippanta- 286.
ṇihelaṇa 206, 266.
nī "to go away" 463, note 4,-"to go" 493 note 4.
ṇīi 493.
nīma, ṇima 248.
ṇīmī 261.
ṇīsaṇiā, °ṇī 149.
nīsāe 593.
ṇumaï 118, 261.
ṇumajjaï 118.
ṇumaṇṇa 118.
ṇeura, °la 126.
ṇedaṁ 174.
neẏāuẏa 60,118.
ṇelaccha 66.
nevacchĕttā 582.
ṇeha, neha 313.
ṇŏllaï 244.
ṇohala 260.
ṇhāru 255.
ṇhāruṇī 255.
ṇhāvia 210,313.
ṇhāviẏā 210.
ṇhusā 148,313.

ta- 425.
taïa, taïjja, taïẏa, tadia 82,91, 134,449.
tacca 281,299.
taṭṭha 308.
tattilla 595.
tattu 293.
tatto 197.
tattha 293.
tatthabhavaṁ 293.
tamāḍaï 554.
tamba = tāmra 295.
tamba = stamba 307.
tambakimī 295.
tambarattī 295.
Tambavaṇṇī 295.
tambasiha 295.
tambā 295.
tambira 137,295.
tambirā 137.
tambola 127.
taraccha 123.
talavŏṇṭa 53.
talāra 167.
taḷāva 231.
talima 248.
tava = stava 307.
tahiẏa 281.
tā = tāt 425.
tāṭhā 76, 304.
tāṃa 261.
tāmahī 261.

dehaï 66.
dogaṁchi- 74.
dŏgga 215.
doṇṇi, donni for all genders 436.
dodhāra 167.
dŏppadī 61.
dosa 129.
dosākaraṇa 129.
dosāṇia 215.
dosiṇā 133,215.
dosiṇī 215.
dohaḷa 222,244.
dramma 268.
draha 268,354.
drehi 66.

dhaa 299.
Dhaṭṭhajjuṇa 278.
dhaṇuha 263.
dhammuṇā 104,404.
dhā, flexion of 500.
dhāi 165.
dhārī 292.
dhippaï 209.
dhi-r-atthu 353.
dhidā, dhīyā 65,148,392.
dhuṇi 299.
dhuuvaï 536.
dhūā, dhūdā, dhūẏā 65, 148,212,392.
dhruṁ 268.

n see ṇ

paï° = prati 220.
paï 300.
paüttha 564.
paüma 139.
paero 36.
paogasā 364.
paosa, padosa 129.
pagambhaï 296.
paṁkhi-, °ṇī 74.
paṅguraṇa 213.
pacīsa 273.
paccatthima 602.
paccatthimilla 595.
paccappiṇaï 557.
paccūsa 263.
paccūha 263.
paccosakkaï 302.
pacchitta 165.
pacchī 293.
pacchekamma-112.
pajjava 254.
pajjharaï 326.
paṭimā 218.
paṭṭhī, piṭṭhī, puṭṭhī 53,194.
paḍaï 218.
paḍaṁsuā 115.
paḍāā, °gā, °ẏā 218.
paḍāyāṇa 163, 258.
paḍilehāe 593.
paḍilehittā 593.
paḍilehiẏā 593.
paḍīṇa 165.
paḍucca 163,202,590.
paḍucciẏa 163.
paḍuppanna 163.
paḍoẏāra 163.
paḍhama, °ḍhu °221.
paṇa = pañca 273.
paṇiẏattha 564.
paṇuvīsaṁ 104,273.
paṇuvīsā 273.
paṇṇa = pañca 273.
pattiaï, pattiẏaï, pattiā adi 281,487.
patteẏa 281.
patthī 293.
padissā 334.
papalīṇu 567.
pabbhāra 270, note 4.
pamhusaï 210.
paravvasa 196.
parasuhatta 194.
pariuttha 564.
parighĕttavva 570.
paricchūḍha 66.
parijhūsiẏa 209.
paripihĕttā 582.
pariẏāga 254.
pariẏāla 257.
parivuttha 564.
parisakkaï 302.
parisaṇha 315.
parihissāmi 530.
parŏppara 195,311.
palakkha 132.
palāa 567.
palāṇa 567.
palāha 262.
pali = pari 257.
paliucchūḍha 66.
palila 244.
palīvei 244.
pallaṅka 285.
pallaṭṭa 130,285.
pallaṭṭaï 130,285.
pallattha 285.
pallāṇa 285.
palhattha 285.
palhatthaï 285.
palhattharaṇa 285.
pavaṭṭha 129.
pavuttha 564.
pasiṇa 133.
pasuhatta 194.
paseḍhi 66.
pahuccaï 286,299.
pahuḍi 218.
pahuppaï 286.
pā (to drink), flexion of 483.
pāikka 165,194.
pāuṇittā 582.
pāuraṇa 104.
pāuraṇī 104.
pāulla 595.
Pāḍaliutta 292.
pāḍikka 163.
pāḍihera 176.
pāṇia, °iẏa 91.
pāṇu 105.
pāmaddā 291.
pāẏae 578.
pāẏaṁ 342.
pāra 167.
pāraa 167.
pārakka 598.
pāraddha 249.
paraddhi 249.
pārāa 167.
pārevaẏa 112.
pāvaḍaṇa 165.
pāvāliā 167.
pāvīḍha 165.
pāsa (eye) 9.
pāsa (side) 63.
pāhaṇāo 141,354.
pāhaṁ 524.
pāhāṇa 263.
pāhāmi 524.
pi 143.
piavi 588.
piucchā 148.
piusiẏā, piussiā °iẏā 148.
pikka 101.

viẏo 143, 336.
viruva 80.
vilia 151.
viva 336,337.
vivalhattha 285.
visaḍha 67.
viseḍhi 66.
viha 263.
vihatthi 207.
vihala 206,332.
vihasanti 206.
vihuṁḍua 9,275.
vihaṇū 120.
vīmaṁsā 251.
vīlī 107.
vīsuṁ 152.
vuccaï *337,544*.
vuccattha 337.
vuccā 587.
vucchāmu 516.
vuñaï 104,237, 488.
vuñĕppi 588.
vuḍḍhi 52.
vuṇṇa 276.
vutta 337.
vuttha 303,337,564.
vubbhaï 266, 337,541.
vūḍha 337.
vūhae 76.
veuvviẏa 565.
vĕcchaṁ 529.
veḍa 122,240.
veḍisa 101.
veḍujja 241.
veḍha 304
veḍhaï 304.
veḍhaṇa 304.
veḍhima 304.
vĕṇṭa 53.
vĕttuṁ 574.
vĕttūṇa 586
Vĕbbhāra 266.
Vebhāra 266.
vera = vajra 166.
verulia, °liẏa 80.
veḷu 243.
vĕlla 107.
vĕllaï 107.
vĕllarī 107.
vĕllā 107.
vĕlli 107.
vĕllira 107.
Vesamaṇa 261.
vŏccattha 337.
vŏcchaṁ 529.
vŏṇṭa 53.
vŏttavva 570.
vŏttuṁ 574.
vŏttūṇa 586.
vodraha 268.
vosiraï 235.
Vrāsa 268.
vva 143.

śak, flexion of 505.
śam, flexion of 489.
śi 145, 498.
śuṇahaka 206.
śeṇaṁ 176.
śri, flexion of 473.
śru, flexion of 503.
śvas, flexion of 496.
sa-423.
saaḍha 207.
saṃlatta 564.
sakka 566.
sakkaa, sakkada, sakkaẏa 76.
sakkaï 302.
sakkaṇomi, °kku° 140, 505.
sakkā 465.
saṅkala °lā 213.
saṅkaliẏa 213.
saṅkhalā 213.
saṃghaaṇa 267.
saṃghadi 267.
saṃghāra 267.
saccavaï 559.
sajjhasa 299.
saḍaï 222.
saḍḍhā 333.
saḍhā 207.
saḍhila 115.
saṇapphaẏa 148.
saṇicchara 84.
saṇiṁcara 84.
saṇḍeẏa 213.
saṇha 315.
sattari 245.
sattāvīsaṁjoaṇo 9.
saddahaï 333.
saddhā 333.
saddhiṃ 103.
santi, pleonastically used 417.
saṃdatta 304.
saṃdāva. 275.
saṃdhiuṃ 575.
saṃdhissāmi 530.
samaccharehim 328.
samaṇāuso 396.
samara 250.
samassaïa 590.
samāḍhatta 223, 286.
samāṇa 561.
samijjhāi 326.
samilā 247.
samupehiẏā 323,590.
samupehiẏāṇaṃ 592.
samosaḍha 67.
saṃpehāe 323,593.
sapehiẏā 323,590.
saṃbharaṇa 313.
saraa, °ẏa 355.
saraḍuya 259.
salilā 244.
savvaṅgia 598.
savvattha 293.
sassiria 195.
sahia 150.
sahü 206.
sāmaccha 281.
sāmattha 281,334.
sāmarī 88, 109, 259.
sāmalī 88.
sāẏavāhaṇa 244.
sālavāhaṇa 244.
sālāhaṇa 244.
sālivāhaṇa 244.
sāha 64, 262.
sāhaï 264.
sāhaṭṭu 577.
sāhāra 167.
si 145, 498.
sikka 566.
siṅkhalā 213.
siṁgha 267.
siṁghala 267.
siṁghalī 267.
siṅghāḍaga 209.
siṁghāṇa 267.
sijjā 101.
siṇāṇa 133.
sippa 211.
sippaï 286.
sippī 286.
sippīra 211.
simiṇa 133,177,248.
simpaï 286.
simbalī 109.
simbha- 267.

APPENDIX III

INDEX OF PRĀKRIT WORDS

The references are to the paragraph-numbers of the grammar. The following contractions are employed:

A. = Apabhraṁśa.
Ā. = Āvanti.
AMg. = Ardhamāgadhī.
CP. = Cūlikāpaiśācī.
D. = Dākṣiṇātyā.
Ḍh. = Ḍhakkī.
JM. = Jaina-Māhārāṣṭrī.
JŚ. = Jaina-Śaurasenī.
M. = Māhārāṣṭrī.
Mg. = Māgadhī.
P. = Paiśācī.
PG = Pallava grant
Pkt. = Prākrit.
Ś. = Śaurasenī.
Skt. = Sanskrit.
VG. = Vijayabuddhavarman grant (§ 10).

a

ā

i

j

th

d

n

pa

va